Early Motion Pictures

EARLY MOTION PICTURES

The Paper Print Collection in the
Library of Congress

by

KEMP R. NIVER

Edited by Bebe Bergsten

With an Introduction by Erik Barnouw

Motion Picture, Broadcasting, and Recorded Sound Division

LIBRARY OF CONGRESS   WASHINGTON   1985

Library of Congress Cataloging in Publication Data

Library of Congress. Motion Picture, Broadcasting,
  and Recorded Sound Division.
  Early motion pictures.

  Includes indexes.
  1. Silent films—Catalogs. 2. Library of Congress.
Motion Picture, Broadcasting, and Recorded Sound Division.
I. Niver, Kemp R. II. Bergsten, Bebe. III. Title.
IV. Title: Paper print collection in the Library of
Congress.
Z5784.M9L5 1985 [PN1995.75] 016.79143'75 84–600185
ISBN 0-8444-0463-2

ENDPAPERS: *A scene from* The Great Baltimore Fire *(1904).*

For sale by the Superintendent of Documents,
U.S. Government Printing Office
Washington, D.C. 20402

Contents

Foreword

Librarians and archivists always hope that the care they take in organizing, cataloging, and preserving the collections in their charge will result in a growing demand for their materials. Their ultimate reward comes when they can see the usefulness of their collections reflected in the works produced by researchers. Over the years it has been very gratifying to watch the Paper Print Collection in the Library of Congress change from an obscure curiosity to a resource used regularly by film producers, historians of the motion picture industry, and other researchers who have found these images from the turn of the century to be a valuable resource.

When the Paper Prints were rediscovered in the basement of the Library in the mid-1930s they seemed to be nothing more than a curiosity—peculiar rolls of positive photographs which looked like movies, but could not be projected; a record of people and events of a bygone generation, made by a movie industry still in its most primitive state. In the 1940s Library staff member Howard Walls, realizing the importance of this resource, made the first detailed inventories which revealed the collection's scope and variety. The Paper Prints range from social history to vaudeville, from twenty-second shorts to hour-long features, and from actuality footage of the Spanish-American War and the Boxer Rebellion to reenactments of boxing matches. He was so impressed with their potential value that he continued to champion a project to rephotograph them even after he left the Library of Congress in the late 1940s to work at Hollywood's Academy of Motion Picture Arts and Sciences. At the Academy, Mr. Walls's Paper Print project found a new friend in Margaret Herrick, the Academy's Executive Director—a person of great persistence, skill, and imagination. Mrs. Herrick found money to begin the copying of the collection and she dispatched the Academy's dedicated librarian, Elizabeth Franklin, to Washington to help complete the organization of the collection. She also found a remarkable person to do the copying—a Hollywood jack-of-all-trades, Kemp Niver. Mr. Niver was a lawyer and a detective with a good knowledge of photography, an instinct for solving problems, a passion for history, and an endless fund of friends and associates to turn to for advice. It was Mr. Niver

who found a way to refilm the Paper Prints without damaging the originals.

For more than a decade, Mr. Niver and his staff, especially William Alt, painstakingly copied these old films, frame-by-frame-by-frame, pausing regularly to readjust the paper to make the copies as clear as possible. This immense task was completed in the early 1960s, when the films became available to scholars for the first time.

His work in restoring the Paper Prints became so much a part of Mr. Niver's life that he began to make his own studies of the early years of film history based upon his copying work, detailed viewing of the copies he made of the films, and his growing personal collection of movie memorabilia. With his editorial assistant, Bebe Bergsten, in 1967 he completed his catalog of the Paper Print Collection, *Motion Pictures from the Library of Congress Paper Print Collection, 1894–1912*. Until the revision, expansion, and updating in this publication, it was the only detailed catalog of the Paper Print Collection and a tool used by thousands of researchers.

Since 1967 several important resources have become available which have enabled Mr. Niver to add invaluable information about film production before World War I in this edition. These sources include the Museum of Modern Art's and Mr. Niver's own collection of publicity bulletins for films made by the Biograph Company, American Mutoscope and Biograph Company's description of its films, annotations of the Biograph Company's bulletins done by Billy Bitzer (D. W. Griffith's cameraman), AM&B's production log dating from 1899 to 1912, production catalogs of Georges Méliès's and Thomas Edison's films, and such early trade publications as *Moving Picture World, Motion Picture News*, and *Motography*.

This new edition also profits from the countless hours Mr. Niver and Ms. Bergsten have spent over the past few years viewing the films from the collection to record the names of performers, add production information, and expand the summaries of the contents. They have been particularly successful in identifying actors and actresses who appear in films made by the Biograph Company, Klaw and Erlanger, the Keystone Company, the New York Motion Picture Company, and the Great Northern Film Company.

They have even identified a few performers appearing in very early productions. Mr. Niver, who was born in the Hollywood area, has also been able to give very specific locations for a number of films shot in Hollywood and surrounding communities. He has also expanded his film coverage from 1912 to 1915 and added over fifty more titles, many of them produced by the Keystone Company.

The 1967 catalog listed the films alphabetically within several genres (such as advertising, cartoons, comedy, documentary, and drama). In this new edition all of the entries are arranged in a single alphabetical sequence, followed by a credit list and an index. Most of the genres used in the original catalog have been retained and are included in the index, with the exception of Newsreels, Newsreels (Catastrophies), and Newsreels (Human Interest), which have been combined together in the index as Documentaries—films showing actual people, places, and events. The index provides many new useful research entries, particularly for credits and the films' shooting locations.

We anticipate that this catalog will be an invaluable aid for the growing numbers of researchers who come to Washington to study the collection, as well as for persons and institutions around the world who will want to order copies of the films. Providing this increased accessibility will be a source of great satisfaction to all of us who work with this collection.

PAUL SPEHR
Assistant Chief
Motion Picture, Broadcasting,
and Recorded Sound Division

Preface

History shows that early in man's existence he attempted to capture his image and make it permanent. By the time the last half of the nineteenth century rolled around, he not only had reached that goal but had gone considerably beyond it by inventing a way to make his image move through motion pictures.

Within a few short years after the invention of motion picture photography — which seems to have occurred simultaneously in England, France, and America — films were being exhibited in almost every country in the world. Characters moved. That was sufficient to enchant all manner of audiences, and silent pictures presented no language barrier.

In 1894 motion pictures were a novelty, but they rapidly became a lucrative business, and producers naturally sought a way to protect their work from usurpers. Film producers in the United States arrived at a system of sending a paper copy of their films to the Library of Congress in Washington, D.C., for copyright under the existing still picture act, the only means available then. It is fortunate for us that this

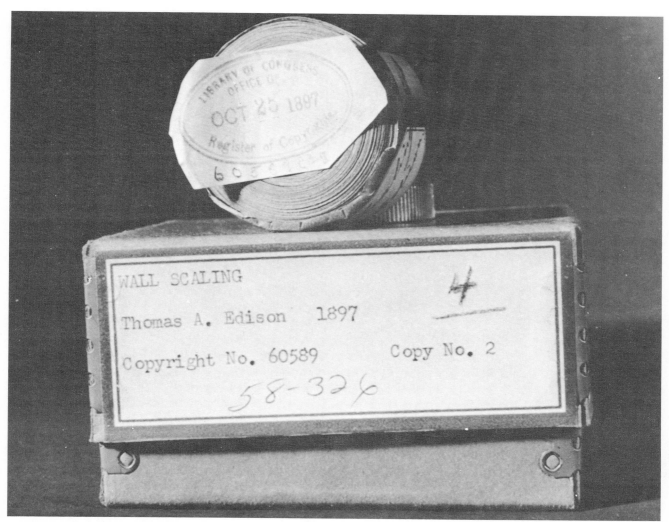

A roll of paper prints, showing the copyright seal.

method of protection was chosen or a great number of these forerunner productions would no longer be around.

The practice of sending paper copies made from the original nitrate negatives to the Library of Congress started with a copyright application for *Edison Kinetoscopic Record of a Sneeze, January 7, 1894,* and continued through at least 1912, when a copyright law specifically covering motion pictures went into effect. The paper negatives forwarded to the Library of Congress during that period remained undisturbed in the archives until 1950. It was then that officials in Washington asked the Academy of Motion Picture Arts and Sciences in Los Angeles to try to find a method to preserve, restore, and transfer the paper copies to modern safety film. Happily, the Academy realized that these paper duplicates were all that was left of something unique.

The Renovare Company of Los Angeles, under my direction, was presented with the challenge of working out the many problems the project entailed. Eastman Kodak Company generously donated the raw stock for the project, while both General and Consolidated film laboratories assisted in the developing.

After underwriting the costs of what became known

Note the center perforations used by the American Mutoscope & Biograph Company on this roll of paper (a contact print) of one of the earliest advertising films—The Gold Dust Twins (1903).

as the "Paper Print Program" for two years, the Board of Governors of the Academy understandably found it a bit too expensive to continue and decided the task would have to be completed with other funds. When they were unsuccessful in securing a grant for the conversion program from any foundation, both Charles Brackett, then president of the Academy, and his successor, George Seaton, approached Senator Kuchel of California. Through their combined efforts, a bill was enacted making it possible to complete most of the remaining years of the Paper Print Program with government funds.

What were the paper prints? Before 1912, when a motion picture was completed, edited, and ready for final release to the public, most producers had a paper contact print made of the final version. Sensitized paper which was exactly the same width and length as the completed negative was used. The paper print was developed, in much the same way as still photographs are made today. Then the finished paper print was forwarded to the Library of Congress in Washington as proof of copyright. But not all motion picture makers availed themselves of copyright protection; as a consequence, we know too little of their work. By the time the Paper Print Program began, perhaps as many as a third of the paper copies in the Library of Congress archives had been damaged by time, making the remaining paper prints (converted into safety film) described in this book extremely valuable.

For several decades, motion pictures were photographed on nitrate stock. Nitrate film seems determined to destroy itself. Sometimes prints or negatives burned up of their own volition. Other hazards that limited the life of nitrate film were inferior raw stock, crude projection equipment that often damaged prints beyond repair, and friction that caused many a print to vanish in flames. Still other prints outlived their usefulness as money-makers and were destroyed purposely. With all these forces working against nitrate films of that period, few were left in their original release form by the time the Paper Print Program started.

The collection of over three thousand films described in detail in this book, all of which were converted from the remaining paper prints in Washington, represents one of the primary sources for the study of the beginning of movement in photography in America, as well as in England, France, and Denmark, since paper copies of quite a few motion pictures produced in those countries somehow found their way to the U.S. Copyright Office.

Once the transference of images to safety film from all the remaining paper duplicates had been completed, the next step was to make it possible for the film

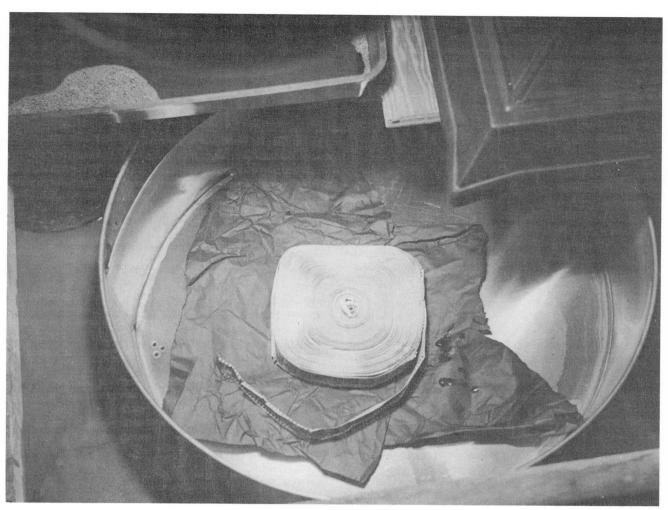

A paper roll as it looked before processing.

to be used. We knew that unless this great hoard of film was properly classified and cross-referenced, it would remain as little known as the paper prints had been, and that there was no way to make such an index except to view each film again and then assign a category. So we began.

In our over two-year study of these films, we took into consideration what the producer, who at that time was often the cameraman and director as well, had in mind. At first, the product of a camera could not be projected on a screen but could only be viewed through an aperture in a boxlike device, animated by a hand-turned crank or by a crude electric motor. Between 1894 and the turn of the century, the results of the cameramen's efforts often turned out to be footage of a burning house, a horse race, a human-interest situation, or a boxing match. It was not until some time later that motion pictures based on a prepared story came into being.

As we went along with the classification, it became increasingly apparent to us that recorded film history was not always consistent with what had actually

The same paper print, photographed and processed and ready to be returned to the Library of Congress.

occurred. Because of a fortuitous circumstance, we had the opportunity to see the films themselves, something not previously granted to many film historians. When we looked at these first moving pictures, it became clear that too much that had been written about the use of a moving picture camera as a tool for conveying an idea to an audience was inaccurate. Many motion picture historians also were not aware of how common the use of special effects was. It was not until some years after the Paper Print Program was finished that any mention was published anywhere of the custom of sending the paper copies to the Library of Congress, even though this had been a commonplace practice for the first twenty years of filmmaking.

As the ending of the film conversion program motivated the classification, so the classification inspired never-ending research. We learned that directors, players, and cameramen were seldom, if ever, given credit on the film itself or anywhere else. We tried to establish their names whenever possible, as well as the locales where the motion pictures had

been photographed. We talked with many players who had appeared in these films and were disappointed to discover it was not uncommon for them, after all these years, not to recall appearing in particular films. Usually, however, they remembered the period and some of their coactors. And we were happy to be able to supply them with titles of films they had appeared in which they evidently had forgotten entirely.

Somehow or other, credit for being the first in any endeavor seems to be all important. The motion picture industry is no exception. When we studied the films in the Paper Print Collection we found that may "firsts" credited to a pioneer cameraman, director, or actor turned out not to be firsts at all. One day a man still active as a film director, once employed by a famous moving picture company before 1910, was shown one of the restored films. He was considerably surprised when he noticed that a camera technique always credited to his former director as a first had been used a couple of years earlier. The Paper Print Collection also contains an amazing number of little-

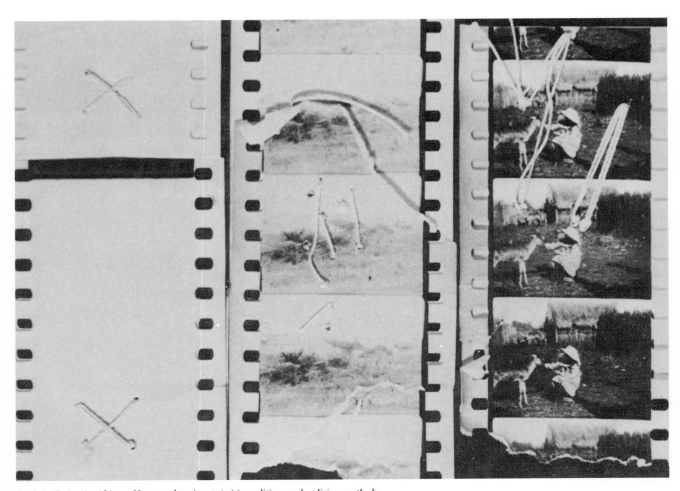

Paul J. Rainey's African Hunt undergoing primitive editing and splicing methods.

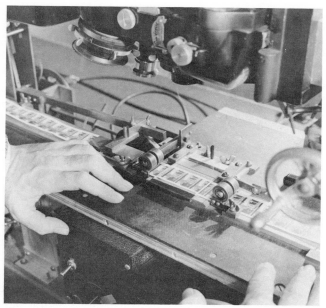
Photographing paper prints.

known uses of a story line to convey comedy or suspense, and it has been a joy to watch how it all began, as well as to observe the rapid development of these singular motion pictures.

By using this book, students of motion pictures and film history can now avail themselves of films made all over the world and draw their own conclusions.

During the work period leading to the publication of this book, I received a great deal of invaluable assistance from Bebe Bergsten, my associate in this classification venture. I also want to thank Donald R. Malkames of Yonkers, New York, for lending me research material from his extensive collection of motion picture memorabilia. And it would not be right to end this preface without acknowledging the assistance rendered by one of Biograph's earliest employees, the late William Beaudine, who helped to identify many Biograph players.

KEMP R. NIVER
Los Angeles, California

This picture is especially interesting because in the front row (from right to left) are Mack Swain, Ford Sterling, and "Fatty" Arbuckle; and in the second row (also from right to left) are Al St. John and Charles Chase. They all became well-known in the moving picture industry, but in this picture they were only extras.

An early chase scene photographed from atop a downtown Los Angeles office building.

Introduction

The three thousand films described in this catalog, representing the earliest years of filmmaking, are an extraordinary, unique collection. Their very existence is a miracle, which has been made possible by a series of mini-miracles, sometimes approaching the bizarre.

Consider the beginning of the story. In 1894 there was no way to copyright a motion picture. Film copyright provisions would not be enacted until 1912. But the Edison company was producing films for its Kinetoscope peep-show machine, which made its commercial debut that year, and was anxious to protect them against piracy.

So the Library of Congress began receiving copyright applications from the Edison company, each accompanied by the fifty-cent copyright fee of that day. Also enclosed, in each case, was what the application called a "photograph." The law *did* provide for the copyrighting of photographs. But these enclosures were not photographs in any familiar sense. What Edison called a photograph was really a complete motion picture, frame after frame, reproduced on photographic paper. The copyright examiner must have been puzzled, and may well have considered it a bit of questionable Edison trickery. Should the material be returned, with the explanation that the law had clearly not been intended for such a purpose?

On the other hand, the law did not decree the permissible dimensions of a photograph. There was apparently no legal reason why it might not be 35mm wide and a hundred yards long. So a cautious bureaucratic decision was made — which probably seemed of trivial significance at the time but turned out to be momentous. The first Kinetoscope motion picture submitted by Edison as a photograph was accepted, a precedent was set, and over the next two decades thousands of motion pictures were registered by producers in the same way. The applications generally came with strips of paper rolled up, often held together by a rubber band. The rolls got bigger and bigger as films got longer. By 1912 the rolls might be eight, ten, or twelve inches in diameter. Most represented complete films; some producers sent only illustrative sequences.

In either case, nothing could really be done with the rolls. They could not be projected. They were a kind of legal record but in almost useless form. As long as the films themselves existed, there seemed little reason to consult the paper rolls.

After the copyright law was revised in 1912, specifically providing for the copyrighting of films, the depositing of paper prints came to a halt, and the existing accumulation was largely forgotten. Now and then a Library of Congress archivist, coming across them, must have wondered what on earth should be done with them. The rolls gradually dried and shriveled, and many twisted out of shape.

Around mid-century comes chapter two. Decades had passed, and the paper rolls were still there. It occurred to an archivist that they represented films that must, by that time, have largely disappeared from the face of the earth. The early films, made on nitrate stock, were chemically unstable. Over the years most nitrate prints had subsided into blobs of jelly or highly combustible powder, or had gone up in flames, or been discarded as obsolete, out of style. A few of the early films, duplicated repeatedly because of unusual popularity, had survived the ravages of the years. But by and large, those early years of filmmaking — the first steps of an infant industry — had vanished. Film history books had accounts of them, but they were based on recollections of veteran filmmakers, not on documentary evidence. Here, forgotten, lay precise and voluminous evidence.

Meanwhile the motion picture, once considered a trivial diversion — not very respectable — had changed in status. It had come to be accepted as a major element in our social history and in the history of human communication.

The dried, wrinkled rolls became the focus of a project. The Library of Congress interested the Academy of Motion Picture Arts and Sciences. The Academy turned to a film technician, Kemp R. Niver. First involved in Hollywood as a studio detective, he had often pursued piracy cases and had become interested in copyright problems, film history, film technology, and film preservation problems. The paper prints now became his crusade. Experimenting with the rolls, he found ways to soften them, restoring their old pliancy. Then he devised special equipment for frame-by-frame reproduction of the old films. Lack of standardization in early equipment posed a host of problems. One by one they were solved. Long months of effort finally established the feasibility of the project. New negatives — then projection prints — *could* be made from the paper rolls. The old films could, in short, be brought back from the dead. But funds had run out. Where to turn?

Now a new miracle. Congress came to the rescue. It appropriated funds that served to duplicate the three thousand paper prints that apparently represented complete films — in other words, to bring back from oblivion some three thousand short films made a half-century earlier and long forgotten. This work was completed in the 1960s, and the Paper Print Collection of pioneer films became available to researchers at the Library of Congress, along with a detailed catalog written by Kemp Niver, who alone knew every frame in the extraordinary collection. For his multiple role in the restoration miracle, Niver received an Oscar. He had created his own niche in film history. He has now prepared a new edition of the catalog for many good reasons.

The impact of the Paper Print Collection and its first catalog turned out to be significant and varied. In the first place, many ideas about film history, based on reminiscences, were shown to be mistaken. The work of setting the record straight began at once and continues. Researchers have been astonished and charmed by the ingenuity of the creators — known and unknown — of these early films. They often achieved effects antedating the "firsts" proclaimed in film histories. Study of the films has also made it possible to identify in the new catalog performers not previously identifiable, and to document the early careers of a number of artists of later importance. But the historic value of the films goes far beyond film industry documentation. The early film entrepreneurs shot hundreds of events — parades, battleship launchings, political rallies, village fairs, railroad disasters, floods. They recorded countless people at work — fighting a fire, building a skyscraper, digging a tunnel, driving a subway, piloting a ferry, building an "el." They showed people at play — at beach, park, stadium, fairground, cafe. The nonfamous, infamous, and famous are here — innumerable figures of the turn of the century were recorded on film, and their identification has likewise been a continuing activity. The geographic range of the material is astonishing. Early filmmakers literally roamed the world with their cameras, providing us with the precise look of innumerable places at particular moments of the past. Architects, historians, sociologists, and graphic artists have been especially fascinated by this aspect of the films. The collection comprises a living atlas of another era. Many special interests — dance, theater, railroads, canals, automobiles, sports, fashion, military history, politics — are illuminated by these incunabula of the film world. On almost any such topic the Paper Print Collection offers a scattering of items, a mini-anthology.

It is ironic that, because of the Paper Print Collection, the film years before 1912 now seem better documented than the years immediately following. After 1912 producers began depositing *films* — nitrate prints — with their copyright applications. But these were regarded as too dangerous for the Library of Congress to store at that time. Therefore, for several decades the Library followed a policy of retaining synopses and other related materials but returning the films — most of which have, of course, vanished.

But the earliest years, the years before 1912, are represented by an historic time capsule — the Paper Print Collection.

ERIK BARNOUW
Benson, Vermont

Key to Abbreviations

Producing companies are indicated as follows:

American Film Manufacturing Company © in full
American Mutoscope & Biograph Company © AM&B
Belcher and Waterson © in full
Biograph Company © Biograph
Walter G. Chase © in full
Columbia Photograph Company © in full
M. H. Crawford © in full
Jack Curley © in full
William K. L. Dickson © in full
Thomas A. Edison © Edison
Engadine Amusement Company © in full
Eureka Feature Film Company © in full
Famous Players Film Company © in full
Feature Films Sales Company, Ltd. © in full
L. Gaumont & Company © Gaumont
Imp Films Company © Imp
Kalem Company © Kalem
Klaw and Erlanger © in full
Laemmle, Carl © Laemmle
Lubin, Siegmund © Lubin
Lubin Manufacturing Company © Lubin Mfg. Co.
Luca Comerio © in full
Macfee, Edward Daniel, Jr. © in full
Méliès, Georges © Méliès
Miles Brothers © in full
New York Motion Picture Co. © N.Y. Motion Picture
Great Northern © Oes, Ingvald C. © Oes
Oklahoma Natural Mutoscene Company © in full
Paley & Steiner © in full
Paul J. Rainey © in full
Savoy Film Exchange © Luca Comerio
George Scott and Company © in full
William N. Selig © Selig
Star Film Company © Méliès
Thanhouser Film Corporation © Thanhouser
Universal Film Manufacturing Company © Universal
Vitagraph Company of America © Vitagraph
Percival L. Waters © in full
James H. White © in full
Winthrop Moving Picture Co. © in full
The Winthrop Press © in full

How to Use the Catalog

This volume is intended as a guide to the many more than 3,000 films restored from the Library of Congress Paper Print Collection, most of which contain a great deal of information for film and other historians. When we wrote this book, it was our intention to provide a simple tool so that any interested person could easily avail himself of the contents of the films.

There is more than one method of obtaining information about a paper print film. If you know the title, look at the alphabetical list entitled "The Paper Print Collection" and which constitutes the main body of the book. If you are seeking a motion picture on a particular subject, turn to the index at the back of the book.

Each film in the collection is described in some detail in the entries arranged alphabetically by title. The data recorded for each title may contain some or all of the following elements: title; producer and/or distributor (usually listed as the copyright claimant); copyright claimant (if different from producer and/or distributor); copyright number and date of copyright; production credits; cast; location and date of production; alternate title(s); length in feet; Library of Congress shelf location number; added identification information; summary; and notes.

Sample Entry

Title—In the Border States

Copyright/or distributor-producer—
Biograph © J142348 June 15, 1910

Production credits—*Director:* D. W. Griffith
Cameraman: G. W. Bitzer

Cast: W. Chrystie Miller, Adele De Garde, Gladys Egan, William J. Butler, Henry B. Walthall, Alfred Paget, Tony O'Sullivan

Location and date of production—Delaware Water Gap, N.J.; Studio, N.Y.C. *Photographed:* May 3-14, 1910

Length and LC shelf location number—413 ft. FLA

Identification information—[America's Cup Races]

Summary—The opening scene of this Civil War film takes place in the interior of a home where a Union soldier is bidding his family goodbye. The scene shifts to the exterior of the house where the soldier joins some troops marching off, presumably to war. The plot revolves around one of the soldiers' daughters who reluctantly hides a wounded Confederate soldier and who later calls upon the same soldier to spare her Union father, also wounded, who has made his way home, but is discovered by several members of the Confederate army.

Notes—There are many camera changes and a lot of activity.

Title—Titles are given as they appear in Copyright Office records published in *Motion Pictures, 1894–1912* or *Catalog of Copyright Entries, Cumulative Series, Motion Pictures, 1912–1939.* Whenever a different title was written or appeared in a title frame on the original paper print it is included in the synopsis. Occasionally a mishap occurred when a producer sent in two films at the same time, and it is quite obvious from the content of the film that the titles became transposed. Each such instance is mentioned in the synopsis. Film titles listed in *Motion Pictures, 1894–1912* sometimes include added identification information. Such identification has been removed from the title and placed at the beginning of the synopsis if the information was necessary for understanding the film. A few entries are done by series titles when this was the appropriate main entry. Alternate titles and the names of films that are part of the series are listed elsewhere in the entry. Foreign films are usually listed by their U.S. release title, but some of George Méliès's films are listed by their original French titles since they were occasionally copyrighted with both French and English titles. There are cross-references from alternate titles.

Examples

In the Border States
The Kleptomaniac
Faust aux Enfers
[Westinghouse Works]

Producer/distributor, copyright claimant, copyright number, and copyright date—Production companies and/or distributors that sent paper duplicates to the Library of Congress for copyright protection are in the alphabetical list entitled "Key to Abbreviations." These short forms are used in the main entries for the American Mutoscope & Biograph Company (AM&B) and for several others. Usually these firms are also the copyright claimants for the works. If this is the case, the copyright symbol © will be placed preceding the copyright number. If the work was produced by one company and copyrighted by another company (or individual), the name of the producer will appear first, followed by the copyright claimant. In this case, the copyright symbol © will precede the name of the claimant, the copyright number will follow the name of the claimant, and the date of copyright registration will appear last.

Note: An oddity that came to light was the lack of consistency between date of production, date of copyright, and date of film release. For most entries, the production and copyright dates are both listed. The release date is not listed. Generally, the period between the date of production and release rarely exceeded thirty days.

Examples   Edison   © H4085 May 6, 1901
AM&B   © H26851 January 9, 1903
Hepworth   © AM&B H52231 October 28, 1904
Famous Players   no registration 1913

Production credits—Production credits are listed insofar as they are known to us. Modern filmgoers are accustomed to seeing cast and production credits included in screen credits. Twenty years of film production passed before this became common practice. The only reliable information about the people making these films must therefore come from other sources, such as film periodicals and the few surviving production records kept by the companies. For the earliest years (before 1906 or 1907) these records frequently list only the camera operator. At that time there was not always a clear distinction between his work and that now done by a director or even a writer. Although a number of terms were used to describe the person operating the movie camera, we have usually used the term *cameraman*. For the few films that were copyrighted after 1912, the term *author* is sometimes used in the legal sense, describing the author of the screenplay as recorded with the registration. The multitalented Georges Méliès—who wrote, directed, designed sets and special effects, and acted in his own productions—is described as *creator*.

Examples Director: D. W. Griffith *Cameraman:* G. W. Bitzer
Producer and Author: Mack Sennett
Creator: Georges Méliès

Cast—As noted above, performers were rarely credited during this period. Identification has been made after carefully viewing the films and comparing known casts from many sources. Since the performers frequently wore makeup, it is difficult to identify some performers and mistakes may have been made, although we have been viewing films from this period for many years and are skilled in identifying even obscure players.

Example   See the sample entry.

Location and date of production—From April 1899 through November 1911, AM&B maintained hand-written records, of production dates and locations. A few records also exist for some Edison productions made during and after 1903. We have recorded this information when we could identify it as pertaining to titles in the Paper Print Collection. Since the entries are hand-written they are not always clear and easy to read. Also, over the years the names of some communities in Connecticut, New York, and New Jersey have changed or disappeared from current maps, causing us to guess what they might be now (indicated by a question mark enclosed in brackets).

After July 30, 1903, AM&B usually recorded the date that the film was photographed. When available, we have used this date and indicated that it is specific by using the term *photographed*. Other records only record a date without indicating whether it was date of photography, date of developing the film, or a release date. In such cases we used the term *date*. Since quite specific location information was available for some titles, such as the street location, we have included it.

Examples   *Location:* Delaware Water Gap, N.Y.; Studio, N.Y.C. *Photographed:* May 3-14, 1910
Location: Greenfield Fishery, Edenton, N.C. *Date:* May 2, 1901
Location: Roof studio, N.Y.C. *Date:* May 1900
Location: Balboa Park, San Diego

Alternate titles—When known, other titles under which a film may have been released or shown are listed. No effort has been made to search out every possible title for each film. The original title for foreign works or the U.S. release title will be given if it is known. For a few films, the working title used by the producer will be listed if it adds some information about the film. The second part of a two-part title—such as, The Evil Art or Gambling Exposed—will not be listed as an alternate title unless it is known to have been used separately.

Examples   *Original title:* Illusions Fantasmagoriques
U.S. title: The Master Magician Alcrofrisbas

Alternate title: The Sneeze

Length—The footage listed is for the 16mm copy made from the original paper print. If the footage is from a 35mm version the entry will say so.

Examples   413 ft.
23 ft., 35mm

Shelf Location—The shelf numbers of the 16mm prints in the Library of Congress are listed. Entries with the letter prefix FLA followed by a number are viewing copies. Shelf numbers beginning with the letter prefix FRA are negative copies. Researchers wishing to view films at the Library of Congress should use the FLA number and the title in their request. Persons wishing to order copies of the films should list the title and the FRA number.

Examples   FLA 5527 FRA 2397
FLA 5878 (copy 1) FLA 5943 (copy 2) FRA 2751

Identification information—Information added to the entry to clarify the location or the event described will appear in brackets just before the summary. Most of these entries are extracted from the information added to the title listed in *Motion Pictures, 1894–1912.*

Examples [Alaska Gold Rush]
[Spanish-American War; New York City Welcome to Admiral Sampson's Fleet after Battle of Santiago Bay]
[McKinley Inaugural Parade]

Summary—Every time we looked at a film, a summary was made, but in no instance was the synopsis intended as a critique of the film. The synopsis represents only what we actually saw in the film and not what others may have said the film contained. For example, in doing research we discovered some contemporary handbills and trade publications with advertisements intended for the film buyer. In most instances, these comprised typical sales puffery rather than facts, and once in a while even the captions under the photographs used as illustrations were incorrect. The summary may include information about film production techniques as well as contents.

Examples See the sample entry.

Notes—Any additional useful information not appearing elsewhere will be added as a note at the end. These notes may relate the film to another film (*See also:* . . .) or describe information recorded on the original paper print which does not appear on the copies made from the original.

Example   *See also:* Review of Russian Artillery

This title was previously listed as Gatling Gun—Firing by Squad. The full title according to the AM&B production records is: C. Von Waldersee Reviewing 2nd & 14th Russian Artillery & 3rd Siberia.

See also: Cossack Cavalry

The Paper Print Collection

The "Abbot" & "Cresceus" Race

Edison © H7988 Aug. 21, 1901

55 ft. FLA4458 (print) FRA0001 (neg.)

The film begins in an area with horse stables in the background. In the foreground a horse being harnessed to a sulky can be seen. The harnessed horse is led away from the preparation area to a racecourse. In the background is a grandstand with more than twenty thousand spectators. The next camera position is a back shot from the track, panning over the heads of the crowd, both standing and seated. There is also footage of horses running in competition, pulling the sulkies.

The Abductors

AM&B © H63799 July 24, 1905

Cameraman: G. W. Bitzer

Location: Studio, N.Y.C. *Photographed:* July 13, 1905

22 ft. FLA3814 (print) FRA0002 (neg.)

The first scene shows a set of an apartment house with a front door and porch, and a staircase on the rear wall away from the camera position. Two men approach the front door from outside. Inside, a woman in a white dress and a large picture hat stands listening at the door. She turns and goes up the stairs. The two men force their entry into the house, run up the stairs, seize the woman, and attempt to drag her from the house. A third man enters, and a terrific fight ensues. He defeats the two abductors and the last scene shows the woman and her savior embracing.

Academy of Music Fire

AM&B © H39143 Dec. 7, 1903

Cameraman: A. E. Weed

Location: Brooklyn, N.Y. *Photographed:* Nov. 30, 1903

37 ft. FLA4459 (print) FRA0003 (neg.)

The film was photographed from many camera positions. The first scenes show two firemen on the roof of a blazing building directing water downward with a hose. The next scene shows the street floor and the remains of a marquee. The camera begins to pan, showing the doorways of the building with flames and smoke pouring through each. As the film ends, it shows the New York Fire Department's hook-and-ladder equipment extended from the street to the top of the building.

An Acadian Elopement

AM&B © H99704 Sept. 16, 1907

Cameramen: O. M. Gove, O. L. Poore

Location: Portsmouth and Rye Beach, N.H. *Photographed:* Aug. 1907

312 ft. FLA4433 (print) FRA0004 (neg.)

American Mutoscope & Biograph felt the film deserved a leading title, complete with copyright number and date of copyright. Each scene is also preceded by a title giving an indication of the plot. There are no actor credits. The first title indicates there is to be an elopement and the opening scene shows just that. The second scene is of the marriage ceremony. The film proceeds to show the bridegroom in various physical encounters: he gets into fist fights with two or three people waiting for a streetcar, with a waiter and a restaurant proprietor, and with clam diggers who throw him bodily into the water, etc. There is an unexplained chase of an escapee from an insane asylum. As the picture ends, the honeymooners are shown coming home to their small country town where they are greeted by at least a dozen people. The title is given as it is listed on the copyright application and copyright record; title on the film appears as An Arcadian Elopement.

Accidents Will Happen

AM&B © H27981 Feb. 7, 1903

Cameraman: Arthur Marvin

Photographed: Aug. 28, 1900

17 ft. FLA3172 (print) FRA0005 (neg.)

A man in workman's clothes, wearing a derby hat and carrying a coal shovel, approaches a coal chute in a set of the front of a barbershop. He removes the lid and climbs into the chute, leaving only his head and neck visible. Another man steps out of the barbershop, sees the derby hat, and gives it a kick. By the use of stop action photography, the hat and the man's head fly off. The second man picks up the head, brushes it carefully, replaces the hat, and restores both to the shoulders of the man who is just climbing out of the coal chute. The head replacement completed, the two men enter the barbershop arm in arm.

The Accommodating Cow

AM&B © H23777 Nov. 11, 1902

Cameraman: Robert K. Bonine

Location: Fair Haven, N.J. *Photographed:* June 25, 1902

14 ft. FLA3443 (print) FRA0006 (neg.)

Two cows are eating from buckets in an outdoor area; one is being milked by a tramp. The tramp continues to milk the cow and, as the film ends, someone off camera throws a bucket of milk over him, causing him to run off in the opposite direction. The title in AM&B's production records is A Hobo Milking A Cow.

Acrobatic Monkey

Edison © 17709 Mar. 15, 1898

19 ft. FLA3347 (print) FRA0007 (neg.)

As the film begins, a man dressed in a poorly designed monkey costume can be seen hanging from some ropes. Judging from the position of the ropes from which he is suspended, the act was planned. For the entire film, the "monkey" does tricks on the ropes, using only his hands.

Across the Subway Viaduct, New York

AM&B © H56521 Feb. 8, 1905

Cameraman: F. S. Armitage

Location: 125th Street viaduct, N.Y.C. *Photographed:* Feb. 5, 1905

65 ft. FLA4954 (print) FRA1951 (neg.)

The film was photographed from a camera platform at the rear of a subway train that starts a trip that ends in a tunnel. No point of departure or destination is indicated.

The Adjustable Bed

AM&B © H61112 May 19, 1905

Cameraman: G. W. Bitzer

Location: Studio, N.Y.C. *Photographed:* May 10, 1905

21 ft. FLA3786 (print) FRA0009 (neg.)

A young man escorts a young woman into a living room of people in moderate circumstances. After she removes her hat, he persuades her to aid him in demonstrating a new reclining chair. She sits down in the chair, he sits on the arm, the chair reclines and they both fall over backward. In the confusion, the man kisses the woman and continues to do so until the film ends.

Admiral Cigarette
Edison © 44332 Aug. 5, 1897
25 ft. FLA4367 (print) FRA1506 (neg.)

The film shows a large, poster-type backdrop with the words "Admiral Cigarettes." Sitting in front of the backdrop are four people in costume: Uncle Sam, a clergyman, an Indian, and a businessman. To the left of the screen is an ashcan size box that breaks apart and reveals a girl, attired in a striking costume, who goes across the stage toward the seated men and hands them cigarettes. Then she unfolds a banner that reads, "We All Smoke."

Admiral Dewey at State House, Boston
Edison © 69558 Oct. 25, 1899
120 ft. FLA4460 (print) FRA0011 (neg.)

The cameraman who photographed this special event was constantly thwarted by people standing between him and the celebrity, Admiral Dewey. However, there are about fifteen feet of good film as the admiral and his party walk toward the camera.

Admiral Dewey Landing at Gibraltar
Edison © 62823 Sept. 27, 1899
67 ft. FLA4461 (print) FLA5963 (35mm print) FRA0012 (neg.)
[Spanish-American War]

A camera located on shore photographed Admiral Dewey's flagship at anchor in the bay. A motor whaleboat approaches in front of the camera position. The motor whaleboat docks, and Admiral Dewey goes ashore.

Admiral Dewey Leading Land Parade
Edison © 64681 Oct. 5, 1899
Location: N.Y.C. Photographed: Sept. 30, 1899
88 ft. FLA4462 (print) FLA5965 (35mm print) FRA0013 (neg.)
[Spanish-American War; Dewey Homecoming, New York City]

The single camera position shows several companies of military troops, marines, soldiers, and cadets walking in a parade in which Admiral Dewey takes part. He is seen as he rides by in an open carriage.

Admiral Dewey Leading Land Parade no. 2
Edison © 65369 Oct. 7, 1899
118 ft.
[Spanish-American War; Dewey Homecoming, New York City]

A land parade made up of American sailors and marines is led by Admiral Dewey. The admiral is seen only once at the beginning of the picture.

Admiral Dewey Passing Catholic Club Stand
Edison © 64680 Oct. 5, 1899
Location: N.Y.C. Photographed: Sept. 30, 1899

30 ft. FLA3061 (print) FRA0015 (neg.)
[Spanish-American War; Dewey Homecoming, New York City]

The single camera position was in front of the Catholic viewing stand and shows spectators watching Admiral Dewey. Little more than horses' legs and carriage wheels can be seen.

Admiral Dewey Receiving the Washington and New York Committees
Edison © 63830 Oct. 2, 1899
Location: New York Harbor Photographed: Sept. 27, 1899
53 ft. FLA4463 (print) FRA0016 (neg.)
Spanish-American War; Dewey Homecoming, New York City]

The single camera position is the deck of Admiral Dewey's flagship while at anchor. Admiral Dewey and an aide are awaiting the arrival of dignitaries from shore.

Admiral Dewey Taking Leave of Washington Committee on the U.S. Cruiser Olympia
Edison © 63831 Oct. 2, 1899
Location: New York Harbor Photographed: Sept. 27, 1899
40 ft. FLA4360 (print) FRA1499 (neg.)
[Spanish-American War; Dewey Homecoming, New York City]

The single camera position is the deck of the flagship Olympia and shows the starboard gangway. Admiral Dewey is seen bidding goodbye to a committee.

Admiral Sampson on Board the Flagship
Edison © 52057 Sept. 3, 1898
Location: New York Harbor Photographed: Aug. 20, 1898 [?]
33 ft. FLA4285 (print) FRA0018 (neg.)
[Spanish-American War; New York City Welcome To Admiral Sampson's Fleet after Battle of Santiago Bay]

The first scenes were photographed on board a vessel that was at a sufficient distance to cause inclusion of the hull of a harbor tug that obscured a considerable portion of Admiral Sampson's flagship. A large part of the film shows the after portion of the flagship at anchor. The camera includes the hull from the water line to just above the awninged quarter deck. There is good detail of the after portion of the ship. Following the title, there is an American Mutoscope & Biograph title frame, with no title shown in the space ordinarily used for it.

Advance Guard, Return of N.J. Troops
Edison © 59211 Oct. 7, 1898

24 ft. FLA3734 (print) FRA0020 (neg.)
[Spanish-American War]

The film was photographed from a camera positioned high above an intersection lined with people who apparently were spectators at a parade of mounted individuals. Most of the riders shown are on excellent horses with nonmilitary tack. However, all the riders visible carry a blanket roll over their shoulders. About a hundred horses can be seen, and there are some two- and three-story buildings in the background.

Advance of Kansas Volunteers at Caloocan

Edison © 37443 June 5, 1899

24 ft. FLA3987 (print) FRA0021 (neg.)

[Spanish-American War]

The first scene was photographed through thick foliage. Approximately two dozen men have rifles pointed at the camera position. As the film progresses, the men advance toward the camera, firing. From the left and right of the camera are men wearing American Army uniforms, who walk away, firing at the first group of men. A man carrying an American flag follows; he is shot, and another soldier picks up the flag. As the picture ends, the soldier waves the flag triumphantly.

Adventure While Strolling

See: The Two Convicts

Adventures of Dollie

AM&B © H13248 July 10, 1908

Director: D. W. Griffith *Cameraman:* Arthur Marvin

Cast: Linda Arvidson, Arthur Johnson, Charles Inslee, Mrs. Gebhardt

Location: Sound Beach, Conn. *Photographed:* June 18–19, 1908

294 ft. FLA5263 (print) FRA0022 (neg.)

A man, a woman, and a little girl are out for a day in the woods. The woman and the little girl are sitting by a stream when a gypsy attempts to sell some baskets. Failing in this, he attempts to steal the woman's purse and is caught. He begins molesting her, and her husband comes to the rescue. The gypsy, gesturing as if swearing vengeance, returns to his wife and wagon. The following scenes show the gypsy kidnapping the little girl, the getaway in his wagon after hiding her in a barrel, the gypsy trying to ford the stream in his wagon, and the loss of the barrel. The barrel floats downstream and over a small waterfall. It is eventually pulled from the water by two small boys who were fishing in the first scene. The film ends as the little girl is extricated from the barrel and reunited with her father. This was the first picture directed by D. W. Griffith.

The Aeroplane Inventor

Great Northern © Oes J168388–168389 Apr. 20, 1912

Director: August Blom *Script:* Otto V. Fich

Cast: Einar Zangenberg, Clara Wieth, Otto Lagoni, Lauritz Olsen

Date: July 5, 1911

Produced in Denmark by Nordisk Film Co. *Danish title:* En Opfinders Skaebne

755 ft. FLA5841-5842 (print) FRA2908 (neg.)

This feature-length motion picture is patterned after the basic plot of the poor-but-honest inventor in competition with unscrupulous financiers. The inventor, faced with the problem of raising money, flies the aeroplane until it crashes. He is carried off on a stretcher.

The Affair of an Egg

Biograph © J144968 Sept. 6, 1910

Cameraman: Arthur Marvin

Cast: Gertrude Robinson

Location: Fort Lee, N.J.

108 ft. FLA4956 (print) FRA0024 (neg.)

A whimsical farm girl writes a message on an egg that finds its way to a city restaurant where it is served to a young man. Intrigued, the young man sets out to locate the message writer. He makes the long and arduous trip by train to the country and confronts the young woman, who, much to his dismay, doubles up her fist and hits him. The next scene shows the young man boarding a train, and the young woman on her knees beseeching him to return to her.

An Affair of Hearts

Biograph © J141593 May 23, 1910

Director: D. W. Griffith *Cameraman:* Arthur Marvin

Cast: Florence Barker, Mack Sennett, Billy Quirk, Jeanie Macpherson

Location: Verdugo, Calif. *Photographed:* Mar. 2, 16–17, 1910

366 ft. FLA3082 (print) FRA2669 (neg.)

The film is built around a contest between two eccentric Frenchmen for the hand of an eligible American girl, who, at the end of the film, finally discourages both of them by introducing her betrothed. Mack Sennett and Billy Quirk, playing the Frenchmen, provide the comedy relief. Their antics include attempting to get into an automobile, riding a bicycle, dueling with shotguns, and eventually matching to see who will kill the other. Florence Barker, the love interest, and Jeanie Macpherson, her maid, play straight for the comics as well as dramatic roles.

An Affair of Honor

AM&B © H23803 Nov. 11, 1902

19 ft. FLA3508 (print) FRA0026 (neg.)

This was photographed as if from the audience at a theater. Four women approach the center of the stage in front of a forest backdrop. Two of the women remove the jackets of their dresses, take fencing swords, and proceed to fence with one another. The film ends as one loses.

"Africander" Winning the Suburban Handicap, 1903

Edison © H33004 June 27, 1903

44 ft. FLA4464 (print) FRA0027 (neg.)

The camera is about the height of a standing spectator and shows a large racecourse with approximately eight horses approaching at a full gallop. The distance makes the horses' numbers indistinguishable. The second camera position is a repeat of the first. The third is a slow pan of the area between the grandstand and the race track railing. Many people are milling about.

After Launching

Edison © 16426 Mar. 10, 1898

25 ft. FLA3995 (print) FRA0028 (neg.)

The title indicates that a ship was launched. A boat bearing the name *Unadila* on the stern is shown as it passes the camera.

After Many Years

AM&B © H117541 Oct. 28, 1908

Director: D. W. Griffith. *Cameramen:* G. W. Bitzer, Arthur Marvin

Cast: Florence Lawrence, Charles Inslee, Herbert Prior, Linda Arvidson, Gladys Egan

Location: Studio, Sea Bright, N.J.; Atlantic Highland, N.J.
  Photographed: Sept. 22, Oct. 8 and 10, 1908
390 ft. FLA3776 (print) FRA0029 (neg.)

The story follows the classic Enoch Arden plot. The camera establishes the relationship of the man and woman and where they live. The next camera position conveys the idea of an impending separation. Then the remainder of the film shows the man being shipwrecked, his survival on a desert island, his rescue, and his eventual return. His wife, during his absence, has remarried; however, the film ends showing the survivor reunited with his wife and family. The AM&B copyright insignia is visible in the background of one of the scenes.

After the Ball

Biograph © J150107 Jan. 3, 1911
Cameraman: Arthur Marvin
Cast: Florence LaBadie, Tony O'Sullivan, Eddie Dillon, Mack Sennett
Location: Studio *Photographed:* Nov. 25, 1910
121 ft. FLA3817 (print) FRA0030 (neg.)

This film was photographed entirely on one set of the living room of a house or an apartment. The plot is built around a wife waiting up for her fun-loving husband who is late returning from a club masquerade. There are three scenes: the arrival of the husband and his two companions; their hilarity in creating a diversionary incident to transform the wife's wrath into compassion; and the final scene showing the wife, aware of their joke, with a rolling pin in her hand suggesting to the conspirators one by one that they leave the house. The last scene shows her hitting her husband on the head.

After the First Snow

AM&B © H33408 July 13, 1903
20 ft. FLA3410 (print) FRA0031 (neg.)

The single camera position, located on the edge of a road in a park, photographed approximately twenty-five preadolescent children riding on sleds down an incline that appears to be a frozen-over thoroughfare.

After the Race—Yachts Returning to Anchorage

Edison © 68177 Oct. 20, 1899
Cameraman: Edwin S. Porter
Location: Off Sandy Hook, N.J. *Photographed:* Oct. 1899
43 ft. FLA4465 (print) FRA0032 (neg.)
[America's Cup Races; Columbia and Shamrock I]

The camera's position was on a boat that was in motion as the America's Cup Race (sailboats) was photographed as the sailboats were returning to their moorings after the race was over. The film shows both contenders in profile in full rig condition.

Afternoon Tea on Board S. S. Doric

Edison © 38227 June 22, 1898
28 ft. FLA4229 (print) FRA0033 (neg.)

A group of people can be seen clustered about tables, while some are sitting on the deck. The single camera position is on a level that includes all of them. No one moves about except to retrieve three small children who were obscuring the group from the camera's view.

See also: S.S. Doric, S.S. Doric in Mid-ocean, and Game of Shovel [sic] Board on Board S.S. Doric

Aguinaldo's Navy

AM&B © H16737 Apr. 18, 1902
Cameraman: Raymond Ackerman
Location: Pasig River near Manila, Philippine Islands
  Photographed: May 9, 1900
11 ft. FLA3205 (print) FRA0034 (neg.)
[Spanish-American War]

The cameraman placed his equipment on the bank of a river to film sampans and outrigger boats going back and forth. Some of the vessels carry as many as ten passengers. Most of the boats are poled along, although they are equipped with masts and furled sails. The quality of the film does not permit any further description.

Airy Fairy Lillian Tries on Her New Corsets

AM&B © H68182 Nov. 3, 1905
Cameraman: G. W. Bitzer
Location: Studio, N.Y.C. *Photographed:* Oct. 24, 1905
33 ft. FLA3962 (print) FRA0035 (neg.)

The scene opens with an obese woman attempting to put on a corset several sizes too small. A man, apparently her husband, comes to help her. Between the two of them they manage to get the stays hooked, but he becomes hysterical and falls on the bed.

See also: Fat Girl's Love Affair and Rat Trap Pickpocket Detector

Al Treloar in Muscle Exercises

AM&B © H60228 May 3, 1905
Cameraman: G. W. Bitzer
Location: Studio, N.Y.C. *Photographed:* Apr. 21, 1905
32 ft. FLA3778 (print) FRA0036 (neg.)

The routine of a physical culturist using barbells, muscle traction, back bends, etc., is photographed from a single camera position as if in the audience.

See also: Treloar and Miss Marshall, Prize Winners at the Physical Culture Show in Madison Square Gardens

Alcrofrisbas, the Master Magician

  See: L'Enchanteur Alcrofrisbas

Algy, the Watchman

Biograph © J170133 June 8, 1912
Director: Mack Sennett
Cast: Dell Henderson, Fred Mace, Charles Hill Mailes
207 ft. FLA3912 (print) FRA0037 (neg.)

This humorous melodrama concerns a farm and the mortgage which is about to be foreclosed. The mother, who needs money to pay the mortgage, sends her two sons out to earn some. One goes to the city and the other to a mining camp. Most of the film is devoted to the mishaps of the son who goes to the city, where he takes a job as a bank guard. He succeeds in locking the president of the bank in his office thinking he is a bank robber. The foreclosure is delayed long enough for the other son to return home from the mines with the news that he has struck it rich and can pay off the mortgage.

Algy's Glorious Fourth of July
AM&B © H18744 June 7, 1902
Cameraman: F. S. Armitage
Location: Roof studio, N.Y.C. *Photographed:* July 5, 1901
16 ft. FLA4151 (print) FRA0038 (neg.)

There are three sets in this film. One is a store front, the second a brick wall with a gate, and the third the interior of a small boy's bedroom. In the first scene, the proprietor of the grocery store loads up a small boy with firecrackers. The boy ignites them in front of the brick wall. The firecrackers, instead of exploding singly, explode simultaneously, completely obliterating everything on the set. Scene three shows the small boy, heavily bandaged, being attended by a physician and fanned by his mother.

All on Account of the Milk
Biograph © J137280 Jan. 15, 1910
Director: Frank Powell *Cameraman:* Arthur Marvin
Cast: Mary Pickford, Blanche Sweet, Mack Sennett, Kate Bruce, Flora Finch, Mrs. Smith, Arthur Johnson
Location: Fort Lee, N.J.; Studio, N.Y.C. *Photographed:* Dec. 9–11, 1909
400 ft. FLA3932 (print) FRA0039 (neg.)

The plot is based on a misconception as to the true identity of the hero and the heroine. The hero, a young contractor, is mistaken by the heroine for a laborer, while he thinks she is the maid although she is the daughter of the manor. The hero continues to represent himself as a laborer in order to see the maid, and the daughter, in order to continue her impersonation, borrows the maid's clothing. But, at the end, the two main characters are brought together in their true light, with the blessing of their respective mothers. This was the first film Frank Powell directed.

Allabad; the Arabian Wizard
AM&B © H23812 Nov. 11, 1902
Cameraman: Arthur Marvin
Location: Roof studio, N.Y.C. *Photographed:* July 26, 1900
42 ft. FLA4466 (print, copy 1) FLA5984 (print, copy 2) FRA0040 (neg.)

Here the producers made the best of stop-action photography to elaborate upon the work of an actor-magician. The complete film is devoted to the magician as he conjures out of space eggs, chickens, trees, animals, etc., and then makes them disappear.

Almost a King
AM&B © H39906 Dec. 23, 1903
Cameraman: A. E. Weed
Location: Studio, N.Y.C. *Photographed:* Dec. 9, 1903
90 ft. FLA4957 (print) FRA0041 (neg.)

All of the action takes place in one room furnished as the dining room of a modest house. A maid is setting the table. She leaves and a messenger brings a suit in, puts it over the back of a chair and leaves. A tramp enters and starts to put food from the table into a pack. But he sees the suit and decides to wear it. He steps behind a screen, removes his tattered garments and drapes them over the screen. The maid returns and removes both the new suit and the tramp's clothing, and the screen. The tramp is seen wearing a barrel as the police escort him from the room.

Alone
AM&B © H48624 July 28, 1904
Cameraman: G. W. Bitzer
Location: Coney Island, N.Y. *Photographed:* July 20, 1904
34 ft. FLA3209 (print) FRA0042 (neg.)

A sandy beach with small waves washing up is shown in the foreground. In the background is a pier extending out into the ocean. A small boy enters the scene from camera right and runs from the waves as they approach him. This game of tag with the water continues. There is no one but the child in the film.

Alphonse and Gaston
AM&B © H23787 Nov. 11, 1902
Cameraman: Robert K. Bonine
Location: Fair Haven, N.J. *Photographed:* June 25, 1902
13 ft. FLA3702 (print) FRA0043 (neg.)

The film opens outside a house with a picket fence. A heavily veiled woman approaches the camera position and hesitates at the edge of the curbing because of mud. Two men appear and after much bowing and swaying to one another, finally put an article of clothing down in the mud in front of the woman who steps on it and proceeds on her way as the film ends.

Alphonse and Gaston, no. 1
AM&B © H37437 Oct. 31, 1903
Cameraman: A. E. Weed
Location: Studio, N.Y.C. *Photographed:* Oct. 16, 1903
5 ft. FLA4434 (print) FRA0044 (neg.)

This was photographed from a single camera position and shows a bar in which a cowboy makes Alphonse and Gaston dance by shooting at their feet.
See also: Alphonse and Gaston, No. 3 for a longer version.

Alphonse and Gaston, no. 2
AM&B © H37438 Oct. 31, 1903
Cameraman: A. E. Weed
Location: Studio, N.Y.C. *Photographed:* Oct. 16, 1903
4 ft. FLA4436 (print) FRA0045 (neg.)

A single camera position shows Alphonse and Gaston against a painted backdrop as a man carrying a log of wood appears and drops something. Both attempt to help him and all three end up in a heap on the ground.

Alphonse and Gaston, no. 3
AM&B © H37366 Oct. 27, 1903
Cameraman: A. E. Weed
Location: Studio, N.Y.C. *Photographed:* Oct. 16, 1903
30 ft. FLA4467 (print) FRA0046 (neg., copy 1) FRA1561 (neg., copy 2)

This one-camera position film is of a vaudeville act that starts in a saloon with the saloon keeper behind the bar. The first action shows two costumed characters approaching the bar. They back up and go forward and gesture over who is to take the first drink until they annoy a cowboy who is also in the saloon. He takes a gun from his holster and shoots at the floor near the two comics. They begin to dance. As the film ends, they are dancing off camera position. The film was taken off 70mm Mutoscope paper.

Alphonse and Gaston Helping Irishman
AM&B © H23785   Nov. 11, 1902
Cameraman: Robert K. Bonine
Photographed: June 25, 1902
12 ft.   FRA3475 (print)   FRA0047 (neg.)

The camera was positioned in the center of a road edged with trees. In the distance, a workman carrying several large planks on his shoulder can be seen approaching. A sack of tools is on one end of the planks as a balance. Two men in top hats and frock coats follow him closely. They rush to his aid as the sack of tools slides from the planks to the ground. Each bows to the other stating, "I'll do it," until the workman can no longer wait. He bends over to retrieve the tools and hits Alphonse and Gaston on the head with the plank. The film is in poor condition and quite grainy.

Always Room for One More
AM&B © H65316   Sept. 11, 1905
Cameraman: G. W. Bitzer
Location: Studio, N.Y.C.   *Photographed:* Aug. 24, 1905
22 ft.   FLA3909 (print)   FRA0048 (neg.)

A young woman and a young man, both dressed in formal attire, walk toward camera position. In the foreground is a high-backed leather chair. The young man indicates that the young lady sit down, which she does. He attempts to share the chair with her but there is no room. To surmount the problem, he picks her up, seats himself, and places her on his lap. As the film ends, they are kissing.

Ambrose's Fury
Keystone © LP4871   Mar. 25, 1915
Producer and Author: Mack Sennett
Cast: Billie Bennett, Louise Fazenda, Alice Davenport, Dave Morris, Mack Swain
Location: Keystone studio, Venice and Santa Monica, Calif.
423 ft.   FLA4214 (print)   FRA0049 (neg.)

A situation comedy, typical of the mistaken identity concept, together with husbands interested in cheating on their wives. But they get caught. There are scenes involving a roller coaster in Venice, as well as beach scenes in Santa Monica, and some taken in and around the Keystone studio.

Ambrose's Little Hatchet
Keystone © LP4746   Mar. 15, 1915
Producer and Author: Mack Sennett
Cast: Don Barclay, Eddie Cline, Louise Fazenda, Bobby Dunn, Dave Morris, Mack Swain
Location: Areas around Keystone studio, Echo and Hollenbeck Parks
400 ft.   FLA4407 (print)

This lively film revolves around a young woman who wants some new clothes, her reluctant husband, her male dressmaker, and one or two other principals who manage to cause considerable confusion involving a hatchet and the curious neighbors. Neighbors see in silhouette what they

believe is the young wife being chopped to pieces. A chase results. The picture ends happily for all concerned.

Ambrose's Lofty Perch
Keystone © LP4956   Apr. 3, 1915
Producer and Author: Mack Sennett
Cast: Louise Fazenda, Harry McCoy, Dave Morris, Mack Swain, Dora Rogers, Dixie Chene, Estelle Allen, Joe Swickard
Location: Keystone studio and Immaculate Heart College in Los Angeles
430 ft.   FLA4411 (print)   FRA0050 (neg.)

A king, played by Mack Swain, seeks a queen to help him rule his kingdom. Finally he selects Louise Fazenda, one of the maidens in his kingdom. After they are married, Robin, a young man the queen had known earlier, attempts to steal her from her royal husband. In the following scenes arrows with notes attached and a bomb play important parts in the attempt to separate the queen from her king.

Ambrose's Nasty Temper
Keystone © LP5063   Apr. 17, 1915
Producer and Author: Mack Sennett
Cast: Cecile Arnold, Louise Fazenda, Harry McCoy, Dave Morris, Mack Swain, Dixie Chene, Frank Hayes
403 ft.   FLA4412 (print)

Another in a series of Ambrose pictures featuring Louise Fazenda and Mack Swain (Ambrose). This time the locale is a garment factory with Louise Fazenda as the owner, Mack Swain as the manager, Dave Morris as the foreman, and Cecile Arnold as the owner's lovely young daughter. The film is devoted to rivalry between Mack Swain and Dave Morris for the hand of Cecile Arnold, which leads to several truly ridiculous situations.

Ambrose's Sour Grapes
Keystone © LP4567   Feb. 27, 1915
Producer and Author: Mack Sennett
Cast: Cecile Arnold, Mae Busch, Chester Conklin, Louise Fazenda, Frank Hayes, Harry Gribbon, Edgar Kennedy, Dora Rogers, Mack Swain, unidentified identical twins
Location: Keystone studio and Hollenbeck Park, Los Angeles and area surrounding park and studio
805 ft.   FLA5838 (print)   FRA2724 (neg.)

One of the twins is married, the other is not, and the comedy is devoted to the unwitting confusion the two identical young ladies inflict upon a husband (Edgar Kennedy) and the two suitors (Harry Gribbon and Mack Swain) of the unmarried twin.

Ambulance at the Accident
Edison © 60592   Oct. 25, 1897
Location: New Jersey [?]
26 ft.   FLA3062 (print)   FRA0053 (neg.)

A man is lying across the cowcatcher of a halted streetcar bearing a sign saying "West Orange." Many people are watching in the background. A horse-drawn ambulance arrives, and the driver and his helper in uniform remove the injured man from the ground, put him in the ambulance, and depart.

See also: Ambulance Call

Ambulance Call

Edison © 60591 Oct. 25, 1897

Location: New Jersey [?]

23 ft. FLA3578 (print) FRA0054 (neg.)

From a single camera position, the camera shows a building. As the film begins, large doors on the street level open, and a horse-drawn vehicle appears, makes a turn, and approaches the camera position. The two-wheeled horse-drawn vehicle passes in front of the camera and, in the distance, a large van with the label "Storage" on the side can be seen.

See also: Ambulance at the Accident

American Falls, Goat Island

AM&B © H30733 Apr. 24, 1903

Location: Niagara Falls, N.Y.

17 ft. FLA3151 (print) FRA0055 (neg.)

The film, photographed from a single camera position, shows Goat Island on the American side of Niagara Falls, New York.

American Falls, Luna Island

AM&B © H30732 Apr. 24, 1903

Location: Niagara Falls, N.Y.

15 ft. FLA3414 (print) FRA0056 (neg.)

This is a single camera position view of what was then called Luna point (it is now nonexistent), on the American side of Niagara Falls, New York.

American Flag

Edison © 17705 Mar. 15, 1898

27 ft. FLA4380 (print) FRA0057 (neg.)

From a single camera position an American flag with thirty stars in the field can be seen in the foreground. The flag is moving in a breeze, and there are houses in the background.

American Flag

Edison © 18130 Mar. 17, 1898

27 ft. FLA4381 (print) FRA0058 (neg.)

This is a single camera position close-up of a small American flag and staff. There are thirty stars in the field. The flag moves as though in a breeze inside a room.

The American Fleet in Hampton Roads, 1909, After Girdling the Globe

Edward Daniel Macfee, Jr. © H124864 Mar. 26, 1909

Location: Hampton Roads, Va.

285 ft. FLA4414 (print, copy 1) FLA2934 (print, copy 2, incomplete) FRA0059 (neg.)

The Columbia Photograph Company of Petersburg, Virginia, was the coproducer of this film, which consists of photographs taken on a voyage around the Hampton Roads Harbor in Virginia. It shows all the battle cruisers, ships, etc., of the U.S. Navy that were at anchor in the harbor at that time.

The American Soldier in Love and War, no. 1

AM&B © H33641 July 21, 1903

Cameraman: G. W. Bitzer

Photographed: July 9, 1903

32 ft. FLA3447 (print) FRA0060 (neg.)

A woman is sitting at a table with her head on her arms in a set of a living room. She moves when a man in military uniform comes into the room from behind a curtain. He walks toward her and begins to comfort her. The film ends as the man in military uniform is embracing the woman.

The American Soldier in Love and War, no. 2

AM&B © H33642 July 21, 1903

Cameraman: G. W. Bitzer

Photographed: July 9, 1903

31 ft. FLA3446 (print) FRA0061 (neg.)

A painted backdrop depicts a jungle. From camera right, a man in the uniform of a Spanish-American War soldier enters. He acts as if he is wounded or exhausted and falls to the ground. Two actors, a man and woman dressed as natives, enter from camera left. The male native immediately sets upon the fallen American soldier and attempts to kill him. There is a scuffle. The woman begs for the life of the soldier as the film ends.

The American Soldier in Love and War, no. 3

AM&B © H33643 July 21, 1903

Cameraman: G. W. Bitzer

Photographed: July 9, 1903

27 ft. FLA3445 (print) FRA0062 (neg.)

This was filmed from the point of view of a theater audience. The set and surroundings convey the impression of a jungle or a desert island, with heavy foliage and an ocean nearby. The only on-stage piece of equipment is a doorway to a hut. A white man in an Army uniform with a large bandage around his head is sitting in front of the hut. Standing alongside, facing the camera, is an actor made up to resemble a large black woman. She is fanning the man with a palm fan. Another native is holding a bowl from which the wounded soldier is eating. The next action shows a man with a beard and pith helmet arriving accompanied by a white woman wearing a large picture hat. The woman rushes into the arms of the soldier. After much embracing, the soldier indicates that the black woman had saved his life, and the picture closes with the white woman removing her necklace and handing it to the other woman.

Ameta

AM&B © H30752 Apr. 24, 1903

Cameraman: F. S. Armitage

Location: Studio, N.Y.C. *Photographed:* Apr. 1, 1903

16 ft. FLA3419 (print) FRA0063 (neg.)

As the film begins, from a camera positioned from the viewpoint of a theater audience, the head of a woman can be seen through an opening formed by two poles on which gossamer material has been stretched. As it progresses, the two crossed poles form a circle and become a gyrating spectacle causing the gossamer material to move in many attractive shapes and directions. "Ameta," the performer, periodically becomes visible through the whirling material.

The Amorous Militiaman

AM&B © H54666 Dec. 10, 1904

51 ft. FLA4468 (print) FRA0064 (neg.)

Three men dressed as women are scrubbing clothes in washtubs on boxes in the backyard of a residence. A man in military dress uniform approaches them and attempts to embrace the youngest of the three. The two older women chase him away but he persists, returns, and falls on his knees as if proposing. One of the older women wraps some wet wash around his head and the three of them dump him head first into a barrel. At this point, trick effects are used and a dummy is substituted for the man in the barrel. The three women remove the dummy from the barrel and wring it out. A live actor is exchanged for the dummy and sits up in bewilderment.

Ancient and Honourable Artillery of London on Parade

Edison © H36946 Oct. 20, 1903
Location: Boston *Photographed:* Oct. 15, 1903
58 ft. FLA4958 (print) FRA0065 (neg.)

The "Ancient & Honourables" is the name given to the volunteer home guard that has guarded the city of London from intruders from the sea for almost a thousand years.

See also: Ancient & Honourables of London Homeward Bound, and The Honourable Artillery Company of London

Ancient and Honourables of London Homeward Bound

Edison © H36947 Oct. 20, 1903
Location: Boston *Photographed:* Oct. 15, 1903
51 ft. FLA4469 (print) FRA0066 (neg.)

The single camera position is on the dockside. Small tugs warping a large transport alongside the dock are shown. Good film on dockside in the early years of the century.

See also: Ancient and Honourable Artillery of London on Parade, and The Honourable Artillery Company of London

And a Little Child Shall Lead Them

AM&B © H123958 Mar. 13, 1909
Director: D. W. Griffith *Cameraman:* G. W. Bitzer
Cast: Arthur Johnson, Marion Leonard
Location: Studio, N.Y.C. *Photographed:* Feb. 22 and 24, 1909
141 ft. FLA4415 (print) FRA0067 (neg.)

The three important scenes of this melodrama were filmed on two different sets: one is a child's bedroom and the other is the living room of a house requiring at least four servants. The film takes place after the illness and death of a child, and shows the incompatibility of the husband and wife as they bicker. The husband (Arthur Johnson) and wife (Marion Leonard) attempt to establish by gestures that they not only do not like one another but have also lost interest in their remaining child, a little girl. The scene before the final one shows the husband and wife irritated with one another after a squabble, while the little girl, toy in hand, tries to interest one of her parents in playing with her. The final scenes show that the persistence of the child, and her personality, has overshadowed the parents' feelings, and the film ends with the father and mother embracing with the child between them.

And Pat Took Him at His Word

AM&B © H40816 Jan. 12, 1904
Cameraman: A. E. Weed
Location: Studio, N.Y.C. *Photographed:* Jan. 5, 1904
28 ft. FLA3665 (print) FRA0918 (neg.)

The film opens on a backdrop painted as a liquor store where all sorts of alcoholic liquors are for sale. A man is carrying a large sign extolling free lunch and Meyer's beer for three cents a mug. He leans the sign against the window of the liquor store and obscures the advertisement on the window. A man dressed in a top hat and a tailcoat and carrying a cane comes by and reads the sign. Judging by his gestures, he loses his temper, hits the sign carrier over the head with his cane, and proceeds to tear the sign to bits.

An Animated Luncheon

Edison © D4731 Feb. 28, 1900
25 ft. FLA4168 (print) FRA0069 (neg.)

A waiter is sitting at a table in the immediate foreground of a set of a restaurant. A well-dressed young woman and a man wearing a top hat and tails enter and are seated at the table by the waiter. During the remainder of the film, stop action photography is employed to cause objects to move from place to place. The hats of the two diners leave their heads and deposit themselves on the fireplace mantel. Then two pigeons appear from the sugar bowl placed on the table by the waiter. As the film ends, the young lady and her escort reach for their teacups and the cups are transformed into white rabbits which they place on the floor to allow them to hop about.

Animated Painting

Edison © H42209 Feb. 16, 1904
Cameraman: Edwin S. Porter
Location: Studio, N.Y.C. *Photographed:* Feb. 12, 1904
30 ft. FLA4002 (print) FRA0070 (neg.)

An artist is sitting in his studio painting a picture of the sun as it either sets or rises. As soon as the painting is complete, he puts down his brushes. To his amazement, the sun in his painting starts not only to rise from behind the horizon, but also to spin, and it rises and spins until it is higher than the easel itself. The artist throws his painting into a bucket of water, where it explodes.

Animated Picture Studio

AM&B © H38401 Nov. 20, 1903
80 ft. FLA4470 (print) FRA0071 (neg.)

The picture opens in a photographic studio, the walls of which are lined with mounted photographs. A camera on a tripod stands on the floor. The camera closely resembles and probably is a French Gaumont, known in Great Britain as a Prestwich. A photographer and his assistant are busying themselves about the studio when a lovely young lady enters. She removes her cloak and begins to dance. While the assistant operates the camera, the photographer embraces the dancer and encourages her to sit on his knee. The film is then projected into a picture frame which the outraged dancer hurls to the floor. Much to her chagrin, miniature images of herself and the photographer continue to move. The dancer has been identified as Isadora Duncan by several dance authorities. The film was made in Great Britain and purchased by AM&B for distribution in the United States.

The Animated Poster
Edison © H37395 Oct. 28, 1903
Cameraman: Edwin S. Porter
Location: Studio, N.Y.C. *Photographed:* Oct. 20, 1903
44 ft. FLA4471 (print) FRA0072 (neg.)

This is a peep show farce showing a man putting up a poster advertising a burlesque show. The poster is in three sections and as the third or bottom section is pasted on the wall, the top part is removed by stop action. A woman is substituted for the head and shoulders shown on the poster.

Anna Held
AM&B © H16386 Apr. 12, 1902
Cameraman: F. S. Armitage
Location: Roof studio, N.Y.C. *Date:* May 24, 1901
24 ft. FLA4472 (print) FRA0073 (neg.)

A one-quarter view of Anna Held drinking a glass of champagne during a photographic interview.

Annual Baby Parade, 1904, Asbury Park, N.J.
Edison © H50382 Sept. 12, 1904
Cameraman: A. C. Abadie
Location: Asbury Park N.J. *Photographed:* Aug. 31, 1904
157 ft. FLA4416 (print) FRA0074 (neg.)

Some small boys dressed in policemen's uniforms approach the camera, which was located on a pier. In the background are amusement stands, concessions, etc., decorated with bunting and flags, indicating a public event of some sort. Following the small boys is an assortment of baby carriages and perambulators decorated with flags, bunting, or crepe paper. The parade includes more than a hundred adults leading or escorting children in decorated baby carriages. The infant parade is followed by several horse-drawn floats.

Annual Parade, New York Fire Department
Edison © H46128 May 17, 1904
Cameraman: Edwin S. Porter
Location: N.Y.C. *Photographed:* May 14, 1904
115 ft. FLA4959 (print) FRA0075 (neg.)

Dignitaries are shown as they alight from a horse-drawn brougham and enter the speakers' bleachers. Next, personnel of the New York Fire Department walk by the camera. One of every piece of fire-fighting equipment then used by the department passes.

Another Job for the Undertaker
Edison © H4369 May 15, 1901
42 ft. FLA4473 (print) FRA0076 (neg.)

The film begins with the opening of a door facing the camera. A small boy and a bearded gentleman dressed as a "rube" come in. As the small boy, who plays the part of a bellboy, starts to leave, he is made to disappear by stop action photography. The remainder of the film conveys the idea that the old man dies because of the disappearance, piece by piece, of his umbrella, valise, hat, clothing, shoes, etc. The film ends with exterior pictures of a funeral procession headed by a hearse drawn by plumed horses and followed by three carriages of mourners.

Another Name Was Maude
AM&B © H76575 May 2, 1906
Cameraman: G. W. Bitzer [?]
Location: Laddin's Rock Farm [?] *Photographed:* Apr. 24, 1906 [?]
207 ft. FLA4417 (print) FRA0077 (neg.)

This film features a vaudeville team of a trained donkey and two comics, one the farmer type and the other the Happy Hooligan type. All the scenes were photographed outdoors in a barnyard. The action consists of the farmer's attempts to get rid of the obstreperous, stubborn little donkey who, when ridden or driven, apparently would go in circles or figure eights only. At no time is the farmer successful in making the donkey do anything except what it wants to do. The film ends abruptly when the farmer ties the donkey to a tree and blows it up with dynamite.

The Apparition, or Mr. Jones' Comical Experience with a Ghost
See: Le Revenant

Les Apparitions Fugitives
Méliès © H42523 Feb. 23, 1904
Cast: Georges Méliès
Location: Montreuil, France *Photographed:* Winter 1903–4
U.S. title: The Fugitive Apparitions
56 ft. FLA4422 (print) FRA0078 (neg.)

The scene opens on an elegantly appointed drawing room. M. Méliès, in dinner clothes, enters, makes two chairs appear, holds a piece of material in front of him and dissolves a woman into the scene. She sits on one chair and he on another. Both dissolve and reappear seated on different chairs. The picture continues with people transforming themselves into pieces of furniture, and it ends when M. Méliès causes himself to disappear through a picture frame.

Appointment by Telephone
Edison © H17675 May 15, 1902
48 ft. FLA4474 (print) FRA0079 (neg.)

The film begins in the office of a broker, where two men are engaged in office business. One makes a telephone call and then leaves. He is next seen waiting outside a restaurant. A woman approaches, he tips his hat, and they go inside. After they are seated at a table by a waiter, they become engrossed in one another. A woman in a large hat notices them through the window and enters the restaurant and begins beating the man. He falls to his knees and begs for forgiveness, while his female friend runs away.

An April Fool Joke
AM&B © H32494 June 11, 1903
Cameraman: F. S. Armitage
Location: Roof studio, N.Y.C. *Date:* June 7, 1901
21 ft. FLA3505 (print) FRA0080 (neg.)

This film begins on a set of a sidewalk in front of a wall with a grilled iron gate; there is a sky cyclorama in the background. Two men, dressed as boys, come through the gate and place a top hat with a brick under it on the sidewalk. The first passerby is a man with a top hat, frock coat, long black hair, and a mustache. He pauses by the silk hat, makes a pass as if he is a conjurer, picks it up and extracts several

pieces of jewelry from the interior, to the amazement of the watching boys. He replaces the hat, makes a few deft passes over it and proceeds on his way. The two pranksters, still amazed, start to pick up the hat but it explodes in their faces.

Arab Act, Luna Park

AM&B © H36553 Oct. 6, 1903
Cameraman: G. W. Bitzer
Location: Coney Island, N.Y. *Photographed:* Sept. 26, 1903
29 ft. FLA3815 (print) FRA0081 (neg.)

Photographed from a one-camera position, as if in the audience there are four tumblers performing for a crowd of customers in the midway of an entertainment area.

Arabian Gun Twirler

Edison © 20770 Mar. 20, 1899
26 ft. FLA4315 (print) FRA0082 (neg.)

The film, photographed from a one-camera position in the audience, shows a bearded man dressed in the costume of an Arab infantryman. He demonstrates his skill at twirling a standard army rifle in front of a painted backdrop on a stage.

Arabian Jewish Dance

Edison © H32802 June 17, 1903
Cameraman: A. C. Abadie
Location: Beirut, Syria *Photographed:* Mar. 13, 1903
33 ft. FLA4475 (print) FRA0083 (neg.)

The photographer filmed a group of people in a circle around an area in which six men are dancing to the accompaniment of a tune played on a musical instrument resembling a flute. The dancers are dressed in the costumes of Arabs and Jews at the turn of the century.

The Arbitrator

AM&B © H40742 Jan. 8, 1904
Cameraman: A. E. Weed
Location: Studio, N.Y.C. *Photographed:* Dec. 24, 1903
20 ft. FLA3768 (print) FRA0084 (neg.)

Two young men are sitting on a sofa in front of a painted backdrop. They appear to be having a heated discussion and rise to their feet and start hitting one another. From camera right, an elderly man, much shorter than either of the two boys, enters and attempts to break up the altercation. The remainder of the film concerns the indirect

Some trick shots from American Mutoscope & Biograph Company's The Animated Picture Studio (1903). The scene inside the picture frame is also a moving picture.

punishment inflicted on the arbitrator by the two boys as they accidentally hit him while trying to hit one another.

An Arcadian Maid

Biograph © J143884 Aug. 3, 1910

Director: D. W. Griffith *Cameraman:* G. W. Bitzer

Cast: Mary Pickford, Mack Sennett, Kate Bruce, George Nicholls

Location: Westfield, N.J.; Studio, N.Y.C. *Photographed:* June 22–23 and 25, 1910

397 ft. FLA4423 (print) FRA0085 (neg.)

A rural area can be seen with a path through a field. A pair of children walk away from the camera position. Between the children and the camera, entering from camera left, is the heroine (Mary Pickford), a servant girl seeking work. She has an interview with the farmer's wife (Kate Bruce), and then is seen hard at work. The villain (Mack Sennett) is an itinerant drygoods drummer who flatters her into believing she is something more than a farmer's serving maid. The drummer turns out to be a wastrel, a drunkard, and a thief. After his money has been dissipated and his creditors are pressing him, he influences the maid into stealing money from the farmer for him, promising her marriage. Instead of meeting her at their trysting place, he leaves town by train. The villain is thrown from the train because of his drunken, outrageous behavior. The servant accosts him, gets the stolen money and returns it to its place under the sleeping farmer's pillow. The last scene shows the servant girl fingering her beads and cross and praying.

The Armenian Archbishop, Rome

AM&B © H35646 Sept. 12, 1903

Location: Rome

19 ft. FLA3355 (print) FRA0661 (neg.)

This single camera position film shows a religious procession consisting of lay priests preceding the archbishop.

Armour's Electric Trolley

Edison © 43409 July 31, 1897

Location: Chicago

25 ft. FLA4027 (print) FRA0087 (neg.)

As the film begins, a large wall of a building can be seen in the background. Progressing from that wall toward the camera are train tracks. A small electric train pulling eight small four-wheeled flat cars, laden with boxes and barrels and labeled "Armour" approach the camera position.

Around New York in 15 Minutes

Paley & Steiner © H56326 Jan. 31, 1905

23 ft. FLA3671 (print) FRA0088 (neg.)

The film begins from a camera position over the heads of people waiting for the arrival of a large but unidentified ocean liner at the New York City docks. The film continues and, in small segments, shows various busy intersections. The length does not allow many points of interest to be seen.

Around the Flip-Flap Railroad

AM&B © H16733 Apr. 18, 1902

Cameraman: F. S. Armitage

Location: Coney Island, N.Y. *Photographed:* Sept. 18, 1900

21 ft. FLA3266 (print) FRA0089 (neg., copy 1) FRA0069 (neg., copy 2, incomplete)

The film shows a device that appears to be a railroad track that makes a loop and continues on. This was one of the most popular attractions at a beach resort. A small car with about ten occupants proceeds toward the camera position down the incline, up and over the loop and out of camera sight. Only one revolution of the amusement ride is shown.

Around the Mulberry Bush

AM&B © H21503 Sept. 5, 1902

Cameraman: Robert K. Bonine

Photographed: Aug. 4, 1902

22 ft. FLA3343 (print) FRA0090 (neg.)

The film appears to be of a lawn party attended by children. Holding hands, they form a circle about a baby boy barely able to stand. The children then go around in a circle.

Arrest in Chinatown, San Francisco, Cal.

Edison © 60596 Oct. 25, 1897

Location: San Francisco

27 ft. FLA4006 (print) FRA0091 (neg.)

A street scene in the business district of San Francisco was photographed. Two policemen with a Chinese coolie between them proceed toward the camera. The next camera position is a profile view of a horse-drawn vehicle labeled Police Department on the side. The Chinese man is seated in the wagon, and then the vehicle, with the two policemen who arrested him, starts up the street away from the camera.

Arrest of a Shoplifter

AM&B © H35649 Sept. 12, 1903

Cameraman: Arthur Marvin

Photographed: July 16, 1900

35 ft. FLA3568 (print) FRA0092 (neg.)

The first scene takes place in an outside set of a department store, lighted by the sun, with many people in front of the camera. One woman carrying a large bag removes articles from the counter and stuffs them into the bag. Although she is not aware of it, the house detective has her under surveillance and as she starts out the door, he apprehends her.

Arrival of Emigrants [i.e. Immigrants], Ellis Island

AM&B © H77049 May 9, 1906

Cameraman: G. W. Bitzer

Location: Ellis Island, N.Y. *Photographed:* Apr. 27, 1906

87 ft. FLA4960 (print) FRA2841 (neg., copy 1) FRA6402 (neg., copy 2)

The opening scenes were photographed from a waterfront dock where a boat arrived with recently admitted immigrants. The next camera position is a profile of the passengers going down the gangway for their first step on American soil. The third camera position shows them with their luggage boarding streetcars to their destinations.

Arrival of McKinley's Funeral Train at Canton, Ohio

Edison © H9082 Sept. 26, 1901

Location: Canton, Ohio *Photographed:* Sept. 16, 1901 [?]

24 ft. FLA3997 (print) FRA0095 (neg.)

It is apparent that the camera was placed on a platform of a train station. A steam locomotive pulling several passenger cars can be seen nearing the camera position and coming to a stop. The remainder of the film is concerned with the people who get off the train and walk off the platform.

Arrival of Prince Henry [of Prussia] and President Roosevelt at Shooter's Island

Edison © H14607 Mar. 1, 1902

Location: Townsend and Downey Ship Building Co., Shooter's Island, N.Y. *Photographed:* Feb. 25, 1902

47 ft. FLA4476 (print) FRA0096 (neg.)

The film records the arrival of a foreign dignitary of sufficient stature for President Theodore Roosevelt to personally meet him. The camera was positioned on a pier and Prince Henry, President Roosevelt, and Mr. Wallace Downey with their immediate entourage approach the camera position, pass it, and continue on. The remainder of the film shows the welcoming committee of dignitaries and the honor guard of U.S. Navy and Army personnel.

Arrival of the Governor General, Lord Minto, at Quebec

Edison © H14291 Feb. 17, 1902

Location: Quebec

49 ft. FLA4477 (print) FRA0097 (neg.)

Approximately fifty men are hauling a landing boat about fifty yards over ice and snow. Inside the boat are a warmly dressed man and two women. There is no way of identifying these individuals from the picture.

Arrival of Tokyo Train

Edison © 38208 June 26, 1898

Cameraman: James H. White

Location: Tokyo

26 ft. FLA3106 (print) FRA0093 (neg.)

The arrival of a train of cars was photographed from a single camera position located on the platform of a railroad station. A small engine, hooked to another engine, comes along, and behind them are many passenger cars. The long train comes to a stop. Passengers can be seen through the windows, as well as some people waiting on the station platform.

Arrival of Train at Muskoka Wharf

AM&B © H29004 Mar. 6, 1903

Cameraman: G. W. Bitzer

Location: Lake Muskoka, Ont. [?], Canada *Date:* Aug. 13, 1900

45 ft. FLA4478 (print) FRA0098 (neg.)

The film is concerned with the arrival and departure of a large lake steamer and a railroad train. The camera was positioned at the end of a dock above the heads of the people who come off the train and embark on the boat. Most of the activity that can be seen is on the dock area between the train and the boat. The distance does not permit definite identification.

Arrival of Train, Cheyenne

AM&B © H32294 May 29, 1903

Cameraman: G. W. Bitzer

Location: Cheyenne, Wyo. *Date:* July 5, 1901

25 ft. FLA3653 (print) FRA0099 (neg.)

The camera was positioned at a place above the railroad station platform to include a portion of the railroad station that faced the railroad tracks. A locomotive pulling a string of passenger cars can be seen approaching and there are many people on the platform awaiting its arrival. As the train nears the camera position, it comes to a full stop. Scenes follow of the loading and unloading of the baggage, and of the passengers getting on or off.

Arrival of Train, Tien-Tsin

AM&B © H18044 May 23, 1902

Cameraman: Robert K. Bonine

Location: Tien-Tsin, China *Date:* Sept. 1901

16 ft. FLA3339 (print) FRA0100 (neg.)

The camera was located above the platform in a railway station, looking down on the track. Approaching the camera position is a locomotive pulling several freight cars, passenger cars, etc. Many people are on the platform awaiting the arrival of the train.

Arrival of Train, Tokio, Japan

AM&B © H36867 Oct. 19, 1903

Cameraman: Robert K. Bonine

Location: Tokyo *Date:* July 26, 1901

17 ft. FLA3297 (print) FRA0101 (neg.)

The camera was positioned to encompass all of the platform area adjacent to the arrival track of the station. In the background are train sheds, the arrival platform covering, and brick buildings of more than one story in height. Orientals in a variety of dress crisscross in front of the camera. Some man-propelled means of transportation also can be seen. These include rickshas, messenger services, etc.

Arriving at Police Station

See: The Kleptomaniac

Arriving at Police Station in Patrol Wagon

See: The Kleptomaniac

Arriving at Store

See: The Kleptomaniac

The Art of Making Up

AM&B © H16726 Apr. 18, 1902

Cameraman: Arthur Marvin

Cast: Kathryn Osterman

Location: Roof studio, N.Y.C. *Date:* May 24, 1900

25 ft. FLA3264 (print) FRA0103 (neg.)

A single camera position shows a woman sitting at a table on which there are several jars. She holds a large mirror in her left hand and is engaged in making up her face, her eyelashes, and her mouth, using the contents of the jars and bottles on the table. The photography was made possible by artificial lighting.

Art Studies

AM&B © H29003 Mar. 6, 1903

Cameraman: F.S. Armitage

Date: Nov. 20, 1900

21 ft. FLA3522 (print) FRA0104 (neg.)

The complete film was photographed from one camera position. The only scene is of two men sitting at a table and turning the pages of a magazine. It is evident from their grimaces and gestures that the pictures they see are risqué.

The Artist's Dilemma
Edison © H11475 Dec. 14, 1901
Cameraman: Edwin S. Porter
57 ft. FLA4479 (print) FRA0105 (neg.)

The first scene is of a set representing an artist's studio. There are an easel and other artist's paraphernalia. A man with a flowing tie and beret is sitting on a stool. A door opens and an attractively gowned young woman enters. The artist escorts her to a position, turns to his easel and begins to paint. At that moment, a man dressed as a clown enters carrying a bucket. He looks around, and sees the easel and the young woman. He gestures to the artist, goes to the easel and with a large brush paints off the dark color. A picture of the young female model emerges. The clown holds up his hand to the picture and a very much alive young woman steps out of the portrait and begins to dance. She is joined by the original model. As the artist touches one of the dancing figures, it disappears. He then makes a lunge for the other and it also disappears but is immediately replaced by the body of the clown. The picture ends the way it opened, with the artist sitting on his stool in repose.

An Artist's Dream
Edison © D6369 Mar. 21, 1900
Cameraman: Edwin S. Porter
33 ft. FLA4176 (print) FRA0106 (neg.)

The whole of this film is devoted to fantasy and the use of stop action photography to create the illusion of the appearance and disappearance of people and objects. The beginning shows two large picture frames in which there are two young women instead of paintings. There is also a man dressed as an artist who seems surprised at his ability to bring life or movement to his subjects by mere admiration. The film is completely dedicated to the actions of the artist, who causes the models to appear and disappear. The film ends when everything is put right and the artist is back to being a mere artist again.

The Artist's Dream
AM&B © H28555 Feb. 24, 1903
Cameraman: F.S. Armitage
Location: Roof studio, N.Y.C. *Date:* July 14, 1899
17 ft. FLA3170 (print) FRA0107 (neg.)

An artist is painting a picture of a woman clothed in a full-length leotard, but he appears weary and falls asleep. By either stop action photography or a quick dissolve, the full figure of the woman is changed to a similarly costumed one with the skeleton visible. The artist wakes as though from a bad dream and the skeleton is transformed back again into an attractive woman.

See also: His Masterpiece

Artist's Point
AM&B © H31668 May 11, 1903
Cameraman: Robert K. Bonine
Location: Yosemite Valley, Calif. *Date:* Nov. 15, 1901
15 ft. FLA3409 (print) FRA0108 (neg.)

A view of scenic grandeur amid rugged hills is shown. The camera pans for at least 180 degrees to show mountain crags, forests, stands of timber, glacial scars on the mountainside, etc. The film was photographed in the Yosemite Valley.

The Artist's Studio
AM&B © H32295 May 29, 1903
Cameraman: G.W. Bitzer
Location: Roof studio, N.Y.C
25 ft. FLA3638 (print) FRA0109 (neg.)

The film begins in an artist's studio. There is an easel, and a woman in a smock is working at it. A man in evening clothes comes in. The artist indicates he is to take a position on bended knee, with his hand on his heart, as if proposing. Another man comes in and becomes upset at seeing them. The film ends as the artist introduces the model to the third man, who sits down and watches while she continues painting.

As In a Looking Glass
AM&B © H32297 May 29, 1903
Cameraman: F.S. Armitage
Photographed: May 21, 1903
34 ft. FLA3603 (print) FRA0110 (neg.)

The film was photographed from one camera position as if in the audience. It shows two rooms, in one of which an old man sits in a rocking chair. A chest of drawers and a mirror on the wall separate the two rooms. A teen-age boy runs a cord or string from the drawer in the bureau through the wall to the back of the rocking chair and arranges it so that when the drawer is opened, the chair will be pulled over. A woman enters, opens the drawer and causes the chair to thump over, spilling out the old man.

As It Is In Life
Biograph © J140186 Apr. 6, 1910
Director: D. W. Griffith *Cameraman:* G. W. Bitzer
Cast: George Nicholls, Gladys Egan, Mack Sennett, Marion Leonard, Mary Pickford, William J. Butler, Charles West, Tony O'Sullivan, Kate Bruce
Location: Los Angeles *Photographed:* Feb. 22–23, 1910
392 ft. FLA5250 (print) FRA0111 (neg.)

This film is built around the actions of an unhappy widower (George Nicholls) who feels that his daughter should not marry and leave him alone after he had sacrificed love to bring up his motherless daughter. The film begins as he bids farewell to an old girl friend (Marion Leonard) and returns to his pigeon farm and his child (Gladys Egan). The child grows up (played now by Mary Pickford), comes home from school, almost at once falls in love, and wants to leave her father. In spite of her father's objection, she marries her suitor (Charles West), has a child, and wins back her father by putting the infant in his lap. The last scene shows their reunion and the man's pride in his new grandchild. Most of the film was photographed on a pigeon farm in the arroyo of the Los Angeles River.

As Seen On the Curtain
AM&B © H41044 Jan. 20, 1904
Cameraman: A. E. Weed

Location: Studio, N.Y.C. *Photographed:* Dec. 30, 1903
25 ft. FLA3595 (print) FRA0112 (neg.)

The exterior of a house with a window is seen. A scantily attired woman comes to the window, looks all around, and then pulls down the window shade. She then proceeds to dress, as shown in silhouette on the shade.

As the Bells Rang Out

Biograph © J143501 July 23, 1910
Director: D. W. Griffith *Cameraman:* G.W. Bitzer
Cast: Charles West, Eddie Dillon, George Nicholls, Verner Clarges, Mack Sennett, Grace Henderson, Dell Henderson, Gertrude Robinson, Charles Craig, Gladys Egan, Adele De Garde, Stephanie Longfellow, Alfred Paget
Location: Studio, N.Y.C. *Photographed:* June 18, 1910
199 ft. FLA4424 (print) FRA0113 (neg.)

The scenes in this film, following in rapid succession, are of the father and his co-conspirators (described in the preceding title as stockbrokers), his daughter meeting her fiance, one of the engaged couples with the girl's father, another showing the police wanting to take the dishonest father away (a cutaway from the wedding preparations), and the final scene of the wedding with the police leading the father off in handcuffs.

Asakusa Temple, Tokio, Japan

AM&B © H36868 Oct. 19, 1903
Cameraman: Robert K. Bonine
Location: Tokyo *Date:* Sept. 27, 1901
17 ft. FLA3121 (print) FRA0114 (neg.)

The view of the Asakusa Temple in Tokyo was photographed from across the main thoroughfare leading to the entrance at a distance of about two hundred yards. The idols protecting the entrance can be seen, as well as the entrance to the main building itself, but the full outline profile is not shown. Several individuals in various types of Japanese clothing pass in front of the camera.

Asia in America, St. Louis Exposition

AM&B © H46575 May 28, 1904
Cameraman: A. E. Weed
Location: St. Louis, Mo. *Photographed:* May 20, 1904
31 ft. FLA3673 (print) LFRA0115 (neg.)

The film begins with a wide shot of an area crowded with people, some riding an elephant, others marching in procession in front of a structure with the sign "Asia" on it. The people are wearing various costumes.

Assembling a Generator, Westinghouse Works

See: Westinghouse Works

Assembling and Testing Turbines, Westinghouse Works

See: Westinghouse Works

Astor Battery On Parade

Edison © 8651 Jan. 27, 1899
Location: N.Y.C.
20 ft. FLA3022 (print) FRA0116 (neg.)

The lead-off color guard of a military regiment can be seen heading a parade that consists of several companies of army reserves. The men, in company-front order, march past the camera position. Included in the parade are a group of officers on horseback and a band in uniform. The parade appears to have been held on lower Broadway in New York City.

The Astor Tramp

Edison © 77520 Nov. 27, 1899
46 ft. FLA4480 (print) FRA0117 (neg.)

There are two sets in this film; one of a very plush bedroom and the other of a sidewalk in front of the building. As the film begins, a tramp is pacing up and down the floor of the bedroom. He poses, looks at himself in the mirror, sprays on some perfume and then proceeds to retire to the bed. The lady of the house, accompanied by her maid, enters the bedroom, sees the tramp and calls the police who throw the tramp into the street. The film ends as the tramp takes a newspaper away from a small boy, refuses to pay him, and kicks at him. He is seen gesturing as if something he is reading in the stolen paper upsets him. This film was offered with words and music or without either.

At the Altar

AM&B © H123389 Feb. 26, 1909
Director: D.W. Griffith *Cameraman:* Arthur Marvin, G. W. Bitzer
Cast: Linda Arvidson, John Cumpson, Mack Sennett, Dorothy West, Clara T. Bracey, Herbert Yost, Robert Harron, Harry Salter, Arthur Johnson, D.W. Griffith, Marion Leonard, Florence Lawrence, Kate Bruce, James Kirkwood
Location: Edgewater, N.J.; Studio, N.Y.C. *Photographed:* Jan.30 and Feb. 8, 1909
383 ft. FLA4425 (print) FRA0120 (neg.)

The picture starts with an engagement party attended by the villain, a rejected suitor. He designs a device to murder the bridal couple as they are about to be married and installs it in the foot platform of the church. (There is an excellent close-up of the triggering device, which adds to audience understanding of the action.) While the bride and groom and their guests are in church, the rejected suitor commits suicide and leaves a confession note. When it is discovered, a policeman starts off for church to warn the couple, but he falls several times en route and arrives exhausted, barely in time to avert the murder. Mack Sennett plays two parts: one of the suitors and a policeman.

At the Crossroads of Life

See: Crossroads of Life

At the Dressmaker's

AM&B © H36557 Oct. 6, 1903
Cameraman: G. W. Bitzer
Location: Studio, N.Y.C. *Photographed:* Sept. 21, 1903
25 ft. FLA3099 (print) FRA0118 (neg.)

The subject matter of this naughty but nice comedy was built around the possibility that if one looked, perhaps an unclothed or a semiclothed woman could be seen. The set had a full-length mirror set at angles to the camera. A dressmaker is examining the fit of a dress of a female customer. The customer removes her dress for alteration and remains in front of the mirror while scantily clad. The picture ends as a messenger boy enters, frightening away the young customer. He is promptly ousted from the dressmaker's establishment for his impertinence.

At the Foot of the Flatiron

AM&B © H37499 Nov. 2, 1903
Cameraman: A. E. Weed
Location: Broadway and 23rd Street, N.Y.C. *Photographed:* Oct. 26, 1903
61 ft. FLA 4963 (print) FRA0119 (neg.)

The single camera position, at the foot of the building and at a diagonal of the front of the building, shows a large window with a display of merchandise. Between the camera position and the store front, many persons of various descriptions pass by. It is an excessively windy day.

At the Fountain

AM&B © H22093 Sept. 27, 1902
Cameraman: Robert K. Bonine
Location: N.Y.C.[?] *Date:* Aug. 4, 1902
19 ft. FLA3836 (print) FRA0121 (neg.)

The film was photographed from a single camera position. Six children ranging in age from three to twelve hold hands while wading in a pool that surrounds a cobblestone fountain about six feet high. They dance around the fountain.

At the French Ball

AM&B © H112127 June 20, 1908
Director: Wallace McCutcheon *Cameraman:* G. W. Bitzer
Cast: D. W. Griffith, Eddie Dillon, Robert Harron
Location: Studio, N.Y.C. *Photographed:* May 28–29, 1908
247 ft. FLA4429 (print, copy 1) FLA5974 (print, copy 2) FRA0123 (neg.)

At the French Ball is a comedy about a husband, played by D. W. Griffith, and wife, who are caught in the toils of their own deceit when both attend the same masquerade ball in costume without telling the other and each accidentally becomes aware of the other's true identity. The same split set idea used in The Great Jewel Mystery in 1905 of placing a timber vertically to simulate a wall dividing two rooms, permitting simultaneous independent action, is utilized here. There are also three head-and-shoulder close-ups of each of the principals, one of whom was Griffith. The paper copy bore the title Over the Hills to the Poorhouse, but it is definitely At the French Ball.

See: Over the Hills to the Poorhouse

At Work

See: The Kidnapper

The Athletic Girl and the Burglar, no. 1

AM&B © H60295 May 3, 1905
Cameraman: G.W. Bitzer
Location: Studio, N.Y.C. *Photographed:* Apr. 26, 1905
42 ft. FLA4481 (print) FRA0125 (neg.)

The film was photographed from a single camera position. The first scene takes place on a set of the interior of a house with some gymnasium equipment visible on the wall. The door opens and a woman enters, removes her hat and coat, and begins doing calisthenics with the wall pulleys, weights, and hand barbells. She continues her exercises by reclining on the floor. While she is in this position, a man dressed in the rough clothing of burglar appears. The woman interrupts her calisthenics and proceeds to beat the burglar into insensibility. Instead of calling the police, she calmly returns to her exercises.

The Athletic Girl and the Burglar, no. 2

AM&B © H60296 May 3, 1905
Cameraman: G. W. Bitzer
Location: Studio, N.Y.C. *Photographed:* Apr. 26, 1905
27 ft. FLA4049 (print) FRA0126 (neg.)

A set of part of a bedroom and living room of a modest house can be seen as the film begins. A rather large woman enters through a door, walks to the next room and removes her first two layers of clothing. She then walks over to a spring-and-pulley exercise machine on the wall. She proceeds to do several exercises with the machine. When she completes the course, she stretches out on the floor and begins doing leg exercises. A man dressed as a burglar is seen stealthily approaching. The woman is startled, but picks up a barbell and beats the burglar into insensibility. She leaves him lying prone on the floor, presumably unconscious, as she nonchalantly continues with her exercises.

Atlantic City Fire Department

AM&B © H17043 Apr. 26, 1902
Photographed: Aug. 1897[?]
20 ft. FLA3869 (print) FRA0127 (neg.)

The film shows a public demonstration of the fire-fighting apparatus available to the citizens in Atlantic City, New Jersey. The camera was placed on a street and, as the equipment approached the camera position, as much film as possible was run through the camera. On the opposite side of the street, many people are watching the demonstration.

Atlantic City Floral Parade

Percival L. Waters © H47449 June 22, 1904
Location: Atlantic City, N.J.
50 ft. FLA4482 (print) FRA0128 (neg.)

The picture was photographed from a single camera position and, as it begins, crowds of people can be seen lining the boardwalk watching small floral floats being pulled or pushed past the camera position. Two uniformed bands go by and one unidentifiable fraternal order.

An Attack by Torpedo Boats

AM&B © H30184 Apr. 4, 1903
15 ft. FLA3643 (print) FRA0129 (neg.)

This film was photographed from a single camera position and shows six steam-driven torpedo boats passing the camera. Three of the ships fire torpedos. The ships are approximately 150 feet long and less than 500 tons.

See also: A Flying Wedge

Attack on Fort Boonesboro

AM&B © H79819 June 23, 1906
Cameraman: G. W. Bitzer
Location: Louisville, Ky. *Photographed:* June 15, 1906
152 ft. FLA4964 (print) FRA1952 (neg.)

The film concerns a historic event in Kentucky. The cameraman placed his camera high above the locale of the reconstructed historic site. In and around the fort and its compound are approximately one hundred people, some dressed as American frontiersmen, and others dressed as Indians. They seem to be getting instructions on what to do. The remainder of the film shows a sham battle between those inside the fort and the Indians outside. All of the persons comport themselves generally as if they were at a picnic or public gathering.

The Attack on Port Arthur
Selig © H43183 Mar. 12, 1904
17 ft. FLA3931 (print) FRA0131 (neg.)
[Russo-Japanese War]

The poor condition and short length of the film make it difficult to describe the action. However, it is possible to see some miniature ships floating on a table-top lake and moving back and forth.

Attempt to Escape That Led to Misfortune
AM&B © H33418 July 13, 1903
Cameraman: Raymond Ackerman
Date: July 9, 1899
20 ft. FLA3544 (print) FRA0132 (neg.)

Two people can be seen sitting and embracing on a sofa in a drawing room. A window opens and an intruder enters and frightens the man away from the sofa. The man climbs up the chimney. The intruder places a dynamite stick in the fire, and the ensuing explosion brings the cowardly man back into the room in tatters. The commotion draws two other people, both of whom are hysterical.

Au Clair de la Lune
Méliès © H40879 Jan. 15, 1904
Cast: Georges Méliès.
Location: Montreuil, France
U.S. title: A Moonlight Serenade; or The Miser Punished.
Original title: Au Clair de la Lune ou Pierrot malheureux.
106 ft. FLA4483 (print) FRA0133 (neg.)

This Georges Méliès spectacular begins in a garden where a man costumed a Pierrot sings through the next twenty feet of film while seated on the ground beside a tree. A backdrop lighted by indirect lighting appears and moves from left to right across the stage. A new moon, in double exposure, can be seen in the sky. As the superimposed moon comes closer, a reclining woman is dissolved into it and, again using stop action, the clown jumps up into the moon to join the woman. There are several additional trick-camera effects, including one extreme close-up of a human eye double exposed over the top of a traveling matte.

L'Auberge du Bon Repos
See: The Inn Where No Man Rests

Aunt Jane and the Tobasco [sic] Sauce.
AM&B © H18747 June 7, 1902
10 ft. FLA4443 (print) FRA0134 (neg.)

A man dressed as an old woman is sitting at a small table and being served a dish of food by a waiter. During the course of the meal, the food is heavily seasoned with Tabasco, so that the woman gasps for breath. The waiter helpfully squirts soda water from a bottle into the woman's open mouth.

Aunt Jane's Experience with Tobasco [sic] Sauce
AM&B © H27772 Jan. 30, 1903
Cameraman: F. S. Armitage
Date: Nov. 9, 1900
11 ft. FLA3353 (print) FRA0135 (neg.)

A man dressed as a waiter brings a plate of food to a woman seated at a table in a set of a restaurant. The woman tastes the food, indicates it lacks something and the waiter leaves to get it. He returns with a bottle of Tabasco sauce which the woman shakes vigorously over her food. After sampling the concoction, it is evident from her facial expression that she has made a terrible mistake, and the film ends with the waiter squirting seltzer water in her mouth.

Aunt Sallie's Wonderful Bustle
Edison © H7640 Aug. 14, 1901
Cameraman: Edwin S. Porter
19 ft. FLA4234 (print) FRA0136 (neg.)

A man and a woman are walking on a set of a bridge. The woman is gesturing and apparently describing the grandeur of the sight below her. She loses her balance and falls over the wall, landing on the stones beneath. By the use of reverse camera action, it appears as if she lands on her bustle and bounces back up to the bridge. The film ends as the woman, who is actually a man dressed as a woman, is being soothed after her fall.

Auto Boat Race on the Hudson
AM&B © H47332 June 18, 1904
Cameraman: G. W. Bitzer
Location: Columbia Yacht Club, Hudson River, N.Y.C.
Photographed: June 11, 1904
68 ft. FLA4965 (print) FRA0137 (neg.)

The single camera position was from the point of view of the judge of the course. The film shows a boat race between small, motor-driven speed boats, which were approximately twenty feet long with the inboard engine decked over. Many boats of various designs and spectators can be seen as if the locale were a yacht club basin or yacht mooring. Participants in the race were W. K. Vanderbilt, Jr.'s *Hard Boiled Egg; The Standard,* which won the championship and had never been beaten; the *Vingt et Un;* the *F.I.A.T.;* the *Shooting Star;* the *Japansky,* the *Kotic,* and the *Nada.*

The Automatic Weather Prophet
Edison © H2475 Mar. 21, 1901
32 ft. FLA3655 (print) FRA0138 (neg., copy 1) FRA0909 (neg., copy 2)

This is an attempt at comedy. Two small boys have constructed a device over a fence camouflaged by a poster. A rose is painted on the poster as well as the words "The Automatic Weather Prophet." As the film progresses, three people are intrigued by the sign. One is a large fat man who attempts to catch the two boys but is unable to get through the narrow slot in the fence. The other two men also receive red paint through a squirt mechanism behind the rose as well as a punch in the nose from a boxing glove on a pole.

Automobile Parade

Edison © D3293 Feb. 6, 1900

Location: N.Y.C.

51 ft. FLA4484 (print) FRA0139 (neg.)

A parade of automobiles is photographed from a single camera position as they drive by the camera. At least ten different makes and models of the era are shown.

Automobile Parade on the Coney Island Boulevard

Edison © H10870 Nov. 29, 1901

Location: Brooklyn, N.Y.

52 ft. FLA4485 (print) FRA0140 (neg.)

This film, taken from a single camera position, shows a parade of approximately thirty automobiles of different types approaching the camera.

Automobile Race for the Vanderbilt Cup

AM&B © H51702 Oct. 17, 1904

Cameraman: G. W. Bitzer, A. E. Weed

Location: Long Island, N.Y. *Photographed:* Oct. 8,1904

80 ft. FLA4966 (print) FRA0141 (neg.)

This automobile race was filmed from many camera positions. Several different types of motor cars from all parts of the world are seen. A series of interconnecting roads was used as the racecourse.

Automobiling Among the Clouds

AM&B © H51121 Oct. 1, 1904

Cameraman: G. W. Bitzer

Location: Mt. Washington, N.H. *Photographed:* July 11, 12, 14 and 15, 1904

220 ft. FLA4430 (print) FRA0142 (neg.)

The terrain, as the film begins, is mountainous and a narrow, undulating road ascending the mountain can be seen. The first visible action consists of an automobile with black-and-white numbers traveling toward the camera. The remainder of the film is devoted to automobiles either ascending or descending the road at high speeds. The title does not indicate that this is a race.

The Auto-somnambulist

The Winthrop Press © H75818 Apr. 18, 1906

9 ft.

The Winthrop Press sent in only a few frames of their products for copyrighting. Therefore, not even a cursory description of this film is possible.

Avenging a Crime, or Burned at the Stake

Paley & Steiner © H53418 Nov. 19. 1904

51 ft. FLA4486 (print) FRA1562 (neg.)

The film was set in a rural community. The first scene shows four men shooting dice in front of a grocery store. The next scene is of a man struggling with a woman whom he chokes to death. The following scenes are the townspeople being notified of the discovery of the body, the organization of a posse, the escape of the villain, and his apprehension by the mob. The picture ends as the mob is about to lynch him.

The Aviator's Generosity

Great Northern © Oes J168002-168003 Apr. 10, 1912

Director: Urban Gad. Author: Christian Nobel.

Cast: Poul Reumert, Einar Zangenberg, Christel Holck, Ellen Kornbeck.

Date: June 1, 1911

Produced in Denmark by Nordisk Film Co. *Danish title:* Flyveren og Journalistens Hustru

821 ft. FLA5892 (print, copy 1) FLA5916 (print, copy 2) FRA2725 (neg.)

This one-reel film encompasses most of the camera effects later considered mandatory for a film to be a success. The plot combines the poor but honest boy, the self-sacrifice of a daughter, the greed of a rich man, the benevolence of another who sees the error of his ways, and the newest suspense device available—the airplane. There are unusual in flight shots of the Glent, built by Danish pioneer aviator Robert Svendsen.

The Awakening

Biograph © J132453 Oct, 2 1909

Director: D. W. Griffith *Cameraman:* G. W. Bitzer

Cast: Arthur Johnson, Mary Pickford, Owen Moore, Florence Lawrence, Kate Bruce, Tony O'Sullivan, Mack Sennett

Location: Edgewater, N.J.; Studio, N.Y.C. *Photographed:* Aug. 16, 17 and 20, 1909

248 ft. FLA4431 (print) FRA0145 (neg.)

The leading man (Arthur Johnson) is a member of an officer's club, where he is seen doing considerable drinking. In the next scene, he signs a contract and is introduced to a young lady (Mary Pickford); they are soon married. After the wedding, the new husband spends most of his time at the officer's club, ignoring his bride entirely. One day he sees her climbing a stone wall in an attempt to pick a flower growing there. She loses her footing, he catches her, and suddenly becomes aware of how lovely she is. The film ends as he is kissing her.

Awakening of Rip

See: Rip Van Winkle

An Awful Moment

AM&B © H119490 Dec. 10, 1908

Director: D. W. Griffith *Cameraman:* Arthur Marvin

Cast: Linda Arvidson, Marion Leonard, Kate Bruce, Adele De Garde, Dorothy West, Dorothy Bernard, Mack Sennett, Florence Barker

Location: Studio, N.Y.C. *Photographed:* Nov. 19, 1908

302 ft. FLA4413 (print) FRA0147 (neg.)

This is the story of a vindictive gypsy who attempts to get revenge on a judge for a jail sentence. After leaving the court, the gypsy enters the judge's home, finds his wife asleep, and gives her gas from an overhead lighting fixture. The gypsy then ties the judge's wife to a chair and arranges a shotgun with a string from its trigger to a doorknob, so that when the judge opens the door, he will trigger the gun and kill his wife. Fortunately, their small daughter awakens and removes the string from the doorknob just as the judge reaches for it. The film was photographed by Arthur Marvin in the studio and the exterior shots were taken on Fourteenth Street in New York City.

Babe and Puppies

Edison © H44669 Apr. 21, 1904
Cameraman: Edwin S. Porter
Location: Studio, N.Y.C. *Photographed:* Apr. 13, 1904
31 ft. FLA4129 (print) FRA0148 (neg.)

The film opens on a constructed set. Two infants, one standing and one seated, can be seen in front of the backdrop. The one standing goes off camera and immediately the seated infant is surrounded by a litter of puppies, attracted by something the seated child has in its hand. The child, besieged by still more puppies, stands up in obvious bewilderment.

The Babies' Quarrel

AM&B © H16350 Apr. 10, 1902
Cameraman: F. S. Armitage
Location: Roof Studio, N.Y.C. *Date:* July 24, 1899
18 ft. FLA4124 (print) FRA0149 (neg.)

This poorly lighted film shows two infants of opposite sex in high chairs facing each other. The little girl shows much displeasure, while the infant boy eats and ignores the tantrum.

Babies Rolling Eggs.

Edison © H16124 Apr. 7, 1902
Location: White House, Washington, D.C. *Photographed:* Mar. 31[?] 1902
33 ft. FLA3782 (print) FRA0150 (neg.)

Some small children in winter clothing face the camera in a semicircle. They throw what appear to be eggs down the incline toward the camera position. From left and right of the camera, a great number of young boys scramble for the eggs. Many close-ups and mass photographs of the activities are then shown.

The Baby

AM&B © H35396 Sept 4, 1903
Cameraman: A. E. Weed
Location: Studio, N.Y.C. *Photographed:* Aug. 21, 1903
21 ft. FLA4106 (print) FRA0151 (neg.)

The film was photographed from a single camera position. The subject is a baby in a decorated bassinet with a woman sitting beside it, gently rocking the bassinet. She picks up the baby, holds it tenderly, then puts it back. The film is badly lighted: everything is black but the woman, the baby and the bassinet.

The Baby

AM&B © H36654 Oct. 9, 1903
Cameraman: G. W. Bitzer
Location: Studio, N.Y.C. *Photographed:* Sept 19, 1903
25 ft. FLA3098 (print) FRA0152 (neg.)

The film, photographed from a single camera position lighted only from the front, shows a basket that has been converted into a bassinet. A young, well-dressed woman carrying an infant in her arms enters the scene from camera left, places the baby in the bassinet, and seats herself nearby. She rocks the bassinet and croons to the baby.

The Baby and the Puppies

AM&B © H48985 Aug. 9, 1904
Cameraman: G. W. Bitzer
Location: Seagate, Coney Island, N.Y. *Photographed:* Aug. 3, 1904
51 ft. FLA4487 (print) FRA0153 (neg.)

An infant sits on the sand, surrounded by at least ten puppies. The cameraman photographed only the child and the puppies.

Baby Class at Lunch

Edison © H35376 Sept. 3, 1903
Cameraman: Edwin S. Porter
Location: Coney Island, N.Y. *Photographed:* Aug. 10, 1903
52 ft. FLA4488 (print) FRA0154 (neg.)

Approximately a hundred children under the age of five are seated in rows on the steps of a building that is not shown. The children are drinking out of large mugs and eating what appears to be sandwiches or cookies. A man enters the scene. The children hand him their cups or mugs. With great difficulty, he walks out of camera range, carrying several mugs, while the children stand up, turn their backs to the camera, and start climbing up the stairs.

Baby in a Rage

AM&B © H21510 Sept. 5, 1902
Cameraman: G. W. Bitzer
Location: Roof studio, N.Y.C. *Date:* July 7, 1902
26 ft. FLA3955 (print) FRA0155 (neg.)

The film, photographed from a single camera position, shows an infant standing at the foot of a stair of what appears to be a house. He is removing objects from a basin and throwing them. A woman dressed as a housewife or a nurse enters and attempts to induce the baby to pick up the thrown objects. Her actions enrage the child, who turns toward the camera and throws the remainder of the objects in the basin. The woman picks things up while the baby screams and stamps his feet.

Baby Lund and Her Pets

AM&B © H32867 June 20, 1903
Cameraman: F. S. Armitage
Location: Detroit *Date:* July 6, 1899
17 ft. FLA4387 (print) FRA0156 (neg.)

The camera was placed close to the ground in what appears to be the backyard of a house. Two ponies tied to stakes appear, cropping the grass on which they are standing. The hind quarters of a large mastiff dog can be seen. A child carrying a basket enters from camera left and starts feeding her pets.

Baby Lund and Her Pets

AM&B © H33537 July 18, 1903
Cameraman: F. S. Armitage
Location: Detroit *Date:* July 6, 1899
16 ft. FLA4388 (print) FRA0157 (neg.)

A little girl with a basket on her arm is feeding a Shetland pony. She gives the pony something, turns about, reaches in the basket, and throws into the air some food that is caught by a large mastiff.

Baby Merry-Go-Round

AM&B © H33540 July 18, 1903

Location: Coney Island *Photographed:* 1898 [?]
27 ft. FLA3432 (print) FRA0158 (neg)

The film, photographed from a single camera position, shows a small eight-seat carousel located on the grounds of an amusement park. Small children are riding on the carousel, and behind it is the elaborately carved proscenium of a large merry-go-round.

Baby Playing in Gutter

AM&B © H21509 Sept. 5, 1902

Cameraman: G.W. Bitzer

Location: Roof studio, N.Y.C. *Date:* July 7, 1902

29 ft. FLA3893 (print) FRA0159 (neg.)

A baby sits on a curb with his feet in the gutter. He is industriously working with a small shovel to pick up sand from the gutter and put it into a paper bag.

The Baby Review

Edison © H35328 Sept. 1, 1903

Cameraman: A. C. Abadie

Location: Wilmington, Del. *Photographed:* Aug. 24, 1903

67 ft. FLA4489 (print) FRA0160 (neg.)

A band begins to play a tune. In the background are a lot of spectators. The next camera position shows a covered platform where several people are seated. Parents carry their children to the platform for judging in either a beauty or a costume contest.

Baby's Day

AM&B © H56068 Jan. 18, 1905

Cameraman: G. W. Bitzer

Location: Studio, N.Y.C. *Photographed:* "Various dates" Dec. 1904–Jan. 1905

436 ft. FLA4689 (print) FRA0161 (neg.)

The subject is a day in the life of an infant supervised by a nurse. The film illustrates the various tasks necessary to properly enhance the growth and security of a small child, such as awakening, supervised play, companionship with other children, exposure to sights and scenes other than those of a nursery, bathing, and sleeping. The cameraman moved his camera to better exemplify each situation.

A Baby's Shoe

AM&B © H126827 May 10, 1909

Director: D. W. Griffith *Cameramen:* G. W. Bitzer, Arthur Marvin

Cast: Florence Lawrence, Owen Moore, Linda Arvidson, Arthur Johnson, Mack Sennett, Clara T. Bracey, George Nicholls, Harry Salter

Location: Studio and Central Park, N.Y.C. *Photographed:* Apr. 5–6 and 12, 1909

386 ft. FLA4690 (print) FRA0162 (neg.)

The story is of a distraught woman who is forced by economic circumstances to abandon her little girl in a basket on the front stoop of a wealthy home. She removes one of the baby's shoes and returns home with it. Her anguish over the loss of her little girl causes her death. A minister is called and he adopts the remaining child, a boy. As the picture continues, it shows both of the children, now grown to marriageable age, meeting through an inevitable accident involving a runaway horse and carriage in the park.

The romance begun in such exciting fashion becomes serious and marriage is considered. One of the last scenes shows the full cast assembled in the home of the rich man who is showing the basket and her baby garments. The minister removes a baby shoe from his pocket and it is found to match the one the little girl had been wearing when found. The about-to-be-married youngsters learn they are brother and sister. As the film ends, the boy has entered the clergy while his sister has become a nun. The title on the film is The Baby's Shoe.

Baby's Tooth

AM&B © H19657 July 2, 1902

Cameraman: F. S. Armitage

Location: Roof studio, N.Y.C. *Photographed:* July 14, 1899

26 ft. FLA3159 (print) FRA0163 (neg.)

Despite the title, the film is something else again. A young woman dressed in a negligee is seated in a rocker, bending over a baby's bath with a metal hood. The woman removes the child from the bath, dries it, and puts on its diapers. Nothing else is shown.

The Bad Boy and the Grocery Man

AM&B © H56152 Jan. 23, 1905

Cameraman: G. W. Bitzer

Location: Studio, N.Y.C. *Photographed:* Jan. 15, 1905

108 ft. FLA4967 (print) FRA0164 (neg.)

Two sets were used in this comedy, one of a workmen's kitchen and the other of the store front of a grocer. The two scenes seem to have no connection with each other, but a mischievous boy, wearing the same costume, appears in both. In the first, a mechanical dishwasher goes awry because of a prank arranged by the mischievous boy. In the second, the grocer is left with his display shelves demolished after an altercation with the same bad boy.

The Bad Boy's Joke on the Nurse

Edison © H7636 Aug. 14, 1901

19 ft. FLA3321 (print) FRA0166 (neg.)

The locale of this film is outdoors in a park. A sleeping old man and a nursemaid with a baby on her lap occupy benches on opposite sides of a walk. Two young boys approach and decide to play a prank. They remove the baby from the nursemaid's lap and place it on the lap of the man and withdraw to watch. The old man wakens, discovers the baby, becomes hysterical and tries to hide the infant. The nurse wakes and begins striking him. At the end of the film, a policeman can be seen leading the two combatants off camera while the baby is left to its own devices on the parkway.

Bad Boy's Joke on the Nurse

Edison © H54487 Dec. 9, 1904

Cameraman: Edwin S. Porter

Location: N.Y.C. *Photographed:* Dec. 5, 1904

26 ft. FLA4490 (print) FRA0165 (neg.)

The locale of this film is a public park, with two benches facing one another. An old man is asleep on one, while on the other a nursemaid has fallen asleep holding an infant. Two small boys come along, size up the situation and remove the baby from the lap of the nurse and put it in the lap of the sleeping old man. The nurse wakens and discovers the infant in the lap of the old man; she takes it back and proceeds to beat him about the head and shoulders. At this moment a policeman arrives and saves the man from the nurse by leading him away, to the amusement of the small boys who watched the entire proceedings.

A Bad (K)Night
AM&B © H23800 Nov. 11, 1902
Cameraman: F. S. Armitage
Location: Roof studio, N.Y.C. *Date:* June 9, 1899
14 ft. FLA3709 (print) FRA0167 (neg.)

The opening scene shows what appears to be a portion of a house with a large staircase, to the left of which is a medieval suit of armor. A man in a top hat and tailcoat staggers into the scene and bows deeply to the suit of armor. He then attempts to climb the stairs but they prove too much. He loses his balance and sits down on a chair. At that moment, a woman in a nightgown descends the stairs, takes the cudgel from the mailed fist of the suit of armor and begins hitting the seated man on the head. She is still hitting him when the film ends.

The Badger Game
AM&B © H60656 May 9, 1905
Cameraman: G. W. Bitzer
Location: Studio, N.Y.C. *Photographed:* Apr. 28, 1905
32 ft. FLA4491 (print) FRA0168 (neg.)

The first scene takes place in a set of the dressing room of an apartment. A man and a woman are having a discussion and the man indicates by gestures that the woman is to do certain things involving the sofa. He then hides. A man dressed as an elderly gentleman enters, and he and the woman sit on the couch and begin to embrace. They continue until she sits on his lap. While this is going on, the woman can be seen removing articles from the pockets of the older man and handing them to her confederate in the background. At a signal, the confederate makes himself known and the elderly gentleman, afraid, runs out of the room. As the picture ends, the two confederates can be seen embracing on the couch.

Balked at the Altar
AM&B © H114598 Aug. 15, 1908
Director: D. W. Griffith *Cameraman:* Arthur Marvin
Cast: Harry Salter, Mabel Stoughton, Mack Sennett, Frank Gebhardt, Linda Arvidson, Arthur Johnson, D. W. Griffith
Location: Studio, N.Y.C., Fort Lee, N.J. *Photographed:* July 29–30, 1908
276 ft. FLA4691 (print) FRA0169 (neg.)

The first scene shows a gawky and giggly woman of marriageable age seated on a bench in front of a house reading a popular novel, *Three Weeks.* There is quite a traffic of eligible young men passing by and one in particular attracts her, but he leaves in a nervous condition. Her father goes down to the post office and inveigles the postman into coming home. The hero embraces the young woman and her father comes out of the house with a shotgun. The following scenes concern the preamble to the marriage, the church scene, the bridegroom jumping out of a church window, and the chase by the whole congregation.

He is apprehended and returned to the church. The picture ends as the bride is now reluctant in her turn and leaves the assemblage. The final scene shows her giggling over the novel.

The Ball Game
Edison © 31442 May 20, 1898
25 ft. FLA4331 (print) FRA0023 (neg.)

Photographed from one camera position behind home plate, the film shows a baseball game in progress. The action includes two players running toward the camera; one uniform is distinguishable as Newark, New Jersey.

The Ballet Master's Dream
Méliès © H38792 Dec. 4, 1903
Cast: Zizi Papillon, Georges Méliès
Location: Montreuil, France
Original title: Le reve d'un Maitre de Ballet
70 ft. FLA4492 (print) FRA0170 (neg.)

The film begins in the bedroom of a dancing master who seems to be trying out dance steps. He indicates to his servant that he lacks new ideas. He removes his trousers and gets into bed. Two dancing girls in full-length dresses appear on a projection screen. They seem to be dancing on top of the ballet master's bed. During one of the turns, they step off the bed and come to life, performing several different dance steps. The ballet master awakens to find the maid performing the steps of the dancers in his dream. The last scene shows him wrestling with pillows on the floor.

The Ballet of the Ghosts
See: Neptune's Daughters

The Ballet Rehearsal
AM&B © H38860 Dec. 5, 1903
Cameraman: A. E. Weed
Location: Studio, N.Y.C. *Photographed:* Nov. 28, 1903
48 ft. FLA4493 (print) FRA0171 (neg.)

The first visible indication of what is to happen is a stage with undecorated backs of flats. A man, dressed as a choreographer and accompanied by four women in dancer's practice clothes, enters. The ballet master attempts to teach all of them to dance some steps in unison. The film ends as though he has given up in despair because one of the dancers, who is especially large and ungainly, cannot follow the pattern. All of the scenes were photographed from one position.

Balloon Ascension, Marionettes
Edison © 59206 Oct. 7, 1898
25 ft. FLA4289 (print) FRA0172 (neg.)

In front of a city backdrop is a puppet in a clown suit. Beside him is a prop balloon with a carrying basket. Another puppet enters the scene and both get into the basket and the balloon ascends. Almost immediately, the puppet in the clown suit falls out of the basket and lands on stage.

See also: Dancing Chinaman, Marionettes; and Skeleton Dance, Marionettes

Balloon Race
AM&B © H34980 Aug. 22, 1903

Cameraman: Wallace McCutcheon
Photographed: Aug. 11, 1903
34 ft. FLA4437 (print) FLA5947 (35mm print) FRA0173 (neg.)

The subject is the ascension of two balloons. The inability of the cameraman to direct the lens of his machine in the proper direction of the ascension makes it impossible to give any details. There is very little film of the actual ascension itself. However, it is possible to see both balloons in the distance.

A Ballroom Tragedy

AM&B © H62508 June 22, 1905
Cameraman: G. W. Bitzer
Location: Studio, N.Y.C. *Photographed:* June 14, 1905
26 ft. FLA3914 (print) FRA0174 (neg.)

This film, a drawing room drama, was photographed from a single camera position. It opens on a set with a sofa and a curtain backdrop as if it is a sitting room off a dining or ball room. The actors, two men and three women, are in formal attire. As the action begins, one woman approaches the camera position toward the two standing men. One of them notices her. She stops, and there is a conversation. The man gestures to the couch, and she walks over and sits down where he joins her. He leans over as if to kiss her. At that moment, a woman can be seen in the background approaching the drape in back of the sofa. She has a knife in her hand. As the lips of the two on the couch meet, the woman behind the sofa strikes with the knife. The picture ends as the seated woman rises to her feet and falls dead as the murderess slinks into the background.

Bally-Hoo Cake Walk

AM&B © H32078 May 21, 1903
Cameraman: Arthur Marvin
Location: Pan-American Exposition, Buffalo, N.Y. *Date:* June 17, 1901
17 ft. FLA4107 (print) FRA0175 (neg.)

A mixed group of black dancers does a "cake walk," a popular step developed in minstrel shows. Approximately ten dancers pass the camera position. The extreme shortness of the film does not permit much description.

The Bamboo Slide

AM&B © H32384 June 4, 1904
Cameraman: G. W. Bitzer
Location: Luna Park, Coney Island, N.Y. *Date:* June 1, 1903
31 ft. FLA4208 (print) FRA0176 (neg.)

The film was photographed from a camera positioned over the heads of a crowd of people, visible in the foreground, who are watching an amusement park ride called "the Bamboo Slide." The camera was centered on the end of the slide. The spectators obscure a great deal of the action.

The Bandit King

Selig © H92502 Apr. 11, 1907
25 ft. FLA4405 (print, copy 1) FLA5983 (print, copy 2) FRA0177 (neg.)

The first scene is a bank robbery. The actors are dressed as cowboys and are seen coming out of the side of a building that has been blown open by dynamite. The remaining scenes are vignettes or individual scenes that resemble a still photograph of an occasion rather than one that can move. The individual scenes are: the blowing up of the strong box, the holdup of the stage coach, the robbery of another bank in another city, the reporting to the sheriff of the robbery, the summoning of the posse, the chase, the capture and killing of the bandits, as well as the return of the loot to its owners.

The Bandit's Waterloo

AM&B © H113969 July 28, 1908
Director: D. W. Griffith *Cameraman:* Arthur Marvin
Cast: Florence Lawrence, Marion Leonard, Arthur Johnson, Harry Salter
Location: Studio, N.Y.C.; Shadyside, N.J. *Photographed:* July 6 and 8, 1908
320 ft. FLA4692 (print) FRA0178 (neg.)

The picture is made up of many scenes, both exterior and interior, beginning with an establishing scene of some actors dressed as Latin-type bandits. The bandits are hiding behind some large rocks and waiting to rob passersby. Their victims are two habited monks, a young woman taking produce to market, and a coach drawn by two horses. The bandits drag a young and beautiful woman from the coach. The chief takes her off to his lair in the forest, where he binds her hands and feet. His female companion protests when he allows the captive to remain by the fireside. The bandit takes the heroine to town for ransom, but she changes costumes with the serving girl at the inn. She entices the captain of the guards stationed there to a bedroom, gets him intoxicated and leaves. She next entices the bandit into tying up the guard captain and proceeds to get him drunk. She pins a note on him saying that the guard captain is tied up in the next room, and picks up the loot. The picture ends as she is leaving the drunken bandit with the note pinned to his chest.

The Bank Robbery

Oklahoma Natural Mutoscene Co. © H120453 Dec. 28, 1908
Cameraman: J. B. Kent
Cast: Al Jennings
Location: Cache and Wichita Forest and Game Reserve, Okla.
907 ft. FLA5843 (print) FRA2852 (neg.)

This film set the pattern for the stereotyped Western. The movie begins by establishing the locale and type of living of the desperados. The camera brings them into town in such a way as to establish not only the town but what they are seeking—the bank. The bank is then robbed, and the bandits pick up their wounded and flee. Loyalty to their wounded comrade is shown as they go out of their way to leave him with a woman to be cared for. The bandits continue their flight and are followed by a woman. They set up a new camp and hide their horses. The posse comes upon the hidden horses and sets up an ambush and waits. The woman arrives in the new camp and tells the bandits of the close pursuit of the posse. They attempt to saddle their horses but are set upon by the posse, and the film ends in a manner that became traditional—the good guys get the bad guys and the money is returned to the bank. This picture was made by Al Jennings, a convicted bank and train robber who had tried to pattern his life as well as those of his brothers after the notorious Dalton brothers. Mr. Jennings lectured on the evils of sin after his release from the penitentiary. "Quanah promised to aid them. Heck Thomas was chief of police at Lawton. He would help. And Al Jennings, then living in that city, was eager to get in. . . . The film as finally worked out included a holdup of the bank at the little town of Cache, by Al Jennings and his gang. This was staged just at the close of business, by agreement with the banker. But a citizen who was present, and not 'in the know' jumped out of the window and ran to give the alarm, adding a bit of excitement that was entirely real."—William Matthew Tilghman, *Marshall of the Last Frontier.*

The Banker's Daughters
Biograph © J146849 Oct. 22, 1910
Director: D. W. Griffith *Cameraman:* G. W. Bitzer
Cast: Verner Clarges, Stephanie Longfellow, Dorothy West, Gladys Egan, Eddie Dillon, Alfred Paget, Henry Walthall, Robert Harron, Tony O'Sullivan
Location: Studio, N.Y.C. *Photographed:* Sept. 8–9, 1910
402 ft. FLA4693 (print) FRA0179 (neg.)

This melodrama is based on the attempt by an organized gang of thieves to use the Trojan horse method of entry into a banker's house to steal a diamond necklace, the banker's gift to his convalescent daughter. The household servants accept a trunk where one of the bandits has secreted himself. While the trunk is in the boudoir of one of the sisters, she discovers the presence of the burglar and sends a note via her very young sister to the invalid. The police are called, and they arrive and capture the robber.

The Barbarian Ingomar
AM&B © H116387 Oct. 1, 1908
Director: D. W. Griffith *Cameraman:* G. W. Bitzer
Cast: Florence Lawrence, Harry Salter
Location: Cos Cob, Conn.; Little Falls, N.J. *Photographed:* Sept. 5 and 8, 1908
Adapted from Friedrich Halm's "Son of the Wilderness"
305 ft. FLA4694 (print) FRA0180 (neg.)

The plot is built around a noble Roman family: a mother, father, and beautiful daughter. The opening scenes indicate a betrothal conversation, then the elderly man and the younger man start out on a journey. They are set upon and kidnapped by barbarians (actors dressed in skins and with beards). Feeling secure in their triumph, the barbarians return to the home of the nobles, capture the heroine, and take her to their camp. Their chief issues orders for his men not to molest the young woman in any way. But that does not deter them. They pounce upon her, run off into the woods, and tie her to a tree. The chief of the barbarians comes upon them and setting about him with his sword, kills the kidnappers. He then returns the heroine to her family and starts to leave when the heroine calls him, realizing that she loves him. The film ends as the heroine and the barbarian embrace.

The Barber's Dee-light
AM&B © H60292 May 3, 1905
Cameraman: G. W. Bitzer
Location: Studio, N.Y.C. *Photographed:* Apr. 25, 1905
27 ft. FLA4105 (print) FRA0181 (neg.)

The set is of a basement barbershop, the upper quarter of which has sidewalk-level windows that allow the customers a view of legs passing by. During the film, several pairs of legs, apparently belonging to women, walk by the window to the delight of the men below. Suddenly a pair of legs can be seen at the head of the stairs; they turn and come down into the barbershop. Much to the disappointment of the customers, the multi-colored stockings and legs belong to a man wearing kilts.

See also: What Demoralized the Barber Shop

The Barber's Pretty Patient
AM&B © H61111 May 19, 1905
Cameraman: G. W. Bitzer
Location: Studio, N.Y.C. *Photographed:* May 10, 1905
21 ft. FLA3788 (print) FRA0182 (neg.)

The set represents a barbershop where a barber chair and the accoutrements of that trade can be seen. A man and a young woman enter from opposite sides of the set and the young woman reluctantly sits in the barber chair. As the film continues, there is much struggling and kicking of feet by the young woman, and at the end, the man, with a gesture of great exertion, is seen holding an outsize tooth in a pair of forceps.

The Barber's Queer Customer
AM&B © H19018 June 14, 1902
Cameraman: Arthur Marvin
Location: Roof studio, N.Y.C. *Date:* Aug. 28, 1900
21 ft. FLA3787 (print) FRA0183 (neg.)

The action begins on a barbershop set. A man comes in, sits down, and the proprietor starts to lather his shaving brush. As he turns to his customer, the customer's face, by the use of stop action photography, is changed into that of an owl and from then until the end of the film when the barber throws him out, the face continues to change into various animals, such as a monkey and so forth.

The Bargain
N.Y. Motion Picture © LP5157 Dec. 3, 1914
Producer: Thomas H. Ince *Director:* Reginald Barker *Script:* William H. Clifford and Thomas H. Ince *Cameraman:* Robert Newhard
Cast: William S. Hart, J. Frank Burke, Clara Williams, J. Barney Sherry, James Dowling
Location: Grand Canyon, Ariz.
2,036 ft. FLA5844-5845 (print) FRA2782-2783 (neg.)

This Western was photographed outdoors at the Arizona side of the Grand Canyon. It is the story of a stagecoach bandit who falls in love, gets married, and attempts to go straight. But he is apprehended as he is returning the loot taken in his last illegal act. He is able to do the marshal a favor, and the marshal gives him a two-hour head start for the border. The picture ends as the bandit confesses his past to his new wife, who decides to go with him and help him start an honest life.

Bargain Day
AM&B © H27979 Feb. 7, 1903
Cameraman: Arthur Marvin
Photographed: July 16, 1900
19 ft. FLA3132 (print) FRA0184 (neg.)

The length of the film prevented the producer from presenting the full scope of his attempt at humor. The film begins on a set of a department store. Signs on the rear wall indicate a sale of articles of women's clothing and the sale prices. In the foreground is a counter heaped with merchandise which attracts the attention of women passersby. The set was constructed outdoors and all light was natural. As the action begins, the first two women seen in the picture move off the set, but several more, in groups of twos, can be seen passing the camera position. A man dressed as a country bumpkin or "rube" walks up to the counter. The woman who accompanies him decides on an item, makes the purchase, turns around facing the camera and, at that moment, pandemonium breaks loose. About eight women want only that item. The picture ends showing the conflict that ensues.

Bargain Day, 14th Street, New York

AM&B © H59778 Apr. 20, 1905
Cameraman: F. S. Armitage
Location: 14th Street, N.Y.C. *Photographed:* Apr. 1, 1905
35 ft. FLA4494 (print) FRA0185 (neg.)

The camera position was a second-floor establishment across the street from a sign "Rothschild Five & Ten." The entire film shows hundreds of tightly packed people all trying to get in the front door of the store at once. They are so closely packed it is impossible to tell one from another.

The Barnstormers

AM&B © H68796 Nov. 16, 1905
Cameraman: G. W. Bitzer
Location: Palisades Park, N.J.; Studio, N.Y.C. *Photographed:* Nov. 2–3, 1905
239 ft. FLA4695 (print) FRA0186 (neg.)

The opening scene shows a railroad station in a farming community. The train arrives, a group of about twenty people alight and unfurl a banner that reads, "Uncle Tom's Cabin." From the point of arrival of the group onto a set of the lobby of Brown's Palace Hotel, Bar & Grill, etc., the antics are slapstick. The actress portraying Little Eva, out of character, strikes her mother. After the performance, the entire troupe is run out of town by the audience. The film ends as they miss their train and are trudging down the tracks toward New York.

Bartho

See: A Nymph of the Waves

Basket Ball, Missouri Valley College

AM&B © H45596 May 10, 1904
Cameraman: A. E. Weed
Location: Marshall, Mo. *Photographed:* Apr. 26, 1904
23 ft. FLA4217 (print) FRA0187 (neg.)

The subject is a basketball game played between teams of girls. The film shows a section of a basketball court in the foreground, the backboard, and the basket. In the background is a three-story brick schoolbuilding. The short length of the film does not allow too much description of the activities.

Bass Fishing

AM&B © H26843 Jan. 3, 1903

Cameraman: Arthur Marvin
Cast: Henry Talbot
Location: Road bridge, Va. *Date:* May 2, 1901
31 ft. FLA3283 (print) FRA0188 (neg.)

A man in fashionable sporting attire is standing on some large rocks at the edge of a stream. He is holding a short fishing rod in his hands and casting into the running stream. The film ends as the fisherman kneels at the edge of the water, holding the reel in his left hand while he hauls in the fish with a net held in his right hand. There are several occasions when the fisherman cannot be seen, as he walks out of camera range.

Bathing at Atlantic City

Edison © H7984 Aug. 21, 1901
Location: Atlantic City, N.J.
34 ft. FLA4495 (print) FRA0189 (neg.)

The film shows the bathing beach at Atlantic City, New Jersey. The camera position was from a tower or some platform high over the heads of the people on the sand adjoining the water. The camera pans approximately 180 degrees, taking in hundreds of people sitting on the sand between the boardwalk and the ocean, part of the boardwalk, and a great deal of the ocean area where people are swimming.

Bathing Girls Hurdle Race

AM&B © H33209 July 2, 1903
Location: Coney Island *Date:* 1898
18 ft. FLA3356 (print) FRA0190 (neg.)

At first, all that can be seen on a sandy beach, marred by several boxes, are the legs and lower portion of a woman in bathing attire as she runs toward the camera. She is followed by four other women. Each of them falls upon a sand pile in the foreground, and they start to tussle.

Bathing in Samoa

AM&B © H35641 Sept. 12, 1903
Cameraman: A. E. Weed
Location: Studio, N.Y.C. *Photographed:* Aug. 26, 1903
28 ft. FLA3522 (print) FRA0191 (neg.)

The film begins and ends on the same scene–a close-up of the bare legs, from below the knee to the feet, of a woman who is apparently lying on a beach mat or blanket. The action shows a trick bird or an insect of some kind constantly flying around the legs and causing them to cross and uncross steadily during the film.

Battery B Arriving at Camp

Edison © 31435 May 20, 1898
28 ft. FLA3989 (print) FRA0192 (neg.)
[Spanish-American War]

The entire film was photographed from a camera position overlooking an army encampment. The only things visible during the film are horses being led or ridden by men in army uniforms.

Battery B Pitching Camp

Edison © 31437 May 20, 1898
22 ft. FLA3259 (print) FRA0193 (neg.)
[Spanish-American War]

The condition of the film and the position of the camera with relationship to the subject matter do not allow the establishment of much detail. The film shows white tents pitched in thick, waist-high foliage, and one person can be seen walking between the camera position and the tents.

Battery K Siege Guns

Edison © 65371 Oct. 17, 1899
Location: N.Y.C. *Photographed:* Sept. 30, 1899
24 ft. FLA3036 (print) FRA0194 (neg.)

[Spanish-American War; Dewey Homecoming, New York City]

From a camera position above the heads of the spectators standing along a main thoroughfare in a large city, eight harnessed horses pull a four-wheel gun carriage on which is mounted a large artillery field piece. Approaching and passing the camera is another of the same sort of team drawing the same type of military field piece.

Battery Park

AM&B © H30725 Apr. 24, 1903
Location: N.Y.C. *Date:* 1897 [?]
26 ft. FLA3400 (print) FRA0195 (neg.)

The camera was placed on the deck of a boat that was following the shoreline closely. The cement mall that lines the edge of the bank and piers and docks in various stages of disrepair can be seen. Also visible are a paddle-wheel ferryboat and several other smaller vessels tied to wharfs. The film ends looking uptown toward New York, showing a large round building and one multistory building in the background.

The Battle at Elderbush Gulch

Biograph © LP1807 July 15, 1913
Director and Author: D. W. Griffith *Cameraman:* G. W. Bitzer
Cast: Mae Marsh, Lillian Gish, Robert Harron, Charles Hill Mailes, Kate Bruce, W. Chrystie Miller, Alfred Paget, Vergie Clarke, Henry B. Walthall.
Location: San Fernando, Calif. *Photographed:* July 1913
874 ft. FBB2271 (print) FRA2882 (neg.)

A pair of orphans and their puppies are the innocent cause of a terrifying battle between settlers and Indians. The film was written and directed by D. W. Griffith, who considered it one of his three best pictures.

Battle Flags of the 9th Infantry

AM&B © H33881 July 28, 1903
Cameraman: A. E. Weed
Location: N.Y.C. *Date:* July 22, 1903
28 ft. FLA3572 (print) FRA0196 (neg.)

In the foreground is a large, flat area resembling a drill field. In the background are some trees and shrubs at a distance of about two hundred yards. Walking along in front of the camera, at camera right, are six men in American Army fatigue uniforms in rout-step formation. Immediately following the squad of men can be seen a color guard of men dressed in army dress uniforms. The color guard is carrying a United States flag and the flag of the battalion. Following the two squads of color guard, in columns of fours, are two companies of United States

volunteers in dress uniforms. The group was under the command of Capt. E. V. Bookmiller.

See also: Bayonet Exercises; Musical Bayonet Exercises; Musical Calisthenics, and Shelter Tent Drill

Battle of Chemulpo Bay

Edison © H44434 Apr. 12, 1904
Cameraman: Edwin S. Porter
Location: Studio, N.Y.C. *Photographed:* Apr. 18, 1904
84 ft. FLA4968 (print) FRA1953 (neg.)

[Russo-Japanese War]

This film is a reproduction of a battle scene that presumably occurred in the Russo-Japanese War. The film producer constructed a set to represent the deck of a Japanese battleship. The men operating the large deck gun wear the uniform of the Japanese Navy. Miniature Russian battleships are in the water tank to add perspective to the foreground. The film actually is a simulated attack by the large naval weapon in the foreground on the miniatures floating in the reproduced bay.

Battle of Confetti at the Nice Carnival

Edison © H30407 Apr. 8, 1903
Location: Nice
54 ft. FLA4496 (print) FRA0198 (neg.)

The first camera position was in back of crowds viewing a parade of floats. The remainder of the film was photographed from several camera positions and shows a town square and costumed people crisscrossing in front of the camera. Other scenes are of children running and jumping in circles holding hands and adults in masks and odd dress.

Battle of Flowers at the Nice Carnival

Edison © H30410 Apr. 8, 1903
Location: Nice
135 ft. FLA4969 (print) FRA0199 (neg.)

The camera was placed over the heads of the crowds lining the streets along the route of the carnival procession. The film was photographed from one position, and the subject matter is basically one horse-drawn wagon after another filled with people who are throwing roses at the spectators. It is estimated that seventy-five decorated carriages of various sizes and types are in the parade.

Battle of Mafeking

Edison © D9117 Apr. 28, 1900
41 ft. FLA4497 (print) FRA1563 (neg.)
[Boer War]

The camera was placed high above a field selected for the staged battle. Most of the action is a charge up a small hill by the infantry soldiers to attack the entrenched enemy, who can be seen in the background. Apparently the attack is successful as a flag can be seen waving as the film ends.

Battle of Mt. Ariat

AM&B © H34100 Aug. 3, 1903
Location: Mt. Arayat, Philippine Islands
20 ft. FLA3606 (print) FRA0201 (neg.)

A mounted cavalry appears to be getting ready for a charge across a large field filled with stacked hay. Approximately halfway through the film and until it ends, the only thing visible is the uniformed mounted troops dashing through the haystacks. There is a silhouette of a mountain in the background.

The Battle of the Yalu, No. 1–4
AM&B © H43618–20, H44025 Mar. 23 and 29, 1904
Cameraman: G. W. Bitzer
Cast: Students of St. John's Military Academy
Location: Manlius, near Syracuse, N.Y. *Photographed:* Mar. 16 and 18, 1904
217 ft. FLA4970 (print) FRA1954 (neg.)

The first scenes are of a snow-covered wooded area. The first action shows a company of men in military uniforms consisting of white tunics and white caps pulling two approximately 75mm two-wheeled artillery field pieces toward the camera position. As the film continues, the uniformed men assemble the field pieces and begin firing into the wooded area, approximately five hundred yards distant. The camera was positioned above the heads of the artillery crew and in the distance, through the trees, at least two companies of men approaching the artillery position can be seen. The remainder of the film was photographed from two camera positions and shows Japanese troops approaching the Russian artillery position and putting the crew to rout. The remainder of the film shows a large snow-covered field on which bodies are lying, and the last scene is a close-up of the Japanese flag.

AM&B's handbill of November 27, 1905, says "Note.—The complete production of 'The Battle of the Yalu' is sold in either 626 or 400 foot [35mm] lengths."

Battleship "Indiana" in Action
AM&B © H55395 Jan. 3, 1905
Cameramen: G. W. Bitzer, Wallace Mc Cutcheon
Location: Glen Island, N.Y. [?] *Photographed:* Nov. 11, 1903
19 ft. FLA4103 (print) FRA0204 (neg.)

From a camera positioned on a small boat, the film shows an American battleship as it passes abeam.

Battleship "Odin"
AM&B © H30183 Apr. 4, 1903
19 ft. FLA3757 (print) FRA0205 (neg.)

From a single camera position, the German battleship *Odin* can be seen as it approaches at a three quarter angle on the bow at approximately a thousand yards. Both port and starboard turrets begin firing and continue until the end of the reel.

Battleships in Action
AM&B © H22207 Oct. 3, 1902
Cameraman: G. W. Bitzer
Location: Off Fishers Island, N.Y. *Photographed:* Sept. 8, 1902
36 ft. FLA4498 (print) FRA0206 (neg.)

Four U.S. Navy battleships are shown passing the camera position. All ships fire a salute. The distance from the camera position is too great to permit description of detail.

Battleships "Iowa" and "Massachusetts"
AM&B © H25965 Dec. 31, 1902
25 ft. FLA3612 (print) FRA0207 (neg.)

The film was photographed from a moving "smallboat" that passes the starboard side of the battleship *Iowa*, showing most of her structure just below the main deck to her truck. There is not much film on the battleship *Massachusetts*.

Bayonet Exercises
AM&B © H33883 July 28, 1903
Cameraman: A. E. Weed
Location: N.Y.C. *Date:* July 22, 1903
27 ft. FLA3569 (print) FRA0208 (neg.)

The calisthenics seen in the film are performed in unison by a full company of U.S. Army cadets on a drill field. In order to photograph a full company from the front, the cameraman placed his camera at such a distance that details of the exhibition cannot be described. However, the exercises are from arms port to arms overhead and from arms port to arms at rest. The film ends on the maneuver of close ranks.

See also: Battle Flags of the 9th U.S. Infantry

Be Good
AM&B © H30462 Apr. 11, 1903
20 ft. FLA3631 (print) FRA0209 (neg.)

The film begins on a close waist-high "two shot" of a man and a woman sitting on a wrought iron bench. The woman has her back turned to the man who is facing the camera. Her actions indicate she is unhappy or crying. The movement of the man's head and hands indicates that he is scolding or admonishing her. Shortly afterward, her demeanor changes and she smiles. She turns toward the man who holds her hand and then kisses her elbow, her upper arm, and then her lips. As the film ends, they are embracing.

Be Good
AM&B © H31666 May 11, 1903
20 ft. FLA3397 (print) FRA0694 (neg.)

As the picture begins, one is aware of the close proximity of the actors to the camera. The action is between a man in evening clothes and a woman sitting on a bench. No other portion of the set or any props are visible. The woman feigns tears while the man admonishes her for misconduct. It becomes apparent from his gestures and facial expressions that he is not as angry as he would like her to assume. Before the picture ends, the young lady is no longer in tears; she has turned toward the man and they are embracing with much enthusiasm.

Beach Apparatus—Practice
Edison © 60573 Oct. 25, 1897
24 ft. FLA3025 (print) FRA0210 (neg.)

The film opens on a sandy beach where some men in the uniform of the Coast Guard lighthouse service are bringing a two-wheel vehicle into camera view. They unpack some boxes, and one man fires a line from a gun affixed to a tree trunk away from the camera to a dead-man anchor in the foreground. The rescue drill is completed by the breeches buoy rescue apparatus being put into action. The other titles in this documentary are: Boat Wagon and Beach Cart, Capsize of Lifeboat, Launch of Lifeboat, Launch of Surf Boat, Rescue—Resuscitation, and Return of Lifeboat.

The Beach at Coney Island

AM&B © H48623 July 28, 1904
Cameraman: G. W. Bitzer
Location: Coney Island, N.Y. *Photographed:* July 19, 1904
84 ft. FLA4974 (print) FRA0211 (neg.)

From a single camera position about one hundred yards from the shore of a seaside resort, at least one hundred persons are shown bathing in a roped-off area. As the camera begins to pan, a rowboat with the words "Life Boat" on the back is rowed toward an individual splashing in the water. Both the lifeguards jump into the water, swim to the evidently disabled person, and return with the person to the lifeboat. The lifeboat makes its way to shore through the many bathers and spectators. The film was released as Beyond the Surf.

A Beast at Bay

Biograph © J169785 May 29, 1912
Director: D. W. Griffith *Cameraman:* G. W. Bitzer
Cast: Mary Pickford, Edwin August, Alfred Paget, Mae Marsh, Marguerite Loveridge, Charles Hill Mailes, Elmer Booth
Location: In or near Los Angeles. *Photographed:* Mar. 1912
426 ft. FLA4696 (print) FRA0212 (neg.)

The story line is built around an escaping convict who captures and exchanges clothing with one of his pursuers. The heroine (Mary Pickford) has lost respect for the hero because he would not enter into a street fight. The convict, after a chase scene, abducts the heroine and holds her as a hostage. But he is defeated by the hero in a fight. The film includes scenes of conversation between heroine and the hero, traveling shots in an automobile, and excellent "chase" photography taken from a camera car preceding the abducted heroine and the convict who are in a large automobile that is being pursued by a locomotive.

Beating Hearts and Carpets

Keystone © LP4722 Mar. 13, 1915
Producer and Author: Mack Sennett
Cast: Billie Bennett, Charles Murray, Peggy Pearce, Harry McCoy, Frank Hayes
Location: Keystone studio and vicinity
405 ft.

Charles Murray portrays a sewing machine demonstrator who responds to a telephone call from a woman (Billie Bennett) who needs one. He becomes enamored of the lovely daughter (Peggy Pearce), but she is in love with Harry McCoy. When Peggy becomes annoyed with his advances, he flirts with Billie. The father (Frank Hayes), who has been resting outside, notices Murray and chases him away. Murray hires a pair of bums to abduct the daughter, but instead they make off with Billie. Murray intercepts them, puts the hooded woman over his shoulder, and hurries to the justice of the peace, where he is surprised to find Peggy and Harry being wed. Father brings up the rear with his shotgun.

The Beauty Bunglers

Keystone © LP5401 Apr. 12, 1915
Producer and Author: Mack Sennett
Cast: Polly Moran, Charles Murray, Slim Summerville

Location: Edendale studio, Los Angeles
425 ft. FLA4762 (print) FRA0214 (neg.)

An active comedy in which Charles Murray and Polly Moran play the parts of a couple who operate a beauty salon. Delayed action gags involving hair dryers, a piece of slippery soap, beauty aids, physical culture equipment, and a swimming pool complete with bathing beauties in leotards are all part of this motion picture.

Beginning of a Skyscraper

AM&B © H16723 Apr. 18, 1902
Cameraman: Robert K. Bonine
Location: N.Y.C. *Date:* Jan. 18, 1902
14 ft. FLA3398 (print) FRA0215 (neg.)

The film, photographed from a single camera position, shows approximately a hundred workmen equipped with shovels, scrapers, and mule-drawn excavation equipment as they start digging the foundation area for a skyscraper.

Behind the Scenes

AM&B © H115211 Aug. 29, 1908
Director: D. W. Griffith *Cameraman:* Arthur Marvin
Cast: Kate Bruce, Florence Lawrence, George Nicholls
Location: Studio, N.Y.C. *Photographed:* Aug. 10 and 13, 1908
199 ft. FLA4697 (print) FRA0216 (neg.)

The film is built around an actress-mother whose child is ill and near death, but she must go to work as she is appearing in a dramatic presentation. There are scenes of the sick room in the apartment of the actress (Florence Lawrence), showing her attempting to comfort her child, of her mother (Kate Bruce) indicating it is time to go to work, of the stage entrance with the actress going in and out, of her mother going in and out. Then there are scenes behind the stage, including all of the cast of the dramatic presentation, and there are at least two camera positions taken in the theater during the stage presentation itself. The actress is told of her daughter's death, and she battles with herself as to whether she should rush home or go on the stage. She decides in the tradition of the theater to continue her act. Afterward, still in costume, she reaches home. The film ends as she clutches her daughter's small body to her bosom.

Behind the Screen

AM&B © H43571 Mar. 22, 1904
Cameraman: A. E. Weed
Location: Studio, N.Y.C. *Photographed:* Mar. 3, 1904
25 ft. FLA4293 (print) FRA0217 (neg.)

The film opens on a one-camera position scene of a wall and a screen. A woman appears, steps behind the screen, and begins placing one article of clothing after another on the chair next to the screen. Another actress appears. She is costumed as a maid and accidentally knocks over the screen, disclosing the unclothed woman in a bathtub.

Belles of the Beach

AM&B © H22203 Oct. 3, 1902
14 ft. FLA3832 (print) FRA0218 (neg.)

An elevated camera angle establishes a body of water in which two female heads can be seen at approximately fifty yards from the camera position. For the whole of the film, the only thing visible are the heads of the women and the water in which the women are sitting or swimming.

Ben Hur

See: The Chariot Race

The Bench in the Park

AM&B © H40808 Jan. 12, 1904

Cameraman: A. E. Weed

Location: Studio, N.Y.C. *Photographed:* Dec. 1, 1903

20 ft. FLA3802 (print) FRA0220 (neg.)

The film was photographed from one camera position as if in the audience. Two young ladies can be seen seated on a park bench in front of a painted park scene backdrop. They both appear to be reading. A young man in summer clothing comes up behind their bench and engages them in conversation. As he talks, he tilts the bench, frightening the young women, one of whom jumps to her feet. The other remains seated and is kissed by the young man. Then they both scold him for his outrageous conduct.

The Bengal Lancers

AM&B © H34519 Aug. 13, 1903

Cameraman: Raymond Ackerman

Location: Peking *Photographed:* Jan. 14, 1901

15 ft. FLA3587 (print) FRA0221 (neg.)

The film, photographed from a single camera position, shows a company of Bengal Lancers passing at a review trot from right to left in front of the camera.

See also: Charge by First Bengal Lancers

Bertha Claiche

AM&B © H65077 Sept. 1, 1905

Cameraman: G. W. Bitzer

Location: Brighton Beach, N.Y.; Studio, N.Y.C. *Photographed:* Aug. 15, 1905

71 ft. FLA4489 (print) FRA0222 (neg.)

The set is of a living room-kitchen where a man is sleeping with his feet on the table. A vivacious young woman enters and begins playfully tweaking his ears and pulling his hair, awakening him. She hides until he goes back to sleep and then resumes. The man gets to his feet, gestures toward her purse, and then starts choking her and throws her to the floor. The next scene takes place in a business district, where the heroine is asking two male friends for help. Her assailant arrives and repeats his demands for money. He begins choking and striking the heroine again, but her male friends appear and take him into custody. The heroine then pulls a revolver from her purse and shoots her assailant in the back. The film ends as he dies.

The Bessemer Steel Converter in Operation

Edison © H16123 Apr. 7, 1902

26 ft. FLA3799 (print) FRA0223 (neg.)

From a single camera position some large buildings can be seen against the overcast sky. Directly in the foreground are two large pipes with either steam or white smoke issuing from them. To the right, flame under pressure is coming out of a stone structure or blast furnace.

Betrayed by a Hand Print

See: Betrayed by Hand Prints

Betrayed by Hand Prints

AM&B © H115136 Aug. 27, 1908

Director: D. W. Griffith *Cameramen:* G. W. Bitzer, Arthur Marvin

Cast: Florence Lawrence, Harry Salter, Linda Arvidson

Location: Studio, N.Y.C. *Photographed:* Aug. 6 and 19, 1908

316 ft. FLA4900 (print) FRA0224 (neg.)

The plot, unusual for the time, concerns the identification of a thief by her palm print. The film begins at a party where an entertainer makes palm prints of the guests, one of whom is a very dejected and unhappy young woman. The party over, the hostess and the unhappy young woman retire to their rooms. The guest opens her window, crawls along a ledge into the hostess's room, steals her jewelry, and returns. When the hostess wakes, she finds her jewelry gone and a hand print on the bureau. The palm print, identified from the party favors of the night before, belongs to the unhappy young woman. There is a struggle and the jewelry drops from a bar of soap that had been hollowed out to conceal it. In the last scene, the guest departs after the hostess offers her money and she refuses it. The film and copyright are under the above title, but it was released on September 1, 1908, as Betrayed by a Handprint. Two unusual uses of the camera are the camera movement to show the difficulty of crawling along the window ledge, and the extreme close-up insert of a pair of hands carving out a cake of soap in which to hide the stolen jewelry.

Betsy Ross Dance

AM&B © H32944 June 25, 1903

Cameraman: G. W. Bitzer

Cast: Little Anita

Date: June 18, 1903

36 ft. FLA3413 (print) FRA0225 (neg.)

A backdrop painted to represent the column and stairs of a theater can be seen at the beginning of this film and, as it progresses, a young lady with long curls enters and dances vigorously. A Biograph Bulletin identifies the dancer as "Little Anita."

See also: Cosy Corner Dance.

The Better Way

Biograph © J130564 Aug. 13, 1909

Director: D. W. Griffith *Cameraman:* G. W. Bitzer

Cast: Stephanie Longfellow, Kate Bruce, James Kirkwood, Henry B. Walthall, Arthur Johnson, Mack Sennett, Owen Moore

Location: Coytesville, N.J.; Studio, N.Y.C. *Photographed:* July 9, 10 and 12, 1909

373 ft. FLA4905 (print) FRA0226 (neg.)

This drama, which takes place in the days of the Pilgrims, is of a young woman who is loved by two men, marries one, and finds she is in love with the other. After her marriage, the second suitor continues his courting, and finally persuades her to run away with him. However, her conscience will not allow her to go through with leaving her husband, and she makes her temptor take her to her parents' home. The parents take her back to her husband, who forgives her.

Between the Dances

AM&B © H62450 June 20, 1905

Cameraman: G. W. Bitzer
Location: Studio, N.Y.C. *Photographed:* June 13, 1905
22 ft. FLA3900 (print) FRA0227 (neg.)

The opening scene shows a couch in front of a drape that separates one part of a house from another. A formally dressed young couple enters through the drape, the man talking rapidly as if attempting to convince the young woman of something. He then becomes annoyed and leaves. The young woman sits down on the couch, then reclines and apparently goes to sleep. Another man arrives and notices her. He decides, after walking up and down a few times in hesitation, to kiss her. She responds by putting her arms tightly around his neck and returning his kiss.

Beverly of Graustark

Klaw & Erlanger © LP3218 Aug. 13, 1914
From the novel by George Barr McCutcheon
Cast: Linda Arvidson, Gertrude Robinson, Robert Drouet, Charles Perley, Jack Brammall, William J. Butler, Charles West
Location: Pasadena, Calif.
1,293 ft. FLA5922 (print) FRA2791 (neg.)

According to the *Random House Dictionary of the English Language, Graustark* is "a novel (1901) by George Barr McCutcheon about the romantic and melodramatic adventures of military and courtly figures in the fictional kingdom of Graustark." Mr. McCutcheon's novel was turned into a stage play almost at once and since that time countless plays and motion pictures have been based on its theme. The picture was shot in Pasadena, and the photography is excellent. The costumes were expensive and the sets well done. Although Klaw & Erlanger had sent a paper copy to Washington on August 13, 1914, Biograph also copyrighted a three-reel film of the same title in May of 1916. We do not know if this is the K&E production as no paper copy accompanied Biograph's copyright application.

The Bewitched Traveller

AM&B © H49049 Aug. 12, 1904
Directors: Lewin Fitzhamon, Cecil Hepworth
Produced in England by Hepworth & Co.
106 ft. FLA4975 (print) FRA0229 (neg.)

The story records the frustrations encountered by a man from the time he rises in the morning until he finally gives up at the end of the day. The first scene is of the man dressing in a set of a bedroom. He is nearly ready for the street when he starts to tie his shoe and all his outer clothes dissolve. He retrieves them somehow, enters the dining room, sits down, and begins eating. The serving girl who brings his food can be seen in two images. She, the table, food, etc. are dissolved from one side of the room, reappearing on the other, leaving our hero alone in his chair. For the full extent of the film suitcases appear and disappear, as well as public conveyances and even the actor's wife. The train at the station just is not there when he starts to board it. In the end, even when he has given up attempting to take any sort of transportation and is walking down the road, things continue to happen to him through the use of camera effects. This picture was made in England. Note that the horse-drawn stagecoach reads: "Surrey Farmers Ltd. and H. Dale & Co., Wilton on Thames."

Beyond the Surf
See: The Beach at Coney Island

The Bibulous Clothier

Edison © 41137 June 23, 1899
25 ft. FLA3081 (print) FRA0230 (neg.)

The proprietor is standing in front of his impromptu outdoor secondhand clothing store set up against a corrugated metal building. While he drinks from a bottle, a rather well-dressed man appears and is measured for a coat. The proprietor finishes measuring, takes another drink from his bottle, looks at the customer and finds he has increased in size. During the course of the film, the proprietor drinks from his bottle four times. Three times the customer grows larger, but with the fourth drink the customer returns to normal. Apparently the emotion engendered by all these changes is too much for the proprietor for he falls to the ground in a faint.

Bicycle Paced Race

Edison © H7635 Aug. 14, 1901
26 ft. FLA3924 (print) FRA0231 (neg.)

The straightway section of a bicycle race track can be seen. During the course of the film, tandem bicycles that precede the single-rider bicycles to break the wind for them pass the camera six times.

See also: Professional Handicap Bicycle Race

Bicycle Trick Riding, no. 2

Edison © 20771 Mar. 20, 1899
20 ft. FLA3850 (print) FRA0232 (neg.)

This was photographed from one camera position as if in the audience. During the film, a bicycle rider demonstrates his skill by executing several rather difficult feats of balance while the bicycle circles the stage.

Ein Bier

AM&B © H17489 May 8, 1902
Cameraman: F. S. Armitage
Location: Roof, N.Y.C. *Photographed:* Mar. 23, 1900
20 ft. FLA3828 (print) FRA1056 (neg.)

This vaudeville turn was photographed from a single camera position as if in the audience. A man is sitting on a barrel as he eats food from a basket. A sign on the wall indicates that beer is available in the off-stage area. The man gets off the barrel and goes off stage. A young boy enters the scene, turns the barrel upside down, and covers the open end with a piece of cloth from the food basket. The man returns and sits on what he believes to be the barrel head and of course falls in.

The Bigamist

Paley & Steiner © H60030 Apr. 25, 1905
13 ft. FLA4408 (print) FRA1533 (neg.)

This film consists of a series of very short scenes to suggest that a group of women took the law into their own hands. Each scene lasts for only a few frames, the first of which shows two mature women entering the courtyard of a house. Another shows two women escorting a policeman down the steps of a police station. Then several women chase a man in striped pajamas into a dog house or chicken coop, and several women tar and feather the same man.

The film ends as the man is standing covered with tar and feathers with his arms around two women who seem very pleased to have him there.

The Bigamist's Trial
AM&B © H60291   May 3, 1905
Cameraman: G. W. Bitzer
Location: Studio, N.Y.C. *Photographed:* Apr. 25, 1905
32 ft.   FLA4500 (print)   FRA0234 (neg.)

As the film begins, a set of a courtroom can be seen, with a bailiff, then the judge, and then several women walking in. Two other men arrive. The appearance of one of them causes great consternation among the women and they individually and collectively approach him in a belligerent manner. The attitude of hostility continues and, as the film ends, the man is shown on his knees with the crowd of women tearing off his clothes and beating him about the head and shoulders while the judge bangs his gavel on the bench to no avail.

The Billionaire
Klaw & Erlanger   © LP2467   Mar. 2, 1914
Based on the novel Brewster's Millions by George Barr
   McCutcheon.
Cast: Vivian Prescott, Dave Morris, Charles Hill Mailes, Gertrude Bambrick, Joseph McDermott
1,229 ft.   FLA5923 (print)   FRA2792 (neg.)

Klaw & Erlanger's film is loosely based on another George Barr McCutcheon novel, *Brewster's Millions*. There are scenes of the billionaire on a ship, in a biplane, at a boxing match, in the interiors of night clubs and theaters. The sets and costumes are extraordinarily lavish; the cast is exceptionally large for the time. Charles Hill Mailes is the billionaire and Dave Morris his valet.

Biograph's Improved Incubator
AM&B © H23788   Nov. 11, 1902
Cameraman: Robert K. Bonine [?]
Date: June 25, 1902 [?]
8 ft.   FLA3492 (print)   FRA0247 (neg.)

The film opens on a scene that appears to be in the back yard of a house. A man is standing by a table with a small box containing eggs. He takes an egg and breaks it. As it leaves his hand, it appears to be a raw egg yolk, but when it lands on the table, it changes into a baby chick. This is done by stop action photography. The quality of the film is so poor that it is difficult to make out the detail.

A Bird's a Bird
Keystone   © LP4415   Feb. 8, 1915
Producer and Author: Mack Sennett
Cast: Chester Conklin, Minta Durfee, Alice Davenport, W. C. Hauber
Location: Edendale studio, Los Angeles
44 ft.   FLA6060 (print)   FRA2207 (neg.)

Chester Conklin loses all his money playing a game of chance in an effort to make enough cash to buy a turkey. Very worried, he goes home to an irate wife, played by Minta Durfee, who scolds him as her parents are coming to dinner. Most of the balance of the picture is devoted to Conklin's unsuccessful efforts to find a substitute for the turkey. Finally he resorts to thievery, stealing the neighbors' turkey, unaware that someone has put a bomb in it. Minta invites the neighbors, and when they recognize their turkey an argument starts. Before it can get very far, the turkey explodes and the rest of the dinner goes with it.

Bird's-Eye View of Dock Front, Galveston
Edison © D18561   Sept. 24, 1900
Location: Galveston, Tex.
35 ft.   FLA4068 (print)   FRA1252 (neg.)
[Galveston Hurricane and Tidal Wave, Sept. 8, 1900.]

This is a 180-degree panorama motion picture of the destruction of the dock area of Galveston, Texas.

Bird's-Eye View of San Francisco, Cal., From a Balloon
Edison © H13040   Jan. 11, 1902
Location: San Francisco
81 ft.   FLA4501 (print)   FRA0249 (neg.)

The film was exposed from a camera position in a captive balloon. The balloon is allowed to ascend. Short sections of the picture are of the business district of San Francisco from various heights during the ascent and descent of the balloon.

Birth of the Pearl
AM&B © H27773   Jan. 30, 1903
Cameraman: F. S. Armitage
Location: Roof Studio, N.Y.C. *Date:* June 14, 1901
33 ft.   FLA4332 (print)   FRA0250 (neg.)

This was photographed from a single camera position as if in the audience and shows a rather elaborately appointed sideshow "turn." As it starts, two women wearing white leotards and turbans pull open a drape and expose to view a large oyster shell. The shell starts to open slowly, revealing a young woman attired only in a leotard. The young woman arises very dramatically, as though facing life for the first time.

Black Diamond Express
See: Uncle Josh at the Moving Picture Show

The Black Hand
AM&B © H74805   Mar. 24, 1906
Cameraman: G. W. Bitzer
Location: Seventh Avenue and studio, N.Y.C. *Photographed:* Mar. 15–16, 1906
269 ft.   FLA4962 (print)   FRA0251 (neg.)

This film was based on an actual Mafia kidnapping that occurred in New York City. Some of the scenes were photographed on sets while others were taken on the streets in the neighborhood where the illegal act took place. The film shows the conspirators writing a threatening letter and mailing it, the receipt of the letter, the kidnapping of the little girl, and the subsequent capture of the gang by the police. The story was filmed in documented sequences, each described by a block lettered title.

The Black Sheep
Biograph © J171872   Aug. 1, 1912
Director: D. W. Griffith *Cameraman:* G. W. Bitzer

Cast: Dorothy Bernard, William Carroll, Alfred Paget, Charles West

Location: Calif. Photographed: May 1912

391 ft. FLA4961 (print) FRA0252 (neg.)

An altercation between the ranch foreman's ne'er-do-well son and a Mexican ranch hand causes the Mexican to seek revenge. The Mexican steals a large sum of money after he slugs the foreman. When he is suspected of being the thief, the foreman's son flees in fright and a posse pursues him. The Mexican loses his stolen money gambling, gets in a fight with other gamblers, and is shot. As he is dying, he confesses to the theft of the money just in time to save the foreman's son from being lynched by the posse.

A Black Storm

AM&B © H30180 Apr. 4, 1903

Cameraman: Arthur Marvin

Date: July 6, 1900

11 ft. FLA3641 (print) FRA0253 (neg.)

A woman is sleeping on a bench in a garden set. Two young boys come along and fill her closed umbrella with soot. The boys then get in back of the wall and sprinkle water on her, so that she opens her umbrella and covers herself with the soot, to the amusement of the boys.

The Black Viper

AM&B © H113479 July 16, 1908

Cameraman: G. W. Bitzer

Cast: D. W. Griffith

Location: Shadyside, N.J. Photographed: June 6 and 22, 1908

292 ft. FLA4988 (print) FRA0254 (neg.)

A lone figure (D. W. Griffith) waits outside a factory where many people are leaving at the end of the day's work. A young woman comes out and resists his attentions, but he follows her until another man drives him away. The disgruntled suitor goes to a tavern and enlists the aid of two unsavory types who use a carriage to follow the pair. They attack the couple, tie and bind the escort, take him to a house, put him inside, and set fire to the house. The young woman runs for help, and the last scenes show the suitor's rescue, while the evil conspirators die in the smoke of the burning house.

Blackmail

AM&B © H65052 Aug. 30, 1905

Cameraman: G. W. Bitzer

Location: Studio, N.Y.C. Photographed: July 20, 1905

20 ft. FLA4032 (print) FRA0258 (neg.)

The set is of an outer and an inner office. A man is working at a roll-top desk in the inner part of the office. Two women enter the outer office and the younger of the two goes into the inner office and sits on the lap of the man and begins kissing him. The door opens and her companion comes in with a camera and photographs the compromising situation. The man then pays the woman for the picture. The film ends as the two women are seen in the outer office dividing the proceeds of their blackmail.

Blanket-Tossing a New Recruit

Edison © 38240 June 22, 1898

25 ft. FLA4368 (print) FRA0259 (neg.)

Approximately fifty men dressed in the uniform of the U.S. Army are crowded around some men who have the edges of a blanket grasped in their hands as they toss a man into the air. The man being tossed can be seen at least six times in the course of the film. Some of the men are aware of the motion picture camera, as they stare at it constantly. Identified in an Edison Catalog as Company F, 1st Ohio Volunteers.

Blessed Is the Peacemaker

AM&B © H36677 Oct. 10, 1903

Cameraman: G. W. Bitzer

Location: Studio, N.Y.C. Photographed: Oct. 5, 1903

29 ft. FLA3748 (print) FRA0260 (neg.)

The first scene takes place in a set of a living room, where a man is sitting at a table and playing patience while his wife is bending over a washtub scrubbing clothes. From her gestures, it is apparent that she is encouraging him to help her but he is not interested. As the film continues, the woman hits the man, he returns the blow, and a violent free-for-all commences that ends when a policeman enters and attempts to break it up. At that moment, the husband and wife turn, beat up the policeman, and throw him out of the house. The film ends as the couple embraces.

A Blessing from Above

AM&B © H41859 Feb. 5, 1904

Cameraman: A. E. Weed

Location: Studio, N.Y.C. Photographed: Jan. 25, 1904

21 ft. FLA4339 (print) FRA0261 (neg.)

One man is standing in a loft and another on the ground of a set of a hay-and-feed barn when a young man carrying a bucket of beer hands it to the man in the loft. He drinks from it and returns to work, after handing the bucket to his companion below. As the man on the ground is drinking, a woman dressed as a charity sister solicits money from them. While she is standing under the hoist, a sack of flour from the loft breaks and spills the contents over her hat and dress.

See also: Clarence, the Cop, on the Feed Store Beat

Blind Man's Buff

AM&B © H42042 Feb. 11, 1904

Cameraman: A. E. Weed

Location: Studio, N.Y.C. Photographed: Jan. 26, 1904

23 ft. FLA4502 (print) FRA0262 (neg.)

The subject is a game of blind man's buff played by three young women on a set of a bedroom, with a cast-iron bed in the center. Two of the girls are being chased by a third who is blindfolded. Each in turn is blindfolded, until the mother enters the room with a stick and persuades them to stop playing and get back into bed.

The Blizzard

AM&B © H25966 Dec. 31, 1902

Location: N.Y.C. Date: Feb. 1899

17 ft. FLA4166 (print) FRA0263 (neg.)

The camera was placed close by Central Park in New York City during a heavy snowfall, and panned for 360 degrees. The quality of the film is poor. However, it is possible to see people walking, horses pulling carriages, streetcars going by, men shoveling snow, and a hansom cab standing by the curb.

A Bluff From a Tenderfoot

AM&B © H26846   Jan. 9, 1903
Cameraman: F. S. Armitage
Date: July 10, 1899
11 ft.   FLA3275 (print)   FRA0264 (neg.)

Three men are sitting at a table playing cards. Soon, two of the men indicate their displeasure with the third. They rise from the table as if to do him bodily harm. He pulls two pistols from under his coat and points them at his would-be attackers who flee in panic. He discharges the pistols which prove to be only paper fans.

The Boarding House Bathroom

AM&B © H60287   May 3, 1905
Cameraman: G. W. Bitzer
Location: Studio, N.Y.C. *Photographed:* Apr. 21, 1905
21 ft.   FLA3790 (print)   FRA0265 (neg.)

A woman in a bathrobe walks up to a door marked "Bathroom" in a set of a boarding house hallway. After she enters and closes the door, two men in sleeping attire each attempt to get into the bathroom but without luck. They begin to show signs of annoyance, look through the keyhole, and show signs of excitement. The camera then shows the transom over the door opening and the woman pouring a large crockery vase filled with water over the heads of the Peeping Toms.

Boarding School Girls

Edison © H65085   Sept. 1, 1905
Location: Coney Island
403 ft.   FLA4998 (print)   FRA0266 (neg.)

Some girls from a boarding school take an unauthorized excursion to Coney Island. The headmistress pursues them through most of the concessions at the amusement park, such as the shoot-the-chute, horse rides, barrel rolls, camel rides, etc. The girls later go swimming, and the second part of the film shows them come out of the bath house onto the sand and enter the water.

A Boarding School Prank

AM&B © H33649   July 21, 1903
Cameraman: A. E. Weed
Photographed: July 11, 1903
21 ft.   FLA3437 (print)   FRA0267 (neg.)

Two grown women are sitting on a bench adjacent to the front door of a set of a two-story frame house. Two young girls come out of the front door and notice that one of the two seated women has an umbrella. They take it and fill it with soot, and then replace it. The film ends when the woman, in leaving, opens the umbrella and dumps soot all over her white hat and dress.

Boat Race

AM&B © H55396   Jan. 3, 1904
Cameramen: G. W. Bitzer, Wallace McCutcheon
Location: Glen Island, N.Y. [?] *Photographed:* Nov. 11, 1903
37 ft.   FLA4503 (print)   FRA0268 (neg.)

Two standard U.S. Navy eight-oar pulling boats, each commanded by a coxswain at the steering position in the stern, are seen abeam of one another. At a signal, both pulling boats begin moving and it can be seen that the camera was positioned on a vessel following the two competing pulling boats. The camera stays with the two boats until their destination is disclosed as a navy battle cruiser at anchor. The cruiser, unidentified, is flying an American flag. The film ends as the two pulling boats come abeam of the cruiser *Indiana* with their oars in the "boat oar" position.

See also: Battleship "Indiana" in Action

Boat Wagon and Beach Cart

Edison © 60574   Oct. 25, 1897
23 ft.   FLA3030 (print)   FRA0269 (neg.)

The scene opens on a large house, alongside of which is a smaller one, like a garage or stable. The doors of the garage open and a four-wheeled vehicle pulled and pushed by seven men appears. The vehicle is carrying a surf lifeboat and, as it passes the camera, a two-wheeled vehicle propelled by five men emerges from the same structure. This vehicle contains sea rescue equipment.

Boating Carnival, Palm Beach

AM&B © H56665   Feb. 13, 1905
Cameraman: G. W. Bitzer
Location: Palm Beach, Fla. *Photographed:* Feb. 3, 1905
85 ft.   FLA3976 (print)   FRA0270 (neg.)

Photographed from a single camera position, the film shows an inlet or bay area. Approximately thirty vessels of all types pass the camera position. First is a large excursion "tonnage" boat; the final boat to go by is a small inboard-motor-powered dinghy about ten feet long. All of the vessels are draped with signal bunting flags, pennants, etc., and all carry passengers.

Boats Under Oars

AM&B © H18742   June 7, 1902
Cameraman: G. W. Bitzer
Location: Annapolis, Md. [?] *Photographed:* Apr. 29, 1901
13 ft.   FLA4150 (print)   FRA0302 (neg., copy 1)   FRA6401 (neg., copy 2)

Photographed from a single camera position, the film shows seven rowboats, each containing eight oarsmen in the uniform of the U.S. Navy (whites). It is difficult to tell from the position of the boats whether they are racing or just passing a review stand since they are in columns of two and equidistant.

Bob Kick, l'Enfant Terrible

Méliès © H37665   Nov. 6, 1903
Creator: Georges Méliès
Cast: Georges Méliès
Photographed: Fall 1903
50 ft.   FLA4504 (print)   FRA0274 (neg.)

This is a typical example of Méliès's use of a short film to demonstrate his talent in the spectacular use of stop action photography. Mr Méliès plays the part of a fat little obstreperous boy who is led into camera position by his two nursemaids, one of whom gives him a big ball to play with. For the remainder of the film, heads appear and disappear through the use of double exposure and projection, stage props blow up and turn themselves into other objects or people and, finally, Mr. Méliès, as a last gesture, causes himself to disappear.

See also the U.S. version: Bob Kick, the Mischievous Kid

Bob Kick, the Mischievous Kid
Méliès © H37667 Nov. 6, 1903
Creator: Georges Méliès
Cast: Georges Méliès
Photographed: Fall 1903
53 ft. FLA4505 (print) FRA0275 (neg.)

This is a frame-for-frame duplicate of the original issued for the French-language world, under the title Bob Kick, L'Enfant Terrible.

Bobby's Kodak
AM&B © H105983 Feb. 7, 1908
Director: Wallace McCutcheon *Cameraman:* G. W. Bitzer
Cast: Robert Harron, Eddie Dillon
Location: Studio, N.Y.C. *Photographed:* Jan. 24 and 30, 1908
210 ft. FLA4999 (print) FRA0276 (neg.)

The picture opens in a dining room where a family is gathered; a boy in his early teens is taking photographs of those present, including the children and a bearded gentleman. Another scene is set in the kitchen where the cook is preparing food; a man in a policeman's uniform enters, sits down and takes the cook on his lap. The boy photographs them. Then there is a scene in the bedroom; the father is sleeping and the mother is going through the pockets of his trousers. This is followed by an office scene, with the boss kissing his secretary, and another scene where big sister and her beau are embracing. The finale shows the group gathered in the living room: the boy projects the pictures to the consternation of all. As the film ends, the father, furious, spanks the teen-age cameraman, and smashes the camera into small pieces with a hammer.

Boer Commissary Train Treking
Edison © D9118 Apr. 28, 1900
20 ft. FLA4470 (print) FRA0277 (neg.)

From a single camera position, horse-drawn vehicles are shown coming toward the camera; the distance makes them unidentifiable.

The Boer War
AM&B © H65560 Sept. 15, 1905
Cameramen: G. W. Bitzer, F. A. Dobson
Location: Boer War Park, Brighton Beach, L.I., N.Y.
  Photographed: Aug. 19 and 22, 1905
156 ft. FLA4977 (print) FRA0278 (neg.)

The film was photographed from several camera positions and shows what appears to be authentic combat action. If the action was staged, however, it was done very well, inasmuch as the deployment of weapons and personnel shows definite knowledge of technique.

Boers Bringing in British Prisoners
Edison © D7810 Apr. 14, 1900
38 ft. FLA4506 (print) FRA0279 (neg.)

A military group approaches the camera, some walking and some mounted on horseback. Those on horseback wear the uniform of the Boer Army. The film was photographed from a single camera position.

Bold Bank Robbery
Lubin Mfg. Co. © H48436 July 25, 1904
Cameraman: Jack Frawley
Location: Philadelphia
227 ft. FLA4581 (print) FRA0280 (neg.)

Several sets and outdoor facilities were used to show a conspiracy to rob a bank, the bank robbery, the getaway of the robbers, the division of the money, the chase, the cooperation between police and railroad authorities, the ultimate capture of the robbers as a result of help from the railroad authorities, and the final scene of the three burglars breaking rocks in a prison yard.

The Bold Soger Boy
AM&B © H42242 Feb. 18, 1904
Cameraman: A. E. Weed
Location: Studio, N.Y.C. *Photographed:* Feb. 11, 1904
85 ft. FLA4978 (print) FRA0281 (neg.)

This film is a comedy in four scenes; it was photographed as if in the audience of a vaudeville theater. The first scene takes place in a garden or a portion of a park. Seated on a bench is an attractive young girl and a baggy-pants comic, trying to persuade her to accept his kisses. While he is on his knees, the woman jumps up and runs into the embrace of a man in a soldier's uniform. As the scene ends, they are sitting on the bench embracing. The remainder of the film shows the comic renting a costume and going back to the park. He attempts to impress a young girl with his prowess with a saber and a military rifle, when along come several soldiers in uniform. He is arrested and taken off to the guard house. The scene ends as the captain of the battalion approaches the young woman on the bench. The next scene shows the comic with his head and hands through the holes of a prison stock while his colleagues blow smoke in his face, and the film ends.

Bombardment of Taku Forts, by the Allied Fleets
Edison © D16704 Aug. 16, 1900
81 ft. FLA4979 (print) FRA0282 (neg.)
[Boxer Uprising, China]

For the full extent of this "table top" film, a battle between shore batteries and seagoing batteries is in progress. The background is a set resembling the hills surrounding Taku, China. In the foreground at least thirty different types of vessels, both sailing and steam, military craft as well as merchant marine, can be seen steaming in circles, executing military battle maneuvers, firing their guns, etc. The set, the water upon which the ships are floating, and the ships themselves are scale miniatures.

Une Bonne Farce Avec Ma Tete
See: Un Prêté Pour un Rendu; ou, Une Bonne Farce Avec Ma Tête

A Boomerang
AM&B © H34814 Aug. 19, 1903
Cameraman: F. S. Armitage

9 ft. FLA4130 (print) FRA0284 (neg.)

In a set of the interior of a Chinese laundry, two men in Chinese costumes with queues down their backs are ironing. The door opens, a small boy enters and plays a trick on one of the laundrymen. In retaliation, the laundryman places a bucket of water over the door in anticipation of the boy's return. The picture ends as the recipient of the water turns out to be the other laundryman who, instead of staying at his task, starts out the door and is drenched by the contents of the bucket.

The Borrowing Girl

AM&B © H40942 Jan. 16, 1904
Cameraman: A. E. Weed
Location: Studio, N.Y.C. *Photographed:* Jan. 7, 1904
27 ft. FLA3823 (print) FRA0285 (neg.)

The action takes place in front of a set constructed of canvas painted to resemble the boudoir of a young woman. As the first scene begins, a young lady is sitting on the edge of a bed, while another is at a sewing machine. The door opens and another young lady in pajamas comes in. She borrows something in a bottle and walks out. As soon as she is off camera, the two young girls take a toilet water bottle from a dressing table, fill it full of ink and put it back. The door of set opens and the same pajama-clad girl returns, picks up the bottle of toilet water to shake on herself. The ink comes out all over her pajama front. The scene ends as she leaves in anger.

Borrowing Girl and the Atomizer

AM&B © H41860 Feb. 5, 1904
Cameraman: A. E. Weed
Location: Studio, N.Y.C. *Photographed:* Jan. 26, 1904
33 ft. FLA4507 (print) FRA0286 (neg.)

The action takes place in front of a set constructed of canvas painted to resemble the boudoir of a young woman. The first scene begins with one young woman sitting on a bed while another is sitting at a table. The door opens and a third young woman enters. She borrows something in a bottle and walks out. The two young girls take a bottle from a dressing table, fill it with ink and replace it. The door opens and the other girl returns, picks up the bottle and sprays it on herself. The ink squirts in her face and scene ends as she leaves the set in anger.

The Boston Horseless Fire Department

Edison © 59372 Sept. 15, 1899
Location: Battery March St., Boston
77 ft. FLA4508 (print) FRA0287 (neg.)

The first scenes are of a city street and, at a distance of approximately one block, a horse-drawn vehicle is seen approaching. As the vehicle nears the camera, it can be identified as some kind of fire-fighting equipment, such as a pumping engine. Immediately behind it is a mechanically driven pumping engine with large steel-tired wheels. Three pieces of horse-drawn equipment and two pieces of mechanically driven equipment pass the camera. The camera shifts to a large building and six horse-drawn vehicles exiting from the large street-level doors.

Boston School Cadets, 3rd Regiment

AM&B © H16925 Apr. 22, 1902
Cameraman: G. W. Bitzer
Location: Beacon St, Boston *Date:* May 13 or 15, 1899
15 ft. FLA3689 (print) FRA0289 (neg.)

From a camera positioned over the heads of crowds of people lining the streets six military groups can be seen passing in review. They are made up of young boys in military uniforms—some navy and some army.

Le Bourreau Turc

See: The Terrible Turkish Executioner

A Bowery Cafe

AM&B © H32871 June 20, 1903
Cameraman: Arthur Marvin
Date: Oct. 9, 1900
14 ft. FLA3357 (print) FRA0290 (neg.)

This was photographed from a single camera position as if in the audience at a vaudeville show. A bartender in a set of a saloon is cleaning the bar top. A door at the back of the set opens, a young woman enters, leans against the bar and the bartender pours her a drink. As she is drinking it, the door opens again and a formally attired man, apparently inebriated, enters the saloon and begins drinking everything in sight from the bottles and glasses on the table. The woman kisses the bartender and departs. The intoxicated man comes over to the bar and drinks from the neck of a bottle. The bartender squirts seltzer water on the drunk customer and the picture ends.

The Bowery Kiss

AM&B © H24883 Dec. 9, 1902
Cameraman: Robert K. Bonine
Date: June 19, 1902
20 ft. FLA4465 (print) FRA0068 (neg.)

A couple made up to appear as Bowery characters Kid Foley and Sailor Lil are the subjects here. The camera was placed close enough so that only the upper half of the two people can be seen. During the entire film, the man kisses the woman. The film was artificially lighted and no background can be seen.

Bowery Waltz

Edison © 53736 Sept. 24, 1897
18 ft. FLA4030 (print) FLA (35mm print) FRA0292 (neg.) FPA0097 (35mm neg.)

This is a burlesque of the waltz, performed by a young man and woman. The dancing couple overemphasize every standard movement of the exhibition. Considering the date of the film and its lighting (from above), there is every reason to believe it was photographed in the Black Maria, the Edison studio in East Orange, New Jersey.

Boxing for Points

Edison © 60588 Oct. 25, 1897
28 ft. FLA4026 (print) FRA0293 (neg.)

Because of its age, this film is especially interesting. It shows students, either of a military school or some military organization, as they box. The camera was operated by one of Edison's earliest cameramen. At that time, the speed at which the camera was cranked was not standard. The camera Edison used in 1897 was so large and so cumbersome that it was difficult to move.

Boxing Horses, Luna Park, Coney Island

Edison © H48519 July 25, 1904

Cameraman: A. C. Abadie

Location: Luna Park, Coney Island, N.Y. *Photographed:* July 19, 1904

68 ft. FLA4509 (print) FRA0295 (neg.)

A large tanbark ring is shown from a single camera position. Beyond the ring are covered spectator boxes. Inside the ring are two horses; attendants put white baglike objects on their forefeet. At a signal from the ringmaster, the two horses stand on their hind legs; they execute this maneuver several times and then one horse feigns being knocked down.

The Boy Detective

AM&B © H107074 Mar. 7, 1908

Director: Wallace McCutcheon *Cameraman:* G. W. Bitzer *Cast:* Robert Harron (messenger)

Location: Hoboken, N.J.; Studio, N.Y.C. *Photographed:* Feb. 26 and 28, 1908

90 ft. FLA4540 (print) FRA0296 (neg.)

Two men in long black overcoats, who are following an attractive young woman with the apparent intent of robbing her, are noticed by a newsboy and a messenger boy who are playing dice on the street. The film shows the detective work of the young newsboy (played by a women) and ends in the capture of the two culprits by the police. The picture has an unusual ending: the camera moves in to a waist shot of the newsboy who points a pistol directly at the lens. The pistol, on closer examination, turns out to be a cigarette case, and the newsboy takes a cigarette from the case and lights it.

The Boy in the Barrel

AM&B © H33414 July 13, 1903

Cameraman: G. W. Bitzer

Photographed: July 3, 1903

17 ft. FLA3521 (print) FRA0297 (neg.)

This was photographed as if from the audience at a vaudeville show. The subject is a comedy-vaudeville turn about a young boy trying to act like a man. He is out in the back yard behind a barrel smoking a cigarette. The back door of the set opens and a comic old gentleman comes down the stairs. The boy, in his guilt, jumps into the barrel with his lighted cigarette and catches on fire. The old gentleman sees the smoke rising from the barrel, runs back in the house, and a woman with a dishpan full of water comes out and empties it over the barrel. The film ends as the young man, drenched by the water, is standing dripping in the barrel.

The Boy Under the Table

AM&B © H40752 Jan. 11, 1904

Cameraman: A. E. Weed

Location: Studio, N.Y.C. *Photographed:* Dec. 30, 1903

25 ft. FLA3239 (print) FRA0298 (neg.)

An adult man and woman and an adolescent boy are sitting at a dining table. The set surrounding the table was constructed out-of-doors. The three people are eating. The boy stands up as if to excuse himself. The two adults turn their heads having apparently heard a knock at the door. Seizing the opportunity of not being under observation, the boy gets under the dining room table and ties the hem of the woman's flowing skirt to the table cloth. As the woman gets up to answer the door, she pulls the tablecloth with all of the dishes and silverware off the table onto the floor. She admits her guest, turns, lifts up the table and with her other hand holds the hair of the young boy and lifts him to his feet.

Boys Diving, Honolulu

AM&B © H16361 Apr. 10, 1902

Cameraman: Robert K. Bonine

Location: Honolulu *Date:* Aug. 1, 1901

14 ft. FLA4242 (print) FRA0299 (neg.)

A large group of small boys stand on a pier, looking up at what probably is the railing of a ship and hoping pennies will be thrown into the water for them to retrieve. The boys are clothed only in swim trunks. At a distance of approximately a mile, six large seagoing clipper ships can be seen at anchor.

The Boys Help Themselves to Foxy Grandpa's Cigars

AM&B © H18038 May 23, 1902

Cameraman: Robert K. Bonine

Cast: Joseph Hart as Foxy Grandpa

Location: Roof studio, N.Y.C. *Date:* May 17, 1902

20 ft. FLA4358 (print) FRA0300 (neg.)

On a set of a garden, two small boys are sitting on a bench and smoking a cigar. As the film progresses, they continue smoking until apparently they become ill. At that moment, an old gentleman (Foxy Grandpa) escorting a lovely young woman enters and the boys jump up from the bench. They run off the set as the old gentleman offers them another cigar. Although the quality of the film is poor, the action is distinguishable.

The Boys, Still Determined, Try It Again on Foxy Grandpa, with the Same Result

AM&B © H18037 May 23, 1902

Cameraman: Robert K. Bonine

Cast: Joseph Hart as Foxy Grandpa

Location: Roof studio, N.Y.C. *Date:* May 17, 1902

44 ft. FLA4510 (print) FRA1564 (neg.)

On a set of a garden at the side of a house, two large boys are conspiring to play a trick on Foxy Grandpa. As the old gentleman enters the scene, the two boys are busily engaged in attempting to do tricks with strings. The film ends as the old gentleman outshines them by doing magic tricks and conjuring up a rabbit from behind his handkerchief.

The Boys Think They Have One on Foxy Grandpa, but He Fools Them

AM&B © H18036 May 23, 1902

Cameraman: Robert K. Bonine

Cast: Joseph Hart as Foxy Grandpa

Location: Roof studio, N.Y.C. *Date:* May 17, 1902

26 ft. FLA4357 (print) FRA0301 (neg.)

A man made up to appear as an old, grey-haired gentleman can be seen sitting on a bench in a set of a garden. Two small boys, one carrying a banjo, appear and hand the banjo to the old gentleman who begins playing it. The two boys start to dance to his accompaniment and when they finish, they indicate that he cannot equal their skill at dancing. The old gentleman rises from the bench, goes to the center of the stage, and executes some very intricate steps while playing his own accompaniment on the banjo, to the amazement and astonishment of the boys.

The Boys Try to Put One Over on Foxy Grandpa

AM&B © H18035 May 23, 1902

Cameraman: Robert K. Bonine

Cast: Joseph Hart as Foxy Grandpa

Location: Roof studio, N.Y.C. *Date:* May 17, 1902

32 ft. FLA4511 (print) FRA0303 (neg.)

On a set of a penny arcade or an amusement zone two rather large boys can be seen tampering with one of the devices. A man, who is dressed and walks as if he were elderly, appears on the scene. Judging from the gestures of the two boys, they attempt to convince him to try the device with which they have tampered. He does, but the trick backfires and the boys are the butt of their practical joke. The remainder of the film shows "Grandpa" working other devices, to the amusement of the two boys.

Boyville Fire Brigade

AM&B © H32388 June 4, 1903

36 ft. FLA4279 (print) FRA0304 (neg.)

A simulated fire is shown in a house that appears to be a two-story building; it actually is a miniature house. Children dressed as adults can be seen coming out of the door waving their arms. Several boys bring their fire department, consisting of miniature fire apparatus, to the scene, remove furniture, and squirt water on the fire.

Branding Cattle

Edison © 13529 Feb. 24, 1898

62 ft. FLA4512 (print) FRA0306 (neg.)

The poor condition of the film allows little opportunity for good description. However, it is possible to see in the foreground a white steer being branded by four men. It is being held by a back leg, its horns, and lassos.

See also: Calf Branding

Brannigan Sets Off the Blast

AM&B © H83102 Sept. 27, 1906

Cameraman: F. A. Dobson

Location: Studio and environs, N.Y.C. *Photographed:* Aug. 30, 1906

87 ft. FLA4980 (print) FRA0305 (neg.)

The film is made up of photography of an excavation site combined with a film using actors and a set. This is a farcical situation of excavation workmen splitting rocks with dynamite. One of the workmen leaves and the dynamite crew sets an explosive charge. The workman returns, strikes the rock with a sledge hammer and there is an explosion. When the smoke clears, there is a hole in the ground, which the falling workman soon fills. Stop action photography was employed to allow the substitution of a dummy for the actor.

The Brave Hunter

Biograph © J168476 Apr. 22, 1912

Director: Mack Sennett

Cast: Mack Sennett, Mabel Normand, Fed Mace, Dell Henderson

182 ft. FLA5264 (print)

The opening scene shows a hunting lodge in a small community where the lodge keeper (Dell Henderson) greets his guests. One of the actors (Mack Sennett), dressed in top hat, swallowtail coat, etc., indicates he is a great hunter and exhibits his animal-skin trophies. He starts out hunting alone, notices movement in the bushes and encounters a large black bear that chases him up a tree. The balance of the picture is devoted to the dilemma of the man in the tree, and his chagrin when a guest (Mabel Normand) entices the bear back into camp with food, after he arrives with self-inflicted wounds and torn clothing and a story of having been attacked by a bear.

A Break for Freedom

AM&B © H70058 Dec. 15, 1905

Cameraman: G. W. Bitzer

Location: Studio, N.Y.C. *Photographed:* Dec. 6, 1905

22 ft. FLA3968 (print) FRA0308 (neg.)

The subject of this film, a prison break, was filmed from a single camera position. The action is of a guard being overpowered by the inmates as he brings them food. The second guard is shot as he comes to the aid of the first, and the prisoners escape.

Breaking of the Crowd at Military Review at Longchamps

Edison © D18580 Aug. 29, 1900

Location: Paris

16 ft. FLA4104 (print) FRA0309 (neg.)

The film was photographed in a paddock in front of the grandstand at a large racecourse. Immediately in front of the camera position many persons can be seen walking about. Some are aware of the camera while others are not. From their movements, it is evident that the military review has just finished.

The Bridal Chamber

AM&B © H63798 July 24, 1905

Cameraman: G. W. Bitzer

Location: Studio, N.Y.C. *Photographed:* July 13, 1905

25 ft. FLA4513 (print) FRA0310 (neg.)

The film begins in a set of a hotel lobby where a maid is dusting, a room clerk is at the desk, and one or two guests are standing around. A man and a woman acting as newlyweds enter and are given a room off the lobby. The set is so constructed that the interior of the bedroom can also been seen. The bridegroom, sensing the presence of a Peeping Tom, climbs up on the door, looks over the transom, and pours water over the head of the desk clerk who was peering through the keyhole.

Bridal Veil Falls

AM&B © H17492 May 8, 1902

Location: Yosemite Valley, Calif.

15 ft. FLA3168 (print) FRA0311 (neg.)

The waterfall was filmed from a single camera position at a distance of approximately a thousand yards. All that is visible are the trees on either side of the falls and the falls itself. The height of the falls is approximately three hundred feet.

Bridge Traffic, Manila

AM&B © H18043 May 23, 1902
Cameraman: Robert K. Bonine
Location: Manila, Philippine Islands *Date:* Aug. 14, 1901
16 ft. FLA4135 (print) FRA0312 (neg.)

The photographer placed his camera on the edge of an entrance to a bridge in order to film the different types of vehicles that passed his point of view. The area, the year, and the locale confined the transportation to nothing more efficient than many two-wheeled, ox-drawn carts. However, there are some two-wheeled, donkey-powered carts in the film.

Bringing Up a Girl in the Way She Should Go, no. 1

AM&B © H69122 Oct. 30. 1905
Cameraman: G. W. Bitzer
Location: Studio, N.Y.C. *Photographed:* Oct. 17, 1905
25 ft. FLA4514 (print) FRA0314 (neg.)

From a single camera position, a young woman can be seen sitting in a rocking chair in her living room. She is reading a book. A man in a nightshirt comes down the stairs and attempts to get the girl to stop reading and rocking and go upstairs. A woman joins him, they all talk some more, and then the father, losing patience, picks up the girl and carries her up the stairs.

Bringing Up a Girl in the Way She Should Go, no. 2

AM&B © H68123 Oct. 30, 1905
Cameraman: G. W. Bitzer
Location: Studio, N.Y.C. *Photographed:* Oct. 19, 1905
63 ft. FLA4515 (print) FRA0315 (neg.)

The entire film was photographed from one camera position. A young girl is sitting in a rocking chair, reading. Her father winds the clock and indicates that she should go to bed, which she refuses to do. Her mother comes downstairs and also indicates that she should go to bed. Again she refuses. Both the man and woman, after cuffing the girl, carry her bodily up the stairs.

British Light Artillery

AM&B © H34101 Aug. 3, 1903
19 ft. FLA3325 (print) FRA0316 (neg.)

The camera was placed on a drill field to film the activities of a British light horse artillery group. Approaching the camera at a distance of approximately fifty yards is an officer mounted on a horse. Directly behind him is a light-artillery weapon drawn by six horses, on the first team of which a mounted rider can be seen. Three identical units follow the first.

Broadway & Union Square, New York

AM&B © H33290 July 8, 1903
Cameraman: Arthur Marvin
Location: Broadway and 14th Street, N.Y.C. *Date:* Aug. 19, 1901

16 ft. FLA4403 (print) FLA5951 (35mm print) FRA0317 (neg.)

This short film, photographed from a single camera position, shows a horse-drawn streetcar approaching and another passing and departing. Both cars are filled with passengers.

The Broadway Massage Parlor

AM&B © H65054 Aug. 30, 1905
Cameraman: G. W. Bitzer
Location: Studio, N.Y.C. *Photographed:* July 20, 1905
28 ft. FLA4102 (print) FRA0318 (neg.)

The set for this film was constructed so that, from the camera's point of view, two rooms are visible. One is an office and a massage parlor; the other, to the right of the camera, is a physical culture gymnasium. The action begins with a woman and a man seated in the office. The woman gets up, goes through into the other section and opens the door to admit two prospective customers. One, a young woman, is sent in the office to have a face massage. The other, her mother, is a woman of large proportions. The mother remains in the gymnasium and starts doing calisthenics. But while she is performing with the dumbbells, she realizes that the man giving the facial is making advances to her daughter. She rushes in and hits him on the head. The final scene shows her admonishing her daughter for allowing it to happen, while the other half of the set shows the wife hitting her husband on the head.

The Broken Broom

See: A Kiss and a Tumble

The Broken Doll

Biograph © J146623 Oct. 19, 1910
Director: D. W. Griffith *Cameraman:* G. W. Bitzer
Cast: Gladys Egan, Kate Bruce, Alfred Paget, Linda Arvidson, Owen Moore, Mack Sennett, Dell Henderson, W. Chrystie Miller
Location: Coytesville, N.J.; Cuddebackville, N.Y. *Photographed:* Sept. 2 and 7, 1910
406 ft. FLA5265 (print) FRA0319 (neg.)

An unsolicited kindness by a white girl toward an Indian girl saves the lives of the white settlers. Members of an Indian tribe come to the settlement to buy food and find the white settlers unfriendly. An Indian is killed, and the Indians plan to attack the settlement. But the little Indian girl, who had been given a doll by the white girl, runs to her friend and warns her of the uprising. The settlers are able to prepare themselves, and they beat off the Indians. The Indian girl is wounded during the attack and, as the film ends, she slowly and painfully makes her way back to the doll she had been given.

The Broken Locket

Biograph © J131862 Sept. 17, 1909
Director: D. W. Griffith *Cameraman:* G. W. Bitzer
Cast: Henry B. Walthall, Billy Quirk, Frank Powell, Mack Sennett, Mary Pickford, Lottie Pickford, Kate Bruce, Arthur Johnson, Marion Leonard, Dell Henderson
Location: Edgewater, N.J.; Studio, N.Y.C. *Photographed:* Aug. 10, 11 and 19, 1909
422 ft. FLA5266 (print) FRA0320 (neg.)

The misbehavior of an alcoholic causes his sweetheart to have a stroke and go blind. A reformed alcoholic begins work on a construction job, carrying half a locket as a talisman. Soon after he arrives, he is again tempted by alcohol, and he becomes involved with a woman he meets in the saloon. The woman writes to his sweetheart and tells her of their infatuation. This causes the heroine to have a stroke which leaves her blind. The hero, now a complete derelict, makes his way home. Learning of his sweetheart's condition proves too much for him, and he is shown in dirty and ragged clothes walking down the dirt road away from the home of the blind heroine.

The Broker's Athletic Typewriter
AM&B © H60654 May 9, 1905
Cameraman: G. W. Bitzer
Location: Studio, N.Y.C. *Photographed:* Apr. 27, 1905
38 ft. FLA4516 (print) FRA0321 (neg.)

The set resembles an office where a woman is typing. A young man is at a desk across the room. The action begins when the young man leaves his desk, crosses the room and kisses the stenographer on the back of her neck. An old gentleman comes through the door in the back of the set, admonishes his employees and continues walking toward the stenographer as the young man leaves the room. The employer starts dictating a letter and then makes advances to the stenographer. She resents this, stands up, takes hold of his lapels and starts throwing him around the room. This is done by the use of stop action photography so that a dummy is substituted for the actor.

After several circuits of the room, the stenographer throws her employer to the floor and, with trick photography, he comes to life. At that moment, the employer's wife comes in and the film ends as she is striking him on the head with an umbrella.

Broncho Busting Scenes, Championship of the World
Edison © H24359 Nov. 26, 1902
80 ft. FLA4981 (print) FRA0322 (neg.)

A flat area surrounded by bleachers where several thousand people are watching men astride bucking horses is shown. During the course of the film, several horses with several different riders can be seen at a distance, while some are as close to the camera position as fifty feet.

Brook Trout Fishing
AM&B © H16650 Apr. 16, 1902
Cameraman: F. S. Armitage
Location: Grand Trunk R.R. *Date:* June 6, 1900
29 ft. FLA4276 (print) FRA0323 (neg.)

The camera shows a small waterfall and a stream. Across the stream on the bank is a man with a fishing pole in one hand and a retrieving net in the other. During the course of the film, he makes the normal movements of a man accustomed to trout fishing. High on the bank to the right is a spectator. At the end of the film, the fisherman catches, nets, and lands a fish.

The Brooklyn Handicap—1904
AM&B © H46715 June 3, 1904
Cameraman: G. W. Bitzer
Location: Gravesend, N.Y. *Photographed:* May 26, 1904
44 ft. FLA5267 (print) FRA0324 (neg.)

To film this event, the camera was placed inside the rail, on the track surface itself. As the film begins, in the foreground a gate opens and a horse ridden by a jockey is escorted across the track, followed by several men who appear to be fans of the race horse. Following the first horse are six in succession, and then there is a large group of men surrounding another horse that appears to be a favorite. The horses head for the starting position, moving away from the camera. In the background at a distance of several hundred yards is a grandstand filled with people. The film ends with a view of the race track paddock with two horses with riders walking around.

Brothers of the Misericordia, Rome
AM&B © H35647 Sept. 12, 1903
21 ft. FLA3401 (print) FRA0325 (neg.)

Photographed from a single camera position, the film shows a crowd of approximately a hundred persons watching a procession of individuals clothed in black-hooded robes. The group in the forefront is carrying what looks like a black-draped coffin on their shoulders and in the background, judging by its architecture, is a cathedral.

Brush Between Cowboys and Indians
Edison © H46138 May 18, 1904
Cameraman: A. C. Abadie
Location: Bliss, Oklahoma Territory *Photographed:* May 7, 1904
39 ft. FLA4517 (print) FRA0326 (neg.)

From a single camera position, a river is shown. Some men on horseback enter the scene from the right. The mounted men shoot rifles at some other men, supposed to be Indians, who are also on horseback at some distance. The total cast consists of about twenty men and horses, and the film seems to have been staged.

Bubbles!
AM&B © H41757 Feb. 2, 1904
Cameraman: A. E. Weed
Location: Studio, N.Y.C. *Photographed:* Jan. 16, 1904
30 ft. FLA4518 (print) FRA0327 (neg.)

The film was photographed from a single camera position and it shows three young women sitting around a small table blowing bubbles. In the center of the table is a bowl in which each of the young ladies is dipping a clay pipe. After they dip the pipe into the bowl, they blow bubbles from the end of the pipe. They then shake the pipes, allowing the bubbles to float into the air.

Buck Dance
Edison © 13556 Feb. 24, 1898
32 ft. FLA3385 (print) FRA0329 (neg.)

The film shows American Indian tents and some Indians who are seated on the ground in a circle around some male dancers.

A Bucket of Cream Ale
AM&B © H42001 Feb. 10, 1904
Cameraman: A. E. Weed
Location: Studio, N.Y.C. *Photographed:* Feb. 2, 1904
28 ft. FLA4519 (print) FRA0330 (neg.)

A man is sitting at a table in front of a wall in a room of a house. Another actor, costumed as a black woman servant, appears with a bucket of beer and pours a glass for the man at the table. When his back is turned, she takes a drink out of the bucket. He discovers her drinking, which enrages him, and he throws his glass of beer at her. She, in turn, picks up the bucket of beer and empties the contents over him.

A Bucking Broncho

AM&B © H29002 Mar. 6, 1903
Rider: William Jennings
Photographed: 1899
27 ft. FLA3624 (print) FRA0331 (neg.)

The locale of the film appears to be either an athletic field or a fair grounds area, as it is surrounded by bleachers. These are empty. In the foreground can be seen four men, three of whom are holding a horse while the fourth is attempting to mount. As he succeeds, the animal is released, and starts to run and buck and otherwise act as though he resented being saddled and ridden. The man riding the bucking horse is wearing sheepskin leg protectors.

Bucking Broncos

Edison © H46139 May 18, 1904
Cameraman: A. C. Abadie
Location: Bliss, Oklahoma Territory *Photographed:* May 9, 1904
27 ft. FLA3659 (print) FRA0332 (neg.)

The locale of the film was a large, flat area resembling an athletic field. Spectators surround the area and watch three men, two of whom are holding a horse while the other is mounting. When the horse is released, it immediately starts to buck, jump, twirl, and otherwise endeavor to unseat the rider. Two mounted riders come alongside the horse and subdue it.

Bucking the Blizzard

AM&B © H25960 Dec. 31, 1902
Location: Watertown, N.Y. *Photographed:* 1899
15 ft. FLA4050 (print) FRA0337 (neg.)

This short film shows snow-covered fields and, in the distance, a locomotive with a snowplow on the front is spraying snow all over. The film was photographed near Watertown, New York, during the 1899 blizzard.

Buffalo Bill's Wild West Parade

AM&B © H19660 July 2, 1902
Cameraman: F. S. Armitage
Location: Fifth Avenue, N.Y.C. *Date:* Apr. 1, 1901
41 ft. FLA4520 (print) FRA0328 (neg., copy 1) FRA1565 (neg., copy 2)

The film, photographed from a single camera position, shows a parade down what seems to be the main street of a small city, judging from the crowds that followed the participants in the parade (Indians, etc.). There were no photographs of Buffalo Bill.

Buffalo Fire Department

AM&B © H17038 Apr. 26, 1902
Cameraman: F. S. Armitage
Location: Buffalo, N.Y. *Date:* June 27, 1899
23 ft. FLA3211 (print) FRA0535 (neg.)

From a single camera position, several horse-drawn fire-fighting vehicles are shown passing the camera. The many spectators indicate that this was either a false alarm or a staged event.

Buffalo Fire Department in Action

Edison © 43411 July 31, 1897
Location: Buffalo, N.Y.
18 ft. FLA3042 (print) FRA0339 (neg.)

The short length plus the poor condition of the film do not permit a detailed explanation.

Buffalo Police on Parade

Edison © 43417 July 31, 1897
Location: Buffalo, N.Y.
21 ft. FLA3032 (print) FRA0340 (neg.)

Photographed from a single camera position, several companies of marching men dressed in policemen's uniforms are shown passing the camera obliquely.

Buffalo Stockyards

Edison © 43408 July 31, 1897
Location: Buffalo, N.Y.
57 ft. FLA4521 (print) FRA1566 (neg.)

The film was photographed from a single camera position with the camera directed toward the opening in a large barn from which horses in groups of twos, threes, and fours are led past the camera position. Following the horses are two coaches drawn by four horses. The film ends as the horses and the carriage return and enter the barn.

Building a Harbor at San Pedro

Edison © H11749 Dec. 19, 1901
91 ft. FLA4982 (print) FRA0342 (neg.)

The film was photographed from a single camera position on a small boat, which is bobbing up and down at the beginning of the breakwater at San Pedro, California. The action consists of large granite boulders being thrown into the water by a steam crane.

The Bull and the Picnickers

Edison © H23243 Oct. 29, 1902
Cameraman: Edwin S. Porter
31 ft. FLA4522 (print) FRA0343 (neg.)

The setting for this comedy was the edge of a cow pasture. In the immediate foreground, two men and two women are sitting on the ground around a picnic spread and enjoying themselves. In the background are two tramps who are walking toward the picnickers. The tramps gesture toward the lunch, confer, turn and walk out of the scene. Shortly before the end of the film, a papier-maché bull enters the scene and frightens away the picnickers. The animal proves to be the tramps, who set about eating the hastily abandoned luncheon.

Bull Fight, no. 1
Edison ⓒ 16431 Mar. 10, 1898
Location: Durango, Mexico
26 ft. FLA4391 (print) FRA0344 (neg.)

The film was photographed as if in the audience at a bull fight. The first thing that can be seen in the foreground is the bull fighter holding a cape. His close proximity to the camera does not allow the bull to be seen at the same time. As the film progresses, it can be noted that the fight has reached the stage of the picador and the bandillero. In the foreground people are sitting and standing behind a fence and watching the activities.

See also: Bull Fight, no. 2 and 3; Train Hour in Durango, Mexico; and Washday in Mexico

Bull Fight, no. 2
Edison ⓒ 16432 Mar. 10, 1898
Location: Durango, Mexico
26 ft. FLA4392 (print) FRA0345 (neg.)

From a single camera position as if in the audience, a bull fight is shown. The fight has progressed to the point of the bandilleros. The film does not show the kill.

Bull Fight, no. 3
Edison ⓒ 16433 Mar. 10, 1898
Location: Durango, Mexico
26 ft. FLA4393 (print) FRA0346 (neg.)

A Mexican bull fight was photographed from a single camera position. The bull is immense, black and white, and rather confused, as he lies down in the middle of the ring.

The Burd [i.e. Bund], Shanghai
AM&B ⓒ H34806 Aug. 19, 1903
Cameraman: Robert K. Bonine
Location: Shanghai *Date:* Aug. 31, 1901
16 ft. FLA4404 (print) FRA0349 (neg.)

The film shows the activity on the Bund (a main thoroughfare of a large Oriental city) and includes a large section of a wide street. On the side away from the camera position, buildings and dwellings can be seen. Between the buildings and the camera, various means of transportation, such as one- and two-wheeled vehicles, some horse-drawn and some drawn by coolies, can be seen.

The Burglar
AM&B ⓒ H35073 Aug. 27, 1903
Cameraman: A. E. Weed
Location: Studio, N.Y.C. *Photographed:* Aug. 13, 1903
42 ft. FLA4523 (print) FRA0352 (neg.)

A woman and a man are in bed in a set of a bedroom. A window in the center of the wall next to the bed slowly opens. The woman awakens her companion and indicates there is a burglar in the house because she has heard a noise. The burglar enters through the window and hides behind some furniture. The woman, tired of waiting for her husband, gets a gun and wanders around the room endangering all and sundry. The husband fetches a policeman who arrests the burglar. The burglar is taken away by the policeman, the woman swoons, and the husband stands in a proud pose as the picture ends.

The Burglar
Edison ⓒ 31443 May 20, 1898
17 ft. FLA3998 (print) FRA0350 (neg.)

A set of an office can be seen as the film begins. The principal object on the set is a big black safe. Approaching the safe is a man dressed in rough clothing with his face covered by a mask. He begins to use some tools he has with him to open the safe but is interrupted by the arrival of another man and hides. The second man goes up to the safe, uses the combination and opens it. He removes all the money, doesn't bother to lock it and walks off, leaving a very unhappy burglar.

The Burglar
Edison ⓒ 40021 July 18, 1898
19 ft. FLA3386 (print) FRA0351 (neg.)

A burglar is seen attempting to open a safe on a set of a business office. While he is engaged in his nefarious activity, he hears someone coming and he hides in a closet. A man carrying a satchel enters through the door, opens the safe by the simple expedient of turning the handle, removes the money and leaves the set. The film ends showing the burglar standing staring at the safe and scratching his head in bewilderment.

The Burglar and the Bundle
AM&B ⓒ H29158 Mar. 11, 1903
14 ft. FLA3648 (print) FRA0353 (neg.)

The film begins on a set of the exterior of a two-story house. A man wearing a mask and carrying a carpetbag can be seen attempting to climb up to the second floor of the house. He finds a bench and starts the climb, but loses his footing and falls on to a table.

The Burglar in the Bed Chamber
Edison ⓒ 73461 Dec. 16, 1898
17 ft. FLA4088 (print) FRA0348 (neg.)

The set is designed as a bedroom in a modest house and a man and a woman can be seen sleeping in the double bed. A man wearing rough clothing and a mask over his face enters the room and begins ransacking everything. This noise wakens the woman and she gets up and leaves the room. She returns with a policeman who has a nightstick which he waves about. The policeman takes the burglar into custody. The man who was asleep in the bed becomes frightened by all the commotion and hides behind the bed, ending the film.

The Burglar on the Roof
Edison ⓒ 72468 Dec. 12, 1898
25 ft. FLA3249 (print) FRA0354 (neg.)

This single camera position film begins with a scene of a rooftop. A man climbs through the skylight. He turns to pick up his carpetbag or tool sack when he is set upon by several women with brooms. The picture ends with his being subdued by two men who come to the aid of the women.

The Burglar-Proof Bed
AM&B ⓒ H16340 Apr. 10, 1902
Cameraman: Arthur Marvin
Location: Roof studio, N.Y.C. *Date:* June 27, 1900

10 ft. FLA3610 (print) FRA0355 (neg.)

The main prop in this film is a Murphy bed. The set, of a man's bedroom, has pictures on the wall, articles of clothing about the room, and, as the film begins, a man asleep in the Murphy bed. A door to the set opens and a man dressed as a burglar enters the room. The burglar points a gun at the man who wakes and raises his head in surprise at the actions of his unwanted visitor. He releases a mechanism, the Murphy bed folds up, and explosions begin through the holes in the bottom of the bed. The burglar is subdued and, as the film ends, the occupant of the Murphy bed is seen jumping around and waving an American flag in glee.

See also: Subub Surprises the Burglar, copyright by Edison in 1903.

A Burglar's Mistake
AM&B © H124687 Mar. 25, 1909
Director: D. W. Griffith *Cameramen:* G. W. Bitzer, Arthur Marvin
Cast: Charles Inslee, Harry Salter, Marion Leonard, Owen Moore, Mack Sennett, Robert Harron
Location: Studio, N.Y.C. *Photographed:* Feb. 16 and 18, Mar. 3 and 5, 1909
356 ft. FLA5268 (print) FRA0356 (neg.)

The story is built around what happens when a man is pushed too far. The hero, a professional man with a large family, is coerced into giving money for "protection" to a thief and burglar. Finally, he tells the burglar he has no intention of paying any more money. The burglar mistakenly burglarizes his home and is caught in the act by the hero, who deliberately shoots the intruder and calls the police. The film was taken in three locations: the living room of a house, the hero's business office, and the burglar's headquarters. Mack Sennett played the part of an associate of the burglar as well as the police captain.

The Burglar's Slide for Life
Edison © H60117 Apr. 28, 1905
Cameraman: Edwin S. Porter
Location: Studio, N.Y.C. *Photographed:* Apr. 14 and 17, 1905
133 ft. FLA4983 (print) FRA0357 (neg.)

Most of the action takes place in a set of the backyard of a three-story tenement house. However, it begins in an apartment house where a burglar is interrupted by the arrival of two women. He jumps out of the window and clings to the cross-hatching of clotheslines in the backyard. He is pursued down the clothesline escape route by a bulldog that hangs on to him by its teeth, while annoyed residents of the building pelt him with objects. The burglar finally arrives on the ground at the same time as the dog, which grabs him by the seat of the pants and prevents his escape. This allows several women time to add to the confusion by bringing their brooms and beating the poor burglar.

The Burglary
See: The Ex-Convict

Burial of the "Maine" Victims
Edison © 25325 Apr. 21, 1898
69 ft. FLA4525 (print) FRA0359 (neg.)

[Spanish American War]

From a single camera position, the film shows a dusty street and across it a picket fence that surrounds a wooden structure. Approaching the camera on a diagonal are horses drawing a two-horse vehicle on which is placed what appears to be a casket. On either side of the vehicle are four men dressed in uniforms of the U.S. Navy. Following this group are six two-horse vehicles, some identifiable as carriages, and upon each is a flag-draped coffin. Each is escorted by an eight-man guard dressed in the uniform of U.S. Navy enlisted personnel. As the last vehicle approaches the camera position, about a hundred unidentifiable mourners march past in a column. The locale does not appear to be in the United States.

Burlesque Suicide
Edison © H16121 Apr. 7, 1902
Cameraman: Edwin S. Porter
33 ft. FLA3939 (print) FRA0360 (neg.)

The camera was placed close to the actor who looks directly into it. He is sitting at a table on which there are a revolver, a glass, and a decanter half filled with some unidentifiable liquor. His actions indicate that he is intoxicated and that he is attempting to kill himself. The film ends as he takes the gun from his temple, lays it on the table near the glass, points his finger at the lens of the camera, and laughs. There is an interesting photographic separation between the background, made of showy wallpaper, and the subject.

The Burning of Durland's Riding Academy
Edison © H14437 Feb. 24, 1902
78 ft. FLA4526 (print) FRA0361 (neg.)

The subject is the complete destruction of a large brick building by fire. The film shows part of one brick wall left standing, large piles of rubble, and, as the camera pans, it includes more piles of rubble, a stalled streetcar, and occasionally one of the several fire hoses playing on the fire.

Burning of St. Pierre
Edison © H18371 May 31, 1902
31 ft. FLA3809 (print) FRA0362 (neg.)
[Martinique]

The condition of the film is very poor and it is almost impossible to see the outline of the constructed mountain and the miniature city below it. The subject concerns a catastrophe, but the condition of the film does not permit description of detail.

Burning of the Standard Oil Co.'s Tanks, Bayonne, N.J.
Edison © D14429 July 12, 1900
Location: Bayonne, N.J. *Photographed:* July 5, 1900
48 ft. FLA4396 (print) FRA1567 (neg.)

The film was photographed from a single camera position sighting down the main street of Bayonne, New Jersey, during the fire that almost completely destroyed the city. Flames and fire are shown in the background, and people escaping in wagons, etc., with their belongings can be seen.

Burning of the Standard Oil Co.'s Tanks, Bayonne, N.J.
Edison © D14429 July 12, 1900
37 ft.

From a camera placed on the street at eye level, the cameraman photographed a fire. Approximately one-quarter mile distant, in the background, a fire is burning that emits very black columns of smoke over a large area. In the foreground, between the camera position and the fire, several buildings can be seen, but they do not seem to be in jeopardy. Judging from the people who are walking along the street and the many horse-drawn carts, one could assume no one was anxious about the fire.

Buster and Tige Put a Balloon Vendor Out of Business
See: Buster Brown Series

Buster Brown and the Dude
See: Buster Brown Series

Buster Brown Series: Buster and Tige Put a Balloon Vendor Out of Business
Edison © H43074 Mar. 9, 1904
Cameraman: Edwin S. Porter
Location: Studio, N.Y.C.
34 ft. FLA5269 (print) FRA8281 (neg.)

The story line in this picture is built around Buster Brown, his "mommy," several dogs, and a balloon vendor. The first action that can be seen is the balloon vendor walking back and forth on a stage with a backdrop of a large city. Buster Brown, his dog, and his mother approach the vendor. Buster orders his dog to bite the vendor and soon the noise attracts several other dogs. The balloon vendor, in fear for his life and his property, attempts to fight off the dogs, but they destroy his balloons one by one.

See also: Pranks of Buster Brown and His Dog Tige; Buster Brown and the Dude; Buster Makes Room for His Mama at the Bargain Counter; Buster's Joke on Papa; Buster's Dog to the Rescue; Buster and Tige Puts(s) a Balloon Vendor out of Business

Buster Brown Series: Buster Brown and the Dude
Edison © H43074 Mar. 9, 1904
Cameraman: Edwin S. Porter
Location: Studio, N.Y.C.
33 ft. FLA5269 (print) FRA8278 (neg.)

This is about "Buster," his dog "Tige," two young ladies, and a young man and his dog. The action takes place in front of a set of the front of a dry goods or small department store. Buster enters the scene with his dog, which he orders to sit. From camera right come two young ladies dressed in the mode of the day. A well-dressed young "dude" leading a small bulldog enters from camera left. He approaches the two young ladies and tips his hat. This apparently upsets Buster as he orders his dog to fight with the small dog. The picture ends as the two dogs are seen going round and round in the center of the stage.

Buster Brown Series: Buster Makes Room for His Mama at the Bargain Counter
Edison © H43074 Mar. 9, 1904

Cameraman: Edwin S. Porter
Location: Studio, N.Y.C.
41 ft. FLA5269 (print) FRA8279 (neg.)

The action and the plot are built around a bargain counter in a department store. The set shows the counter and the displayed merchandise. The first action is a little boy, "Buster," and his dog "Tige" entering the scene. Immediately behind the boy are approximately twenty women who crowd around the merchandise at the bargain counter. Buster's mother appears and cannot get to view the merchandise. Buster orders his dog to cause a commotion. The film ends as Tige is jumping, barking, and grabbing the legs of stools, which cause all of the women at the bargain counter to leave, allowing Buster's mother to select her purchases unhindered.

Buster Brown Series: Buster's Dog to the Rescue
Edison © H43074 Mar. 9, 1904
Cameraman: Edwin S. Porter
42 ft. FLA5269 (print) FRA0365 (neg.)

A buxom woman can be seen sitting by the kitchen table and feigning sleep. A small boy, "Buster" and his dog enter the room. The boy, seeing the cook asleep, ties her apron over her head. He then goes into the closet and helps himself to jam. At that moment, a tramp in torn clothes enters through the window in the set. Buster seats him at the table and begins feeding him. His mother comes in and Buster sicks his dog on the tramp. He is complimented for his bravery and given large portions of cookies and jam. This ends the film.

Buster Brown Series: Pranks of Buster Brown and His Dog Tige
Edison © H43074 Mar. 9, 1904
Cameraman: Edwin S. Porter
Location: Studio, N.Y.C.
68 ft. FLA5269 (print) FRA8280 (neg.)

The plot is built around the activities of Buster Brown, a small, mischievous boy. The complete film was photographed from a single camera position. It begins by showing a kitchen where a buxom woman is busy at work. The small boy enters, asks for something and is refused. As the woman leaves the room, it is evident from her gestures that she is admonishing him to behave himself. As the door closes behind her, Buster places a ladder so as to reach something on a top shelf. He is caught ascending the ladder by his mother and soundly spanked. His mother leaves the room, shaking her finger at him, and his dog Tige enters. Buster orders him to climb the ladder, steal the object and return it to his master. The film ends as the dog is being rewarded by pats on the head.

Buster Makes Room for His Mama at the Bargain Counter
See: Buster Brown Series

Buster's Dog to the Rescue
See: Buster Brown Series

Buster's Joke on Papa
Edison © H37396 Oct. 28, 1903
63 ft. FLA4528 (print) FRA0366 (neg.)

The action begins in the kitchen where the cook is handling some live crabs that have just been purchased. The next scene is in a bedroom where a man can be seen sitting in a rocker reading a newspaper. He leaves the room to prepare for bed and our hero, "Buster," is seen placing crabs in his bed. Father returns, gets into bed and right out again, with some crabs attached to his anatomy. The last scene shows Buster being led to a chair by his mother. He is wearing a large, soft pillow tied to his posterior.

Buster's Joke on Papa
Edison © H39775 Dec. 21, 1903
53 ft. FLA4529 (print) FRA0367 (neg.)

The first scene shows Mother buying crabs from a vendor. The second shows Father preparing for bed while Buster places crabs in the bed. Father retires and leaps from the bed in agony at the pain inflicted by the crabs. The last scene shows Buster standing up to eat his breakfast rather than sit on a pillow.

A Busy Day for the Corset Models
AM&B © H42037 Feb. 11, 1904
Cameraman: A. E. Weed
Location: Studio, N.Y.C. *Photographed:* Jan. 29, 1904
30 ft. FLA3407 (print) FRA0368 (neg.)

This risqué film of women trying on corsets over voluminous slips and other undergarments was photographed in a set of the showroom or salesroom for ladies' undergarments. During the film, several young women stand on a pedestal and remove one garment at a time until there is a large pile of clothing beside them.
See also: The Way to Sell Corsets

Butt's Manual, St. John's School
AM&B © H44026 Mar. 29, 1904
Cameraman: G. W. Bitzer
Location: Manlius, N.Y. *Photographed:* Mar. 17, 1904
44 ft. FLA4530 (print) FRA1568 (neg.)

Men in army uniforms are facing the camera. Behind the three companies can be seen a band of about fifty pieces. The men in uniform are doing calisthenic exercises with a standard U.S. Army rifle.
See also: Company Drill, St. John's Military Academy; Dress Parade, St. John's Academy; Manual of Arms, St. John's Military Academy; and Small Gun Drill, St. John's Academy

Buying Stamps from Rural Wagon, U.S.P.O.
AM&B © H34985 Aug. 22, 1903
Cameraman: A. E. Weed
Location: Westminster, Md. *Photographed:* Aug. 10, 1903
22 ft. FLA4058 (print) FRA0369 (neg.)
[United States Post Office]

The film shows a man carrying a mail sack. He climbs the stairs of a front porch, rings a doorbell, and a woman comes to the door. The postman hands her something, turns around, and walks down the stairs.

By Right of Sword
See: Duel Scene, "By Right of Sword"

C. Von Waldersee Reviewing 1st Chita & Reg. Cossacks
See: Cossack Cavalry

C. Von Waldersee Reviewing 2nd & 14th Russian Artillery & 3rd Siberia
See: Review of Russian Artillery

A Cable Road in San Francisco
Edison © H13038 Jan. 11, 1902
52 ft. FLA4531 (print) FRA0370 (neg.)

Scenes of the city were photographed from the front of a cable car as it went up and down the hills of San Francisco.

Cake Walk
AM&B © H31674 May 11, 1903
Cameraman: F. S. Armitage
Cast: Americus Quartet
Location: Philadelphia *Date:* Sept. 18, 1900
11 ft. FLA3381 (print) FRA0371 (neg.)

The opening scene shows three black men and two black women formally attired standing with their backs against an unpainted backdrop. The man at the center moves toward the camera from the line and performs a dance step. He returns to his position in line, and for the remainder of the film the others do a strutting type of Cake Walk dance.
See also: Comedy Cake Walk

A Cake Walk on the Beach at Coney Island
AM&B © H49072 Aug. 13, 1904
Cameraman: G. W. Bitzer
Location: Coney Island, N.Y. *Photographed:* Aug. 7, 1904
52 ft. FLA4984 (print) FRA0372 (neg.)

On the sand at the seashore, organized rows of men and women attired in bathing suits dance, run, jump, and walk past the camera position several times.

A Calamitous Elopement
AM&B © H113967 July 28, 1908
Director: D. W. Griffith *Cameramen:* Arthur Marvin, G. W. Bitzer
Cast: Linda Arvidson, John Cumpson, Tony O'Sullivan, Frank Gebhardt, D. W. Griffith
Location: Studio, N.Y.C. *Photographed:* July 9 and 11, 1908
274 ft. FLA5270 (print) FRA0373 (neg.)

The theme of this film is the troubles of an eloping couple. The first scene takes place in a living room and the camera is then shifted to show the exterior, complete with second-story balcony. While the hero seeks a ladder, a nondescript character with a rope ladder appears, apparently with the intention of burglarizing the house. He hides and sees the luggage come hurtling over the banister. A policeman comes along and, misunderstanding the situation, takes the lovers off to the police station, leaving their luggage attended only by the burglar. The young couple, freed by the magistrate, go to their apartment, unlock their luggage, and leave. The burglar, who had hidden in their trunk, lets himself out, helps himself to clothing and everything else of value, and walks out the door smoking a cigar. One of the two policemen in the film is D. W. Griffith, and the police precinct is the front door of the Biograph Studio at 11 East Fourteenth Street, New York.

Calf Branding
Edison © 13531 Feb. 24, 1898
62 ft. FLA4532 (print) FRA1569 (neg.)

The cameraman placed his camera near a fire where some branding irons were being heated. As the film begins, three men can be seen going through the various operations of branding calves. In the background is a large herd of cattle.

See also: Branding Cattle

California Limited, A.T. & S.F. R.R.
Edison © 13553 Feb. 24, 1898
Location: "Lucky" Baldwin's Ranch, Santa Anita, Calif.
30 ft. FLA3067 (print) FRA0379 (neg.)

A four-car passenger train was photographed from a single camera position as it passed a station.

California Oil Wells in Operation
Edison © H11750 Dec. 19, 1901
Location: Inglewood, Calif.
42 ft. FLA4533 (print) FRA1570 (neg.)

The film begins close to the machine house of an oil well. Beyond the structure in the foreground can be seen several other oil wells in operation—either drilling, pulling drill pipe, or pumping. The activity and the camera position do not allow absolute identification of the locale but, considering the year, the area was about where the city of Inglewood stands today.

California Orange Groves, Panoramic View
Edison © 13552 Feb. 24, 1898
27 ft. FLA3023 (print) FRA0381 (neg.)

The film, photographed from a single camera position, shows what appears to be the front end of a train traveling over a single track through the orange groves next to some foothills in California. Judging from the shadows, the train is heading east.

California Volunteers Marching to Embark
Edison © 38249 June 22, 1898
24 ft. FLA4375 (print) FRA1513 (neg.)
[Spanish-American War]

The film shows U.S. Army troops leaving for the Spanish-American War. However, the camera position was at shoulder level in back of a crowd of people standing along the parade route, and so very little of the passing army contingent can be seen. In the background, over the heads of the crowds, are some business district buildings, but not enough can be seen to identify them.

Calisthenic Drill, Missouri Commission
AM&B © H46818 June 3, 1904
Cameraman: A. E. Weed
Location: Kirksville, Mo. *Photographed:* May 23, 1904
30 ft. FLA3669 (print) FRA0383 (neg.)

A formation of young men and women of college age is standing in front of a backdrop that says "Missouri State Normal School, Kirksville." As the action begins, the

movements done in unison by the group can be identified as an Irish jig.

The Call
Biograph © J137557 Jan. 22, 1910
Director: D. W. Griffith *Cameraman:* G. W. Bitzer
Cast: James Kirkwood, Billy Quirk, Mary Pickford, Florence Lawrence, Marion Leonard, Henry B. Walthall, Mack Sennett, Florence Barker, Jeanie Macpherson, Fred Mace, W. Chrystie Miller
Location: Fort Lee, N.J.; Studio, N.Y.C. *Photographed:* Dec. 7–9, 1909
422 ft. FLA5271 (print) FRA0385 (neg.)

A circus performer, ill from overexertion, collapses during a performance. The circus manager fires her, but a farmer who had seen her collapse offers her help. She marries him and regains her health and is happy as his wife. Then the circus returns to town, and she decides to join it and take up her life as a circus performer again. But confronted with the easy living and the untidiness of the circus and her life as the farmer's wife, she chooses to go back to her husband and gets home before he discovers the note she had left for him.

The Call of the Heart
Lubin Mfg. Co. © J132448 Sept. 6, 1909
Location: Studio, Philadelphia
267 ft. FLA5272 (print) FRA0384 (neg.)

The story is of a love triangle between a widowed mother, her fiancé of many years standing, and the widow's daughter. A letter to the widow from her secret fianceé is used to establish the relationship, and also to show that the young daughter has just returned from Europe where she was being educated. Most of the film shows the growing love between the fiancé and the daughter. He tells the daughter that he must give her up and she is heartbroken. But the mother nobly decides to sacrifice her love for her daughter, so she renounces her fiancé. The picture ends by showing the daughter and the fiancé rejoicing in their good fortune.

The Call of the Wild
AM&B © H117205 Oct. 19, 1908
Director: D. W. Griffith *Cameramen:* Arthur Marvin, G. W. Bitzer
Cast: Florence Lawrence, Charles Inslee, Mack Sennett
Location: Coytesville, N.J.; Studio, N.Y.C. *Photographed:* Sept. 17–25, 1908
376 ft. FLA5273 (print) FRA0386 (neg.)

The first scene of this tale of an Indian's unrequited love for a white girl takes place at a party in the house of a well-to-do person. After the guests depart, the Indian proposes to his hostess. She declines, and the Indian angrily tears off his evening clothes and puts on his Indian attire and returns to his tribe. Later, the heroine, on a horseback ride in the woods, is captured by the Indians. They are about to kill her when her former suitor intervenes. The heroine then returns to her home, while the Indian rides off sadly.

The Call to Arms
Biograph © J143780 July 28, 1910
Director: D. W. Griffith *Cameraman:* G. W. Bitzer

Cast: Marion Leonard, Linda Arvidson, Mary Pickford, Henry B. Walthall, Lottie Pickford, James Kirkwood, Owen Moore, Mack Sennett, Dell Henderson

Location: Paterson, N.J.; Studio, N.Y.C. *Photographed:* June 1, 6, 15 and 21, 1910

402 ft. FLA5274 (print) FRA0387 (neg.)

The actors wear medieval costumes. Several mounted men in armor carry lances as well as two-handed swords and foot soldiers have shields as well as two-handed swords. The plot concerns the greed of a cousin of the lord of the manor who covets a ruby of great value, which he plans to steal while the lord is away battling his enemies. The cousin harasses the mistress of the house to tell him where the ruby is hidden. In her frantic attempt to escape his anger when she will not cooperate, she falls from a balcony and is killed. The lord of the manor, having been summoned by messenger, returns, and finds his wife dead. The picture ends as the lord is about to chop off the head of his erring cousin.

The Camel at Luna Park

AM&B © H32385 June 4, 1903

Cameraman: G. W. Bitzer

Location: Coney Island, N.Y. *Photographed:* June 1, 1903

16 ft. FLA4206 (print) FRA0388 (neg.)

The film, photographed from a single camera position, shows a large throng standing around a kneeling, single-hump camel. A woman is helped aboard the camel's back by an attendant. As soon as she is seated, the driver leads the camel away, past the camera, out of the scene, and then back into the scene. The woman is helped off the camel, and the crowd disperses.

The Camera Fiend, no. 1

AM&B © H35875 Sept. 21, 1903

Cameraman: Wallace McCutcheon

Location: The Adirondacks, N.Y. *Photographed:* Sept. 9, 1903

105 ft. FLA4985 (print) FRA0389 (neg.)

The camera was placed to best view a corner of a pond or lake in front of many trees. Standing on a small dock at the edge of the pond is a man holding a box camera in his hand. While he is taking pictures, a person falls out of a rowboat and starts drowning. The photographer makes no attempt to aid the stricken swimmer but continues to take pictures of the unfortunate person in the water. A rescuer appears, dives in the water, saves the swimmer, and then pushes the photographer into the lake. He is also rescued and, as the film ends, is being carted away soaking wet in a wheelbarrow.

The Camera Fiend, no. 2

AM&B © H36561 Oct. 6, 1903

Cameraman: G. W. Bitzer

Location: Studio, N.Y.C. *Photographed:* Sept. 28, 1903

60 ft. FLA4986 (print) FRA0390 (neg.)

There are two scenes in this film. One takes place in the living room of a modest house, and the second in the same room after an explosion. A photographer prepares his camera and his subjects in order to take their picture. He lights a match to ignite the flash powder in the trough and inadvertently drops the still-lighted match into the can of flash powder, which explodes. The last scene shows the photographer and his subjects hanging from various jagged sections of the room, while the police and the fire department extricate pieces of furniture from their persons.

Cancelling Machine, U.S.P.O.

AM&B © H34974 Aug. 22, 1903

Cameraman: A. E. Weed

Location: Washington, D.C. *Photographed:* July 29, 1903

28 ft. FLA3884 (print) FRA0392 (neg.)

The camera that photographed this film, built around the operation of cancelling mail, was placed high enough to include not only the machine and its operation but also the man who was making it work. During the film, a large number of envelopes are worked through the machine by an operator.

The Cannon Ball

Keystone © LP5578 June 14, 1915

Producer and Author: Mack Sennett

Cast: Chester Conklin, Charles Arling, Rosemary Theby, Harry Myers, Harry Booker, Al St. John

Location: Keystone studio and vicinity, Los Angeles, Venice, and Ocean Park, California

751 ft.

This film is built around Chester Conklin, who plays the part of a spy who pretends to work for the "Department of Exterior" in order to discover the ingredients in gunpowder manufactured by the Boom Powder Company. He soon becomes enamored of the owner's daughter, who is in love with the manager of her father's company. The usual violent and destructive antics arise from the kidnapping of the owner's daughter and her rescue.

Canoeing at Riverside

AM&B © H28677 Feb. 26, 1903

Cameraman: G. W. Bitzer

Location: Charles River, Boston *Date:* July 7, 1899

27 ft. FLA3185 (print) FRA0394 (neg.)

The camera is mounted on a moving boat. Judging from the foliage, the locale is a fresh-water river or lake. Approximately twenty canoes approach from a distance. They are of various sizes and are paddled by crews. The camera boat proceeds through the group of canoes. When the film ends, there are no canoes in sight.

Canoeing on the Charles River, Boston, Mass.

Edison © H48348 July 21, 1904

Cameraman: Edwin S. Porter *Photographed:* July 18, 1904

21 ft. FLA4534 (print) FRA1571 (neg.)

About fifty canoes filled with people on an outing in the summertime were photographed from a single camera position from a bridge overlooking the Charles River in Boston, Massachusetts.

Canoeing Scene

Edison © H7712 Aug. 16, 1901

Location: Charles River, Boston

58 ft. FLA4535 (print) FRA0396 (neg.)

At the side of a body of water, a large number of canoes can be seen. They have from two to six passengers each and are paddled in the usual fashion by one or all of the occupants.

The canoes come close enough to the camera to identify the wearing apparel and the features of the passengers.

Cañon of the Rio Grande

Edison © 13570 Feb. 24, 1898

Location: Denver and Rio Grande R.R.

18 ft. FLA4081 (print) FRA0397 (neg.)

The camera was placed alongside a railroad track laid at the base of a sheer wall of a canyon. A locomotive can be seen in the distance. As it approaches, the full train, consisting of two locomotives pulling some freight and passenger cars, becomes visible.

Canton River Scene

Edison © 38253 June 22, 1898

Location: Canton

26 ft. FLA3116 (print) FRA0398 (neg.)

The film shows scenes of a congested area close to the docks somewhere on a river in China. The quality of the film is such that details of the landscape and the action are barely visible. One sampan being sculled can be made out against the background.

Canton Steamboat Landing Chinese Passengers

Edison © 38251 June 22, 1898

Location: Canton

26 ft. FLA3358 (print) FRA0399 (neg.)

The camera was positioned on a dock to show the landing platform in the foreground as well as the paddlewheel passenger ship tied to the dock. Walking toward the camera position from the vessel are many Chinese people in various forms of dress and carrying all sorts of packages, bags, bundles, cases, etc. The distance between the camera and the ship does not permit better description of detail.

Capsize of Lifeboat

Edison © 60571 Oct. 25, 1897

Location: Pacific Coast Life Saving Service, San Francisco

27 ft. FLA3045 (print) FRA0291 (neg.)

From the first camera position, a large coast guard self-righting lifeboat that has capsized can be seen. The crew in the demonstration is holding onto the thwarts of the boat. The second camera position shows a front view from the bow of the lifeboat as it begins to right itself. At the completion of the picture, all the crew is inside the boat and the boat has righted itself and is ready to move in any direction.

See also: Launching the Surf Boat and Rescue—Resuscitation

Capsized Boat

Edison © H46580 May 28, 1904

Cameraman: A. C. Abadie

Location: Toronto *Photographed:* May 21, 1904

25 ft. FLA3684 (print) FRA0934 (neg.)

The subject matter is a man's agile handling of a canoe. During the course of the film, he is seen skillfully paddling a canoe in the wake of the camera boat. Later, he is seen standing up and paddling, and it can be seen that he is wearing a bathing suit. In the background is a considerable number of people who are about to be instructed in the

proper way to capsize a canoe, right it, and climb back into it, all of which is demonstrated in the film.

Capt. Boynton Feeding His Pets

AM&B © H16927 Apr. 22, 1902

Cameraman: F. S. Armitage

Location: Coney Island, N.Y. *Date:* Sept. 12, 1899

26 ft. FLA3192 (print) FRA0518 (neg.)

The film, photographed from a single camera position, shows a body of water similar to a swimming pool, with a cement walkway. Standing on the walkway is a man in the clothing of a seafarer. He has in his hands a bucket from which he takes fish to throw to several seals immediately in the foreground. Behind the man feeding the seals are spectators, some riding in small boats, others standing on the edge of the water area. There is a pavilionlike building in the background with a sign reading "Capt. Boynton." The man falls into the water with the seals. The working title was Capt. Boynton and Seals.

Captain Nissen Going Through Whirlpool Rapids, Niagara Falls

Edison © H9961 Oct. 22, 1901

59 ft. FLA4536 (print) FRA1572 (neg.)

The film was photographed on the bank of the river below Niagara Falls at a point called the Whirlpool Rapids. A specially designed boat, approximately twenty feet in length, is shown leaving the area and attempting to go through the whirlpool rapids. The film ends as the boat passes out of camera view. According to an Edison catalog, Captain N. P. Nissen was formerly known as Captain Bowser. His craft is called the *Fool Killer.*

Capture and Death

See: Capture of Yegg Bank Burglars

Capture of Boer Battery

Edison © D7876 Apr. 16, 1900

Cameraman: James H. White

Location: West Orange, N.J.

42 ft. FLA4538 (print) FRA1573 (neg.)

Photographed from a single camera position the film shows what definitely appears to have been a staged skirmish.

Capture of Boer Battery by British

Edison © D7811 Apr. 14, 1900

Cameraman: James H. White

Location: West Orange, N.J.

43 ft. FLA4539 (print) FRA1574 (neg.)

The subject is a skirmish between men dressed as Boers and men dressed as British Highland soldiers. The camera was placed directly behind two small artillery pieces, manned by approximately ten men in the uniform of the Boers. After two rounds have been fired from the artillery pieces, the Boers break and run toward the camera position. In the background are some British soldiers in kilts. The film ends as the kilted men pass the camera position.

Capture of the Biddle Brothers

Edison © H14434 Feb. 24, 1902

Cameraman: Edwin S. Porter

55 ft. FLA5275 (print) FRA2649 (neg.)

This short melodrama, using a single camera position, was taken in a heavily forested area after a heavy snowfall. In the distance, approaching the camera at a rapid rate, are approximately ten men on horseback. A sleigh drawn by two horses comes within camera view headed in the opposite direction from the riders. The sleigh halts and two men with rifles alight. They start shooting at the oncoming riders who return the fire. The two men, hit by the gunfire, fall to the ground. Some of the riders dismount, pick up the men, place them in the sleigh, and leave the scene.

Capture of Trenches at Candaba [Canda Bar]

Edison © 38515 June 10, 1899

40 ft. FLA4045 (print) FRA1232 (neg.)

[Spanish-American War,]

Several men in white uniforms are visible. They hold and fire rifles into the heavy foliage that surrounds them. This continues for a short period of time. The men then retreat, their position being filled by men in American uniforms of the Spanish-American War period, who fire at the retreating soldiers.

Capture of Yegg Bank Burglars: Capture And Death (H50924); Cellar Scene (H50925); Dive Scene (H50927); Tracked (H50926)

Edison © H50924 Sept. 28, 1904

Cameraman: Edwin S. Porter

Location: Studio and vicinity, N.Y.C. *Photographed:* Aug. 15 – Sept. 10, 1904

99 ft. FLA4537 (print) FRA2896 (neg.)

This film is made up of a series of active tableaux, instead of an establishing scene. All but one of the tableaux take place on sets. The first action consists of someone dressed as an old woman who enters a room in which four roughly clad men are playing cards. Before the scene ends, the woman, now disclosed as a man, has killed all four of the thugs. The remaining three scenes are somewhat confusing since they are similar and involve the man disguised as a woman. The one outdoor scene takes place on a street with a saloon. Two men approach the camera position and just before passing it, turn into the saloon. Apparently they are being followed for they pull up their coat collars, pull down their hats, and hasten into the saloon. There is no explanation for their actions.

Capuchin Monks, Rome

AM&B © H35634 Sept. 12, 1903

21 ft. FLA3344 (print) FRA0653 (neg.)

From a single camera position, a procession of bearded men of a religious order is photographed passing the camera. The title indicates they are of the Capuchin order, but there is no identifiable insignia.

Cardinal Gibbons

AM&B © H27387 Jan. 22, 1903

Photographed: 1898 (?)

31 ft. FLA3274 (print) FRA0592 (neg.)

The reception for Cardinal Gibbons was photographed from a single camera position. The cardinal and his aide are shown coming out of a building and walking down the steps, passing by the camera. The reception committee was entirely religious.

The Cardinal's Conspiracy

Biograph © J129525 July 12, 1909

Director: D. W. Griffith *Cameraman:* G. W. Bitzer

Cast: Frank Powell, Florence Lawrence, Harry Salter, Linda Arvidson, Mack Sennett, Mary Pickford

Location: Studio, N.Y.C.; Greenwich, Conn. *Photographed:* June 3, 4 and 12, 1909

358 ft. FLA5276 (print) FRA2208 (neg.)

A princess will have nothing to do with a neighboring prince her father, the king, has chosen for her. The Cardinal suggests that the prince disguise himself as a guard, and arranges for him to save the princess from three thugs. She falls in love with him, and the Cardinal underscores his advantage by having the prince imprisoned. The princess, of course, does all she can to aid him escape and then defiantly presents him to her father as the man she will wed. The "guard" is then revealed as the prince. The king is happy at having his way, while the princess is delighted with having gained her way. All of the actors wear early eighteenth-century French costumes.

A Career of Crime, no. 1

AM&B © H23795 Nov. 11, 1902

Cameraman: Arthur Marvin

Location: Studio, N.Y.C. *Date:* June 19, 1900

A bald stout man in the apron of a storekeeper is arranging vegetables in front of a set of a grocery store with a "Help Wanted" sign on it. A boy in a straw hat and linen duster with an umbrella appears on the scene. He and the proprietor talk, and the proprietor invites him into the store. As soon as they go inside, a thief begins stealing the produce displayed outside. The grocer and his new assistant notice the thief and the picture ends as the grocer's new assistant and the thief roll around fighting on the sidewalk in front of the store.

A Career of Crime, no. 2

AM&B © H23796 Nov. 11, 1902

Cameraman: Arthur Marvin

Location: Studio, N.Y.C. *Date:* June 19, 1900

9 ft. FLA4019 (print) FRA2900 (neg.)

A tout board listing at least a dozen horses is visible as this film begins. A man wearing a derby hat and a grey suit is making entries on the board while to the right is a young man in a dark suit and a straw hat who is apparently reading the names of the horses and acting as if he is very unhappy. The film ends as several of the male spectators are holding the young man to prevent him from running away.

A Career of Crime, no. 3

AM&B © H23797 Nov. 11, 1902

Cameraman: Arthur Marvin

Location: Studio, N.Y.C. *Date:* June 19, 1900

10 ft. FLA3020 (print) FRA2899 (neg.)

A set of an office furnished with a table, a chair, and a safe can be seen. A young man in a dark suit and straw hat enters through the window and walks up to the safe, while another man still outside the window encourages him. The young man manipulates the knob and handle of the safe, opens the door and stuffs his pockets with what appears to be money. Just then he is accosted by a large man whom he strikes and knocks to the floor.

A Career of Crime, no. 4
AM&B © H23798   Nov. 11, 1902
Cameraman: Arthur Marvin
Location: Studio, N.Y.C *Date:* June 27, 1900
10 ft.   FLA4021 (print)   FRA2898 (neg.)

The set is of a private dining room in an expensive restaurant, where a young man in a tuxedo is romancing a young woman in an evening dress. A waitress is serving them wine. The young man pulls his companion to his lap and kisses her as a policeman and two plainclothes policemen enter through the curtain and arrest the young man.

A Career of Crime, no. 5
AM&B © H23799   Nov. 11, 1902
Cameraman: Arthur Marvin
Location: Studio; N.Y.C. *Date:* June 21, 1900
10 ft.   FLA4021 (print)   FRA2897 (neg.)

Several prison guards, a priest, and some witnesses have gathered to take part in an execution. One of the group is placed in a chair, tied hand and foot, and a bandage is placed over his eyes. He can be seen struggling against his bonds, as if charges of electricity are coursing through his body.

A Caribou Hunt
See: Moose Hunt in New Brunswick; Stalking and Shooting Caribou, Newfoundland

Carmen
Feature Films Sales Company   © J169531   May 28, 1912
212 ft.   FLA5277 (print)   FRA2209 (neg.)

This picture follows a story line that does not compare with the opera. In two of the scenes at least five hundred people are visible. All action is played parallel to the lens plane. The story is of a bandit chief with a daughter but not a son. At his death, the daughter attempts to run the gang with very little success. In one of the situations, she is actually captured and in danger of being killed or jailed. One of the leading men sees her and is attracted to her. He manages to raise her bond so she is paroled in his custody. The picture ends as they embrace. Several of the scenes involve spectacles where hundreds of people watch either a parade or a mardi gras, and there are two or three scenes of large floats. At the end of the picture, the actors in the foreground are supported by many, many spectators who are watching the floats parade by. There is every indication that this film was made in Europe and only distributed in the United States.

Carrie Nation Smashing a Saloon
AM&B © H23802   Nov. 11, 1902
Cameraman: F. S. Armitage
Location: Studio, N.Y.C. *Date:* Apr. 18, 1901
29 ft.   FLA3504 (print)   FRA0784 (neg.)

This was photographed from a single camera position as if in the audience of a theater. A bartender is serving a drink to a man at a table, when two women, obviously in high dudgeon, enter from stage right. They immediately begin dismantling the saloon. The film ends when the larger of the two women knocks the tap out of a keg of beer and the force of the fermented malt liquor drenches her completely.

Carriers at Work, U.S.P.O.
AM&B   © H34978   Aug. 22, 1903.
Cameraman: A. E. Weed
Location: Washington, D.C. *Photographed:* Aug. 10, 1903
72 ft.   FLA4541 (print)   FRA1575 (neg.)

The subject is the handling and sorting of the U.S. mail. The sorting bags and the alphabetizing pigeonhole equipment are visible in a scene photographed from an altitude of approximately twenty-five feet. The placement of the equipment and its use by the post office personnel can be seen.

Carriers Leaving Building, U.S.P.O.
AM&B   © H34973   Aug. 22, 1903
Cameraman: A. E. Weed
Location: Washington, D.C. *Photographed:* Aug. 5, 1903
20 ft.   FLA3873 (print)   FRA1084 (neg.)

Male letter carriers of the U.S. Post Office are the subject of this series on the Postal Department. The camera was placed to show a large number of uniformed mail carriers as they leave the main post office to deliver letters. They can be seen walking down the steps of the building toward the camera position. Some mount bicycles and ride away, while others just walk. There are also some women in the film.

Carriers Leaving Building, U.S.P.O.
AM&B   © H34989   Aug. 22, 1903
Cameraman: A. E. Weed
Location: Washington, D.C. *Photographed:* July 28, 1903
20 ft.   FLA3874 (print)   FRA1085 (neg.)

The opening scene shows the steps of a large public building. Above the steps is a door out of which, coming toward the camera position, are approximately a hundred and fifty mail carriers of the postal service. They are in uniform and are all carrying mail bags. They continue down the steps in formation for the full length of the film.

Carrying Out the Snakes
Edison   © H11270   Dec. 12, 1901
Cameraman: James H. White [?]
31 ft.   FLA4120 (print)   FRA1296 (neg.)

The film, photographed from a single camera position, shows Indians of the Walpapi tribe during a tribal ceremony. The Indians carry snakes. One of a lecture series of five short films that were offered with a "Lecture synopsis with each film or upon application."

See also: Line-up and Teasing the Snakes, The March of Prayer and Entrance of the Dancers, Panoramic View of Moki-land, and Parade of Snake Dancers Before the Dance.

Cascade Near Wawona, California
AM&B   © H29156   Mar. 11, 1903
Cameraman: Robert K. Bonine
Location: Wawona, Calif. *Date:* Nov. 15, 1901
18 ft.   FLA3617 (print)   FRA0877 (neg.)

The camera was positioned to allow a cascade to be viewed. The film is of this water eruption and nothing else.

See also: Wawona, Big Tree and Tourists Arriving at Wawona Hotel.

Casey and His Neighbor's Goat

Edison © H36501 Oct. 3, 1903
Cameraman: Edwin S. Porter
Location: Studio, N.Y.C. *Photographed:* Sept. 26, 1903
47 ft. FLA4542 (print) FRA1576 (neg.)

The plot of this comedy is based on the attempts of a man to get rid of a neighbor's goat who eats plants in his garden. The man enters his backyard and the goat gets away through the fence. The irate man goes into his house and returns with a box marked dynamite. While he is tying some of the dynamite on the plants, the goat returns, bites into a stick, and blows up the yard. By the use of stop action photography, a dummy replaces the man, who comes back to life as if nothing had happened. The billy goat also reenters the scenes nonchalantly.

Casey at the Bat

Edison © 27968 Apr. 22, 1899
Location: Thomas Edison estate, West Orange, N.J.
22 ft. FLA4283 (print) FRA1436 (neg.)

The film was photographed from the umpire's position facing the pitcher's mound. The locale was a back lawn on the estate of Thomas A. Edison in West Orange, New Jersey. The film is on a parallel with home movies, with a comedy format.

Casey's Christening

AM&B © H68878 Nov. 20, 1905
Cameraman: F. A. Dobson
Location: Studio, N.Y.C. *Photographed:* Oct. 28, 1905
53 ft. FLA4987 (print) FRA1955 (neg.)

The film is built around the substitution of a small dog dressed as a baby for a real infant. The baby is in a crib in a kitchen while his parents are guests of the dog owners. The guests are sitting at a table and drinking beer when the host gets up and substitutes the dog for the baby. When the prank is discovered by the baby's parents, a fight starts. By the end of the film the room is a shambles and every article of furniture has been broken.

Casey's Frightful Dream

Edison © H42203 Feb. 16, 1904
Cameraman: Edwin S. Porter
Location: Studio, N.Y.C. *Photographed:* Jan. 19, 1904
42 ft. FLA5278 (print) FRA2645 (neg.)

The opening scene shows a set of the interior of a man's bedroom. A man in a nightshirt walks across the room and opens a window. The camera shifts to show the exterior of the house, and the man in the nightshirt is seen as he opens the window, gets out on the roof, and walks up and down on the ledge until he falls. As his body falls off the roof, the camera shifts to the interior of the bedroom just as the man hits the floor, having fallen out of his bed.

Casting a Guide Box, Westinghouse Works

See: Westinghouse Works

A Catastrophe in Hester Street

AM&B © H40814 Jan. 12, 1904
Cameraman: A. E. Weed
Location: Studio, N.Y.C. *Photographed:* Dec. 11, 1903
57 ft. FLA5279 (print) FRA2646 (neg.)

From a single camera position, a set of the front of a confectionery store is seen. A man stands in front of the store and peers right and left down the street. Two men, acting intoxicated, appear; they are carrying blasting powder. As a result of their collective carelessness, there is an explosion. When the smoke clears away, it is possible to see parts of bodies (dummies) lying about. A policeman, attracted by the explosion, begins to assemble the pieces, and finally gets one man put together. Stop action photography was used to effect the trick assemblage.

Catch-as-Catch-Can Wrestling

AM&B © H33648 July 21, 1903
Cameraman: G. W. Bitzer
Location: Studio, N.Y.C. *Date:* July 11, 1903
87 ft. FLA4989 (print) FRA1956 (neg.)

A wrestling match between two teen-aged boys wearing the wrestling costume of the period is shown. A man in shirt sleeves can be seen on a lighted stage, against a painted backdrop simulating spectators. During the wrestling match the camera did not move, as if the participants had been told to stay in one area.

A Catch of Hard Shell Crabs, part 1

AM&B © H36564 Oct. 6, 1903
Cameraman: G. W. Bitzer
Location: Studio, N.Y.C. *Photographed:* Sept. 22, 1903
49 ft. FLA5280 (print) FRA2647 (neg.)

The comedy flavor of this film begins as a man dressed in street clothes, acting intoxicated, approaches the camera position through a doorway of a set of a bedroom. There is a three-quarter bed, a dresser, and a chair in the set. The intoxicated man attempts to disrobe and go to bed. He takes his nightclothes and wanders out of the room long enough for a young boy carrying a peach basket to enter, turn down the bed covers, and deposit several crabs in the bed. The man, now dressed in a night shirt, comes back, gets into bed and out again, shaking and jumping to rid himself of the crabs clinging to him. As the picture ends, he is on the floor. This is part one of two parts. Part two, however, was not found in inventory.

Catching an Early Train

Edison © H10604 Nov. 9, 1901
Cameraman: Edwin S. Porter
23 ft. FLA3700 (print) FRA0949 (neg.)

The complete action of this film is devoted to utilizing trick camera effects to aid a man in a comic situation to get out of the house in a hurry. The camera was placed so that the photographer could capture a bedroom scene in which a man leaves his bed with a jump that lands him in the middle of the room. He reaches out his hand to pick up his trousers, shoes, collar, coat, etc., and each item jumps into his hand. In the short span of the film, he is completely dressed and on his way out the door.

Cat's Cradle

AM&B © H36556 Oct. 6, 1903

Cameraman: G. W. Bitzer

Location: Studio, N.Y.C. *Photographed:* Sept. 22, 1903

28 ft. FLA3747 (print) FRA0994 (neg.)

As the film begins, two well-dressed people are sitting on pieces of furniture arranged so they are facing one another. The woman has a loop of string around the fingers of both hands. As the film progresses, they play a parlor game called "Cat's Cradle." This requires them to create geometrical designs with the looped thread by using their fingers. The man and woman modify the game slightly by using their teeth as well as their hands and, as they pull their hands apart, the string pulls their heads together and they kiss. The film was photographed from a single camera position with overhead lighting. The camera was near enough to the actors for the film to be considered a close-up.

Cattle Driven to Slaughter

Edison © 43405 July 31, 1897

Location: Stockyards, Chicago

25 ft. FLA3048 (print) FRA0313 (neg.)

Wooden splat fences can be seen from a single camera position. A gate, approximately twenty-five feet away from the camera position, opens, and a herd of horned cattle is driven in the direction of the camera and on by it. As the last of the animals passes, the empty stock pen and a man in the foreground closing a gate can be seen.

Cattle Fording Stream

Edison © 13549 Feb. 24, 1898

64 ft. FLA5281 (print) FRA2648 (neg.)

The film shows the manner in which three men and a boy, all mounted on horseback, drive a herd of cattle across a small river. The action was photographed from a single camera position and shows the cattle always being herded in the direction of the camera.

Cattle Leaving the Corral

Edison © 13542 Feb. 24, 1898

25 ft. FLA3228 (print) FRA0552 (neg.)

The single camera shows a fenced area, a large gate, two men on the fencepost above the gate, and a large herd of cattle behind the gate. The gate is opened and the cattle stream through the opening, herded by four men on horseback. As the film ends, all of the herd of cattle have passed through the gate and by the camera position. Only the empty corral is visible.

Caught by Wireless

AM&B © H107672 Mar. 18, 1908

Director: Wallace McCutcheon *Cameraman:* G. W. Bitzer

Location: Studio, N.Y.C. *Photographed:* Mar. 11 and 13, 1908

370 ft. FLA5282 (print) FRA2210 (neg.)

The story concerns a man who is forced to flee from his country because of an altercation with a rent collector. He becomes a policeman in New York and sends for his wife and children, who come by boat. On the same boat is the villain, the rent collector, who has absconded with his employer's funds. The wife recognizes him and helps the New York police, who had been alerted by a telegram, to capture him. The film was photographed from a single camera position as if from the audience of a theater. All of the scenes show use of sets, props, special effects, etc.

Caught in a Park

Keystone © LP4417 Feb. 6, 1915

Producer and Author: Mack Sennett

Cast: Phyllis Allen, Cecile Arnold, Sydney Chaplin, Slim Summerville, Mack Swain

Location: Vicinity of the Keystone studio and Echo Park in Los Angeles

411 ft. FLA6063 (print) FRA2212 (neg.)

Syd Chaplin is a playboy with a dull wife, who becomes bored with her snoring beside him on a park bench. While she sleeps, he proceeds to get into trouble with a beautiful young woman seated nearby. When his wife and her boyfriend become aware of what is going on, considerable pandemonium breaks loose, with Chaplin ending up the loser.

Caught in the Act

Keystone © LP4877 Mar. 27, 1915

Producer and Author: Mack Sennett

Cast: Polly Moran, Cecile Arnold, Charles Murray, Slim Summerville, Eddie Cline

Location: Studio and downtown Los Angeles, on top of buildings at the First and Broadway area

440 ft. FLA6064 (print) FRA2215 (neg.)

Charlie Murray plays the part of a janitor who discovers that one of the tenants, a painter, intends to paint some attractive young ladies as they pose en déshabillé. In the painter's absence, Murray pretends he is the painter until his wife, played by Polly Moran, discovers what is going on. Just then the painter returns, and a chase over the rooftops of office buildings ensues, with Polly Moran and her broom bringing up the rear.

Caught in the Undertow

AM&B © H23783 Nov. 11, 1902

Cameraman: G. W. Bitzer [?]

Location: Atlantic City, N.J. [?] *Photographed:* Aug. 18, 1902 [?]

62 ft. FLA4990 (print) FRA1957 (neg.)

The subject is the rescue of a swimmer caught by the undertow at a bathing beach. The camera was placed high on a pier overlooking an area where many bathers can be seen in the surf. One apparently begins to drown. The lifeguards launch a rowboat and row through the surf to where the stricken swimmer is floundering. The lifeguards return with the tired swimmer and administer first aid. At the end, the spent swimmer is lying on his back on the sand and the lifeguards are working over him when a woman appears out of the crowd and throws herself on the swimmer.

The Cavalier's Dream

Edison © 73464 Dec. 16, 1898

26 ft. FLA3980 (print) FRA1188 (neg.)

The subject of this film is the purported dream of a man dressed as a cavalier in knee breeches. He is first seen with his head on his arm as if asleep. The surrounding set represents a baronial hall. By the use of stop action photography, food and table decorations appear and disappear, as well as many different types of people, such as the devil, the spectre of death, persons in ecclesiastical costumes, and some young women. As the film ends, the room where the cavalier is asleep is filled with these individuals, all of whom disappear, leaving him as he was, with his head on his arm, apparently asleep.

A Cavalry Charge
AM&B © H23774 Nov. 11, 1902
Photographed: 1897 [?]
19 ft. FLA3478 (print) FRA0759 (neg.)

The poor condition and the short length does not permit a detailed description. The barely visible subject was approximately three companies of cavalry riding by the camera position.

Cellar Scene
See: Capture of Yegg Bank Burglars

Central High School, Gymnastic Drill
AM&B © H45154 May 2, 1904
Cameraman: A. E. Weed
Location: Kansas City, Mo. *Photographed:* Apr. 18, 1904
19 ft. FLA4007 (print) FRA1207 (neg., copy 1)
  FRA1208 (neg., copy 2)

The cameraman placed his equipment at the edge of a school yard where supervised gymnastics were being conducted by high school students. Male students can be seen doing the long and short "horse" exercises to the left of the camera position. In the center, a group of young girls are engaged in using the parallel bars and to the right of the camera, some older boys in white clothing are executing several difficult exercises on the high parallel bars. Across the extent of the visibility of the camera is a blackboard with the words "Kansas City, Mo."

Central Park After Dark
AM&B © H35648 Sept. 12, 1903
Cameraman: Arthur Marvin
Location: Roof studio, N.Y.C. *Photographed:* Apr. 24, 1900
18 ft. FLA3359 (print) FRA0662 (neg.)

The scene opens on a backdrop of foliage and trees. In front of this backdrop a man and woman are sitting on a park bench embracing fervently. An actor dressed as a policeman arrives and shines his hand light on the couple, who immediately become circumspect and arrange their clothing. The policeman walks away to continue his rounds, and the two resume their embrace. Note the unusual use of a spotlight to show the policeman's hand lantern.

A Champion Beer Drinker
AM&B © H30737 Apr. 24, 1903
Cameraman: Arthur Marvin
Location: Roof studio, N.Y.C. *Photographed:* June 6, 1900
48 ft. FLA5283 (print) FRA2650 (neg.)

The hero of this filmed comedy is a man made up to appear like the later famous comic strip character "Happy Hooligan." He is sitting at a table in front of a backdrop painted to look like the interior of a restaurant. The action begins with one waiter after another bringing our hero glasses of beer, which he drinks in rapid succession. Time after time the waiters carry in trays filled with glasses of beer. Finally, two waiters arrive and the beer drinker turns into a beer barrel.

Champion Pony "Midget"
AM&B © H32786 June 17, 1903
27 ft. FLA3740 (print) FRA0986 (neg.)

A well-conditioned pony ridden by a teen-age boy approaches the camera position. A fence and a judge's stand on what appears to be a fairgrounds can be seen in the background. The horse is put through his paces, including whirls, jumps, and footwork.

Champs de Mars
Edison © D16382 Aug. 9, 1900
Location: Paris
40 ft. FLA3940 (print) FRA1152 (neg.)

From a single camera position, the cameraman photographed in a 300-degree pan the exhibit buildings of the Paris Exposition and the traffic. People can be seen walking and riding, and the base of the newly built Eiffel Tower is shown.

Champs Elysees
Edison © D16384 Aug. 9, 1900
Location: Paris
39 ft. FLA3210 (print) FRA0534 (neg.)

The film was photographed from a camera positioned on what appears to be a street-centered abutment. Various methods of surface transportation can be seen: double-decker horse-drawn buses, one-horse two-wheeled shays, one- and two-horse carriages, and various drayage vehicles. Most of the movement is toward the camera position. However, traffic can be seen on both sides.

A Change of Heart
Biograph © J133141 Oct. 14, 1909
Director: D. W. Griffith *Cameraman:* G. W. Bitzer
Cast: Owen Moore, Billy Quirk, Arthur Johnson, James
  Kirkwood, W. Chrystie Miller, Kate Bruce
Location: Greenwich, Conn. *Photographed:* Sept. 2 and 4,
  1909
391 ft. FLA5284 (print) FRA2211 (neg.)

A wealthy young man from the city makes the acquaintance of a lovely young daughter of a farmer. By promising marriage, he entices her into accompanying him to the city. There is a fake wedding. She inadvertently learns the truth and in great anguish sets out for her home. The rich young man is holding a drinking party when his mother stops in and advises him to give up drinking and become an upstanding young man. He takes her advice, realizes the error of his ways, and begins searching for the girl he wronged. His search is successful and, as the film ends, he is being married legally to the farmer's fair daughter.

Changing Horses at Glen
AM&B © H31689 May 5, 1903
Cameraman: G. W. Bitzer
Location: Glen, N.J. *Date:* Apr. 27, 1903
30 ft. FLA3384 (print) FRA0684 (neg.)

The camera was positioned on a roadway, and a vehicle drawn by two horses can be seen approaching. The vehicle comes to a stop about ten yards from the camera position, the horses are unhitched and immediately replaced by two more. The vehicle can be described as a coach carrying passengers and baggage, and appears to be one that was used between towns in rural areas during the late 1890s.

See also: Changing Horses at Linden

Changing Horses at Linden
AM&B © H31688 May 5, 1903
Cameraman: G. W. Bitzer
Location: Linden, N.J. *Date:* Apr. 27, 1903
46 ft. FLA5285 (print) FRA2651 (neg.)

The changing of a team of horses at a coach station is shown. The public conveyance is a coach, known as Mr. Hyde's Liberty coach, drawn by four horses. The full transfer of the animals and the departure of the coach with the fresh team can be seen.

See also: Changing Horses at Glen

"Chappie" and "Ben Bolt"
AM&B © H16732 Apr. 18, 1902
Cameraman: F. S. Armitage
Location: Manhattan Field, N.Y. *Date:* May 18, 1899
10 ft. FLA3487 (print) FRA0768 (neg.)

A rail fence with two diagonal approaches can be seen. Standing beside the fence are two men wearing riding habits. A horse and rider trot up to the wing fence, the top rail of which is approximately four feet high; they continue, and the horse is urged to jump over the top rail, which it clears. A second horse makes the same approach; however, as it jumps, it hind feet knock off the top rail.

Charge by 1st Bengal Lancers
AM&B © H27774 Jan. 30, 1903
Cameraman: Raymond Ackerman
Location: Peking *Date:* Jan. 14, 1901
18 ft. FLA3143 (print) FRA0476 (neg.)

Almost on the horizon of flat territory are approximately fifty mounted horses in company front formation. They approach the camera at a full gallop, continue in the same direction, and pass by the camera position. The poor condition of the film, coupled with the speed of the horses, provide little opportunity for identification beyond stating that the riders wear turbans and carry lances.

See also: The Bengal Lancers

Charge of Boer Cavalry
Edison © D7812 Apr. 14, 1900
Cameraman: James H. White
25 ft. FLA4204 (print) FRA1367 (neg.)

The photographer placed his camera above a flat area between two hills. In the distance, approaching the camera, are approximately fifty mounted men wearing a uniform resembling that of the Boer Army. As they come nearer to the camera position, it is possible to see that some of the riders are brandishing cavalry sabers. The film seems to be a reproduction.

Charge of Boer Cavalry
Edison © D7877 Apr. 16, 1900
Cameraman: James H. White
25 ft. FLA4203 (print) FRA1366 (neg.)

Approximately fifty mounted men in the uniform of the Boers are riding toward the camera position from a distance. Most of the film shows their approach. Just as the main body of riders passes the camera position, two horses leisurely walk past the camera from the opposite direction. This film seems to be a reproduction.

Charge of the Light Brigade
AM&B © H32499 June 11, 1903
25 ft. FLA3591 (print) FRA2136 (neg.)

The film, photographed from a single camera position, shows many small boys throwing snowballs at one another. A horse-drawn delivery wagon passes, and the boys pelt the driver with snowballs.

The Chariot Race
Kalem © H102798 Nov. 22, 1907
Directors: Frank Oaks Rose, Sidney Olcott *Scenario:* Gene Gauntier
Location: Manhattan Beach, N.Y.
[Based on the novel Ben Hur by Lew Wallace]
93 ft. FLA4991 (print) FRA0219 (neg.)

The actors are dressed as early Romans and each of the five chariots is drawn by three horses. There are large sets that are photographed from several camera positions. The spectators do not sit in a grandstand or bleacher but stand on the side of the roadway and move back as the chariots near the camera position. Indications are that this film is all that is left of the Ben Hur made by Kalem in 1907.

Charity Ball
Edison © 53737 Sept. 24, 1897
24 ft. FLA4370 (print) FRA1508 (neg., copy 1) FRA1509 (neg., copy 2)

A man in dinner clothes with a young lady in a long white dress and white shoes as his partner execute various dance steps designed as exhibition dancing. The film was photographed from a single light source and single camera position. There are no props or backdrops.

The Charity Ball
Klaw & Erlanger © LP3037 June 11, 1914
Cast: Franklin Ritchie, Vola Smith, Jack Drumeir, Violet Reid, Robert Drouet, Robert Nolan
[Based on the play by David Belasco and Henry DeMille]
1,034 ft. FLA5847-5848 (print) FRA2727-2728 (neg.)

The story concerns an ambitious man who intends to marry the daughter of an economic rival, although he has "betrayed another under promise of marriage." Circumstances later force him "to realize the full horror of the situation," and he marries instead the woman he had deceived. The background is of people of wealth in a large city. There are numerous well-constructed sets, and a considerable number of persons take part in two of the scenes.

Charleston Chain-Gang
Edison © H16714 Apr. 18, 1902

Location: Charleston, S.C.

29 ft. FLA3237 (print) FRA0561 (neg.)

Apparently, the film was photographed from a compound bordered by high walls and buildings. At a distance of fifty yards in the direction that the camera is pointed a column of men can be seen walking backwards and holding a chain under their arms. All the men are dressed the same. Two men carrying shotguns gesture to indicate the chain gang should move. They walk toward camera position, continuing until the last man in the column passes the camera.

Le Chauldron [i.e., Chaudron] Infernal

Méliès © H37508 Oct. 12, 1903

Creator: Georges Méliès

Location: Montreuil, France

Cast: Georges Méliès

Photographed: Summer 1903

U.S. title: The Infernal Caldron

52 ft.

The set looks like some sort of torture chamber with a large tub or caldron. An actor dressed as the devil appears, followed by a second who is forcing a woman to march in front of him. She is put into a sheet and thrown into the caldron, causing a large explosion and much smoke. This is repeated. The smoke rises to the top of the set where it turns into ghostlike figures who seem to float around. The picture ends as the devil transforms the floating apparitions into falling, burning embers. He then turns and jumps into the caldron, which blows up and, when the smoke clears, there is nothing left on the stage.

Chauncey Explains

AM&B © H65320 Sept. 11, 1905

Cameraman: G. W. Bitzer

Location: Studio, N.Y.C. *Photographed:* Aug. 18, 1903

19 ft. FLA3946 (print) FRA1157 (neg.)

An elderly gentleman with white hair and full mutton chop whiskers, clad in white tie and tails, can be seen from the waist up. The actor indicates by gestures that he is sincerely attempting to convey an idea. He augments his gestures by showing a large piece of paper on which the words "Equitable Life" can be seen plainly. The film ends as the man is holding up the policy and laughing heartily. The backdrop moves back and forth all during the actor's discourse.

Chest and Neck Development

Winthrop Press © H75807 Apr. 18, 1906

12 ft. FRA6410 (neg.)

The only action visible in this short piece of film is a large muscular woman standing on a pedestal doing calisthenics to develop her neck and chest.

Chicks to Order

AM&B © H33207 July 2, 1903

Cameraman: G. W. Bitzer

Cast: Kathryn Osterman

Date: June 24, 1901

40 ft. FLA4543 (print) FRA1577 (neg.)

The producer of this comedy made use of stop-action photography to implement his plot. A table with a bowl of eggs, a plate, and other utensils can be seen directly in front of the camera. Behind the table, facing the camera, is a woman who breaks an egg and spills the contents into the plate in front of her. As the egg reaches the plate, it is transformed into a baby chick. This egg breaking is repeated approximately a dozen times until the end of the film. Released under the title Strictly Fresh Eggs.

The Ch-ien-men Gate, Pekin

AM&B © H16647 Apr. 16, 1902

Cameraman: Robert K. Bonine

Location: Peking *Date:* Sept. 1901

19 ft. FLA4257 (print) FRA1413 (neg.)

The camera was positioned to show traffic leaving and entering the gate of the great wall surrounding the Forbidden City in Peking, China. Single-wheeled, two-wheeled, and multiwheeled vehicles can be seen drawn by horses, donkeys, and human beings.

The Child of the Ghetto

Biograph © J142132 June 8, 1910

Director: D. W. Griffith *Cameraman:* G. W. Bitzer

Cast: Dorothy West, Henry B. Walthall, Kate Bruce, George Nicholls

Location: Studio, N.Y.C.; Westfield, N.J. *Photographed:* Apr. 29–30, and May 2–4, 1910

379 ft. FLA5287 (print) FRA2218 (neg.)

A destitute young orphan is forced to do contract sewing in order to survive. The evil son of her employer accuses her of theft and calls the police. She flees to the country and a young farmer finds her exhausted on the road. He takes her home, where she regains her health and falls in love with him. Meanwhile one of her original police pursuers decides to go fishing, and while he is out in the country he finds the young woman. She pleads with him not to take her back to the city and not to disclose her past. He agrees not to tell anybody, and the young woman and the farmer are shown embracing in the last scene.

The Child Stealers

AM&B © H46917 June 9, 1904

Produced in England by Gaumont

170 ft. FLA5288 (print) FRA2213 (neg.)

This British-made movie was distributed by American Mutoscope & Biograph Company. A gypsy woman finds unattended children, steals them, and takes them to her headquarters. The children are dressed in old clothes and become part of a street begging team and aid in enlisting sympathy from passersby. Three different children are stolen during the film. It ends when a mother recognizes her stolen child and summons the police. There is a chase, the gypsies are apprehended, and all the kidnapped children are returned to their parents.

Children Bathing

Edison © H11494 Dec. 16, 1901

29 ft. FLA3093 (print) FRA0432 (neg.)

A scene of the ocean is shown, with one adult woman and a small child, both attired in bathing suits, splashing in the water. Another adult joins them; she is wearing a large brimmed straw hat, as well as a bathing suit, and they continue bathing in the water.

Children Feeding Ducklings

AM&B © H25962 Dec. 31, 1902

Cameraman: G. W. Bitzer

Location: Somewhere in Mass. *Date:* June 26, 1899

16 ft. FLA3991 (print) FRA1197 (neg.)

Long rows of pens with hundreds of not quite full-grown ducks can be seen. Two children carrying baskets with food that is attractive to the ducks approach the camera from a distance of approximately fifty feet. The short length of the film does not permit a more detailed explanation.

Children in the Surf, Coney Island

AM&B © H49062 Aug. 12, 1904

Cameraman: G. W. Bitzer

Location: Sea Gate, Coney Island, N.Y. *Photographed:* Aug. 3, 1904

81 ft. FLA4992 (print) FRA1958 (neg.)

Seven small children can be seen from the low angle camera position; the camera is pointed out to sea. The children are holding hands and wading in the surf. Beyond them can be seen three adults. At the end of the film, there is only one child in a white bathing costume holding a sailboat. Beyond the child toward the ocean is a large sailing craft.

Children Rolling Down Hill

AM&B © H51258 Oct. 4, 1904

18 ft. FLA3245 (print) FRA0568 (neg.)

The camera was positioned at the bottom of a steep incline or hill where a large group of children has congregated, perhaps for a picnic. They entertain themselves by sliding down the incline, but the grainy condition of the film limits interpretation of detail.

The Children's Friend

Biograph © J131611 Sept. 14, 1909

Director: D. W. Griffith *Cameraman:* G. W. Bitzer

Cast: Frank Powell, Marion Leonard, Gladys Egan, Adele De Garde

Location: Sea Breeze and Edgewater, N.J. *Photographed:* July 30 and Aug. 12, 1909

138 ft. FLA5289 (print) FRA2214 (neg.)

Several children of various ages are leaving a house on the beach to walk in the sand. One of the children is carrying a pet pigeon. The children become lost and fall into a sand pit and cannot extricate themselves. A little dog pulling a cart returns without them and the search begins. After many hours of searching, the parents return to the house just as the pigeon arrives with a note. The children are finally rescued by the adults from the deep sand pit.

Children's Hour on the Farm

AM&B © H58985 Apr. 7, 1905

Cameramen: F. S. Armitage, G. W. Bitzer

Location: Lexington, Mass. *Photographed:* Mar. 13 and 24, 1905

Contents; The Burro's Babies, The Watchdog's Family, Among the Shetland Ponies

168 ft. FLA5290 (print) FRA2217 (neg.)

The subject of the film is animals. The first scene shows a newly born burro and, as the scene ends, its mother is brought before the camera. In the second scene a litter of bulldogs is eating around a pan of food; close-ups of the head of one of the animals as well as a head-and-shoulder picture of a full-grown English bulldog are shown. The remainder of the film is devoted to Shetland ponies. They are harnessed or saddled, and either driven or ridden in a wooded area with snow on the ground.

A Child's Faith

Biograph © J143291 July 16, 1910

Director: D. W. Griffith *Cameraman:* G. W. Bitzer

Cast: Florence Barker, Alfred Paget, Mack Sennett, Billy Quirk, Owen Moore, Gladys Egan, George Nicholls

Location: Studio, N.Y.C. *Photographed:* June 7 and 11, 1910

397 ft. FLA5291 (print) FRA2216 (neg.)

The daughter of a rich man marries a man he doesn't approve of and he refuses to see her any more. Time passes and the marriage brings a daughter as well as ill health to the husband, who eventually dies. The father, who has become a miser, sells his house and unwittingly moves into meager quarters above his recently widowed daughter. He hides his money in a hole over the chimney. It falls through the chimney and land at the feet of his granddaughter who has been praying while her mother is out vainly seeking work. The frantic miser obtains access to the apartment below and finds the praying child with the money. The rich old man is reconciled with his daughter and granddaughter.

A Child's Impulse

Biograph © J142715 June 30, 1910

Director: D. W. Griffith *Cameramen:* G. W. Bitzer, Arthur Marvin

Cast: Dell Henderson, Charles West, Mary Pickford, Verner Clarges, Robert Harron, Gladys Egan, Eddie Dillon, Charles Craig, William J. Butler, George Nicholls, Dorothy West

Location: Westfield, N.J. *Photographed:* May 19, 26 and 27, 1910

389 ft. FLA5292 (print) FRA2219 (neg.)

An eligible young man is smitten by a loose-living adventuress who, while professing to love him, continues to see other men. His friends suggest a trip to the country to forget her. While enjoying the fresh air and sunshine, he meets the daughter of a farmer, falls in love with her and proposes marriage. Determined to marry the rich young man, the adventuress follows him and convinces him he should return to the city with her. The shock to his country love is great. Fear for her life motivates her little sister to make a trip alone to the city, and she succeeds in bringing the young man back to her sister. The film ends as the two young lovers are reunited.

A Child's Remorse

Biograph © J172322 Aug. 17, 1912

Director: D. W. Griffith *Cameraman:* G. W. Bitzer

Cast: Edwin August, Claire McDowell, Gladys Egan, George Hennessy

Location: N.Y.C. *Photographed:* June 1912

381 ft. FLA5293 (print) FRA2220 (neg.)

The story is about a test of character of a little girl who is not accepted by her peers. A group of children are having a picnic at a park. Some of them climb into a leaky motorboat. The little girl who was spurned by them sees them take the boat. She worries for a long time over the possibility of their drowning and finally goes to her parents and tells them of the children in the leaky motorboat. The children are saved and the film ends with the reconciliation of all the children.

A Child's Stratagem
Biograph © J148630 Dec. 9, 1910
Director: D. W. Griffith *Cameraman:* G. W. Bitzer
Cast: Linda Arvidson, Claire McDowell, Lottie Pickford, Jack Pickford, Gladys Egan
Location: Studio, N.Y.C.; Westfield, N.J. *Photographed:* Oct. 5 and 26, 1910
398 ft. FLA5294 (print) FRA2221 (neg.)

A little girl, anguished and unhappy at the thought of her parents' impending divorce, puts a plan into action that brings them back together. The child writes notes to both her mother and father that she has been kidnapped and starts out for her aunt's home. On arrival there, she finds the aunt has moved, and she becomes lost. Some friendly people send her back home with a newsboy to guide her. The film ends as the child, the mother, and the father are seen embracing in gratitude for her safe return.

Chimmie Hicks at the Races
AM&B © H16734 Apr. 18, 1902
Cameraman: F. S. Armitage
Cast: Charles E. Grapewin as Hicks
Date: Oct. 26, 1900
22 ft. FLA3189 (print) FRA0515 (neg.)

The first scene, filmed from the audience, shows a man, dressed in an ordinary business suit, overcoat, and hat, standing on the stage. He indicates by pantomime that he is watching a horse race, and by enthusiastic gestures conveys the idea that he won a bet. An associate in the act walks in, hands him some paper money and he, in turn, makes another bet. It is soon obvious from his pantomimed gestures that he has lost all. The picture ends as he hands his watch and belongings to the bookmaker; he drops to his knees, and prays for forgiveness, promising that he will never bet again.

See also: Jimmie Hicks in Automobile

The Chimney Sweep and the Miller
AM&B © H16334 Apr. 10, 1902
Cameraman: Arthur Marvin
Location: Roof studio, N.Y.C. *Date:* Apr. 24, 1900
12 ft. FLA4240 (print) FRA1397 (neg.)

The camera was placed as if it were a spectator in a vaudeville show and, as the picture begins, a backdrop painted to appear as an outdoor scene is visible. Walking in front of the camera, but in opposite directions, are two men. One is dressed in white overalls and is carrying a white bag, presumably of flour. The other man is in black, dirty clothes and carries the tools of a chimney sweep. They meet head on in the center of the stage and challenge one another. For the remainder of the film , the chimney sweep is being beaten with the bag of flour, while thrashing the miller with a bag of soot.

Chinese Procession, no. 12
Edison © 13534 Feb. 24, 1898
25 ft. FLA3833 (print) FRA1060 (neg.)

The camera was positioned over the heads of spectators that lined the street watching a parade of Orientals carrying banners, papier-mâché dragon heads, floats, etc. The procession consists of approximately a hundred people. On the side of the street opposite the camera position, several hundred persons can be seen watching the parade from bleachers.

The Chinese Rubbernecks
AM&B © H34813 Aug. 19,1903
Cameraman: Arthur Marvin
Location: Roof studio, N.Y.C. *Date:* Aug. 30, 1900
10 ft. FLA4149 (print) FRA1319 (neg.)

Two men wearing pigtails and dressed as Chinese laundrymen are busying themselves about the ironing boards and tubs in their establishment. Then one of the laundrymen turns and burns his companion on the posterior with the hot iron he has been using. His companion becomes irate and chases his attacker around the establishment and out the door. As the pursued laundryman crosses the threshold, his pursuer seizes his head and, using a dummy head and an accordion-pleated cloth neck, it appears as though the neck is being stretched to approximately five feet. When the hold on the neck is released, the head snaps back into place, and both laundrymen are seen in the room, one holding his neck as though it really had been painfully stretched.

Chinese Shaving Scene
Edison © H13037 Jan. 11, 1902
35 ft. FLA4544 (print) FRA1578 (neg.)

A Chinese man is seated on a chair directly in front of the camera. An "old world" Chinese, he still has his queue. A second Chinese, dressed identically in a black, pajamalike garment, appears. This man also has his hair braided in a queue. He begins to shave the seated man.

Ching Ling Foo Outdone
Edison © D4735 Feb. 28, 1900
17 ft. FLA4219 (print) FRA1378 (neg.)

A set of a living room appears first. By the use of stop-action photography, a man dressed in black silk knee breeches and a tail coat appears. He makes a pass and a table appears from which he removes a heavy brocaded cloth. Then, by using the brocaded cloth as a screen to work with, the man conjures up a washtub, fills it with water, makes ducks appear, and, at the end of his act and the film, a small boy appears as the tub disappears.

Choosing a Husband
Biograph © J136613 Jan. 3, 1909
Director: D. W. Griffith *Cameraman:* G. W. Bitzer
Cast: Florence Barker, Mack Sennett, Billy Quirk, Kate Bruce, Blanche Sweet, Henry B. Walthall
Location: Studio, N.Y.C. *Photographed:* Nov 27, 1909
210 ft. FLA5295 (print) FRA2223 (neg.)

A bewildered young woman, overwhelmed by the force of numbers of young men eager to marry her, decides to test their sincerity. As the film begins, one after another, four young men propose. To each she says she will let him know tomorrow. Then, she hides behind a screen while leaving a very attractive young woman in the drawing room to greet them. One at a time, the suitors arrive, find her absent, and each makes advances to her substitute. The young woman comes out from behind the screen and orders her philandering suitors out of the room. At the end of the film, a man she really does love returns from abroad, and she is seen sitting on his lap embracing him.

The Chorus Girl and the Salvation Army Lassie

AM&B © H35630 Sept. 12, 1903
Cameraman: A. E. Weed
Location: Studio, N.Y.C. *Photographed:* Aug. 25, 1903
21 ft FLA4545 (print) FRA1579 (neg.)

The film opens on a backstage area where two girls are smoking. A Salvation Army lassie is attempting to convert them, or at least talk them out of smoking cigarettes and drinking. One of the two chorus girls becomes angry and chases the Salvation Army lassie out of the room.

Christening and Launching Kaiser Wilhelm's Yacht "Meteor"

Edison © H14548 Feb. 28, 1902
Location: Townshend and Downey Shipyard, Shooter's Island, N.Y. *Photographed:* Feb. 25, 1902
129 ft. FLA4993 (print) FRA1959 (neg.)

The film shows a long dock in what appears to be a shipyard. Approaching the camera position are people in formal attire, both military and civilian, followed by men in formation dressed in German naval enlisted personnel uniforms. The next scene shows the launching platform; the dignitaries attending the ceremonies can be seen over the heads of the spectators. Among the dignitaries are Prince Henry of Prussia, Pres. Theodore Roosevelt, and Alice Roosevelt. The bow of a large sailing yacht with a sign *Meteor* can be seen. A bottle is smashed against the bow and the boat begins to slide down the launching rails into the water.

The Christmas Burglars

AM&B © H120042 Dec. 17, 1908
Director: D. W. Griffith *Cameraman:* G. W. Bitzer
Cast: Florence Lawrence, Adele De Garde, Gladys Egan, Mack Sennett, Arthur Johnson, Marion Leonard, Charles West
Location: Studio and Eighth Avenue at 14th Street, N.Y.C. *Photographed:* Nov. 28 and 30, 1908
258 ft. FLA5296 (print) FRA2224 (neg.)

A woman drops a note from her small daughter to Santa Claus on the floor of a pawnshop where she goes in desperation to pawn her shawl, starting a drama that ends happily. The pawnbroker becomes interested and enlists the aid of a group of disreputable habitués of his shop to break into the apartment of the mother and child. While the two sleep, the "burglars" decorate a Christmas tree, put food and presents under it, and sneak out. The child awakens in the morning to find all the things she had asked for, and the film ends as she dances around the tree and

opens her presents. An optical dissolve was used to indicate what one of the characters was thinking.

Christmas Morning

AM&B © H25018 Dec. 15, 1902
Photographed: 1897 [?]
10 ft. FLA3772 (print) FRA1016 (neg.)

During this short film, the only action is that of an adult and four youngsters of various ages who enter a set of the living room of a house with a fireplace on Christmas morning. The children open their gifts and generally jump about in delight. All of the children are wearing sleeping garments.

See also: The Christmas Party, Hanging Stockings on Christmas Eve, and Santa Filling Stockings

The Christmas Party

AM&B © H25019 Dec. 15, 1902
Photographed: 1897[?]
20 ft. FLA4184 (print) FRA1348 (neg.)

There is a set of the living room of a large house on Christmas morning, with stockings hung on the fireplace, and a well-decorated Christmas tree. Gathered about a man in a Santa Claus costume are approximately twenty small children jumping up and down nervously awaiting their turn to receive a gift from Santa's well-stocked bag. The film is quite grainy. However, the action of the film's participants can be readily understood. Released under the title The Christmas Tree Party.

See also: Christmas Morning, Hanging Stockings on Christmas Eve, and Santa Filling Stockings

Christy Mathewson, N.Y. National League Baseball Team

Winthrop Moving Picture Company © H94486 May 24, 1907
14 ft. FLA3775 (print) FRA1019 (neg.)

Christy Mathewson, the great baseball pitcher of the early years of this century, is shown pitching.

Chums

AM&B © H26844 Jan. 9, 1903
Cameraman: Robert K. Bonine
Photographed: Dec. 5, 1902
44 ft. FLA4546 (print) FRA1580 (neg.)

The quality of the film is so poor that detailed description is not possible. A small boy is seated in a chair feeding a rather large spotted dog. There is no other action.

Church "Our Lady of Grace," Hoboken

AM&B © H33289 July 8, 1903
Cameraman: Robert K. Bonine
Location: Hoboken, N.J. *Photographed:* Nov. 25, 1902
76 ft. FLA4994 (print) FRA1960 (neg.)

The camera position was across the street from a building that appears to be a church. The film shows many persons emerging through the large doors. From a different camera position, still more members of the congregation are photographed leaving the church. At one time, a milk truck passes between the camera and the congregation.

Circle Dance

Edison © 13566 Feb. 24, 1898

20 ft. FLA3378 (print) FRA0679 (neg.)

A ritual dance performed by American Indians is shown. Approximately fifty male Indians can be seen shoulder-to-shoulder in a circle with their backs to the camera. There are some spectators to the event. The circle of men revolves slowly in a dance. Two tepees are also visible. About halfway through the film, the words "Copyright 1897, Patented August 1, 1898" are stenciled on one frame.

See also: Carrying Out the Snakes, Line-up and Teasing the Snakes, March of Prayer and Entrance of Dancers, Panoramic View of Moki-land, and Parade of Snake Dancers Before Dance

Circular Panorama of Electric Tower

Edison © H7633 Aug. 14, 1901

Cameramen: Edwin S. Porter, Arthur White

Location: Pan-American Exposition, Buffalo, N.Y.

54 ft. FLA4547 (print) FRA1581 (neg.)

The film, photographed from a single camera position, shows the total exposition and its buildings. The film contains a 360-degree pan.

Circular Panorama of Housing the Ice

Edison © H14440 Feb. 24, 1902

Location: Ice fields, Groton, Mass.

29 ft. FLA3352 (print) FRA0659 (neg.)

The camera photographed an area of industrial activity. Against a hill approximately one hundred feet in height, ten escalatorlike conveyors have been constructed. The film indicates that the system was designed to lift ice that had been cut from a lake to the top of a hill where it was either stored or shipped. The camera pans from the mechanized area to the right 150 degrees to show the total operation.

Circular Panorama of Suspension Bridge and American Falls

Edison © H7627 Aug. 13, 1901

Location: Niagara Falls, N.Y.

42 ft. FLA3735 (print) FRA0981 (neg.)

This 180-degree pan of Niagara Falls area starts from a position that shows the suspension bridge, buildings along the bank, and both the American and Canadian Falls.

Circular Panorama of the Horse Shoe Falls in Winter

Edison © H40909 Jan. 15, 1904

Cameraman: Edwin S. Porter

Location: Niagara Falls, N.Y. *Photographed:* Jan. 11, 1904

57 ft. FLA4548 (print) FRA1582 (neg.)

The film, photographed from a single camera position, shows a winter scene, beginning on the bank and including the spill (not the drop) of Niagara Falls covered with snow and ice.

Circular Panoramic View of Jones & Laughlin's Steel Works Yard

Edison © H16118 Apr. 7, 1902

Location: Pittsburgh

34 ft. FLA3835 (print) FRA1096 (neg.)

In this single-camera-position film, there is a 180-degree pan of a large construction company's steel fabrication yard, showing hoists, overhead cranes, and a switch engine.

Circular Panoramic View of Whirlpool Rapids

Edison © H7626 Aug. 13, 1901

Location: Niagara River Gorge, N.Y.

51 ft. FLA4549 (print) FRA1583 (neg.)

The camera was positioned high on the edge of a bank alongside of rapids caused by the movement of the water and the unevenness of the terrain. The cameraman's shadow can be seen in silhouette against the swirling water.

City Hall to Harlem in 15 Seconds via the Subway Route

Edison © H51950 Oct. 22, 1904

Cameraman: Edwin S. Porter

Location: N.Y.C. *Photographed:* Oct. 17–19, 1904

73 ft. FLA4995 (print) FRA1961 (neg.)

The film begins with an exterior scene of a man approaching a subway entrance. The next camera position shows him descending a staircase onto the loading ramp. From the loading ramp, he goes down the track to a construction area in the subway. The next camera position shows him attempting to ignite an explosive. When he reexamines the fuse, an explosion occurs, propelling him through the tunnel to Harlem. The picture ends as he descends through a roof and lands on a woman who is washing her hands and face.

Clarence, the Cop

AM&B © H39905 Dec. 23, 1903

Cameraman: A. E. Weed

Location: Studio, N.Y.C. *Photographed:* Dec. 11, 1903

49 ft. FLA4996 (print) FRA1962 (neg.)

The opening scene shows a set of the front of a jewelry store. A uniformed policeman and his sergeant appear and the sergeant instructs his subordinate to guard the store. The policeman becomes sleepy, gets a box, sits on it and falls asleep. A pair of burglars arrive, see the policeman asleep, and pour glue on his shoes. Then they proceed to rob the store. As the film ends, the sergeant returns, finds the empty store and the policeman, glued to the sidewalk, and leads him off in high dudgeon.

Clarence, the Cop, on the Feed Store Beat

AM&B © H41858 Feb. 5, 1904

Cameraman: A. E. Weed

Location: Studio, N.Y.C. *Photographed:* Jan. 25, 1904

24 ft. FLA4330 (print) FRA1478 (neg.)

On a set of the floor and loft of a feed-and-grain store, two men are engaged in tying bags of flour together and readying them to be hoisted to the loft. A policeman walks by, stops, and begins a conversation. Another man, not watching where he is going, bumps into the policeman. The policeman scolds him and one of the feed-store employees fastens the hoist hook in the policeman's belt while the other employee pulls the policeman into the air. The film ends as the employees are emptying the contents of a flour bag over the policeman who is dangling in the air.

See also: A Blessing From Above

Classmates

AM&B © H105590 Jan. 27, 1908

Director: Wallace McCutcheon

Cameraman: G. W. Bitzer

Cast: Linda Arvidson, D. W. Griffith, Eddie Dillon

Location: Studio, N.Y.C.

310 ft. FLA5297 (print) FRA2237 (neg.)

This film is an assemblage of pictures of a 1903 football game between two major universities, a 1902 installation ceremony at another major university, and a sequence of scenes of college life. The scenes show a cheering section outside a football dressing room, dancing after the game, and conversations in palm-lined rooms. One young man attempts to force his attentions upon a young lady who knocks him down the stairs. Another young man enters the scene, and they fight. The film ends as the fight ends.

See also: Harvard-Pennsylvania Football Game and Installation Ceremonies of President Butler [Columbia University]

Classmates

Klaw & Erlanger © LP2468 Feb. 23, 1914

f1Supervisor: D. W. Griffith *Director:* James Kirkwood

Cast: Blanche Sweet, Henry B. Walthall, Lionel Barrymore, Marshall Neilan, Gertrude Robinson, Thomas Jefferson

Based on the play by William C. DeMille

1,633 ft. FLA5849-5850 (print) FRA2729-2730 (neg.)

This Klaw & Erlanger film is based on a triangle. A weak-charactered-but-wealthy young man and a poor-but-honest young man both love the same beautiful girl. The poor man wins an appointment to West Point, and a year later, the wealthy boy follows him. But then he attempts to discredit the poor boy's father. The resulting fight culminates in the dishonorable discharge of both. There is a trip through the jungles of the Amazon to find one of the young men, and the picture ends with the exposure of the true character of the jealous wealthy boy, while the poor boy is cleared of disgrace and weds the heroine.

Clerks Casing Mail for Bags, U.S.P.O.

AM&B © H34972 Aug. 22, 1903

Cameraman: A. E. Weed

Location: Washington, D.C. *Photographed:* Aug. 10, 1903

30 ft. FLA3875 (print) FRA1086 (neg.)

The subject is an operation of mail handling called "casing." The camera was placed so that two men can be seen demonstrating the method. The demonstrators, with stacks of letters in their hands, place them in one of many apertures built into a cabinet or "case."

Clerks Tying Bags, U.S.P.O.

AM&B © H34975 Aug. 22, 1903

Cameraman: A. E. Weed

Location: Washington, D.C. *Photographed:* Aug. 10, 1903

26 ft. FLA3877 (print) FRA1088 (neg.)

Two employees of the Post Office Department are removing stacks of letters from the apertures in the "case" or cabinet and tying them into bundles. They then throw the tied envelopes into the appropriate sacks.

Clerks Tying Up for Bags, U.S.P.O.

AM&B © H34977 Aug. 22, 1903

Cameraman: A. E. Weed

Location: Washington, D.C. *Photographed:* Aug. 7, 1903

24 ft. FLA4401 (print) FRA1530 (neg.)

The film shows two postal employees as they tie into bundles stacks of letters they have just removed from a destination "case."

Cleveland Fire Department

AM&B © H32791 June 17, 1903

Cameraman: G. W. Bitzer

Location: Cleveland *Date:* Oct. 18, 1900

37 ft. FLA4550 (print) FRA1584 (neg.)

The subject is the activities of a fire department that can be seen coming out of the fire engine house located across the street from the camera position. The action must have been a drill or rehearsal as the street is lined with people awaiting the arrival of the three pumpers, the two hook-and-ladder wagons, and the four personnel wagons that made up the contingent of fire equipment.

Clever Horsemanship

AM&B © H30178 Apr. 4, 1903

Location: Dresden

37 ft. FLA3614 (print) FRA0874 (neg.)

The film, photographed from a single camera position, shows several mounted horses at the crest of a steep embankment. The horses are ridden down the steep slope. The distance of the subjects from the camera, plus its poor condition, does not permit more description.

Climbing the American Alps

AM&B © H69545 Dec. 6, 1905

Cameramen: F. A. Dobson, G. W. Bitzer

Location: Studio, N.Y.C.; Peekskill, N.Y. *Photographed:* Nov. 20–21, 1905

258 ft. FLA5298 (print) FRA2225 (neg.)

The story the cameraman followed in order to make this picture was preposterous. Utilizing strange camera positions and stop action photography, as well as running the camera backward, the photographer shows a man and a woman planning to climb what they call the "American Alps." The two are studying a map when a stop-action typographical projection of the Great Divide appears on the door. Then the two people and their guide, each carrying an umbrella, hop backward up a hill. The film ends as all three stand on the summit and wave an American flag.

The Clock Maker's Dream

Méliès © H42528 Feb. 23, 1904

Creator: Georges Méliès

Cast: Georges Méliès

Photographed: Winter 1903–4 *Location:* Montreuil, France

Original *Title:* Rêve de L'Horloger

75 ft. FLA5299 (print) FRA2657 (neg.)

The film opens on a set decorated as the interior of a clockmaker's shop with several large clocks. An actor is repairing a clock and is encountering difficulty. He walks off stage with the clock, comes back and sits in a large chair and falls asleep. The remainder of the film is centered around clocks dissolving into people, people being dissolved to reappear in new costumes, group poses dissolved into other group poses. The background interior of the shop dissolves into an exterior with different people. The scene dissolves back to the shop as it was in the first scene with the clockmaker's work still undone.

The Cloister's Touch

Biograph © J137957   Feb. 2, 1910

Director: D. W. Griffith *Cameramen:* Arthur Marvin, G. W. Bitzer *Cast:* Marion Leonard, Linda Arvidson, Verner Clarges, Henry B. Walthall, Mack Sennett, Arthur Johnson, Frank Powell, Kate Bruce, W. Chrystie Miller, George Nicholls

Location: Studio, N.Y.C. *Photographed:* Dec. 20–21, 1909

381 ft.   FLA5300 (print)   FRA2226 (neg.)

The film is set in the feudal era when a lord could press into service any of his tenant serfs. A happy little family of three is divided when the duke of the realm decides to take the wife as one of his courtesans. The beautiful young woman is not happy at court; she pines for her child and becomes ill. Her husband and son find refuge in a monastery, where the serf becomes a postulant. The duke, remorseful at the result of his selfish action, joins the monastic group, where he meets the serf he has wronged. The picture ends as the duke vows to the serf that he will help rear the boy and provide him with every advantage.

A Close Call

Biograph © J169460   May 22, 1912

Director: Mack Sennett

Cast: Sylvia Ashton, William Beaudine, Kate Bruce, Frank Evans, D. W. Griffith, Fred Mace, Dell Henderson, Charles Hill Mailes, Alfred Paget

222 ft.   FLA5301 (print)   FRA2227 (neg.)

A street hawker feels his banjo playing will be more effective and attract more customers if he makes himself up as a black. While he is blackening his face, a black gardener is fired for insubordination. The child of the house wanders away and the parents fear the gardener is guilty. A mob collects and mistakenly chases the black-faced street hawker. He hides in a tool shed; the mob fires guns at him and sets fire to the shed in an attempt to dislodge him. At this point, the child is found safe and sound, and the poor street hawker is forgiven.

A Close Shave

AM&B © H24892   Dec. 9, 1902

Cameraman: F. S. Armitage

Location: Roof studio, N.Y.C. *Date:* June 4, 1901

19 ft.   FLA3184 (print)   FRA0511 (neg.)

The film begins on a set of a barbershop with a man standing by a barber chair stropping a razor. The door opens and a customer comes in, seats himself in the chair, and the barber begins to prepare him for shaving. The door opens again, this time admitting a man dressed as a boy, carrying a large bucket and a brush. The boy begins to slop the contents of the bucket on the man in the barber chair. Judging by the man's actions, this annoys him. He rises from the chair and begins to fight with the barber. The film ends as the customer picks up the bucket and puts it on the barber's head.

Close View of the "Brooklyn" Naval Parade

Edison © 52054   Sept. 3, 1898

Location: Harbor and Hudson River, N.Y.C. *Photographed:* Aug 20, 1898

28 ft.   FLA3299 (print)   FRA0613 (neg.)

[Spanish-American War: New York City Welcome to Admiral Sampson's Fleet]

In order to photograph this film, the camera was positioned on a boat that was part of the reception committee for a U.S. Navy battle cruiser. The action begins as the boat conveying the camera moves parallel to the *Brooklyn*, close enough to identify good details of the turrets and superstructure of the ship. However, the composition and the closeness of the camera do not allow for much detail of the superstructure, which rests on the main deck. The film lasts long enough to see the full length of the ship. The *Brooklyn* was under the command of Winfield Scott Schley and was part of Admiral Sampson's North Atlantic Squadron.

See also: U.S. Cruiser Brooklyn Naval Parade

The Clown and the Alchemist

Edison © D21657   Nov. 16, 1900

Cameraman: Edwin S. Porter

31 ft.   FLA3854 (print)   FRA1066 (neg.)

For the full extent of the film, the producer supplies the viewer with a series of illusions, made possible by the use of trick photography. The actors are mainly costumed as clowns. They gesture in an exaggerated manner, fall down, etc., as grotesque apparitions appear and reappear from empty barrels and lampshades. The cast consists of five people, each of whom takes part in at least one illusion.

Club Swinging, Carlisle Indian School

AM&B © H19019   June 14, 1902

Cameraman: Arthur Marvin

Location: Carlisle, Pa. *Date:* Apr. 17, 1901

34 ft.   FLA3791 (print)   FRA1028 (neg.)

An elevated single camera position enabled the lens to take in about two hundred boys and girls in their early teens swinging Indian clubs in unison. Buildings are in the background.

The Clubman and the Tramp

AM&B © H118716   Nov. 21, 1908

Director: D. W. Griffith *Cameraman:* G. W. Bitzer

Cast: Jeanie Macpherson, Linda Arvidson, Florence Lawrence, Mack Sennett, John Cumpson, Arthur Johnson

Location: Studio and West 12th Street, N.Y.C. *Photographed:* Oct. 21–29 Nov. 16, 1908

374 ft.   FLA5302 (print)   FRA2228 (neg.)

The film begins when a tramp by a ruse gets the cook in the house of a wealthy clubman to leave. While the cook is out, the tramp takes advantage of the availability of the food in the kitchen. Then he continues upstairs where he bathes and dresses in the clothing of his unsuspecting host. During the remainder of the film, the tramp wanders about town where he is continually mistaken for the clubman whose clothes he is wearing. Three young women invite him to join them in a private dining room, and the picture ends when the wife of the clubman discovers the tramp with the young women, thinks he's her husband, and beats him with her umbrella.

Coach at Rural Post Office, U.S.P.O.
AM&B © H34991 Aug. 22, 1903
Cameraman: A. E. Weed
Location: Washington, D.C. *Photographed:* July 30, 1903
29 ft. FLA3480 (print) FRA0761 (neg.)

This section of the postal film is concerned with a stagecoach pulled by four horses arriving and delivering a pouch of mail to a rural post office for rerouting. Also visible is the post office delivery wagon.

Coaches Arriving at Mammoth Hot Springs
Edison © 2468 Jan. 4, 1899
Location: Mammoth Hot Springs Hotel, Yellowstone Park, Wyo.
28 ft. FLA3253 (print) FRA0575 (neg.)

The single camera position seems to be the loading or unloading platform of a resort. The action shows people alighting from horse-drawn vehicles.

Coaches Going to Cinnabar from Yellowstone Park
Edison © 2466 Jan. 4, 1899
Location: Yellowstone Park, Wyo.
26 ft. FLA3362 (print) FRA0991 (neg., copy 1) FRA0992 (neg., copy 2)

The film was photographed from the side of a road on which several types of horse-drawn transportation pass. The camera was positioned lower than the crown of the road, so little beyond the carriages is visible.

Coaching for a Record
AM&B © H17626 May 10, 1902
Camera: Arthur Marvin
Location: Princeton, N.J. *Photographed:* Oct. 9, 1901
23 ft. FLA6175 (print copy 1) FRA1098 (neg., copy 1) FLA3838 (print, copy 2) FRA0903 (neg., copy 2)

The camera was positioned to overlook an area resembling a picnic grounds. A large group of men and women is shown milling about. Further action shows a coach pulled by four horses arriving and stopping close to the camera position. The horses are changed, and the passengers reenter the coach and are driven away.

Coaching for a Record
See: Coaching Party

Coaching Party
AM&B © H33288 July 8, 1903
25 ft. FLA3649 (print) FRA0902 (neg., copy 1) FRA0904 (neg., copy 2)

Groups of people are seen leaving from the front of a large private residence in several different types of horse-drawn vehicle. There are two-wheeled open cabs, two-wheeled closed cabs, coaches, etc. There is some confusion here. This film is believed to be Coaching Party, produced by American Mutoscope & Biograph in 1903 and having the

same copyright number, but Coaching for a Record is the title on the original paper print film.

Coaching Party, Yosemite Valley
AM&B © H30734 Apr. 24, 1903
Cameraman: Robert K. Bonine
Location: Yosemite Valley, Calif. *Date:* Nov. 15, 1901
17 ft. FLA3374 (print) FRA0374 (neg.)

The poor quality of the film does not allow identification of many details. However, it is evident that the camera was taken into a heavily wooded area near a roadway to photograph horse-drawn vehicles as they passed by. Movement was apparent but very little detail can be established.

Coal Heavers
AM&B © H52230 Oct. 28, 1904
54 ft. FLA4551 (print) FRA1585 (neg.)

In order to capture all of the action in this film, several camera positions were required. The first shows several men shoveling coal from a horse-drawn coal wagon into a chute. The second camera position shows the same group still working when a man in a white suit joins them. His gestures indicate he is admonishing them for doing their work incorrectly. The third camera position shows the coal heavers throwing coal dust all over the man in the white suit. The fourth position shows them throwing him into a nearby canal. The scene ends as he is fished out of the water with a pole, and the workers propose to pour more coal dust over him. He is seen departing hastily.

The Coal Strike
AM&B © H69963 Dec. 12, 1905
Cameraman: F. A. Dobson
Location: Studio, N.Y.C. *Date:* Dec. 1, 1905
66 ft. FLA4997 (print) FRA1963 (neg.)

From a single camera position, a set of a kitchen can be seen. A man dressed as a charwoman is working over a washtub. The door opens and a small boy comes in. He attempts to eat a piece of pie. The charwoman catches him by the scruff of the neck and rubs pie in his face. He runs out. A policeman enters and is embraced by the woman who gives him some food and a bottle of beer. One of the windows in the set opens and a load of coal comes in through the coal chute, landing all over them.

The Coal Strike
See: Lady Bountiful Visits the Murphys on Wash Day

Coaling a Steamer, Nagasaki Bay, Japan
AM&B © H16648 Apr. 16, 1902
Cameraman: Robert K. Bonine
Location: Nagasaki, Japan *Date:* Sept. 23, 1901
18 ft. FLA3308 (print) FRA0622 (neg.)

The camera was positioned on a steamship dock at a distance that allowed photographing the process of coaling a ship. Primitive scaffolding reached to the deck of the ship from the dock. Many women and children standing on the dock passed the coal piece by piece from hand to hand to the deck of the ship. Since the camera did not move, no operations are visible other than the lifting of the coal pieces.

Coasting

Edison © 12175 Feb. 17, 1898

Location: Court Street hill, Newark, N.J.

27 ft. FLA4207 (print) FRA1369 (neg.)

The subject that interested the cameraman was a group of people of all ages coasting on sleds down a sloping, snow-covered street in a residential district of a city. The quality of the photography, because of the camera position with relationship to the light, does not permit a more detailed description.

Coasting Scene at Montmorency Falls, Canada

Edison © H14292 Feb. 17, 1902

Location: Montmorency Falls, P.Q., Canada

42 ft. FLA4552 (print) FRA1586 (neg.)

A constructed incline, on which people are placing their sleds and sliding down toward the camera position, can be seen.

Cohen's Advertising Scheme

Edison © H42210 Feb. 16, 1904

Cameraman: Edwin S. Porter

Location: Studio, N.Y.C. *Photographed:* Feb. 2, 1904

24 ft. FLA3847 (print) FRA1107 (neg.)

Only the set of the front of an inexpensive clothing store is visible as the film begins. The windows, window frames, and doorways are painted in, and some articles of clothing hang outside with a banner saying "Fire Sale." The proprietor comes out, appears discouraged and goes back inside. A tramp arrives and looks over the garments on display. The proprietor comes out to try to sell him a suit. When he is unsuccessful, the proprietor goes in the shop and returns with a full-length overcoat which he hands to the tramp. As the tramp walks away, it can be seen that the overcoat has a sign on the back advertising the clothing store.

Coil Winding Machines, Westinghouse Works

See: Westinghouse Works

Coil Winding Section E, Westinghouse Works

See: Westinghouse Works

A Cold Supper with a Hot Finish

AM&B © H33024 June 20, 1903

20 ft. FLA4344 (print) FRA1488 (neg.)

The film begins in a set of a combination kitchen-living room where a man is sitting in a rocking chair and reading a newspaper while a woman is doing housework. A door opens and a young boy with a dog on a leash enters. He commands the dog to sit on a chair while he ties the leash to the back of the chair where the man is reading. The woman prepares some food, places it on the floor across the room from the dog, and calls it. When the dog obeys, he pulls the rocking chair over, spilling the man to the floor and, as the film ends, he is seen waving his arms and legs helplessly.

Collecting Mail, U.S.P.O.

AM&B © H34968 Aug. 22, 1903

Cameraman: A. E. Weed

Location: Washington, D.C. *Photographed:* Aug. 10, 1903

24 ft. FLA3883 (print) FRA2877 (neg.)

The subject is the movement of mail by the U.S. postal service. As the film begins, two types of mail boxes on a pole on the corner of a street can be seen. In the background, away from the camera position, are people going by on foot, as well as horse-drawn and electric streetcar transportation. At the end of the film, a man wearing the uniform of a mailman is seen approaching the mail boxes. He unlocks the boxes and removes the mail from both the small and large boxes.

A College Girl's Affair of Honor

AM&B © H79737 June 19, 1906

Cameraman: G. W. Bitzer

Location: Studio, N.Y.C. *Photographed:* May 25, 1906

20 ft. FLA3593 (print) FRA2138 (neg.)

The locale of this film is a gymnasium where two women are being trained in the fine points of wrestling by a male instructor. During the film, the women struggle with one another, and the film ends with one fall being awarded. The Library of Congress catalog gives 1906 as the copyright date, but 1903 appears as the copyright date on the film.

Colonel Funstan [i.e., Funston] Swimming the Baglag River

Edison © 61838 Sept. 23, 1899

48 ft. FLA4553 (print) FRA1587 (neg.)

The film reproduces an incident in the Spanish-American War when an American officer swam a river despite the enemy soldiers on the opposite shore. The film shows a man removing his clothing and jumping into a river under cover of fire directed by his colleagues at the enemy who can be seen across the river. As the film ends, the American flag is unfurled.

Colored Troops Disembarking

Edison © 31436 May 20, 1898

28 ft. FLA4301 (print) FRA2850 (neg.)

[Spanish-American War]

The film shows troops disembarking. The camera was placed to enable the cameraman to film the forward section of a large, wooden-hulled transport tied to a dock. From the gangway, approximately twenty uniformed troops, with rifles and bedrolls, can be seen disembarking.

Colored Villainy

Keystone © LP4305 Jan. 25, 1915

Producer and Author: Mack Sennett

Cast: Mae Busch, Charles Chase, Nick Cogley, Frank Opperman, Mack Sennett

Location: Keystone studio and vicinity, as well as some footage photographed on a farm east of Los Angeles

440 ft. FLA5303 (print) FRA2230 (neg.)

This film, played by actors in blackface, concerns a very lazy and overweight young man (Nick Cogley), his employer (Frank Opperman), the employer's flirtatious daughter (Mae Busch), and a young traveler (Charles Chase). The father tries hard to keep his daughter from associating with the young men, and she tries just as hard to thwart him. A cigar box containing some money is stolen by one of the suitors, observed by the other (Nick Cogley) who is anxious for revenge. He sees where Chase has hidden the stolen box, removes the money and replaces the cash with angry bees. The balance of the film shows Chase's battle with the bees and his eventual flight on his bicycle clad only in a gunny sack, having been forced to discard his natty attire in order to rid himself of the bees.

"Columbia" and "Defender" Rounding Stake-Boat
AM&B © H17487 May 8, 1902
Cameraman: F. S. Armitage
Location: Long Island Sound *Date:* July 10, 1899
30 ft. FLA3318 (print) FRA0632 (neg.)
[America's Cup Races]

The camera position is on a moored vessel on the weather side of the turning marker buoy. One of the sailboats in the race for the America's Cup can be seen on the starboard tack. The boat approaching the camera tacks her rigging and makes a right-hand turn round the marker buoy. The remainder of the film shows the second contender making her approach, tacking, and turning close to the camera position.

"Columbia" and "Shamrock II" Finishing Second Race
Edison © H9409 Oct. 7, 1901
38 ft. FLA4555 (print) FRA1589 (neg.)
[America's Cup Races]

The camera that photographed this film was positioned on one of the spectator boats. At a distance of approximately half a mile, one of the two entries in the America's Cup Race can be seen. The course of the sailboat is directly toward the camera. All of the film was photographed on the starboard body of the approaching vessel. At the end of the film, the racing vessel has just passed the camera position.

"Columbia" and "Shamrock II" Jockeying and Starting
Edison © H9408 Oct. 7, 1901
34 ft. FLA4556 (print) FRA1590 (neg.)
[America's Cup Races]

The start of the America's Cup sailboat race was photographed from what appears to be the judge's boat. The film shows the two contenders tacking back and forth before the start of the race. The film shows both vessels on all points: starboard, port, bow, stern, and full sail.

"Columbia" and "Shamrock II" Start of Second Race
Edison © H9410 Oct. 7, 1901
24 ft. FLA4554 (print) FRA1588 (neg.)
[America's Cup Races]

The camera seems to have been positioned on the judge's boat. The beginning scenes show both contenders for the America's Cup, close-hauled under full sail, passing the camera position and going away. The best sequence was abaft the beam on the starboard side.

"Columbia" and "Shamrock II" Starting in the Third Race
Edison © H9497 Oct. 9, 1901
73 ft. FLA4557 (print) FRA1591 (neg.)
[America's Cup Races]

The camera position was on a boat at a considerable distance from the start of the race between the two sailboats. The opening scenes show the two vessels at a distance of about a mile, bending their sails and getting ready to tack, using different sailing maneuvers. There are several scenes showing both vessels under full sail and making at least two sailing maneuvers each.

"Columbia" and "Shamrock II" Turning the Outer Stake Boat
Edison © H9496 Oct. 9, 1901
33 ft. FLA3990 (print) FRA1196 (neg.)
[America's Cup Races]

One of the two sailboat contenders for the America's Cup is visible. The distance from the camera to the ship is about a mile. However, the crew of the leading vessel can be seen preparing her to come about. The film shows the leading vessel making her turn at about the time the second vessel becomes visible to the camera. Her crew brings her about also. The film ends as the sails begin to bite and the sailboat is under way again.

"Columbia" Close to the Wind
AM&B © H26955 Jan. 14, 1903
37 ft. FLA3282 (print) FRA0599 (neg.)
[America's Cup Races]

As the film begins the American contender *Columbia* can be seen at a distance of about a mile as she prepares to round a turning buoy. The film shows her tacking, turning, resetting her sails, and coming to a course directly approaching the camera position. As the film ends, the *Columbia* is within two hundred yards of the camera position, on a starboard tack, her sails in a close-hauled position.

"Columbia" vs. "Defender"
AM&B © H30746 Apr. 24, 1903
Cameraman: F. S. Armitage
Location: Long Island Sound *Date:* July 10, 1899
23 ft. FLA3383 (print) FRA0683 (neg.)
[America's Cup Races]

Two large sailing vessels of the America's Cup Defender class can be seen close-hauled on the port tack about a mile from the camera position. The camera platform was a boat that stayed with the racing boats until the film ended. The relative position of the two ships under full racing sails did not alter perceptibly.

"Columbia" Winning the Cup
Edison © 69350 Oct. 24, 1899
Cameraman: Edwin S. Porter
37 ft. FLA4558 (print) FRA1592 (neg.)
[America's Cup Races; Columbia and Shamrock I]

The camera was positioned on a boat approximately two thousand yards from where the two large America's Cup racing sailboats were competing for the cup. The barely visible action shows the two sailboats jockeying for position to begin the race.

"Columbia" Winning the Cup
Edison © H9495 Oct. 9, 1901
25 ft. FLA4100 (print) FRA1281 (neg.)

[America's Cup Races; Columbia and Shamrock II]

The film of the two large racing sailboat cup defenders was photographed from a camera position on board a vessel approximately a thousand yards from the finish line. The action shows both sailboats approaching the finish line close-hauled on the port tack.

Comata, the Sioux

Biograph © J131568 Sept. 13, 1909

Director: D. W. Griffith *Cameraman:* G. W. Bitzer

Cast: James Kirkwood, Marion Leonard, Arthur Johnson, Florence Lawrence, Linda Arvidson, Verner Clarges

Location: Cuddebackville, N.Y. *Photographed:* Aug. 6–7, 1909

360 ft. FLA5228 (print) FRA2828 (neg.)

A white man (Arthur Johnson) convinces an Indian maiden (Marion Leonard) to abandon her Indian village and accompany him to his small house on the edge of some cleared land. In time, they have a child. In the background, from the beginning, an Indian (James Kirkwood) can be seen as though guarding the young Indian girl. In time, the white man becomes enamored of a white girl. He leaves the Indian girl, and the last scene shows her with her child in her arms, going off into the hills with the Indian brave who had always loved her.

Comedy Cake Walk

AM&B © H31675 May 11, 1903

Cameraman: F. S. Armitage

Cast: Americus Quartet

Location: Philadelphia [?] *Date:* Sept. 18, 1900 [?]

11 ft. FLA3391 (print) FRA0689 (neg.)

Four blacks, two male and two female, dressed in formal attire are dancing the preliminaries to the Cake Walk in front of a wall. For the duration of the film, a man and a woman of the group proceed toward the camera from the wall and then turn and return.

See also: Cake Walk

Comedy Set-to

Edison © 31430 May 20, 1898

16 ft. FLA4377 (print) FRA1515 (neg.)

During the short course of this film, an attractive young girl and a boy of approximately the same age are seen acting out the routine of comedy boxers. The young girl approaches the young man as if she knows what will happen next, and the bout ends when the boy is knocked to the floor. This film was photographed with artificial light placed so that the shadows of the two participants are small and beneath them.

Committee on Art

AM&B © H42804 Feb. 27, 1904

Cameraman: A. E. Weed

Location: Studio, N.Y.C. *Photographed:* Feb. 17, 1904

32 ft. FLA4559 (print) FRA1593 (neg.)

A man dressed as a burlesque rube comes out on stage and is impressed by the risqué poster he sees advertising a burlesque show. He looks off-stage and then runs off. Women, dressed in the fashion of the era but obviously "do-gooders," enter and busily pin skirts and blouses on the drawings of the unclothed women. The picture ends when the rube returns, slaps his knee, and exits laughing.

Common Beasts of Africa

Paul J. Rainey © MP224 June 22, 1914

282 ft. FLA5304 (print) FRA2662 (neg.)

This is a series of close-up and long-range views of common African animals, including water buffaloes, zebras, rhinoceroses, and several varieties of antelopes. The film quality varies between poor and fair.

Company Drill, St. John's Military Academy

AM&B © H43410 Mar. 17, 1904

Cameraman: G. W. Bitzer

Location: St. John's Military Academy, Manlius, near Syracuse, N.Y. *Photographed:* Mar. 4, 1904

22 ft. FLA3054 (print) FRA0395 (neg.)

A flat, snow-covered area can be seen. The first action consists of a company of men in military dress in columns of four passing in front of the camera. The next scene is of the same group executing three different close-order drill commands, all in double time. The film ends as they leave the camera position.

Concealing a Burglar

AM&B © H117340 Oct. 22, 1908

Director: D. W. Griffith *Cameraman:* G. W. Bitzer

Cast: Florence Lawrence, Linda Arvidson, Arthur Johnson, Mack Sennett, Jeanie Macpherson

Location: Studio, N.Y.C. *Photographed:* Sept. 26 and 28, 1908

254 ft. FLA5305 (print) FRA2231 (neg.)

A burglar threatens a young woman that if she reveals his presence in her boudoir, he will say he is her lover. Her husband, who arrives in an intoxicated condition, makes several humorous scenes possible as the wife, frightened and desperate, tries to hide the burglar in the closet, under the bed, and so on. The husband finally discovers the burglar and begins shooting at him, but the police arrive and remove the culprit before he is injured.

Condensed Milk

AM&B © H32872 June 20, 1903

20 ft. FLA3424 (print) FRA0712 (neg.)

A barnyard was photographed from a single camera position. The cast consists of two men and a woman milking a cow. One of the men takes the bucket of milk from the milkmaid, places it under the water pump, and pumps water into the pail that presumably contains milk. This seems to annoy the other man who picks up the pail and throws the contents on the man who watered it.

Coney Island at Night

Edison © H62761 June 29, 1905

Cameraman: Edwin S. Porter

Location: Coney Island, N.Y. *Photographed:* June 3–4, 1905

104 ft. FLA5000 (print) FRA1964 (neg.)

The film, taken at night when the only source of light for the photographer was the concessions themselves, shows both close-up and distance shots, elevated and at street level, of the various concessions in Coney Island. The titles of the film could have been photographed on the spot.

However, they seem to have been contrived for the film by the use of stop-action photography.

The Coney Island Beach Patrol

AM&B © H49071 Aug. 13, 1904

Cameraman: G. W. Bitzer

Location: Coney Island, N.Y. *Photographed:* Aug. 6, 1904

60 ft. FLA5001 (print) FRA1965 (neg.)

Two small boys with policemen's hats and nightsticks are struggling with another small boy. The object of their struggle seems to be to arrest him. Approaching the camera from a distance are two men in bathing suits, pretending they are horses, and pulling what is supposed to be a patrol cart. The small culprit is put in the wagon and taken back to a tent on the sand. The tent bears the sign "Police Patrol Headquarters."

The Coney Island Bikers

AM&B © H28550 Feb. 24, 1903

20 ft. FLA3169 (print) FRA0498 (neg.)

Approaching the camera position is a young woman riding a bicycle on the sand of a beach. She is dressed for bathing. She is followed closely by three women, two of whom are holding the third on the seat of a bicycle as though teaching her to ride. The film ends as she falls.

Coney Island Police Court

AM&B © H115087 Aug. 25, 1908

Director: D. W. Griffith [?] *Cameraman:* G. W. Bitzer

Cast: John Cumpson, Harry Salter

Location: Studio, N.Y.C. *Photographed:* Aug. 7, 1908

162 ft. FLA5306 (print) FRA2249 (neg.)

From a single camera position a set of a police court can be seen. This picture, a burlesque of the day's activities of a police court, begins with two sleeping policemen being awakened by a charwoman who wants to scrub the floor. One after another, males and females, young and old, are brought in by police officers and submitted to the legal scrutiny of a man on the bench. The disposition of each case is, of course, handled in a comic fashion. At the end of the film, two pugilists are brought in. Their fight involves everyone in the court, wrecks the police station, and results in complete pandemonium. This is a good example of the type of motion picture production being made at Biograph when D. W. Griffith arrived. Released as Monday Morning in a Coney Island Police Court.

Confidence

AM&B © H125501 Apr. 8, 1909

Director: D. W. Griffith *Cameramen:* G. W. Bitzer, Arthur Marvin

Cast: Florence Lawrence, John Cumpson, Kate Bruce, Linda Arvidson, Arthur Johnson, Charles Inslee, Jeanie Macpherson

Location: Studio, N.Y.C. *Photographed:* March 12, 13, and 20, 1909

378 ft. FLA5307 (print) FRA2232 (neg.)

A fight between a saloon gambler and his enemies in which the young heroine, his girl friend, is involved causes her to become a nurse. She falls in love with a doctor she meets at the hospital, and they are married. The gambler, learning of her good marriage, blackmails her. She pays him off once

and on his second visit to her home to get money, the gambler is caught by the doctor. The doctor demonstrates his love for his wife by throwing the evidence of her past into the fire and the villain out the door.

Congress of Nations

Edison © D21659 Nov. 16, 1900

Cameramen: Edwin S. Porter, James H. White

45 ft. FLA4560 (print) FRA1594 (neg.)

This film was photographed over stage footlights from a single camera positioned in the audience. A man in the center of the stage seems to suspend in the air over his head a large circular paper hoop similar to a drum head. By the use of stop-action photography, people appear when a piece of material is removed from a hole punched in the paper hoop. Each person wears a uniform of a different nation. The man then conjures up an American flag, causes it to unfurl on the stage backdrop, and the picture ends with people of all nations standing in a tableau, indicative of friendship.

Contrary Wind

AM&B © H28559 Feb. 24, 1903

Cameraman: F. S. Armitage

Location: Roof studio, N.Y.C. *Date:* Nov. 30, 1900

12 ft. FLA3135 (print) FRA0468 (neg.)

The film was photographed by overhead incandescent light. Three small children are grouped around a large water-filled washtub, in which two sailboats float. The children attempt to make the little sailboats move across the surface of the water by blowing on the sails.

The Converts

AM&B © J139195 Mar. 16, 1910

Director: D. W. Griffith *Cameraman:* G. W. Bitzer

Cast: Linda Arvidson, Arthur Johnson, Marion Leonard, Henry B. Walthall, Owen Moore, Mack Sennett, Kate Bruce, W. Chrystie Miller

Location: San Gabriel, Calif.; Studio, Los Angeles *Photographed:* Feb. 8–9, 1910

373 ft. FLA5308 (print) FRA2229 (neg.)

Three men are discussing religion and its effect. A wager is made and the hero dons the frock of a priest, goes out on the street, and preaches a sermon. A drunken dance-hall girl hears him, and is so impressed she becomes a settlement worker, unbeknown to the hero. In the meantime, the hero is tormented and seeks to establish if there is any truth in the sermon he preached. In his wanderings about the town, an old derelict falls at his feet. The pseudo-priest kindly starts to pick him up and realizes he is being helped by the settlement worker whose conversion resulted from the sermon he preached in jest.

The Convict and the Curate

See: The Convict's Escape

The Convict's Bride

AM&B © H81754 Aug. 9, 1906

Cameraman: F. A Dobson

Location: Studio, N.Y.C. *Photographed:* July 25, 1906

22 ft. FLA3613 (print) FRA2889 (neg.)

The set represents the interior of a jail with two cells visible. One of the cells contains a man in the striped suit of a convict, while a guard paces up and down in front of the cells. As the film continues, a young woman dressed for the street approaches the guard who grants her permission to talk with the prisoner. She embraces the prisoner, and then turns to the guard and pleads with him for mercy, justice, or pardon. While her pleadings are being denied by the guard, the prisoner removes a gun from the woman's stocking. The prisoner shoots the guard and they both escape.

See also: In the Tombs

The Convict's Escape

Produced by a British company, Clarendon, in France, and
    distributed in the United States by AM&B
AM&B © H50327 Sept. 10, 1904
Original *Title:* The Convict and the Curate
Director: Percy Stow
96 ft. FLA5002 (print) FRA1966 (neg.)

This film is based on a story of an escaped convict who enters a vicar's home, steals his clothing, and continues to flee. The vicar wakes, dons the convict's uniform, and sets out after him. The police mistakenly arrest the vicar and take him off to the police station. The police also find the escaped convict in a haystack and haul him off to be confronted by the vicar.

A Convict's Punishment

AM&B © H27980 Feb. 7, 1903
Cameraman: Arthur Marvin
Location: Roof studio, N.Y.C. *Date:* July 26, 1900
11 ft. FLA3162 (print) FRA0492 (neg.)

The set is constructed to appear as the interior of a prison and in front of a wall is a man dressed in the striped uniform of a prisoner. He is being accosted by two men wearing prison guard uniforms. The prisoner is attempting to fight the guards, who subdue him, tie his hands with rope to a hook on the prison wall, and begin lashing him with a whip. The prisoner receives seven lashes before the film ends.

The Convict's Sacrifice

Biograph © 1909
Director: D. W. Griffith *Cameraman:* G. W. Bitzer
Cast: James Kirkwood, Stephanie Longfellow, Henry B.
    Walthall, Harry Salter, Gladys Egan, Tony O'Sullivan,
    Owen Moore, Mack Sennett
Location: Studio, N.Y.C.; Fort Lee, N.J. *Photographed:* June 10
    and 16 1909
359 ft. FLA5251 (print) FRA2814 (neg.)

The first scene shows a prisoner (James Kirkwood) being processed for release. The next scene is of a group of laborers at an excavation site where a young girl is bringing her father (H. B. Walthall) his lunch pail. The exconvict appears and the laborer shares his lunch and helps him get a job. But the exconvict gets into a fight with a drunken laborer and is returned to jail. This time he escapes. He steals clothing from a scarecrow and ends up at the house of the laborer who had befriended him. There he finds his friend anguished because his daughter is ill and he has no money for medicine. The exconvict calls to the prison guards who have trailed him to the house and submits to the laborer so that he can get the reward for the capture, and the film ends here.

The Cook in the Parlor

AM&B © H32908 June 23, 1903
Cameraman: G. W. Bitzer
Location: Studio, N.Y.C. *Photographed:* June 17, 1903
26 ft. FLA3439 (print) FRA0724 (neg.)

This comedy begins on a set of the living room of a large house. There are pictures on the wall, a piano, a portrait on an easel and, directly in front of the camera, a glass fishbowl on a stand. A buxom woman dressed as a cook is scrutinizing the fishbowl. From time to time she attempts to catch the fish in her bare hands. While this is going on, another servant, a maid, carrying a feather duster, enters and scolds the cook for annoying the fish. A fight begins, during which every standing piece of furniture in the room is either knocked over or broken. The fight between the two lasts until the end of the picture. The last few frames of the film disclose that the parts of the maid and the cook were taken by men because in the scuffle both lose their wigs. Released as The Cook Visits the Parlor.

The Cook in Trouble

Méliès © H45466 May 9, 1904
Creator: Georges Méliès
Cast: Georges Méliès
Location: Montreuil, France *Photographed:* Spring 1904
Original title: La Sorcellerie Culinaire
106 ft. FLA5309 (print) FRA2655 (neg.)

In a large kitchen, two pots are cooking on the large stove. Three persons, apparently the cook's helpers, are sitting around a tub and preparing vegetables. One large pot on the stove starts to smoke. The cook pours something into it and the pot stops smoking. He turns his back, and it starts smoking again and then pandemonium breaks loose. The cook's helpers run around in circles, bump into one another and try to help the cook prevent people dressed as devils either from jumping into the cooking pots or coming out through the oven doors. This film shows some interesting application of tumbling and stop action photography.

The Cook in Trouble

See: La Sorcellerie Culinaire

The Cop and the Nurse Girl

Edison © 72467 Dec. 12, 1898
18 ft. FLA3227 (print) FRA0551 (neg.)

A policeman is standing on the bank of a stream or lake. A short distance from him, a young woman dressed as a maid or governess is pushing a four-wheeled baby pram. The policeman walks up to the maid and begins kissing her. Someone off camera gives the pram a push and both baby and perambulator go into the water. The policeman grapples with the man but he gets away. The last of the film shows the policeman staring belligerently in the direction taken by the fleeing culprit.

The Cop Fools the Sergeant

Edison © H45037 Apr. 29, 1904
Cameraman: Edwin S. Porter

Location: Studio, N.Y.C. *Photographed:* Apr. 22, 1904
69 ft. FLA5003 (print) FRA1967 (neg.)

The cameraman placed his equipment across the street from a bakery with an entrance to the basement. A policeman appears and goes down the stairs and into the basement bakery. While he is there, he is warned that his sergeant is pacing up and down outside the entrance hoping to catch him. The bakers put the policeman in a bread basket, cover him with loaves of bread, and then cart the basket up the stairs and past the waiting sergeant. They load it onto a horse-drawn bakery wagon which drives off. At the end of the film, the policeman strolls up to his sergeant, much to the sergeant's surprise.

The Cord of Life

AM&B © H121877 Jan. 22, 1909

Director: D. W. Griffith *Cameramen:* G. W. Bitzer, Arthur Marvin

Cast: Linda Arvidson, Dorothy Bernard, Marion Leonard, Charles Gorman, Charles Inslee, Adolphe Lestina, Guy Hedlund, Harry Salter, Mack Sennett, John Cumpson, Charles French, Clara T. Bracey

Location: Studio, N.Y.C.; Palisades, N.J. *Photographed:* Jan. 6, 9 and 13, 1909

302 ft. FLA5310 (print) FRA2247 (neg.)

The actors in this melodrama are dressed to indicate their Italian derivation while the sets and street scenes show a poor section of a large city. In the first scene, the villain approaches a woman and asks directions. He goes to an apartment and finds the hero with his wife, and child at dinner. There is an altercation over what appears to be money, and the villain is knocked down and ordered out of the apartment. The villain puts the sign of death on the door with his knife. The remainder of the film shows the villain either trying to collect the debt or attempting to kill the debtor. On one call, he finds the debtor's child unattended. He ties the child's feet, places him in a basket, and hangs the basket from a rope out the window so that if the window sash is raised, the child will fall. Then the villain attempts to kill the hero, who is saved by the opportune arrival of a policeman. The villain confesses what he has done with the child and the hero chases off through the park to rescue his baby. He reaches home and is lowered head down through the window to remove the basket. The final scene shows the family safely reunited.

Cornell-Columbia-University of Pennsylvania Boat Race at Ithaca, N.Y., Showing Lehigh Valley Observation Train

Edison © H4935 June 6, 1901

Location: Ithaca, N.Y.

63 ft. FLA4561 (print) FRA1595 (neg.)

The opening camera position shows a boat-train carrying spectators to an eight-car shell boat race. The second camera position shows spectators standing and some on the river on various types of floating equipment. The third camera position shows the racing shells at the finish.

A Corner in the Play Room

AM&B © H33291 July 8, 1903

Cameraman: Robert K. Bonine

Date: Dec. 5, 1902

20 ft. FLA3729 (print) FRA0976 (neg.)

Two small children play with a hobby horse, a train, and a ball. They wear paper soldier hats and have wooden swords in their belts.

A Corner in Wheat

Biograph © J135969 Dec. 15, 1909

Director: D. W. Griffith *Cameraman:* G. W. Bitzer

Cast: Linda Arvidson, Kate Bruce, W. J. Butler, Adele De Garde, Gladys Egan, Grace Henderson, Arthur Johnson, James Kirkwood, Jeanie Macpherson, Owen Moore, Frank Powell, Mack Sennett, Blanche Sweet, Henry B. Walthall, Charles West

Location: Jamaica, Long Island, N.Y. *Photographed:* Nov. 3 to 13, 1909

396 ft. FLA5311 (print) FRA2233 (neg.)

Based on Frank Norris's writings, this film was unusual for its time in its emphasis on social significance. The two elements, established at the beginning of the film, are a poor farmer planting his crop and a Wall Street broker out to corner the wheat market. The director contrasts their situations throughout and ends with the asphyxiation of the broker in a grain pit, where he has taken some friends to see the wheat he has accumulated.

Corner Madison and State Streets, Chicago

Edison © 43410 July 31, 1897

Location: Chicago

24 ft. FLA3038 (print) FRA0245 (neg.)

The film, photographed from a single camera position, shows the intersection of Madison and State streets in Chicago, Illinois, on a holiday or a Sunday. A streetcar passes, as well as horse-drawn vehicles and people carrying placards. The film was exposed at approximately thirty-six frames-per-second. The Chicago Transit Authority says of this film that it is the "only known movie of a cable car in Chicago."

Corpus Christi Procession, Orvieto

AM&B © H35635 Sept. 12, 1903

Location: Orvieto, Italy

19 ft. FLA3348 (print) FRA0656 (neg.)

The camera overlooks a town square. Immediately as the film begins, a crowd of people is visible. It is a procession led by persons in the robes of a religious order, carrying a large cross on which is an effigy of a crucified individual. The distance does not permit a more detailed description.

"Corsair" in Wake of Tugboat

AM&B © H26952 Jan. 14, 1903

Cameraman: F. S. Armitage

Location: America's Cup Race *Photographed:* Oct. 16, 1899

21 ft. FLA3287 (print) FRA0603 (neg.)

The single camera position was from the stern of some vessel. The film shows a large seagoing yacht under way. The angle of approach to the yacht was broad on the port bow. The *Corsair* was owned by J. P. Morgan.

The Corset Model

AM&B © H32866 June 20, 1903

Cameraman: F. S. Armitage

Date: June 9, 1899
31 ft. FLA3463 (print) FRA0745 (neg.)

In a dressmaker's shop, a woman can be seen standing behind a dummy. The dummy is dressed in a corset and other undergarments. The woman is standing behind the dummy in such a way as to be indistinguishable from it. However, she moves, and the viewer becomes aware of the illusion. The manager proceeds to dismantle the dummy. Other people enter the shop, and a live woman models the corset.

Cossack Cavalry

AM&B © H34102 Aug. 3, 1903
Cameraman: Raymond Ackerman
Location: Tientsin, China *Date:* Jan. 1901
24 ft. FLA3331 (print) FRA0642 (neg.)

The first camera position shows a large group of mounted riders at a distance of five hundred yards. As they approach the camera, they can be identified as a Russian Cossack cavalry regiment. They proceed in formation at inspection trot. The second camera position shows the riders approaching, and the regimental colors are easily established. However, the condition of the film leaves a lot to be desired. If anything in the film is of value, film-laboratory chemistry can bring out the more pertinent details. The full title according to AM&B records is *C. Von Waldersee Reviewing 1st Chita & Reg. Cossacks.*

See also: Review of Russian Artillery

Cosy Corner Dance

AM&B © H32943 June 25, 1903
Cameraman: G. W. Bitzer
Date: June 18, 1903
42 ft. FLA4562 (print) FRA1596 (neg.)

A young girl (Little Anita) dressed in a short white dress goes through various dance steps in front of an unlighted dark backdrop.

See also: Betsy Ross Dance

Cotton Spinning

AM&B © H29001 Mar. 6, 1903
Cameraman: Arthur Marvin
Location: Pan-American Exposition, Buffalo, N.Y. *Date:* May 25, 1901
16 ft. FLA3621 (print) FRA2849 (neg.)

A single camera position shows what appears to be an exhibit for a fair: a constructed log cabin in front of which is a spinning wheel operated by a black woman. Two adult blacks and three adolescents are watching her.

Council Bluffs Bridge Station

AM&B © H29152 Mar. 11, 1903
Cameraman: G. W. Bitzer
Location: Omaha, Neb. *Date:* Nov. 28, 1900
40 ft. FLA4563 (print) FRA1597 (neg.)

The approach to a cantilever bridge is shown. The camera is on the front of the car traveling over the rails. The car crosses the cantilever bridge, makes two turns, and goes through a station. This is part of a series of eight films made for the Union Pacific Railroad. Other titles are: Devil's Slide, Georgetown Loop, One Thousand Mile Tree, Overland Limited, Sherman Hill Tunnel, Steamboat and Great Eastern Rock, and Tunnel Number Three.

The Count of Monte Cristo

Famous Players Film Company © LP188 Dec. 10, 1912
Director and Cameraman: Edwin S. Porter
Cast: James O'Neill
2,160 ft. FLA5924-5925 (print) FRA2793-2794 (neg.)

This film is James O'Neill's version of the famous Dumas historical novel and follows the story as closely as possible under the circumstances of the time. The production was an ambitious one and is unique, as it was the first film made by Famous Players under Adolph Zukor's production responsibility, and the first film directed by Edwin S. Porter while in his employ. Although it was made in 1912, it was not released until November 1, 1913. Motion pictures achieved legal status when Famous Players won a lawsuit against William N. Selig for infringement of their rights to the above film. The Selig picture was subsequently destroyed.

Country Couple

See: Uncle Josh at the Moving Picture Show

A Country Courtship

AM&B © H67887 Oct. 25, 1905
Cameraman: G. W. Bitzer
Location: North Beach, Long Island, N.Y. *Photographed:* Oct. 17, 1905
235 ft. FLA5312 (print) FRA2234 (neg.)

The locale of this comedy is a rural community. A protective father negotiates a marriage for his daughter with a man he considers suitable, but she runs off with the boy she wants instead. A chase, involving two horse-drawn vehicles, results, and the elopers reach the parson and get married before the other suitor arrives. There is a mild altercation, but everybody climbs in the wagons and returns to the bride's home, where the father and the new bridegroom pick up the suitor bodily, throw him into his wagon, and pack him off.

The Country Doctor

Biograph © J129513 July 9, 1909
Director: D. W. Griffith *Cameraman:* G. W. Bitzer
Cast: Frank Powell, Florence Lawrence, Mary Pickford, Stephanie Longfellow, Kate Bruce, Gladys Egan, Adele De Garde
Location: Greenwich, Conn.; Studio, N.Y.C. *Photographed:* May 29 and 31, June 7, 1909
354 ft. FLA5313 (print) FRA2235 (neg.)

The opening scene presents a quiet, serene, bucolic vista and, as the picture begins, the camera starts to pan slowly across a river and cultivated fields and comes to rest on the front of a house. At the end, the camera also pans from the front of the same house slowly over the same acreage and stops on the identical scene where it began. The plot concerns a country doctor faced with the dilemma of whether to save his own ill child or the daughter of one of his patients. In spite of the entreaties of his wife and servant, he lives up to his Hippocratic oath and sacrifices his own child that another might live.

The Country Schoolmaster
AM&B © H83541 Oct. 6, 1906
Cameraman: G. W. Bitzer
Location: Studio, N.Y.C.; Sound Beach, Conn. *Photographed:* Sept. 13, 14 and 16, 1906
289 ft. FLA5314 (print) FRA2236 (neg.)

The picture starts with the mother of a little boy and girl urging them off to school. When they get there, the two cause a complete breakdown of the school discipline. Their teacher spanks them. The three following scenes end the same way. In the last scene, the schoolmaster is shown sleeping in a hammock. The children build a fire under him and his coat catches on fire. He runs off down the road until he reaches a firehouse where the firemen douse the fire by squirting water on him.

A Couple of Lightweights at Coney Island
AM&B © H48620 July 28, 1904
Cameraman: G. W. Bitzer
Location: Coney Island, N.Y. *Photographed:* July 20, 1904
31 ft. FLA3214 (print) FRA0538 (neg.)

The film, photographed from a single camera position located on a sandy beach, shows two small children in bathing dress and boxing gloves sparring. Many exchanges of blows are shown.

The Course of True Love
AM&B © H66191 Sept. 26, 1905
Cameraman: F. A. Dobson
Location: Bayonne and High Bridge, N.J.; Studio, N.Y.C. *Photographed:* Sept. 13–15, 1905
225 ft. FLA5315 (print) FRA2238 (neg.)

An unscheduled embrace during a parlor game of blind-man's buff leads to a kiss and causes a young woman to break her engagement. She then sets out to destroy her life by jumping off a bridge, lying down on a railroad track in front of an oncoming train, and, finally, jumping off a ferryboat into the water. In each of her suicide attempts, she is thwarted by policemen, track walkers, or men on the ferryboat. The last scene shows the young woman in the hospital being attended by doctors and nurses. When her exfiancé comes to see her and gave her a kiss, the young woman responds with enthusiasm. When AM&B issued a bulletin describing this picture, it said, "This film is clear, sharp and distinct, and projects as steady as a clock ticks. The subject moreover is not of passing interest, but *will be good for all time.*" (Italics added.)

The Course of True Love
AM&B © J138088 Feb. 8, 1910
Director: D. W. Griffith *Cameraman:* Arthur Marvin
Cast: Owen Moore, Florence Barker, Dell Henderson, Eleanor Kershaw
Location: Fort Lee, N.J.; Studio, N.Y.C. *Photographed:* Dec. 23 and 31, 1909
396 ft. FLA5316 (print) FRA2239 (neg.)

When an artist's innocent kindness to a hungry, poverty-stricken flower girl causes a misunderstanding with his fiancée, she breaks their engagement. The film begins with the artist at work in his studio, when the poor flower girl enters. The artist feels sorry for her and feeds her. As she is eating, his fiancée and her friends pay an unexpected call, and the fiancée, misunderstanding the situation, breaks the engagement. The artist, distraught, destroys his paintings, packs his clothing, and prepares to leave town. The flower girl learns of the havoc she has inadvertently wrought and goes to the fiancée. At the end of the film, the artist and his betrothed are embracing while the flower girl tiptoes out, leaving a flower as a talisman.

Court House Crooks
Keystone © LP5777 July 5, 1915
Producer and Author: Mack Sennett
Cast: Minta Durfee, Harold Lloyd, Billie Bennett, Ford Sterling, Charles Arling
Location: Keystone studio and vicinity, Los Angeles
842 ft. FLA5851 (print) FRA2731 (neg.)

A judge, Charles Arling, is married to a flirtatious young woman, Minta Durfee, who manages to wind her husband around her finger while carrying on a flirtation with the district attorney, Ford Sterling. She demands a piece of jewelry for their second wedding anniversary, and from there on things go all wrong. Harold Lloyd, as an innocent bystander, ends up in jail, but soon escapes, and there is the usual Keystone nonsense in getting him back. All ends well, though, for everybody except Ford Sterling.

Court Room Scene
See: The Kleptomaniac

The Cowboy and the Lady
AM&B © H36402 Oct. 1, 1903
Cameraman: G. W. Bitzer
Location: Studio, N.Y.C. *Photographed:* Sept. 24, 1903
45 ft. FLA4564 (print) FRA1598 (neg.)

The first scene takes place in a saloon where a man and a woman are sitting at a table having a drink and a man is playing the piano. An obviously intoxicated cowboy enters and pounds on the table for attention. The waiter does not appear immediately, so he takes out two revolvers and starts to shoot up the place. Pandemonium reigns. The woman panics and goes through the ceiling. Her feet and legs (a dummy is used) in circular knitted stockings appear through the ceiling. The cowboy gets a screen, puts it around the clearly embarrassed woman, sits down, and the waiter serves him. Stop action photography was used and the camera was turned upside down as well.

Cowboy Justice
AM&B © H40754 Jan. 11, 1904
Cameraman: G. W. Bitzer
Location: Studio, N.Y.C. *Photographed:* Dec. 30, 1903
45 ft. FLA5047 (print) FRA2833 (neg.)

The film starts with a scene in a saloon and then enacts a hanging on a set of a tree in front of a painted backdrop. All the actors are in identical Western clothing except for the man who was hung who is wearing Indian clothing.

Cowboys and Indians Fording River in a Wagon
Edison © H46141 May 18, 1904
Cameraman: A. C. Abadie
Location: Bliss, Oklahoma Territory *Photographed:* May 7, 1904
30 ft. FLA3678 (print) FRA0928 (neg.)

The film, photographed from a single camera position, shows a wagon pulled by four mules as it fords a river. The passengers' attire indicates they are Indians.

The Creators of Foxy Grandpa

AM&B © H18032 May 23, 1902
Cameraman: Robert K. Bonine
Cast: Joseph Hart, Carrie DeMar, Charles E. Schultz
Date: May 7, 1902
26 ft. FLA4354 (print) FRA0347 (neg.)

The camera was positioned as if in a front seat in a vaudeville house. The film shows a painted backdrop and a constructed fence, arbor, etc. The action consists of the participants being introduced to the audience. There is a woman in a large picture hat and summer dress, a man in an ordinary business suit, two boys dressed as twins, and last but not least, a young man made up to appear as an old gentleman. This series illustrates scenes from William A. Brady's musical production.

The Cricket on the Hearth

Biograph © H127599 May 26, 1909
Director: D. W. Griffith *Cameramen:* G. W. Bitzer, Arthur Marvin
Cast: Charles Inslee, Owen Moore, Violet Mersereau, Herbert Prior, Linda Arvidson, Mack Sennett, George Nicholls, Harry Salter, Dorothy West, John Cumpson
Location: Studio, N.Y.C.; Fort Lee, N.J. *Photographed:* Apr. 8, 9 and 21, 1909
379 ft. FLA5317 (print) FRA2250 (neg.)

The film is about a toymaker with two daughters of marriageable age. One has a suitor (Owen Moore) who first appears in a sailor suit and announces he must go to sea. The father of the two daughters, seizing the opportunity, tries to marry off the sailor's sweetheart to a rich old man. The sailor learns of the plan from a friend (Mack Sennett) and conspires to defeat the father. The film ends in a scene depicting the jubilance of all and sundry for, as a result of the plan to thwart the father, they inadvertently get the toymaker's second daughter married to the rich old man.

The Criminal Hypnotist

AM&B © H121531 Jan. 12, 1909
Director: D. W. Griffith *Cameraman:* G. W. Bitzer
Cast: Owen Moore, Marion Leonard, Arthur Johnson, Florence Lawrence, Mack Sennett, Harry Salter
Location: Studio, N.Y.C. *Photographed:* Dec. 8 and 21, 1908
239 ft. FLA5318 (print) FRA2240 (neg.)

The story concerns a sinister character, a hypnotist, and a young woman he meets at a party. Under his hypnotic influence, the young woman is sent to steal money. She is left at the scene of the crime to take the blame, and the hypnotist plans to leave town. The girl's father senses something is wrong and follows her. He engages the hypnotist in a fight but is defeated and tied up. A household servant finds the mesmerized young woman, and a doctor is sent for, who brings her back to consciousness. The hypnotist is captured and led away by the police.

Cripple Creek Bar-Room Scene

Edison © 31770 May 10, 1899
25 ft. FLA4187 (print) FRA1351 (neg.)

The film begins in what seems to be the back room of a shed that has been converted into a bar by the simple expedient of painting such words as "Redeye" or "Corn Liquor" on large jugs. The action starts with actors being served by a barmaid. When the guests become intoxicated, she opens the door and throws them out.

Cripple Creek Floats

Edison © 13539 Feb. 24, 1898
20 ft. FLA4258 (print) FRA1414 (neg.)

The poor condition of the film does not allow much detail to be considered. However, the cameraman placed his equipment at the side of a wide road used for a parade. One or two floats go by the camera but the details are not distinct.

Crissie Sheridan

Edison © 60590 Oct. 25, 1897
27 ft. FLA4157 (print) FRA1325 (neg.)

From one camera position, a woman is shown in a voluminous costume that allows her, by the gyration of her arms, to cause the skirt to perform circles. The artist was a professional and was invited to perform by Mr. Edison's earliest film people. All evidence indicates that the film was shot in the Black Maria, the nickname given to Edison's first moving picture studio.

The Critic

AM&B © H72184 Jan. 22, 1906
Cameramen: G. W. Bitzer, F. A. Dobson
Location: Studio, N.Y.C. *Photographed:* Jan. 10–11, 1906
307 ft. FLA5319 (print) FRA2241 (neg.)

The camera, placed as though in the audience, shows several seats with spectators in the immediate foreground and a box to the right. The stage acts are burlesques of regular vaudeville acts. A critic, a member of the audience, writes an honest opinion of the lack of ability of the performers. The article annoys the performers who plan to go to his office and attack him. The last scene takes place in the critic's office where he can be seen throwing the "strong" man and the juggler from the vaudeville act through the window. Two items of interest are the use of an insert of a newspaper column as well as a close-up of a man seated at a desk.

Cross Country Running on Snow Shoes

Edison © H14293 Feb. 17, 1902
47 ft. FLA4565 (print) FRA1599 (neg.)

The opening scenes show a large field covered with snow outside a large city. Approaching the camera position are ten men on snowshoes running in single file. Following the men on snowshoes is a sled pulled by dogs. The scene from the second camera position shows the men on snowshoes forming a circle and tossing one of their group into the air. The third scene, from another camera position, shows a close-up of the group approaching the camera.

Crossed Love and Swords

Keystone © LP5312 May, 13, 1915
Producer and Author: Mack Sennett

Cast: Louise Fazenda, Al St. John, James T. Kelly, Cecile Arnold, Estelle Allen, Dave Morris, Dora Rogers

Location: Keystone studio and vicinity, Los Angeles

483 ft.   FLA5320 (print, copy 1)   FLA6068 (print, copy 2)   FRA2242 (neg.)

The film begins with a party intended as a satire on social register conduct. The host and his guests are being entertained by a nautch dancer when the fashionably dressed guest of honor (played by Louise Fazenda) arrives carrying a small French poodle. Their arrival sets off a series of comedic events that end with the rescue of her bedraggled poodle from a raft floating in a lake.

Crossing Ice Bridge at Niagara Falls

Edison © H40910   Jan. 15, 1904

Cameraman: Edwin S. Porter

Location: Niagara Falls, N.Y. *Photographed:* Jan. 10, 1904

61 ft.   FLA4566 (print)   FRA1600 (neg.)

The camera was positioned on or near the ice frozen over the top of the rapids created by Niagara Falls. A 360-degree pan takes in the falls, the area frozen over, both banks, and the full cantilever suspension bridge between Canada and the United States. People can be seen walking on the ice.

Crossing the Atlantic

Edison © H32796   June 17, 1903

Cameraman: A. C. Abadie

Date: May 10, 1903

124 ft.   FLA5004 (print)   FRA2844 (neg.)

The film begins in a harbor area. At a distance a large seagoing vessel with three smoke stacks can be seen. The next section of film is taken from the bridge wing of a paddle-wheel pilot vessel as it approaches the port side of the large vessel. After that comes scenes of various people boarding and of crew members loading mail, cargo, baggage, etc. The next camera position is from the deck of the liner and shows the pilot vessel leaving the side of the large ship. The last scenes are of people on board the liner playing deck games.

Crossroads of Life

AM&B © H112128   June 20, 1908

Cameramen: Arthur Marvin, G. W. Bitzer

Cast: Marion Leonard, D. W. Griffith, C. K. French

Location: Studio, N.Y.C. *Photographed:* June 2 and 4, 1908

279 ft.   FLA5321 (print)   FRA2248 (neg.)

The film is about two young daughters of a clergyman who want to become actresses and their father's revulsion to the idea. They go to great lengths to hide their activities from their father, who nevertheless finds out and goes to the theater to watch their act. Several scenes show young women in various stages of undress in their dressing room. One of the girls decides to return home with her father. The man she spurns, along with a career on the stage, is played by D. W. Griffith. His one scene with the heroine begins with his kissing her before her decision, and their goodbye handshake as the film ends. The film was copyrighted under the above title, but it was released on July 3, 1908, as At the Crossroads of Life.

Crowd Entering, Futurity Day

AM&B © H21775   Sept. 17, 1902

Cameraman: Robert K. Bonine

Location: Belmont Park, L.I., N.Y. *Date:* Sept. 2, 1902

22 ft.   FLA4567 (print)   FRA1601 (neg.)

The subject is the arrival of the crowd at a notable race meeting. The camera was placed in the compound adjacent to the grandstand. Just as the film opens, a horse-drawn cart with a sign "Evening Telegram" painted on it, passes the camera position. The whole film is devoted to the arrival of spectators who come by automobile, public streetcars, and horse-drawn conveyances of all types.

See also: The Futurity

Cruelty to Horses

AM&B © H51117   Oct. 1, 1904

45 Ft.   FLA4568 (print)   FRA1602 (neg.)

The film begins in an alley behind a stable where a horse is tied up. A man who seems to be intoxicated is molesting the horse. Another person, evidently the owner of the horse, stops him and a fight begins between the two. This sets off a chase involving approximately ten people who catch the culprit and dunk him in a horse's water trough.

The Cruise of the "Gladys"

AM&B © H82299   Aug. 25, 1906

Cameraman: F. A. Dobson

Location: City Island, N.Y. *Photographed:* Aug, 10–11, 1906

265 ft.   FLA5322 (print)   FRA2246 (neg.)

This film shows the problems and difficulties encountered by four people who, although unequipped to sail a small boat, decide to go on an outing aboard one. The film begins with a scene of two men and two women outfitting themselves to go to sea. Then the group boards the small sailboat. One falls into the water; the boat is run aground and capsized. The group is rescued by another boat. The final scene shows the landlubbers at home again in bed with hot-water bottles and covered with bandages.

Cruiser "Cincinnati"

Edison © 25327   Apr. 21, 1898

22 ft.   FLA3440 (print)   FRA0725 (neg.)

[Spanish-American War]

The platform on which the camera was placed was a small vessel. The film begins by showing a large Spanish-American War battle cruiser at anchor in an unidentifiable waterway. The starboard side of the cruiser is seen as the boat carrying the camera passes by. The film is short and the quality is poor.

Cruiser "Detroit"

Edison © 25326   Apr. 21, 1898

23 ft.   FLA3547 (print)   FRA0822 (neg.)

[Spanish-American War]

The battle cruiser *Detroit* at anchor is the subject of this film. It was photographed from a single camera position on a small boat that cruised alongside the anchored vessel.

Cruiser "Marblehead"

Edison © 25564   Apr. 22, 1898

23 ft.   FLA4300 (print)   FRA1450 (neg)

[Spanish-American War]

The title indicates that the vessel was a cruiser in the U.S. Navy. The film, photographed from a single camera position on a dock, shows only a small section of the starboard side of a large ship moored to the dock. There are one mast and two wind scoops visible and three people, apparently a gangway watch, on the dock in the foreground.

The Crushed Hat

AM&B © H44030 Mar. 29, 1904

Cameraman: A. E. Weed

Location: Studio, N.Y.C. *Photographed:* Mar. 17, 1904

19 Ft. FLA3510 (print) FRA0788 (neg.)

A man is dressing on a set of a bedroom. A delivery boy enters the room and hands him a box containing a new top hat which the man puts on his head. Apparently he drops his collar button, for he gets down on his hands and knees and is searching for it when a woman opens the door so it bangs against him and crushes his new hat. The film ends as the man stands up, admonishes the woman, and jerks the hat from his head.

Cuban Ambush

Edison © 46695 Aug. 5, 1898

Cameraman: William Paley

25 ft. FLA3236 (print) FRA0560 (neg.)

[Spanish-American War]

The first thing visible is a vine-covered wall of a stone building in need of repair. A man in military uniform, carrying a sword, stealthily approaches the building. He is followed by two men armed with rifles and in different military uniforms. Out of one of the windows in the building comes gunsmoke. The three men on the ground return the fire, and a man in the window falls to the ground. He is fired on repeatedly by two of the men and hit on the head with the sword of the other.

See also: Shooting Captured Insurgents

Cuban Refugees Waiting for Rations

Edison © 31439 May 20, 1898

27 ft. FLA4286 (print) FRA1438 (neg.)

[Spanish-American War]

A few men dressed in white trousers and coats with bandoleers wander around on a flat area or compound that appears to be connected with public buildings. The title seems derived only from their dress or the fact that they have pots or pans in their hands.

See also: Cuban Volunteers Marching for Rations

Cuban Volunteers Embarking

Edison © 38246 June 22, 1898

24 ft. FLA4298 (print) FRA1448 (neg.)

[Spanish-American War]

The camera that photographed the film was placed on a dock so that the action of the men in uniform going up a zigzag gangway onto a large ship could be seen. The short length of the film allows but twenty men to be seen boarding the ship, and there is nothing to indicate the locale.

Cuban Volunteers Marching for Rations

Edison © 31434 May 20, 1898

25 ft. FLA4211 (print) FRA1373 (neg.)

[Spanish American War]

The short length of the film does not permit much action to be seen other than a long line of men in white clothing being kept in line by several men in American Army uniforms of the period. In the background, a portion of a building that resembles an army barracks can be seen.

See also: Cuban Refugees Waiting for Rations

The Cup of Life

N.Y. Motion Picture © LP5112 Apr. 26, 1915

Producer: Thomas H. Ince

Cast: Bessie Barriscale, Enid Markey, Charles Ray, Frank Borzage, J. Barney Sherry, Howard Hickman, Louise Glaum, Arthur Maude, Jerome Storm

1,825 ft. FLA5852-5853 (print) FRA2732 2733 (neg.)

The film portrays two sisters with totally opposite ideas of life. One believes in marriage, home, and children while the other belives in leading a gay life as a kept woman. At the end of the film, one sister has a husband and children who love her, while the other lives in poverty in a cheap hotel. This film carries the seal of approval of the National Board of Censors of New York.

Cupid and Psyche

Edison © 60560 Oct. 25, 1897

Cast: The Leander Sisters

Location: Sutro Baths, San Francisco

20 ft. FLA4346 (print) FRA1490 (neg.)

The film was photographed on the edge of what appears to be the stage of a gymnasium or auditorium where two young ladies, one dressed as Cupid and the other as Psyche, are dancing, which is what they do for the entire film. In the background are several rows of seated spectators. Written on two frames is "T.A. Edison, Patented August 31, 1897." The film was photographed at a speed greater than 16 frames per second.

See also: The Leander Sisters

Cursed by His Beauty

Keystone © LP3636 Oct. 31, 1914

Producer and Author: Mack Sennett

Cast: Alice Davenport, Charles Murray, Nick Cogley, Charles Chase, Slim Summerville, Phyllis Allen, Glen Cavender, Harry McCoy, Alice Howell, Cecile Arnold, Dixie Chene

Location: Keystone studio and downtown Los Angeles

411 ft. FLA6069 (print) FRA2243 (neg.)

Alice Davenport is a matron who takes up art but cannot find a suitable male model until she sees Charles Murray who has come to her house to deliver ice. Before the picture is over, her husband, Murray's wife, and quite a few of their neighbors become involved in a chase, with much shooting and a lot more smoke.

Curses! They Remarked

Keystone © LP3654 Nov. 5, 1914

Producer and Author: Mack Sennett

Cast: Chester Conklin, Frank Opperman, Norma Nichols, Billie Bennett, Edgar Kennedy

Location: Keystone studio and Griffith Park, Los Angeles

506 ft. FLA5323 (print, copy 1) FLA6070 (print, copy 2) FRA2244 (neg.)

A beautiful young lady (Norma Nichols), ward to a legal firm, now becomes the ward of Frank Opperman, who plays Chester Conklin's father. When the two learn that the young woman is also an heiress, whose money passes to her husband's control, father and son conspire to see that she marries Conklin, despite the bother that he already has a wife, Billie Bennett. But the young woman has met Edgar Kennedy, far more appealing to her. There is a desperate chase between a car containing Conklin and Nichols on their way to a justice of the peace and Edgar Kennedy on his trusty horse, photographed in Griffith Park in Los Angeles.

The Curtain Pole

AM&B © H120977 Jan. 2, 1909

Director: D. W. Griffith *Cameraman:* G. W. Bitzer

Cast: Linda Arvidson, Mack Sennett, Jeanie Macpherson, Arthur Johnson, Florence Lawrence, Harry Salter, Clara T. Bracey

Location: Fort Lee, N.J.; Studio, N.Y.C. *Photographed:* Oct 16 and 22, 1908

293 ft. FLA5324 (print) FRA2245 (neg.)

The film consists of a series of situations, each pandemonium in itself, which starts when an interior decorator goes downtown to purchase a curtain pole. He buys the pole, and in his hurry to get back with it, takes a horse-drawn cab. He goes hell for leather down the streets of the town, wreaking havoc with the long curtain pole. Everything in his path is either broken or knocked over, and more and more townspeople join in chasing him. When he finally arrives with the curtain pole, he finds the maid has already replaced the broken one, and all his rushing was for naught. The picture was taken on the streets of Fort Lee, New Jersey, and many of the people involved in the chase were local citizens. To add to the confusion of the film, the director had the camera run backward during some scenes.

A Customer Drops In

AM&B © H30749 Apr. 24, 1903

Cameraman: F. S. Armitage

Date: Nov. 9, 1900

12 ft. FLA3408 (print) FRA0701 (neg.)

The set, of a photographer's studio, was photographed from a single camera position. The studio has a camera, a chair, and what appears to be a glass roof. A man dressed in a black suit and flowing tie paces up and down as if waiting for someone when the roof caves in on him. He appears delighted to find a human being among the debris and props the poor man, still in a stupor, in a chair, photographs him, takes his money, and sends him on his way. The film ends at this point.

Cutting and Canaling Ice

Edison © H14436 Feb. 24, 1902

Location: Groton Ice Fields, Mass.[?]

42 ft. FLA4569 (print) FRA1603 (neg.)

The camera shows what appears to be a frozen-over lake on which men are driving teams of horses pulling a device similar to a plow. The second camera position shows that the horses are being driven in a straight line across the ice,

with the device chiseling a groove, called canaling, into the ice. This action precedes removal of the ice for storage so it can be used during the summer.

See also: Circular Panorama of Housing the Ice, and Loading the Ice on Cars, Conveying it Across the Mountains and Loading it into Boats.

Cutting Sugar Cane

AM&B © H18040 MAy 23, 1902

Cameraman: Robert K. Bonine

Location: Honolulu *Date:* Aug. 1, 1901

14 ft. FLA4132 (print) FRA1304 (neg.)

The poor condition of the film, its short length, and the distance of the subject matter from the camera position do not permit much description other than saying some workers are in a field. In the foreground, it can be seen that workers have been harvesting a crop of the cane family.

See also: Loading Sugar Cane and Train of Sugar Cane

The Dairy Maid's Revenge

AM&B © H21311 Aug. 25, 1902

Cameraman: F.S. Armitage

Location: Roof studio, N.Y.C. *Date:* July 24, 1899

10 ft. FLA3206 (print) FRA0531 (neg.)

A young man is sitting on a bench in a set of the back of a farm house. A young woman dressed conventionally but carrying two galvanized pails suspended from a neck-and-shoulder yoke approaches him. As she nears the house, the young man rises and attempts to help her. The young woman resents this and finally swings one end of the yoke at him. The man loses his balance. The young woman sets down the pails, picks them up one at a time, and empties them over the young man.

Daly of West Point Winning Hurdle Race

AM&B © H24881 Dec. 9, 1902

18 ft. FLA4048 (print) FRA1235 (neg.)

The film, photographed from a single camera position, shows a hurdle race at West Point, New York. The athletes run toward the camera. It is a good example of how form has since improved.

Damnation du Docteur Faust

See: Faust et Marguerite

The Damnation of Faust

Méliès © H39290 Dec. 11, 1903

Creator: Georges Méliès

Location: Montreuil, France *Date:* Fall 1903

Original title: Faust aux Enfers

182 ft. FLA5005 (print) FRA2863 (neg.)

This film makes use of the usual Méliès "tableau" formula. The story of Faust is followed for it allows Méliès to make good use of his special effects work. The film has wipes, fades, split screen, camera movement, both dolly in and dolly out, stop action, and double, triple, and quadruple exposures.

See also: Faust aux Enfers

Dance, Franchonetti Sisters

AM&B © H30723 Apr. 24, 1903

8 ft. FLA3376 (print) FRA0678 (neg.)

Three young ladies dressed in costumes for dancing can be seen on a stage artificially lighted for this film. Then in unison, they go through the routine of acrobatic dancers.

A Dance in Pajamas
AM&B © H39142 Dec. 7, 1903
Cameraman: A. E. Weed
Location: Studio, N.Y.C. *Photographed:* Nov. 25, 1903
23 ft. FLA4216 (print) FRA1376 (neg.)

Three young women wearing pajamas and high heeled shoes can be seen as the film begins. One of the women is sitting on a table and clapping her hands while the other two perform several tap dance routines. Soon the two dancers are joined by the third young woman and they continue their dance routine to the end of the film.

A Dance on the Pike
AM&B © H43560 Mar. 22, 1904
Cameraman: A. E. Weed
Location: Studio, N.Y.C. *Photographed:* Feb. 27, 1904
25 ft. FLA4560 (print) FRA1604 (neg.)

This film was photographed from the audience's point of view at a vaudeville act. A woman dressed as a Spanish dancer enters from the wings, camera right, and starts to dance. Her dancing consists of a series of high kicks, followed by a routine of handsprings, splits, and some contortionist positions. At the end, she takes a bow.

Dancing Boxing Match, Montgomery and Stone
Winthrop Moving Picture Co. © H93358 May 7, 1907
Cast: David Craig Montgomery, Fred Stone
9 ft. FlA3777 (print) FRA1020 (neg.)

Part of a vaudeville turn of the famous team of Montgomery and Stone. The short length of the film does not permit much description of the performance.

Dancing Chinaman, Marionettes
Edison © 59208 Oct. 7, 1898
25 ft. FLA4302 (print) FRA1451 (neg.)

The film begins as if the viewer were watching a puppet show. The area encompassed by the camera lens is the only puppet show. On the stage, two puppets in identical costumes execute a jumping sort of dance, consisting of one basic movement.

See also: Balloon Ascension, Marionettes and Skeleton Dance, Marionettes

Dancing Darkey Boy
Edison © 60568 Oct. 25, 1897
16 ft FLA3021 (print) FRA0094 (neg.)

The film, photographed from a single camera position, shows a black boy as he dances on the hatch cover of a ship or boat. An audience of approximately twenty adults encourages him.

The Dancing Girl of Butte
Biograph © J136851 Jan. 8, 1910
Director: D. W. Griffith *Cameraman:* G. W. Bitzer
Cast: Florence Barker, Owen Moore, Mack Sennett, John Cumpson, W. Chrystie Miller, Linda Arvidson

Location: Edgewater, N.J.; Studio, N.Y.C. *Photographed:* Dec. 2–4, 1909
373 ft. FLA5326 (print) FRA2251 (neg.)

A man of good standing, an artist on a newspaper, falls in love with a dance-hall girl. He is unaware of her occupation. When confronted with the facts of the girl's reputation as well as occupation, he is angry and frustrated. However, the final scenes show him and the dance-hall girl pushing a baby carriage, and the inference is that it all worked out for the best. All the scenes, both interior and exterior, were photographed from a single camera position.

The Dancing Skeleton
See: Davey Jones' Locker

The Dandy Fifth
AM&B © H21512 Sept. 5, 1902
Cameraman: F. S. Armitage
Location: N.Y.C. *Date:* Sept. 30[?] 1899
22 ft. FLA3217 (print) FRA0541 (neg.)
[Spanish-American War]

The film was photographed from a camera positioned above the heads of crowds gathered to watch a parade of military infantry companies. The infantry platoons are marching company front and their rifles are at port. Several companies pass the camera position. The quality is rather poor and does not permit a detailed description of the soldiers' apparel. However, each is wearing a hussar type of headgear, and white crossed sashes over gray uniforms. The "Dandy Fifth" was the fifth regiment of Maryland.

The Danger of Dining in Private Dining Rooms
AM&B © H32408 June 5, 1903
Cameraman: G. W. Bitzer
Location: Studio, N.Y.C. *Date:* June 3, 1903
72 ft. FLA5006 (print) FRA1968 (neg.)

This melodrama has an interesting twist for the times, and a warning that it was not safe to dine in private dining rooms. The first scene shows two couples frolicking and having a good time. They go into a private dining room where they start to gamble and drink. The waiter brings them a drugged drink. They fall unconscious onto the floor and are robbed.

A Dangerous Play
Great Northern © Oes J168439-40 Apr. 19, 1912
Director: Edward Schnedler-Sørensen
Cast: Robert Dinesen, Dagny Schyberg, Frederik Jacobsen, Aage Hertel, Hilmar Clausen
Location: Copenhagen and vicinity *Photographed:* Jan. 5, 1912
Danish title: Et Farligt Spil
825 ft. FLA5854 (print, copy 1) FLA5855 (print, copy 2) FRA2734 (neg.)

The beginning of the picture establishes a relationship between two gentlemen who are obviously prominent and of some social stature. There is an exchange of papers and handshakes. Before the film ends, one of the two men realizes that his daughter has married the wrong man—a spy who has stolen and sold military secrets of his country—because the father believed in an old friend who deceived him. When he realizes that the man in the beard is actually his alleged friend in disguise, a chase begins over the winter snow in Denmark. These chases occupy a large portion of the film and are done very well. As in all melodramas of this type, the villain gets his just deserts and is brought to justice and the picture ends.

The Darkening Trail

N.Y. Motion Picture © LP5426 May 31, 1915

Producer: Thomas Ince *Director:* William S. Hart *Story and Screenplay*: C. Gardner Sullivan

Cast: William S. Hart, Enid Markey, George Fisher, Nona Thomas, Milton Ross, Louise Glaum, Roy Laidlaw

1,532 ft.   FLA5856-5857 (print)   FRA2737-2738 (neg.)

This story in five reels begins in the East and then comes West to Inceville, where sets represent the Alaska gold-fields. A cad, to escape doing the honorable thing and marrying the girl, gives up his inheritance and migrates to Alaska. There he turns the head of, and is forced to marry, the daughter of a storekeeper. The hero (William S. Hart) is secretly in love with the same girl. The young wife, in an effort to rescue her husband from the cold one night when he returns from a drinking bout, catches pneumonia and dies as the result of her husband's premeditated delay in getting her medical aid. The hero, aware of the cad's act of negligence, shoots him and buries him beside his wife. The picture implies that the hero spends the rest of his life alone with his bitter memories.

The Darling of the Gallery Gods

AM&B © H63379 July 15, 1905

19 ft.   FLA3937 (print)   FRA1149 (neg.)

The film was photographed from a position above the young lady, who is the only person to appear in it. The distance from the lens to the camera was quite short so the full extent of the film shows only a small area above her head to just below her chin. The actress directs her recitation into the lens of the camera as if it were in a balcony above her. Judging from her expression and her gestures, she is reciting a poem or reading part of a play.

A Dash Through the Clouds

Biograph © J170666 June 28, 1912

Director: Mack Sennett

Cast: Mabel Normand, Fred Mace, Jack Pickford, Kate Bruce, Alfred Paget, Sylvia Ashton, and the pilot, Philip Parmalee

Location: Culver City, Calif.

278 ft.   FLA5327 (print)   FRA2252 (neg.)

This film is an assembly of unconnected erratic scenes. However, the heroine (Mabel Normand) and the hero (Fred Mace) begin the film by leaving the front door of their house and traveling to what now would be considered an airdrome. The second scene opens on a dual-propellered biplane of very early vintage. The husband takes his wife home and leaves for a nearby town. While there, he is kidnapped and fears for his life. He manages to get a note to his wife who effects his rescue by the use and aid of the pilot and his airplane. There is a considerable amount of film of the airplane taking off, landing, and in the air. Philip Parmalee, a member of the first group of aviators taught to fly by Wilbur Wright, was killed in a plane crash less than two years later.

Davey Jones' Locker

AM&B © H30728 Apr. 24, 1903

Cameraman: F. S. Armitage

Date: Dec. 8, 1900

12 ft.   FLA3418 (print)   FRA0707 (neg.)

The opening scene shows a schooner, approximately one hundred feet in length, foundering on a beach where incoming waves are washing over it. As the film continues, a superimposed film shows a puppet skeleton directed to wander over the dead ship. At the end, the skeleton takes off into the air. The production was made by combining two films shot in 1897, The Wreck of the Steamer Richmond Off the Coast of New Jersey, and The Dancing Skeleton.

The Day After

Biograph © J136612 Jan. 3, 1910

Director: D. W. Griffith *Cameraman:* G. W. Bitzer

Cast: Marion Leonard, Henry B. Walthall, W. Chrystie Miller, Arthur Johnson, Mack Sennett, Blanche Sweet, George Nicholls, Tony O'Sullivan, Jeanie Macpherson, James Kirkwood, Gertrude Robinson, William J. Butler

Location: Studio, N.Y.C. *Photographed:* Nov. 24 and 26, 1909

189 ft.   FLA5328 (print)   FRA2253 (neg.)

The story line of this humorous film is built around the expression, "the day after," inferring that those who attend parties and drink intoxicating beverages to excess awaken the next day with such symptoms as headaches, dryness of skin, dehydration, etc. All the sets are of the rooms of a fashionable dwelling. All the actors are dressed for a costume party and, as the film progresses, behave as if they have been drinking. A parlor scene with great hilarity and frenzied dancing is shown. The next day, the host and hostess are suffering from the pangs of remorse for their activities of the previous night. The last scene closes with their embrace and their vow never to do it again.

A Day at the Circus

Edison © H4418 May 17, 1901

Location: The Great Forepaugh and Sells Bros. Combined Four-Ring Circus

57 ft.   FLA4571 (print)   FRA1605 (neg.)

The film, photographed from a single camera position inside a circus tent, shows animals and various acts.

The Deadwood Sleeper

AM&B © H61361 May 26, 1905

Cameraman: G. W. Bitzer

Location: Studio, N.Y.C. *Photographed:* May 17, 1905

89 ft.   FLA5007 (print)   FRA1969 (neg.)

All of the action takes place in the passageway and in the berths of a set of a Pullman sleeping car. Humorous situations arise when some people attempt to retire and are inconvenienced by others not yet ready. The picture ends as a train robber is set upon by a woman wearing a nightgown and bed cap who has been annoyed so many times she resorts to violence.

Deaf Mute Girl Reciting "Star Stangled Banner"

AM&B © H18743 June 7, 1902

Cameraman: Arthur Marvin

Location: Washington, D.C. Date: Apr. 2, 1901
31 ft. FLA4138 (print) FRA1308 (neg.)

This single camera position film shows a young woman executing sign language positions. The title indicates that she is reciting the "Star Spangled Banner." The backdrop is the American flag.

The Death Disc

Biograph © J135518 Dec. 3, 1909

Director: D. W. Griffith *Cameraman:* G. W. Bitzer

Cast: Marion Leonard, Arthur Johnson, Mack Sennett, James Kirkwood, Jeanie Macpherson, Frank Evans, Gertrude Robinson, Linda Arvidson

Location: Coytesville, N.J.; Studio, N.Y.C. *Photographed:* Oct. 26–28, 1909

375 ft. FLA5329 (print) FRA2359 (neg.)

The period film was based on the religious persecutions of Oliver Cromwell in seventeenth-century England and the actors were costumed accordingly. A little girl is selected to choose which of three soldiers, arrested because they would not forsake the Catholic faith and embrace the Church of England, is to die. She is first taken to Oliver Cromwell. She so charms him that he gives her a signet and tells her that she has only to present it and he will do as she commands. The small child, unaware of the meaning of her task, selects her father, and just as he is about to be executed, the signet is sent to Cromwell, who pardons all three soldiers.

Death of Little May

See: Ten Nights in a Bar-Room

Death of Slade

See: Ten Nights in a Bar-Room

The Deceived Slumming Party

AM&B © H113968 July 28, 1908

Cameramen: G. W. Bitzer, Arthur Marvin

Location: Studio and 42nd Street, N.Y.C. *Photographed:* May 27 and July 14, 1908

189 ft. FLA5330 (print) FRA2254 (neg.)

The film is a satire on sightseers in New York City. Each of the several scenes ends by showing that the man conducting the tour and the people in the opium den, the Chinese restaurant, and the Bowery saloon are all part of a conspiracy to shock and defraud the tourists. Each of the scenes, photographed from a single camera position, shows either the premises being raided and the tourists paying off the fake police, or the tourists being involved in brawls that stop as soon as they depart.

The Deception

AM&B © H123959 Mar. 13, 1909

Director: D. W. Griffith *Cameraman:* G. W. Bitzer

Cast: Florence Lawrence, Herbert Yost, Mack Sennett, Linda Arvidson, Dorothy West, Arthur Johnson

Location: Studio, N.Y.C. *Photographed:* Feb. 5–6, 1909

245 ft. FLA5331 (print) FRA2256 (neg.)

There are three scenes in this film. The first is in an artist's studio where the artist and his wife, completely out of food, are being dunned for back rent. The wife, in the second scene, is working in a laundry and is shown washing clothes over a scrubbing board, while her husband is under the impression she has taken a job in a music conservatory. While she is at work, the artist sells a picture and rushes off to the conservatory to tell his wife of his good fortune. When he discovers she does not work there, he goes home totally disillusioned. At the same time, his wife falls at the laundry and breaks her arm. A doctor and some of the other scrubwomen escort her home. Her husband learns the truth, and the film ends as he realizes her deception was based on love.

Decorated Carriages, no. 11

Edison © 13535 Feb. 24, 1898

25 ft. FLA3403 (print) FRA0697 (neg.)

The film was photographed from a camera positioned across the roadway from a bleacher or grandstand at what appears to be a fairgrounds. Immediately below the camera position, entering from camera left, are four- and two-wheeled horse-drawn carriages decorated with bunting, crepe tissue, flowers, etc. The horses, as well as the passengers, are in fancy dress. The distance does not allow a definite description of details, and the quality of the film is poor.

See also: Horticultural Floats, no. 9 and Parade of Coaches

Decoyed

Produced in Great Britain by the Hepworth Company and released there under the title Lost, Stolen or Strayed AM&B © H52231 Oct. 28, 1904

Director: Lewin Fitzhamon

Cast: Lewin Fitzhamon, Dolly Lupone.

108 ft. FLA5008 (print) FRA1970 (neg.)

A horse-drawn omnibus can be seen as it nears the camera. The omnibus comes to a stop and a young girl gets off and starts asking passers-by for directions. A disreputable man volunteers to guide her. Instead, he takes her to a basement in a poor section of town where he makes her change to the tattered clothes of a beggar. Her captor forces her into the streets, where she is noticed by the hero. He follows the two to their basement hovel, and starts a fight in an attempt to rescue the young woman. At the end of the film, the hero is administering a sound thrashing to the bad guy.

Deer Stalking with Camera

AM&B © H71527 Jan. 3, 1906

Cameraman: C. W. Bitzner

Location: Pinehurst, N.C. *Photographed:* Nov. 21–22, 1905

216 ft. FLA5332 (print) FRA2265 (neg.)

The opening scenes show a grove of trees similar to those in a cared-for park area. Two deer pass in front of the camera at a distance of approximately one hundred yards. As the picture progresses, a man clad in outdoor clothes is seen stalking the two animals. He carries a still camera in his hand. The remainder of the film shows moving pictures of both a doe and a buck profile, head photographs, close-ups, as if they were the pictures the man with the camera was taking. One of several films made by AM&B for the New England Forest, Fish and Game Association, and exhibited at the Sportsman Show in Boston.

See also: Moose Hunt in New Brunswick, Quail Shooting at Pinehurst, Salmon Fishing on the Nipissiguit River, Trout Fishing, Rangeley Lakes, and A Wild Turkey Hunt

Delivering Mail From Sub-Station

AM&B © H36398 Oct. 1, 1903

Cameraman: A. E. Weed

Location: Philadelphia *Photographed:* Sept. 19, 1903

27 ft. FLA3519 (print) FRA2876 (neg.)

The subjects seen by the camera are a portion of a large building with columns in front that indicates it is a government building and three small shuttle streetcars across the street from the camera position. As the film progresses, the shuttle cars leave. Twice during the film a larger streetcar passes in front of the camera position.

Delivering Newspapers

AM&B © H30745 Apr. 24, 1903

Cameramen: G. W. Bitzer, Arthur Marvin

Location: N.Y.C. *Date:* May, 1, 1899

27 ft. FLA3387 (print) FRA2874 (neg.)

Judging from the surrounding buildings, this film was photographed in Union Square, New York. In the immediate foreground approximately fifty preadolescent boys can be seen. In the background, an electric streetcar crosses the camera view. As it disappears, a one-horse paneled van draws up. When the van reaches the immediate foreground, the driver turns it, revealing on the side a sign reading "New York World." A great commotion and a struggle to be first occurs as all of the boys gather around the rear gate of the vehicle. Two small boys can be seen fighting for a position in line.

A Delusion

AM&B © H22088 Sept. 27, 1902

Cameraman: Robert K. Bonine

Location: Studio, N.Y.C. *Date:* July 16, 1902

9 ft. FLA3218 (print) FRA0542 (neg.)

A young woman dressed in a diaphanous costume strikes a pose as she stands on a pedestal in front of a camera, which is part of a set of a photographer's studio. Through the use of stop action photography, the young model is replaced by a rather large woman dressed as a tramp. This photographic illusion apparently causes the photographer much consternation. The photographer grabs the tramp by the hand and pulls him off the pedestal and immediately he is transformed into the young woman. As the film ends, the young woman is still striking her pose while the photographer is sitting in a chair acting as though he has fainted.

Democratic National Commitee at Esopus

AM&B © H48851 Aug. 4, 1904

Cameraman: G. W. Bitzer

Location: Esopus, N.Y. *Photographed:* July 29, 1904

41 ft. FLA4572 (print) FRA1606 (neg.)

The elevated camera position shows a train platform where almost thirty men of some political significance at the time are standing awaiting the arrival of the train. When the train gets there, they board it, and the picture ends.

See also: Judge Alton B. Parker & Guests

Denver Fire Brigade

Edison © 13532 Feb. 24, 1898

Location: Denver

62 ft. FLA4573 (print) FRA1607 (neg.)

The entire film is devoted to a parade of passing fire equipment: pumpers, personnel vehicles, hook-and-ladders of at least three different fire stations of the City of Denver, Colorado. The camera was stationed above a street selected for the demonstration. Crowds of spectators on each side of the street are visible. In the background, perhaps a mile distant, one large building can be seen to stand against the horizon.

Departure of Peary [and the] "Roosevelt" from New York

AM&B © H63906 July 28, 1905

Cameraman: G. W. Bitzer

Location: Dock at West Houston Street, N.Y.C. *Photographed:* July 12, 1905

129 ft. FLA5009 (print) Fra1971 (neg., copy 1) FRA1972 (neg., copy 2)

The film was photographed from many camera positions, and includes a dolly shot of a full-rigged topsail schooner, the *Roosevelt*, tied up at what appears to be the waterfront in New York City. The ship is being loaded with stores, and the ship's master explorer, Robert Peary, can be seen standing at the gangway greeting guests as they come aboard.

Desdemona

Great Northern © OesJ168207-08 Apr. 16, 1912

Director: August Blom *Script:* Louis Møller

Cast: Valdemar Psilander, Henny Lauritzen, Zanny Petersen, Svend Bille, Otto Dethlefsen, Frederik Skondrup, Nicolai Brechling, Thyra Reymann

620 ft. FLA5858 (print, copy 1) FLA5859 (print, copy 2) FRA2780 (neg.)

This film, with a very slight variation, follows the story of Desdemona very closely. The director utilized the camera to convey the story in a manner that would be considered highly professional even today had he used more reverse shots and inserts. He used two. The story can be followed easily despite the absence of titles. The sets are convincingly done and the lighting and photography are acceptable.

Desperation

See: The Ex-Convict

Detected

See: The Divorce

"Deutschland" Leaving New York at Full Speed

Edison © H15199 Mar. 15, 1902

Location: New York Harbor

51ft. FLA4575 (print) FRA1609 (neg.)

[With Prince Henry of Prussia]

The camera was positioned on the deck of either a pilot vessel or a supporting tug. The film shows the beam of a large liner flying the German flag. Next the full profile of the liner can be seen, and then closer scenes of the starboard quarter and of her port beam going away. There is a small pilot vessel visible on her port beam at the end of the film. Prince Henry of Prussia is supposed to be on board.

The Devil

AM&B © H116154 Sept. 25, 1908

Director: D. W. Griffith *Cameraman:* G. W. Bitzer

Cast: Jeanie Macpherson, Florence Lawrence, Harry Salter, Frank Gebhardt

Location: Studio, N.Y.C. *Photographed:* Sept. 12, 1908

233ft. FLA5333 (print) FRA2257 (neg.)

The story is about an artist influenced by the devil to see his model as a beautiful woman. He makes love to her and is caught in the act by his wife. During the course of the film, the devil is seen influencing the four actors, the artist, his model, his wife, and the wife's male friend, into behaving badly. The film ends when the devil has succeeded in persuading the artist, angry and jealous of attentions paid to his wife by her friend, to shoot her, while the devil laughs in the background. The devil is brought in and out of scenes by the use of stop-action photography. There are no other uses of stop action.

The Devil

N.Y. Motion Picture © LP4907 Apr. 1, 1915

Producer: Thomas H. Ince *Director:* Reginald Barker

Cast: E. J. Connelly, Bessie Barriscale, Arthur Maude, Rhea Mitchell, Clara Williams, J. Barney Sherry, A. Hollingsworth

Based on the play by Ferenc Molnár

1,661 ft. FLA5860-5861 (print) FRA2735-2736 (neg.)

This five-reel film was based on a famous play about the devil's interference in some lives. There are many scenes photographed from three camera positions. The main characters are a successful artist, his model, his betrothed, and a married woman with whom he has had an affair. Under ordinary circumstances, they would have led uncomplicated lives. However, the devil, by the use of dissolves, discourages and encourages the characters, pits one against another, and plays on their emotions, all to their detriment.

Devil's Slide

AM&B © H18046 May 23, 1902

Camerman: G. W. Bitzer

Location: Union Pacific R.R., Devil's Slide, Utah *Date:* Dec. 2, 1899

22 ft. FLA4362 (print) FRA1501 (neg.)

The camera was placed on the front of a car descending on railroad tracks on the steep side of a mountain. The rugged terrain, cantilever bridges over washes, etc., are shown, as part of a trip photographed on the Union Pacific Railroad through the Rocky Mountains.

The Dewey Arch

AM&B © H32835 June 18, 1903

Cameraman: F. S. Armitage

Location: Madison Square, N.Y.C. *Photographed:* Sept. 30, 1899

30 ft. FLA4288 (print) FRA1440 (neg.)

[Spanish-American War; Dewey Homecoming, New York City]

The camera was stationed in such a position and at such a distance that the full span of the construction of the Dewey Arch is visible. The distance is about two hundred yards. Between the arch and the camera position, spectators walking and riding in all manner of vehicles, including streetcars, can be seen.

Dewey Arch—Troops Passing Under Arch

Edison © 64682 Oct. 5, 1899

Location: Madison Square, N.Y.C. *Photographed:* Sept. 30, 1899

49 ft. FLA4576 (print) FRA1610 (neg.)

[Spanish-American War; Dewey Homecoming, New York City]

The camera is directed on a major thoroughfare and shows soldiers marching toward the camera position, as well as the crowds lining the street. The second scene, from another camera position, shows horse-drawn carriages in front of the reviewing stand; the carriages then pass between the camera and the reviewing stand. None of the dignitaries is seen.

Dewey Parade, 10th Pennsylvania Volunteers

Edison © 65373 Oct. 7, 1899

Location: Riverside Drive, N.Y.C. *Photographed:* Sept. 30, 1899

27 ft. FLA3380 (print) FRA0681 (neg.)

[Spanish-American War; Dewey Homecoming, New York City]

The camera was positioned over the heads of a myriad of spectators standing on both sides of a street in the Riverside Drive area of New York City. From camera left in the picture can be seen the beginning of a parade of men in the uniform of the U.S. Army. They are marching in company-front order. Several companies pass the camera position, and just before the film ends, mounted soldiers can been seen following the parading foot soldiers.

Deyo

AM&B © H92889 Apr. 22, 1907

22 ft. FLA5334 (print) FRA2711 (neg.)

This film was photographed outdoors and shows a young girl giving an acrobatic- and toe-dancing exhibition. The film was possibly a film test. The action is very slow, indicating that the camera was turned rapidly.

Dial's Girls' Band, Luna Park

Eugene Dial © H67888 Oct. 25, 1905

Location: Coney Island, N.Y.

112 ft. FLA5010 (print) FRA1973 (neg.)

The first camera position shows girls in uniform marching in double file down a curved flight of stairs in an amusement zone. The remainder of the film is from several camera positions and shows the band wearing two different types of uniforms, and either going through tunnels, down passageways, or down stairways. The background architecture of the amusement zone is clearly visible. Copyright application lists Eugene Dial as the copyright owner and AM&B as an agent in registration.

Dick Croker Leaving Tammany Hall

Edison © D3543 Feb. 9, 1900

Location: 14th Street Wigwam, N.Y.C.

26 ft. FLA3992 (print) FRA2872 (neg.)

The camera was positioned so that nearly a full block and the street floor of a building can be seen. Two men approach the camera and stop about twenty-five feet away to converse for a few seconds. They then proceed, followed

by another man who tips his hat. Richard Croker

owner's daughter and his cash. The villain finally succeeds

Location: Sound Beach, Conn.; Studio, N.Y.C. *Photographed:* Sept. 3, 4 and 10, 1906

291 ft. FLA5336 (print) FRA2262 (neg.)

This farce concerns a young man who is hired as a guardian in an insane asylum. He is introduced to the patients who then commence to harass him until he flees for his life. The balance of the film is devoted to the chase. The camera takes the viewer over a considerable portion of the countryside while the pursuit is in progress and shows the guard being subjected to an enormous amount of abuse. He is finally captured by the inmates, tied to a wall, and knives are thrown at him. The director of the asylum arrives and distracts the violent patients by giving each of them a pie. Each sits down to eat his pie and forgets all about the poor guard.

The Doctor's Bride

Lubin Mfg. Co. © J132442 Aug. 30, 1909

Location: Philadelphia

230 ft. FLA5337 (print) FRA2260 (neg.)

In this melodrama, a big city physician ministers to a woman whom he later marries. There are several scenes of the couple attending and giving parties and other social functions. However, the doctor is given to philandering, which causes his wife to have hysterics and to throw herself on the living room floor. The doctor leaves home, and his wife and little baby wander out on a country road where she collapses. Another doctor happens along, stops, and helps her.

The Doctor's Favorite Patient

AM&B © H32560 June 12, 1903

Cameraman: G. W. Bitzer

Location: Studio, N.Y.C. *Date:* June 8, 1903

24 ft. FLA3581 (print) FRA0853 (neg.)

The film begins by showing a man wearing a goatee and a swallowtail coat in a set of a doctor's office. The page from the outer office enters and informs the doctor he has a patient, who turns out to be a very well-dressed and lovely young woman. The doctor takes her hand, seats her in a comfortable chair, and begins to embrace her. During this intimate scene, the door opens and the page indicates there are more visitors. Two middle-aged women burst into the room and sit down to wait for the attractive patient to leave. She departs and one of the two women walks around the desk and is met by the doctor, who takes her hand and begins embracing her.

Dog Factory

Edison © H44668 Apr. 21, 1904

Cameraman: Edwin S. Porter

Location: Studio, N.Y.C. *Photographed:* Apr. 15, 1904

98 ft. FLA5011 (print) FRA1974 (neg.)

This is a nearly three-minute film of a vaudeville turn. There is a contraption approximately the size of a piano, with a sign stating it is a "dog transformer." On the wall behind the machine are pegs or hangers with various kinds of wursts or sausages. Someone comes in, sees the signs, points to one that reads "bull pups, spaniels, etc.," and the sausage is put into the machine, the crank turned, and out comes the dog of his choice.

See also: Sausage Machine and Fun in a Butcher Shop

A Dog Fight

AM&B © H28562 Feb. 24, 1903

Cameraman: Arthur Marvin

Photographed: Sept. 1, 1900

23 ft. FLA3144 (print) FRA0477 (neg.)

From a camera positioned from the point of view of a spectator, two dachshund dogs of immature growth are shown. The dogs roll about the floor of the stage prepared for the moving picture until, near the end of the film, a man separates them, keeping one and handing the other to another man. The working title was "Impromptu Scrap."

Dogs Playing in the Surf

Edison © 12172 Feb. 17, 1898

24 ft. FLA3053 (print) FRA0380 (neg.)

The film, photographed from a single camera position, shows the ocean front with several dogs of various breeds playing about in the waves. They are joined by more dogs of assorted breeds. They all run, bark, and splash in the water. Nothing else is visible.

A Donkey Party

AM&B © H32788 June 17, 1903

18 ft. FLA4083 (print) FRA2868 (neg.)

This is a primitive attempt at capturing hilarity from what at the time was perhaps quite humorous. Three women ride a small donkey while two other women lead and push the animal.

The Donkey Party

Edison © H2342 Mar. 16, 1901

25 ft. FLA3743 (print, copy 1) FLA5967 (print, copy 2) FRA0989 (neg.)

The camera was positioned as if it were a guest watching other guests play a game of "Pin the Tail on the Donkey." Across the set of a room in a house is a donkey painted on a piece of material. Gathered around the donkey are ten young women and one person dressed as a fat old woman. As the film progresses, two girls pin tails in the wrong place on the donkey, and the actor playing the fat old woman is blindfolded and given a tail to pin on the donkey. The film ends as the tail is pinned on the donkey. His head and neck fall down and the left rear leg kicks out, striking the old woman who falls to the floor. The girls laugh uproariously.

Do-Re-Mi—Boom!

Keystone © LP5039 Apr. 15, 1915

Producer and author: Mack Sennett

Cast: Chester Conklin, Charles Arling, Rosemary Theby, Vivian Edwards, Harry Booker

Location: Keystone studio, Los Angeles, and environs

418 ft. FLA5338 (print, copy 1) FLA6073 (print, copy 2) FRA2261 (neg.)

Chester Conklin becomes involved in a series of events that frustrate his attempt to become engaged to a lovely young girl, Rosemary Theby, as well as his attempts to eliminate the music teacher, Charles Arling, with whom she is in love. To aid his plans, Chester steals a monkey and an organ from an organ grinder. Then he puts a large bomb in a piano with an automatic device that will set off the bomb if the piano is played. When the young lady goes to the piano,

Chester has to admit what a terrible thing he has done. Tossed out the window with the piano, the last scene shows Chester, accompanied by the little monkey, riding on top of the smoking piano, with the organ grinder in close pursuit.

Double Ring Act, Luna Park

AM&B © H36555 Oct. 6, 1903

Cameraman: G. W. Bitzer

Location; Coney Island, N.Y. *Photographed:* Sept. 26, 1903

40 ft. FLA4583 (print) FRA1616 (neg.)

A circus ring located outdoors next to the pavilion at Luna Park is shown. Two performers work with a large circus horse, doing acrobatics on and off his back. There is also a ringmaster. The horse goes around the ring, carrying the performers on its back while they exhibit their agility. A large number of spectators can be seen in the background at the pavilion railing.

Dough and Dynamite

Keystone © LP3724 Oct. 24, 1914

Producer and Author: Mack Sennett

Cast: Charles Chaplin, Chester Conklin, Fritz Schade, Norma Nichols, Vivian Edwards, Cecile Arnold, Phyllis Allen, Charles Chase, Wallace MacDonald, Slim Summerville, Nick Cogley, Glen Cavender

Location: Keystone studio, Los Angeles

900 ft. FLA5339-5340 (print, copy 1) FLA6074-6075 (print, copy 2) FRA2739 (neg.)

All of the action of this comedy takes place in a restaurant where Charles Chaplin and Chester Conklin are waiters. When a strike by the bakers occurs, the owner of the restaurant, Nick Cogley, coerces the two into turning into bakers, at which point pandemonium sets in. And when the striking bakers conceive of the idea of putting a stick of dynamite in a loaf of bread, returning it to the restaurant on the basis that it is underbaked, even more confusion occurs. Close-ups were not common in early Keystone moving pictures, but this film boasts two.

Down Kicking Horse Grade, Can. R. R.

See: Down Western Slope

Down the Hotel Corridor

AM&B © H33887 July 28, 1903

42 ft. FLA4584 (print) FRA1617 (neg.)

The first thing visible is a set with a wall that has two numbered doors, suggesting a hotel corridor. A bellhop escorts a man and a woman to one of the rooms. Something they hear in the room next door intrigues them and, on a pretext, they get the bellhop to open the door where they discover a gambling game in progress. The first two people attempt to apprehend the criminals and grapple with them, when the police arrive and take the culprits away.

Down the Hudson

AM&B © H36559 Oct. 6, 1903

80 ft. FLA5012 (print) FRA1975 (neg.)

The film was photographed from the deck of a boat that, indicated by the many changes of angle, was steering in and out of coves, inlets, etc., while journeying down the Hudson River. Many means of transportation are shown, including paddle wheels, sailing vessels, and steamers.

Down Western Slope

AM&B © H26946 Jan. 14, 1903

Cameraman: G. W. Bitzer

Location: Canadian Pacific Railway, Kicking Horse Canyon, Canada *Photographed:* Oct. 18, 1899

39 ft. FLA4585 (print) FRA1618 (neg.)

The camera was mounted on the front of a railroad train traveling over a single track through mountainous country. On both sides of the track is the slope of the mountains, covered with snow; the river running alongside the grade can also be seen. The title is given as it is listed on the copyright application and copyright record. But the title on the original paper print film is Down Kicking Horse Grade, Can. R.R.

Down Where the Wurzburger Flows

Edison © H35062 Aug. 26, 1903

Cameraman: Edwin S. Porter

Location: Atlantic City, N.J. *Photographed:* Aug. 17, 1903

31 ft. FLA4586 (print) FRA1619 (neg.)

The film begins on a set of a beer garden. In the background is a table in front of a brick wall. A customer comes in and sits down and the proprietor brings him a glass of beer. The heads and shoulders of two disreputable-looking characters can be seen above the brick wall. One takes a long, thick tube, puts it in the glass and drinks it dry. The customer notices his glass is empty and summons the proprietor who brings another. The second tramp uses a device to dip the beer from the glass for his share. The customer, again seeing the empty glass, pounds on the table. The proprietor returns, there is a commotion, and the customer is thrown out of the beer garden.

The Downward Path: The Fresh Book Agent

AM&B © H23807 Nov. 11, 1902

Cameraman: Arthur Marvin

Location: Roof studio, N.Y.C. *Date:* May 16, 1900

10 ft. FLA4011 (print) FRA2905 (neg.)

The set represents a sharecropper's cabin. A boy in his early teens wearing overalls but no shirt or shoes is leaning against a slapdash drainboard teasing a young girl who is preparing food. In the middle of the room, a barefoot, bearded old man in overalls is facing the camera. The old man gestures to the boy to stop his teasing. The door of the cabin opens and a man in a white linen suit and straw hat carrying a briefcase enters. He pushes the boy around, seats himself on a chair in the center of the room, and pulls the young girl onto his lap.

The Downward Path: She Ran Away

AM&B © H23810 Nov. 11, 1902

Cameraman: Arthur Marvin

Location: Roof studio, N.Y.C. *Date:* May 16, 1900

10 ft. FLA4014 (print) FRA2902 (neg.)

A young man dressed in summer clothes is putting a ladder up to the second floor window of a set of the exterior of a farmhouse. A young woman appears and tosses a suitcase and some clothing down to the waiting man and, without further ceremony, follows her possessions. They waste no time rushing off. They are followed by a man and a woman who are both brandishing weapons while an old, bearded man peers at them from the second-story window.

The Downward Path: The Girl Who Went Astray
AM&B © H23808 Nov. 11, 1902

Cameraman: Arthur Marvin

Location: Roof studio, N.Y.C. *Date:* May 16, 1900

10 ft. FLA4012 (print) FRA2904 (neg.)

A set of a business street in a small city is seen as the film begins. A young lady passes in front of the camera and it is evident that she is trying to attract the attention of men walking by. She is successful in provoking the interest of a well-dressed man just as she sees her aged mother and father approaching. She rushes to embrace her parents, but the man she has accosted is bent on her attentions. He pulls her roughly away, hits her father on the jaw, and drags the young woman down the street. The old gentleman holds his wife, who has fainted, and gestures for help. A policeman leisurely swinging a night-stick passes them by without even a cursory glance.

The Downward Path: The New Soubrette
AM&B © H23806 Nov. 11, 1902

Cameraman: Arthur Marvin

Location: Roof studio, N.Y.C. *Date:* May 16, 1900

11 ft. FLA4010 (print) FRA2906 (neg.)

Several people are sitting at tables in a set of a disreputable saloon. A young woman in a tutu and ballet slippers enters, dances a few steps, accepts the applause of the male spectators, and joins them for a drink. As the film ends, she is shown dancing on the top of the table.

The Downward Path: The Suicide
AM&B © H23809 Nov. 11, 1902

Cameraman: Arthur Marvin

Location: Roof studio, N.Y.C. *Date:* May 16, 1900

11 ft. FLA4013 (print) FRA2901 (neg.)

The first scene takes place in a set of a disreputable saloon furnished with plain tables and chairs. A young woman violently pounds the table apparently trying to convince the man seated across from her of something. The young man becomes annoyed and stamps out of the saloon. The young woman takes a vial from her blouse, drinks the contents, and immediately falls on the floor as though dead, to the consternation of the other patrons. The film ends as the door of the saloon opens and the young woman's parents enter and kneel beside her still form.

The Draped Model
AM&B © H22089 Sept. 27, 1902

Cameraman: Robert K. Bonine

Location: Roof studio, N.Y.C. *Date:* July 16, 1902

22 ft. FLA3951 (print) FRA1162 (neg.)

From a single camera placed so as to include all of a set of a photographic studio, a man can be seen adjusting the hair of a model on the stand. The model is wearing a full-length white leotard, the man a smock and a flowing tie. Also visible is a large, bellows-type still plate camera. After the photographer has carefully arranged the coiffure of the model, he goes over to his camera. As the film ends, the photographer's model is turned toward the camera in a way that shows her figure to the best advantage.

Drawing a Lobster Pot
AM&B © H25970 Dec. 31, 1902

Cameraman: Arthur Marvin

Location: Kittery, Maine *Date:* Mar. 8, 1901

20 ft. FLA4004 (print) FRA1205 (neg.)

One man can be seen inspecting a cratelike device known as a lobster pot from a two-man rowboat. The film is too short to permit further discussion.

See also: Unloading Halibut

The Drawing Lesson; or, The Living Statue
Méliès © H33237 July 6, 1903

Location: Montreuil, France *Date:* Spring 1903

Creator: Georges Méliès

Original title: La Statue Animée

74 ft. FLA5341 (print) FRA2643 (neg.)

The backdrop represents a courtyard or garden of a chateau, with the actors dressed in period costumes and wigs. Méliès again combines his ability as a magician with the suitability of a motion picture camera for this kind of work, and causes people and props to appear and disappear.

Dream of the Race-Track Fiend
See: How Millionaires Sometimes Entertain Aboard Their Yachts

Dress Parade of Scouts, St. Louis Exposition
AM&B © H47293 June 17, 1904

Cameraman: A. E. Weed

Location: Louisiana Purchase Exposition, St. Louis, Mo. *Photographed:* June 5, 1904

40 ft. FLA4587 (print) FRA1620 (neg.)

A flat area surrounded by trees is photographed from a single camera position. A military contingent comprised of Boy Scouts and men dressed in regular army fatigue uniforms pass the camera. A band of approximately fifty pieces proceeds directly toward the camera; at about twenty-five feet, they do a complete left turn. They are followed by several companies of Boy Scouts and soldiers from the Philippines.

Dress Parade, St. John's Academy
AM&B © H43621 Mar. 23, 1904

Cameraman: G. W. Bitzer

Location: St. John's Academy, Manlius, N.Y. near Syracuse *Photographed:* Mar. 12, 1904

22 ft. FLA4276 (print) FRA1430 (neg.)

The camera was positioned on a parade ground of a military academy. The full length of the film shows the corps of cadets in uniform and equipped with rifles passing in review by the camera in columns of fours.

The Dressmaker's Accident
AM&B © H39141 Dec. 7, 1903

Cameraman: A. E. Weed

Location: Studio, N.Y.C. *Photographed:* Nov. 25, 1903

20 ft. FLA4294 (print) FRA1444 (neg.)

Three women dressed in the ordinary street clothes of the era can be seen busily engaged in the various tasks of dressmaking in a set of a dressmaker's workroom. A woman, walking rapidly, enters and stumbles over a footstool, injuring her right shin. The other women pick her up from the floor, place her on a chair, and lift her dress above her knees to administer first aid, exposing her legs from below the knee. The film ends at this point.

See also: Her New Party Gown

Drill, Ambulance Corps

AM&B © H32790 June 17, 1903

Cameraman: F. S. Armitage

Location: Franklin Field, Philadelphia *Date:* May 18, 1899

23 ft. FLA4001 (print) FRA1203 (neg.)

The camera was placed on the drill field of a military base. At the start of the action, four men run into camera view, put a stretcher on the ground, and administer first aid to a man lying there. In the distance and approaching the camera is a four-wheeled vehicle drawn by four horses. It is flying two flags, one the colors of the United States and the other a large white flag with a red cross in the center. The vehicle comes up to the four men who have placed the injured person on a stretcher. It stops, and the stretcher is placed in the wagon. The first-aid men climb aboard and drive off.

Drill by Naval Militia

AM&B © H17044 Apr. 26, 1902

Cameraman: G. W. Bitzer

Location: Fall River, Mass. *Date:* Dec. 8, 1900

25 ft. FLA3469 (print) FRA0751 (neg.)

The poor condition of the film does not permit a detailed description of the action. However, a company of what appears to be young boys can be seen nearing the camera position. They are carrying rifles with fixed bayonets on their shoulders and are pulling a small cannon with two wheels. As the film progresses, it is evident that a drill is being performed. The film ends with the company leaving the scene in formation.

Drill by the Providence Police

AM&B © H38866 Dec. 5, 1903

Cameraman: F. S. Armitage

Location: Providence, R.I. *Photographed:* Nov. 23, 1903

35 ft. FLA4588 (print) FRA1621 (neg.)

In the center of a town square, a company of uniformed policemen equipped with nightsticks is standing at attention. The policemen execute several close-order drill maneuvers similar to those of any army infantry company. They end as they began, company front.

Drill, Ye Tarriers, Drill

AM&B © H16091 Apr. 5, 1902

Cameraman: Arthur Marvin *Date:* Sept. 26, 1900

10 ft. FLA4267 (print) FRA1422 (neg.)

A man is holding a single jack spike while two other men are pounding on it. They are working on a set of an outdoor area. Papier-mâché rocks or boulders are in front of a backdrop of the sky. The two men with sledges cease pounding on the spike and the spike holder places a charge of explosives behind the rocks. The explosives go off and blow him into the sky. At that moment, the camera is stopped and a dummy is substituted, which flies up out of

range and falls to the stage. As it hits the floor, a live actor replaces the dummy. The film ends as the two companions return to congratulate the man on his survival. Based on a song made famous by the Four Shamrocks.

Drilling an Awkward Squad

AM&B © H55398 Jan 3, 1905

33 ft. FLA4589 (print) FRA1622 (neg.)

The film, photographed on an area of drill field at a naval training station for recruit sailors, shows a drill master attempting to teach uniformed civilians the rudiments of close-order drill and the manual of arms. Approximately two hundred bluejackets wander around, more like a herd than a company of men.

Drills and Exercises, Schoolship "St. Mary's"

Edison © H62108 June 17, 1905

Cameraman: A. E. Weed

Location: New London, Conn. *Photographed:* May 31, 1905

164 ft. FLA5343 (print) FRA2263 (neg.)

The subject is a series of drills and exercises performed by recruits in training at a U. S. Naval Training School. A full-rigged ship is visible and, during the course of the film, trainees completely dress the ship with bunting and sail. Other exercises shown are swimming, rowing, and first aid.

Driving Cattle to Pasture

Edison © H46137 May 18, 1904

Cameraman: A. C. Abadie

Location: Bliss, Oklahoma Territory *Photographed:* May 9, 1904

37 ft. FLA3713 (print) FRA0960 (neg.)

The camera was placed to get the best view of the many cattle being driven toward grazing land. Edison Foundation records (envelope 135): "photographed by A. C. Abadie, May 9, 1904, Bliss, Oklahoma Territory. Showing a large number of cattle being rounded up in a pasture."

A Drop of Ink

AM&B © H40815 Jan. 12, 1904

Cameraman: A. E. Weed

Location: Studio, N.Y.C. *Photographed:* Jan. 5, 1904

25 ft. FLA3767 (print) FRA1012 (neg.)

From a single camera position, two men, one smoking and the other reading, can be seen sitting at a table facing the camera. The reader indicates that he has found something humorous in the magazine and hands it to the other man. While the smoker is reading the magazine, the man pours ink into the bowl of his pipe. The film ends as the man who was smoking spits a mouthful of ink into the other man's face.

Droppington's Devilish Deed

Keystone © LP4954 Apr. 5, 1915

Producer and Author: Mack Sennett

Cast: Chester Conklin, Minta Durfee, Clary Lyndon, Charles Arling, Billie Brockwell, James T. Kelly, Vivian Edwards

Location: Studio, Los Angeles

426 ft. FLA5345 (print, copy 1) FLA6076 (print, copy 2) FRA2264 (neg.)

This one-reel comedy was photographed on a set built to resemble the back stage of a vaudeville house. In the back shots of the audience, some later famous comics can be identified. Chester Conklin and James T. Kelly play stage hands responsible for most of the progressive situations. Their job was to do the bidding of one and all. They were willing but far from able, and the consequences of their inability to perform even the simplest task without ruining something are the basis for the film.

Droppington's Family Tree

Keystone © LP4991 Apr. 10, 1915

Producer and Author: Mack Sennett

Director: J.F. Macdonald.

Cast: Chester Conklin, Dora Rogers, Billie Brockwell, Al St. John, James T. Kelly, Frank Hayes, Dixie Chene, Billie Bennett, H. T. Booker, Minta Durfee, Joe Swickard, Mrs. Griffith

818 ft. FLA6077-6078 (print)

Chester Conklin is the cause of a considerable amount of disturbance when he goes to a restaurant and sees a beautiful Spanish dancer, Dora Rogers, to whom he makes advances. Later his son asks his permission to marry the dancer. Father protests this would be a disgrace to their fine family; and mother, Billie Brockwell, becomes distraught. But when son discovers father is enamored of the same girl, he decides to trick father into giving his consent. Son asks Dora Rogers to invite his father to the restaurant and then takes his mother there, having first arranged for a judge with a marriage license to be there too. When Chester's wife arrives, he really has no choice but to agree to his son's marriage to the dancer, and the ceremony takes place in the restaurant.

Drunkard's Child

Lubin Mfg. Co. © J132443 Aug. 9, 1909

251 ft. FLA5346 (print) FRA2267 (neg.)

An act of honesty by a crippled newsboy, the son of a drunkard, sets off the chain of events portrayed in this film. The scenes are: the newsboy selling his papers on a busy street, the act of honesty, the reward from the benefactor, the death of the newsboy's mother, the attempt by the drunkard father to steal the benefactor's money, the killing of the father when he attempts the burglary, and the final scene when the benefactor adopts the crippled newsboy. All but three of the scenes take place on sets lighted by incandescent light. The others were taken outdoors on the street.

The Drunkard's Reformation

AM&B © H125114 Mar. 31, 1909

Director: D. W. Griffith *Cameraman:* G. W. Bitzer

Cast: Linda Arvidson, Arthur Johnson, Adele De Garde, Owen Moore, Mack Sennett, Florence Lawrence, Marion Leonard, David Miles

Location: Studio, N.Y.C. *Photographed:* Feb. 25–27 and Mar. 1, 1909

394 ft. FLA5347 (print) FRA2268 (neg.)

This is a story of a drunkard, sent to see a temperance play—*L'Assommoir*, based on Emile Zola's 1877 novel of the same name—by his wife. He is so impressed that he vows to stop drinking. The five scenes, all lighted by incandescent light, are the saloon where the husband gets drunk, the living room of his home where he arrives and abuses his wife and child, the audience in the theater where the temperance play is given, the return home showing the husband making a vow never to touch liquor again, and the last scene showing the family group illuminated by light from the fireplace, which creates a tranquil atmosphere in the home.

The Dude and the Bathing Girls

AM&B © H33417 July 13, 1903

17 ft. FLA3525 (print) FRA0801 (neg.)

Several attractive young ladies are bathing in the surf. They appear to be waving to someone behind the camera position. Very soon a man in summer attire whizzes by on a bicycle into the water after the bathing girls. The film ends as the man, knee-deep in the surf and still fully clothed, is playing ring-around-the-rosy with the bathing girls.

The Dude and the Burglars

AM&B © H34510 Aug. 13, 1903

Cameraman: G. W. Bitzer

Photographed: July 30, 1903

23 ft. FLA3565 (print) FRA0841 (neg.)

This film was photographed on a set of the drawing room and entrance of a house of some consequence. Two men dressed as burglars and wearing eye masks enter from camera right and immediately gesture as if someone is approaching. A young woman comes in from the opposite side of the set and begins arranging objects on the table at camera center. One of the burglars comes up stealthily behind her and starts choking her. At this moment, a tall man wearing evening clothes enters from around the corner. He sees the burglar assaulting the woman, nonchalantly puts down his hat, coat, and gloves before walking over and striking the burglar behind the head, knocking him to the floor. The second burglar joins the fray. The man casually removes a large pistol from his back pocket, and supporting the fainting woman on his shoulder, holds the burglars at bay but is finally forced to shoot one of them. He orders the other to pour a glass of wine for the swooning woman and, as the picture ends, the police are shown arriving to take charge.

Duel Scene, "By Right of Sword"

AM&B © H40943 Jan. 16, 1904

Cameraman: A. E. Weed

Cast: Ralph Stuart

Location: Studio, N.Y.C. *Photographed:* Jan. 7, 1904

40 ft. FLA4590 (print) FRA1623 (neg.)

This was photographed as if from the audience at a theater. Four men dressed in military uniforms of Prussian design (circa 1890) are on stage in front of a backdrop of a forest. Two of the men remove their cloaks, draw cavalry sabers, and begin a duel. After a short period of swordplay, one is cut across the arm and the dueling stops. The two duelers and their seconds leave in opposite directions, ending the film. Ralph Stuart, a stage actor, was one of the duelers.

Duel Scene from "Macbeth"

AM&B © H63805 July 24, 1905

Cameraman: G. W. Bitzer

Location: Studio, N.Y.C. *Photographed:* July 15, 1905

21 ft. FLA4591 (print) FRA1624 (neg.)

This was photographed as if from the audience at a theater. The scene begins at the end of a duel between a man wearing armor and another in kilts who falls in front of the camera, as if dead. Another man in kilts carrying a sword enters and begins dueling with the winner of the first encounter. The man in kilts is the winner and the film ends here. All of the action occurs in front of a painted backdrop.

Duke and Duchess of Cornwall and York Landing at Queenstown, Ontario

Edison © H9962 Oct. 22, 1901
Location: Queenstown, Ont., Canada
71 ft. FLA4592 (print) FRA1625 (neg.)

The film was photographed from several different positions to show the arrival of the celebrities at Queenstown. The first camera position was from a dock, showing the approach of a paddle-wheel steamer. The second scene shows mooring procedures. The third position, from the dock directly at the gangway, shows the duke and duchess, their family, and their entourage disembarking and proceeding toward the city. The last scene shows the complete assemblage of spectators, as well as the arrivals, and was photographed from the city side. The sign on the ferry landing reads "Lewiston."

Duke of York at Montreal and Quebec

Edison © H9310 Oct. 4, 1901
93 ft. FLA5013 (print) FRA1976 (neg.)

This film shows the citation, presentation, and dedication of a bridge by the Duke of York, later King of England and grandfather of Queen Elizabeth. Many high-ranking military officials of both England and Canada are with him.

The Duke's Plan

Biograph © J138229 Feb. 12, 1910
Director: D. W. Griffith *Cameraman:* G. W. Bitzer
Cast: Frank Grandon, Marion Leonard, Kate Bruce, W. Chrystie Miller, James Kirkwood, Tony O'Sullivan, Jack Dillon, Wilfred Lucas, Owen Moore
Location: Studio, N.Y.C. *Photographed:* Dec. 27–28, 1909
385 ft. FLA5348 (print) FRA2269 (neg.)

The action in each of the five sets was photographed from a single camera position. All entrances and exits of the many actors, in seventeenth-century costumes, are from camera left. The story is about a rich and powerful member of the aristocracy who wants to marry his daughter to a politically suitable man although she is in love with a poor man. The poor suitor is incarcerated on false charges of being a traitor. His sweetheart disguises herself as a boy and attempts to rescue him, but she is caught. She then attempts to die in his place and again her identity is discovered. Her father, the duke, relents and, as the picture ends, the poor-but-honest suitor and the duke's daughter are being married.

A Dull Razor

Edison © D4732 Feb. 28, 1900
17 ft. FLA3892 (print) FRA1114 (neg.)

This short film is devoted to a man lathering his face, then shaving with a straight razor. Incandescent lights were used for the photography. The actor was seated at a table so that only the upper part of his body is visible. The film is so short that the man does not finish shaving.

Dumping Iron Ore

AM&B © H38859 Dec. 5, 1903
Cameraman: G. W. Bitzer
Location: Cleveland, Ohio *Date:* Oct. 27, 1900
34 ft. FLA4593 (print) FRA6405 (neg.)

A steel cantilevered construction resembling a support for an overhead railway can be seen about a hundred yards away from the single camera position. At camera right is a boxlike contraption moving obliquely to camera. In the foreground is a large pile of a black substance that might be coal, coke, or pig iron. During the course of the film, this boxlike car travels the full length of the overhead railway and, at a given spot, the bottom opens, dumping the black substance onto the pile. The car then returns for another load.

Eagle Dance, Pueblo Indians

Edison © 13541 Feb. 24, 1898
Cameraman: James H. White
27 ft. FLA3377 (print) FRA2871 (neg.)

An Indian chief with a full-feathered war bonnet is shown from a single camera position as he executes a step-and-a-half dance. Approximately twenty other Indians watch him, and two tents can be seen in the background.

The Early Morning Attack

Edison © 61216 Sept. 22, 1899
65 ft. FLA4594 (print) FRA1626 (neg.)
[Spanish-American War]

Men in white uniforms emerge from a thickly wooded terrain. They start firing toward the camera position. Almost immediately after, from under the camera position, men in khaki uniforms carrying an American flag can be seen firing in the general direction of the men in white. The men in khaki charge, causing those in white to retreat. A volley from the white-uniformed men changes the strategic position; now the men in khaki retreat toward the camera. Next the khaki-clad men rally and the men in white uniforms are shown being led off.

An East River Novelty

Edison © H37247 Oct. 22, 1903
Cameraman: Edwin S. Porter
Location: From Brooklyn Bridge, New York, N.Y. *Photographed:* Oct. 18, 1903
54 ft. FLA4595 (print) FRA1627 (neg.)

The film was photographed from a high place, such as a bridge, under which ships, barges, etc., can be seen moving. The camera was panned to cover an area of waterfront that encompassed at least two land miles. While the camera was too far away to permit reading the signs on the warehouses on the docks, the general conformation can be seen clearly. At the beginning of the film, a tug pushing a barge laden with railroad cars can be seen.

East Side Urchins Bathing in a Fountain

Edison © H36495 Oct. 3, 1903
Cameraman: Edwin S. Porter

Location: N.Y.C. *Photographed:* Sept. 11, 1903
35 ft. FLA4596 (print) FRA1628 (neg.)

A large water fountain with a water depth of approximately three feet can be seen from a single camera position. Beyond the water fountain are unidentifiable New York City buildings. Twenty small boys come from behind the camera, go to the fountain, and climb in the pool where they splash about. The film ends as two or three men show disapproval of these antics and chase the little boys from the fountain.

The Easy Chair

AM&B © H40723 Jan. 8, 1904

Cameraman: A. E. Weed

Location: Studio, N.Y.C. *Photographed:* Dec. 24, 1903

34 ft. FLA4597 (print) FRA1629 (neg.)

A set of the interior of an artist's studio can be seen. A man is working on a painting when a prospective customer arrives. The artist seats him in a chair. The artist's assistant offers the customer some suggestions about the paintings that are for sale. The customer gets up and again is asked to sit down. He sees a chair, tries to sit upon it, but falls through a painting. The assistant makes him pay for the damage. As the customer leaves the atelier, the painter and his assistant are shown tossing paper money into the air and dancing about in glee.

Eating Force

AM&B © H32107 May 22, 1903

33 ft. FLA3976 (print) FRA1184 (neg.)

The camera was placed so close to the subject that only the top of the table where a child is sitting and a short distance above his head are visible. The child is in profile and is crying bitterly. Then he faces the camera, eating something from a bowl with obvious relish.

Eating Macaroni in the Streets of Naples

Edison © H32452 June 8, 1903

Cameraman: A. C. Abadie

Location: Naples, Italy *Photographed:* Apr. 8, 1902

37 ft. FLA3726 (print, copy 1) FLA5968 (print, copy 2)
0973 (neg.)

The film begins across the street from some young boys who are lined up against a curbing eating spaghetti or macaroni. The only other action occurs when a small child runs across the picture and is yanked out of camera sight by someone.

The Eavesdropper

AM&B © H126278 Apr. 28, 1909

Director: D. W. Griffith *Cameramen:* G. W. Bitzer, Arthur Marvin

Cast: Marion Leonard, Linda Arvidson, David Miles

Location: Studio, N.Y.C. *Photographed:* Mar. 5 and 8, 1909

235 ft. FLA5349 (print) FRA2270 (neg.)

The actors are in Spanish costumes. Two men in love with the heroine both make gestures describing their undying love. The heroine is in love with one, but her father insists she marry the other. She tells her lover that she cannot marry him, and their conversation is overheard by the man her father has chosen for her. The film ends as he does the noble thing and releases her from her agreement to marry him.

Eccentricities of an Adirondack Canoe

AM&B © H16337 Apr. 10, 1902

Cameraman: Arthur Marvin

Date: Aug. 13, 1900

16 ft. FLA4448 (print) FRA1553 (neg.)

A lake can be seen with canoes and rowboats. As the action begins, a man, a boy, and several women of various ages walk out onto a float where a canoe is tied up. The man bends, unties the canoe, and helps a woman and her teenage daughter into it. He then gets in himself and the canoe tips over, spilling the three of them into the water. As the film ends, they are being helped back onto the float by the others.

Eclipse Car Fender Test, no.1–2

AM&B © H35652 Sept. 12, 1903

Cameraman: F. S. Armitage

Date: May 22, 1903

25 ft. FLA4365 (print) FRA1504 (neg.)

This is a photographic record of the safety features of the Eclipse Electric Streetcar Fender (cowcatcher). The inventor really believed it would work, and he permits the streetcar to run into him to prove the value of the invention.

Edgar Allen [i.e., Allan] Poe

AM&B © H122509 Feb. 3, 1909

Director: D. W. Griffith *Cameraman:* G. W. Bitzer

Cast: Linda Arvidson, Herbert Yost, Clara T. Bracey, Arthur Johnson, Charles Perley

Location: Studio, N.Y.C. *Photographed:* Jan. 21 and 23, 1909

162 ft. FLA5014 (print) FRA2993 (neg.)

Two sets were used in this drama of a supposed incident in the life of Edgar Allan Poe. One set is the interior of his home, and the other is two rooms in a publishing house. The film begins by showing a desperately ill woman in bed. A man with flowing hair and a mustache enters, attempts to comfort his wife, and then sits down at a table to write. By the use of stop-action photography, a raven appears and perches on top of a bookcase. His manuscript completed, Poe reads it to his wife and then rushes off to sell it. His poem is rejected by several individuals in the publisher's office, until, as a last resort, he forces his way into the editor's office. The editor buys the poem. Poe hurries home only to find that he is too late and his wife is dead.

Edison Kinetoscopic Record of a Sneeze, January 7, 1894

Edison © W. K. L. Dickson 2887 Jan. 9, 1894

Cameraman: W. K. L. Dickson

Cast: Fred Ott

Location: Edison studio affectionately called the "Black Maria," West Orange, N.J. *Photographed:* Jan. 7, 1894

Alternate *Title:* The Sneeze

45 frames FLA6049 (print) FRA0255 (neg.)

This film is considered to be the first motion picture given legal status by copyright acceptance. The forty-five frames it contains were sent in for copyright as a still picture. The action consists of a man, Fred Ott, sneezing. Application for copyright was filed by William K. Laurie Dickson, Edison's assistant and supervisor of the new motion picture project. The frames were rephotographed from the still picture and turned back into a motion picture which thus exists for people to see only because of the Paper Print Restoration Program.

The Educated Chimpanzee
Edison © H7331 July 31, 1901
58 ft. FLA4598 (print) FRA1630 (neg.)

The cameraman placed his equipment to show the area of a table where a chimpanzee is seated. The chimp is dressed as a man and changes its clothes several times. The film was intended to show the achievements of the animal and to prove it could perform several tricks, such as ring a bell, eat with a fork, sit at a desk, pound the keys of a typewriter with both hands, and strike the keys of a miniature piano. For each trick, the chimp wore an appropriate costume.

Eeling Through Ice
AM&B © H16724 Apr. 18, 1902
Cameraman: Robert K. Bonine
Location: Shrewsbury River, N.J. *Date:* Jan 20, 1902
16 ft. FLA3195 (print) FRA0521 (neg.)

The film, photographed from a single camera position located either on or near a frozen-over lake, shows a great deal of activity. There are people skating, a portion of an iceboat rig is visible, and several spectators are watching a man in the foreground. He has an axe and is chopping a hole in the ice on which he is standing. As soon as the ice is pushed away to form a hole, one of the spectators brings a long pole that he pokes down through the ice, rolling it about between his hands. One of four films. Others in the series are: Ice Yacht Racing, A Mile in 56 Seconds, and A Spill.

Effecting a Cure
Biograph © J148460 Dec. 2, 1910
Director: D. W. Griffith *Cameraman:* Arthur Marvin
Cast: Linda Arvidson, Mack Sennett, Florence Barker, Stephanie Longfellow, Kate Bruce
Location: Studio, N.Y.C. *Photographed:* Oct. 20–21, 1910
384 ft. FLA5350 (print) FRA2271 (neg.)

This comedy is built around a man who takes advantage of the absence of his wife and daughter by going to his club and excessively imbibing intoxicants to the general annoyance of club members who have to bring him home in an obstreperous condition. The clubmen and his wife then conspire to play a trick on him, hoping to cure him of drinking. They enlist the aid of an attractive young lady who writes him a note stating she will accept his proposal of marriage of the night before. At least half of the film is devoted to his frantic efforts to keep his wife from learning of what he believes he did while drunk. The film ends as he is offered a drink, refuses it, and pledges abstention.

Eggs Hatching
AM&B © H16922 Apr. 22, 1902
Cameraman: Raymond Ackerman
Date: Sept. 1, 1899
31 ft. FLA3473 (print) FRA0755 (neg.)

The single camera position shows an exterior shot of a tray containing chicken eggs in the last stages of hatching. At the head of the tray is a sign, "The Monitor Incubator."
See also: Two Hours After the Chickens Leave the Shells

Egyptian Boys in Swimming Race
Edison © H32486 June 10, 1903
Cameraman: A. C. Abadie
Location: Nile River, Luxor, Egypt *Photographed:* Mar. 26, 1903
39 ft. FLA3632 (print) FRA0889 (neg.)

The best view is of an area of a small tributary, across which a group of boys runs down the embankment, jumps into the water, and swims toward the camera position. They stand unclothed, with their hands outstretched, awaiting a reward for their efforts.

Egyptian Fakir with Dancing Monkey
Edison © H32453 June 8, 1903
Cameraman: A. C. Abadie
Location: Cairo *Photographed:* Mar. 29, 1903
50 ft. FLA4599 (print) FRA1631 (neg.)

A small monkey dressed in a costume of bangles and beads performs on a platform to the beat of a cymbal played by its owner. The monkey does several tricks and jumps about.

Egyptian Market Scene
Edison © H32804 June 17, 1903
Cameraman: A. C. Abadie
Location: Cairo *Photographed:* Mar. 26, 1903
51 ft. FLA4600 (print) FRA1632 (neg.)

The camera, in the center of a large, crowded area, pans to show a variety of people wearing turbans and burnooses, carrying objects on their heads, and merchandise spread out on mats. A few sheds and other buildings are also visible.

Eiffel Tower from Trocadero Palace
Edison © D16387 Aug. 9, 1900
Location: Paris
37 ft. FLA3252 (print) FRA0574 (neg.)
[Paris Exposition]

The single camera position is from the top of a building identified as the Trocadero Palace; the camera is pointed toward the Eiffel Tower. The film shows only up to the first arch of the Eiffel Tower.

18th Pennsylvania Volunteers
AM&B © H32495 June 11, 1903
27 ft. FLA3583 (print) FRA0855 (neg.)
[Spanish-American War]

The film shows a battalion of infantry marching in company-front formation toward the camera position. The platform where the camera was operated was high above the heads of the soldiers. The marching infantrymen wear field packs and are preceded by officers on horseback.

Electric Locomotive Tests, Schenectady
AM&B © H53668 Nov. 23, 1904
Cameraman: G. W. Bitzer

Location: Schenectady, N.Y. Photographed: Nov. 12, 1904
104 ft. FLA5015 (print) FRA2888 (neg.)

The film is of tests, which were open to the public, of the electric locomotive. Apparently the man in charge of the filming wanted to emphasize that the electric locomotive did not smoke because every time the locomotive goes by the camera, there is a heavily smoking steam engine on the track beside it.

The Electric Mule

Edison © H64996 Aug. 29, 1905

Cameraman: Edwin S. Porter

Location: Schenectady, N.Y. *Photographed:* May 29, 1905

220 ft. FLA5351 (print) FRA2895 (neg.)

The locale is a barge canal. The camera was located on one side of the canal to photograph the opposite bank and the roadway beside it. Shortly after the film begins, a span of mules drawing a barge appear and cross in front of the camera. The scenes of the mules towing barges are repeated three times. There is a scene with no action, and then a small electric car with a trolley and two passengers, accompanied by a man walking can be seen. The electric car is towing two large barges. Just as the film ends, the electric mule is again seen as it comes to a stop in front of the camera, but this time it is headed in the opposite direction.

Electric Tower

AM&B © H29469 Mar. 18, 1903

Cameraman: G. W. Bitzer

Location: Pan-American Exposition, Buffalo, N.Y. *Date:* May 7, 1901

34 ft. FLA4601 (print) FRA1633 (neg.)

Taken from a single camera position, the first scenes visible are of the large exhibit buildings housing some of the electrical wonders on display at the fair. The camera begins to move across the exhibit area, taking in the large electric tower and continuing its movement until the fountain at the center of the square can be seen. The camera pans in the opposite direction until the large electric tower is in the full center frame of the moving picture. The camera rests in that position, but when the sun goes down and the sky darkens, the bare outline of the electric tower becomes visible. The tower starts to light up as banks of electric-light globes completely outline it against the night sky.

See also: Esplanade by Night

Electrocuting an Elephant

Edison © H26890 Jan. 12, 1903

35 ft. FLA4205 (print) FRA1368 (neg.)

The film begins on what appears to be the yard of an engineering plant. Approaching the camera are two men leading a large elephant in a specially built harness to a special steel plate. Smoke arises from between the plate and the elephant's feet just before it falls over on its side, apparently dead.

The Elephant's Bath

AM&B © H30179 Apr. 4, 1903

29 ft. FLA3650 (print) FRA0905 (neg.)

The film, photographed from a single camera position, shows a water tank with a slanting ramp leading into it. A large elephant is on the ramp walking away from the camera into the water. The elephant performs two pirouettes, then leaves the water. Several children watch.

Elephants Shooting the Chutes at Luna Park

Edison © H46916 June 8, 1904

Cameraman: Edwin S. Porter

Location: Luna Park, Coney Island, N.Y. *Photographed:* May 26, 1904

40 ft. FLA4602 (print) FRA2878 (neg.)

The camera was placed to show a small body of water. Across this body of water, approximately a hundred feet away, a large slide can be seen. Leading up to the slide on an incline is a walkway of heavy construction. An elephant is seen at the top of the slide. It goes down the slide into the water. The elephant swims across the water and its mahout leads it away.

Elephants Shooting the Chutes, Luna Park, Coney Island, no. 2

Edison © H48780 July 30, 1904

Cameraman: A. C. Abadie.

Location: Luna Park, Coney Island, N.Y. *Photographed:* July 20, 1904

40 ft. FLA4082 (print) FRA1265 (neg.)

A large slide can be seen that begins on the bank and leads into a small lake. A large elephant comes out at the top of the slide and descends into the water. It is followed by another elephant. Both are seen getting out of the water and walking away with their attendants.

Elevated Railroad, New York

AM&B © H28548 Feb. 24, 1903

36 ft. FLA4603 (print) FRA2865 (neg.)

All the scenes were photographed from the moving front platform of a train traveling over the elevated tracks. While the train turns on the curves, a great deal of the New York City business district can be seen beyond the railings of the elevated tracks.

Ella Lola, a la Trilby

Edison © 59209 Oct. 7, 1898

Cast: Ella Lola

Location: Black Maria Studio, West Orange, N.J.

26 ft. FLA4378 (print) FRA1516 (neg.)

NOTE: The author believes that this film was made in the Black Maria at a camera speed in excess of thirty frames per second. Ella Lola was a stage star of note before the turn of the century, and was given this opportunity to show her ability as a dancer.

See also: Turkish Dance, Ella Lola

The Elopement

AM&B © H23794 Nov. 11, 1902

Cameraman: Arthur Marvin

Location: Roof studio, N.Y.C. *Date:* May 16, 1900

10 ft. FLA4457 (print) FRA1560 (neg.)

A young man wearing a straw hat and an ordinary business suit is approaching the window of a set of a dwelling. As he nears the window, a young woman dressed for the street is eagerly attempting to climb out. The young man tries to curb her enthusiasm until he fetches a ladder and he leaves to do so. The young woman, evincing great confidence, climbs out the window and in doing so, catches her skirt on something. She is seen suspended by her dress, now practically over her head, revealing her undergarments, garters, etc.

The Elopement

AM&B © H37381 Oct. 28, 1903

Cameraman: G. W. Bitzer

Location: Studio, N.Y.C. *Photographed:* Oct. 20, 1903

23 ft. FLA4604 (neg.) FRA1634 (neg.)

A set of the wall of a house can be seen as the picture begins. There is a doorway, a door, and a second-story window. Two well-dressed young men in top hats, contrasting overcoats, gloves, and spats walk over to the window. A young woman appears and hands them the edge of a trunk, which they lower to the ground. One of the young men stands on the trunk to help the girl over the sill and onto the ground. The three start to leave when the trunk opens and the young woman's father steps out. Her mother comes out of the house, takes the young woman inside, and then begins beating one of the young men with a broomstick, while the father knocks him to the ground with his fist.

The Elopement

AM&B © H103097 Nov. 29, 1907

Cameraman: G. W. Bitzer

Location: Studio, N.Y.C.; Asbury Park, N.J. *Photographed:* Nov. 14, 18 and 20, 1907

266 ft. FLA5352 (print) FRA2288 (neg.)

The film shows an elopement and a chase that ends as the two young people are legally married just as her parents, still in their night clothes, arrive moments too late. The film has many exterior scenes that were filmed along the roadway. After the father refuses the young couple permission to marry, they decide to elope. The young man calls for the girl in his speedy open roadster, and they start out for the preacher. Her parents, in their chauffeur-driven great touring car pursue them. The roadster breaks down, the young couple take to the woods and find a motorboat on the edge of a lake but it blows up and they are forced to swim. One of the last scenes shows the bride-to-be, utterly exhausted, draped over her suitor's arm as they wait for the preacher to open the door.

Elopement on Horseback

Edison © 69081 Nov. 26, 1898

18 ft. FLA3047 (print) FRA0307 (neg.)

A young woman, dressed only in her nightgown, leaves her house through the window. A man standing beneath the window assists her in getting up on a large box, where she remains for a moment. Another man, in riding clothes, astride a black horse appears and helps her mount in back of him. They then ride out of camera range. The first man is attempting to close the shutters on the window when a man is seen sliding down the cellar door directly beneath the window. When he reaches the ground, he gets to his feet and scuffles with the man who had aided the couple with their elopement.

The Elopers Who Didn't Elope

AM&B © H43622 Mar. 23, 1904

Cameraman: A. E. Weed.

Location: Studio, N.Y.C. *Photographed:* Feb. 26, 1904

19 ft. FLA3511 (print) FRA0789 (neg.)

The opening scene is of a set of the front of a two-story apartment building or house. A young man walks up to the window, places a ladder against the house, and climbs up to the second-story window where a young lady awaits him. He begins to help her down the ladder but as she gets halfway down, two men come out of a door on the first floor, tip over the ladder, and carry away the young lady suspended in a horizontal position on the ladder.

Eloping with Aunty

Biograph © H127383 May 22, 1909

Cameramen: G. W. Bitzer, Arthur Marvin

Cast: Florence Lawrence, Mack Sennett, Clara T. Bracey, Arthur Johnson

Location: Studio, N.Y.C. *Photographed:* Apr. 6, 7 and 21, 1909

231 ft. FLA5353 (print) FRA2272 (neg.)

A father does not wish his daughter to continue seeing the young man of her choice. To insure that she does not, he enlists the aid of a rather homely maiden aunt as the girl's constant chaperone. The young suitor disguises himself as the maiden aunt and reports to the father to take the young girl on a presumed shopping trip. Instead, he takes her to a preacher where they get married. The film ends with the father reluctantly accepting the inevitable. In one unusual comedy scene, the glass from a mirror is removed and the aunt and the disguised suitor face one another, and the suitor is forced to mimic the aunt's gestures so that she will believe she is seeing herself.

Emerson School Calisthenics

AM&B © H45151 May 2, 1904

Cameraman: A. E. Weed

Location: Kansas City, Mo. *Photographed:* Apr. 18, 1904

19 ft. FLA3103 (print) FRA0440 (neg.)

As the film begins, four rows of preadolescent girls in white dresses are facing the camera position. The film was photographed outdoors, and the youngsters demonstrate several calisthenic exercises in unison. A blackboard immediately behind the rows of students has chalk lettering saying, "Kansas City, Missouri."

Emigrants [i.e., Immigrants] Landing at Ellis Island

Edison © H33775 July 24, 1903

Cameraman: A. C. Abadie

Location: Ellis Island, N.Y. *Date:* July 9, 1903

63 ft. FLA4605 (print) FRA2839 (neg., copy 1) FRA6408 (neg., copy 2)

The ferryboat *William Meyers* is approaching a landing at an embarkation dock used by the American government for a landing point at Ellis Island. The film includes the docking of the vessel, the placing of the gangway, and the debarkation of passengers.

Empire State Express

AM&B © H20217 July 25, 1902

Photographed: 1896

28 ft. FLA3837 (print) FRA1097 (neg.)

The film opens on a scene of a railroad section gang mending tracks on a curved area. In the distance a locomotive can be seen approaching the camera position. As it goes by the camera, four cars can be counted, in addition to the locomotive. The track workers wave and cheer, and the white-coated Pullman porters standing on the steps of each car wave back. Although this film bears a 1902 copyright date, there is no doubt it is one of the films shown as a package when the Biograph projector was introduced to the public in October of 1896. See articles in "Biograph Bulletins," compiled by Kemp R. Niver.

Empire State Express, the Second, Taking Water on the Fly
Edison © H62109 June 17, 1905
Cameraman: Edwin S. Porter
Location: Schenectady, N.Y. *Photographed:* May 30, 1905
35 ft. FLA4114 (print) FRA1290 (neg.)

The film was photographed from a single camera position. It demonstrates a new principle of a locomotive taking water for the boiler by scooping it out of a trough alongside the tracks as the train moves.

The Enchanted Drawing
Edison © D21656 Nov. 16, 1900
Cast: J. Stuart Blackton
37 ft. FLA4606 (print) FRA1635 (neg.)

A man with a pleasant expression on his face and wearing a tailcoat can be seen standing alongside a large easel that has been placed outdoors. He draws with a crayon a one-line caricature of a man. Then he draws a wine bottle and a champagne glass, reaches for them, and they become real in his hands. As he pours himself a drink, the expression on the man in the cartoon goes from bland to unhappy. The artist then pours another drink, simulates giving it to the cartoon, who now smiles. For the remainder of the film, the artist draws top hats, cigars, etc., causing the cartoon face to look happy. When he takes them away, the man in the drawing becomes downcast and unhappy. As the film ends, the man in the cartoon has been given a cigar which he smokes while he smiles happily. The cartoonist was J. Stuart Blackton, an early pioneer in films, and an employee of Edison's. He later became the full partner in the development of the world-renowned Vitagraph Moving Picture Company, now part of Warner Bros.

The Enchanted Well
Méliès © H32937 June 25, 1903
Creator: Georges Méliès *Cast:* Georges Méliès
Location: Montreuil, France *Photographed:* Spring 1903
Original title: Le Puits Fantastique
98 ft. FLA5354 (print) FRA2641 (neg.)

This is a Méliès film of unusual proportion. Scenes shift, people are transformed by stop action photography from props and vice versa, and emerge from holes in the ground that appear to be made by something that disappears. Enlarged mechanical animals also appear, which is rare in Méliès's productions. The film represents his usual excellent work.

L'Enchanteur Alcrofrisbas
Méliès © H38292 Nov. 19,1903
Creator: Georges Méliès *Cast:* Georges Méliès
Location: Montreuil, France *Photographed:* Fall 1903

U.S. title: Alcrofrisbas, the Master Magician
101 ft. FLA5355 (print) FRA2656 (neg.)

A magician leads another actor into a series of caverns. At first, the magician shows the actor a large vase, and then turns it into a woman clothed in a dress of organdy or tulle. She becomes air-borne as the sorcerer leads his guest into another section of the cave, where he sees more of Méliès, fantasies, such as double exposures of waterfalls superimposed over live action and vice versa, and props that explode and are transformed into people. In two instances, moving sets are used. There is an interesting close-up of a woman's head set in a sunburst, which was unusual for that time.

The Engagement Ring
Biograph © J167110 Mar. 11, 1912
Director: Mack Sennett
Cast: Mabel Normand, Dell Henderson, Kate Bruce, Fred Mace
192 ft. FLA5356 (print) FRA2273 (neg.)

This comedy is about a young lady who is wooed by two young men, one of whom is wealthy while the other is poor. Each buys her an engagement ring; the rich man pays for his in cash while the poor young man buys on time. A series of humorous incidents arise from the poor suitor's inability to meet the payments. The rich suitor constantly harasses the jeweler to repossess the ring. But the indigent young man is knocked down by an automobile, and the money he receives as damages enables him to pay in full for his ring just in time to prevent his girl, who is being influenced by her mother, from accepting his rival's ring.

English Lancers Charging
Edison © D9116 Apr. 28, 1900
Cameraman: James H. White
44 ft. FLA44308 (print) FRA1457 (neg.)
[Boer War]

The camera was located on a small hill overlooking an area that had been selected for a sham battle between men dressed as Boer volunteers and as British lancers. As the film progresses, the company of men closest to the camera begins firing rifles, and a small cannon is seen to emit smoke. At a distance, coming out of a gully, are approximately two companies of men dressed in British Army uniforms who charge their opponents. The film ends by showing many of the defeated soldiers lying on the battlefield while the victors enthusiastically wave their flag and march away.

The Englishman and the Girl
Biograph © J138587 Feb. 21, 1910
Director: D. W. Griffith *Cameraman:* G. W. Bitzer
Cast: Mary Pickford, Mack Sennett, Frank Grandon, Gertrude Robinson, Charles Craig, George Nicholls, Kate Bruce, Tony O'Sullivan
Location: Studio, N.Y.C. *Photographed:* Jan. 4–5, 1910
364 ft. FLA5357 (print) FRA2274 (neg., copy 1) FRA6431 (neg., copy 2)

All the scenes were photographed indoors. The sets resemble a country store, the living quarters behind the store, and the living room of a relative of the proprietor. The first scene is of a rehearsal of the small town drama group. The rehearsal is interrupted by the delivery of a letter informing the recipient of the imminent arrival of an English relative. The relative arrives, and his stuffiness causes him to be the butt of some pranks. The theater group dons Indian costumes and makes believe they are going to scalp him. He turns the tables on them by pulling out a pistol and chasing them. After a considerable number of pieces of furniture is broken, and the shelves and contents of the store are demolished, the picture ends.

An Englishman's Trip to Paris From London

Hepworth (England) © AM&B H52229 Oct. 28, 1904
Director: Lewin Fitzhamon
144 ft. FLA5016 (print) FRA1977 (neg.)

The opening scenes show an Englishman in tweed knickers at a railway station preparing to take the boat train. Inside the station the crowd is shown pushing through the turnstile of a ticket agency. The boat train is shown leaving the station for the steamship docks. Then, there are scenes of the promenade deck of a paddle-wheel steamer, and of the Englishman becoming ill on board the boat. He arrives in Paris and views the streets around the administrative buildings, the Chamber of Deputies, and the Champs Elysees. The picture ends with a scene based on "once an Englishman, always an Englishman," for our hero sits down at a sidewalk cafe and orders a glass of British stout.

Epileptic Seizure, nos. 1–9

Walter G. Chase © H68449-54, H68797, H71845, H75692 Nov. 10, 1905
Location: Craig Colony, Sonyea, N.Y.
792 ft. Individual chapters:

No. 1	FLA5017 (print)	FRA1978 (neg.)
No. 2	FLA5018 (print)	FRA1979 (neg.)
No. 3	FLA5019 (print)	FRA1980 (neg.)
No. 4	FLA5020 (print)	FRA1981 (neg.)
No. 5	FLA5021 (print)	FRA1982 (neg.)
No. 6	FLA5022 (print)	FRA1983 (neg.)
No. 7	FLA5023 (print)	FRA1984 (neg.)
No. 8	FLA5024 (print)	FRA1985 (neg.)
No. 9	FLA5025 (print)	FRA1986 (neg.)

This Walter G. Chase film about epileptic seizures was photographed from a single camera position against a backdrop of dark canvas. The patients were placed on the ground in front of the backdrop and then their seizures were photographed. The subjects were both males and females of various ages. Patients are shown enduring muscle strictures. According to the *Motion Picture World* of March 23, 1907, this footage, photographed at the Craig colony of epileptics at Sonyea, New York, took two months to complete.

Eradicating Aunty

Biograph © H127700 May 28, 1909
Director: D. W. Griffith *Cameramen:* G. W. Bitzer, Arthur Marvin
Cast: Florence Lawrence, Owen Moore, Stephanie Longfellow, Arthur Johnson, Florence Auer
Location: Studio, N.Y.C.; Fort Lee, N.J. *Photographed:* Apr. 15, 16 and 26, 1909
207 ft. FLA5358 (print) FRA2275 (neg.)

There are five scenes in this picture. There is the exterior of what seems to be a large inn, two interior scenes, a chase scene in a wooded area, and a scene in a railroad station showing a departing train. In the film two young lovers wish to be alone so they can embrace but are constantly frustrated by a maiden aunt and a clergyman who spy on them. A friend of the frustrated lovers arrives and they conspire to frighten their unwanted chaperones. The friend dresses himself as a wild west cowboy, with chaps, two guns, and a mustache. He then proceeds to fire his revolvers at the feet of the unwanted guardians. The last scene shows the two chaperones running toward the train as they are pursued by the gun-waving pseudo-cowboy.

Eruption of Mt. Vesuvius

AM&B © H76577 May 2, 1906
Cameraman: G. W. Bitzer
Location: Studio, N.Y.C. *Photographed:* Apr. 25, 1906
58 ft. FLA4607 (print) FRA1636 (neg.)

It is possible to identify a tabletop model construction of the supposed area around the foot of Mount Vesuvius. There is a mountain and terrain as well as the bay area and a backdrop with a full moon. As the action begins, the miniature mountain begins to smoke slightly. Then there is a miniature explosion in which a burning substance runs down the side and sets fire to the city below. There are several explosions, each larger, followed by black smoke.

The Escalta, Manila

AM&B © H34817 Aug. 19, 1903
Cameraman: Raymond Ackerman
Location: Manila, Philippine Islands *Date:* Dec. 21, 1899
18 ft. FLA4144 (print) FRA1314 (neg.)

The camera was placed so that a much-traveled thoroughfare with three- and four-story buildings on each side can be seen. During the course of the film, all manner of vehicles pass the camera position. There are horse-drawn two- and four-wheeled vehicles as well as public transportation, such as horse-drawn trams.

Escape from Sing Sing

AM&B © H27977 Feb. 7, 1903
Cameraman: Arthur Marvin
Location: Roof, N.Y.C. *Date:* June 26, 1900
35 ft. FLA3120 (print) FRA0455 (neg.)

As the film begins, a rope is dropped against an obviously painted stone wall. An actor dressed as a prisoner slides down the rope, and then another follows him. Their attempt to climb over an outer wall is thwarted by prison guards, ending the film.

An Escape from the Flames

AM&B © H44208 Apr. 6, 1904
Cameraman: A. E. Weed
Location: Studio, N.Y.C. *Photographed:* Mar. 18, 1904
20 ft. FLA3710 (print) FRA0957 (neg.)

The set in this film was constructed so that it appears as though the camera was placed at the edge of a roof of a building. Smoke can be seen billowing out of the vents in the roof. Two people dressed in sleeping garments come out of the skylight and run along the edge of the smoking roof. A third person in a nightgown emerges from the skylight, runs to the edge of the building, and climbs down a ladder.

The Escaped Lunatic

AM&B © H40805   Jan. 12, 1904

Cameraman: A. E. Weed

Location: Studio and Bronx, N.Y.C. *Photographed:* Various dates, circa Nov. 1903

271 ft.   FLA5359 (print)   FRA2276 (neg.)

Three guards of a comic mental institution chase after an inmate who thinks he is Napoleon. Napoleon does not like his surroundings and wants to prove he can escape. By using many camera positions to show the rugged countryside, foot bridges, cliffs, and roads, the producer is able to capture the feeling of an exciting pursuit. The film ends as Napoleon proves to his captors that he can escape, run over hill and dale, and get back into his cell before they can catch him. Stop action photography was used in one scene.

See also: Maniac Chase

Esplanade des Invalides

Edison © D16379   Aug. 9, 1900

Location: Paris

56 ft.   FLA4608 (print)   FRA1637 (neg.)

[Paris Exposition]

From a single camera position, a nearly 200-degree pan shows the World's Fair in Paris in 1900. The film gives a good indication of what was available for tourists to see.

Esquimaux Game of Snap-the-Whip

Edison © H7499   Aug. 9, 1901

Cameramen: Edwin S. Porter, Arthur White

Location: Pan-American Exposition, Buffalo, N.Y.

17 ft.   FLA3759 (print)   FRA1004 (neg.)

The film, photographed from a single camera position, shows a large tent of animal skins in front of which are two spectators watching two participants perform a game of skill. Each participant holds a long whip with which he attempts to snare his opponent's whip.

Esquimaux Leap-Frog

Edison © H7500   Aug. 9, 1901

Cameramen: Edwin S. Porter, Arthur White

Location: Pan-American Exposition, Buffalo, N.Y.

23 ft.   FLA3760 (print)   FRA1005 (neg.)

The film, photographed from a single camera position, shows buildings resembling igloos on ice floes, in front of which persons clothed as Eskimoes play a game of leapfrog.

Esquimaux Village

Edison © H7327   July 31, 1901

Cameramen: Edwin S. Porter, Arthur White

Location: Pan-American Exposition, Buffalo, N.Y.

27 ft.   FLA3761 (print)   FRA1006 (neg.)

The first of three camera positions shows a low building resembling an igloo beside a small pool, and an ice floe. Dark-complexioned people dressed as Eskimoes run up and down alongside the pool, and a dog pulls a sled. Next, some sled dogs are led in front of the camera. The last camera position shows the same dogs running into a tent made from animal skins.

European Rest Cure

Edison © H49807   Sept. 1, 1904

Cameraman: Edwin S. Porter

Cast: Joseph Hart

Location: N.Y.C. *Photographed:* Aug. 31, 1904

402 ft.   FLA5360 (print)   FRA2277 (neg.)

This humorous film follows an especially written story about an old gaffer (played by Joseph Hart), who is sent by his family on a sea voyage and European tour for his health. Every scene is directed to give the hero of the story a bad time and to see that rest is one thing he does not get. Sets were built to resemble a cabin of a ship at sea, Italian ruins, Egyptian pyramids, etc., and all added to our hero's dilemma. Instead of the customary painted backdrops of the day, all of the sets have dimension and are practical by today's standards. Newsreel film photographed in 1897 and 1898 was edited into the ship departure and arrival scenes photographed especially for the film. In one scene, the camera is rocked to give the illusion of rough going at sea for the passenger, possibly an innovation. Porter also employed stop-action special effects whenever it seemed to add to the humor of the story.

Everybody Works But Father (Blackface)

AM&B © H68149   Nov. 1, 1905

Cameraman: G. W. Bitzer

Location: Studio, N.Y.C. *Photographed:* Oct. 20, 1905

69 ft.   FLA5026 (print)   FRA1987 (neg.)

The set is of the interior of a log cabin, with a fireplace on the rear wall. There are four people in the cast: an old black man, his wife, their daughter and a grown son. The father, wearing a silk hat and raggedy clothes, enters, yawns, and seats himself in a rocking chair. His wife comes in with a bag of clothes, puts them in a washtub and begins to scrub them. All during the film, the father enjoys himself in his rocking chair, the wife is bent over the washtub scrubbing, the son brings wood for the fireplace, and the daughter carries in more clothes to be washed. The last scene shows all three standing around the rocking chair making menacing gestures at the father. This film was a novelty and was intended as a replacement for slides for a song hit of the same name by Lew Dockstader.

Everybody Works But Father (Whiteface)

AM&B © H68124   Oct. 13, 1905

Cameraman: G. W. Bitzer

Location: Studio, N.Y.C. *Photographed:* Oct. 20, 1905

66 ft.   FLA5027 (print)   FRA1988 (neg.)

The story of this film concerns a father who will not work and his wife, daughter, and son, all of whom work hard. The film begins when father enters a set built as the interior of a poor man's cabin, walks to a rocking chair, and sits down. His wife comes in and begins washing clothes. His daughter brings in more clothes, and the son brings an armload of wood. All during the film, the woman is busy at the washtub, the young girl brings in more washing, and the son carries in wood he has chopped. At the end of the film, the whole family stands angrily around father, who ignores them completely. The cast of this film played without makeup, while the other version, using the same set and props, was played in blackface. This film was a novelty intended to replace slides for singing Lew Dockstader's song hit of the same name.

Everybody Works But Mother

AM&B © H71424 Dec. 30, 1905
Cameraman: F. A. Dobson
Location: Studio, N.Y.C. *Photographed:* Dec. 23, 1905
20 ft. FLA3856 (print) FRA1068 (neg.)

A man is sitting in a chair and reading a newspaper. On one side of him is a piano and on the other side, closest to the camera position, is a bench with a washtub and wringer on it. A robust woman of ample proportions enters the room and gestures to the man that he is to start working on the washtub. She seats herself at the piano and begins playing. The man at the washtub stops his work and the woman stops playing the piano, comes over, takes him by the scruff of the neck and dunks his face in the soapy water. As the film ends, it shows consternation on the man's face and amusement on the woman's.

The Eviction

Gaumont (England) © AM&B H47465 June 23, 1904
Director: Alfred Collins
84 ft. FLA5028 (print) FRA1989 (neg.)

The film begins with an insert of a legal eviction notice written by the King's court. The film is built around the tenants resisting the police when they attempt to enforce the eviction. The neighbors of those about to be evicted also join in the fight, and all of them chase and fight the police continually. The film ends with the man who served the eviction notice being hauled away unconscious in a wheelbarrow.

The Evidence Secured

See: The Divorce

The Evidence Was Against Him

AM&B © H16343 Apr. 10, 1902
Cameraman: F. S. Armitage
Date: Dec. 7, 1900
10 ft. FLA4175 (print) FRA1340 (neg.)

A man hangs a suit of clothes outside a set of a store front where there is a sign reading "Used Clothing for Sale." While the proprietor is arranging the merchandise, a man in a derby hat and a dark suit comes along. They talk and enter the store. A moment before they go in the store, the customer drops a cigar on the sidewalk, and a tramp spies it. The tramp attempts to relight his rescued cigar butt and the customer comes out of the store and notices him. The customer makes a magician's pass causing a suit hanging on the "For Sale" rack to transfer itself to the ragged tramp. When the proprietor sees the tramp wearing his suit, he calls the police. The evidence being what it is, the policeman goes off with the tramp in his new suit.

The Evil Art, or, Gambling Exposed, parts 1–3

Eureka Feature Film Company © J172399 Aug. 7, 1912
1,173 ft. FLA5926 (print) FRA2795 (neg.)

Gambling with cards, roulette, faro, and a number wheel is shown in this film. The producer attempted to introduce a story involving a man who loses a great deal of money to a gambler who tricks him into entering a crooked gambling establishment. The film ends with a statement that the man who lost so much money would never gamble again because he has now seen the various devices added to different pieces of gambling equipment to reduce the element of chance for the gambling house proprietor.

The Ex-Convict

Edison © H53489-53496 Nov. 19, 1904
Cameraman: Edwin S. Porter
Location: N.Y.C.; Orange, N.J. *Photographed:* Nov. 2–16, 1904
293 ft. Individual chapters:
  Leaving Home FLA4701 (print)
  Looking for Employment FLA4707 (print)
  Discharged FLA4577 (print)
  The Rescue FLA4845 (print)
  Discouraged FLA4578 (print)
  Desperation FLA4574 (print)
  The Burglary FLA4524 (print)
  A Friend at Last FLA4633 (print)

This film is made up of eight separate parts, each with a title, and each with a separate copyright number. The picture is significant because it was produced and directed by Edwin S. Porter, who also made the Great Train Robbery. It has all the elements that make a film successful today, but in primitive form. Lacking the medium of sound, one sentence titles were used to indicate the contents of each chapter. The story is of an ex-convict who finds it difficult to obtain work, so that his wife and child are starving. In desperation, he turns to crime. He looks for a likely place to rob and, in the process, rescues a rich man's daughter from sure death under the wheels of an automobile. Later that night he burglarizes the rich man's house, is captured, and is identified by the young daughter. The wealthy man prevents the police from arresting him, and the film ends with the ex-convict now employed in a decent job.

Examination Day at School

Biograph © J145990 Sept. 30, 1910
Director: D. W. Griffith *Cameraman:* G. W. Bitzer
Cast: Kate Bruce, William J. Butler, Verner Clarges, Adele De Garde, Eddie Dillon, Robert Harron, Lottie Pickford, W. Chrystie Miller, Jack Pickford, Mary Pickford, Gertrude Robinson, Mack Sennett, Dorothy West
Location: Studio, N.Y.C.; Westfield, N.J. *Photographed:* Aug. 23 and 27, 1910
371 ft. FLA5361 (print) FRA6432 (neg.)

This mildly nostalgic comedy is about a country teacher in a one-room school who is discharged by the county school board on the grounds that he is too old to discipline the class. The charges are brought when some of the children draw a picture of the head of the school board on the blackboard while the schoolteacher is telling them to behave. The climax of the picture comes when the children refuse to cooperate with his replacement and instead go to the school board where they demand that their teacher be reinstated. When the school board approves, they go en masse to the house of the old teacher to ask him to return. There are two interiors in the picture. The balance of the scenes were photographed outside.

Excavating for a New York Foundation

AM&B © H38561 Nov. 25, 1903
Location: N.Y.C.
68 ft. FLA5029 (print) FRA1990 (neg.)

The film, photographed from a single camera position, shows the method of digging and removing dirt for the basement foundation of a building under construction in New York City.

Excavating Scene at the Pyramids of Sakkarah

Edison © H32799 June 17, 1903
Cameraman: A. C. Abadie
Location: Sakkarah, Egypt *Photographed:* Mar. 27, 1903
32 ft. FLA3533 (print) FRA0809 (neg.)

The film was photographed from a single camera position. In the background approximately fifty natives are carrying baskets of sand and dumping them into a pile. A pyramid can be seen in back of the laborers.

Excavation for Subway

AM&B © H29161 Mar. 11, 1903
Cameraman: Robert K. Bonine
Location: Union Square, N.Y.C. *Date:* Nov. 11, 1902
32 ft. FLA3375 (print) FRA0677 (neg.)

The film was photographed from a single camera position, elevated to make possible a good view of the excavation of what appears to be a large tunnel. There are cranes, horse-drawn vehicles, as well as electrical and internal combustion machines.

Exchange of Mail at Rural P.O., U.S.P.O.

AM&B © H34982 Aug. 22, 1903
Cameraman: A. E. Weed
Location: Westminster, Md. *Photographed:* Aug. 10, 1903
28 ft. FLA3878 (print, copy 1) FLA5982 (print, copy 2) FRA1089 (neg.)

The opening scene shows a yard in front of what seems to be a two-story house. A small boy is standing in front of the house near a post box fastened to one of the columns supporting the roof of the building. A horse-drawn rural delivery wagon drives up and a man gets out, delivers mail, gets back in, and drives the wagon out of the scene.

Excursion Boats, Naval Parade

Edison © 52052 Sept. 3, 1898
Location: New York Harbor, N.Y. *Photographed:* Aug. 20, 1898
30 ft FLA4284 (print) FRA1437(neg.)

[Spanish-American War; New York City Welcome to Admiral Sampson's Fleet After Battle of Santiago Bay]

While the condition of the film is fair, its short length, plus the confusion caused by the many vessels passing the camera, does not permit a detailed description. The first thing seen in the film is a steam motor-sailer in the foreground. It steams on a course past the camera position. However, excursion boats and large ferry boats obscure the camera's view.

An Execution by Hanging

AM&B © H69962 Dec. 12, 1905

Cameraman: F. A. Dobson
Location: Studio, N.Y.C. *Photographed:* Dec. 1, 1905
32 ft FLA3223 (print) FRA0547 (neg.)

This film, photographed from a single camera position, shows what appears to be a public execution of a woman. The set looks legitimate and so does the execution. However, there is some stop action photography before the actual springing of the trap. To be on the safe side, the producer, AM&B, photographed two films: An Execution by Hanging and Reprieve from the Scaffold. Mrs. May Rogers, convicted murderess, actually was granted a reprieve at the last moment.

See also: Reading the Death Sentence and Reprieve from the Scaffold

Execution of a Spy

AM&B © H24896 Dec. 9, 1902
Cameraman: Arthur Marvin
Location: Roof studio, N.Y.C. *Date:* July 18, 1900
18 ft FLA3769 (print) FRA1013 (neg.)

This shows an execution by gun fire, photographed from a single camera position. In the presence of a priest, American Army troops in standard military position fire upon a man who is bound and blindfolded.

Execution of Czolgosz, with Panorama of Auburn Prison

Edison © H10605 Nov. 9, 1901
Location: Studio, N.Y.C.; Auburn, N.Y.
84 ft FLA4609 (print) FRA1638 (neg.)

[Leon Czolgosz, President McKinley's Assassin]

The film begins by showing railroad cars in the foreground with the overshadowing walls of a state prison in the background. The second camera position, from a higher elevation, pans slowly showing the yard interior of the prison and some of the large buildings. There is a dissolve from the exterior to the interior, a set of a stone wall with an iron barred door. Uniformed men are visible; they open the door and remove a man in civilian clothes. The camera then dissolves to another set in which there is a chair with wires attached. The man in civilian clothes is brought in and strapped to the chair. At the end of the film, two of the six witnesses examine him with stethoscopes.

"Exempt" of Brooklyn, N.Y.

AM&B © H30747 Apr. 24, 1903
Cameraman: F. S. Armitage
Location: Brooklyn, N.Y. *Date:* Aug. 1899
16 ft FLA3141 (print) FRA0474 (neg.)

There is no reason discernible from the film title for the estimated fifty persons teamed into two groups working an alternate man-powered pumper unit.

See also: "Oceans" Fire Company

Exhibition Drill, New York Firemen, Union Square

AM&B © H47294 June 17, 1904
Cameraman: Arthur Marvin
Location: Union Square, N.Y.C. *Photographed:* June 8, 1904
40 ft FLA4610 (print) FRA1639 (neg.)

The film begins from a camera position over the heads of spectators standing on the sidewalk in Union Square, New York City, watching a fire drill. Three pieces of equipment can be seen from the first camera position. The next scene, from another camera position, shows the equipment at the station, and water can be seen coming out of the nozzles held by firemen. Beyond them, spectators can be seen on the other side of the square.

Exhibition of Prize Winners
Edison © 60595 Oct. 25, 1897
Location: Oceans Ave. Long Branch, N.J.
24 ft FLA3870 (print) FRA1081 (neg.)

The camera position was across the track from a spectators' stand at what was either a horse show or a fair ground. Approaching the camera can be seen a large carriage drawn by three horses followed by two- and four-wheeled vehicles, each being drawn by a horse demonstrating a gait to the people in the stands.

Expert Bag Punching
AM&B © H33886 July 28, 1903
Cameraman: G. W. Bitzer
Cast: Gus Keller
Date: July 20, 1903
48 ft FLA4611 (print) FRA1640 (neg.)

The camera was positioned as if it were a spectator watching a vaudeville act. Gus Keller is punching a single bag suspended over his head. During the course of the film, he hits the punching bag with his knees, his head, his elbow, and also punches three bags simultaneously. Each action was connected by a photographic dissolve.

The Expiation
Biograph © J133582 Oct. 23, 1909
Director: D. W. Griffith *Cameraman:* G. W. Bitzer
Cast: Marion Leonard, Owen Moore, Arthur Johnson, Mack Sennett
Location: Studio, N.Y.C. *Photographed:* Sept. 15–16, 1909
42 ft FLA5362 (print) FRA2278 (neg.)

The story, photographed on three sets, shows a husband, very drunk, being brought home by two male friends, one of whom is enamored of his wife. The friend, a man of character, decides to go away rather than be a source of friction to the couple he regards highly. He goes to say goodbye, and the wife rushes toward him for consolation. The inebriated husband misunderstands the gesture and thinks they are in love. He takes a last drink, toasts them, writes a note wishing them well, and shoots himself. The film ends with a scene of the anguished wife who believes her involuntary indiscretion and not his alcoholic indulgence has been the cause of her husband's suicide.

Exploding a Whitehead Torpedo
Edison © D10161 May 12, 1900
Location: Newport, R.I.
18 ft FLA3928 (print) FRA1142 (neg.)

The title indicates that this film is of a torpedo exploding. However, there is no water wake shown to indicate that this is so.
See also: Discharging a Whitehead Torpedo

Exterior of Klingsons's Castle
See: Parsifal

The Extra Turn
Edison © H36496 Oct. 3, 1903
Cameraman: Edwin S. Porter
Location: Studio, N.Y.C. *Photographed:* Sept. 16, 1903
34 ft FLA4612 (print) FRA1641 (neg.)

This film was photographed as if from a vaudeville audience. A young woman in a short white dancing dress is on stage. To the left of the stage where she is dancing is a theater box with four occupants in evening clothes. The spectators in the box enjoy the young woman's performance to such an extent that they throw her a bouquet of flowers. After her act is completed and she leaves, a man in evening clothes comes out on the stage and starts to sing, but is pelted with vegetables, programs, and hats. He leaves the stage but returns with an umbrella which he holds over his head to fend off the produce that is being thrown at him by the displeased audience. Two members of the stage crew finally drag the reluctant singer from the stage.

Extraordinary Illusions
See: Illusions Fantasmagoriques

The Face at the Window
Biograph © J142395 June 18, 1910
Directors: D. W. Griffith *Cameraman:* G. W. Bitzer
Cast: Linda Arvidson, Harry Cashman, Verner Clarges, Joe Graybill, Grace Henderson, James Kirkwood, Alfred Paget, Billy Quirk, Gertrude Robinson, Mack Sennett, Henry B. Walthall, Charles West
Location: Studio, N.Y.C. *Photographed:* May 10–14, 1910
421 ft FLA5364 (print) FRA2280 (neg.)

The story line is built around a complete cycle of events. The son of a wealthy man is invited to become a member of an exclusive social club. He soon meets and marries an artist's model who had spent much of her time in drinking and riotous living. They have a son. The husband deserts her and, as the film progresses, he becomes a drunken derelict and outcast from his social level. His wife dies, and their son is brought up in rich and luxurious surroundings by the grandfather. The film ends as the grandfather, derelict son, and grandson are reunited at the same exclusive social club. The derelict, in his sodden wanderings, looks in the window of the club and his erstwhile friends invite him to join them. He comes in and dies in the arms of his son while his father looks on.

Facial Expression
Edison © H13362 Jan. 27, 1902
29 ft FLA3975 (print) FRA1182 (neg.)

This film was photographed so close to the actress that only her face is visible. For the whole film, she distorts her face and makes grimaces.

Faded Lilies
Biograph © H128253 June 12, 1909
Director: D. W. Griffith *Cameraman:* G. W. Bitzer
Cast: Mary Pickford, Billy Quirk, Herbert Yost, Frank Powell, Jeanie Macpherson, Owen Moore
Location: Studio, N.Y.C. *Photographed:* May 15–26, 1909
175 ft FLA5365 (print) FRA2279 (neg.)

The opening scene is of a party, with several well-dressed persons being entertained by a violinist. The musician falls in love with his hostess, who gives him some lilies. The violinist takes this to mean more than it really does, and when he learns of her engagement to another, is taken ill. From his hospital room, he summons her, and she arrives just in time to see him die.

A Fair Exchange

Biograph © J132094 Sept. 22, 1909

Director: D. W. Griffith *Cameraman:* G. W. Bitzer

Cast: James Kirkwood, Mack Sennett, Tony O'Sullivan, Verner Clarges, Billy Quirk, Kate Bruce, Gladys Egan, Owen Moore, George Nicholls, Adele De Garde

Location: Cuddebackville, N.Y.; Studio, N.Y.C. *Photographed:* Aug. 14 and 23, 1909

377 ft. FLA5366 (print) FRA2667 (neg.)

This free adaptation from George Eliot's novel *Silas Marner*, tells the story of a cobbler (James Kirkwood) who is accused of robbing a dying friend. Embittered, he moves to another section of the country, and hoards his money, which he buries on the hearth. He, too, is robbed. A starving little girl, whose mother has died, wanders into his hut through the open door, and he finds her asleep where the gold had been. Recompensed for the loss of his gold, the misanthrope reverts to his former kindly self. There are some outdoor scenes, and artistically lighted interiors.

A Fair Exchange Is No Robbery

Edison © 42265 June 28, 1899

37 ft. FLA4613 (print) FRA1642 (neg., copy 1) FRA1643 (neg., copy 2)

As the film begins, a horse and carriage can be seen in front of a porch outside a house. A man is asleep in the carriage. Two young boys appear, unhitch the horse from the vehicle and lead it away. They return leading a full-grown male goat which they hitch to the shafts of the carriage. The man who had been sleeping in the wagon now wakes and gets out, unhitches the goat, and walks away.

A Fair Rebel

Klaw & Erlanger © LP3039 May 21, 1914

Based on a play by Harry Mawson

Cast: Charles West, Charles Perley, H. Elsky, Linda Arvidson, Clara T. Bracey, Walter Lewis, Dorothy Gish, G. Pierce, Robert Drouet, Jack Brammall, Florence Ashbrook, Frank Opperman

1,228 ft. FLA5927 (print) FRA2796 (neg.)

The story is of a conflict between love and duty when two young men, good friends at West Point, find themselves on opposite sides during the Civil War. The southerner's cousin is engaged to the northern young man and when he is captured and jailed, she conspires to free him. She disguises herself as a sentry and is wounded by her cousin, but succeeds in helping her lover escape from prison.

The Fairyland: or, The Kingdom of the Fairies

Méliès © H35851 Sept. 3, 1903

Creator: Georges Méliès

Cast: Georges Méliès, Bleuette Bernon

Location: Montreuil, France *Photographed:* Summer 1903

Original title: Le Royaume des Fées

403 ft. FLA5368 (print) FRA2282 (neg.)

"The Kingdom of the Fairies" is one of Georges Méliès's foremost contributions to the early film world. The film runs the full gamut of photographic trick effects, from stop action through lap dissolves, fades, wipes, table-top miniatures, etc. Méliès did not use chapters for his films but instead had a tableau of each scene; and he ended each scene with a dissolve that opened into the succeeding scene. In this film, he extended himself both in unusual camera uses and costumes.

Faithful

Biograph © J139617 Mar. 28, 1910

Director: D. W. Griffith *Cameramen:* G. W. Bitzer, Arthur Marvin

Cast: Florence Barker, Arthur Johnson, Mack Sennett

Location: Hollywood, Calif.; Studio, Los Angeles *Photographed:* Feb. 10, 11, 12 and 16, 1910

408 ft. FLA5369 (print) FRA2287 (neg.)

This film is based on the old Chinese belief that if you save a person's life, he is your responsibility forever. In this instance, the hero (Arthur Johnson) attempts to become engaged to the heroine (Miss Barker). On the way home from one of their meetings, his chauffeur-driven automobile runs down a poor, simple-minded type (Mack Sennett). The hero feels guilty, so he buys him clothing and feeds him. For the remainder of the film, Mr. Johnson cannot get away from Mr. Sennett, who obviously adores him. Sennett continues to make a pest of himself until Miss Barker's house catches on fire, and he saves her. She is now willing to marry Arthur Johnson, even though Mack Sennett seems to be part of the bargain.

Fake Beggar

Edison © 46697 Aug. 5, 1898 20 ft. FLA4198 (print) FRA1361 (neg.)

The cameraman placed his camera on the sidewalk of a section of a busy business district in order to photograph this film. The establishing scene is of a legless beggar leading a man with a sign on his chest reading "Help the Blind." They stop near the camera and, as the film progresses, several people pass by and drop coins in the blindman's cup. One passer-by drops a coin that hits the sidewalk instead of the cup and a policeman standing nearby notices that the blindman reaches out and picks it up. The policeman attempts to arrest the blindman and takes hold of his coat, but the blindman wriggles out of it and runs down the street with the policeman in close pursuit.

The Fall of Black Hawk

American Film Manufacturing Co. © J170709 June 20, 1912

Director: William Lee

Cast: Harry Launsdale

23 ft. FLA5370 (print) FRA2703 (neg.)

All of the scenes were shot outdoors. They are very short, consist of tableaux rather than action or movement of actors, and show the conflict between the whites and the Indians. One scene is of a conference around a campfire that is attended by both white men and Indians.

Falls of Minnehaha

Edison © 43416   July 31, 1897
Location: Minneapolis, Minn. [?]
24 ft   FLA3024 (print)   FRA0130 (neg.)

A full view of the complete spillway of the waterfall can be seen. Between the waterfall and the camera position is a railing. Several people, watching the movement of the waterfall, are standing at the railing.

A False Alarm in the Dressing Room

AM&B © H35627   Sept. 12, 1903
Cameraman: A. E. Weed
Location: Studio, N.Y.C. *Photographed:* Aug. 26, 1903
19 ft   FLA4121 (print)   FRA1297 (neg.)

A set of a combination bedroom and living room, furnished with a bed, tables, chairs, and a dressing screen is visible. A woman enters the room, puts on false whiskers, a man's hat and coat, and goes behind the screen. The picture continues as two young women enter the room and begin removing their clothes. When they have nearly finished, the head and shoulders of the person with the whiskers, coat, and hat appear over the top of the screen, causing the two to run screaming from the room to summon help. The picture ends as they return with a man, who accosts the person behind the screen. The prankster removes her hat and false whiskers, revealing a member of the family.

Family Troubles

AM&B © H30719   Apr. 24, 1903
Cameraman: Arthur Marvin
Location: Roof studio, N.Y.C. *Date:* Sept. 11, 1900
7 ft   FLA3149 (print)   FRA0482 (neg.)

A man and a woman are sitting at what appears to be a breakfast table in a set of the kitchen of a modest house. The man unfolds a newspaper, begins to read, drinks from a cup, spits out the mouthful, puts the cup down and shakes his finger in annoyance at the woman. He then stands up and throws down the newspaper. The woman on the other side of the table gets up, picks up what apparently is a pie, and shoves it into the face of the man.

A Famous Escape

AM&B © H108356   Apr. 3, 1908
Cameraman: G. W. Bitzer
Location: Studio, N.Y.C. *Photographed:* Mar. 27 and 30, 1908
290 ft.   FLA5371 (print)   FRA2282 (neg.)

The story, an incident in the Civil War, begins by showing some Union troops saying goodbye to their families as they march off to war. This is followed by scenes showing their capture in battle and their incarceration in a military prison in the South. The prisoners dig a tunnel to make their escape, and the film ends with a scene of them embracing their families, having reached home safely.

Fancy Diving

AM&B © H21495   Sept. 5, 1902
Cameraman: Raymond Ackerman
Location: Mt. Tom Bath House, N.Y.C. *Date:* Aug. 10, 1899
20 ft.   FLA4252 (print)   FRA1408 (neg.)

The film, photographed from a single camera position, shows what appears to be a public swimming pool. Several persons with little or no diving ability jump off a three-foot diving board in a disorganized fashion. The film was registered for copyright with the title "Fancy Driving," but it was released as "Fancy Diving."

Fancy Driving

AM&B © H17628   May 15, 1902
Cameraman: F. S. Armitage
Location: Bay Shore, L.I., N.Y. *Date:* Dec. 2, 1901
20 ft.   FLA4253 (print)   FRA1409 (neg.)

Six horses, harnessed to a vehicle of the stagecoach type, are driven in circles and figure eights around white posts. The film was photographed from a single camera position. The driver was Morris Howlett.

Et Farligt Spil

See: A Dangerous Play

The Farmer and the Bad Boys

Edison © H8014   Aug. 22, 1901
19 ft.   FLA3699 (print)   FRA0948 (neg.)

Four boys, grouped in a circle in front of a large appliance store, are matching pennies. A man dressed as a country rube stops to view the items on display in the store window. The boys begin molesting him and the picture ends as a policeman breaks up the fight.

Farmer Kissing the Lean Girl

Edison © 52061   Sept. 3, 1898
20 ft.   FLA3564 (print)   FRA0840 (neg.)

In the center of a set of an unfurnished front room of a modest house, an old man wearing a beard and costumed as a rube or country bumpkin is standing while beside him is a tall, slender young woman made up to appear equally grotesque. The young woman leans over and kisses the old man; he shakes himself until his hat falls off his head and a handkerchief flies out of his pocket.

Farmer Oatcake Has His Troubles

AM&B © H16356   Apr. 10, 1902
Cameramen: G. W. Bitzer, Arthur Marvin
Photographed: Apr. 25, 1899
10 ft.   FLA4259 (print)   FRA1415 (neg.)

Two young women, one old man, and one young man are working in front of a set of the interior of a barn. The young women are collecting hay and the two men are tying a bag of flour to an overhead pulley rope. The old man gestures to the two women to help him and the young boy lift the bag to the overhead loft, but as the bag reaches a point directly overhead, it breaks, spilling flour over all four, thereby ending the film.

A Farmer's Imitation of Ching Ling Foo

AM&B © H24894   Dec. 9, 1902
Cameraman: Arthur Marvin
Location: Roof studio, N.Y.C. *Date:* Aug. 2, 1900
14 ft.   FLA3484 (print)   FRA0765 (neg.)

In a rural area, a small man dressed as a farmer with a white bandana around his head is jumping up and down. Under his arm is a quilt which he holds up, displaying both sides as if he were a magician. He lowers the quilt revealing a young woman in a middy blouse and black bloomers. She becomes his assistant and picks up one end of the quilt. This time, a young lady and a white donkey appear as they drop the quilt. They raise and lower the quilt again; the donkey disappears, and in its stead are two more young ladies, who perform acrobatic tricks, handsprings, etc., for the balance of the film.

The Fascinating Mrs. Francis
AM&B © H121876 Jan. 22, 1909
Director: D. W. Griffith *Cameraman:* G. W. Bitzer
Cast: Mack Sennett, Linda Arvidson, Marion Leonard, Charles West, Florence Lawrence, John Cumpson
Location: Studio, N.Y.C. *Photographed:* Jan. 9, 1909
161 ft.   FLA5372 (print)   FRA2286 (neg.)

The leading woman is a fascinating and attractive young woman who enjoys high society life, parties, and large groups of admirers. Her actions are a constant source of irritation and discouragement to her family who want her to lead a respectable, settled married life. During the course of the film, her father warns her constantly as to what will happen eventually if she persists in such behavior. The film ends by showing the heroine alone in a chair holding a faded rose, while all her friends have forsaken her and no longer seek her company.

Fast Mail, Northern Pacific R.R.
Edison © 68009 Dec. 6, 1897
27 ft.   FLA3059 (print)   FRA0404 (neg.)

The single camera position shows a locomotive pulling a baggage car and six passenger cars past some people standing alongside the track. They obscure a sign reading "Fast Mail Northern Pacific" on the train as it goes by.

Fastest Wrecking Crew in the World
AM&B © H32498 June 11, 1903
Cameraman: Wallace McCutcheon [?]
Location: N.Y., N.H. and H.R.R., Roxbury, Mass. *Photographed:* Fall 1897
23 ft.   FLA3711 (print)   FRA0958 (neg.)

The photographer placed his camera in such a position that it encompassed a steam locomotive, a coal car, and a large derrick on a flat car. As the film progresses, the locomotive begins to move, and men are seen running toward it and getting on the large crane on the flat car. The film is too short to permit further description except that the locale was a railroad yard.

The Fat and Lean Wrestling Match
Edison © H11474 Dec. 14, 1901
Cameraman: Edwin S. Porter
36 ft   FLA4131 (print)   FRA1303 (neg.)

The camera was placed as if in the audience at a vaudeville show. First seen are a stage and a backdrop painted to resemble a garden wall. A large, fat man in white wrestling trunks, and a short, slender man in the same costume enter from the wings. The entire film consists of special camera effects. The fat man falls on the slender man and mashes him flat, then he rolls the slender man up and, before the eyes of the audience, the slender man unrolls and becomes a man again. Several special effect tricks culminate with the parts of a dismembered body rejoining one another and coming to life.

Fat Bather and Treacherous Springboard
AM&B © H33545 July 18, 1903
10 ft.   FLA3586 (print)   FRA0858 (neg.)

The first scene takes place at a large reservoir with a springboard in the immediate foreground. A woman in a long dress and a hat walks out to the end of the springboard, kneels down, and apparently talks to someone in the water. The head and shoulders of a man appear; he swims toward the board. The swimmer reaches up from the water and takes hold of the diving board. His weight causes it to bend. The woman loses her balance and falls into the water.

The Fat Girl's Love Affair
AM&B © H68184 Nov. 3, 1905
Cameraman: G. W. Bitzer
Location: Studio, N.Y.C. *Photographed:* Oct. 24, 1905
20 ft.   FLA3918 (print)   FRA1134 (neg.)

The story line of this film is based on the ridiculous possibilities of the romance of an excessively fat woman. A man of small stature in evening dress enters a set of a living room, sits down, and starts to read. A particularly large woman joins him, and he stretches out his arms in a futile attempt to embrace her. The fat woman seems willing but the man gives up in frustration and is seen leaving to the considerable dismay of the fat woman.

See also: Airy Fairy Lillian Tries on Her New Corsets and Rat Trap Pickpocket Detector

The Fatal Blow
See: Ten Nights in a Bar-Room

The Fatal Hour
AM&B © H114372 Aug. 8, 1908
Director: D. W. Griffith *Cameraman:* Arthur Marvin
Cast: Frank Gebhardt, Linda Arvidson
Location: Fort Lee, N.J.; Studio, N.Y.C. *Photographed:* July 21 and 27, 1908
309 ft.   FLA5373 (print)   FRA2287 (neg.)

An attractive young woman is kidnapped by some Chinese white slavers. Another young woman, a police operative, is determined to rescue her. Successful in her attempt, the rescuer ends by being made a prisoner herself. The white slavers, as punishment for calling the police, plan to make her the victim of a pistol shot to be triggered by the hands of a clock. The heroine is rescued by the police seconds before the hands of the clock reach the "fatal hour."

The Fatal Wedding
Klaw & Erlanger © LP2469 Jan. 19, 1914
Director: Lawrence Marston
Cast: Walter Miller, Claire McDowell, Charles Hill Mailes, Irene Howley, Millicent Evans, Elaine Ivans, Mrs. L. Marston
From the play by Theodore Kremer
1,274 ft.   FLA5928 (print)   FRA2797 (neg.)

This three-reel melodrama is built around a conspiracy between a man and a woman who wants to become the wife of her cousin, already married to her best friend. The villainous pair arrange to compromise the wife, and a divorce follows. After a reasonable number of years, the exhusband promises to marry his cousin if she can locate his children who were hidden by his estranged wife. The cousin succeeds in finding the children, and the wedding ceremony is starting in the church, when the divorced wife locates a promissory note that proves she was compromised. The film ends as the little family is happily reunited. This was the first of the Klaw & Erlanger productions.

Fate of a Gossip

AM&B © H33647 July 21, 1903

Cameraman: G. W. Bitzer

Photographed: July 11, 1903

30 ft. FLA3461 (print) FRA0743 (neg.)

Three pajama-clad girls are filling a lamp chimney with soot on a set of a bedroom. They put the soot-filled lamp chimney back in its place near the ceiling and then hide. An older woman enters, places a chair in a position to retrieve the lamp, strikes a match, and lifts the chimney, showering herself with soot.

The Fate of the Artist's Model, parts 1 through 5

AM&B © H37315-H37319 Oct. 26, 1903

Cameraman: G. W. Bitzer

Location: Studio, N.Y.C. *Photographed:* Oct. 7 and 8, 1903

100 ft. part 1 FLA4614 (print) FRA1644 (neg.)
100 ft. part 2 FLA4615 (print) FRA1645 (neg.)
100 ft. part 3 FLA4616 (print) FRA1646 (neg.)
100 ft. part 4 FLA4617 (print) FRA1647 (neg.)
100 ft. part 5 FLA4618 (print) FRA1648 (neg.)

This melodrama in five parts begins with an artist painting at an easel in front of a painted park scene. Passers-by stop to look at his work. A young lady is particularly impressed with his work, and he is impressed with her beauty. The first part ends with the artist and the young woman walking off together. The next three scenes take place in the artist's studio. The young woman has become his model and, as the film progresses so does the ardent love affair between the two. However, by the end of the fourth chapter the artist is no longer interested in his beautiful model and orders her out of the studio, even after she pleads with him on her bended knee. The last chapter shows a set of the exterior of a house during a snowstorm, where the model, now a mother, is walking unsteadily as she clutches her baby to her bosom. She is footsore and weary. She knocks on the door and collapses. A woman comes out of the house, puts her arms around the young woman and her baby and takes them inside.

Fate's Interception

Biograph © J197954 Apr. 8, 1912

Director: D. W. Griffith *Cameraman:* G. W. Bitzer

Cast: Mary Pickford, Wilfred Lucas, Charles Hill Mailes, Harry Hyde, Robert Harron, W. J. Butler

Location: Southern California

400 ft. FLA0004 (print) FLA0116 (neg.)

The opening title indicates the locale of the picture is Mexico, while a second title explains that an American engineer, played by Wilfred Lucas, has been sent there by his firm. Lucas boards in the same house as Mary Pickford, a Mexican maiden. He begins to see her socially, and she falls in love with him. When the American is recalled to the States, he refuses to take her along. Angered, she promises marriage to one of her suitors if he will murder the engineer. She soon realizes what she has done and attempts to stop the engineer from being killed. There is a frantic carriage ride. Mary arrives to find her suitor dead from the effects of gas inhalation from a gas jet he blew out instead of turning off, but the American engineer is safe. When the engineer understands just how much the Mexican girl really loves him, he decides to take her back to the United States with him.

Fate's Turning

Biograph © J151150 Jan. 25, 1911

Director: D. W. Griffith *Cameraman:* G. W. Bitzer

Cast: Dorothy Bernard, Claire McDowell, Linda Arvidson, Lottie Pickford, Charles West, Dorothy West, Donald Crisp, Arthur Johnson

Location: Studio, N.Y.C. *Photographed:* Dec. 3-6, 1910

388 ft. FLA5375 (print) FRA2283 (neg.)

The son of a wealthy and prominent socialite has a nervous breakdown and his father sends him out West to recuperate. He meets a young waitress, becomes enamored, and has an affair with her. He is then summoned home by his attorney, and reaches home just before his father dies. He writes a letter to the waitress breaking their engagement and takes up with the young woman to whom he had been engaged before his illness. They proceed with their marriage plans. But during the ceremony, the waitress, with his child in her arms, shows up at the church. Instead of marrying him to his fiancée, the minister marries him to the waitress, who is still holding the child.

Father Gets in the Game

AM&B © H116386 Oct. 1, 1908

Director: D. W. Griffith *Cameraman:* G. W. Bitzer

Cast: Mack Sennett, Linda Arvidson, Charles Gorman, Jeanie Macpherson, Harry Salter

Location: Studio and Central Park, N.Y.C. *Photographed:* Sept. 3, 1908

283 ft. FLA5376 (print) FRA2285 (neg.)

The story line is built around the rejuvenation of a dejected and dispirited old man. He is incapable of accepting any suggestions for happiness from his friends and just stays home and broods. One day his barber suggests that his beard be removed, his hair dyed black, and a mustache added. When this is accomplished, the remodeled old man goes out on the town to test the results. After several social encounters in which he is hit by women's umbrellas and beat up by their escorts, he finally retreats to his home, where the female members of his family seem impressed enough with his new appearance to satisfy his ego. This is probably the first moving picture in which Mack Sennett had the principal role.

Fatty and Mabel at the San Diego Exposition

Keystone © LP4282 Jan. 23, 1915

Author: Mack Sennett

Cast: Roscoe Arbuckle, Minta Durfee, Harry Gribbon, Edgar Kennedy, Harry McCoy, Mabel Normand, Vivian Edwards

Location: San Diego, Calif.

385 ft. FLA5377 (print, copy 1) FLA6079 (print, copy 2) FRA2289 (neg.)

A gay comedy that begins on one of the main streets of San Diego in front of the U. S. Grant Hotel and continues at the fair grounds of the San Diego Exposition. The film sequences were photographed in the various concessions of the Exposition. One of the concessions shown is a demonstration of the rack and tank method of developing motion picture films. There is an incident involving the Royal Hawaiian dancers at the Hawaiian Village, as well as a fight around a large fountain on the Exposition grounds in which Mabel Normand, Roscoe Arbuckle, Minta Durfee, and some policemen all take part.

Fatty and Mabel's Simple Life

Keystone © LP4237 Jan. 16, 1915

Producer and Author: Mack Sennett

Cast: Roscoe Arbuckle, Mabel Normand, Al St. John, Joe Bordeaux

Location: Studio and farm in Los Angeles

807 ft. FLA6080-6081 (print) FRA2740 (neg.)

The plot of the comedy concerns a farmer with an overdue mortgage and a lovely daughter. The man who holds the mortgage has an awkward son. The rich man attempts to marry off his unattractive son to the farmer's beautiful daughter, in exchange for the mortgage payments. But the beautiful daughter, Mabel Normand, has other ideas, and after a great many comic adventures, she succeeds in getting Fatty Arbuckle for her husband instead of Al St. John.

Fatty's Chance Acquaintance

Keystone © LP4654 Mar. 8, 1915

Producer and Author: Mack Sennett

Cast: Roscoe Arbuckle, Minta Durfee, Billie Bennett, Harry McCoy, Frank Hayes, Estelle Allen, Glen Cavender

Location: Hollenbeck Park, Los Angeles

440 ft. FLA5378 (print, copy 1) FLA6082 (print, copy 2)

A tangled story of what happens when a married couple (Fatty Arbuckle and Billie Bennett) go to the park for the afternoon, and the husband starts a flirtation with a young woman (Minta Durfee) who has also come to the park to enjoy the fine weather with her boyfriend (Harry McCoy), a thief. McCoy steals Billie Bennett's purse as she sleeps, extracts the money, and goes off. While this is going on, Fatty has become involved with Minta, so he does not know his wife's purse has been rifled. But a policeman, Frank Hayes, who has been hiding in the bushes, has watched McCoy remove the money from the purse, and a chase begins. Almost at the end of the film, McCoy and Arbuckle engage in a sort of duel, using canes.

Fatty's Faithful Fido

Keystone © LP4872 Mar. 20, 1915

Producer and Author: Mack Sennett

Cast: Roscoe Arbuckle, Minta Durfee, Al St. John, Frank Hayes, Dixie Chene, Joe Bordeaux, Fido

Location: In and around the Keystone studio and Griffith Park, Los Angeles

858 ft. FLA6083 (print) FRA2290 (neg.)

In this comedy, Fatty and Al St. John are rivals for the hand of Minta Durfee. Fatty attempts to trap Al St. John. They throw rocks at one another, quite a few of which crash through the window of a nearby Chinese laundry. At a dance that night, Al St. John attempts to eliminate his rival by putting a chalk X on the back of Fatty's jacket, after he has conspired with hoodlums to beat up the person so identified. Al St. John accidentally acquires a chalk X on his back, and from there until the end of the picture, the two hoodlums, plus Fatty, St. John, and the rest of the guests at the dance participate in a gigantic brawl. By the end of the film, Fatty, Al St. John, the Chinese laundryman (Frank Hayes), and Fido all are immersed in the laundry's washtub, with Fatty cuddling the faithful Fido.

Fatty's New Role

Keystone © LP4385 Feb. 1, 1915

Producer and Author: Mack Sennett *Director:* Charles Avery

Cast: Roscoe Arbuckle, Billy Dunn, Bobby Dunn, Al St. John, Slim Summerville, Mack Swain, Joe Bordeaux, Frank Hayes, Edgar Kennedy

Location: Studio and Edendale Boulevard south of the Keystone studio, Los Angeles

409 ft. FLA6084 (print) FRA2291 (neg.)

The film begins with a scene of Fatty attired as a tramp awakening from a nap in a hayloft. After arising from bed, Fatty proceeds to the free lunch counter of a nearby saloon but is forcibly ejected when he attempts to take too much food. Customers of the saloon decide to play a joke on the owner, Mack Swain, and his bartender, Slim Summerville, by inferring that Fatty is a mad bomber who blows up saloons, and the remainder of the film is devoted to incidents that make the proprietor believe that Fatty really plans to blow up his establishment.

Fatty's Plucky Pup

Keystone © LP5776 June 28, 1915

Producer and Author: Mack Sennett

Cast: Roscoe Arbuckle, Josephine Stevens, Phyllis Allen, Al St. John, Edgar Kennedy, Joe Bordeaux, and Fido

Location: Around the Edendale studio in Los Angeles; Venice, Calif.

428 ft. FLA6068 (print) FRA2741 (neg.)

Fatty and his pet, Fido, live with his mother, Phyllis Allen, a laundress. Mother tries unsuccessfully to get some help from her son, but all he manages to do is set fire to his bed, drop her freshly washed laundry in the mud, and perform other similar antics. Fatty takes his girl, Josephine Stevens, to an amusement park, steals money from some con men who, to get even, kidnap Fatty's girl who has become separated from him. She is tied up, with a gun aimed at her head, and set to go off and kill her at a certain time. Fatty on his bicycle, Fido on all four feet, and members of the Keystone police department rush to the rescue. There is extensive use of special effects throughout the picture.

Fatty's Reckless Fling

Keystone © LP4639 Mar. 4, 1915

Producer and Author: Mack Sennett *Director:* Roscoe Arbuckle

Cast: Roscoe Arbuckle, Minta Durfee, Edgar Kennedy, Frank Hayes, Mrs. Griffith, Glen Cavender, Harry McCoy

Location: Keystone studio, Los Angeles

395 ft. FLA6087 (print) FRA2242 (neg.)

This film starts with a scene in a hotel lobby, where Fatty is seen apparently arriving home in a drunken condition. Edgar Kennedy, who later in the film plays an outraged husband, can be seen drinking in a bar off the hotel foyer. Fatty's outraged wife, Mrs. Griffith, enters the scene and herds her inebriated husband up to his room. She then puts on street clothes, locks the door, and leaves. Fatty manages to get out and join a nearby poker game. The remainder of the film is a series of sequences involving the poker players who are interrupted by the police as they play. The finale of the film shows an exhausted Fatty under water in a bathtub where he has just landed.

Fatty's Tintype Tangle

Keystone © LP5966 July 26, 1915
Producer and Author: Mack Sennett *Director:* Roscoe Arbuckle
Cast: Roscoe Arbuckle, Louise Fazenda, Norma Nichols, Edgar Kennedy, Joe Bordeaux.
Location: Echo Park Boulevard, Los Angeles
858 ft.   FLA6088-6089 (print)   FRA2742 (neg.)

This farce is made up of a series of situations that begin with the intolerable position in which Fatty finds himself vis-à-vis his mother-in-law. He can no longer stand living with her. On his way to the train station, he meets a young woman sitting on a bench (Louise Fazenda) whose husband (Edgar Kennedy) has gone to buy a newspaper. Fatty is unaware that he is being photographed by a sidewalk photographer as he talks with Louise Fazenda. Edgar Kennedy returns, sees the picture, and the chase is on. The film ends with both Fatty and Kennedy being rescued by their wives from a rain barrel into which they have fallen.

Faust and Marguerite

Edison © D4734 Feb. 28, 1900
Cameraman: Edwin S. Porter
23 ft.   FLA4218 (print)   FRA1377 (neg.)

As the film begins, two people, each in period costumes, can be seen. The man is standing, and the woman is seated in a set of a stone castle. Stop-action photography was utilized throughout to make people, such as another man and a skeleton, appear and disappear, and the seated woman becomes a standing woman while a man appears seated in her chair. The film ends as the Devil and Marguerite take part in a marriage ceremony.

See also: Faust et Marguerite

Faust aux Enfers

Méliès © H39289 Dec. 11, 1903
Creator: Georges Méliès *Cast:* Georges Méliès
Location: Montreuil, France *Photographed:* Fall 1903
U.S. title: The Damnation of Faust
188 ft.   FLA5033 (print)   FRA1994 (neg.)

This film follows the pattern of Méliès's work. In telling the story, he takes advantage of special effects and trick photography. It is similar to his first story of Faust; however, there are a few more scenes in this film, such as a different finale, and the Devil leads Faust through a few more sets.

See also: The Damnation of Faust

Faust et Marguerite

Méliès © H44096 Mar. 31, 1904

Creator: Georges Méliès *Cast:* Georges Méliès
Location: Montreuil, France *Photographed:* Spring 1904
Alternate title: Damnation du Docteur Faust
U.S. title: Faust and Marguerite
151 ft.   FLA5031 (print)   FRA1992 (neg.)

This film is another version of one made by Méliès with the same title, but there are some scenes here that do not appear in the other. The quality of the photography is much better than in copyright no. H44097 (see following film). For study and reproduction purposes, copyright no. H44096 is preferred.

Faust et Marguerite

Méliès © H44097 Mar. 31, 1904
Creator: Georges Méliès *Cast:* Georges Méliès
Location: Montreuil, France *Photographed:* Spring 1904
Alternate title: Damnation du Docteur Faust
U.S. title: Faust and Margeurite

Méliès follows the original closely. Here again he runs the gamut of stop-action photography to make devils, angels, etc., appear and disappear.

Faust Family of Acrobats

Edison © H8690 Sept. 16, 1901
34 ft.   FLA3853 (print)   FRA1065 (neg.)

The camera is located above athletic mats placed in the yard of what appears to be a school. Then a group of acrobats perform many varied tumbling tricks, individually and in pairs. At the end, the largest man is supporting the weight of six of the members of the troupe.

Feeding Geese at Newman's Poultry Farm

Edison © H13360 Jan. 27, 1902
Location: Long Island, N.Y.
31 ft.   FLA3327 (print)   FRA0639 (neg.)

The film, photographed from a single camera position, shows a large flat area adjacent to some buildings. In the background, in front of the buildings, approximately a hundred people are facing the camera and apparently watching a large flock of geese waddling nervously about. The geese make left and right turns, as if someone off camera were directing them.

Feeding Pigeons in Front of St. Mark's Cathedral, Venice, Italy

Edison © H32451 June 8, 1903
Cameraman: A. C. Abadie
Location: Venice, Italy *Photographed:* Apr. 15, 1903
38 ft.   FLA3553 (print)   FRA0829 (neg.)

The pigeons are shown as they are fed in front of the fountain. There are a great many birds, and the fountain and buildings are in the background.

Feeding Sea Gulls

Edison © 16429 Mar. 10, 1898
Location: San Francisco Bay from Oakland ferryboat
25 ft.   FLA4232 (print)   FRA1390 (neg.)

The camera was placed on the stern of a vessel progressing through the water and followed by a large flock of sea gulls.

The gulls can be seen in the wake of the vessel, as if they were being fed or were expecting to be fed.

Feeding the Bear at the Menagerie

Edison © H16655 Apr. 16, 1902

29 ft. FLA3886 (print) FRA1095 (neg.)

A caged bear is being fed by a man in street clothes. The film was photographed from single camera position. The only action occurs when the man takes food from a small paper bag and hands it through the bars to the bear.

Feeding the Russian Bear

AM&B © H37497 Nov. 2, 1903

Cameraman: G. W. Bitzer

Location: Glen Island, N.Y. *Photographed:* Oct. 25, 1903

25 ft. FLA4270 (print) FRA1425 (neg.)

The film was photographed from a single camera position over the heads of some little children who are attracted by and are feeding a large black or brown bear in a cage with other bears.

Female Crook and Her Easy Victim

AM&B © H65078 Sept. 1, 1905

Cameraman: G. W. Bitzer

Location: Studio, N.Y.C. *Photographed:* Aug. 17, 1905

17 ft. FLA3898 (print) FRA1119 (neg.)

This film concerns an attractive young woman, her male companion, and the elderly gentleman who is their victim. The set represents a downtown business district with store fronts and a bank. An old gentleman comes out of the bank and puts his wallet in his pocket, when a young woman stumbles and falls into his arms. She feigns faintness and he gallantly supports and fans her. While this is going on, the young woman steals his wallet, and, as soon as it is in her possession, her coconspirator, pretending to be an irate husband, appears and makes a scene. The film ends as the young pair go off down the street while the victim realizes he has been robbed, picks up his cane, and starts in pursuit of the nefarious pair.

The Female of the Species

Biograph © J168165 Apr. 13, 1912

Director: D. W. Griffith *Cameraman:* G. W. Bitzer

Cast: Dorothy Bernard, Claire McDowell, Mary Pickford, Charles West

Location: Calif.

369 ft. FLA5379 (print) FRA6439 (neg.)

All of this film was photographed outdoors. The first scene shows three women, a man, and a burro walking laboriously through the California desert. The man, obviously in poor health, makes advances to one of the three women who repulses him. His wife separates the two and shortly thereafter, for a reason not explained in the film, the man dies. The widow attempts to kill the young woman with a hand axe, but stops when she hears a baby crying. An infant is discovered in the arms of a dead Indian woman who has just been shot by a prospector. The last scene shows the widow embracing the child as if it were her own and, enmity forgotten, the three women continue their trek. Mary Pickford made this picture during her second period with Biograph.

Fencing Class, Missouri Valley College

AM&B © H45595 May 10, 1904

Cameraman: A. E. Weed

Location: Marshall, Mo. *Photographed:* Apr. 26, 1904

23 ft. FLA4325 (print) FRA1473 (neg.)

The camera shows an area of a playground that is part of a school. Two young women wearing protective clothing for fencing are being watched by several other young women in gymnasium attire. The young women fence throughout the extent of the film.

Ferryboat Entering Slip

AM&B © H24887 Dec. 9, 1902

20 ft. FLA3182 (print) FRA0509 (neg.)

The camera was placed at the land end of a large slip used for mooring ferries. A ferry boat with the name *Montclair* makes her approach to the slip. The *Montclair* enters the slip, approaching the camera position. Several people can be seen standing on the carriage deck of the ferryboat.

The Feud and the Turkey

AM&B © H119109 Dec. 3, 1908

Director: D. W. Griffith *Cameramen:* Arthur Marvin, G. W. Bitzer

Cast: Florence Lawrence, Linda Arvidson, Herbert Miles, Violet Mersereau, Eddie Dillon, Mack Sennett, Frank Gebhardt, Clara T. Bracey

Location: Studio, N.Y.C.; Shadyside, N.J. *Photographed:* Nov. 4, 6 and 17, 1908

333 ft. FLA5380 (print) FRA2305 (neg.)

This story of a feud between two families starts with a scene photographed on the street of a small town. A fight starts when two young girls stop to talk to two young boys, members of a family on the opposite side of the feud. The feud continues when a black farmhand steals a turkey and progresses through a love affair between the son of the leader of one clan and the daughter of the leader of the other, ending with the banishment of both the young people.

The Fickle Spaniard

Biograph © J168889 May 3, 1912

Director: Mack Sennett

Cast: Mabel Normand, Fred Mace, Claire McDowell, William J. Butler, Eddie Dillon, Dell Henderson

Location: Calif.

178 ft. FLA5398 (print)

This farce comedy revolves around a young woman (Mabel Normand), who is known in her village as an attractive young lady and a competent barber. She is enamored of a guitar-playing caballero (Fred Mace) who vows his undying love. While plying her trade, she overhears her lover wooing another señorita (Claire McDowell). Enraged, she starts a chase which ends with her petrified and fickle lover locked in his room. The camera shifts to the barbershop where an incapacitated barber hires her to take his place. The caballero comes in to get a shave and is confronted with his angry girlfriend, razor in hand. He sends for a padre and they are married as he sits in the barber chair with his face covered with lather.

15th Infantry

AM&B © H17970 May 21, 1902
Cameraman: F. S. Armitage
Location: Governors Island, N.Y. *Date:* July 24, 1900
33 ft. FLA4619 (print) FRA1649 (neg.)

Photographed from a single camera position, the film shows infantry troops as they march by. Judging from the bandoliers and khaki uniforms, the period is after the Spanish-American War.

The Fight

See: The Unfaithful Wife

A Fight for a Bride

AM&B © H69579 Dec. 7, 1905
Cameraman: F. A. Dobson
Location: Studio, N.Y.C. *Photographed:* Nov. 24, 1905
23 ft. FLA3915 (print) FRA1131 (neg.)

A young woman is sitting on a chair or bench next to the wall of a set of a living room. Kneeling in front of her are two young men in dinner clothes. Each of the young men has one of the girl's hands in his. She gets up, walks over to the table in the corner of the room and returns with two pairs of boxing gloves. The two young men put these on and begin boxing. The bout continues until one of the men is knocked down, and the winner is embraced by the young woman.

The Fight for Freedom

AM&B © H113480 July 16, 1908
Director: D.W. Griffith *Cameraman:* G. W. Bitzer
Location: Shadyside, N.J.; Studio, N.Y.C. *Photographed:* June 23–24, 1908
272 ft. FLA5381 (print) FRA2293 (neg.)

The film opens with a fight in a saloon in which a man is murdered. The unfortunate killer flees and arrives home wounded. He is hidden in the attic by his wife and mother. The posse soon arrives and takes the wife off to jail as a hostage. The hero comes down from the attic, dresses in his mother's clothes, goes to jail, and represents himself as a relative bringing food to the prisoner. While the guard checks the basket, our hero hands his wife a gun through the bars. The guard is overcome and bound and they begin their escape. A posse starts after them, and the two plan an attack and steal three horses from the posse and gallop off. But the posse approaches from another direction, and the woman is killed by their gunfire, ending the picture.

Fight in the Dormitory

AM&B © H42805 Feb. 27, 1904
Cameraman: A. E. Weed
Location: Studio, N.Y.C. *Photographed:* Feb. 17, 1904
25 ft. FLA4620 (print) FRA1650 (neg.)

The picture begins in a set of a girls' dormitory where two girls are asleep in each of the two beds. One wakes, takes her pillow, and begins hitting her companion with it. As the film continues, all four young girls become involved in the pillow fight which goes on until feathers start coming out of the cases. A tall woman in a nightgown and nightcap enters through the door and attempts to stop the fight. She is successful only in directing their enthusiasm at herself, and, as the film ends, the four girls are hitting the house mother with their pillows.

Fighting the Flames

AM&B © H48619 July 28, 1904
Cameraman: G. W. Bitzer
Location: Coney Island *Photographed:* July 21, 1904
125 ft. FLA5034 (print) FRA1995 (neg.)

The camera was placed at the head of a street so that the photographer could film the scheduled demonstration of the routine of a fire-fighting organization. The film begins with a parade down the street toward the camera position. Spectators can be seen applauding the firemen. Apparently at a signal all the spectators cross the street away from a large brick building. The remainder of the film is devoted to filming the various activities required for a fire-fighting unit to extinguish a fire.

Fighting the Flames, Dreamland

AM&B © H49061 Aug. 12, 1904
Cameraman: G. W. Bitzer
Location: Dreamland, Coney Island, N.Y. *Photographed:* July 21, 1904
110 ft. FLA5035 (print) FRA1996 (neg.)

In order to cover this story, which culminates in a series of related but not connected scenes, the cameraman had to place his equipment in many positions. There are scenes photographed at street level of people watching antique fire-equipment being drawn along the roadway by men in firemen's uniforms, as well as scenes fairly close-up of spectators applauding parading firemen. The last scenes were of a hook-and-ladder wagon and a personnel carrier arriving at a fire, which was primarily a demonstration. Men can be seen squirting water on a four-story brick building that was supposedly burning.

Fights of Nations

AM&B © H90564 Feb. 18, 1907
Cameraman: G. W. Bitzer
Location: Studio, N.Y.C. *Photographed:* Jan. 17, 19, 23 and 28, 1907
308 (print) FRA5382 (print) FRA2845 (neg.)

This is a series of vignettes or vaudeville acts directed toward a connected final scene. The producer apparently was seeking to convey the idea of the United States as a melting pot by showing a series of altercations connected with specific nations, such as a knife fight in Spain, a fist fight between Irishmen, Scots fighting with broadswords, etc. The final scene shows one or two members of all of the previous acts in front of the camera in a tableau. The tableaux are titled "Mexico vs. Spain," "Our Hebrew Friends," "A Scottish Combat," "Sunny Africa," "Eighth Avenue, New York," "Sons of the Ould Sod," and "America, Land of the Free."

A Filipino Cock Fight

AM&B © H17972 May 21, 1902
Cameraman: Robert K. Bonine
Location: Manila, Philippine Islands *Date:* Aug. 15, 1901
18 ft. FLA3830 (print) FRA1058 (neg.)

The photographer placed his camera at a low angle and directed his camera over the top of a pit designed for cock fighting. The opening scenes of the film show two fighting cocks being held sufficiently close to become aroused. They are released, and the last of the film shows the two cocks very busily engaged in fighting one another.

Filipino Scouts, Musical Drill, St. Louis

AM&B © H47292 June 17, 1904

Cameraman: A. E. Weed

Location: St. Louis, Mo. *Photographed:* June 5, 1904

74 ft. FLA5036 (print) FRA1997 (neg.)

From a single camera position, located over the heads of an assembly of musicians in the foreground, approximately three companies of uniformed troops can be seen going through a series of calisthenics in time to the music. The locale is an outdoor clearing or parade ground at the Louisiana Purchase Exposition.

Filipinos Retreat From Trenches

Edison © 37444 June 5, 1899

37 ft. FLA4369 (print) FRA1-07 (neg.)

[Spanish-American War]

The cameraman placed his equipment to convey the impression of a trench in a jungle. Many Filipino infantry troops are firing at the Americans. As the film progresses, there is a volley from rifles off camera causing a great deal of smoke. The men in the trenches adjacent to the camera fall down as if wounded or dead. At the end of the film, the trench is overrun with American troops carrying a flag.

The Final Settlement

Biograph © J138843 Mar. 3, 1910

Director: D. W. Griffith *Cameramen:* G. W. Bitzer, Arthur Marvin

Cast: Arthur Johnson, James Kirkwood, Dorothy Bernard, Tony O'Sullivan

Location: Coytesville and Fort Lee, N.J.; Studio, N.Y.C.

Photographed: Jan. 5 and 8, 1910

361 ft. FLA5385 (print) FRA2294 (neg.)

This film was photographed both indoors and out. The exteriors were taken in the winter and the camera was moved many times to photograph the various scenes. The story concerns a young woman who breaks her engagement to a young man because he drinks too much. She marries another. Years later, the former fiancé attempts to rob and molest a woman in her cabin home and then discovers she is the woman who had spurned his love because of his addiction to alcohol. An earlier altercation with her husband forces him to fight a duel. Motivated by his disgust at his wasted life, he files the projectiles from the cartridges of his revolver rather than kill the husband of the woman he had loved and lost.

Fine Feathers Make Fine Birds

Clarendon © AM&B H64926 Aug. 25, 1905

Director: Percy Stow

210 ft. FLA5383 (print) FRA2295 (neg.)

All of the scenes were photographed outdoors. The film begins as a large touring car of British manufacture arrives at the front gate of a country estate. The passengers remove their outer traveling garments, hand them to the chauffeur, and enter the gate. Shortly afterward, the maid calls the chauffeur away. Four itinerants come along, take command of the clothing and the car, and drive away. The chauffeur returns, finds the car gone, and chases them on a motorcycle. For the remainder of the film, the automobile is pursued by the chauffeur. The chase ends when the car goes into a small lake, and the occupants are apprehended by the police. The title on the original paper print is Fine Feathers Make Fine Friends. It was released in Great Britain under still another title: Willie and Tim in the Motor Car.

Fine Feathers Make Fine Friends

See: Fine Feathers Make Fine Birds

The Finish of Bridget McKeen

Edison © H1493 Mar. 1, 1901

Cameraman: Edwin S. Porter

30 ft. FLA4621 (print) FRA1651 (neg., copy 1) FRA2849 (neg., copy 2)

A fat woman can be seen fussing with an old cast-iron stove. She turns and reaches for a gallon can, removes the stopper, and pours the contents into the stove. There is an explosion, and pieces of stove and the woman descend back onto the set after the smoke clears. The next scene is a painting of a cemetery and in the foreground is a large tombstone with a jingle that reads: "Here Lie the Remains of Bridget McKeen, Who Started a Fire with Kerosene."

Finish of Futurity, 1901

AM&B © H17971 May 21, 1902

Cameraman: F. S. Armitage

Location: Sheepshead, L.I., N.Y. *Date:* Sept. 3, 1901

11 ft. FLA3783 (print) FRA1024 (neg.)

The camera was positioned in the grandstand overlooking the heads of the spectators at a horse race. During the film, approximately ten horses running at full gallop can be seen approaching and passing the camera position. The film ends showing the finish line and some of the horses in the paddock. The tote board is also visible.

Finish of the First Race, Aug. 22

AM&B © H35070 Aug. 27, 1903

Cameraman: A. E. Weed

Location: Sandy Hook, N.J. *Photographed:* Aug. 22, 1903

43 ft. FLA4622 (print) FRA1652 (neg.)

[America's Cup Races: Reliance vs. Shamrock III]

Judging by the movement of the camera, it was positioned on a small boat. There are two large sailing vessels under full racing sails maneuvering for position to come about at a turning buoy. The two yachts are such a distance from the camera that little can be seen.

Finish of Yacht Race, Aug. 25th

AM&B © H35397 Sept. 4, 1903

Cameraman: A. E. Weed

Location: Sandy Hook, N.J. *Photographed:* Aug. 25, 1903

58 ft. FLA4623 (print) FRA1653 (neg.)

[America's Cup Races: Reliance vs. Shamrock III]

The camera that filmed the two sailboats racing was in the position of the judge's boat. The distance was approximately five hundred yards, and both yachts can be seen in three sailing positions as they approach the camera.

Finishing Touches

AM&B © H19017 June 14, 1902

Cameraman: F. S. Armitage

Location: Roof studio, N.Y.C. *Date:* June 11, 1901

15 ft. FLA3688 (print) FRA0938 (neg.)

As the action starts, two rather buxom women can be seen on the stage. They are clad in leotards and are grasping the edges of a stage curtain, and then opening it. The parted curtain reveals a backdrop of a large easel with a painting on it, and a nude woman kneeling before the painting applying the finishing touches to the artwork.

Fire, Adams Express Office

AM&B © H44210 Apr. 6, 1904

Cameraman: A. E. Weed

Location: Lower Broadway, N.Y.C. *Photographed:* Mar. 26, 1904

21 ft. FLA3749 (print) FRA0995 (neg.)

The film is of poor quality and very short, so little detail can be described. The scene is heavily clouded with smoke; two or three pieces of fire-fighting apparatus squirt water into the smoke and haze.

Fire and Flames at Luna Park, Coney Island

Edison © H49193 Aug. 15, 1904

Cameraman: Edwin S. Porter

Location: Luna Park, Coney Island, N.Y. *Photographed:* Aug. 12, 1904

80 ft. FLA5037 (print) FRA1998 (neg.)

In order to photograph this film, the camera was placed far enough back from the scene and high enough from the ground to allow the lenses to pick up the scenes of the arrival of several different pieces of fire-fighting equipment, such as hook-and-ladder wagons, pumpers, personnel carts, hose carts, etc. At the beginning of the action, a simulated fire in a five-story building constructed as a tourist attraction in an amusement park, the camera photographed the arrival of the fire engines. The film records a demonstration of every form of fire apparatus known at the time, and includes people jumping from the building into rescue nets. As the film ends, a curtain is drawn to obscure the action from the spectators and the camera.

The Fire-Bug

AM&B © H64038 Aug. 5, 1905

Cameraman: G. W. Bitzer

Location: Studio, N.Y.C.; Fort Lee, N.J. *Photographed:* July 24 and 28, 1905

246 ft. FLA5384 (print) FRA2296 (neg.)

The film begins with a camera positioned very close to an actor portraying a demented pyromaniac. He stands in front of a neutral-colored wall lit by incandescent lights. The several scenes, both indoors and out, culminate in a chase through a wooded area. The fire-bug sets fire to a house, kidnaps the small daughter, and runs into the woods with her. The household guests, her father, and the servants, all armed, start after them. For the remainder of the film, the photographer captures the running fight between the fire-bug, who uses the little girl as a shield, and his pursuers. The film ends with a very lively fight between the father and the kidnapper, who gets shot.

Fire Department, Fall River, Massachusetts

AM&B © H32501 June 11, 1903

Cameraman: G. W. Bitzer

Location: Fall River, Mass. *Photographed:* Dec. 8, 1900

26 ft. FLA3972 (print) FRA1180 (neg.)

The film shows several pieces of fire-fighting equipment on a demonstration trip down a main street of the city of Fall River, Massachusetts. Several pumper wagons, hook-and-ladder wagons, personnel carriers, etc., are seen passing. In the background are several commercial buildings or factories. There are a few people standing around watching the exhibition.

A Fire in a Burlesque Theatre

AM&B © H43565 Mar. 22, 1904

Cameraman: A. E. Weed

Location: Studio, N.Y.C. *Photographed:* Feb. 18, 1904

23 ft. FLA3630 (print) FRA0880 (neg.)

This was photographed as if from the audience at a vaudeville house. The first scene shows a constructed flat depicting the back or alley side of a burlesque theater. There is a door on either side of which is a poster advertising the burlesque show. Smoke can be seen issuing from the door. Two men dressed in firemen's uniforms and carrying ladders rush from the wings to one of the windows where several scantily clad women can be seen. The remainder of the film concerns itself with the women climbing down the ladder and running off stage.

The Fire of Life

Great Northern © Oes J168484-168485 Apr. 23, 1912

Director: Edward Schnedler-Sorensen *Script:* Xenius Rostock

Cast: Valdemar Psilander, Julie Henriksen, Else Fröhlich, Frederik Christensen, Poul Reumert, Frederik Skondrup, Elith Pio, Axel Boesen, Arnold Jensen, Jon Iversen, Tage Hertel

Location: Denmark *Photographed:* Nov. 4, 1911

Danish title: Livets Baal

807 ft. FLA5865 (print, copy 1) FLA5866 (print, copy 2) FRA2743 (neg.)

A research chemist or doctor has a young and beautiful wife and a playboy friend. The chemist spends too much time in his laboratory, and a triangle results. The scientist announces a formula for eternal life, and sets up a demonstration, but then discovers his wife and friend embracing. He is so distraught he cannot recall the formula and frantically tries to reconstruct the elixir. He gives up, puts some ingredients in a jug, and lights it in an attempt to destroy himself. His wife finds the lost formula and rushes to her husband, but arrives as he dies. As the husband is being cremated, his wife peers through the door of the oven. The heat ignites her husband's concoction for eternal life, which kills her.

Fireboat "New Yorker" Answering an Alarm

Edison © H32036 May 20, 1903

Cameraman: J. B. Smith

Location: Battery, N.Y.C. *Photographed:* May 10, 1903

30 ft. FLA3755 (print) FRA1007 (neg.)

This single-camera position film was photographed from the edge of a boat dock. It shows the departure of a boat, approximately eighty feet long, with water nozzles. The film ends when the boat leaves the range of the camera.

Fireboat "New Yorker" in Action
Edison © H32035 May 20, 1903
Cameraman: J. B. Smith
Location: New York Harbor, N.Y. *Photographed:* May 10, 1903
111 ft. FLA5038 (print) FRA1999 (neg.)

This film shows a fireboat demonstration, and it was photographed from a camera mounted on some type of floating craft. The picture shows the fireboat with all its nozzles spurting water as it goes back and forth in front of the camera.

Firing by Squad, Gatling Gun
Edison © 71220 Dec. 20, 1897
26 ft. FLA4454 (print) FRA1557 (neg.)

This film is of a military demonstration. The Gatling gun crew appear and fire by squad to demonstrate the firing power of an eight-man squad. Smokeless powder was not yet being used.

See also: Gatling Gun Crew in Action and Mount and Dismount, Gatling Gun

Firing 10 Inch Gun
AM&B © H30721 Apr. 24, 1903
Location: Sandy Hook, N.J. [?] *Photographed:* 1897 [?]
19 ft. FLA3303 (print) FRA0617 (neg.)

The film is a demonstration of the system of firing a ten-inch disappearing gun. It shows a profile of the weapon as it elevates, fires, and retires. A Mutograph picture from this film appears on page 505 of *Magic: Stage Illusions and Scientific Diversions* as well as in the April 17, 1897, issue of *Scientific American.*

Firing the Cabin (The Pioneers)
AM&B © H35880 Sept. 21, 1903
Cameraman: Wallace McCutcheon
Location: Adirondack Mts., N.Y. *Photographed:* Sept. 11, 1903
76 ft. FLA4624 (print) FRA1654 (neg.)

As the picture begins, a rustic cabin with a door and two windows can be seen at camera center. The door opens and a young girl carrying a bucket comes toward the camera position. Shortly after she exits from camera position, she returns running and waving her arms wildly. The door of the cabin opens and, as she goes through, two actors dressed as Indians appear. A tomahawk thrown by them sticks in the door just as it closes. A rifle barrel is seen sticking out of one of the windows, and someone begins firing it. The Indians set fire to the cabin, driving out a woman and the young girl. As the picture ends, the Indians have killed the adults and are leading away the young girl. We have reason to believe that this film was the first part of a series of five released by American Mutoscope & Biograph in August of 1904 under the title THE PIONEERS.

See also: Discovery of Bodies, Rescue of Child from Indians, and Settler's Home Life.

Firing the Cook
AM&B © H37500 Nov. 2, 1903
Cameraman: A. E. Weed
Location: Studio, N.Y.C. *Photographed:* Oct. 25, 1903
43 ft. FLA3635 (print) FRA1655 (neg.)

In order to properly convey the humor and violence of this film, the cameraman placed his camera in three different positions: a kitchen, another position in the kitchen, and outside the house. The first scene takes place in the kitchen where the lady of the house is attempting to admonish the cook for breaking china. The lady of the house summons a policeman who tries, without success, to take the cook off to jail. The cook picks up the policeman and, with the aid of stop action photography, a dummy is substituted for him and thrown out of the window. The camera is moved to the outside position to film the dummy crashing through the window. As the dummy lands on the ground in front of the camera, a man is substituted who crawls away feigning near-unconsciousness.

First Avenue, Seattle, Washington
Edison © 60554 Oct. 25, 1897
Location: Seattle, Wash.
25 ft. FLA4035 (print) FRA2851 (neg.)

Photographed from a single camera position, the film shows a section of a business district, where a banner stretched between columns of a building indicates gold-mining equipment is for sale. In the background a small electric streetcar can be seen.

The First Baby
AM&B © H48626 July 28, 1904
Cameraman: G. W. Bitzer
Location: Coney Island, N.Y. *Photographed:* July 20, 1904
20 ft. FLA3207 (print) FRA0532 (neg.)

A man and a woman are lying on the sand by the seashore. They wear bathing costumes. They display adoration and attention to the infant seated on the sand between them. In the background is a portion of a pier, and an occasional wave rolls up on the beach.

The Fisherman and His Sweetheart
Great Northern © Oes J167403-167405 Mar. 22, 1912
Cast: Ebba Thomsen, Einar Zangenberg, Christel Holck, Zanny Petersen
Location: Denmark
Danish title: Fiskeren og hans Brud
1,183 ft. FLA5930 (print) FRA2798 (neg.)

The opening scenes establish the plot. There is a fisherman with a girl friend; they are happy with their surroundings and circumstances. The locale is an island. Then a man and two women arrive from the city. One of the women is older and it can be presumed she is the mother. The fisherman is instantly attracted to the city girl, a countess, portrayed by Ebba Thomsen, and, in very short order, not only ceases being a fisherman but moves to the city to live with the girl. The film shows the elaborate surroundings to which the fisherman has now become accustomed and, judging from the officer's uniform he is wearing, he has something to do with shipping. The scene shifts from the rich city dwelling back to the island, where the fisherman's former sweetheart and her father have learned of his marriage. The father takes his daughter to the city where they confront the former fisherman. The film ends as the father and weeping daughter are thrown out of the mansion, while the ex-fisherman and his wealthy wife embrace.

Fisherman, Eels or Snakes

Paley & Steiner © H56277 Jan. 20, 1905
12 ft. FLA4406 (print) FRA1532 (neg.)

The producing company, without concern for the future of its product, sent in for copyright only three scenes from its film. The scenes cannot be connected by either action or interest. The first scene shows four men standing in a swamp next to a horse and buggy; the second, a man walking through water fully clothed, and the third, men getting into a boat on the water.

Fisherman's Luck

Edison © 52618 Sept. 20, 1897
25 ft. FLA3044 (print) FRA0283 (neg.)

Two fishermen are on the end of a small dock freshwater fishing. One is standing and the other is seated. The seated man pulls in what he thinks is a strike but what is actually a length of stovepipe that hits his companion on the head, knocking him into the water. The remainder of the film is concentrated on the comedy antics of the two men during the attempt at rescue. During this time, a rowboat containing four people passes by.

Fisherman's Wharf

Edison © 60562 Oct. 25, 1897
27 ft. FLA4028 (print) FRA1218 (neg.)

The camera position appears to be from a dock directly bordering a slip where fishing craft tie up. The only action is a small sailboat approaching the camera position and lowering it sails.

Fishing at Faralone Island

Edison © H12584 Jan. 6, 1902
Location: Farallon Islands, Calif.
140 ft. FLA5039 (print) FRA1000 (neg.)

The film was photographed from a small boat a short distance from a larger boat where several men are hand-hauling a large fishing net toward the stern of their vessel. The film is almost impossible to watch because it jumps so badly. However, it is possible to see the fishing vessel, the men actively engaged in working with the net, and large numbers of birds attracted by the fish.

Fishing Smacks

Edison © 60563 Oct. 25, 1897
25 ft. FLA4044 (print) FRA1231 (neg.)

From a single camera position located on a wharf, several small fishing vessels can be seen tied to the wharf. Several men unload fish from the hold of the boat nearest the camera.

Fiskeren og Hans Brud

See: The Fisherman and His Sweetheart

A Five Cent Trolley Ride

See: [On] a [Good Old] Five Cent Trolley Ride

Five Minutes to Train Time

AM&B © H16388 Apr. 12, 1902

Cameraman: F. S. Armitage
Location: Roof Studio, N.Y.C. *Photographed:* June 28, 1901
28 ft. FLA3485 (print) FRA0766 (neg.)

This short film begins on a living room set. In the foreground is a large steamer trunk, and a woman and man are standing beside it. Their actions indicate they are in somewhat of a hurry. They begin to pack the trunk with all manner of clothes that are lying on the floor. As the sequence continues, the woman goes to the door and admits the baggage man, who waits while they rapidly finish packing the trunk. When they are through, the couple turn to look for their child. The film ends as they unlock the trunk, quickly unpack it, and uncover the child at the bottom.

The Flag

AM&B © H32942 June 25, 1903
Photographed: 1897 [?]
17 ft. FLA3999 (print) FRA1201 (neg.)

A single camera position shows a relatively close picture of a silk flag at the top of a mast waving in a rather strong breeze.

Flag Dance

AM&B © H32079 May 21, 1903
14 ft. FLA3406 (print) FRA0700 (neg.)

A girl, approximately fourteen years of age, dressed in a costume resembling the American flag, performs a dance. She also waves an American flag, and her actions show she has had very little training.

Flagship "New York"

Edison © 25562 Apr. 22, 1898
26 ft. FLA3096 (print) FRA0435 (neg.)
[Spanish-American War]

The single camera position was on board a boat. The film shows the battle cruiser *New York* at anchor. The short, poorly exposed film shows only the starboard side of the cruiser as the camera passes by.

La Flamme Merveilleuse

See: The Mystical Flame

A Flash of Light

Biograph © J143387 July 20, 1910
Director: D. W. Griffith *Cameraman:* G. W. Bitzer
Cast: Charles West, Dorothy Bernard, Vivian Prescott, Verner Clarges, George Nicholls, Joe Graybill, Mack Sennett, Jeanie Macpherson, Blanche Sweet
Location: Studio, N.Y.C. *Photographed:* June 14, 16-17, 1910
394 ft. FLA5387 (print) FRA2298 (neg.)

A young chemist is in love with and marries the youngest daughter of a household, unaware that the older sister loves him too. During an experiment, an explosion occurs that leaves him blinded and handicapped. His young wife abandons him for a gay social whirl, while her older sister remains at home and nurses him. Eventually an operation is performed in an effort to restore his sight, but a flash of light, too soon after the surgery, causes permanent blindness. It is then that he learns he had been attended by the older sister, rather than by his wife.

The Fleet Steaming Up North River

Edison © 52047 Sept. 3, 1898

Location: Hudson River, N.Y. *Photographed:* Aug. 20, 1898

64 ft. FLA4626 (print) FRA1656 (neg. copy 1) FRA1657 (neg., copy 2)

[Spanish-American War; New York City Welcome to Admiral Sampson's Fleet After Battle of Santiago Bay]

As the film begins, naval battleships and cruisers can be seen in line steaming up the North River, escorted by several steam tugs awaiting permission to act as mooring aides. The New York Palisades are visible. The film shows New York City's welcome to Admiral Sampson.

A Flirtation

AM&B © H16336 Apr. 10, 1902

Cameraman: Arthur Marvin

Location: Roof Studio, N.Y.C. *Photographed:* Oct. 14, 1900

12 ft. FLA4238 (print) FRA1395 (neg.)

As the film begins, a woman holding a newspaper (*The Morning Telegraph)* in front of her face as though reading it is sitting in front of a backdrop of the interior of a restaurant. As the film continues, a man with a mustache and goatee and wearing street clothes approaches the table at which the young woman is seated, bows slightly, sits down, and attempts to start a conversation. The woman lowers the newspaper and looks at the gentleman who has accosted her. Her face is all distorted, she has a large putty nose, and her eyes are crossed. Even though she appears well-dressed, the self-appointed Lothario finds her a little too much for him and he leaves. AM&B's original title was "Such a Flirtation"

A Flock of Export Sheep

AM&B © H31669 May 11, 1903

Cameraman: F. S. Armitage

Location: Buffalo, N.Y. *Photographed:* June 28, 1899

15 ft. FLA3415 (print) FRA0704 (neg.)

A flock of sheep moves toward a corral fence. There are approximately one hundred sheep passing the camera position. In the background two men walk slowly behind them. The corral fence is the only other object to be seen.

Flock of Sheep

AM&B © H19016 June 14, 1902

Cameraman: G. W. Bitzer

Location: Union Pacific Railroad, A. S. Kuellen Co. Ranch, Wyo. *Photographed:* July 5, 1901

28 ft. FLA3789 (print) FRA1027 (neg.)

A large flock of sheep passes by the camera for the entire length of the film. For a few fleeting frames at the end, a dog and two men can be seen.

Flood Scene in Paterson, N.J.

Edison © H36824 Oct. 16, 1903

Cameraman: A. C. Abadie

Location: Paterson, N.J. *Photographed:* Oct. 13, 1903

51 ft. FLA4627 (print) FRA1658 (neg.)

The camera position covers a flood in a business district. Many people and horse-drawn vehicles can be seen passing the camera.

Flour and Feed

AM&B © H41857 Feb. 5, 1904

Cameraman: A. E. Weed

Location: Studio, N.Y.C. *Photographed:* Jan. 25, 1904

40 ft. FLA4628 (print) FRA1659 (neg.)

Photographed from the point of view of the audience, this film takes place on a loft set where a man lowers sacks of flour to a companion below. The companion places the flour sacks in a wheelbarrow and trundles them out of the camera range. As the film progresses, a man and woman appear on the stage and stand talking beneath the loft window. The man in the loft slips and a bag of flour is emptied on the couple below who immediately start an altercation as if one or the other were at fault. A third person joins them, for no apparent reason, and the film ends there.

Flying Train

AM&B © H30736 Apr. 24, 1903

Location: Bremen, Germany

46 ft. FLA4619 (print) FRA1660 (neg.)

All of the film was photographed from the forward part of the gondola of an electric car suspended beneath arches fifty feet above the ground. The monorail electric car travels about twenty miles during the course of the film, making several turns and stops. Beneath the car can be seen a landscape with buildings and vehicles. The film was photographed from the suspension railway in Bremen, Germany.

A Flying Wedge

AM&B © H30177 Apr. 4, 1903

15 ft. FLA3596 (print) FRA0861 (neg.)

Photographed from a single camera position, the film shows six German naval gunboats steaming by in formation. The formation is now classified as form oblique, right, left, and off-leader.

See also: An Attack by Torpedo Boats

Flyveren og Journalistens Hustru

See: The Aviator's Generosity

Follow the Leader

Edison © H1403 Feb. 23, 1901

24 ft. FLA3744 (print) FRA0990 (neg.)

The film begins with a gathering of five women whose gestures indicate they are agreeing to do something suggested by one of their party who seats them and gives each a dish. Their leader alternately eats and rubs on her face a brown substance similar to chocolate from the dish. The others follow suit. Soon the four women rebel, grab the leader and, as the film ends, can be seen putting the substance on her face.

Fools of Fate

Biograph © J132811 Oct. 7, 1909

Director: D. W. Griffith *Cameraman:* G. W. Bitzer

Cast: Marion Leonard, Frank Powell, James Kirkwood

Location: Cuddebackville, N.Y.; Studio, N.Y.C. *Photographed:* Aug. 27-30, 1909

363 ft. FLA5783 (print) FRA2823 (neg.)

"A life story showing how foolish it is to rebel against the designs of Fate. A young woman, tired of her lot, elopes with a man, who is himself innocent of any wrong, only to find in him the person to whom her husband owes his life, he having previously saved him from drowning. The husband follows his wife and her unknown companion, and is amazed to find the unwitting wrecker of his home the man to whom he has sworn eternal friendship." This synopsis was taken from a handbill printed in *The Moving Picture World* of October 9, 1909. There is an unusual camera effect in the film of the woman walking into a darkened room with the only source of light the lantern that returns the room to darkness when it is extinguished. Pippa Passes, the film associated with the first use of this type of photography, was advertised for release on the same handbill.

A Fool's Revenge

AM&B © H123743 Mar. 8, 1909
Director: D. W. Griffith *Cameramen:* G. W. Bitzer, Arthur Marvin
Cast: Florence Barker, Owen Moore, Linda Arvidson, Vivian Prescott, John Cumpson, Fred Mace, Mack Sennett
Location: Studio, N.Y.C. *Photographed:* Feb. 11-12, 1909
378 ft. FLA5388 (print) FRA2300 (neg.)

The story, taken from Hugo's *Le Roi s'Amuse*, shows the accidental murder of a young woman instead of the duke who was slated for death. The actors are in period costumes, and the film was photographed entirely on interior sets.

Football Game: West Point vs. Annapolis

AM&B © H18125 May 26, 1902
Cameraman: Congdon
Location: Philadelphia *Photographed:* Dec. 2, 1901
25 ft. FLA4017 (print) FRA1213 (neg.)

The camera was placed at approximately the fifty yard line and at standard eye level to photograph this athletic event. More than one type of lens was used to cover the field. In the background are bleachers for spectators and buildings.

For a Wife's Honor

AM&B © H114858 Aug. 19, 1908
Director: D. W. Griffith *Cameraman:* Arthur Marvin
Cast: Charles Inslee, Linda Arvidson, Arthur Johnson, Harry Salter
Location: Studio, N.Y.C. *Photographed:* July 28 and 30, 1908
181 ft. FLA5389 (print) FRA2297 (neg.)

The build up of suspense in this picture is centered around an argument between a maid and the lady of the house which results in the maid's dismissal. Out of spite, the maid locks her former mistress in a room with a male visitor. The maid then runs and tells the husband that his wife is being unfaithful, and informs two other men that the husband is going to murder his wife. The husband rushes home, finds the front door locked, and attempts to break it down. The other two men arrive and intervene in time to keep the husband from doing physical harm to the man locked inside the room with his wife.

For Better—But Worse

Keystone © LP5390 May 22, 1915
Producer and Author: Mack Sennett
Cast: Nick Cogley, Mae Busch, Dell Henderson, Hugh Fay, Harry McCoy
Location: Keystone studio in the Edendale section of Los Angeles and Glendale Boulevard, Los Angeles
466 ft. FLA6090 (print)

Police chief Nick Cogley bids goodbye to his beautiful daughter, Mae Busch, and sets off for work. Down the street one of their neighbors orders her husband, played by Harry McCoy, to take their poodle to the park for a walk. In the park, McCoy meets and becomes enchanted with Mae Busch who has gone there in response to a note from her boyfriend Dell Henderson. McCoy makes advances to Busch, and when Henderson arrives he is understandably annoyed. McCoy returns home where he conceives the idea of kidnapping Mae Busch. He returns to the park, hires two park bums to "bag" her, and then the inevitable occurs. The bums bag his wife instead. Dell Henderson and Mae Busch, about to meet again, observe the kidnapping and each hurries to save her. The Keystone cops rush to the rescue in a horse-drawn cart, while McCoy, his hostage, and the bums take off in a trolley car. When McCoy discovers it is his wife who has been "bagged," he faints. A 1910 Packard and a Saxon automobile are used in this picture.

For Love of Gold

AM&B © H114479 Aug. 11, 1908
Director: D. W. Griffith *Cameraman:* Arthur Marvin
Cast: Harry Salter, Charles Inslee
Location: Studio, N.Y.C. *Photographed:* July 21, 1908
208 ft. FLA5391 (print) FRA2299 (neg.)

The plot, from a Jack London story, is built around two burglars who rob a safe belonging to a rich man. They return with their spoils to their hideout. Each suspects the other of contemplating his murder. In the dramatic conclusion, photographed from a single camera position, each burglar poisons the other's coffee, and each falls to the floor dead. All three scenes were photographed with incandescent light.

The Forbidden City, Pekin

AM&B © H34805 Aug. 19, 1903
Cameraman: Ackerman
Location: Peking, China *Date:* Jan. 31, 1901
16 ft. FLA4142 (print) FRA1312 (neg.)

The film was photographed from a single camera position overlooking the principal area of the Forbidden City in Peking. The camera pans 360 degrees and includes the rooftops and a section of the Great Wall in its scope. The film is short.

See also: General Chaffee in Pekin

Fording the River Nile on Donkeys

Edison © H32506 June 11, 1903
Cameraman: A. C. Abadie
Location: Upper Cairo, Egypt *Photographed:* June 4, 1903
71 ft. FLA4630 (print) FRA1661 (neg.)

The photographer positioned his camera on the bank of a ford of the river. Approximately a dozen little donkeys are being pulled, pushed, ridden, and driven across the ford toward the camera by drivers who wear turbans and burnooses, or by naked little boys riding them across.

The Forecastle of the "Kearsarge" in a Heavy Sea

AM&B © H55393 Jan. 3, 1905

Cameraman: G. W. Bitzer

Photographed: Aug. 30, 1903

28 ft. FLA4118 (print) FRA1294 (neg.)

The camera was positioned on the starboard bridge wing of the ship in order to photograph these scenes of the ship heading into a storm of about force 8—C, judging by the height of the waves and the residual water coming back over the deck.

48th Highlanders Regiment

AM&B © H33406 July 13, 1903

Cameraman: Arthur Marvin

Location: N.Y.C. *Date:* Mar. 26, 1902

26 ft. FLA3430 (print) FRA0717 (neg.)

A street corner in a town is shown. People indicate their interest toward something coming by moving down the street. The Highlanders of Toronto then come into camera view and march by.

The Foster Mother

AM&B © H16385 Apr. 12, 1902

Cameraman: F. S. Armitage

Location: Roof Studio, N.Y.C. *Date:* Oct. 28, 1899

23 ft. FLA3199 (print) FRA0525

A young girl nurses a white puppy with a black spot from a bottle of milk with a nipple. The newborn puppy is on a table covered with a pressed flannel tablecloth.

Fougere

AM&B © H18745 June 7, 1902

Cameraman: F. S. Armitage

Cast: Eugenie Fougère

Date: Nov. 25 [?], 1899

16 ft. FLA4108 (print) FRA1283 (neg.)

Against a backdrop painted to represent the rolling waves of an ocean, a young lady in the costume of a can-can dancer performs her act. The young woman seems to have developed a rather awkward side-knee step which she uses continually throughout this short film. Eugenie Fougère was a famous Parisian chanteuse and this film represents her version of the ragtime cakewalk "Hello Ma Baby" with which she made a sensation at the New York Theater.

Four Beautiful Pairs

AM&B © H42043 Feb. 11, 1904

Cameraman: A. E. Weed

Location: Studio, N.Y.C. *Photographed:* Jan. 28, 1904

36 ft. FLA4631 (print) FRA1662 (neg.)

The film begins by showing a department store stocking counter set. Behind the counter are four young women preparing merchandise for sale. Directly in front of each girl, as a part of the set, is a pair of false legs encased in stockings. From the camera position, the false legs appear to be joined to the women behind the counter. A grim-faced, severely dressed woman carrying an umbrella enters with her henpecked husband. While his wife makes a purchase, the man becomes interested in the stockinged legs. Suddenly the wife notices his interest, and the film ends as she is dragging him away, hitting him with her umbrella.

See also: Shocking Stockings

The Four Seasons

AM&B © H41758 Feb. 2, 1904

Cameraman: G. W. Bitzer

Location: Studio, N.Y.C. *Photographed:* Jan. 12, 1904

73 ft. FLA5040 (print) FRA2001 (neg.)

This film was divided into four tableaulike scenes that depict the span of human life. All were photographed in silhouette by using a strong light behind the actors to cause a sharp shadow on diffused material. The shadows of the actors were then photographed from the diffused material. The first of the four scenes shows a seated woman attending an infant. During her moment before the camera, she leans forward, picks up the baby, diapers, powders, and dresses it. The next three scenes are "Summer," "Autumn," and "Winter." Each is identified by letters, also in silhouette, that spell out the season.

The 14th Sikhs

AM&B © H16740 Apr. 18, 1902

Cameraman: Raymond Ackerman

Location: Shanghai *Date:* Jan. 31, 1901

14 ft. FLA3664 (print) FRA1076 (neg.)

The buildings that surround the area indicate that the film was photographed on the drill field of an army garrison. Several companies of Sikh infantry troops can be seen being put through close-order drill. Most of the film is of the battalion marching by in company-front order.

14th U.S. Infantry Drilling at the Presidio

Edison © 38217 June 22, 1898

Location: San Francisco

25 ft. FLA3094 (print) FRA0433 (neg.)

[Spanish-American War]

Military troops are shown training in close-order drill in preparation for the Spanish-American War. They are training on the parade ground of the Presidio. The film was photographed from a single camera position and therefore it is difficult to estimate the number of soldiers involved.

The Fourth Ghorkhas

AM&B © H34520 Aug. 13, 1903

Cameraman: Raymond Ackerman

Location: Shanghai *Date:* Feb. 1, 1901

21 ft. FLA3577 (print) FRA0850 (neg.)

Photographed from a single-camera position, the film shows nearly two companies of foot soldiers practicing a bayonet-thrust drill.

The Fox Hunt

AM&B © H83896 Oct. 16, 1906

Cameramen: F. A. Dobson, G. W. Bitzer

Location: Orange, N.J.; Bartell's Animal Farm *Photographed:* Aug. 23 and Sept. 29, 1906

267 ft.   FLA5392 (print)   FRA2301 (neg.)

In this film, a satire on fox hunting, an actor carries a fox in a basket across the countryside in front of a full pack of hounds and the hunt club members. (The actor is a man costumed as a woman.) The film starts with his placing the fox in the basket and continues through the fox hunt, until the actor carrying the fox ends up on top of a haystack. Each camera change is preceded by a title describing the next scene. This film was made with the cooperation of the Union County Hounds of Orange, New Jersey, Sidney Holloway, master.

Foxy Grandpa and Polly in a Little Hilarity

AM&B © H18034 May 23, 1902

Cast: Joseph Hart as Foxy Grandpa, Carrie DeMar as Polly

Cameraman: Robert K. Bonine

Location: Roof Studio, N.Y.C. *Date:* May 17, 1902

12 ft.   FLA4356 (print)   FRA1497 (neg.)

The camera was positioned over the head of people watching a vaudeville act. First we see a constructed stone fence and a stage backdrop painted as a garden scene. A man made up to appear as a fat old man enters from stage left. He is escorting an attractive young lady dressed in the fashion of the era. The two of them then demonstrate their ability as dancers by executing several different routines in unison.

Foxy Grandpa Shows the Boys a Trick or Two With the Tramp

AM&B © H18033 May 23, 1902

Cast: Joseph Hart as Foxy Grandpa

Cameraman: Robert K. Bonine

Location: Roof Studio N.Y.C. *Date:* May 17, 1902

21 ft.   FLA4355 (print)   FRA1496 (neg.)

Two boys carrying a dummy dressed in men's clothing between them can be seen in front of a set of an outdoor scene. The boys place the dummy on the bench in the foreground and leave. A tramp comes along, notices the dummy, tosses it away, and lies down himself. The two boys reappear with a man dressed as an old gaffer. The tramp gets to his feet and attempts to fight with the old man who returns his blows and chases him away. The films ends as the old gentleman stands with his thumbs stuck in his vest in a gesture of bravado.

Foxy Grandpa Tells the Boys a Funny Story

AM&B © H18039 May 23, 1902

Cast: Joseph Hart as Foxy Grandpa

Cameraman: Robert K. Bonine

Location: Roof Studio, N.Y.C. *Date:* May 17, 1902

15 ft.   FLA4359 (print)   FRA1498 (neg.)

An old gentleman with grey hair is sitting on a bench with two small boys on either side of him as the film begins. The set is a backdrop of a garden scene. The old man is telling the youngsters a story that causes them to break into peals of laughter, which continue for the remainder of the film.

Foxy Grandpa Thumb Book

AM&B © H36862 Oct. 19, 1903

Cast: Joseph Hart as Foxy Grandpa

Cameraman: A. E. Weed

Location: Studio, N.Y.C. *Photographed:* Oct. 9, 1903

7 ft.   FLA4353 (print)   FRA1495 (neg.)

A set of a two-story apartment house front can be seen. An old man is peering out a window at two boys approaching the front porch carrying a bucket of water and a ladder. The boys place the ladder against the front door, climb up, and arrange the bucket of water to fall on the next person to leave the house. As the boys climb down the ladder, the old gentleman (Foxy Grandpa) reaches out and releases the contents of the bucket on the heads of the two young pranksters. The film ends as the old gentleman is standing above the boys shaking his finger at them in admonishment.

Frank J. Gould's Dogs

AM&B © H28547 Feb. 24, 1903

Location: Lyndhurst, N.Y. *Photographed:* c. Apr. 1899

17 ft.   FLA3138 (print)   FRA0471 (neg.)

Several St. Bernard dogs are shown milling about on a lawn surrounded by trees. The only other moving object is a man, apparently the kennel man, who wanders among the dogs, urging them to move around.

Frankenstein's Trestle

AM&B © H17964 May 21, 1902

Cameraman: G. W. Bitzer

Location: Frankenstein, N.H. *Date:* July 26, 1899

10 ft.   FLA4024 (print)   FRA1216 (neg.)

The camera was placed at a distance from a trestle to photograph the full span. The trestle is of a unique design. A steam locomotive, which does not appear to be of American manufacture, pulls four cars toward the camera position and crosses the trestle. The film was photographed in Frankenstein, New Hampshire, in the White Mountains.

Frazer Canon

AM&B © H17966 May 21, 1902

Cameraman: G. W. Bitzer

Location: Frazer Canyon, east of Yale, B.C., Canada *Date:* Oct. 28, 1899

30 ft.   FLA3127 (print)   FRA0461 (neg.)

The camera platform was the front of a railroad car proceeding on a single track railroad located in mountainous country. The track winds, going in and out around spurs of land and gulches caused by the river alongside. As the train continues along the track, telegraph or telephone poles can be seen alongside. The film was photographed on the Canadian Pacific Railroad, near Banff.

Free Arm Movement, All Schools, Missouri Commission

AM&B © H45456 May 7, 1904

Cameraman: A. E. Weed

Location: Garfield School, St. Joseph, Mo. *Photographed:* April 22, 1904

21 ft.   FLA3105 (print)   FRA0442 (neg.)

The camera photographed a group of preadolescent children standing in rows facing the camera. During the film, all of the boys and girls demonstrate several different calisthenic exercises. Behind the children is a wall constructed to resemble the interior of a schoolroom. The film was photographed outdoors.

Free-for-All Race at Charter Oak Park
Edison © 43418 July 31, 1897
Location: Charter Oak Park, Hartford, Conn.
18 ft. FLA3896 (print) FRA1117 (neg.)

The film shows a sulky race. The camera was stationed at the edge of the track. Six sulkies are driven by the camera position. Several hundred people can be seen watching the race. One of the horses was described in the Edison catalog as "The Fastest Harness Horse in the World, John R. Gentry."

Free Show on the Beach
AM&B © H78530 June 1, 1906
Cameraman: G. W. Bitzer
Photographed: May 9, 1905
38 ft. FLA3961 (print) FRA1171 (neg.)

A man wearing a bathing suit is on a beach with a beach umbrella. He puts it on the fake sand, disappears, and returns with a young woman. They both sit down on the sand and the umbrella obscures them from camera view. Another young woman, also clad in a bathing suit, appears, looks over the umbrella, and then writes "Free Show" in the sand. The man spooning behind the umbrella becomes annoyed, picks up the intruder, and carries her out of sight.

Freight Train
Edison © 16428 Mar. 10, 1898
Location: Southern Pacific Railway
43 ft. FLA4632 (print) FRA0375 (neg.)

From the camera position to infinity, the curve of a track emerging from a tunnel in the side of a mountain can be seen. There is snow on the ground. Heading toward the camera position from the tunnel is a large steam locomotive pulling a freight train. As the train approaches, a second locomotive is visible. Approximately twenty cars go by the camera position. The box cars have signs on the side reading "Special Train, HOPS, Sunset Route." A third locomotive is pushing the freight train.

French Acrobatic Dance
AM&B © H27771 Jan. 30, 1903
10 ft. FLA3178 (print) FRA0505 (neg.)

This was photographed as if the camera were in the audience. As the curtain rises, three young women dressed in conventional ballet costumes and another in a French peasant costume are holding hands and bowing on the stage. Then they demonstrate their ability as acrobatic dancers by doing backbends, handsprings, and so forth.

The French Duel
Biograph © H127177 May 18, 1909
Director: D. W. Griffith *Cameramen:* G. W. Bitzer, Arthur Marvin
Cast: Owen Moore, Herbert Yost, Arthur Johnson, Mack Sennett, John Cumpson, Linda Arvidson
Location: Coytesville, N.J.; Studio, N.Y.C. *Photographed:* Feb. 23 and Mar. 11, 1909
154 ft. FLA5393 (print) FRA2302 (neg.)

The film is set in the late eighteenth century, and all of the actors are dressed as members of the elite of that period. The opening scene is in the lobby of a gentleman's club, where a fight between two men ends in a challenge to a duel. The next scene shows horse-drawn carriages containing doctors, seconds, nurses, witnesses, and contestants arriving for the affair of honor. The duelists are offered a choice of weapons, including large flintlock rifles. They decide to use sabers. The film ends as all of the spectators get into a melee over the legality of one of the duelers' actions—placing a metal plate inside his jacket—while the two erstwhile antagonists embrace one another.

The Fresh Book Agent
See: The Downward Path

The Fresh Lover
AM&B © H17490 May 8, 1902
Cameraman: F. S. Armitage
Location: Roof Studio, N.Y.C. *Date:* June 29, 1901
14 ft. FLA3834 (print) FRA1061 (neg.)

The set is a one-dimensional, two-story house, with a painted backdrop to convey the impression of trees around the house. A young woman is at the downstairs window when a man dressed in a top hat and tailcoat strolls by. The young woman waves to him; he turns and walks over and kisses her outstretched hand again and again. She apparently encourages him, for soon they are kissing. At this point, an old man comes to the upper window, and shouts at them to stop. A passerby notices the situation, picks up the young man by the ankles, holds him in the air and, as the picture ends, the old man is pummeling the young man about the head and shoulders.

A Friend at Last
See: The Ex-Convict

A Friend in Need Is a Friend Indeed
AM&B © H73108 Feb. 9, 1906
Cameraman: G. W. Bitzer
Location: New York City Streets and Studio, N.Y.C. *Photographed:* Jan. 24 and 27, 1906
223 ft. FLA5394 (print) FRA2303 (neg.)

The first scene takes place in a set of the disreputable living quarters of a ragged old man who is sharing his food with his boxer dog. The next title indicates that the dog, impressed by this unselfishness, goes out to steal food for his master. But the dog is stolen and sold to a sausage factory to become an ingredient. However, it breaks away and rushes home to its master with a length of sausage, even though it is chased all through the streets. This film is unusual in that, at the title separation at the beginning of the last scene, the camera moves in from a full establishing shot of the poor man's quarters to a waist close-up of the old man and the dog eating.

From Patches to Plenty
Keystone © LP4640 Mar. 6, 1915
Producer and Author: Mack Sennett
Cast: Cecile Arnold, Dave Morris, Charles Murray, Joe Bordeaux, Minta Durfee, Alice Davenport, Harry Booker

Location: Hollywood, Midwick Country Club polo field, Los Angeles, and the bay in front of the Yacht Club at San Pedro, Calif.

FLA6091 (print)

A girl (Cecile Arnold) is accidentally knocked down by an automobile as she waits for a streetcar. Dave Morris has just come from the bank with a suitcase full of bonds, sees the accident, drops his valise, and hurries across the street to help. A bum (Charlie Murray) stumbles over the bag, opens it, and comments, "My word, a mislaid million." He picks it up and sneaks off down the alley where he encounters Joe Bordeaux who is looking for empty beer bottles. They strike up a friendship. While Cecile Arnold and Dave Morris are enjoying a romance, Murray has cashed some of the bonds, bought a polo pony, plays an excellent game, and is the hero of the day. He invites a group of people to a party on his yacht. When he goes to cash more bonds, he is caught by bank detectives but puts up such a fight that he is wrapped in a tablecloth like a straitjacket, and the scene ends with both Charlie Murray and Joe Bordeaux being taken into custody.

From Show Girl to Burlesque Queen

Am&B © H35629 Sept. 12, 1903
Cameraman: A. E. Weed
Location: Studio, N.Y.C. *Photographed:* Aug. 25, 1903
30 ft. FLA3563 (print) FRA0839 (neg.)

A young woman is standing next to some screens, either behind or in the wings of a stage or a dressing room on a stage. She begins to remove her clothing—first the dress, then a slip, another slip and another—down to her fourth petticoat. With a very fetching smile, she goes behind a screen. Several other articles of clothing fall to the floor, having been tossed over the screen. In the last scene, the young woman emerges. She is half-clothed but is wearing long stockings. The dressing room door opens and a man in a band costume looks approvingly at what he sees.

A Frontier Flirtation

AM&B © H36403 Oct. 1, 1903
Cameraman: G. W. Bitzer
Location: Studio, N.Y.C. *Photographed:* Sept. 24, 1903
19 ft. FLA3540 (print) FRA0816 (neg.)

The cameraman who photographed this film placed his equipment over the heads of the audience. The painted backdrop is a scene in a park. On a bench in front of the backdrop is a heavily veiled young woman. A roughly dressed man appears and attempts to make her acquaintance. She encourages him and, as he sits down beside her, her veil drops revealing a mask with the face of a billy goat, which frightens him away. A well-dressed man comes in, sits down, removes her mask, and they embrace and laugh.

The Fugitive

Biograph © J147671 Nov. 14, 1910
Director: D. W. Griffith *Cameraman:* G. W. Bitzer
Cast: Edwin August, Kate Bruce, Lucy Cotton, Eddie Dillon, Joe Graybill, Dorothy West
Location: Fishkill, N.Y.; Studio, N.Y.C. *Photographed:* Sept. 24-29, 1910
393 ft. FLA5397 (print) FRA0240 (neg.)

The dramatic conclusion of this Civil War story occurs when the mother of a slain Confederate soldier harbors a hunted Union soldier, and learns that he is the man who killed her son. But the Southern mother, thinking of the other mother, sends the Union soldier back, and the picture ends in a happy reunion with his mother and sweetheart.

The Fugitive Apparitions

See: Les Apparitions Fugitives

Full Rigged Ship at Sea

AM&B © H26953 Jan. 14, 1903
Cameraman: F. S. Armitage
Location: America's Cup Race *Date:* Oct. 24, 1899
15 ft. FLA3288 (print) FRA0604 (neg.)

The camera position was the deck of a vessel. As the film begins, it shows a full-rigged American cruiser under way.

Fun in a Bakery Shop

Edison © H15916 Apr. 3, 1902
Cameraman: Edwin S. Porter
37 ft. FLA4634 (print) FRA1664 (neg.)

The plot is only a pretext to utilize the ability of a rapid sculptor. The set is of the interior of a bakery. A man in a baker's hat and costume enters and begins kneading some dough on a table by the oven. He notices a make-believe rat crawling up the side of a nearby barrel and throws the dough at the rat, covering it completely. He then goes over to the dough and begins to pummel it with his hands. His back is to the camera, which obscures the actual manipulation of the dough, but when he steps away there is now a sculptured mask to admire. He sculpts another mask, and two other men, also dressed as bakers, come in, see what he is doing, pick him up bodily, and stick him head first into the flour barrel.

Fun in a Butcher Shop

Edison © H4089 May 6, 1901
Cameraman: Edwin S. Porter
26 ft. FLA3983 (print) FRA1191 (neg.)

The camera was placed as if in the audience at a vaudeville house, where the set on the stage is a butcher shop. On the stage, directly in front of the camera, is a contraption labeled "Sausage Machine." As the action begins, a small boy carries a puppy to the operator of the machine and hands it to him. The puppy is placed in the machine, and the handle is turned until a string of sausages emerge. In rapid succession, several dogs of various sizes and breeds are brought into the shop, put into the machine, and the butcher, to the amazement of the audience, delivers sausages. This continues to the end of the film.

See also: Dog Factory and Sausage Machine

Fun in a Photograph Gallery

AM&B © H21497 Sept. 5, 1902
Cameraman: Robert K. Bonine
Location: Roof Studio, N.Y.C. *Date:* July 3, 1902
15 ft. FLA3235 (print) FRA0559 (neg.)

This was filmed from the point of view of an audience seeing a vaudeville turn of a photographer preparing to photograph a bearded man. The photographer goes into the darkroom and during his absence two small boys enter, open the camera, do something to it, and leave. When the photographer returns and prepares to snap the picture, there is a large explosion which demolishes the shop.

Fun in Camp

Edison © 77518 Nov. 27, 1899
27 ft. FLA3965 (print) FRA1174 (neg.)

Several men in military uniform are seated around a campfire. There are two white pyramid tents in the immediate background. Large tame bears with little children riding on their backs are led around the campfire.

Fun on a Sand Hill

AM&B © H30181 Apr. 4, 1903
17 ft. FLA3629 (print) FRA0886 (neg.)

The film was photographed from the bottom of a steep sand hill. Boys, girls, and some adults are shown sliding and rolling down the incline toward the camera position. They pick themselves up, run up the hill, and repeat the action.

Fun on the Joy Line

AM&B © H66271 Sept. 28, 1905
Cameraman: G. W. Bitzer
Location: Studio, N.Y.C. *Photographed:* Sept. 20, 1905
141 ft. FLA5041 (print) FRA2002 (neg.)

The subject is a series of situations that occur in the lobby between cabins on a set of an excursion steamer. When the action starts, people can be seen being shown to their rooms; the ship's band has formed and has begun to play. Some of the guests indicate that they enjoy the music while others do not. When the band leader is given one drink and then another, the band does not cease playing. However, when a keg of beer arrives, the whole band rises and follows the man with the keg. In the last humorous situation, one of the female guests who is tipsy attempts to play the tuba. This causes other guests to open the door of their rooms and pelt her with pillows. She is seen being carried off as the film ends.

Funeral Leaving the President's House and Church at Canton, Ohio

Edison © H9015 Sept. 25, 1901
Location: Canton, Ohio *Date:* Sept. 19, 1901
79 ft. FLA5042 (print) FRA2003 (neg.)

In order to film the funeral of President McKinley, the photographer placed his camera in three locations. The first scene shows the casket being carried from his home by the honor guard and placed in the hearse. The second scene shows the hearse, the honor guard, and people lining the streets. The third scene shows the celebrities who attended the funeral preceding the casket out of the church. The final scenes are of the people watching the casket being placed in the hearse again.

Funeral of Hiram Cronk

AM&B © H61323 May 25, 1905
Cameraman: G. W. Bitzer
Location: Brooklyn, N.Y.; N.Y.C. *Photographed:* May 17–18, 1905
104 ft. FLA5043 (print) FRA2004 (neg.)

The film shows a large city thoroughfare with crowds of people watching a parade of military personnel (army, navy, and marine), fraternal organizations, ecclesiastical groups, and civic leaders. There are more than a thousand paraders. Following them are four horse-drawn open carriages and then a large hearse drawn by four black horses. The camera position shifts and most of the paraders can be seen for a second time. The film ends on a wide-angle profile shot of the hearse and four black horses standing still. Hiram Cronk, a veteran of the War of 1812, died at the age of 105; he was thought to be the last surviving veteran of that war and so was given an elaborate funeral.

The Furs

Biograph © J169193 May 13, 1912
Director: Mack Sennett
Cast: Mabel Normand, Dell Henderson, Kate Bruce, Mack Sennett
Location: Los Angeles
178 ft. FLA5399 (print) FRA2304 (neg.)

This "split reel" farce is about a wife (Mabel Normand) who attempts to get a fur muff and a stole despite her mother-in-law's objections. She steals money from her sleeping husband's (Dell Henderson) trousers, buys the furs, and pawns them at the Panama Loan Office, 410 South Main Street, Los Angeles. She then takes the pawn ticket to her husband for him to redeem for her. Instead the husband takes his mother (Kate Bruce) to the pawnshop, gives her the furs, and brings his wife a ratty little fur stole in its place.

The Futurity

AM&B © H21776 Sept. 17, 1902
Cameraman: Robert K. Bonine
Location: Sheepshead Bay, N.Y. *Date:* Sept. 2, 1902
24 ft. FLA4635 (print) FRA1665 (neg.)

The condition of this film does not permit much explanation of the detail. However, it is possible to see that the photographer placed his camera over the heads of a crowd of people leaning on a railing watching a horse race. During the remainder of the film, several horses with jockeys astride speed by the camera position. No identification is possible.

See also: Crowd Entering Gates, Futurity Day

The Gambler of the West

Klaw & Erlanger © LP3118 July 30, 1914
Cast: Linda Arvidson, Charles West, Alfred Paget, Charles Perley, Jack Brammall, Robert Drouet
1,213 ft. FLA5400 (print, copy1) FLA5401-5402 (print, copy 2) FRA2659 (neg., copy 1) FRA2660 (neg., copy 2) FRA2661 (neg., copy 3)

Four of the original Biograph group of actors appear in this drama set just after the Civil War. Most of the picture records the search for a young man, separated from his family following an Indian massacre, who was adopted by Indians and reared as one. The film ends, when the sister, Linda Arvidson, succeeds in locating her brother.

Game of Cards

See: How Jones Lost His Roll

Game of Shovel Board on Board S.S. "Doric"

Edison © 38225 June 22, 1898
25 ft. FLA4312 (print) FRA1461 (neg.)

The camera was positioned on a section of a deck of a sea-going steamer where some passengers are engaged in a game of shuffleboard. Four people can be seen pushing a disc-shaped object with shovel-shaped poles across the deck toward the camera.

Gans-Nelson Contest, Goldfield, Nevada, September 3rd, 1906

Miles Brothers © H83436 Oct. 4, 1906

Location: Goldfield, Nevada *Photographed:* Sept. 3, 1906

2,350 ft. FLA5867-5868 (print) FRA2789-2790 (neg.)

The Joe Gans-Battling Nelson prize fight was filmed in its entirety from a single camera position. The film condition is fair. However, the camera was at such a distance from the center of the ring that identification or enjoyment of the fight is limited.

Gap Entrance to Rocky Mountains

AM&B © H16728 Apr. 18, 1902

Cameraman: G. W. Bitzer

Location: Canadian Pacific Railway, Canada *Date:* Oct. 17, 1899

37 ft. FLA3198 (print) FRA0524 (neg.)

A single camera placed on a train photographed the area on either side of a single-track railroad. The film shows the track crossing a trestle and winding through very mountainous terrain. The picture ends as the train makes a turn. In the background are the peaks of the Rocky Mountains.

The 'Gater and the Pickanniny

AM&B © H29473 Mar. 18, 1903

Cameraman: Arthur Marvin

Date: Aug. 15, 1900

12 ft. FLA3647 (print) FRA0901 (neg.)

The opening scene takes place on a set of a mangrove swamp. In the foreground a young black boy is fishing, unaware that a huge alligator is creeping up on him from the rear. As the film continues, the alligator swallows him in one swallow. Then a black man, equipped with an axe, hits the alligator many times, chopping it in two, and extricating the child. The alligator was man-propelled and stop action photography was used.

Gatling Gun Crew in Action

Edison © 71218 Dec. 18, 1897

18 ft. FLA4453 (print) FRA1556 (neg.)

Following the demonstration of the eight-man squad firing intermittently, the same crew shows the inadequacy of squad fire against the six hundred rounds-per-minute of the Gatling gun.

See also: Firing by Squad, Gatling Gun; and Mount and Dismount, Gatling Gun.

Gatling Gun—Firing by Squad

See: Firing by Squad, Gatling gun

A Gay Old Boy

AM&B © H27830 Jan. 22, 1903

Cameraman: F. S. Armitage

Date: Aug. 18, 1899

26 ft. FLA3284 (print) FRA0600 (neg.)

The poor quality of the film is due to the shade of the actress' dresses being too similar to the wall paper of the set of the living room in this production. There are four characters: three women and a man. One of the women, dressed as a maid, is dusting with a feather duster while the man is attempting to kiss her. She is annoyed by his actions and leaves the room. The man sits down in a chair and starts to read the paper when a woman enters accompanied by another who appears to be his wife. The wife takes him by the lapels of his coat and begins throwing him about the room.

Gay Shoe Clerk

Edison © H34389 Aug. 12, 1903

Cameraman: Edwin S. Porter

Location: Studio, N.Y.C. *Photographed:* July 23, 1903

28 ft. FLA3468 (print) FRA0750 (neg.)

A man is arranging the stock in a shoe store set when an elderly woman accompanied by a young girl enters the store. The older woman seats herself and begins reading while the younger woman sits on the shoe-demonstration chair and puts up her foot. At that moment, the camera is moved in to an insert close-up covering only the woman's foot, the shoe clerk's hand, and the hem of her skirt. As the film continues, the hem of the woman's skirt rises exposing her ankle, and the area below the knee. The remainder of the film is photographed from a different camera position. The clerk kisses the young woman. Her chaperone notices their embrace, gets up, and beats the shoe clerk on the head with her umbrella.

Geisha Girls

AM&B © H29164 Mar. 11, 1903

Photographed: 1897[?]

16 ft. FLA3361 (print) FRA0664 (neg.)

The camera was positioned as if in the audience. Three small Caucasian girls dressed in Japanese kimonos perform some twists and turns in unison, simulating a Japanese geisha dance.

Gen. Bell's Pack Train Swimming the Agno River

See: An Historic Feat

General Chaffee in Pekin

AM&B © H34811 Aug. 19, 1903

Cameraman: Raymond Ackerman

Photographed: Jan. 1901

25 ft. FLA3330 (print) FRA0641 (neg.)

The camera was positioned at the side of a road. In the background is a brick wall of Chinese architecture. Approaching the camera position are men on horseback. Leading the mounted riders is an American general in uniform, accompanied by two civilians in embassy attire and one foreign general of Oriental appearance. These four are followed by what appears to be a staff, also mounted, and behind them is a full company of U.S. cavalry. The film ends as the last riders pass the camera position. It was photographed at the time of the Boxer Rebellion.

See also: The Forbidden City, Pekin [China]

Thomas A. Edison's film, Gatling Gun Crew in Action (1897).

General Cronje & Mystic Shriners

AM&B © H65559 Sept. 15, 1905

Cameraman: G. W. Bitzer

Location: Boer War Park, Brighton Beach, N.Y. *Photographed:*
Aug. 22, 1905

59 ft. FLA4637 (print) FRA1667 (neg.)

From a single camera position, a two-wheeled cart drawn by
four matched horses, is shown approaching the camera.
The cart comes to a halt and then proceeds. It is followed
closely by a large file of men wearing civilian clothes.
However, some of the men wear the fez of the Shriners
organization.

General Lee's Procession, Havana

Edison © 7259 Jan. 20, 1899

49 ft. FLA4638 (print) FRA1668 (neg.)

[Spanish-American War]

Judging from the distance to the subject and the camera
angle, the film was photographed from a balcony. The
subject is foot soldiers marching in procession behind some
mounted troops that appear to be ranking officers. In the
background beyond the marching troops can be seen what
appears to be a public park with trees and portions of
public buildings.

General Wheeler and Secretary Alger

AM&B © H28551 Feb. 24, 1903

Location: Camp Wikoff *Photographed:* 1898[?]

13 ft. FLA3134 (print) FRA0467 (neg.)

[Spanish-American War]

As the film begins, three men are seen standing on the side
of the road. One of them, without a hat, has a white beard.
He wears the uniform of a general of the U.S. Army. There
are two other men, one in American military uniform, the
other in civilian attire. A contingent of American mounted
troops passes between the camera position and the three
principals who, judging by their gestures, are inspecting the
military establishments visible in the background. As the
film ends, the three men turn and walk toward the camera.
Two of the men are Gen. Joseph Wheeler (1836-1906) and

Russell A. Alger, Secretary of War, who resigned his post in July 1899, under public criticism.

The Genius

Klaw & Erlanger © LP3036 June 25, 1914

Director: Dell Henderson

Cast: Dell Henderson, James Kirkwood, Charles West, Isabel Rea, Mrs. LaVarnie, Gertrude Bambrick

1,176 ft. FLA5931 (print) FRA2744 (neg.)

In this comedy, a young man must become an artist in order to win the hand of a young lady with whom he is in love. He is wealthy, but no painter, so he hires a genuine artist to produce paintings which he presents as his own. The critics hail him as a genius. Dell Henderson, the make-believe artist, falls in love with his model (Gertrude Bambrick) and decides to confess. He is understandably annoyed when his confession is considered to be just another sign of a true artist's eccentricity.

The Gentlemen Highwaymen

AM&B © H56069 Jan. 18, 1905

Cameraman: G. W. Bitzer

Location: Fort Lee, N.J. *Photographed:* Jan. 13, 1905

123 ft. FLA5044 (print) FRA2005 (neg.)

This film, a chase from beginning to end, was all filmed on a road in a wooded area. A two-seater Oldsmobile with a man and woman in it comes down the road. A man wearing a full-length fur coat steps out of the bushes, stops the car, and attempts to remove the woman. The driver runs into the attacker, knocks him to the road, and continues. The man in the fur coat climbs into a much larger French automobile in which another man is waiting, and the chase is on. The villain's car breaks down, so the pursued couple has time to get to the police, who take the culprits into custody. The film ends with the hero towing the villain's car, with the two policemen as passengers.

Gentlemen of Nerve

Keystone © LP3632 Oct. 29, 1914

Producer and Author: Mack Sennet

Cast: Charles Chaplin, Mabel Normand, Chester Conklin, Phyllis Allen, Alice Davenport, Mack Swain, Dixie Chene, Norma Nichols, Harry McCoy, Peggy Pearce, Joe Bordeaux, Vivian Edwards, Glen Cavender, Joseph Swickard, Slim Summerville

Location: Auto racetrack located at the edge of Beverly Hills, Calif.

401 ft. FLA6092 (print)

Walrus (Chester Conklin) escorts Mabel Normand to the auto races. Their grandstand seat is next to Phyllis Allen to whom Walrus is attracted, much to the annoyance of Mabel. Chaplin and Swain, both broke, join forces to try to sneak into the grandstand area. This leads to several ridiculous situations when slim Charlie gets through a small opening, while fat Mack Swain gets caught halfway between. Mabel Normand, deserted by Walrus, takes up with Chaplin, and together they watch the races, including a propeller-operated automobile. The picture ends with a policeman taking both Walrus and Swain off the premises.

The Georgetown Loop

AM&B © H32383 June 4, 1903

Cameraman: G. W. Bitzer

Location: Georgetown, Colo. *Date:* July 11, 1901

80 ft. FLA5045 (print) FRA2006 (neg.)

The camera was placed on a car attached to an excursion train of five cars and a steam engine. Over the tops of the preceding cars, the engine can be seen as it goes under a trestle on which there is another train. People are waving from the excursion train as it goes around a mining community of about a hundred structures. This little piece of film was later used in June of 1906 by AM&B as part of a popular series offered as "attractive railroad pictures which have been found highly successful with tour car schemes."

German and American Tableau

Edison © H14870 Mar. 14, 1902

39 ft. FLA3985 (print) FRA1193 (neg.)

[The Visit of Prince Henry of Prussia to America]

As the film begins, two people are visible. One is an American soldier and the other a German soldier. They are standing beside a large double picture frame. As the film progresses, through the use of projected slides, photographs of both the German and American hierarchy are seen in the frames. At the end of the film, the American and German soldier turn, step forward, face one another, and shake hands. At that moment, a curtain consisting of an American and German flag closes out the scene from the camera lens.

German Railway Service

AM&B © H30436 Apr. 10, 1903

19 ft FLA3619 (print) FRA0879 (neg.)

The photographer placed his camera on the station platform of a German railroad depot. A locomotive pulling six passenger cars can be seen approaching the camera from a distance of approximately half a mile. The train reaches the station platform and stops. The doors of the passenger cars open. Many people alight and walk across the station platform and out of camera range.

German Torpedo Boat in Action

AM&B © H30176 Apr. 4, 1903

Photographed: 1905[?]

17 ft. FLA3576 (print) FRA0849 (neg.)

The poor condition of the film and the distance of the subject from the camera does not allow much interpretation of detail. However, in the distance, what appears to be a model of a ship can be seen approaching the camera. Two puffs of smoke can be seen as though some sort of mechanism was being discharged.

The Gerry Society's Mistake

AM&B © H39907 Dec. 23, 1903

Cameraman: A. E. Weed

Location: Studio, N.Y.C. *Photographed:* Dec. 10, 1903

22 ft. FLA4262 (print) FRA1418 (neg.)

Four young women are sitting at make-up tables in a backstage dressing room. They are in various stages of undress and are evidently preparing to perform. One of the young ladies rises, tightens her dancing shoes, and performs some pirouettes. While she is dancing, the door opens and a policeman in uniform and two men in street clothes come in and attempt to arrest the women for indecent conduct. The girls plead with the policeman, and finally remove their jewelry, take more out of trunks, and give it all to him and push the man out of the door. As the film ends, the women are expressing their jubilation at their triumph over the law. The Gerry Society was a group that tried to keep children under sixteen years of age off the stage.

See also: Scrap in the Dressing Room

A Gesture Fight in Hester Street
AM&B © H34815 Aug. 19, 1903
Cameraman: Arthur Marvin
Photographed: June 8, 1900
18 ft. FLA4134 (print) FRA2843 (neg.)

The camera was positioned as if it were in the audience of a vaudeville theater. A necktie salesman with a tray of neckties arrives on the scene first. Behind him is a painted backdrop depicting a store, a saloon, etc. As the film continues, the necktie salesman accosts a passing woman who refuses to buy his merchandise. Then a pushcart peddler bumps into him and a fight ensues. As the film ends, the pushcart has been overturned, and a policeman is beating the two warring salesmen on their heads with a nightstick.

Getting Even
Biograph © J131612 Sept. 14, 1909
Director: D. W. Griffith *Cameraman:* G. W. Bitzer
Cast: Edwin August, Florence Barker, John Cumpson, James Kirkwood, Florence LaBadie, Tony O'Sullivan, Mary Pickford, Billy Quirk, Mack Sennett, Mrs. Smith
Location: Edgewater, N.J.; Studio, N.Y.C. *Photographed:* Aug. 9, 10 and 12, 1909
213 ft. FLA5404 (print) FRA6436 (neg.)

The hero (Billy Quirk) is being harassed in an embarrassing sort of way in front of his girl friend (Mary Pickford). He vows to get even and so arrives at a costume party that night disguised in extraordinarily impressive female attire. Before the end of the evening, all of his cowboy friends who had administered the spanking pay him some attention, not as a man, but as a woman. The last scene of the film shows him dancing with his girl after he makes his identity known to his chagrined cowboy friends.

Getting Ready to Entertain Harvesters
AM&B © H26845 Jan. 9, 1903
Cameraman: F. S. Armitage
Location: Roof studio, N.Y.C. *Date:* May 19, 1899
24 ft. FLA3271 (print) FRA0590 (neg.)

The camera was positioned as if in the audience. The opening scene shows a set located outdoors. The set appears to be the back door of a house and the yard. Seated to the right of the camera position is a man made up as an elderly gentleman who is sound asleep in his chair. The first action shows a young teen-age girl rolling in a keg, which she stands on end. She then awakens the sleeping old man, and the two of them place the barrel on a table. The young girl leaves the set, goes into the house and returns with a bung starter. She uses it incorrectly and the barrel blows up, and the table tips over. As the film ends the man is seated on the ground covered from head to foot with suds.

Getting Strong
AM&B © H41750 Feb. 2, 1904
Cameraman: A. E. Weed
Location: Studio, N.Y.C. *Photographed:* Jan. 7, 1904
20 ft. FLA3396 (print) FRA2133 (neg.)

A woman is sitting at a dressing table in front of the wall of a bedroom set. While she is combing her hair, two women in pajamas enter. They engage the seated woman in conversation, and encourage her to remove her dress and clothing and join them in calisthenics. While she is doing her calisthenics, one of the visitors manages to kick her in the posterior and the film ends.

Getting Up in the World
AM&B © H32834 June 18, 1903
Location: Roof studio, N.Y.C. *Date:* May 9, 1899
10 ft. FLA3541 (print) FRA0817 (neg.)

The action shows three young women, two of whom are preparing to walk up a ladder that is leaning against a fence. One stays at the bottom of the ladder as a counterweight, while the other climbs up and over the ladder, tipping it so that it becomes a seesaw. The young woman nearest the camera falls through the aperture caused by the rungs of the ladder and in doing so, her skirt and petticoat remain caught in the ladder, revealing her legs covered by pantalets.

The Ghost Train
AM&B © H27984 Feb. 7, 1903
Photographed: Jan. 5, 1901
9 ft. FLA3148 (print) FRA0481 (neg.)

The novelty of this film of a locomotive pulling four cars around a turn was made possible by developing the film as a negative rather than as a print. When projected, those items in the film ordinarily white are black, while those usually black are white.

Giant Coal Dumper
Edison © 43407 July 3, 1897
24 ft. FLA3017 (print) FRA0017 (neg.)

The first of the two camera positions shows a large barrel-type device sufficient in size to completely encompass a railroad freight car. The cylindrical device can be seen rolling sideways. The second camera position shows coal-filled railroad cars entering the device one at a time to be emptied.

The Gibson Goddess
Biograph © J134044 Nov. 1, 1909
Director: D. W. Griffith *Cameraman:* G. W. Bitzer
Cast: Marion Leonard, Mack Sennett, Arthur Johnson, Billy Quirk, James Kirkwood, Frank Evans, George Nicholls, Tony O'Sullivan
Location: Highlands, N.J.; Studio, N.Y.C. *Photographed:* Sept. 11 and 17, 1909
225 ft. FLA5057 (print) FRA2829 (neg.)

An attractive young lady (Marion Leonard) arrives at a beach resort and is harassed by several unattached young men seeking a conquest. In desperation, she conceives a plan to get some peace. She adds padding to her figure, especially her legs, puts on a long beach coat and proceeds to the beach, followed by all the young men. When she gets there, she removes her coat and displays herself to the dismayed young men, all of whom laugh derisively and walk away. But there is one rather plain sailor who likes her no matter what. The last scene in the film shows the beautiful young woman, restored to normal, promenading through the crowd of gasping young men on the arm of her stalwart friend.

The Giddy Dancing Master

AM&B © H32503 June 11, 1903
Cameraman: G. W. Bitzer
Location: Studio, N.Y.C. *Date:* June 5, 1903
22 ft. FLA3496 (print) FRA0776 (neg.)

The opening scene takes place on a set of the drawing room of a modest home. One young lady is standing while the other is seated at a piano. The door opens and a small man with a mustache and a goatee and dressed in a tailcoat enters and begins instructing the young ladies how to dance. At the end of each portion of the lesson, the dancing master bends over the young lady's hand and kisses it. During the course of the film, a rather large woman, apparently a chaperone, watches the instruction. As the film ends, the woman is propelling the dancing master through the door, holding the lobe of his ear.

The Girl and Her Trust

Biograph © J167566 Mar. 28, 1912
Director: D. W. Griffith *Cameraman:* G. W. Bitzer
Cast: Wilfred Lucas, Dorothy Bernard, Edwin August, Alfred Paget, Charles Hill Mailes, Robert Harron, W. C. Robinson.
Location: Southern Calif.
369 ft. FLA5405 (print) FRA2307 (neg.)

The elements of this film are two thousand dollars, a woman telegraph operator, two bandits who attempt to kill her and steal the money, and a race between a train and a car rushing to her aid. There are several uses of close-ups to convey suspense and establish point of view, and a rare close-up of a pistol cartridge being exploded by a hammer. Several camera positions on and about speeding trains make up the unusual camera uses in this film. The film shows the arrival of a construction company's payroll, and then the two bandits who try to steal it from the custody of the young woman telegraph operator.

The Girl and the Cat

AM&B © H42040 Feb. 11, 1904
Cameraman: A. E. Weed
Location: Studio, N.Y.C. *Photographed:* Jan. 9, 1904
21 ft. FLA4639 (print) FRA1669 (neg.)

A young woman is sitting up in bed with a black-and-white cat in her lap on the set of a woman's boudoir. During the film, the young lady picks the cat up from her lap and fondles and pets it. A maid enters carrying a tray. She pours a saucer of milk and hands it to the young lady who puts it in her lap for the cat. The picture ends as the cat begins to lap the milk.

The Girl and the Outlaw

AM&B © H115212 Aug. 29, 1908
Director: D. W. Griffith *Cameraman:* Arthur Marvin

Cast: Florence Lawrence, Charles Inslee
Location: Fort Lee, N.J. *Photographed:* July 31 and Aug. 2-4, 1908
316 ft. FLA5407 (print) FRA2308 (neg.)

All of the scenes were taken outdoors, and they show a contest between the chief of a band of renegade Indians and his cast-off girl friend. He leaves her beside the road, presumably dead, after severely beating her. She is found by the daughter of a local settler. After she is revived, the two start out for the settlement, but they are set upon by the outlaw band, who hold them captive. The girl friend helps her rescuer make her escape. As the film ends, one of the Indians can be seen placing a blanket over the body of the girl who sacrificed her life to save the settler's daughter.

Girl at the Window

AM&B © H34810 Aug. 19, 1903
Cameraman: Wallace McCutcheon
Cast: Kathryn Osterman
Photographed: Aug. 4, 1904
28 ft. FLA3291 (print) FRA0607 (neg.)

A girl at a window is looking through binoculars. She attracts a man who comes over to the window. The girl hands him the binoculars and, as he turns his back to use them the young lady kisses him.

See also: "He Cometh Not," She Said; He Loves Me, He Loves Me Not

The Girl From Montana

Selig © H91440 Mar. 14, 1907
49 ft. FLA5046 (print) FRA2007 (neg.)

The film concerns the heroics of a competent Western horsewoman who saves her lover from being hanged by shooting the suspension rope in two. The film ends as several mounted men approach the camera, while the heroine is holding a gun on the villains, who are holding their arms up in surrender. The scenes leading to the finale show fighting between horsemen, a group of mounted men chasing a bandit, three men in the costumes of early California Spaniards, and very primitive barns and cabins.

The Girl Who Went Astray

See: The Downward Path

Girls' Acrobatic Feats

AM&B © H22557 Oct. 14, 1902
Photographed: 1898[?]
18 ft. FLA3506 (print, copy 1) FLA5969 (print, copy 2) FRA0785 (neg.)

The poor condition and the shortness of this film do not permit a great deal of detail to be described. However, from a single camera position, a considerable amount of activity is shown of young girls in the gym clothing of the time performing various feats of dexterity, such as running, jumping, climbing, and pushing a swing.

The Girls and Daddy

AM&B © H122510 Feb. 3, 1909
Director: D. W. Griffith *Cameramen:* G. W. Bitzer, Arthur Marvin
Cast: Florence Lawrence, Dorothy West, Charles Inslee, Dorothy Bernard, Harry Salter, D. W. Griffith, Robert

Harron, Mack Sennett, Arthur Johnson, Wilfred Lucas, Clara T. Bracey, Gladys Egan

Location: Fort Lee, N.J.; Studio, N.Y.C. *Photographed:* Dec. 31, 1908 and Jan. 1-4 1909

340 ft. FAB0505 (print) FLA5406 (print) FRA2306 (neg.)

Two young ladies (Lawrence and West), observed by a burglar (Inslee) as they cash a money order at the post office, are followed home. Their happy chatter about plans to buy their father a gift is overheard by a drunken sneak thief (Salter) who has sought refuge under their porch steps. Within a few minutes of one another, the thief and the burglar enter the home. The burglar leaves with his loot. The drunken thief makes so much noise he awakens the two young girls. An exciting time ensues with the drunken man following the girls from room to room, battering down doors. One of the girls is forced up on the roof where she encounters the burglar emerging from a trapdoor. She screams for help, and after considering shooting her, the burglar comes to her aid. The police are alerted, and all ends well.

The Girls and the Burglar

AM&B © H43564 Mar. 22, 1904

Cameraman: A. E. Weed

Location: Studio, N.Y.C. *Photographed:* Mar. 8, 1904

19 ft. FLA4321 (print) FRA1469 (neg.)

The opening scene takes place in a bedroom set of a modestly furnished house, where two young girls dressed in pajamas are apparently expecting someone. They go the door and discover it cannot be locked. They return to the bed and create a dummy, which they place in the bed while they climb under the bed. A burglar enters and creeps stealthily about the room seeking valuables. He comes up to the bed, sees the dummy, and flees in terror.

Girls Dancing Can-Can

AM&B © H23791 Nov. 11, 1902

Photographed: 1898[?]

7 ft. FLA3395 (print) FRA0693 (neg.)

Eight women, four dressed in full-length skirts and four in bloomers and boots, go through an organized dance routine in front of a painted backdrop on the stage.

See also: Girls Playing See-Saw and Girls Swinging

Girls Jumping the Rope

AM&B © H40809 Jan. 12, 1904

Camera: A. E. Weed

Location: Studio, N.Y.C. *Photographed:* Dec. 7, 1903

22 ft. FLA5779 (print) FRA2822 (neg.)

From a single camera position a dining room set can be seen. Four young women are seated around a table with a tea service on it. The action begins when the young women clear off the table and get out a jump rope. After that, the girls jump rope one at a time.

Girls Playing See-Saw

AM&B © H23790 Nov. 11, 1902

Photographed: 1898[?]

17 ft. FLA3442 (print) FRA0927 (neg.)

A large seesaw is in the foreground of an area surrounded by trees. Standing in the center of the board are two young girls in gymnasium attire. On either side of the seesaw are eight or ten young girls in various types of outdoor clothing. Apparently they are enjoying themselves, working the seesaw up and down. Several bicycles are leaning against the seesaw support.

See also: Girls Dancing Can-Can and Girls Swinging

Girls Swinging

AM&B © H23804 Nov. 11, 1902

Photographed: 1897[?]

18 ft. FLA3451 (print) FRA0732 (neg.)

The entire film was photographed from the viewpoint of the audience at a vaudeville show. The subject was two girls pushing the third in a swing out over the audience. There was a backdrop. However, the poor condition of the film does not allow detail to be seen.

See also: Girls Dancing Can-Can and Girls Playing See-Saw

Girls Taking Time Checks, Westinghouse Works

See: Westinghouse Works

The Girls, the Burglar, and the Rat

AM&B © H60290 May 3, 1905

Cameraman: G. W. Bitzer

Location: Studio, N.Y.C. *Photographed:* Apr. 24, 1905

38 ft. FLA4640 (print) FRA1670 (neg.)

Two young women prepare for bed and get into it. The bedroom door opens and two men dressed as burglars enter and ransack the apartment. The burglars hear a noise and jump under the bed. This wakes the two girls who jump out of bed and beat up the burglars who leave the apartment. Shortly thereafter, a large mouse or rat appears in the bedroom, and the picture ends as the two young women stand on chairs, apparently frantic with fright.

Girls Winding Armatures

See: Westinghouse Works

Glacier Point

AM&B © H28546 Feb. 24, 1903

Cameraman: Robert K. Bonine

Location: Yosemite Valley, Calif. *Date:* Nov. 15, 1901

16 ft. FLA3140 (print) FRA0473 (neg.)

The cameraman placed his camera at a spot overlooking the vast area now called Yosemite National Park. The substance of the film consists of the fissures and trees, as well as outcroppings caused by glacial movement, as the camera pans 180 degrees.

The "Glen Island" Accompanying Parade

Edison © 52056 Sept. 3, 1898

Location: Hudson River, N.Y.C. *Photographed:* Aug. 20, 1898

31 ft. FLA4246 (print) FRA1402 (neg.)

[Spanish-American War; New York City Welcome to Admiral Sampson's Fleet After the Battle of Santiago Bay]

Photographed from a single camera position located on a pier, a large paddle wheel excursion ship can be seen passing the camera. The ship was supposed to be part of a welcoming committee for Admiral Sampson. The film only shows the passenger ship as it goes by.

A Glimpse of the San Diego Exposition
Keystone © MP293 Feb. 18, 1915
Author: Mack Sennett
Location: Balboa Park, San Diego
160 ft. FLA6093 (print)

The film begins from a single-camera position high above the Exposition grounds. The camera begins to pan from left to right, following the horizon. The picture includes all of the spires and buildings of the fair. Then the camera is moved to the Exposition midway and footage is taken of the California exhibit, the Panamanian exhibit, and many others. The emphasis is on the permanent exhibits which, at the time of this writing, still exist.

Glimpses of Yellowstone Park
Lubin Mfg. Co. © J132440 Sept. 9, 1909
Location: Yellowstone National Park, Wyo.
79 ft. FLA5049 (print) FRA2008 (neg.)

As the film begins, one of the geographical phenomenon for which Yellowstone National Park is known comes into view. The remainder of the film concentrates on such points of interest as the waterfalls and the geysers. These scenes include: the Devil's Firehole; Senator Miles of Montana feeding an elk; Yellowstone Falls, 305-feet high; and a giant geyser (Old Faithful). One of the elements of particular interest is the scene of Senator Miles feeding an elk.

Gloomy Gus Gets the Best of It
AM&B © H32783 June 17, 1903
Cameraman: G. W. Bitzer
Location: Studio, N.Y.C. *Date:* June 12, 1903
15 ft. FLA3580 (print) FRA0852 (neg.)

The set is part of a wall adjoining the back door of a house. The door opens, and a woman carrying a pie enters the scene. She places the pie on a table next to the wall and goes back through the door. Two men dressed as tramps appear, notice the pie, and attempt to purloin it. They are set upon by a small white dog and, while one of the tramps is wrestling on the ground with the dog, the other tramp picks up the pie, climbs up on the wall, and eats the pie.

The Goddess of Sagebrush Gulch
Biograph © J167455 Mar. 23, 1912
Director: D. W. Griffith *Cameraman:* G. W. Bitzer
Cast: Blanche Sweet, Dorothy Bernard, Harry Hyde, Alfred Paget, Charles West, Charles Hill Mailes, Walter Chrystie Cabanne, W. C. Miller, Tony O'Sullivan
Location: Southern Calif.
401 ft. FLA5409 (print) FRA2692 (neg.)

A beautiful blond young woman (Blanche Sweet), resident of a mining camp where she is known as "the Goddess," is visited by her city sister (Dorothy Bernard), who uses her wiles to steal her sister's boy friend (Charles West). The alternate love interest (Harry Hyde), who eventually wins "the Goddess," appears in the beginning but is not seen again until the end. The suspense occurs when the city girl is tied up in a cabin by some robbers who accidentally set it

on fire, and the Goddess must make a decision about calling for help. She does, and the posse overwhelms the robbers and saves her sister. There is a considerable amount of camera movement, and several times the camera is moved in for a single-person close-up.

Going Through the Tunnel
Edison © 13533 Feb. 24, 1898
Location: Southern Pacific Railway, Calif.
45 ft. FLA4641 (print) FRA1671 (neg.)

The camera was placed on the forward part of a train at the beginning of the film and shows the cars moving through a switchyard alongside some freight cars and into a tunnel. As the film ends, a train pulling three passenger cars approaches the camera.

Going to Market, Luxor, Egypt
Edison © H32807 June 17, 1903
Cameraman: A. C. Abadie
Location: Luxor, Egypt *Photographed:* Mar. 27, 1903
27 ft. FLA3429 (print) FRA0716 (neg.)

The film shows a large group of people in what appears to be a market place. They are milling about, and the camera holds the interest of some as they stand and stare into it. During the filming, a camel is led close by the camera.

Going to the Hunt, Meadowbrook
AM&B © H21310 Aug. 25, 1902
Cameraman: G. W. Bitzer
Location: Meadowbrook Hunt Club, Long Island, N.Y. *Date:* Apr. 24, 1899
20 ft. FLA3948 (print) FRA1159 (neg.)

The subject is a fox hunt. The camera takes in the club house and stables. As the film progresses, approximately twenty horseback riders accompanied by a group of dogs can be seen through the archway of one of the buildings. These horse-drawn, four-wheeled vehicles filled with passengers can also be seen at the end of the film.

See also: The Meadowbrook Hunt

Going to the Yokohama Races
Edison © 38223 June 22, 1898
Location: Yokohama, Japan
27 ft. FLA3112 (print) FRA0448 (neg.)

The film, photographed from a single-camera position, shows middle-class Japanese people passing by the camera on their way to the races. They ride mainly in rickshas.

See also: Returning from the Races

The Gold Dust Twins
AM&B © H32367 June 4, 1903
Cameraman: Robert K. Bonine
Photographed: Nov. 12, 1902
3 ft. FLA3774 (print) FRA1018 (neg.)

In front of a signboard set, two small black children can be seen. One holds a dishpan, while the other polishes the bottom of it with a cleanser that is being advertised as Gold Dust Scouring Powder.

Gold Is Not All
Biograph © J139986 Apr. 1, 1910

Director: D. W. Griffith *Cameraman:* G. W. Bitzer

Cast: Linda Arvidson, Marion Leonard, Dell Henderson, Florence Barker, George Nicholls, Mack Sennett, Gladys Egan, Kate Bruce, Alfred Paget, W. Chrystie Miller

Location: Pasadena, Calif.; Studio, Los Angeles *Photographed:* Feb. 18-19, 21 and 24, 1910

369 ft. FLA5410 (print) FRA2670 (neg.)

The film contrasts the lives of two families, one rich and the other poor. The first scene is of a mansion in the distance, with a long driveway and a handsome iron fence. Two poorly dressed women (Linda Arvidson and Kate Bruce) appear, and it is obvious that they envy the residents of the mansion. The gate of the mansion opens, and the mistress (Marion Leonard) comes out. The film shows the unhappy life led by the wealthy woman, whose husband (Dell Henderson) deserts her, and whose only child dies, while the poor woman (Linda Arvidson), who is married to a gardener (Mack Sennett), is surrounded by love and happiness. The exteriors were photographed on an estate in Pasadena, California.

A Gold Necklace

Biograph © J146227 Oct. 8, 1910

Director: D. W. Griffith *Cameraman:* Arthur Marvin

Cast: Mary Pickford, Kate Bruce, Jeanie Macpherson, Lottie Pickford, Mack Sennett, Florence LaBadie, Eddie Dillon, Violet Mersereau, Charles West

Location: Cuddebackville, N.Y.; Studio, N.Y.C. *Date:* Aug. 26, 29-31, 1910

321 ft. FLA5412 (print) FRA0007 (archival print)

A mix-up about a piece of jewelry lent by the owner (Mary Pickford) to her friend (Jeanie Macpherson) is the basis for this comedy. The friend loses the necklace and confesses the loss to her boyfriend (Mack Sennett) and sets off a series of comic incidents. He buys the necklace from the owner and gives it to his girlfriend, who returns it to the owner. But she already has her necklace back because the governess had found it where it was lost originally. The final scene shows all of the participants in one place, each blaming the others for the mishap. Most of the scenes were photographed out-of-doors.

The Gold Seekers

Biograph © J141120 May 5, 1910

Director: D. W. Griffith *Cameramen:* G. W. Bitzer, Arthur Marvin

Cast: Henry B. Walthall, Florence Barker, Tony O'Sullivan, Dell Henderson, Alfred Paget, Charles West, George Nicholls, W. Chrystie Miller, Kate Bruce, Mack Sennett

Location: Sierra Madre, Calif.; Studio, Los Angeles

Photographed: Mar. 18, 19 and 21, 1910

392 ft. FLA5411 (print) FRA2309 (neg.)

This melodrama begins with a scene showing a disgruntled and unhappy man, woman, and child who have spent about as much time in the gold fields as their emotional state will allow. In a stormy scene, the man swears to try just once more and if he fails he promises they will return to civilization. He is seen making a half-hearted search. In sheer disgust, he throws down his pick and, at that moment, realizes he has found gold. He stakes out a claim and sends his wife and child into the settlement to record it. The villains in the piece, two men, seek to thwart the wife's efforts to record the claim. They lock both wife and child in an empty room. The film ends showing the supreme effort of the wife and child to prevent the villains from recording the claim themselves. The wife boosts the little boy up and out of the transom over the door of her prison. He runs for aid, which is forthcoming barely in time to catch the claim jumpers redhanded.

The Golden Chariots

Edison © H16716 Apr. 18, 1902

Location: Charleston Exposition, Charleston, S. C. *Photographed:* Apr. 1902

27 ft. FLA3203 (print) FRA0529 (neg.)

From a single camera position, at a distance of about a hundred feet, what seems to be a section of an amusement park can be seen. A modified carousel is seen at camera center. The machine is in operation, and several persons are sitting in it.

Golden Louis

AM&B © H123059 Feb. 17, 1909

Director: D.W. Griffith *Cameraman:* Arthur Marvin

Cast: Kate Bruce, Adele De Garde, Wilfred Lucas, Owen Moore, Mack Sennett, Marion Leonard

Location: Bleecker Street and Studio, N.Y.C. *Date:* Jan. 28-30, 1909

181 ft. FLA5413 (print) FRA2310 (neg.)

This film is based on a version of the "The Little Match Girl" story. All of the actors wear eighteenth-century French costumes. A woman bandages the foot of a small girl and sends her out on the snow-covered streets to beg. The child falls asleep on the stairs of a church. A cavalier passes by and puts a gold coin in her wooden shoe. Another cavalier, who has lost his fortune gambling, sees the child and the golden louis. There is a dramatic scene as the noble wrestles with his conscience, but finally greed wins, and so does he on the gambling table. Enriched, he seeks out the child to return her money, but finds her frozen to death. There are two insert close-ups: one of the coin in the palm of a hand, and the other of the same coin in the heel of a wooden shoe.

The Golden Supper

Biograph © H148744 Dec. 15, 1910

Director: D. W. Griffith *Cameraman:* G. W. Bitzer

Cast: Edwin August, Alfred Paget, Dorothy West, Charles West, Claire McDowell

Location: Greenwich, Conn.; Studio, N.Y.C. *Date:* Oct. 19–29, 1910

376 ft. FLA5414 (print) FRA2311 (neg.)

This film, based on Tennyson's poem "Lover's Tale," shows a young man as he makes a farewell visit to the tomb of his unrequited love. However, he finds her alive, and courageously sets out to find her husband for her since after the death of his beloved wife, the grief-stricken husband had abandoned civilization. The film ends as the husband and wife are reunited by her admirer's unselfish act. All of the actors wear fifteenth-century Italian costumes. The film was photographed on a Greenwich, Connecticut, estate. The title is followed by a line reading "Adaptation from Alfred Lord Tennyson's poem."

Goo Goo Eyes

Edison © H26889 Jan 12, 1903

Cast: Gilbert Sarony

29 ft. FLA4226 (print) FRA1385 (neg.)

The picture begins with a tight head close-up of a man made up to resemble an ugly woman. Throughout the film, the man costumed as a woman grimaces and contorts his face continually. He conveys the impression of a rapidly talking woman who is attempting to describe an incident. In order to better illustrate the story, he crosses his eyes and twists his mouth until the film ends.

A Good Joke With My Head

See: Un Prêté Pour un Rendu; ou, Une Bonne Farce Avec Ma Tête

A Good Shot

AM&B © H16380 Apr. 12, 1902

Cameraman: F. S. Armitage

Location: Roof studio, N.Y.C. *Date:* May 18, 1899

10 ft. FLA3571 (Print) FRA0845 (neg.)

The camera was positioned in what appears to be the backyard of a modest house. The camera view encompasses a window and a shielding wall constructed at right angles to the side of the house. A large man dressed as a laundress can be seen standing behind the wall and scrubbing clothes. As the film continues, a young couple approaches the wall that hides the laundering from view, and the young girl holds up a target at which the boy fires with a rifle. Evidently the bullet was supposed to have penetrated the wall and hit the washer woman because immediately after the rifle is discharged, she dives head first into the tub. The commotion causes the youngsters to flee, followed closely by the irate laundress.

A Good Time with the Organ Grinder

AM&B © H28674 Feb. 26, 1903

Cameraman: Arthur Marvin

Location: Roof studio, N.Y.C. *Date:* May 24, 1900

10 ft. FLA3173 (print) FRA0499 (neg.)

A man dressed as the general conception of an organ grinder is the first person seen in this film. He is standing by a large, two-wheeled street organ, when a man escorting two rather gay young ladies appears. The man flips a coin into the air, the organ grinder bends down to retrieve it, and one of the young women performs an acrobatic trick over his back. The man who flipped the coin starts turning the crank of the street organ, while the two women take hold of the organ grinder and dance around with him. A few frames before the picture ends, a policeman appears on the scene.

"Goodby John"

Winthrop Moving Picture Co. © H94484 May 24, 1907

Cast: David Craig Montgomery, Fred A. Stone

11 ft. FLA5415 (print) FRA2712 (neg.)

The producer of this film made a practice of sending in only a few pieces of a film for copyright purposes. This piece is a close-up of the comedy team of Montgomery and Stone. It is too short for further description.

Gordon Sisters Boxing

Edison © H4083 May 6, 1901

51 ft. FLA4642 (print) FRA1672 (neg.)

Two women engage in hitting one another with boxing gloves in front of a painted backdrop of a garden. They give a good account of themselves.

The Gossipers

AM&B © H71529 Jan 3, 1906

Cameraman: G. W. Bitzer

Location: Studio, N.Y.C. *Photographed:* Dec. 14, 1905

40 ft. FLA4643 (print) FRA1673 (neg.)

The camera was placed so that we see three people sitting at a dining room table. A woman is serving some food to the man on her left, while the man on her right waits patiently holding his plate. All during the picture, the woman chatters, paying no attention to the man on her right. He finally becomes exasperated and throws the contents of his plate on the other man.

Government House at Hong Kong

Edison © 38233 June 22, 1898

30 ft. FLA4317 (print) FRA1465 (neg.)

The single-camera position encompasses three columns of the front of the Government House in Hong Kong. Several bearers with shoulder yokes and poles walk by during the film.

Governor Roosevelt and Staff

AM&B © H17968 May 21, 1902

Cameraman: Francis S. Armitage

Location: Dewey Homecoming, N.Y.C. *Photographed:* Sept. 30, 1899

35 ft. FLA3800 (print) FRA1036 (neg.)

A parade led by Theodore Roosevelt was photographed from a single-camera position, and Governor Roosevelt can be seen only in the first few feet of film. The remainder shows his staff and military escort.

Governor Roosevelt and Staff

Edison © 65370 Oct. 7, 1899

Location: Land parade honoring Admiral Dewey, N.Y.C. *Photographed:* Sept. 30, 1899

32 ft. FLA3800 (print) FRA1036 (neg.)

[Spanish-American War; Dewey Homecoming]

The camera was placed too far away to permit much detail. However, Theodore Roosevelt can be seen astride a horse and several other people, also on horseback, follow him along streets lined with individuals who wave, as if watching a parade.

Governor's Foot Guards, Conn.

AM&B © H17969 May 21, 1902

Cameraman: Francis S. Armitage

Location: Land parade honoring Admiral Dewey, N.Y.C. *Photographed:* Sept. 30, 1899

21 ft. FLA4025 (print) FRA1217 (neg.)

The camera was stationed high over the heads of crowds of spectators on the street watching a parade of marching men. The men, dressed in the uniform of the Revolutionary

War, are in close-order drill as they march by the camera position.

Grand Hotel to Big Indian

AM&B © H75637 Apr. 12, 1906

Cameraman: G. W. Bitzer

Location: Ulster & Delaware R.R., N.Y.; Studio, N.Y.C.
Photographed: Apr. 5–6, 1906

160 ft. FLA5416 (print) FRA2314 (neg.)

This film consists of a combination of indoor photography on a set of the interior of a railroad passenger car and scenes of the actual railroad right-of-way. The first third of the film is devoted to a pan shot and pictures of the train as it goes around corners, through tunnels, and over trestles. Then the interior of the passenger car is cut into the film. A fight over seating takes place in the interior, and the film reverts to exterior shots taken from the front of the moving train, which slowly comes to a stop for a stalled horse and buggy. The engineer and firemen get off the train and fight with the horse and owner, and lose. But the horse, of its own volition, pulls the cart off the track.

Grandfather as a Spook

AM&B © H43406 Mar. 17, 1904

Cameraman: A. E. Weed

Location: Studio, N.Y.C. *Photographed:* Feb. 24, 1904

33 ft. FLA4644 (print) FRA1674 (neg.)

This film is built around a series of pranks directed at an old gentleman, who is sleeping in a chair in the living room of a large house. A woman made up as a precocious little girl enters, sees the man asleep, goes out, and returns with someone disguised as a ghost with a skeleton face. They soon realize that the old man is not affected by their tricks and they remove the sheet and drape it over the sleeping man, placing the skeleton mask on his bald pate. A middle-aged woman arrives, sees the mask, becomes frightened, and falls down, thus waking the old man who slides from his chair. The film ends as the two of them are seated on the floor.

Grandma and the Bad Boys

Edison © D23260 Dec. 21, 1900

23 ft. FLA4197 (print) FRA1360 (neg.)

A woman is puttering about a table against the wall of living room set of a modest house. On the wall above her head is a coal oil lamp in its bracket. The woman leaves the set, and two small boys appear, place a chair against the wall, climb up, and remove the lamp. They proceed to fill the lamp chimney with flour and replace it. They then scurry away and hide. When the woman returns and prepares to light

Two scenes from American Mutoscope & Biograph Company's The Great Baltimore Fire (1904). This fire destroyed forty-two square blocks of Baltimore.

the lantern, the flour spills all over her head and shoulders. She discovers the two boys and chastises them. During this episode, the violence of her actions causes her to lose her wig, revealing that the part was played by a man.

Grandpa's Reading Glass

AM&B © H22204 Oct. 3, 1902

Cameraman: Robert K. Bonine

Date: July 25, 1902

34 ft. FLA4645 (print) FRA1675 (neg.)

A group of small children is clustered about an old gentleman who is seated at a library table reading through a hand-held magnifying glass. The children, intrigued with the possibilities of the glass, take it from him and point it at objects that interest them. During the remainder of the film, the cameraman moved his camera to a close-up of a bird, a printed page, the eye of a child, the head of a grown woman, the head of an infant, the head of a little girl holding a kitten, and a monkey. Each of these close-ups was vignetted by a matte frame in the camera.

"Grandrepublic" Passing "Columbia"

AM&B © H31672 May 11, 1903

Cameraman: F. S. Armitage

Date: Oct. 5, 1899

19 ft. FLA3467 (print) FRA0749 (neg.)

[America's Cup Races]

As the film begins, America's Cup defender, *Columbia*, can be seen. From camera right comes a large sidewheel propelled passenger excursion boat, completely obscuring the *Columbia*; but, as the film ends, the *Columbia*, under full sail, is again in view.

Greaser's Gauntlet

AM&B © H14338 Aug. 6, 1908

Director: D. W. Griffith *Cameraman:* Arthur Marvin

Cast: Wilfred Lucas, Marion Leonard, Arthur Johnson, Frank Gebhardt, Kate Bruce, Linda Arvidson

Location: Studio, N.Y.C.; Shadyside, N.J. *Photographed:* July 14–15, 1908

386 ft. FLA5417 (print) FRA2315 (neg.)

A blessing by a gypsy and an amulet given to a Spanish caballero save the life of the heroine as well as that of the man to whom it was originally given. The film opens and closes with a gypsy seated by the side of a road. She reads the fortune of the caballero as he kneels beside her. The subsequent events are the caballero being suspected of robbery and being saved from hanging; transferring of the amulet to his benefactress, quarreling with her spurned lover who kidnaps her, and her rescue because of the amulet. The final scene shows the caballero returning to the site of the first scene, where he gives the amulet back to the gypsy.

The Great Baltimore Fire

AM&B © H42176 Feb. 15, 1904

Cameraman: A. E. Weed

Location: Baltimore, Md. *Photographed:* Feb. 9, 1904

69 ft. FLA5050 (print) FRA2009 (neg.)

The camera pans for approximately 360 degrees to show the ruins of the city of Baltimore, Maryland, after the great fire of 1904. There are good scenes of old fire-fighting equipment, firemen in action, and the charred ruins of a city.

The Great Bull Fight

Edison © H15912 Apr. 2, 1902

Location: Mexico City *Photographed:* Feb. 1, 1902

417 ft. FLA5418 (print) FRA2312 (neg.)

As the title indicates, the subject is a bull fight, which took place in Mexico City on February 2, 1902. Among those in the audience were President Diaz and his cabinet. The complete fight was filmed, starting with the arrival of the matador at the bull ring and ending with the carcass of the dead bull being towed away. Some of the film shows good detail while other sections were incorrectly exposed. However, for the three minutes the film runs, most of the action is visible and understandable.

The Great Fire Ruins, Coney Island

Edison © H37834 Nov. 10, 1903

Cameraman: A. C. Abadie *Location:* Coney Island, N.Y. *Photographed:* Nov. 2, 1903

82 ft. FLA4646 (print) FRA1676 (neg.)

In order to photograph the catastrophe, the cameraman placed his camera in several positions throughout the devastated area. The opening scenes, as the camera pans, show the remains of a number of buildings destroyed by fire and workmen wrecking the dangerous standing walls. Other camera positions show closer views of fires still burning because of shorted power lines, demolition of brick walls left standing, etc.

The Great Jewel Mystery

AM&B © H67834 Oct. 23, 1905

Cameramen: G. W. Bitzer, F. A. Dobson

Location: Sound Beach, Conn.; Studio, N.Y.C. *Date:* Oct. 5, 6, 11–13, 1905

268 ft. FLA5419 (print) FRA2685 (neg.)

The film begins with a medium close-up of an open jewel box, with strings of pearls, brooches, and other jewelry in it. The next scene is preceded by a title and shows some people discussing robbery plans. One man gets in a coffin, and the mourners accompany it as it is put aboard the same railroad car as the jewel casket. As the picture continues, the man gets out of the coffin, slugs the postal guard, and takes the jewelry into the coffin with him. The coffin is removed, accepted by a hearse, and delivered to a room where his confederates await him. While the robbers are exulting over their success, the police break down the doors and capture them. There is a good example of a traveling matte as the scenery goes by the train window. The film was considered by the producer to be the most plausible theory as to the manner of theft of $100,000 in jewels that actually took place between New York and Newport. The film carries the title The Mystery of the Missing Jewel Casket.

The Great Toronto Fire, Toronto, Canada, April 19, 1904

George Scott and Company © H46445 May 27, 1904

Location: Toronto, Canada *Photographed:* Apr. 19, 1904

85 ft. FLA5051 (print) FRA2010 (neg.)

The film shows the arrival of fire-fighting equipment and actual fire fighting in a large city in Canada. The several camera positions show street scenes with the fire equipment passing by, streams of water playing on the blaze, and buildings being blown up. One hundred fourteen buildings were destroyed in a eight-hour period.

The Great Train Robbery

Edison © H38748 Dec. 1, 1903

Cameraman: Edwin S. Porter

Cast: "Broncho" Billy Anderson, Marie Murray, George Barnes, Frank Hanaway

Location: Orange Mountains, N.J..

302 ft. FLA5421 (print, copy 1) FLA4912 (print, copy 2) FLA 5949 (35mm print) FRA2313 (neg.)

This is the complete version, starting with the conspiracy scenes through the station agent's office to the switch engine hold-up of the train, the robbery of the passengers, and the capture of the bandits by the posse as they are burying their ill-gotten gains.

The Great Train Robbery

Lubin © H47533 June 27, 1904

Cameraman: Jack Frawley [?]

Location: Philadelphia

300 ft. FLA 2794 (print) FRA 3922 (neg.)

A frame-for-frame copy of Edison's famous film, The Great Train Robbery.

A Guardian of the Peace

AM&B © H38015 Nov. 12, 1903

Cameraman: A. E. Weed

Location: Studio, N.Y.C. *Photographed:* Oct. 29, 1903

27 ft. FLA3667 (print) FRA0919 (neg.)

The scene begins in what appears to be the backyard of a house. The back porch is shown, together with a set of a brick wall. A man and a woman are walking about making gestures as if they are arguing. They begin fighting, and a policeman appears who attempts to break up the fight by separating the two. Both the man and the woman begin beating the policeman. At this time, a dummy is substituted for the policeman. The couple throw the dummy over the wall of their yard. The camera is then turned around to show the other side of the wall and the dummy as it is propelled over the fence toward the camera position, landing on the sidewalk. Via stop action photography, the live actor now replaces the dummy. The policeman gets up and walks away, making gestures as if vowing never again to interfere between husband and wife.

See also: Off His Beat

The Guerrilla

AM&B © H118186 Nov. 11, 1908

Director: D. W. Griffith *Cameramen:* Arthur Marvin, G. W. Bitzer

Cast: Mack Sennett, Herbert Yost, Harry C. Myers, Harry Salter

Location: Coytesville, N.J.; Studio, N.Y.C. *Photographed:* Oct. 12 and 14, 1908

330 ft. FLA5422 (print) FRA2316 (neg.)

The period of this film is the Civil War, and it involves a young man, a Union soldier, and the girl he leaves behind, as well as a Confederate soldier and a black servant. The Confederate soldier dons a uniform and decides to call on the woman of the manor. He is unwelcome, and a tense series of scenes show her repulsing his advances as he forces her from room to room. She manages to write a note and gives it to her black servant, who succeeds in delivering the note to her lover, although he sacrifices his life in the attempt. There is a long chase with the Union soldier breaking away from Confederate soldiers just in time to save his betrothed from her drunken pursuer. Suspense is built up by frequent cutbacks and the camera is panned early in the picture.

Gun Drill by Naval Cadets at Newport Training School

Edison © D22021 Nov. 22, 1900

Location: Newport, R.I.

27 ft. FLA3993 (print) FRA1198 (neg.)

The subject is the training program of the naval recruits at Newport, Rhode Island. The action, from a single-camera position, shows the company-front formation of sailors dressed in training whites, leggings, gun belts, etc., as they fire their rifles. The second camera position shows a company of men firing rifles, fixing bayonets, and then charging by the camera position. This maneuver is repeated three times by the trainees.

See also: Gymnasium Exercises and Drills at Newport Training School, Naval Apprentices at Sail Drill on Historic Ship Constellation, and Naval Sham Battle at Newport

Gussle Rivals Jonah

Keystone © LP5038 Apr. 24, 1915

Producer and Author: Mack Sennett

Cast: Sydney Chaplin, Phyllis Allen, Eleanor Fields, Henry "Pathe" Lehrman, Peggy Pearce

Location: First reel: A passenger steamer that went between San Pedro and Catalina Island, Calif. Second reel: The dock at Avalon, Catalina Island

797 ft. FLA6094-6095 (print)

A married couple (Sydney Chaplin and Phyllis Allen), loaded down with packages, takes an outing on an excursion steamer. A rather heavy man and two attractive female friends also board the boat. The minute Syd Chaplin discovers one of the particularly pretty young ladies (Peggy Pearce) and begins a flirtation with her, the trouble begins. It is one of the most physically rough of all the Keystone films. The picture ends with Gussle (Sydney Chaplin) flat on his back on the dock spouting water as if he were a whale pulled in from the bay.

Gussle the Golfer

Keystone © LP4066 Dec. 28, 1914

Producer and Author: Mack Sennett

Cast: Sydney Chaplin, Dixie Chene, Mack Swain, Slim Summerville, Joe Swickard, Eddie Cline, Henry "Pathe" Lehrman

Location: Midwick Country Club, Los Angeles

FLA6096 (print)

A highly amusing film in the Gussle series. Syd Chaplin, as Gussle, has an opportunity to display his ability as an acrobat when he does a headspin, followed by an antic involving a piece of paper that insists on clinging like flypaper to his golf club as he plays a game with Mack Swain and his wife, Dixie Chene. Disgusted, Gussle gives up golf for gambling at the club house, loses all his money in spite of cheating, and then informs the police of an illegal card game. The police raid the club and take Swain off to jail, leaving Gussle free to court Swain's wife. Swain catches him when he is released the next day. The picture ends in typical Gussle style with Syd Chaplin silhouetted against the sky as he tries to escape from Mack Swain's shotgun.

Gussle Tied to Trouble

Keystone © LP5285 May 6, 1915

Producer and Author: Mack Sennett *Director:* Charles Avery

Cast: Sydney Chaplin, Phyllis Allen, Eleanor Fields, Peggy Pearce

Location: Big Bear Lake area of Calif.

416 ft. FLA6097 (print)

This comedy begins in an alpine setting with a group of people preparing to make a mountain climb when one of the wives, Phyllis Allen, catches her husband, Syd Chaplin, flirting with a barmaid. This makes her furious and she starts after him, beginning a chase that continues throughout the picture with Phyllis shooting at him at every opportunity. Gussle (Syd Chaplin) double-crosses his friends by robbing them but is caught. As he backs away from the irate group, he loses his balance, falls over a cliff into a rushing river. Phyllis Allen throws a rock at her errant husband, hitting him on the head. The picture ends with the still unconscious Gussle floating down the river toward certain disaster.

Gussle's Backward Way

Keystone © LP5252 May 3, 1915

Producer and Author: Mack Sennett *Director:* Charles Avery

Cast: Sydney Chaplin, Phyllis Allen, Cecile Arnold, Eleanor Fields

Location: Big Bear Lake, Calif.

410 ft. FLA6098 (print)

The film concerns the adventures of Gussle, played by Sydney Chaplin, in the Big Bear Lake area of California. The picture opens with our hero riding a mule through a creek bed, when he is set upon by some robbers. Gussle outsmarts them and he and the mule make their way to a resort inn where he becomes a hero after recounting his experiences. The balance of the film is devoted to Gussle and the rest of the guests at the inn playing games, all the result of something Gussle has done. One of the scenes shows Gussle drinking a glass of beer belonging to Phyllis Allen through a long-stemmed clay pipe.

Gussle's Day of Rest

Keystone © LP4874 Mar. 27, 1915

Producer and Author: Mack Sennett

Cast: Phyllis Allen, Sydney Chaplin, Eddie Cline, Cecile Arnold, Slim Summerville

Location: Echo Park and Griffith Park; Santa Monica Boulevard in Los Angeles.

768 ft.   FLA6099-6100 (print)

An action-packed account of what happens when Gussle (Sydney Chaplin) and his wife (Phyllis Allen) spend a day at a California ocean resort. There are many delightful situations in it. When Phyllis Allen is knocked down by a model-T Ford in which Cecile Arnold and Slim Summerville are riding, Gussle pushes, hits, and kicks the automobile, forcing it backwards down the street. Slim and Cecile settle down to enjoy a picnic, and Phyllis Allen decides on a nap, leaving Gussle free to flirt with Cecile Arnold. A wild fight erupts between the two couples, ending with Cecile and Gussle taking off in the model-T. Gussle runs into a cliff at the same moment a construction crew sets off some dynamite, burying Gussle and Cecile Arnold under mountains of dirt.

Gussle's Wayward Path

Keystone   © LP5040   Apr. 10, 1915

Producer and Author: Mack Sennett

Cast: Estelle Allen, Billie Bennett, Sydney Chaplin, Phyllis Allen, Peggy Pearce

Location: Los Angeles

442 ft.   FLA6101 (print)

Gussle, home from a hunting trip, hangs his hunting dog—a small puppy—on a coat rack. His wife, Phyllis Allen, hands him a telegram advising him of troubles at his factory. A preacher and his wife drop in and notice Gussle embracing the maid, Estelle Allen. Gussle's wife gives him her picture and says, "When you are tempted, look at my picture." When Gussle reaches the station, he is tempted by a lovely young lady, and his wife's picture helps him to stay out of trouble. Not so when a second young woman (Peggy Pearce) flirts with him. This time he tears up his wife's picture and they board the train together. In the meantime, his wife has learned of his activities and hurries to the train station, boards the train, and becomes involved with a masher. When Gussle discovers them, he rams a suitcase over their heads.

Gymnasium Exercises and Drill at Newport Training School

Edison   © D22022   Nov. 22, 1900

Location: Newport, R.I.

37 ft.   FLA4647 (print)   FRA1677 (neg.)

From a single-camera position located on the parade-and-drill grounds of a naval recruit training center approximately five hundred men in navy whites can be seen performing calisthenics. The film includes the sailors in the immediate foreground up to an area approximately one hundred yards away where the superstructure of a steam vessel tied to a dock is visible in the background.

See also: Gun Drill by Naval Cadets at Newport Training School, Naval Apprentices at Sail Drill on Historic Ship Constellation, and Naval Sham Battle at Newport.

A Gypsy Duel

AM&B   © H34098   Aug. 3, 1903

Cameraman: G. W. Bitzer

Photographed: July 15, 1903

22 ft.   FLA3723 (print)   FRA0970 (neg.)

A woman dressed as a gypsy is reading the palm of a man also dressed as a gypsy. Another man enters and indicates by his gestures that he is displeased at the association. A fight starts and one of the two men is seen with a knife protruding from his chest when the picture ends.

Haevnen, or Haevnet

See: Vengeance

The Hairdresser

AM&B   © H32106   May 22, 1903

Cameraman: G. W. Bitzer

Location: Studio, N.Y.C. *Date:* May 14, 1903

35 ft.   FLA3605 (print)   FRA0869 (neg.)

The picture begins in a living room set. Among the furniture is a large mirror. Two adult actors, a man and a woman, embrace. The man is dressed for the street. He leaves and the woman sits down in front of the mirror. The door opens, and another man enters. The woman embraces him. Just then the door opens and the first man reappears. The woman removes the pins from her hair, sits in front of the mirror, and the door opens once again to admit still another man. Two of the men leave, and the hairdresser and the woman resume their embrace as the picture ends.

Halloween

AM&B   © H68125   Oct. 30, 1905

Cameraman: G. W. Bitzer

Location: Studio, N.Y.C. *Photographed:* Oct. 19, 1905

20 ft.   FLA3861 (print)   FRA1073 (neg.)

The set resembles a basement with shelves around the walls and a staircase in the center. A man in a dark suit and a derby comes down the stairs into the basement and rehearses a prank he is about to play. It consists of pulling a make-believe mouse across the floor. As the film continues, a young woman holding a mirror in front of her backs down the stairway. As she reaches the bottom, she sees the fake mouse, drops the mirror and starts up the stairs. Then she turns around and runs down the stairs and into the arms of the prankster.

Halloween Night at the Seminary

Edison   © H42204   Feb. 16, 1904

Cameraman: Edwin S. Porter

Location: Studio, N.Y.C. *Date:* Feb. 8, 1904

50 ft.   FLA4648 (print)   FRA1678 (neg.)

The set represents the entrance hall of a large house. A man in the tattered garments of a tramp creeps slowly into the room. When he gets to the center, he notices something like an apple hanging from a string. He is scrutinizing it when he is set upon by four young girls in pajamas, who appear to be hilarious as they push him from the room. They return to their Halloween games, which include dunking for apples, etc., when one of the young ladies notices the tramp again. The film ends as the four young women seize the tramp, dunk him in the tub of water, and cover him with flour.

Hammock Over Water

AM&B   © H35874   Sept. 21, 1903

Cameraman: M. Casler
Location: Canastota, N.Y. Date: Oct. 1901
48 ft.   FLA4649 (print)   FRA1679 (neg.)

A hammock is stretched over an inlet section of water. The background indicates it is a shaded, wooded area. A fashionably dressed young woman and her escort can be seen through the foliage, moving toward the camera. They make their way to the edge of the water, climb into the hammock, and begin embracing. The hammock breaks, and they land in the water. Two men in shirt-sleeves appear at the edge of the water and help the now very thoroughly soaked young man and woman out of the water. This film was considered experimental and was not originally intended for exhibition.

Hanging Stockings Christmas Eve
AM&B © H25016   Dec. 15, 1902
17 ft.   FLA3795 (print)   FRA1032 (neg.)

As the film begins, one can see a living room set. There is a fireplace on the back wall, and next to the fireplace is a doorway covered by a drape. An adult and two children carrying Christmas decorations come through the drape and proceed to hang stockings on the mantelpiece; then they go off camera. The picture ends; however, there is a sequel.

See also: Christmas Morning. Santa Filling Stockings and The Christmas Party. Released under the title: Night Before Christmas.

Happy Hooligan
AM&B © H33025   June 20, 1903
Cameraman: G. W. Bitzer
Date: June 15, 1903
19 ft.   FLA3435 (print)   FRA0721 (neg.)

A tramp is watching an organ grinder at work in front of a two-story house set. As the picture progresses, the music attracts an unsympathetic woman to the second-floor window. The tramp spies a policeman and warns the organ grinder, who runs away. The policeman apprehends and admonishes the tramp for his actions. While the policeman is ordering the tramp to vacate the area, the woman returns to the window and dumps a bucket of water on the policeman. When she sees what she has done, she hangs half way out the window in a faint.

Happy Hooligan April-Fooled
Edison © H3107   Apr. 6, 1901
24 ft.   FLA3712 (print)   FRA0959 (neg.)

The backdrop is painted to resemble the front of a saloon, and a man dressed as a bartender is standing in front of it. Two small boys walk up to him and attempt to sell him newspapers. He does not want any. The small boys begin wrestling over a tall silk hat lying on the sidewalk. The bartender separates the youngsters just as a man dressed as a tramp enters the scene. The tramp starts to pick up the silk hat, decides it is a trick, and the bartender picks it up. Underneath the hat is a bottle, which the bartender picks up, and drinks from. The tramp falls down in a faint, ending the scene.

Happy Hooligan in a Trap
AM&B © H33399   July 6, 1903

Cameraman: G. W. Bitzer
Photographed: June 25, 1903
20 ft.   FLA3618 (print)   FRA0878 (neg.)

Two young ladies are sitting on a bench in a yard in front of a structure representing a modest house. While they are busy at their work, Happy Hooligan in his tramp costume appears, sticks his head between the young women, and frightens them away. He then walks over to the house, climbs on a box, and puts his head through the window. The window closes on him, leaving him hanging by his neck. He is rescued by his tramp friend, Gloomy Gus. The film ends with Happy Hooligan prostrate on the ground while resuscitation methods are employed.

Happy Hooligan Surprised
Edison © H3108   Apr. 6, 1901
24 ft.   FLA4651 (print)   FRA1681 (neg.)

Three boys are matching pennies in front of a grocery store set. Happy Hooligan, standing on the sidewalk close to the building, observes them. The grocer notices the boys at their game and interrupts them to show them a new game involving a funnel and a coin. The funnel is placed inside the belt of a man's trousers and a coin is placed on his forehead. The trick is to catch the coin in the funnel. This is played two, or three times when Happy's curiosity gets the better of him and he asks to join in. When the funnel is tucked in his belt and a coin is put on his forehead, the grocer pours water into the funnel.

Happy Hooligan Turns Burglar
Edison © H13157   Jan. 16, 1902
Cameraman: Edwin S. Porter
47 ft.   FLA4652 (print)   FRA1682 (neg.)

This comedy begins on a set of the sitting room of a wealthy person, where the maid is entertaining a policeman. She seats him and serves him refreshments. A face appears in the window behind them, frightening the maid who hides the policeman in a cabinet. Happy comes in through the door and begins removing furniture and bric-a-brac. The cabinet door opens a crack and Happy sets about blowing it up with dynamite. Pieces of the policeman land on the set and the maid assembles them. With the use of stop-action photography, a live policeman replaces the dummy. The policeman, with an agonized expression on his face, stands there, realizing the maid has put him back together incorrectly. He has a hand for a foot and a foot where his hand should be.

Happy Hooligan's Interrupted Lunch
AM&B © H36631   Oct. 8, 1903
Cameraman: A. E. Weed
Location: Studio, N.Y.C. Photographed: Oct. 1, 1903
37 ft. FLA4650 (print)   FRA1680 (neg.)

The opening scene is a set of a dining room in a modest house where a well-dressed woman, and a woman dressed as a maid, enter and busy themselves setting a table. They leave, and the head of Happy Hooligan appears at an open window. He surveys the room, enters, sits at the table, and begins gobbling food as rapidly as both hands can work and his mouth tolerates. While he is gorging himself, the two women return and begin chasing him around the table. In order to create the impression of great speed, the cameraman slowed down his photography. After a few turns around the table, Happy jumps out the window, leaving the two women looking out the window after him.

Happy Jack, A Hero

Biograph © J148649   Dec. 10, 1910

Cameraman: Arthur Marvin

Cast: Mack Sennett, Joe Graybill, Lottie Pickford, William J. Butler, Grace Henderson, Dell Henderson, Edwin August, Kate Bruce, Florence Barker, Frank Evans

Location: Fort Lee, N.J.; Studio, N.Y.C. *Photographed:* Oct. 29, 1910 and Nov. 1–3, 1910

221 ft.   FLA5073 (print)

Two thieves gain entrance to a high-fashion social event by a trick and are caught by a roustabout friend (Mack Sennett) stealing an engagement present. The friend is coerced into standing in a suit of armor as a replacement for a broken stand by the promise of some food after the party. He becomes a hero when he captures the two thieves as they open the safe in which the present was placed. All of the scenes were photographed from a single camera position.

A Hard Wash

AM&B © H26945   Jan. 14, 1903

Photographed: c. 1896

10 ft.   FLA3307 (print)   FRA0621 (neg.)

The film begins with a close-up of a black infant being given a bath. The bath continues for the full length of the film.

Harry Thompson's Immitations of Sousa

Edison © H11491   Dec. 16, 1901

19 ft.   FLA3167 (print)   FRA0497 (neg.)

A group of men, each holding a different musical instrument, can be seen sitting in front of a backdrop painted to represent an outdoor park scene. A man with a false beard and the cap of a U.S. Navy bandleader takes the podium in the midst of the men and, for the extent of the film, simulates conducting a band concert. At the end of the film, he bows to unseen applauders.

Harvard-Pennsylvania Football Game

AM&B © H38239   Nov. 16, 1903

Cameramen: G. W. Bitzer, W. McCutcheon, A. E. Weed

Location: Franklin Field, Philadelphia *Photographed:* Nov. 7, 1903

180 ft.   FLA5053 (print)   FRA2011 (neg., copy 1) FRA2072 (neg., copy 2)

The camera was placed on about the five-yard line. The two football teams are scrimmaging midfield about the ten-yard line. A period ends, and the teams go by the camera position. The film includes what can be identified as team play but the distance is such that individual action is not discernible.

See also: Classmates

A Hash House Fraud

Keystone © LP5620   June 10, 1915

Producer and Author: Mack Sennett

Cast: Louise Fazenda, Nick Cogley, James T. Kelly, Chester Conklin, Hugh Fay

The American Mutoscope & Biograph Company sent the then unheard of number of three cameramen to photograph The Harvard-Pennsylvania Football Game (November 1903).

Location: Hollywood and Santa Monica pier, Calif.
432 ft. FLA6102 (print)

Louise Fazenda is a cashier in the Busy Bee Restaurant which is in desperate straits. When a customer comes in and orders a steak and then becomes rough when it is inedible, a fight takes place between the waiter-owner and the cook. The discouraged owner, Hugh Fay, puts his restaurant up for sale, sees a prospective customer coming, and invites a group of itinerants in for a free meal to make his restaurant appear profitable. He instructs his cashier to pretend to charge the group, but when the new owner's wife takes over as cashier, much trouble ensues. The police are called and the chase begins, ending up with the car in the ocean.

Hash House Mashers

Keystone © LP4235 Jan. 16, 1915
Producer and Author: Mack Sennett
Director: J. Farrell Macdonald
Cast: Charles Chase, Vivian Edwards, Joe Swickard, Billie Bennett, Nick Cogley, Frank Opperman, Eddie Cline, Estelle Allen, Billie Brockwell, W. C. Hauber
Location: Keystone Studio and surrounding area
401 ft. FLA5946 (35mm print) FLA6103 (16mm print)

Two male boarders are enamored of the lovely daughter (Vivian Edwards) of their landlord. She prefers Chase to Cogley. The landlord makes every effort to bring Cogley and his daughter together, much to his daughter's dismay. Instead, she tries to encourage Charles Chase, the suitor not approved of by her father. One situation leads to another, and the daughter elopes with Chase. They take

part in a wedding scene, ostensibly part of a moving picture being shot nearby, but which turns out to be the real thing, providing a "love will find a way" ending for the picture. The camera seen on the movie set is a British Williamson camera, and the man who played the part of the director was W. C. Hauber.

Hauling a Shad Net

AM&B © H19020 June 14, 1902
27 ft. FLA3804 (print) FRA1039 (neg.)

The subject is the hauling in of a large fishnet. As the film begins, about a dozen men are visible with the haul-in line of a large net in their hands. Throughout the film they tug on the net in unison.

The Haunted Hat

Lubin Mfg. Co. © J131733 July 29, 1909
117 ft. FLA5054 (print) FRA2013 (neg.)

The story is built around a growing mob hysteria caused by a man who sees a straw hat moving down the street, apparently under its own power. From the first time the straw hat is seen, the action progresses, gathering more and more momentum and more and more people so that at the climax of the film, when one of the city fathers is brave enough to attack the straw hat, nearly everybody in town has been involved. The film ends as the by-now large group of people surround the city official, as he picks up the hat and finds it was propelled by a kitten instead of the monster they feared. The last scene in the film is a close-up of the kitten sitting on top of the straw hat on the ground.

131

Haverstraw Tunnel

AM&B © H30724 Apr. 24, 1903

Location: Haverstraw, N.Y. *Date:* 1897[?]

27 ft. FLA3394 (print) FRA0692 (neg.)

The camera was positioned on the front of a train traveling along one of the two tracks in an unpopulated section of country. As the train progresses, the film encompasses the surroundings on each side of the tracks, such as trees, telephone poles, cattle breaks, farmhouses, etc. The train tracks enter a tunnel. The film continues, showing the entry and the exit through the tunnel, and ends as the train is once again on a long, straight track.

Having Her Gown Fitted

See: Her New Party Gown

"He Cometh Not," She Said

AM&B © H34508 Aug. 13, 1903

Cameraman: Wallace McCutcheon

Cast: Kathryn Osterman

Location: Studio, N.Y.C. *Photographed:* July 31, 1903

21 ft. FLA3706 (print) FRA0954 (neg.)

A well-dressed woman is sitting at a table unhappily gazing at a photograph of a man. After several seconds, indicating her sadness at the possibility that the man in the picture will never return, another woman dressed as a maid, enters with a calling card. Immediately our heroine perks up as she powders her nose, plumps up her hair, and destroys the photograph. At the end of the film, a man in dinner clothes is seen kissing her.

See also: He Loves Me, He Loves Me Not, and Girl At The Window

He Forgot His Umbrella

AM&B © H16347 Apr. 10, 1902

Cameraman: F. S. Armitage

Location: Roof Studio, N.Y.C. *Date:* June 29, 1901

12 ft. FLA4191 (print) FRA1355 (neg.)

A man and a woman are sitting at a table in a restaurant set. The man was made up to look past middle age. He is drinking from a coffee cup. Then he gets up, kisses the young woman, puts on his silk top hat, and leaves. A young man enters, kisses the young woman's hands, and prepares to sit down when they are startled by the return of the older gentleman who had forgotten his umbrella. The young man hides under the table, but the older man notices his protruding hands. He jumps on them, then picks up a plate from the table and breaks it over the young man's head. The young man wrenches himself free and overturns the table. The young woman swoons.

He Got Into the Wrong Bath House

AM&B © H63382 July 15, 1905

Cameraman: G. W. Bitzer

Location: Studio, N.Y.C. *Photographed:* June 28, 1905

21 ft. FLA4034 (print) FRA1222 (neg.)

Three young women in bathing suits are playing leap frog. The set has been constructed to appear as a row of dressing rooms at the seashore. The three finish their game and each enters a separate dressing room. At this juncture, a man dressed in summer clothes with a towel and a bathing suit over his arm is seen looking for an empty dressing room. He enters one already occupied by one of the three young women. The film ends as the three girls combine their efforts to drag the man bodily from the dressing room. They throw him on the sand and beat him.

He Loves Me, He Loves He Not

AM&B © H34821 Aug. 19, 1903

Cameraman: Wallace McCutcheon

Cast: Kathryn Osterman

Location: Studio, N.Y.C. *Photographed:* Aug. 3, 1903

20 ft. FLA3323 (print) FRA0636 (neg.)

The film begins with a close-up of a well-dressed young woman who is engaged in pulling the petals from a daisy, one at a time. Her mouth forms the words, "He loves me, he loves me not." The first daisy, from her expression, comes out "He loves me not" so she starts on a second. As the film ends, she is pleased and her lips form the words, "He loves me."

See also: "He Cometh Not," She Said, and Girl At The Window

He Wouldn't Stay Down

Keystone © LP5388 May 20, 1915

Producer and Author: Mack Sennett

Cast: Ford Sterling, Minta Durfee, Charles Chase, Frank Hayes, Dixie Chene, James T. Kelly

Location: Keystone Studio, Los Angeles, and surrounding area, San Pedro, Calif.

410 ft. FLA6104 (print)

Minta Durfee is Ford Sterling's wife in this comedy. An insurance man, Frank Hayes, persuades Sterling to take out a life insurance policy, and Minta's boyfriend, Charles Chase, who is also there, notices an immediate payment clause in the policy. He plots to drown Ford Sterling, so he can get the money and the lovely widow. Chase persuades Sterling to pretend to commit suicide so he can learn what his wife is really like. Sterling, a heavy piece of metal around his neck, jumps off the pier, supposing Chase will not let go of the rope. Instead, Chase rushes off, the insurance man is notified and reluctantly pays over the money, but Minta refuses to give it to Chase. Sterling, who has been rescued by a passing fisherman, also goes home and joins in the skirmish. The final scenes show Minta Durfee and Ford Sterling rolling in and out of the wall in a Murphy bed. At last Sterling gets his neck caught in the wall, while Minta, also in the bed, pulls hard to free him.

Head-On Collision at Brighton Beach Race Track July 4th, 1906

Miles Brothers © H82213 Aug. 14, 1906

Cameraman: H. J. Miles [?]

Location: Brighton Beach, N. Y.

Date: July 4, 1906

379 ft. FLA5424 (print) FRA2317 (neg.)

The subject is a man-made collision between two steam locomotives. The tracks were laid across the back fields at an amusement park. The film was photographed with two cameras, and most of it shows the surrounding countryside, the bleachers and grandstand, amusement rides, etc. From a distance of approximately half a mile, one of the two cameras filmed the full run of the two trains before they collided.

Heart of Oyama

AM&B © H115483 Sept. 9, 1908
Director: D. W. Griffith. *Cameraman:* Arthur Marvin
Cast: Florence Lawrence, D. W. Griffith, Harry Salter
Location: Studio, N.Y.C. *Photographed:* Aug. 14, 1908
333 ft. FLA5425 (print) FRA2318 (neg.)

This melodrama was filmed on five different sets. The actors were dressed in Japanese costumes. The opening scene shows four young Japanese girls fluttering about a set portraying joy and happiness. A door slides open and the hero arrives and embraces the heroine (Florence Lawrence). The balance of the film is based on the problems of the heroine who must marry the man her father has chosen for her, rather than the man she loves. The villain, a warlord, is determined that the heroine will marry him. There are scenes of Oriental torture, ending with the death of the hero. The film ends as the heroine, firm in her resolve not to marry the villain, takes a dagger from her sleeve, kills the villain and then kills herself.

Hearts and Planets

Keystone © LP4508 Feb. 20, 1915
Producer and Author: Mack Sennett
Cast: Chester Conklin, Minta Durfee, Joe Swickard
Location: Keystone Studio, Los Angeles
409 ft. FLA6105 (print)

Chester Conklin and Minta Durfee are in love and plan to get married. Minta's father, Joseph Swickard, an astronomer, is against the idea. In revenge, Chester and Minta paint a fake scene of the sky on a piece of canvas and put it outside the window of her father's observatory. Then they set off fireworks. Swickard thinks he has discovered some new comets and calls some colleagues. He is very excited about his discovery until he sees Chester's hand holding the end of a pinwheel. The fireworks start a fire on the roof, and the fire department responds, chasing Chester around the roof with a fire hose.

The Heathen Chinese and the Sunday School Teachers

AM&B © H40721 Jan. 8, 1904
Cameraman: A. E. Weed
Location: Studio, N.Y.C. *Photographed:* Dec. 17, 1903
104 ft. FLA5055 (print) FRA2014 (neg.)

There are five scenes in this film: in a laundry, in a schoolroom, two in a Chinese opium den, and in a jail. The action begins when three young women pick up their laundry from a Chinese laundry. The next scene shows the schoolroom with the same young women teaching Chinese students, with a significant bit of "business" when one of the Chinese holds the hand of a schoolteacher. The schoolroom scene is followed by one in an opium den. Two of the school teachers, who are heavily veiled, enter, lie down, and begin smoking opium. During the opium smoking scene, there is a dissolve showing the teachers progressing from their introduction to opium to their delight with it and the Chinese men. The last two scenes show a raid with the police arresting the Chinese and the schoolteach-

ers, but jailing only the Chinese. The film ends with the teachers attempting to get bail for the Chinese.

Heaven Avenges

Biograph © J171535 July 23, 1912
Director: D. W. Griffith *Cameraman:* G. W. Bitzer
Cast: Dorothy Bernard, W. Chrystie Miller, Kate Toncray, Charles West
Location: Southern Calif.
377 ft. FLA5426 (print) FRA2320 (neg.)

The scion of a wealthy orange-grove owner trifles with the affections of an attractive daughter of a fruit picker. They meet clandestinely, but she is unable to talk him into marriage and, ashamed, she runs away from home. Her outraged father, accompanied by the girl's farmer fiancé, go to the home of the wealthy young man to demand some kind of consideration for the loss of the young girl. Both are armed with rifles. The young man will not listen to their pleas, so they wait outside his home to ambush him. Their guns go off, and he falls to the ground. The doctor discloses that the young man's death resulted from a heart condition and not from their bullets. The final scene shows the young woman reunited with her father and boy friend.

The Heavenly Twins at Lunch

Edison © H36780 Oct. 14, 1903
Cameraman: Edwin S. Porter
Location: Newark, N.J. *Photographed:* Oct. 2, 1903
38 ft. FLA4653 (print) FRA1683 (neg.)

The subject of this human-interest film is identical twins. The camera is placed across the table from the small children to observe them as they eat mush from a bowl. One of the small boys sometimes eats from the other's bowl. Another camera position was then used to show the two children as they smoke corncob pipes, which they continue to do until the end of the film.

See also: The Heavenly Twins at Odds

The Heavenly Twins at Odds

Edison © H36781 Oct. 14, 1903
Cameraman: Edwin S. Porter
Location: Newark N.J. *Photographed:* Oct. 2, 1903
31 ft. FLA3746 (print) FRA0993 (neg.)

The locale of this film is the bank of a lake. In the immediate foreground, between the water and the camera position, are two small boys dressed alike. Judging from their actions, they were coached from the sidelines to fight one another, and they hit, push, and kick for the full extent of the film.

See also: The Heavenly Twins at Lunch

Heaving the Log

Edison © 25334 Apr. 21, 1898
25 ft. FLA3047 (print) FRA1224 (neg.)

Retrieving the taffrail log, an event that occurs frequently in the merchant marine, is shown. The camera was positioned on the afterdeck of a large ship, evident by the size of the superstructure shown in the film. Two men in oilskins are at work bringing in the line.

Helen's Marriage

Biograph © J169461   May 22, 1912

Director: Mack Sennett.

Cast: Mabel Normand, Fred Mace, Dell Henderson, William J. Butler, Charles West, Mack Sennett, Eddie Dillon, Sylvia Ashton, D. W. Griffith

Location: Hollywood, Calif.

165 ft.   FLA5427 (print)   FRA2324 (neg.)

The substitute bride gambit was used in this picture. A young couple are thwarted by her irate father in their attempts to get married. The young man decides to make use of a motion picture company as a means to marry the girl of his choice, and his friends aid him. At the wedding ceremony, the "bride" feigns illness and the heroine takes her place. The preacher is real as is the bridegroom, and the wedding ceremony takes place without interruption. The picture ends with the father forgiving the newly married couple.

Help! Help!

Biograph © J168044   Apr. 10, 1912

Director: Mack Sennett.

Cast: Mabel Normand, Fred Mace, Dell Henderson, Alfred Paget

Location: Los Angeles, Calif.

192 ft.   FLA5428 (print)   FRA2323 (neg.)

A dog trying to get out from behind a velvet drape causes a neurotic young wife to telephone her husband at his office and tell him that burglars are breaking into the house. The husband rushes home in a car with two of his employees. The remainder of the picture shows the frustration of the husband as the automobile breaks down on several occasions. The husband and his employees arrive at the house, break down the door and find the dog. All of the chase scenes were photographed from moving automobiles in and around suburban Los Angeles.

Help Wanted

Biograph © J150815   Jan. 16, 1911

Cameraman: Arthur Marvin

Cast: Joe Graybill, Violet Mersereau, Spike Robinson, Donald Crisp, William J. Butler, George Nicholls

Location: Studio, N.Y.C. *Photographed:* Dec. 7–8, 1910

239 ft.   FLA5429 (print)   FRA2322 (neg.)

In an attempt to get money from a rich uncle who has stopped his allowance, a young man writes a note threatening to commit suicide by a certain hour unless the uncle restores his allowance. The uncle, preoccupied by his duties as a host, forgets the nephew's note. The nephew, in the meantime, tries various methods of suicide, including rope, poison, etc. In the middle of his party, the uncle recalls his nephew's note, takes it out of his pocket, and discusses it with his family. They recommend that he aid the young man just one more time. The uncle rushes off to his nephew's apartment, where a doctor has been summoned. The doctor tells the uncle that the suicide attempt was a farce, and they decide to give the nephew an emetic. The rich uncle leaves, after handing his nephew the want ad page from the newspaper.

The Helping Hand

AM&B © H120043   Dec. 17, 1908

Director: D. W. Griffith *Cameraman:* Arthur Marvin

Cast: Linda Arvidson, Robert Harron, Arthur Johnson, Dorothy Sunshine, Mack Sennett, Harry Salter, Clara T. Bracey, Grace Henderson, Charles Avery, Kate Toncray, Gladys Egan, Adele De Garde

Location: Central Park and Studio, N.Y.C. *Photographed:* Nov. 23 and 27, 1908

316 ft.   FLA5430 (print)   FRA2321 (neg.)

An altercation in a public saloon starts when a masher successfully attempts to kiss a young woman. He is then herded out of the place. His resentment at this treatment causes him to try to prevent her marriage from taking place later in the film. The film was photographed both indoors and out, and in some scenes as many as twenty actors were employed.

The Henpecked Husband

AM&B   1905

Cameramen: G. W. Bitzer, F. A. Dobson

Location: Studio, N.Y.C. *Photographed:* Dec. 8, 1905

97 ft.   FLA5235 (print)   FRA2183 (neg.)

This is a multicamera position comedy with several scenes. The first scene shows a woman haranguing her husband. The second scene is in the living room where the man seats himself comfortably when the same woman arrives, admonishes him, and puts him to work with a carpet sweeper. The husband, tired of his wife's harassment, pulls the hose from a gas jet, puts it in his mouth, and attempts suicide. The wife enters in time to save her husband, who then goes to the barn and tries to hang himself. His wife saves him again. The final scene is in the living room with the husband sitting with his leg in a splint, his head in a bandage, his arm in a cast, and his wife still nagging until he falls over dead.

This film was copyright under the name Threshing Scene © H70259 Dec. 19, 1905 but was released on January 27, 1906 under the title The Henpecked Husband, which apparently was not copyrighted.

Her Face Was Her Fortune

Lubin Mfg. Co. © J132447   Sept. 13, 1909

323 ft.   FLA5431 (print)   FRA2325 (neg.)

A dejected, impoverished writer who is unable to sell his stories meets a friend and admirer on the street. The admirer has two thoughts in mind: to encourage the writer and, to marry off an unattractive niece. Over a bottle of beer, the writer and the well-to-do-man reach an agreement that the writer will marry the niece, and the benefactor will pay him. The wedding takes place, and for the remainder of the film, the writer attempts to run away from his new wife. The picture ends when telephone linemen hoist the bride up a telephone pole, and the groom escapes.

Her Father's Pride

Biograph © J144012   Aug. 6, 1910

Director: D. W. Griffith *Cameraman:* G. W. Bitzer

Cast: Florence Barker, Charles West, Alfred Paget, Kate Bruce, W. Chrystie Miller

Location: Coytesville, N.J. & Studio, N.Y.C. *Photographed:* June 28–30, 1910

376 ft.   FLA5432 (print)   FRA2326 (neg.)

The closeness of a Quaker family is disrupted when the girl falls in love with a wealthy young man, the victim of an automobile accident, who is brought into her home to recuperate. Her father, very upset because the young man is a concert singer, disowns his daughter and sends her from her home. After she has begun her new life as a young married socialite, ill fortune forces her parents to become inmates of the local poor farm. The daughter learns of their plight, and she and her husband hurry to alleviate it. The father, still obdurate, refuses to talk to her. In the last scenes, the young woman plays her father's favorite hymn on the organ, and the old man leaves his floor scrubbing to embrace her. The film ends with the little family reconciled once more.

Her First Adventure

AM&B © H107372 Mar. 13, 1908

Director: Wallace McCutcheon *Cameraman:* G. W. Bitzer

Location: Studio, N.Y.C.; Leonia Junction, N.J. *Photographed:* Mar. 9, 1908

201 ft. FLA5433 (print) FRA2327 (neg.)

A little girl is attracted by two gypsies and the music of a hurdy-gurdy. She follows them from place to place in and about the streets of the town where the film was taken. When her parents miss her, they send the collie dog to track her down and they follow it. The dog and the parents are joined by other townspeople; the group following the dog is shown by cutbacks. The film ends after a long series of chase sequences in which many camera positions were used. When the gypsies stop to eat a meal, the pursuers catch up with them, and the parents are reunited with their little girl. The film ends as the camera moves to an extreme close-up of the dog, the hero of the day.

Her First Biscuits

Biograph © H128254 June 12, 1909

Director: D. W. Griffith *Cameraman:* G. W. Bitzer

Cast: Dorothy Bernard, Clara T. Bracey, John Cumpson, Charles Craig, Flora Finch, Guy Hedlund, Arthur Johnson, Florence Lawrence, Marion Leonard, Owen Moore, George Nicholls, Tony O'Sullivan, Mary Pickford, Harry Salter, Mack Sennett

Location: Studio, N.Y.C. *Photographed:* Apr. 20, 1909

195 ft. FLA5434 (print) FRA2328 (neg., copy 1) FRA6437 (neg., copy 2)

The opening scene is of a kitchen where, from a single-camera position, the heroine of the film (Florence Lawrence) removes a pan filled with biscuits from the oven and puts them on a plate. She attempts to convince her father of her success in her first try at baking and, as the film progresses, more and more people for various reasons eat some of the biscuits. The final scene shows a group of ill people pointing menacingly at the cook who insists that they partake again of her culinary mishap.

Her First Cigarette

AM&B © H27378 Jan. 22, 1903

Cameraman: F. S. Armitage

Date: June 5, 1899

22 ft. FLA3306 (print) FRA0620 (neg.)

From a single-camera position, two young women are photographed lighting a cigarette. After several puffs, one of the young ladies becomes faint, and the other one tries to revive her fallen friend.

Her Morning Exercise

AM&B © H23775 Nov. 11, 1902

10 ft. FLA3493 (print) FRA0773 (neg.)

During the extent of this short film, the only person visible is a woman dressed in what appears to be a sheer nightgown. She is standing in front of a weight-and-pulley exerciser placed in front of a backdrop on a stage. The woman exhibits her grace in three different types of exercises using the mechanical contrivance. The film was photographed under artificial light.

Her New Party Gown

AM&B © H39140 Dec. 7, 1903

Cameraman: A. E. Weed

Location: Studio, N.Y.C. *Photographed:* Nov. 25, 1903

21 ft. FLA4337 (print) FRA1483 (neg.)

Four women can be seen on a set of a dressmaker's cutting room. One woman is seated at a sewing machine, one is standing on a dressmaker's pedestal, another is measuring her, while the fourth is putting materials away. As the film progresses, they begin removing the clothing of the woman who is being measured for a dress. The woman unfastens and drops her skirt, then she coyly picks it up and holds it in front of her as if she does not want to be seen in such an undressed state. AM&B production records show the title of Her New Party Gown as Having Her Gown Fitted.

See also: The Dressmaker's Accident.

Her Terrible Ordeal

Biograph © J137169 Jan. 13, 1910

Director: D. W. Griffith *Cameraman:* G. W. Bitzer

Cast: Owen Moore, Florence Barker, George Nicholls, W. Chrystie Miller, Charles Craig, Tony O'Sullivan

Location: Studio, N.Y.C.; Fort Lee, N.J. *Photographed:* Dec. 6 and 9, 1909

367 ft. FLA5435 (print) FRA2330 (neg.)

A fit of temper directed at a peddler by the leading man results in his sweetheart's being locked in a walk-in safe. The owner of the business, who must go on a trip, leaves his son in charge of the office. The owner's son is in love with his father's secretary. The peddler returns, finds the secretary alone, remembers the earlier harsh treatment given him, and locks her in the safe. The remainder of the film is made up of many scenes, indoors and out, as the frantic young man attempts to find his father who has the combination of the safe. Finally, the father is located. He opens the safe none too soon, and the young woman is embraced by the son.

Herd of Cattle

AM&B © H18896 June 12, 1902

Cameraman: G. W. Bitzer

Location: J. B. Hord's Ranch, Central City, Neb. *Date:* July 5, 1901

30 ft. FLA3805 (print) FRA1040 (neg.)

The sole subject is a herd of cattle passing the camera position. Through an opening in a fence near a railroad track, the cattle can be seen streaming by the camera position as they are driven by a man on horseback. He passes the camera just as the film ends.

Herd of Sheep on the Road to Jerusalem

Edison © H32808 June 17, 1903

Cameraman: A. C. Abadie

Location: Jordan, Palestine *Photographed:* Mar. 16, 1903

25 ft. FLA3422 (print) FRA0710 (neg.)

The poor condition of the film is not conducive to proper establishment of the subject matter, but from the single-camera position, alongside a road, a large flock of sheep can be seen approaching the camera. They are escorted by four men on foot. The four men are dressed in the costume of desert shepherds of Jerusalem. The details of the costumes are not too clear.

Herding Horses Across a River

Edison © H46142 May18, 1904

Cameraman: A. C. Abadie

Location: Bliss, Oklahoma Terr. *Photographed:* May 9, 1904

33 ft. FLA3692 (print) FRA0941 (neg.)

Approximately forty horses can be seen in the distance across a river. They are being driven into the water by men on horseback. The horses approach the camera position as they ford the river. The film ends as the horses are seen passing the camera and being herded by five men on horseback.

The Hero of Liao Yang

AM&B © H50675 Sept. 22, 1904

Cameraman: G. W. Bitzer

Location: Col. Verbeck's Japanese garden, St. John's Military Academy, Manlius, N.Y. *Photographed:* Sept. 1904

531 ft. FLA5869 (print) FRA2774 (neg.)

This two-reel film begins by showing a Japanese family living tranquilly, playing games and arranging flowers. They are interrupted by a man in a military uniform who reads an edict. The camera shifts to the older son, now in uniform. Part one ends as he goes off to war. Part two shows troop maneuvers, small arms fire, and the young Japanese soldier being pursued by men in Russian uniforms. He is wounded, captured, and placed in a hospital, where he feigns death. He is thrown in a hole for burial, and an Oriental gravedigger aids him to escape. An early use of camera movement, including several pans, to enhance the story.

High Diving

AM&B © H21511 Sept. 5, 1902

Location: Avon, N.J.

25 ft. FLA3953 (print) FRA1164 (neg.)

The film was photographed from a small boat near the shore line at the Avon, New Jersey, bathing beach. It shows children either jumping or diving into the water from the end of a pier. The distance of the children from the camera position does not permit further detail.

High Diving by A. C. Holden

Edison © D12834 June 20, 1900

Cast: Arthur C. Holden, champion high diver and water exhibitor

Location: Vailsburg, N.J.

42 ft. FLA4654 (print) FRA1684 (neg.)

Divers are shown jumping, falling, and diving from what appears to be the spreader on a telephone pole into a lake or pond. No form or training is evident.

High School Field Exercises, Missouri Commission

AM&B © H45455 May 7, 1904

Cameraman: A. E. Weed

Location: St. Joseph, Mo. *Photographed:* Apr. 22, 1904

20 ft. FLA3935 (print) FRA1147 (neg.)

The cameraman placed his equipment on the side of an athletic field adjacent to a high school. During the course of the film, teen-age boys exhibit their skill at high jumping, pole vaulting, shot putting, discus throwing, and broad jumping. These events take place in the immediate area of the camera range. All the events are supervised by an adult who is visible on the field at all times.

The Hindoo Dagger

AM&B © H123060 Feb. 17, 1909

Director: D. W. Griffith *Cameraman:* G. W. Bitzer

Cast: Marion Leonard, Arthur Johnson, Robert Harron, John Cumpson, Frank Gebhardt

Location: Fort Lee, N.J.; Studio, N.Y.C. *Photographed:* Dec. 23 and 29, 1908

214 ft. FLA5436 (print) FRA2341 (neg.)

The plan of a married couple to compromise another man ends in disaster. The attractive wife bids her husband adieu and waits for the victim. A Hindoo dagger that arrives by messenger is used to set the trap. When the lover arrives, he finds the wife stretched out on the floor, presumably near death. He summons a doctor, and when he discovers he has been tricked, his anger is so great that he kills the woman. The husband returns home, finds his wife dead, and his grief and anguish cause him to kill himself.

Hindoo Fakir

Edison © H14252 Feb. 15, 1902

78 ft. FLA5036 (print) FRA2015 (neg.)

The substance of this film is a series of magic tricks performed by a man costumed as a Hindu fakir and his assistant, a woman. All of the tricks were made possible by the use of stop-action and double-exposure photography. The performer exhibits his efforts at levitation, disappearing, reappearing, and conjuring up one object and then transforming it into another. Apparently this film was made in Europe and distributed by an American firm.

Hippodrome Races, Dreamland, Coney Island

Edison © H62762 June 29, 1905

Cameraman: Edwin S. Porter

Location: Coney Island, N.Y. *Date:* June 4, 1905

20 ft. FLA5058 (print) FRA2016 (neg.)

The first sight is the straightaway portion of a small hippodrome with a dirt-covered track. On each side of the track are grandstands used for seating spectators. As the film progresses, people costumed with helmets and breast-plates, carrying shields and spears of the Roman era, can be seen coming down the street section of the track. They are followed by women in togas festooned with flowers, then a large group of men leading horses goes by. The remainder of the film was photographed from the same camera position, and it shows horses ridden Roman style, chariot races, cowboys rescuing a woman from a runaway horse, etc. The film ends with an exhibition ride between two horse-drawn chariots.

See also: Mystic Shriners' Day, Coney Island

His Day of Rest

AM&B © H110428 May 9, 1908
Cameraman: G. W. Bitzer
Location: Studio, N.Y.C. *Photographed:* Apr. 20–21, 1908
153 ft. FLA5437 (print) FRA2331 (neg.)

The film consists of a series of disasters that happen when a wife, determined that her husband is not going to read the paper and enjoy himself on his day off, sets him to work doing chores. He attempts to fix the stovepipe and pulls it down on himself, breaks the water tap, and finally blows up the house while trying to locate a gas leak with a lighted candle.

His Duty

Biograph © H127701 May 28, 1909
Director: D. W. Griffith *Cameramen:* G. W. Bitzer, Arthur Marvin
Cast: Frank Powell, Kate Bruce, Owen Moore, Arthur Johnson, Marion Leonard
Location: Edgewater, N.J.; Studio, N.Y.C. *Photographed:* May 10–12, 1909
161 ft. FLA5438 (print) FRA2890 (neg.)

The theme of this movie is a policeman placing his duty before his love for his brother. The three principal characters (the mother, a son who is a policeman, and a younger, spoiled son) are shown in the first scene. The younger brother has just been given a new cap, and the policeman teases him a little and then goes off to work. As the film progresses, the younger brother enters a jewelry store and steals from the safe. In his haste to leave the premises, he leaves his new cap behind, and it is found by his brother when he is called to investigate the burglary. The last scenes in the film are of the policeman confronting his brother with the evidence and attempting to take him off to jail, while the mother pleads for his release.

His First Ride

Selig © H92120 Mar. 29, 1907
21 ft. FLA3346 (print) FRA0655 (neg.)

This film, photographed from several camera positions, was made with humorous intent and shows a boy who actually is a skillful bicycle rider. Nevertheless, he feigns inability to ride the bicycle properly and allows it to run amuck through the streets. He knocks over several persons who, in turn, join in the chase after him. It is a good example of Selig's early work.

His Last Burglary

Biograph © J138678 Feb. 26, 1910
Director: D. W. Griffith *Cameraman:* G. W. Bitzer
Cast: Dorothy West, Henry B. Walthall, Kate Bruce, Claire McDowell, James Kirkwood, George Nicholls
Location: Coytesville, N.J.; Studio, N.Y.C. *Photographed:* Jan. 7, 1910
376 ft FLA5439 (print) FRA2673 (neg.)

A destitute inventor (H. B. Walthall) and his wife (Dorothy West) must abandon their starving infant. They leave it with a note in a rich man's house, where it is found by a burglar (James Kirkwood). The burglar takes the infant home to his wife (Kate Bruce) who is grieving over the death of their child. The inventor receives a large check, and the excited parents rush to the rich man's home to regain their child. He is confused and cannot help them. The mother becomes desperately ill when they cannot find the child. The burglar meanwhile has taken a job as a coachman for a doctor, and while the doctor is visiting the ill mother, the burglar learns the identity of the child he stole. He restores the baby, with his wife's blessing, to its real mother.

His Last Dollar

Biograph © J140314 Apr. 4, 1910
Cameraman: Arthur Marvin
Cast: Marion Leonard, Billy Quirk, Charles West
Location: Glendale, Calif. *Photographed:* Feb. 9, 1910
166 ft. FLA5440 (print) FRA2333 (neg.)

A young man with only one dollar takes a young lady to luncheon at a fashionable restaurant. The scenes show his constant worry as he continuously looks at his remaining silver dollar. They finish their meal and leave the restaurant, and encounter an old friend of the young lady's. She goes off with the friend, leaving the young man who has just spent his last dollar on her. The last scene shows him in an orange grove picking oranges.

His Lesson

Biograph © J169289 May 16, 1912
Director: D. W. Griffith
Location: Southern Calif.
Cast: Edwin August, Dorothy Bernard, Kate Toncray, Charles West
384 ft. FLA5441 (print) FRA2332 (neg.)

This story is based on the lesson to be learned from "All Work and No Play." A farmer has a lovely wife, but he denies her even the small luxuries or items of finery that the other farmers' wives have. Her life of constant drudgery, combined with her husband's apparent lack of interest in her appearance, make her ripe for the flattery of a young man from the city. The attention he pays her makes her feel brave enough to leave her husband. She is seated at the table writing him a farewell note when he drives up in the horse and buggy bringing her a new hat and a servant to help her in the kitchen. When the film ends, they are embracing.

His Lost Love

Biograph © J133276 Oct. 19, 1909
Director: D. W. Griffith *Cameraman:* G. W. Bitzer
Cast: James Kirkwood, Mary Pickford, Owen Moore, Kate Bruce, Lottie Pickford, Mack Sennett, Marion Leonard
Location: Studio, N.Y.C. *Photographed:* Sept. 7, 8 and 10, 1909
380 ft. FLA5442 (print) FRA2335 (neg.)

A father is denied the love of his daughter when they meet in his brother's home after many years of separation. The reason for the denial, the picture brings out, was the father's inability to control his emotions when the child was yet unborn. While his wife was pregnant, he sought the company of her sister. When his wife confronts her sister and her husband with her suspicions, they go off together, and leave the wife alone. She dies as a result of their actions; and the husband's brother rears the child.

His Luckless Love

Keystone © LP4870 Mar. 18, 1915
Producer and Author: Mack Sennett
Cast: Billie Brockwell, Nick Cogley, Vivian Edwards, Cecile Arnold, Edgar Kennedy
Location: Keystone Studio and vicinity, Los Angeles.
377 ft. FLA6106 (print)

The main characters in this comedy are a husband and wife (Billie Brockwell and Nick Cogley), their daughter (Vivian Edwards), their maid (Cecile Arnold), and her boyfriend (Edgar Kennedy). The husband makes several attempts to flirt with the maid, which both his wife and her boyfriend resent. Each time, the husband is punished for his actions. There is a wild fight, involving nearly the entire cast, as well as a pie-throwing scene.

His Madonna

Universal © J171729 July 26, 1912
45 ft. FLA4655 (print) FRA2021 (neg.)

The picture is made up of the following scenes: the female lead sits on the edge of a well; the male lead, an artist, sits at his easel in a field on new-mown hay; the young woman approaches a shock of hay. There are many short scenes of people going into and coming out of a church; and scenes of the frustration of an artist unable to produce the type of picture he sees in his mind. Near the end of the film, the artist sees the simple maid he met in the hayfield in church holding a baby. This inspires him to paint a great picture called "The Madonna." The film ends here.

His Masterpiece

AM&B © H28679 Feb. 26, 1903
Cameraman: F. S. Armitage
Date: Aug. 21, 1899
16 ft. FLA3156 (print) FRA0489 (neg.)

The film begins on a set designed to be an artist's studio. A man wearing a smock and flowing tie, with an artist's palette in one hand and a brush in the other, is studying a three-dimensional full-length painting of an unclothed woman. The artist backs away, as if to get a better perspective, and the figure comes to life, stretching out her arms to him. He approaches the now live figure of the woman and falls to her feet.

See also: The Artist's Dream

His Move

AM&B © H65318 Sept. 11, 1905
Cameraman: G. W. Bitzer
Location: Studio, N.Y.C. *Photographed:* Aug. 24, 1905
19 ft. FLA4016 (print) FRA1212 (neg.)

A young man in dinner clothes and a young woman in formal dress are sitting at a small table and playing chess. The set is of the living room or den of a well-to-do family. As the chess game progresses, it is evident from the young lady's gestures that she has defeated her opponent. The young man stands up, takes the young woman's face in his hands, and kisses her as the film ends.

His Name Was Mud

AM&B © H27978 Feb. 7, 1903
Cameraman: Arthur Marvin
Date: July 16, 1900
9 ft. FLA3142 (print) FRA0475 (neg.)

Two men stealthily approach the wall of a constructed two-story house. One man carries a bucket and a long-handled paint brush while the other carries a pole with a loop at the end. The bucket carrier bangs on the door of the house and an old man in a nightcap and nightgown opens the window on the second floor. The man with the pole puts the loop over the old man's head and pulls him out of the window, while the other splashes paint on his face with his long-handled brush. The picture ends as a policeman arrives on the scene and attempts to stop the prank, but the old man falls out of the second-story window.

His New Lid

Biograph © J148146 Nov. 26, 1910
Director: D. W. Griffith *Cameraman:* Arthur Marvin
Cast: Thomas Ince, Lucille Lee Stewart
Location: Westfield, N.J.; Studio, N.Y.C. *Photographed:* Oct. 4, 6 and 14, 1910
216 ft. FLA5443 (print) FRA2337 (neg.)

An altercation in a restaurant between a man who has just lost his new straw hat and a man he believes took it, but who did not, is the first situation in this film. The man who actually took the hat wears it out of town to the seashore, where it blows off into the water. The finder believes the owner dead and delivers the hat to the address inside it. His story apparently convinces the wife because memorial services are in progress when the very-much-alive man turns up, wearing a felt hat. His appearance frightens the mourners but brings happiness to his wife.

His Own Fault

Biograph © J171533 July 23, 1912
Director: Mack Sennett
Cast: Fred Mace, Kate Bruce
204 ft. FLA5444 (print) FRA2336 (neg.)

An expansive gesture by the hero toward a friend whose wife is celebrating her birthday starts a series of events that leads to his being discredited as a borrower of money and a gambler. He buys his friend's wife an expensive handbag, and, as an afterthought, a cheaper one for his wife. His wife grudgingly accepts the cheap bag when the friend and his wife arrive and show off his gift to the wife. His furious wife demands a handbag of equal quality. Her husband attempts to extricate himself from the situation by gambling in the hope of making enough to pay for it. The casino is raided by the Purity League, of which his wife and her friends are members. He is the only person caught in the casino.

H.R.H. the Prince of Wales Decorating the Monument of Champlain and Receiving Addresses of Welcome from the Mayor of Quebec, the Governor General of Canada and Vice-President Fairbanks, Representative of the United States.

Vitagraph © H114183 Aug. 3, 1908

43 ft. FLA5136 (print) FRA2721 (neg.)

The cameraman placed his camera in several positions to cover the ceremonies of the then Prince of Wales placing a wreath on the monument commemorating Champlain. One position shows the actual placing of a wreath on the monument, another shows the prince entering an automobile, and another the Prince of Wales standing under an awning and reviewing the troops.

H.R.H. the Prince of Wales Viewing the Grand Military Review on the Plains of Abraham, Quebec.

Vitagraph © H114184 Aug. 3, 1908

Location: Quebec, Canada

22 ft. FLA5136 (print) FRA2721 (neg.)

The camera was placed in the position of the reviewing stand to take the salute of a passing battalion of cavalry. The second camera position photographed the light-horse artillery that followed the battalion.

His Sister-in-Law

Biograph © J149038 Dec. 20, 1910

Director: D. W. Griffith *Cameraman:* G. W. Bitzer

Cast: Lottie Pickford, Gladys Egan, Eddie Dillon, Claire McDowell, William J. Butler

Location: Westfield, N.J.; Studio, N.Y.C. *Photographed:* Oct. 14–18, 1910

401 ft. FLA5221 (print) FRA2826 (neg.)

When a suitor (Eddie Dillon) begins calling on her attractive older sister (Lottie Pickford), a little girl (Gladys Egan) is jealous and behaves badly. The older sister marries her suitor, and they take the younger sister to live with them, but she becomes a problem. Used to being the center of attention, she resents the new situation and does all sorts of things to annoy the adults. Finally she decides to return to her aunt's home and leaves a note for the newlyweds. The last scene in the film, preceded by a title, shows the little girl happily holding a new baby just born to her older sister.

His Trust

Biograph © H150968 Jan. 19, 1911

Director: D. W. Griffith *Script:* Emmett Campbell Hall

Cameraman: G. W. Bitzer

Cast: Dell Henderson, Claire McDowell, Adele De Garde, Kate Bruce, Wilfred Lucas, Linda Arvidson, Alfred Paget, Mack Sennett

Location: Fort Lee, N.J.; Studio, N.Y.C. *Photographed:* Nov. 5–18, 1910

386 ft. FLA5445 (print) FRA2338 (neg.)

This film, part one of two, is the story of a Confederate soldier of considerable means who goes off to the Civil War and leaves instructions with his most trusted slave to look after his wife and little daughter. He is killed in battle, and, as arranged, his sword is sent to the slave. In the last scenes, the Union troops sack and burn the manor house and leave the widow and her small daughter homeless. The slave acknowledges the trust his master placed in him and takes the widow and the little girl to his cabin. The last scene shows him going to sleep on a blanket outside the cabin door.

His Trust Fulfilled

Biograph © J151126 Jan. 24, 1911

Director: D. W. Griffith *Script:* Emmett Campbell Hall

Cameraman: G. W. Bitzer

Cast: Claire McDowell, Wilfred Lucas, Dorothy West, Verner Clarges, Gladys Egan, Harry Hyde, Grace Henderson, Jack Pickford

Location: Fort Lee, N.J.; Studio, N.Y.C. *Photographed:* Nov. 5–18, 1910

388 ft. FLA5446 (print) FRA0241 (neg.)

This is the second part of a two-reel picture. However, it is a complete story in itself as was the first part. There is a time lapse of four years, during which the widow of a Confederate soldier has been living in the former cabin of their black slave. Now she dies, leaving her daughter to be educated. The slave uses his own savings and impoverishes himself. Just as he is desperate as to how to pay for her further education, a cousin of the young lady arrives from England, falls in love with her, and marries her. The film ends as the slave is shown entering his quarters with his master's saber held tightly in his arms. The family lawyer, a white man and his co-conspirator, enters and shakes his hand. Between each scene there is a noticeable camera dissolve. In both pictures, the actors wear make-up, and in His Trust Fulfilled, the aging of the characters is accomplished by the use of make-up.

His Ward's Love

AM&B © H122930 Feb. 13, 1909

Director: D. W. Griffith *Cameraman:* G. W. Bitzer

Cast: Arthur Johnson, Florence Lawrence, Owen Moore

Location: Studio, N.Y.C. *Photographed:* Jan. 29, 1909

87 ft. FLA5059 (print)

The opening scene of this melodrama is in the study of a minister (Arthur Johnson) who is sitting at a desk as his ward, a lovely young girl (Florence Lawrence) comes down the stairs and goes through his study out onto the flower-decked porch where her suitor (Owen Moore) is awaiting her. The film continues through the tête-à-tête where the suitor proposes, and the young lady goes to get her guardian's permission, which he gives. However, before the picture ends, she finds that she really loves her guardian who apparently returns her love, for the last scene shows the guardian and his ward embracing.

His Wife's Mother

Biograph © H123539 Mar. 1, 1909

Director: D. W. Griffith *Cameramen:* G. W. Bitzer, Arthur Marvin

Cast: Florence Lawrence, John Cumpson, Mack Sennett, Charles Inslee, Mrs. Herbert Miles, Arthur Johnson

Location: Bleecker Street and Studio, N.Y.C. *Photographed:* Jan. 25–26, 1909

195 ft. FLA5447 (print) FRA2334 (neg.)

A happily married man and his attractive wife receive a letter from her mother informing them that she is arriving for a visit. The mother-in-law stops the husband from smoking or drinking or from leading his accustomed life. Complaining to his young wife gets him nowhere, so he decides to handle matters for himself. He lavishes attention, flowers, food, and alcohol on his mother-in-law to such an extent that his wife becomes jealous and insists that her mother go home, to the delight of the husband. The film ends as the wife forgives her husband and they embrace.

His Wife's Sweethearts
Biograph © J150108 Jan. 3, 1911
Cameraman: Arthur Marvin
Cast: Mack Sennett, Kate Bruce, W. Chrystie Miller, Grace Henderson
Location: Leonia, N.J.; Studio, N.Y.C. *Photographed:* Nov. 23–30, 1910
257 ft. FLA5448 (print) FRA2339 (neg.)

A man buys his wife a complete new wardrobe and then starts off on a business trip. En route to the station, he sees some of the new clothes on a woman he assumes to be his wife. He proceeds to beat up the man she had been standing with. He returns home and finds his wife asleep. Puzzled, he starts out again only to encounter a similar situation. This is repeated a third time, with the husband getting the worst of the fight. At this point, the harassed husband realizes that the woman is one of his servants and demands the garments back. In the meantime, his wife awakens, finds the clothes missing, and reports the loss to the police. They arrest the husband as he is returning home with the new clothes. The film was photographed from many camera positions, both inside and out-of-doors.

His Wife's Visitor
Biograph © J130779 Aug. 19,1909
Director: D. W. Griffith *Cameraman:* G. W. Bitzer
Cast: Mary Pickford, Owen Moore, James Kirkwood, George Nicholls, Frank Powell, Billy Quirk
Location: Studio, N.Y.C. *Photographed:* July 13, 1909
196 ft. FLA5449 (print) FRA2340 (neg.)

A pregnant woman, resentful that her husband has gone out on the town, plans a trick to make him jealous and to call attention to his responsibilities. The abandoned wife partially fills two glasses with liquor, partially smokes a cigar, and then retires to the bedroom to wait for her husband's return. The husband becomes irate when he discovers the glasses and cigar butt, and threatens to shoot his wife. The film ends as she shows him some knitted baby garments. The complete film was shot on two sets, the home and his club, and both were artificially lighted.

An Historic Feat
AM&B © H16738 Apr. 18, 1902
Cameraman: Raymond Ackerman
Location: Salaea, Philippine Islands *Date:* Feb. 5, 1900
30 ft. FLA3865 (print) FRA1077 (neg.)

The first scene is photographed over the shoulder of a man on horseback. The locale is a river and in the distance, approaching the camera, is a large number of what later can be identified as mules. The film ends as the mules come out of the water and pass the camera position. AM&B production records identify the subject as General Bell's pack train swimming the Agno River.

Hjemløs
See: Homeless

A Hobo Milking a Cow
See: The Accommodating Cow

Hockey Match on the Ice
Edison © 13572 Feb. 24, 1898
24 ft. FLA3051 (print) FRA0364 (neg.)

The camera was placed on the edge of a frozen-over pond. Immediately in the foreground is a man on skates with a hockey stick in his hands. He is in the defense position. As the film progresses, more men on ice skates with hockey sticks can be seen actively engaged in what appears to be an ice hockey game.

Hogan Out West
Keystone © LP4568 Feb. 27, 1915
Producer and Author: Mack Sennett
Cast: Charles Murray, Billie Brockwell, Bobby Dunn, Frank Hayes
Location: Glendale, Keystone Studio and Santa Ynez Canyon, Calif.
400 ft. FLA5450 (print, copy 1) FLA6107 (print, copy 2)

Hogan is given a warm reception when he ventures into the Wild West, including a battle with Indians, an attack on a stagecoach in which he is a passenger, dancing as his feet are being shot at, a scene in a Western dance hall with the "Cactus Queen," and other incidents, all a burlesque of Western dramas. Billie Brockwell, the Cactus Queen, who has become enamored of Murray, rescues him from one dilemma, only to discover the authorities are preparing to lynch him because they mistakenly take him for a bandit. The last scene in the picture shows Murray floating to the ground with an umbrella, from a church steeple onto which he had been propelled when a dynamite storage building blew up.

Hogan the Porter
Keystone © LP4416 Feb. 4, 1915
Producer and Author: Mack Sennett *Director:* Charles Avery
Cast: Charles Murray, Vivian Edwards, Frank Hayes, Joe Swickard, Mae Busch, Eddie Cline, Bobby Dunn
Location: Keystone Studio, Los Angeles
418 ft. FlA6108 (print)

All of the scenes were taken on a set designed to appear as parts of a hotel—lobby, hallways, bedrooms, or bathrooms. It is a busy hotel, with only one porter (Charles Murray) who must also double as the barber, the bellhop, the cook, or whatever is necessary to meet a request by one of the hotel guests. Murray spends his time running to and fro in an attempt to carry out management's orders but never quite completes any task. By the end of the picture, there are a lot of unhappy guests.

Hogan's Aristocratic Dream
Keystone © LP4455 Feb. 13, 1915
Producer and Author: Mack Sennett
Cast: Charles Murray, Bobby Dunn, Teddy (Keystone's famous dog), Frank Hayes, Vivian Edwards, Billie Brockwell, and a large number of unidentified extras who take part in the garden party
Location: The no longer extant DeLongpre gardens in Hollywood
803 ft. FLA6109-6110 (print)

The film consists of a series of ridiculous circumstances arising from a dream a tramp (Charles Murray) and his companion, (Bobby Dunn) have of a life of luxury in the period of Louis XIV, following a dinner of alfalfa, a stolen egg, and milk from the cow whose quarters they share. The lovely dream ends when they are rudely awakened by a farmer (Frank Hayes) brandishing a pitchfork.

Hogan's Mussy Job
Keystone © LP4271 Jan. 21, 1915
Director: Charles Avery *Author:* Mack Sennett
Cast: Charles Murray, Bobby Dunn, Al St. John, Estelle Allen, Vivian Edwards, Eddie Cline, Frank Hayes, Billie Brockwell
Location: Hollywood Boulevard, Echo Park Boulevard, and around the Keystone Studio, Los Angeles
331 ft. FLA6111 (print)

One of the tenants is giving a "rag" party for his dancing friends causing the plaster from the ceiling to fall on a couple (Frank Hayes and Billie Brockwell) who are eating dinner in their apartment below. The irate couple call the manager, Bobby Dunn, who sends a plasterer, Charles Murray, to repair the ceiling. He arrives immediately and the balance of the picture is devoted to the destruction wreaked by the plasterer who is not only extremely careless but inebriated as well.

Hogan's Romance Upset
Keystone © LP4454 Feb. 13, 1915
Producer and Author: Mack Sennett
Cast: Charles Murray, Bobby Dunn, Billie Brockwell, Vivian Edwards, Joe Swickard; crowd at the ringside included Ford Sterling, Mack Swain, Roscoe Arbuckle, Al St. John, Charles Chase, and at least fifty other male spectators
Location: Keystone Studio, Los Angeles; Echo Park, Hollywood
408 ft. FLA6112 (print)

A pair of bums (Charles Murray and Bobby Dunn) find some money dropped by an attractive young woman (Billie Brockwell) who is waiting for a friend, Joe Swickard. She discovers her loss, they give her purse back, and Swickard leaves. The young woman is attracted to Bobby Dunn, and they leave together much to the annoyance of Murray, who follows them. They go out in a rowboat, but discover it is leaking because Murray has bored a hole in the bottom. Murray rescues the young lady. Dunn is furious, and the two men get into a fight. Bystanders suggest they settle their differences in a boxing ring, which they do.

Hold-Up in a Country Grocery Store
Edison © H45036 Apr. 29, 1904
Cameraman: Edwin S. Porter
Location: Studio, N.Y.C. *Photographed:* Apr. 23, 1904
63 ft. FLA5060 (print) FRA2018 (neg.)

The set was built to look like the interior of a country store. From the action, it appears that a polite debate is going on between some of the townspeople. The debate winds up in a physical fight. During the debate but before the fighting starts, a well dressed man carrying a suitcase calmly watches the fight materialize. When the fight is at its peak, the drummer opens his bag, takes out an Edison phonograph

and starts playing it. Soon the brawlers are holding hands and dancing in a circle about the little music machine.

The Hold-Up of the Rocky Mountain Express
AM&B © H75633 Apr. 12, 1906
Cameraman: G. W. Bitzer
Location: Ulster and Delaware Railroad, Phoenicia, N.Y. *Photographed:* Apr. 4–6, 1906
230 ft. FLA5451 (print) FRA2678 (neg., copy 1) FRA2679 (neg., copy 2)

The story line is built around the mock hold-up of a train. The film ends as the bandits or train robbers are captured at a railroad crossing. Building up to the capture is a chase filmed from the front of the train following the four-wheeled pump car the fleeing train robbers are using. But, preceding the train hold-up is a scene filmed in a constructed set of the interior of a railroad car. There is a comedy sequence involving three women and two men, a Pullman porter, and a freeloading tramp. What relationship this scene has to the hold-up is not indicated. Nevertheless, it is the transition from the beginning locale of a railroad station to the hold-up.

Holland Submarine Boat Tests
AM&B © J48223 July 18, 1904
Cameraman: G. W. Bitzer
Location: New Suffolk, N.Y. *Photographed:* June 16, 1904
175 ft. FLA5452 (print) FRA2342 (neg., copy 1) FRA2343 (neg., copy 2)

The film shows a mechanically operated, man-controlled submarine. As the film begins, the forward part of the craft can be seen resting on the surface of the water. The forward hatch opens and a torpedo approximately ten feet long is lowered into an aperture. As the film progresses, a bubble wake from the fired torpedo is visible and for the remainder of the film, the conning tower and some super-structure of the submarine appear and disappear as the craft is put through its maneuvers. According to a contemporary handbill, "the very boat shown in the picture was purchased by the Japanese Government a few days after the film was made, to be used in the Russo-Japanese War."

The Home Breakers
Keystone © LP4355 Jan. 30, 1915
Producer and Author: Mack Sennett
Cast: Alice Davenport, Chester Conklin, Mack Swain, Dora Rogers, Slim Summerville, Estelle Allen
Location: Keystone Studio and vicinity, Los Angeles
745 ft. FLA6113-6114 (print)

Mack Swain is a bank president married to Alice Davenport but enamored of the wife (Dora Rogers) of his chief clerk (Chester Conklin) who is in love with Alice Davenport. The picture is a series of problems between the clandestine lovers, complicated by the janitor, Slim Summerville. The picture ends with the two original couples being reunited.

A Home-Breaking Hound
Keystone © LP5576 June 14, 1915
Producer and Author: Mack Sennett
Cast: Rosemary Theby, Joe Swickard, Frank Opperman

Holland Submarine Boat Tests (1904). In the photo on the left, the man on the extreme left is John Philip Holland. He is supervising the boarding of a torpedo which was discharged successfully. The submarine's crew is shown in the photo on the right.

Location: Both the hotel and Angel's Flight funicular, where this comedy was photographed, are gone now, but they were on Hill Street in Los Angeles.

390 ft.   FLA6115 (print)

A one-reel story of the troubles that beset a young man who attempts to check into a hotel with his little dachshund. When he is refused a room, he notices a couple (Theby and Swickard) arriving and manages to secrete his dog in the wife's suitcase. Then he manages to check into the room directly across from the couple, and the balance of the picture shows his desperate attempts to recover his dog. He is mistaken for a burglar and later for the wife's paramour, but eventually succeeds in retrieving his pet, after a wild chase down a fire escape.

The Home-Made Turkish Bath

AM&B   © H40867   Jan. 14, 1904

Cameraman: A. E. Weed *Photographed:* December 6, 1903
Location: Studio, N.Y.C.

32 ft.

From a single-camera position, a bedroom set can be seen. The door in the wall opens and an old gentleman escorted by a young woman enters. She puts the old man into a steam cabinet. As soon as the young woman closes the cabinet, it begins to smoke and then it blows up. The young woman returns, affixes a ladder to the side of the set, and the old gentleman comes down the ladder from the floor above, ending the film.

See also: A Hot Time at Home

Home of Thief

See: The Kleptomaniac

Homefolks

Biograph   © J170147   June 10, 1912

Director: D. W. Griffith

Cast: Mary Pickford, Robert Harron, Kate Bruce, Wilfred Lucas, Charles Hill Mailes. Small roles: Mae Marsh, Blanche Sweet, Henry B. Walthall, Mack Sennett

381 ft.   FLA5453 (print)   FRA2319 (neg., copy 1)   FRA6438 (neg., copy 2)

A family in a rural community is dominated by the father who is a tyrant and will not allow his two children (Mary Pickford and Robert Harron) any kind of social intercourse with the neighbors. In defiance of his father's wishes, the son goes to a square dance and when he returns, the father orders him to move out. As the film continues, a blacksmith who loves the young girl brings her a present and sees her embracing a young man. Not knowing it is her brother, he

suspects she has another suitor. The picture ends when the young woman induces her father to allow her brother to come home, and the suitor realizes that his jealousy was totally unfounded.

Homeless

Great Northern © Oes J168436-168438 Apr. 18, 1912

Producer: Fotorama, Aarhus, Denmark *Script:* Edward Schnedler-Sørensen

Cast: Marie Nidermann, Philip Bech, Aage Schmidt, Peter Nielsen, Kamma Creutz Natansen, Zanny Petersen.

Date: Nov. 18, 1912

Danish title: Hjemløs

1,127 ft. FLA5932 (print, copy 1) FLA5933 (print, copy 2) FRA2745 (neg.)

The opening scene establishes that the heroine is from a well-to-do background. She is courted by two men, one of whom she rejects. The wedding is shown, and subsequently a child is born. The husband is a dominant type, and when the rejected suitor notices the wife's unhappiness, he embraces her, but they are caught by the husband. Encouraged by his success with the wife, the one-time suitor robs the bank where he works and elopes with the heroine. The police find him, and she is left alone. Her purse is stolen by a female pickpocket who is struck by an automobile; she is taken to a hospital where she dies. When the husband learns of his wife's supposed death, he immediately remarries. The heroine, at a loss for money, turns to singing in the streets and is heard by an impresario who makes her famous. She returns home to blackmail her husband, who gives her a large sum of money to leave the country. Instead she kidnaps her own child. However, when she realizes that the child does not know her and loves the stepmother, she attempts to drown herself in the ocean but is saved by the impresario.

Hong Kong Regiment, no. 1

Edison © 38237 June 22, 1898

Cameraman: James H. White

Location: Hong Kong, China

29 ft. FLA4389 (print) FRA1522 (neg.)

Military troops were photographed from a single-camera position as they passed in review. Some of the troops wear turbans.

Hong Kong Regiment, no. 2

Edison © 38236 June 22, 1898

Cameraman: James H. White

Location: Hong Kong, China

27 ft. FLA4690 (print) FRA1523 (neg.)

Photographed from a single-camera position, the film shows a company of British infantry at bayonet and rifle drill. Their distance from the camera does not permit much detail to be seen.

Hong Kong, Wharf-Scene
Edison © 38247 June 22, 1898
Cameraman: James H. White
Location: Hong Kong, China
24 ft. FLA3213 (print) FRA0536 (neg.)

Photographed from a single-camera position from a dock or warehouse area, are a great number of people, ranging from "bobbies" in full police uniform to Chinese potentates being carried in sedan chairs. Many Chinese laborers, with pigtails, can be seen.

Honolulu Street Scene
Edison © 38226 June 22, 1898
Cameramen: James H. White, W. Bleckyrden
Location: Honolulu
26 ft. FLA3231 (print) FRA0555 (neg.)

The first scenes are of a business district in Honolulu. The camera covers an area beginning at an intersection of the major business district. Approaching and passing the camera position are a horse-drawn streetcar, followed by a conveyance pulled by one man and pushed by another. The conveyance is loaded with large bags of what appears to be copra. At the end of the film, another horse-drawn streetcar crosses in front of the camera, and the details of the streetcar are quite clear.

The Honor of His Family
Biograph © J137729 June 26, 1910
Director: D. W. Griffith *Cameramen:* G. W. Bitzer, Arthur Marvin
Cast: Henry B. Walthall, James Kirkwood, William J. Butler, Gus Pixley, Verner Clarges, W. Chrystie Miller, Tony O'Sullivan
Location: Coytesville, N.J.; Studio, N.Y.C. *Photographed:* Dec. 10, 17 and 18, 1909
387 ft. FLA5454 (print, copy 1) FLA5781 (print, copy 2) FRA0243 (neg.)

This is the story of the father of a Confederate Army officer who shoots his cowardly son and carries his body to the battlefield to make it appear that he died in combat. The film begins as the father shows the son paintings of his forebears who had won honors on the field of battle. The scene shifts to the battlefield; there are many camera positions of troop movements, artillery and rifle fire, trench warfare, and cavalry maneuvers. Near the end, a general and his staff confront the father with a statement that his son was seen running from the battle. The father strikes the general and offers to find his son. They proceed to the battlefield where the Confederate officers find the body of the cowardly son where the father had placed it.

The Honor of Thieves
AM&B © J120976 Jan. 2, 1909
Director: D. W. Griffith *Cameraman:* G. W. Bitzer
Cast: Florence Lawrence, Owen Moore, Harry Salter, Frank Powell, Mack Sennett
Location: Hudson Street and Studio, N.Y.C. *Photographed:* Dec. 4 and 10, 1908
286 ft. FLA5455 (print) FRA2344 (neg.)

The story line is built around the relationship of a young woman and her dishonest boyfriend who conspires with another burglar to rob her father's pawnshop. As a ruse to gain entry, the boyfriend suggests an elopement. The young woman prepares to leave her father's store, after her father has gone upstairs to bed. She admits her boy friend, who then lets his friend in, and they burglarize the safe, knock the father unconscious, beat the girl and tie her up, and finally set fire to the store. After the burglars leave, one suffers a twinge of conscience and returns with the police in time to put out the fire and save the lives of the pawnbroker and his daughter.

Hon. Theo. Roosevelt, Asst. Sec'y, U. S. Navy Leaving White House
See: Theodore Roosevelt Leaving the White House

The Honourable Artillery Company of London
AM&B © H36632 Oct. 8, 1903
Cameraman: G. W. Bitzer
Location: Providence, R.I. *Photographed:* Oct. 3, 1903
36 ft. FLA4114 (print) FRA1292 (neg.)

The subject was a parade honoring a group of people called the "Ancient Honorables." It was filmed in an area resembling a public square. In the background is a large building similar to a railroad station. In front of it are many spectators watching a company of several different brigades of British military passing in review. They are all marching on a diagonal course in front of the camera position.

See also: Ancient & Honourables Artillery of London on Parade and Ancient Honourables of London Homeward Bound

Hooligan as a Safe Robber
AM&B © H36676 Oct. 10, 1903
Cameraman: G. W. Bitzer
Location: Studio, N.Y.C. *Photographed:* Oct. 5, 1903
18 ft. FLA3831 (print) FRA1059 (neg.)

A burglar is busily engaged in opening the combination knob of a big black safe in an office set. As the film continues, the burglar is seen drilling holes and setting fuses. The shade in the window goes up and the face of Happy Hooligan appears. Hooligan, seeing the burglar at work, is inspired to do his duty as a citizen and he jumps into the room, scaring off the burglar. Just then, the safe explodes, and the police arrive and take the innocent Hooligan away, certain he is the culprit.

Hooligan Assists the Magician
Edison © D21658 Nov. 16, 1900
39 ft. FLA4656 (print) FRA1685 (neg.)

A magician performs in front of a backdrop resembling the rear wall of a concert hall. His act consists of making barrels appear and disappear, conjuring up apparitions that grow in size and then disappear, and causing furniture to vanish or break in pieces. For the finale of the act, the magician causes himself to disappear.

Hooligan in Jail
AM&B © H36551 Oct. 6, 1903
Cameraman: G. W. Bitzer
Location: Studio, N.Y.C. *Photographed:* Sept. 25, 1903
30 ft. FLA4657 (print) FRA1686 (neg.)

The film begins on a set of the interior of a jail where Happy Hooligan, dressed in tattered garments and wearing a tin hat, is occupying a cell. A grotesque and burlesque version of a policeman enters and hands Happy a bowl of food. Happy begins to eat and, as he does so, the camera starts to move toward him. By the time the film ends, the camera has moved in to a tight close-up of Happy.

Hooligan to the Rescue

AM&B © H36550 Oct. 6, 1903

Cameraman: G. W. Bitzer

Location: Studio, N.Y.C. *Photographed:* Sept. 25, 1903

3 ft. FLA5456 (print) FRA2708 (neg.)

The painted set of the front of a house was photographed from a one-camera position, and smoke can be seen coming from the window. Happy Hooligan runs into the scene, picks up a bucket of water, and throws it into the window just as the occupant of the house appears and is covered with water. A policeman arrives and arrests Happy.

Hooligan's Christmas Dream

AM&B © H38687 Dec. 1, 1903

Cameraman: G. W. Bitzer

Location: Studio, N.Y.C. *Photographed:* Nov. 5, 1903

150 ft. FLA5457 (print) FRA2345 (neg.)

Happy Hooligan falls asleep in the snow after looking through the window of a house. He dreams that he is asleep in a warm bed as Santa Claus delivers gifts. A servant serves him breakfast in bed, helps him dress, and lights his cigar. The last scene, before a policeman wakens him from his lovely dream, shows Happy Hooligan hitting one of the servants who hides under a table. Happy then stamps on the servant's fingers.

Hooligan's Roller Skates

AM&B © H36863 Oct. 19, 1903

Cameraman: A. E. Weed

Location: Studio, N.Y.C. *Photographed:* Oct. 9, 1903

20 ft. FLA3754 (print) FRA1000 (neg.)

The action begins in front of a set of a house-front. Two boys are tying roller skates on to a sleeping tramp. Then, they wake the tramp, who proceeds to give an involuntary exhibition of a poor skater. The skating tramp frantically attempts to catch the culprits but instead skates into a policeman, who is seen escorting him off the set as the film ends.

Hooligan's Thanksgiving Dinner

AM&B © H37833 Nov. 10, 1903

Cameraman: A. E. Weed

Location: Studio, N.Y.C. *Photographed:* Oct. 30, 1903

12 ft. FLA5458 (print) FRA2707 (neg.)

Shown from a single-camera position, the cartoon character Happy Hooligan and a buxom woman are sitting at a table. Underneath the table is a small boy who is fussing with the feet of the woman. She becomes annoyed, thinks Happy is guilty, picks up the roast turkey on the table, and hits him on the head with it. He tips over the table and finds the little boy and his companion; each adult grabs a boy and spanks him.

The Hoop and the Lovers

AM&B © H43575 Mar. 22, 1904

Cameraman: A. E. Weed

Location: Studio, N.Y.C. *Photographed:* Mar. 8, 1904

18 ft. FLA4277 (print) FRA1431 (neg.)

A young woman is sitting in a hammock and swinging back and forth in front of a painted backdrop of an outdoor scene. She is joined by a young man, who sits down beside her. A little boy and girl run in back of them rolling a hoop. The children stop, see the couple in the hammock, drop the hoop over their heads, and unceremoniously dump the couple on the ground. The young man jumps to his feet and chases the two children, while the young lady dusts herself off.

The Hoopskirt and the Narrow Door

AM&B © H44031 Mar. 29, 1904

Cameraman: A. E. Weed

Location: Studio, N.Y.C. *Photographed:* Mar. 17, 1904

28 ft.

This farce is built around the efforts and frustrations of a woman who attempts to get through a narrow door while wearing a hoopskirt. She finally succeeds by tilting the hoop, thereby exposing her pantaloons.

The Horse Market

AM&B © H33279 July 8, 1903

Cameraman: G. W. Bitzer

Date: December 3, 1902

32 ft.

The camera was positioned high above the heads of a large group of spectators or participants at a public horse auction. The animals can be seen coming out of a large barn door on which there is a sign: "Auction Barn." During the last part of the film, horses are led around in circles through the crowd of possible purchasers.

Horse Parade at the Pan-American Exposition

Edison © H10087 Oct. 26, 1901

Location: Buffalo, N.Y.

59 ft. FLA4658 (print) FRA1687 (neg.)

There is a paved street in the foreground and on the curbing on the opposite side spectators have gathered to watch a parade. In the background are several large exposition buildings. A band in uniform passes the camera, and following that are many show horses of various types led by their handlers.

The Horse Thief

AM&B © H65361 Sept. 13, 1905

Cameraman: G. W. Bitzer

Cast: Laura Burt, Sidney Holloway

Location: Hartsdale, N.Y. *Photographed:* Aug. 31, 1905

287 ft. FLA5459 (print) FRA2346 (neg.)

The film begins with a close-up "two shot" of a beautiful saddle horse held by the reins by a young woman as though being introduced to the audience. This is followed by a scene of the young woman riding through the countryside. She stops at a farmhouse for a glass of water, and returns to the stable. One of the two men who had seen her at the farmhouse decides to steal the horse, which he does. The remainder of the film, photographed from many camera positions, is devoted to the pursuers on horseback and on foot chasing the horse thief; he is finally captured and led off to jail. The heroine was played by Laura Burt, who had been a leading lady with Sir Henry Irving. It was photographed on the Westchester estate of Sidney Holloway, using his champion horses Radium and Buck, and other blue-ribbon winners. Mr. Holloway also appeared in the picture.

Horses Drawing in Seine

AM&B © H34988   Aug. 22, 1903
Cameraman: Herbert J. Miles
Location: Altona, Wash. *Date:* Aug. 11, 1903
37 ft.   FLA4659 (print)   FRA1688 (neg.)

The photographer placed his camera on an ocean beach. He panned the camera approximately 150 degrees. During the camera movement it is possible to see two horses standing on the beach harnessed to a doubletree to which ropes leading to a large seine are attached. As the camera continues to turn, it is possible to see approximately ten men on the beach, in or out of the water, preparing the net to be dragged onto the beach by the horse. Fish that have been removed from the portion of the net up on the beach can be seen.

See also: Horses Drawing Salmon Seine and Men Taking Fish From Salmon Seine

Horses Drawing Salmon Seine

AM&B © H34986   Aug. 22, 1903
Cameraman: Herbert J. Miles
Location: Altona, Wash. *Date:* Aug. 11, 1903
19 ft.   FLA3645 (print)   FRA0899 (neg.)

The camera was placed on the beach above the activity of several men driving at least six horses attached to a fishnet harness. The fishnet is spread out on the ocean beach and the men and horses are engaged in hauling the net and its cargo up on the shore.

See also: Horses Drawing in Seine and Men Taking Fish from Salmon Seine.

Horses Loading for Klondike, no. 9

Edison © 60558   Oct. 25, 1897
Cameraman: Robert K. Bonine
Location: Seattle, Wash.
24 ft.   FLA3068 (print)   FRA0410 (neg.)
[Alaska Gold Rush]

The single-camera position is over the heads of spectators watching wooden-box lift vans for horses. The action shows two boxes being lifted aboard and lowered into the hold of a ship. The film shows the cargo boom but not the windlass or the power source.

See also: Loading Baggage for Klondike, no. 6

Horticultural Floats, no. 9

Edison © 13530   Feb. 24, 1898
64 ft.   FLA4660 (print)   FRA1689 (neg.)

The subject is a parade. The cameraman placed his equipment above the spectators that lined both sides of a street watching horse-drawn vehicles with costumed passengers pass by. The vehicles are decorated with all manner of real and artificial flowers, bunting, crepe paper, etc.

See also: Decorated Carriages and Parade of Coaches

Hot Meals at All Hours

AM&B © H26947   Jan. 14, 1903
Cameraman: Raymond Ackerman
Location: New Castle *Date:* June 26, 1899
19 ft.   FLA3476 (print)   FRA0757 (neg.)

The subject is a sow and her litter. They are shown in one corner of a split-rail-fenced pen. The sow stands and eats while the piglets run around her feet.

Hot Mutton Pies

AM&B © H21513   Sept. 5, 1902
Cameraman: F. S. Armitage
Location: Roof Studio, N.Y.C. *Date:* June 5, 1901
17 ft.   FLA3956 (print)   FRA1166 (neg.)

A store front set in a business district is seen as the film begins. A man dressed in a Chinese costume, complete with queue, stands in a doorway behind a little stand with a sign "Hot Mutton Pies." Two men dressed as boys appear and see the sign. Each buys a pie and starts eating it while facing the camera. In back of them, the Chinese vendor manipulates the sign and it now reads "Alle Samee Cat Pies." The two customers finish their pies and now see the change of sign and clutch their stomachs. The film ends as they fight with the Chinese vendor.

Hot Stuff

Biograph © J167393   Mar. 21, 1912
Director: Mack Sennett
Cast: Mabel Normand, Dell Henderson, Mack Sennett, Kate Bruce, Eddie Dillon, Fred Mace
191 ft.   FLA5460 (print)   FRA2347 (neg.)

A slick cigar salesman from the city makes such an impression on a small town boy's girlfriend and her family that they give a party in his honor and do not invite her boyfriend. The unhappy boy attempts to get even with the city fellow by taking advantage of some taffy put on the window sill to cool, sprinkling it generously with Tabasco. When the party goers begin to pull and eat the taffy, the Tabasco turns their happiness to anger and they chase the cigar salesman from the locality. The film ends as the small town boy is welcomed by his friends again.

A Hot Time at Home

AM&B © H41749   Feb. 2, 1904
Cameraman: A. E. Weed
Location: Studio, N.Y.C. *Photographed:* Jan. 6, 1904
20 ft.   FLA4333 (print)   FRA1479 (neg.)

The picture begins by showing a bedroom set where a man dressed as a woman crosses the room in front of the camera, fluffs up "her" hair, and goes behind the screen and removes a kimona. The film ends as the "woman" comes out from behind the screen and gets into a box that resembles a steam cabinet from which steam emanates.

Hotel Del Monte

Edison © 60586   Oct. 25, 1897
Location: Carmel, Calif.
25 ft.   FLA3039 (print)   FRA0246 (neg.)

From a single-camera position, the film shows a roadway and in the background a large wooden structure. Passing between the wooden building and the camera is a large stagecoach pulled by six white horses followed by three horse-drawn transportation vehicles of different types filled with passengers.

Hotel Vendome, San Jose, Cal.

Edison © 60584 Oct. 25, 1897

Location: San Jose, Calif.

28 ft. FLA4123 (print) FRA6406 (neg.)

The circle drive leading out of the old Vendome Hotel was photographed from a single camera position. The elegant means of transportation provided at the time includes a six-horse stagecoach and a one-seater sulky. Five wagons with horses are shown.

The House with Closed Shutters

Biograph © H144163 Aug. 11, 1910

Director: D. W. Griffith *Cameraman:* G. W. Bitzer

Cast: Dorothy West, Henry B. Walthall, Charles West, Joe Graybill, Grace Henderson

Location: Coytesville, N. J. and studio, N. Y. C. *Photographed:* June 25 and 27, July 1 and 2, 1910

393 ft. FLA5461 (print) FRA0244 (neg.)

The story concerns a young female member of a proud Southern family who saves the family's honor by taking over her brother's military mission. She is killed and buried under her brother's name. Many camera positions were used for scenes of Confederate soldiers leaving home, combat scenes of the infantry behind butresses firing their rifles, and scenes of cavalry skirmishes. The last scenes take place twenty-five years later and show the brother who has been imprisoned to keep others from learning of his cowardly behavior. It is interesting that make-up was used to age the principal actors in this film.

How a French Nobleman Got a Wife Through the New York Herald Personal Columns

Edison © H49524 Aug. 26, 1904

Cameraman: Edwin S. Porter

Location: New York, N.Y.; Englewood, N.J. *Photographed:* Aug. 23–24, 1904

287 ft. FLA5462 (print) FRA2349 (neg.)

The title of the film sets the plot of this early comedy. A man places an advertisement in the *New York Herald* in an attempt to find a wife, and more than twenty women, all anxious to marry, answer it. The poor French nobleman cannot decide among the many possibilities, and in panic runs from the steps of Grant's Tomb through the New York countryside, over ditches and fences, and through the woods. He finally ends up in a lake or river with the women standing on the bank crying out for him. One stalwart woman wades into the water, and the two walk through the water hand in hand, ending the film. There is a close-up of the *New York Herald* page.

See also: Personal

How a Nearsighted Man Read the Sign

See: Springtime in the Park

How Bridget Made the Fire

AM&B © H16339 Apr. 10, 1902

Cameraman: Arthur Marvin

Location: Studio, N.Y.C. *Date:* June 8, 1900

9 ft. FLA4173 (print) FRA1338 (neg.)

A woman in a house dress and checkered apron is kneeling in front of a small cast-iron stove with a chimney that reaches the ceiling. She is unsuccessfully attempting to kindle a fire. She shows discouragement as she tries many measures and finally leaves the room, returning with a gallon can. She pours the contents into the stove, and the picture ends as the smoke is clearing away from the room after the explosion.

How Brown Got Married

Lubin Mfg. Co. © J133964 Aug. 16, 1909

Location: Philadelphia [?]

261 ft. FLA5463 (print) FRA2348 (neg.)

A member of a bachelor's club decides to get married, and his fellow club members plan to play some pranks on him. The first of these shows the clubmen dressed in mourning as they lament the loss of one of their ranks. Later, they kidnap the bridegroom as he is on his way to the church, take him by automobile to an abandoned house, and dress him in the knickerbockers, flowing tie, and straw hat of a small boy. They tie him securely and leave him there to be released by the police. He hurries to the church, where he startles the gathering of well-dressed guests with his ridiculous costume.

How Buttons Got Even With the Butler

AM&B © H33455 July 15, 1903

Cameraman: G. W. Bitzer

Date: July 3, 1903

19 ft. FLA3566 (print) FRA0842 (neg.)

The set represents the dining room in the house of a wealthy family. A man is sitting at the table and being served by a butler in uniform. A young boy enters the room and speaks to the man at the table. The boy goes behind the butler and ties his tailcoat to the shelf on the sideboard and leaves. As the butler is summoned to attend his master, his coat tail pulls a large vase off the shelf onto the floor.

How Buttons Got Even With the Butler

AM&B © H34509 Aug. 13, 1903

Cameraman: G. W. Bitzer

19 ft. FLA3567 (print) FRA0843 (neg.)

The film begins in a dining room set of a well-to-do family. An old gentleman is sitting at the table and being served by a butler. A boy in a bellhop's uniform brings him a message. After delivering the message, the bellhop goes behind the butler and ties his coat tails to the sideboard. He then proceeds to get the hat and coat for the old gentleman and returns to him. The man gets up, and the butler moves toward him, pulling the sideboard over on top of him and breaking several pieces of china.

How Charlie Lost the Heiress

AM&B © H29470 Mar. 18, 1903

Cameraman: Arthur Marvin

Photographed: July 3, 1900

10 ft. FLA3608 (print) FRA0871 (neg.)

A black woman is pushing a baby carriage with twin black children in it. A white man comes along and she asks him to mind the children until she returns. He graciously complies and, while he is standing there, a woman who is evidently his fiancee comes down the street and notices the two children. She looks aghast, turns and rushes away. When the black woman returns, she finds her helper has fainted.

How Ducks Are Fattened

AM&B © H31676 May 11, 1903
Cameraman: G. W. Bitzer
Location: Mass. *Date:* June 26, 1899
19 ft. FLA3393 (print) FRA0691 (neg.)

The first scene shows a large pen with a considerable number of ducks in it. Two men with buckets empty out what appears to be mash or corn into troughs built on the ground. As they leave the pens, the ducks descend on the troughs and completely obscure them from the sight of the camera.

How Hubby Got a Raise

Biograph © J146226 Oct. 8, 1910
Cameraman: Arthur Marvin
Cast: Grace Henderson, Tony O'Sullivan, Kate Bruce
Location: Studio, N.Y.C. *Photographed:* Aug. 27 and Sept. 2, 1910
160 ft. FLA5464 (print) FRA2350 (neg.)

A wife feels that a good meal, well-served to her husband's boss, will help her husband get a raise, and she persuades her reluctant husband to invite his employer to dinner. When the boss accepts, she scurries around to various neighbors and succeeds in borrowing a fine tablecloth, silverware, fine china, flowers, and even a maid. The employer comes to dinner and is entertained royally. However, the impression the wife makes is exactly the opposite from that she intends. The boss becomes suspicious and has a letter hand-delivered to his employee discharging him because he lives beyond his means.

How Jones Lost His Roll: Jones Meets Skinflint (part 1 of 7)

Edison © H58567 Mar. 27, 1905
Cameraman: Edwin S. Porter
Location: Studio, N.Y.C. *Date:* Mar. 15–16, 1905
23 ft. FLA4680 (print) FRA1708 (neg.)

The title of the picture starts the film. It is followed by letters that scramble to spell out "You Meet Mr. Skinflint, a Suburban Neighbor." The second scrambled title reads "And He Gave You the Glad Hand," and at that moment two fabricated hands slide across the screen and end in a handclasp. After this, the steps and front of a public building are photographed. A man wearing a top hat and a long black greatcoat comes out of the building. He is met by another man dressed the same, and they walk off together, ending the first episode in this series.

How Jones Lost His Roll: Skinflint Treats Jones (part 2 of 7)

Edison © H58568 Mar. 27, 1905
Cameraman: Edwin S. Porter
Location: Studio, N.Y.C. *Date:* Mar. 15–16, 1905
13 ft. FLA4881 (print) FRA1886 (neg.)

The film begins with the assembly of jumbled white letters on a black background that move by stop action photography. When the letters come to rest, they read "And Much to Your Surprise Asked You to Have a Drink." The next scene takes place on a street in a business district of a city. Two men in top hats and long dark overcoats walk toward the camera and stop about half way between the camera position and where they were first seen and begin a conversation. Their gestures indicate they have decided on something and they then enter a building through a storm door, ending the film.

How Jones Lost His Roll: Invitation to Dinner (part 3 of 7)

Edison © H58570 Mar. 27, 1905
Cameraman: Edwin S. Porter
Location: Studio, N.Y.C. *Date:* Mar. 15–16, 1905
17 ft. FLA4882 (print) FRA1887 (neg.)

The film starts with a series of scrambled letters that form a sentence reading "When Invited to Dinner You Almost Dropped Dead," which is followed by a scene photographed alongside the grass walk in front of a house in a good residential section of a city. In the distance, walking toward the camera, are two men wearing top hats and long black overcoats. Their gestures indicate they are friends and, as they approach the camera position adjacent to the stairs of the house, they stop, and one of the two indicates the other is welcome to enter. The film ends when the two men go up the steps and disappear into the house.

How Jones Lost His Roll: Skinflint's Cheap Wine (part 4 of 7)

Edison © H58569 Mar. 27, 1905
Cameraman: Edwin S. Porter
Location: Studio, N.Y.C. *Date:* Mar. 15–16, 1905
62 ft. FLA4670 (print) FRA1698 (neg.)

The film begins showing the movement across the screen of some jumbled letters that, when they come to rest, spell: "After Filling You Up On Cheap Wine." The first scene is in the dining room of a well-to-do person, where a maid is being supervised by the lady of the house in setting the table. The door opens and one of the two men from the last scene enters and holds a conversation with the lady of the house who apparently agrees with his suggestion. The man leaves the room and returns with his friend, who is seated at the table and, for the remainder of the picture, is seen drinking one glass of wine after another.

How Jones Lost His Roll: Game of Cards (part 5 of 7)

Edison © H58571 Mar. 27, 1905
Cameraman: Edwin S. Porter
Location: Studio, N.Y.C. *Date:* Mar. 15–16, 1905
60 ft. FLA4636 (print) FRA1666 (neg.)

At the start of the film, an introductory title, done with a revolving stop action camera, puts into syntheses several scrambled letters to read "He Proposed a Friendly Game of Cards." After the title, the camera shows a set of a dining room in the house of a well-to-do person, where a woman is instructing her maid to move a mirror behind a chair. The chair is one of three around a table where there are cards and some poker chips. The host, accompanied by a guest, enters and seats the guest at a chair with his back to the newly moved mirror. The film ends when the host, the guest, and the lady of the house begin playing a game of cards.

How Jones Lost His Roll: Jones Loses (part 6 of 7)
Edison © H58572 Mar. 27, 1905
Cameraman: Edwin S. Porter
Location: Studio, N.Y.C. *Date:* Mar. 15–16, 1905
58 ft. FLA4679 (print) FRA1707 (neg.)

The film starts with a group of mixed letters that eventually form the words "Losing All Your Money, You Bet Everything You Had." The set is a drawing room of a house of a wealthy man, where two men and one woman are sitting at a table in the center of the room playing cards. There are poker chips as well as cards on the table. There is a mirror behind the man who faces the camera and, as the film continues, he loses all his chips. He then starts removing articles of clothing, and the film ends when the loser begins to take off his trousers.

How Jones Lost His Roll: Jones Goes Home in a Barrel (part 7 of 7)
Edison © H58573 Mar. 27, 1905
Cameraman: Edwin S. Porter
Location: Studio, N.Y.C. *Date:* Mar. 15–16, 1905
58 ft. FLA3994 (print) FRA1199 (neg.)

The film begins with a set of titles of white letters on a black background that form the words "And You Were Compelled To Go Home Like This. Didn't It Make You Mad?" by stop action photography. The opening scene takes place in a residential district where a man can be seen approaching the camera. He is wearing long underwear and a barrel and walks rapidly. The film ends as he passes the camera. However, there is another stop action title that ends the film: "Didn't It Make You Mad?"

How Little Willie Put a Head on His Pa
AM&B © H16379 Apr. 12, 1902
Cameraman: F. S. Armitage
Location: Roof Studio, N.Y.C. *Date:* May 13, 1899
15 ft. FLA3204 (print) FRA0530 (neg.)

The opening scene shows a bald man sleeping in a chair which is part of the furnishing of a set of the sitting room of a modest house. The man's head is so placed in the chair that just the top is visible. A young boy enters and begins painting a face on the bald pate. When he finishes his work of art, the boy hides. A rather large woman enters the room, sees the face on the man's bald head and promptly swoons, causing the sleeping man to awaken. The remainder of the film is pandemonium, with much falling down, pushing of furniture, etc. All apparently caused by the bewilderment of the man awakened from a sound sleep.

How Millionaires Sometimes Entertain Aboard Their Yachts
AM&B © H67107 Oct. 9, 1905
Cameraman: G. W. Bitzer
Location: Yacht "Taro" anchored in the East River, N.Y.
  Photographed: Sept. 26, 1905
20 ft. FLA3844 (print) FRA1104 (neg.)

The camera was placed amidship on an anchored yacht. The action consists of two men, with a woman seated on the lap of one, watching the antics of another woman who is dancing on the afterdeck of the boat. The woman who is dancing finally stops and the other woman takes her place. As the film ends, the second dancing woman becomes intoxicated or dizzy and falls on to the deck of the boat. Note: This is a scene from a film named Dream of the Race-Track Fiend released October 14, 1905.

How Old is Ann?
Edison © H39575 Dec. 15, 1903
Cameraman: Edwin S. Porter
Location: Studio, N.Y.C. *Date:* Dec. 11, 1903
34 ft. FLA4661 (print) FRA1690 (neg.)

This film shows the effect of the mental strain a man suffers when he tries to answer a puzzle based on the age of a girl named Ann. The film begins by showing a man sitting at a table. He is wearing a dressing gown and reading a newspaper with the headline "How Old is Ann?" As the film continues, the actor is shown getting more and more frantic, nervous, and hysterical as he figures and refigures the problem, always tearing up the results. The last scene shows him in a padded cell, still attempting to solve the riddle of Ann's age.

How the Athletic Lover Outwitted the Old Man
AM&B © H33541 July 18, 1903
10 ft. FLA3421 (print) FRA0709 (neg.)

A set of two rooms of a house can be seen as the film starts. On a small sofa in the room to the left of the camera is a young couple embracing. In the room to camera right an older gentleman is reading the newspaper. Suddenly he gets up and places a tall stool near the door to enable him to see over the transom. This apparently frightens the young man, who rises from the sofa and runs through the door, knocking the old man from his high perch.

How the Cook Made Her Mark
AM&B © H43407 Mar. 17, 1904
Cameraman: A. E. Weed.
Location: Studio, N.Y.C. *Photographed:* Feb. 24, 1904
69 ft. FLA5062 (print) FRA2020 (neg.)

The story concerns the annoyance of the lady of the house at a romance between the policeman on the beat and her cook. The film begins showing the cook hard at work kneading dough when a uniformed policeman enters. He is enthusiastically received by the cook, who very carefully cleans her hands, seats the policeman, and pours him a drink. The tête-à-tête is in full swing when the lady of the house enters and orders the cook back to work and the policeman to leave. The policeman puts the jacket of his uniform back on and goes. The next scene shows the policeman on his beat confronted by the precinct captain who inspects him and finds two white handprints on the back of his uniform.
  See also: Why Mrs. Jones Got a Divorce

How the Dutch Beat the Irish
Edison © H4371 May 15, 1901
29 ft. FLA3464 (print) FRA0746 (neg.)

A man smoking a pipe is leaning out of the window of a set of a two-story house in a city. A large barrel stands in the center of the sidewalk below. A policeman comes along and stops when he reaches the barrel. He looks up and waves his nightstick to admonish the man in the window, and knocks the barrel off the sidewalk. The policeman goes on his way while the man comes out and puts a dog inside the barrel, which he returns to the center of the sidewalk. The policeman returns, notices the barrel again and scolds the man in the window. The dog in the barrel gets out and bites the policeman. The film ends as they roll around on the sidewalk.

See also: Tramp's Strategy That Failed

How the Old Woman Caught the Omnibus
AM&B © H39710 Dec. 19, 1903
Produced in England by Hepworth
Director: Percy Stow
Location: England
69 ft. FLA5063 (print) FRA2022 (neg.)

This comedy is based on a farcical situation involving a contest between an old woman and a horse-drawn omnibus. The locale is the intersection of two streets, where the old woman can be seen waving frantically at an omnibus headed her way. She carries a large box which she puts down. The driver ignores her entirely and proceeds right by her. She holds on to the trace chains of the horse and, by the use of stop action photography, she is replaced by a dummy that is run over by the omnibus. She gets up, brushes herself off and chases the bus. She catches up with it, hooks the handle of her umbrella over the back of it, and pulls the bus to the location of her box. The remainder of the film is a constant altercation between the old woman and the driver of the bus who has no intention of letting her aboard. However, the old woman eventually wins.

How the Young Man Got Stuck at Ocean Beach
AM&B © H33538 July 18, 1903
Cameraman: F. S. Armitage
Location: Roof Studio, N.Y.C. *Date:* May 2, 1900
15 ft. FLA3449 (print) FRA0730 (neg.)

The set is a backdrop painted as an ocean scene. The camera was positioned as if in the audience at a vaudeville act. Immediately in front of the painted backdrop is a park bench with a sign "No Love Making Allowed." A man dressed as a policeman enters; he is carrying a large brush and a bucket marked "Glue." He paints the park bench with the glue and leaves. A young man and a young woman enter; the man sits on the bench and the young woman sits on his lap and they begin kissing. The policeman reenters, frightening the woman who turns and runs. The man attempts to rise, realizes he is stuck, and makes a supreme effort. As he turns to leave, it is obvious that the seat of his trousers is missing.

How They Do Things on the Bowery
Edison © H23280 Oct. 31, 1902
56 ft. FLA4662 (print) FRA2894 (neg.)

The opening scene is of a street in New York's Bowery section, with business fronts of restaurants and shoestores, etc. Into the camera and walking away from it can be seen a man. Judging from his clothing and the type of luggage he is carrying, he is definitely from the country. Approaching the camera is a fairly well-dressed woman, who, as she passes the country "rube," drops her handkerchief. He retrieves it for her. Gestures indicate she thanks him for it and suggests a drink. They both walk away from the camera and through a restaurant storm door. The next camera position is of a set of the inside of the restaurant. After the woman and the rube are seated, the woman lights and smokes a cigarette. The waiter pours them a drink that renders the man unconscious. After a short interval, the woman picks his pocket, pays for the drinks, and leaves. The film finishes with an exterior scene. A patrol wagon arrives, and the rube and his luggage are thrown out into the street by the tavern keeper.

How They Fired the Bum, Nit
AM&B © H32627 June 13, 1903
Cameraman: Arthur Marvin
Location: Roof Studio, N.Y.C. *Date:* May 14, 1900
15 ft. FLA3732 (print) FRA0979 (neg.)

The scene opens on a set of a wooded area next to a lake, with a park bench where a tramp is reclining. Another man comes along and the tramp accosts him for some money. He refuses and summons a policeman. When the policeman arrives, he cannot awaken the tramp by hitting him on the feet with his club so he chooses an alternate method and sticks matches in the sole of his shoe and lights them. The tramp wakes and squirts water on the matches from a perfume atomizer. The title of the film is How They Fired the Bum-Nit.

How They Rob Men in Chicago
AM&B © H16335 Apr. 10, 1902
Cameraman: Arthur Marvin
Location: Roof Studio, N.Y.C. *Date:* Apr. 24, 1900
10 ft. FLA4192 (print) FRA2893 (neg.)

The set represents a street with several different types of businesses on it. A man in a top hat and tailcoat walks by the camera at the same time as an attractive young woman goes by in the opposite direction. Each gives the other a careful appraisal. The man stops, turns around and watches the young woman walking away. As he does this, a man dressed as a thug and brandishing a club appears from behind some boxes and hits the bewitched man over the head several times, knocking him to the pavement. After rifling his pockets, the thug leaves. The film ends as a man dressed as a policeman walks by, looks down at the robbery victim, bends over, removes his watch and continues on his way.

How to Disperse the Crowd
Gaumont © H44522 Apr. 18, 1904
7 ft. FLA3110 (print) FRA0446 (neg.)

This fragment, only a portion of what was photographed, shows a street scene. A man strumming a guitar is surrounded by a small group who seems to be paying more attention to the camera position than they are to the performer. As the film is incomplete, it is impossible to say what was in the minds of the producers.

How Would You Like a Wife Like This?
AM&B © H93237 May 4, 1907
Cameraman: G. W. Bitzer
Location: Studio, N.Y.C. *Photographed:* Feb. 14–16, 1907

How Would You Like a Wife Like This? (1907) provides an example of early time and stop-action photography. A bowling ball goes completely through the pins without knocking any of them down, much to the mystification of the audience.

287 ft.   FLA5465 (print)   FRA 2351 (neg.)

A husband lounges on a couch with his feet up and reads a magazine when a man made up as a woman appears, grabs the contented little man, and mops up the floor with him. She then puts him to work with a carpet sweeper and a feather duster. As soon as he can, the husband sneaks out, and the chase is on. The irate wife chases him from a poker game, a bowling alley, a pool hall, and finally catches up with him as he watches a dance of the seven veils in a burlesque house. She drags him from the theatre, takes him home, ties him to a chair, and proceeds to perform the same dance, stopping occasionally to beat him on the head. During the bowling sequence, the camera once moved in for an extreme close-up of trick photography as the ball went completely through the pins without knocking one down. Released as If You Had a Wife Like This.

How'd You Like to Be the Iceman?

AM&B   © H16357   Apr. 10, 1902
Cameraman: F. S. Armitage
Location: Roof Studio, N.Y.C. *Date:* Mar. 10, 1900
12 ft.   FLA4320 (print)   FRA1468 (neg.)

A young woman dressed in the style of the era is busying herself about a kitchen set. The door opens and a stalwart man with a piece of ice enters. He puts the ice on the table and gives the young lady a kiss. Then he puts the ice in the water cooler, receives and drinks something the young woman pours in a glass for him and kisses her again. He receives another drink, tips his hat, picks up his ice tongs, and departs.

Hulda's Lovers

AM&B   © H109471   Apr. 16, 1908
Cameraman: G. W. Bitzer *Script:* Gene Gauntier
Cast: Eddie Dillon, Tony O'Sullivan, Guy Hedlund
Location: Studio, N.Y.C. *Photographed:* Apr, 10, 1908
158 ft.   FLA5466 (print)   FRA2352 (neg.)

A young lady is sitting at a table preparing vegetables when her parents embrace her and admonish her to behave in their absence. Hardly have they departed when a series of young men arrive singly and each embraces the young girl. Each time there is another knock, Hulda is forced to hide her present suitor. Finally she has one hidden in the oven, one in the wood box, one in the attic, and another in a pickle barrel. A shy young man dressed as a hired hand intermittently enters with wood that he nonchalantly drops on the man hidden in the woodbox. At this point, Hulda's parents return and pandemonium breaks loose as all the suitors try to make their escape simultaneously. The script was written by Gene Gauntier, later famous as an actress and producer with Kalem.

Human Apes From the Orient
AM&B © H77050   May 9, 1906
Cameraman: G. W. Bitzer
Location: Aboard the S.S. Werdenfels docked in Brooklyn, N.Y. *Photographed:* Apr. 28, 1906
118 ft.   FLA5064 (print)   FRA2023 (neg.)

The subject is two grotesque-looking human beings who are sitting on the deck of a ship. The two weird individuals sit crosslegged and do the bidding of a man in Oriental costume. The point of the film seems to be directed at the fact that the bone structure of the two subjects makes them look like monkeys or apes, and the spectators seem to be trying to get them to behave like monkeys, that is, scratch themselves, etc. At the end of the film, the two subjects stand up.

A Human Hound's Triumph
Keystone © LP5311   May 8, 1915
Producer and Author: Mack Sennett
Cast: Mae Busch, Harry McCoy, Frank Opperman, Mack Swain, Nick Cogley, Joe Swickard
Location: Vicinity of and in Keystone Studio, and Van Nuys Boulevard, Los Angeles
422 ft.   FLA6116 (print)

This is a summer boarding house scramble in which a crook (Mack Swain), a detective disguised as a woman (Nick Cogley), and two lovers (Mae Busch and Harry McCoy) figure prominently. When the lovers elope, the chase starts, and it involves a horse, an automobile and a motorcycle. It ends with the young couple being married by the justice of the peace (Joe Swickard), and the detective departing with the city slicker in his custody.

Humorous Phases of Funny Faces
Vitagraph © H75272   Apr. 6, 1906
Animation: J. Stuart Blackton
A few frames   FLA5978 (print)   FRA8072 (neg.)

The extent of the film sent in for copyright is only a few frames. However, it is possible to detect actual progressive movement from frame to frame. The film has its place as a pure cartoon, even though the production is not very extensive. The cartoon is believed to have been drawn by J. Stuart Blackton.

The Hungry Actor
Lubin Mfg. Co.   © J132276   Aug. 16, 1909
Location: Philadelphia
93 ft.   FLA5065 (print)   FRA2024 (neg.)

A hungry actor tries by craftiness to remain an actor and eat while not doing any physical labor whatsoever. At first he tries to eat some biscuits and a pie set out to cool on a window sill, but they prove too tough. He then sees a "Man Wanted" sign on a construction site. He takes the sign and hangs it on the front of a bakeshop, and enters and talks to the baker about the sign. While the baker is removing it, the actor eats bakery goods from the display counter. When the baker returns, they start to fight, and several other people become involved. The police are called and as the film ends, the actor nonchalantly walks away.

Hunting the Largest Game in the World
See: Whaling in the Far North Off the Coast of Alaska in the Treacherous Bering Sea

A Hustling Soubrette
AM&B   © H42239   Feb. 18, 1904
Cameraman: [A. E. Weed]
Location: Studio, N.Y.C. [?] *Photographed:* Dec. 18, 1903 [?]
18 ft.   FLA4438 (print)   FRA1544 (neg.)

Two women dressed as maids are seen in a set of a backstage dressing room. A third young woman, dressed in street clothes, enters and is immediately set upon by the two women who begin removing her clothing until she is wearing only a black leotard over which she puts a costume. She immediately leaves the dressing room, only to return soon. The succession of events is repeated. As soon as this costume is changed, she leaves the dressing room in a hurry and the film ends.

Hyde Park School Graduating Class
AM&B   © H45150   May 2, 1904
Cameraman: A. E. Weed
Location: Kansas City, Mo. *Photographed:* Apr. 18, 1904
19 ft.   FLA3969 (print)   FRA1177 (neg.)

Two rows of girls and one of boys are facing the camera as the film begins. Immediately in the background is a blackboard with the words "Kansas City, Mo." As if on signal, the three rows of young people begin demonstrating their ability to twirl Indian clubs in unison; for the full extent of the film, the students do just that.

Hyde Park School, Room 2
AM&B   © H45149   May 2, 1904
Cameraman: A. E. Weed
Location: Kansas City, Mo. *Photographed:* Apr. 18, 1904
20 ft.   FLA3111 (print)   FRA0447 (neg.)

Four rows of preadolescent children, both boys and girls, are standing in front of a blackboard on which the words "Kansas City, Missouri" can be seen. Each boy and girl has a pair of Indian clubs and for the extent of the film the group demonstrates in unison different exercises, using the clubs.

The Hypnotist's Revenge
AM&B   © H97644   Aug. 3, 1907
Camerman: G. W. Bitzer *Photographed:* April 18, 19 and 23, 1907
Location: Studio and N.Y.C.
400 ft.   FLA5468 (print)

This film consists of a series of scenes based on the revenge inflicted by a hypnotist on a skeptic. The hypnotist becomes so irritated by the unbeliever that he follows the man around and mesmerizes him into acting like a monkey, dancing wildly at a party, becoming a waiter and eating from an emty plate, as well as trying to take the place of a groom at a wedding.

The police are called and the skeptic is taken off to an insane asylum where he is cured of his hallucinations and convinced of the efficacy of hypnotism.

Some of the scenes were photographed on the streets of New York. There is one instance of a camera pan to follow an actor from a carriage to a front door, an uncommon camera use in those years. Each scene was preceded by a descriptive title.

I Did It, Mamma

AM&B © H123871 Mar. 11, 1909
Director: D. W. Griffith *Cameraman:* G. W. Bitzer
Cast: Gladys Egan, Clara T. Bracey
Location: Studio, N.Y.C. *Photographed:* Feb. 15, 1909
139 ft. FLA5469 (print) FRA2354 (neg.)

This is the story of a little boy and little girl who have not been getting along too well in the playroom. The film was photographed on a set of the dining room of a well-appointed home and on a set of the children's playroom. The little girl helps herself to a large portion of cake from the dining room table and starts eating it. The mother enters, assumes the boy took the cake, and spanks him. The camera shifts between scenes of the mother spanking the boy and the little girl in the playroom where she is eating the cake and wrestling with her conscience. After several shifts of the camera from the chastisement scene to the little girl eating the cake, she breaks down and admits to her mother that she is the culprit. The camera moves in for a tight close-up of the mother and the two children, which ends the film.

I Had to Leave a Happy Home for You

AM&B © H30729 Apr. 24, 1903
Cameraman: Wallace McCutcheon
Location: Roof Studio, N.Y.C. *Date:* Jan. 23, 1900
14 ft. FLA3130 (print) FRA0464 (neg.)

A man with his suspenders hanging over his trousers is shaving in front of a mirror in a set of a man's bedroom. While he is shaving, a woman dressed as a maid enters the room and begins dusting. The man walks over and kisses the maid, who protests. He forces the issue and they are interrupted by the arrival of another woman, presumably the wife. She points to the shaving soap on the maid's face and orders her out of the room with a gesture of her arm and a pointed finger.

Ice-Boat Racing at Redbank, N.J.

Edison © H1492 Mar. 1, 1901
Location: Shrewsbury River, Red Bank, N.J.
49 ft. FLA4664 (print) FRA1682 (neg.)

The camera was placed on the ice of a frozen-over river. The maneuvers of several different size ice boats sailing back and forth in front of the camera position and around a turning pylon can be seen. The distance of the boats from the camera does not permit detail of the rigging of the boats or the personnel aboard to be seen.

Ice Boating on the North Shrewsbury, Red Bank, N.J.

Edison © H42208 Feb. 16, 1904

Cameraman: Edwin S. Porter
Location: Shrewsbury River, Red Bank, N.J. *Date:* Jan. 17, 1904
57 ft. FLA4663 (print) FRA1691 (neg.)

The subject is ice boating. The cameraman placed his equipment to show the crew of a boat making it ready, the passengers boarding, and then the ice boat on the frozen river. The remainder of the film shows the maneuvers of the boat as it goes back and forth in front of the camera.

An Ice-Covered Vessel

AM&B © H42801 Feb. 27, 1904
Cameraman: A. E. Weed
Location: Sandy Hook, N.J. *Photographed:* Feb. 16, 1904
37 ft. FLA3750 (print) FRA0996 (neg.)

The camera was positioned at a distance that made it possible for the photographer to encompass a small trawler under way in a sound or coming in from the ocean. The photographer's interest was in the fact that the ship was completely covered by ice which came from the spray made by the vessel as it made its way through the water.

Ice Skating in Central Park, N.Y.

Edison © H40944 Jan. 16, 1904
Cameraman: Edwin S. Porter
Location: Central Park, N.Y. *Date:* Jan. 17, 1904
42 ft. FLA4665 (print) FRA1693 (neg.)

The photographer placed his camera in such a position that while he panned, it filmed many hundreds of people actively engaged either in skating, putting on their skates, or removing them. The altitude of the camera took in just the skaters on the ice, not the surrounding territory.

Ice Yacht Racing

AM&B © H16360 Apr. 10, 1902
Cameraman: Robert K. Bonine
Location: Shrewsbury River, N.J. *Date:* Jan. 20, 1902
19 ft. FLA4236 (print) FRA1393 (neg.)

The photographer placed his camera a distance that does not permit much detailed description of the several ice boats. During the short length of the film, the boats pass back and forth in front of the camera.

Ice Yachting

AM&B © H26853 Jan. 9, 1903
Date: 1899 [?]
21 ft. FLA3733 (print) FRA0980 (neg.)

The film was photographed from a position above the heads of some people watching race-boat enthusiasts prepare to start and run their race boats on an iced-over lake. There is some foreground footage of a man attempting to get his boat properly started.

Ice Yachting

AM&B © H32945 June 25, 1903
14 ft. FLA3294 (print) FRA0610 (neg.)

The short length of the film did not permit the subject, an ice boat, to pass the camera position more than once. Little else can be seen except two large houses in the background.

The Iconoclast

Biograph ⓒ H146130 Oct. 5, 1910

Director: D. W. Griffith *Cameraman:* G. W. Bitzer

Cast: Henry B. Walthall, Claire McDowell, Adele De Garde, Verner Clarges, Charles West, Jeanie Macpherson, Kate Bruce, Gladys Egan, Grace Henderson, George Nicholls, Alfred Paget, W. J. Butler, Tony O'Sullivan, Guy Hedlund

Location: Studio, N.Y.C. *Photographed:* Aug. 25–26, 1910

387 ft. FLA5470 (print) FRA2353 (neg.)

A printer with anarchistic tendencies becomes rude and outright violent when his wealthy employer invites his dinner guests to inspect his publishing plant. The printer is discharged and decides upon revenge. Armed with a gun, he goes to his employer's house. Here he finds his boss with his small daughter, a permanent cripple. Touched by the child's plight and her courage, he finds himself unable to take the revenge he had planned. His employer realizes that his ex-employee has undergone a change of attitude, and rehires him. The film was made on four sets: the wealthy man's house, the print shop, the laborer's apartment, and the exterior of the rich man's house.

Illusions Fantasmagoriques

Melies ⓒ H37664 Nov. 6, 1903

Creator: Georges Méliès

Cast: Georges Méliès

Location: Montreuil, France *Date:* Fall 1903

Original title: Illusions Funambulesque

58 ft. FLA5471 (print) FRA2644 (neg.)

The first scene takes place on what appears to be a stage with a table on it. The actor (Georges Méliès) dissolves himself into the scene and stands on the table dressed in Oriental attire. He jumps off the table, dissolves himself out of the Oriental costume and into knee breeches before he lands on the floor. He then causes tables to turn over, people to appear and disappear, and, in general, makes use of some interesting stop action photography.

Illusions Funambulesque

See: Illusions Fantasmagoriques

The Impalement

Biograph ⓒ J141757 May 31, 1910

Director: D. W. Griffith *Cameramen:* G. W. Bitzer, Arthur Marvin

Cast: Dell Henderson, Stephanie Longfellow, Florence Barker, Frank Powell, Kate Bruce, Arthur Johnson, Verner Clarges, Charles West

Location: Stamford, Conn.; Studio, N.Y.C. *Photographed:* Apr. 21–23 and 28, 1910

389 ft. FLA5472 (print) FRA2355 (neg.)

A socially prominent man and his wife attend a party where they meet a frivolous female dancer. The husband is intrigued and sets out to make a conquest of her. His wife becomes jealous and threatens to take poison. The husband contemptuously pours the poison in a glass, hands it to his wife, and goes to a dinner given in his honor by the dancer. After he leaves, the wife falls to the floor in a faint. During the party, the husband becomes remorseful. He leave the party and rushes home, and finds his wife on the floor. He thinks she is dead and returns to the party, where he suffers a heart attack and dies, presumably because of his bad conscience.

An Impartial Lover

AM&B ⓒ H37498 Nov. 2, 1903

Cameraman: G. W. Bitzer

Location: Glen Island, N.Y. *Photographed:* Oct. 25, 1903

29 ft. FLA4666 (print) FRA1694 (neg.)

The camera was located to show a little boy seated between two little girls on the bottom step of a staircase. All during the picture, the little boy looks directly at the camera or kisses one of the two girls. There is no other action.

Impersonation of Britt-Nelson Fight

Lubin ⓒ H66293 Sept. 29, 1905

Reel 9: 1,202 ft. Reel 10: 177 ft. FLA5934 (print) FRA2808 (neg.)

As the title indicates, this picture is a restaging of a prize fight. The camera was mounted in the center of the ring, before either a boxing or wrestling match. Then, two men who resembled the famous "Battling" Nelson and Jimmy Britt were substituted. The film was photographed from a single-camera position to make it look as though this were the actual prize fight.

The Impossible Convicts

AM&B ⓒ H70260 Dec. 19, 1905

Cameraman: G. W. Bitzer

Location: Studio, N.Y.C. *Photographed:* Dec. 6, 1905

70 ft. FLA5066 (print) FRA2025 (neg.)

An unusual film-making technique was used to make this picture. All of the action and movement of the participants is accomplished by having them walk backwards in and out of doorways, or up and down stairs while the camera turned backwards as well. People in the striped uniforms of prisoners and others dressed as prison guards can be seen from a single-camera position on a set of a penitentiary cell block. The action of the film resembles a picture made with the same cast on the same set but done in a normal manner.

Impromptu Scrap

See: A Dog Fight

In a Boarding School Gym

AM&B ⓒ H43569 Mar. 22, 1904

Cameraman: A. E. Weed

Location: Studio, N.Y.C. *Photographed:* Feb. 25, 1904

18 ft. FLA4210 (print) FRA1371 (neg., copy 1) FRA1372 (neg., copy 2)

In the center of a gymnasium set, a large woman wearing gym clothing is standing on a tumbling mat. She is surrounded by a circle of young girls she encourages to run, jump, and skip around her. For the full extent of the film, the young girls, who are dressed in ordinary street attire, continue to circle their instructress. In the last scene, two of them, feigning dizziness, fall over on the instructress, who is seen flat on her back with her feet in the air as the film comes to a conclusion.

See also: School Girl Athletes and School Girl Gymnastics.

In a German Bath

AM&B ⓒ H30182 Apr. 4, 1903

20 ft. FLA3628 (print) FRA0885 (neg.)

The photographer placed his camera on the edge of a large swimming area. During the film, young boys, some clothed, some unclothed, dive and jump into the water.

In a Hempen Bag

Biograph © J136054 Dec. 20, 1909

Director: D. W. Griffith *Cameraman:* G. W. Bitzer

Cast: Kate Bruce, Gladys Egan, Adele De Garde, Mack Sennett, Linda Arvidson, Robert Harron, Grace Henderson

Location: Edgewater, N.J.; Studio, N.Y.C. *Photographed:* Nov. 2–9, 1909

180 ft. FLA5473 (print) FRA2356 (neg.)

This picture begins when the lady of the house orders a servant to put a cat in a bag and drown it. Two children come in and let the cat out of the bag. Their mother puts her infant on the floor beside the cat and leaves the room. While she is gone, a drunken nursemaid, recently discharged, sees the baby and puts it in the cat's bag. The bag is given to a hired man with instructions to throw it in the river. The mother returns, finds the infant missing, and a chase starts. The hired man, en route to the river, encounters some boys with a rifle who offer to shoot the cat. They make several efforts, but the rifle does not discharge, they are out of ammunition, etc. Just as they are about to make a final attempt, the mother halts them, and the baby is saved.

In a Manicure Parlor

AM&B © H22087 Sept. 27, 1902

Cameraman: Robert K. Bonine

Location: Roof studio, N.Y.C. *Date:* July 10, 1902

22 ft. FLA3220 (print) FRA0544 (neg.)

The set is divided by a wall in order to resemble two sections of a manicure parlor. A young woman manicurist and a young man having a manicure are seated at tables on each side of the wall. Just as the film begins, a young man starts to hug and kiss the various manicurists. Judging from their reactions, the women do not seem to find this annoying nor do they resist. The embracing continues throughout the film.

In a Massage Parlor

AM&B © H22090 Sept. 27, 1902

Cameraman: R. K. Bonine

Location: Roof studio, N.Y.C. *Date:* July 21, 1902

10 ft. FLA3947 (print) FRA1158 (neg.)

As the film begins, only the face of a young woman and the hands of a man standing behind her are visible. The camera was placed for the best view of the woman's face as the man caresses and massages her throat and neck. He kisses the young woman twice during the course of the film.

In a Raines Law Hotel

AM&B © H63806 July 24, 1905

Cameraman: G. W. Bitzer

Location: Studio, N.Y.C. *Date:* July 13, 1905

24 ft. FLA3919 (print) FRA1135 (neg.)

The set is of the lobby, a staircase, a split wall, and a bedroom of a small hotel. A large sign behind the bar says "No Drinks Served at the Bar Today." The first action shows men, women, and couples entering the hotel, reporting to the desk clerk, and being ushered by him into the bedroom part of the set. He unlocks the door and locks it after them on each occasion. After several customers have been let into the locked room, a policeman enters and is let into the room filled with people who are drinking. As the film ends, several people appear to be pleading with the policeman. "The Raines Law, 1896 . . . provided that liquor could be sold on Sundays in New York State only in those hotels possessing both a license and at least ten bedrooms," *The Columbia Encyclopedia.*

In Life's Cycle

Biograph © J145612 Sept. 19, 1910

Director: D. W. Griffith *Cameraman:* G. W. Bitzer

Cast: Stephanie Longfellow, Henry B. Walthall, George Nicholls, Linda Arvidson, W. Chrystie Miller, William J. Butler, Alfred Paget, Adele De Garde, Tony O'Sullivan, Jack Pickford, Charles West

Location: Cuddebackville, N.Y.; Fort Lee, N.J.; Studio, N.Y.C. *Photographed:* July 18–21 and Aug. 18, 1910

401 ft. FLA5474 (print) FRA2363 (neg.)

A brother and sister make a pact that one will always keep flowers on their dead mother's grave. The boy becomes a priest, but his sister runs away with a ne'er-do-well and bears him a child out of wedlock. They are finally married by a priest who is called to administer last rites to the ne'er-do-well when he is injured in a barroom brawl. The sister starts home with her small daughter. She stops at her mother's grave, where her brother finds her as she is kneeling in prayer. He takes them both home to reunite them with their aged father. There are several camera movements from full shots to close-ups, with dissolves between scenes.

In Little Italy

Biograph © J136491 Dec. 29, 1909

Director: D. W. Griffith *Cameraman:* G. W. Bitzer

Cast: Marion Leonard, W. Chrystie Miller, Tony O'Sullivan, Henry B. Walthall, Mack Sennett, Gladys Egan, Adele De Garde, John Cumpson, George Nicholls, Florence Barker, Charles Craig

Location: Fort Lee, N.J.; Studio, N.Y.C. *Photographed:* Nov. 17–20, 1909

384 ft. FLA5475 (print) FRA2364 (neg.)

Two men, one a gentle, kindly man, the other a brutal, jealous drunkard, want to marry an attractive widow. The film shows the courting, the announcement of the marriage plans, the wedding supper, and the stabbing of the successful suitor by the rejected one. The rejected suitor takes advantage of the convalesence of the injured man to press his suit with the widow. A great deal of suspense is built up when the rejected lover attempts to attack the widow. She locks herself in a room and moves furniture against the window and over the trap door in the floor, while he tries to enter every possible way. She sends her little daughter for the police, who arrive at the crucial moment.

In My Lady's Boudoir

AM&B © H34822 Aug. 19, 1903

Cameraman: Wallace McCutcheon

Cast: Kathryn Osterman

Location: Studio, N.Y.C. *Photographed:* Aug. 3, 1903

28 ft. FLA3762 (print) FRA1007 (neg.)

The camera work is quite imaginative. The actions encompassed are those of a young woman facing a mirror as she makes up her face and puts up her hair. All during the film, she has her back to the camera. Only her face can be seen as she looks into the mirror.

In Old California

Biograph © J139101 Mar. 12, 1910

Director: D. W. Griffith *Cameraman:* G. W. Bitzer

Cast: Marion Leonard, Frank Grandon, Arthur Johnson, Henry B. Walthall, Mack Sennett, W. Chrystie Miller, Charles West

Location: Hollywood *Photographed:* Feb. 2–3, 1910

415 ft. FLA5476 (print) FRA2365 (neg.)

A son is born out of wedlock to a woman who, twenty years later, is destitute and contacts the father of her son. The father, now governor of California, is impressed by the size and appearance of his son and appoints him to the palace guards. The son soon proves to be a wastrel. He is in constant disfavor with his superiors, and his post is in jeopardy. However, at no time does his ailing mother learn of this. The film ends dramatically when the dying mother asks to see her son once again, and the governor has him dressed in the uniform of a bemedaled hero, and then accompanies him to his mother's bedside. Immediately after the mother's death, the governor orders his wastrel son stripped of medals and honors.

In Old Kentucky

Biograph © J131613 Sept. 14, 1909

Director: D. W. Griffith *Cameraman:* G. W. Bitzer

Cast: Henry B. Walthall, Owen Moore, Kate Bruce, Verner Clarges, William J. Butler, Mary Pickford, Linda Arvidson, Mack Sennett, Frank Powell

Location: Cuddebackville, N.Y.; Studio, N.Y.C. *Photographed:* July 29 and Aug. 3, 5 and 6, 1909

367 ft. FLA5477 (print) FRA6435 (neg.)

This film is set in the pre-Civil War era and begins on a set of the sitting room of a mansion where four people are having a heated discussion. The discussion culminates as the father (Verner Clarges) raises an American flag and holds it in the air. His son (H. B. Walthall) angrily leaves the room to join the Confederate troops. Several battle scenes follow. The son becomes frightened and deserts. He runs home pursued by soldiers of his company. His mother hides him in her bed and, when the pursuers have gone, the unhappy warrior leaves. The last scenes show him returning to his father's home where they are celebrating the end of the war, and he embraces the Union flag in the presence of his father's guests. There is a good example of early camera use when the point of view of the soldier on picket duty is shown by panning the camera.

In the Border States

Biograph © J142348 June 15, 1910

Director: D. W. Griffith *Cameraman:* G. W. Bitzer

Cast: W. Chrystie Miller, Adele De Garde, Gladys Egan, William J. Butler, Henry B. Walthall, Alfred Paget, Tony O'Sullivan

Location: Delaware Water Gap, N.J.; Studio, N.Y.C. *Photographed:* May 3–14, 1910

413 ft. FLA

The opening scene of this Civil War film takes place in the interior of a home where a Union soldier is bidding his family goodbye. The scene shifts to the exterior of the house where the soldier joins some troops, presumably marching off to war. The plot revolves around one of the soldier's daughters who reluctantly hides a wounded Confederate soldier, and who later calls upon the same soldier to spare her Union father, also wounded, who has made his way home, but is discovered by several members of the Confederate army. There are many camera changes and a lot of activity.

In the Den

See: The Kidnapper

In the Dressing Room

AM&B © H35628 Sept. 12, 1903

Cameraman: A. E. Weed

Location: Studio, N.Y.C. *Photographed:* Aug. 25, 1903

25 ft. FLA4201 (print) FRA1364 (neg.)

The opening scene is in a set of the dressing room of a burlesque show, where four young women are in various stages of undress. The door opens admitting a messenger boy, who leaves almost immediately and a fat man in a dark suit. The young women rush about attempting to exercise a certain amount of modesty, and one of them hides behind a screen. One of the young women pulls a negligee from the top of the screen, and knocks it over revealing the other girl, who has very little clothing on.

In the Haunts of Rip Van Winkle

AM&B © H75634 Apr. 12, 1906

Cameraman: G. W. Bitzer

Location: Ulster and Delaware R.R., Catskill Mountains N.Y. *Photographed:* Apr. 5, 1906

130 ft. FLA5067 (print) FRA2026 (neg.)

As the film begins, the camera starts to move. It is located on the front of a railroad engine that is traveling through a farming area. The train rounds a bend and in the distance a woman is running between the rails. She waves her apron frantically in an attempt to flag down the locomotive. The track makes another turn, disclosing a tramp asleep or reading a newspaper on the tracks. The train stops very close to the nonchalant tramp. The engineer and fireman get off and physically escort him from the roadbed. After the train has departed, the tramp returns to the roadbed where he reclines flat on his back and resumes reading the newspaper.

See also: In the Valley of the Esopus and Into the Heart of the Catskills.

In the Springtime, Gentle Annie!

AM&B © H40941 Jan. 16, 1904

Cameraman: A. E. Weed

Location: Studio, N.Y.C. *Photographed:* Jan. 4, 1904

72 ft. FLA5068 (print) FRA2027 (neg.)

A man and a woman are sitting in front of a smoking fireplace in a set of the living room of a modest home. They summon a housemaid, who comes in and pokes at the fire. Using stop action photography, the smoke leaves the room and the fireplace is emptied. The maid is instructed to clean the chimney and, when she leaves to get her tools, the man of the house brings in a chimney sweep who climbs inside the chimney. The housemaid returns and starts her task, unaware of the presence of the chimney sweep, and is completely covered by the soot she brushes down.

In the Tombs
AM&B © H81753   Aug. 9, 1906
Cameraman: F. A. Dobson
Location: Studio, N.Y.C. *Date:* July 25, 1906
25 ft.   FLA3609 (print)   FRA0872 (neg.)

The film begins by showing a set of the interior of a jail. A young man with his head in his hands can be seen through the bars of one of the doors to a cell. A man dressed as a guard walks back and forth in front of the cell. The door opens and a large woman dressed in mourning approaches the cell door and shakes hands with the young man inside. The women in black leaves, and a woman in white appears, accompanied by another guard. The man in the cell holds a conversation with the prison guard who opens the door to his cell. The film ends as the prisoner and the young lady in white embrace. The original Paper Print film has a copyright date of 1903 but the correct copyright date is Aug. 9, 1906.

The AM&B production records give the title for this little film as Reproduction of Harry Thaw in the Tombs.

[See also:]The Convict Bride

In the Valley of the Esopus
AM&B © H75636   Apr. 12, 1906
Cameraman: G. W. Bitzer
Location: Ulster & Delaware R.R., Catskill Mountains, N.Y.
   Photographed: Apr. 5, 1906
145 ft.   FLA5479 (print)   FRA2664 (neg.)

The film is of a ride the cameraman took on the front of a train traveling on a single track through the Esopus Valley. The trip starts at the railroad yards at the edge of a small town, continues through the cultivated farm land, and approaches a bridge over a small river beyond the township. A man is standing on the bridge and feigning intoxication. The platform on which the camera is positioned stops, but the camera continues to turn. Two men, dressed as engineer and fireman, run ahead of the train, wrestle the drunk off the bridge, and get back on the train which continues on down the track.

See also: In the Haunts of Rip Van Winkle and Into the Heart of the Catskills

In the Watches of the Night
Biograph © J133855   Oct. 27, 1909
Director: D. W. Griffith *Cameraman:* G. W. Bitzer
Cast: Marion Leonard, Gladys Egan, George Nicholls, Tony O'Sullivan, Mary Pickford, Kate Bruce, Mack Sennett
Location: Edgewater, N.J.; Studio, N.Y.C. *Photographed:* Sept. 13, 14 and 20, 1909
407 ft.   FLA5480 (print)   FRA2370 (neg.)

In the early scenes, a desperate father seeks work to buy food for his ailing and hungry child and wife. He goes to the home of a wealthy manufacturer where he is refused work. At his wit's end, the father decides to steal from the manufacturer. He is successful in his burglary but his wife convinces him he should return the loot. He is captured in

the act of honesty, and the police allow him to say goodbye to his family. He decides then to murder his wife and child and to commit suicide himself. Before he can carry out this plan, the man he robbed arrives, gives him money, and promises him a job.

In the Window Recess
Biograph © J135516   Dec. 3, 1909
Director: D. W. Griffith *Cameraman:* G. W. Bitzer
Cast: Marion Leonard, Adele De Garde, George Nicholls, Mack Sennett, James Kirkwood, Arthur Johnson
Location: Fort Lee, N.J.; Studio, N.Y.C. *Photographed:* Oct. 15, 16 and 28, 1909
125 ft.   FLA5481 (print)   FRA2358 (neg.)

An escaped convict takes refuge in the home of a policeman while he is at work, seizes the policeman's child as a hostage, and retires to a curtain-covered alcove. He tells the mother he will kill the child if she divulges his whereabouts. The policeman returns home, asks for his daughter, and his wife is unable to tell him what has happened. However, she does manage to signal him. He captures the convict after a furious fight, and the film ends as the policeman's colleagues take the convict away.

In the Woods
See: Parsifal

The Inauguration of President Roosevelt
AM&B © H57515   Mar. 10, 1905
Cameraman: Wallace McCutcheon
Location: Washington, D.C. *Photographed:* Mar. 4, 1905
92 ft.   FLA5069 (print)   FRA2028 (neg.)

The opening scene, from a camera position over the heads of assembled spectators lining the street, shows Pres. Theodore Roosevelt passing on his way to his inauguration. The second camera position was from the balcony, again over the heads of the crowd, and the scene shows several military contingents parading ahead of the carriage bearing President Roosevelt and group.

The Indian
Klaw & Erlanger © LP3432   Sept. 24, 1914
Cast: Linda Arvidson, Charles Perley, Alfred Paget, Bert Williams, Lewis Wells, Violet Reid
1,200 ft.   FLA5482 (print)   FRA2360 (neg., reel 1)
   FRA2361 (neg., reel 2)   FRA2362 (neg., reel 3)

This three-reel film starts with a battle a tribe of Indians and the cavalry in which twin sons of the Indian chief become separated. One of the sons is raised as a white man and becomes an American soldier, while the other grows up with his father. Conflict arises when dishonest Indian agents sell supplies intended for the Indians. One of the agents then kidnaps the daughter of the American general who raised one of the twin Indians. She is rescued by troops led by the Americanized twin and supported by the Indians themselves. However, the other twin is killed during the skirmish. There are at least three companies of cavalry in the picture, and approximately two hundred and fifty adult Indians and an Indian village.

Indian Day School
Edison © 13560   Feb. 24, 1898

Location: Isleta, N.M.

30 ft. FLA4248 (print) FRA1404 (neg.)

The film was photographed from a single-camera position and shows the doorway of a building with a sign in front indicating it is the Isleta Indian School. Children less than ten years of age come out of the door of the school and pass in front of the camera.

The Indian Runner's Romance

Biograph © J130843 Aug. 24, 1909

Director: D. W. Griffith *Cameraman:* G. W. Bitzer

Cast: James Kirkwood, Owen Moore, Marion Leonard, Arthur Johnson, Mary Pickford

Location: Cuddebackville, N.Y. *Photographed:* June 29–30 and July 2–3, 1909

379 ft. FLA5557 (print) FRA2357 (neg.)

The film begins with a love affair and subsequent marriage between an Indian brave and the daughter of a chief. The marriage ceremony and a dance following it are shown. Shortly after the marriage, three white men abduct the bride, gamble for her; and the winner rides off with her on his saddle. The Indian brave finds his wife missing, and starts to search for her. Eventually he locates her and, as the picture ends, he is seen killing the white man and walking off into the sunset with his arm around his wife.

An Indian Summer

Biograph © J171149 July 12, 1912

Director: D. W. Griffith

Cast: Kate Bruce, W. Chrystie Miller, Mary Pickford, Mae Marsh, Jack Pickford, Harry Hyde

Location: Calif.

413 ft. FLA5485 (print) FRA6430 (neg.)

This is the story of a romance between an elderly widower with very little hair and a widow of equal age who runs a boarding house. Their budding romance is held in abeyance because a letter from a hair-restoring company solicited by the old man is misconstrued by the widow as being from another woman. The film consists of series of such situations that keep the two people (Kate Bruce and Walter Chrystie Miller) apart. It ends when each falls asleep on rocks at the seashore and is marooned when the tide comes in. The letter falls out of the old gentleman's pocket when he waves his handkerchief for help, and the widow sees it. The two old people embrace happily as the film ends.

Indiana Whitecaps

AM&B © H24874 Dec. 9, 1902

Cameraman: Arthur Marvin

Date: Sept. 7, 1900

20 ft. FLA3981 (print) FRA1189 (neg.)

The camera was placed as if in the audience at a vaudeville house. On the stage are a painted backdrop and a wooden wall that looks like the door of a cabin. As the action begins, four men armed with squirrel rifles approach the door. They are accompanied by a man with a bag, and a man with a small barrel. They open the door, drag a man out, force him to the floor of the stage, pour the contents of the barrel over him, and dump a large bag of feathers over that. The film ends as the armed men turn and walk off the stage.

Indians Leaving Bald Mountain

AM&B © H35881 Sept. 21, 1903

Cameraman: Wallace McCutcheon

Location: The Adirondack Mountains, N.Y. *Photographed:* Sept. 12, 1903

34 ft. FLA4667 (print) FRA1695 (neg.)

The camera position shows three men clothed as mountaineers and carrying rifles walking toward the camera.

See also: Trappers Crossing Bald Mountain

Infancy

See: The Seven Ages

The Infernal Caldron

See: Le Chauldron [i.e., Chaudron] Infernal

The Ingrate

AM&B © H118294 Nov. 14, 1908

Director: D. W. Griffith *Cameramen:* G. W. Bitzer, Arthur Marvin

Cast: Florence Lawrence, Arthur Johnson

Location: Cos Cob, Conn.; Studio, N.Y.C. *Photographed:* Oct. 2–28, and Nov. 2, 1908

342 ft. FLA5486 (print) FRA259 (neg.)

A trapper finds a man lost in the woods and brings him home. He and his wife help the wanderer to regain his health, only to have him make advances to the trapper's wife. The opening scene shows a portion of a lake in front of a rustic cabin. The trapper, axe over his shoulder, can be seen in the distance. A woman emerges from the cabin to greet him. The camera pans to follow the two of them, then moves in for a close "two shot" to better identify them. The picture concludes dramatically when the wife rescues her trapper husband from a bear trap placed in his path by the ungrateful woodsman who had been their guest.

The Inn Where No Man Rests

Melies © H32938 June 25, 1903

Creator: Georges Méliès

Cast: Georges Méliès

Location: Montreuil, France *Date:* Spring 1903

French title: L'auberge du bon repos

147 ft. FLA5070 (print) FRA2029 (neg.)

This is a classic example of the capabilities of Georges Méliès. The set is a hotel room, and an obviously intoxicated guest is shown the room. In the best Méliès tradition, odd things begin to happen to the guest, such as pictures coming to life and biting, boots walking up walls, clothes-horses kicking and wrestling, etc. The film ends with all of the guests of the inn chasing the intoxicated guest.

The Inner Circle

Biograph © J172323 Aug. 17, 1912

Director: D. W. Griffith

Cast: Mary Pickford, Adele De Garde, Alfred Paget, Charles Hill Mailes, Robert Harron, Mae Marsh, "Spike" Robinson, Jack Pickford

368 ft. FLA5487 (print) FRA6429 (neg.)

A secret society bent on surviving through blackmail decided to blow up the house of one of their victims in order to teach him a lesson. They choose a member who is

The Inn Where No Man Rests shows the magic effects of French filmmaker Georges Méliès.

a widower with a small child to carry out their decision. He goes to bomb the house, looks through the window, and sees his only child who had been brought into the house after she had been struck by a hit-and-run driver.

An Innocent Conspirator

AM&B © H32298 May 29, 1903
26 ft. FLA3539 (print) FRA0895 (neg.)

The real meaning of this film is difficult to follow. The set represents a foyer of a theater or a club, or perhaps the living room of a large house. A woman is sitting on a bench next to the wall and a man in evening clothes is sitting in a chair reading a newspaper. Across the room from him a young woman and a young man on a sofa are kissing. As the film continues, the man who was reading the newspaper gets up and leaves and the two on the sofa continue embracing.

An Innocent Victim

AM&B © H32557 June 12, 1903
11 ft. FLA3497 (print) FRA0777 (neg.)

A man is displaying his wares in front of a wall that seems to be part of a barn decorated as a grocery store front. He is painting a sign which is not entirely visible. The storekeeper puts down his paintbrush, leaves the unfinished sign, and goes in the store. A prankster appears, picks up the paintbrush, and touches up the sign. Whatever he did was

not photographed. He hides to wait for a passerby; one comes along and is caught by the grocer staring at the sign. A fight occurs that continues to the end of the film.

Inside Car, Showing Bag Catcher

AM&B © H36400 Oct. 1, 1903
Cameraman: A. E. Weed
Location: St. Georges, Md. *Photographed:* Sept. 21, 1903
28 ft. FLA3370 (print) FRA0673 (neg.)

The camera was placed inside a baggage car that is approaching a railroad station. The film shows a recent innovation for nonstop pick-up of mail bags, and includes the catch from its location at the station. The hands of the baggage-car man are shown, hooking the mailbag and the last few feet of film show the device close up.

Installation Ceremonies of President Butler

AM&B © H23813 Nov. 11, 1902
Cameraman: Arthur Marvin
Location: Columbia Univ., N.Y.C. *Date:* Apr. 21, 1902
90 ft. FLA4669 (print) FRA1697 (neg.)

The film shows the installation of Nicholas Murray Butler as Dean and President of Columbia University. The occasion was a triple-threat ceremony of the dedication of a building, the graduation of students, and the installation of the new president of the university. Many educators and politically significant persons were present, among them Theodore Roosevelt, Andrew Carnegie, and of course, Nicholas Murray Butler.

See also: Classmates

The Insurance Collector

AM&B © H36354 Sept. 30, 1903

Cameraman: G. W. Bitzer

Location: Studio, N.Y.C. *Photographed:* Sept. 21, 1903

26 ft. FLA3602 (print) FRA0867 (neg.)

This film takes place in a set of the kitchen of a house of modest means where two women are working. The younger is washing dishes in a dishpan, while the other scrubs clothes at a washtub. The older woman abruptly stops and goes to the door. She lets in a man dressed in dark clothes who removes a straw hat from his head and goes over and takes the hand of the young lady. He attempts to kiss her hand, which provokes the older woman and she pushes him into a tub filled with water. The older woman continues to demonstrate her hostility by picking up a bucket, also filled with water, and pouring it on the man's head. At this point, the young woman helps her by emptying the contents of her dishpan on the already badly soaked young man.

The Insurance Solicitor

AM&B © H72714 Feb. 1, 1906

Cameraman: G. W. Bitzer

Location: Studio, N.Y.C. *Photographed:* Jan. 19– 21, 1906

260 ft. FLA5488 (print) FRA2367 (neg.)

A young man accepts a position as a salesman of life insurance and the film shows the situations, some humorus and some disastrous, that he gets into when he tries to make good. He enters an office at the wrong time and is thrown out, a cook piles all the furniture in the kitchen on top of him, and a man in a feed-and-grain store dumps the contents of a chute all over him. The last scene shows the young man back on the farm, happily accepting the routine life there. The title on the film reads The Insurance Solicitor or The Story of a Blasted Ambition.

Inter-Collegiate Athletic Association Championships, 1904

Edison © H46906 June 7, 1904

Cameramen: Edwin S. Porter, A. C. Abadie

Location: Franklin Field, Philadelphia *Photographed:* May 27–28, 1904

242 ft. FLA5489 (print) FRA2366 (neg.)

Installation Cermonies of President Butler (1902) at Columbia University. Theodore Roosevelt is in the center and Nicholas Murray Butler is to the right.

The camera was placed in many positions to photograph an intercollegiate track meet in Philadelphia in 1904. The film is excellent to use in comparing progress between then and now. The following events are shown: shot-put, one-mile run, 440-yard run, 120-yard hurdles, running high-jump, 100-yard dash, two-mile run, 16 pound hammer throw, 220-yard hurdles, 220-yard run, and the pole vault.

Inter-Collegiate Regatta, Poughkeepsie, New York, 1904

Edison © H47665 July 2, 1904

Cameraman: Edwin S. Porter *Photographed:* June 25–28, 1904

Location: Poughkeepsie, N.Y.

283 ft. FLA5490 (print) FRA2368 (neg.)

The camera coverage of these boat races was from many vantage points: atop the incline where the shells were put into the water by their crews, during the races from the judge's motor boat as they pushed off from the floats, panoramic pictures from the bank including the whole race course, and aboard the judge's boat at the finish line. The film also includes scenes of four-oar shells as well as eight-oar shells.

Interior N.Y. Subway, 14th St. to 42nd St.

AM&B © H61570 June 5, 1905

Cameraman: G. W. Bitzer

Location: Interborough Subway, 14th St. to 42nd St., N.Y.C.

  Photographed: May 21, 1905

53 ft. FLA5071 (print) FRA2030 (neg.)

The camera platform was on the front of a New York subway train. The camera train is behind a train on the same track, and the film is lighted by a work car on the opposite track. As the trains progress through the subway, the film records a train operator's view of the subway during operating hours: starts, stops, platforms, people getting on, and people getting off. This documentary was printed by AM&B together with a Rube in the Subway and was released as a comedy by them in 1905.

Interior of Department Store

  See: The Kleptomaniac

Interior of Temple

  See: Parsifal

International Contest for the Heavyweight Championship: Squires vs. Burns, Ocean View, Cal., July 4th, 1907

Miles Brothers © H96711 July 18, 1907

Cameraman: Herbert J. Miles [?]

International Contest for the Heavyweight Championship: Squires vs. Burns, Ocean View, Cal., July 4th, 1907. Tommy Burns was the victor in this very short fight.

The Italian was produced by Thomas H. Ince, one of D. W. Griffith's early actors, who became an important producer but met an untimely death. On the right we see an uncommon way of providing screen credits, even in 1915.

Location: Ocean View, Calif. *Photographed:* July 4, 1907
73 ft. FLA5491 (print, copy 1) FLA5976 (print, copy 2) FRA5976 (master pos.) FRA2698 (neg., copy 1) FRA2699 (neg., copy 2) FRA2700 (neg., copy 3)

This is an actual film of the heavyweight championship prize fight. The fight was labeled the shortest and fiercest prize fight on record up to that time.

The Interrupted Bathers

Edison © H22833 Oct. 22, 1902
29 ft. FLA3455 (print) FRA0737 (neg.)

Three young ladies are splashing about in a section of a small pool or lake. Another young woman is reclining against a vine-covered tree on the bank in the background. Two tramps come out of the foliage and trees. They frighten the young ladies into running away and steal their clothing from the water's edge. The last scene in the film shows one of the young women walking off camera clothed in a barrel.

An Interrupted Elopement

Biograph © J172320 Aug. 17, 1912

Director: Mack Sennett
Cast: Eddie Dillon, Mabel Normand, William J. Butler, Alfred Paget, Ford Sterling
195 ft. FLA5492 (print) FRA2369 (neg.)

This split reel comedy is about a suitor who is prevented from marrying the girl of his choice because he is not athletic. He and his friends plan an elopement by automobile to the minister's home. Mabel, on her way to her wedding, nervously drops the note and it is found by her father. The suitor and his friends learn that the father is also headed for the minister's so they decide to kidnap the minister. There is a mix-up and the father is kidnapped instead, and when he is released from the bag, the embarrassment of all is great. The suitor is so annoyed that he hits one of his friends. The girl's father is so impressed by the suitor's strength that he agrees to the marriage and all ends happily.

An Interrupted Honeymoon

Hepworth © AM&B H53767 Nov. 28, 1904
Director: Lewin Fitzhamon
Location: Walton-on-Thames, England

137 ft. FLA5072 (print) FRA2032 (neg.)

There are some sets, and the outdoor and indoor scenes were combined to show an interrupted honeymoon. There is a chase in which the bride and groom exchange clothing, and she assumes the role of head of the house before the pursuers arrive. This ruse is successful in diverting their attention from the honeymooners.

An Interrupted Kiss

AM&B © H33416 July 13, 1903
Date: 1898 [?]
10 ft. FLA3652 (print) FRA0907 (neg.)

The camera was placed as if in the audience at a vaudeville theater. A park bench stands in front of a painted backdrop of a park. A man and a woman enter the set and sit down on the bench, and he starts holding her hand. Another man comes along and sits down by them. He manages to push something off the lap of the other man, who bends down to pick it up. As he does so, the young woman leans across him and gives the second man a kiss, and all of them fall over backward.

The Interrupted Picnic

Edison © H22834 Oct. 22, 1902
30 ft. FLA3456 (print) FRA0738 (neg.)

The poor condition of this film does not permit a detailed description of the action. However, it is possible to see that four people are sitting on the bank of a lake or a river and having a picnic. A tramp frightens them and they run away. The two men return, grab the tramp, and throw him into the water. The film ends as the four picnickers throw objects at the tramp who is standing waist deep in the water.

Into the Heart of the Catskills

AM&B © H75635 Apr. 12, 1906
Cameraman: G. W. Bitzer

Location: Ulster & Delaware R.R., Catskill Mountains, N.Y.
  Photographed: Apr. 5, 1906
158 ft. FLA5493 (print) FRA2371 (neg.)

A railroad station is visible from the camera position. The camera then begins to move as if it were mounted on the front of a railroad train. The camera proceeds along a railroad track through rural countryside. The sides of many houses and barns are seen as the train continues along the track. Bridges, trestles, overpasses. wagon and cattle crossings are seen but nothing shown in the film permits positive identification of either the track or the locale.

See also: In the Haunts of Rip Van Winkle and In the Valley of the Esopus.

Invisible Fluid

AM&B © H111674 June 11, 1908
Cameraman: G. W. Bitzer
Location: Studio, N.Y.C.; Grantwood, N.J. *Photographed:* May 16, 1908
255 ft. FLA5494 (print) FRA2372 (neg.)

Stop action photography plays a principal part in the film. In the first scene, in a broker's office, a doltish messenger boy discovers that the article in his hand has the capacity to make objects and persons disappear. He takes a pushcart from a peddler, a groom from a bride, a sweetheart from his girl, and a cash register from a restaurant, and then the chase begins. All of the people from whom he has taken something begin to chase him while he is carrying the cash register. He stops at an intersection and causes the people chasing him to disappear one at a time. A policeman captures him by the simple expedient of removing the magic object from his hand, and takes him off to jail where the messenger boy causes himself to disappear. The original Paper Print film bears the title The Man in the Box. Obviously an error, as both were sent in for copyright at the same time.

See also: Man in the Box

Invitation to Dinner

See: How Jones Lost His Roll

Iola's Promise

Biograph © J167112 Mar. 11, 1912
Director: D. W. Griffith *Cameraman:* G. W. Bitzer
Cast: Mary Pickford, Alfred Paget, Joe Swickard, George Nicholls, William J. Butler, Dorothy Bernard
Location: Near Los Angeles
400 ft. FLA5870 (print) FRA6433 (neg.)

Photographed in California, this story is about an Indian maiden (Mary Pickford) who is rescued from cruel captors by a kind prospector (Alfred Paget). He convinces her that most white people are like him. Before she returns to her tribe, her benefactor shows her some gold-bearing rock and asks her to let him know if she finds any. Her tribe attacks a covered wagon. The prospector's fiancee is captured and about to be burned at the stake when Iola acts as a decoy and is fired on by her own people. She dies in the arms of the prospector, but not before she shows him where she has found some gold-bearing rock.

The Italian

N.Y. Motion Pictures © LP5156 Jan. 7, 1915
Producer: Thomas H. Ince *Director:* Reginald Barker

Cast: Clara Williams, George Beban
2,157 ft. FLA5871-5872 (print) FRA2746-2747 (neg.)

An Italian gondolier with high hopes emigrates to the United States, becomes a bootblack, and sends for his betrothed. When she arrives, they get married and have a son. The infant becomes ill from lack of pure milk. The father, on his way to buy the desperately needed milk, is robbed of his last few cents and is arrested when he brawls with the thugs. He is taken off to jail, and his baby dies while he is there. Later, crazed with grief, he learns that a politician who treated him cruelly has an ill child, and he goes to the house intending to revenge himself, but lacks the courage to carry out his plan. The picture contrasts his former happy life in Italy with his present hard and bitter existence in a big city slum.

The Italian Barber

Biograph © J150748 Jan. 11, 1911
Director: D. W. Griffith *Cameraman:* G. W. Bitzer
Cast: Mark Pickford, Joe Graybill, Mack Sennett, Kate Bruce, Robert Harron, Marion Sunshine
Location: Fort Lee, N.J.; Studio, N.Y.C. *Photographed:* Nov. 15–16, 1910
365 ft. FLA5495 (print) FRA6434 (neg.)

A barber becomes enamored of the little newsgirl (Mary Pickford) on the corner near his shop. She allows him to escort her home. They become close friends until the barber sees her sister. A complicated problem arises and is eliminated when another young man enters the scene. He (Mack Sennett) becomes interested in the heartbroken and jilted young woman, and his attentions mend her emotional wounds.

It's a Shame to Take the Money

AM&B © H61110 May 19, 1905
Cameraman: G. W. Bitzer
Location: Studio, N.Y.C. *Photographed:* May 9, 1905
23 ft. FLA3806 (print) FRA1041 (neg.)

On a set of a street, a young boy is waiting for a customer for his shoeshine stand. A policemen comes along and hides behind a wall when he sees a young lady approaching to have her shoes shined. She sits down and pulls her skirts up above her ankles. When the shine is completed, the young lady attempts to pay the boy who refuses to accept money, so she walks off camera. The policeman, who has been watching, shakes the shoeshine boy's hand.

It's Unlucky to Pass Under a Ladder

AM&B © H16352 Apr. 10, 1902
Date: Apr. 22, 1899
10 ft. FLA4243 (print) FRA1399 (neg.)

On a set of a two-story apartment house, a man can be seen putting a ladder against one of the second-floor windows. As he starts up the ladder carrying a bucket, a young lady leans out a lower window and talks to him. The man comes down from the ladder and has a tête-à-tête with the young woman who comes out of the house. He returns to the ladder with his bucket. A well-dressed young man walks into the scene and starts talking to the young woman to the annoyance of the man on the ladder. To show his displeasure, he empties the contents of his bucket on the well-

Stage actor George Beban in The Italian, *which was purportedly filmed in Italy, but was actually shot on the canals and bridges of Venice, California, which were patterned after those in Italy. (See illustrations on pages 166 and 167 also.)*

dressed young man. The film ends as a fight is in progress between the two men.

Jack and Jim

Méliès © H38791 Dec. 4, 1903

Creator: Georges Méliès

Location: Montreuil, France *Photographed:* Fall 1903

Original title: Jack et Jim

Alternate French title: Jacques et Jim

76 ft. FLA4671 (print) FRA1699 (neg.)

This farce of special effects consists of a series of magical sequences in which people appear and disappear into tubs, and are changed into pigs, etc.

Jack and the Beanstalk

Edison © H19221 June 20, 1902

Director: Edwin S. Porter *Cameraman:* Edwin S. Porter

Cast: Small boy is Thomas White, son of Edison employee Arthur White

250 ft. FLA5496 (print) FRA2373 (neg.)

The film is based on the famed fairy tale, Jack and the Beanstalk, with the addition of trick effects and unusual camera uses. All of the story was filmed: trading the family cow for beans, the beanstalk growing, the altercation with the giant, the chase, chopping down the beanstalk, the fall and death of the giant, etc. All were effectively conveyed.

Jack et Jim

See: Jack and Jim

Jack Jaggs & Dum Dum

Méliès © H37292 Oct. 26, 1903

Creators: Georges Méliès

Cast: Georges Méliès

Location: Montreuil, France *Date:* Summer 1903

Original title: Tom Tight et Dum Dum

75 ft. FLA5497 (print) FRA2641 (neg.)

A panoramic backdrop of a garden is used in the first scene. Georges Méliès, in costume, enters with an unidentifiable bundle under his arm. When it is assembled, the bundle turns out to be a large mannequin, which he causes to become alive by stop-action photography. A man enters and starts displaying his ability as a dancer. This annoys Méliès who pounds on the man's head with an overlarge hammer, driving him into the stage. The remainder of the film is devoted to people appearing and disappearing and being transformed from flags into human beings, etc.

165

Jack Johnson vs. Jim Flynn Contest for Heavyweight Championship of the World, Las Vegas, New Mexico, July 4, 1912

Jack Curley © U171968 July 18, 1912

Location: Las Vegas, N.M. *Date:* July 4, 1912

600 ft. FLA5874 (print) FRA2788 (neg.)

Nine rounds of the Johnson-Flynn prize fight are shown from a single-camera position. The film clearly shows the ability of the great Jack Johnson. The fight, held July 4, 1912, in Las Vegas, New Mexico, was stopped by the police, and Johnson won on points.

Jacques et Jim

See: Jack and Jim

Jamestown Exposition

See: Opening Day, Jamestown Exposition

Japanese Acrobats

Edison © H45038 Apr. 29, 1904

Cameraman: Edwin S. Porter

Location: Studio, N.Y.C. *Date:* Apr. 20, 1904

55 ft. FLA4672 (print) FRA1700 (neg.)

On a stage with a backdrop depicting a garden scene, two men, obviously Orientals, enter from the wings and begin a tumbling act. One acrobat juggles the other on his feet. At the completion of their routine, the acrobats take two bows, leaving the stage as the film ends.

Japanese Fencing

AM&B © H17973 May 21, 1902

Cameraman: Robert K. Bonine

Location: Kyoto, Japan *Date:* July 28, 1901

17 ft. FLA3827 (print) FRA1055 (neg.)

Several students demonstrate the Japanese manner of fencing, which is holding a broomsticklike sword and wielding it as a club. All of the participants wear face masks and shoulder and breast protectors. The background consists of a wall that surrounds the practice yard.

Japanese Sampans

Edison © 38248 June 22, 1898

Cameraman: James H. White

24 ft. FLA3328 (print) FRA0271 (neg.)

Proceeding toward the camera position are some small rowboat-style Japanese boats being propelled by two men on either side of the boat, each with a sculling oar. They are

in a parade line and the film ends as the last boat is rowed past the camera position. Across the horizon are some marine-size steam vessels.

Japanese Village

Edison © H7330 July 31, 1901

Location: Pan-American Exposition, Buffalo, N.Y.

65 ft. FLA4673 (print) FRA1701 (neg.)

At the beginning of the film, at a distance of about one-hundred feet, is a two-story building with a balcony, some tropical plants, and a telephone pole. A young Japanese man appears directly in front of the camera. He is accompanied by two small Japanese boys attired in tight knee britches and rather loose sleeved blouses. The three of them exhibit their gymnastic powers by performing back handsprings, back flips, unusual handstands, etc. There are two spectators in Occidental clothing. Nothing shown in the film indicates Japanese surroundings.

The Jealous Monkey

Edison © 60569 Oct. 25, 1897

18 ft. FLA3080 (print) FRA0421 (neg.)

Three men are sitting around a table holding a monkey and a dog apart. The men attempt to induce the monkey and the dog to become acquainted, but from their actions, the animals do not seem to think much of the idea.

Jealousy and the Man

Biograph © J129609 July 21, 1909

Director: D. W. Griffith *Cameraman:* G. W. Bitzer

Cast: James Kirkwood, Florence Lawrence, W. J. Butler, Arthur Johnson

Location: Fort Lee, N.J.; Studio, N.Y.C. *Photographed:* Mar. 31 and June 15, 1909

152 ft. FLA5498 (print) FRA2375 (neg.)

A husband, several years older than this attractive wife, misinterprets a set of circumstances and becomes jealous over what appears to him to be too much attention paid by his wife to their young, stalwart boarder. His suspicions grow stronger, and he decides to shoot them both. He goes home, hides behind a curtain with a pistol in his hand, and waits for his young wife. The wife and the boarder enter, the husband steps out, and they hand him gifts of a hat and socks as a surprise for his birthday. The last scene in the film shows the jealous husband embracing his wife and shaking hands with the boarder behind her back with a sheepish expression on his face.

Jeffreys in His Training Quarters

Edison © H109L7 Dec. 2, 1901
155 ft. FLA5500 (print) FRA2696 (neg.)

The film is devoted to the various activities of a professional prize fighter in his training quarters. He can be seen skipping rope, boxing with sparring partners, and utilizing specialized equipment for developing muscle. The film ends with Jim Jeffries sparring with one of his trainers.

Jernbanens Datter

See: The Little Railroad Queen

A Jersey Skeeter

AM&B © H16644 Apr. 16, 1902
Cameraman: Arthûr Marvin
Location: Roof studio, N.Y.C. *Date:* July 26, 1900
15 ft. FLA4265 (print) FRA1421 (neg.)

The set represents the back of a house in a rural area. An old man is sitting at the table with a large barrel on it. The barrel is labelled "Jersey Applejack," and the man seems to have been imbibing freely from it. A model insect of considerable size appears and flies around the old man's head. The presence of the insect disturbs him greatly and he swats at it with a broom. At the end of one mighty swing, he loses his balance and falls to the ground. The mosquito picks him up by the seat of the trousers and carries him out of camera view.

Jerusalem's Busiest Street, Showing Mt. Zion

Edison © H32794 June 17, 1903
Cameraman: A. C. Abadie
Location: Jerusalem, Palestine *Photographed:* Mar. 15, 1903
35 ft. FLA4674 (print) FRA1702 (neg.)

The cameraman placed his camera to show living quarters, the Wall, streets, stone structures, the natives, and some pack animals in the middle of the business district of the city of Jerusalem. The camera attracted the attention of the natives and some of the subjects can be seen staring at it.

A Jewish Dance at Jerusalem

Edison © H32487 June 10, 1903
Cameraman: A. C. Abadie
Location: Jerusalem, Palestine *Photographed:* Mar. 15, 1903
28.5 ft. FLA3707 (print) FRA0955 (neg.)

Thirteen persons are shown dancing a hora, a traditional dance, on a street alleged to be in Jerusalem.

The Jilt

AM&B © H126828 May 10, 1909
Director: D. W. Griffith *Cameramen:* G. W. Bitzer, Arthur Marvin
Cast: Arthur Johnson, Owen Moore, Tony O'Sullivan, Florence Lawrence, Marion Leonard, Mack Sennett, George Nicholls

Location: Riverside Drive and Studio, N.Y.C. *Photographed:* : Apr. 13 and 16, 1909
367 ft. FLA5501 (print) FRA2376 (neg.)

A rich young stock broker (Arthur Johnson) is despondent over this unrequited love for a socialite (Marion Leonard) and he loses his money. He becomes a bum, but is encouraged to regain his self-respect by a crippled young woman (Florence Lawrence). The film begins with a fight in the park, and the hero beats several thugs who attack his friend (Owen Moore). The following scenes show the grateful young man thanking his rescuer. Complications arise between the two over the affections of the socialite. Author's note: This was one of the first two films advertised under the corporate name Biograph Company.

Jim Jeffries on His California Ranch

Miles Brothers © H94997 June 8, 1907
Cameraman: Herbert J. Miles [?]
Location: Calif.
35 ft. FLA4675 (print) FRA1703 (neg.)

The first scene preceded by the title: Greeting Visitors, is taken across a dirt road that runs in front of the Jeffries' home. Approaching the house is an automobile with four passengers. As the car stops in front of the house, Jim Jeffries and his wife come out to greet the visitors. All then enter the house, the camera was at such a distance that subjects are not easily identifiable. The next scene, Mrs. Jeffries and Jim Feeding the Chickens, shows Jim and his wife feeding the chickens.

Jimmie Hicks in Automobile

AM&B © H32500 June 11, 1903
Cast: Charles E. Grapewin
Cameraman: G. W. Bitzer
Location: Galveston, Tex. *Date:* Sept. 25, 1900
29 ft. FLA3730 (print) FRA0977 (neg.)

A paved intersection can be seen in the foreground while in the background are foliage and what appears to be a public building. A motor-driven vehicle with four wheels and of buggy size approaches the camera. Accompanying it is a smaller motor-driven vehicle with two passengers. The larger of the two cars is put through a demonstration maneuver to show that it could go forward, turn left, right, go backward turning right and left, and start and stop easily.

See also: Chimmie Hicks at the Races

Jockeying and Start of Yacht[s], Aug. 25th

AM&B © H35392 Sept. 4, 1903
Cameraman: A. E. Weed
Location: Sandy Hook, N.J. *Photographed:* Aug. 25, 1903
87 ft. FLA5074 (print) FRA2032 (neg.)
[America's Cup Races; Reliance and Shamrock III]

From camera right to camera left, two of the American contenders can be seen in profile at a distance of about a thousand yards. Both their position in relation to one another and their rigging are clearly shown. From the action on the boats, it is evident that they are preparing to come about. The remainder of the film shows the two contenders close up with their crews at work. In one of these scenes, Thomas Lipton can be seen standing by the wheel of his yacht.

Jockeying for the Start, Aug. 20
AM&B © H35096 Aug. 28, 1903
Cameraman: A. E. Weed
Location: Sandy Hook, N.J. *Photographed:* Aug. 20, 1903
51 ft. FLA4676 (print) FRA1704 (neg.)
[America's Cup Races; Reliance and Shamrock III]

The film was photographed from the deck of a boat to show the America's Cup Race. The film begins at a distance of about a thousand yards from the two contenders, which are under full sail and approaching a marker buoy. Later in the film, both vessels can be seen as they pass close to the camera vessel. They are all sailing on different courses. The crew's activity is clearly visible.

Jockeying for the Start, Aug. 22
AM&B © H35072 Aug. 27, 1903
Cameraman: A. E. Weed
Photographed: Aug. 22, 1903 *Location:* Sandy Hook, N.J.
56 ft. FLA5075 (print) FRA2033 (neg.)
[America's Cup Races: Reliance and Shamrock III]

The camera was positioned on a boat cruising over the racecourse for the America's Cup Race. As the film begins, the bowsprit of one of the contenders can be seen, and then the rest of the vessel passes the other contender. Crew activity is clearly visible. The remainder of the film shows both racing vessels in close-hauled sailing positions turning about marker buoys, approaching and going away from camera.

Joe, the Educated Orangoutang
AM&B © H21308 Aug. 25, 1902
Date: 1898 [?]
16 ft. FLA3208 (print) FRA0533 (neg.)

A standard size child's high chair can be seen. Seated in the high chair is a baby orangutang, and on the tray of the high chair is a large glass dish containing food. The animal picks up a spoon and starts eating whatever is in the glass dish. The film was photographed outdoors, but nothing in the background is in focus.

John Paul Jones Ceremonies
AM&B © H76576 May 2, 1906
Cameraman: G. W. Bitzer
Location: Annapolis, Md. *Photographed:* Apr. 24, 1906
222 ft. FLA5502 (16mm print) FLA5957 (35mm pos.) FRA2504 (neg.)

The film records the reinterment of the body of John Paul Jones in the crypt of the U.S. Naval Academy at Annapolis, Maryland. All of the celebrities, dignitaries, and military personages from two continents were photographed from many camera positions as they paid homage to the celebrated naval hero. Every branch of the French and American governments was represented and can be seen passing in review before the camera position. Pres. Theodore Roosevelt represented the U.S. government at the ceremonies while France sent its ambassador.

The Johnie and the Telephone
AM&B © H39904 Dec. 23, 1903
Cameraman: A. E. Weed
Location: Studio, N.Y.C. *Photographed:* Dec. 10, 1903
36 ft. FLA4677 (print) FRA1705 (neg.)

The camera was placed to encompass a set of the backstage dressing room of a burlesque show. There are three chorus girls and one featured dancer in the dressing room as the film starts. A man in evening attire, accompanied by a waiter with a tray, several glasses, and a bottle of champagne, is ushered in by the doorman. The rest of the film is devoted to the group as they drink and carouse until the man walks over to a wall telephone and makes a call. While he is talking on the phone, one of the chorus girls throws the champagne bucket at him, ending the film.

Johnny's in the Well
AM&B © H32868 June 20, 1903
Cameraman: F. S. Armitage
Location: Roof studio, N.Y.C. *Date:* Aug. 11, 1899
20 ft. FLA3438 (print) FRA0723 (neg.)

The film begins on a set of the backyard of a house. Immediately in front of the camera is a belfry of a well where two children, a boy and a girl, are playing. The boy falls into the well; the little girl runs into the house and fetches an adult woman who proceeds, with the aid of the windlass, to extricate the boy from the well. When the film ends, the woman can be seen soundly spanking the boy.

A Joke at the French Ball
AM&B © H42038 Feb. 11, 1904
Cameraman: A. E. Weed
Location: Studio, N.Y.C. *Photographed:* Feb. 4, 1904
36 ft. FLA4678 (print) FRA1706 (neg.)

The set shows two rooms. Two young women and one man, all dressed in costumes and wearing dominoes, enter, seat themselves around a table, and begin drinking. The young man gets up, asks one of the young women to join him, and they go into the adjoining room. Some more people come into the first room and conspire to play a trick on their friends. The man from the first scene disguises himself as a woman and flirts with another man who attempts to embrace him. At that moment, all of the pranksters enter the room, laughing.

Joke on Grandma
Edison © H1401 Feb. 23, 1901
16 ft. FLA3698 (print) FRA0947 (neg.)

A group of women are sitting in a living room set. Their actions indicate they are discussing the rather obese old woman who is sitting in a rocking chair. (The person playing the part of the old woman is a man.) All six young women leave their seats, cross the room to the old lady's chair, pick her up, hold her over their heads, and let her drop to the floor. The film ends as grandma sits up in amazement or bewilderment.

A Joke on Whom?
AM&B © H16730 Apr. 18, 1902
Cameraman: F. S. Armitage
Location: Roof Studio, N.Y.C. *Date:* June 25, 1901

9 ft. FLA3188 (print) FRA0514 (neg.)

A man dressed as an aged gentleman is sleeping in a hammock, which is part of a set of an outdoor garden. Two small boys are watching the old man intently as if to make certain he is asleep. When they are sure that he is, the boys approach and begin tickling him. One of the boys climbs under the hammock as if to stick a pin in the sleeper when the hammock latch lets go, and the old man and the hammock land on the little boy.

The Jolly Bill Poster

AM&B © H40750 Jan. 11, 1904
Cameraman: A. E. Weed
Location: Studio, N.Y.C. *Photographed:* Dec. 23, 1903
24 ft. FLA4183 (print) FRA1347 (neg.)

On a set of the front of an opera house are two men pasting advertisements of a coming attraction into the poster frames. The man on the ladder carelessly bumps his coworker who accepts the apologies with a smack in the face from the wet pastebrush. This act of violence annoys his companion, and for a considerable amount of the film the two workmen are seen punching one another and using the paste-filled buckets and brushes as weapons. A man in a formal business suit comes onto the set through one of the doors and attempts to stop the brawl. As the film ends, both of the workers have turned on him and are covering him with paste.

The Jolly Monks of Malabar

AM&B © H71758 Jan. 10, 1906
Cameraman: F. A. Dobson
Location: Studio, N.Y.C. *Photographed:* Dec. 29, 1905
257 ft. FLA5467 (pos.)

The first scene is a head-and-shoulder view of a group of men dressed as monks or friars, singing and laughing at stories in a small book their superior is reading to them. The camera shifts to a room furnished as a dining room. A servant with an apron is drinking wine from a large barrel. The remainder of the film shows the group going fishing. They encounter a fisherman, and one of the order persuades him to donate some fish to them, as they have not been successful. He is later punished when the other monks realize he did not catch the fish himself.

See also: The Simple Life and Wine, Women and Song

Jones and His New Neighbors

AM&B © H124891 Mar. 26, 1909
Director: D. W. Griffith *Cameraman:* G. W. Bitzer
Cast: Florence Lawrence, John Cumpson, Flora Finch, Mack Sennett
Location: Perry Street and Studio, N.Y.C. *Photographed:* Feb. 24–25, 1909
173 ft. FLA5503 (print) FRA2377 (neg.)

All of the incidents in this humorous one-reel picture are related to the preoccupation of neighbors who live on a street where the front doors are identical. A husband comes home, his wife embraces him and leaves the room. When she returns, she finds a strange man reading the newspaper and generally making himself at home. She is disturbed. The unwelcome intruder flees in terror, accidentally taking his host's hat and overcoat. The film shows three such incidents. The final scenes show all the neighbors, bran-

dishing kitchenware and pounding on the door of the man who caused all the trouble by wandering into the wrong apartment. A policeman arrives and straightens everything out, ending the film.

Jones and His Pal in Trouble

Edison © 15264 Feb. 25, 1899
Cast: James H. White
16 ft. FLA4196 (print) FRA1359 (neg.)

Two men wearing hats and overcoats and using walking sticks approach the camera. Judging from their unsteady gait through the snow-covered ground, they are inebriated. A policeman approaches and stops them. One of the two men gets on his hands and knees behind the policeman, and the other pushes the officer who falls on the snow. The man who did the pushing runs off, leaving his companion to face the consequences of the policeman's anger.

See also: Jones Interrupted Sleighride and Jones Return from the Club.

Jones and the Lady Book Agent

AM&B © H126829 May 10, 1909
Director: D. W. Griffith *Cameraman:* G. W. Bitzer
Cast: Florence Lawrence, Flora Finch, John Cumpson, Mack Sennett, Robert Harron
Location: Studio, N.Y.C. *Photographed:* Jan 12–20, 1909
205 ft. FLA5504 (print) FRA2378 (neg.)

A most persistent but unsuccessful female book agent returns to an office where she had failed to sell a book. She overhears her prospective customer ridiculing her and she becomes angry. She substitutes a corset she has in her handbag for a pair of evening gloves her prospective customer had bought as a present for his wife and leaves. The victim of her practical joke goes home, and the inevitable happens. The wife opens her gift, becomes furious, beats up her husband, and then locks, herself in her bedroom where she begins packing to go home to mother. The husband is finally forgiven, but not until he has taken a lot of punishment.

Jones at the Ball

AM&B © H120041 Dec. 17, 1908
Director: D. W. Griffith *Cameraman:* G. W. Bitzer
Cast: John Cumpson, Florence Lawrence, Jeanie Macpherson, Mack Sennett, Arthur Johnson
Location: Studio, N.Y.C. *Photographed:* Sept. 23–24, 1908
200 ft. FLA5505 (print) FRA2379 (neg.)

Mr. and Mrs. Jones attend a formal ball where Mr. Jones has the misfortune to split his trousers. The remainder of the film is a series of comical incidents arising from this mishap. He removes his trousers so that Mrs. Jones can repair them and hides behind a screen in the ladies' dressing room. Several young ladies want to powder their noses and pound on the door. Mr. Jones is forced to leave via the window. A policeman who thinks Mr. Jones is a burglar takes him off to jail, still without his trousers. Before his arrest, there are several occasions where other guests land in a pile on top of one another because doors do not open soon enough or open too quickly.

Jones Entertains

AM&B © H120835 Dec. 30, 1908

Director: D. W. Griffith *Cameraman:* G. W. Bitzer

Cast: John Cumpson, Florence Lawrence, Flora Finch, Jeanie Macpherson

Location: Studio, N.Y.C. *Photographed:* Oct. 31 and Nov. 2, 1908

234 ft.   FLA5506 (print)   FRA2380 (neg.)

Mrs. Jones is to be the hostess for members of her club. This pleases Mr. Jones because he thinks he will have an afternoon and evening away from home. However, his wife's will prevails, and he agrees to serve as a waiter. The prim and proper guests arrive, seat themselves around a table, and the maid serves them. Mr. Jones decides to spike their second cup of tea with rum. The film ends as Mrs. Jones orders her female guests out of the house because in their intoxication they all find her husband so attractive they hug and kiss him. The film was copyright under the above title but it was released on January 7, 1909, as Mrs. Jones Entertains.

Jones Goes Home in a Barrel

See: How Jones Lost His Roll

Jones' Interrupted Sleighride

Edison   © 15266   Feb. 25, 1899

Cast: James H. White

19 ft.   FLA3027 (print)   FRA0146 (neg.)

The camera was set up in the snow at the edge of a clearing in a group of pine trees where the back of a horse-drawn sleigh can be seen as it moves away from the camera position. A man wearing a black overcoat and a top hat is hanging half out of the back of the sleigh and, after progressing about twenty yards, the sleigh stops and the driver insists his passenger leave. He does. The sleigh drives off, and a man is seen walking up to the top-hatted man, who appears to be inebriated, as the film ends.

See also: Jones and His Pal in Trouble; and Jones' Return from the Club

Jones Loses

See: How Jones Lost His Roll

Jones Makes a Discovery

Edison   © 17838   Mar. 8, 1899

Cameraman: James H. White

15 ft.   FLA3028 (print)   FRA0197 (neg.)

A young couple is kissing on a sofa, which is part of the furnishings of a living room set. The young people continue with their love-making but are interrupted by the arrival of a man clad in a nightgown and bed cap. He proceeds to take the young man by the scruff of the neck and then by the seat of his trousers, and throws him bodily out the window. The film ends as the night-shirted man is about to chastise the young girl.

Jones Meets Skinflint

See: How Jones Lost His Roll

Jones' Return from the Club, parts 1, 2 and 3

Edison   © 14371, 14372, 15265   Feb. 20 and 25, 1899

Cast: James H. White

64 ft.   FLA0581 (print, part 1)   FRA0581 (neg., part 1)   FLA3271 (print, part 2)   FRA0582 (neg., part 1)   FLA3262 (print, part 3)   FRA0583 (neg., part 3)

The photographer placed his camera in the snow to photograph the uneven path of a man simulating drunkenness as he walks through the snow-covered field. The man is dressed in a top hat and heavy wrap-around overcoat. As the man approaches a tree in the immediate foreground, he is met by another man who apparently attempts to assist him; the first man hits his benefactor and knocks him into the snow. He repeats this action three times before wandering off past the camera position. Although these three films have separate copyright numbers, they are essentially the same and merely repeat the performance.

See also: Jones' Interrupted Sleighride and Jones and His Pal in Trouble

The Joneses Have Amateur Theatricals

AM&B   © H122929   Feb. 13, 1909

Director: D. W. Griffith *Cameraman:* G. W. Bitzer

Cast: Florence Lawrence, John Cumpson, Clara T. Bracey, Harry Salter, Marion Leonard, Mack Sennett, Owen Moore

Location: Studio, N.Y.C. *Photographed:* Jan. 19–20, 1909

147 ft.   FLA5507 (print)   FRA2381 (neg.)

A single-camera position shows a living room and a married couple (John Cumpson and Florence Lawrence). Several people enter the room and proceed to have an amateur night, as the title indicates. As the film ends, the host and hostess are sitting in the same chairs at the same table as at the beginning. They are yawning and acting bored.

The Judge

See: The Seven Ages

Judge Alton B. Parker and Guests

AM&B   © H48850   Aug. 4, 1904

Cameraman: G. W. Bitzer

Location: Esopus, N.Y. *Photographed:* July 29, 1904

36 ft.   FLA4681 (print)   FRA1709 (neg.)

The film, photographed from three camera positions, depicts a man apparently showing a waterfront or dock to his friends. Among the guests was Mayor George B. McClellan, of New York City, and other Democratic celebrities. "The Democratic National Convention met at St. Louis (July 6, 1904) and nominated Judge Alton B. Parker (N.Y., 1852-1926) for President." Richard B. Morris, *Encyclopedia of American History*, p. 268

See also: Democratic National Committee at Esopus

Judge Parker Receiving the Notification of His Nomination for the Presidency

Edison   © H49192   Aug. 15, 1904

Cameraman: A. C. Abadie

Location: Esopus, N.Y. *Photographed:* Aug. 10, 1904

75 ft.   FLA4682 (print)   FRA1710 (neg.)

The film begins by showing an approximately thousand-ton ferry boat bringing delegates to what looks like a boat landing. Nearly two hundred delegates disembark and surround a park area where the judge and his friends accept the nomination for the presidency as a candidate against Theodore Roosevelt.

Judging Tandems

Edison © 60565   Oct. 25, 1897

29 ft.   FLA3952 (print)   FRA1163 (neg.)

The camera was placed at the edge of a reviewing stand next to the course where the trial for tandem harness horses is being held. Five different two-wheeled vehicles pass the camera position during the film.

Judith of Bethulia

Biograph   LP1660   Oct. 31, 1913

Director: D. W. Griffith *Cameraman:* G. W. Bitzer

Cast: Blanche Sweet, Henry B. Walthall, Kate Bruce, Charles Hill Mailes, Mae Marsh, Robert Harron, Alfred Paget, Lillian Gish, J. J. Lañoe, Harry Hyde

Location: Los Angeles *Photographed:* 1913

1,647 ft.   FLA5875-5876 (print)   FRA2748-2749 (neg.)

This Biograph production, directed by D. W. Griffith, was photographed in Los Angeles in 1913, and was released one reel at a time in 1914.

Jumbo, Horseless Fire-Engine

AM&B © H17042   Apr. 26, 1902

Date: 1897[?]

19 ft.   FLA4077 (print)   FRA1261 (neg.)

The film, photographed from a single-camera position, shows a large steam-driven fire engine proceeding along a road in a rural community.

June's Birthday Party

Edison © H63406   July 17, 1905

278 ft.   FLA5508 (print)   FRA2383 (neg.)

The film shows the activities of approximately two dozen children under the age of ten at the seashore. There are several scenes of supervised play, beginning with a maypole dance. There are foot races, wading in the surf, swimming, and picnicking. A close-up shows two small children filling their buckets with sand by using little tin shovels. A sign in the background reads "Bailey's," and the silhouette of an amusement pier can also be seen.

Jupiter's Thunderbolts; or, the Home of the Muses

See: Le Tonnerre de Jupiter

Just Before the Raid

AM&B © H40810   Jan. 12, 1904

Cameraman: A. E. Weed

Location: Studio, N.Y.C. *Photographed:* Dec. 7, 1903

21 ft.   FLA3675 (print)   FRA0925 (neg.)

Four young women en dêshabille are sitting around a table in a set representing a hotel suite sitting room. They pour drinks from champagne bottles and throw the bottles on the floor. As the film continues, the four rise from the table, join hands, and dance around the table. Before the film ends, one of the young women climbs up on the table top and dances a jig as the others stand about and applaud.

Just Like a Girl

Paley & Steiner © H52169   Oct. 27, 1904

5 ft.   FLA4421 (print)   FRA1583 (neg.)

The camera was placed on the bank of a small lake or stream. Two women can be seen, against the very dark foliage, standing on a small pier out over the water. One of them jounces the boards and falls into the water, to the consternation of her companion who, as the film ends, can be seen making gestures indicating concern over the welfare of her friend in the water.

Just Like a Woman

Biograph © J168396   Apr. 20, 1912

Director: D. W. Griffith *Cameraman:* G. W. Bitzer

Cast: Mary Pickford, Wilfred Lucas, Mae Marsh, Charles Hill Mailes, Grace Henderson, Kate Bruce

Location: Calif.

490 ft.   FLA5510 (copy 1)

A woman who has lost all her money attempts to marry her young daughter to a wealthy older man. Confronted with unpaid bills and discontinuance of credit, the young girl decides to follow her mother's suggestion. After the marriage, the older man finds to his dismay that his young bride does not really love him. He buys his mother-in-law's worthless stock, tells the girl her mother can now afford to support her, and leaves. His generosity causes the young bride to fall in love with him. Each scene is preceded by a lettered title as well as a drawing that symbolizes the scene.

Juvenile Elephant Trainer

AM&B © H38318   Nov. 19, 1903

Cameraman: Wallace McCutcheon

Location: Glen Island, N.Y. *Photographed:* Nov. 9, 1903

152 ft.   FLA5511 (print)   FRA2384 (neg.)

The film was photographed from a single-camera position and shows two full-sized elephants as they are put through their tricks by a child who appears to be not more than five years of age. The child wanders in, about, and under the tails and trunks of the two animals. On two occasions, the elephants obey his command to lie down.

Juvenile Stakes

AM&B © H31756   May 13, 1903

Cameraman: G. W. Bitzer

Location: Morris Park, N.Y. *Photographed:* May 7, 1903

31 ft.   FLA3627 (print)   FRA0884 (neg.)

The short length of the film and its condition do not permit more than a cursory description of the details. However, it is possible to see that the film was of a horse race on a recognized track, but beyond that there is nothing from which to identify the location or the event.

Kaerlighedens Magt

See: The Power of Love

Kaiser Wilhelm's Yacht, "Meteor," Entering the Water

Edison © H14606   Mar. 1, 1902

Location: Townsend and Downey Ship Building Co., Shooters Island, N.Y. *Photographed:* Feb. 25, 1902

102 ft.   FLA3842 (print)   FRA1102 (neg.)

The camera position was a small boat in the vicinity of two large unidentifiable sailing yachts. In the beginning of the film, and at a distance of approximately a thousand yards, are two sailing vessels of virtually the same design and size. Using a spinnaker sail, they execute the maneuver of coming about and bending.

Kanakas Diving for Money, no. 1

Edison © 38214 June 22, 1898
Cameramen: James H. White, W. Bleckyrden
Location: Honolulu
27 ft. FLA4222 (print) FRA1381 (neg.)

In the foreground, it is possible to see eight small boys swimming in what appears to be a harbor area. Several large steamships tied to a dock, either loading or unloading cargo, are visible in the background across the water in which the boys are swimming. The boys just splash about in the foreground.

Kanakas Diving for Money, no. 2

Edison © 38215 June 22, 1898
Cameramen: James H. White, W. Bleckyrden
Location: Honolulu
27 ft. FLA4223 (print) FRA1382 (neg.)

Several native boys swimming in what appears to be a harbor area can be seen in the foreground. In the background several seagoing ships are loading and unloading cargo. During the course of the film, a man in an outrigger canoe paddles by the camera.

Kansas Saloon Smashers

Edison © H1404 Feb. 23, 1901
31 ft. FLA4194 (print) FRA1357 (neg.)

The camera was positioned as if from the audience in a theater. The set resembles the interior of a saloon. A man in an overcoat and derby hat stands at the bar drinking. Another man, made up as a woman, enters and gets a bucket of beer. A third person comes in; he has a beard and a tall hat. He leans a shovel against the bar and has a drink. Two women appear and proceed to chase everybody from the place. They hit people on the head, break mirrors, and generally demolish the place. When the police arrive, the women chase them off, too.

Karina

AM&B © H22556 Oct. 14, 1902
11 ft. FLA3448 (print) FRA0729 (neg.)

A woman dressed as a can-can dancer stands in the center of the stage and, for the full extent of the film, she raises the hem of her dress as she twirls around.

Katchem Kate

Biograph © J170618 June 25, 1912
Director: Mack Sennet
Cast: Mabel Normand, Fred Mace, Jack Pickford, Vivian Prescott, Tony O'Sullivan
261 ft. FLA5512 (print)

Mabel Normand works in a laundry, but she pines to do other and better things. She reads and answers an ad in a newspaper about learning to become a private detective. Apparently her instructor conveys the idea that she has the authority to arrest people, for the balance of the film is a series of situations where Mabel follows a group of plotters who have put a bomb in an old barn, and then not only attempts to learn more of their activities but also tries to capture them. She succeeds after she disguises herself with a mustache and a man's suit.

Katzenjammer Kids and School Marm

AM&B © H33542 July 18, 1903
Cameraman: G. W. Bitzer
10 ft. FLA3425 (print) FRA0713 (neg.)

The film starts on a set of a school room where ten boys and girls are sitting at desks. Their teacher gestures that she plans to leave the room and that the children should study. She goes out and, instead of studying, the youngsters throw books and erasers at one another. This continues until the teacher returns and, while she is admonishing them for their obstreperousness, she trips over a chair and falls to the floor.

The Katzenjammer Kids Have a Love Affair

AM&B © H29471 Mar. 18, 1903
Cameraman: G. W. Bitzer
11 ft. FLA3636 (print) FRA0893 (neg.)

Two young children, a boy and a girl, are sitting in a porch swing in front of a wall, part of a garden set. A larger boy comes through the gate and the two boys begin fighting. A grown woman, fortified with a kitchen broom, attempts to break up the melee by the judicious application of the broom to the boys' posteriors.

Kent House Slide

AM&B © H17226 May 1, 1902
Cameraman: Robert K. Bonine
Location: Quebec, Canada *Date:* Feb. 14, 1902
13 ft. FLA4152 (print) FRA1320 (neg.)

The cameraman placed his equipment at the end of a toboggan slide runway. Throughout the film, one toboggan after another approaches the camera position. Some have as many as four passengers. There is nothing in the picture to indicate the locale of the slide.

See also: Quebec Fire Department on Runners and Skee Club

Kentuckian

AM&B © H112470 June 27, 1908
Cameramen: G. W. Bitzer, Arthur Marvin
Cast: D. W. Griffith
Location: Coytesville, N.J.; Studio, N.Y.C. *Photographed:* June 9 and 11, 1908
311 ft. FLA5513 (print) FRA2386 (neg.)

This drama is built around an episode involving a card game during which one of the aristocratic players is caught cheating. A duel occurs and results in the death of one of the players and the exile of another. The exiled man is seen dressed in rough clothing in a saloon, and from the gestures of two Indians it is evident that they plan to rob him. When he leaves the saloon, the Indians follow him, carry out their plan, and leave him for dead. However, an Indian squaw saves the wounded man's life by dragging him back to her tepee and nursing him back to health. The white man regains his health and asks the chief for the hand of the young woman who was his savior. There is a wedding ceremony. The remaining scenes show their happy life together and their little boy. But the last scene shows the suicide of the Indian woman because she cannot face the loss of her child and husband who are returning to society.

A Kentucky Feud

AM&B © H68323 Nov. 7, 1905
Cameraman: G. W. Bitzer
Location: Sound Beach, Conn. *Photographed:* Oct. 26, 1905
285 ft. FLA5514 (print) FRA2387 (neg.)

This film is a series of scenes documenting the historic feud between two families, the Hatfields and the McCoys, in the Kentucky mountains. Each scene is preceded by extensive titles explaining it. There is a considerable amount of fighting in each scene, and the picture ends with the Hatfields and the McCoys fighting with Bowie knives.

The Kentucky Squire

AM&B © H42035 Feb. 11, 1904
Cameraman: A. E. Weed
Location: Studio, N.Y.C. *Photographed:* Jan. 28, 1904
80 ft. FLA5076 (print) FRA2034 (neg.)

The basic plot for this comedy concerns a man, invited into a marriage mill to act as a witness, who ends up getting married himself. There is lots of activity involving four young women and one older man, besides the preacher at the marriage mill. The sets are unusually well-constructed in that they have signs all over them advertising other items besides quick marriage.

Kicking Football—Harvard

AM&B © H62446 June 20, 1905
13 ft. FLA5515 (print) FRA2709 (neg.)

This is a reduction print from an American Mutoscope & Biograph Company 75 mm paper print. The photographs were of two different men wearing football uniforms and kicking footballs. One man faces the camera while kicking, and the other is in right profile. This film originally was used as a flip-card peep show.

The Kid

Biograph © J140598 Apr. 14, 1910
Director: Frank Powell *Cameraman:* Arthur Marvin
Cast: Florence Barker, Henry B. Walthall, Jack Pickford
Location: Fullerton, Calif.; Studio, Los Angeles *Photographed:* Feb. 16–18 and Mar. 2–8, 1910
387 ft. FLA5516 (print) FRA2624 (neg.)

A widower (Henry B. Walthall) is trying to read the paper when his small son (Jack Pickford) pesters him to join in his games. The scene shifts outside and shows a young woman (Florence Barker) so intrigued by an old windmill that she climbs to the top. The young boy, now playing outside, notices her and removes the ladder. His father, looking for him, rescues the young woman and is impressed by her. The succeeding scenes show that the two are attracted to each other, but she returns to the windmill tower. The widower again rescues her, and this time they embrace, with his small boy between them.

The Kidnapper: At Work [part 1]

AM&B © H34095 Aug. 3, 1903
Cameraman: G. W. Bitzer
Date: July 23, 1903
19 ft FLA4350 (print) FRA0124 (neg.)

The opening scene shows the set of a living room and entrance hall of a house of a person of means. The first person visible is a man dressed in rough clothing. He skulks about the room, and finally goes through a door and comes out struggling with a woman who attempts to prevent his leaving with a small child. He holds the child with his left arm while he beats the woman off with his right. The kidnapper successfully repels the woman, puts a sack over the child's head, and slinks around the corner of the set. The film ends as a man comes in, revives the woman who had fainted, and they both start after the kidnapper.

The Kidnapper: In the Den [part 2]

AM&B © H34096 Aug. 3, 1903
Cameraman: G. W. Bitzer
Date: July 23, 1903
20 ft. FLA4351 (print) FRA1493 (neg.)

The door opens on the set of a disreputable room. A large man dressed in rough clothing is seen carrying a small child. He puts the child down, and begins mistreating him, and throws him on a rag pallet in the corner of the room. The man turns to pour himself a drink, and the child attempts to leave the room. The man catches him, removes his clothing, and starts beating him with a large whip. The film ends as the man picks up the child, throws him into the corner, and leaves the room with the child's clothing under his arm.

The Kidnapper: The Rescue [Part 3]

AM&B © H34097 Aug. 3, 1903
Cameraman: G. W. Bitzer
Date: July 23, 1903
20 ft. FLA4352 (print) FRA1494 (neg.)

The set represents the interior of a disreputable dwelling. A small boy can be seen sleeping in the corner on a pile of rags. A big man drinking from a bottle enters. He continues drinking, and then walks to the child sleeping on the pallet of rags and begins mistreating him. At that moment, the door opens again, admitting a fashionably dressed woman and a man who apparently is a plainclothes policeman. The woman picks up the child and holds him while her companion manages to subdue the child's captor with several blows from a billy club, thus ending the film.

The Ki-Ki Dance

AM&B © H23793 Nov. 11, 1902
Date: 1898[?]
10 ft. FLA3474 (print) FRA0756 (neg.)

Four young women dressed in harem costumes are visible. They dance several steps in unison, none of them very difficult, in front of a black backdrop. The scene is lighted artificially. The working title was The Ki Yi Dance by Nautch Maidens.

Kindergarten Ball Game

AM&B © H45156 May 2, 1904
Cameraman: A. E. Weed
Location: Kansas City, Mo. *Photographed:* Apr. 18, 1904
19 ft. FLA3107 (print) FRA0443 (neg.)

A row of approximately twenty-five children under the age of six can be seen facing the camera. They stand in front of a long blackboard with the words "Kansas City, Mo." written on it. As the film continues, the children bounce the balls they have in their hands, then form a circle and march around the bouncing balls.

Kindergarten Dance

AM&B © H45155 May 2, 1904

Cameraman: A. E. Weed

Location: Kansas City, Mo. *Photographed:* Apr. 18, 1904

19 ft. FLA3102 (print) FRA0439 (neg.)

A group of boys and girls of kindergarten age is doing directed group dancing. The children bow, take hands, and walk around in unison in a circle. A flag-decorated wall in the background appears to be the side of a building. A blackboard with the words "Kansas City, Mo." is fastened to the wall of the building.

King and Queen Diving Horses

AM&B © H16382 Apr. 12, 1902

Cameraman: F. S. Armitage

Location: Coney Island, N.Y. *Date:* Sept. 12, 1899

19 ft. FLA3558 (print) FRA0834 (neg.)

A specially constructed diving tower, approximately fifty feet high, is shown from one camera position. One white horse and then another appear and jump from the top of into the water below.

King Edward and President Loubet Reviewing French Troops

Edison © H32396 June 4, 1903

Cameraman: A. C. Abadie

Location: Vincennes, France *Photographed:* May 2, 1903

32 ft. FLA4683 (print) FRA1711 (neg.)

As the film begins, a carriage drawn by four horses passes the camera. The carriage is photographed from a second camera position as it stops, and Edward, King of England, alights. The remaining film consists of pictures of cavalry passing in review.

King Edward's Visit to Paris

Edison © H32395 June 4, 1903

Cameraman: A. C. Abadie

Location: Paris *Photographed:* May 1, 1903

82 ft. FLA4684 (print) FRA1712 (neg.)

The film was photographed from a single-camera position over the heads of the crowds watching the arrival in Paris of King Edward of England. At least two companies of mounted cavalry in full formal military array preceded King Edward's carriage, which is followed by a number of carriages filled with dignitaries. After they pass, another group of mounted cavalry follow, also in full military formal regalia.

The King of Detectives

AM&B © H23781 Nov. 11, 1902

Cameraman: Robert K. Bonine

Date: Aug. 25, 1902

22 ft. FLA3479 (print) FRA0760 (neg.)

The plot and outcome of this film are confusing. A man and a woman are standing in the snow talking to one another. A second man appears and knocks the first one to the ground and then shoots him. The woman searches the wounded man and then leaves. Another woman, without a coat, approaches the injured man, kneels, rolls him over, and is immediately surrounded by many people who seem to have been summoned by either the altercation or by the police. All of the action takes place on a stage in front of a backdrop painted to appear as the business district of a metropolitan city. This is an early version of another film by the same name, copyrighted by American Mutoscope & Biograph in 1903.

The King of the Cannibal Island

AM&B © H109315 Apr. 11, 1908

Cameraman: G. W. Bitzer

Location: Fort Lee, N.J.; Hudson River and studio, N.Y.C. *Photographed:* Apr. 3, 4 and 6, 1908

256 ft. FLA5517 (print) FRA2388 (neg.)

The cast is dressed as Dutch burghers. The film was photographed on constructed sets and then combined with film photographed outdoors of houses and country roads during the "chase" sequence. The plot is about a hen-pecked violinist who plays in taverns where he receives free drinks in payment, and his constantly nagging wife. There is a combination of phantasy and reality when the violinist has a dream that he is running away from home. Scenes show him getting on board a sailing vessel and arriving on a desert island where he is made king. He is enjoying his new life mightily when his shrewish wife is brought in by his cannabalistic subjects and dumped head first into a stew pot. Some sets had dimensions, while others were simply painted backdrops.

King of the Detectives

AM&B © H34526 Aug. 13, 1903

Cameraman: G. W. Bitzer

Location: Studio, N.Y.C. *Photographed:* Aug. 3, 1903

30 ft. FLA3589 (print) FRA0860 (neg., copy 1) FRA2134 (neg., copy 2)

A well-dressed man and woman can be seen standing stage center against a backdrop painted to resemble a gospel mission front in a slum area of a city. The man draws a dagger from beneath his cape and shows it to the woman and then slinks off leaving her standing as if waiting for someone. Another man, wearing an overcoat and a homburg, and carrying a cane, approaches the woman and begins talking to her. The first man returns and stabs the second man who falls to the snow covered ground. The woman immediately kneels down and removes something from underneath the overcoat of the stabbed man. A short man with a beard, who had been standing partially hidden behind a clothing store dummy in the background, accosts the woman and gestures to her that he will help if he can. As the film continues, a woman dressed in a long grey cloak and a large hat enters upon the stage and kneels by the wounded man to aid him. As she does this, she is surrounded by many people who point accusingly at her.

See also: King of Detectives for another version, copyright by American Mutoscope & Biograph in 1902.

The King's Messenger

AM&B © H109927 Apr. 28, 1908

Cameraman: G. W. Bitzer

Location: Asbury Park, N.J. *Photographed:* Apr. 15 and 17, 1908

345 ft. FLA5518 (print) FRA2389 (neg.)

The film involves the trials of a king's messenger when the king's enemies do all they can to prevent his delivering an important message. There are several scenes in the throne room, some in the armorer's room where men practice dueling, and a scene involving drawing lots for the dangerous task of delivering the king's message. By the end of the film, the messenger has accomplished the nearly impossible feat and his enemies are shown being captured and killed.

The Kiss

Edison © D5532 Mar. 9, 1900

23 ft FLA4065 (print) FRA1249 (neg., copy 1)
FRA1333 (neg., copy 2)

The complete film is a three-quarter view of a man and woman embracing and kissing.

A Kiss and a Tumble

Clarendon © AM&B H50323 Sept. 10, 1904

Director: Percy Stow

42 ft. FLA4685 (print) FRA1713 (neg.)

A maid is leaning out of a second-story window. She attempts to embrace a man who has climbed up a telephone pole. The distance between the telephone pole and the window proves too much, so the maid tries to make it shorter by supporting the weight of her ardent suitor on the end of a broom. This does not work and the man falls into a horse-drawn vehicle similar to a garbage collection wagon. He climbs out of the wagon and waves to the maid. The film was made in Great Britain and was released there under the title The Broken Broom.

A Kiss in the Dark

AM&B © H40866 Jan. 14, 1904

Cameraman: A. E. Weed

Location: Studio, N.Y.C. *Photographed:* Dec. 30, 1903

20 ft. FLA3663 (print) FRA0916 (neg.)

The set represents the front of a two-story house. In a lower window, a young woman in a negligee is sitting. A young man comes along and attempts to kiss her. She puts her hands over his eyes and substitutes a fat black mammy. The remainder of the film shows the black woman holding her hands over the young man's eyes while she kisses him enthusiastically.

Kiss Me

AM&B © H42803 Feb. 27, 1904

Cameraman: A. E. Weed

Location: Studio, N.Y.C. *Photographed:* Feb. 17, 1904

26 ft. FLA4686 (print) FRA1714 (neg.)

The film beings on a set of a street; a nearby fence is covered with theater and burlesque posters. The woman in one of the posters is real. As the action begins, a young woman, accompanied by an older one, passes the row of posters and stops to admire them. As she does so, her chaperone yanks her away by the lobe of her ear. An older man comes along and he, too, is entranced with the real-life poster, and is pulled away from the scene by the woman seen earlier with the young girl.

Kit Carson

AM&B © H35872, H35873, H35876, H35883-8, H36653 Sept. 21 and Oct. 9, 1903

Cameraman: Wallace McCutcheon

Location: The Adirondack Mountains, N.Y. *Photographed:* Sept. 3, 4, and 7, 1903

527 ft. No. 1 FLA5077 (print) FRA2035 (neg.)

No. 2 FLA5078 (print) FRA2036 (neg.)

No. 3 FLA5079 (print) FRA2037 (neg.)

No. 4 FLA5080 (print) FRA2038 (neg.)

No. 5 FLA5081 (print) FRA2039 (neg.)

No. 7 FLA5082 (print) FRA2040 (neg.)

No. 8 FLA5083 (print) FRA2041 (neg.)

No. 9 FLA5084 (print) FRA2042 (neg.)

No. 10 FLA5085 (print) FRA2043 (neg.)

No. 11 FLA5086 (print) FRA2044 (neg.)

Scene 1. A single-camera position shows a campfire smoking in the wilderness and two people asleep by a body of water. One man arises, washes his hands and face, and kicks his companion to awaken him. They pick up their gear and walk out of the scene. *Scene 2.* The same camera position shows some Indians apparently tracking Kit Carson. *Scene 3.* Kit and his companion enter the scene camera left, make camp, cook food, eat, and retire. *Scene 4.* While Kit and his companion are asleep, they are set upon by the Indians, overwhelmed, tied up, and lead off, while one remaining Indian ransacks their equipment. *Scene 5* opens in deep woods with Kit's captors leading him toward their destination. By a ruse, Kit shoves one into a stream they are crossing and attempts to make his escape. There is no Scene 6. *Scene 7* opens with a single-camera position of a canoe paddled into the scene by Kit, followed closely by two canoes containing Indians shooting at him. *Scene 8.* Another camera position in the deep woods shows Kit paddling a canoe. Before the scene ends, it shows other Indians lying in wait, preparing to pursue him with their canoe. *Scene 9* opens in the deep woods. Kit can be seen paddling his canoe toward the ambush. As Kit approaches the bank, Indians fire at him, jump into water, and again take him captive. *Scene 10* opens in the Indian village. Kit's captors bring him in and tie him to a tree. The Indians harass him by brandishing firebrands and throwing stones at him. After making certain he is securely tied to the tree, the Indians retire, leaving one man to sleep at Kit's feet. An Indian maiden emerges from the women's tepee and sets Kit free. *Scene 11*, the last scene, opens from a camera position with a man in front of a shingled-roof house chopping wood. Kit appears, a woman runs out of the house, they embrace, and sit down as though enjoying his return.

See also: Firing the Cabin, Discovery of Bodies, Rescue of Child from Indians and Settler's Home Life

The Kleptomaniac

Edison © H56408-H56418 Feb. 4, 1905

Cameraman: Edwin S. Porter *Photographed:* Jan 19–31, 1905

Location: Studio, N.Y.C. and N.Y.C.

Contents:

Arriving at Police Station. H56408

Court Room Scene. H56409

Tableau. H56410

Home of Thief. H56411

Stealing Bread. H56412

Leaving Store. H56413

Superintendent's Office. H56414

Interior of Department Store. H56415

Arriving at Store. H56416

Leaving Home. H56417

Arriving at Police Station in Patrol Wagon. H56418
315 ft. FLA4687 (print) FRA0102 (Neg.)

All eleven parts of this film of social injustice are preceded by a title explaining the scene that follows. The story is of a destitute woman with an ill and starving child. She steals a loaf of bread and is dragged off to jail in a police patrol wagon, where she waits to be sentenced for her misdeed. This treatment is contrasted with a wealthy woman, caught by a store detective stealing, who is allowed to proceed to the magistrate in her own conveyance and who is in no way humiliated or embarrassed. The last scene shows the scale of justice titled in favor of the monied class.

A Knot in the Plot
Biograph © J141733 May 28, 1910
Cameraman: Arthur Marvin
Cast: Mack Sennett, Fred Mace, Kate Bruce, Florence Barker, Billy Quirk, Frank Powell
Location: Verdugo, Calif. *Photographed:* Apr. 5–6, 1910
380 ft. FLA5519 (print) FRA2390 (neg.)

A young lady is wooed by a Mexican caballero and an extremely well-dressed cowboy. She has a row with the Mexican suitor and is found crying by some of the other men at the camp. They misunderstand and think it is the cowboy dandy who has caused here tears, and the self-appointed vigilantes take him into custody and escort him to her front porch, with the intention of seeing that he marries her. At this moment, the girl and the Mexican come out of the house, and she explains to the embarrassed group that they have the wrong man, and that she has just married the Mexican. The last scene shows the two men making peace with one another.

"Kronprinz Wilhelm" Docking
AM&B © H18898 June 12, 1902
Cameraman: Congdon
Location: N.Y.C. *Date:* Feb. 25, 1902
34 ft. FLA3257 (print) FRA0579 (neg.)

The camera was in a boat in the vicinity of two large sailing yachts. There is no identification on either of the two yachts to distinguish one from the other. The yachts approach the camera position, come about, and proceed in the opposite direction.

"Kronprinz Wilhelm" With Prince Henry on Board Arriving in New York
Edison © H14496 Feb. 26, 1902
Cameraman: James H. White
Location: N.Y.C. *Date:* Feb. 25, 1902
96 ft. FLA5177 (print) FRA2123 (neg.)

The opening scene of this film on the arrival of Prince Henry of Prussia shows the large four-stacked ocean liner *Kronprinz Wilhelm*. The remainder of the film is of scenes of the liner as it proceeds up the channel to the dock, escorted by an undetermined number of harbor tugs. The arrival of the celebrities is not shown. However, a full pan photograph of the German steam yacht that was their living quarters is shown.

Ladies' Saddle Horses
AM&B © H29157 Mar. 11, 1903
Cameraman: F. S. Armitage
Location: Manhattan Field, N.Y. *Date:* May 19, 1899
18 ft. FLA3055 (print) FRA0400 (neg.)

The locale of the film is a large, flat area. Horses are being ridden back and forth in front of the camera by women. All of the horses have docked tails. Some of the women ride sidesaddle while the balance are astride. A tallyho coach and four horses can be seen in the background at the edge of the exhibit area.

Ladies' Saddle Horses
Edison © 60567 Oct. 25, 1897
22 ft. FLA3623 (print) FRA0881 (neg.)

The first scenes are of a small grandstand filled with spectators. The grandstand faces a track. Nearing the camera position are women on saddle horses, all of them using a sidesaddle. They pass the grandstand as if in show competition.

Lady Bountiful Visits the Murphys on Wash Day
AM&B © H35395 Sept. 4, 1903
Cameraman: A. E. Weed *Photographed:* Aug. 19, 1903
Location: Studio, N.Y.C.
35 ft. FLA3548 (print) FRA0823 (neg.)

A single-camera position shows a kitchen set. It is a flat set with a door and three windows. As the action begins, a rather obese female is working over a kitchen stove and a washer, laundering clothes. The door opens. A young boy enters and attempts to purloin one of the two pies cooling on the sideboard. He is caught in the act of taking a large bite from one of them, and the cook-laundress proceeds to wash his face with the pie. She then physically propels him from the set with a resounding kick in the seat of his trousers. Almost immediately, large amounts of snow descend through the window onto the cook who busies herself straightening up the kitchen. Then, camera right, an actor dressed as a policeman enters the set; he is embraced by the cook and given food and drink. After he eats, the policeman and his hostess sit on a bench beneath the other window in the set and begin embracing. Suddenly, the contents of a sack of coal are emptied upon them, causing considerable action, falling down, etc. The scene ends.

See also: the following film, same title, same copyright number, but entirely different plot.

Lady Bountiful Visits the Murphys on Wash Day
AM&B © H35395 Sept. 4, 1903
Cameraman: A. E. Weed
Location: Studio, N.Y.C. *Photographed:* Aug. 19, 1903
35 ft. FLA3548 (print) FRA0823 (neg.)

The film was photographed form a single-camera position. The subject is the arrival of Lady Bountiful at the home of the Murphys. The opening scenes show father seated on a rocking chair reading and smoking, a son approximately ten years old seated on another chair, and mother bending over a scrubbing board adjacent to the boy's chair. The door opens and a lady wearing a white dress and a large picture-hat enters. She is greeted cordially, and the chair formerly occupied by the boy is brushed off for her to sit on. She declines, and while the conversation continues, the small boy puts the train of her dress into the wringer and starts the crank. This pulls Lady Bountiful into the washtub. The film ends as the tub tips over and Mr. and Mrs. Murphy are attempting to extricate the dress from the wringer.

See also: the film of the same title, with the same copyright number, but an entirely different plot.

Lady Helen's Escapade
AM&B © H125727   Apr. 14, 1909
Director: D. W. Griffith *Cameraman:* G. W. Bitzer
Cast: Florence Lawrence, Dorothy West, Clara T. Bracey, Mack Sennett, Arthur Johnson, John Cumpson, Herbert Miles, Jeanie Macpherson, Owen Moore
Location: Studio, N.Y.C. *Photographed:* Feb. 10–11, 1909
288 ft.   FLA5520 (print)   FRA2391 (neg.)

A socially prominent and wealthy young lady becomes bored with her lot and decides to answer an advertisement for a housemaid. The next scene shows her preparing to serve dinner. A violinist has been hired to entertain the guests, who leave the table in boredom. By the time he has finished his rendition, only the maid has remained to listen. She returns to her home, and comes back to the house of her former employers escorted by an impresario who hires the violinist. The violinist repays his benefactress by falling in love with her, and she accepts him. Each scene was photographed from a single-camera position.

Lake Lucerne, Switzerland
Edison © H32793   June 17, 1903
Cameraman: A. C. Abadie
Location: Lucerne, Switzerland *Photographed:* Apr. 23, 1903
35 ft.   FLA3582 (print)   FRA0854 (neg.)

Snow-covered mountains are visible in the distance from a single-camera position. As the camera begins to pan, it shows a lake in the foreground. It continues to pan, and buildings appear at the foot of the mountain. There is an excursion vessel on the lake, and the end of the pan shows a floating dock with a ramp coming from the shore. There are people, and in the background, a city can be seen.

The Lamp Explodes
AM&B © H21498   Sept. 5, 1902
Cameraman: Robert K. Bonine
Location: Roof studio, N.Y.C. *Date:* July 10, 1902
15 ft.   FLA3930 (print)   FRA1144 (neg.)

This film is a comedy skit worked out following the pattern of the later-famous cartoon characters Alphonse and Gaston. The two men are seated in their club or living room and one notices that the lamp is smoking. While they bow to one another in deferment, the lamp explodes. The film ends showing the two men in rags and tatters and the tables and chairs demolished.

Landing of U.S. Troops Near Santiago
AM&B © H25968   Dec. 31, 1902
Date: 1898 [?]

27 ft.   FLA4054 (print)   FRA1239 (neg.)
[Spanish-American War]

The film, photographed from a single-camera position, shows what looks like Spanish-American War troops crossing a river under heavy fire. This could be a reproduction.

Landing Wharf at Canton
Edison © 38234   June 22, 1898
Cameraman: James H. White
Location: Canton
26 ft.   FLA3029 (print)   FRA0200 (neg.)

The first scenes were taken from a camera positioned on a vehicle moving along the edge of a bridge. The camera was positioned to look down on the sampan-mooring area of the wharf district in an Oriental city. As the film progresses, the camera begins to move and several different types of water craft of the country and era can be seen. The camera changes to a stationary position and shows some of the sampans and their occupants at closer range.

La Lanterne Magique
See: The Magic Lantern

A Large Haul of Fish
AM&B © H26949   Jan. 14, 1903
Cameraman: Arthur Marvin
Location: Greenfield Fishery, Edenton, N.C. *Date:* May 2, 1901
20 ft.   FLA3289 (print)   FRA0605 (neg.)

A dock and wharf area where several men and a cargo boom are busily engaged emptying a huge net of fish into bins can be seen from a single-camera position. The length and condition of the film, coupled with the single-camera position, do not allow description of further detail.

Larks Behind the Scene
Edison © 13535   Feb. 17, 1899
24 ft.   FLA3117 (print)   FRA0452 (neg.)

Three young women are visible in a locale that suggests they are behind stage or in the dressing room of a theater. One of the women is brushing her hair while the other two talk. A door opens and a fourth woman carrying a small tambourine joins them. Two of the first three women attempt to kick the tambourine from the hand of the fourth woman who holds it above her head.

Las Vigas Canal, Mexico
Edison © H16656   Apr. 16, 1902
Location: Mexico City
22 ft.   FLA3812 (print)   FRA1047 (neg.)

The camera was placed on a canal bank. Boats of various sizes poled by boatmen pass the camera, and in the background at a distance of one hundred and fifty yards is a bridge over the canal and a woman walking on it.

Las Vigas Canal, Mexico City
Edison © 13554   Feb. 24, 1898
Location: Mexico City
27 ft.   FLA4444 (print)   FRA1547 (neg.)

The subject is the arrival and departure of boats, poled by boatmen, carrying produce to a market place seen in the foreground. Several boats arrive and depart during the short length of the film.

Lassoing Steer
Edison © 13567 Feb. 24, 1898
25 ft. FLA3128 (print) FRA0462 (neg.)

The first action is a steer, at a distance of about fifty yards, running across the camera's field of view. The steer is closely followed by a rider on horseback swinging a lariat or lasso. As the film continues, the animal is first lassoed around the neck and set free, and then around the back legs. The film ends after the steer, lying on its side, is approached by one of the dismounted riders, who has a branding iron.

The Last Deal
Biograph © J137856 Jan. 29, 1910
Director: D. W. Griffith *Cameraman:* G. W. Bitzer
Cast: Owen Moore, Linda Arvidson, James Kirkwood, Joe Graybill, Dell Henderson, George Nicholls, Billy Quirk, Adele De Garde
Location: Studio, N.Y.C. *Photographed:* Dec. 15–16, 1909
394 ft. FLA5141 (print)

This film is built around a bank employee (Owen Moore) whose addiction to gambling causes him to appropriate bank funds. The bank president (George Nicholls) allows him time to make restitution. The employee pawns his wife's jewelry and with the proceeds gets in a poker game. His brother-in-law (James Kirkwood), whom he has never met, learns what has happened, joins the poker game, and wins all the money. He turns his winnings over to the compulsive gambler to make restitution at the bank, but his employer fires him anyway. He dejectedly returns home to his wife (Linda Arvidson), and the last scene shows him with his family as he tears up the playing cards and vows never to gamble again.

The Last Round Ended in a Free Fight
AM&B © H27384 Jan. 22, 1903
Date: 1898 [?]
18 ft. FLA3290 (print) FRA0606 (neg.)

Four women dressed in clothing of the era are standing in a line facing the camera. To the right and left of the camera two women in gym clothing are wearing boxing gloves. They are seated. At a signal from one of the standing women, the two with boxing gloves begin sparring, which apparently causes the spectators to meddle in the melee. The last scene shows the women wrestling.

The Late Senator Mark Hanna
AM&B © H42495 Feb. 20, 1904
20 ft. FLA4280 (print) FRA1433 (neg.)

The film shows a large group of people gathered in front of what appears to be one of the federal buildings in Washington, D.C. They are awaiting the arrival or departure of Sen. Mark Hanna.

Lathrop School, Calisthenics
AM&B © H45152 May 2, 1904
Cameraman: A. E. Weed
Location: Kansas City, Mo. *Photographed:* Apr. 18, 1904
19 ft. FLA3104 (print) FRA0441 (neg.)

A group of preadolescent boys and girls is standing in a row facing the camera position. In back of them is a wall on which is written "Kansas City, Mo." As the film progresses, the students go through a series of calisthenics, performing them in unison, and continue this throughout the film.

Latina, Contortionist
AM&B © H68883 Nov. 21, 1905
Cameraman: G. W. Bitzer
Location: Studio, N.Y.C. *Photographed:* Nov. 15, 1905
33 ft. FLA3215 (print) FRA0538 (neg.)

We see a woman in tights, attempting to maneuver her body through a hoop that seems too small. However, she does it since her body is double-jointed.

Latina, Dislocation Act
AM&B © H68886 Nov. 21, 1905
Cameraman: G. W. Bitzer
Location: Studio, N.Y.C.
17 ft. FLA3867 (print) FRA1079 (neg.)

Taken from the audience's point of view, the film shows a contortionist demonstrating that she can completely revolve her arms in the shoulder sockets. The exhibition was a waist-high front view, side view, and rear view.

Latina, Physical Culture Poses, no. 1
AM&B © H68884 Nov. 21, 1905
Cameraman: G. W. Bitzer
Location: Studio, N.Y.C.
19 ft. FLA3855 (print) FRA1067 (neg.)

A full-length view, photographed from the audience, of a woman dressed in tights doing calisthenics. She demonstrates arm and waist movements.

Latina, Physical Culture Poses, no. 2
AM&B © H68885 Nov. 21, 1905
Cameraman: G. W. Bitzer
Location: Studio, N.Y.C.
15 ft. FLA3868 (print) FRA1080 (neg.)

Photographed from one camera position, a robust woman demonstrates physical culture exercises.

Laughing Ben
AM&B © H16727 Apr. 18, 1902
Cameraman: Arthur Marvin
Location: Pan-American Exposition, Buffalo, N.Y. *Date:* May 25, 1901
9 ft. FLA3194 (print) FRA0520 (neg.)

The photographer placed his camera so close to the subject that only his head is visible. The subject is a toothless, white-haired black man who is laughing heartily. He continues laughing for the full length of the film.

Launch of Battleship "Connecticut"
AM&B © H51257 Oct. 4, 1904
Cameramen: G. W. Bitzer, Wallace McCutcheon, A. E. Weed.
Location: Brooklyn Navy Yard, N.Y. *Photographed:* Sept. 29, 1904
217 ft. FLA5522 (print) FRA2394 (neg.)

The subject is the launching of the battleship *Connecticut*. The site of the construction and launching of the ship's hull was Brooklyn, New York (the bridge can be seen plainly in the background). The activities, ceremonies, and labor connected with the launching of the vessel are seen from several camera positions. One was underneath the hull where the workmen were pulling out the wedges. The second was at the christening platform with the celebrities, and the third was from the waterside, showing the hull as it entered the water. The hull reputedly was christened by Mrs. Theodore Roosevelt.

Launch of Japanese Man-of-War "Chitosa"
Edison © 16427 Mar. 10, 1898
Location: Union Iron Works, San Francisco
23 ft. FLA4099 (print) FRA1280 (neg.)

The camera that photographed this film was located overlooking the water in which the hull of a large ship can be seen. In the foreground are small boats containing workmen attending the launching. The hull of the ship is seen, then the bow is visible, marking the completion of the launching.

Launch of Life Boat
Edison © 60570 Oct. 25, 1897
Location: Pacific Coast Life Saving Service, San Francisco
24 ft. FLA3069 (print) FRA0401 (neg.)

The first scenes are of a long dock from the waterside. The boathouse, about a hundred yards away, has a pyramid-shaped roof. As the action begins, the door of the boathouse opens and an eight-oar life boat can be seen as it starts down the ramp toward the water. As the film ends, the boat has completed its descent into the water, the eight oarsmen have wet their oars, and the boat can be seen in profile.

See also: Capsize of Lifeboat, Launch of Surf Boat, and Rescue—Resuscitation

Launch of Surf Boat
Edison © 60575 Oct. 25, 1897
Location: Pacific Coast Life Saving Service, San Francisco
23 ft. FLA3084 (print) FRA0423 (neg.)

The camera was positioned so that the action of a full lifeboat crew launching a lifeboat into the surf could be seen. As the scene begins, the lifeboat is afloat with the eight men preparing to board. The film shows the maneuvers, from boating to shipping the oars, to preparing to go through the surf. The last scenes are of the lifeboat, approximately two hundred yards from the camera position, being rowed through some large waves.

See also: Capsize of Lifeboat, Launch of Life Boat and Rescue—Resuscitation

Launch, U.S. Battleship "Kentucky"
AM&B © H32833 June 18, 1903
Location: Newport News, Va. *Date:* 1898 [?]
28 ft. FLA3550 (print) FRA0826 (neg.)

The camera that filmed the launching was located on land far enough away from the launching skids to encompass the whole yard in which the hull was built. As the film begins, the ship starts down the skids into the water and, as the film ends, the whole of the hull is afloat.

Launching, no. 2
Edison © 16435 Mar. 10, 1898
25 ft. FLA4225 (print) FRA1384 (neg.)

The film begins by showing the recently launched hull of a large naval vessel. The camera distance is such that the whole hull can be seen. Between the hull and the camera are several small boats with launching attendants in them.

Launching a Stranded Schooner From the Dock
Edison © D18562 Sept. 24, 1900
15 ft. FLA4698 (print) FRA1716 (neg.)
[Galveston, Texas, Hurricane and Tidal Wave]

As the title indicates, the film shows the launching of a schooner from the docks in Galveston, Texas, after a tidal wave and hurricane had washed it up on the beach.

Launching U.S.S. "Illinois"
AM&B © H28676 Feb. 26, 1903
Date: 1898 [?]
30 ft. FLA3181 (print) FRA0508 (neg.)

The camera was positioned at the christening end, or bow end, of the ship to be launched. As the film begins, a large black shiny hull starts to slide down the runway away from the camera position. The film continues until the ship is completely afloat and away from anything but her mooring lines.

Laura Comstock's Bag-Punching Dog
Edison © H4086 May 6, 1901
47 ft. FLA4699 (print) FRA1715 (neg.)

The beginning scene shows the head and shoulders of a woman and the head and paws of a dog sitting at a table near the camera. Immediately in the foreground is a sign stating her name and that she owns a dog that can punch a bag. The remainder of the film shows the dog jumping and butting a punching bag suspended from a rope over its head. The film ends as the dog succeeds in catching the punching bag and shaking it violently. The dog was named Mannie.

Lawn Party
AM&B © H21505 Sept. 5, 1902
Cameraman: Robert K. Bonine
Photographed: August 5, 1902
18 ft. FLA3921 (print)

The short length of this film does not permit much description of the action that appears to be taking place on the lawn in front of a large house. Some tables are in the immediate foreground. Approximately ten people, ranging in age from four years to adulthood, approach the tables and seat themselves. As the film ends, they are eating.

The Leading Man
Biograph © J168888 May 3, 1912
Director: Mack Sennett
Cast: Dell Henderson, Fred Mace, Kate Bruce, Claire McDowell
226 ft. FLA5523 (print) FRA2392 (neg.)

An out-of-work actor attempts to swindle his landlord out of a few days' board and sends himself a postal card indicating he has been hired at $200 a week. There are several interior scenes in the boarding house with the female guests paying the hero (Dell Henderson) much attention, to the annoyance of the landlord. The film ends when the landlord and landlady escort their female boarders to an amusement park and encounter their leading man with a large megaphone calling to the passersby to ride on the merry-go-round.

Leander Sisters
Edison ©️ 60561 Oct. 25, 1897
Location: Sutro Baths, San Francisco
20 ft. FLA4291 (print) FRA1442 (neg.)

In order to photograph the scenes of two children dancing, the cameraman placed his equipment on the edge of a spacious room that probably was a gymnasium or a dance recital hall. The two young girls give an exhibition of their ability to interpret musical comedy characters and continue dancing throughout the film. Approximately a hundred boys and girls of various ages can be seen along a railing in the background watching the exhibition.

See also: Cupid and Psyche

Leaping Dogs at Gentry's Circus
Edison ©️ H11489 Dec. 16, 1901
51 ft. FLA4700 (print) FRA1717 (neg.)

The condition of the film is too poor to permit a detailed description of events. However, against the white interior of the tent, it is possible to see a vaudeville act in session. The act consists of an attendant piling chairs on top of tables, gradually increasing the height of the barrier, and ordering several dogs of various sizes to leap over them.

Leather Stocking
Biograph ©️ J132315 Sept. 29, 1909
Director: D. W. Griffith *Cameramen:* G. W. Bitzer, Arthur Marvin
Cast: James Kirkwood, Linda Arvidson, Mack Sennett, Billy Quirk, George Nicholls, Owen Moore, Henry B. Walthall
Location: Cuddebackville, N.Y. *Photographed:* Aug. 24–27, 1909
372 ft. FLA5524 (print) FRA2393 (neg.)

This version of James Fenimore Cooper's story of the early settlers and their problems with Indians was photographed almost entirely outdoors. A few scenes were photographed inside a stockade. A party of settlers, consisting of two men, two women, and a small child, led by a friendly Indian and escorted by a British soldier set out on a journey. En route they are stalked and attacked by Indians. There is a fight and one man goes for aid. At the crucial moment, soldiers from the fort arrive and beat off the unfriendly Indian tribe.

Leaving Home
See: The Ex-Convict, and The Kleptomaniac

Leaving Store
See: The Kleptomaniac

A Legal Hold-Up
AM&B ©️ H16346 Apr. 10, 1902
Cameraman: F. S. Armitage
Location: Roof studio, N.Y.C. *Photographed:* June 7, 1901
20 ft. FLA4260 (print) FRA1416 (neg.)

A brick wall with a wrought-iron gate can be seen against a painted park backdrop. A man wearing a top hat and tails wends his way along the wall; he is apparently intoxicated. He staggers to the gate in the wall, sees the bench, and proceeds to recline at full length upon it. The head of a uniformed policeman is seen above the wall and, when he reaches the gate, he sees the sleeper. He awakens the man, removes several cigars from his person, pushes him in the stomach with his nightstick, lights a cigar he has taken from him, and proceeds on his way.

Lehigh Valley Black Diamond Express
Edison ©️ H32241 May 23, 1903
Cameraman: Edwin S. Porter
Location: Sayre, Pa. *Date:* May 13, 1903
39 ft. FLA3685 (print) FRA0935 (neg.)

Photographed from a single camera position, the film shows a section of curved railroad track. A sign indicates the road belongs to the Lehigh Valley Railroad. The last half of the film shows a locomotive and four cars approaching the camera, and a locomotive and three cars going away from the camera.

See also: New Black Diamond Express

Lena and the Geese
Biograph ©️ J170619 June 25, 1912
Director: D. W. Griffith *Cameraman:* G. W. Bitzer *Script:* Mary Pickford
Cast: Mary Pickford, Claire McDowell, Charles Hill Mailes, J. Lañoe, Grace Henderson, Kate Bruce, Lottie Pickford, Mae Marsh
Location: In or near Los Angeles
385 ft. FLA5525 (print) FRA2395 (neg.)

For reasons of state, a baby girl is taken from her mother and given up with a peasant woman to raise as her own. She grows up with the peasant's real daughter, who tends a flock of geese. Her real mother becomes ill, decides her daughter should be reinstated in the royal household, and sends for her. The peasant woman substitutes her own daughter instead, and the next several scenes show the young woman being instructed in protocol and proper behavior. Soon she has had enough, and runs home to her mother, the geese, and her country suitor. Her mother confesses and the rightful heir is sent to court, while the goose girl is seen happily embracing her suitor. This picture was written by Mary Pickford, who acted the part of Lena.

The Lesser Evil
Biograph ©️ J168738 Apr. 27, 1912
Director: D. W. Griffith *Cameraman:* G. W. Bitzer
Cast: Blanche Sweet, Edwin August, Charles West, Alfred Paget, Mae Marsh, Charles Hill Mailes, Owen Moore, Harry Hyde
409 ft. FLA5526 (print) FRA2396 (neg.)

A young girl goes to meet her fisherman lover and inadvertently discovers the identity of a group of smugglers who take her with them on their schooner out to sea. The fisherman arrives at the rendezvous and finds his sweetheart missing. He appeals to the authorities and they all set out after the schooner in a motor boat. The suspense builds up as the smugglers mutiny, intending to kill their captain and attack the fisherman's sweetheart. The captain bravely holds them off and, as the authorities arrive and capture the schooner, he jumps overboard and swims safely to shore, while the reunited lovers embrace.

The Lesson

Biograph © J149318 Dec. 22, 1910

Director: D. W. Griffith *Cameraman:* G. W. Bitzer

Cast: Stephanie Longfellow, Joseph Graybill, W. Chrystie Miller, Charles West, Verner Clarges, Jeanie Macpherson, Edwin August

Location: Fort Lee, N.J.; Studio, N.Y.C. *Photographed:* Oct. 26, 28 and Nov. 2, 1910

389 ft. FLA5527 (print) FRA2397 (neg.)

The ne'er-do-well son of a minister refuses to accept the faith of his father and turns instead to riotous living and drinking. The father believes he is dying and sends his daughter for the son, who at that moment is quite drunk in a saloon. The sister swallows her pride and begins to search, going from saloon to saloon and finally finds her completely intoxicated brother. She enters the saloon, and the bartender attempts to push her out. Her drunken brother comes to her aid and strikes the bartender who falls to the floor, hits his head, and dies. The film ends as the sister brings her brother home in time to say goodbye to their dying father, and the last scene is of the brother being led off to jail by the police.

Let Uncle Reuben Show You How

AM&B © H41999 Feb. 10, 1904

Cameraman: A. E. Weed

Location: Studio, N.Y.C. *Photographed:* Feb. 1, 1904

29 ft. FLA4702 (print) FRA1719 (neg.)

A woman and a teen-age boy industriously attempt to assemble a stove and stovepipe in a set of a kitchen. The door opens, admitting a man in a top hat and tails, who kicks the young boy in the posterior and indicates that he will take over the job. While he and the woman attempt to complete the task, the boy fills the top hat with soot. After several futile attempts at assembling the stove, the visitor gives up and starts to leave in a huff. When he gets to the door, he puts on his hat, spilling soot all over himself.

Levi & Cohen, the Irish Comedians

AM&B © H33281 July 8, 1903

Cameraman: G. W. Bitzer

Date: June 30, 1903

24 ft. FLA3725 (print) FRA0972 (neg.)

The camera was placed as if in the audience, and a number of spectators were seated between it and the stage. Two men, introduced as comedians, walk out on the stage and begin their act. Apparently their act is not acceptable to the members of the audience who begin to pelt the men with vegetables for the remainder of the film.

Li Hung Chang and Suite: Presentation of Parlor Mutoscope

AM&B © H16924 Apr. 22, 1902

Cameraman: Raymond Ackerman

Location: Peking *Date:* Jan. 14, 1901

12 ft. FLA3279 (print) FRA0596 (neg.)

A Chinese dignitary and aide in the courtyard of the Palace of Roses watch the demonstration of the viewing device manufactured by the American Mutoscope & Biograph Company. Li Hung Chang was known as the "Grand Old Man of China" and cooperated with General Gordon in suppressing the Taiping rebellion. At one time in his career, he became Grand Chancellor. When Li Hung Chang visited his country in 1898, a moving picture was made at Grant's Tomb. This view shows him looking at it through a Parlor Mutoscope.

Liberty Belles

Klaw & Erlanger © LP3031 May 14, 1914

Director: Dell Henderson

Cast: Dorothy Gish, Gertrude Bambrick, Reggie Morris, Dave Morris, Jack Pickford, Spottiswoode Aitken, Vola Smith

1,216 ft. FLA5877 (print) FRA2750 (neg.)

The film has three interconnecting plots. One revolves around two young ladies and two young men who try to see one another but who are thwarted by their fathers or by the various school mistresses. The second is of the father of one of the girls who finds a treasure map, then finds the treasure, and returns home with it, bringing along the long-lost husband of one of the school mistresses. The third story is about the father of the second girl. He is an inventor who attempts to invent an airplane. The fathers of the girls are made up to look ridiculous.

Lick Observatory, Mt. Hamilton, Cal.

Edison © 60585 Oct. 25, 1897

Location: Mt. Hamilton, Calif.

25 ft. FLA3070 (print) FRA0411 (neg.)

From the single-camera position, a portion of a large building constructed of brick can be seen. The only action is when a coach drawn by four horses enters the picture and stops in the foreground in front of the camera. The lighting is bad, consequently very little is visible, except for outlines.

Life of an American Fireman

Edison © H27362 Jan. 21, 1903

Cameraman: Edwin S. Porter

Cast: Arthur White, Vivian Vaughan

Location: Newark and Orange, N.J.; Studio, N.Y.C.

169 ft. FLA5087 (print) FLA5954 (35mm print) FRA2095 (neg.)

This classic documentary-drama starts with a fireman sitting in a fire station. In the same scene, but shown in double exposure, are a woman and a baby in a burning building. This is followed by a close-up of a fire alarm box and a hand operating it. Until the end of the picture, the scenes consist of the various operations a fireman of that period went through in order to extinguish a fire. The picture was along the same lines as The Still Alarm and was obtained with the cooperation of the Newark and Orange, New Jersey, fire departments. The outdoor scenes were all taken at Newark and Orange, while the studio work was done at the Edison studio on Twenty-first Street in New York.

Life Rescue at Long Branch

Edison © H8692 Sept. 16, 1901

Location: Long Branch, N.J.
64 ft. FLA4703 (print) FRA1720 (neg.)

The several scenes are about the rescue of a female bather by two lifeguards. The first camera position is from the end of a pier and shows the woman swimming, faltering, and sinking. The second camera position shows the lifeguards going to the rescue. One of them jumps from a rowboat into the water and saves the swimmer. The next camera position is on the sand and shows the boat, the two lifeguards, and the rescued woman approaching the camera. The remainder of the film shows the crowd watching as the revival exercises are begun by the lifeguards. As the film ends, the woman has revived completely and is embracing her rescuers.

Lifting the Lid
AM&B © H63696 July 12, 1905
Cameraman: G. W. Bitzer
Location: Broadway and 38th Street and studio, N.Y.C.
  Photographed: June 19, 20 and 27, 1905
204 ft. FLA5528 (print) FRA2398 (neg.)

The film was made up of photographs of interior sets combined with exteriors to establish the beginning and the end of the film. The first scene is of a New York street where a sightseeing bus is about to start off on a trip. Then the interiors, using actors, begin. A guide with a megaphone escorts a country couple through a vaudeville show-restaurant and an opium den. The country bumpkins are enthusiastic about the tour. The last scene shows the bus loaded with tourists returning to its starting point.

The Light That Came
Biograph © J134658 Nov. 13, 1909
Director: D. W. Griffith *Cameraman:* G. W. Bitzer
Cast: Mary Pickford, Marion Leonard, Linda Arvidson, Herbert Yost, Guy Hedlund, Tony O'Sullivan, Billy Quirk, Mack Sennett, Kate Bruce, Arthur Johnson, George Nicholls, Owen Moore
Location: Studio, N.Y.C. *Photographed:* Sept. 30 and Oct. 2–4, 1909
395 ft. FLA5529 (print) FRA2613 (neg.)

The story line is built around the unselfishness of the homely one of three sisters who falls in love with a blind musician and then learns his sight can be restored by expensive surgery. Torn between her fear of losing the musician if he sees her and helping to restore his sight, the homely girl pays for the surgery. When the doctor removes the bandages, the no-longer-blind musician immediately selects the homely girl rather than either of her two lovely sisters who attempt to attract his attention. All the scenes were shot indoors with incandescent light, and the camera was not moved in any scene.

The Light That Didn't Fail
AM&B © H24882 Dec. 9, 1902
Cameraman: Robert K. Bonine
Location: Roof studio, N.Y.C. *Date:* June 18, 1902
13 ft. FLA3770 (print) FRA1014 (neg.)

The action begins in a hotel room set where a white-haired man in a nightshirt is standing in front of an electric light attempting to blow it out. When he is unsuccessful, he reaches under the bed and retrieves a big carpetbag and puts it around the electric light, causing the room to become dark.

Line-Up and Teasing the Snakes
Edison © H11271 Dec. 12, 1901
Cameraman: James H. White
38 ft. FLA3087 (print) FRA0426 (neg.)
[Walpapi Indians, Snake Dance]

This single-camera position film is part of a series of films of tribal rituals involving snakes. This one shows Indians in costume, harassing snakes with sticks and pieces of brush. One of five short films that were offered with "Lecture Synopsis with each film or upon application."

See also: Carrying Out of the Snakes, the March of Prayer and Entrance of the Dancers, Panoramic View of Moki-Land, and Parade of Snake Dancers Before the Dance

The Linen Draper's Shop
AM&B © H50325 Sept. 10, 1904
39 ft. FLA5423 (print)

From a single-camera position, a set of the interior of a dry goods store is seen. There are two women passersby visible as the door opens and a man with an overcoat enters and begins to remove dresses from display dummies and hide them under his overcoat. This is noticed by one of the salesladies who assumes the attitude and position of a display dummy and catches the thief as he tries to steal her drape. The remainder of the film shows the three salesladies attempting to apprehend the thief; in doing so they completely demolish the store interior.

See also: Arrest of a Shoplifter

Lines of White on a Sullen Sea
Biograph © J133854 Oct. 27, 1909
Director: D. W. Griffith *Cameraman:* G. W. Bitzer *Script:* Stanner E. V. Taylor
Cast: Linda Arvidson, James Kirkwood, Marion Leonard, Dorothy West, Kate Bruce, Frank Powell, George Nicholls, W. Chrystie Miller, Arthur Johnson, Owen Moore, Billy Quirk, Harriet Quimby (famous aviatrix)
Location: Highland, N.J.; Studio, N.Y.C. *Photographed:* Sept. 11 and 18, 1909
372 ft. FLA5530 (print) FRA2399 (neg.)

Linda Arvidson, daughter of a fisherman, is romantically involved with a sailor, James Kirkwood. He goes off to sea, but not before giving her a bracelet, with a promise of marriage on his return. We next see him in a foreign port, where he becomes involved with another woman (Marion Leonard). They get married and have a child. In the meantime, although courted by another, Linda waits for her sailor. Several years pass and she is on her deathbed when the sailor comes home accompanied by his wife and child. The sailor is persuaded to go through a mock marriage ceremony with his former sweetheart, and she dies happily, unaware of his deceit.

Linwood School, Calisthenics
AM&B © H45153 May 2, 1904
Cameraman: A. E. Weed
Location: Kansas City, Mo. *Photographed:* Apr. 18, 1904
19 ft. FLA3100 (print) FRA0437 (neg.)

Four rows of small children face the camera as the film begins. They are standing in front of a blackboard that says "Kansas City, Missouri." Judging from the direction the children are facing, they were awaiting instructions and, at a signal, all of them began doing arm-waving exercises, which they continued throughout the film. As the film ends, the children nearest the camera in the front of each row bend down.

Little Angels of Luck
Biograph © J145184 Sept. 9, 1910
Director: D. W. Griffith *Cameraman:* G. W. Bitzer
Cast: Alfred Paget, Gladys Egan, Adele De Garde, William J. Butler, Dell Henderson, Grace Henderson, George Nicholls
Location: Studio, N.Y.C. *Photographed:* Aug. 5–6, 1910
390 ft. FLA5531 (print) FRA2400 (neg.)

This film combines outdoor photography with interior sets. A sugar tycoon loses his money. While he explains to his wife that he is broke, his remarks are overheard by his two little girls who feel they should help daddy. They leave home, and wander about New York looking for the man who took their father's money. When they finally locate him, he turns out to be a man of compassion who enjoys children. The little girls' remark, "We have brought our money to give you instead of the money you took from Daddy," melts the sugar-trust president's heart and he gives the children a note to take home to Daddy, hiring their father at a considerable annual salary.

A Little Bit Off the Top
AM&B © H40819 Jan. 12, 1904
Cameraman: A. E. Weed
Location: Studio, N.Y.C. *Photographed:* Dec. 18, 1903
21 ft. FLA4182 (print) FRA1346 (neg.)

Three women in rather brief stage costumes can be seen doing limbering-up exercises in front of a set of a theater dressing room. A very short, fat man dressed in a toreador's outfit appears in the dressing room and begins waltzing with one of the young ladies who is much taller than he. To aid him in his attempt, the other two girls unfold a ladder. The film ends as the little man climbs to the top of the ladder and kisses the woman.

The Little Darling
Biograph © J131223 Sept. 3, 1909
Director: D. W. Griffith *Cameraman:* G. W. Bitzer
Cast: Verner Clarges, Robert Harron, Arthur Johnson, Owen Moore, George Nicholls, Lottie Pickford, Mary Pickford, Billy Quirk, Mack Sennett, Mrs. Charlotte Smith, Kate Toncray, H. B. Walthall, Dorothy West
Location: Cuddebackville, N.Y.; Studio, N.Y.C. *Photographed:* July 27 and Aug. 3, 1909
73 ft. FLA5088 (print) FRA2046 (neg.)

The story line of this film follows the mistaken idea a group of people have about the age of a relative coming to visit them. The first scene shows a group enjoying one another's company in a set of the living room of a modest house. A maid brings in a letter indicating that "a little darling" is coming to visit. Mass hysteria influences the group to rush out to the stores and buy a perambulator, a crib, and all manner of toys. The last scene in the picture shows two of

the group (Mack Sennett and Arthur Johnson) dressed in top hats and tails waiting on the station platform for the arrival of the "little darling," who, instead of being an infant, turns out to be a young lady (Mary Pickford).

Little German Band
Edison © H42205 Feb. 16, 1904
Cameraman: Edwin S. Porter
Location: Studio, N.Y.C. *Date:* Feb. 5, 1904
71 ft. FLA5089 (print) FRA2047 (neg.)

The three scenes that make up this comedy are: one, in front of a saloon; two, the interior of a saloon; and, three, the alley behind the saloon. All are sets. The action begins with a four-piece German band in front of the saloon. The saloon-keeper, apparently disturbed by the noise, invites the band in for a drink of beer if they will promise to go away afterward. During the course of having the drink, the tuba player empties the contents of the beer barrel into his large horn. The scene ends as the band leaves the saloon. The film ends as the members of the band drink the beer from their instruments and the saloon-keeper arrives brandishing a club.

Little Lillian, Danseuse
Warwick © Edison H34329 Aug. 8, 1903
Location: England *Date:* April 1902
57 ft. FLA5090 (print) FRA2048 (neg.)

By the use of stop-action photography, a young woman changes her costumes five times during the course of her interpretive dancing. All of the action was photographed from one camera position. In the background there was a set intended to be a Turkish mosque.

This film was produced in England by Warwick Trading Company and imported by Edison.

A Little Man
AM&B © H23776 Nov. 11, 1902
21 ft. FLA3444 (print) FRA0728 (neg.)

The film apparently was photographed in the yard of a house where a porch swing is standing, with a small boy in the center of it. He is holding onto the support of the swing and rocking himself to and fro. There is no other action but the child operating the swing.

A Little Mix-Up in a Mixed Ale Joint
AM&B © H23780 Nov. 11, 1902
Cameraman: Robert K. Bonine
Date: Aug. 13, 1902
17 ft. FLA3676 (print) FRA0926 (neg.)

The film begins on a set of the interior of a saloon where a man dressed as a woman is sitting at a table with a man. A waiter serves them a drink. The waiter walks away, and the two people begin fighting; they continue until the picture ends. Because of the film's condition, no further description can be given.

A Little Piece of String
AM&B © H16387 Apr. 12, 1902
Cameraman: F. S. Armitage
Location: Roof studio, N.Y.C. *Date:* June 4, 1901
9 ft. FLA3202 (print) FRA0528 (neg.)

A well-dressed young woman can be seen coming out of the door of a set of a store in a metropolitan city. As she reaches the sidewalk, a man comes up, tips his hat, and begins admiring her dress and hat. Another man walks up from the other direction, greets the young woman, and repeats the gestures of admiration. The first young man notices a bit of fluff at the waistband of her dress. He goes to brush it off, but apparently it is the binding belt of her skirt because as he pulls, the skirt falls to the sidewalk revealing her petticoat and legs. She picks up the skirt, holds it about her and runs back into the store.

The Little Railroad Queen

Great Northern © Oes J168598–168600 Apr. 25, 1912

Director: August Blom *Script:* Alred Kjerulf

Cast: Valdemar Psilander, Else Fröhlich, Karen Lund, Richard Christensen, Axel Ström, Elna From, Johannes Krum Hunderup, Frederik Skondrup

Photographed: May 1911

Danish title: Jernbanens Datter

1,100 ft. FLA5878 (print, copy 1) FLA5943 (print, copy 2) FRA2751 (neg.)

The simplicity of the beginning of the picture in no way indicates the complexity of the plot. As the picture begins, a man and a woman carrying an infant can be seen in an obviously unhappy situation, for the man denies the woman. The woman abandons the infant on a train; the infant is discovered and taken to a railroad magnate who adopts her. She grows into a beautiful young woman. In a connecting scene, the mother of the foundling is selling flowers in a restaurant where the foundling, now grown up, is a guest of the villain, her true father, although they are unaware of it. The flower vender recognizes her daughter and attempts to save her when the villain makes advances. Later, the heroine marries the boy next door who goes to work in a bank owned by the villain. The villain, motivated by jealousy, steals money and frames the husband. The heartbroken couple leave home and, unable to earn a living, join a circus. The wife, now a bareback rider, is thrown from a horse and killed. When her mother learns of this, she goes to the home of the villain, confronts him in the presence of his wife, and shoots him.

A Little Ray of Sunshine After the Rain

AM&B © H16384 Apr. 12, 1902

Cameraman: F. S. Armitage *Date:* Sept. 1899

11 ft. FLA3471 (print) FRA0753 (neg.)

The set resembles a street in front of a store. A couple carrying unfurled umbrellas can be seen. The door of the store opens, and a man comes out and lets down the awning, dumping the collected rainwater over the people standing there.

The Little Teacher

Biograph © J132812 Oct. 7, 1909

Director: D. W. Griffith *Cameramen:* G. W. Bitzer, Arthur Marvin

Cast: Mary Pickford, Arthur Johnson, George Nicholls, Gladys Egan, Kate Bruce, Eddie Dillon, Billy Quirk, Adele De Garde, Tony O'Sullivan, Dorothy West

Location: Greenwich, Conn.; Leonia, N.J.; Studio, N.Y.C. *Photographed:* Sept. 1, 3 and 8, 1909

364 ft. FLA5532 (print) FRA6421 (neg.)

The film begins in a one-room rural school, filled with children of various ages, where discipline has broken down completely. A member of the school board introduces the new teacher (Mary Pickford), who is too young to cope with some of the over-age students, and during recess she goes outside to cry. A surveyor (Arthur Johnson) sees her and volunteers to help. He knocks some of the larger students about and warns them to behave. The little schoolteacher becomes enamored of the surveyor and is rudely awakened from her romantic dreams when the surveyor introduces her to his fiancée. The last scene shows one of the older students trying to comfort the teacher. There are both interior and exterior scenes, all photographed from a single-camera position.

The Little Teacher

Keystone © LP5660 June 21, 1915

Producer and Author: Mack Sennett

Cast: Mabel Normand, Owen Moore, Roscoe Arbuckle, Mack Sennett, Joe Bordeaux, Frank Opperman, Vivian Edwards, Frank Hayes, Billie Brockwell

Location: Keystone studio and Hollenbeck (Eastlake) Park, Los Angeles

725 ft. FLA6117–6118 (print)

Mabel Normand is a school teacher with such obstreperous students as Mack Sennett and Fatty Arbuckle. When her boyfriend, Owen Moore, stops by to say hello, she insists he wait outside in his chain-driven Fiat until classes are over. During recess, Mack Sennett makes himself extremely obnoxious to the waiting Owen Moore. In the meantime, Fatty Arbuckle pushes one of his fellow students, Joe Bordeaux, off a bridge and then falls in himself. Since neither one can swim, Mabel makes a spectacular dive into the water to rescue both. She returns to school to change her clothes, after sending both youngsters home to do the same. Mack Sennett, who has been spying, sees Owen Moore waiting for Mabel, runs to tattle on them, even though Moore and Mabel are in separate rooms. Fortunately, the mother (Billie Brockwell) of one of the rescued children arrives just in time to clear both Mabel and her boyfriend of any wrongdoing.

A Little Teaze

AM&B © H35098 Aug. 28, 1903

Cameraman: A. E. Weed

Location: Coney Island, N.Y. *Photographed:* Aug. 18, 1903

13 ft. FLA4386 (print) FRA1521 (neg.)

To make this film, the cameraman placed his equipment on the pier near a seashore. The complete action consists of a man in a bathing suit sitting on the sand while a small boy piles sand on top of him and throws sand at him. The quality of the film is poor but the action is distinguishable. One of a series. The others are: The Sand Baby, The Sand Fort, and What Are the Wild Waves Saying, Sister?

The Little Train Robbery

Edison © H65086 Sept. 1, 1905

Cameraman: Edwin S. Porter

Location: Versailles, Pa. *Photographed:* Aug. 3–23, 1905

283 ft. FLA5533 (print) FRA2401 (neg.)

This melodrama, patterned after its famous predecessor, The Great Train Robbery, is probably the first time in the

Inspired by the success of The Great Train Robbery (1903), Edison produced The Little Train Robbery (1904); it had a similar plot, child actors, and a miniature railroad.

history of motion pictures where another version with all the characters played by children was made. The plot of the adult version is followed fairly closely. However, in view of lack of ability, and probably because of high production costs, not every detail was photographed. The child bandits ride horses, stop and capture a narrow-gauge railroad train, and take the loot to a hideout to divide. They are caught after a chase by boy police officers in uniform.

Lively Brushes on Speedway
AM&B © H33286 July 1903
Cameraman: Robert K. Bonine
Date: May 15, 1902
25 ft. FLA3534 (print) FRA0810 (neg.)

Ten or fifteen persons seem to be standing on a sidewalk and watching horse-drawn carriages. Both four-wheeled and two-wheeled carriages pass by in close order. The traffic is congested. In the background are two spans of a large support bridge.

See also: Parade of Horses on Speedway

Livets Baal
See: The Fire of Life

Living Pictures
AM&B © H32628 June 13, 1903
Cameraman: G. W. Bitzer
Location: Studio, N.Y.C. *Date:* June 8, 1903
OR
Cameraman: F. S. Armitage

Location: Roof studio, N.Y.C. *Photographed:* May 13, 1899
41 ft. FLA4704 (print) FRA1721 (neg.)

The camera was positioned as if in the audience watching a series of tableaus on a stage. The first scene shows two women clothed in white spangled leotards beginning to open a curtain on a staged scene of a nearly nude woman. This scene is followed by several more, each framed as though to simulate a large painted picture. Each shows a pseudoartistic but actually risqué scene.

The Llamas at Play
AM&B © H37496 Nov. 2, 1903
Cameraman: G. W. Bitzer
Location: Glen Island, N.Y. *Photographed:* Oct. 25, 1903
58 ft. FLA4705 (print) FRA1722 (neg.)

The film shows two llamas in a pen being fed by a boy between four and six years of age. The entire film is devoted to the animals as they walk about in their chicken-wire cage.

The Loaded Cigar
AM&B © H43561 Mar. 22, 1904
Cameraman: A. E. Weed
Location: Studio, N.Y.C. *Photographed:* Mar. 2, 1904
19 ft. FLA4305 (print) FRA1455 (neg.)

The picture begins on a set of the living room of a conventional dwelling. A young boy enters, sits down next to a table, selects a cigar, lights it, and begins smoking. A man in a dressing gown walks in, takes the cigar from the little boy, admonishes him, and sends him to his room. The man sits down and relights the cigar. It blows up in his face, tipping his chair over backward. The boy runs to his aid but the man spanks him for his efforts.

Loading a Vessel at Charleston
Edison © H16719 Apr. 18, 1902
Location: Steamship Edgar, Charleston, S. C.
37 ft. FLA3197 (print) FRA0523 (neg.)

As the film begins, several men with axes and adzes in their hands are working on large timbers that are part of an auxiliary dock fendering the hull of a large steam cargo ship visible in the foreground. Judging from the size of the cargo ship that can be seen from the single camera position, she was in excess of 5,000 tons. Only a portion of her bridge area and the port side to the water line are shown. There are about forty workmen in the film. A rowboat is seen wending its way through the workmen, and the passenger in the boat is later seen standing as if inspecting the work.

Loading Baggage for Klondike, no. 6
Edison © 60553 Oct. 25, 1897
Cameraman: Robert K. Bonine [?]
Location: "Williamette," Seattle, Wash.
25 ft. FLA3031 (print, copy 1) FLA5958 (print, copy 2) FRA0202 (neg.)
[Alaska Gold Rush]

From a single-camera position a steamship can be seen at a dock loading cargo by using the main mast boom. The power source is not shown. There are many spectators. A large horse-drawn baggage carrier from a hotel passes between the camera position and the loading ship.

Loading Horses on Transport
Edison © 38241 June 22, 1898
25 ft. FLA3372 (print) FRA0675 (neg.)
[Spanish-American War]

From the single-camera position, the side of a large ship can be seen. A cargo hatch in the side of the ship is open. From the cargo opening toward the camera position is a bridge or walkway with a hand railing about five feet high. A man in U.S. cavalry fatigue uniform leads a horse across the bridge into the cargo hold of the ship. Six more horses are led into the hold.

Loading Mail Car, U.S.P.O.
AM&B © H34993 Aug. 22, 1903
Cameraman: A. E. Weed
Location: Washington, D.C. *Photographed:* July 30, 1903
24 ft. FLA3894 (print) FRA1115 (neg.)

This film, part of series on the various activities of the Post Office, starts with a scene of a large railroad mail car on a siding. A horse-drawn, four-wheeled vehicle with a sign 'U.S. Mail' on the side proceeds away from the camera toward the mail car. The vehicle stops, the driver gets out, and, as the film ends, he is seen unloading the cart and putting mail bags in the train.

Loading Sugar Cane
AM&B © H21496 Sept. 5, 1902
Cameraman: Robert K. Bonine
Location: Honolulu *Date:* Aug. 1, 1901

18 ft. FLA3920 (print) FRA1136 (neg.)

The short length of this film leaves much to be desired to give a proper description. However, it is possible to see a large receiving car in a cane brake where several people are visible chopping cane and carrying it to the receiver. There is one person wearing white trousers, a blue coat, and a straw hat who comes from behind the camera position and starts up the incline. This film was photographed in Hawaii.
See also: Cutting Sugar Cane and Train of Sugar Cane

Loading the Ice on Cars, Conveying It Across the Mountains and Loading It Into Boats
Edison © H14435 Feb. 24, 1902
Location: Groton, Mass.
77 ft. FLA4706 (print) FRA1723 (neg.)

The film covers four operations involved in shipping ice: sawing the ice from frozen-over lakes, transferring it by means of specially constructed freight cars to a dock some distance away, unloading it, and then transloading it onto a waiting ship. This is one of three films.
See also: Circular Panorama of Housing The Ice and Cutting and Canaling Ice

A Lodging for the Night
Biograph © J169195 May 13, 1912
Director: D. W. Griffith *Cameraman:* G. W. Bitzer
Cast: Mary Pickford, Charles West, Frank Opperman, Charles Hill Mailes, Tony O'Sullivan, Alfred Paget
Location: San Gabriel, Calif.
367 ft. FLA5534 (print) FRA6420 (neg.)

Two thugs notice a well-dressed young man (Charles West) as he gets off the stage coach in a small town. The man takes a room in a hotel, wins a considerable amount of gold in a card game, and returns to his room for the night. Feeling that he is being spied upon, he takes his gold and seeks a night's lodging elsewhere. Overhearing her father planning to rob the new roomer, a young girl (Mary Pickford) goes to the saloon, gets the marshall and his posse and returns in time to save the young man and his money. The young man kisses the girl on the cheek in gratitude. The final scene shows both of them seated in their separate rooms, each with a smile of anticipation on his face. The camera is moved a number of times, and the film is a good example of cutback editing.

Logging in Maine
AM&B © H79740 June 19, 1906
Cameraman: G. W. Bitzer
Location: Maine *Photographed:* June 1 and 3, 1906
414 ft. FLA5535 (print) FRA2402 (neg.)

The subject is the movement of cut timber from the forest to the mill. The few scenes that make up the film are of loggers performing the various operations necessary to prevent logs from jamming together. The men keep them headed with the flow of the water toward the lake on which the mill is located. The activities of approximately a dozen men were photographed.

The Lone Highwayman
AM&B © H82501 Aug. 31, 1906
Cameraman: F. A. Dobson

Cast: Gordon Burby

Location: Palisades Park, N.J.; Studio, N.Y.C. *Photographed:* Aug 16, 17 and 20, 1906.

296 ft.   FLA5536 (print)   FRA2403 (neg.)

The subject is a bandit who robs passersby at gunpoint. Escaping from one of his holdups, the highwayman comes upon a burning house and rescues a trapped woman and a little girl. He continues his life of crime, and one of the last scenes shows him retreating from a posse. He again comes upon the farmhouse, enters and can be seen firing at the posse from a set of the interior of the farmhouse. In the final scene, the highwayman is in the room with the woman and her child; he has been shot and is dying. There were two unusual camera uses in this film: one was a cutback and the other a close-up of the sign offering a reward for the capture of the highwayman.

Lonely Villa

Biograph   © H128182   June 10, 1909

Director: D. W. Griffith *Cameraman:* G. W. Bitzer

Cast: Marion Leonard, Mary Pickford, Adele De Garde, Owen Moore, James Kirkwood, Mack Sennett, John Cumpson, Gladys Egan

Location: Fort Lee, N.J.: Studio, N.Y.C. *Photographed:* Apr. 29 and May 4–6, 1909

283 ft.   FLA5537 (print)   FRA2405 (neg., copy 1)   FRA6419 (neg., copy 2)

The scenes in this film were photographed both indoors and out. The story, written by Mack Sennett, is of a suspenseful situation when a man leaves his wife and children alone in an isolated house while he starts out on a business trip by automobile. Some burglars see him leaving. The man attempts to let his wife know the car has broken down, and when he finally reaches her, she tells him that burglars are attempting to break in. He makes a frantic effort to return to her aid, and the camera shifts back and forth to show the burglars chasing the retreating family from room to room, and the husband's troubles in getting home. The scenes become shorter and shorter until the husband, who has comandeered a gypsy wagon, arrives just as the burglars have broken down the last door. The story is supposedly based on newspaper clippings. However, the plot probably was borrowed from André de Lorde's play, *At the Telephone.*

Lonesome Junction

AM&B   © H105288   Jan. 20, 1908

Cameraman: G. W. Bitzer

Location: Studio, N.Y.C. *Photographed:* Jan. 8, 1908

227 ft.   FLA5538 (print)   FRA2404 (neg.)

The set is of a railroad station waiting room and ticket office. Although the title is *Lonesome Junction,* implying that few people ever enter the premises, approximately twelve people, all dressed in a comic fashion, are entering or exiting through the one door. They are photographed from a single-camera position that includes all of the available floor space. Each person manages to place a suitcase or other piece of luggage in the way of the other actors. There is some harmless shooting.

Looking for Employment

See: The Ex-Convict

Looking for John Smith

AM&B   © H81472   July 31, 1906

Director: Wallace McCutcheon *Cameraman:* F. A. Dobson

Location: Sound Beach, Conn.; Studio, N,Y,C. *Photographed:* July 11–14, 1906

296 ft.   FLA5539 (print)   FRA2680 (neg.)

The sequences in this picture were evidently designed to make use of various photographic devices. The picture begins with two men talking, and their conversation appears, by means of stop-action photography, in balloons on the black wall behind them. All of the remaining scenes contain some element of stop-action photography; the last scene shows a rogue's gallery photograph of a sought-after man, which moves as if he were alive. The title on the original paper print film is Si Jones Looking for John Smith.

Lord Chumley

Klaw & Erlanger   © LP2487   Mar. 16, 1914

Director: James Kirkwood *Cameraman:* Henry Cronjager Original play by Henry C. DeMille

Cast: Henry B. Walthall, W. Chrystie Miller, Lillian Gish, Charles West, William J. Butler, Charles Hill Mailes, Gus Pixley, Mary Alden, Thornton Cole, Mrs. LaVarnie, Jose Ruben

1,399 ft.   FLA5879-5880 (print)   FRA2752-2753 (neg.)

This four-reel film concerns an English family with a son in the army. He is afraid of being publicly disgraced for absconding with regimental funds that he did not steal. A professional gambler attempts to blackmail the sister into marrying him by threatening to claim her brother is a thief. There are a considerable number of military arrivals and departures throughout the film. Eventually the professional gambler is exposed as the actual culprit, and the army officer is exonerated.

The Lost Child

AM&B   © H51655   Oct. 15, 1904

Director: Probably Wallace McCutcheon *Cameraman:* G. W. Bitzer

Cast: Kathryn Osterman

Location: Fort Hamilton, Brooklyn, N.Y. *Photographed:* Oct. 1 and 3, 1904

231 ft.   FLA5540 (print)   FRA2406 (neg.)

A single-camera position shows the backyard of a house in a suburban community. A buxom woman brings a small boy outside, puts him on the ground, and returns considerably later to find him missing. Unaware that the baby has crawled into the dog house, she admonishes a little man who is putting something into a good-sized peach basket. The little man becomes frightened and begins to run. The woman thinks he has her baby and chases him. As she goes down the street, more and more people join in the chase, until there are approximately fifty people of all types and ages involved. The little man is finally captured, and all he has in the basket is a guinea pig. At the moment of capture, the camera moves in for a close-up, which includes the head and shoulders of a policeman, the mother, and some bystanders.

Lost, Stolen or Strayed

See: Decoyed

Love Among the Roses

Biograph © J141266 May 12, 1910

Director: D. W. Griffith *Cameramen:* G. W. Bitzer, Arthur Marvin

Cast: Marion Leonard, Mary Pickford, Claire McDowell, Arthur Johnson, Mack Sennett

Location: Hollywood *Photographed:* Mar. 22, 23 and 25, 1910

384 ft. FLA5541 (print)

A great lady (Marion Leonard) becomes enamored of the gardener (Mack Sennett), while the lord of the land (Arthur Johnson) falls in love with a lowly lacemaker (Mary Pickford). All of the scenes were photographed outdoors in the famous de Longpre gardens in Hollywood, California, and all the actors and actresses wore late seventeenth-century costumes.

Love and Friendship

Great Northern © Oes J168564-168565 Apr. 24, 1912

Cast: (Mrs.) Felumb-Friis, Clara Wieth, Olaf Fønss, Aage Hertel, Tage Hertel, Zanny Petersen, Frederik Jacobsen, Knud Rasow, Tronier Funder, Elith Pio, Frederik Skondrup, Agnete Blom, Axel Boesen, H. C. Nielsen, Johannes Krum Hunderup

Location: Denmark *Date:* Sept. 27, 1911

Danish title: Venskab og Kaerlighed

932 ft. FLA5881 (print, copy 1) FLA5944 (print, copy 2) FRA2754 (neg.)

The film concerns two young girls, very close friends at a private school, who grow up in different circumstances. One marries and has a child while the other becomes a successful music hall singer. The film shows the private school that brought them together and cemented their friendship through the marriage of, and subsequent birth of a child to one friend. When the singer becomes unhappy over a professional situation, she is invited to the home of her friend. The friend has married a military officer who is a fencing instructor. The husband becomes enamored of his wife's best friend; the wife finds them embracing during a fencing class. The picture ends with a dramatic sequence when the wife removes the tip from a fencing foil and challenges her friend to a duel to the death, while the husband is locked in the dressing room. The last scenes are of the wife in her husband's arms after she has been mortally wounded.

Love and Jealousy Behind the Scenes

AM&B © H40720 Jan. 8, 1904

Cameraman: A. E. Weed

Location: Studio, N.Y.C. *Photographed:* Dec. 4, 1903

101 ft. FLA5091 (print) FRA2049 (neg.)

A young woman gets a job in the chorus and becomes acquainted with the other actors on the bill, one of whom is a clown who falls in love with her. The clown sees a stage-door Johnny paying attention to the chorus girl, and it is too much for his sensitive soul—he shoots the usurper. The picture was done in two scenes: the first was in the booking office of a talent agent while the remainder was on a set of the backstage area of a vaudeville theater.

Love and War

James H. White © 77713 Nov. 28, 1899

Director: James H. White

71 ft. FLA4708 (print) FRA1725 (neg.)

The first scene shows the dramatic departure for the battlefield of the only son of a closely knit family. The second shows the battlefield action between American troops and insurrectionists during the Spanish-American War. The third shows the arrival of the wounded hero at a hospital tent and his subsequent release. The fourth and final scene takes place as the hero returns home to his joyful family. The set used for the first and last scenes was the interior of a house, and the cameraman overshot the top of the wall of the house. Otherwise the scenes were complete. Love and War was distributed by the Edison Company. Describing the film, Edison's catalog says, "We have at last succeeded in perfecting synchronizing music and moving pictures. The following scenes are very carefully chosen to fit the words and the songs, which have been especially composed for these pictures."

Love at 55

AM&B © H33543 July 18, 1903

Cameraman: Arthur Marvin

Location: Roof studio, N.Y.C. *Date:* June 23, 1900

11 ft. FLA3436 (print) FRA0722 (neg.)

A middle-aged man and woman are seated on the sofa next to the back wall of a living room set. From their actions, it appears they are attempting to become intimately acquainted. During the preliminary courting, his wig becomes entangled with hers, and both wigs fall to the floor. They bend to retrieve them and, in their haste, each puts the other's wig on. As the film ends, a third man enters the room, gestures admonishingly, and the woman swoons when she discovers she has put on the man's hairpiece while the man seems bewildered.

Love by the Light of the Moon

Edison © H2341 Mar. 16, 1901

Cameraman: Edwin S. Porter

26 ft. FLA3696 (print) FRA0945 (neg.)

The film begins on a set of a park on summer evening. There are a fence railing, some foliage, and a park bench as well as a moon, with a painted face, in the sky. A young couple enter and lean on the railing; they look up at the sky. The face on the moon begins to smile. The young couple continues to embrace, and the smile on the moon's face grows wider. They walk over and sit down on the bench, obscuring the moon's view of them, so the smile on the moon's face becomes a disappointed frown. As the picture ends, the young man is fanning the young woman with his straw hat because the moon, like a jack-in-the-box, has left the sky and is hanging over their shoulders.

Love Finds a Way

AM&B © H121529 Jan. 12, 1909

Director: D. W. Griffith *Cameramen:* G. W. Bitzer, Arthur Marvin

Cast: Marion Leonard, Arthur Johnson, Charles West, Mack Sennett

Location: Studio, N.Y.C. *Photographed:* Dec. 31, 1908 and Jan. 4, 1909

126 ft. FLA5542 (print) FRA2407 (neg.)

The substitution of another man for the groom in a marriage ceremony, and the later acceptance of the substitute by the bride's father, who was originally reluctant to grant permission for him to marry his daughter, is the story of this film. The actors all wear period costumes. The sets were constructed, and all of the scenes were interior.

Love in a Hammock

AM&B © H31671 May 11, 1903
Cameraman: F. S. Armitage
Date: July 18, 1899
10 ft. FLA3177 (print) FRA0504 (neg.)

A young lady and a young man are swinging in a hammock rigged in a set of the back part of a house. The couple is embracing and swinging through most of the film when one of the support ropes of the hammock breaks, spilling them both to the ground.

Love in a Hammock

Edison © H375 Jan. 12, 1901
21 ft. FLA3697 (print) FRA0946 (neg.)

A woman is sitting in a hammock strung between two trees in a wooded area. Two adolescent boys can be seen in the background walking toward the camera position. A man comes up to the woman, bows deeply, removes his hat, and joins her in the hammock. They swing the hammock, jostle and embrace, to the amusement of the two young boys. One of the youngsters climbs one of the supporting trees and goes out on a branch; it breaks, catapulting him into the hammock, and all three land on the ground in a heap.

Love in Armor

Keystone © LP4723 Mar. 11, 1915
Producer and Author: Mack Sennett
Cast: Billie Brockwell, Estelle Allen, Billie Bennett, Nick Cogley, Mae Busch, Charles Chase, W. C. Hauber, Frank Opperman, Bert Hunn
Location: Eastlake Park and Keystone studio, Los Angeles
433 ft. FLA5543 (print)

When a young lady (Mae Busch) has a birthday, her parents give her a party and surprise her with an expensive gift. But before this happens, Mae has a clandestine meeting with her boyfriend, Charles Chase. While they are talking together, a "Baron" (Nick Cogley) sees her and devises a scheme to make himself appear a hero. He approaches two bums and asks them to pretend to kidnap the young lady. Then he rushes in to "save" her. Her parents (Billie Bennett and Frank Opperman) observe his heroic act and the "Baron" is invited to her birthday party, while her boyfriend is not. Chase sneaks in, hides in a suit of armor, and succeeds in making the Baron appear a thief, at the same time frustrating two actual thieves who have come to steal the necklace. All ends well with Charles Chase and Mae Busch together.

Love in Quarantine

Biograph © J147937 Nov. 21, 1910
Cameraman: Arthur Marvin
Cast: Mack Sennett, Grace Henderson
Location: Fort Lee, N.J.; Studio, N.Y.C. *Photographed:* Sept. 28–29, 1910
195 ft. FLA5543 (print) FRA2408 (neg.)

This split-reel comedy begins with a single-camera position of a house exterior; a man and a woman are seated on the front porch, evidently courting. A title indicates that one of the household servants is ill. A doctor is summoned. Her illness proves to be contagious and the couple on the front porch is quarantined. They begin to fight, and the mother of the young lady writes a note to the young man and suggests he become ill as soon as possible so her daughter can take care of him. He takes the hint and, despite the discomfort of their vaccinations, the couple makes up.

Love in the Cornfield

AM&B © H16342 Apr. 10, 1902
Date: 1899
10 ft. FLA4328 (print) FRA1476 (neg.)

A young man and a young woman are sitting in a hollowed-out place in a stack of cornstalks; the surroundings indicate the locale is a farmyard. The young couple is embracing and kissing when a third person comes around the pile of cornstalks. She watches the embracing with disapproval and then tips several stalks over on top of the couple. They are oblivious of her presence. The surprised young people extricate themselves from the cornstalks, and the man sets off in pursuit of the tormentor.

Love in the Dark

AM&B © H26948 Jan. 14, 1903
10 ft. FLA3268 (print) FRA0587 (neg.)

A young woman and a young man are standing in a set of the living room of a modest house. The young man looks at the girl, then reaches up and turns out the flame of the gas jet. They sit down on the couch and begin kissing. As they continue embracing, the heads of an old man, a woman, and a young boy begin to appear in the gloom of the darkened room. The boy, who is watching from over the top of a screen, knocks it over, hitting the old man. The lovers jump to their feet and turn on the light. The suitor, in high dudgeon, hits the old lady, puts on his hat, shakes his finger under the nose of his inamorata, and is seen striding off, leaving the young woman in tears scolding her family.

Love in the Suburbs

AM&B © H27381 Jan. 22, 1903
Cameraman: G. W. Bitzer
Location: Guttenberg, N.J. *Date:* Sept. 11, 1900
13 ft. FLA3269 (print) FRA0588 (neg.)

The camera was placed in the center of a street in a suburban area where a woman dressed as a maid is walking. Two men in summer apparel follow her and apparently try to attract her attention. By turning, the camera follows their course from the center of the street to the edge of the street and down it. A local policeman sees the trio, shoos the two annoyers away, and kisses the maid himself.

Love in the Tropics

Great Northern © Oes J168482–168483 Apr. 23, 1912
Director: August Blom *Script:* Helga Stewens
Cast: Valdemar Psilander, Else Frohlich, Edith Buemann, Aage Hertel, Frederik Christensen
Location: Denmark *Date:* Sept. 29, 1911
Danish title: Tropisk Kaerlighed
741 ft. FLA5882 (print) FRA2755 (neg.)

The film begins with a scene indicating a tropical area where a successful planter has acquired a native girl, either as a wife or a mistress. The principals are the planter, the native girl, and the girl back home whom we meet only at the end of the picture. Before the end of the first scene, a messenger arrives with a cable for the planter summoning him home. A flashback shows a European home and the family's joy at learning the planter is returning. The next scene shows a large liner being warped by tugs into the dock, indicating the arrival home. The planter takes the native girl to a beauty salon and a store, and has her completely outfitted in the latest mode. She is then introduced to his friends at supper clubs, country clubs, etc. The native girl is not happy and longs for her home. The planter saves a female swimmer who is brought to his house to recover. The planter falls in love with her. The native girl discovers them embracing and plans revenge. She prepares a poison from a supply she had brought with her. Discovered by the planter and overcome with guilt and remorse, as well as homesickness, she rushes from the house and throws herself under a train, thus ending the film.

Love, Loot and Crash

Keystone © LP5179 Apr. 24, 1915

Producer and Author: Mack Sennett

Cast: Joe Swickard, Dora Rogers, Nick Cogley, Charles Chase, W. C. Hauber

Location: Keystone studio and surrounding territory, Los Angeles; Ocean Park, Calif.

397 ft. FLA6120 (print)

Father (Joe Swickard) and his daughter (Dora Rogers) go through a long routine trying to operate the kitchen range, although Dora has her mind on her boyfriend, Charles Chase, who is waiting for her outside. In the meantime, one crook (W. C. Hauber) persuades another (Nick Cogley) to dress as a woman and apply for the job of cook in the household. Swickard hires him. While Swickard is out of the house trying to break up the romance between his daughter and Chase, Cogley packs some valuables. He is interrupted by the arrival of a policeman who is expecting a free meal. Instead, he is pushed down in the basement while Cogley makes his escape. Chase has arranged to elope with Dora, and by a coincidence, their signal is the same as that of the crooks, so Dora is abducted by one of the burglars while the other thief mistakenly joins Chase on his motorcycle. Nearly the entire cast, plus the Keystone police take off in pursuit. The picture comes to an end with most of the actors driving off the pier and into the water at Ocean Park, California.

Love Me, Love My Dog

AM&B © H35093 Aug. 28, 1903

Cameraman: Wallace McCutcheon

Location: Studio, N.Y.C. *Date:* Aug. 14, 1903

20 ft. FLA3333 (print) FRA0644 (neg.)

A young couple is sitting on a couch in front of a painted backdrop of the wall of a house. The woman has a little white poodle beside her. The man attempts to embrace or kiss the young woman who, as a diversionary tactic, picks up the dog, to the annoyance of the young man. The dog senses the man's unfriendliness and bites him. The young woman looks distressed as she saves her little animal from being struck by the man.

The Love Microbe

AM&B © H101443 Oct. 21, 1907

Director: Wallace McCutcheon

Cameramen: G. W. Bitzer, F. A. Dobson

Location: Studio, N.Y.C. *Photographed:* Sept. 12, 19, 21; Oct. 5, 1907

267 ft. FLA5544 (print) FRA2409 (neg.)

A chemist or a professor attempts to develop a love serum that will make people automatically attractive to one another. There are several sets in the film, which begins by showing the scientist walking through a park searching for lovers. As he finds a couple embracing, he takes a sample with a hypodermic from the neck of each. He returns to his laboratory, develops his serum, and the remainder of the film shows how it brings people together or stops fighting between people already married. There is one special effect in the film, an insert done by revolving stop-action photography.

The Love of Lady Irma

Biograph © J139353 Mar. 22, 1910

Director: Frank Powell *Cameraman:* Arthur Marvin

Cast: Florence Barker, Dell Henderson, Owen Moore, Mack Sennett

Location: Studio, N.Y.C. *Photographed:* Jan. 5–7, 1910

397 ft. FLA5231 (print) FRA2809 (neg.)

The story concerns a jealous wife (Florence Barker) who has the face of her handsome husband (Dell Henderson) disfigured because she wants to possess him completely. The first scene shows the husband and his wife at a party where he is lionized. His wife, upset by the attention paid to him, hires two thugs (Owen Moore and Mack Sennett) to disfigure his face. After his recovery, the couple attends a musicale where nobody pays any attention to the husband. The two thugs demand more money from the wife and she, in despair, confesses to her husband. He realizes her action was based on love and forgives her. All the actors wore late eighteenth-century costumes. This was one of the first pictures directed by Frank Powell.

Love, Speed and Thrills

Keystone © LP4238 Jan. 18, 1915

Producer and Author: Mack Sennett

Cast: Minta Durfee, Chester Conklin, Mack Swain

Location: Vicinity of the Keystone studio and Pasadena bridge, Los Angeles

383 ft. FLA5545 (print)

Mack Swain and Minta Durfee play the parts of a husband and wife. The husband goes hunting and rescues another hunter, after accidentally shooting him. He takes the wounded hunter (Chester Conklin) home and gives his wife instructions to take good care of him and then leaves. Conklin rewards his benefactor by making advances to Minta. Swain returns home but is knocked off his feet by a thrown chamber pot. By the time he gets to his feet, Chester has made off with Minta as a passenger in the sidecar of an Excelsior motorcycle. Swain follows on horseback, a chase that ends with the motorcycle and passengers going off the bridge. Both are rescued, with Conklin being taken off by the police.

The Lover

See: The Unfaithful Wife

The Lovers

See: The Seven Ages

The Lovers, Coal Box and Fireplace

Edison © H9309 Oct. 4, 1901

Cameraman: Edwin S. Porter

38 ft. FLA4709 (print) FRA1726 (neg.)

The film begins on a set of a combination dining-living room. A young woman opens the door, and a young man wearing white flannels and a straw boater comes in. The two embrace but apparently hear somebody coming, for the young man jumps into a coal bin adjacent to the fireplace. The visitor is not the husband they apparently expected but the coal man, who pours coal on top of the lover. The coal man departs and the young woman extricates her lover, only to have the husband arrive. This time the lover hides in the fireplace. The husband sits down and starts to eat, then decides to light a fire in the fireplace, flushing out the lover. The husband throws the lover in his torn and smoking clothes out through the door.

See also: An Unlucky Lover

The Lover's Knot

AM&B © H22085 Sept. 27, 1902

Cameraman: Robert K. Bonine

Location: Fair Haven, N.J. *Date:* June 25, 1902

8 ft. FLA3950 (print) FRA1161 (neg.)

The quality of the film does not permit too much detail. However, it appears to have been photographed outside. It shows a porch where a young girl is leaning over the rail and accepting the kisses of a young man standing on the lawn in front of the porch. To the right of the lovers is a small boy with a rope in his hands. He sneaks underneath the porch and ties the feet of the young man together. The film ends as the boy with his feet tied together attempts to walk and falls over backward.

A Lover's Lost Control

Keystone © LP6075 Aug. 2, 1915

Producer and Author: Mack Sennett

Cast: Sydney Chaplin, Phyllis Allen, Peggy Pearce, Billie Bennett, Frank Hayes, Joe Swickard, Eleanor Fields, Henry (Pathe) Lehrman, Hugh Fay, Wayland Trask

Location: Hollywood and Sunset Boulevards, Hollywood and Pacific Palisades

821 ft. FLA6122–6123 (print)

Sydney Chaplin and his wife Phyllis Allen go to a department store where a bored husband spies a lovely young lady trying on shoes, and for the whole two reels, he succeeds in becoming involved in fights with the clerks, other customers, and his wife. After Chaplin has caused a riot in the store, he and the young lady take off in his family car. They are pursued by his wife, some policemen, and some of the store officials in another car. Eventually Chaplin and the young lady (Peggy Pearce) wind up in the ocean, car and all.

The Lover's Ruse

Hepworth & Co. © H53765 Nov. 28, 1904

Director: Lewin Fitzhamon

Location: Walton-on-Thames, England

Original title: Poison or Whiskey

22 ft. FLA3305 (print) FRA0619 (neg.)

Judging from the grass, trees, and the cared-for walks, the locale of this film was a park or public place. The action begins when a young, well-dressed woman approaches the camera position from the right. She is followed closely by a man who is attempting to convince her that he loves her. The man gets down on his knees, places his hands over his heart, and holds his hat in his hands, while the young woman shakes her head and twirls her umbrella. In desperation, he takes out a bottle, drinks the contents, and falls to the ground and, as the picture ends, the woman holds his head in her lap.

A Lover's Yarn

AM&B © H16651 Apr. 16, 1902

Cameraman: F. S. Armitage

Location: Roof studio, N.Y.C. *Date:* May 17, 1901

10 ft. FLA4251 (print) FRA1407 (neg.)

A young woman is unwinding yarn from the hands of a young man who has his arms outstretched to her. As the unwinding continues, the young man begins kissing the young woman, but they are interrupted by an older woman who evidently does not approve of their amorous actions. As the young man jumps to his feet, the yarn he is holding catches on the hem of the young lady's skirt, pulling it up to show both her ankles and one knee, causing her to become indignant.

Love's Perfidy

AM&B © H63376 July 15, 1905

Cameraman: G. W. Bitzer

Location: Studio, N.Y.C. *Photographed:* June 29, 1905

27 ft. FLA4710 (print) FRA1727 (neg.)

A maid is helping her mistress to dress. The set is so designed that the living room and a hallway can be seen at the same time. The maid leaves, goes to the door and lets in a man. Before entering the living room, he spends some time in the hallway making advances to the maid, hugging and kissing her. The young man, in evening attire, then joins the young woman in the living room and begins making advances to her, much to the consternation of the maid who not only overhears the conversation but surreptitiously watches what is going on. The film ends when the maid can no longer contain herself and walks into the living room, interrupting her mistress and the visitor as they are embracing.

Love's Young Dream

AM&B © H23773 Nov. 11, 1902

Cameraman: Arthur Marvin

Date: July 6, 1900

9 ft. FLA3507 (print) FRA0786 (neg.)

Two young people are sitting on a couch in a drawing room set. The young man continues kissing the young girl in between futile efforts to leave her company. During one of his attempts to go, a door of the set opens and an older man in a nightcap and nightgown enters and throws the young man bodily out the window. The young woman attempts to avoid the physical punishment she fears is due her by running around the room and finally out through the door. The man attempts to kick his daughter, misses, and is seen landing on his back.

Lower Broadway

AM&B © H32629 June 13, 1903

Cameraman: Robert K. Bonine

Location: N.Y.C. *Date:* May 15, 1902

42 ft. FLA4711 (print) FPA0097 (35mm neg.) FRA2848 (neg.)

The film was photographed from a single-camera position looking down Broadway toward the Battery. A horse-drawn streetcar passes in front of the camera, with a sign giving its destination as the "Courtland and Fulton Street Ferry."

Lower Falls, Grand Canyon, Yellowstone Park

Edison © 2469 Jan. 4, 1899

Location: Yellowstone Park, Wyo.

24 ft. FLA3050 (print) FRA0363 (neg.)

The film shows the grandeur of a waterfall against the heavy growth of timber on each side. The distance of the waterfall from the camera did not permit the complete fall of the water to be shown.

Lucky Jim

AM&B © H125728 Apr. 14, 1909

Director: D. W. Griffith *Cameramen:* G. W. Bitzer, Arthur Marvin

Cast: Marion Leonard, Charles French, Charles Craig, Mack Sennett, Arthur Johnson, John Cumpson, Harry Salter

Location: Studio, N.Y.C. *Photographed:* Mar. 17, 1909

182 ft. FLA5546 (print) FRA2410 (neg.)

This split-reel comedy uses three sets—the room of the rejected suitor, the dining room of the accepted suitor's house, and a church. The heroine (Marion Leonard) is seated in a chair listening to a man (Mack Sennett) propose marriage. Another man enters, she stands up and kisses him, to the consternation of her other suitor who is still on his knees. The film shows the subsequent wedding and the newlyweds seated at the table. The husband objects to the coffee, and his bride loses her temper. She beats her new husband unmercifully, and the scene ends. The remaining scenes show Mack Sennett noticing an obituary; he immediately rushes over and proposes to the lovely young widow. This time he is accepted. As the film ends, the new groom is on his knees, and his wife is beating him on the head with a vase for objecting to the quality of the coffee.

Lucky Kitten

AM&B © H34517 Aug. 13, 1903

Cameraman: G. W. Bitzer

Cast: Kathryn Osterman

Location: Studio, N.Y.C. *Photographed:* Aug.3, 1903

27 ft. FLA3738 (print) FRA0984 (neg.)

The film is a close-up of a fashionably dressed woman holding a small kitten against the skin above her low-cut dress. She is photographed only from the waist up. The full extent of the film shows the woman fondling the kitten. The title is given as it appears on film and in the copyright application.

A Lucky Leap

Keystone © LP4524 Feb. 22, 1915

Producer and Author: Nick Cogley

Cast: Frank Opperman, Billie Bennett, Dixie Chene, Charles Chase, Nick Cogley, W. C. Hauber, Harry McCoy

Location: Keystone studio, Los Angeles; Inceville, Calif.

FLA6124 (print)

Frank Opperman and his wife, Billie Bennett, operate a small grocery store. Their daughter, Dixie Chene, is enchanted with a young man, Charles Chase. When Nick Cogley, an employee, arrives in a burrow-drawn cart, he is sent to the basement to draw some "fizzy vinegar." He cannot stop the barrel from spraying and soon everybody upstairs comes down, one at a time, and becomes soaked and unhappy. In the meantime, a pair of burglars have observed the store owners secrete some cash in their safe for their daughter's education, and while all the commotion is going on in the basement, they take off with the safe. Almost instantly their departure is discovered and the authorities are involved, plus Nick Cogley who has been reading a book on buried treasure and inadvertently finds the loot. The authorities think he is the burglar, but it is soon straightened out when he jumps through the roof of the shack where the real burglars have taken refuge, and the confusion is cleared up.

A Lucky Toothache

Biograph © J146453 Oct. 14, 1910

Cameraman: Arthur Marvin

Cast: Mary Pickford, Mack Sennett, Kate Bruce, Linda Arvidson, W. Chrystie Miller, Billy Quirk, Charles West, Claire McDowell, Eddie Dillon, Fred Mace

Location: Westfield, N.J. *Photographed:* Sept. 7, 1910

246 ft. FLA5547 (print) FRA5886 (neg., copy 1) FRA6416 (neg., copy2)

This split-reel comedy is about a young schoolteacher (Mary Pickford) who arrives in a rural community where all the males attempt to ingratiate themselves. She develops a toothache; her admirers offer various remedies, and one (Mack Sennett) hands her a note reading "If you follow my directions, your toothache will be cured." His "cure" consists of a kiss. The schoolteacher is outraged and the rest of the men capture him and intend to hang him to avenge the insult. The schoolteacher rushes to his aid and persuades them to leave him to her to administer punishment. The film ends with no hanging, no toothache, but with a new sweetheart for the schoolteacher. All the scenes were taken outdoors.

The Lucky Wishbone

Paley & Steiner © H63158 July 12, 1905

19 ft. FLA3945 (print) FRA1156 (neg.)

The entire film consists of a series of unconnected nonsensical scenes. For example, a group of men are seated on a pier. Along comes a large umbrella and, through the use of stop-action photography, the umbrella disappears and is replaced by a man and a woman fighting with boxing gloves. There are many such humorous tableaus. The scenes were filmed on a pier, on a boardwalk in an amusement zone, and in a congested area of a metropolitan city.

Ludlow's Aerodrome (1905) shows the plane designed and built by wealthy sportsman Israel Ludlow being towed by a car in order to take off. Ludlow was not seriously injured when the plane crashed.

Ludlow's Aerodrome

AM&B © H65080 Sept. 1, 1905

Cameraman: G. W. Bitzer

Location: Boer War Park, Brighton Beach Velodrome, Coney Island, N.Y. *Photographed:* Aug. 22, 1905

54 ft. FLA4712 (print) FRA1728 (neg.)

The first scenes show a biplane being carried onto a field. A rope is hooked to an automobile, and the plane is towed much like a kite into the air. There is a man in the plane, and there is a good close-up of the plane on the ground, as well as in the air. Then, the plane cracks up. The man in the plane is Israel Ludlow, a wealthy sportsman.

Ludlow's Aeroplane, no. 2

AM&B © H68148 Nov. 1, 1905

Cameraman: G. W. Bitzer

Location: Boer War Park, Brighton Beach Velodrome, Coney Island, N.Y. *Photographed:* Aug. 1905

84 ft. FLA5092 (print) FRA2050 (neg.)

The film begins with the camera positioned about two-hundred yards away from a large group of people who are watching preparations for a man to be pulled off the ground in a contraption resembling an airplane. The next scene is from a different camera position and shows the device being pulled into the air by a long rope in much the same manner as one would fly a kite. There are a few seconds of film showing the man-laden biplane in the air. Another camera position shows the plane gliding free down toward the water. The plane lands on the water. The remainder of the film is devoted to attempts to rescue both the flyer and his biplane by the use of motor boats and a tug.

Lukens, Novel Gymnast

Edison © H8691 Sept. 16, 1901

49 ft. FLA4713 (print) FRA1729 (neg.)

The entire film, photographed from one camera position, is of a high bar act of four men. One man is a security man, two are catchers, and the fourth is the star of the troupe. Lukens, the star, demonstrates his ability to do twists, turns, and somersaults in the air while swinging with or between the two catchers.

Lure of the Gown

AM&B © H123872 Mar. 11, 1909

Director: D. W. Griffith *Cameramen:* G. W. Bitzer, Arthur Marvin

Cast: Clara T. Bracey, Florence Lawrence, Marion Leonard, Owen Moore, Charles Inslee, John Cumpson, Mack Sennett

Location: Fort Lee, N.J.; Studio, N.Y.C. *Photographed:* Feb. 9, 10 and 18, 1909

207 ft. FLA5548 (print) FRA2411 (neg.)

Some of the scenes were photographed from a single-camera position on interior sets of the living quarters of Italian immigrants, and the actors were costumed accordingly. Several scenes were taken on the streets of a small town, and the spectators appear in conventional American clothes. As the film begins, a young man is in love with one of two sisters who are hurdy-gurdy operators. They introduce him to a young woman in a spectacular dress, coat, and hat. He falls in love with her and discards his original girl friend. She borrows a beautiful evening gown from a wealthy woman who had noticed her crying on the street, attends a dance, and makes a tremendous impression on her former boy friend. She no longer cares and accepts the attentions of another young man instead.

Lurline Baths

Edison © 60578 Oct. 25, 1897

Location: San Francisco

24 ft. FLA3077 (print) FRA0418 (neg.)

A large indoor swimming pool can be seen. The camera was directed toward a slide from which people can be seen entering the pool in rapid succession. Only about three quarters of the pool is included in the film so only the people enjoying the slide are visible.

See also: Sutro Baths and Sutro Baths, No. 1

Mabel and Fatty Viewing the World's Fair at San Francisco, Cal.

Keystone © MP313 Apr. 22, 1915

Producer and Author: Mack Sennett

Cast: Mabel Normand, Roscoe Arbuckle

Location: San Francisco

400 ft. FLA5549 (print) FRA2416 (neg.)

The opening scene is on the foredeck of a ferryboat approaching the foot of Market Street ferry landing in San Francisco. The subjects in the scene are Mabel Normand and Fatty Arbuckle, who are next shown leaving the ferryboat. They burlesque their walk as they approach the camera. The remainder of the film shows the pair being welcomed by Mayor James Rolph, Jr, and the World's Fair Committee, as well as touring the midway. One scene is preceded by a lengthy title explaining one of the showplaces of the fair—the authentic British slave ship *Success.* Fatty also tries, without success, to impress Metropolitan Opera star Mme. Schumann-Heink with his singing ability.

Mabel and Fatty's Married Life

Keystone © LP4437 Feb. 11, 1915

Producer and Author: Mack Sennett

Cast: Mabel Normand, Roscoe Arbuckle, Glen Cavender, Al St. John, Mae Busch, Cecile Arnold

Location: Keystone studio, Echo Park and Edendale Boulevard, Los Angeles

413 ft. FLA5948 (35mm pos. print) FPA0095 (35mm neg.)

Newlyweds Mabel and Fatty are sitting in the park. They are visited by an organ grinder's monkey. Fatty is so annoyed by the intrusion that he chases the monkey away, which upsets the organ grinder (Glen Cavender). A fight results, at the end of which the organ grinder puts a curse on Fatty. Mabel and Fatty return home; Fatty goes out on business; and Mabel, left alone, suddenly becomes aware of a movement behind her drapes. She panics, and calls the police, who eventually arrive but are hindered by a number of spectators. Fatty returns home and is frantic about the safety of his wife. The police, inside the house, bumble about but finally discover the culprit is the organ grinder's monkey. The film ends with an embrace between Fatty and Mabel.

Mabel and Fatty's Wash Day

Keystone © LP4201 Jan. 14, 1915

Producer and Author: Mack Sennett

Cast: Mabel Normand, Harry McCoy, Roscoe Arbuckle, Alice Davenport, Joe Bordeaux, W. C. Hauber, Teddy (Keystone dog)

Location: Keystone studio and Hollenbeck Park in Los Angeles

402 ft. FLA6126 (print)

Mabel Normand is doing the laundry while her husband, Harry McCoy, still sleeps. Mabel becomes angry when he does not want to get out of bed to help her. When she goes outside to hang up the clothes, she finds a neighbor, Fatty Arbuckle, has been put to work wringing clothes by his wife, Alice Davenport. Fatty helps Mabel by putting her laundry through his wringer and when their respective spouses find out, arguments ensue. Both couples go off separately to the park where they sit on benches not too far apart. Alice Davenport drops off to sleep, and Mabel continues to fight with her husband, then walks away. She encounters Fatty and they go to a little outdoor cafe. Fatty has no money, a situation he solves by stealing his sleeping wife's purse. McCoy discovers Mabel has gone off somewhere, so he picks up her purse and begins to look for her. About this time, Alice Davenport awakens, finds her purse gone, and calls the police (Hauber and Bordeaux). When the confusion is cleared up, each couple returns home together, a little reluctantly.

Mabel, Fatty and the Law

Keystone © LP4318 Jan. 28, 1915

Author: Mack Sennett

Cast: Roscoe Arbuckle, Mabel Normand, Harry Gribbon, Minta Durfee, Estelle Allen, Frank Hayes, Joe Bordeaux, W. C. Hauber, Al St. John, Glen Cavender, Joe Swickard, Alice Davenport, Billie Bennett

Location: Keystone studio, Hollenbeck and Echo Park in Los Angeles

432 ft. FLA6127 (print)

The first husband (Arbuckle) gets fresh with the maid and is caught by the first wife (Normand). After an argument they go to the park together. The second husband (Harry Gribbon) flirts with the second maid (Estelle Allen) and is caught by the second wife (Minta). After an argument, they too go to the park. While there, each couple becomes involved with the other's spouse. Each couple sits on a bench under a sign, "No Spooning Allowed." Sharp-eyed cop Frank Hayes sees them from his perch in a tree. The result is Fatty Arbuckle and Minta Durfee are taken off to jail, while Gribbon and Normand elude the police and go home. Fatty and Minta both phone home and Gribbon and Normand come down to the jail to bail out their respective spouses.

Mabel Lost and Won

Keystone © LP5577 June 3, 1915

Producer and Author: Mack Sennett

Cast: Mabel Normand, Owen Moore, Alice Davenport, Dora Rogers, Mack Swain, Estelle Allen, Frank Hayes, Dixie Chene

Location: Keystone studio, Los Angeles

400 ft. FLA5550 (print)

Mabel Normand and her boyfriend are sitting alone in the darkened parlor. Moore slips an engagement ring on her

Dora Rogers in Keystone's Mabel Lost and Won (1915).

finger, much to the delight of her mother (Alice Davenport), who has been peeking in from time to time. There are a number of guests dancing in the living room. Mother announces the engagement to her guests, one of whom, Dora Rogers, seems devastated by the news. Dora pretends to have a terrible headache and succeeds in getting the newly engaged man to spend some time alone with her. Mother discovers them and insists the engagement be broken, much to Mabel's distress. Just then, Mack Swain

and four children arrive and claim the flirtatious Dora as their mother and his wife. She leaves with them. Mabel and Owen make up and even Alice Davenport is happy now.

Mabel's Wilful Way

Keystone © LP5233 May 1, 1915

Producer and Author: Mack Sennett

Cast: Mabel Normand, Roscoe Arbuckle, Edgar Kennedy, Alice Davenport, Glen Cavender, Joe Bordeaux, Bobby Dunn

Location: Ocean Park and Venice, Calif.

408 ft.

A daughter (Mabel Normand) is in a restaurant with her parents, Alice Davenport and Glen Cavender, listening to a band. Suddenly the smell of the onions her mother is eating with gusto, and the noise of the band is too much for her so she leaves. Outside she becomes acquainted with Fatty Arbuckle. They take several slides down the famous "Bamboo Slide" at Venice and try to get an ice cream cone without paying for it. While their friendship is growing, his pal, Edgar Kennedy, is getting into trouble on his own, including becoming unhappily involved with Mabel's father who is out looking for her. There is a scene of Kennedy riding on a carousel, while Glen Cavender runs around after him. Mabel becomes irritated with Fatty and goes off, only to start talking with her father's nemesis, Kennedy. When her parents find Mabel, they give her a spanking, ending the picture.

Macbeth

See: Duel Scene from "Macbeth"

McKinley and Party

AM&B © H27386 Jan. 22, 1903

Date: 1898 [?]

29 ft. FLA3295 (print) FRA0391 (neg.)

This single-camera position film was photographed from a point overlooking an unknown army encampment of several hundred tents. President McKinley and his staff can be seen as they approach the camera.

McKinley Funeral on Way to Church

AM&B © H27388 Jan. 22, 1903

Cameraman: Arthur Marvin

Location: Canton, Ohio *Photographed:* Sept. 18, 1901

23 ft. FLA4115 (print) FRA1291 (neg.)

Photographed from a single-camera position, the film shows the military escort of the horse-drawn hearse carrying the body of the assassinated president of the United States.

McKinley Funeral: Panorama of McKinley Home

AM&B © H23805 Nov. 11, 1902

Cameraman: Congdon

Location: Canton, Ohio *Photographed:* Sept. 19, 1901

27 ft. FLA3441 (print) FRA0726 (neg.)

Photographed from a single-camera position, the film shows a long line of civilian mourners awaiting a chance to pass through President McKinley's house to view his casket. The camera pans approximately 180 degrees.

McKinley's Funeral Entering Westlawn Cemetery, Canton

Edison © H9084 Sept. 26, 1901
Location: Canton, Ohio *Photographed:* Sept. 19, 1901
84 ft. FLA5093 (print) FRA2051 (neg.)

Photographed from several camera positions, the film shows the funeral procession both preceding and following the body of the assassinated president before he is interred at Canton, Ohio.

Madison Square, New York

AM&B © H33285 July 8, 1903
18 ft. FLA3926 (print) FRA2854 (neg.)

Madison Square, New York, is shown just after the turn of the century. There is normal traffic consisting of streetcars and horse-drawn vehicles.

Magic Garden

See: Parsifal

The Magic Lantern

Méliès © H39153 Dec. 9, 1903
Creator: Georges Méliès
Location: Montreuil, France *Date:* Fall 1903
Original title: La Lanterne Magique
132 ft. FLA5551 (print) FRA2710 (neg.)

The scene opens on a nondescript but oddly appointed room. Two characters in clown costumes enter from left and right and take stage scenery (flats) from which they assemble a box about four feet by six feet. When assembled, the box appears to be a magic lantern. Without any more action on the part of the two clowns, the magic lantern projects moving pictures on the back wall of the set, and to further confuse, the moving pictures projected become the faces of the two clowns who assembled the lantern. While trying to examine the lantern, ballet dancers from the Folies Bergere in tutu costumes arrive and perform a ballet. This continues until they close the box and more people come out.

The Magician

Edison © D4733 Feb. 28, 1900
22 ft. FLA4162 (print) FRA1330 (neg.)

A man dressed in top hat and tails appears camera center in a set of a drawing room. He removes his hat, throws it in the air and it does not return. The man removes his coat, folds it, throws it up in the same fashion, and it, too, disappears. He unfolds his pocket handkerchief, and shows there is nothing in the sleeve of his coat or the leg of his trouser. Then he gestures and, with the use of stop-action photography, conjures up a table with a vase and a plate on it. He then shakes the plate, and rabbits fall out onto the floor as the film ends.

Mailing Platform, U.S.P.O.

AM&B © H34969 Aug. 22, 1903
Cameraman: A. E. Weed
Location: Washington, D.C. *Date:* Aug. 10, 1903
28 ft. FLA4056 (print) FRA1241 (neg.)

As the film begins, several four-wheeled, horse-drawn vans designed to distribute mail throughout a metropolitan city can be seen backed up against a loading platform. Two wagons are loaded with mail sacks during the film and are driven away out of camera range.

Major General Shafter

Edison © 46694 Aug. 5, 1898
Location: Cuba
26 ft. FLA3242 (print) FRA0565 (neg.)
[Spanish-American War]

This is a single-camera position film of a military bivouac. General Shafter comes into camera view mounted on horseback with his escort walking alongside. The Edison catalog describes the commander of the 5th Army Corps in the following words: "He wears a white helmet, a broad expanse of shirt bosom and a general air of avoirdupois."

Making a Welch Rabbit

See: A Welsh Rabbit

Making an Impression

AM&B © H27376 Jan. 22, 1903
10 ft. FLA3281 (print) FRA0598 (neg.)

The film begins on a street scene in a rural community where two women are walking down the sidewalk. A man in working clothes carrying a ladder is proceeding down the street when he is run into by a man on a bicycle, who gets to his feet and starts a fight. The two women leave the sidewalk and attempt to break up the fight.

The Man

Biograph © J139354 Mar. 22, 1910
Director: D. W. Griffith *Cameraman:* G. W. Bitzer
Cast: Wilfred Lucas, Frank Powell, Stephanie Longfellow
Location: Sierra Madre and studio, Los Angeles *Photographed:* Feb. 4 and 5, 1910
390 ft. FLA5552 (print) FRA2414 (neg.)

This drama, filmed in the Verdugo hills of California, is the story of a miner who lives with his wife in an isolated area. A stranger appears, asks for and is given a meal by the miner's lonely wife. He suggests they elope, and they go off together. The miner trails them and finds the stranger suffering from ptomaine poisoning. He takes the man to the cabin to recover. The miner waits for the stranger to regain his health, and then takes him out in the front yard and shoots him. The last scene shows him escorting his wife outside and leaving her with the dead man.

The Man and the Woman

AM&B © H114339 Aug. 6, 1908
Director: D. W. Griffith *Cameramen:* G. W. Bitzer, Arthur Marvin
Cast: Linda Arvidson, Frank Gebhardt
Location: Fort Lee, N.J.; Studio, N.Y.C. *Photographed:* July 17–18, 1908
281 ft. FLA5553 (print) FRA2415 (neg.)

All of the scenes in this film were photographed from a single-camera position. A woman talks a man into marrying her, and he persuades a friend to perform a fake marriage ceremony. In a short time, he abandons the woman who by now has a child. The young woman, baby in arms, goes home to her family. Her mother welcomes her, but her father will not allow her in the house. She wanders the streets, eventually reaching the home of the father of the man she believes is her husband. In the last scene, the father orders his son to accept the responsibility of his wife and child. The last scene shows the young couple embracing on the steps of the house.

Man in the Box

AM&B © H111673   June 11, 1908
Cameramen: G. W. Bitzer, Arthur Marvin
Cast: D. W. Griffith
Location: Studio, N.Y.C. *Photographed:* May 22 and 24, 1908
221 ft.   FLA5554 (print)   FRA2413 (neg.)

Most of the action in the film takes place on a split set. The film begins by showing one of a gang on thieves nailing a confederate into a large box for shipping. Then a Wells Fargo strong box is placed next to the box containing the thief, who is waiting for the proper time to knock out the guard and admit his confederates. Once this is accomplished, and the thieves are engaged in burglarizing the money box, the guard succeeds through superhuman effort in sending for help via his telegraph instrument. The final scenes show the arrival of the police, a terrific fight between the police and the bandits, the bandits being tied up and led off to jail. The original Paper Print film bears the title Invisible Fluid, obviously an error; both have the same copyright date.

See also: Invisible Fluid

Man Overboard

AM&B © H55394   Jan. 3, 1905
Cameramen: G. W. Bitzer, Wallace McCutcheon
Location: Battleship *Indiana Photographed:* Nov. 11, 1903
31 ft.   FLA4715 (print)   FRA1731 (neg.)

The film starts as a "man overboard" rescue drill begins. The exercise is performed by bluejackets of the U.S. Navy who are part of the crew of a battle cruiser.

Maneuvering a Small Motor Boat

AM&B © H78533   June 1, 1906
Cameraman: G. W. Bitzer
Location: Stamford, Conn. *Photographed:* May 18, 1906
27 ft.   FLA3611 (print)   FRA0873 (neg.)

The camera was placed to encompass an inlet area of a lake surrounded by trees, boat houses, and piers. A small boat approaches the camera from a distance. As the boat nears the camera, it can be seen to be an open rowboat. However, the boat was unique as it was powered by an inboard motor. A man on the after seat guides the motor boat with a tiller.

See also: White Fox Motor Boat

The Maniac Barber

AM&B © H19658   July 2, 1902
Cameraman: F. S. Armitage
Location: Roof studio, N.Y.C. *Photographed:* Aug. 10, 1899
46 ft.   FLA4714 (print)   FRA1730 (neg.)

The poor quality of the film does not permit much separation between the actors and the furniture on a set of a barbershop. Stop-action photography allowed the barber to sever the head of his customer, complete shaving him in a more advantageous position, and then replace his head.

The customer gets up from the barber chair, compliments the barber, and then leaves.

Maniac Chase

Edison © H51386   Oct. 7, 1904
Cameraman: Edwin S. Porter
Location: N.Y.C. *Photographed:* Sept. 27–30, 1904
206 ft.   FLA5555 (print)   FRA2418 (neg.)

The film begins on a set of the confinement quarters in a mental institution, where a man dressed in a Napoleonic costume nervously paces the floor. A guard in white brings the patient a meal he does not like, and a fight begins. Two more guards help subdue the patient who is left on the floor. "Napoleon" makes his escape by prying the bars from the windows, goes to a wooded area, and starts running. For the remainder of the film, and until he returns to his cell, the patient is photographed crossing streams, running through rivers, climbing trees, and sliding down roofs. The last scene shows Napoleon back in the institution with three exhausted guards staring at him.

See also: The Escaped Lunatic

The Maniac Cook

AM&B © H120836   Dec. 30, 1908
Director: D. W. Griffith *Cameraman:* G. W. Bitzer
Cast: Marion Leonard, Clara T. Bracey, Mack Sennett, David Miles, Harry Salter
Location: Studio, N.Y.C. *Photographed:* Nov. 25 and 27, 1908
206 ft.   FLA5556 (print)   FRA2412 (neg.)

An angry cook is breaking dishes and generally wrecking the kitchen. The man of the house attempts unsuccessfully to subdue her, then calls the police. The cook hides, and the family settles down for the night. The cook sneaks back into the house, creeps upstairs, removes an infant from its crib, and decides on a diabolical plot of putting the baby in the oven so that when the family lights the stove, they will be responsible for the baby's death. The man of the house awakens, and his wife goes to the kitchen to light the stove. But the husband misses the baby, and rushes downstairs in time to catch the cook and save the baby. The police arrive and take the mentally deranged cook away.

The Manicure Fools the Husband

AM&B © H32108   May 22, 1903
Cameraman: Robert K. Bonine
Date: July 10, 1902
18 ft.   FLA3728 (print)   FRA0975 (neg.)

The first scene shows a woman sitting at a table with the accoutrements of a manicurist in front of her. A door in the set of the beauty shop opens, and a man comes in and sits at the table. The woman begins to manicure his nails. Very soon she gets up from her chair and sits on his lap. The door opens, and a large man wearing an overcoat enters, removes the manicurist from the man's lap, and kicks him out the door.

Man's Enemy

Klaw & Erlanger © LP3038   May 8, 1914
Cast: Lillian Gish, Franklin Ritchie, Vivian Prescott, Hector V. Sarno, William Jefferson, Frank Newburg, Thornton Cole, Louise Orth, George Robinson
1,186 ft.   FLA5589-5591 (print)   FRA2419-2421 (neg.)

A large cast and many sets were employed to make this three-reel drama concerning intrigue between a temptress and titled noblemen who are opportunists and wastrel sons of good families. By the last scene, the villian has been punished and the hero and heroine justly rewarded.

Man's Genesis

Biograph © J171534 July 23, 1912
Director: D. W. Griffith *Cameraman:* G. W. Bitzer
Cast: Mae Marsh, Robert Harron, Wilfred Lucas, Charles Hill Mailes, W. C. Robinson, W. Chrystie Miller
Location: Calif.
414 ft. FLA5558 (print) FRA2417 (neg.)

The actors in this film, which was photographed outdoors, wore primitive man costumes. "Weakhands" (Robert Harron) sees "Lilywhite" (Mae Marsh), who seems to be totally alone in the world, and takes her to his cave. She accepts his protection, which proves inadequate when "Bruteforce" (Wilfred Lucas) takes "Lilywhite" away. The two primitive men meet on the field of battle for the possession of "Lilywhite" and "Weakhands" wins by virtue of brains rather than brawn, for he invents a club that allows him to subdue "Bruteforce." The last scene shows him heading off toward his cave with "Lilywhite."

Man's Lust for Gold

Biograph © J170958 July 10, 1912
Director: D. W. Griffith *Cameraman:* G. W. Bitzer
Cast: Blanche Sweet, William J. Butler, Robert Harron, Frank Opperman
Location: San Fernando, Calif.
386 ft. FLA5559 (print) FRA2422 (neg.)

The film was photographed outside in rugged, uncultivated territory. A claim jumper kills a miner and later is saved from thirst and fatigue by the miner's son-in-law. As payment, and to ease his conscience, the claim jumper gives his benefactor a map to a gold mine. They are overheard by a greedy Mexican helper, who rushes off to reach the mine first. He finds some gold, digs it up, and hides. The daughter and son-in-law who are also seeking the gold are set upon by Indians, but the film ends happily with the young couple returning from the mine with a mule-drawn covered wagon and gold.

Manual of Arms, St. John's Military Academy

AM&B © H43409 Mar. 17, 1904
Cameraman: G. W. Bitzer
Location: Manlius (near Syracuse), N.Y. *Photographed:* Mar. 14, 1904
56 ft. FLA5094 (print) FRA2052 (neg.)

From a single-camera position, approximately two companies of men dressed in pre-World War I army uniforms, execute close-order drill. Under command, they pass back and forth in front of the camera. There is snow on the ground.

Marceline, the World-Renowned Clown of the N.Y. Hippodrome

Winthrop Moving Picture Co. © H93044 Apr. 26, 1907
17 ft. FAA1769 (print) FRA2722 (neg.)

The film is of a man who, judging from his face and the part of his costume that is visible, is made up as a clown. The shortness of the film permits little other than just identification. The photographic composition is a tight one-shot (close-up), and just the head and shoulders of the subject are visible.

The March of Prayer and Entrance of the Dancers

Edison © H11268 Dec. 12, 1901
Cameraman: James H. White [?]
Location: Ariz.
44 ft. FLA4716 (print) FRA2870 (neg.)
[Walpapi Indians; Snake Dance]

The film, photographed from a single-camera position, shows some American Indians wearing ceremonial tribal dress, preliminary to an ancient dance of appeal to some force of nature.

See also: Carrying Out the Snakes, Line-up and Teasing the Snakes, Panoramic View of Moki-land, and Parade of Snake Dancers Before Dance

Marching Scene

Edison © 13548 Feb. 24, 1898
Location: State Street, Chicago
30 ft. FLA4376 (print) FRA1514 (neg.)
[7th Regiment, Illinois National Guard]

A company of military troops can be seen passing the camera position. All are wearing summer white uniforms and carrying lances with pennants instead of rifles. They execute several close-order drill maneuvers. As the film ends, they are still marching by the camera position. On the opposite side of the street are some buildings.

The Marked Time Table

Biograph © J142590 June 25, 1910
Director: D. W. Griffith *Cameraman:* G. W. Bitzer
Cast: George Nicholls, Grace Henderson, Alfred Paget, W. Chrystie Miller, Mack Sennett, Dell Henderson, Joe Graybill, Verner Clarges, Wilfred Lucas, Charles West
Location: Studio, N.Y.C. *Photographed:* May 17, 18 and 25, 1910
383 ft. FLA5560 (print) FRA2676 (neg.)

The three principal actors in this film are a businessman (George Nicholls), his wife (Grace Henderson), and their profligate son (Joe Graybill) who is in trouble with professional gamblers. The son steals his father's wallet, thinking it contains a large sum of money entrusted to his father by his firm. However, his mother, fearful for her son, has already extracted the money. The father awakens, finds money and wallet missing, and goes to the police. While there, his son is brought in, and the father identifies the wallet as his by a marked timetable. He cannot bring himself to place charges against his son, and goes home where his wife returns the money. The film ends as the son leaves a note telling his parents he is going off to make himself worthy of the name he bears.

Market Scene, City of Mexico

Edison © 13540 Feb. 24, 1898
Location: Mexico City
25 ft. FLA3233 (print) FRA0557 (neg.)

The film was photographed from a single-camera position and shows a large group of people in a Mexican city.

Children and adults stare at the camera as they are being photographed. In the background is the arch of a building support.

Market Scene in Old Cairo, Egypt

Edison © H32795 June 17, 1903
Cameraman: A. C. Abadie
Location: Cairo *Photographed:* Mar. 28, 1903
33 ft. FLA3543 (print) FRA0819 (neg.)

The camera was placed in the center of an area used as a marketplace. As the picture starts, the camera begins panning and shows natives dressed in burnooses, turbans, and fezzes and other types of clothing indigenous to that country.

Market Street Before Parade

AM&B © H32390 June 4, 1903
Cameraman: H. J. Miles
Location: San Francisco *Date:* May 26, 1903
49 ft. FLA4717 (print) FRA1732 (neg.)

The film begins as the streetcar on which the camera is placed starts to move down the principal street of a large city, showing the buses and the transportation of the era. The street is gaily decorated for a parade on the occasion of Theodore Roosevelt's visit.

Married for Millions

AM&B © H88152 Dec. 26, 1906
Cameraman: G. W. Bitzer
Location: Studio, N.Y.C. *Photographed:* Nov. 27–28, 1906
310 ft. FLA5561 (print) FRA2671 (neg.)

A series of comic situations begins with the wedding of a man who is so poor that he has to borrow money from the bride to pay the fee. Each episode is preceded by a title suggesting the following scene. The second episode starts with the wife putting her husband to work washing a considerable amount of dirty clothes. He objects. She up-ends him in the tub and from there on until the last scene, the poor groom suffers all sorts of indignities: bookshelves fall on him, he is thrown out the window, etc. The final scene shows him working as a waiter after a divorce. The restaurant is full of laborers who beat him up because he is so slow in serving them.

The Martyred Presidents

Edison © H9412 Oct. 7, 1901
Cameraman: Edwin S. Porter
20 ft. FLA3114 (print) FRA0450 (neg.)

This film is difficult to classify. It opens on a scene showing a mourner with bowed head sitting in front of what appears to be a tombstone. Shortly afterwards, the face of Abraham Lincoln and then of two other presidents, Garfield and McKinley, can be seen on the monument and then they disappear. There is a figure huddled at the foot of a statue of Justice, as if asking forgiveness.

The Masher

Biograph © J146452 Oct. 14, 1910
Director: Mack Sennett *Cameraman:* Arthur Marvin
Cast: Kate Bruce, Charles West, Alfred Paget, Grace Henderson

Location: Coytesville, N.J. *Photographed:* Sept. 9–10, 1910
167 ft. FLA5562 (print) FRA2426 (neg.)

A man and his wife, who is wearing a checkered blouse, are sitting on a park bench. They start to fight, and he stamps off. After a short while, the husband decides to return and make up with his wife, and he goes to the area where he had last seen her. He rushes up to a woman in a checkered blouse and embraces her; she screams. She has him arrested, and the last scene of the film shows him in front of the police bailiff, charged with mashing. His wife arrives, the two women find they are dressed exactly alike, and the case is dismissed.

Masked Procession

Edison © 13571 Feb. 24, 1898
18 ft. FLA3298 (print) FRA0612 (neg.)

The single-camera position was over the heads of a crowd watching a procession of people of various ages wearing masks. There is no identification of the group.

The Masqueraders

AM&B © H80887 July 17, 1906
Cameraman: G. W. Bitzer
Location: Sound Beach, Conn.; Studio, N.Y.C. *Photographed:* June 26–29, 1906
256 ft. FLA5563 (print) FRA2427 (neg.)

A young lady receives notes from two of her suitors that each will be wearing a clown's costume to a masquerade party they are all attending. This is followed by a ballroom scene where approximately twenty people are dancing. The two men costumed as clowns start a fight and one challenges the other to a duel. The young lady desperately attempts to stop the duel, and even goes to the dueling grounds, where she surreptitiously unloads the pistols. The two men, by this time very frightened by the whole thing, fire their pistols and are much relieved to find they are not loaded. The film ends as all three embrace happily.

The "Massachusetts" Naval Parade

Edison © 52053 Sept. 3, 1898
Location: Hudson River, N.Y.C. *Photographed:* Aug. 20, 1898
25 ft. FLA3277 (print) FRA0594 (neg.)
[Spanish-American War; New York City Welcome to Admiral Sampson's Fleet After Battle of Santiago Bay]

The camera was positioned on the deck of a vessel in the vicinity of the anchorage area of the *U.S.S. Massachusetts* and shows the hull and superstructure of the vessel. The camera boat cruised and photographed the length of the naval vessel from her bridge structure aft, taking in the smoke-stacks, armament, etc. As the camera vessel neared the stern position of the *Massachusetts,* a large sailing yacht with canvas awnings obstructed the camera's visibility. As the film ends, another vessel of the harbor tug variety comes between the camera position and the naval vessel.

Mass. State Militia Encampment

AM&B © H63907 July 28, 1905
Cameraman: G. W. Bitzer
Location: Camp Bartlett, Westfield, Mass. *Photographed:* July 1905
292 ft. FLA5564 (print) FRA2424 (neg.)

This film recorded a full inspection of a military encampment in Massachusetts. The camera photographed the inspection of the infantry from its assembly in the morning through its maneuvers during a battle action that included the firing of two-wheeled artillery pieces. The artillery and the cavalry performed various drills for the reviewing staff who can be seen occasionally in an automobile that was ultra-modern for the period. There is an unidentified celebrity in the inspection group.

The Massacre

Biograph © LP104 Sept. 20, 1912

Director and Author: D. W. Griffith *Cameraman:* G. W. Bitzer

Cast: Wilfred Lucas, Charles West, Blanche Sweet, Eddie Dillon, Claire McDowell, Charles Hill Mailes, Alfred Paget, Dell Henderson, W. Chrystie Miller, Charles Craig, Robert Harron

Location: Fort Lee, N.J.

834 ft. FLA5883 (print) FRA2756 (neg.)

The daughter of a farmer (Blanche Sweet), left an orphan, is raised by a man who later seeks to marry her. Instead, she marries an adventurer (Charles West) and they make their way west with a wagon train, taking their infant along. En route they are attacked by Indians. The battle is filmed from many camera positions with long shots from the top of bluffs, and exceptional close-ups of action. The climax of the film comes when the cavalry has run off the Indians and the hero searches the battlefield for his wife and baby. He finds them alive under a pile of bodies of plainsmen who had stood back to back to protect the woman and her child.

The Matron Stakes

AM&B © H19655 July 2, 1902

Cameraman: Wallace MuCutcheon

Date: Oct. 8, 1901

15 ft. FLA3679 (print) FRA9029 (neg.)

The cameraman placed his equipment on the outside rail of a race track and photographed the horses racing. Three of the camera positions were used to show the horses competing and approaching the camera. The race was won by Clarence Mackay's Heno.

Maude's Naughty Little Brother

Edison © D21660 Nov. 16, 1900

33 ft. FLA4718 (print) FRA1733 (neg.)

A woman is sitting at a table fanning herself in front of a wall constructed to represent a dining room of a modest house. A young man enters the room and sits at the table beside the young woman. He is followed by a young boy who crawls under the table and ties the visitor's tailcoat to the tablecloth. The door opens and a man gesturing angrily enters and begins to chase the young man who gets up to run, pulling the table over on top of him.

May and December

Biograph © J142449 June 22, 1910

Director: D. W. Griffith *Cameraman:* Arthur Marvin. *Script:* Mary Pickford

Cast: Mary Pickford, Billy Quirk, Kate Bruce, Charles Hill Mailes

Location: Verdugo, Calif. *Photographed:* Mar. 12, 1910

140 ft. FLA5565 (print) FRA2382 (neg.)

A middle-aged woman proposes to a young man while a middle-aged man proposes to a young girl. The first scene shows the older man becoming engaged to the young woman, and then the other couple becoming engaged. The older woman gestures that she expects a kiss to seal the bargain and is disappointed when she does not get it. This gesture of hers continues throughout the film and always without results. As the film continues, the two engaged couples meet here and there by chance. The two younger ones inevitably end up talking to each other, while the other two separate them. The film ends when the two young people give up hope of being happy with their elders, and go off together, leaving the two old people embracing.

See also: Never Again

Mayor Van Wyck and General Miles

AM&B © H17041 Apr. 26, 1902

Cameraman: F.S. Armitage

Location: N.Y.C. *Date:* May 30, 1899 (Memorial Day)

18 ft. FLA3862 (print) FRA1074 (neg.)

The poor condition of the film does not permit much description of detail. However, it is possible to see a horse-drawn carriage in which a gray-haired man in military uniform is seated next to a man in a top hat and formal clothes. Across the street from the carriage is a reviewing stand decorated with bunting.

Maypole Dance

Edison © H35329 Sept. 1, 1903

Cameraman: A. C. Abadie

Location: Wilmington, Del. *Date:* Aug. 26, 1903

32 ft. FLA4719 (print) FRA1734 (neg.)

In the center of a playground for children, a maypole was set up, and approximately twenty children circle it holding ribbons in their hands. For the entire film, the children dance around and around the pole, entwining the ribbons about it as they go.

Me and Jack

AM&B © H16333 Apr. 10, 1902

Date: 1898 [?]

11 ft. FLA4355 (print) FRA1411 (neg.)

A young woman dressed in summer attire is sitting on a bank at the edge of a reservoir. She is bathing a large dog. The young woman and the dog fall into the water, and the film ends as she is seen pulling herself to safety.

The Meadowbrook Hunt

AM&B © H21309 Aug. 25, 1902

Cameraman: G. W. Bitzer

Location: Westbury, Long Island, N.Y. *Date:* Apr. 24, 1899

27 ft. FLA3949 (print) FRA1160 (neg.)

The subject of this short film is a fox hunt. At the beginning, several dogs approach the camera position as they come through the rails of a post-and-rail fence. They are followed by people on horseback jumping the fence. In the background are a farmhouse and a windmill.

See also: Going to the Hunt, Meadowbrook

Meadowbrook Steeplechase

AM&B © H31758 May 13, 1903

Cameraman: G. W. Bitzer
Location: Morris Park, N.Y. *Date:* May 7, 1903
50 ft. FLA3687 (print) FRA0937(neg.)

The film was photographed at the Morris Park track, and the camera was positioned at some of the barriers or jumps during the course of a race. The poor condition of the film does not permit much description. However, several jockeys and their horses can be seen approaching the starting area, and one unmounted jockey walks by the camera position.

See also: Metropolitan Handicap

The Mechanical Toy

AM&B © H40813 Jan. 12, 1904
Cameraman: A. E. Weed
Location: Studio, N.Y.C. *Photographed:* Dec. 10, 1903
24 ft. FLA4185 (print) FRA1349 (neg.)

The camera was placed as if in the audience and shows a set of the living room of a residence, with a large doorway at the end farthest from the camera position. To the right of the set, seated around a table, are three young women, showing amusement over some written material. Through the doorway come a man and woman dressed for the street. The woman engages the other three in conversation while the man puts a mechanical mouse on the floor. Apparently this causes great consternation as all four women appear frightened and climb up on chairs. The man reappears, picks up the mechanical toy, and the four women chase after him as he leaves the room.

The Medicine Bottle

AM&B © H124890 Mar. 26, 1909
Director: D. W. Griffith *Cameraman:* G. W. Bitzer
Cast: Florence Lawrence, Adele De Garde, Marion Leonard, Linda Arvidson, Jeanie Macpherson, Clara T. Bracey, Dorothy West, Owen Moore
Location: Studio, N.Y.C. *Photographed:* Feb. 3, 4, 10 and 16, 1909
177 ft. FLA5566 (print) FRA2425 (neg.)

In the first scene, a mother cuts her finger, and a nurse who is caring for her ill mother offers first aid. A bottle of poison is accidentally substituted for the medicine usually given to the old lady. The nurse leaves, and so does the mother, after carefully instructing her little girl to give her grandmother her medicine. The next scenes show the mother attending a party and her discovery that the two bottles must have been mixed up. She tries frantically to reach the child by telephone and is prevented by some gossiping telephone operators. After a long delay, she gets through in time to prevent her child from feeding the old lady the poison.

Mellin's Food, no. 1

AM&B © H44655 Apr. 18, 1904
Cameraman: G.W. Bitzer
Location: Studio, N.Y.C. *Photographed:* Jan. 12, 1904
18 ft. FLA4327 (print) FRA1475 (neg.)

An infant can be seen seated on a high chair. Over the child's head is a sign that says, "Six Months Old When First Started on Mellin's Food." The film progresses to a title insert that reads, "Same Baby Six Months Later." The

healthy baby is still sitting on the stool but appears much larger in size because the camera was moved closer to fill more of the screen.

Mellin's Food, no. 2

AM&B © H44657 Apr. 18, 1904
Cameraman: G. W. Bitzer
Location: Studio, N.Y.C. *Photographed:* Jan. 12, 1904
24 ft. FLA4720 (print) FRA1735 (neg.)

A baby is sitting on a chair that has been placed on a pedestal. Above and below him are signs that read "Mellin's Food." The baby simply sits in the chair and amuses himself until a child of approximately four or five years enters the scene. She kisses the baby, walks in front of him, and deposits some packages behind the chair. At that moment, the camera is stopped and a photograph of the seated child is substituted for the live one. The older child finally turns the photograph sideways, exposing the trick.

Le Mélomane

See: The Melomaniac

The Melomaniac

Méliès © H33097 June 30, 1903
Creator: Georges Méliès *Cast:* Georges Méliès
Location: Montreuil, France *Date:* Spring 1903
Original French title: Le Mélomane
75 ft. FLA4721 (print) FRA1736 (neg.)

Another Méliès vaudeville act involving magic on the screen. A bandmaster brings out his band, removes his head, throws it onto the telegraph wires above, throws the treble clef beside it, and then directs the band to play the notes as they are formed by his head on the telegraph wires.

Men and Women

Klaw & Erlanger © LP3035 Apr. 23, 1914
Supervisor: D. W. Griffith *Director:* James Kirkwood *Script:* Based on a play by Henry C. DeMille
Cast: Lionel Barrymore, Blanche Sweet, Gertrude Robinson, Marshall Neilan, Frank Crane, F. Kerzog, Frank Norcross, F. Hearn, Hattie de Loro
1,317 ft. FLA5592-5594 (print) FRA2432-2434 (neg.)

This three-reel melodrama involves a father who became a state governor after having been convicted of the embezzlement of bank funds many years before. While in prison, his wife dies and his child is sent to an orphanage. When he is released, he takes the young girl out of the orphanage and sends her to a private school where she makes friends with socially prominent classmates. The brother of her classmates works in a bank and is also wrongfully suspected of embezzlement. Her father, now a governor, makes restitution for the missing bonds, later discovered to have been reported missing through an auditing error and not a theft. The boy suspected of stealing them is restored to his rightful position and marries the daughter of the governor.

Men Taking Fish From Salmon Seine

AM&B © H34987 Aug. 22, 1903
Cameraman: H. J. Miles
Location: Altona, Wash. *Date:* Aug. 11, 1903
23 ft. FLA3691 (print) FRA0940 (neg.)

This single-camera position film shows several men hauling a seine from the edge of what appears to be the ocean.

See also: Horses Drawing Salmon Seine and Horses Drawing in Seine

The Mended Lute

Biograph © J130411 Aug. 7, 1909

Director: D. W. Griffith *Cameraman:* G. W. Bitzer

Cast: James Kirkwood, Florence Lawrence, Owen Moore, Mack Sennett, Arthur Johnson, James Young Deer, Princess Red Wing

Location: Cuddebackville, N.Y. *Photographed:* June 28–30 and July 2, 1909

375 ft. FLA5568 (print) FRA2430 (neg.)

All of the actors are in Indian costumes. The plot is based on a conflict between two Indian braves over the hand of the chief's daughter. The first scene takes place around the chief's tepee, as he is trading his daughter to the highest bidder, who is not the man she loves. Shortly after her arrival at her new husband's tepee, she makes her escape and goes off to the man she loves. The remaining scenes show the couple being chased in canoes by the tribe of the Indian who owned her by fair trade. Finally they are captured, tied together, and apparently going to be burned to death. But something in the attitude of the captured male Indian impresses the other brave, and he sets both free.

Merely a Married Man

Keystone © LP5621 June 12, 1915

Producer and Author: Mack Sennett

Cast: Mae Busch, Harry McCoy, Dave Morris

Location: Keystone studio, Hollywood and surrounding area

420 ft. FLA6129 (print)

Mae Busch leaves home in her car and her mother decides her son-in-law (Harry McCoy) should be kept busy every instant. She devotes most of the film to making his life unbearable by constantly nagging and finding new chores for him to do, none of which he does well. A bum, Dave Morris, happens by, and Harry McCoy talks him into helping, but Morris is almost as inept as McCoy. Mae Busch does not get too far from home before her car breaks down. After a valiant attempt to repair it, she returns home to find her mother waiting up for McCoy. McCoy, who knows his mother-in-law is sitting there waiting to belabor him, persuades Morris to take his place in bed. His mother-in-law sleeps through the tramp's trip upstairs. When dishevelled Mae returns, she finds Morris in her bed and calls the police. McCoy sees a policeman enter his home, joins him, and helps to capture the confused Morris. McCoy denies knowing the hapless bum, who is taken off to jail.

The Mermaid

Méliès © H46129 May 18, 1904

Creator: Georges Méliès *Cast:* Georges Méliès

Location: Montreuil, France *Date:* Spring 1904

Original title: La Sirene

99 ft. FLA5096 (print) FRA2053 (neg.)

The film starts in a room where there is a large aquarium. Beside it is an ordinary hammock. Georges Méliès enters, takes off a silk hat, dips water out of the fish tank and pours it into the hat. He gets a fish pole from the hammock and

catches live fish from the hat, which he puts into the tank. The live fish dissolve away as the camera dollies back, a mermaid appears, and the live fish swim around. With the use of other trick photography, Méliès transfers the mermaid back onto the stage with him.

Merry-Go-Round

Edison © 52058 Sept. 3, 1898

23 ft. FLA4230 (print) FRA1388 (neg.)

A single-camera position film of a merry-go-round at an unidentified location. The carousel makes about ten revolutions during the film.

Mesmerist and Country Couple

Edison © 40080 June 17, 1899

41 ft. FLA4722 (print) FRA1737 (neg.)

The film is of poor quality and there is very little separation between the characters and the background. However, the action can be followed. The entire film consists of trick camera effects made possible by stopping the camera and substituting or removing people, articles of clothing, or furniture.

The Message

Biograph © J129505 July 6, 1909

Director: D. W. Griffith *Cameramen:* Arthur Marvin, G. W. Bitzer

Cast: James Kirkwood, Florence Barker, Baden Powell, Frank Powell, Robert Harron

Location: Greenwich, Conn.; Studio, N.Y.C. *Photographed:* June 1, 7–18, 1909

344 ft. FLA5569 (print) FRA2431 (neg.)

A young woman is shown choosing between two suitors, and she decides on a farmer. They have a child, and subsequent scenes show both the tranquility as well as the drudgery and dullness of her new life. Her other suitor, a city man, comes calling and attempts to convince her to run away with him. She writes a note to her husband, and starts off to meet the city man. Her baby follows her to the rendezvous point, and she realizes that she cannot leave the child. She returns and confesses to her husband, who forgives her. The film ends with a tranquil, pastoral scene.

The Message of the Violin

Biograph © J147013 Oct. 26, 1910

Director: D. W. Griffith *Cameraman:* G. W. Bitzer

Cast: Stephanie Longfellow, Charles West, George Nicholls, Grace Henderson, Alfred Paget, Eddie Dillon, W. J. Butler

Location: Studio, N.Y.C. *Photographed:* Sept. 13–14, 1910

408 ft. FLA5570 (print) FRA2423 (neg.)

A young violinist, the son of a drunken father in poor circumstances, is refused permission to marry the girl of his choice. Oil is discovered on the property belonging to the young girl's father, and the lovers are separated by economic circumstances, as she moves into a new social circle. She meets a titled man and becomes engaged to him. Her father gives a party and the violinist is hired as part of the entertainment. The young lady recognizes the violin solo he plays and, as the film ends, their gestures indicate that the gap in their lives has been closed.

The Messenger Boy and the Ballet Girl

AM&B © H60294 May 3, 1905

Cameraman: G. W. Bitzer

Location: Studio, N.Y.C. *Photographed:* April 26,1905

22 ft. FLA3897 (print) FRA1118 (neg.)

Two young ladies dressed as ballet dancers are doing warm-up exercises in front of a set of a dressing room. A stage hand comes in and performs a favor for one of them. He is followed by a small boy in a messenger's uniform who is carrying a bouquet; the boy gives it to one of the dancers, asking her to sign a receipt. He seems fascinated by the ballet dancers as they bend over and their tutu skirts flare. One of the dancers discovers his interest and boots him out of the dressing room.

The Messenger Boy's Mistake

Edison © H36779 Oct. 14, 1903

Cameraman: Edwin S. Porter

Location: Studio, N.Y.C. *Photographed:* Sept. 29, 1903

35 ft. FLA4723 (print) FRA1738 (neg.)

A messenger boy delivers a package to well-dressed and attractive young woman on a drawing-room set. A note with the package, included as a close-up insert, indicates the sender wants the recipient to wear the contents of the box, which turn out to be a pair of pajamas. A young man, apparently the sender, arrives as the young woman is pacing up and down in anger. She is berating him when the messenger returns and explains he made an error. The new box proves to contain flowers, and the film ends with the two young people embracing.

The Meteor

AM&B © H25957 Dec. 31, 1902

Cameraman: Robert K. Bonine

Date: Apr. 2, 1902

30 ft. FLA4167 (print) FRA1334 (neg.)

The camera position was from a boat. A schooner-rigged sailing vessel approximately a hundred and fifty feet in length can be seen. The film shows the sailboat in three positions, and then turns to a large single-stack steam-driven ocean liner (unidentifiable).

Metropolitan Handicap

AM&B © H31757 May 13, 1903

Cameraman: G. W. Bitzer

Location: Morris Park, N.Y. *Photographed:* May 7, 1903

30 ft. FLA4724 (print) FRA1739 (neg.)

All of the film was photographed in and around a race course during a meet. However, the poor condition of the film does not permit detailed description.

See also: Meadowbrook Steeplechase

Mexican Fishing Scene

Edison © 13537 Feb. 24, 1898

Location: Mexico

24 ft. FLA1300 (print) FRA1300 (neg.)

The poor condition of the film does not permit much detail to be described. However, it is possible to see dimly two people who appear to be young boys standing on a flat-bottomed punt and fishing. Both of the boys jump into the water and then swim back and climb aboard the punt.

Mexican Rurales Charge

Edison © 13559 Feb. 24, 1898

Location: Mexico

25 ft. FLA3986 (print) FRA1194 (neg.)

A large flat area resembling a military drill field is seen. In the distance is a large group of Mexican *rurales* (cavalry) who approach the camera. The mounted men pass by the camera, turn, and, as the film ends, gallop away.

Mexican Sweethearts

Biograph © H128738 June 24, 1909

Director: D. W. Griffith *Cameraman:* G. W. Bitzer

Cast: Lottie Pickford, James Kirkwood, Billy Quirk, Charles Gorman, Mack Sennett

Location: Studio, N.Y.C. *Photographed:* May 28, 1909

120 ft. FLA5097 (print) FRA2054 (neg.)

The entire film was photographed in a set of a Spanish or Mexican *cantina* (saloon). The furniture consists of a table, some chairs, and a small bar. There are two unidentified cowboys, an actor dressed as a Mexican, and the leading woman, who is either a waitress or the proprietess of the saloon. The story line follows the conquests, fights, and intrigues of the various people who enter the *cantina* in the course of a business day. The final scenes are built around a fight motivated by the attentions paid by the leading lady to an American soldier (Billy Quirk). There is much waving of arms and flashing of guns. The picture ends as the man dressed in the Spanish costume and the leading lady appear to have solved their difficulties and embrace.

Mexico Street Scene

Edison © 17708 Mar. 15, 1898

Location: Mexico city

28 ft. FLA4316 (print) FRA1464 (neg.)

The subject is activities in a town square. The camera was placed to show the movements of the people going to and fro across the area. Many burros or pack animals are led by natives and there are two small electric streetcars to be seen.

A Midnight Adventure

Biograph © J135022 Nov. 20, 1909

Director: D. W. Griffith *Cameramen:* Arthur Marvin, G. W. Bitzer

Cast: Mary Pickford, Billy Quirk, Dorothy Bernard, Kate Bruce, Mack Sennett, Jeanie Macpherson

Location: Studio, N.Y.C. *Photographed:* Oct. 5, and 8, 1909

209 ft. FLA5571 (print, copy 1) FLA0035 (print, copy 2) FLA2708 (archival print) FRA2880 (neg.)

A young woman (Dorothy Bernard) orders her boyfriend (Billy Quirk) to prove his love for her by stealing her photograph from a friend's house. He dresses as a burglar, but is caught by the friend (Mary Pickford) and becomes enchanted by her. He comes back to call, she summons the police, and this time he explains his reasons for visiting. The last scene shows the young lady who started it all, disconsolate at the loss of her boyfriend.

A Midnight Cupid

Biograph © J143007 July 9, 1910

Director: D. W. Griffith *Cameraman:* G. W. Bitzer

Cast: Charles West, Alfred Paget, William J. Butler, Grace Henderson, Dorothy West, Gertrude Robinson, W. Chrystie Miller, Billy Quirk, Florence Barker, George Nicholls, Mack Sennett

Location: Coytesville, N.J. *Photographed:* June 3–4, 1910

395 ft. FLA5572 (print) FRA2428 (neg.)

A bored rich young man removes a letter from the pocket of a tramp who broke into his house and fell asleep after drinking too much wine. The young man decides to take the tramp's place. He goes out to the country and presents himself to the friends and relatives of the tramp, one of whom is an attractive young woman. After he has ingratiated himself with these people, the tramp appears and challenges him. The last scene of the film shows the rich young man back at home being married to the young lady he met while pretending to be a tramp.

Midnight Intruder

Edison © H42207 Feb. 16, 1904

Cameraman: Edwin S. Porter

Location: Studio, N.Y.C. *Photographed:* Feb. 1, 1904

21 ft. FLA3118 (print) FRA0453 (neg.)

The photographer placed his camera at the foot of a bed in order to show a man asleep in a bed. The man's facial contortions indicate he is breathing hard or snoring laboriously, but he sits up abruptly as though he hears a noise. He takes a pistol from the night stand and brandishes it about. At this point, a large grey cat climbs up on the bed and is welcomed by his master who goes back to sleep. The film was lighted by incandescent lights.

The Midnight Marauder

Biograph © J150814 Jan. 16, 1911

Cameraman: Arthur Marvin

Cast: Eddie Dillon, Jeanie Macpherson, Wilfred Lucas, Kate Bruce, Flora Finch, Lottie Pickford, Owen Moore, Harry Hyde

Location: Fort Lee, N.J.; Studio, N.Y.C. *Photographed:* Nov. 16–18 and 23, 1910

157 ft. FLA5573 (print) FRA2429 (neg.)

A cowardly blow-hard type is given credit for capturing a burglar when all he does is fall out of the window and land on top of the burglar. The first scene shows a living room where an old gentleman is explaining how he shot the bear whose skin has become a rug. One by one, his listeners, unable to stand his tall tales, leave the room. Later in the film, after the accidental capture of the burglar, there is an insert followed by a closer insert of a newspaper account of the accidental deed. The film ends as his wife, who knows the man's character, fires a pistol, and Mr. Blow Hard hides under the table.

A Midnight Phantasy

AM&B © H32493 June 11, 1903

Cameraman: F. S. Armitage

Location: Roof studio, N.Y.C. *Date:* Sept. 23, 1899

15 ft. FLA3256 (print) FRA0578 (neg.)

The film begins by showing a set of a picket fence with posters painted on it. A cigar-store Indian is standing in front of the picket fence and next to it is a poster of a ballerina; it, too, has dimension. A man in a top hat and tails appears on the scene, scrutinizes the cigar-store Indian, steals his cigar, and wanders over to the ballerina poster, removes his hat and bows from the waist. The girl acknowledges his salute and steps from the poster to ground beside him. The man starts to escort her off the set when the cigar-store Indian hits him on the head with a tomahawk, scalps him, and hands the scalp to the astonished ballet dancer.

Midsommer

See: Midsummer-Tide

Midsummer-Tide

Great Northern © Oes J168688–90 Apr. 27, 1912

Director: August Blom *Author:* Axel Garde

Cast: Valdemar Psilander, Cajus Bruun, Frederik Skondrup, H. C. Nielson, Frederik Christensen, Augusta Blad, Thorkild Roose, Zanny Petersen, Elith Pio, Frederik Jacobsen, Julie Henriksen, Tage Hertel, Johanne Dinesen

Location: Denmark *Date:* Oct. 23, 1911

Danish title: Midsommer

956 ft. FLA5884 (print, copy 1) FLA5885 (print copy 2) FRA2757 (neg.)

In the Midsommer-Tide, the owner of a general store, unable to meet a note that is coming due, convinces his handsome playboy son (Valdemar Psilander) that he must marry a wealthy woman, even though he knows his son has chosen another. The son reluctantly agrees and goes off to the country estate of the woman his father has selected for him. There he finds that his beloved is also a guest, and many unhappy scenes take place between the two lovers. Before the announcement of the coming marriage of the playboy to the rich woman can be made, he is accidentally shot by another guest, apparently also a suitor of the girl the playboy really loved. A Danish critic of 1911 described Midsummer-Tide as 'a very entertaining film.' The number of times the camera is moved in rapid sequence from one position to another, and from one point of view to another, makes the story flow easily and gives the simple plot added interest. In the very first scene, the camera is moved from the interior where the father has been unhappily scanning his bills to the exterior as he dispatches a messenger to the polo field to summon his son. There are good action shots of the polo game in Midsummer-Tide, as well as a great many fine interiors. The lighting is so well matched in this moving picture that the change from outside to inside constructed sets is unnoticeable, a feat not always accomplished in the early years of filmmaking.

Midway of Charleston Exposition

Edison © H16713 Apr. 18, 1902

Location: Charleston, S.C. *Photographed:* Apr. 1902

12 ft. FLA3190 (print) FRA0516 (neg.)

The film, photographed from a single-camera position, shows people walking on the midway at the Charleston Exposition. Very few objects are discernible because of the distance.

Midwinter Bathing, L Street Bath, Boston

AM&B © H57949   Mar. 20, 1905

Cameraman: G. W. Bitzer

Location: L Street Bath, South Boston *Photographed:* Feb. 25, 1905

197 ft.   FLA5574 (print)   FRA2435 (neg.)

This film was photographed in the winter, much of it during an actual snowstorm, and snow can be seen on the ground in all scenes. The subject is a group of men, clothed only in swimming trunks, who demonstrate their physical prowess by doing calisthenics, playing handball, and swimming during freezing weather.

A Mid-Winter Brush

Edison   © 13569   Feb. 24, 1898

28 ft.   FLA3825 (print)   FRA1053 (neg.)

The film was photographed from a single-camera position next to a road. Several one-horse sleighs are pulled past the camera.

Mike Got the Soap in His Eyes

AM&B © H32792   June 17, 1903

Cameraman: G. W. Bitzer

Location: Studio, N.Y.C. *Date:* June 10, 1903

28 ft.   FLA351 (print)   FRA0827 (neg.)

A woman with her back to the camera is kneeling in what appears to be a kitchen set furnished with a table, a small sink, and a small wood-burning stove with a stovepipe that reaches the ceiling. A man dressed in work clothes enters, and the woman pours some water in a basin and hands him a piece of soap with which he begins washing his face and hands. Apparently, soap gets in his eyes and, while stumbling about the room trying to locate a towel, he succeeds in upsetting the basin and knocking over a bucket of water. As the film ends, he is seen on the edge of the stove, having also crashed into the stovepipe. The racket resulting from the havoc he has wreaked attracts the attention of his wife who returns and starts beating him. He returns the blows.

A Mile in 56 Seconds

AB&B © H32870   June 20, 1903

Cameraman: Robert K. Bonine

Location: Shrewsbury River, N.J. *Date:* Jan. 20, 1902

19 ft.   FLA3450 (print)   FRA0731 (neg.)

The film, photographed from a single-camera position, shows the start of an ice boat maneuver. The craft makes a one-pylon turn.

Miles Canyon Tramway

Edison   © H4090   May 6, 1901

Location: Yukon Terr., Canada

34 ft.   FLA3670 (print)   FRA0922 (neg.)

This picture was filmed from a single-camera position and shows what appers to be the beginning of a mining area inasmuch as the only buildings to be seen are canvas-covered tentlike structures. There is considerable activity among the men in the picture but, because of its poor condition, it is not possible to describe exactly what they are doing. Some farm wagons mounted on railroad-train wheels and drawn by horses in the direction of the camera position can be seen.

Military Camp at Tampa Taken From Train

Edison   © 31446   May 20, 1898

Location: Tampa, Fla.

22 ft.   FLA3345 (print)   FRA0654 (neg.)

[Spanish-American War]

As the film begins, it is evident that the camera is moving. The first scenes visible are of rough terrain in the foreground and of army tents in the background. The moving camera platform allows the photographer to encompass scenes of an army receiving center that was constructed for the Spanish-American War. The distance from the subject to the camera is such that little detail can be established.

Military Drill of Kikuyu Tribes and Other Native Ceremonies

Paul J. Rainey   © MP223   July 4, 1914

Author: Carl E. Akeley

Location: Africa

879 ft.   FLA5886 (print)   FRA2777 (neg.)

The first part of the film follows the title, while the second is devoted to the hunting of leopards and cheetahs, interspersed with a few views of natural wonders, such as turbulent rivers, steaming springs, and some close-ups of members of the hunting party holding hunting dogs.

Military Maneuvers, Manassas, Va.

Edison   © H50559   Sept. 17, 1904

Location: Manassas, Va. *Photographed:* Sept. 1904

114 ft.   FLA5098 (print)   FRA2055 (neg.)

This is a reconstruction of the Civil War Battle of Manassas. The camera shots include the artillery area and infantry attack positions, as well as the firing of several artillery pieces of Civil War vintage. There are four scenes of men in U.S. Army officer's uniforms directing troops. The last few feet of film consist of closeups of the spectators. The Edison catalog of 1904 identifies Generals Grant, Corbin, Bell, and Chaffee among those filmed.

Military Parade, St. Louis Exposition

AM&B © H50482   Sept. 14, 1904

Cameraman: A. E. Weed

Location: St. Louis, Mo. *Date:* Aug. 17, 1904

105 ft.   FLA5099 (print)   FRA2056 (neg.)

[Louisiana Purchase Exposition]

Photographed from a single-camera position, the film shows marching companies of men in uniform, some of whom can be identified as U.S. military men. Certain of the marchers play band instruments, while others carry them. There are two mounted troops. The background leads one to believe this was the forming-up area for a parade.

Military Tactics

AM&B © H47466   June 23, 1904

90 ft.   FLA5100 (print)   FRA2057 (neg.)

The opening scene shows a sentry box and a sentry walking his post wearing a full-length greatcoat and a helmet with a plume. The second camera position shows a woman creeping up behind the sentry box. She is clothed in a long white dress, but not a hat. Surreptitiously she maneuvers to get into the sentry box out of view of the sentry, but he discovers her on his return tour and they embrace happily.

During the embrace, the sentry sees an officer circuitously approaching. He quickly unbuttons his greatcoat and rebuttons it around the woman to obscure her from view. There is an exchange of salutes and the officer walks off camera. The next camera position shows a man in a sergeant's uniform seated with the young woman on a park bench. Their tête-à-tête is interrupted by an officer who, after an exchange of salutes, sends the sergeant on an errand. The officer immediately makes shy advances to the young woman. The next scene shows the officer and the young woman promenading in the park. As the film ends, the young woman and the soldier push the officer into a pile of dirt that just happens to be there. After covering the protesting officer with the dirt, they run away.

Milking Time

AM&B © H24884 Dec. 9, 1902
Cameraman: Robert K. Bonine
Location: Fair Haven, N.J. *Date:* June 25, 1902
14 ft. FLA4000 (print) FRA1202 (neg.)

This single-camera position film shows a woman milking a cow. A man joins them, and she squirts milk on him.

The Mills of the Gods

Biograph © J131133 Aug. 31, 1909
Director: D. W. Griffith *Cameraman:* G. W. Bitzer
Cast: Linda Arvidson, John Cumpson, Marion Leonard, Tony O'Sullivan, Henry B. Walthall, Arthur Johnson, Mack Sennett
Location: Studio, N.Y.C. *Photographed:* July 17, 1909
248 ft. FLA5575 (print) FRA2436 (neg.)

A household servant (Linda Arvidson) who is in love with a struggling writer (Arthur Johnson) attempts to improve his unhappy financial situation by selling one of his stories to a publisher. She is successful and returns to the author's quarters, where she writes him a note telling him of the acceptance of his story. The author rushes off to the editor who describes the serving girl. He returns home and tells her he knows of her good deed. While she is still glowing from the unwonted praise, the author tells her of his love for another woman. The last scene shows the maid being embraced by the grocer's delivery boy (Mack Sennett), who has a new suit and some money in his pocket.

Miniature Railway

Edison © H16718 Apr. 18, 1902
Location: Charleston Exposition, Charleston, S.C. *Photographed:* Apr. 1902
23 ft. FLA3191 (print) FRA0517 (neg.)

Photographed from a single-camera position, the film shows either a fairground or a public gathering place where a miniature locomotive pulls four open cars filled with people. The train approaches the camera at a diagonal. The film ends when a second train comes into view.

Miniature Railway at Wilmington Springs, Del.

Edison © H33293 July 8, 1903
Cameraman: A. C. Abadie
Location: Wilmington Springs, Del. *Photographed:* June 30, 1903
41 ft. FLA3637 (print) FRA0894 (neg.)

A miniature steam locomotive is pulling a car loaded with children. The train stops in front of the camera, and as one group of children disembarks another replaces them.

See also: Razzle Dazzle

Mining Operations, Pennsylvania Coal Fields

Edison © H54720 Dec. 23, 1904
Cameraman: Jamison
Location: Drifton, Pa. *Photographed:* Dec. 17, 1904
63 ft. FLA5101 (print) FRA2058 (neg.)

The film opens on an area covered with snow where the following operations are visible: track laying, and dirt moving by explosion, grader, steam shovel, and steam engine.

The Minister's Hat

AM&B © H35626 Sept. 12, 1903
Cameraman: A. E. Weed
Location: Studio, N.Y.C. *Photographed:* Aug. 26, 1903
19 ft. FLA4128 (print) FRA1302 (neg.)

The set is of the interior of a house of modest means where a man dressed as a minister enters and is seated on a chair by a woman dressed as a maid. After taking his hat, the maid motions for him to follow her, which he does; as soon as he is out of the area, the face and shoulders of a young lady with a mischievous expression are seen. She enters the room and is followed by two other young women who immediately begin playing a game with the preacher's hat. They hold it up in the air and compete with one another in trying to kick a hole in it. One is successful and can be seen prying the hat off her foot.

The Minister's Wooing

AM&B © H32562 June 12, 1903
12 ft. FLA3554 (print) FRA0830 (neg.)

The film begins with a set of the front of a house, outside of which is a conventional park bench. A man dressed as a parson walks up to the bench and picks up a magazine that apparently interests him. He holds it up; a scantily-clad woman can be seen on the cover. The door in the set opens and a young woman comes out; her gestures show she is delighted to see the parson and she sits down beside him. A teen-age boy appears with a large insect dangling from a fishing pole; he drops this in front of the young woman who appears frightened and jumps up from the bench causing it to overturn, spilling the parson to the ground, and thus ending the film.

Mischievous Monkey

AM&B © H32556 June 12, 1903
21 ft. FLA3499 (print) FRA0779 (neg.)

A set furnished as a bedroom is seen, with a man asleep on the bed. A man disguised as a monkey enters through a window of the wall farthest from the camera and begins to harass the sleeping man by pulling off the bed cloths, biting his feet, etc. When the man is sufficiently awakened to protect himself, the picture ends.

Mischievous Willie's Rocking Chair Motor

AM&B © H22091 Sept. 27, 1902
18 ft. FLA3216 (print) FRA0540 (neg.)

An old man is sleeping in a rocking chair with his feet on a table in a set of the living room of a modest house. As the film continues, the face of a little boy is seen peering in through the window. He enters the house, stands up on a chair, and ties a string from the rocking chair to a fishbowl that is suspended directly over the sleeping man's head. He then begins to tickle the sleeper, causing him to lean back, which pulls the string and empties the water from the fishbowl over his head, much to the amusement of the little boy. The film ends as a woman comes in and admonishes the old man for spilling the water out of the fishbowl.

A Misdirected Ducking
AM&B © H43572 Mar. 22, 1904
Cameraman: A. E. Weed
Location: Studio, N.Y.C. *Photographed:* Mar. 5, 1904
18 ft. FLA3704 (print) FRA0952 (neg.)

The camera was positioned at a distance from a set of the front of a two-story flat-roofed building with windows and doors on both floors. A young couple comes out of the house, sits down on the bench in front, and starts to embrace. A man with an umbrella comes along. The youngsters go inside, get water, and start pouring it on the man with the umbrella. At that moment, a window directly over them on the second floor opens and someone pours water on them.

The Mis-Directed Kiss
AM&B © H40756 Jan. 11, 1904
Cameraman: A. E. Weed
Location: Studio, N.Y.C. *Photographed:* Jan. 4, 1904
28 ft. FLA4725 (print) FRA1740 (neg.)

The plot is based on a case of mistaken identity. A well-dressed young woman enters her home and gives her wraps to a black maid. The maid ushers in a rather old and frail man. He is seated; the lady of the house accepts the flowers and present he brought her and allows him to kiss her hand. She then gets up to put the flowers in the vase. The black maid returns. The old gentleman mistakenly kisses her hand, looks up, puts his glasses on, and becomes aware of his error. The film ends here.

The Misplaced Signs
AM&B © H42241 Feb. 18, 1904
Cameraman: G. W. Bitzer
Location: Studio, N.Y.C. *Photographed:* Feb. 6, 1904
43 ft. FLA4726 (print) FRA1741 (neg.)

The film starts in front of a store-front set with two doors. Over one door is a sign reading "Shoemaker," while over the other the sign says "Tailor." Two women appear and each enters one of the shops. They soon come out and are joined by a third young woman. The three conspire to play a prank on the shopkeepers by reversing the storefront signs. This leads to much irritation on the part of subsequent customers, and for the tailor and the shoemaker as well, all of which culminates in confusion and violence. Eventually the tailor and the shoemaker discover what has happened to them, and at the end of the film, the two shake hands.

Miss Fatty's Seaside Lovers
Keystone © LP5389 May 15, 1915
Producer and Author: Mack Sennett *Director:* Roscoe Arbuckle
Cast: Roscoe Arbuckle, Billie Bennett, Walter Reed, Edgar Kennedy, Harold Lloyd, Joe Bordeaux, Billy Gilbert.
Location: Hollywood; Keystone studio, Los Angeles; Venice, Calif.
420 ft. FAA6537 (print)

A rich mothball magnate (Walter Reed), his wife (Billie Bennett), and their very large "daughter" (Fatty Arbuckle) arrive at a seaside resort. They are met by a trio of "lounge lizards" wearing white flannel pants and sport coats (Edgar Kennedy, Harold Lloyd without his famous spectacles, and Joe Bordeaux). A series of pratfall situations get the family and the lounge lizards upstairs into the suite of the mothball magnate. In one scene "Miss Fatty" uses one of "her" suitors (Joe Bordeaux) as a dust mop. Later Miss Fatty has a craving to go to the beach and all of her suitors join the family. Miss Fatty falls asleep on a rock as the tide comes in and is rescued by the overpowered suitors.

Miss Jessie Cameron, Champion Child Sword Dancer
Edison © H35622 Sept. 11, 1903
Cameraman: Edwin S. Porter
Location: N.Y.C. *Photographed:* Sept. 7, 1903
44 ft. FLA4727 (print) FRA1712 (neg.)

The photographer placed his camera at the edge of a floor laid for exhibition dancing, and the film shows a young girl wearing kilts performing a Scottish Highlander dance. Throughout the film, the girl dances around and between a pair of crossed swords placed flat on the dance floor. A group of people, also wearing kilts, can be seen in the immediate background watching the performance.

See also: Miss Jessie Dogherty, Champion Female Highland Fling Dancer, and Old Fashioned Scottish Reel

Miss Jessie Doghtery, Champion Female Highland Fling Dancer
Edison © H35623 Sept. 11, 1903
Cameraman: Edwin S. Porter
Location: N.Y. *Photographed:* Sept. 7, 1903
35 ft. FLA3529 (print) FRA0805 (neg.)

The film was photographed from a single-camera position on what appears to be the floor of an exhibition hall of considerable size. A young woman dressed in kilts and wearing a tartan is seen in the immediate foreground dancing the Highland Fling to the music of some bagpipers in the background. These are spectators seated on bleacher seats.

See also: Miss Jessie Cameron, Champion Child Sword Dancer, and Old Fashioned Scottish Reel

Miss Lillian Shaffer and Her Dancing Horse
Edison © H52145 Oct. 26, 1904
Cameraman: Edwin S. Porter
Location: Danbury, Conn. *Photographed:* Oct. 15, 1904
82 ft. FLA5102 (print) FRA2054 (neg.)

This film appears to have been taken in a fairgrounds or a similar cleared area. A woman mounted on her horse is seen guiding it through a number of difficult tricks, such as various paces, crossing one foot in front of another, side stepping, and "dancing." The film ends while the horse is executing a bow.

Mr. Butt-In

AM&B © H73401 Feb. 14, 1906

Cameraman: G. W. Bitzer

Location: Studio, N.Y.C. *Photographed:* Feb. 1-2, 1906

286 ft. FLA5576 (print) FRA2437 (neg.)

The comedy consists of a series of tableaus, each preceded by a title. The action shows a particularly obnoxious man who gets himself into trouble by showing other men their businesses. Mr. Butt-In is shown telling the plumber how to mend a pipe, which breaks and squirts water all over himself, his wife, and her new hat. In the three following scenes, he attempts to stop a fight between bricklayers, interfere in a prize fight, and, because of his injuries, tell the doctor how to practice medicine. The film ends as he is put away in a home for the mentally deranged. The character, Mr. Butt-In, was used by special arrangement with the *New York World.*

Mr. Easymark

AM&B © H39908 Dec. 23, 1903

Cameraman: A. E. Weed

Location: Studio, N.Y.C. *Photographed:* Dec. 9, 1903

22 ft. FLA3562 (print) FRA0838 (neg.)

The picture begins in a set of the living room of a modest house where a young man and a young woman in a negligee can be seen embracing in a large armchair. Their romantic interlude continues for a considerable period of the film, and during this time the woman smokes a cigarette. Evidently there is a knock on the door, for the two jump to their feet, and the young man hides behind the door as it is opened. The young woman pulls a man into the room by his lapels, giving her first suitor an opportunity to leave. The second arrival appears delighted and extracts a small box containing a large piece of jewelry from under his coat and drapes it around the young woman's neck. As the film ends, she kisses him.

Mr. Gay and Mrs.

AM&B © H104043 Dec. 24, 1907

Cameraman: Arthur Marvin

Location: Studio, N.Y.C. *Photographed:* Dec. 3-4, 1907

306 ft. FLA5577 (print) FRA2438 (neg.)

The plot is about a gay and philandering old man whose wife becomes rough with him each time she finds him embracing the maid, his office girls, or the manicurist. During the film, the husband is thwarted in his attempts to cheat on his wife by her constant surveillance. During the last scenes, the husband flirts with a manicurist, and his wife watches his activities over the top of a screen. She falls onto the table, giving her husband time to escape her wrath. The final scene shows the husband arriving home in an intoxicated state. His wife awakens and begins to harangue him. She is in a Murphy bed which her long-suffering husband nonchalantly folds up against the wall.

Mr. Hurry-Up of New York

AM&B © H89824 Jan. 31, 1907

Cameraman: G. W. Bitzer

Location: Studio and Central Park, N.Y.C. *Photographed:* Dec. 6, 7, 10 and 12, 1906

265 ft. FLA5578 (print) FRA2439 (neg.)

The theme of the film is a day in the life of a New York businessman who seems to be in a hurry and the consequences of such haste. He rushes to eat, to work, to keep appointments, and then to drink. His drinking sets the stage for the use of trick effects that reduce our hero to complete submission. Furniture moves, appears, and disappears; a circular staircase revolves, etc. A camera position above the set where the hero is sleeping in a drunken stupor shows the bed spinning on its axis, finally defying gravity, and taking off into the air. By the time the film ends, most of the special camera uses known at the time have been employed.

Mr. Jack Caught in the Dressing Room

AM&B © H44029 Mar. 29, 1904

Cameraman: A. E. Weed

Location: Studio, N.Y.C. *Photographed:* Mar. 17, 1904

20 ft. FLA3517 (print) FRA0796 (neg.)

A man enters the door of a set of a woman's backstage dressing room. There are mirrors on the wall, chairs with articles of women's clothing, and a screen. The man amuses himself by looking at the stockings and corsets that are lying around, hears someone approaching, and goes behind the screen. Three young women in stage costumes enter the dressing room, notice the uninvited man's top hat, and conspire to play a trick on him. One pulls the screen away, while the other throws a basin of water over their guest.

Mr. Jack Entertains in His Office

AM&B © H44027 Mar. 29, 1904

Cameraman: A. E. Weed

Location: Studio, N.Y.C. *Photographed:* Mar. 16, 1904

21 ft. FLA3516 (print) FRA0795 (neg.)

The set was constructed to look like two rooms, with the division panel directly at camera center. It is furnished as a business office. A man is sitting at a desk when an office boy enters and informs him that he has callers. Three women are ushered in, and they are just getting acquainted with the businessman when the office boy rushes in and whispers something in his employer's ear. There is much commotion as the three young women try to disguise themselves as office employees, or hide in closets. A tall, cross-looking woman enters and starts beating the man about the head and shoulders with her umbrella.

Mr. Jack in the Dressing Room

AM&B © H44028 Mar. 29, 1904

Cameraman: A. E. Weed

Location: Studio, N.Y.C. *Photographed:* Mar. 16, 1904

22 ft. FLA3113 (print) FRA0449 (neg.)

Three young ladies, all dressed in either leotards or brief costumes, can be seen with their backs to the camera as they peer into mirrors attached to a wall of a backstage dressing room set. A rather corpulent man enters and begins pouring drinks for the young women and otherwise disporting himself by putting on pieces of their costumes and cavorting about the room. The door opens, and a severely dressed woman carrying an umbrella enters, grabs the man, and begins beating him about the head and shoulders as she ushers him out of the presence of the chorus girls.

Mr. Jones' Burglar

Biograph © J130484 Aug. 10, 1909

Director: D. W. Griffith *Cameramen:* G. W. Bitzer, Arthur Marvin *Script:* Frank Woods

Cast: Florence Lawrence, John Cumpson, Arthur Johnson, Frank Powell, Harry Salter, Owen Moore, William J. Butler, Tony O'Sullivan, Mack Sennett

Location: Coytesville, N.J.; Studio, N.Y.C. *Photographed:* June 26 and July 1909

141 ft. FLA5579 (print) FRA2693 (neg.)

The first scene is in the living room of a modest home where a woman (Florence Lawrence) is scolding her husband (John Cumpson) for going to his club and leaving her alone. This is followed by scenes from three camera positions of a poker game that Mr. Jones wins. On his way home, he notices a man (Mack Sennett) with a pistol trying to enter his home. Mr. Jones seizes the opportunity to become a hero and also to escape his wife's ire, so he forces the burglar to enter through the window while he runs in through the door. His wife finds him holding the burglar at bay, with the nervous burglar's own pistol. The last scene shows the wife hugging her heroic husband.

Mr. Jones Has a Card Party

AM&B © H121796 Jan. 19, 1909

Director: D. W. Griffith *Cameraman:* G. W. Bitzer *Script:* Frank Woods

Cast: Florence Lawrence, John Cumpson, Arthur Johnson, Mack Sennett, Flora Finch, Jeanie Macpherson

Location: Grand Central Station and Studio, N.Y.C. *Photographed:* Dec. 16, 17–23, 1908

219 ft. FLA5580 (print) FRA2440 (neg.)

Mr. Jones, delighted that his wife and her club plan to leave town for a few days, holds a card party that turns into a drunken brawl. The host and his guests start their revelry at the same time their wives miss the train. The women return and find a considerable number of men in various stages of inebriation and the host missing. The drunken guests realize they could ruin their host's standing with his wife so they create a diversion by pretending to capture a burglar. They get Mr. Jones dressed and out the window so that he can return through the front door. The film ends as Mrs. Jones is embracing him for being a nice man even after a wicker hamper of liquor bottles is discovered under the table.

Mrs. Jones Entertains

See: Jones Entertains

Mrs. Jones' Lover

Biograph © J130780 Aug. 19, 1909

Director: D. W. Griffith *Cameraman:* G. W. Bitzer *Script:* Frank Woods

Cast: Florence Lawrence, Dorothy Bernard, John Cumpson, Tony O'Sullivan

Location: Studio, N.Y.C. *Photographed:* May 27 and June 18, 1909

175 ft. FLA5581 (print) FRA2441 (neg.)

A maid dusting the furniture and bric-a-brac in the living room of a modest house accidentally breaks a vase. She sends for a repairman to fix it, and when he leaves he forgets to take his black derby. The man of the house comes home, and it is evident that he is spoiling for a fight. He spies the black derby, knows it is not his, and begins to berate his wife for being a cheat. The wife crawls under a chair for safety, and the husband continues with his tantrum. At this juncture, the repairman comes back for his hat. The maid seizes the opportunity to break up the fight between her employers. The film ends with the couple embracing as he realizes his wife is faithful, and she is delighted because he loves her.

Mixed Babies

AM&B © H111646 June 10, 1908

Cameraman: G. W. Bitzer

Location: Studio and vicinity, N.Y.C. *Photographed:* Apr. 27, 1908

215 ft. FLA5582 (print) FRA2442 (neg.)

This split-reel comedy is a chase by a group of irate women after a uniformed doorman who switches baby carriages while the mothers are in a store. The camera was set up outside a department store where a sale on hats is in progress, and women are checking baby carriages before going in. A mischievous boy switches tags on perambulators, and the women redeem the wrong babies. All of the women return to the front of the store, and the uniformed checker flees for his life, but the women apprehend him as the film ends. There is a close-up of a black and a white woman, each holding her respective baby. The camera is in tight to a "two shot." During the picture, spectators can be seen watching the movie being made.

Mixed Bathing

AM&B © H51628 Oct. 14, 1904

104 ft. FLA5003 (print) FRA2060 (neg.)

A man and a woman are sitting on the sand at the seashore. The man notices women bathing, waits until his wife falls asleep, and joins them after renting a bathing suit from a bathhouse on wheels. His spouse wakes, discovers her husband missing, and notices he is in bathing with other women. She seizes her umbrella and rushes into the surf after him.

The Mob Outside the Temple of Music at the Pan-American Exposition

Edison © H8590 Sept. 11, 1901

Location: Buffalo, N.Y. *Photographed:* Sept. 6, 1901

37 ft. FLA4364 (print) FLA5229 (neg., copy 1) FPA0093 (35mm neg.) FRA1503 (neg., copy 2)

[Site of President McKinley's Assassination]

The camera was positioned at such a height behind a large group of people outside an exhibit building that mainly hats are visible.

Model Posing Before Mirror

AM&B © H28554 Feb. 24, 1903

17 ft. FLA3139 (print) FRA0472 (neg.)

The first scene shows a set with a large full-length mirror at a one-quarter angle from the camera position. The first action is of a buxom woman dressed in a full, white leotard approaching the mirror. During the remainder of the film, the woman continually looks at her reflection in the mirror. It is difficult to decide whether she is viewing herself with alarm or approbation. Her pirouette and gestures are limited.

The Model That Didn't Pose
AM&B © H43567 Mar. 22, 1904
Cameraman: A. E. Weed
Location: Studio, N.Y.C. *Photographed:* Feb. 18, 1904
39 ft. FLA3957 (print) FRA1167 (neg.)

This farce opens on a scene where an artist is posing two models in leotards. Two fully clothed women enter and apparently attempt to convince the artist to use them rather than his present models. An older woman carrying an umbrella and wearing a hat tied on with a scarf attempts to convince the late arrivals not to pose.

The Modern Prodigal
Biograph © J144748 Aug. 30, 1910
Director: D. W. Griffith *Cameraman:* G. W. Bitzer
Cast: Guy Hedlund, George Nicholls, Kate Bruce, Jack Pickford, Alfred Paget, W. Chrystie Miller
Location: Cuddebackville, N.Y. *Photographed:* July 28 and 30, 1910
399 ft. FLA5583 (print) FRA2444 (neg.)

This picture was shot entirely outdoors. A young man of the community, now an escaped convict, returns to see his aged mother. Prison guards can be seen searching thoroughly for him while he hides in the bushes near a creek where two boys are swimming. One boy gets out in deep water, and the current begins to carry him away. The criminal jumps into the water and rescues him, just as the boy's father, the sheriff, appears on the scene. The sheriff thanks the convict profusely but takes him into custody. He arms his wife and leaves the convict in her charge while he harnesses a horse. The wife pretends to fall asleep, and the last scene shows the prisoner picking up the bundle of clothes she has provided for him and kissing her brow.

A Modern Sappho
AM&B © H63378 July 15, 1905
Cameraman: G. W. Bitzer
Location: Studio, N.Y.C. *Photographed:* June 30, 1905
30 ft. FLA3821 (print) FRA1051 (neg.)

A masked man creeps down a flight of stairs, part of a set. The farthest wall from the camera position contains a door, it opens and an aged, bearded man enters with a young and attractive woman. As they approach the stairs where the masked man is hiding, he hits the bearded man on the head with a club. The old man falls to the floor where he remains motionless. The young woman searches him and removes his wallet. The masked man picks her up and carries her up the stairs.

A Mohawk's Way
Biograph © J145352 Sept. 14, 1910
Director: D. W. Griffith *Cameraman:* G. W. Bitzer
Cast: Dorothy Davenport, George Nicholls, Alfred Paget, Mack Sennett, Claire McDowell, W. J. Butler
Location: Delaware Water Gap, N.J. *Photographed:* Aug. 9 – 12, 1910
398 ft. FLA5584 (print) FRA2443 (neg.)

The plot revolves around early American settlers and the Indians and a conflict between good and evil. A white doctor refuses to treat a sick Indian child, so his wife ministers in his stead. Later, due to the settlers' indiscretions and cruelties, the Indians take to the warpath and kill many of the settlers, including the white doctor. The only survivor is his wife who is spared because of her earlier kindness to the ailing Indian child. The white woman is returned to another settlement by the Indians.

Moki Snake Dance by Wolpi [Walpapi] Indians
Edison © H11269 Dec. 12, 1901
Camera: James H. White [?]
Location: Ariz.
24 ft. FLA3388 (print) FRA0685 (neg.)

A snake dance was photographed from a single-camera position. The condition of the film is very poor.

Money Mad
AM&B © H118991 Nov. 28, 1908
Director: D. W. Griffith. *Cameraman:* G. W. Bitzer
Cast: Arthur Johnson, Harry Salter, Mack Sennett, Charles Inslee, Florence Lawrence
Location: Studio and nearby streets, N.Y.C. *Photographed:* Oct. 28 and Nov. 2 and 16, 1908
263 ft. FLA5585 (print) FRA2445 (neg.)

The opening scene is of a beggar imploring people to give him money. He robs a young woman passerby and runs off to his basement hideaway, where he avariciously counts his money. He is observed as he changes some stolen money in a bank, and two rough-looking men follow him home and kill him. They take his money to their shack, send the old woman there out, and divide the loot. Each lies down on a blanket and feigns sleep. Both are armed, and suddenly each gets up and strikes the other at the same instant and both fall dead. The old woman comes back, sees the two men dead, and hungrily starts counting the money. She knocks over a candle and sets fire to the place, and the last scene shows the three of them burning up.

Monitor "Terror"
Edison © 25563 Apr. 22, 1898
26 ft. FLA4224 (print) FRA1383 (neg.)
[Spanish-American War]

The short length of this single-camera position film makes anything but a cursory identification impossible. The film, photographed from a dockside, shows a little of the below-deck structure of a large naval vessel. Judging from the mooring lines, the tide is out. However, the superstructure and part of one turret are readily distinguishable. Before the film ends, two American sailors in white uniforms approach the dock.

Monkey Business
AM&B © H62750 June 29, 1905
Cameraman: G. W. Bitzer
Location: Studio, N.Y.C. *Photographed:* June 16, 1905
20 ft. FLA3826 (print) FRA1054 (neg.)

A woman in a light-colored dress is sitting cross-legged on a table directly in front of the camera. Behind her is a potted palm. In her lap she has a banana. She attempts to impersonate a monkey by distorting her face, scratching herself, and eating the banana.

Monkey's Feast
AM&B © H33544 July 18, 1903
Date: 1896
19 ft. FLA2462 (print) FRA0744 (neg.)

The entire film shows two rhesus monkeys chained together on a perch. Each has a banana, but during the short length of the film does nothing but hold it.

M. Lavelle, Physical Culture, no. 1
AM&B © H59311 Apr. 11, 1905
Cameraman: F. S. Armitage
Location: Studio, N.Y.C. *Photographed:* Apr. 1, 1905
32 ft. FLA4728 (print) FRA1743 (neg.)

This is a single-camera position film of muscle-flexing exercises by a professional physical culturist. The expansion, contraction, and flexing of the muscles and chest were done to display not only the prowess but also the control of the demonstrator.

M. Lavelle, Physical Culture, no. 2
AM&B © H59312 Apr. 11, 1905
Cameraman: F. S. Armitage
Location: Studio, N.Y.C. *Photographed:* Apr. 1, 1905
29 ft. FLA4729 (print) FRA1744 (neg.)

This single-camera position film shows a professional physical culturist displaying his ability to separate his muscles by flexing them. He goes through all of the competitive positions.

The Monster
Méliès © H33098 June 30, 1903
Creator: Georges Méliès *Cast:* Georges Méliès
Location: Montreuil, France *Date:* Spring 1903
Original title: Le Monstre
72 ft. FLA4730 (print) FRA2864 (neg.)

The first scene shows a backdrop of the Sphinx and one or two pyramids. Two actors walk out and salaam to the Sphinx and to one another. One goes off stage and drags back with him a casketlike box from which he removes a human skeleton. He seats the skeleton and drapes it in material. The skeleton them becomes alive and jumps around until one of the actors throws it into the arms of the other, whereupon it becomes a skeleton again.

Le Monstre
See: The Monster

Montreal Fire Department on Runners
Edison © H2443 Mar. 19, 1901
Location: Montreal
50 ft. FLA4731 (print) FRA1745 (neg.)

The subject is the fire apparatus of a large city. During the film, personnel trucks, hook-and-ladder wagons, pumper engines, boilers, etc., go by the camera, which was positioned on a street in Montreal, Canada. All of the fire equipment was mounted on sled runners.

Moonlight on Lake Maggiore
Edison © H16717 Apr. 18, 1902
Location: Northern Italy
33 ft. FLA3186 (print) FRA0512 (neg.)

The first scenes were photographed through the leaves of a tree high above a lake. Nearing the camera, in the area covered, is a gondola complete with gondolier and three passengers. The first gondola leaves the viewing area, but is succeeded by another with four female passengers. The title indicates that the film was photographed by the light of the moon. However, this is questionable. Nevertheless, there is a bright path of light, as if from the moon, on the water.

A Moonlight Serenade; or The Miser Punished
See: Au Clair de la Lune

The Moonshiner
AM&B © H49329 Aug. 19, 1904
Director: Wallace McCutcheon *Cameraman:* G. W. Bitzer
Cast: Wallace McCutcheon, Harold Vosburg
Location: Scarsdale, N.Y. *Photographed:* June 28 and July 5, 1904
394 ft. FLA5232 (print) FRA8317 (neg.)

The story concerns some people who are suspected of making illicit alcoholic beverages—their surveillance, capture, and subsequent death as a result of resisting Federal Revenue officers. The camera was positioned outdoors for all scenes, and each scene is preceded by a title that describes it. The film shows the front of a country house, the barter of raw materials for the finished product, jugged whiskey, and the operation of the still. There are two close-ups and some camera panning in this motion picture.

The Moonshiner
AM&B © H49329 Aug. 19, 1904
Director: Wallace McCutcheon *Cameraman:* G. W. Bitzer
Cast: Wallace McCutcheon, Harold Vosburg
Location: Scarsdale, N.Y. *Photographed:* June 28, July 2 and 5, 1904
394 ft. FLA5232 (print) FRA8317 (neg.)

The story concerns some people who are suspected of making illicit alcoholic beverages and comprises their surveillance, capture, and subsequent death as a result of resisting Federal Revenue officers. The camera was positioned outdoors for all scenes, and each scene is preceded by a title that describes it. The film shows the front of a country house, the barter of raw materials for the finished product, jugged whiskey, and the operation of the still. There are two close-ups and some camera panning in this film.

Moose Hunt in New Brunswick
AM&B © H71528 Jan. 3, 1906
Cameraman: G. W. Bitzer
Location: Portland, Maine, and New Brunswick, Canada *Photographed:* Sept. 9–10 and 15–16, 1905
355 ft. FLA5586 (print) FRA2684 (neg.)

The picture begins at a railroad station where a camp guide, Bill Rider, of the camp of the same name, is waiting for his guests. There is a scene of a small switch engine on a narrow-gauge railroad track leading into the interior. This is followed by scenes of wagon trains and of a portage. The guides prepare meals, and the hunting party shoots two moose. This film probably is the first part of a picture released in June 1907 under the title of A Caribou Hunt

See also: Stalking and Hunting Caribou, Newfoundland

Morning Colors on U.S. Cruiser "Raleigh"

Edison © 29259 Apr. 28, 1899

24 ft. FLA4053 (print) FRA1238 (neg.)

[Spanish-American War]

The film shows the after deck of a military vessel, including the flagstaff and the American flag. There are two persons, visible: a Marine raising the colors to the top of the mast, and one saluting the flag.

Morro Castle, Havana Harbor

Edison © 25324 Apr. 21, 1898

Location: Havana

26 ft FLA4060 (print) FRA1244 (neg.)

[Spanish-American War]

Photographed from aboard a ship, the film has good 180 degree coverage, from a single-camera position, of Morro Castle during the Spanish-American War.

Mother's Angel Child

AM&B © H63531 July 19, 1905

Cameraman: F. A. Dobson

Location: Studio, N.Y.C. *Date:* July 11, 1905

47 ft. FLA5105 (print) FRA2061 (neg.)

The set represents the sitting room and foyer of a two-story house, and is arranged so that a portion of a child's bedroom is visible. When the film starts, a woman is leading a reluctant young girl, in a nightgown, away from a window and into the bedroom. The woman goes to the outer door and lets in a well-dressed man who hands her his top hat. He sits down and they begin to talk. The young girl looks over the top of the transom and uses a bean shooter to annoy the visitor. She is admonished and ordered to go to bed. The tête-à-tête continues while the young girl empties ashes into the visitor's top hat. When the visitor starts to put on his hat, the ashes spill all over him.

Moulin Rouge Dancers

AM&B © H23792 Nov. 11, 1902

Date: 1898 [?]

19 ft. FLA3849 (print) FRA1108 (neg.)

Four women dressed in the costume of the era perform a can-can. They were photographed from a single camera position.

Mount and Dismount, Gatling Gun

Edison © 71219 Dec. 18, 1897

24 ft. FLA4455 (print) FRA1558 (neg.)

This single camera position film shows an officer and six enlisted men of the Army as they demonstrate the assembly drill of a Gatling gun

See also: Gatling Gun-Firing by Squad, and Gatling Gun Crew in Action

Mt. Pelee in Eruption and Destruction of St. Pierre

Edison © H18370 May 31, 1902

45 ft. FLA4732 (print) FRA1746 (neg.)

This single-camera position film shows a miniature working set of an island with a volcano that erupts, causing the city at the foot of the miniature mountain to be destroyed by simulated lava and fire.

Mt. Pelee Smoking Before Eruption

Edison © H18369 May 31, 1902

33 ft. FLA4733 (print) FRA1747 (neg.)

This shows a miniature scene constructed to make the viewer believe that it was an event a long distance away. The camera shows a small area of water (table-top), a miniature city next to it, and, behind the city, a tiny mountain belching man-made smoke as if it were about to erupt. There are indications that possibly this film was only distributed by an American film company and not made here.

Mount Stephen

AM&B © H17965 May 21, 1902

Cameraman: G. W. Bitzer

Location: Canadian Pacific R. R. near Field Station, B.C., Canada *Date:* Oct. 18, 1899

29 ft. FLA3816 (print) FRA1047 (neg.)

The camera was mounted on the front of a railroad train traveling over a single track that wound in and around land points in mountainous country. The camera photographed the side areas of the track, showing trees, telegraph poles, and some running water by the roadbed.

Mount Tamalpais R.R., no. 1

Edison © 16437 Mar. 10, 1898

Location: Marin County, Calif.

29 ft. FLA4271 (print) FRA1426 (neg.)

The camera was mounted on the back of a railroad train traveling up Mt. Tamalpais, and the camera was on one train photographing another as it started the scenic route.

Mount Tamalpais, R.R., no. 2

Edison © 16438 Mar. 10, 1898

Location: Marin County, Calif.

29 ft. FLA4272 (print) FRA1427 (neg.)

The camera was mounted on a flat car directly behind an engine as it proceeded along a single track built up the side of Mt. Tamalpais. The short length of the film does not permit any further description.

Mount Taw R.R., no. 3

Edison © 17707 Mar. 15, 1898

Location: Mount Tamalpais, Marin County, Calif.

58 ft. FLA4734 (print) FRA1748 (neg.)

The camera was placed on the back of a railroad train proceeding down the grade of Mt. Tamalpais. Directly in front of the train bearing the camera is another steam locomotive backing down the grade. An excursion car, laden with tourists, can be seen on the turns.

The Mountaineer's Honor

Biograph © J135135 Nov. 26, 1909

Director: D. W. Griffith *Cameraman:* G. W. Bitzer

Cast: Mary Pickford, Arthur Johnson, James Kirkwood, Kate Bruce, Owen Moore, George Nicholls, Mack Sennett, Tony O'Sullivan

Location: Cuddebackville, N.Y.; Studio, N.Y.C. *Photographed:* Oct. 14, 19 and 20, 1909

388 ft. FLA0036 (print, copy 1) FLA5611 (print, copy 2) FRA2811 (neg.)

This film was made in a mountainous area. A young mountain woman (Mary Pickford) falls in love with a valley visitor (Arthur Johnson), who jilts her. Her brother (James Kirkwood) attempts to make the valley man marry her, but is laughed at for his effort. He then takes the law into his own hands and kills the man. The valley people form a posse, go to the mountain home, and capture the brother. The mother (Kate Bruce) learns that they intend to hang her son and, under the guise of giving him some water, shoots him so that the family honor will not be stained by a hanging. The last scene shows "Harum-Scarum" (the daughter), the cause of all the tragedy, going off with her mountain admirer (Owen Moore).

Move On

Edison © H37369 Oct. 27, 1903

Cameraman: A. C. Abadie

N.Y.C. *Photographed:* Oct. 22, 1903

38 ft. FLA4735 (print) FRA2840 (neg.)

The cameraman placed his equipment on the street near the curbing where several pushcarts and street peddlers had stopped to display their wares. Vegetable pushcarts are in the immediate foreground, while in the background is an elevated railroad that crosses the street on which the camera is placed. A policeman wearing a tall hat and carrying a nightstick appears and orders all the peddlers and pushcarts to move from their locations.

A Moving Picture

AM&B © H16355 Apr. 10, 1902

Date: Circa 1898

17 ft. FLA4244 (print) FRA1400 (neg.)

From a single-camera position an old-fashioned stove used for heating is visible on a set. A man is busy repairing it when the door opens and another man enters and starts to help the first man. The door opens again; a woman with a large laundry basket walks in and begins to harangue the two men repairing the stove. The picture ends as the stovepipe on which they are working breaks, releasing black soot all over them and the laundry.

Muggsy Becomes a Hero

Biograph © J144969 Sept. 6, 1910

Director: D. W. Griffith *Cameraman:* Arthur Marvin.

Cast: Mary Pickford, Billy Quirk, Eddie Dillon, Kate Bruce, Mack Sennett, Grace Henderson, Jack Pickford, Edwin August

Location: Cuddebackville, N.Y.; Coytesville, N.J. *Photographed:* July 21, 26 and 27 and Aug. 2-3, 1910

283 ft. FLA5588 (print) FRA2446 (neg.)

A young lady sends a note to her boyfriend asking him to meet her after church. While he is waiting for the services to end, another note is handed to him, requesting him to escort two old maids through a bad area. Though the boy friend is disappointed, he resolutely starts to escort the two women home. They are set upon by two thugs whom our hero manages to thrash soundly. Our hero becomes the town hero, with the young lady proudly standing beside him.

Mules Swimming Ashore at Baiquiri, Cuba

Edison © 46691 Aug. 5, 1898

Cameraman: William Paley

Location: Baiquiri, Cuba *Photographed:* June 28, 1898

34 ft. FLA3556 (print) FRA0832 (neg.)

[Spanish-American War]

The first sight is of an ocean area with a large ship at anchor. A rowboat escorting two mules approaches the camera. The film ends as the mules walk, unescorted, out of the waves onto the beach.

Multicycle Race

AM&B © H26850 Jan. 9, 1903

11 ft. FLA3313 (print) FRA0627 (neg.)

The first scene shows an outdoor area surrounded by factory buildings in the background, while in the foreground is part of the straightaway and most of a turn of a bicycle race track. A specially constructed two-wheeled bicycle comes toward the camera. Five men are riding it, all of them working the pedals in unison. They are followed by four more similarly constructed vehicles carrying the same number of persons. Judging by the activity, it must have been a race. The complete competitive group passes the camera two times.

See also: Paced Bicycle Race

Murder

See: The Wages of Sin

Murder and Suicide

See: The Unfaithful Wife

Murder of Willie

See: Ten Nights in a Bar-Room

Murphy's Wake

AM&B © H38153 Nov. 14, 1903

74 ft. FLA5106 (print) FRA2062 (neg.)

The picture is made up of three scenes. The first is in a yard where a group of people dressed in Irish costumes are dancing. It ends in a fight in which a man is killed. The second scene is the final church services, and the third is the wake. Several people are seated around the bier drinking and making gestures of lamentation. The "dead" man sits up, reaches for a nearby pitcher, takes several drinks, and lies back down. This drinking by the "deceased" continues until the keeners notice him. They rush out in alarm. The last scene shows the alleged deceased in his shroud eating, drinking, dancing, and laughing alone.

Musical Bayonet Exercises

AM&B © H33882 July 28, 1903

Cameraman: A. E. Weed

Date: July 22, 1903

42 ft. FLA4736 (print) FRA1749 (neg.)

From a single-camera position, at a distance not conducive to good identification, approximately fifty men can be seen executing company front facing the camera and doing calisthenics with military rifles. The distance and the condition of the film do not allow identification of the terrain or the individuals.

See also: Battle Flags of the 9th U.S. Infantry, Musical Calisthenics, and Shelter Tent Drill

Musical Calisthenics

AM&B © H33885 July 28, 1903
Cameraman: A. E. Weed
Date: July 22, 1903
44 ft. FLA4737 (print) FRA1750 (neg.)

The camera was positioned on a drill field at a distance from a company of military cadets or recruits doing calisthenics in unison. The camera was too far from the subjects to make further description possible.

See also: Battle Flags of the 9th U.S. Infantry Musical Bayonet Exercises, and Shelter Tent Drill

The Musical Ride

Edison © H8695 Sept. 16, 1901
50 ft. FLA4738 (print) FRA1751 (neg.)

The entire film was devoted to showing the maneuvers and drills of an especially skilled group of horses and their riders executing several drills with great precision.

Must Be in Bed Before Ten

AM&B © H28553 Feb. 24, 1903
10 ft. FLA3124 (print) FRA0458 (neg.)

A young girl enters a room furnished as a woman's boudoir. She stands on one side of the room, faces the camera, and begins removing her clothing, piece by piece. When she has removed all except one or two pieces of apparel, she sits on the edge of the bed and starts unlacing her shoes, just as the film ends. The film was photographed with artificial light.

Mutiny on a Russian Battleship

See: Mutiny on the Black Sea

Mutiny on the Black Sea

AM&B © H63385 July 12, 1905
Cameraman: F. A. Dobson
Location: Studio, N.Y.C. *Date:* July 8, 1905
79 ft. FLA5107 (print) FRA2063 (neg.)

This film reconstructs a mutiny aboard the armored Russian cruiser *Potemkin.* All of the action occurs on a set of the deck of the battleship. Several actors dressed as Russian sailors have a lively discussion over their unhappy condition. They draw lots, and one of the sailors is designated to take a message to the naval officers. He hands a piece of paper to one of three officers grouped on the foredeck of the ship. After reading the note, the officer pulls out his pistol and shoots the sailor, killing him. All of the officers are immediately set upon by the sailors and murdered, and the victorious enlisted men are shown hoisting a black flag. Also released under the titles Mutiny on a Russian Battleship, and Mutiny on the Potemkin.

Mutiny on the Potemkin

See: Mutiny on the Black Sea

The Mysterious Cafe

Edison © H11495 Dec. 16, 1901
Cameraman: Edwin S. Porter
37 ft. FLA4739 (print) FRA1752 (neg.)

The poor quality of this film does not permit much description of the detail. However, it was built around a series of incidents made possible by the use of stop-action photography. People, furniture, and objects materialize and disappear, move, turn upside down, and reappear continually throughout the picture.

The Mysterious Midgets

AM&B © H52703 Nov. 8, 1904
74 ft. FLA5108 (print) FRA2064 (neg.)

The film is of a combination magic and puppet act, with the magician seated at a table. The camera was close enough to photograph only from the top of his table to the top of the black velvet drape that hid his assistant. The magician's associate aided him by making the props move and dance about the table. All of the magician's tricks were made possible by the use of stop-action photography. The puppeteer stuck his head through the black velvet drape and used black gloves which would not photograph to manipulate the puppets. The film ends when both of the magicians shake hands in front of the camera.

The Mystery of the Missing Jewel Casket

See: The Great Jewel Mystery

A Mystic Re-Incarnation

AM&B © H25971 Dec. 31, 1902
Cameraman: Arthur Marvin
Location: Roof studio, N.Y.C. *Date:* May 18, 1901
24 ft. FLA4363 (print) FRA1502 (neg.)

The camera was placed as if it were a member of the audience at a vaudeville act. The act shows a man dressed in the clothes of the Louis XIV era. He enters stage center, waves his wand and conjures up a sheet that he places on the floor of the stage in front of him. He gestures with arms outstretched, and a leg with a woman's shoe appears in each hand and is placed on the sheet. The torso, the head, and the arms of a woman appear and are also placed on the sheet. The magician rolls up the sheet, claps his hands, and a woman in white leotards appears before him. Artificial light was used to photograph this film, and no background is visible.

Mystic Shriners' Day, Dreamland, Coney Island

Edison © H64177 Dec. 31, 1902
Location: Coney Island, N.Y.
95 ft. FLA5109 (print) FRA2065 (neg.)

The Shriners' Convention in Coney Island was the motivating purpose of this film. The first camera position shows the delegates from various lodges parading along a boardwalk. Some are riding camels, others carrying parts of floats, banners, or signs. The second camera position shows the exhibit ring and race track. The same persons who were seen earlier parading on the boardwalk now walk around a portion of the exhibit ring for the benefit of the spectators in the grandstand.

See also: Hippodrome Races, Dreamland, Coney Island

The Mystic Swing

Edison © D6368 Mar. 21, 1900
Cameraman: Edwin S. Porter
22 ft. FLA3248 (print) FRA0571 (neg.)

This vaudeville act was photographed from the audience. As it begins, two men dressed in formal tail coats and knee breeches are standing by a swing in front of a painted backdrop of an outdoor scene. The man at camera left makes a magician's gesture and a young woman in a nightgown is suddenly sitting in the swing. The conjurer nods to the other man who makes a gesture, and the young lady disappears. Another young woman is made to appear and disappear. A human skeleton is conjured up and made to vanish. As the film ends, the two young ladies reappear and hold hands with the magicians as they all take a bow.

The Mystical Flame

Méliès © H33236 July 6, 1903
Creator: Georges Méliès
Cast: Georges Méliès
Location: Montreuil, France *Date:* Spring 1903
Original title: La Flamme Merveilleuse
52 ft. FLA4740 (print) FLA5962 (35mm pos.) FPA0096 (35mm neg.) FRA1753 (neg.)

Before a painted backdrop, a man (Méliès) appears in period costumes and does tricks with a handkerchief, stretching it into the size of a bed sheet. He snaps it and makes a man appear who helps him move stage props and cause things to appear and disappear, burst into flame, or explode into smoke. The projection over live action is interesting.

The Narrow Road

Biograph © J171930 Aug. 5, 1912
Director: D. W. Griffith *Cameraman:* G. W. Bitzer
Cast: Mary Pickford, Elmer Booth, Charles Hill Mailes, Jack Pickford, Alfred Paget, Tony O'Sullivan
Location: N.Y.C.
400 ft. FLA0038 (print) FLA0134 (neg.)

The picture begins by showing a happy young woman (Mary Pickford) tidying up a one-room apartment. The establishing title indicates she is on the way to visit her prison inmate husband (Elmer Booth). Several scenes of prison life, introducing her husband and the man who was responsible for his being there, follow.

After the release of the two inmates, the husband vows never to return to his old ways and obtains a construction job, while his friend immediately goes back to his counterfeiting activities. When the counterfeiter realizes he is under surveillance, he begs his former prison mate to hide a suitcase containing his tools, which he agrees to do. The suitcase is stolen by a pair of thieves, who have also been keeping track of his activities. When the police apprehend the counterfeiter, they also capture the pair of thieves. The picture ends with a scene of the husband back at his construction job, happy to be respected for his honesty.

Native Daughters

Edison © 16434 Mar. 10, 1898
19 ft. FLA4235 (print) FRA1392 (neg.)

The camera was positioned in back of a crowd standing on streets and watching a parade. During the extent of the film, attractively dressed women riding sidesaddle on horses pass the camera position. Just as the picture ends, a large horse-drawn float with several young ladies in long dresses and wearing picture hats supporting a five-pointed star approximately ten feet high can be seen.

Native Woman Washing a Negro Baby in Nassau, B.I.

Edison © H30397 Apr. 8, 1903
38 ft. FLA3635 (print) FRA0892 (neg.)

The cameraman placed his camera on the sand and photographed a rather large black woman washing a rather small black boy in a conventional galvanized iron washtub. As the job of bathing progresses, the cameraman pans his camera to show other natives who apparently resent being photographed as they scatter in all directions.

Native Women Coaling a Ship and Scrambling for Money

Edison © H30406 Apr. 8, 1903
Location: St. Thomas, V.I.
56 ft. FLA4741 (print) FRA1754 (neg.)

The film shows a group of women employed to replenish the coal supply of a large steam vessel. Only a portion of the vessel, tied to a dock, is shown. Several women scramble on the dock for money thrown to them by the ship's passengers. Another view shows native women lining up to take coal into the baskets on their heads and then walking up the gangway provided for the delivery of the coal.

Native Women Coaling a Ship at St. Thomas, D.W.I.

Edison © H30403 Apr. 8, 1903
Location: St. Thomas, V.I.
41 ft. FLA4742 (print) FRA1755 (neg.)

The camera was placed on a dock near the bottom of a gangway provided for the women, and a few men, employed to carry coal in baskets onto the ship, which can be seen tied alongside the dock. During the course of the film, approximately a hundred women and a few men, with baskets on their heads, are seen walking up the gangway.

Native Women Washing Clothes at St. Vincent, B.W.I.

Edison © H30399 Apr. 8, 1903
Location: St. Vincent, V.I.
35 ft. FLA3651 (print) FRA0906 (neg.)

Several native women are laundering clothes in a stream. They vigorously pound the clothes on a rock. The women wear no garments from the waist up.

Naval Apprentices at Sail Drill on Historic Ship Constellation

Edison © D22020 Nov. 22, 1900
Location: Naval Training School, Newport, R.I.
60 ft. FLA4743 (print) FRA1756 (neg.)

The *U.S.S. Constellation,* a full-rigged topsail sailing vessel, can be seen at anchor with her deck crew in position to furl sail. As the film progresses, the crew sets the topsails, the mains, the jib, and spinnakers. The film appears to have been taken at intervals while the crew was setting the ship's canvas.

See also: Naval Sham Battle at Newport, Gun Drill by Naval Cadets at Newport Training School, and Gymnasium Exercises and Drill at Newport Training School.

Naval Battle, St. Louis Exposition
AM&B © H50483   Sept. 14, 1904
Cameraman: A. E. Weed
Location: St. Louis *Date:* Sept. 6, 1904
83 ft.   FLA5110 (print)   FRA2066 (neg.)
[Louisiana Purchase Exposition]

This single-camera position film shows a large water tank designed to look like either the Havana Harbor or Manila Bay. Approximately twenty ship models of the American and Spanish navies are moving about on the water. There are simulated explosions, gunfire, etc., to give the impression of a moving picture of a full-scale naval battle.

Naval Parade
AM&B © H19654   July 2, 1902
Cameraman: F. S. Armitage
Location: N.Y.C. *Date:* June 18, 1900
30 ft.   FLA3693 (print)   FRA0942 (neg.)

A parade of large naval vessels of battleship class can be seen steaming in column formation up a river. The view of the moving naval vessels is constantly obscured throughout the film by many other vessels of various types, from large steam yachts to small harbor tugs, some carrying spectators.

Naval Sham Battle at Newport
Edison © D22019   Nov. 22, 1900
Location: Naval Training School, Newport, R.I.
46 ft.   FLA4744 (print)   FRA1757 (neg.)

The camera is overlooking terrain that slopes toward a body of water. In the foreground, approximately a battalion of enlisted naval personnel repelling invaders approaching in small boats in the adjacent water. Troop movements, gunfire from the boats, and the land troops can all be seen but are not easily identifiable.

See also: Naval Apprentices at Sail Drill on Historic Ship Constellation, Gun Drill by Naval Cadets at Newport Training School, and Gymnasium Exercises and Drill at Newport Training School

Nearsighted Mary
Lubin Mfg. Co.   © J131734   July 29, 1909
Location: Philadelphia
194 ft.   FLA5587 (print)

A maid (played by a man), presumably nearly blind without her glasses, applies for and gets a job in the house of a well-to-do family. Her mistress shows the maid to her quarters and the kitchen. For an unexplained reason, the maid sneezes (the sneeze is a close-up) which causes her to lose her glasses. She starts breaking dishes, spills food over her employer, falls over a broken appliance, and otherwise makes such a mess of matters that the family throw her bodily out of the house.

The Necklace
Biograph   © J129504   July 3, 1909
Director: D. W. Griffith *Cameramen:* Arthur Marvin, G. W. Bitzer
Cast: Rose King, Charles Inslee, Mack Sennett, Billy Quirk, Mary Pickford, Arthur Johnson, James Kirkwood, Owen Moore, Lottie Pickford, Frank Powell, Caroline Harris (Mrs. Richard Barthleness)
Location: Studio, N.Y.C. *Photographed:* May 12-27, 1909
355 ft.   FLA5567 (print)   FRA2688 (neg.)

This film is a free adaptation of Guy de Maupassant's story of the same name. The first scene shows a young couple rejoicing at receiving an invitation to a ball. The young woman buys a new gown and borrows a necklace from a wealthy friend. At the ball, the necklace is stolen, and the remainder of the film shows the couple growing older and older until, by the end of the film, they are near death from overwork and deprivation in their efforts to pay for the replacement of the lost necklace. In the last scene, they are presented with the necklace they had spent their lives paying for, the owner having found out what they had done. They also learn that the stolen necklace was of little value.

The Necromancer
AM&B © H32561   June 12, 1903
Cameraman: G. W. Bitzer
Location: Studio, N.Y.C. *Photographed:* June 8, 1903
61 ft.   FLA4745 (print)   FRA1758 (neg.)

The set is of the interior of a cave. A man, seemingly in a trance, and dressed in a pointed cap and a gown decorated with symbols, is seated in front of a painted backdrop, when a young man in evening dress comes through the door of the cave. The young man spends a considerable amount of time explaining exactly what he has in mind to the magician and then hands him a large sum of money. The rest of the film shows the magician conjuring up several attractive young women, each of whom is rejected by the young man. Finally, the young man asks the magician to bring one of them back and, as the film ends, they embrace and leave the cave together. All of the illusions were accomplished by the use of stop-action photography.

Neighbors
Biograph   © J170617   June 25, 1912
Director: Mack Sennett
Cast: Mabel Normand, Sylvia Ashton, Fred Mace, Mack Sennett, Frank Evans, William Beaudine, Charles Avery
Location: Redondo Beach, Calif.
150 ft.   FLA5595 (print)   FRA2448 (neg.)

This farce is a series of scenes that involve a chase intermittently interrupted by titles that describe each event. The film starts when two women on bicycles collide. The husbands decide to fight a duel, but one of the husbands then decides duels are not for him and he takes off, with the rest of the cast in pursuit. The film ends when the pursuers catch up with the pursued as he is having a drink at a sidewalk cafe, and they join him in a friendly drink, the reason for the duel forgotten.

Nellie, the Beautiful Housemaid

Vitagraph © H110099 May 4, 1908
33 ft. FLA4428 (print) FRA1541 (neg., copy 1) FRA2837 (neg., copy 2)

The sequence of events in the finished film is awry. However, the story is self-evident. The plot is built around three elderly gentlemen who place an advertisement in a newspaper for a domestic servant. It is answered, and the three men go to great lengths to improve their appearance in order to make a good impression on the new maid. The film ends as the three gentlemen are seated at their dining room table, and the door opens admitting Nellie, an obese black woman in a plaid dress.

Nelson-Britt Prize Fight

Miles Brothers © H66202—Preliminaries and First Round; H66204—Rounds 6, 7, 8, 9 and 10; H66205—Rounds 11, 12, 13 and 14; H66206—Rounds 16, 17 Sept. 27, 1905
Location: Colma, Calif.
1,549 ft.

Preliminaries and First Round: FLA5596 (print) FRA2715 (neg., copy 1) FRA2716 (neg., copy 2)

Rounds 6, 7, 8, 9 and 10: FLA5597 (print) FRA2717 (neg.) Rounds 11, 12, 13 and 14: FLA5598 (print) FRA2719 (neg.) Rounds 16, 17, 18 and Finish: FLA5599 (print) FRA2718 (neg.)

The camera was positioned in the center of the prize fight ring. As the film progresses, the camera is panned to include all of the people present inside the fences of the boxing stadium. The camera was then moved to show the entire ring and for the remainder of the film, the officials—timekeeper, the two principals, referee, handlers, etc.—were photographed as they came into and out of the ring.

Neptune's Daughters

AM&B © H30750 Apr. 24, 1903
Cameraman: F. S. Armitage
Location: New Jersey in part Date: Dec. 8, 1900 Combination of The Wreck of the Steamer Richmond off Coast of New Jersey (1897), The Sad Sea Waves (1897), and The Ballet of the Ghosts (1899)—respectively productions 349, 351, and 1161.
10 ft. FLA3420 (print) FRA0708 (neg.)

The subject of this film was conveyed by the use of trick photography, in particular, by superimposed double exposure. The first scene shows a sailing vessel at sea riding rather heavy waves. Directly over that film can be seen what appear to be specters which, as the film continues, dissolve into four young women costumed as dancers and wearing garlands of flowers. For the remainder of the film, the four women dance in unison.

Nervy Nat

See: A Tramp on the Roof

Nervy Nat Kisses the Bride

Edison © H51067 Sept. 30, 1904
Cameraman: Edwin S. Porter
54 ft. FLA4746 (print) FRA1759 (neg.)

There are three scenes: the interior of a railroad waiting room and ticket office, the interior of the passenger section of a train, and an exterior showing a train going by the camera. The first scene shows a man in top hat, tailcoat, and spats stealing a train ticket from the pocket of a man sleeping in the waiting room. The second scene is in the train where the newlyweds are seated, with the thief directly behind them. The groom leaves the bride alone, and the villain makes advances to her. He is caught by her husband who asks the conductor to help. The masher is thrown bodily from the observation platform of the moving train, but instead of the actor, a dummy is used. At the end of the film, the live actor is seen walking down the tracks toward the camera.

Nevada Falls

AM&B © H30740 Apr. 24, 1903
Cameraman: G. W. Bitzer
Location: Yosemite Valley, Calif. Date: Sept. 29, 1901
17 ft. FLA3174 (print) FRA0501 (neg.)

The title indicates the film is of the Nevada Falls. It was photographed in the Yosemite Valley from a single-camera position and shows neither the beginning nor the entire falls.

Never Again!

Biograph © J142450 June 22, 1910
Director: D. W. Griffith Cameraman: Arthur Marvin
Cast: Mary Pickford, Mack Sennett, Billy Quirk
Location: Brentwood and Venice, Calif.
Photographed: Mar. 9, 10 and 18, 1910
239 ft. FLA5600 (print) FRA6418 (neg.)

Boy gets girl, boy loses girl, and boy finds girl again is the basis for this comedy. A girl (Mary Pickford) sees her boyfriend (Billy Quirk) with his head close to her sister's as they are engrossed in a book and this causes her to flirt with her boyfriend's friend (Mack Sennett). He takes her for a rowboat ride on the grand canal of Venice, California, and somehow falls in the water. During the period he is under the water, the young girl's first suitor rescues her with another rowboat, which causes a great deal of consternation when the abandoned young man surfaces and finds the girl missing. There is a considerable amount of camera movement, both panning as well as closer approach. All scenes were taken outdoors.

See also: May and December, copyright June 22, 1910

Never Touched Him

AM&B © H37380 Oct. 28, 1903
Cameraman: A. E. Weed
Location: Studio, N.Y.C. Photographed: Oct. 17, 1903
25 ft. FLA3664 (print) FRA0917 (neg.)

The picture opens in a saloon set where four men are playing cards at a table in the foreground. Suddenly three of the players begin beating the fourth. Using stop action photography, a dummy is substituted for the fourth player, and the three men continue beating and kicking it. As the picture ends, the dummy comes back to life. Without too much effort, he thrashes the three men and then is seen at the bar having a drink by himself.

New Black Diamond Express

Edison © D11027 May 26, 1900
Location: Wysock, Pa.

31 ft. FLA4171 (print) FRA1336 (neg.)
[Lehigh Valley Railroad]

The length of the film and the poor quality of the photography do not permit description other than to say that a train can be seen nearing the camera position. In the foreground of this short film are some workmen but it is impossible to discern what they are doing.

See also: Lehigh Valley Black Diamond Express

New Brooklyn Bridge

AM&B © H21955 Mar. 11, 1903
Camera: G. W. Bitzer *Date:* Nov. 12, 1902
Location: N.Y.C.
28 ft. FLA3675 (print) FRA0875 (neg.)

The camera was placed on a structure overlooking the Brooklyn Bridge and, as the picture begins, the camera pans slowly taking in the first arch and cable supports. The pan stops, and the cameraman directs the camera from top to bottom of the span support, and then the film stops. The title on the production record sheet is New Brooklyn Bridge Panorama.

New Brooklyn Bridge Panorama

See: New Brooklyn Bridge

New Brooklyn to New York Via Brooklyn Bridge, no. 1

Edison © 61217 Sept. 22, 1899
Location: Brooklyn Bridge, N.Y.C.
58 ft. FLA4747 (print) FRA1760 (neg.)

The film was photographed from a single-camera position from the front of a railroad train as it crossed the bridge from Brooklyn to Manhattan.

New Brooklyn to New York Via Brooklyn Bridge, no. 2

Edison © 61218 Sept. 22, 1899
Location: Brooklyn Bridge, N.Y.C.
64 ft. FLA4748 (print) FRA1761 (neg.)

The film begins as the vehicle on which the camera is placed begins to move across the Brooklyn Bridge, making a turn on the Manhattan side. Nothing can be seen except what is immediately in front of the car.

The New Maid

AM&B © H32946 June 25, 1903
Cameraman: F. S. Armitage
Location: Roof studio, N.Y.C. *Date:* May 25, 1901
9 ft. FLA3634 (print) FRA0891 (neg.)

The set is of a dining room in a modest home; it was photographed from a single-camera position. A man is sitting at the dining room table and watching the maid prepare the silver and china before setting the table. As the maid approaches him, he grabs her and kisses her. Another woman making gestures of annoyance enters the dining room, removes the maid from the man's lap, and begins beating and shaking him. The film was underexposed, and it is therefore difficult to see much detail.

The New Soubrette

See: The Downward Path

New Sunset Limited

Edison © H16657 Apr. 16, 1902
Location: Southern Pacific R.R., Beaumont, Tex.
38 ft. FLA3942 (print) FRA1153 (neg.)

The photographer placed his camera beside some railroad tracks in order to film the passing of a train, which is not visible as the film begins. What can be seen, though, are the tracks in the foreground, a roadway running parallel to the tracks, and some houses in the distance. As the film progresses, a large steam locomotive pulling eight passenger cars approaches the camera position. As the last of the passenger cars passes by the camera, the film ends.

A New Trick

Biograph © H128181 June 10, 1909
Director: D. W. Griffith *Cameraman:* G. W. Bitzer
Cast: Marion Leonard, Arthur Johnson, Mack Sennett
Location: Edgewater, N.J. *Photographed:* May 11, 1909
78 ft. FLA5111 (print) FRA2067 (neg.)

The story, photographed in the countryside, concerns the efforts of two nice young men to help a young woman recover her stolen purse. The heroine (Marion Leonard) becomes so engrossed in reading a letter that her purse falls unnoticed to the ground. It is picked up by a man in a dark suit and a derby (Mack Sennett) who then denies all knowledge of it. Two well-dressed young men, one of whom is Arthur Johnson, come to the young lady's rescue and help her. Red paint and a sharp stick are used to convey the impression that one of the heroes has been murdered, and when the villain walks into their trap, his naturally dishonest instincts prompt him to offer the heroine's purse as a bribe. They accept it, and Arthur Johnson returns it to her, and she rewards him by giving him her name and address.

New Year's Mummers Parade

See: New Year's Mummies Parade

New Year's Mummies Parade

Edison © H13163 Jan. 17, 1902
Location: Philadelphia *Photographed:* Jan. 1, 1902
28 ft. FLA4446 (print) FRA1551 (neg.)

The camera was positioned beside a wide street to film the participants in a costume parade. Several groups of costumed people pass the camera position during this short film. The title on the original paper print film is New Year's Mummers Parade.

New York Athletic Club at Phila., Pa.

AM&B © H63384 July 15, 1905
Location: Philadelphia
79 ft. FLA5112 (print) FRA2068 (neg.)

The first scene is of a wooden dock low to the water. As the film progresses, eight men carrying a racing shell place the boat in the water alongside the dock. All eight of the oarsmen and the coxswain get in the pulling boat and row away. The remaining scenes are of a man and a woman carrying a parasol being rowed away from the dock in a single-place shell. In the background, canoes paddle by, and rowboats pass the camera.

New York Athletic Club Games, Travers Island
AM&B © H62771 June 30, 1905
Cameraman: G. W. Bitzer
Location: Travers Island, N.Y. *Photographed:* June 10, 1905
206 ft. FLA5601 (print) FRA2450 (neg.)

The subject is a day's outing that interested a considerable number of people, judging from the number of automobiles in the parking area. The cameraman moved his equipment about the area and filmed people as they walked by, automobiles as they passed by, the athletic events—running, jumping, pole vaulting, etc.—and people dining both indoors and outdoors. Whatever the reason for the meet, the film shows it was of considerable interest, and it evidences good management.

New York Caledonian Club's Parade
Edison © H35620 Sept. 11, 1903
Cameraman: Edwin S. Porter
Location: N.Y.C. *Photographed:* Sept. 7, 1903
18 ft. FLA3549 (print) FRA0825 (neg.)

Some people in columns of fours approach the single-camera position from a distance. As the film progresses, they can be identified as members of the Caledonian Club from a banner they bear, as well as their kilts. There are approximately a hundred and fifty persons of all ages so attired.

New York City Dumping Wharf
Edison © H32030 May 20, 1903
Cameraman: J. B. Smith
Location: N.Y.C. *Photographed:* Apr. 28, 1903
40 ft. FLA4749 (print) FRA2847 (neg.)

The single-camera position film shows a pier. A barge tied to the pier is being loaded with trash from two-wheeled, horse-drawn trash and garbage wagons.

New York City "Ghetto" Fish Market
Edison © H32029 May 20, 1903
Cameraman: J. B. Smith
Location: N.Y.C. *Photographed:* May 1, 1903
91 ft. FLA5113 (print) FRA2873 (neg.)

This film, photographed from an elevated camera position, shows a very crowded New York City street. Rows of pushcarts and street venders' vehicles can be seen.

New York City Police Parade
Edison © H32028 May 20, 1903
Cameramen: J. B. Smith, Edwin S. Porter
Location: Madison Square, N.Y.C. *Photographed:* May 2, 1903
145 ft. FLA5115 (print) FRA2859 (neg.)

The subject is the Police Department of the City of New York, and the film shows the presentation of citations by dignitaries, the reviewing stand and its occupants, and a parade past the camera position of a considerable part of the policemen employed by the City of New York. The parading policemen march in company-front order, and, between each group, one policeman can be seen carrying a flag. Several bands also appear in the parade.

New York City Public Bath
Edison © H36497 Oct. 3, 1903
Cameraman: Edwin S. Porter
Location: Lower East Side, N.Y.C. *Photographed:* Sept. 11, 1903
35 ft. FLA4750 (print) FRA1762 (neg.)

From a single-camera position, the film shows about a quarter of a public swimming pool. The area closest to the camera is a roped-off section where nearly two dozen small children paddle about. The remainder of the film shows portions of the deeper water where adults are swimming.

N.Y. Fire Department Returning
AM&B © H32003 May 19, 1903
Cameraman: G. W. Bitzer
Location: City Hall, N.Y.C. *Date:* May 11, 1903
24 ft. FLA3857 (print) FRA1062 (neg.)

Various pieces of horse-drawn fire-fighting equipment are shown as they pass the single-camera position.

New York Harbor Police Boat Patrol Capturing Pirates
Edison © H32027 May 20, 1903
Cameramen: J. B. Smith, Edwin S. Porter
Location: New York Harbor, N.Y. *Photographed:* May 10, 1903
60 ft. FLA4751 (print) FRA1763 (neg.)

The subject is a simulated capture by a police gunboat of three men, either pirates or smugglers, who are in a rowboat in New York Harbor. The gunboat is 150 feet long and approximately 250 tons. The camera that photographed the drill was on the stern of another vessel to film the gunboat approaching the men in the rowing boat. The copyright number is given as it is listed on the copyright application and copyright record.

N.Y. Journal Despatch Yacht "Buccaneer"
Edison © 25330 Apr. 21, 1898
Location: N.Y.C.
17 ft. FLA4278 (print) FRA1432 (neg.)

This film is so short and its condition is so poor that it is not possible to give details. However, the silhouette of a steam yacht can be seen coming about and passing by the camera.

New York Police Parade, June 1st, 1899
Edison © 38517 June 10, 1899
Location: 14th Street and Broadway, N.Y.C. *Photographed:* June 1, 1899
58 ft. FLA4752 (print) FRA1764 (neg.)

Members of the Police Department were photographed from a single-camera position as they paraded by an intersection. The crowd is interspersed with such vehicles as horses, bicycles, and both mounted and driven horses.

The Newest Woman
Lubin Mfg. Co. © J132444 Aug. 9, 1909
Location: Philadelphia
82 ft. FLA5116 (print) FRA2069 (neg.)

The film concerns the conflict between a man and his wife over her high-style clothing. The set, constructed outdoors, resembles a dining room, where an attractive woman gets up from the table to model a dress for her husband. Judging by his expression, he certainly does not like it. She leaves the room and returns wearing a dress with a skirt like a harem bloomer, which aggravates her husband further. He ponders, then leaves the room too, reappearing in a dark suit with the trousers rolled halfway to the knee with lace cuffs. He prances around, and his wife understands his point. They throw their ridiculous garments out of the window. As the film ends, a pair of tramps pick up the garments, put them on, and fall in a faint when they see each other.

The Newlyweds

Biograph © J138954 Mar. 7, 1910

Director: D. W. Griffith *Cameramen:* G. W. Bitzer, Arthur Marvin

Cast: Arthur Johnson, Florence Barker, Jeanie Macpherson, Kate Bruce, Charles West, Lottie Pickford, George Nicholls, Gladys Egan, Alfred Paget, W. Chrystie Miller, Mack Sennett, Tony O'Sullivan, Charles Craig, Frank Powell

Location: Studio and surrounding areas, Los Angeles *Photographed:* Jan. 14 and 26, 1910

388 ft. FLA5602 (print) FRA2449 (neg.)

A title indicates that a married couple is getting a divorce. The husband is then sworn into a bachelor's club that prohibits marriage. On his way home, he bumps into a little girl carrying a package of rice, and some spills over him. The next scene shows the divorced man on a train where he is seated next to a lovely young woman who had discouraged several other passengers from sitting beside her. One of the passengers notices the rice on the man, assumes they are newlyweds, and this starts a series of events, which ends when the two people who were brought together on the train agree to marry one another. This is one of the earliest Biograph films made in California.

Next

AM&B © H38317 Nov. 19, 1903

Cameraman: A. E. Weed

Location: Studio, N.Y.C. *Photographed:* Nov. 4, 1903

37 ft. FLA4753 (print) FRA1765 (neg.)

The story line of this comedy was built around the cartoon characters Alphonse and Gaston. The film begins by showing them waiting their turn in a barbershop. The barber has an empty chair and signals to the waiting customers. A considerable portion of the film is devoted to Alphonse and Gaston bowing to one another, each insisting the other go first, to the annoyance of the other customers. The camera was moved to another location to show the outside of the barbershop, and both Alphonse and Gaston can be seen as they are propelled headlong through the window by the angry customers. They land on the sidewalk outside, and the film ends as they continue bowing to one another.

See also: Alphonse and Gaston films

Niagara Falls, Winter

AM&B © H30744 Apr. 24, 1903

16 ft. FLA3373 (print) FRA0676 (neg.)

This film, photographed from a single-camera position, contains a 50-degree pan of Niagara Falls when it was frozen over.

Nicholas Nickleby

AM&B © H38252 Nov. 17, 1903

91 ft. FLA5117 (print) FRA2071 (neg.)

This segment of Dickens's novel was photographed from a single-camera position. The film shows a school room where a schoolmaster is trying to discourage the headmaster from beating one of the children.

A Nigger in the Woodpile

AM&B © H44250 Apr. 8, 1904

Cameraman: A. E. Weed

Location: Studio, N.Y.C. *Photographed:* Mar. 29, 1904

102 ft. FLA5118 (print) FRA2836 (neg.)

The first action is of a man sawing wood and piling it in cords in a set farmyard. Another man appears with a box labelled "dynamite." They manage to drill a hole in one of the sticks of wood and then insert a stick of dynamite. They place the loaded stick of wood on the cord with the rest and leave. Two blacks appear, help themselves to double armloads of wood, and take them to the interior of their cabin. They put some wood in the stove, it blows up and takes both of the men with it. The film ends as the original owner of the wood searches the debris for the two black men.

A Night at the Haymarket

AM&B © H33029 June 29, 1903

Cameraman: G. W. Bitzer

Date: June 20, 1903

126 ft. FLA5602 (print) FRA2451 (neg.)

The first scene shows a set of the front of a music hall; the second scene, photographed from a single-camera position, shows a number of people dancing, and the third is of the section where beer and food are served. As the film progresses, there is an altercation, ending with two couples being evicted by a policeman. The final scenes show apache-type dancing, which is interrupted by the police, who herd the dancers into a patrol wagon.

Night Duty

AM&B © H52100 Oct. 26, 1904

46 ft. FLA4754 (print) FRA1766 (neg.)

This film, taken outdoors, shows the relationship of a policeman with the hired help in one of the houses on his beat. The policeman stamps on a manhole cover, removes it, and the head and shoulders of a woman in a maid's uniform appear. She gives the policeman a bottle, which he pockets and then kisses her. The scene shifts to the interior of the house where the lady of the house is angrily trying to find the maid. Unsuccessful, the woman pulls a poker from the stove and is next seen handing it to the policeman through the manhole aperture. The policeman takes the hot end of the poker, jumps up and down several times waving his burned hand in pain, and the film ends.

A Night of Terror

See: A Terrible Night

The Night of the Party
AM&B © H80447 July 10, 1906
Cameraman: G. W. Bitzer
Location: Studio, N.Y.C. *Photographed:* June 19, 1906
195 ft. FLA5604 (print) FRA2452 (neg)

The film shows two obstreperous children who resent having to go to bed while their parents are giving a party downstairs. They are caught at the punch bowl, and sent back upstairs, only to return and pour some punch down their mother's neck. Once again, they are sent upstairs where they drill a hole and pour water onto the party. Their antics continue, and finally all of the guests are involved in a chase which winds up in the cellar. The film ends with the children, now covered with coal dust, engaged in a pillow fight.

The Nihilists
AM&B © H58604 Mar. 28, 1905
Cameraman: F. S. Armitage
Location: Grantwood, N.J.; Studio, N.Y.C. *Photographed:* Feb. 28, 1905
390 ft. FLA5605 (print) FRA2453 (neg.)

The picture begins by showing a family seated around a table and eating. Their meal is interrupted by a man wearing a Russian army uniform of the prerevolutionary period. The grey-haired man seated at the head of the table is removed, taken to a prison, chained to a wall, and beaten. He is later driven, with other prisoners, through the snow to exile in Siberia. His daughter joins a nihilist organization and becomes part of a conspiracy to assassinate a provincial governor. The last scene shows a ballroom with many uniformed people present and the young lady concealed behind a pillar. There is a terrific explosion, which obliterates the set with smoke. When the smoke clears away, the young woman is seen among the rubble, still alive, and she makes a gesture of victory. *Author's note:* Both Nihilists and Tom, Tom, The Piper's Son evince production standards, direction, costumes, and sets of creative nature not shown at American Mutoscope & Biograph either before March of 1905 or again until the arrival of D. W. Griffith some three years later.

9th and 13th U.S. Infantry at Battalion Drill
Edison © 38245 June 22, 1898
32 ft. FLA4038 (print) FRA1225 (neg.)
[Spanish-American War]

The exercises or drill of two battalions of U.S. Army infantry were filmed from a single-camera position along the path of march. The film shows the troops marching by in full field pack in an area of first-growth forest.

9th Infantry Boys' Morning Wash
Edison © 31444 May 20, 1898
30 ft. FLA4343 (print) FRA1487 (neg.)
[Spanish-American War]

Many of the members of the 9th Infantry are seen at personal fatigue. The complete film shows the soldiers washing, shaving, and bathing in the primitive facilities afforded by the encampment territory.

The 9th Infantry, U.S.A.
AM&B © H34103 Aug. 3, 1903

Cameraman: Raymond Ackerman
Location: Peking *Date:* Jan. 31, 1900
44 ft. FLA4755 (print) FRA1767 (neg.)

A column of infantry of the U.S. Army is marching toward the camera position. As long as the film continues, the troops pass the camera. There are approximately ten companies. In the distance is an archway in a wall of a fortresslike building. However, the distance is such that detailed description is not possible.

9th U.S. Cavalry Watering Horses
Edison © 31433 May 20, 1898
48 ft. FLA4756 (print) FRA2857 (neg.)
[Spanish-American War]

Despite the title, which indicates watering horses, the only scenes, filmed from a single-camera position, show the approach of mounted cavalry on a road. The cavalry moves at a walk. In the background are buildings which look like those of a military establishment.

No Liberties, Please
AM&B © H32386 June 4, 1903
10 ft. FLA4237 (print) FRA1394 (neg.)

The camera was positioned so as to show only the actions of a young man and a a young woman seated at a manicurist's table. During the course of the manicure, the man continuously annoys the manicurist who tries to restrain him by gently rapping his knuckles or tapping his face. The film ends as the man takes the manicurist's face to his hands and kisses her, and she does not resist.

No Salad Dressing Wanted
AM&B © H24893 Dec. 9. 1902
10 ft. FLA4189 (print) FRA1353 (neg.)

The set was constructed as a kitchen and dining room with an inter-connecting door between the two. As the film begins, one woman is preparing a salad in the kitchen while a young lady sets the table in the dining room. The woman in the kitchen apparently finds it too warm and removes most of her clothing. A young man appears in the dining room and is seated at the table. The older woman leaves the kitchen with the salad bowl and walks into the dining room and is horrified to see a young man there. She throws up her arms and rushes back into the center of her kitchen.

No Wedding Bells for Him
AM&B © H81473 July 31, 1906
Cameraman: F. A. Dobson
Location: Sound Beach, Conn.; Studio, N.Y.C. *Photographed:* July 18–19, 1906
234 ft. FLA5606 (print) FRA2456 (neg.)

The set used as the film begins is of a bachelor's den, where a contented man is seen reclining on a couch reading and enjoying a drink. He is interrupted by a bombastic little man who insists that the bachelor join him in the country for the weekend, and they are shown making the long journey out to the country. A large number of children meet them and make the bachelor's life miserable by climbing in his lap, spilling food over him, and making a great deal of noise. The bachelor jumps up from the dining table, runs from the house and is seen chasing a streetcar.

The last scene shows him in his own den drinking whisky as fast as possible.

The Non-Union Bill-Poster
Paley & Steiner © H57771 Mar. 17, 1905
5 ft. FLA3310 (print) FRA0624 (neg.)

The only scenes in this very short film show two men dressed in overcoats walking up to a man putting up a theater bill. The next scene is of a group of men beating the bill-poster about the head and shoulders and tearing his sign to bits.

A Non-Union Paper Hanger
AM&B © H16344 Apr. 10, 1902
Cameraman: F. S. Armitage
Location: Roof studio, N.Y.C. *Date:* June 5, 1901
10 ft. FLA4169 (print) FRA1335 (neg.)

A man and a woman are busily engaged in pasting wallpaper and hanging it on a set of a room in a modest house. The woman is preparing the paper by putting paste on it while the man stands on a plank placed on sawhorses against the wall. She hands him a piece of paper prepared for hanging and directs him to move sideways. He goes too far on the plank, steps on its short end and falls into a barrel, which throws the bucket of paste into the air. The bucket descends upon him, ending the film.

Noon Hour, Hope Webbing Co.
AM&B © H38864 Dec. 5, 1903
Cameraman: F. S. Armitage
Location: Pawtucket, R.I. *Photographed:* Nov. 23, 1903
35 ft. FLA4264 (print) FRA1420 (neg.)

The single-camera position shows the employees of a manufacturing company as they pass by during the noon hour.

Nora's Fourth of July
AM&B © H16389 Apr. 12, 1902
Cameraman: F. S. Armitage
Location: Roof studio, N.Y.C. *Date:* July 5, 1901
10 ft. FLA3488 (print) FRA0769 (neg.)

A woman is kneading dough on a table in front of a kitchen set. There are another table and an ice box in the kitchen. The door opens and a small boy enters, immediately followed by a man wearing a policeman's uniform. When the small boy sees the policeman, he ducks under the table and is seen lighting some fire-crackers, while the cook opens two bottles of beer—one for the policeman and one for herself. The film ends when an explosion occurs and fills the kitchen with smoke.

Not So Bad As It Seemed
Biograph © J148145 Nov. 26, 1910
Cameraman: Arthur Marvin
Cast: Violet Mersereau, Grace Henderson, Mack Sennett, William J. Butler, Verner Clarges, Robert Harron, Dorothy West
Location: Fort Lee, N.J.; Studio, N.Y.C. *Photographed:* Oct. 4–14, 1910
179 ft. FLA5607 (print) FRA2455 (neg.)

This short comedy film is about a married couple being called out of town. The husband writes to a friend giving him permission to use the library in his absence, while his wife writes to a friend asking her to feed their bird while they are away. The recipients of the notes follow their instructions and go to the house at the same time. Each hears the other and thinks the sound is caused by an intruder. In addition, their respective spouses assume an illicit rendezvous is taking place and break into the house. But everything is cleared up by the arrival of the man and woman who sent the notes when they are forced to return home on foot because their car breaks down.

The Note in the Shoe
AM&B © H126279 Apr. 28, 1909
Director: D. W. Griffith *Cameraman:* G. W. Bitzer
Cast: Marion Leonard, Florence Lawrence, Owen Moore, Arthur Johnson, Tony O'Sullivan, John Cumpson, Mack Sennett, Clara T. Bracey, Robert Harron, Frank Powell
Location: Studio, N.Y.C. *Photographed:* Mar. 13 and 16, 1909
262 ft. FLA5608 (print) FRA2454 (neg.)

The film begins by showing several young women packing shoes in a shoe manufacturing plant. The next scene takes place in a shoe store; a customer comes in and buys a pair of shoes. He goes home, tries them on, and is very annoyed by a note in the box. He returns the shoes and admonishes the clerk for his audacity. The next scene is in the shoe factory again, where the young woman (Florence Lawrence) who packed the shoes is being scolded by the manager. At the end of his harangue, she is dismissed, but apparently he is smitten by her charms, for he sends her a note and asks her to return. He calls on her at home and begins to scold her again with his arms outstretched, and the longer he talks, the closer she gets until finally she is enclosed in his arms.

A Novel Way of Catching a Burglar
AM&B © H43574 Mar. 22, 1904
Cameraman: A. E. Weed
Location: Studio, N.Y.C. *Photographed:* Mar. 7, 1904
18 ft. FLA4296 (print) FRA1446 (neg.)

A man is asleep on a bench in front of a set of a two-story apartment house. Another man, wearing rough clothes, approaches the first man and goes through his pockets, removing some articles. While this is going on, a young woman comes to the window above with a flower pot and sees what is happening. She leaves the window and returns with a specially constructed loop at the end of a rope which she drops over the thief and his victim. She is seen pulling in the slack in the rope as a policeman arrives and takes the culprit off to jail.

See also: A Snare for Lovers

Nurse Wanted
See: Wanted—A Nurse

Nursing a Viper
Biograph © J134294 Nov. 5, 1909
Director: D. W. Griffith. *Cameraman:* G. W. Bitzer
Location: Englewood, N.J. and Studio, N.Y.C.
Cast: Arthur Johnson, Marion Leonard, Billy Quirk, Owen Moore, Henry "Pathe" Lehrman, Dorothy West, Mack

Sennett, Frank Powell, Gertrude Robinson, George Nicholls

379 ft. FLA5609 (print) FRA2457 (neg.)

This picture was set in the period of the French Revolution. The first scene shows a great number of revolutionists descending upon a chateau, brandishing clubs and other weapons. One of the noblemen escapes their fury, and is given refuge in another chateau and permitted to pose as a servant. He repays his host by attempting to attack the lady of the house but is caught in the act by her husband. At pistol point, the husband forces the "viper" in his house to leave its protection and go out and face certain death at the hands of the revolutionaries.

A Nymph of the Waves
AM&B © H30731 Apr. 24, 1903
Cameraman: F. S. Armitage
Location: Studio, N.Y.C. *Date:* Dec. 8, 1900
Combination of productions 70, Upper Rapids [Niagara Falls] From Bridge (1896-7), and 1210, Bartho (Sept. 1899)
10 ft. FLA3417 (print) FRA0706 (neg.)

During the entire film, a young lady who is a competent dancer can be seen dancing on what appear to be ocean waves. The effect was obtained by double exposure; evidently the producer of this film photographed the ocean waves and then photographed the dancer on the same negative. The dancer was Cathrina Bartho performing her celebrated "Speedway" dance.

The Oath and the Man
Biograph © J145784 Sept. 26, 1910
Director: D. W. Griffith *Cameraman:* G. W. Bitzer
Cast: Henry B. Walthall, W. Chrystie Miller, Alfred Paget, George Nicholls, Frank Powell, Billy Quirk, Claire McDowell, Florence Barker, Gertrude Robinson, Jack Pickford
Location: Paterson, N.J.; Studio, N.Y.C. *Photographed:* Aug. 16–19, 1910
392 ft. FLA5610 (print) FRA2675 (neg.)

There are indoor and outdoor scenes in this film, and a considerable number of camera positions were used to create suspense and clarify the action. The story is of a perfumer (Henry B. Walthall) whose wife (Florence Barker) is invited by a nobleman to become his mistress. The perfumer becomes so angry at the loss of his wife that he organizes a rebellion and overthrows the guards at the chateau. His wife and her lover are forced to flee for their lives. The village priest prevents the outraged husband from murdering them both. In fact, the perfumer ends up aiding them to escape the anger of the peasants he had set against them. The film bears the subtitle "A Story of the French Revolution."

O'Brien-Burns Contest, Los Angeles, Cal., Nov. 26th, 1906
Miles Brothers © H86763 Dec. 17, 1906
Cameraman: Herbert J. Miles [?]
Location: Los Angeles *Photographed:* Nov. 26, 1906
1,864 ft. FLA5942 (print) FRA8277 (neg.)

The boxing contest between O'Brien and Burns was photographed from a single-camera position. As the film

begins, the usual preliminaries by the managers of the two fighters, the press interview, and the still photographers can be seen. The remainder of the fight and the periods between rounds are all shown. The heavyweight championship ended in a draw after twenty rounds.

Observation Train Following Parade
Edison © 52051 Sept. 3, 1898
Location: N.Y.C. [?] *Photographed:* Aug. 20, 1898 [?]
33 ft. FLA4221 (print) FRA1380 (neg.)
[Spanish-American War; New York City Welcome To Admiral Sampson's Fleet after Battle of Santiago Bay]

The film shows a large group of people sitting on fences and roof tops along a railroad track. A steam locomotive and five freight cars with one caboose are on the railroad. On the tops of these various cars are more people. At the end of the film, the train begins to move.

Obstacle Race
AM&B © H55397 Jan. 3, 1905
Cameraman: G. W. Bitzer
Location: On board U.S.S. Minneapolis, Portsmouth Navy Yard, Portsmouth, N.H. *Photographed:* Dec. 4, 1903
24 ft. FLA3851 (print) FRA1063 (neg.)

An obstacle race held on board a U.S. naval ship is shown. Various appurtenances of the ship were used to inhibit the speed and direction of the crew of bluejackets in the race. The film is too short to permit elaboration of detail.
See also: Scrubbing Clothes

"Oceans" Fire Company
AM&B © H30748 Apr. 24, 1903
Cameraman: F. S. Armitage
Location: Brooklyn, N.Y.C. [?] *Date:* Aug. 21, 1899
16 ft. FLA3382 (print) FRA0682 (neg.)

Approximately twenty men are hard at work pumping water. The film shows what appears to be either a competition between volunteer fire-fighting units or a demonstration of a water pump or fire-fighting apparatus. Spectators appear in the last part of the film.
See also: "Exempt" of Brooklyn, N.Y.

Off for the Rabbit Chase
Edison © 12173 Feb. 17, 1898
22 ft. FLA3977 (print) FRA1185 (neg.)

The camera was placed across the street from a large building. Judging from the architecture, it could be a hotel or a club. In the foreground is a street and in the distance approaching the camera are mounted riders and dogs. They continue on and pass the camera at a gallop. There is nothing further in the film to explain their actions.

Off His Beat
AM&B © H38014 Nov. 12, 1903
Cameraman: A. E. Weed
Location: Studio, N.Y.C. *Photographed:* Oct. 29, 1903
26 ft. FLA4190 (print) FRA1354 (neg.)

A man dressed as a policeman and a young woman in street clothes are sitting very close together in the corner of a set of a back yard with a brick wall. Occasionally, they kiss. A man with a hod appears in back of the wall and seems distressed by what he sees so he dumps the bricks on the policeman. He then jumps over the wall and starts beating the policeman. The camera is moved from its original position to the other side of the wall and, with the use of stop-action photography, a dummy is substituted for the policeman. The hod carrier picks up the dummy and slams it to the sidewalk several times. A live policeman is now substituted for the dummy, and the hod carrier pulls him to his feet and sends him about his business with a swift kick.

See also: Guardian of the Peace

Office Boy's Revenge
AM&B © H47315 June 18, 1904
64 ft. FLA5120 (print) FRA2072 (neg.)

An office boy is busy dusting the various pieces of furniture with a feather duster in a set of a business office. He sits down and begins playing with the typewriter and is caught by his employer who spanks him. Later, when the office is operating as usual and the secretary is at her desk and the employer at his, the office boy comes in and ties a string between the employer and secretary who sit back to back. The film ends as a severely dressed woman carrying an umbrella enters the office, notices the connection between her husband and the secretary, and bats him with the umbrella, to the glee of the office boy.

The Offices Boy's Revenge
Edison © H39174 Dec. 9, 1903
Cameraman: Edwin S. Porter
Location: Studio, N.Y.C. Photographed: Dec. 5, 1903
38 ft. FLA3527 (print) FRA0803 (neg.)

A woman is seen sitting at a desk while a boy dressed as an office boy in uniform kneels before her in an office set. The office boy is still pleading with her when a man wearing a top hat, tailcoat, and morning trousers enters through the side door. He hauls the office boy to his feet, shakes him, and scolds him. Then he takes his place at a large desk and the office boy can be seen tying pieces of furniture together with string. A visitor comes in and closes the door which pulls the top of the employer's desk crashing down on another piece of furniture. When the film ends, the boss has the office boy over his knee and is spanking him soundly. The Thomas A. Edison copyright notice on the back wall of the set very closely resembles the wall that was used in the telegraph office in The Great Train Robbery.

Oh, Those Eyes!
Biograph © J167693 Apr. 1, 1912
Director: Mack Sennett
Cast: Mabel Normand, Edwin August, Eddie Dillon, Dell Henderson, Raymond Hatton
204 ft. FLA5801 (print) FRA2460 (neg., copy 1) FRA2461 (neg., copy 2)

A father attempts to teach his very attractive but flirtatious daughter a lesson by conspiring with two of her suitors to fight a duel. They agree that both are to feign death as a result of the encounter. Thus the duel would not only teach her a lesson, but would show which of her suitors she really favored. Things proceed according to plan. The two men stand face to face with drawn pistols while the young lady turns her back to them. Both men fire and both fall down as if dead. The flirt runs away, and her father and suitors find

her unconcernedly attempting to make friends with a large brown bear.

Oh, Uncle!
Biograph © J130911 Aug. 27, 1909
Director: D. W. Griffith Cameraman: G. W. Bitzer
Cast: Mary Pickford, Billy Quirk, James Kirkwood
Location: Studio, N.Y.C. Photographed: July 21–22, 1909
100 ft. FLA5612 (print)

A young man (Billy Quirk), newly married, attempts to play a trick on an uncle (James Kirkwood) who comes for a visit and who had not wanted his nephew to marry. He relegates his young wife (Mary Pickford) to the kitchen and has her dress as a maid. The uncle becomes suspicious and begins a violent flirtation with the "maid," which lasts throughout the picture to the annoyance of the bridegroom. In the end, the uncle approves of the marriage. The film was photographed indoors on two sets, one of a living room and the other of a kitchen.

The Old Actor
Biograph © J168900 May 4, 1912
Director: D. W. Griffith Cameraman: G. W. Bitzer
Cast: W. Chrystie Miller, Kate Bruce, Mary Pickford, Edwin August, Claire McDowell, Frank Opperman, Vivian Prescott, Charles Hill Mailes
Location: Southern Calif.
400 ft. FLA0042 (print) FRA0137 (neg.)

The opening scene takes place in the living room of an inexpensive apartment where an old man (W. Chrystie Miller), his wife (Kate Bruce), and his young daughter (Mary Pickford) are elated that the old actor has been given a role in a Shakespearean drama. But when the actor arrives at the theater, he is told his part has been given to another because he is too old. The bewildered old man starts home. On the way he encounters an ill beggar. He helps the dying man into a house, where the actor is astounded when he discovers how much money the beggar had collected. Unable to face his family after the loss of his livelihood, the old actor decides to become a beggar and assumes the beggar's disguise. Soon the actor's daughter and her boyfriend pass him on the street but do not recognize him. The young man tosses the beggar a coin but almost immediately realizes it was a five-dollar gold piece. When the two young people return to retrieve the coin, the young woman sees the beggar is her father. All three return home, where a message recalling the old actor to his Shakespearean role is waiting.

An Old Bachelor
AM&B © H42800 Feb. 27, 1904
Cameraman: A. E. Weed
Location: Studio, N.Y.C. Photographed: Feb.15, 1904
52 ft. FLA5121 (print) FRA2073 (neg.)

The whole film was photographed from a single medium-camera position. It shows a man wearing long underwear sitting on the side of a bed and going through the motions of sewing a button on a pair of trousers. The full extent of the film is devoted to his difficulty in threading the needle and sewing on the button. The film ends when he severs the thread from the button with his teeth.

Old Faithful Geyser

Edison © H4082 May 6, 1901
Location: Yellowstone Park, Wyo.
48 ft. FLA4757 (print) FRA1769 (neg.)

The geyser, a phenomenon of nature in the Yellowstone National Park, was photographed from a single-camera position. Clouds of steam and water are seen shooting into the air. None of the background is visible.

Old Fashioned Scottish Reel

Edison © H35621 Sept. 11, 1903
Cameraman: Edwin S. Porter
Location: N.Y.C. *Photographed:* Sept. 7, 1903
30 ft. FLA3925 (print) FRA1140 (neg.)

The photographer placed his camera at the edge of a clearing of what appears to be a picnic grounds in order to photograph four men dressed in kilts as they dance several types of Scottish reels. During the film, the four men dance collectively, individually. and in pairs.

See also: Miss Jessie Cameron, Champion Child Sword Dancer, and Miss Jessie Dogherty, Champion Female Highland Fling Dancer.

Old Gentleman Spinkles

AM&B © H32631 June 13, 1903
11 ft. FLA3731 (print) FRA0978 (neg.)

At the beginning of this film, two people are sitting in front of a set of a two-story house. Someone starts pouring water from a pitcher on the heads of the two people below, and the film ends.

Old Glory and Cuban Flag

Edison © 17706 Mar. 15, 1898
30ft. FLA4160 (print) FRA1328 (neg.)

At the beginning of the film, an American flag is visible. By the use of stop-action photography, the American flag is replaced by a Cuban flag half way through the film. The Cuban flag remains until the film ends. There is nothing to be seen in the background that is associated in any way with the two flags.

Old Glory and Cuban Flag

Edison © 18131 Mar. 17, 1898
27 ft. FLA4159 (print) FRA1327 (neg.)

The subject matter of this short film is unfurled flags. As the film begins, there is a Cuban flag; half way through the film, through the use of stop-action photography, the American flag appears, and it remains until the film ends. There is nothing else to be seen, with the exception of a house with a peaked roof in the distance.

Old Isaacs the Pawnbroker

AM&B © H107936 Mar. 26, 1908
Author: D. W. Griffith *Cameraman:* G. W. Bitzer
Location: Studio, N.Y.C. *Photographed:* Mar. 17–19, 1908
271 ft. FLA5613 (print) FRA2464 (neg.)

A little girl living with her ill mother in a tenement is faced with tremendous responsibilities when they are served with eviction papers. The child goes the rounds of the various agencies, seeking help. Driven to despair by the indifference of the charity agencies, she then attempts to pawn her mother's last valuables but without success. She goes home, gets her doll, and takes it to the pawnbroker, who is so impressed by the little girl's unselfishness that he gives her some money. Later he goes to the address she had given and arrives just in time to prevent their furniture from being removed. The pawnbroker brings food, clothing, a nurse for the ill mother, and returns the doll to the child.

Old Maid and Fortune Teller

Edison © H42206 Feb. 16, 1904
Cameraman: Edwin S. Porter
Location: Studio, N.Y.C. *Photographed:* Feb. 9, 1904
30 ft. FLA4758 (print) FRA1769 (neg.)

The cameraman placed his camera close enough to show the gestures made during a conversation between a man made up as a very homely woman and a young woman costumed as a gypsy fortune teller. For the full extent of the film, we see the two intent on the palm reading. The film ends when the old maid looks directly at the camera with a look of absolute amazement as she holds up nine fingers.

The Old Maid and Pet Cat

See: The Seven Ages: What Age?

The Old Maid and the Burglar

AM&B © H34514 Aug. 13, 1903
Date: 1898 [?]
10 ft. FLA3579 (print) FRA0851 (neg.)

The poor quality and graininess of this film conspire to prevent much detail from being seen. Some action is discernible, however. The set was designed as a bedroom where a woman in nightclothes can be seen preparing for bed. She blows out the candle, climbs in bed, and finds to her amazement and fright that there is a man under her bed who crawls out and leaps through the window. Two other women come into the room and attempt to calm the nerves of the first, and the film ends.

The Old Maid Having Her Picture Taken

Edison © H1494 Mar. 1, 1901
Cast: Gilbert Saroni
38 ft. FLA3753 (print) FRA0999 (neg.)

This is a single-camera position comedy film of a photographer's studio where the photographer is preparing to take a picture of a not too attractive young woman. The woman looks into one of the prop mirrors to tidy herself and a picture falls off the wall. Calmed down by the photographer, she looks at a clock and it, too, falls off the wall. The photographer seats her, she looks into the camera, and it explodes.

The Old Maid in the Horsecar

Edison © H1496 Mar. 1, 1901
Cast: Gilbert Saroni
35 ft. FLA4759 (print) FRA1770 (neg.)

The composition of the picture consists of a waist shot of an angularly built man costumed as a woman. Make-up was used to create an impression of ugliness. The only action seen in the film is the "woman" talking rapidly, and giggling behind a fan. The gestures are repeated over and over again as if it were a monologue.

The Old Maid's Disappointment
AM&B © H19651 July 2, 1902
14 ft. FLA3794 (print) FRA1031 (neg.)

In order to photograph this film, the cameraman placed his equipment close to the subject to get a picture from the waist up. An overhead single source of light shows a table with a lamp on it and a seated woman. It is difficult to understand exactly what she is trying to convey, but during the course of the film, she opens a letter, reads it, and tears it up. The expression on her face shows great annoyance and disappointment.

The Old Maid's Picture
AM&B © H34809 Aug. 19, 1903
Date: 1898 [?]
10 ft. FLA4101 (print) FRA1282 (neg.)

A severely dressed young woman fussing with her hair can be seen standing in front of a mirror which is part of a photographic studio set. A plate camera on a tripod is in the immediate foreground. A man wearing a dark suit and a flowing tie enters, and the young woman seats herself in a chair directly in front of the camera. The photographer arranges and adjusts the camera, squeezes the bulb attached to the camera shutter, and an explosion occurs that blows the camera to bits, ending the picture.

Old Mail Coach at Ford, U.S.P.O.
AM&B © H34990 Aug. 22, 1903
Cameraman: A. E. Weed
Location: Washington, D.C. *Photographed:* July 30, 1903
24 ft. FLA3882 (print) FRA1093 (neg.)

The film begins by showing a river approximately fifty yards wide. The opposite bank from the camera position is wooded. Shortly after the beginning of the film, four horses, drawing a standard passenger-and-mail coach, head for the camera position. The horse-drawn vehicle proceeds into the water, crosses the river, and passes the camera.

An Old Story With a New Ending
Biograph © J144498 Aug. 19, 1910
Cameraman: Arthur Marvin
Cast: Joe Graybill, Tony O'Sullivan, Lottie Pickford, Gertrude Robinson, W. Chrystie Miller, Robert Harron
Location: Coytesville, N.J. and Studio, N.Y.C. *Photographed:* July 14, 1910
221 ft. FLA5614 (print) FRA2463 (neg.)

The young women in the assembly department of a factory decide to play a prank on the austere and elegant forelady by enclosing her card with a note addressed to any young man in a pair of trousers. The beau brummel of the village buys the trousers, reads the note, and writes a letter to the forelady proposing marriage. The young woman, somewhat mystified and considerably annoyed, answers the beau brummel to the effect that she is not interested in a man who would propose marriage to a girl he has not met, and certainly not in one who could pay only forty-seven cents for a pair of breeches.

The Old Swimming Hole
AM&B © H81471 July 31, 1906
Cameraman: F. A. Dobson

Location: North Beach [?] *Photographed:* July 12, 1906
50 ft. FLA4760 (print) FRA1771 (neg.)

Approximately twenty young boys are shown as they swim, jump, and splash in the shallow water of a stream. The film was photographed from a single-camera position.

Old Volunteer Fire Department
AM&B © H32831 June 18, 1903
Cameraman: Robert K. Bonine
25 ft. FLA3413 (print) FRA0711 (neg.)

A parade of men in civilian garb who are pulling some antiquated fire-fighting apparatus are shown from a single-camera position.

[On] a [Good Old] Five Cent Trolley Ride
Edison © H61056 May 16, 1905
Cameraman: Edwin W. Porter
Location: Forest Hills, N.Y.; Studio, N.Y.C. *Photographed:* May 2–3, 1905
224 ft. FLA5386 (print) FRA2686 (neg.)

In order to make the film, the cameraman was required to start on a set of a movable streetcar, and then to transfer his camera outside and photograph a real streetcar on the tracks. In general, the story line revolves around a series of comic vaudeville gags put into sequences. The movie begins in the interior of a trick streetcar, where a series of comic characters arrive and depart. The last person to board is a man with a basket full of snakes which get loose and cause all and sundry to abandon the streetcar to get off and chase the owner of the snakes. A goose gets involved in the chase and is stolen by a tramp. This provides added reason to continue the chase a little longer. The film ends as the group arrives on the bank of a small stream that the fleeing tramp has already crossed, with the goose under his arm. The title listed on the copyright application and records is A Five Cent Trolley Ride; but in the catalog it is [On] a [Good Old] Five Cent Trolley Ride.

On the Beach at Brighton
AM&B © H63380 July 15, 1905
Cameraman: G. W. Bitzer
Location: Studio, N.Y.C. *Photographed:* June 28, 1905
30 ft. FLA3934 (print) FRA1146 (neg.)

As the film opens, a section of a bath house can be seen. Three women in bathing attire pass the camera and enter the bath house doors marked "Shower" and "Dressing Rooms". A man wearing street clothing and a top hat comes along and enters into a conversation with a male bath-house attendant who infers that if the man creeps under the floor of the bath house he might see something not otherwise visible. The man follows the instructions and is caught in the act by the women who empty buckets of water over him as the film ends.

On the Benches in the Park
AM&B © H35640 Sept. 12, 1903
Cameraman: F. S. Armitage
Location: Roof studio, N.Y.C. *Date:* June 15, 1901
18 ft. FLA3353 (print) FRA0665 (neg.)

This film was photographed as if from the audience at a vaudeville show. It opens on a stage set with a painted backdrop of sky and trees, etc. In the foreground to the right of the camera is a park bench where a young woman is seated. She is reading from a book and declaiming. A man wearing tattered garments peers through the foliage at her. The tramp approaches the bench, sits down, and places his arm about the young woman. She jumps up from the bench and yells for a policeman, who arrives. The policeman takes the tramp by his tattered garments, shakes him, and hits him on the head with a club. Just then, a little pug dog enters the scene. He grabs the tramp by the seat of his trousers. The picture ends as the tramp, with the dog firmly affixed to his coat tail, is seen running off through the bushes. The final scene is of the policeman comforting the young woman by putting his arm around her and fanning her with his hat.

On the Flying Rings

AM&B © H34522-H34524 Aug. 13, 1903
Cameraman: G. W. Bitzer
Cast: Silveon and Emerie
Photographed: July 30, 1903
81 ft.
Pt. A: FLA4761 (print) FRA1772 (neg.)
Pt. B: FLA4762 (print) FRA4761 (neg.)
Pt. C: FLA4763 (print) FRA4761 (neg.)

This shows a trapeze act consisting of one man and two women, who demonstrate their skill and ability by performing various well- known feats on the flying ring and parallel bar. The women are contortionists as well as ring and bar gymnasts; consequently, there are variations on each of the acts.

On the Night Stage

New York Motion Picture Corp. © LP4961 April 15, 1915
Producer and Author: Thomas H. Ince *Director:* Reginald Barker
Cameraman: Robert Newhard
Cast: William S. Hart, Rhea Mitchell, Robert Edeson, Gladys Brockwell, Herschel Mayall, Shorty Hamilton
Location: Santa Ynez Canyon (Santa Monica), Calif.
2,150 ft. FAAL538-6542

According to contemporary accounts, C. Gardner Sullivan collaborated with Thomas H. Ince on the story line of this western drama. On the Night Stage proved to be the prototype of what later became the standard William S. Hart westerner. Both the new parson in a small western town and William S. Hart are in love with a dance hall girl, and when there is a barroom melee, the parson is forced to come to the aid of his rival against their common enemy.

On the Reef

Biograph © J137450 Jan. 19, 1910
Director: D. W. Griffith *Cameraman:* G. W. Bitzer
Cast: Marion Leonard, Henry B. Walthall, Gladys Egan, W. Chrystie Miller, Tony O'Sullivan, John Cumpson, Grace Henderson
Location: Studio, N.Y.C. *Photographed:* Dec. 13–14, 1909
408 ft. FLA5615 (print) FRA2465 (neg.)

A dying woman, endeavoring to take care of her attractive daughter, arranges for her to marry a family friend, an older widower with a young daughter. The wedding is performed at the sickbed and the mother dies almost immediately. As the film continues, the young wife becomes enamored of a handsome young friend of her husband's. Realizing the hopelessness of their love, the young man writes a note, which is seen by the husband. The shock kills him. The young widow now seeks the man she loves, only to learn she is too late, as he has gone off for parts unknown. The last scene is preceded by a title reading "The Only Thing Left to Live For" and shows the young widow embracing her weeping stepdaughter.

On the Road

AM&B © H31690 May 5, 1903
Cameraman: G. W. Bitzer
Location: Linden, N.J. *Date:* Apr. 27, 1903
19 ft. FLA4154 (print) FRA0487 (neg.)

The camera was positioned at the side of a road lined with trees on both sides. At a distance of approximately a quarter of a mile, approaching the camera, are a tallyho coach and four horses, followed by a man on a bicycle. The only action in the picture is of the coach continuing toward the camera and passing it. The quality of the film is grainy and very contrasty and little detail is distinguishable.

See also: Changing Horses at Linden

On the Trail

See: The Divorce

On the Window Shades

AM&B © H41756 Feb. 2, 1904
Cameraman: A. E. Weed
Location: Studio, N.Y.C. *Photographed:* Jan. 16, 1904
30 ft. FLA3751 (print) FRA0997 (neg.)

As the film opens, two windows can be seen. Backlighted between the light and the camera position are the silhouettes of two women dressing. It is evident from their silhouettes on the window shade that they are donning various articles of clothing. The picture ends as a door opens in the front of the set of the outside of a house, and one of the two women emerges fully clothed. She walks down the street out of sight of the camera while the remaining woman watches her from the window.

On to Brooklyn, no. 1

AM&B © H37651 Nov. 5, 1903
63 ft. FLA4764 (print) FRA1773 (neg.)

The backdrop depicts a river with a bridge, similar to the Brooklyn Bridge. A man in a plaid suit with a lantern hung around his neck comes out on stage, followed by another man who also carries a lantern. They turn as if to view the work and then turn toward the camera. Another person in frock coat and stovepipe hat appears on stage, carrying a sign that reads, "Fusion, On to Brooklyn." The three men march around in an attempt to convey a political idea, for in addition to the placard, they are carrying bags with dollar signs on them.

On to Brooklyn, no. 2

AM&B © H37650 Nov. 5, 1903
50 ft. FLA4765 (print) FRA1774 (neg.)

There is a painted backdrop with a wooden fence in front of it and three steps leading to a porch. A man seated on the steps is approached by two men, costumed as frock-coated, stovepipe-hatted politicians who ask for and receive money. Soon a person dressed in a tiger skin appears and chases the three men away and then mounts the stairs and acts as if he were monarch of all he surveys.

One Busy Hour

AM&B © H126642 May 6, 1909

Director: D. W. Griffith *Cameramen:* G. W. Bitzer, Arthur Marvin

Cast: Mack Sennett, Eddie Dillon, John Cumpson, Robert Harron

Location: Fort Lee, N.J.; Studio, N.Y.C. *Photographed:* Apr. 2, 1909

90 ft. FLA5122 (print) FRA2074 (neg.)

This film takes place at four different locations: a country store interior, the exterior, the local newspaper office, and a house owned by the principal of the film, a grocer. The grocer, who apparently wants to sell his store, places an ad in the local paper. So great is the response to his ad, in fact, that his store is nearly wrecked, and the film ends as the grocer receives a letter that causes him to faint. However, the contents of the letter are not disclosed to the viewers of the film.

104th Street Curve, New York, Elevated Railway

Edison © 27964 Apr. 22, 1899

Location: N.Y.C.

68 ft. FLA4766 (print, copy 1) FLA5975 (print, copy 2) FRA1775 (neg.)

The first camera position was on an elevated railroad platform and shows passing steam and electric cars and some of the New York skyline. Another camera position was from the front of a train making the full curve at 104th Street, showing the track and also a nearly full sweep of the New York skyline, including Columbia University and the Cathedral of St. John the Divine.

One Is Business, the Other Crime

Biograph © J168597 Apr. 24, 1912

Director: D. W. Griffith *Cameraman:* G. W. Bitzer

Cast: Charles West, Dorothy Bernard, Blanche Sweet, Edwin August, Kate Bruce, Mae Marsh, Alfred Paget

416 ft. FLA5617 (print) FRA2458 (neg.)

The film begins by showing a poor but honest workman attempting to get work. Failing, he decides to turn to crime, and he chooses to steal from a rich man who has just received a large sum of cash as a bribe for his vote. The workman is caught by the rich man's wife, who finds the letter to her husband with the bribe. The rich man returns home in time to witness the poor man pleading for his freedom. The rich man's wife points out to her husband that stealing is no worse a crime than that of which he is guilty, namely, accepting a bribe. The rich man returns the bribe (shown by an insert of his letter), and gives the poor man a job as a construction worker. Most of the scenes were photographed indoors and were lighted artificially.

One Night and Then

Biograph © J138316 Feb. 16, 1910

Director: D. W. Griffith *Cameraman:* G. W. Bitzer

Cast: Henry B. Walthall, Mack Sennett, Charles West, Kate Bruce, Adele De Garde, W. J. Butler, Billy Quirk, Blanche Sweet

Location: Studio, N.Y.C. *Photographed:* Dec. 30, 1909

125 ft. FLA5616 (print) FRA2462 (neg.)

Only part of this film is in existence. It begins in the living room of a wealthy man where a gay party is in progress, with many people drinking, eating, or dancing. The host (H. B. Walthall) stands up while waiting for his wine glass to be refilled, and suffers a heart attack. The doctor who is summoned tells him he has only one more night to live and the host sends his guests away. There is a flashback to acquaint the viewers with another type of life. It shows a poverty stricken woman playing a game of tag with two small girls. A later scene shows the same woman attending one of the children who is ill, while she sends the other for medicine. The last scene of this fragment shows the rich man exchanging his clothing with a workman, evidently with the idea that he will do some good with his last remaining hours of life.

A One Night Stand

Keystone © LP4873 Mar. 22, 1915

Producer and Author: Mack Sennett

Cast: James T. Kelly, Chester Conklin, Harry Booker, Charles Arling, Mae Busch, Bobby Dunn, Charles Chase, Harry Gribbon

Location: Keystone studio, Los Angeles

410 ft. FLA6131 (print, copy 1) FLA6132 (print, copy 2)

Chester Conklin and James Kelly play basketball instead of tending to their jobs as stage hands, infuriating the stage manager, Harry Booker. A trouper (Charles Arling) arrives, followed by a second (Mae Busch). It is evident they have had a quarrel. Conklin immediately falls for Mae Busch and gets into considerable trouble trying to impress her. He and Kelly continue to disrupt the proceedings by playing football with the manager's hat and performing other antics. When they finally succeed in disrupting a performance, they are really in trouble. Conklin remains convinced that Mae Busch feels exactly the same way about him as he does about her. When the film ends, Arling and Busch are having a reconciliatory embrace, with Chester stretched out on the floor between their feet. Poor Chester is the victim of somebody's carelessly aimed brick.

One-Round O'Brien

Biograph © J171148 July 12, 1912

Director: Mack Sennett

Cast: Fred Mace, William J. Butler, Frank Evans

185 ft. FLA5618 (print) FRA2459 (neg.)

Two down-and-out but enterprising bums get the idea of staging a boxing match, challenging all comers to stay one round for twenty-five dollars. One bum will do the boxing, and the other will stand behind a curtain and hit the challenger on the head with a mallet. An enthusiastic audience encourages any and all of its members to take on the challenger. Three men respond to the challenge. The first two meet defeat by the mallet route. The third, a large man, takes the effects of the mallet blow with no apparent effects. Realizing what has happened, the challenger picks up his opponent and places him against the curtain. His cohort, thinking it is the enemy, strikes a hard blow, causing the defeat of this partner.

One Thousand Mile Tree
AM&B © H26854 Jan. 9, 1903
Cameraman: G. W. Bitzer
Location: Union Pacific R.R. *Date:* Dec. 2, 1899
31 ft. FLA3285 (print) FRA0601 (neg.)

A winding railroad track was photographed from a moving vehicle passing over it. The film was photographed in the Rocky Mountains on the Union Pacific Railroad.

One Touch of Nature
AM&B © H120834 Dec. 30, 1908
Director: D. W. Griffith *Cameramen:* G. W. Bitzer, Arthur Marvin
Cast: Arthur Johnson, Florence Lawrence, Gladys Egan, Adele De Garde, Frank Gebhardt, Charles Inslee, Dorothy West
Location: Studio, N.Y.C. *Photographed:* Nov. 13–18, 1908
276 ft. FLA5619 (print) FRA2466 (neg.)

Two groups of people and four sets appear in the film. A young policeman and his wife have a beautiful little girl, but tragedy strikes their happy home and she dies. The mother suffers a nervous breakdown and must have a nurse with her constantly. As the film continues, it shows another little girl, under the control of a pair of beggars, who constantly beat and mistreat her. The policeman notices their cruelty, raids the cellar where they live, and rescues the little girl. He takes her home to his wife, who seems delighted.

One Way of Taking a Girl's Picture
AM&B © H40807 Jan. 12, 1904
Cameraman: A. E. Weed
Location: Studio, N.Y.C. *Photographed:* Dec. 1, 1903
23 ft. FLA3764 (print) FRA1009 (neg.)

This is a single-camera position film of a set designed as a photographer's studio. A woman comes in accompanied by another woman. They remove her blouse and she turns her back to the camera. The film ends with the woman looking over her shoulder and exposing her back. The completed picture was intended to convey the impression of a still photograph.

See also: The Picture the Photographer Took.

The Open Gate
Biograph © J135125 Nov. 24, 1909
Director: D. W. Griffith *Cameraman:* G. W. Bitzer
Cast: Kate Bruce, George Nicholls, Gertrude Robinson, Owen Moore, Adele De Garde
Location: Coytesville, N.J.; Studio, N.Y.C. *Photographed:* Oct. 9 and 12, 1909
404 ft. FLA5620 (print) FRA2467 (neg.)

A young woman, saddled with a sudden responsibility of her dead sister's child, breaks her engagement. Many years later, the child, now a grown woman, attempts to break her engagement because she feels responsible for the welfare of her aging aunt. The aunt and her long ago suitor attempt to straighten out the young people, who as a result are brought together again. The gate, left open when the first engagement was broken, is once more closed.

Opening Ceremonies, New York Subway, Oct. 27, 1904
Edison © H52333 Oct. 29, 1904
Cameraman: Edwin S. Porter
Location: City Hall, N.Y.C. *Photographed:* Oct. 27, 1904
126 ft. FLA5123 (print) FRA2075 (neg.)

The film shows the crews crossing the street toward the subway stair entrance by City Hall. The next scene shows the crews awaiting the arrival of dedicating dignitaries. The next camera position was down in the subway and on the platform where a car is photographed arriving and then leaving.

Opening Ceremonies, St. Louis Exposition
AM&B © H45954 May 13, 1904
Cameraman: A. E. Weed
Location: St. Louis *Photographed:* Apr. 30, 1904
102 ft. FLA5124 (print) FRA2076 (neg.)
[Louisiana Purchase Exposition]

The principal buildings surrounding the square at the St. Louis Exposition are shown in a nearly 360-degree pan. The last portion of the film was photographed over the heads of spectators cheering the dedication speaker.

Opening Day, Jamestown Exposition
AM&B © H94003 May 18, 1907
Cameraman: G. W. Bitzer
Location: Jamestown, Va. *Photographed:* Apr. 26, 1907
203 ft. FLA5621 (print) FRA2468 (neg.)
[Jamestown Tercentennial]

The subject is the dedication ceremonies of an exposition of sufficient importance for the president of the United States and representatives of thirty-seven nations to officially open it. Most of the film concerns the arrival of Pres. Theodore Roosevelt and entourage, as well as the military representatives of the guest nations. There are, however, some scenes of the size of the crowd and the bunting-decorated grandstand. Among those present, besides the president, were Mrs. Roosevelt, Major General Grant, Rear Admiral Evans, Lieutenant Fitzhugh Lee, William Loeb, Jr. and Miss Ethel Roosevelt. The subtitle on the film is: President Roosevelt and Family Arriving at Discovery Landing: Naval and Military Representatives of 37 Nations. President Roosevelt Opening Exposition. The film was released on May 11, 1907, as *Jamestown Exposition.*

Opening of Belmont Park Race Course
Edison © H60646 May 8, 1905
Cameraman: Edwin S. Porter
Location: Belmont Park, Elmont, N.Y. *Photographed:* May 4, 1905
68 ft. FLA5125 (print) FRA2077 (neg.)

Horses mounted by jockeys can be seen in a paddock. The second camera position is from the grandstand. As the camera begins to pan, horses approach the camera at a full gallop, rounding the turn counterclockwise. As the horses pass the camera position, the camera pans again to show the packed grandstand. Other scenes of horses in a paddock, racing, horses being rubbed down after a race, horses blanketed and led away were photographed from two other camera positions. Reported to be "The only motion picture in existence of the greatest race horse, Sysonby, ever produced in America." It was owned by James R. Keene. The race was the Metropolitan Handicap which ended in a dead heat between Sysonby and Race King.

Opening of New East River Bridge, New York

Edison © H40151 Dec. 28, 1903
Cameraman: J. B. Smith
Location: East River, N.Y.C. *Photographed:* Dec. 19, 1903
86 ft. FLA5126 (print) FRA2078 (neg.)

A large portion of the bridge can be seen. Judging by their dress, the people passing the camera are dignitaries about to dedicate the structure. A second camera position shows parading individuals led by a standard bearer (standard unidentified). From a third camera position, taken over the heads of the crowd, can be seen buildings customarily found around waterfronts and then a covered platform, draped in flag bunting, where the people previously seen have gone to begin the ceremonies. One of the dignitaries was Seth Low, then mayor of New York.

Opening, Pan-American Exposition

Edison © H4637 May 28, 1901
Location: Buffalo, N.Y. *Photographed:* May 20, 1901
60 ft. FLA4767 (print) FRA1776 (neg.)

A group of dignitaries from various countries was photographed from a single-camera position participating in a parade marking the opening of the Pan-American Exposition.

Opening the Williamsburg Bridge

AM&B © H42039 Feb. 11, 1904
Cameraman: G. W. Bitzer
Location: East River, N.Y.C. *Photographed:* Dec. 19, 1903
38 ft. FLA3360 (print) FRA0663 (neg.)

From a single-camera position located on the newly constructed Williamsburg Bridge, a parade of dignitaries and military representatives is photographed passing the camera position on the way to the reviewing stand.

En Opfinders Skaebne

See: The Aeroplane Inventor

L'Oracle de Delphes

See: The Oracle of Delphi

The Oracle of Delphi

Méliès © H33234 July 6, 1903
Creator: Georges Méliès *Cast:* Georges Méliès
Location: Montreuil, France *Date:* Spring 1903
47 ft. FLA4768 (print) FRA1777 (neg.)
French title: L'oracle de Delphes

This film evidently was intended as a peep show as its one-minute length has little else to offer. The play is about a vase or treasure of some great value in a storehouse broken into by a thief. By the use of trick photography, a bearded figure emerges from the darkness and frightens the thief into returning his ill-gotten loot.

Ore the Banster

AM&B © H63381 July 15, 1905

Cameraman: G. W. Bitzer
Location: Studio, N.Y.C. *Photographed:* June 30, 1905
22 ft. FLA5113 (print) FRA1289 (neg.)

A set of the inside entrance to a house, with a staircase leading to the second floor, can be seen. A well-dressed young couple comes through the door into the house and repeatedly kisses. As they approach the bottom of the staircase, the young man embraces the young woman who begins to climb the stairs. She is detained by the man who seeks to kiss her once more so she leans over the banister. In doing so, she knocks over an object which crashes to the floor, awakening an old man who runs down the stairs in his pajamas. The old man seizes the suitor by the scruff of the neck and kicks him repeatedly toward the door. The film ends as the young man is seen going through the door propelled by the old man's foot. AM&B production records give the title as Over the Banister, but it was copyrighted as Ore the Banster.

Ormond, Fla. Auto Races

AM&B © H56520 Feb. 8, 1905
Cameraman: G. W. Bitzer
Location: Ormond Beach, Fla. *Photographed:* Jan. 24, 25, 26 and 30, 1905
114 ft. FLA5127 (print) FRA2080 (neg.)

To record the automobile race, the cameraman placed his equipment to best film the cars as they raced by. Some of the photography was of the direct approach, some overhead, but most of the scenes were photographed above the heads of the crowd watching the event.

Orphan Children on the Beach at Coney Island

AM&B © H49073 Aug. 13, 1904
Cameraman: G. W. Bitzer
Location: Coney Island, N.Y.C. *Photographed:* Aug. 6, 1904
30 ft. FLA3557 (print) FRA0833 (neg.)

The camera was situated on an ocean beach. The only action visible is a large number of children bathing in the surf. For the full extent of the film, the group can be seen splashing about in the surf.

Orphans in the Surf

Edison © H35375 Sept. 3, 1903
Cameraman: Edwin S. Porter
Location: Coney Island, N.Y. *Photographed:* Aug. 10, 1903
36 ft. FLA3089 (print) FRA0428 (neg.)

An area of a public bathing beach is shown. Passing the camera on both sides and running toward the beach are approximately fifty preadolescent boys in bathing suits. They continue on into the surf and splash about. Then, as if by direction, they return, approach the camera, and pass it by.

"Osler"-ising Papa

AM&B © H60054 Apr. 26, 1905
Cameraman: G. W. Bitzer
Location: Studio, N.Y.C. *Photographed:* Apr. 21, 1905
23 ft. FLA4769 (print) FRA1778 (neg.)

The set of this film was intended to represent the library or living room of a better-than-average dwelling. An older man and a young woman are seated at a table reading when a young man comes in and attempts to embrace the girl. The old man prevents them from so much as even touching hands. Several pretexts later, the frustrated young man shakes chloroform on a handkerchief and then holds it over the old man's nose. As the film ends, the old man is sound asleep in his chair, and the couple is embracing. According to Webster's Biographical Dictionary, "A chance allusion in a public address referring to the relative uselessness of men over sixty [by Sir William Osler, M.D.] was interpreted as a suggestion that all men over this age should be choloroformed," and his remark became the inspiration for this little comedy.

'Ostler Joe

AM&B © H111373 June 4, 1908
Cameraman: G. W. Bitzer *Script:* D. W. Griffith, based on a
  poem by George R. Sims
Cast: D. W. Griffith
Location: Studio, N.Y.C. *Photographed:* May 7 and 9, 1908
329 ft. FLA5622 (print) FRA2469 (neg.)

A young girl marries a man whose occupation is taking care of carriage horses. The first part of the film shows the wedding, the subsequent arrival of a baby, and their happy home life. But the wife meets a man of substance who begins paying attention to her. He offers her a life of luxury, and she runs off with him. The next scenes show her enjoying a social whirl of gay parties. The final scene shows the wife, old beyond her years, lying in a bed in disreputable surroundings, deserted by the man she ran away with, as her husband kneels beside her, praying for her as she dies. The sets were inconsistent in period.

Ostrich Farm

AM&B © H19650 July 2, 1902
Cameraman: Arthur Marvin
Location: Pan-American Exposition, Buffalo, N.Y. *Date:* June
  24, 1901
24 ft. FLA3793 (print) FRA1030 (neg.)

A fenced enclosure, with approximately a dozen full-grown ostriches, can be seen. During the course of the film, an attendant harasses the ostriches in order to make them move about.

Ostrich Farms at Pasadena

Edison © H11745 Dec. 19, 1901
Location: Pasadena, Calif.
31 ft. FLA4148 (print) FRA1318 (neg.)

The film shows a large fenced area where about fifty ostriches are confined. Many of the big birds pass close to the camera.

Ostriches Feeding

Edison © 13547 Feb. 24, 1898
Location: A.T. and S.F. R.R., Calif.
57 ft. FLA4209 (print) FRA1370 (neg.)

The camera was positioned to view at close range approximately a dozen full-grown ostriches busily feeding. Their attendant had thrown food on the ground, and during the course of the film the ostriches can be seen picking up the food from the ground. One of a series made with the cooperation of the A.T. and S.F.R.R.

Ostriches Running, no. 1

Edison © 13545 Feb. 24, 1898
Location: Pasadena, Calif.
32 ft. FLA4227 (print) FRA1386 (neg.)

The camera was placed on what appears to be the inside of a fenced enclosure similar to that of a race track. At a distance of approximately a hundred yards, nearly two dozen ostriches can be seen running at high speed. As they near the camera position, it is apparent that they are being herded by a man on horseback. Part of a series made with the cooperation of the A.T. and S.F.R.R.

Ostriches Running, no. 2

Edison © 13546 Feb. 24, 1898
Location: Pasadena, Calif.
30 ft. FLA4228 (print) FRA1387 (neg.)

The first thing visible is a large flat uncultivated area with a three-story house at a distance of approximately half a mile. As the film progresses, three full-grown ostriches pass by the camera. They are being chased by a running man. The ostriches pass back and forth in front of the camera twice before the film ends. One of the five films photographed in Southern California with the cooperation of the A.T. and S.F.R.R.

The Other Side of the Hedge

AM&B Hepworth © H53766 Nov. 28, 1904
Director: Lewin Fitzhamon
Location: Walton-on-Thames, England
40 ft. FLA4770 (print) FRA1779 (neg.)

There are two camera positions in this film, the first of which is in a rural area with a hedge in the background. A picnic is in progress in front of the hedge, attended by two young people chaperoned by a rather obese older woman. All of them eat food from a blanket spread on the ground. The young couple constantly attempts to hold hands, hug, or kiss, but is thwarted by the stern gaze of their companion. The second scene takes place on the other side of the hedge, after the youngsters have succeeded in making the fat woman overeat. As a consequence, she becomes sleepy and lies down to take a nap, whereupon the young couple run around the hedge, sits down on the grass, and embraces. Released as Over the Hedge.

Our Dare Devil Chief

Keystone © LP5253 May 8, 1915
Producer and Author: Mack Sennett
Cast: James T. Kelly, Minta Durfee, Ford Sterling, Eddie
  Cline, Al St. John, Vivian Edwards
Location: Keystone studio and surrounding areas, Los
  Angeles
805 ft. FLA5623-5624 (print)

Mayor James T. Kelly is married to a flirtatious young woman, (Minta Durfee) who is enamored of the chief of police (Ford Sterling). The mayor goes to his office, adjacent to the police station, and finds the police chief asleep at his desk. Sterling, an easy prey for some crooks, becomes involved when he helps Minta take home a number of packages. The crooks, planning to rob the mayor's home in his absence, find Minta and Sterling playing hide and seek. Minta, who has hidden in a closet, is joined by a frightened Sterling. From there until the end of the film, things just become worse for the pair. Eventually Minta is forgiven by her husband, the mayor.

Our Deaf Friend, Fogarty
AM&B © H42002 Feb. 10, 1904
Cameraman: A. E. Weed
Location: Studio, N.Y.C. *Photographed:* Feb. 2, 1904
35 ft. FLA4771 (print) FRA1780 (neg.)

Two people can be seen bending over a cast iron stove in a set of an Irish hod carrier's kitchen. When the visitor starts to put on his hat, the the host offers him a seat. The hostess brings a pitcher and pours each of them a glass of beer. While the beer drinking is in session, the host goes to the stove, out of sight of the alderman, pours cinders into the alderman's top hat, and then returns to the table. When the social amenities have ended, the host hands the alderman his top hat. When the visitor starts to put on his hat, the cinders fall all over the host instead of the alderman.

Out in the Street
See: The Waif

An Outcast Among Outcasts
Biograph © J169786 May 29, 1912
Director: D. W. Griffith *Cameraman:* G. W. Bitzer
Cast: Blanche Sweet, W. Chrystie Miller, Tony O'Sullivan, W. C. Hauber, William J. Butler, Frank Opperman, Charles West
Location: Santa Inez Canyon, near Santa Monica, Calif.
399 ft. FLA5625 (print) FRA2471 (neg.)

A rural postmaster becomes ill and his daughter (Blanche Sweet) takes his place. She is attacked by a group of tramps who attempt to rob her of the registered mail sack she is delivering. She runs into an abandoned house, locks herself in, and finds she is trapped. A one-armed tramp, who had refused to join in the holdup, notifies the authorities and they arrive just in time to rescue her. The young woman is so grateful for her deliverance that she kisses the little tramp, and the last scene shows him with a happy smile on his face as he walks down the railroad track into the sunset.

Outing, Mystic Shriners, Atlantic City, New Jersey
Edison © H48344 July 20, 1904
Cameraman: A. C. Abadie
Location: Atlantic City, N.J. *Photographed:* July 14, 1904
57 ft. FLA4772 (print) FRA1781 (neg.)

A large number of men wearing bathing suits march quick step by the camera. As the men continue, the seashore can be seen. Behind the marching men is an amusement pier out over the ocean. The film ends as the men can be seen in the distance marching into the water.

The Outlaw
AM&B © H111672 June 11, 1908
Cameraman: G. W. Bitzer
Location: Coytesville, N.J. *Photographed:* May 19 and 25, 1908
268 ft. FLA5626 (print) FRA2470 (neg.)

The story concerns a young woman who falls in love with a bandit at a stagecoach stop and helps him hide from his pursuers. After the holdup, approximately twelve mounted men form a posse and track the bandit to a barn where he has taken refuge. They set the barn on fire, and when the bandit attempts to escape he is shot, dying in the arms of the young woman who is in love with him. All of the scenes were photographed outdoors from many camera positions.

The Over-Anxious Waiter
AM&B © H38863 Dec. 5, 1903
Cameraman: A. E. Weed
Location: Studio, N.Y.C. *Photographed:* Nov. 27, 1903
25 ft. FLA4329 (print) FRA1477 (neg.)

Two people are sitting at a table on a set of a private dining room. A waiter continually comes in and interrupts the young couple at their tête-a-tête which obviously annoys the young man. When the young man can no longer tolerate the intrusions of the waiter, he rises from the table, picks up a bottle of seltzer water and squirts it at the waiter, emptying the entire contents on him.

Over Route of Roosevelt Parade in an Automobile
AM&B © H32391 June 4, 1903
Cameraman: H. J. Miles
Location: San Francisco *Date:* May 26, 1903
181 ft. FLA5128 (print) FRA2081 (neg.)

As the title indicates, this film was photographed from an automobile. It shows the route of the parade over which Pres. Theodore Roosevelt was to travel. Several turns and good views of buildings are shown.

Over Silent Paths
Biograph © J141397 May 18, 1910
Director: D. W. Griffith *Cameraman:* G. W. Bitzer
Cast: Marion Leonard, W. Chrystie Miller, Frank Powell, Arthur Johnson
Location: San Fernando, Calif. *Photographed:* Apr. 5–6, 1910
392 ft. FLA5627 (print) FRA2472 (neg.)

A young woman attempts to convince her aged father to give up gold mining and return to civilization. She goes off on an errand and returns to find her father dead and robbed of the gold. The daughter swears vengeance. En route to the nearest town, she encounters the murderer who has collapsed from exhaustion. She revives him and takes him along with her, and when she reaches town she tells the marshall that she suspects the man of having murdered her father. The marshall cautions her to say nothing for the present. The desert wanderer, now in love with the girl, proposes marriage and offers her a sack of gold, which she recognizes as her father's. She draws out a gun and marches him off to the marshall's office. The San Fernando Mission is seen from three different camera positions, as is a San Fernando road intersection with a sign.

Over the Banister
See: Ore the Banster

Over the Hedge
See: The Other Side of the Hedge

Over the Hills to the Poorhouse
AM&B © H112129 June 20, 1908
Cameramen: G. W. Bitzer, Arthur Marvin *Script:* D. W. Griffith

Location: Studio, N.Y.C. *Photographed:* May 15–21, 1908
281 ft. FLA5628 (print, copy 1) FLA0270 (print, copy 2) FRA2473 (neg.)

This film tells the story of an old woman who is saved from the rigors of a scrubbing board and washtub in the poorhouse by the timely arrival of a wealthy son. The events that lead up to this climax start after the old woman has divided her money between her children. She then goes to live with one son. There is a disagreement over what her daughter-in-law feels is undue influence over the grand-daughter. Grandmother is banished from the house and ends up in a squalid room, from which she is ousted by a cruel landlord for nonpayment of rent. There is a scene showing her trudging down the road and stopping in front of a sign reading "To the Poor-house." The original paper print film bears the title At the French Ball, but has been identified as Over the Hills to the Poorhouse.

Overland Express Arriving at Helena, Mont.
Edison © D7247 Apr. 4, 1900
Location: Northern Pacific R.R., Helena, Mont.
20 ft. FLA4008 (print) FRA209 (neg.)

The camera was placed close to the siding between the train platform and the track to record the arrival of a steam locomotive and passenger cars. As the engine nears the camera position, it stops. The remainder of the film, from the same camera position, shows people either getting on or off the passenger cars.

Overland Limited
AM&B © H18897 June 12, 1902
Cameraman: G. W. Bitzer
Location: Grand Island, Neb. *Date:* July 6, 1901
23 ft. FLA3683 (print) FRA0933 (neg.)

The camera was positioned alongside the track of an approaching steam locomotive pulling nine passenger cars. As the locomotive passes, the passengers wave at the camera or at something close to the camera.

Ox Carts, Tokio, Japan
AM&B © H36866 Oct. 19, 1903
Cameraman: Robert K. Bonine
Location: Kyoto, Japan *Date:* July 28, 1901
15 ft. FLA3085 (print) FRA0424 (neg.)

At first, all that can be seen is a village street. Approaching the camera position along the street are two-wheeled carts drawn by oxen and guided by men dressed in farmers' clothing. Four different types of vehicles are shown.

Paced Bicycle Race
AM&B © H26851 Jan. 3, 1903
Location: Charles River Park, Boston [?] *Photographed:* Oct. 1897 [?]
18 ft. FLA3250 (print) FRA0572 (neg.)

The opening scenes show factory buildings in the background and in the foreground part of a straightaway and curve of an outdoor track. Men riding bicycles of the two-wheeled variety can be seen. However, the bicycles are so constructed that they can be ridden by five men simultaneously. The bicycles are used as wind breakers or pacers for a one-man bicycle following close behind. The bicycles pass the camera position three times.

See also: Multicycle Race

Pack Mules With Ammunition on the Santiago Trail, Cuba
Edison © 46693 Aug. 5, 1898
Cameraman: William Paley
Location: Cuba *Photographed:* June [?] 1898
24 ft. FLA3337 (print) FRA0648 (neg.)
[Spanish-American War]

A full "brigade" of pack animals used in the Spanish-American War is shown approaching the camera position. Good details are visible of the type of packs worn as well as the size and position. Several men can be seen, some of whom are riding while others are walking. Some of the men wear military uniforms while others are in civilian clothing.

Pack Train, Gen. Bell's Expedition
AM&B © H16358 Apr. 10, 1902
Cameraman: Raymond Ackerman
Location: Philippine Islands *Date:* Feb. 6, 1900
15 ft. FLA4256 (print) FRA1412 (neg.)

The short length of this film, together with its poor condition, does not permit much description. About the only thing discernible is that the film was taken outdoors in a hilly or mountainous terrain.

Pack Train on the Chilcoot Pass
Edison © H4085 May 6, 1901
Cameraman: Robert K. Bonine
Location: Chilkoot Pass, Canada
34 ft. FLA3872 (print) FRA1083 (neg.)
[Alaska Gold Rush]

A single-camera position discloses snow-covered mountainous terrain. From around a point of land, a rider comes leading about ten mules, each carrying a pack. The remainder of the film, from the same camera position, shows approximately thirty more mules, each with a pack.

Packers on the Trail
Edison © H4575 May 24, 1901
Cameraman: Robert K. Bonine
Location: Klondike, Canada
35 ft. FLA3472 (print) FRA0754 (neg.)
[Alaska Gold Rush]

As the film begins, one sees a wooded terrain covered with heavily packed snow. Approaching the camera position is a team of dogs drawing a sled with a driver in white furs. Following the sled are approximately twelve men laden with digging implements and dressed in heavy clothing. The balance of the film, from the same camera position, shows the sled returning over the same trail accompanied by the same people.

Packing Ammunition on Mules, Cuba
Edison © 46692 Aug. 5, 1898
Cameraman: William Paley [?]
Location: Cuba
26 ft. FLA4371 (print) FRA1510 (neg.)
[Spanish-American War]

Photographed from a single-camera position, the film shows a mule being loaded with boxes by men in American Army uniforms. Beyond the mule, American transport ships can be seen in a bay.

A Pair of Queens

AM&B © H32907 June 23, 1903

Cameraman: G. W. Bitzer

Location: Studio, N.Y.C. *Date:* June 17, 1903

21 ft. FLA3434 (print) FRA0720 (neg.)

The film opens on a kitchen set where a woman costumed as a cook is preparing food, while a second woman, dressed as a maid, watches her. The maid annoys the cook who spills the contents of a bowl on the maid's uniform. This causes the maid to retaliate by throwing her feather duster, and a brawl starts. When the film ends, no piece of furniture is intact and even the window has been broken.

The Pajama Girl

AM&B © H32109 May 22, 1903

Cameraman: G. W. Bitzer

Location: Roof studio, N.Y.C. *Date:* May 15, 1903

29 ft. FLA3737 (print) FRA0983 (neg.)

This film shows a woman clothed in pajamas who demonstrates several different types of calisthenic exercises. She performs her exercises in front of an outdoor set.

The Pajama Statue Girls

AM&B © H38861 Dec. 5, 1903

Cameraman: A. E. Weed

Location: Studio, N.Y.C. *Photographed:* Nov. 25, 1903

31 ft. FLA4186 (print, copy 1) FLA5970 (print, copy 2) FRA1350 (neg.)

The camera was placed as if it were a spectator in a vaudeville house. The show consists of three young ladies clad in pajamas playing "bean bag" with a handkerchief on a stage in front of a backdrop. One throws the handkerchief to one of the other girls and, as it is caught, all three "freeze" in that position. The game continues for the entire length of the film.

Palace of Electricity

Edison © D16380 Aug. 9, 1900

Location: Paris

29 ft. FLA3296 (print) FRA0611 (neg.)

[Paris Exposition]

This single-camera position film employs a 360-degree pan that starts with a view of the electric building and includes most of the principal buildings at the exposition (World's Fair), held in Paris, France, although the title of the film does not indicate the location.

Pan-American Exposition by Night

Edison © H9784 Oct. 17, 1901

Cameramen: Edwin S. Porter, Arthur White

Location: Buffalo, N.Y.

27 ft. FLA4009 (print) FRA1210 (neg.)

The film begins with a slow pan over the tower building of the exposition, which was lighted by electric lights. The pan goes from a daylight shot of the grounds to what appears to be a special effects situation involving back lighting of the scene.

Panorama at Grant's Tomb, Dewey Naval Procession

Edison © 64322 Oct. 4, 1899

Location: N.Y.C. *Photographed:* Sept. 29, 1899

83 ft. FLA4773 (print) FRA1782 (neg.)

[Spanish-American War; Dewey Homecoming, New York City.]

Photographed from a single-camera position, the deck of a boat, the film shows the Naval Parade welcoming Admiral Dewey's flotilla as it passes Grant's Tomb in New York City. Faces are not discernible.

Panorama Exterior Westinghouse Works

See: Westinghouse Works

Panorama from Canoe, no. 6

AM&B © H35871 Sept. 21, 1903

52 ft. FLA4774 (print) FRA1783 (neg.)

The film begins from a camera platform that the title indicates is a canoe. The camera was directed from the canoe to the adjacent foliage and overhanging the bank of whatever water the canoe is floating upon.

Panorama from German Building, World's Fair

AM&B © H49803 Sept. 1, 1904

Cameraman: A. E. Weed

Location: St. Louis *Date:* August. 26, 1904

57 ft FLA5129 (print) FRA2082 (neg.)

Although the film was photographed from a single-camera position, the photographer panned the camera approximately 150 degrees. Most of the major buildings, grounds, waterways, and fountains of the St. Louis World's Fair are shown.

Panorama from Gondola, St. Louis Exposition

AM&B © H46226 May 19, 1904

Cameraman: A. E. Weed

Location: St. Louis *Photographed:* May 10, 1904

124 ft. FLA5130 (print) FRA2083 (neg.)

The first scenes were photographed from a boat that was either rowed or sculled along the waterway of the St. Louis Exposition. The film shows the principal exhibit buildings lining the mall, as well as statues and bridges. The next camera position was stationary. The scenes show decorated rowboats and motorboats laden with costumed people as though part of a parade. The lead boat in the parade contains a single occupant in military uniform.

See also: Parade of Floats

Panorama from Incline Railway

AM&B © H22205 Oct. 3, 1902

Cameraman: Robert K. Bonine

Location: Mt. Beacon, N.Y. *Date:* Sept. 18, 1902

78 ft. FLA5131 (print) FRA2084 (neg.)

The camera platform was a car on a funicular track that ran from the top of a mountain and ended at a depot at the bottom. The film was photographed from a train descending the side of a mountain.

See also: Panorama From Running Incline Railway

Panorama from Running Incline Railway
AM&B © H22206 Oct. 3, 1902
Cameraman: Robert K. Bonine
Location: Mt. Beacon, N.Y. *Date:* Sept. 18, 1902
64 ft. FLA5132 (print) FRA2085 (neg.)

A large barn and some mechanical facilities to attend a small railroad are visible in the first scene, photographed from a camera on a car that was part of an incline railroad. As the film progresses, the camera begins to move and photographs the area on either side of the track. During the descent of the car, a man on a small track inspector's cart can be seen.

See also: Panorama From Incline Railway

Panorama From the Moving Boardwalk
Edison © D16381 Aug. 9, 1900
Location: Paris
50 ft. FLA4775 (print) FRA1784 (neg.)
[Paris Exposition]

The camera was positioned on a moving sidewalk built especially for the interest of the tourist at the Paris Exposition. As the mechanical conveyance progresses over its route, the scope of the camera takes in many of the buildings, decorations, trees, shrubbery, and the concessions set up for the exposition.

See also: Panorama of the Moving Boardwalk

Panorama from the Tower of the Brooklyn Bridge
AM&B © H35636 Sept. 12, 1903
Cameraman: G. W. Bitzer
Location: N.Y.C. *Date:* Apr. 18, 1899
19 ft. FLA3366 (print) FRA0668 (neg.)

The film was photographed from a single-camera position, the tower of Brooklyn Bridge. There is an approximately 180-degree pan that shows the Staten Island and Manhattan Island waterfronts.

Panorama from Times Building, New York
AM&B © H59310 Apr. 11, 1905
Cameraman: Wallace McCutcheon
Location: N.Y.C. *Date:* Apr. 1905
115 ft. FLA5133 (print) FRA2862 (neg.)

The camera position is at the top of the Times Building (approximately twenty stories high). The camera action starts from a depressed camera position and changes to an elevated one, while the photography encompasses a section of New York buildings looking north. The photographer then made a pan to the right over the tops of the buildings to Bryant Park and continued south. It is possible to distinguish the old Hippodrome Building, and the marquee of the Girard Hotel can be seen. The view continues down to the 23rd Street intersection and the Flatiron Building.

Panorama, Golden Gate
AM&B © H30735 Apr. 24, 1903
Cameraman: Robert K. Bonine
Location: San Francisco *Date:* Nov. 19, 1901

28 ft. FLA3399 (print) FRA0695 (neg.)

Using primitive equipment, the camera was panned from one position to show the area seaward of the Golden Gate in San Francisco. There are very few frames of the actual Golden Gate.

Panorama, Great Gorge Route over Lewiston Bridge
Edison © H9963 Oct. 22, 1901
Location: Niagara River, N.Y.
80 ft. FLA5134 (print) FRA2086 (neg.)

The camera was positioned on the front of an electric railroad car. Another electric car on another track can be seen approaching the camera position. As the car approaches, the camera platform starts to move. The film shows a mountainous countryside, filled with ravines, and as the track turns, a suspension bridge can be seen over the gorge. The gorge is estimated as 250 feet deep. The remainder of the film shows the scenery on both sides of the gorge.

Panorama of Beach and Cliff House
AM&B © H36355 Sept. 30, 1903
Cameraman: H. J. Miles
Location: San Francisco *Date:* Sept. 23, 1903
43 ft. FLA4776 (print) FRA1785 (neg.)

At the moment the film begins, the camera starts to pan and during the course of the film, it photographs a great number of people who are in a beach area at the foot of the famed San Francisco hotel, the Cliff House. The crowd seems to be casual and unorganized. In the last few scenes, the camera lingers on some children wading in the surf.

Panorama of Blackwell's Island, N.Y.
Edison © H32034 May 20, 1903
Cameraman: Edwin S. Porter
Location: East River, N.Y. *Photographed:* May 9, 1903
71 ft. FLA5135 (print) FRA2087 (neg.)

This film was photographed from a camera position on the deck of a boat circumnavigating Blackwell's Island. All of the buildings, the land under cultivation, the streets, utilities, etc., visible from the East River were photographed.

See also: Panorama of Riker's Island, N.Y., and Panorama Water Front and Brooklyn Bridge From East River

Panorama of East Galveston
Edison © D18567 Sept. 24, 1900
Location: Galveston, Tex. *Date:* Sept. 1900
50 ft. FLA4777 (print) FRA1786 (neg.)
[Galveston, Texas, Hurricane and Tidal Wave]

The title describes the subject matter of this film. It contains a 180-degree pan of the destruction of the city of Galveston, Texas, by tidal wave and hurricane in 1900.

Panorama of Eiffel Tower
Edison © D16385 Aug. 9, 1900
Location: Paris
45 ft. FLA3246 (print) FRA0569 (neg.)
[Paris Exposition]

The supporting arch of one side of the Eiffel Tower is shown. Many people walk to and fro in front of the camera. It is apparent from the film that the camera was elevated to take in almost the full height of the tower. It is elevated and then declined from the same position. Along about this time, many of the spectators or tourists became aware of the camera and they gesticulate, make funny faces, etc., as they show off.

Panorama of Esplanade by Night

Edison © H10633 Nov. 11, 1901
Cameramen: Edwin S. Porter, Arthur White
Location: Buffalo, N.Y.
27ft. FLA4040 (print) FRA1227 (neg.)
[Pan-American Exposition]

The first objects visible in this film, which was taken at night, are the glowing light globes that outline the buildings closest to the camera position. The camera slowly pans, encompassing the complete area of the exhibit buildings, and the outlines of all the buildings are clearly discernible. Edwin S. Porter maintained that this was the first motion picture ever taken at night by incandescent light in America.

See also: Electric Tower

Panorama of Excursion Boats

AM&B © H35650 Sept. 12, 1903
Cameraman: A. E. Weed
Location: Sandy Hook, N.J. *Photographed:* Aug. 25, 1903
25 ft. FLA3367 (print) FRA0669 (neg.)
[America's Cup Races; Reliance and Shamrock III]

Spectator boats watching the America's Cup sailing races were photographed. There are various sizes of sailing and motor-driven craft shown, ranging from an estimated twenty to a hundred and fifty feet in length. There are also some commercial tugboats.

Panorama of Field Street, St. Joseph

AM&B © H45459 May 7, 1904
Cameraman: A. E. Weed
Location: St. Joseph, Mo. *Photographed:* Apr. 22, 1904
28 ft. FLA3255 (print) FRA0577 (neg.)

The camera, positioned on a piece of moving equipment such as a horse-drawn wagon, shows a wide, congested street of the business district of St. Joseph. There are horse-drawn carts, two-wheeled and four-wheeled carriages, and people strolling about. Some of the buildings have advertisements. AM&B production records have been corrected to read "Felix Street," rather than "Field Street."

Panorama of Flatiron Building

AM&B © H32387 June 4, 1903
Cameraman: Robert K. Bonine
Location: N.Y.C. *Date:* Oct. 8, 1902
30 ft. FLA4778 (print) FRA1787 (neg.)

This shows a New York City street, photographed from a single-camera position looking across the street from the then-famous Flatiron Building. The cameraman elevated his camera, going from the street level to the roof. The picture's main interest is the lack of other buildings around the Flatiron Building.

Panorama of 4th St., St. Joseph

AM&B © H45458 May 7, 1904
Cameraman: A. E. Weed
Location: St. Joseph, Mo. *Photographed:* Apr. 23, 1904
28ft. FLA4042 (print) FRA1229 (neg.)

The camera was positioned on a moving vehicle as it proceeded down a business district street. The subjects photographed were buildings on either side of the street and a few horse-drawn vehicles.

Panorama of Galveston Power House

Edison © D18563 Sept. 24, 1900
Location: Galveston, Tex. *Photographed:* Sept. 1900
28 ft. FLA3840 (print) FRA1100 (neg.)
[Galveston, Texas, Hurricane and Tidal Wave]

The opening scenes show the devastation and damage to buildings caused by the hurricane and tidal wave. The debris piled up by the backwash of water is shown, and the camera slowly pans for approximately 90 degrees to take in scenes of further destruction.

Panorama of Gorge Railway

Edison © D11028 May 26, 1900
Location: Niagara River, N.Y.
49 ft. FLA4779 (print) FRA1788 (neg.)

The water that cascaded down the sheer cliffs of a gorge so interested the photographer that he filmed approximately a mile run of it from a train platform as the train wound along the bank. Aside from the water, very little else is visible except for some protection railings and one short span of a bridge.

Panorama of Kobe Harbor, Japan

AM&B © H36864 Oct. 19, 1903
Cameraman: Robert K. Bonine
Location: Kobe, Japan *Photographed:* July 29, 1901
18 ft. FLA3752 (print) FRA0998 (neg.)

The short length of the film included the water of the harbor, where there is a large steam vessel floating, another at anchor and, in the immediate foreground, a small sampan with three passengers being sculled by a boatman using a single oar. The camera was positioned on a boat, which caused an undulating movement throughout the film.

Panorama of Machine Co. Aisle Westinghouse Co. Works

See: Westinghouse Works

Panorama of Morro Castle, Havana, Cuba

Edison © H30401 Apr. 8, 1903
Location: Havana, Cuba
32 ft. FLA3657 (print) FRA0911 (neg.)

The camera platform for this film was a boat proceeding past the lighthouse point of Morro Castle, Cuba. The distance from the camera to the subject was such that no detail is shown.

Panorama of Orphans Home, Galveston

Edison © D18564 Sept. 24, 1900
Location: Galveston, Tex. *Photographed:* Sept. 1900

28 ft. FLA4395 (print) FRA1525 (neg.)
[Galveston, Texas, Hurricane and Tidal Wave]

The camera focuses on the building indicated as the Orphans Home, showing damage created by either the wind of the hurricane or the backwash from the tidal wave, and including debris around the yard. As the camera begins to pan for about 25 degrees, it shows further damage of the buildings.

Panorama of Place de L'opera

Edison © D16389 Aug. 9, 1900
Location: Paris
31 ft. FLA3221 (print) FRA0545 (neg.)

All the scenes were photographed from a camera positioned on a street curbing to show the residents of Paris going about the business of the day. People are shown walking toward the camera, away from the camera, getting on and off public vehicles, driving in vehicles, and being transported in vehicles, sitting at sidewalk cafes, etc. All was encompassed by an 180-degree panoramic exposure of the film by the camera.

Panorama of Race Track Crowd, St. Louis

AM&B © H47705 July 6, 1904
Cameraman: A. E. Weed
Location: St. Louis *Photographed:* June 25, 1904
51 ft. FLA4780 (print) FRA1789 (neg.)
[Louisiana Purchase Exposition]

The first scenes are high over the heads of a large crowd of people milling about in the interior area of a horse race track. As the camera begins to pan, in the background across the turf, private boxes can be seen in the grandstand, which is decorated with bunting. As the camera continues to move, more of the crowd in the center of the race track is visible. Striped tents can be seen here and there throughout the crowd and, as the film ends, a large building can be seen in the background.

Panorama of Riker's Island, N.Y.

Edison © H32031 May 20, 1903
Cameraman: Edwin S. Porter
Location: N.Y.C. *Photographed:* May 9, 1903
58 ft. FLA4781 (print) FRA1790 (neg.)

The camera was placed on the platform of a swiftly moving boat going around the island. The film shows heavy construction equipment in use, either moving caissons or digging.

See also: Panorama of Blackwell's Island, New York, and Panorama Water Front, and Brooklyn Bridge from East River

Panorama of Ruins from Baltimore and Charles Street

Edison © H42054 Feb. 12, 1904
Cameraman: A. C. Abadie
Location: Baltimore *Photographed:* Feb. 9, 1904
116 ft. FLA4782 (print) FRA1791 (neg.)
[Baltimore Fire]

This film was photographed from a single-camera position but the camera executed a pan of approximately 300 degrees to include the devastation of fire on the principal streets of Baltimore. Film coverage reveals building damage, street damage, and debris from buildings that have collapsed or were destroyed by blasting.

Panorama of Ruins from Lombard and Charles Street

Edison © H42055 Feb. 12, 1904
Cameraman: A. C. Abadie
Location: Baltimore *Photographed:* Feb. 9, 1904
26 ft. FLA4783 (print) FRA1792 (neg.)
[Baltimore Fire]

Views photographed from several camera positions show the fire damage with buildings gutted by fire, vehicles burning, and debris being moved and searched through by volunteers.

Panorama of Ruins from Lombard and Hanover Streets, Baltimore

Edison © H42310 Feb. 19, 1904
Cameraman: A. C. Abadie [?]
Location: Baltimore *Photographed:* Feb. 9, 1904
57 ft. FLA4402 (print) FRA1531 (neg.)
[Baltimore Fire]

This 360-degree panoramic picture shows devastation caused by fire: buildings gutted, walls collapsed, piles of bricks from buildings that have caved in, volunteers standing guard duty during the fire, and volunteer workers searching the ruins.

Panorama of Ruins from Water Front

Edison © H42056 Feb. 12, 1904
Photographed: A. C. Abadie *Date:* Feb. 9, 1904
Location: Baltimore, Md.
56 ft. FLA4784 (print) FRA1793 (neg.)
[Baltimore Fire]

A 360-degree pan is photographed, beginning with a water-filled street. As the camera continues to turn on a horizontal plane, it shows gutted buildings, piles of brick, sections of buildings still standing where other walls have caved in, burning telephone poles, and people inspecting the devastation and examining the debris. When the film ends, the camera has returned to the same scene from which it began.

See also: Panorama of Ruins from Baltimore and Charles Street, Panorama of Ruins from Lombard and Charles Street, and Panorama of Ruins from Lombard and Hanover Streets, Baltimore.

Panorama of the Moving Boardwalk

Edison © D16383 Aug. 9, 1900
Location: Paris
42 ft. FLA4785 (print) FRA1771 (neg.)
[Paris Exposition]

The camera was positioned to show a mechanical transportation device called a moving boardwalk. People of various ages get on and off the moving sidewalk. The locale is not identified.

See also: Panorama From the Moving Boardwalk

Panorama of the Paris Exposition, from the Seine

Edison © D16388 Aug. 9, 1900
Location: Paris

143 ft. FLA5137 (print) FRA2088 (neg.)

Contrary to the title, most of this film was taken from an excursion boat as it traveled down the river for about a mile. However, about 15 percent of the film is devoted to the two buildings the cameraman could photograph from the river.

Panorama of the Paterson Fire

Edison © H14295 Feb. 17, 1902

Location: Paterson, N.J.

27 ft. FLA3964 (print) FRA1173 (neg.)

Instead of burning buildings, the cameraman photographed the ruins, devastation, etc., caused by the fire. The film shows twenty-five or thirty completely ruined structures.

See also: Paterson Fire, Showing the Y.M.C.A. and Library, and Ruins of City Hall, Paterson

Panorama of 3rd Street, St. Joseph

AM&B © H45457 May 7, 1904

Cameraman: A. E. Weed

Location: St. Joseph, Mo. *Photographed:* Apr. 22, 1904

53 ft. FLA5138 (print) FRA2089 (neg.)

The camera was placed on a moving vehicle as it progressed down the main street of St. Joseph, Missouri. The film is very unsteady.

Panorama of Tivoli, Italy, Showing Seven Falls

Edison © H32507 June 11, 1903

Cameraman: A. C. Abadie

Location: Tivoli, Italy *Photographed:* Apr. 14, 1903

48 ft. FLA4786 (print) FRA1795 (neg.)

As the camera begins to pan, from its position in the hills below the city of Tivoli, waterfalls are seen at a distance of approximately three hundred yards. Buildings of the city, as well as an occasional waterway or fall, can be seen throughout the film.

Panorama of Willemstadt, Curacao, Taken from the River

Edison © H30400 Apr. 8, 1903

Location: Willemstadt, Curaçao

74 ft. FLA4787 (print) FRA1796 (neg.)

The photographer mounted his camera on the deck of a large vessel as it proceeded down river toward the open sea. The film shows the waterfront area, buildings, names of steamship lines. There are a great many spectators on the docks throughout the film. The film ends as the ship passes a lighthouse on the sea wall and enters the open sea. The film begins with the Edison warning against patent infringement.

Panorama of Wreckage of Water Front

Edison © D18560 Sept. 24, 1900

Location: Galveston, Tex.

30 ft. FLA4788 (print) FRA1797 (neg.)

[Galveston, Texas, Hurricane and Tidal Wave]

From a single-camera position, a 180-degree pan was effected, showing the devastation left by a hurricane and tidal wave that hit Galveston, Texas. The film shows damaged structures and vehicles. Along the docks are capsized boats.

Panorama, St. Louis Exposition

AM&B © H46820 June 3, 1904

Cameraman: A. E. Weed

Location: St. Louis *Photographed:* May 10, 1904

38 ft. FLA4789 (print) FRA1798 (neg.)

[Louisiana Purchase Exposition]

The camera was positioned on a section of a building high above the exhibit area of the St. Louis Fair so that the lens could encompass the largest building. As the film progresses, the camera begins to pan and continues for 180 degrees. During the period of camera movement, all buildings, walkways, exhibit areas, warehouses, etc., become visible.

Panorama, Union Square, San Francisco

AM&B © H32394 June 4, 1903

Cameraman: H. J. Miles

Location: San Francisco *Date:* May 26, 1903

88 ft. FLA5139 (print) FRA2858 (neg.)

Judging from the area included by the taking lens, the camera was placed at about the third floor of a building overlooking the area of Union Square. The camera was panned from its original position approximately 180 degrees and shows the buildings lining the square as well as several hundred people walking about under the bunting decorations. After reaching 180 degrees left pan, the cameraman began a pan to the right, encompassing a repeat of the previous scenes of the people and the buildings.

See also: The President's Carriage

Panorama View Street Car Motor Room

See: Westinghouse Works

Panorama Water Front and Brooklyn Bridge From East River

Edison © H32037 May 20, 1903

Cameraman: Edwin S. Porter

Location: N.Y.C. *Photographed:* May 9, 1903

69 ft. FLA4790 (print) FRA1799 (neg.)

The camera was positioned from the deck of a vessel proceeding down the East River toward the Brooklyn Bridge. The beginning scenes are abeam of the camera vessel and show all of the existing methods of docking a vessel and loading or unloading, as well as sailboats and steamships of all sizes.

See also: Panorama of Blackwell's Island, New York, and Panorama of Riker's Island, New York

Panoramic View Aisle B., Westinghouse Works

See: Westinghouse Works

Panoramic View, Albert Canyon

Edison © H11093 Dec. 9, 1901

Location: Albert Canyon, B.C., Canada

76 ft. FLA5142 (print) FRA2090 (neg.)

The photographer mounted his camera on a railroad train traveling on a nonstandard-gauge single-track rail along a gorge in very mountainous terrain. Mountain peaks, stands of timber, and telegraph poles alongside the track are all visible.

Panoramic View Between Palliser and Field, B.C.
Edison © H13036 Jan. 11, 1902
Location: British Columbia, Canada
82 ft. FLA4791 (print) FRA1800 (neg.)

The camera platform was located on one end of a train traveling over a single-track railroad outside a populated area. Mostly scrub brush, and foothill type countryside are seen.
See also: Panoramic View of the Canadian Pacific R.R. Near Leauchoil, B.C.

Panoramic View from Pittsburgh to Allegheny
Edison © H16120 Apr. 7, 1902
Location: Pittsburgh
49 ft. FLA4792 (print) FRA1801 (neg.)

The film was photographed from the front of a streetcar as it proceeded down its track through a city. People can be seen walking or riding in different types of vehicles. Several buildings can be also be seen.

Panoramic View, Horseshoe Curve From Penna. Ltd.
Edison © 40946 June 22, 1899
Location: Near Altoona, Pa.
23 ft. FLA4793 (print) FRA1802 (neg.)

The film was photographed from the front end of a railroad train that was traveling down a curved track. An oncoming train and one small railroad station can be seen.

Panoramic View, Horseshoe Curve, Penna. R.R., no. 2
Edison © 44243 July 7, 1899
Location: Near Altoona, Pa.
58 ft. FLA4794 (print) FRA1803 (neg.)

Moving photography from the front end of a railroad train or car as it proceeded down a curved length of track is seen. A station and a water tower are visible.

Panoramic View, Kicking Horse Canyon
Edison © H11091 Dec. 9, 1901
Location: Kicking Horse Canyon, Canada
87 ft. FLA5142 (print) FRA2092 (neg.)

The camera platform was a train proceeding over a single-track railroad. The track winds along a river at the side of a mountain. The railroad goes through two tunnels and crosses over two bridges of cantilever construction and one of general support construction.

Panoramic View, Lower Kicking Horse Canyon
Edison © H11089 Dec. 9, 1901
Location: Kicking Horse Canyon, Canada
83 ft. FLA5144 (print) Fra2092 (neg.)

The camera is located on one end of a vehicle, presumably a railroad train, moving over a single-track railroad through terrain that requires the track to wind in and out around the slopes. Sometimes running water can be seen, and an occasional pole with four wires is visible. As the film ends, a railroad siding with a few railroad cars, a water tower, and a few one-story wooden buildings can be seen.

Panoramic View, Lower Kicking Horse Valley
Edison © H11092 Dec. 9, 1901
Location: Kicking Horse Canyon, Canada
82 ft. FLA5145 (print) FRA2043 (neg.)

All of the film was photographed from a platform moving over a single-track railroad winding through mountainous terrain. Occasionally, rapidly moving water can be glimpsed. Telegraph poles have been established all along the right of way. Buildings are not visible.

Panoramic View Near Mt. Golden on the Canadian Pacific R.R.
Edison © H13039 Jan. 11, 1902
Location: Kicking Horse Canyon, Canada
80 ft. FLA4795 (print) FRA1804 (neg.)

The camera used to photograph this film was mounted on the leading end of a train traveling over a single-track railroad winding through mountainous terrain. The train tracks cross two cantilever construction trestles, go through one tunnel, and proceed alongside a rapidly running stream for approximately a third of the film. There are no people or structures visible.

Panoramic View of an Egyptian Cattle Market
Edison © H32803 June 17, 1903
Cameraman: W. L. Jamison
Location: upper Cairo, Egypt *Photographed:* June 13, 1903
63 ft. FLA4796 (print) FRA1805 (neg.)

A 360-degree pan was made from a single-camera position over the heads of many people milling about in the yards of a livestock market place. A few buildings are visible.

Panoramic View of Beyrouth, Syria, Showing Holiday Festivities
Edison © H32800 June 17, 1903
Cameraman: A. C. Abadie
Location: Beyrouth, Syria *Photographed:* Mar. 12, 1903
50 ft. FLA4797 (print) FRA1806 (neg.)

A large group of people is milling about in an area that resembles a fairground or amusement area. In the foreground are men wearing fezzes, and women with their faces covered with veils. In the background are small ferris wheels, swings, and carousels on which children are disporting themselves.

Panoramic View of Boston Subway from an Electric Car
Edison © H11492 Dec. 16, 1901
Location: Boston
33 ft. FLA4798 (print) FRA1807 (neg.)

This shows a short streetcar ride through a section of the Boston subway during its construction in 1901.

Panoramic View of Brooklyn Bridge
Edison © 10650 Feb. 4, 1899
Location: N.Y.C.
27 ft. FLA3224 (print) FRA0548 (neg.)

The camera was positioned on the front of a streetcar as it crossed the Brooklyn Bridge, but the cameraman apparently ran out of film before he completed the trip. Only the superstructure of the passageway is visible. The film is of poor quality.

Panoramic View of Charleston Exposition

Edison © H16720 Apr. 18, 1902
Location: Charleston, S.C. *Photographed:* Apr. 1902
80 ft. FLA5146 (print) FRA2094 (neg.)

The camera was placed in almost the center of the compound area by the exhibit buildings, and the cameraman began to photograph and pan his camera simultaneously. The film consists of pictures of the walkways, pools of water, bridges over the pools, exhibit buildings, bandstands, statuary, and decorations of all nature that, put together, made up the Exposition in Charleston in 1902.

Panoramic View of Electric Tower From a Balloon

Edison © H7634 Aug. 14, 1901
Cameramen: Edwin S. Porter, Arthur White
Location: Buffalo, N.Y.
38 ft. FLA4059 (print) FRA1243 (neg.)
[Pan-American Exposition, Buffalo]

The title indicates that this film was taken from a balloon. However, there is no aerial photography. Instead it is an up and down or elevation of the camera on the then-famous Electric Tower built for the exposition at Buffalo, New York.

Panoramic View of Floral Float "Olympia"

Edison © 64679 Oct. 5, 1899
Location: N.Y.C. *Photographed:* Sept. 29, 1899
27 ft. FLA3781 (print) FRA1023 (neg.)
[Spanish-American War, Dewey Homecoming, New York City]

The photographer mounted his camera on a boat in order to photograph a float built on a barge in honor of the arrival of Admiral Dewey. During the film, the float comes near enough to the camera for the details to be clearly visible.

Panoramic View of Moki-Land

Edison © H11266 Dec. 12, 1901
Location: Arizona
24 ft. FLA3165 (print) FRA0495 (neg.)

The camera was panned from the single-camera position to show the dry, arid butte land that was the home of the Moki Indians.

See also: Circle Dance, Carrying Out the Snakes, Line-up and Teasing the Snakes, March of Prayer and Entrance of Dancers, and Parade of Snake Dancers Before Dance

Panoramic View of Monte Carlo

Edison © H30408 Apr. 8, 1903
Location: Monte Carlo
52 ft. FLA4799 (print) FRA1808 (neg.)

The subject is the city of Monte Carlo. Most of the important buildings of Monte Carlo can be seen.

Panoramic View of Mt. Tamalpais

Edison © H13035 Jan. 11, 1902
Location: San Francisco
105 ft. FLA5147 (print) FRA2095 (neg.)

The film shows the curves of a single-track railroad as it wends its circuitous way up Mt. Tamalpais. The camera view is obstructed by the excavation and winding of the track.

Panoramic View of Mt. Tamalpais Between Bow Knot and McKinley Cut

Edison © H13034 Jan. 11, 1902
Location: San Francisco
83 ft. FLA4800 (print) FRA1809 (neg.)

The film was photographed from a single-camera position mounted on a railway car traveling over a single-rail track that winds and turns around the mountainous terrain of Mt. Tamalpais.

Panoramic View of Newport

Edison © D10163 May 12, 1900
Location: Newport, R.I.
37 ft. FLA4801 (print) FRA1810 (neg.)

The camera platform is on the deck of a seagoing steam-driven vessel or tugboat. The camera captured little more than the activity immediately by the bridge of the boat. Several men can be seen walking to and fro on the deck. They appear to be in American Navy uniforms. In the background are some unidentifiable buildings.

Panoramic View of Niagara Falls

AM&B © H35638 Sept. 12, 1903
Cameraman: F. S. Armitage
Location: Niagara Falls, N.Y. *Date:* June 28, 1899
23 ft. FLA3523 (print) FRA0799 (neg.)

The rapids above Niagara Falls and the falls themselves are shown in a 25-degree pan from the single-camera position.

Panoramic View of Rubio Canyon, Mt. Low R.R.

Edison © H11746 Dec. 19, 1901
Location: Mt. Lowe, Calif.
51 ft. FLA4802 (print) FRA1811 (neg.)

The camera was positioned on the front of a moving vehicle traveling over a single-track railroad winding in and around various points of land at the summit of Mt. Lowe, a Southern California tourist attraction.

See also: Panoramic View of the Great Cable Incline, Mt. Low

Panoramic View of St. Pierre, Martinique

Edison © H30395 Apr. 8, 1903
Location: St. Pierre, Martinique
130 ft. FLA5148 (print) FRA2096 (neg.)

The subject is the havoc and destruction wreaked by a volcanic eruption in St. Pierre on the island of Martinique. The camera was located on a boat that circumnavigated the island at a distance of 200 yards off the shore.

Panoramic View of the Canadian Pacific R.R. Near Leauchoil, B.C.

Edison © H13042 Jan. 11, 1902
Location: British Columbia
79 ft. FLA4803 (print) FRA1812 (neg.)

The camera was positioned on what seems to be the front of a train traveling over a single-track railroad through mountainous terrain. The track winds around points of land, and there is one straight stretch for what appears to be almost a mile. There are no structures seen; however, there are telegraph poles alongside most of the track.

See also: Panoramic View Between Palliser and Field, B.C.

Panoramic View of the Champs Elysees

Edison © D18581 Aug. 29, 1900
Location: Paris
24 ft. FLA4174 (print) 12FRA1339 (neg.)

The camera was mounted on a moving vehicle on a main street of Paris, France. The Arc de Triomphe can be seen in the distance. The vehicle carrying the camera makes an abrupt turn and proceeds down a street heavily congested with horse-drawn vehicles, both public and private.

Panoramic View of the Fleet After Yacht Race

Edison © H9411 Oct. 7, 1901
Location: Sandy Hook, N.J. *Photographed:* Sept. or Oct. 1901
46 ft. FLA4804 (print) FRA1813 (neg.)
[America's Cup Races: Columbia and Shamrock II]

The film, photographed at the time of the America's Cup Races, shows both contenders sailing back to their moorings. Three large dispatch cruisers come between the camera and the sailing vessels. During the maneuvering period of the camera-carrying vessel, other auxiliary craft that were part of the racing administration can be seen.

Panoramic View of the Golden Gate

Edison © H13041 Jan. 11, 1902
Location: San Francisco
69 ft. FLA5149 (print) FRA2097 (neg.)

The camera was positioned on the front of a vehicle, presumably a steam train. The picture begins as the vehicle moves down a single, narrow-gauge track. The next sixty feet of film are of the terrain adjacent to the track. It includes some scenes of the San Francisco Bay area. It is difficult to discern the Golden Gate.

Panoramic View of the Gorge R.R.

Edison © H7625 Aug. 13, 1901
Location: Niagara River, N.Y.
92 ft. FLA5150 (print) FRA2098 (neg.)

This film was taken from a platform on a train traveling over a two-track railroad bed located alongside a body of running water between some rather sheer cliffs. Visible in the film are two platforms on which people are standing looking at a view not shown in the film.

Panoramic View of the Great Cable Incline, Mt. Low

Edison © H11748 Dec. 19, 1901
Location: Mt. Lowe, Calif.
106 ft. FLA5150 (print) FRA2098 (neg.)

The camera was positioned on a platform of an incline railroad as it ascended Mt. Lowe, California. The film shows the track construction except when the descending train passes the ascending camera train.

See also: Panoramic View of Rubio Canyon, Mt. Low R.R.

Panoramic View of the Hohenzollern

Edison © H14439 Feb. 24, 1902
Location: N.Y.C. *Photographed:* Feb. 1902
30 ft. FLA3350 (print) FRA0658 (neg.)

The camera was placed so it could move along the full length of the moored German ocean liner *Hohenzollern*. However, because of the distance, only an area from the water line to the boat deck can be seen. As the camera moves along the side of the ship, some of the superstructure of the vessel can be seen. Side painters and members of the crew are busying themselves at various tasks.

Panoramic View of the Place de L'Concord

Edison © D18579 Aug. 29, 1900
Location: Paris
37 ft. FLA4805 (print) FRA1814 (neg.)

The camera was placed adjacent to the intersection of several main thoroughfares in Paris. During the film, the camera was panned to show some major buildings, statues, bridges, etc. In the foreground, throughout the film, many people can be seen walking to and fro, as well as quite a number of horse-drawn vehicles.

Panoramic View of the President's House at Canton, Ohio

Edison © H9016 Sept. 25, 1901
Location: Market Street, Canton, Ohio *Photographed:* Sept. 19, 1901
40 ft. FLA4806 (print) FRA1815 (neg.)
[President McKinley's Funeral]

Photographed from a single-camera position, the film's 160-degree pan shows President McKinley's house and the large line of people being controlled by military troops. The crowd had gathered before going through the president's house to view his body.

Panoramic View of the White Pass Railroad

Edison © H4081 May 6, 1901
Location: Alaska; British Columbia, Can. *Photographed:* 1899
32 ft. FLA3656 (print) FRA0910 (neg.)
[Alaska Gold Rush]

The camera was located on a train traveling over a track skirting a rugged, mountainous area. The film shows the tunnels and bridges constructed as part of the railway system.

Panoramic View of Tremont Hotel, Galveston

Edison © D18565 Sept. 24, 1900
Location: Galveston, Tex. *Photographed:* Sept. 1900
28 ft. FLA4807 (print) FRA1816 (neg.)
[Galveston, Texas, Hurricane and Tidal Wave]

The damage wreaked by a hurricane and tidal wave is clearly evident. As the camera pans, more damage to buildings is seen. There is a full shot of a hotel, bearing a painted sign to the effect that the price of beds ranged from fifteen to twenty-five cents per night. The foreground throughout the film records the devastation.

Panoramic View, Upper Kicking Horse Canyon

Edison © H11090 Dec. 9, 1901
Location: Kicking Horse Canyon, Canada
81 ft. FLA5152 (print) FRA2100 (neg.)

The film was photographed by a single camera positioned on the front of a train traveling over a single-track railroad winding through mountainous terrain. It is evident that the tracks are nearly at the summit, as the tops of mountains can no longer be seen in the distance.

Parade, Fiftieth Anniversary Atlantic City, N.J.

Percival L. Waters © H47450 June 22, 1904
Location: Atlantic City, N.J.
60 ft. FLA5153 (print) FRA2101 (neg.)

The subject is a parade made up of civic leaders, dignitaries, military units and military bands, fraternal organizations, fire-fighting apparatus (both ancient and modern), and decorated horse-drawn floats. The camera was positioned along the line of march and photographed the parade as it passed by.

Parade, Mystic Shriners, Atlantic City, New Jersey

Edison © H48345 July 20, 1904
Cameraman: A. C. Abadie
Location: Atlantic City, N.J. *Photographed:* July 13-14, 1904
53 ft. FLA4908 (print) FRA1817 (neg.)

The subject is the Mystic Shriners' convention parade. The photographer placed his equipment at an intersection and photographed the various Shriners as they marched past. The film includes several lodge groups, attired in their singular regalia, doing close-order drill. On two occasions, the paraders are obscured from the camera by a passing electric streetcar and by horse-drawn vehicles.

Parade of Buffalo Bill's Wild West Show, no. 1

Edison © 38211 June 22, 1898
18 ft. FLA4349 (print) FRA1492 (neg.)

Part of a parade can be seen as it passes the single-camera position. Covered wagons, men dressed as cavalrymen, and Indians in full-feathered war bonnets approach and pass the camera.

Parade of Buffalo Bill's Wild West Show, no. 2

Edison © 38212 June 22, 1898
61 ft. FLA4809 (print) FRA1818 (neg., copy 1) FRA18189 (neg., copy 2)

The camera was positioned above the heads of a crowd of people lining the street of an unidentified city. They are watching a parade of people in various costumes mounted on horseback. However, the camera is such a distance from the parade that identification of any individual is practically impossible. The height of the buildings in the background indicates a large city.

Parade of Chinese

Edison © 16439 Mar. 10, 1898
26 ft. FLA4292 (print) FRA1443 (neg.)

A parade through a business district of a large city is shown. The camera was placed on the side of a wide street where a considerable number of spectators are standing and watching the event. A number of horsedrawn floats with Chinese dignitaries as passengers and other floats drawn by people carrying dragon-decorated banners pass by.

Parade of Coaches

Edison © 13555 Feb. 24, 1898
Location: Rose Parade, Pasadena, Calif. *Photographed:* Jan. 1, 1898
15 ft. FLA3095 (print) FRA0434 (neg.)

Two six-horse coaches with approximately twelve women riding on top of each are seen. The camera position does not allow much detail. However, it is clear that the harness of the horses as well as the spokes of the wheels have been decorated as if for a festive occasion.

See also: Decorated Carriages, and Horticultural Floats

Parade of Eagles, New York

AM&B © H35631 Sept. 12, 1903
Cameraman: A. E. Weed
Location: N.Y.C. *Photographed:* Sept. 2, 1903
86 ft. FLA5164 (print) FRA2102 (neg.)

Photographed from a single-camera position above the heads of the crowds watching a parade, the film shows several different chapters of the International Order of Eagles. Some wear civilian attire, others costumes signifying a subdivision of their order.

Parade of "Exempt" Firemen

AM&B © H36401 Oct. 1, 1903
Cameraman: F. S. Armitage
Location: Washington Arch, N.Y.C. *Photographed:* Sept. 21, 1903
37 ft. FLA4810 (print) FRA1820 (neg.)

The entire film was photographed at the edge of a large public square where many people can be seen watching the approach of a color guard followed by a number of marching men pulling ancient fire equipment. The film is too short to permit further detail.

Parade of Floats, St. Louis Exposition

AM&B © H48986 Aug. 9, 1904
Cameraman: A. E. Weed
Location: St. Louis *Date:* Aug. 4, 1904
57 ft. FLA5155 (print) FRA2103 (neg.)
[Louisiana Purchase Exposition]

One of the parades of floating craft held in the waterways of the St. Louis Exposition is shown in this film. The cameraman placed his equipment on shore at a distance to include each of the competing craft. Photographed were twelve small craft, some motor-powered and some rowed, but all decorated with foliage and bunting and containing foreign representatives and dignitaries.

See also: Panorama From Gondola

Parade of Horses on Speedway

AM&B © H33282 July 8, 1903
Cameraman: Robert K. Bonine
Location: N.Y.C. *Date:* May 15, 1902

27 ft. FLA3677 (print) FRA0927 (neg.)

This parade of horse-drawn vehicles was photographed from the spectator side of a thoroughfare called a "speedway." In the background an arched bridge resembling the one at 59th Street in New York City can be seen, and also, in the extreme background, the Brooklyn Bridge is visible. During the film, various types of carriages containing people attired in fashionable riding apparel pass by the camera position.

See also: Lively Brushes on the Speedway

Parade of Marines, U.S. Cruiser "Brooklyn"
Edison © 60143 Oct. 12, 1898
50 ft. FLA4811 (print) FRA1821 (neg.)
[Spanish-American War]

Photographed from a single-camera position, the film shows some public event where the U.S. Marine Corps is passing in review.

Parade of Shriners, Luna Park
AM&B © H49510 Aug. 26, 1904
Cameraman: F. S. Armitage
Location: Luna Park, Coney Island, N.Y. *Photographed:* Aug. 17, 1904
69 ft. FLA5156 (print) FRA2104 (neg.)

A convention of the fraternal order of Shriners was the subject of this film, photographed at Luna Park in Coney Island, New York. During the film, members of the organization can be seen passing the camera position on camels or horses, in horse-drawn vehicles, or walking. All members of the parading group were attired in some sort of distinguishing regalia.

Parade of Snake Dancers Before the Dance
Edison © H11267 Dec. 12, 1901
Location: Ariz.
25 ft. FLA3088 (print) FRA0427 (neg.)
[Walpapi Indians; Snake Dance]

The single-camera position was above some Indians in ceremonial tribal dress who are preparing themselves for a ritual dance involving snakes and water.

See also: Carrying Out the Snakes, Circle Dance, Line-up and Teasing the Snakes, March of Prayer and Entrance of Dancers, and Panoramic View of Moki-Land

Parade of the Pikers, St. Louis Exposition
AM&B © H45955 May 13, 1904
Cameraman: A. E. Weed *Photographed:* April 30, 1904
Location: St. Louis
65 ft. FLA5157 (print) FRA2105(neg.)
[Louisiana Purchase Exposition]

The camera was positioned over the heads of a crowd watching a parade consisting of various kinds of decorated horse-drawn vehicles and marching individuals at the St. Louis Exposition. The floats were wagons and carriages decorated to represent such things as boats, industrial buildings, etc. The pedestrians were members of fraternal orders.

Parade of Women Delegates; World's Fair
AM&B © H49075 Aug.13, 1904

Cameraman: A. E. Weed
Location: St. Louis *Date:* Aug. 8, 1904
35 ft. FLA4812 (print) FRA2855 (neg.)
[Louisiana Purchase Exposition, St. Louis]

As the title implies, the film shows women delegates parading at the St. Louis World's Fair in 1904. They are employees of National Cash Register Company.

La Parapluie Fantastique
See: 10 Ladies in an Umbrella

Paris From the Seine
AM&B © H52232 Oct. 28, 1904
Location: Paris
99 ft. FLA5158 (print) FRA2106 (neg.)

This film was photographed from a small boat traveling down the Seine toward and through Paris. As the film progresses, the boat nears the civic buildings section of the city. All during the film, the landscape changes as the boat moves and many buildings and churches can be seen. The boat travels under bridges on which vehicles and people can be seen crossing the river.

Parisian Dance
See: Uncle Josh at the Moving Picture Show

Parke Davis' Employees
AM&B © H31670 May 11, 1903
Cameraman: F. S. Armitage
Location: Detroit *Date:* July 5, 1899
28 ft. FLA3161 (print) FRA0491 (neg.)

Photographed from a single-camera position, this film encompasses a scene of a large number of people either walking or riding bicycles as they leave what appears to be a factory. The title indicates they are employees of a drug firm.

Parsifal
Edison © H51619–51626 Oct. 13, 1904
Cameraman: Edwin S. Porter *Scenery:* Harley Merry
Cast: Robert Whittier (Parsifal), Adelaide Fitz-Allen (Kundry)
Location: Brooklyn, N.Y.C. *Photographed:* 1904 [?]
611 ft.
Parsifal Ascends the Throne: FLA5162 (print) FRA1991 (neg.)
Ruins of Magic Garden: FLA5164 (print) FRA2107 (neg.)
Exterior of Klingson's Castle: FLA5030 (print) FRA2108 (neg.)
Magic Garden: FLA5161 (print) FRA2109 (neg.)
Interior of Temple: FLA5160 FRA2110 (neg.)
Scene Outside the Temple: FLA5165 (print) FRA2111 (neg.)
Return of Parsifal: FLA5163 (print) FRA2112 (neg.)
In the Woods: FLA5159 (print) FRA2113 (neg.)

Each section had a separate title and was copyrighted individually: Parsifal Ascends the Throne, H51619; Ruins of Magic Garden, H51620; Exterior of Klingson's Castle, H51621; Magic Garden, H51622; Interior of the Temple,

H51623; Scene Outside the Temple, H51624; Return of Parsifal, H51625; In the Woods, H51626. Elaborate sets were used in each scene. All the actors gestured in an exaggerated manner. Interesting trick effects were used in some scenes. All the camera positions were from the audience's point of view. Based on Richard Wagner's opera, this film was intended to be shown with a musical accompaniment.

Parsifal Ascends the Throne
See: Parsifal

Passengers Embarking from S.S. "Augusta Victoria" at Beyrouth
Edison © H32509 June 11, 1903
Cameraman: A. C. Abadie
Location: Beyrouth, Syria *Photographed:* Mar. 12, 1903
39 ft. FLA3758 (print) FRA1003 (neg.)

The film was photographed from a small boat alongside a large anchored steamship whose passengers are leaving and getting on small boats clustered around a ladder that can be seen on the side of the ship. The seas were running to such a degree that the camera undulated. Consequently little detail can be seen.

The Passing of a Grouch
Biograph © J147353 Nov. 5, 1910
Cameraman: Arthur Marvin
Cast: Mack Sennett, Lottie Pickford, Florence Barker, Verner Clarges, Harry Hyde, Dell Henderson, Jack Pickford
Location: Edgewater, N.J.; Studio, N.Y.C. *Photographed:* Sept. 21–22, 1910
213 ft. FLA5629 (print) FRA2474 (neg.)

A man kisses his wife goodbye, starts off to work, meets two attractive young ladies, and, as he turns to greet them, slips and falls down, causing passersby to laugh at him. This makes him grouchy, and the rest of the film shows the chain reaction set off by his bad temper, until by evening it has reached his wife who scolds him when he gets home.

Paterson Fire, Showing the Y.M.C.A. and Library
Edison © H14289 Feb. 17, 1902
Location: Paterson, N.J. *Photographed:* Feb. 9, 1902
41 ft. FLA4813 (print) FRA1822 (neg.)

The film opens from a position about two stories from the ground, showing the devastation caused by a fire. As the camera begins to pan, the damage to the business district of the city becomes evident. There are two camera positions, the second one showing the devastation from about the same level but from another approach to the city. The film also includes a view of an electric streetcar.

See also: Ruins of City Hall, Paterson, and Panorama of the Paterson Fire

Paul J. Rainey's African Hunt
Laemmle © J168443 Apr. 22, 1912
Cameraman: J. C. Hemment
Location: Africa
1,307 ft. FLA5919–5921 (print) FRA2804–2806 (neg.)

The full extent of this six-reel film shows preparations for a trek into the African animal district. It begins with the selection of native bearers and animals to be used for pack and transportation. It shows the arrival of the hunting dogs, and continues with pictures of the safari, with the bearers carrying their burdens and the leaders riding horseback. The remainder of the film is devoted to scenes of trap setting, the capture of small animals, and filming, from a great distance, such animals as elephants and rhinoceroses at water holes.

Pawtucket Fire Department
AM&B © H38865 Dec. 5, 1903
Cameraman: F. S. Armitage
Location: Pawtucket, R.I. *Photographed:* Nov. 23, 1903
35 ft. FLA4814 (print) FRA1823 (neg.)

A good film, photographed from a single-camera position, of the Fire Department of the city of Pawtucket, Rhode Island, and its equipment. For the time, the apparatus was ultramodern.

The Paymaster
AM&B © H79818 June 23, 1906
Director: Mr. Harrington *Cameraman:* G. W. Bitzer
Cast: Gene Gauntier, Jim Slevin, Gordon Burby
Location: Mianus, Conn.; Studio, N.Y.C. *Photographed:* June 12, 1906
274 ft. FLA5630 (print) FRA2475 (neg.)

This film was made up of a series of tableaus, photographed from a single-camera position. Each scene was preceded by a title that indicated the action to follow. All scenes were photographed outdoors in Connecticut. The picture concerns the robbery of a payroll of a mill, the burial of cash by the culprits, the discovery of its whereabouts by a dog, and the subsequent capture of the bandits. The film begins with a close-up of the paymaster as he bends over the table counting money.

Peace Envoys at Portsmouth, N.H.
AM&B © H64599 Aug. 15, 1905
Cameraman: G. W. Bitzer
Location: Portsmouth, N.H. *Date:* July 19, 1905
173 ft. FLA5631 (print) FRA2476 (neg., copy 1) FRA2477 (neg., copy 2)
[Russo-Japanese Peace Conference]

The film documents several events concerning the arrival and departure of the envoys of the Russian and Japanese governments, and arbitration groups from the United States. Neutral areas designated for the conference can be seen. They were the docking area, the streets for the parade, and the building in which the peace conference was held. Most of the film was concerned with the arrival and departure of the dignitaries, in automobiles or horse-drawn vehicles and, in two instances, in large steam yachts.

See also: Scenes and Incidents, Russo-Japanese Peace Conference

The Peach-Basket Hat
Biograph © H128739 June 24, 1909
Director: D. W. Griffith *Cameramen:* G. W. Bitzer and Arthur Marvin

Cast: Mary Pickford, Florence Lawrence, John Cumpson, Jeanie Macpherson, Linda Arvidson, Charles West, Owen Moore, Marion Leonard

Location: Fort Lee, N.J. and studio, N.Y.C.

244 ft. FLA5632 (print) FRA2478 (neg.)

A large paper box falls off a dining room table and lands on top of an infant seated on the floor, completely hiding the baby. The frightened parents suspect that some gypsies who had been in the house reading the maid's palm stole the baby. There are many camera positions of the country town as the frantic parents set off after the gypsies. Each time the camera shows the group of people, the number of pursuers has increased. The distraught parents finally return home and discover the baby safe and sound under the paper box.

Peanuts and Bullets

Keystone © LP4354 Jan. 30, 1915

Producer and Author: Nick Cogley

Cast: Nick Cogley, Charles Chase, Dora Rogers, Billie Bennett, Eddie Cline, Harry McCoy

Location: Keystone studio and hill at rear of studio, Los Angeles

390 ft. FLA6135 (print)

A weight lifter (Nick Cogley) and a musician (Charles Chase) live in a rooming house where Dora Rogers plays a maid. Chase is not only behind in his rent, he has no money at all. When a fruit vendor (Harry McCoy) stops his cart under Chase's window, Chase devises a scheme for stealing fruit by means of a fork attached to a string. The cop on the beat stops by the vendor who accuses him of stealing the fruit. When Dora Rogers comes back from an errand, all the men try to impress her. McCoy gives her an apple, Nick Cogley lifts a 500-pound weight, and Chase just acts debonair. McCoy finally catches Chase stealing his fruit and the fight is on, with all the neighbors joining in. Chase goes back upstairs, takes some bullets from his gun and drops them out the window into a pile of peanuts roasting on the cart. The exploding bullets disperse the crowd but the vibration of the explosions causes the cart to start rolling down the street. When everyone gets to the top of the cliff, they fall over and the cart topples on them just as it explodes. The only two saved are Charles Chase and Dora Rogers who had stayed behind in his room.

Peeping Tom in the Dressing Room

AM&B © H60655 May 9, 1905

Cameraman: G. W. Bitzer

Location: Studio, N.Y.C. Photographed: Apr. 27, 1905

20 ft. FLA3917 (print) FRA1133 (neg.)

The subject of the film is a burlesque of a Peeping Tom who is caught in the act. From the camera position of the audience, a split set shows a rather buxom woman dressing on one side of a wall while a man is kneeling on the other side, watching her and another girl who has just entered. The Peeping Tom is apprehended and brought into the presence of the chorus girls. The film ends as the women beat him about the head and shoulders with powder puffs.

Pennsylvania Tunnel Excavation

AM&B © H65053 Aug. 30, 1905

Cameraman: G. W. Bitzer

Location: Seventh and Eighth Avenues, N.Y.C. Photographed: July 19, 1905

35 ft. FLA5166 (print) FRA2887 (neg.)

This single-camera position film employs an 180-degree pan shot of an excavation project. The film includes pictures of the narrow-gauge railroad that carries excavated material from the tunnel shaft under construction.

A Perilous Proceeding

AM&B © H16639 Apr. 16, 1902

Cameraman: Congdon

Location: Broadway & 13th Streets, N.Y.C. Date: Oct. 21, 1901

20 ft. FLA4188 (print) FRA1352 (neg.)

Centered in the picture are approximately ten men who are grouped in a basket suspended by the cantilever arm of a large crane at the top floor of a building under construction. As the film continues, the crane begins to move. It lifts the basket of men up and out over the interior of the construction site and then begins to lower them toward the ground. For the remainder of the film, the camera follows the basket filled with men as it is lowered down the six floors to the basement of the construction site, where the film ends.

Personal

AM&B © H47623 June 29, 1904

Director: Wallace McCutcheon Cameraman: G. W. Bitzer

Location: Grant's Tomb, N.Y.C.; Paterson and Edgewater, N.J. Photographed: June 8 and 13, 1904

186 ft. FLA5633 (print) FRA2481 (neg.)

The picture opens on the concrete sidewalk in front of Grant's Tomb in New York, where a man in a tall silk hat and a swallowtail coat is pacing up and down as if waiting for someone. A young woman comes up and shakes his hand, and he bows. Soon there are many more young women. The man panics and begins to run, followed by all the young women. They cross bridges, jump ravines, run down roads and over fences, and finally get to the bank of a stream where he can go no further. The woman who has been leading the chase removes a small revolver from her pocket, points it at his head, and he submits. That ends the film, which was directed by Mr. McCutcheon.

See also: How A French Nobleman Got a Wife Through the New York Herald Personal Column

Petticoat Lane on Sunday

Hepworth © AM&B H53768 Nov. 28, 1904

Location: London

80 ft. FLA5167 (print) FRA2114 (neg.)

An area known as the "Bowery" of London, England, was photographed from a single-camera position. The camera pans to show posters and signs indicating items for sale. Large groups of people are shown either buying or selling something.

A Phenomenal Contortionist

Edison © H10635 Nov. 11, 1901

Cameraman: Edwin S. Porter

Cast: St. Elmo

43 ft. FLA4819 (print) FRA1828 (neg.)

The film is made up of a combination of an extremely agile contortionist and his appearance and disappearance by the use of stop-action photography. As it begins, there is a simulated stone fence from which a figure draped in a sheet appears. When the sheet disappears, the figure becomes a man dressed from head to foot in tights. This individual then performs all manner of acts of contortion. When a prop is needed, it appears by stop action photography. At the end the actor disappears in the same manner.

Philadelphia Express, Jersey Central Railway

Edison © 43412 July 31, 1897
15 ft. FLA3895 (print) FRA1116 (neg.)

The locale appears to have been a railroad yard. The camera was positioned low and to the left of a railroad track. A train can be seen approaching. In the background is a railroad overpass. As the train approaching the camera position passes, another train crosses the overpass.

The Photographer's Mishap

Edison © H7329 July 31, 1901
Cameraman: Edwin S. Porter
44 ft. FLA4820 (print) FRA1829 (neg.)

A man is carrying a camera and a tripod as he walks down a railroad track. He sets his camera up to film an oncoming train. The next camera position shows the photographer putting his dark hood on as the train approaches. The train strikes the photographer, demolishes his camera, and he bounds to his feet only to have to jump from the path of an oncoming train on another track. Stop-action photography was used to substitute a dummy for the photographer who was hit by the train. The actor who played the photographer, whose name is not known to us, also appeared in A Romance of the Rail, copyrighted by the Edison firm in October of 1903.

Photographing a Country Couple

Edison © H7639 Aug. 14, 1901
Cameraman: Edwin S. Porter
28 ft. FLA3763 (print) FRA1008 (neg.)

A man is walking toward the camera, carrying a camera and tripod on his shoulder. He sets up the camera. A man and woman walk into the scene and the photographer seats them on a bench. The man becomes intrigued by the camera so the photographer allows him to get under the hood and observe him while the photographer sits with the woman and embraces her.

Photographing a Female Crook

AM&B © H41754 Feb. 2, 1904
Cameraman: A. E. Weed
Location: Studio, N.Y.C. *Photographed:* Jan. 13, 1904
24 ft. FLA4334 (print) FRA1480 (neg.)

The first scene takes place in a photographer's studio in a police station. Two policemen struggle to get a woman seated on a stool in front of a photographer's sign. The camera moves toward the seated woman. She obviously does not wish to be photographed for she grimaces and contorts her face while the camera moves slowly toward her.

See also: Subject for the Rogue's Gallery

The Physical Culture Girl

Edison © H36499 Oct. 3, 1903
Cameraman: Edwin S. Porter
Location: Studio, N.Y.C. *Photographed:* Oct. 1, 1903
65 ft. FLA5168 (print) FRA2115 (neg.)

A woman can be seen reclining on a day bed in one corner of a set of a living room of an ordinary house. The woman, costumed in bloomers, rises, walks over to a punching bag suspended from the ceiling, and begins to hit it. She continues to work out with wall weights, Indian clubs, and fencing foils. She finishes her calisthenics by doing push ups, knee bends and other physical culture exercises. The title is given as listed on copyright application and film; the page in the copyright record is blank.

The Physical Culture Girl, no. 1

AM&B © H33644 July 21, 1903
Cameraman: G. W. Bitzer
Photographed: July 8, 1903
30 ft. FLA3458 (print) FRA0740 (neg.)

The film begins on a set of a woman's bedroom. A barefoot woman clothed in sleeping attire walks from camera left to the back wall, picks up some wooden barbells, and begins a series of calisthenics. As the film progresses, she exercises with springs and Indian clubs, and does deep knee bends, etc. Apparently having finished her course of calisthenics, the film ends.

The Physical Culture Girl, no. 2

AM&B © H33645 July 21, 1903
Cameraman: G. W. Bitzer
Photographed: July 8, 1903
26 ft. FLA3459 (print) FRA0741 (neg.)

A woman can be seen against the rear wall of a set as the film begins. She is facing the camera and exercising on a machine of pulleys and weights. For the entire extent of the film, she can be seen bending, stretching, and pulling the hand grips attached to the weights against the wall.

The Physical Culture Girl, no. 3

AM&B © H33646 July 21, 1903
Cameraman: G. W. Bitzer
Photographed: July 8, 1903
28 ft. FLA3460 (print) FRA0742 (neg.)

The subject is calisthenics done by a woman dressed in a full black leotard. During the film she exhibits her grace in performing several bending and stretching exercises, using a wand or pole. The exercises are performed on a stage in front of a painted backdrop.

Physical Culture Lesson

AM&B © H78531 June 1, 1906
Cameraman: G. W. Bitzer
Date: May 9, 1906
19 ft. FLA3599 (print) FRA0864 (neg.)

The first scene was photographed on a set of a woman's dressing room. A woman in a long black dress is sitting at a dressing table, arranging her hair and fixing her face. A man in a dark suit enters and persuades the woman to follow his calisthenics instructions. She does the knee bend, then an overhead stretch and a few others, including a side kick with the foot. While the foot exercise is in progress, the physical culture instructor grabs her ankle, but then lets go. He sits down on her chair, pulls her into his lap, and begins kissing her as the film ends.

Picking Oranges

Edison © 13557 Feb. 24, 1898
23 ft. FLA4156 (print) FRA1324 (neg.)

The film, photographed from a single-camera position, shows oranges being picked by several persons who use ladders. One man falls down the ladder, but there is little else in the way of action.

The Pickpocket

Gaumont © AM&B H39217 Dec. 10, 1903
Director: Alfred Collins
Location: England
129 ft. FLA5634 (print) FRA2479 (neg.)

This film is made up of a series of incidents beginning with a pickpocket being caught in the act. He breaks away from his would-be captor and a chase begins through the business district of what appears to be London. The camera is moved approximately ten times in order to film the pursuit of the pickpocket by more and more people. He is finally caught on top of a pile of lumber in a contractor's supply yard by three policemen, who manage to handcuff him. During the chase, he breaks away from half a dozen such encounters.

The Picture the Photographer Took

AM&B © H40806 Jan. 12, 1904
Cameraman: A. E. Weed
Location: Studio, N.Y.C. *Photographed:* Nov. 30, 1903
28 ft. FLA3661 (print) FRA0914 (neg.)

This is a single-camera position film of a photographer's studio where the photographer can be seen as he prepares a model for a still picture. The film ends with a close-up of the model in a frame, conveying the impression of a finished still picture.

See also: One Way of Taking a Girl's Picture

Pictures Incidental to Yacht Race

Edison © 72833 Nov. 7, 1899
Cameraman: Edwin S. Porter
Location: Off Sandy Hook, N.J. *Date:* Oct. 1899
49 ft FLA4815 (print) FRA1824 (neg.)

First the bowsprit of a full-rigged ship and then the complete ship are seen as it sails by the camera position. The next scene shows the sailboat at approximately a thousand yards going away from the camera position. Next an unidentified steamship appears, and the remainder of the film is taken aboard what appears to be a military vessel where a sailor can be seen using the Morse code semaphore system with one flag.

Pie Eating Contest

Edison © 60593 Oct. 25, 1897
26 ft. FLA3076 (print) FRA0417 (neg.)

This single-camera position film shows the head and shoulders of two men engaged in a pie-eating contest. They succeed in devouring the pie but not in keeping themselves clean. This production represents a very early American use of artificial light in moving picture photography.

Pie, Tramp and the Bulldog

Edison © H4087 May 6, 1901
Cameraman: Edwin S. Porter
28 ft. FLA3633 (print) FRA0890 (neg.)

The film begins on a set that includes a house, a second-story kitchen window, a dog house, and a garden fence with a gate. A pie is cooling on the shelf outside the second-story kitchen window. A man dressed as a tramp comes through the garden gate, but his presence is violently objected to by a dog in the yard. Noticing the pie, the tramp leaves and returns wearing stilts. He manages to prop himself up against the building and begins consuming the pie. The dog, not to be outwitted, leaves the set, enters the house and, as the film ends, can be seen jumping out through the window onto the back of the tramp.

Pierrot and His Wives

See: Pierrot's Problem

Pierrot, Murderer

Gaumont © H44521 Apr. 18, 1904
7 ft. FLA3108 (print) FRA0444 (neg.)

This film, copyrighted in the United States by the L. Gaumont Company, has only two scenes. In the first, a man dressed as Pierrot (a clown), fires into the brush in a wooded area. After the smoke clears, a man dressed as a French policeman emerges holding a rabbit by the ears. The other scene takes place in a set of a dining room in a large house, and shows two people sitting at a dining room table. The film ends when one of the two people gets up and starts to leave. Evidently, the film is incomplete.

Pierrot's Problem

AM&B © H16338 Apr. 10, 1902
Cameraman: Arthur Marvin
Location: Roof studio, N.Y.C. *Date:* July 27, 1900
9 ft. FLA3226 (print) FRA0550 (neg.)

A stage backdrop painted to appear as an outdoor scene is visible. The first action is a man in a clown's suit landing on his feet after completing a handspring. He makes a gesture as if he hopes for the acceptance of a young woman in leotards who appears as if by magic. The clown moves from camera center to right and stands for a moment, then quickly moves away and another young woman in similar attire appears. He brings the two young women face to face in front of him at stage center, and they are quickly transformed into one woman of huge proportions. The film ends as the clown peers from behind the huge woman. Released as Pierrot and His Wives.

The Pig That Came to Life

Clarendon © AM&B H50326 Sept. 10, 1904
Location: England
105 ft. FLA5169 (print) FRA2116 (neg.)

A butcher is standing in front of his shop in the business district of a city. Then he enters his store, and a woman steals a pig from the display hook, puts in it a sack, and carries it away. She is soon tired and puts the sack down in a field, sitting down beside it and falling asleep. The butcher and his son find her and decide to teach her a lesson. They substitute the boy for the pig which the butcher takes back to the shop. The sleeping woman wakes, and resumes the arduous task of carrying the sack home. She is aided by a passing parson who becomes as frightened as she when the presumably dead pig in the gunny sack begins to move. He drops the sack, which begins to hop and follow the woman who runs into a nearby lake. The butcher and his son throw objects at the woman who is standing knee-deep in the lake.

Pigeon Farm at Los Angeles, Cal.
Edison © H11747 Dec. 19, 1901
Location: Los Angeles
69 ft. FLA4816 (print) FRA1825 (neg.)

The cameraman placed his equipment inside an area of approximately ten acres on which there are structures housing pigeons. He exposed the film and panned the camera approximately 180 degrees to encompass the barns and feed pens. Before the film ends, the camera has been moved four times and panned, using different lenses to cover the complete facility. There are many takes of pigeons, either flying or roosting. The locale was in the river bottom next to the city of Los Angeles.

A Pillow Fight
AM&B © H17629 May 15, 1902
9 ft. FLA4309 (print) FRA1458 (neg.)

The poor quality of the film, coupled with its shortness, gives little opportunity for detailed description. During the film three children dressed in sleeping garments can be seen standing on two beds tossing the contents of the pillows at one another, while a fourth watches with great glee.

The Pillow Fight, no. 2
AM&B © H62445 June 20, 1905
Cameraman: G. W. Bitzer
Location: Studio, N.Y.C. *Photographed:* June 12, 1905
20 ft. FLA3905 (print) FRA1125 (neg.)

Two beds joined together in an L-shape are seen against a brick wall. Kneeling at the edge of the beds are four little girls saying their prayers and being listened to by a woman dressed as a governess. The children are helped into bed and the woman leaves. As soon as the children feel they are really alone, they begin throwing pillows at one another. One of the pillows rips, filling the air and surrounding area with feathers. The governess returns and spanks one of the naughty children as the picture ends.

Pilot Boats in New York Harbor
Edison © 27966 Apr. 22, 1899
Location: N.Y.C.
15 ft. FLA3016 (print) FRA0010 (neg.)

A Marconi-rigged schooner of pilot boat hull-design passes close enough for four members of the crew to be seen from the single-camera position. Following the sailing vessel is a single-masted steamship of approximately 5,000 tons. The full length of the hull is visible at one time.

Pilot Leaving "Prinzessen Victoria Luise" at Sandy Hook
Edison © H30402 Apr. 8, 1903
Location: Sandy Hook, N.J.
35 ft. FLA3720 (print) FRA0967 (neg.)

From a camera positioned on the starboard rail of a large ocean liner, a bosun's ladder can be seen suspended down the side of the ship. As the film progresses, a man descends the ladder. When he reaches the bottom of the ladder, he waits until a small rowing boat comes close. As it does, he steps from the ladder into the boat and is rowed out of the picture.

The Pioneers
See: Discovery of Bodies, Firing the Cabin, Rescue of Child From Indians, Settler's Home Life

A Pipe Dream
AM&B © H62751 June 29, 1905
Cameraman: G. W. Bitzer
Location: Studio, N.Y.C. *Photographed:* June 16, 1905
26 ft. FLA4817 (print) FRA1826 (neg.)

A well-dressed young lady is seen on a bench. She starts to light a cigarette, shakes out the match, and blows on it. She then takes a puff of smoke, stretches out her right hand, and blows some smoke on her hand. At that moment the figure of a miniature man appears on her hand. The man kneels and stretches out his arms to the young woman, who blows more smoke on him, causing him to disappear. The remainder of the film shows the young lady with a look of consternation on her face as she tries unsuccessfully to repeat the trick.

A Pipe for a Cigar
AM&B © H43624 Mar. 23, 1904
Cameraman: A. E. Weed
Location: Studio, N.Y.C. *Photographed:* Mar. 10, 1904
23 ft. FLA3514 (print) FRA0793 (neg.)

It is evident that this was a vaudeville act filmed from the audience's point of view. There is a stage with a backdrop painted to represent the business district of a city. The two participants in the act are dressed as an Irish hod carrier smoking a white clay pipe, and an ordinary businessman smoking a cigar. The two men reach camera center from opposite wings of the stage and one asks the other for a match. They then exchange pipe, cigar, and matches until the film ends.

A Pipe Story of the Fourth
AM&B © H22094 Sept. 27, 1902
Cameraman: G. W. Bitzer
Location: Roof studio, N.Y.C. *Date:* July 7, 1902
50 ft. FLA4818 (print) FRA1827 (neg.)

The poor condition of the film caused by excessive grain and the lack of contrast, does not permit detailed description. The separation between the actors and the background is very slight. However, a man smoking a pipe is seen entering and coming out of a store with an armload of what appear to be fireworks. It is possible to see that an explosion occurs after which a white horse-drawn four-wheeled vehicle drives up and some attendants get out and place a body on a stretcher.

Gertrude Robinson in D. W. Griffith's Pippa Passes. *Griffith often based his plots on classics, in this instance, an 1841 poem by Robert Browning.*

Pippa Passes

Biograph No © rd. Oct. 1909

Director: D. W. Griffith *Cameramen:* G. W. Bitzer, Arthur Marvin, Mr. Higgin

Cast: Gertrude Robinson, George Nicholls, Adele De Garde, James Kirkwood, Mack Sennett, Tony O'Sullivan, Linda Arvidson, Billy Quirk, Arthur Johnson, Marion Leonard, Owen Moore, Clara T. Bracey

Location: Edgewater, N.J.; Studio, N.Y.C. *Photographed:* Aug. 17–21, 1909

364 ft. FLA5635 (print) FRA2842 (neg.)

This version of Robert Browning's poem shows the effect of a young girl's singing on at least three groups of people. The film begins in the dark and lights are slowly brought up to create the illusion of the sun rising. A young girl (Gertrude Robinson as "Pippa") awakens, takes her lute, and goes outside, and she is shown singing outside of taverns and houses in the town. She returns home, perhaps to retire, and the picture ends with the lights going down to complete darkness.

The Pirate's Gold

AM&B © H117952 Nov. 6, 1908

Director: D. W. Griffith *Cameramen:* G. W. Bitzer, Arthur Marvin

Cast: Linda Arvidson

Location: Seabright, N.J.; Studio, N.Y.C. *Photographed:* Oct. 8 and 10, 1908

366 ft. FLA5636 (print) FRA2482 (neg.)

The period of the film is the eighteenth century, and the first scene shows a man saying goodbye to his wife in their cottage. The next scene shows a beach where a rowboat lands. Three pirates unload the boat and open a chest, and begin to fight; two are killed. The third makes his way to the cottage with the treasure, which the woman helps him hide behind bricks in the fireplace. He dies of his wounds, and she is killed by lightning. The husband returns home, finds his wife dead, and eventually remarries. He gets into dire financial straits and is about to shoot himself when his wife rushes in and diverts the gun; the bullet hits the fireplace and exposes the pirate's treasure.

Pity the Blind, no. 2

AM&B © H41755 Feb. 2, 1904

Cameraman: A. E. Weed

Location: Studio, N.Y.C. *Photographed:* Jan. 15, 1904

20 ft. FLA4324 (print) FRA1472 (neg.)

The camera was placed as though over the heads of spectators at a vaudeville show. As the action begins, a young boy leads a man to the center of the stage. The man kneels down and the boy puts a sign reading "Pity the Blind" around his neck. Several people pass by and drop money in the blind man's cup. Three attractive women walk by the blind man but apparently they have no change for they raise their skirts to remove money from change purses next to their garters. While this is going on, it is very obvious that the blind man can see and that he is watching every move the young women make.

A Plain Song

Biograph © J148441 Dec. 1, 1910

Director: D. W. Griffith *Cameraman:* G. W. Bitzer

Cast: Mary Pickford, Dell Henderson, Gertrude Robinson, Robert Harron, Charles West, Kate Bruce, W. Chrystie

Miller, Eddie Dillon, Gladys Egan, Jack Pickford, Tony O'Sullivan, William J. Butler

Location: Westfield, N.J.; Studio, N.Y.C. *Photographed:* Oct. 13–17, 1910

400 ft. FLA5637 (print) FRA2483 (neg.)

A young woman (Mary Pickford) who has the responsibility of caring for her aged parents is wooed by a man about town (Dell Henderson), who convinces her that she is entitled to some fun out of life. She leaves a note for her parents and starts out with him. Symbolism is used at the train station when a group of approximately twenty old persons file by while the young woman is still debating with herself whether or not she should desert her parents. In the last scene, it is evident that her sense of duty and love of parents have triumphed, for she goes home before her parents have an opportunity to find the letter she had left.

The Planter's Wife

AM&B © H117027 Oct. 14, 1908

Director: D. W. Griffith *Cameraman:* G. W. Bitzer

Cast: Linda Arvidson, Florence Lawrence, Arthur Johnson, Charles Inslee

Location: Little Falls, N.J.; Studio, N.Y.C. *Photographed:* Sept. 8 and 10, 1908

333 ft. FLA5638 (print) FRA2484 (neg.)

As the picture begins, a small child is being attended by its mother (Linda Arvidson), a farmer's wife. A man in city clothes (Charles Inslee) enters, embraces the wife, and leaves. Her husband (Arthur Johnson) and her sister (Florence Lawrence) arrive. The next scene shows an outdoor rendezvous between the wife and her lover, who convinces her to run away with him. They are followed by her sister, and there is an exciting chase by horseback and rowboat. The sister catches up with the elopers and orders the wife back at gun point. There is a struggle between the three when they return home, but by the time the husband returns, all is tranquil. The farmer embraces his wife, and the sister picks up the baby and puts it between them.

A Plate of Ice Cream and Two Spoons

AM&B © H27379 Jan. 22, 1903

Cameraman: F. S. Armitage

Location: Roof studio, N.Y.C. *Date:* July 27, 1899

10 ft. FLA3273 (print) FRA0591 (neg.)

Two young ladies can be seen sitting on a couch eating ice cream held by one of them. Each of the young ladies dips into the ice cream, using her own spoon. Eventually, one feeds the other. The repetition of this action leads to spilling the ice cream and a fight. The girl holding the plate of ice cream smears it on the face of the other, ending the film.

Play Ball on the Beach

AM&B © H78529 June 1, 1906

Cameraman: G. W. Bitzer

Photographed: May 9, 1906

27 ft. FLA3594 (print) FRA2139 (neg.)

The film begins on a stage in front of a painted backdrop of a seashore locale. Three people, two women and one man, dressed in bathing attire start to play a game of ball using a broom for a bat. The man, who has assumed the role of umpire, appears to have trouble with the players because of his decisions. This results in a free-for-all with one woman holding him by the neck and the other woman beating him on the posterior with the broom. The film ends as all three fall in a heap.

Playmates

See: The Seven Ages

A Poet's Revenge

AM&B © H24890 Dec. 9, 1902

Cameraman: Robert K. Bonine

Location: Studio, N.Y.C. *Date:* May 22, 1902

17 ft. FLA4031 (print) FRA1220 (neg.)

This film is of poor quality. However, a set constructed and furnished as a publisher's or printer's office is discernible in the opening scene. There is a large wood-burning stove in the foreground, and a man is sitting at the desk writing. A man wearing a top hat and tail coat enters and reads from papers he is holding, accompanying his reading with wild gestures. He hands the paper to the seated man, who disdainfully indicates it is of no value. The man in the top hat removes an object from his coat and puts it in the stove, causing a terrific explosion. At the end of the film, the man who was seated at the desk is on his back on the floor with debris falling all about him.

Poison or Whiskey

See: The Lover's Ruse

Poker at Dawson City

Edison © 13536 Feb. 17, 1899

24 ft. FLA3974 (print) FRA1183 (neg.)

[Alaska Gold Rush]

Four people are sitting around a table made by placing a flat board on top of a barrel. They are playing cards and cheating. A fight ensues. The film speed indicates that the film was made in the Black Maria.

Pole Vaulting

AM&B © H16729 Apr. 18, 1902

Cameraman: G. W. Bitzer

Location: Columbia College, N.Y. *Date:* Apr. 21, 1899

23 ft. FLA3848 (print) FRA1062 (neg.)

The camera was placed on what appears to be the workout and recreation area of a college. The subject is an athletic event featuring pole vaulting, performed by one man at a time. There are several spectators and, during the course of the film, three different men approach the camera position and vault over the crossbar.

Police Boats Escorting Naval Parade

Edison © 52046 Sept. 3, 1898

Location: N.Y.C. *Photographed:* Aug. 20, 1898

28 ft. FLA4249 (print) FRA1405 (neg.)

[Spanish-American War; New York City Welcome to Admiral Sampson's Fleet after Battle of Santiago Bay]

The camera position was the deck of a boat that was part of a naval escort for a high-ranking dignitary arriving by ship in New York. Boats of various sizes are seen making headway through the water. In the background is a structure that appears to be the Brooklyn Bridge.

Police Raid at a Dog Fight

AM&B © H73112 Feb. 9, 1906

Cameraman: G. W. Bitzer

Location: Studio, N.Y.C. *Photographed:* Jan. 30, 1906

28 ft FLA3923 (print) FRA1139 (neg.)

The film begins from a single-camera position and shows two white terrier dogs goaded into fighting by two men. The fight progresses for about ten seconds, then two uniformed policemen interrupt the six spectators, arrest the promotors, and carry off the dogs.

Policemen's Prank on Their Comrades

Edison © H33294 July 8, 1903

Cameraman: A. C. Abadie

Location: Wilmington, Del. *Photographed:* June 30, 1903

22 ft. FLA3604 (print) FRA0868 (neg.)

The opening scene shows a woman wearing a sunbonnet and a long dress sitting on a bench at the edge of a swimming pool. A man wearing a policeman's uniform appears and sits down beside her. He tickles her under the chin and then kisses her. He continues embracing her, while other men dressed as policemen can be seen in the background surrounding the pair seated on the bench. Without any apparent warning, the watching police push over the park bench causing the woman and her police suitor to fall into the swimming pool. At the end of the film, they are clinging to the edge of the pool.

Politician's Love Story

AM&B © H123061 Feb. 18, 1909

Director: D. W. Griffith *Cameramen:* G. W. Bitzer, Arthur Marvin

Cast: Mack Sennett, Marion Leonard, Arthur Johnson, Linda Avidson, Alfred Paget, Florence LaBadie, Lee Dougherty, Kathlyn Williams

Location: Central Park and Studio, N.Y.C. *Photographed:* Jan. 18–19, 1909

193 ft. FLA5639 (print) FRA2485 (neg.)

A politician (Mack Sennett) can be seen walking up and down in his office with a newspaper cartoon in his hand. He removes a revolver from the desk and goes to the newspaper office. He threatens all of the employees, and they hide under desks and other forms of cover. Someone directs him to an attractive young lady (Marion Leonard) who is drawing cartoons. She soothes the irate politician, who leaves and sits on a park bench. People, including the young cartoonist, start leaving their offices, and the politician begins to follow her through the park. She is accosted by a masher, and the politician comes to her rescue. The last scene shows the politician and the young lady arm in arm. The insert of the newspaper cartoon was rather unusual and very clear.

Politimesteren

See: The Two Convicts

Pollywogs 71st Regiment, N.G.S.N.Y. Initiating Raw Recruits

Edison © H47969 July 13, 1904

Location: Peekskill, N.Y. *Photographed:* July 7, 1904

62 ft. FLA4821 (print) FRA1830 (neg.)

The name "Pollywog" in the title of this film is a term given to a new recruit for the National Guard, State of New York, at summer encampment. The first scene shows veteran National Guard personnel in field fatigue attire hazing several recruits in uniform. The second camera position shows a road with uniformed military personnel on each side watching the "Pollywogs," who are on their hands and knees, race. There is a hurdle constructed of boxes, and when the recruits pass the position, they are rewarded by splashes from buckets of water thrown by spectators.

Polo Game: Myopia vs. Dedham

AM&B © H35632 Sept. 12, 1903

Cameraman: G. W. Bitzer

Location: Prospect Park, Brooklyn, N.Y. *Date:* July 10, 1899

31 ft. FLA3902 (print) FRA1122 (neg.)

The film shows a game of polo. During the film, the cameraman placed his equipment to show goals being made by one of the teams. There are buildings in the background but the distance does not permit a definite description.

Pompey's Honey Girl

AM&B © H63377 July 15, 1905

Cameraman: G. W. Bitzer

Location: Studio, N.Y.C. *Photographed:* June 29, 1905

20 ft. FLA3820 (print) FRA1050 (neg.)

A young man and a woman can be seen sitting on a couch in a set of a living room. They are embracing. A rather large woman enters and admonishes them for their actions. She sends the young man out of the room and threatens the young lady and then leaves. While the young lady is sitting there dejectedly, a black servant comes in and indicates that if she will part the curtains she will have a surprise. She does and finds her young man. As the film ends, they are embracing once more.

Pontoon Bridge Building

AM&B © H24898 Dec. 9, 1902

Cameraman: Arthur Marvin

Location: Bronx Park, N.Y. *Photographed:* Apr. 8, 1902

32 ft. FLA3160 (print) FRA0490 (neg.)

The camera was positioned so as to view the activities of what seems to be West Point cadets in an exercise of building a bridge on the top of boats. This type of pontoon construction is designed to allow military forces to ford a body of water, and the film illustrates this.

Poor Girl, It Was a Hot Night and the Mosquitos Were Thick

AM&B © H35642 Sept. 12, 1903

Cameraman: A. E. Weed

Location: Studio, N.Y.C. *Photographed:* Aug. 26, 1903

23 ft. FLA3364 (print) FRA0666 (neg.)

We see a backdrop showing the edge of a lake; at stage right is a painted, one-dimensional bath house. Three well-dressed young women come on stage, notice the bath house, change into bathing attire, and then walk off behind the stage blind. A man dressed in a black leotard with black make-up on comes on stage carrying a club. He sees the women's clothes, and as the film ends, is dancing around in some of the undergarments topped with a large picture hat.

Poor Hooligan, So Hungry Too

AM&B © H37474 Nov. 2, 1903

Cameraman: G. W. Bitzer

Location: Studio, N.Y.C. Photographed; Oct. 20, 1903

21 ft. FLA4442 (print) FRA1548 (neg.)

From a single-camera position, we see a set of the side of a house. A woman comes through the door of the set and begins feeding the two small dogs with her. Her actions interest two tramps, one of whom steals the dogs' food as soon as the woman returns to the house. The act of theft is repeated when the woman replenishes the stolen food, but this time a policeman notices it and arrests the first tramp and removes him from the scene. The film ends as the happy second tramp takes over the plate of dog food.

Poor John

Belcher and Waterson © H90029 Feb. 1, 1907

Cast: Vesta Victoria

77 ft. FLA5170 (print) FRA6404 (neg.)

A young man dressed in a tuxedo walks to camera center in front of a wall that is very dark and not conducive to much description of the ornamentation on it. He introduces a young woman dressed formally in a satin dress topped by an ermine jacket and feather hat and then leaves. From her gestures, it would appear that the young woman is reciting a poem of giving a lecture. She continues doing just that until the end of the film when she bows and walks off camera. The young woman is probably Vesta Victoria, a well-known English entertainer, who introduced the song "Poor John" in the United States.

See also: Waiting at the Church

A Poor Place for Love Making

AM&B © H63383 July 15, 1905

Cameraman: G. W. Bitzer

Location: Studio, N.Y.C. *Photographed:* June 28, 1905

34 ft. FLA3958 (print) FRA1168 (neg.)

Two young people are sitting on the sand in front of the open doors of a bath house. Two fun-loving girls in bathing suits apparently are hoping someone will sit under the sprinkler provided by the management to wash the sand off bathers. The pranksters pull the sprinkler chain, causing the young woman in her large picture hat and her companion to be soaked. They leave in a hurry, but return and seat themselves in the same spot with a beach umbrella for protection.

A Poor Relation

Klaw & Erlanger © LP3430 Sept. 24, 1914

Cast: Millicent Evans, Robert Nolan, Vola Smith, Adele De Garde, Joseph McDermott

1,098 ft. FLA5889 (print) FRA2758 (neg.)

The film begins with a man abandoning his wife and children; throughout the film, he continues his evil ways. He gets a job in a manufacturing plant and rises to partner. In the meantime, his children become acquainted with their neighbor, a poor inventor, who attempts to sell an invention to the factory owner. Instead, the plans are stolen by the man who is now a partner. Eventually, the mechanical engineer gets his plans back and is paid for them. All the scenes were expensively produced and the sets were well made. There were a considerable number of extras in the strike scenes at the factory. Each scene was preceded by a title and was broken up by least two more.

The Poor Sick Men

Biograph © J151208 Jan. 27, 1911

Cameraman: Arthur Marvin

Cast: Dell Henderson, Grace Henderson, Donald Crisp, Jack Pickford, Kate Bruce, Marion Sunshine, William J. Butler

Location: Fort Lee, N.J.; Studio, N.Y.C. *Photographed:* Nov. 30 and Dec. 19, 1910

389 ft. FLA5640 (print) FRA2486 (neg.)

Two married men lie about their health to their wives to avoid accompanying them to the opera when they really want to attend a poker game. The wives go off alone and the two men go to the poker game, which is raided. The two men escape by going out on the fire escape, and the remainder of the picture shows the series of escapades in which they become entangled. The film ends as both men finally succeed in reaching home seconds before their wives arrive.

Pope in His Carriage

AM&B © H35643 Sept. 12, 1903

Cameraman: W. K. L. Dickson

Location: St. Peter's, Rome *Photographed:* 1898

12 ft. FLA3526 (print) FRA0802 (neg.)

The camera was placed inside the walls of the Vatican City adjoining a roadway where the Pope (Leo XIII) was planning to pass. Preceding the carriage transporting the Pope are armed horsemen. After they pass the camera, the horses pulling the Pope's carriage appear. The carriage stops immediately in front of the camera, and one of the Pope's entourage points to the camera. The Pope bestows his blessing, and then drives on.

See also: Renovare Production Company "Special"

Pope Leo XIII Being Carried in Chair Through Upper Loggia

See: Renovare Production Company "Special"

Pope Leo XIII Being Seated Bestowing Blessing Surrounded by Swiss Guards

See: Renovare Production Company "Special"

Pope Leo XIII in Canopy Chair

See: Renovare Production Company "Special"

Pope Leo XIII in Carriage

See: Renovare Production Company "Special"

Pope Leo XIII Leaving Carriage and Being Ushered into Garden

See: Renovare Production Company "Special"

Pope Leo XIII Seated in Garden

See: Renovare Production Company "Special"

Pope Leo XIII Walking Before Kneeling Guards

See: Renovare Production Company "Special"

Pope Passing Through Upper Loggia

AM&B © H35633 Sept. 12, 1903

Cameraman: W. K. L. Dickson
Location: St. Peter's, Rome *Photographed:* 1898
8 ft. FLA3365 (print) FRA0667 (neg.)

The camera was placed in a corridor in the Vatican. At a distance from the camera but proceeding toward it, a group of uniformed men can be seen escorting the Pope and carrying him in a sedan chair. The Pope and his complete entourage continue to walk toward the camera, and the film lasts only until the Pope and the group pass its position.

See also: Renovare Production Company "Special"

The Porous Plaster

AM&B © H38862 Dec. 5, 1903
Cameraman: A. E. Weed
Location : Studio, N.Y.C. *Photographed:* Nov. 27, 1903
22 ft. FLA4297 (print) FRA1447 (neg.)

A man wearing pajamas stands in the middle of a bedroom. He takes his pajama top off and attempts to remove an adhesive plaster that is just out of reach between his shoulder blades. After several abortive attempts, he summons a woman from off stage who removes the patch much to the discomfiture of the man and the amusement of the woman.

Le Portrait Spirite

See: A Spiritualist Photographer

Post Man Delivering Mail, U.S.P.O.

AM&B © H34984 Aug. 22, 1903
Cameraman: A. E. Weed
Location: Washington, D.C. *Photographed:* Aug. 8, 1903
28 ft. FLA4066 (print) FRA1250 (neg.)

This film shows the delivery of the U.S. mail, in a rural area. A two-horse vehicle, with a sign reading "U.S. Mail," appears on the scene. The postal employee gets out of the vehicle and places mail in a standard metal mail box. A woman comes out of her house and removes the mail from the mail box, then buys stamps from the mail carrier as the picture ends.

The Poster Girls

AM&B © H17039 Apr. 26, 1902
Cameraman: F. S. Armitage
Location: Roof studio, N.Y.C. *Date:* Sept. 13, 1899
17 ft. FLA4347 (print) FRA1491 (neg.)

A one-camera position film from a theater audience point of view. A billboard poster hanger puts up posters advertising a burlesque show. When the work is completed, he leaves. A passerby, attracted by the posters, stops to examine the scantily clad women when the center poster comes to life and the girl in it kicks his hat off. The spectator bends to retrieve his hat, and the girl in the poster kicks him on the posterior.

Postman Whitewashed

AM&B © H47316 June 18, 1904
32 ft. FLA4822 (print) FRA1831 (neg.)

The poor quality of this film does not permit detailed description of the action. It is possible to see a man carrying a large bucket filled with a white liquid enter the scene and place it on a badly constructed scaffold onto which he later climbs. It is also possible to see that someone above him hands him something to drink and, in his eagerness to get more, he walks too far out on the scaffolding. This projects the bucket some distance, and its contents are spilled over a man wearing the uniform of a postman. The two men start a fight, some of which can be seen.

A Potato Bake in the Woods

AM&B © H24885 Dec. 9, 1902
Cameraman: Robert K. Bonine
Location: Highwood Park, N.Y. [?] *Date:* Nov. 3, 1902
27 ft. FLA3263 (print) FRA0584 (neg.)

Some preadolescent children and a few adults are gathered around a large camp fire in a wooded area. They appear to be putting objects in the fire to cook in some manner. The distance of the activity from the camera allows only a cursory interpretation; very little detail is distinguishable.

The Pouting Model

AM&B © H18894 June 12, 1902
Cameraman: F. S. Armitage
Location: Roof studio, N.Y.C. *Date:* June 11, 1901
19 ft. FLA3797 (print) FRA1034 (neg.)

This was photographed as if in the audience at a vaudeville show. Two women in white leotards can be seen. They draw the curtains and disclose an aged man with a beard sitting on a chair. At camera left, with her head turned toward the wall as if crying, is a young girl, absolutely nude. The final action in the film is of the curtains closing.

See also: Sleeping Child, and Waiting for Santa Claus

The Power of Authority

AM&B © H40751 Jan. 11, 1904
Cameraman: A. E. Weed
Location: Studio, N.Y.C. *Photographed:* Dec. 23, 1903
26 ft. FLA4181 (print) FRA1345 (neg.)

A man dressed in military uniform and shouldering a musket is standing rigidly at attention in front of a set of a military garrison wall. A young man in an officer's uniform, escorting a young lady, passes by the sentry. The officer halts and inspects the sentry's rifle, then admonishes him for unmilitary behavior. As the film ends, the officer is drenched by a liquid from a hornet's nest which is punctured by the bayonet affixed to the enlisted man's rifle.

The Power of Love

Great Northern © Oes J168562-63 Apr. 24, 1912
Director: August Blom *Script:* Alfred Kjerulf
Cast: Clara Wieth, Carlo Wieth, Axel Strøm, Ella la Cour, Frederik Buck, Carl Lauritzen, Julie Lauritzen
Location: Denmark *Date:* July 19, 1911
Original title: Kaerlighedens Magt
907 ft. FLA5890-5891 (print) FRA2759 (neg.)

The Power of Love is a motion picture with a classic plot of the young man from a well-to-do family who prefers to be a playboy, carouse with wild companions, and drink too much rather than work. He falls in love with a pure young woman who works for his father and who, through his love for her, succeeds in reforming him.

After the young man is dismissed by his father for his continued inattention to work, he joins the fire department, saves the girl he loves, and becomes a hero.

Although the plot of this film verges on the trite, August Blom directed the photography in such a way as to transform it into a wholly absorbing drama.

The Power of the Press
Klaw & Erlanger © LP3057 May 22, 1914
Cast: Lionel Barrymore, Alan Hale, William Russell, Betty Gray, Vivian Prescott, William Jefferson, Mrs. Lawrence Marston, W. C. "Spike" Robinson
1,584 ft. FLA5935 (print) FRA2760 (neg., copy 1) FRA2761 (neg., copy 2)

This four-reel drama takes place in the early part of the twentieth century. The hero of the story (Lionel Barrymore) is promoted to foreman of the shipyard when the villain is fired for incompetency and dishonesty. Later, the discharged foreman frames the hero by taking advantage of his drunken condition to plant some stolen money on him. A great deal of laborious intrigue follows, involving a great number of people. The dishonored and discharged hero is restored to his position when a front-page story affects public opinion, thus exemplifying "The Power of the Press."

Pranks
Biograph © J131132 Aug. 31, 1909
Director: D. W. Griffith *Cameraman:* Arthur Marvin
Cast: Marion Leonard, Arthur Johnson, Billy Quirk, Robert Harron, Henry B. Walthall, Tony O'Sullivan
Location: Little Falls, N.J. *Photographed:* July 19, 20 and 28, 1909
128 ft. FLA5641 (print) FRA2487 (neg.)

A young man (Arthur Johnson) and his girl (Marion Leonard) have a quarrel and part company. The next scene shows the young man arriving dejectedly at a public bath house where he bumps into his equally dejected girl friend. While they are swimming, some mischievous boys switch clothing from one bath house to another. The two return from their bathing, still not on speaking terms, so each, in desperation, dons the other's clothing and attempts to get home. The girl, attractive even in boy's clothing, is attacked by a masher. Her boyfriend, still wearing her clothes, rescues the young woman, and they embrace as the film ends.

Pranks of Buster Brown and His Dog Tige
See: Buster Brown Series

The Prentis Trio
Edison © 50476 Aug. 4, 1899
17 ft. FLA4178 (print) FRA1342 (neg.)

The photographer took his camera outdoors to a flat, grass-covered area and photographed a man, a woman, and a child approximately eight years of age as they did some gymnastics. The young boy is tossed from the man's shoulders to the ground. All three are agile and demonstrate their ability at handsprings, handstands, and back-bends for the full extent of the film.

President McKinley and Escort Going to the Capitol
Edison © H1795 Mar. 8, 1901

Location: Washington, D.C. *Date:* March 1901
67ft. FLA4823 (print) FRA1832 (neg.)
[McKinley Inauguration]

The film begins by showing military personnel on horseback. The camera was positioned on a side street and photographed representatives of several different companies of American cavalry. Just as the film ends, foot soldiers and West Point cadets preceding the two horse-drawn carriages, one containing President McKinley's party, come into view.

President McKinley Leaving Observatory, Mt. Tom, Holyoke, Massachusetts
AM&B © H16349 Apr. 10, 1902
Cameraman: G. W. Bitzer
Location: Holyoke, Mass. *Date:* June 23, 1899
25 ft. FLA3682 (print) FRA0932 (neg.)

The film was photographed from a camera positioned the width of a porch away from the doorway of a large public building. At the beginning of the film, President McKinley, the First Lady, and their entourage can be seen leaving the building. President McKinley stops for the benefit of the spectators and then continues on his way.

President McKinley Reviewing the Troops at the Pan-American Exposition
Edison © H8588 Sept. 11, 1901
Location: Buffalo, N.Y. *Photographed:* Sept. 5, 1901
40 ft. FLA4824 (print) FRA1833 (neg.)

From a single-camera position pointed directly at the reviewing stand, the film shows President McKinley and his entourage as they stand in the reviewing stand and take the salute of the passing American infantry troops.

President McKinley Taking the Oath
Edison © H1794 Mar. 8, 1901
Location: Washington, D.C. *Photographed:* Mar. 1901
26 ft. FLA3126 (print) FRA0460 (neg.)
[McKinley Inauguration]

This film records President McKinley taking the oath of office. The first camera position shows the seating arrangements prepared for the spectators and witnesses on the steps of the Capitol. At the time the film was taken, there were many empty seats. The second camera position shows the inaugural party during the swearing-in ceremonies. All that can be seen is the black-draped balcony and, in the distance, two people standing facing one another, as if they were part of the administration of the oath. The film ends as the newly inaugurated president begins his speech.

President McKinley's Funeral Cortege at Buffalo, New York
Edison © H8914 Sept. 21, 1901
Location: Buffalo, N.Y. *Photographed:* Sept. 1901
165 ft. FLA5171 (print) FRA2117 (neg.)

The photography in this film is from several camera positions. The first position was over the heads of the crowds that lined the street watching the cortege begin. Mounted police precede the escort for the funeral procession. The next camera position is from the other side of the spectators and reveals the escort of various military organizations represented (army, navy, marine corps, West Point and U.S. Naval Academy cadets). Another camera position includes the immediate family in their carriages preceding the hearse carrying the body of the president. The next camera position, high above the heads of the people, is in front of the building where the memorial services were held. It shows the hearse and the casket being removed and taken on the shoulders of the bearers up the steps of the church. In the background are streets crowded with people. The last scene shows large groups of people leaving the memorial services.

President's McKinley's Funeral Cortege at Washington, D.C.

Edison © H8915 Sept. 21, 1901

Location: Washington, D.C. *Photographed:* Sept. 1901

146 ft. FLA5172 (print) FPA0093 (35mm neg.) FRA2118 (16mm neg.)

The photographer covered the subject, the funeral cortege of President McKinley, from many different positions along the line of march. The people shown are those who preceded the hearse and those who followed after it. First come the walking military (army, navy, marine corps, national guard), then the mounted military (army and marine corps), and then the ranking military dignitaries who immediately precede the hearse. Following the escorted hearse are the two closed carriages, containing the president's immediate family. After the carriages, are more mourners on foot, representing the various countries. There is some film taken from one of the wings of the Capitol overlooking the courtyard of that building.

President McKinley's Speech at the Pan-American Exposition

Edison © H8589 Sept 11, 1901

Location: Buffalo, N.Y. *Photographed:* Sept. 5, 1901

40 ft. FLA4825 (print) FRA1834 (neg.)

The film begins by showing the introductory speaker, William Jennings Bryan, at the Pan-American Exposition in Buffalo. Bryan introduces the incumbent-president of the United States, William F. McKinley. The remainder of the film is a straight-on moving photograph of the president during his last public speech.

President Reviewing School Children

AM&B © H32393 June 4, 1903

Cameraman: H. J. Miles

Location: San Francisco *Date:* May 26, 1903

35 ft. FLA4826 (print) FRA1835 (neg.)

The photographer positioned his camera on the side of a broad avenue crowded with people awaiting the arrival of the president of the United States, Theodore Roosevelt. The marching military that preceded the president's carriage can be seen at a distance of about a quarter of a mile. The remainder of the film was photographed from four camera positions along the line of march, and includes the escort, the dignitaries, and, as the film ends, Theodore Roosevelt in his carriage.

See also: The President's Carriage

President Roosevelt Addressing Crew of "Kearsarge"

AM&B © H55389 Jan. 3, 1905

Cameraman: G. W. Bitzer

Location: Oyster Bay, N.Y. *Photographed:* Aug. 18, 1903

28ft. FLA4109 (print) FRA1284 (neg.)

The film was photographed from a camera position on the deck of a U.S. battleship. In the immediate foreground from the camera position are approximately two hundred closely packed American sailors of various ratings wearing summer whites. At a considerable distance from the view of the camera, the president can be seen addressing the group of men. The film ends as the sailors applaud.

President Roosevelt and the Rough Riders

AM&B © H27385 Jan. 22, 1903

22 ft. FLA3483 (print) FRA0764 (neg.)

[Spanish-American War]

The locale is a U.S. Army cavalry horse training area. A group of mounted riders approach the camera from a distance. They continue in the direction of the camera until they are in the immediate foreground, when they dismount and walk away. One of the riders can be identified as Theodore Roosevelt.

President Roosevelt at Army-Navy Football Game

See: President Roosevelt Crossing the Field

President Roosevelt at Lynn, Mass.

AM&B © H24895 Dec. 9, 1902

Cameraman: G. W. Bitzer

Location: Lynn, Mass. *Date:* Aug. 26, 1902

33 ft. FLA4827 (print) FRA1836 (neg.)

The president is seen at a gathering of people in Lynn, Massachusetts. The camera was located in several places to best photograph the ceremonies. President Roosevelt is shown being introduced, leaving the building where he made the address, entering his carriage, and riding through the streets preceded by a military escort. The crowds on the streets are also shown.

President Roosevelt at the Canton Station

Edison © H9085 Sept. 26, 1901

Location: Canton, Ohio *Photographed:* Sept. 18, 1901

44 ft. FLA4828 (print) FRA1837 (neg.)

[President McKinley's Funeral, Canton, Ohio]

The film begins by showing Theodore Roosevelt arriving with other mourners at Canton, Ohio. Mr. Roosevelt is shown leaving the station and getting into his carriage. The remainder of the film was photographed by panning the camera over the large crowd gathered in the area to watch the arrival of celebrities attending the funeral of President McKinley.

Pres. Roosevelt at the Dedication Ceremonies, St. Louis Exposition

Selig © H31552 May 6, 1903

Location: St. Louis *Photographed:* April 30, 1904 [?]

6 ft. FLA4055 (print) FRA1240 (neg.)

[Louisiana Purchase Exposition]

The unusually short length of this film makes it totally impractical for use as a motion picture film. However, the six feet of the film were repeated in printing to equal 22 feet, and it shows a grandstand or speaker's platform from which President Roosevelt may be seen preparing to enter a carriage.

President Roosevelt Crossing the Field

AM&B © H16354   Apr. 10, 1902
Cameraman; Congdon
Location: Philadelphia *Date:* Dec. 2, 1901
22 ft.   FLA3466 (print)   FRA0748 (neg.)

The photographer placed his camera inside the perimeter of a stadium to photograph Pres. Theodore Roosevelt crossing a football field. He can be seen approaching the camera position accompanied by approximately twelve members of his entourage. All are wearing the formal attire of the day. The title on the original paper print film is President Roosevelt at Army-Navy Football Game.

President Roosevelt Reviewing the Troops at Charleston Exposition

Edison © H16715   Apr. 18, 1902
Location: Charleston, S.C. *Photographed:* Apr. 1902
64 ft.   FLA4829 (print)   FRA1838 (neg.)

In order to film Pres. Theodore Roosevelt as he reviewed the army, navy, and marine corps foot soldiers at the opening of the Charleston Exposition, the photographer placed his camera across the street that had been designated as the line of march. The president and the First Lady and their entourage, as well as the military escort, are shown standing on the steps of a large building.

President Roosevelt's Arrival at "Kearsarge"

AM&B © H55391   Jan. 3, 1905
Cameraman: G. W. Bitzer
Location: Oyster Bay, N.Y. *Photographed:* Aug. 17, 1903
29 ft.   FLA4830 (print)   FRA1839 (neg.)

An officer's launch is shown arriving alongside the starboard gangway of the *Kearsarge*. Among the arrivals is Pres. Theodore Roosevelt, followed by a group of men dressed in formal attire. They are greeted by men in full dress naval uniforms.

President Roosevelt's Departure from "Kearsarge"

AM&B © H55390   Jan. 3, 1905
Cameraman: G. W. Bitzer
Location: Oyster Bay, N.Y. *Photographed:* Aug. 18, 1903
20 ft.   FLA3911 (print)   FRA1129 (neg.)

In order to photograph Pres. Theodore Roosevelt, his military escort, and accompanying dignitaries as they were leaving the starboard quarter deck of the *U.S.S. Kearsarge*, the photographer placed his camera on the deck above the main deck of the ship. The film shows the side boys paying their respects as the party of dignitaries passes through their lines and starts down the gangway to leave the ship.

Pres. Roosevelt's Fourth of July Oration

AM&B © H33456   July 15, 1903
Cameraman: G. W. Bitzer
Location: Huntington, L.I., N.Y. *Photographed:* July 4, 1903
74 ft.   FLA5173 (print)   FRA2119 (neg.)

The opening scene, from the first of the two camera positions, shows a covered platform on which Pres. Theodore Roosevelt can be seen eating and then speaking to the people who have congregated to hear him. The second camera position is over the heads of the crowd bidding him goodbye as he and his party enter a horse-drawn carriage and leave the vicinity.

President Roosevelt's Homecoming

AM&B © H47935   July 12, 1904
Cameraman: G. W. Bitzer
Location: Oyster Bay, L.I., N.Y. *Photographed:* July 2, 1904
30 ft.   FLA4832 (print)   FRA1841 (neg.)

Many people can be seen walking around the yard adjacent to a railway station. A train with several passenger cars pulls up to the station. The camera pans, photographing quite a few people and horse-drawn two- and four-wheeled vehicles. The picture ends as a four-wheeled horse-drawn vehicle approaches the camera position. A coachman sits on the box in the front, and in the seat behind him is Pres. Theodore Roosevelt waving at the crowd.

President Roosevelt's Inauguration

Edison © H57365   Mar. 7, 1905
Cameramen: Edwin S. Porter, Robert K. Bonine
Location: Washington, D.C. *Photographed:* Mar. 4, 1905
372 ft.   FLA5642 (print)   FRA2380 (neg.)

Photographed from several camera positions at various locations along the line of march down Constitution Avenue in Washington, D.C., the film shows the spectators at the parade and inauguration festivities. The scenes consist of the open carriage with Theodore Roosevelt and entourage being led by a mounted escort to the front steps of the Capitol building. From the same camera position, the walk from the carriage to the rostrum on the Capitol steps and the actual swearing in of the President is shown. His inaugural address was also photographed from this position. The remainder of the film is of the presidential party leaving the Capitol, and of the various military and fraternal organizations that attended as part of the parade.

President Roosevelt's Visit to Admiral Barker

AM&B © H55400   Jan. 3, 1905
Cameraman: G. W. Bitzer
Location: Oyster Bay, L.I., N.Y. *Photographed:* Aug. 18, 1903
14 ft.   FLA3960 (print)   FRA1170 (neg.)

President Theodore Roosevelt, preceded by a ranking U.S. naval officer in full dress, boards the starboard gangway of either the *Olympic* or the *Kearsarge*. The film is so short that it is not possible to ascertain anything further.

The President's Carriage

AM&B © H32392   June 4, 1903
Cameraman: H. J. Miles
Location: San Francisco *Date:* May 26, 1903
44 ft.   FLA4831 (print)   FRA1840 (neg.)

The subject is a parade, with Pres. Theodore Roosevelt in an open horse-drawn vehicle. The camera was placed at the curb of a street crowded with people. The bunting-decorated business district is seen as the dignitaries approach the camera position. The president can be seen in his open carriage, which passes immediately in front of the

President Theodore Roosevelt in open carriage.

camera position. His carriage is followed by several others, some with passengers and some with only a driver.

See also: President Reviewing School Children

Un Prêté Pour un Rendu, ou, Une Bonne Farce Avec Ma Tête

Méliès © H41415 Jan. 28, 1904

Creator: Georges Méliès

Cast: Georges Méliès

Location: Montreuil, France *Date:* Winter, 1903-4

U.S. title: Tit for Tat, or A Good Joke With My Head

122 ft. FLA4904 (print) FRA1904 (neg.)

This is another Méliès vaudeville act. He makes his own head disappear by putting it in a box. He then harasses his head by smoking. The head in turn leaves the box and spits water on M. Méliès. The cast consists of only Georges Méliès.

The Pretty Typewriter

See: The Typewriter

The Price of a Kiss

AM&B © H16381 Apr. 12, 1902

Cameraman: F. S. Armitage

Location: Roof studio, N.Y.C. *Date:* May 27, 1899

10 ft. FLA3200 (print) FRA0526 (neg.)

An attractive young woman is shaving a man seated in a barbershop chair in a set of a barbershop. A sign, fully visible to the camera, says, "Shave with Bay Rum 15¢." When the shave is finished, the man attempts to embrace the young woman who points to the sign on the wall. The moment she points, a bottom portion is released revealing a sign that says "Kisses $1."

The Prima Donna's Understudy

AM&B © H57146 Feb. 28, 1905

Cameraman: G. W. Bitzer

Location: Studio, N.Y.C. *Photographed:* Feb. 18, 1905

23 ft. FLA3819 (print) FRA1049 (neg.)

The door opens in a set of a backstage dressing room. A woman in costume enters and starts making up her face. Another woman carrying a mop and a bucket comes through the same door. She sits down in a chair and begins to put on some ballerina tights. The picture ends when three people come back in, pick her up bodily, and throw her off the set.

Primitive Irrigation in Egypt

Edison © H32798 June 17, 1903

Cameraman: A. C. Abadie

Location: Upper Cairo, Egypt *Photographed:* Mar. 27, 1903

33 ft. FLA3592 (print) FRA2137 (neg.)

The film begins by showing a small hill. On the top of the hill is a counterbalanced pole with a rope and a bucket attached. An operator wearing a turban and a burnoose dips the bucket into a well. A tethered donkey can also be seen. As the film progresses, the camera is positioned overlooking an irrigation project where an ox-powered water wheel is in operation. The poor condition of the film does not permit further description of detail.

The Primitive Man

Biograph © LP1806 Nov. 14, 1913

Director and Author: D. W. Griffith

Cast: Mae Marsh, Robert Harron, Wilfred Lucas, Alfred Paget, Edwin August, Charles Hill Mailes, William J. Butler

1,170 ft. FLA5914-5915 (print) FRA2786-2787 (neg.)

The first of these three reels begins at a formal dress party where the hero (Robert Harron) falls asleep reading a book by Darwin on primitive man. The scene rises out and dissolves back to a field with primitive men living in caves, and the remainder of the first reel parallels Man's Genesis. The second reel shows "Weakhands" inventing a club. The third reel shows two tribes at war because a shortage of women, vital for propagation of the species, has occurred. This time, "Weakhands" invents a bow and arrow and once more defeats his less intelligent contemporaries. Wings, forked tails, horns, etc., were added to live animals and reptiles to give them a prehistoric appearance. There is one photograph of a moving dinosaur, approximately forty feet high, and several insert close-ups. There is also a considerable amount of camera movement.

Prince Henry Arriving at West Point

Edison © H14854 Mar. 13, 1902

Cameraman: James H. White

Location: West Point, N.Y. *Date:* Mar. 7, 1902

39 ft. FLA4834 (print) FRA1842 (neg.)

The film, photographed from two camera positions, starts with a scene of a snow-covered bridge, which is the entrance to West Point. The corps of cadets on horseback is escorting Prince Henry of Prussia, who follows them in a horse-drawn sleigh. As they round the camera position, the camera pans to show the procession heading toward the administration building at the Point.

Prince Henry Arriving in Washington and Visiting the German Embassy

Edison © H14547 Feb. 28, 1902

Cameraman: James H. White

Location: Washington, D.C. *Date:* Feb. 1902

80 ft. FLA5174 (print) FRA6407 (neg.)

The film was photographed from two camera positions; the opening scenes were photographed across the street from the German Embassy in Washington, D.C. Most of the film shows the uniformed military officers as they leave the canopied area of the embassy and get into open, horse-drawn carriages, complete with coachmen and footmen.

Charles Hill Mailes, Mae Marsh, and Robert Harron appeared in D. W. Griffith's The Primitive Man (1913).

The film ends as a mounted escort leads the group away from the camera position.

Prince Henry at Lincoln's Monument, Chicago, Illinois

Edison © H14821 Mar. 12, 1902

Cameraman: James H. White

Location: Chicago *Date:* Mar. 1902

44 ft. FLA3941 (print) FRA1151 (neg.)

The film was photographed from a single-camera position over the heads of spectators at a procession in Chicago with Prince Henry of Prussia. Poor camera footage, since the heads of visiting dignitaries were not included in the picture. Prince Henry was accompanied by Robert Lincoln, the president's son.

Prince Henry at Niagara Falls

Edison © H14853 Mar. 13, 1902

Cameraman: James H. White

Location: Niagara Falls, Canada, and N.Y.C. *Photographed:* Mar. 1902

37 ft. FLA3845 (print) FRA1105 (neg.)

The film shows a panorama of crowds attracted by Prince Henry of Prussia who follow him as he views the falls and starts up the staircase to go under them. At the end of the film, the cameraman takes a picture of a train on a bridge

Prince Henry at West Point

AM&B © H33284 July 8, 1903

Cameraman: Robert K. Bonine

Location: West Point, N.Y. *Date:* Mar. 7, 1902

44 ft. FLA3537 (print) FRA0813 (neg.)

West Point cadets, mounted on horseback, are escorting Prince Henry of Prussia to the reviewing stand. The complete corps of cadets then passes in review.

Prince Henry Reviewing the Cadets at West Point

Edison © H14855 Mar. 13, 1902

Cameraman: James H. White

Location: West Point, N.Y. *Photographed:* Mar. 7, 1902

88 ft. FLA5175 (print) FRA2121 (neg.)

The full corps of West Point cadets is marching past a reviewing group that includes Prince Henry of Prussia. The ground is covered with snow, and there is a strong wind, evidenced by the flapping of the flags on the reviewing stand.

Prince Henry Visiting Cambridge, Mass. and Harvard University

Edison © H14822 Mar. 12, 1902

Location: Cambridge, Mass. *Date:* Mar. 1902

117 ft. FLA5176 (print) FRA2122 (neg.)

The film starts from a camera position looking down a street in Cambridge, Massachusetts. Approximately a company of mounted troops leading a parade, as an escort to Prince Henry of Prussia, approaches the camera position. The second camera position was across the street from a large building (probably an administration building). The whole group can be seen as they mount horse-drawn carriages and leave.

The Prince of Darkness

AM&B © H18746 June 7, 1902

Cameraman: F. S. Armitage

Location: Roof studio, N.Y.C. *Date:* Apr. 6, 1900

6 ft. FLA4153 (print) FRA1321 (neg.)

The set is a well-decorated living room of a wealthy person. The door opens and admits a rather large and irate man. He walks across to the center of the room, tears off his hat, throws it on the floor, and stamps on it. His coat and vest follow the hat. He is just beginning to remove his shirt when, by the use of stop-action photography, a specter of death with arms outstretched menacingly appears before him. At the instant of the specter's appearance, the man's clothes magically reappear on him. The man throws up his arms in fright and falls lifeless to the floor.

The Princess in the Vase

AM&B © H106575 Feb. 25, 1908

Cameraman: G. W. Bitzer

Cast: D. W. Griffith

Location: Studio, N.Y.C. *Photographed:* Feb. 10 and 14, 1908

364 ft. FLA5643 (print) FRA2488 (neg.)

A young Egyptian princess is holding court, and dismisses everybody to let a man (D. W. Griffith) make love to her. Some armed men enter and kill him; the princess also dies and is cremated. The smoke from the fire, by trick photography, enters a vase which is sealed in a crypt by the priests. A time lag of several years is indicated by a fade, and an archaeologist is seen uncovering the vase. He brings it home, the princess materializes, and several comic incidents follow when he takes her to dinner, and D. W. Griffith appears, sword in hand, and stabs the archaeologist. The last scene shows that it was all the archaeologist's bad dream.

Princess Rajah Dance

AM&B © H46819 June 3, 1904
Cameraman: A. E. Weed
Location: St. Louis *Photographed:* May 23, 1904
28 ft. FLA4835 (print) FRA1843 (neg.)
[Louisiana Purchase Exposition]

A young lady is seen doing several types of dances throughout the film. For the finale, she holds a chair in her teeth and does balancing acts with it. Her dancing seems to draw from the contortions of the Turkish, the pirouettes of ballet, and the body gyrations of burlesque.

Princeton and Yale Football Game

Edison © H38332 Nov. 19, 1903
Cameraman: A. C. Abadie
Location: New Haven, Conn. *Photographed:* Nov. 14, 1903
75 ft. FLA5178 (print) FRA2124 (neg., copy 1) FRA2125 (neg., copy 2)

The camera was moved to many positions throughout the stadium, which contained an estimated 50,000 spectators. The opening scene was a complete pan around the locale, showing the crowd assembled to watch the game. The remaining scenes were photographed from various positions throughout the football field, showing the game in progress. There is line play shown as well as broken-field running.

The Prisoner of Zenda

Famous Players Film Company No © recorded 1913
Director: Edwin S. Porter
Cast: James K. Hackett as the king and his cousin, Beatrice Beckley, as the Princess of Flavia; David Torrence as "Black Michael," Duke of Strelsau; Mina Gale Haines as Antoinette de Mauban; Walter Hale as Rupert of Hensau; Tom Callahan, William P. Randall, Frank Coulter, Frank Shannon
From the novel by Anthony Hope
2,090 ft. FLA5893-5894 (print) FRA2784-2785 (neg.)

The plot of the classic story, *The Prisoner of Zenda*, was followed very closely by the cameraman and director. The details of the story of the impersonation of a kidnapped king by a relative who resembles him are brought out clearly. The film was directed by Edwin S. Porter and was his second picture after leaving his own company and joining Adolph Zukor and Famous Players. This copy was deposited with the Library of Congress in April 1913, but as the conditions of copyright were never fulfilled, the process of registration was never completed, and the title does not appear in the copyright office records except as unfinished business.

A Private Supper at Hellar's [i.e., Heller's]

AM&B © H24888 Dec. 9, 1902
Cameraman: Robert K. Bonine

Location: Roof studio, N.Y.C. *Date:* May 27, 1902
13 ft. FLA4447 (print) FRA1552 (neg.)

A man dressed as a waiter is setting a table in the center of a set of a fashionable restaurant. While he is going about his task, a young woman escorted by a young man appears and, as they make an effort to seat themselves at the table, the table disappears and reappears in another section of the room. The waiter assures them they must be mistaken and assists them to their chairs, but the chairs vanish and both young people fall to the floor. They show annoyance when the normal-sized table becomes a small table right before their eyes. They attempt to sit on the floor to begin their dinner, but the table immediately becomes larger. The young man becomes so exasperated that he kicks the waiter in the posterior, thus ending the film.

Prize Fight

AM&B © H22555 Oct. 14, 1902
Cameraman: F. S. Armitage
Location: Roof studio, N.Y.C. *Date:* May 18, 1899
17 ft. FLA3970 (print) FRA1178 (neg.)

Photographed from a single-camera position, the film shows a rather active prize fight; the youths appear to be approximately eighteen years of age. One of the fighters is knocked down.

Prize Winners at the Country Fair

Edison © H11490 Dec. 16, 1901
65 ft. FLA4836 (print) FRA1844 (neg.)

The subject is a demonstration of horses well enough trained to be exhibited before what appears to be a large grandstand filled with people at a county fair. The horses are shown as they pass the reviewing stand and turn away from the camera position. They are pulling two- and four-wheeled custom-built carriages. There is also one donkey-drawn cart.

Procession of Floats

Edison © 16425 Mar. 10, 1898
Location: Pasadena, Calif.
19 ft. FLA4247 (print) FRA1403 (neg.)

The single-camera position was over the heads of a crowd watching a procession of floats during the Tournament of Roses fete.

Procession of Floats and Masqueraders at Nice Carnival

Edison © H30409 Apr. 8, 1903
Location: Nice, France
38 ft. FLA5179 (print) FRA2126 (neg.)

The single-camera position was at shoulder level, over the heads of the crowds who are watching a procession of floats, clowns, and other people go by. The film is similar to a newsreel of an event such as the Mardi Gras. The title is preceded by a patent notation date of March 14, 1893.

Procession of Mounted Indians and Cowboys

Edison © 13550 Feb. 24, 1898
63 ft. FLA4837 (print) FRA1845 (neg.)

The film was photographed from a single-camera position above the heads of spectators at a parade that is similar to a wild west show. Specially constructed floats and decorated wagons, etc., are shown.

Professional Handicap Bicycle Race
Edison © H7637 Aug. 14, 1901
33 ft. FLA3694 (print) FRA0943 (neg.)

Bicycle racing is the subject. To photograph it, the cameraman took his equipment to the inside of the track on which the bicycle riders were racing. The film shows the start and several turns of the track during the race.

See also: Bicycle Paced Race

The Professor
AM&B © H38152 Nov. 14, 1903
39 ft. FLA4838 (print) FRA1846 (neg.)

A man wearing the mortarboard cap and the gown of a professor is seen standing in front of a set of a brick wall with a heavy wooden door in it. A sign on the door says "Professor J. Ink Will Receive His Classes at . . . " and the professor fills in "7 P.M." in the space provided and then leaves. Two male students appear, look at the sign and, with much giggling, remove the letter "C" from "classes," and then leave. Several young women arrive and seem to resent the sign. The last scene shows the professor returning. When he notices the sign, he rubs out the "L" and stamps off in high glee, ending the film.

The Professor of the Drama
AM&B © H32502 June 11, 1903
Cameraman: G. W. Bitzer
Location: Studio, N.Y.C. *Date:* June 5, 1903
25 ft. FLA4282 (print) FRA1435 (neg.)

This shows the attempted subtleties of a professor of drama who, by the devious approach of instructing one of his young female pupils on how to gesture, is caught in the act of embracing her. He is unceremoniously thrown out of the window by the head of the school.

Projectile From 10 Inch Gun Striking Water
AM&B © H30722 Apr. 24, 1903
Location: Sandy Hook, N.J. *Date:* 1897 [?]
19 ft. FLA3304 (print) FRA0618 (neg.)

The film, photographed from a single-camera position, shows a large artillery cannon in three-quarter profile as it is prepared for an accuracy test. Most of the results are obscured by the smoke from the explosion. A still made from the Mutograph of this film was reproduced in the April 17, 1897, edition of *Scientific American* magazine.

See also: Firing 10 Inch Gun

The Proposal
Biograph © J147352 Nov. 5, 1910
Cameraman: Arthur Marvin
Cast: Tony O'Sullivan, Vivian Prescott
Location: Fort Lee, N.J.; Studio, N.Y.C. *Photographed:* Sept. 15–17, 1910
190 ft. FLA5644 (print) FRA2492 (neg.)

A bachelor in search of a wife calls on a widow, is impressed by her, and returns home. He writes and mails a proposal of marriage. While he is standing by the mailbox, a heavily laden man accompanied by a woman with a screaming infant comes along and stops. The man picks up some packages he has dropped, and they depart. Our hero realizes what he has gotten himself into the waits for the postman, who refuses to return his letter. After a sleepless night, he attempts to intercept the letter but to no avail. Dejected, the bachelor returns to his quarters and considers shooting himself when the postman arrives with his letter which has been returned to him for a more complete address.

The Providence Light Artillery
AM&B © H36633 Oct. 8, 1903
Cameraman: G. W. Bitzer
Location: Providence, R.I. *Photographed:* Oct. 3, 1903
63 ft. FLA4839 (print) FRA1847 (neg.)

Photography for this film was from a single-camera position over the heads of spectators watching a parade of military units. The paraders are led by uniformed officers wearing swallowtail coats with epaulets and plumed "fore and aft" hats. Following them are approximately ten platoons of infantry, each man wearing a spiked-and-plumed European-style black steel helmet. The right guide and standard bearer of each platoon wears a white or silvered helmet, larger than the rest, with white plumes. One company of three platoons wears bearskin shakos. Preceding this company is a band in unidentified uniforms. There are approximately twenty pieces in the band. About five hundred spectators stand in the background in front of a public building that, by its general design, was either the front of a boat landing or a railroad station.

The Prussian Spy
AM&B © H123540 Mar. 1, 1909
Director: D. W. Griffith *Cameraman:* G. W. Bitzer
Cast: Marion Leonard, Arthur Johnson, Owen Moore, Florence Lawrence, Mack Sennett.
Location: Studio, N.Y.C. *Photographed:* Feb. 1, 1909
175 ft. FLA5645 (print) FRA2492 (neg.)

An actor wearing the uniform of a Prussian officer enters a drawing room and makes demands upon an attractive woman, who refuses, and he leaves. A man in a white military uniform of high rank comes in and embraces the young lady. The first officer returns, accompanied by three others. The young woman hides her lover in a large cabinet. The Prussian officers unsuccessfully search the apartment for the officer in the white uniform. But then their leader draws a target on a piece of paper, pins it to the door of the cabinet, and uses it for target practice.

Le Puits Fantastique
See: The Enchanted Well

Pull Down the Curtains, Susie
AM&B © H40803 Jan. 12, 1904
Cameraman: A. E. Weed
Location: Studio, N.Y.C. *Photographed:* Dec. 30, 1903
23 ft. FLA3658 (print) FRA0912 (neg.)

A young lady is shown being escorted home by her male companion. She kisses him goodnight, goes into the house, stands by an unshaded window, and starts to remove her clothing. Outside the house, her male friend can be seen watching her disrobe. After removing several articles of clothing, the young lady pulls the shade down and the picture ends.

Pulling Off the Bed Clothes

AM&B © H32001 May 19, 1903
Cameraman: G. W. Bitzer
Location: Roof studio, N.Y.C. *Date:* May 11, 1903
20 ft. FLA4323 (print) FRA1471 (neg.)

In one of the sections of a set of two rooms is a boy diligently stringing a cord from the door knob of one door up and over the transom and down to the bed covers of the bed in the other room. As the film continues, the boy leaves. A woman gets into the bed and pulls the covers up over her. Soon a man comes through the door, causing the bed clothes to be yanked from the sleeping woman.

Pumpkin Eater

Paley & Steiner © H53977 Dec. 2, 1904
9 ft. FLA4435 (print) FRA1543 (neg.)

The film is too short to permit any interpretation of the story line and very little description of the players. The only plot or action visible is two men sitting at a table in the yard outside a house where they are served something to eat by a woman. The woman wears an apron over her dress. The film does not continue beyond this.

The Punishment

Biograph © J167862 Apr. 5, 1912
Director: D. W. Griffith *Cameraman:* G. W. Bitzer
Cast: Blanche Sweet, Wilfred Lucas, Harry Hyde, George Nicholls, Kate Bruce, Walter Chrystie Cabanne
Location: Calif.
391 ft. FLA5646 (print) FRA2489 (neg.)

An arrogant nobleman with a spoiled son (Walter Chrystie Cabanne) falls in love with the beautiful daughter (Blanche Sweet) of his caretaker and insists on marrying her. She is in love with a local boy (Wilfred Lucas), and this forms the basis of her old husband's jealousy. The young wife meets her former lover accidentally, drops a cross, and when he follows her into the house to return it, the husband and his son see him. The son hides in a spring lock chest. The husband, thinking it is the lover in the chest, locks it, waits until he is certain the man in the chest is dead, and opens it in front of his wife. He is so shocked and angry by his discovery that he suffers a heart attack, ending the film.

The Purgation

Biograph © J142946 July 6, 1910
Cameraman: G. W. Bitzer
Cast: Mack Sennett, Charles West, Dell Henderson, Grace Henderson, Eddie Dillon, William J. Butler, Gertrude Robinson
Location: Westfield, N.J.; Studio, N.Y.C. *Photographed:* May 24, 27 and 28, 1910
393 ft FLA5647 (print) FRA2490 (neg.)

A young man (Charles West), influenced by a confirmed thief into taking part in dishonest acts, reforms, gets a job, and falls in love with his employer's daughter (Gertrude Robinson). Her father gives her an expensive necklace as a wedding present, and it is stolen by the young man's former evil companion (Mack Sennett). The young man gets the necklace back and attempts to return it to the safe, but he is caught, and his past record is held against him. He is believed guilty of the theft. One of the actual thieves confesses, and the hero is absolved of stealing the necklace, but the last scene shows him being led off to jail by the police to pay for his earlier crimes.

Putting Up the Swing

AM&B © H52101 Oct. 26, 1904
58 ft. FLA5180 (print) FRA2127 (neg.)

The backyard of a house and a man asleep in a chair with his face covered by a newspaper can be seen. A woman is bending over a washtub scrubbing clothes. Two adolescent girls enter the scene, wake up the sleeper and get him to build them a swing, much to his irritation. The film continues showing the man building the swing. When the task is completed, he sits in the swing to test it and pulls the support down on top of him. The support appears to be a rainwater trough for a cistern. As the film ends, he is seen standing with his clothes dripping wet.

Quail Shooting at Pinehurst

AM&B © H71526 Jan. 3, 1906
Cameraman: G. W. Bitzer
Location: Pinehurst, N.C. *Photographed:* Nov. 21–22, 1905
408 ft. FLA5648 (print) FRA2493 (neg.)

The entire film is devoted to quail hunting. Judging from the equipment and tack, the hunt was held on an estate of considerable size. The hunters have a picnic lunch, which they eat on the ground, and there is a close-up of a pointer dog holding a quail in his mouth.

The Quarrelsome Washerwoman

AM&B © H50324 Sept. 10, 1904
38 ft. FLA4840 (print) FRA1848 (neg.)

Two women, one hanging out a clean, white wash, the other beating a carpet, try to do both jobs in approximately the same area. The first woman puts up her wash, and the second woman arrives determined to beat her carpets. There is an inevitable altercation. The fight lasts for a considerable part of the film. They can be seen hitting one another, and then land on the ground where they continue wrestling. A man arrives and attempts to separate them, which only makes matters worse. He becomes the recipient of the anger of both of the women, and the film ends.

Quebec Fire Dept. on Runners

AM&B © H25958 Dec. 31, 1902
Cameraman: Robert K. Bonine
Location: Quebec, P.Q., Can. *Photographed:* Feb. 14, 1902
29 ft. FLA3597 (print) FRA0862 (neg.)

The film, photographed during a snowstorm, shows horse-drawn fire apparatus being pulled past the camera position. The wheels of each piece of fire-fighting equipment has been set in runners so that it will slide over the top of the existing snow.

See also: Kent House Slide, and Skee Club

Queen Elizabeth

Famous Players and Engadine Amusement Company © J171705 July 22, 1912

Director: Louis Mercanton

From the play of the same name by Emile Moreau

Cast: Sarah Bernhardt as Queen Elizabeth, Lou Tellegen as the Earl of Essex, Mlle. Romain as the Countess of Nottingham, M. Maxudian as the Earl of Nottingham

Location: France *Date:* 1912

1,059 ft. FLA5941 (print)

From beginning to end, the method used in portraying this story of a period in the lives of Queen Elizabeth and the Earl of Essex was a series of tableaus. First, a title appears, and then the next few scenes illustrate that title, and so on until the picture is completed. The film indicates that the "Dresses, Armor, and Furniture were from the Sarah Bernhardt Theatre, Paris, France."

A Quick Recovery

AM&B © H16731 Apr. 18, 1902

Cameraman: F. S. Armitage

Location: Roof studio, N.Y.C. *Date:* June 28, 1901

10 ft. FLA3265 (print) FRA0585 (neg.)

The film begins on a set of a doctor's office. A young woman can be seen hurrying to hug a man walking toward her, and they embrace several times. The man then lies down on the doctor's examining table while the woman covers him with a sheet. Another man, dressed as a burlesque doctor, enters, removes the head of the man on the table, and places the head on a shelf. The young woman picks up the head from the shelf and replaces it on the body. This restores the young man to life and he begins embracing the young woman once more as the film ends. The removal and replacement of the young man's head was effected by the use of trick photography.

Quick Work for the Soubrettes

AM&B © H42240 Feb. 18, 1904

Cameraman: A. E. Weed

Location: Studio, N.Y.C. *Photographed:* Feb. 4, 1904

20 ft. FLA3913 (print) FRA1130 (neg.)

Three young women can be seen dressing themselves and aiding one another to dress on a set of a bedroom. As the film begins, the young ladies are en dêshabille, and when it ends, they are all in their costumes.

A Race for a Kiss

Hepworth © AM&B H53769 Nov. 28, 1904

Director: Lewin Fitzhamon

Cast: Dolly Lupone, Lewin Fitzhamon (jockey)

Location: Walton-on-Thames, England

88 ft. FLA5181 (print) FRA2128 (neg., copy 1) FRA2129 (neg., copy 2)

A young woman is walking along a wooded area accompanied by a man dressed as a jockey and leading a horse. A man in an automobile joins them and the jockey and the driver of the automobile start an argument. The camera position changes and the young woman is seen drawing a line across the narrow road, and the automobile and the mounted jockey begin to race. The competitors pass the camera several times. The race and the film end when a policyman halts the car and places the driver under arrest, evidently for exceeding the speed limit.

Racing at Sheepshead Bay

Edison © 43414 July 31, 1897

Location: Sheepshead Bay, N.Y.

27 ft. FLA3072 (print) FRA0414 (neg.)

The film begins from a camera position on the rail of the turf at a track where horse racing is in progress. While the camera position is stationary, it is approached at an angle by six horses at full gallop. The remainder of the film was photographed in what appears to be the winner's circle, as two of the horses come to a stop in view of the camera, and their jockeys dismount. "Won by the famous Clifford, Sloane up." (Edison catalog, 1901)

The Racing Chutes at Dreamland

AM&B © H48625 July 28, 1904

Cameraman: G. W. Bitzer

Location: Coney Island, N.Y. *Photographed:* July 20, 1904

38 ft. FLA3213 (print) FRA0537 (neg.)

A small lake can be seen in the foreground; at the opposite end of the lake, approximately a hundred yards aways, is a bridge. People are standing on the bridge watching water sleds of an amusement at Coney Island come down the sheer face of the slides. Six water sleds filled with people in groups of twos make their descent down the slide into the water during the film.

Racing for a Tow

AM&B © H35100 Aug. 28, 1903

29 ft. FLA3714 (print FRA0961 (neg.)

The subject is a large seagoing steam tug, photographed from a single-camera position that seems to have been on the stern of another tug. The footage was taken from directly in front of the tug, shown in profile. There is nothing else in the background or on the horizon.

Raffles, the Amateur Cracksman

Vitagraph © H64825 Aug. 23, 1905

Director: G. M. (Broncho Billy) Anderson

Cast: J. Barney Sherry

13 ft. FLA4199 (print) FRA1362 (neg.)

Throughout the film there are several short scenes, each depicting theft or robbery or some attempt at violence. In every scene a man made up as an old gentleman can be seen. He is shown as a pickpocket, a robber with a gun or club, or as part of a gang. As the film ends, the old gentleman is seen impeccably attired walking down a street; two frames later he has disappeared through a secret panel in the wall of a house. All the tableaus represent scenes from the real-life activities of the "nice old gentleman."

Raffles, the Dog

Edison © H62774 June 30, 1905

Cameraman: Edwin S. Porter

Location: N.Y.C. *Photographed:* June 13, 1905

250 ft. FLA5649 (print) FRA2494 (neg.)

A man, a woman, and a dog are in a living room set. The couple collaborates on teaching the dog to steal on command. The woman dresses for the street and goes out with the man and the dog onto the streets of New York where the dog, when ordered, steals such articles as suitcases and handbags from persons sitting on benches or in carriages. A dice game in which a grocery delivery boy is participating in interrupted when the dog steals an item from the grocery basket. A chase starts, and some twenty-five or thirty people are soon following the dog and its owners across a lot of New York real estate. The picture ends when the dog and his owners are caught.

A Raid on a Cock Fight

AM&B © H73109 Feb. 9, 1906
Cameraman: G. W. Bitzer
Location: Studio, N.Y.C. *Photographed:* Jan. 30, 1906
42 ft. FLA4841 (print) FRA1849 (neg.)

The scene opens on a cock fight with about six spectators who can be seen in the background. The fighting cocks are actively engaged in attempting to kill one another when the fight is broken up by the police, who come in and pick up the money lying on the ground and put it in their pockets.

Raid on a Coiner's Den

Gaumont © AM&B H47463 June 23, 1904
Director: Alfred Collins
Location: England
182 ft. FLA5650 (print) FRA2495 (neg.)

The film begins with an extreme close-up of three pairs of hands; one is holding a pistol, which is pointed at the other two, who are holding handcuffs and British pound notes. A cutaway from the close-up shows the interior of a two-story room where counterfeiters are at work. The scene shifts to the exterior as a man signals for admittance. He is observed by another man, and the police raid the shop. There are scenes of running and fighting until all of the law-breakers are captured. The last two frames of the picture are watermarked "L. Gaumont and Company."

Railroad Panorama Near Spanishtown, Jamaica

Edison © H30396 Apr. 8, 1903
Location: Spanishtown, Jamaica
90 ft. FLA5182 (print) FRA2130 (neg.)

The opening scene shows a railroad track where some laborers are working. As the film progresses, the camera position begins to move, and for the remainder of the film shows what can be seen from the back of a moving train as it travels along the tracks. The shrubbery that had grown up close to the tracks, an occasional tool shed at the side of the track and, in three instances, the transit through tunnels are shown.

Railroad Smashup

Edison © H50587 Sept. 19, 1904
Cameraman: Edwin S. Porter
Location: Revere, Mass. *Photographed:* Aug. 27, 1904
39 ft. FLA3196 (print) FRA0522 (neg.)

The film was photographed from two positions, and begins with a distant shot of two steam locomotives headed toward each other on the same track. They collide. The next camera position shows a closer view of the two nearly demolished locomotives, with steam and smoke rising, and spectators rushing to get a better view.

Railroad View—Experimental

AM&B © H34516 Aug. 13, 1903
Cameraman: Arthur Marvin

Date: July 23, 1903
28 ft. FLA3724 (print) FRA0971 (neg.)

This film was photographed from both the front and rear of a train traveling at extremely high speed over an unidentified railroad. The camera was cranked at a speed that makes it impossible to establish or understand its purpose, but as the title indicates, the film was merely experimental.

Railway Station at Yokohama

Edison © 38228 June 22, 1898
Location: Yokohama, Japan
27 ft. FLA3311 (print) FRA0625 (neg.)

The film, photographed from a single-camera position, shows a level space where ricksha coolies are standing. According to the title, the space is in front of a railway station, but, there is nothing in the film to indicate this.

A Railway Tragedy

Gaumont © AM&B H51118 Oct. 10, 1904
135 ft. FLA5183 (print) FRA2141 (neg.)

A Railway Tragedy is about a robbery and assault on an attractive young woman in a train compartment. During the attack the young woman is thrown from the train. The film ends with the capture of the villain on a station platform as he attempts to make his getaway. Several camera positions were used. When the train door opens during the attack scene, it is obvious that the railway compartment was a constructed set, as the landscape remains stationary.

Rainmakers

Edison © 60594 Oct. 25, 1897
25 ft. FLA3058 (print) FRA0403 (neg.)

A single-camera position film shows the end of a fence with a sign that says, "Drop a Nickel in the Slot and See It Rain." The camera is positioned to show a small boy behind the fence with a garden hose. He squirts water over the fence onto an inquisitive person standing by the sign with an umbrella over his head.

Raising Old Glory over Morro Castle

Edison © 10651 Feb. 4, 1899
25 ft. FLA4046 (print) FRA1233 (neg.)
[Spanish-American War]

The film opens on a constructed miniature of the military fort in Cuba called Morro Castle. In the foreground is a flagstaff flying the Spanish flag. The action of the picture consists of lowering the Spanish flag and replacing it with the American flag, which is then unfurled.

Ramona

Biograph © J141683 May 26, 1910
Director: D. W. Griffith *Cameraman:* G. W. Bitzer
Based on the novel by Helen Hunt Jackson
Cast: Mary Pickford, Henry B. Walthall, Frank Grandon, Kate Bruce
Location: Piru, Camulos and Los Angeles, Calif. *Photographed:* Mar. 30–31 and Apr. 1–2, 1910
432 ft. FLA5651 (print) FRA6422 (neg.)

This film follows an historical incident and concerns a white man's inhumanity to the California Indians. The director moved his camera, changing the composition from a close-up of the lead actress to a dramatic scene of the actors on a hilltop, a movement motivated by the terror in the valley below. This is the only film in the Library on Congress Biograph collection that has a title preceding the picture giving credit to the author of the book. The film also identifies the location as one of those mentioned by the author of *Ramona*. Biograph paid Little, Brown and Company $100 for rights to use the Helen Hunt Jackson novel.

Rapids Below Suspension Bridge

Edison © 13537 Feb. 17, 1899

Location: Niagara River, N.Y., and Canada

25 ft. FLA3015 (print) FRA0008 (neg.)

The single-camera position shows a portion of the whirling water of the rapids below Niagara Falls, immediately beneath the suspension bridge.

The Rat Trap Pickpocket Detector

AM&B © H68183 Nov. 3, 1905

Cameraman: G. W. Bitzer

Location: Studio, N.Y.C. *Photographed:* Oct. 24, 1905

24 ft. FLA3944 (print) FRA1155 (neg.)

A set of a bedroom complete with a big brass double bed can be seen. A man in top hat and pajamas staggers into the room carrying his trousers. He reaches into the pajama pocket and takes out a mouse trap which he puts into the pocket of the trousers, and hangs them on a coat rack near the bed. The man then climbs into the bed. An extremely large woman clad in a nightgown comes into the bedroom, looks about, walks over to the trousers, and begins going through the pockets. She runs afoul of the mouse trap and can be seen spinning about trying to extricate her fingers. When she is free, she turns on the man in the bed and begins to molest him, exposing a great deal of her anatomy in the process.

See also: Airy Fairy Lillian Tries on her New Corsets, and Fat Girl's Love Affair

Razing a Brick Building

AM&B © H17491 May 8, 1902

20 ft. FLA3784 (print) FRA1025 (neg.)

The film begins by showing a five-story brick building that has begun to topple. It continues and concludes with the arc of the fall of the building until it hits the ground. The cameraman also filmed some of the spectators.

Razzle Dazzle

Edison © H33296 July 8, 1903

Cameraman: A. C. Abadie

Location: Wilmington Springs, Del. *Photographed:* June 30, 1903

28 ft. FLA3490 (print) FRA0771 (neg.)

The entire film was photographed from a position that permitted the camera to encompass a peculiar amusement concession named "Razzle Dazzle." It consists of a large circle suspended from cables, giving it the effect of a maypole. Children sit on it and the circle is revolved and undulated in the air.

See also: Miniature Railway at Wilmington Springs, Del.

Reading the Death Sentence

AM&B © H70057 Dec. 15, 1905

Cameraman: G. W. Bitzer

Location: Studio, N.Y.C. *Photographed:* Dec. 6, 1905

26 ft. FLA3963 (print) FRA1172 (neg.)

The opening scene shows a wall with barred doors and a staircase. A man in ordinary civilian attire descends the stairs, accompanied by two prison guards. The man removes a paper from his breast pocket and reads it aloud. The guards open one of the barred doors. A woman dressed completely in black comes out and starts up the stairs. The three men go with her. AM & B, playing it safe, made two endings to their newsreel drama, An Execution by Hanging, and A Reprieve from the Scaffold. As it turned out, Mrs. May Rogers, convicted murderess, was granted a reprieve at the last moment.

Reception of British Fleet

AM&B © H68733 Nov. 13, 1905

Cameraman: G. W. Bitzer

Location: New York harbor and Hudson River, N.Y. *Photographed:* Nov. 9, 1905

221 ft. FLA5652 (print) FRA2499 (neg., copy 1) FRA2500 (neg., copy 2)

The subject is the arrival of the British fleet, its anchorage in the Hudson River, and its exchange of courtesies with the U.S. Navy, which also is anchored there. The camera pans 360 degrees, and the embankments on both sides of the Hudson River are visible.

Reception of President Taft in Petersburg, Virginia, May 19th, 1909

Columbia Photograph Company © J129814 July 29, 1909

Location: Petersburg, Va. *Photographed:* May 19, 1909

365 ft. FLA5653 (print) FRA2691 (neg.)

The film encompasses a dedication of a memorial to the Civil War dead who lost their lives on the battlefields of the State of Virginia, as well as an outdoor luncheon. The Scenes are of the arrival of the spectators and participants in the ceremonies, the unveiling of the obelisk (by Mrs. H. A. Gilbert of Harrisburg, Pennsylvania), the dedication speeches by the president of the United States. William Howard Taft, and an alfresco luncheon. The camera also photographed the picnic grounds, and the parade of both the mounted troops of the U.S. cavalry and the foot soldiers of the infantry Confederate and Union Civil War veterans. The film ends with the departure of President Taft in an open horse-drawn carriage. It is probably a companion piece of part of same film as Unveiling of a Pennsylvania Monument on the Battlefields of Petersburg, Va., May 19, 1909. Information is given as photographed on the original paper print film.

The Reckoning

AM&B © H119108 Dec. 3, 1908

Director: D. W. Griffith *Cameraman:* G. W. Bitzer

Cast: Florence Lawrence, Mack Sennett, Harry Salter

Location: Hoboken, N.J.; Studio, N.Y.C. *Photographed:* Nov. 9–10, 1908

187 ft. FLA5654 (print) FRA2498 (neg.)

The film opens in the apartment of a workman (Harry Salter) who says goodbye to his wife (Florence Lawrence) and goes to work. But he finds a large sign on the gate informing him that the factory will be closed until Saturday. The next scene shows a male visitor (Mack Sennett) embracing the workman's wife and sharing a beer. The workman starts home but is stopped by a friend, and they head for the nearest saloon. One drink is enough, and the workman continues home. When he arrives, he notices that the window blinds are down, which causes him to become suspicious. He enters, finds the stranger with his wife, and shoots them both.

The Recreation of an Heiress

Biograph © J149493 Dec. 24, 1910

Cameraman: Arthur Marvin

Cast: Charles West, Grace Henderson, Verner Clarges, Dorothy West, Claire McDowell

Location: Studio, N.Y.C. *Photographed:* Nov. 14, 1910

166 ft. FLA5655 (print) FRA2501 (neg.)

A fortune-hunting woman influences her son to try to marry a rich heiress who is coming to visit. The heiress, suspicious of the young man's enthusiasm to marry her, sets out to trick him by sending a note indicating that the maid accompanying her is really the heiress. The trick works, and the young man immediately switches his attentions to the maid. The young man and the maid are embracing when the heiress enters and orders the maid to carry her suitcases out, much to the consternation of the young man and his designing mother. All the scenes were filmed indoors from a single-camera position.

Red Cross Ambulance on Battlefield

Edison © D9115 Apr. 28, 1900

53 ft. FLA4842 (print) FRA6402 (neg.)

[Boer War]

A film of a field, photographed from a single-camara position, where several stretchers holding wounded men can be seen. The wounded soldiers are attended by men whose military unform indicates they are part of the Red Cross or a medical squad. Several horse-drawn vehicles enter the scene, and the stretchers are put into the horse-drawn vehicles and driven away.

The Red Girl

AM&B © H115322 Sept. 3, 1908

Director: D. W. Griffith *Cameraman:* Arthur Marvin

Cast: Charles Inslee, Harry Salter, Marion Sunshine, Tony O'Sullivan, Florence Lawrence

Location: Little Falls, N.J.; Studio, N.Y.C. *Photographed:* Aug. 1–12, 1908

392 ft. FLA5656 (print) FRA2497 (neg.)

All of the cast were dressed as westerners, either cowboys, Mexicans, or Indians. The woman who plays the villainess is dressed as a Mexican renegade. She steals a bag of gold from a woman who has just brought it to the settlement, and before she is caught by the owner of the gold, she manages to shoot several people, to enlist the help of other renegades, and to tie up an Indian maiden and suspend her over a river. The film ends when the villainess is captured and order is restored. With the exception of the saloon scenes, all of the action takes place out-of-doors in roadways, cornfields, on in canoes on the river.

The Redman and the Child

AM&B © H113769 July 22, 1908

Director: D. W. Griffith *Cameraman:* Arthur Marvin

Cast: Charles Inslee, John Tansy, Harry Salter, Linda Arvidson

Location: Little Falls, N.J. *Photographed:* June 30 and July 3, 1908

328 ft. FLA5657 (print) FRA2681 (neg.)

The first scene shows a surveyor's tent pitched on the edge of a slow-running river in a heavily wooded area; an Indian and a small boy are walking toward a tree. The Indian shows the child his cache of gold nuggets and takes him home. Later the child is kidnapped by two men who force him to take them to the cache. The Indian observes them through the surveyor's telescope and pursues them as they flee by canoe with the gold and the child. He kills both kidnappers, and the last scene shows the Indian bringing the badly injured little boy home. All the scenes were photographed outdoors in natural light. There is one matte shot from the point of view of the Indian looking through the telescope, watching the kidnappers steal the gold.

The Redman's View

Biograph © J135835 Dec. 11, 1909

Director: D. W. Griffith *Cameraman:* G. W. Bitzer

Cast: James Kirkwood, Arthur Johnson, Owen Moore, Lottie Pickford, Alfred Paget, W. Chrystie Miller

Location: Mt. Beacon, N.Y. *Photographed:* Nov. 4–6, 1909

389 ft. FLA5658 (print) FRA2502 (neg.)

The subject of this film is the movement of reluctant Indians even further west by groups of armed white men. The Chief's daughter is left behind as part of a trade with the white men to prevent a massacre, and the climax of the film occurs when her father dies. The young Indian brave she was not permitted to marry returns to the white men's camp and gets permission to take her to the burial site of her father. The film ends as the two of them stand close to the grave, heads lowered in sorrow.

The Rehearsal

AM&B © H37383 Oct. 28, 1903

Cameraman: G. W. Bitzer

Location: Studio, N.Y.C. *Photographed:* Oct. 22, 1903

23 ft. FLA3672 (print) FRA0923 (neg.)

The camera was positioned as if in the audience at a theater and, as the film begins, three people are standing facing the camera, while the fourth is seated at a piano with his back to the camera. Each of the standing persons has a sheet of music. Judging from the movement of their mouths, they are singing. There is no other action in the film.

Reilly's Light Battery "F"

AM&B © H21507 Sept. 5, 1902

Cameraman: Raymond Ackerman

Location: Peking, China *Date:* Jan. 12, 1901

11ft. FLA3319 (print) FRA0633 (neg.)

The poor condition of the film, its short length, and the distance of the subjects from the camera do not permit detailed description. The film consists of what appears to a large group of military personnel on horseback riding past the camera at about five hundred yards distance.

The Rejuvenation of Aunt Mary

Klaw & Erlanger © LP3096 July 23, 1914

Location: Some scenes were photographed in San Francisco.

Cast: Kate Toncray, Audrey Kirby, Dell Henderson, Reggie Morris, Dave Morris, Tom MacEvoy, Jack Mulhall, William Sloane, Florence Lee, Gertrude Bambrick, Mrs. La Varnie, Clarence Barr.

1,294 ft. FLA5936 (print) FRA2799 (neg.)

All four reels of this film show how a rich and dominant woman who dislikes city life changes her mind and moves from the country and its quiet ways. Aunt Mary has a nephew who goes to the city and gets into one scrape after another. He abandons a woman to whom he had proposed, causing Aunt Mary to disinherit him. His friends invite Aunt Mary to the city, and she begins to enjoy the gay life, even to the extent of changing her will again. There are many indoor and outdoor scenes as she attends all sorts of social functions with her nephew and his friends.

"Reliance" and "Shamrock III" Jockeying and Starting in First Race

Edison © H35047 Aug. 25, 1903

Cameraman: J. B. Smith

Location: Five miles off Sandy Hook, N.J. *Photographed:* Aug. 22, 1903

55 ft. FLA4843 (print) FRA1850 (neg.)

[America's Cup Races]

The opening scene shows the area designated for turning in the America's Cup Races. Two large sailing yachts approach the turning buoy and make their turn. They pass close to the boat carrying the camera. The crew of one of the yachts is clearly visible.

"Reliance" Crossing the Line and Winning First Race

Edison © H35048 Aug. 25, 1903

Cameraman: J. B. Smith

Location: Five miles off Sandy Hook, N.J. *Photographed:* Aug. 22, 1903

34 ft. FLA3718 (print) FRA0965 (neg.)

[America's Cup Races]

The length of the film only permits seeing one racing yacht sailing before the wind as it approaches the finish line. The distance is about a thousand yards from the camera and there is nothing else in sight.

"Reliance" vs. "Shamrock III," Aug. 20

AM&B © H35095 Aug. 28, 1903

Cameraman: A. E. Weed

Location: Sandy Hook, N.J. *Photographed:* Aug. 20, 1903

42 ft. FLA4844 (print) FRA1851 (neg.)

[America's Cup Races]

The camera was approximately 550 yards from the race course track line. The first action is the bowsprit of the leading contender entering the picture. The remainder of the film includes a full photograph of the leading yacht as well as most of the trailing yacht. Both of the vessels are sailing close-hauled and full rigged. The *Reliance* and *Shamrock III* were contenders for the America's Cup.

Renovare Production Company "Special"

Renovare Company, 1953

Contents:

Pope Leo XIII in Canopy Chair © American Mutoscope Co., 73559, Dec. 15, 1898

Pope Leo XIII in Carriage © American Mutoscope Co., 73561, Dec. 15, 1898

Pope Leo XIII Being Carried in Chair Through Upper Loggia © American Mutoscope Co., 73560, Dec. 15, 1898

Pope Leo XIII Being Seated Bestowing Blessing Surrounded by Swiss Guards © American Mutoscope Co., 73566, Dec. 15, 1898

Pope Leo XIII Leaving Carriage and Being Ushered into Garden © American Mutoscope Co., 73563, Dec. 15, 1898

Pope Leo XIII Seated in Garden © American Mutoscope Co., 73564, Dec. 15, 1898

Pope Leo XIII Walking Before Kneeling Guards © American Mutoscope Co., 73562 Dec. 15, 1898

109 ft. FAA 7703 (copy 1) FLA 5980 (copy 2) FRA 3030 (neg.)

Various separate films were incorporated in a special production for the Academy of Motion Pictures Arts and Sciences press showing. Six reels of 1898 Mutoscope "flip cards" were sent from the Library of Congress. They were separated and photographed one at a time (1,500 cards in each reel). When this was completed, the result was a moving picture, which had never before existed, of Pope Leo XIII in the Vatican in the latter part of the nineteenth century. Mr. W. K. Laurie Dickson spent four months in Italy making these photographs.

See also: Pope [Leo XIII] in His Carriage, and Pope [Leo XIII] Passing Through Upper Loggia

The Rent Jumpers

Keystone © LP5037 Apr. 8, 1915

Producer and Author: Mack Sennett

Cast: Mae Busch, Charles Chase, Nick Cogley, Joseph Swickard, Vivian Edwards, Frank Opperman, Billie Bennett

Location: Keystone studio, Los Angeles

400 ft. FLA6136 (print)

Two tenants of a rooming house, Charles Chase and Nick Cogley, are both interested in the daughter of the house, Mae Busch. Her father, Frank Opperman, favors Cogley. Father accidentally steps in a bucket of water, falls down, and gets his pants soaked. He gives them to his daughter to press for him. Chase, always broke, steals Cogley's wallet, not knowing it is empty, and invites Mae Busch out to dinner. Mae leaves her father's trousers on the ironing board and goes off with Chase. Cogley also needs his trousers pressed, and persuades another roomer, Billie Bennett, to do it for him. Somehow the trousers get mixed up; Cogley puts on the wrong pair and heads for the restaurant. Father dons what he thinks is his pants and also goes off to the same restaurant. By this time, Mae and Charles have finished their meal and the waiter presents the bill. Chase then discovers the stolen wallet is empty. Cogley comes along with a handful of cash he has found in the wrong trousers, and says he will take care of Mae Busch. Father arrives, takes his money back from Cogley. Father pays the manager (Joseph Swickard) when he learns his daughter and Chase have become engaged.

The Renunciation
Biograph © J129610 July 21, 1909
Director: D. W. Griffith *Cameraman:* G. W. Bitzer, Arthur Marvin
Cast: Mary Pickford, Arthur Johnson, James Kirkwood, W. Chrystie Miller, Bill Quirk, Edwin August
Location: Shadyside, N.J.; Studio N.Y.C. *Photographed:* June 2, 14 and 18, 1909
365 ft. FLA5659 (print) FRA6411 (neg.)

Two men dressed as miners are sitting in the foreground of what appears to be a mining camp. In the distance several men are digging into the dirt with pickaxes. A man and a young woman walk toward the camera until they, too, are in the foreground, and introductions are made all around. It is obvious that the two young men have been smitten by the charms of the young woman, and the film builds up their enmity over her. The climax comes when the life-long friends fight a bowie knife duel, which might have ended in death, except that the young girl breaks it up by introducing her city fiance. Each scene is taken from a single-camera position, and all the actors walk in and out of the camera position to end the photographic thought.

Repairing Streets in Mexico
Edison © 13558 Feb. 24, 1898
Location: Mexico City
26 ft. FLA4093 (print) FRA1274 (neg.)

This is a single-camera position film of streets being repaired in Mexico City. Apparently the laborers are prisoners, as there are guards watching them.

A Reprieve from the Scaffold
AM&B © H70056 Dec. 15, 1905
Cameraman: F. A. Dobson
Location: Studio, N.Y.C. *Photographed:* Dec. 1, 1905
30 ft. FLA3943 (print) FRA1154 (neg.)

This single-camera position film shows a simulated brick wall, presumably surrounding a scaffold area. A hangman's noose can be seen suspended over a square in the floor. A woman, attired completely in black, with a uniformed guard on each side, is escorted to the trap door. A black hood is placed over her head, and the noose is fitted about her neck. At that moment, a man rushes in waving a piece of paper which is read to the person supervising the execution. The paper is a reprieve. The noose is removed with much visible relief to everyone. To be on the safe side, AM&B photographed two endings; Reading the Death Sentence, and the above. Mrs. May Rogers, convicted murderess, was granted a reprieve at the last moment.

See also: An Execution by Hanging and Reading the Death Sentence.

Reproduction, Coronation Ceremonies—King Edward VII
Warwick & Méliès © AM&B H20562 Aug. 8, 1902
Directors: Georges Méliès, Charles Urban
Location: Montreuil, France
95 ft. FLA5184 (print) FRA2142 (neg.)

This film was copyrighted under AM&B's name, but their advertising indicates that it was made in Montreuil, France, by the French filmmaker, Georges Méliès, for the English firm, Warwick Trading Company. The film was photographed from a single-camera position and shows what is supposed to be the interior of Westminster Abbey.

Reproduction, Nan Paterson's Trial
AM&B © H60289 May 3, 1905
Cameraman: G. W. Bitzer
Location: Studio, N.Y.C. *Photographed:* Apr. 22, 1905
24 ft. FLA3779 (print) FRA1021 (neg.)

The action begins in a courtroom set. First a judge appears: he is followed by a bailiff, attorneys, witnesses, etc. There is a great deal of moving about and gesturing by the men and women who have come to appear before the magistrate. However, the film is too short to allow interpretation of anything they do. Nan Patterson, a chorus girl, was on trial for the murder of her married lover but was acquitted.

Reproduction of Corbett-McGovern Fight
AM&B © H32322 June 2, 1903
Cameraman: F. S. Armitage
Date: May 27, 1903
291 ft. FLA5662 (print) FRA2702 (neg.)

This film is devoted to a boxing match that was a reproduction of a prize fight previously held between young Corbett and Terry McGovern for the featherweight championship of the world. As the film begins, a backdrop painted to represent a large audience is visible. There is a ring smaller than regulation size, in front of the backdrop. Each boxer is represented by a second and an assistant, and there is a referee.

Reproduction of Harry Thaw in the Tombs
See: In the Tombs

Reproduction of Jeffries-Corbett Contest
AM&B © H36013 Sept. 22, 1903
Cameraman: G. W. Bitzer *Date:* Sept. 16, 1903
Location: Studio, N.Y.C.
235 ft. FLA5660 (print)

The film is exactly what the title says—a reproduction of a championship prize fight between the current heavyweight champion James J. Jeffries and the challenger James J. Corbett, who was attempting to regain the title. The actors, who were acceptably skilled boxers, are unknown.

The picture was photographed from one camera position that encompassed the full boxing ring. There is a painted backdrop of a barely visible audience directly behind the ring.

The action closely followed the actual prize fight. Ten rounds of boxing are shown, with the required interval between rounds. One knockdown occurs in the fourth round, one in the sixth, and a final knockdown by Jeffries in the tenth round. There is no lead title, and the film ends abruptly at the completion of the tenth round.

The Rescue
See: The Ex-Convict

The Rescue

See: The Kidnapper

Rescue of Child from Indians

AM&B © H35877 Sept. 21, 1903

Cameraman: Wallace McCutcheon

Location: The Adirondacks, N.Y. *Photographed:* Sept. 10, 1903

86 ft. FLA5185 (print) FRA2143 (neg.)

From a single-camera position, the opening scene shows a wooded area. Several persons dressed as Indians appear from camera right. They are pushing a girl approximately ten years old in front of them as if she were a prisoner. The Indians make a fire, prepare to retire, and tie the young girl to a tree. From camera right, some men dressed as frontiersmen with rifles arrive and shoot the Indians. They set the young girl free and go out of camera position. Author's note: We have reason to believe that this was the last part of a series of five released by American Mutoscope & Biograph in August 1904, under the title The Pioneers.

See also: Firing the Cabin, Discovery of Bodies, and Settler's Home Life

Rescue—Resuscitation

Edison © 60572 Oct. 25, 1897

Location: San Francisco

19 ft. FLA3083 (print) FRA0422 (neg.)

The photographer placed his equipment on the sand close to the water's edge to film four members of the U.S. Coast Guard demonstrating the proper technique for saving and resuscitating a drowning man. At the start of the film, a man can be seen some distance from the shore clinging to a derelict and waving frantically for someone to rescue him. Somehow, not shown in the film, a towing line is transported to him and the four sailors are shown hand-hauling the towing line and the man onto the beach. When he reaches the shore, the four Coast Guardsmen place him face down over a log and begin rolling him back and forth by his feet and arms.

See also: Launch of Life Boat, and Launch of Surf Boat

Rescued by Rover

Hepworth © AM&B H64738 Aug. 19, 1905

Director: Lewin Fitzhamon. *Script:* Mrs. Cecil Hepworth

Cast: Mr. and Mrs. Cecil Hepworth, Mr. and Mrs. Sebastian Smith, May Clark, baby: Barbara Hepworth, Rover: Blair

Location: Walton-on-Thames, England

195 ft. FLA5663 (print) FRA2868 (neg.)

This film was made in London at the Walton Studio of Cecil Hepworth whose wife wrote the story and the acted in it. This was the first time that paid actors were used in a British film. The plot concerns the kidnapping of an infant (the Hepworth's child) by a gypsy (Mrs. Sebastian Smith), and the subsequent rescue by the family dog (the Hepworth's pet). The film opens with a close two-shot of a large collie dog as he stands guard over a sleeping infant. Then it shows the the anxiety of the parents, and the determined efforts of the dog to locate the infant. The dog is photographed as he runs through the London streets, finds the baby, returns home, and leads his master to the gypsy's quarters. The last scene shows the family across the living room. Then the camera moves in one step to a close-up of the mother, father, infant, and dog.

Responding to an Alarm

AM&B © H33415 July 13, 1903

18 ft. FLA3426 (print) FRA714 (neg.)

The opening scenes show a large wall of a building with the aura of a military barracks or garrison about it. Seated in front of the building are approximately ten men with military campaign hats. A man in military clothing walks into the picture between the walls of the building and the camera. Another man, wearing military campaign fatigues, approaches him, salutes, turns on his heel, and runs toward the group of people seated by the large door in the barracks wall. As the film ends, approximately two companies of men in military attire run at double time in military formation across the view of the camera.

The Restoration

Biograph © J134602 Nov. 10, 1909

Director: D. W. Griffith *Cameraman:* G. W. Bitzer

Cast: Marion Leonard, Mary Pickford, Owen Moore, James Kirkwood, George Nicholls

Location: Little Falls, N.J.; Studio N.Y.C. *Photographed:* Sept. 22 and Oct. 1–7, 1909

391 ft. FLA5664 (print) FRA2503 (neg.)

A jealous husband (James Kirkwood) attacks a man (Owen Moore) he believes is betraying him with his wife (Marion Leonard), but the fight causes the husband to lose his mind. The doctor believes that a reenactment of the scene might restore the demented husband to his senses, and the young lovers (Mary Pickford and Owen Moore) agree to help. The scheme works, and the husband regains not only his senses but his loyal wife, who is confused as to why her husband doubts her. The scenes in the film are a combination of interiors and exteriors, with no camera movement.

Resurrection

Biograph © H127268 May 19, 1909

Director: D. W. Griffith. *Cameramen:* G. W. Bitzer, Arthur Marvin

Cast: Florence Lawrence, Arthur Johnson, Clara T. Bracey, Owen Moore, Linda Arvidson, John Cumpson, Mack Sennett

Location: Studio, N.Y.C. *Photographed:* Mar. 26-30 and Apr. 20–23, 1909

371 ft. FLA5665 (print) FRA6423 (neg.)

This drama, based on Tolstoy's novel, was photographed in sets of a tavern and a prison, and outdoors in the snow. There is one insert of a page from the Bible given to the heroine (Florence Lawrence) by the lead (Arthur Johnson), after he has ravished her. She becomes a prostitute and is arrested and sent to Siberia. The last scene shows her abductor handing her a reprieve, but she has become religious and she decides to accompany the prisoners to Siberia so that she can comfort them. Author's note: This was one of the first two films advertised under the corporate name "Biograph Company."

Retribution

See: The Wages of Sin

Return of Lifeboat

Edison © 60576 Oct. 25, 1897

Location: San Francisco [?]

25 ft. FLA3043 (print) FRA0257 (neg.)

This is a single-camera position film with an approximately 25-degree pan of a Coast Guard pulling boat that is manned by a crew and controlled by a coxswain as it comes in through the surf. Probably part of a series advertised by Edison as Pacific Coast Life Saving Series.

See also: Capsize of Lifeboat, Launch of Life Boat, and Launch of Surf Boat

Return of Parsifal

See: Parsifal

Return of 2nd Regiment of New Jersey

Edison © 59212 Oct. 7, 1898

59 ft. FLA4846 (print) FRA1853 (neg.)

[Spanish-American War]

This film was photographed from a single-camera position over the heads of a large group of spectators in what seems to be a public square. Pushing through the crowd and making a turn past the camera are personnel in military uniform carrying the American flag and a regimental standard. The flags and the men who carry them are followed by at least two companies of military personnel in formation.

Return of Troop C, Brooklyn

Edison © 60142 Oct. 12, 1898

Location: Prospect Park, Brooklyn, N.Y.

32 ft. FLA4220 (print) FRA1379 (neg.)

[Spanish-American War]

The film shows a parade. The camera was located at the curb of a wide cobblestoned street lined with spectators cheering the return of a troop of U.S. cavalry from the Spanish-American War. During the film, several companies of mounted troops in close parade order pass the camera position.

Returning from the Races

Edison © 38229 June 22, 1898

Location: Yokohama [?] Japan

26 ft. FLA3238 (print) FRA0562 (neg.)

The camera was positioned alongside a road in a Japanese city, and many Japanese can be seen walking by wearing the clothing of their country and time.

See also: Going to the Yokohama Races

Returning to China

AM&B © H33208 July 2, 1903

Cameraman: G. W. Bitzer

Location: Vancouver, B.C., Can. *Date:* Oct. 19, 1899

33 ft. FLA3535 (print) FRA0811 (neg.)

The cameraman positioned his equipment on what appears to be a large shipping dock. During the film, approximately two hundred Chinese, dressed in the conventional garb of coolie workmen, pass the camera. All of the Chinese are carrying luggage or bags as if about to travel.

Reuben in the Subway

AM&B © H62449 June 20, 1905

Cameraman: G. W. Bitzer

Location: 14th Street, N.Y.C. *Photographed:* June 7, 1905

15 ft. FLA3904 (print) FRA1124 (neg.)

The film was photographed from the edge of a street across from a theatre marquee with the word Keith's on it. Beneath the Keith sign is a subway entrance, and people can be seen going in and out of it. During the film, a streetcar passes from left to right (labeled 22nd Street Ferry) and another is marked "14th Street and 10th Avenue." D. W. Griffith's first picture had its premiere in this theater. From the description and length given in the Biograph bulletin, this little film is only one scene from a 145-foot comedy.

See also: Interior of N.Y. Subway 14th St. to 42nd St.; Rube in the Subway

Rêve de l'Horloger

See: The Clock Maker's Dream

Le Rêve d'un Maitre de Ballet

See: The Ballet Master's Dream

Le Revenant

Méliès © H37509 Oct. 12, 1903

Creator: Georges Méliès

Cast: Georges Méliès

Location: Montreuil, France *Date:* Summer 1903

U.S. title: The Apparition, or Mr. Jones' Comical Experiences with a Ghost

73 ft. FLA4847 (print) FRA1854 (neg.)

This farce opens in a hotel suite where the guest is being helped out of his traveling jacket and into his dressing gown. He opens the newspaper and starts to read by candlelight. The moment he starts to read, the candle moves to the opposite side of the table. In anger, the guest chases the candle from one side of the table to another until, by the use of stop-action, the candle changes into one that reaches the roof of the room. Several little incidents of people popping in and out of the picture by stop-action photography finish the film.

Revenge!

Gaumont © AM&B H51119 Oct. 1, 1904

Director: Alf Collins

Location: England

149 ft. FLA5061 (print) FRA2019 (neg.)

This film depicts nearly every possible conflict between a man, his wife, and his wife's lover that could be put into a film. The lover, a police officer of executive rank, enters the home while the husband is away. The husband arrives home unexpectedly and a fight starts that culminates in the husband being taken off to jail, apparently for striking a policeman. He breaks out of jail, pursued by the police, and rushes home where he seizes his little girl and begins to flee with her in his arms. The police quickly catch him, and during the fight that ensues, both his wife and child are shot and killed by the lover. The police attempt to take the father to jail but he breaks away and one by one throws his captors over a cliff. The father then seeks out the man who has ruined his life and finds the police officer sunning himself on a park bench. The father strangles the police/lover while other police, aware of their leader's acts, hold their guns on the father but do not fire.

The Reversible Divers

Edison © H7987 Aug. 21, 1901

10 ft. FLA3695 (print) FRA0944 (neg.)

The film was photographed from a single-camera position across what appears to be a public swimming pool, with people splashing about in the pool. As the film ends (having been run backward) the people jump out of the water up to the edge of the pool.

Review of Cadets at West Point

AM&B © H33407 July 13, 1903

Location: West Point, N.Y.

27 ft. FLA3524 (print) FRA0800 (neg.)

A 50-degree pan from the single-camera position shows the corps of West Point cadets in regimental front as they prepare for inspection. The panning camera encompasses not only the corps at attention but also the spectators.

Review of Cadets, West Point

AM&B © H33283 July 8, 1903

Location: West Point, N.Y.

55 ft. FLA4849 (print) FRA1856 (neg.)

The subject is a review of West Point cadets at West Point, New York. The cameraman placed his equipment at the edge of a drill field. The whole film was devoted to the corps of cadets passing in review in company-front order.

Review of Cadets, West Point

AM&B © H33287 July 8, 1903

28 ft. FLA3715 (print) FRA0962 (neg.)

The single-camera position shows the drill field at West Point where four companies of West Point cadets pass in review.

Review of Russian Artillery

AM&B © H34820 Aug. 19, 1903

Cameraman: Raymond Ackerman *Date:* Jan. 12, 1901

Location: Teintsin, China

9 ft. FLA4139 (print) FRA1309 (neg.)

The film begins from a single-camera position that overlooks a large, open drill field. Foot troops, apparently on maneuvers, can be seen, as well as one bearded man in uniform carrying an unsheathed sword over his shoulder who rides past the camera position. There is one four-wheel vehicle pulled by seven horses with four uniformed men seated on it, while a single soldier rides in the rear. The full title according to AM&B production records is: C. Von Waldersee Reviewing 2nd & 14th Russian Artillery & 3rd Siberia.

See also: Cossack Cavalry

Reviewing the "Texas" at Grant's Tomb

Edison © 52048 Sept. 3, 1898

Location: New York, N.Y. *Photographed:* Aug. 20, 1898

53 ft. FLA4848 (print) FRA1855 (neg.)

[Spanish-American War, New York City Welcome to Admiral Sampson's Fleet After the Battle of Santiago Bay]

The camera was aboard a vessel going north on the Hudson River. The film opens on Grant's Tomb and in the foreground, approximately two hundred yards distant, is a tugboat heading in the same direction as the camera vessel. The next scenes show the stern of a large ship with an American flag on its flagstaff approaching the camera position. The camera proceeds to photograph along the starboard side of an anchored U.S. battleship, *Texas*, and an excursion steamer passes between the camera position. The *Texas* was part of the fleet returning from service in Cuba during the Spanish-American War.

Rex's Bath

AM&B © H21501 Sept. 5, 1902

Cameraman: Robert K. Bonine

Date: Aug. 4, 1902

10 ft. FLA3891 (print) FRA1113 (neg.)

A boy can be seen scrubbing the back of a dog standing in an outdoor fish pond. For as long as the film continues, the boy can be seen with a scrubbing brush bathing the shaggy St. Bernard dog.

Rhode Island Light Artillery

AM&B © H48418 July 23, 1904

Cameraman: F. S. Armitage

Location: Providence, R.I. *Photographed:* July 14, 1904

102 ft. FLA5186 (print) FRA2144 (neg.)

Mounted troops are approaching the camera at an angle. As the troops get closer, a large artillery piece (approximately 200mm) can be seen as part of the cadre as it makes a turn abreast of the camera position. The camera continues photographing the mounted group, which is executing right-and left-wheel maneuvers. Also at a distance, a group can be seen dismounting, assembling, and firing the artillery piece.

A Rich Revenge

Biograph © 140366 Apr. 11, 1910

Director: D. W. Griffith *Cameraman:* G. W. Bitzer

Cast: Mary Pickford, Billy Quirk, William J. Butler, George Nicholls, Tony O'Sullivan

Location: Edendale, Calif. *Photographed:* Feb. 25–26, 1910

403 ft. FLA5666 (print) FRA6412 (neg.)

A disappointed suitor sets out to destroy the happiness of the young woman who refused to marry him. The young married couple (Mary Pickford and Billy Quirk) settle down on their irrigated farm devoted to truck gardening. The disappointed suitor corners the market, making it impossible for the newlyweds to sell their crop. To further harass the couple, he empties a barrel of chemically treated oil into the irrigation water of the farm. An oil speculator sees the land, thinks it is a rich find, and pays the young couple $10,000 for their now ruined farm. The film ends by showing the happy couple facing the camera from the back of an automobile and waving goodbye to the oil speculator.

Rickshaw Parade, Japan

AM&B © H16646 Apr. 16, 1902

Cameraman: Robert K. Bonine

Location: Kyoto, Japan *Date:* July 28, 1901
22 ft. FLA3927 (print) FRA1141 (neg.)

During this short film, the cameraman photographed approximately two dozen rickshas being pulled by coolies past the camera position. From the design of the buildings, the road on which the rickshas are being pulled borders a shopping district. The title on the original paper print film reads Rickshaw Parade, Kioto, Japan.

Rickshaw Parade, Kioto, Japan
See: Rickshaw Parade, Japan

A Ride Through Pack Saddle Mountains, Penna. R.R.
Edison © 44242 July 7, 1899
Location: Pa.
67 ft. FLA4850 (print) FRA1857 (neg.)

The camera was mounted on a train that began to move over what appears to be a double-track railroad bed. The remainder of the film shows the area to the left and right of the railroad track as the train progresses through a rural community. There is one switch tower to be seen, and some track workers waiting for the train to pass.

The Rights of Youth
Great Northern © Oes J168629-30 Apr. 26, 1912
Director: August Blom *Script:* Alfred Kjerulf
Cast: Valdemar Psilander, Einar Zangenberg, Else Fröhlich, Robert Dinesen, Zanny Petersen, Aage Hertel
Location: Denmark *Photographed:* Sept. 19, 1911
Original *Title:* Ungdommens Ret
849 ft. FLA5898 (print) FRA2762 (neg.)

This film is based on the eternal triangle and has no starring roles. The plot is laid at a country estate where the squire is entertaining his guests, with riding to the hounds followed by a dinner party. The cast consists of the following principals: the squire, his wife, their daughter and her suitor, and a guest enamored of the squire's wife. After the dinner party, the enamored guest contrives through a ruse to be alone with the squire's wife; he attempts to embrace her but is resisted. The squire's wife is interested in her daughter's suitor. The daughter, strolling in the garden with a guest, sees a silhouette of her mother and her suitor in an embrace. With no thought of her own feelings, she returns to the house and places herself in a compromising position to save the dignity of the household. A fire breaks out, there is much running about and lives being saved, etc., which reveals the position of each person at the time of the fire. The squire's wife and her illicit lover are ordered from the house by the irate squire.

Rip and the Dwarf
See: Rip Van Winkle

Rip Leaving Sleepy Hollow
See: Rip Van Winkle

Rip Meeting the Dwarf
See: Rip Van Winkle

Rip Passing Over Hill
See: Rip Van Winkle

Rip Van Winkle
AM&B © see below
Location: Buzzards Bay, Mass. *Photographed:* Aug. or Sept. 1896
Cast: Joseph Jefferson
Contents: Rip Meeting the Dwarf; H25402, 1902; and 68804, 1896;
FLA4416 (print) FRA1536 (neg.) Rip and the Dwarf; H24875, 1902 FLA 4415 (print); FRA 1536 (neg.) Rip Leaving Sleepy Hollow; H24876, Dec. 9, 1902; 69088 Dec. 19, 1896 FLA 4418 (print) FRA 1536 (neg.) Rip's Toast; H25401, Dec. 29, 1902; 69095, Dec, 19, 1896 FLA 4403 (print) FRA 1536 (neg.) Rip's Toast to Hudson and Crew: H25403, Dec. 29, 1902; 9236, Feb. 4, 1897 FLA 4417 (print) FRA 1536 (neg.) Rip's Twenty Year's Sleep; H25404, Dec. 29, 1902; 3551, Jan. 7, 1897 FLA 4414 (print) FRA 1536 (neg.) Awakening of Rip; H25400, Dec. 29, 1902; 9237, Feb. 4, 1897 FLA 4412 (print) FRA 1536 (neg.) Rip Passing Over Hill; H25405, Dec. 29, 1902 FLA 4306 (print) FRA 1536 (neg.)
108 ft. FRA

Each short scene was photographed from a single-camera position. The action seems to follow the subtitles closely so that further description would be redundant. All indications are that the above films were photographed with Joseph Jefferson in 1896 but were not copyrighted until 1902.

Rip's Toast
See: Rip Van Winkle

Rip's Toast to Hudson and Crew
See: Rip Van Winkle

Rip's Twenty Year's Sleep
See: Rip Van Winkle

The Rival Models
AM&B © H43566 Mar. 22, 1904
Cameraman: A. E. Weed
Location: Studio, N.Y.C. *Photographed:* Feb. 18, 1904
24 ft. FLA3342 (print) FRA0652 (neg.)

Three actors can be seen from the single-camera position. One is dressed as a painter while the two women are clad in white leotards with scarves draped around them. The props consist of an easel and a chair. As the action begins, it shows the man outfitted as an artist changing the position of the models' heads by moving their chins with his hands. The film ends shortly after he sits down at the easel and simulates painting their pictures.

The Rivals
AM&B © H25964 Dec. 31, 1902
Date: 1899
7 ft. FLA4091 (print) FRA1272 (neg.)

The cameraman placed his equipment on the turf between two opposite curves of railroad track. During the short length of the film, two locomotives can be seen approaching the camera position at quite a distance away. The film continues until the two locomotives pass the camera position. At one point in the film, the two locomotives are at exactly the same distance from the camera, and the two appear to be identical.

The Rivals
AM&B © H30437 Apr. 10, 1903
12 ft. FLA4092 (print) FRA1273 (neg.)

A young man and a young woman are sitting on a bench. No background is visible. The camera was placed at such a position that only their heads and shoulders can be seen. The two are kissing and petting. Later, another young man walks up and sits down beside the couple. The young woman turns from her companion and begins kissing and embracing the new arrival to the displeasure of the first young man. The picture was made by incandescent light.

The River Pirates
AM&B © H65806 Sept. 20, 1905
Cameraman: G. W. Bitzer
Location: Hastings on Hudson, N.Y.; Studio, N.Y.C. *Date:* Sept 5–7, 1905
358 ft. FLA5667 (print) FRA2505 (neg.)

A man in evening clothes enters a living room, presents a paper to another man, who puts it in a combination safe in the room and leaves. The first man attempts to open the safe but is seen by a woman and ejected from the house. The next set represents a thieves' hideaway under a pier, where the villain is shown negotiating with some disreputable-looking men. One rejects his proposal and is tied and beaten. The remainder of the scenes show the gang stealing the safe, transporting it onto a rowboat, and from there onto a small sailing yacht, where the police are waiting for them, having been alerted by the man left tied in the den. There is a chase and much carnage before the thieves are finally captured. Based on an actual happening, the thieves had not been caught at the time the film was released, even though the capture is portrayed in the picture.

River Scene at Macao, China
Edison © 38254 June 22, 1898
Location: Macao
26 ft. FLA3057 (print) FRA0272 (neg.)

The poor condition of the film does not allow the identification of much of the detail shown. However, it is self-evident that the camera was on board a boat in the water of a Chinese harbor. Occasionally a Chinese junk, either sailing or being sculled, passes the camera position and is photographed. Nothing in the background is visible.

Riverside Geyser, Yellowstone Park
Edison © H4576 May 24, 1901
Location: Yellowstone Park, Wyo.
38 ft. FLA3482 (print) FRA0763 (neg.)

A geyser or stream of steamy water is the subject of this film. The cameraman placed his equipment so close to the natural phenomenon that nothing but billows of steamy water are visible.

The Road to the Heart
AM&B © H125115 Mar. 31, 1909
Director: D. W. Griffith *Cameraman:* Arthur Marvin

Cast: David Miles, Florence Lawrence, Mack Sennett, Anita Hendry, John Cumpson
Location: Studio, N.Y.C. *Photographed:* Mar. 4–5, 1909
241 ft. FLA5668 (print) FRA2507 (neg.)

This comedy, with all the actors dressed in Spanish costumes, begins in a combination dining room and kitchen. A young man (David Miles) enters and proposes marriage to the daughter (Florence Lawrence), but is turned down by her father. There is a heated discussion, and the daughter and mother leave the house. The daughter gets married, and they all set up housekeeping together. The father stubbornly insists he can get along without them. The next scenes show his attempts to do so as he hires and fires an oriental cook, a non-Latin housekeeper, and a cattleman's camp cook who wears chaps and carries two guns. The last scenes show the father attempting to ingratiate himself with his family after his last cook tears up the house because the father refuses to eat his food.

The Road to Yesterday
Klaw & Erlanger © LP3033 June 18, 1914
Cameraman: Henry Cronjager
Cast: Walter Miller, Jack Dillon, Irene Howley, Kenneth Davenport, Joseph McDermott, Mrs. Lawrence Marston
1,276 ft. FLA5937 (print) FRA2800 (neg.)

The plot of this three-reel film is of a romantic young girl who visits a museum and falls in love with the medieval period of history, comes home and has a long and involved dream in which she is the heroine of events that take place at that time. The last scene shows her, now awake, encountering in reality the man she dreamed about and startling him by embracing him. There are many sets of both periods, and the costumes are expensive.

Robbed of Her All
AM&B © H65079 Sept. 1,1905
Cameraman: G. W. Bitzer
Location: Studio, N.Y.C. *Photographed:* Aug. 17, 1905
20 ft. FLA3811 (print) FRA1045 (neg.)

The set of this film resembles a street intersection and on the corner nearest the camera position is a door marked "Bank Closed Today." Two men carrying burglar's tools come up to the door of the bank and one begins to jimmy the lock. Then as if warned by his confederate that someone is approaching, he hides. The someone becomes a young woman who wishes to enter the bank. Since the bank is closed, she puts her money under the garter above her knee. At this point, the two bandits grab the woman, lift up her skirts and remove the money from her garter. When the film ends, the woman is jumping up and down in annoyance. AM&B's original title was She Banked in Her Stocking.

Rock Drill at Work in Subway
AM&B © H32485 June 10, 1903
Cameraman: G. W. Bitzer
Location: Subway, N.Y.C. *Date:* June 3, 1903
31 ft. FLA4851 (print) FRA1858 (neg.)

Men appear to be operating a large steam drill to excavate an area approximately fifty feet deep and a hundred yards wide.

Rock of Ages
AM&B © H18126 May 26, 1902
Photographed: Jan. 5, 1901
9 ft. FLA3173 (print) FRA0500 (neg.)

During the short length of this film, it is possible to see only a close-up of rapidly moving water and an image of a religious nature double exposed over the top of the water.

The Rock of Ages
AM&B © H36562 Oct. 6, 1903
Cameraman: G. W. Bitzer
Location: Studio, N.Y.C. *Photographed:* Sept. 29, 1903
22 ft. FLA4241 (print) FRA1398 (neg.)

The film was photographed as if in the audience of a vaudeville theater. The subject, a parody on the words "Rock of Ages," shows two men, one dressed as a woman, made up to look quite old. They are reclining in a large hammock which they rock back and forth. The film ends as the hammock support breaks and they fall to the ground.

Rock of Ages
Edison © H23342 Oct. 31, 1902
27 ft. FLA3173 (print) FRA0500 (neg.)

As the picture begins, the only thing visible is the turbulent white water in the lower third of the motion picture screen. The remainder of the scene is black. As the film continues, by the use of double exposure, a large cross is seen in the center of the turbulent water. When the water turbulence and the cross against the jet black background are well-established, a woman dressed in flowing garments appears from out of the depths of the tumult and is able to make her way to her feet by using the base of the cross as a support. By holding on to the cross, she is able to stretch her arms out and she remains in this position until the end of the picture.

Rocking Gold in the Klondike
Edison © H4088 May 6, 1901
Cameraman: Robert K. Bonine
Location: Yukon Terr., Canada
31 ft. FLA3065 (print) FRA0408 (neg.)
[Alaska Gold Rush]

From a single-camera position, the film shows sluice boxes as they are operated by gold miners in the Klondike gold fields.

The Rocky Road
Biograph © J136775 Jan. 6, 1910
Director: D. W. Griffith *Cameraman:* G. W. Bitzer
Cast: Frank Powell, Stephanie Longfellow, Adele De Garde, Blanche Sweet, Kate Bruce, Wilfred Lucas, W. Chrystie Miller, George Nicholls, Tony O'Sullivan, Linda Arvidson, Charles Craig
Location: Studio, N.Y.C.; Edgewater and Hackensack, N.J. *Photographed:* Nov. 29–30 and Dec. 1–4, 1909
397 ft. FLA5669 (print) FRA2508 (neg.)

A man (Frank Powell), deserts his wife(Stephanie Longfellow) and daughter (Adele De Garde), goes off to a nearby city, and becomes wealthy. Later, he meets his now-grown daughter (Blanche Sweet), and falls in love with her. He proposes marriage and she accepts, and they are just about

to be married when the mother, who has been out of her mind from the shock of her husband's desertion, recovers her senses just in time to prevent the wedding. All scenes in the film were photographed from a single-camera position; sets were used, as well as outdoor locations, or available buildings.

Roeber Wrestling Match
Edison © H11493 Dec. 16, 1901
Cast: Ernest Roeber, August Faust
149 ft. FLA5187 (print) FRA21245 (neg.)

The film shows a wrestling match that was held before a few spectators. The camera photographed the entire ring. The combatants are escorted to the center of a roped-off enclosure by a referee; they disrobe and begin to wrestle. The remainder of the film shows the wrestling match and ends as the victor is carried off on the shoulders of his backers.

Le Roi du Maquillage
Méliès © H42524 Feb. 23, 1904
Creator: Georges Méliès *Cast:* Georges Méliès
Location: Montreuil, France *Date:* Winter 1903–4
U.S. title: The Untamable Whiskers
61 ft. FLA4852 (print) FRA1859 (neg.)

Georges Méliès plays a magician doing a vaudeville act. The act consists of his drawing a human head without hair and then drawing a hairpiece to fit the head. M. Méliès himself is bald. The pictures he draws of specific hairpieces and whiskers are then transferred from the picture onto M. Méliès' head or chin.

The Roller Skate Craze
Selig © H97845 Aug. 9, 1907
18 ft. FLA4410 (print) FRA1535 (neg.)

During this short film, the cameraman photographed many different people in varied walks of life all of whom are wearing roller skates. Each scene, since the camera changed from individual to individual, is too short to allow any further description.

Romance of a Jewess
AM&B © H117093 Oct. 16, 1908
Director: D. W. Griffith *Cameraman:* G. W. Bitzer
Cast: Florence Lawrence, Mack Sennett, John Cumpson, Frank Gebhardt, Charles Inslee, Guy Hedlund, Gladys Egan, Harry Salter
Location: Studio and streets near Studio, N.Y.C. *Photographed:* Sept. 15 and 25, 1908
369 FLA5670 (print) FRA2310 (neg.)

This film was photographed from a single-camera position on four sets, and is the story of a young Jewess, the daughter of a pawnbroker, who falls in love with a gentile bookstore owner. Her father refuses her permission to marry the man, but she does so anyway, and they are happy with their small girl until the husband has a fatal accident. The wife is forced to sell the bookstore. She becomes ill and sends her daughter with her last possession to the pawnbroker who recognizes it as a gift he had made to his daughter. The film ends with a reconciliation scene.

Romance of an Egg

AM&B © H11068 May 26, 1908

Cameraman: G. W. Bitzer

Location: Little Falls, N.J. *Photographed:* Apr. 27, 1908

248 ft. FLA5671 (print) FRA2509 (neg.)

The opening scene takes place on a set of a barnyard, where a man dressed as a farmer is writing the dates on a basket of eggs. Then he places the eggs and other produce in a horse-drawn, four-wheeled vehicle. The next scenes take place in a large room with beds around the walls and a table in the center at which five women en déshabillé are seated. The following three scenes are the finale of the film. All of the young ladies are now outdoors, all dressed alike in a sort of uniform. One has a gentleman caller. The remaining young ladies conspire to play a prank on him, so they tie him hand and foot to the wall of a barn and pelt him with the eggs he was shown dating in the first scene.

A Romance of the Rail

Edison © H36500 Oct. 3, 1903

Cameraman: Edwin S. Porter

Cast: Marie Murray

Location: Delaware, Lackawana, and Western R.R., Penn. and N.J. *Photographed:* Aug. 30, 1903

108 ft. FLA5188 (print) FRA2886 (neg.)

The subject of this film is the Lackawanna Railroad, and the idea it promotes is that the railroad is immaculate at all times in all locations. The first scene shows an attractive young woman dressed entirely in white seated on a trunk in front of a Lackawanna Railroad station. A man also dressed in white joins her and they board a train, and are photographed as they sit on the observation platform and as they get on and off the train. At the end of their journey, a porter with a whiskbroom sees no need to brush them. Two men in top hats and tails come out from under the railroad cars, pass by the porter with his whiskbroom, and their gestures indicate that not even they need dusting. The woman (Marie Murray) represented a nationally known advertising character named "Phoebe Snow."

A Romance of the Western Hills

Biograph © J140416 Apr. 13, 1910

Director: D. W. Griffith *Cameraman:* G. W. Bitzer

Cast: Mary Pickford, Charles West, Arthur Johnson, Alfred Paget, Kate Bruce, Blanche Sweet

Location: Sierra Madre and Pasadena, Calif. *Photographed:* Feb. 16–18 and Mar. 1–2, 1910

387 ft. FLA5672 (print) FRA2511 (neg.)

The opening scene takes place in an Indian village when an Indian maiden (Mary Pickford) is adopted by a white couple. She falls in love with their nephew (Charles West) who carries on a flirtation with her. Later she sees him embracing a pretty young woman (Blanche Sweet). She feels she has been betrayed by both civilization and the white man so she returns to seek out the Indian boy (Arthur Johnson) who had loved her before her adoption. Together, they return to the city where the Indian brave avenges her wrongs, and the last scene shows them walking hand-in-hand up the mountain toward the Indian village.

A Romp on the Lawn

AM&B © H24886 Dec. 9, 1902

Cameraman: Robert K. Bonine

Location: Highwood Park *Date:* Nov. 3, 1902

17 ft. FLA3312 (print) FRA0626 (neg.)

Visible in the foreground are an adolescent girl and a dog romping with a small child on what appears to be a lawn in front of a house. Beyond the romping people is a gazebo where six spectators are standing. However, they are so far away from the camera that it is possible only to identify them as human beings.

Rooms for Gentlemen Only

AM&B © H69580 Dec. 7, 1905

Cameraman: F. A. Dobson

Location: Studio, N.Y.C. *Photographed:* Nov. 24, 1905

20 ft. FLA3916 (print) FRA1132 (neg.)

A rather distraught young man is excitedly guiding another man who is carrying a trunk on his back, and admonishing him to be careful. The man carrying the trunk loses his balance, and the trunk falls to the floor. From the gestures of the other man, it is clear this upsets him. The baggage man leaves and the other man hurriedly opens the trunk, and a young woman in a long cloak stands up and hugs and kisses him.

Roosevelt's Rough Riders

AM&B © H32832 June 18, 1903

Date: 1898 [?]

14 ft. FLA3332 (print) FRA0643 (neg.)

[Spanish-American War]

The film was photographed from a single-camera position, in what appears to be the review stand of an Army cavalry post. A company of cavalry approaches the camera and, close to the camera, all of the cavalry turns.

Roosevelt's Rough Riders Embarking for Santiago

Edison © 38238 June 22, 1898

32 ft. FLA3978 (print) FRA1186 (neg.)

[Spanish-American War]

The photographer placed his camera on a dock. In the immediate foreground are men in army uniforms of the Spanish-American War period. They are moving boxes and parcels of various sizes toward a large steamship that is some distance away, but tied to the same dock where they are working. Throughout the film, the same action is repeated.

The Root of Evil

Biograph © J167176 Mar. 15, 1912

Director: D. W. Griffith *Cameraman:* G. W. Bitzer

Cast: Dorothy Bernard, Joe Graybill, William J. Butler, Charles Hill Mailes, Harry Hyde, Alfred Paget, Adele De Garde

407 ft. FLA5673 (print) FRA2512 (neg.)

A wealthy man (William J. Butler) has a lovely daughter (Dorothy Bernard) who falls in love with his male secretary (Joe Graybill), but her father disapproves of their marrying. They get married anyway, and the father disinherits her, leaving his money to his financial advisor. The daughter's husband dies, and she and her child visit the ill father. The financial advisor plots to kill the old man before he can change his will. The little girl, imitating the villain, switches a poisoned bottle of wine, so that the villain drinks the poison instead. The film ends with a scene of the old man rejoicing at the return to his home of his daughter and granddaughter.

The Rose

AM&B © H34518 Aug. 13, 1903
Cameraman: G. W. Bitzer
Cast: Kathryn Osterman
Location: Studio, N.Y.C. *Photographed:* Aug. 3, 1903
20 ft. FLA3570 (print) FRA0844 (neg.)

The film begins with a waist camera position or close-up of a young woman wearing an off-the-shoulder dress. Nothing else is visible except for the young woman from her waist to above the top of her head. The film was artificially lighted. She admires some long-stemmed roses she is holding. She smiles and talks during the film as if she were discussing the loveliness of the flowers with another person.

Rose O' Salem-Town

Biograph © J145818 Sept. 27, 1910
Director: D. W. Griffith *Cameraman:* G. W. Bitzer
Cast: Dorothy West, George Nicholls, Alfred Paget, Henry B. Walthall, W. Chrystie Miller, Gladys Egan
Location: Studio, N.Y.C.; Delaware Water Gap, N.J.; Marblehead, Mass. *Photographed:* Aug. 3 and 20, 1910
416 ft. FLA5674 (print) FRA2513 (neg.)

A lovely young maiden attracts the attention of one of the Puritan elders. But when she rejects his proposal, she incurs his animosity. With the aid of a prejudiced trial jury, he has her declared a witch, and the Puritans prepare to burn her at the stake along with her aged foster parent. A young mountain man who loves her realizes he cannot rescue her without help, so he enlists the aid of some friendly Indians. Under the cover of the smoke of the fire set to burn her, he cuts her bonds and sets her free, and they depart for a new life in the forest.

The Roue's Heart

AM&B © H123744 Mar. 8, 1909
Director: D. W. Griffith *Cameraman:* G. W. Bitzer
Cast: Marion Leonard, Herbert Yost, John Cumpson, Florence Lawrence, Linda Arvidson, Dorothy West, Adele De Garde, Mack Sennett, Owen Moore
Location: Studio, N.Y.C. *Photographed:* Jan. 23–24, 1909
288 ft FLA5675 (print) FRA2506 (neg.)

This melodrama was set in the late eighteenth century, and three sets were used. A socially prominent roué accidentally sees a bust sculptured by a blind woman when he and his entourage visit a gallery. He insists on meeting the artist, who is at work on the bust of a little girl. He falls in love with her and decides to reform, and there are scenes of him sending his former playmates away. After some help from the child who was the model, the reformed roué and the blind sculptress are united and are embracing in the last scene.

Rough House in a New York Honky-Tonk

AM&B © H60293 May 3, 1905
Cameraman: G. W. Bitzer
Location: Studio, N.Y.C. *Photographed:* Apr. 25, 1905

31 ft. FLA3906 (print) FRA1126 (neg.)

The film begins from a single-camera position that shows a set consisting of a back wall; against it is a staircase and in front are several tables and chairs. The first action shows people descending the stair and sitting at the tables. A man wearing a waiter's apron and carrying beer glasses enters from stage left. More people come down the stairs and seat themselves at tables. One of the women starts a discussion with the people at a near-by table which her companion seems to resent. A fight ensues, and everyone leaves the place via the staircase.

Rounding Up and Branding Cattle

Edison © H46140 May 18, 1904
Cameraman: A. C. Abadie
Location: Bliss, Okla. Terr. *Photographed:* May 9, 1904
49 ft. FLA4853 (print) FRA1860 (neg.)

During the film there are three different exhibitions of calf branding: one in which two mounted riders simultaneously rope a calf while a third brands the animal; one in which two riders simultaneously rope or lasso the calf and one of the two men brands the calf, and another, where one rider lassos the calf and dismounts and does his own branding. The film ends as the last branded calf is turned loose to rejoin the herd.

Rounding Up of the "Yeggmen"

Edison © H50522 Sept. 16, 1904
Cameraman: Edwin S. Porter
Location: New York, N.Y.; South Orange, N.J. *Photographed:* Aug. 15–Sept. 10, 1904
380 ft. FLA5677 (print) FRA2514 (neg.)

Probably part of Capture of the Yegg Bank Burglars, this film is a reconstruction of a bank robbery. The scenes are: the four conspirators in the woods preparing for the hold-up, the hold-up, the gun battle between the bank guards and the fleeing robbers, a chase via boat and on horseback, and the bandits stealing locomotive no. 666. Some film of two locomotives crashing and exploding is attached.

A Round-up in Oklahoma

Oklahoma Natural Mutoscene Co. © H120452 Dec. 28, 1908
Cameraman: J. B. Kent
Location: Okla.
321 ft. FLA5676 (print) FRA2515 (neg.)

The subject is a cattle drive and barbecue. Two scenes show the operation of a chuck wagon, both from the cook's standpoint and the cowboys who eat around it. There is a staged scene of a group of Indians in full battle feathers as they sneak up on the chuck wagon, kill the cook, and are driven off by the cowboys who apparently kill several of them. The poor condition of the film does not permit too much detail.

Rout of the Filipinos

Edison © 38514 June 10, 1899
34 ft. FLA3251 (print) FRA0573 (neg.)
[Spanish-American War]

Thick jungle foliage is visible in the background. The first action is from camera left as some men uniformed as

Filipino insurrectionists back into the scene as though in retreat. Smoke is emanating from the rifle barrels. As they back out of camera range, men dressed as American military troops of the Spanish-American War appear. They move ahead, firing rapidly. The film ends as the Americans wave flags and hats as though they had won a victory. No casualties are visible.

Routing Mail, U.S.P.O.

AM&B © H34979 Aug. 22, 1903

Cameraman: A. E. Weed

Location: Washington, D.C. *Photographed:* Aug. 7, 1903

33 ft. FLA3881 (print) FRA1092 (neg.)

A man dressed in the attire of a U.S. mail carrier is standing in front of a backdrop painted to represent a projected dimensional schematic of the interior of a post office. The mail carrier is holding a stack of envelopes in his left hand, while with his right hand, he is placing the letters in the pigeonholes of a case especially constructed for the alphabetical sorting of letters. The case, approximately three feet by four feet, is mounted on four legs.

Royal Gorge

Edison © 13565 Feb. 24, 1898

Location: Denver Rio Grand R.R., Colo.

21 ft. FLA4094 (print) FRA1275 (neg.)

The full extent of the film was photographed by a camera positioned on the after part of a train traveling on a triple track through extremely mountainous country. The film shows what can be seen as the train progresses over the winding railroad bed.

Royal Train with Duke and Duchess of York, Climbing Mt. Hector

Edison © H10871 Nov. 29, 1901

Location: Alberta, Can.

38 ft. FLA4195 (print) FRA1358 (neg.)

The film shows a train, photographed from a single-camera positon, presumably bearing the Duke and Duchess of York up Mount Hector. Only two Pullman cars, pulled by three locomotives, are visible. No people can be seen.

Le Royaume des Fées

See: Fairyland; or, The Kingdom of the Fairies

Rube and Fender

Edison © H35326 Sept. 1, 1903

Cameraman: A. C. Abadie

Location: Wilmington, Del. *Photographed:* Aug. 26, 1903

14 ft. FLA3086 (print) FRA0425 (neg.)

The camera was positioned on a street so that an oncoming streetcar could be photographed as it approached the camera. Between the oncoming streetcar and the camera is a man dressed in rough clothing who walks toward the camera. The conductor can be seen ringing the bell and yelling at the man to get off the track, but he does not. Instead, he is scooped up by the front fender of the streetcar, where he is as the picture ends.

Rube and Mandy at Coney Island

Edison © H34528 Aug. 13, 1903

Cameraman: Edwin S. Porter

Location: Coney Island, N.Y.; Studio, N.Y.C.

295 ft. FLA5678 (print) FRA2516 (neg.)

This film records a trip around Coney Island by a couple made up as country bumpkins. The camera placement shows their entrance, exit, and participation in the various concessions. In the next-to-last scene, the two approach a hot dog stand, and each buys a hot dog and eats it in a greedy manner while walking toward the camera. In the final scene, the camera moves in for a close-up, waist shot of the two principals eating the hot dogs and getting mustard and pieces of roll all over their faces.

A Rube Couple at a County Fair

Edison © H52013 Oct. 24, 1904

Cameraman: Edwin S. Porter

Location: Danbury, Conn. *Photographed:* Oct. 13-15, 1904

212 ft. FLA5679 (print) FRA2517 (neg.)

The subject is a county fair. Most of the film consists of scenes of the various concessions and exhibits of trained horses, sulky races, and prize animals. Approximately half way through the film, two actors are brought into the picture. They are made up to appear as country rubes. The camera pans to show that the man wants to see a group of seminude women dance, but his wife, brandishing a cane, leads him off to the preserves counter.

Rube in an Opium Joint

AM&B © H62752 June 29, 1905

Cameraman: G. W. Bitzer

Location: Studio, N.Y.C. *Photographed:* June 20, 1905

20 ft. FLA3818 (print) FRA1048 (neg.)

Four people, two women and two men, can be seen reclining in the bunks of an artist's conception of a Chinese opium den. Two men dressed as Chinese are attending to the opium smokers. The door of the set opens, admitting a man carrying a hand megaphone and wearing a cap labeled "Guide." He is accompanied by a couple dressed as country folk who stand and gape. The Chinese men offer the "rube" a pull on an opium pipe. He accepts, then shakes his head and reaches in his pocket for his own pipe. All the visitors leave the set and, as the film ends, the two Chinese can be seen smoking pipes similar to the one carried by their newly departed guest.

A Rube in the Subway

AM&B © H61988 June 15, 1905

Cameraman: G. W. Bitzer

Location: Studio, N.Y.C. *Photographed:* June 7, 1905

71 ft. FLA5189 (print) FRA2146 (neg.)

The story is built around the confusion that occurs on a set of a subway platform. Several times during the course of the film, groups of people enter and leave subway cars and the platform. On one occasion, several people, one of whom is dressed as a country bumpkin, exit from a car. He is carrying numerous bags and bundles and is accompanied by two equally rustic women. They become confused on the platform; his purse is stolen by pickpockets, and all his bundles disappear. At the end of the film, he is carried away by subway guards as he attempts to chase a subway car that the conductor will not let him board without money.

Rubes in the Theatre

Edison © H8694 Sept. 16, 1901

38 ft. FLA3846 (print) FRA1106 (neg.)

The film was photographed as though the camera were on a vaudeville stage taking pictures of the audience. Immediately in front of the camera and in the center of a group of seated spectators are two men made up to resemble country bumpkins. Throughout the film, the only action visible is the antics of the rubes and the other spectators close to them who are laughing at them. This film has an Edison Patent notice in it.

A Rude Hostess

AM&B © H125116 Mar. 21, 1909

Director: D. W. Griffith. Cameraman: G. W. Bitzer

Cast: Marion Leonard, Frank Powell, Arthur Johnson, Mack Sennett, Owen Moore, Jeanie Macpherson

Location: Studio, N.Y.C. Photographed: Mar. 3, 1909

172 ft. FLA5680 (print) FRA2518 (neg.)

A handsome burglar (Arthur Johnson) dressed in dinner clothes is nearly surprised in the act of burglarizing a safe. He decides to bluff it out, and allows himself to be found as if inebriated. The woman of the house (Marion Leonard) returns from escorting guests out and finds the burglar. At the same time, she notices that the curtains hiding the safe have been moved. In order not to let the burglar escape, she begins to pay unusual attention to him until her butler is signaled to go for help. The film ends as the police arrive and take the handsome burglar into custody. The camera moves to a semiclose-up of the hostess who is in hysterics at losing such a handsome boyfriend. All of the action occurred in one room and, with the exception of the camera movement at the end, was photographed from a single-camera position.

Ruhlin in His Training Quarters

Edison © H10906 Dec. 2, 1901

Cast: Gus Ruhlin

Location: San Francisco [?]

117 ft. FLA5190 (print) FRA2147 (neg.)

The first camera position shows a rural area. In the foreground six people can be seen watching the approach of three running figures dressed in heavy clothing. The second scene, from the same camera position, shows Ruhlin approaching the camera on a bicycle. The next scene shows Ruhlin in boxing attire sparring with a man while another looks on. The next two scenes are the same except that the sparring partner changes.

Ruins of City Hall, Paterson

Edison © H14290 Feb. 17, 1902

Location: Paterson, N.J. Photographed: Feb. 9[?], 1902

24 ft. FLA4047 (print) FRA1234 (neg.)

The single-camera position effects an approximate 60-degree pan to show devastation caused by fire to a large stone building. Portions of the walls are visible, but mainly just the concrete and stone foundations and doorways are seen.

See also: Panorama of the Paterson Fire, and Paterson Fire, Showing the Y.M.C.A. and Library

Ruins of Magic Garden

See: Parsifal

Rumpelstiltskin

N.Y. Motion Picture © LP5251 May 10, 1915

Producer: Thomas H. Ince Director: Raymond B. West

Cast: Clyde Tracy, Elizabeth Burbridge, J. Barney Sherry, Louis Morrison, George Fisher, Margaret Thompson, H. C. Kern, Kenneth Browne

Location: Santa Monica, Calif.

1,702 ft. FLA5899-5900 (print) FRA2763-2764 (neg.)

This four-reel film was based on the Grimm Brothers fairy tale of the same name, and the director followed the story closely. Occasionally, however, he added scenes to better exemplify the art of the cinema. Most of the craft available at the time of this production was used, such as double exposure, stop action, special effects, etc.

Run of N.Y. Fire Department

AM&B © H32002 May 19, 1903

Cameraman: G. W. Bitzer

Location: City Hall, N.Y.C. Date: May 11, 1903

43 ft. FLA4855 (print) FRA1862 (neg.)

A street lined with tall buildings in a downtown area of New York City is shown. On the sidewalk opposite the camera position are people who seem to be aware of an approaching spectacle. Later, horse-drawn fire-fighting equipment arrives. There are hook and ladder, personnel, and pumping units.

Runaway Match

Gaumont © AM&B H38686 Dec. 1, 1903

Director: Alfred Collins

Location: London

120 ft. FLA5681 (print) FRA2520 (neg.)

The film was directed around the elopement of a young couple pursued by the father of the bride-to-be. The locale is a fashionable residential district. The chase begins with the father following the fleeing couple in his automobile. He arrives at the minister's too late to stop the wedding. The film ends with all forgiven. They all depart, friends once more, in the father's car. There is an unusual (for the time) camera use of an insert of the wedding ring being placed on the bride's finger during the ceremony.

Running Through Gallitzen Tunnel, Penna. R.R.

Edison © 44244 July 7, 1899

Location: Gallitzin, Pa.

60 ft. FLA4854 (print) FRA1861 (neg.)

The poor condition of this film does not permit detailed description. However, it is possible to see that the camera was placed on a train that was moving on a track and approaching a tunnel through a mountain. As the film continues, the train carries the camera completely through the excavation and out the other side. The only other thing visible during the film is a freight car traveling in the opposite direction on the other track.

Rural Elopement

AM&B © H121530 Jan. 12, 1909

Cameraman: G. W. Bitzer

Cast: Guy Hedlund, Linda Arvidson, Harry Salter, Mack Sennett

Location: Coytesville, N.J. *Date:* Dec. 16, 1908

206 ft. FLA5682 (print) FRA2519 (neg.)

A young man learns of a couple's plan to elope and waits outside. He ties up the hero and absconds with the girl. She realizes that he is not her fiancé and a struggle begins. The camera position is changed to show the hero loosening his bonds, and then leading a group of pursuers who capture the kidnapper after a violent fight. The two elopers continue on their way, this time with the blessing of the girl's father. The camera was moved many times to show the flight of the villain with the girl, as well as the pursuit. A portion of the original paper print no longer exists.

Rural Wagon Delivering Mail, U.S.P.O.

AM&B © H34981 Aug. 22, 1903

Cameraman: A. E. Weed

Location: Westminister, Md. *Photographed:* Aug. 10, 1903

21 ft. FLA3879 (print) FRA1090 (neg.)

The subject is the delivery of the U.S. mail in a rural area. The camera was positioned in full sight of a standard rural free delivery post box located in front of a well-kept house and garden. A small boy and girl walk past the camera position in front of the mail box. At that moment, a standard rural horse-drawn postal delivery wagon comes into sight. The postman places the mail in the box, and the wagon continues on its way.

Rural Wagon Giving Mail to Branch, U.S.P.O.

AM&B © H34983 Aug. 22, 1903

Cameraman: A. E. Weed

Location: Westminister, Md. *Photographed:* Aug. 10, 1903

21 ft. FLA3880 (print) FRA1091 (neg.)

The first scene shows a rural free delivery mail man standing waiting for the area mail to be delivered to him. As the film continues, a horse-drawn wagon marked "Rural Postal Delivery" passes the camera position. The mail is then handed to the waiting postman who boards a two-wheel wagon and drives away.

Russian Sharp Shooters

AM&B © H43405 Mar. 17, 1904

Cameraman: Raymond Ackerman

Location: Tientsin, China *Date:* Jan. 12, 1901

19 ft. FLA3841 (print) FRA1101 (neg.)

The extent of the production is a scene photographed from a single-camera position, showing troops approaching the camera company front. They are dressed and armed as Russian infantry soldiers of the era.

S.S. "Chippewa"

AM&B © H18891 June 12, 1902

Cameraman: F. S. Armitage

Location: Detroit *Date:* July 8, 1899

15 ft. FLA3680 (print) FRA0930 (neg.)

The camera was positioned on the shore of what seems to be a river. From camera left comes a four-deck excursion vessel, propelled by side wheels powered by a walking-beam steam engine. The distance from the camera as well as its course do not allow much description of either the vessel or the passengers.

S.S. "Columbia" Sailing

AM&B © H24880 Dec. 9, 1902

24 ft. FLA4023 (print) FRA1214 (neg., copy 1) FRA1215 (neg., copy 2)

As the film begins, a large ocean liner with three smokestacks can be seen tied to a dock where there are many people. The film shows the liner getting under way and moving away from the dock. The people on the pier as well as the passengers lining the decks of the ship wave.

S.S. "Coptic"

Edison © 25332 Apr. 21, 1898

Cameramen: James H. White, W. Bleckyrden

Location: Pacific Ocean

22 ft. FLA3073 (print) FRA0413 (neg.)

This single-camera position, single-scene film begins from the deck of a ship at sea. In the immediate foreground is the handrail on which two large life preservers are fastened. Beyond the railing is a turbulent sea. One of eight small films on the *S.S. Coptic.* According to the Edison catalog, eight cameramen were assigned to this series.

S.S. "Coptic" at Dock

Edison © 60580 Oct. 25, 1897

23 ft. FLA3037 (print) FRA0242 (neg.)

The film begins from a camera position located slightly above the heads of a crowd gathered on a pier to watch the departure of a large ocean liner. The tide condition and the height of the dock make only the upper deck and the superstructure of the vessel visible as it gets under way.

S.S. "Coptic" Coaling

Edison © 38231 June 22, 1898

Cameramen: James H. White, W. Bleckyrden

Location: Japan

22 ft. FLA4310 (print) FRA1459 (neg.)

The side of a ship against which crude scaffolding has been erected can be seen from a single-camera position. The locale is apparently a foreign port as the many natives use the "bucket brigade" system of coaling.

S.S. "Coptic" in the Harbor

Edison © 60581 Oct. 25, 1897

21 ft. FLA3056 (print) FRA0402 (neg.)

A scattered crowd is visible as the film begins. At a distance of five hundred yards a large ocean liner with one smokestack and four auxiliary masts can be seen making its way through the harbor area.

S.S. "Coptic" Lying To

Edison © 25331 Apr. 21, 1898

Cameramen: James H. White, W. Bleckyrden

Location: Pacific Ocean

22 ft. FLA4281 (print) FRA1434 (neg.)

The film does not corroborate the title. It was photographed from a single-camera position and shows what appears to be the after part of the vessel because of the curve of the railing in the foreground. A life ring is hung on the rail. Beyond the railing is the ocean, with heavy ground swells.

S.S. "Coptic" Running Against the Storm

Edison © 25333 Apr. 21, 1898
Cameramen: James H. White, W. Bleckyrden
Location: Pacific Ocean
25 ft. FLA4250 (print) FRA1406 (neg.)

The film was photographed from a single-camera position situated on the port bridge wing or superstructure of the liner. The film shows the ship heading into the sea. The movement of the standing and running rigging relative to the horizon does not indicate the ship is making heavy weather.

S.S. "Coptic" Running Before a Gale

Edison © 75820 Dec. 24, 1898
Cameramen: James H. White, W. Bleckyrden
Location: Pacific Ocean
22 ft. FLA3278 (print) FRA0595 (neg.)

The camera was positioned on the boat deck forward of the bridge of a good-sized seagoing vessel heading into a sea. The spray coming back over the camera position is visible in the film.

S.S. "Coptic" Sailing Away

Edison © 60582 Oct. 25, 1897
25 ft. FLA4164 (print) FRA1332 (neg.)

The camera was positioned at head height on a pier. In the foreground is a mixed group of people looking toward a large liner approximately 250 yards from the camera position. The vessel appears to be getting under way; however, the distance does not allow for much detail to be seen.

The S.S. "Deutschland" in a Storm

Edison © H19314 June 25, 1902
Location: Atlantic Ocean
31 ft. FLA4062 (print)

The film was photographed from the promenade deck forward of an ocean liner proceeding through the sea. A number of people are on deck, and since none wears foul-weather clothing, it must have been a very pleasant day. Five short films seem to have been photographed on the same day.

See also: Shuffleboard on S.S. "Deutschland."

The S.S. "Deutschland" in a Storm, no. 2

Edison © H19316 June 25, 1902
Location: Atlantic Ocean
26 ft. FLA4063 (print) FRA1246 (neg.)

The poor condition of the film does not allow the establishment of subject matter beyond something in the foreground that looks like a ship's railing.

S.S. "Deutschland" in Heavy Sea

Edison © H19318 June 25, 1902
Location: Atlantic Ocean
11 ft. FLA4061 (print) FRA1245 (neg.)

The camera was located on the starboard side of the port deck above the engine room. The only things visible are the metal wind scoops in the foreground and a man in the background.

S.S. "Deutschland" Leaving Her Dock in Hoboken

Edison © H19317 June 25, 1902
Location: Hoboken, N.J.
26 ft. FLA3719 (print) FRA0965 (neg.)

A large seagoing liner leaves a pier in Hoboken, New Jersey. The starboard quarter deck area is visible in the foreground. A group of people lining the rail waves to a larger group of people on the dock in the background. As the ship moves from the dock, the camera begins to pan, taking in all of the dock area and a sign that reads "Hamburg-American Line." Two harbor tugs are in the water at the end of the pier.

S.S. "Doric"

Edison © 38216 June 22, 1898
Cameramen: James H. White, W. Bleckyrden
Location: Two miles out from Yokahama, Japan
24 ft. FLA3241 (print) FRA0564 (neg.)

A steam vessel of approximately five thousand tons approaches the camera at a distance of two hundred and fifty yards. The ship closes the distance and passes the camera close enough for the superstructure and deck gear to be seen clearly.

See also: Afternoon Tea on Board S.S. "Doric", S.S. "Doric" in Mid-Ocean, and Game of Shovel [sic] Board on Board S.S. "Doric".

S.S. "Doric" in Mid-Ocean

Edison © 38224 June 22, 1898
Cameramen: James H. White, W. Bleckyrden
Location: Pacific Ocean
24 ft. FLA3341 (print) FRA0651 (neg.)

An ocean liner approaches at a distance of approximately five yards. It progresses through the water faster than the ship carrying the camera; therefore, the complete outline of the hull, mast, superstructure, and deck gear is visible as the ship passes the camera.

S.S. "Gaelic"

Edison © 38221 June 22, 1898
Location: Pacific Ocean
23 ft. FLA3229 (print) FRA0553 (neg.)

The camera was positioned on one of the promenade decks of a seagoing vessel. In the foreground four people are splashing about in a swimming pool. In the background is a ship's railing with a life preserver marked "S.S. Gaelic" attached. Beyond that is the sea.

S.S. "Gaelic" at Nagasaki

Edison © 38255 June 22, 1898
Cameramen: James H. White, W. Bleckyrden
Location: Nagasaki, Japan
24 ft. FLA4314 (print) FRA1463 (neg.)

The camera was positioned on what appears to be a steamship dock. In the immediate foreground, and for a considerable distance from the camera, are workmen and women passing baskets of ship's stores from hand to hand. In the background is the hull of a large vessel.

S.S. "Morro Castle"

AM&B © H42802 Feb. 27, 1904

Cameraman: A. E. Weed

Location: Sandy Hook, N.J. *Photographed:* Feb. 16, 1904

23 ft. FLA4067 (print) FRA1251 (neg.)

The camera, looking out to sea, photographed the bow of a large seagoing vessel approaching at a distance of about two hundred yards. The full hull, superstructure, etc., pass in view.

S.S. "Queen" Leaving Dock

Edison © 60555 Oct. 25, 1897

27 ft. FLA3046 (print) FRA0294 (neg.)

The camera was positioned on a dock looking out to sea. In the immediate foreground is the forward portion of a large steamship. The steamship begins to move and backs away to a position where most of the ship is visible. The words "S.S. Queen" are painted on the bow.

S.S. "Queen" Loading

Edison © 60557 Oct. 25, 1897

23 ft. FLA3041 (print) FRA0256 (neg.)

The film was photographed on a pier. In the immediate foreground are the people and mobile equipment. In the background can be seen the forecastle head and bridge structure of a seagoing vessel. The booms are rigged out, and the people and equipment are unloading the vessel.

S.S. "Williamette" Leaving for Klondike

Edison © 60556 Oct. 25, 1897

Cameraman: Robert K. Bonine

25 ft. FLA4119 (print) FRA1295 (neg.)

[Alaska Gold Rush]

The camera was positioned on the docks to show the heads and shoulders of a group of spectators. They are watching a large, seagoing vessel back away from the dock where they are standing. The ship is too far from the camera to show much of its deck gear, etc.

Sack Race

AM&B © H32497 June 11, 1903

17 ft. FLA3988 (print) FRA1195 (neg.)

The film was photographed from a single-camera position over the heads of a crowd of people. They are engrossed in watching approximately ten men and boys completely enclosed in large sacks competing to cover a specified length of ground.

The Sacrifice

AM&B © H121590 Jan. 14, 1909

Director: D. W. Griffith *Cameraman:* G. W. Bitzer

Cast: Florence Lawrence, Harry Salter, Mack Sennett, Arthur Johnson, Marion Leonard, Owen Moore, Linda Arvidson, John Cumpson

Location: Studio, N.Y.C. *Photographed:* Dec. 11–12, 1908

178 ft. FLA5683 (print) FRA2521 (neg.)

This film is based on O. Henry's well-known story "The Gift of the Magi." The hero has a beautiful watch, of which he is very proud, but no fob. His wife (Florence Lawrence) has a considerable amount of beautiful hair but her comb has no teeth. In their unselfish love for one another, each sacrifices his dearest possession. He sells his watch to buy her a new comb, and she sells her hair to buy him a watch fob. The film, photographed on four sets, had close-ups of the watch without the fob and of the tortoise-shell comb without teeth.

The Sad Sea Waves

See: Neptune's Daughters

Sailing of the "Deutschland" With Prince Henry on Board

Edison © H15200 Mar. 15, 1902

Cameraman: James H. White

Location: Hoboken, N.J.

48 ft. FLA4856 (print) FRA1863 (neg.)

The film shows the departure of a large German steamship. The camera was located on the level of the boat deck. The vessel gets under way and her superstructure can be seen passing the camera position. The complete hull of the ship can be seen in the distance as the film ends.

Sailors Ashore

AM&B © H42806 Feb. 27, 1904

Cameraman: A. E. Weed

Location: Studio, N.Y.C. *Photographed:* Feb. 18, 1904

42 ft. FLA3843 (print) FRA1103 (neg.)

The camera is placed as if in the audience. The set shows a stage door or back of a theater. On each side of the door is a poster of a burlesque bill. In the first action, four men dressed in sailor's uniforms become interested in the posters and attempt to go through the stage door but are stopped. Above the posters and door are two windows. The sailors form a ladder and aid one of their mates in through a window. He in turn hands down the young ladies of the chorus. The picture ends as the sailors, with a girl on each arm, go off stage.

Sailors of Atlantic Fleet, Dewey Parade

AM&B © 16649 Apr. 16, 1902

Cameraman: F.S. Armitage

Location: N.Y.C. *Photographed:* Sept. 27, 1899

31 ft. FLA4079 (print) FRA1262 (neg.)

[Spanish-American War, Dewey Homecoming, New York City]

In order to film the subject (a parade) the cameraman stationed his equipment to view the side of a street. The parade consists of soldiers and sailors in uniform. For the rest of the film, several companies pass by the camera position. Both sides of the street are crowded with spectators.

Sailors Waltzing

AM&B © H22208 Oct. 3, 1902

Cameraman: G. W. Bitzer

Location: On board the "Kearsarge," Fisher's Island, N.Y. *Date:* Sept. 8, 1902

11 ft. FLA3368 (print) FRA0671 (neg.)

The camera was positioned under the awning of an American battleship, judging by the size of the guns protruding from the turrets. As the camera starts to pan, the white hull of another unidentifiable American warship can be seen. The camera continues to pan and about twenty American sailors in tropical whites can be seen dancing together. Approximately a company of marines observes their actions.

St. Patrick's Cathedral and Fifth Avenue on Easter Sunday Morning

Edison © H16116 Apr. 7, 1902

Location: N.Y.C. *Photographed:* Mar. 30, 1902

54 ft. FLA4858 (print) FRA1864 (neg., copy 1) FRA1866 (neg., copy 2)

The single-camera position was located on Fifth Avenue across from St. Patrick's Cathedral in New York City. The camera was positioned high over the heads of crowds that were both part of and watching the Easter Parade. The footage of transportation of the period, both in double-decker buses and hansom cabs, is good. The camera panned left about 20 degrees to include the intersection at 51st Street.

The "St. Paul" Outward Bound

AM&B © H26956 Jan.14, 1903

Cameraman: F. S. Armitage

Location: Philadelphia [?] *Date:* Sept. 26, 1900

20 ft. FLA3180 (print) FRA0507 (neg.)

The camera evidently was positioned on a pier head directed toward the open water, where there is a moving vessel. From the right of the picture, at a distance of about 250 yards, is the bow of a large, seagoing vessel. Without camera movement, the remainder of the ship passes by; sections of the hull, superstructure, and deck gear are clearly visible.

Salmon Fishing Nipissisquit

AM&B © H71524 Jan. 3, 1906

Cameraman: G. W. Bitzer

Location: Nipissiquit River, New Brunswick, Canada *Photographed:* Oct. 6, 1905

182 ft. FLA5684 (print) FRA2522 (neg.)

The subject is fresh water fishing. During the film, the photographer placed his camera in numerous places in a slow-runing fresh water stream. Several fishermen catch and land fish in small, hand-held nets. The film ends as one man lands a fish and holds it up. It is approximately a foot and a half long. There is a woman spectator.

A Salutary Lesson

Biograph © J144207 Aug. 12, 1910

Director: D. W. Griffith *Cameraman:* G. W. Bitzer

Cast: Charles West, Dorothy West, Gladys Egan, Vivian Prescott, Alfred Paget

Location: Studio, N.Y.C.; Keyport and Highlands, N.J. *Photographed:* July 6, 8 and 9, 1910

392 ft. FLA5685 (print) FRA2523 (neg.)

The first scene takes place on a set of a living room of a modest home. A little girl attempts to attract her preoccupied mother's attention but is ignored, so her father takes her to the beach. He becomes interested in talking with an attractive female acquaintance, and the child, once more ignored, wanders off. She falls asleep on some rocks, where her life is endangered when the tide comes in. A stranger, a strong swimmer, saves her and takes her to her home. The film ends with her parents embracing in happiness over the child's safe return.

The Salvation Army Lass

AM&B © H123873 Mar. 11, 1909

Director: D. W. Griffith *Cameramen:* Arthur Marvin, G. W. Bitzer

Cast: Florence Lawrence, Marion Leonard, John Cumpson, Harry Salter, Clara T. Bracey, Mack Sennett, Owen Moore, Dorothy West

Location: Fort Lee, N.J.; Studio, N.Y.C. *Photographed:* Dec. 28-30, 1908, and Jan. 27 and Feb. 18, 1909

322 ft. FLA5686 (print) FRA2524 (neg.)

A young woman, left alone when her husband is sent to jail for killing a man in a barroom brawl, joins the Salvation Army. While out on the street begging with her tambourine, she encounters her husband who has been released from prison. The several interior and exterior scenes that follow show the young woman attempting to reform her husband, with little success. The last scene shows his repentance, and he also becomes a member of the Salvation Army.

Sampans Racing Toward Liner

AM&B © H18042 May 23, 1902

Cameraman: Robert K. Bonine

Location: Kobe, Japan *Date:* July 29, 1901

10 ft. FLA4274 (print) FRA0273 (neg., copy 1) FRA1429 (neg., copy 2)

The film shows man-operated sculled sampans approaching a liner.

Sampans Racing Toward Liner

AM&B © H29160 Mar. 11, 1903

Cameraman: Robert K. Bonine

Location: Kobe, Japan *Date:* July 29, 1901

18 ft. FLA4275 (print) FRA0273 (neg.)

The camera shows a large, single-stacked liner in the background. Approximately fifty sampans, maneuvered by sculling oars, approach the side of the liner directly in front of the camera position.

Sampson-Schley Controversy [parts 1 and 2 of 3]

Edison © H7674 Aug. 15, 1901

68 ft. FLA4857 (print) FRA1865 (neg.)

[Spanish-American War]

As the film opens, the set is constructed to appear as though the camera were placed forward on the bridge of a ship. The background, a painted backdrop, consists of a watchtower and a point of land around which the miniature ships can be seen approaching the camera position. All during this segment of the film, a bearded actor in naval uniform continually observes the approaching ship. The scale and proportion of the two ships are acceptable. The second camera position seems to be over the top of a constructed guardrail. There is a large gun with full crew of men opening and closing the breech and occasionally firing the make-believe weapon. The miniature ships on the ocean return the gunfire and the miniature vessels are blown up.

Sampson and Schley Controversy—Tea Party [part 3 of 3]
Edison © H8753   Sept. 18, 1901
29 ft.   FLA8753   FRA1043 (neg.)
[Spanish-American War]

On a set of a formal drawing room, nine young ladies dressed in period costumes appear to be taking orders from a woman who is evidently their hostess. A tall man clad in an admiral's uniform enters, is seated by the hostess with the young ladies, and is served something from a pot resembling a teapot. As he is being served, the film ends.

San Francisco Disaster
AM&B © H77924   May 19, 1906
Cameraman: G. W. Bitzer
Location: Studio, N.Y.C. *Photographed:* May 5, 1906
125 ft.   FLA5191 (print)   FRA2148 (neg.)

This film was motivated by an American disaster. The producer constructed a miniature city with the idea that the spectator would believe it was San Francisco. From a single-camera position many fires can be seen burning the miniature buildings. Great clouds of billowing smoke obscure the whole area.

The Sand Baby
AM&B © H35394   Sept. 4, 1903
Cameraman: A. E. Weed
Location: Coney Island, N.Y. *Photographed:* Aug. 18, 1903
23 ft.   FLA3561 (print)   FRA0837 (neg.)

An infant is seated on the sand at a bathing beach. The camera was positioned to show only the child and some sand around the place where he is seated. The child fills a sand bucket with sand and empties the sand from the bucket.
See also: A Little Teaze.

The Sand Fort
AM&B © H35393   Sept. 4, 1903
Cameraman: A. E. Weed
Location: Coney Island, N.Y. *Photographed:* Aug. 18, 1903
31 ft.   FLA4269 (print)   FRA1424 (neg.)

A large sand pile decorated with an American flag and seashells is shown. Several infants are seated around the mound busily piling more sand on it to make it larger. In the background on the horizon is a full-masted sailing ship.
See also: A Little Teaze

Sandow
AM&B © H23770   Nov. 11, 1902
12 ft.   FLA3090 (print)   FRA0429 (neg.)

A single-camera position film of a side show strong man flexing his muscles. The movements were standard poses calculated to show good muscle separation. He does one backflip. The film is very contrasty. AM&B copyrighted one Mutoscope card and two films with this title. The Mutoscope card has a copyright date of December 18, 1896, and it is likely that the above, as well as the following short film, also were made at that time.

Sandow
AM&B © H32496   June 11, 1903
16 ft.   FLA3091 (print)   FRA0430 (neg.)

From a single-camera position, the film shows the strong man Sandow striking a pose before performing the various poses designed to show his excellent muscle separation and development. During the course of the demonstration, he does a backflip. There is reason to believe that this film was made several years before the copyright date.

The Sands of Dee
Biograph © J171536   July 23, 1912
Director: D. W. Griffith *Cameraman:* G. W. Bitzer
Cast: Mae Marsh, Robert Harron, Grace Henderson, Charles Hill Mailes, Kate Toncray, Edwin August, Claire McDowell, W. Chrystie Miller, Gladys Egan
Location: Balboa and Long Beach, Calif.
399 ft.   FLA5687 (print)   FRA2525 (neg.)

The first title says that the story was suggested "by the verse of the famous English poet, Charles Kingsley.' The daughter of a simple farmer, whose job is to tend the cows on their rugged island home, meets an artist on one of her trips from the meadows. The artist finds her attractive, makes love to her, and makes an appointment to paint her portrait. Her parents arrange a marriage with another man, which makes her most unhappy, and she goes off to her artist friend to discuss her problem. His wife arrives, and the young woman, disillusioned and terribly unhappy, throws herself into the ocean where she is drowned. There is a scene where her body is carried from the surf to the shore. Instead of titles, lines from the poem "Sands O'Dee" were used.

The Sandwich Man
AM&B © H16351   Apr. 10, 1902
Cameraman: F. S. Armitage
Location: Roof studio, N.Y.C. *Date:* Sept. 20, 1899
17 ft.   FLA4177 (print)   FRA1341 (neg.)

The action of this farce-comedy concerns a small newsboy who finds a cigar butt in front of a tobacconist's shop and a passing sandwich man who takes it from him. As the sandwich man leans over to light the cigar, the newsboy takes the top portion of his sandwich sign, bends it over to the ground and sits on it, thus rendering the sandwich man hors de combat. He is also able to retrieve the cigar end. The small boy is seen smoking the cigar butt as the picture ends.

Santa Filling Stockings
AM&B © H25017   Dec. 15, 1902
25 ft.   FLA4052 (print)   FRA1237 (neg.)

A single-camera position shows a stage on which is a fireplace with Christmas decorations. A man dressed as Santa Claus starts out of the fireplace. He hits his head, which removes his false hair. He goes back into the fireplace and starts to come out all over again. As the short film ends, Santa takes presents from his bag and puts them in the stockings hung on the mantel.
See also: Hanging Stockings on Christmas Eve, Christmas Morning, and Christmas Party

Sarnia Tunnel

AM&B © H38016 Nov. 12, 1903

Cameraman: F. S. Armitage

Location: Sarnia, Ontario, Canada *Date:* Feb. 24, 1900

56 ft. FLA5192 (print) FRA2149 (neg.)

The train on which the camera is placed begins to move on a well-constructed railroad track. An approaching train of approximately ten cars passes; the passengers apparently are aware of being photographed as they wave their hands at the train. The train enters a tunnel made of chipped granite blocks, lined with corrugated pipe, which reflects light. Eventually, the train comes to a stop at a large station over which the Canadian and customs flags are flying.

Saturday's Shopping

Hepworth © AM&B H38154 Nov. 14, 1903

Director: Cecil Hepworth

Location: Walton-on-Thames, England

120 ft. FLA5193 (print) FRA2150 (neg.)

This film, a progressive situation comedy, records a shopping trip of a browbeaten husband and his belligerent, overbearing wife. At the beginning of the picture, the husband places two infants in a perambulator and follows his wife down the street. She tries constantly to hurry him along. After the first stop, a bottle of liquor is hidden among the purchased provisions. The husband soon discovers that if he tips over the pram, it gives him a chance to have another nip from the bottle and, for the full extent of the film, that is just what he does. All during the journey, he is aided by the town constable who helps him pick up the scattered packages and shares the bottle with him.

The Sausage Machine

AM&B © H23772 Nov. 11, 1902

Date: 1897 [?]

17 ft. FLA3701 (print) FRA0950 (neg.)

The subject of this comedy is a mechanical contrivance that converts dogs into sausages. As the film begins, one sees a set with a sign in large letters reading "Sausage Factory." A machine with belts, wheels, entrance apertures, and exit pipes, with a sign on it "Sausage Machine," is between the back of the set and the camera. The action of the film shows derby hatted sausage manufacturers transforming little dogs into sausages by putting them into one side of the machine and taking the sausages out on the other. On the basis of such transformations, the Mutoscope was used as an illustration in the 1901 edition of *Magic*, by Albert E. Hopkins.

See also: **Dog Factory**, and **Fun in a Butcher Shop**

Saved!

AM&B © H40753 Jan. 11, 1904

Cameraman: A. E. Weed

Location: Studio, N.Y.C. *Photographed:* Dec. 30, 1903

47 ft. FLA4859 (print) FRA1866 (neg.)

There are two scenes in this film. One shows a set of the interior of a storehouse for explosives, and the other the front of a backdrop painted to represent the outdoors. A man is sitting on some boxes in the storehouse when a woman in a sunbonnet enters with his lunch and then leaves. The workman lights his pipe which causes a terrible explosion. He disappears. The next scene takes place in front of the painted backdrop where the woman in the sunbonnet and a man are gazing upward in anxiety. As they look up, the workman comes floating down, using an umbrella as a parachute. When he lands, he is congratulated on his good fortune.

Scarecrow Pump

Edison © H54486 Dec. 9, 1904

Cameraman: Edwin S. Porter

Location: Studio, N.Y.C. *Photographed:* Nov. 22, 1904

35 ft. FLA4960 (print) FRA1867 (neg.)

A set of the back yard of a farm house is visible when the film begins. We can see a corner of the house and a picket fence with a gate; immediately in the foreground is a hand-operated water pump. A pre-teen boy in farm clothing carries a hat and some rags over to the pump and disguises it as a scarecrow. When the boy hears someone approaching, he jumps into the tub underneath the nozzle pump. A man dressed in rough clothes, walking as if he is elderly, appears and sees the disguised pump. He reaches out and pumps the handle, causing water to come out and wet the young prankster in the tub. The film ends there.

A Scene Behind the Scenes

AM&B © H40811 Jan. 12, 1904

Cameraman: A. E. Weed

Location: Studio, N.Y.C. *Photographed:* Dec. 7, 1903

20 ft. FLA3662 (print) FRA0915 (neg.)

On a set representing the area behind the stage in a vaudeville theater, two women wearing tights are rehearsing. Shortly after the film starts, several other women in stage costumes appear in front of the camera, and one of the more fun-loving of this group chases the others about the stage, squirting them from a siphon of soda water.

Scene From the Elevator Ascending Eiffel Tower

Edison © D16386 Aug. 9, 1900

Location: Paris

54 ft. FLA4861 (print) FRA1868 (neg.)

[Paris Exposition]

Photographed from a camera in one of the ascending elevators of the Eiffel Tower, the basic structure and the lower level of the tower are plainly visible. As the elevator rises, and the film continues, more and more of the city spreads out below and becomes visible. The film shows the exhibit buildings of the Paris Exposition looking away from the Seine River, Napoleon's Tomb, some of the public buildings, etc.

Scene in a Rat Pit

AM&B © H73111 Feb. 9, 1906

Cameraman: G. W. Bitzer

Location: Studio, N.Y.C. *Photographed:* Jan 30, 1906

34 ft. FLA4862 (print, copy 1) FLA5973 (print, copy 2) FRA1869 (neg.)

A single-camera position shows a board, dirt-floored arena, approximately ten feet by ten feet, with two men and a dog. One of the men has the dog on leash. The other has a wire cage containing rats which he releases and allows the dog to destroy.

Scene in Chinatown

AM&B © H30730 Apr. 24, 1903

Cameraman: Raymond Ackerman

Location: San Francisco *Date:* Sept. 15, 1900

22 ft. FLA3389 (print) FRA0686 (neg.)

The title of the film indicates that it was photographed in the Chinese section of a city. There are, however, very few people dressed in Chinese apparel. The camera did not move, and the area photographed is a short, narrow street. None of the shops can be identified, and the people shown are, with few exceptions, dressed as ordinary Americans in any city.

Scene in Chinese Restaurant

AM&B © H28557 Feb. 24, 1903

Cast: Chuck Connors

Cameraman: F. S. Armitage

Location: Studio, N.Y.C. *Date:* Nov. 7, 1900

18 ft. FLA3155 (print) FRA0488 (neg.)

Three men are shown seated at a table. Two of the men are dressed in Chinese clothing. The third man, facing the camera, is not an Oriental, nor is he dressed like one; he is wearing a derby. All three hold rice bowls in one hand and use chopsticks to convey the food to their mouths. The scene was photographed indoors with studio lights. AM&B production records indicate that the Occidental is Chuck Connors, an entertainer.

Scene in the Swiss Village at Paris Exposition

Edison © D18582 Aug. 29, 1900

Location: Paris

34 ft. FLA4863 (print) FRA1870 (neg.)

The scope of the camera takes in the edge of a grove of trees in the background. Coming toward the camera through the trees, in columns of twos and threes, is a group (approximately fifty) of young girls in the costume of their country. The group approaches the camera, forms a circle, holds hands, and performs what appears to be a dance, going around and around in the circle.

See also: Swiss Village no. 2

Scene Outside the Temple

See: Parsifal

Scenes and Incidents, Russo-Japanese Peace Conference, Portsmouth, N.H.

Edison © H64509 Aug. 14, 1905

Cameraman: Edwin S. Porter

Location: Oyster Bay, N.Y.; Portsmouth, N.H. *Photographed:* Aug. 5–9, 1905

342 ft. FLA5688 (print) FRA2526 (neg.)

The subject is the peace conference between the Russian and Japanese governments, mediated by the U.S. government at the invitation of Theodore Roosevelt, then president of the United States. The film consists of scenes of the dignitaries and celebrities who were part of the conference. The film shows some of the things that occurred to the committees and their associates as they traveled between such locations as Oyster Bay and New York to various spots throughout the grounds at Portsmouth. Several of the scenes show not only the dignitaries but also their mode of transportation by land or water as well as the multitudes of people gathered to watch them arrive or depart. A subtitle in the film indicates Admiral Mead was among those present.

See also: Peace Envoys at Portsmouth, N.H.

Scenes in an Infant Orphan Asylum

Edison © H48640 July 29, 1904

Cameraman: Edwin S. Porter

Location: N.Y.C. *Photographed:* July 25, 1904

209 ft. FLA5689 (print) FRA"527 (neg.)

The subject of this documentary is an orphan asylum for infants. The beginning portion includes the dining facilities for the children. A woman dressed as a nurse leads approximately two hundred small children into the eating area where they stand behind their chairs. At a given signal, each child sits down and begins eating. The remainder of the film is devoted to showing some of the infants, less than a year old, being pushed in baby carriages and bathed, and later having haircuts. All of the children wear similar attire and the nurses wear uniforms.

Scenes in San Francisco

AM&B © H77925 May 19, 1906

Cameraman: Otis M. Gove

Location: San Francisco *Photographed:* May 9, 1906

58 ft. FLA5194 (print) FRA2151 (neg., copy 1) FRA2151 (neg., copy 2)

[San Francisco Earthquake]

The cameraman placed his equipment in various locations to record the disaster shown. The opening scene shows devastation and damage caused by the earthquake and fire. The remains of many buildings can be seen, both in the foreground and in the distance, as the cameraman panned his camera in increments of 40 to 80 degrees at a time. There are pictures of people getting on and off streetcars and walking down thoroughfares.

See also: Views in San Francisco

Scenes in San Francisco

AM&B © H77926 May 19, 1906

Cameraman: Otis M. Gove

Location: San Francisco *Photographed:* May 9, 1906

115 ft. FLA5195 (print) FRA2153 (neg.)

The cameraman placed his camera in various spots throughout the devastated area to record the damage caused by the earthquake. The camera pans from 40 to 180 degrees. In both the foreground and background, remains of buildings can be seen. The film also shows people going about their business of restoring the city, tearing down walls, and scraping up debris. Also shown are living facilities, army outdoor camp stoves, tents, and a line of persons getting their soup from a soup kitchen.

See also: Views in San Francisco

Schneider's Anti-Noise Crusade

AM&B © H125117 Mar. 31, 1909

Director: D. W. Griffith *Cameramen:* G. W. Bitzer, Arthur Marvin

Cast: Florence Lawrence, John Cumpson, Owen Moore, Tony O'Sullivan, Clara T. Bracey

Location: Studio, N.Y.C. *Photographed:* Mar. 8-9, 1909
206 ft. FLA5690 (print) FRA2528 (neg.)

In this film, a woman (Florence Lawrence) married to a composer (John Cumpson) is visited by a large woman and her young son. After enthusiastic greetings, the composer goes back to work and the little boy begins to cause trouble. He teases the parrot until it screeches, plays the trombone, and otherwise disturbs the composer. This goes on until, late at night, the composer can be seen sitting up while the rest of the household sleeps. Two burglars enter, and the composer, pistol in hand, pays them to remove the various noise-making devices from the house. As an afterthought, he gives them the parrot in its cage.

School Girl Athletes

AM&B © H43570 Mar. 22, 1904
Cameraman: A. E. Weed
Location: Studio, N.Y.C. *Photographed:* Feb. 25, 1904
23 ft. FLA4338 (print) FRA1484 (neg.)

Several young ladies wearing gymnasium costumes of the era can be seen enjoying themselves by performing humorous acrobatic feats on flying rings on a gymnasium set. Each of the four girls in turn holds on to the rings and does something to amuse her classmates. The film ends as the last of the impromptu performers falls to the floor.

See Also: In a Boarding School Gym and School Girl Gymnastics

School Girl Gymnastics

AM&B © H43568 Mar. 22, 1904
Cameraman: A. E. Weed
Location: Studio, N.Y.C. *Photographed:* Feb. 25, 1904
18 ft. FLA4304 (print) FRA1453 (neg., copy 1) FRA1454 (neg., copy 2)

The four young girls and the older woman in this film seem to be a teacher and her pupils. However, as the film progresses, it seems likely that the girls are professional dancers attempting comedy gymnastic routines. The instructress encourages them to form human pyramids. Each time they try, the pyramid collapses and they fall in a heap with a great flurry of arms and legs. As the film ends, the instructress picks up the girls one at a time, and piles each on top of the others. When she finishes, they all tumble down again.

See also: In a Boarding School Gym, and School Girl Athletes

School Master's Surprise

AM&B © H16640 Apr. 16, 1902
Photographed: 1898 [?]
19 ft. FLA4864 (print) FRA1871 (neg.)

On a set of a schoolroom are some tables, desks, and a pole at the top of which is a standard oil lamp with a glass chimney. Two boys enter the room through the door. They place a chair to enable them to reach the lamp, remove the chimney and fill it with flour and then return it to its place on the pole. The film ends as the boys run and hide and the door opens admitting a man dressed as a schoolteacher who lifts the chimney off the lamp and covers himself with flour.

The School Teacher and the Waif

Biograph © J170957 July 10, 1912
Director: D. W. Griffith *Cameraman:* G. W. Bitzer
Cast: Mary Pickford, Jack Pickford, Claire McDowell, Kate Bruce, Edwin August, Robert Harron, Charles Hill Mailes, Mae Marsh, Frank Opperman, Alfred Paget
Location: Calif.
407 ft. FLA5691 (print) FRA2496 (neg.)

A rather disreputable farmyard with broken down equipment, pigsties, etc. can be seen where a group of teen-age boys are harassing a sheep protected by a young girl. The next scene shows an old man reading a letter ordering him to send his daughter to school, much against his wishes. The remainder of the film shows the school teacher attempting to teach the young girl, while he also tries to prevent her from running away with an itinerant drummer who promises marriage at a later date. The film ends as the school teacher is shown making progress with the backward young girl. The scenes are preceded by a title of the day of the week, as "Monday," "Tuesday," etc.

Schoolmates

See: The Seven Ages

Scout Yacht Race

AM&B © H27982 Feb. 7, 1903
25 ft. FLA3193 (print) FRA0519 (neg.)

The camera was positioned on a pier overlooking a harbor where a small boat race takes place. In the foreground, approximately one hundred yards from the camera, a buoy can be seen. Three sloop-rigged boats, almost twenty feet in length, approach that buoy; each rounds it and passes directly in front of the camera. The title on the film is Scrub Yacht Race.

Scrambling for Eggs

Edison © H16119 Apr. 7, 1902
Location: White House, Washington, D.C. *Photographed:* Apr. 1, 1902
20 ft. FLA3885 (print) FRA1094 (neg.)

The film, photographed from a single-camera position, shows a large group of boys participating in an egg hunt supervised by adults who throw eggs to the boys, causing them to scrimmage in search of the eggs.

See also: Tossing Eggs

A Scrap in Black and White

Edison © H33295 July 8, 1903
Cameraman: A. C. Abadie
Location: Wilmington, Del. *Photographed:* June 30, 1903
39 ft. FLA4865 (print) FRA1872 (neg.)

Inside an area of a roped-off square, two adult men can be seen with two boys, a young black boy, and a young white one. The boys are dressed in boxing shorts and boxing gloves. At a signal from one of the adults in the ring, the two boys touch gloves and begin to box. The fight lasts two rounds, during which time each of the boys knocks the other down. The boys stop boxing and start wrestling. To break up the fight, one of the adults throws a bucket of water on the boys.

A Scrap in the Dressing Room

AM&B © H40812   Jan. 12, 1904

Cameraman: A. E. Weed

Location: Studio, N.Y.C. *Photographed:* Dec. 10, 1903

16 ft.   FLA3936 (print)   FRA1148 (neg.)

Four women are visible when the film begins. Two are sitting on chairs watching the others roll about the floor, hitting each other and pulling one another's hair. Another young woman, not visible at the beginning of the film, passes the camera position and leaves the set of the backstage dressing room, returning with a man who stops the fight. All of the women are dressed in the scanty costumes of chorus girls.

See also: The Gerry Society's Mistake

Scrub Yacht Race

See: Scout Yacht Race

Scrubbing Clothes

AM&B © H55399   Jan. 3, 1905

Cameraman: G. W. Bitzer

Location: Navy Yard, Portsmouth, N.H. *Photographed:* Dec. 7, 1903

25 ft.   FLA3901 (print)   FRA1121 (neg.)

A large group of naval recruits is shown at a clothes-washing area in a naval training station. Only the many naval recruits wearing summer whites and scrubbing their clothes are shown.

See also: Obstacle Race

The Sculptor's Nightmare

AM&B © H110169   May 4, 1908

Cameraman: G. W. Bitzer

Cast: D. W. Griffith, Mack Sennett

Location: Studio, N.Y.C. *Photographed:* Apr. 18 and 20, 1908

266 ft.   FLA5692 (print)   FRA2530 (neg.)

This comedy is primarily a political satire, and the first scene takes place in a political club where the members are trying to agree on whose bust will replace the one they have of Teddy Roosevelt. Unable to agree, all go to a sculptor's studio, where each bribes the artist to sculpt a bust of his favorite. Instead, the sculptor takes his model to dinner and becomes so inebriated that he is taken off to jail, where he has a nightmare. Three pedestals, each with a pile of sculptor's clay, appear, and, by the use of stop-action photography, the clay turns into excellent likenesses of Bryan, Fairbanks, and Taft. Each becomes animated, and one smokes a cigar. The last scene shows another pedestal with clay, out of which comes an animated bust of Teddy Roosevelt, complete with pince-nez.

Sea Gulls Following Fishing Boats

Edison © H12583   Jan. 6, 1902

Location: San Francisco

58 ft.   FLA4862 (print)   FRA1873 (neg.)

The photographer positioned his camera on the bridge deck of a motor-propelled fishing vessel. One member of the fishing boat's crew is seen throwing fish bait over the stern of the vessel. This attracts a great number of sea gulls; they drag the water to catch the pieces of fish tossed into the wake of the vessel.

Sea Gulls in Central Park

AM&B © H35639   Sept. 12, 1903

Cameraman: F. S. Armitage

Location: The reservoir in Central Park, N.Y.C. *Date:* June 30, 1901

16 ft.   FLA3369 (print)   FRA0672 (neg.)

The film, photographed from a single-camera position, shows an area of approximately one acre covered with sea gulls feeding. The last few feet of film show them starting to fly away.

The Sea Lions' Home

Edison © 60577   Oct. 25, 1897

25 ft.   FLA3074 (print)   FRA0415 (neg.)

The camera was positioned on a boat to show an area selected by sea lions as their habitat. Ten to thirty sea lions of various sizes are seen entering and leaving the water.

Sea Waves

Edison © 16440   Mar. 10, 1898

Location: Long Branch, N.J.

24 ft.   FLA4287 (print)   FRA1439 (neg.)

The camera was positioned above the tide line to show the waves breaking on a wooden stake fence, with the stakes about four feet apart. About ten waves break against the prepared sea wall.

The Sealed Room

Biograph © J131224   Sept. 3, 1909

Director: D. W. Griffith *Cameraman:* G. W. Bitzer

Cast: Henry B. Walthall, Arthur Johnson, Marion Leonard, George Nicholls, William J. Butler, Mary Pickford

Location: Studio, N.Y.C. *Photographed:* July 22–23, 1909

291 ft.   FLA5693 (print)   FRA2529 (neg.)

All the actors and actresses wore period costumes in this drama which was photographed from a single-camera position. A king (Arthur Johnson) suspects that his wife (Marion Leonard) is having an affair with a minstrel (Henry B. Walthall) in his court, and he sets a trap for them. After telling them he is going on a trip, he returns unannounced and finds his wife and the minstrel making love in a room with a single exit. Showing no emotion whatsoever, the noble orders the bricklayers to seal up the doorway. After they have completed their task and gone, the king vents his spleen by beating his sword against the sealed wall. The last scene shows the unfaithful wife and her paramour suffocating together in the sealed room.

A Search for the Evidence

AM&B © H34099   Aug. 3, 1903

Cameraman: G. W. Bitzer

Cast: Kathryn Osterman

Location: Studio, N.Y.C. *Date:* July 16-17, 1903

85 ft.   FLA5196 (print)   FRA2455 (neg.)

A woman and her escort are looking through keyholes in a set of a hotel corridor; they are apparently searching for someone. Their progression down the hall is always from right to left, as the same set is used several times. Each time the woman approaches one of the doors, she bends down and looks through the keyhole. The camera lens was matted to resemble the shape of the key aperture and the scenes are from the point of view of the person looking through the keyhole. To build up suspense, each room discloses a different scene, such as ill people, drunk people, people preparing to retire, people playing cards, and finally, the evidence they seek is found. In the last room are the woman's husband and his paramour. The wife and her escort attempt to break into the room. The camera is turned around and put inside the room to show the terror and excitement of the two transgressors as they try unsuccessfully to hide. The film ends with the broken-hearted wife now certain of her husband's infidelity. Author's note: This film made by a competitive company predates The Great Train Robbery.

Searching Ruins on Broadway, Galveston, for Dead Bodies

Edison © D18566 Sept. 24, 1900
Location: Galveston, Tex. *Photographed:* Sept. 1900
29 ft. FLA4080 (print) FRA1264 (neg.)
[Galveston, Texas, Hurricane and Tidal Waves]

Exactly as its title indicates, the film shows laborers clearing away the wreckage left by the hurricane in the city of Galveston in 1900.

The Seashore Baby

AM&B © H48621 July 28, 1904
Cameraman: G. W. Bitzer
Location: Coney Island, N.Y. *Photographed:* July 20, 1904
36 ft. FLA3292 (print) FRA0608 (neg.)

A small child in baby clothes sits on the sand playing with sea shells and occasionally looking at the camera.

Seashore Frolics

Edison © H35063 Aug. 26, 1903
Cameraman: Edwin S. Porter
Location: Atlantic City, N.J. *Photographed:* Aug. 17, 1903
84 ft. FLA5197 (print) FRA2156 (neg.)

The film illustrates what would be filmed by an itinerant moving picture cameraman of the era at a seaside resort. The intent expressions on the faces of the people photographed is evidence that they were directed in their activities. A mixed group of people in bathing attire performs such games as leapfrog, wrestling, etc., for the benefit of the photographer. One of the scenes shows a still photographer in a white suit attempting to film the revelers, who apparently are in a gay mood, as they are shown accosting the photographer and tossing him bodily into the ocean. As the film ends, they are retrieving him.

A Seashore Gymkana

AM&B © H23779 Nov. 11, 1902
22 ft. FLA3503 (print) FRA0783 (neg.)

The film was photographed on the shore of a beach inlet near the shallow water to show the organized play of several bathers. The activities consist of jousting from rowboats, and a mixed group attempting to race by swimming while propelling wooden tubs.

Second Childhood

See: The Seven Ages

2nd Special Service Battalion, Canadian Infantry, Embarking for So. Africa

Edison © 72832 Nov. 7, 1899
83 ft. FLA4867 (print) FRA1874 (neg.)

The photographer set his camera at shoulder height to film the uniformed troops boarding a ship. There are two camera positions, both showing the infantry troops in columns moving aboard up the gangway.

2nd Special Service Battalion, Canadian Infantry—Parade

Edison © 72831 Nov. 7, 1899
82 ft. FLA5198 (print) FRA2157 (neg.)

The film begins from a single-camera position located to command a view of the crowd-lined street in a business district of an unidentified city. Marching directly toward the camera is a column of infantry, approximately of battalion strength. The distance to the marching infantry is such that identification of any specific individual is impossible.

Secretary Long and Captain Sigsbee

Edison © 25335 Apr. 21, 1898
Location: Washington, D.C.
23 ft. FLA3354 (print) FRA0660 (neg.)
[Spanish-American War]

The camera was placed to keep in view most of the State Department building. In the foreground, people can be seen descending the stairs. One of the men is attired in a frock coat and tall silk hat. Judging from the gestures, the other two are deferring to the Secretary. The film ends as they turn at the bottom of the stairs and walk toward the camera. Captain Sigsbee commanded the *Maine* until it was destroyed in Havana harbor.

Sec'y Taft's Address & Panorama

AM&B © H45956 May 13, 1904
Cameraman: A. E. Weed
Location: St. Louis *Photographed:* Apr. 30, 1904
49 ft. FLA5199 (print) FRA2158 (neg.)
[Louisiana Purchase Exposition]

As the title indicates, Secretary Taft is shown as he addresses a considerable number of people who are crowded around replicas of various state buildings in Washington, D.C.

Section of Buster Brown Series, Showing a Sketch of Buster by Outcault

Edison © H43260 Mar. 12, 1904
Cameraman: Edwin S. Porter
Location: Studio, N.Y.C.
38 ft. FLA3326 (print) FRA0638 (neg.)

The camera shows an office wall against which an easel with a white piece of paper is leaning. Standing in front of the easel is a gentleman in a tailcoat and morning trousers. He nods his head to either the cameraman or the man directing the scene, to indicate that he is ready, picks up a piece of black crayon, and starts to draw a picture of a small boy and his dog. The artist was Mr. Outcault, creator of the comic strip called "Buster Brown and His Dog Tige."

See-Saw Scene

Edison © 31441 May 20, 1898

22 ft. FLA3040 (print) FRA0248 (neg.)

The camera is positioned to overlook a yard area where there are piles of lumber. The yard is surrounded by a fence, and on the other side of the fence can be seen commercial buildings constructed of wood. Two adults are in the foreground on a seesaw made of a long, heavy piece of lumber placed on a fulcrum point made of more large, heavy pieces of lumber. One of the men is approached by a third man with a bucket filled with water. As he jumps on the seesaw, the bucket filled with water splashes on his companion on the other end of the seesaw.

Seeing Boston

AM&B © H72715 Feb. 1, 1906

Cameraman: G. W. Bitzer

Location: Boston *Photographed:* Jan. 8, 1906

175 ft. FLA5200 (print) FRA2866 (neg.)

In 1906 a cameraman boarded a streetcar in Boston and rode around the city wherever that vehicle took him. The film is exceptional because it shows Boston's public buildings, its squares, and subway construction, as well as the large public library.

Seeing New York by Yacht

AM&B © H36560 Oct. 6, 1903

Cameraman: A. E. Weed

Location: N.Y.C. *Photographed:* Sept. 6, 1903

84 ft. FLA5201 (print) FRA2159 (neg.)

The camera platform from which this film was shot was vibrating so badly and the pilot of the boat and/or the cameraman were so unaware of physical problems this caused that very little of what was photographed can be identified. This film was a record of a tour around New York, under bridges and in and out of inlets, etc., but none of the scenes is actually of benefit for viewing purposes.

The Seeress

AM&B © H40755 Jan. 11, 1904

Cameraman: A.E. Weed

Location: Studio, N.Y.C. *Photographed:* Dec. 31, 1903

18 ft. FLA4394 (print) FRA1524 (neg.)

Two people are sitting at a table in front of a drape or curtain. One of the people is a man costumed as a black mammy, while the other is a young lady interested in the intricacies of having her fortune told by cards. The only action is of the young woman watching the cards as they are shuffled and spread on the table before her.

The Serenaders

AM&B © H23801 Nov. 11, 1902

Cameraman: F. S. Armitage

Location: Roof studio, N.Y.C. *Date:* May 25, 1899

18 ft. FLA3667 (print) FRA0920 (neg.)

The film is short and does not permit too much description. However, this vaudeville turn was performed on a set that looks like a two-story building. The camera was positioned as if in the audience. Two men play trombones in front of the building while a woman in the second-floor window shows her disapproval. One of the two troubadors kicks the other in the posterior, and he sails from the stage to the second-floor window. The picture ends there.

Serious Sixteen

Biograph © J143502 July 23, 1910

Cameramen: Arthur Marvin, G. W. Bitzer

Cast: Florence La Badie, Mae Marsh, Mack Sennett, Lottie Pickford, William J. Butler, Billy Quirk

Location: Delaware Water Gap, N.J. *Photographed:* June 8,9 and 13, 1910

220 ft. FLA5694 (print, copy 1) FLA5718 (print, copy 2) FRA2687 (neg.)

A young man (Billy Quirk) and his girl (Lottie Pickford) ask her father (William J. Butler) for permission to marry. He refuses. Brokenhearted, the girl decides to join the Salvation Army, while the boy decides to become a Trappist monk. Their mutual friends are very amused and refuse to take their new plans very seriously. The film ends when the father comes home with a large box containing a new bonnet, and the young girl finds it impossible to resist worldly objects. Instead, she hits her relieved boyfriend over the head with the box. This whole film is played lightly, with an attempt to create humor.

Serving Rations to the Indians, no. 1

Edison © 13561 Feb. 24, 1898

Location: New Mexico or Colorado [?]

27 ft. FLA4382 (print) FRA1517 (neg.)

The single-camera position shows what appears to be a government log cabin. Indians come out of a door of the cabin carrying flour or grain sacks in their arms.

Serving Rations to the Indians, no. 2

Edison © 13562 Feb. 24, 1898

Location: New Mexico or Colorado [?]

19 ft. FLA4382 (print) FRA1518 (neg.)

The film was photographed from a single-camera position. A log house with two doors facing the camera can be seen as the film begins. During the film, several Indians laden with supplies exit through the doors and walk desultorily toward the camera.

Settled at the Seaside

Keystone © LP4876 Mar. 29, 1915

Producer and Author: Mack Sennett

Cast: Mae Busch, Charles Chase, Nick Cogley, W. C. Hauber, Billie Brockwell

Location: Santa Monica and Venice, Calif.

300 ft. FLA5661 (print)

Charlie Chase and his girl (Mae Busch) are sitting on a bench on a boardwalk, and he gives her an engagement ring. Nick Cogley is pushing a sedan chair containing his wife along the boardwalk. Cogley becomes so entranced with the pretty girl he lets go of the cart. The chair rolls downhill, heads for the merry-go-round and follows it round and round. Mae Busch, in the meantime, has gone over to the hot dog stand for something to eat, but when she has no money the vendor will not serve her. Chase comes along then and is very angry because Cogley is paying so much attention to his girl. She becomes angry, they have a fight and she returns his engagement ring. She and Nick Cogley are playing in the water when his wife finds them and goes out on the diving board, yelling at him to come out of the water immediately. He holds his nose and dives under the water to escape her. Charlie and Mae make up, he gives back the engagement ring, and all is well between them.

Settler's Home Life

AM&B © H35878 Sept. 21, 1903

Cameraman: Wallace McCutcheon

Location: The Adirondacks, N.Y. *Photographed:* Sept. 11, 1903

78 ft. FLA5202 (print) FRA2160 (neg.)

A woman in rough clothing is working with some cooking utensils on a stump in front of a cabin in a heavily wooded area. A man dressed in animal skins and carrying a muzzle-loading rifle appears. The cabin door opens and a barefooted young girl comes out, goes over to the man, relieves him of his kill and rifle, and returns to the cabin. The man walks over to the woman who is preparing food, kisses her, removes his jacket, and begins chopping wood. As soon as the wood chopping is completed, he enters the cabin and the film ends.

See also: Firing The Cabin, Discovery Of Bodies, and Rescue of Child From Indians

The Seven Ages

Edison © H57124–31 Feb. 27, 1905

Cameraman: Edwin S. Porter

Location: Studio, N.Y.C. *Photographed:* Feb. 23, 1905

200 ft. Infancy:FLA4069 (print) FRA1253 (neg.)

Playmates:FLA4070 (print) FRA1254 (neg.)

Schoolmates:FLA4071 (print) FRA1255 (neg.)

The Lovers:FLA4072 (print) FRA1256 (neg.)

The Soldier:FLA4073 (print) FRA1257 (neg.)

The Judge:FLA4074 (print) FRA1258 (neg.)

Second Childhood:FLA4075 (print) FRA1259 (neg.)

What Age?:FLA4076 (print) FRA1260 (neg.)

Each segment is preceded by a title and each is followed by a scene depicting the stage in life mentioned. The basic idea of the film is secondary because the producer-director-cameraman, Porter, made the film as a series of short scenes in which to work out some primary photographic problems. These were: reflected light, increasing light intensity, as well as back and side lighting. All of these problems are brought out in the film, such as in the instance of the old couple in front of the fireplace. The only source of light is the sun reflected through the fireplace. The film copyrighted as What Age? was released separately under the title Old Maid and Pet Cat.

Seven Days

Klaw & Erlanger © LP2470 Mar. 23, 1914

Cast: Dave Morris, Charles Hill Mailes, Louise Orth, Florence Lee, Jack Pickford, Walter Miller, Jack Dillon, Mrs. LaVarnie, Charles Fuller, Augusta Anderson

1,266 ft. FLA5938 (print) FRA2801 (neg.)

Approximately a dozen persons of varied social position are quarantined for seven days in the home of a wealthy man whose servant is suspected of having smallpox. The host, recently divorced, has a substitute wife in order to convince his rich aunt he is still married, the cook has a policeman who dropped in for coffee, and all the others have problems they do not wish the others to learn about, and the film shows their constant and humorous anxiety. The film ends when it is discovered that the Japanese servant does not have smallpox after all. A considerable amount of money was spent on the sets and the wardrobe.

1776, or, the Hessian Renegades

Biograph © J131458 Sept. 9, 1909

Director: D. W. Griffith *Cameramen:* G. W. Bitzer, Arthur Marvin

Cast: Kate Bruce, William J. Butler, James Kirkwood, Mary Pickford, Owen Moore, Gertrude Robinson, Arthur Johnson, Billy Quirk, George Nicholls, Dorothy West, Mack Sennett

Location: Cuddebackville, N.Y.; Studio, N.Y.C. *Photographed:* July 26 and Aug.2–3, 1909

371 ft. FLA5695 (print) FRA2531 (neg.)

The story line is built around a skirmish between the British soldiers and the American colonists during the revolutionary war. The interiors were sets but the exteriors were an existing house and the surrounding countryside. The action begins with an attempt by Hessian troops to capture a Colonial army messenger who hides in his father's farmhouse. The farmer, his wife, and daughters are all there when the Hessian troops arrive in hot pursuit. The farmhouse is searched thoroughly. The messenger, hiding in a clotheshamper, is shot by the leader of the British troops. One of the farmer's daughters (Mary Pickford) tricks the outside sentry and changes into his uniform to allow her father (James Kirkwood) to rouse the countryside. The film ends as the neighboring farmers led by the father, defeat and capture the Hessian soldiers.

The Seventh Day

Biograph © J130912 Aug. 27, 1909

Director: D. W. Griffith *Cameraman:* G. W. Bitzer

Cast: Rose King, Frank Powell, Mack Sennett, James Kirkwood, Gladys Egan, Jeanie Macpherson, Arthur Johnson, Owen Moore, Mary Pickford

Location: Studio, N.Y.C. *Photographed:* June 5 and 8, 1909

249 ft. FLA5696 (print) FRA2532 (neg.)

A young socialite (Rose King) is more devoted to social events than to her three children. When her husband (Frank Powell) objects, she seeks a divorce and custody of the children. There is a scene in an attorney's office. The attorney decides the children should make up their minds which parent they prefer and a seven-day trial period is set up. Mother continues her social whirl, the children long for their father, but on the seventh day their nursemaid meets with an accident. The mother is forced to stay home with the children and gradually she becomes so delighted with them that she forgets her appointment in court. The judge and her husband find her and a reconciliation follows.

Seventh Regiment, N.Y.

AM&B © H21312 Aug. 25, 1902

Cameraman: F. S. Armitage

Location: Dewey Parade, N.Y.C. *Photographed:* Sept. 30. 1899

21 ft. FLA3489 (print) FRA0770 (neg.)

The poor condition of the film does not permit much detailed description. The camera was positioned over the heads of marching troops. The men are dressed in special period uniforms consisting of white trousers, gray jackets with crossed white sashes, and revolutionary war hats. They carry what appear to be old-fashioned muskets. Three companies march by.

71st New York Volunteers Embarking for Santiago

Edison © 38239 June 22, 1898
38 ft. FLA4127 (print) FRA1301 (neg.)
[Spanish-American War]

The 71st New York Volunteers are shown as they embark to take part in the Spanish-American War. The film shows very little more than soldiers milling about on the dock.

71st Regiment, Camp Wyckoff

AM&B © H16645 Apr. 16, 1902
Cameraman: F. S. Armitage
Date: Oct. 1899
29 ft. FLA4868 (print) FRA1875 (neg.)

The camera was positioned in an area that appears to be a parade ground of an army encampment. In the background are some standard white U.S. Army canvas tents. Two men in American cavalry uniforms march by. They are followed by a band and several companies of American troops in full military field outfits. AM&B bulletin says it is the 71st Regiment "after their return from the Cuban campaign."

Sham Battle at the Pan-American Exposition

Edison © H10816 Nov. 25,1901
Location: Buffalo, N.Y. *Photographed:* Nov. 2, 1901
128 ft. FLA5203 (print) FRA2161 (neg.)

Large arches and columns are seen surrounding a flat field. In the foreground of the field, some American Indians on horseback ride toward the camera. The Indians are wearing feathers, warpaint, and are carrying frontier rifles across the bare backs of their horses. In the middle of this flat area, men dressed as U.S. Army troops in battle regalia are lined up in the position of skirmishers. They fire at the Indians, who gallop by. The troops move over this flat area while the Indians on horseback circle them.

"Shamrock" After Carrying Away Topsail

AM&B © H26954 Jan. 14, 1903
Cameraman: Francis S. Armitage
Location: Off Sandy Hook, N. J.
Date: Oct. 17, 1899
18 ft. FLA3314 (print) FRA0628 (neg.)
[America's Cup Races]

From a single-camera position, approximately a thousand yards away, a racing yacht with a tug close aboard can be seen. The yacht has lost her topmast but is still under sail, heading to the wind to protect her sail from the broken piece of mast hanging from the stump.

"Shamrock" and "Columbia" Rounding the Outer Stake Boat

Edison © 69349 Oct. 24, 1899
Cameraman: Edwin S. Porter
Location: Off Sandy Hook, N. J.
Photographed: Oct. 1899

44 ft. FLA4869 (print, copy 1) FLA4870 (print, copy 2) FRA1876 (neg.,copy 1) FRA1877 (neg.,copy 2)
[America's Cup Races]

The camera has an unobstructed view seaward. To the right on the horizon is an anchored vessel flying the yacht club colors of a stake boat. Entering the picture from camera left is a racing yacht under full sail, close-hauled. She can be seen rounding the stake boat at the same time that another racing yacht enters the picture.

"Shamrock" and "Columbia" Rounding the Outer Stake Boat

Edison © 69557 Oct. 25, 1899
Cameraman: Edwin S. Porter
Location: Off Sandy Hook, N.J.
Photographed: Oct. 1899
57 ft. FLA4871 (print) FRA1878 (neg.)
[America's Cup Races]

The camera was located on a spectator vessel observing the race between two large racing sloops for the America's Cup. The ships are seen from camera right approaching the stake boat; the yachts are maneuvered to come about, and proceed on a different tack. The distance between the racing yachts and the camera is about one thousand yards.

"Shamrock" and "Columbia" Yacht Race—First Race

Edison © 68178 Oct. 20, 1899
Cameraman: Edwin S. Porter
Location: Off Sandy Hook, N.J.
Photographed: Oct. 1899
80 ft. FLA4871 (print) FRA1878 (neg.)
[America's Cup Races]

An anchored boat can be seen from the camera position. It flies the flags of two yacht clubs and the anchor ball of a turning vessel. Then one of the two contestants for the America's Cup enters the picture. The remainder of the film shows one or the other of the two contenders rounding the stake boat.

"Shamrock" and "Columbia" Yacht Race—1st Race, no. 2

Edison © 72834 Nov. 7, 1899
Cameraman: Edwin S. Porter
Location: Off Sandy Hook, N.J.
Photographed: Oct. 1899
45 ft. FLA5204 (print) FRA2162 (neg.)
[America's Cup Races]

Despite the poor quality of the film, there are some views of both racing yachts, contenders in the America's Cup Races, on a starboard and port tack in racing position. At the end there is a photograph of a coastal trading schooner under full sail.

"Shamrock" and "Erin" Sailing

Edison © 69556 Oct. 25, 1899
Cameraman: Edwin S. Porter
Photographed: Oct. 1899
48 ft. FLA4872 (print) FRA1879 (neg.)
[America's Cup Races]

Photographed from a single-camera position on a boat, the film of both the race and the contenders is good.

Shanghai Police

Edison © 38220 June 22, 1898
Cameraman: James H. White, W. Bleckyrden
Location: Shanghai
20 ft. FLA3230 (print) FRA0554 (neg.)

The photographer placed his camera across the courtyard in front of the main gate of the garrison headquarters of the police force in Shanghai, China. As the film progresses, the gates open and several companies of turbaned, bearded Sikhs dressed in police uniforms march past the camera position.

Shanghai Street Scene, Scene 1

Edison © 38219 June 22, 1898
Cameraman: James H. White, W. Bleckyrden
Location: Shanghai
28 ft. FLA4451 (print) FRA1555 (neg.)

The poor quality and short length of the film do not permit much description. However, it is possible to see Chinese coolies propelling one- and two-wheeled carts; horse-drawn vehicles with produce or passengers on them; and a considerable number of people walking by the camera position. There are some buildings in the background but these cannot be identified.

Shanghai Street Scene, Scene 2

Edison © 38218 June 22, 1898
Cameraman: James H. White, W. Bleckyrden
Location: Shanghai
27 ft. FLA4452 (print) FRA1555 (neg.)

During the course of this rather short film, the cameraman was able to capture a considerable amount of activity on a wide street in Shanghai, China. Several Caucasian men in one- and two-wheeled vehicles can be seen being propelled by Chinese coolies. Many different types of horse- and man-drawn vehicles also pass by the camera position. Several large buildings can be seen in the background.

She Banked in Her Stocking

See: Robbed of Her All

She Fell Fainting Into His Arms

AM&B © H36563 Oct. 6, 1903
Cameraman: G. W. Bitzer
Location: Studio, N.Y.C. *Photographed:* Sept. 29, 1903
22 ft. FLA4239 (print) FRA1396 (neg.)

A man lounges in an armchair while a woman with her back to the camera straightens some articles on a sideboard in a set of a living room of a house. The little man who was reclining in the chair gets up and places a spring-wound mouse on the floor directly behind the woman. She sees the toy and faints. The man attempts to support the weight of the woman, who is much taller and heavier than he, but they land in a heap on the floor as the picture ends.

She Kicked on the Cooking

AM&B © H41752 Feb. 2, 1904
Cameraman: A. E. Weed

Location: Studio, N.Y.C. *Photographed:* Jan. 9, 1904
22 ft. FLA4336 (print) FRA1482 (neg.)

A young woman en dêshabille is standing over a chafing dish on a stool in the center of a set of a woman's bedroom. Another young woman enters the scene and watches the proceedings. She is followed by a third young woman who is very well dressed and who appears to object to what is being prepared in the chafing dish. The cook holds some of the ingredients under the nose of one of the young ladies for approval. The other woman hoists her skirts and kicks the food-filled plate, splashing the contents all over the room.

She Meets With Wife's Approval

AM&B © H21499 Sept. 5, 1902
Cameraman: Robert K. Bonine
Location: Roof studio, N.Y.C. *Date:* July 21, 1902
21 ft. FLA3234 (print) FRA0558 (neg.)

A young woman stenographer and her male employer are sitting at their desks on a set of a business office. A tall woman, severely dressed, and peering through a lorgnette enters through a door marked "Private." She walks toward the man, leans over, kisses him, and apparently satisfies herself that the young woman at the typewriter is nothing more than a stenographer. She turns and leaves through the same door. The man moves over very close to the stenographer and begins kissing her.

She Ran Away

See: The Downward Path

She Wanted to Rise in the World

AM&B © H41751 Feb. 2, 1904
Cameraman: A. E. Weed
Location: Studio, N.Y.C. *Photographed:* Jan. 9, 1904
22 ft. FLA4372 (print) FRA1511 (neg.)

Three young women can be seen in a bedroom set. They apparently are attempting to amuse themselves on a swing suspended from the ceiling of their boudoir. One of the fun-loving young women hooks the end of the swing rope to the belt of one of her companions and hoists her up in the air. The film ends as she is being harassed by her two companions as she is suspended in the air by the belt of her dress.

She Would Be an Actress

Lubin Mfg. Co. © J132445 Aug. 5, 1909
Cast: Lottie Briscoe, Kempton Greene, Leonard Shumway
Location: Philadelphia
167 ft. FLA5697 (print) FRA2533 (neg.)

A young wife wants to be an actress but her husband does not approve. The first scene is a close-up of a woman reading from a book "How to Become and Actress." While she is dancing to a street hurdy-gurdy, an agent sees her and books her into a local beer garden. Her husband disguises himself as a waiter and gets a job at the same place. When she has a backstage tete-a-tete arranged by the management with a stage-door Johnny, the husband-waiter becomes so jealous he throws the suitor through the window. The film ends with a close-up of the husband and wife embracing, as they realize how much they mean to each other.

Shearing a Donkey in Egypt

Edison © H32806 June 17, 1903
Cameraman: A. C. Abadie
Location: Cairo *Photographed:* Mar. 25, 1903
42 ft. FLA4873 (print) FRA1880 (neg.)

The subject is a group of approximately ten men standing around a small Egyptian donkey. They are shearing the animal by the use of various cutting implements such as shears, short and long bladed knives, etc. All are attired in burnooses and turbans.

Sheep and Lambs

AM&B © H25961 Dec. 31, 1902
Cameraman: G. W. Bitzer [?]
Location: Brooklyn, N.Y. [?] *Date:* May 20, 1899 [?]
15 ft. FLA4161 (print) FRA1329 (neg.)

The film was photographed in a meadow near a river. A small flock of sheep, shepherded by two men and three dogs, pass the camera position.

Sheep Run, Chicago Stockyards

Edison © 43406 July 31, 1897
Location: Chicago
25 ft. FLA3071 (print) FRA0412 (neg.)

A large group of fully grown sheep is shown approaching the camera, which was located at the head of a sheep run in a stockyard.

Sheik Artillery, Hong Kong

Edison © 38232 June 22, 1898
Cameramen: James H. White, W. Bleckyrden
Location: Hong Kong
27 ft. FLA4303 (print) FRA1452 (neg.)

The poor quality of the film, coupled with its shortness, does not permit much description. However, during the course of the film, a group of Sikh soldiers may be seen at the base of a large artillery piece. One of the soldiers mounts the gun and begins to train it by working its mechanism.

Shelter Tent Drill

AM&B © H33884 July 28, 1903
Cameraman: A. E. Weed
Location: N.Y.C. *Date:* July 22, 1903
43 ft. FLA4874 (print) FRA1881 (neg.)

The subject is a contest between two infantry companies to see which unit can erect a row of shelter tents in the shortest length of time. However, the cameraman placed his equipment at too great a distance to permit a detailed view. It is only possible to see the two companies of infantry engaged in erecting the tents in a proper military manner.

See also: Battle Flags of the 9th U.S. Infantry

Sherlock Holmes Baffled

AM&B © H28561 Feb. 24, 1903
Cameraman: Arthur Marvin
Location: Roof studio, N.Y.C. *Date:* Apr. 26, 1900
18 ft. FLA3145 (print) FRA0478 (neg.)

A man dressed in rough clothes and wearing a face mask is seen tossing items in a sack he has placed on a table in the center of a set of a living room of a house. As he continues to fill the sack, the door opens and a man attired in a full-length dressing gown appears, taps the burglar on the shoulder and, with the use of stop-action photography, the man disappears. Apparently bemused by this, the man in the dressing gown sits down at the table, lights a cigar that blows up, and through the smoke he can see the burglar now sitting on the edge of the table. For the remainder of the film, the burglar appears and reappears several times. As the film ends, he reappears for the last time outside the house with the sack of loot in his hand.

Sherman Hill Tunnel

AM&B © H29153 Mar. 11, 1903
Cameraman: G. W. Bitzer
Location: Sherman Hill, Wyo. *Date:* July 8, 1901
57 ft. FLA4875 (print) FRA1882 (neg.)

The camera was positioned on the front of a railroad car traveling over a single track built on flat land that appears to be the "wash" land found mostly in the western part of the United States. Most of the film was taken on the approach to the tunnel and ends as the train emerges. Part of a series done for the Union Pacific Railroad.

See also: Council Bluffs Bridge Station

The Shocking Stockings

AM&B © H42034 Feb. 11, 1904
Cameraman: A. E. Weed
Location: Studio, N.Y.C. *Photographed:* Jan. 28, 1904
28 ft. FLA3654 (print) FRA0908 (neg.)

A set of a department store stocking counter is first visible. It is so arranged that the stockinged dummies' legs in the showcase appear to be part of the clerks behind the counter. A man and a woman approach the counter. The man sees the stockings, assumes they are on the legs of the clerk behind the counter, and puts on his glasses to get a better view. His wife, taken in by the same illusion, rushes over and stands in front of the dummy's legs with her skirt outstretched.

See also: Four Beautiful Pairs

Shoo Fly

AM&B © H32564 June 12, 1903
Cameraman: Arthur Marvin
Location: Studio, N.Y.C. *Date:* Aug. 28, 1900
10 ft. FLA3703 (print) FRA0951 (neg.)

A man can be seen sitting in a chair at a table in a set of a living room. An insect of some kind flits about his bald head. The man vainly attempts to catch or kill the insect. During the course of one of his most violent swings, a woman walks in through the door and is the recipient of his swing. She reacts by hitting him in return, and, as the film ends, the man is on his knees while the woman is striking him about the head and shoulders.

Shoot the Chutes Series

Edison © 61840 Sept. 23, 1899
Location: Coney Island, N.Y.
111 ft. FLA5205 (print) FRA2163 (neg.)

A shoot-the-chute ride in an amusement park is shown. People are riding in the little boats that go up and back down the slide. The film was photographed from four camera positions: at the bottom of a slide across the water; at the top of the slide showing people entering the boats and sliding down into the water; from one of the boats as it goes down the slide into the water and crosses the little pond to the opposite side. The last position shows the spectators watching the people slide down the chute.

Shooters' Parade, Philadelphia

AM&B © H55673 Jan. 6, 1905

Cameraman: G. W. Bitzer

Location: Philadelphia *Photographed:* Jan. 2, 1905

83 ft. FLA5206 (print) FRA2164 (neg.)

The film shows a parade through the downtown district of a large American city. Several large and eleborate floats are pulled through the streets by members of the organization. Spaced between the floats are numbers of people dressed in various costumes bordering on the ridiculous. They wear face masks, stilts, large noses, etc. Also in the parade are two minstrel bands.

Shooting Captured Insurgents

Edison © 46696 Aug. 5, 1898

Cameraman: William Paley

Location: Cuba

26 ft. FLA3063 (print) FRA0406 (neg.)

[Spanish-American War]

The first object visible is the remains of a large, brick-walled building covered with foliage, as though in a jungle. From camera right, approaching camera position, is a man dressed in the military uniform of an officer of the U.S. army carrying a saber. Behind him are marching men dressed in American enlisted men's uniforms carrying guns and escorting four men in civilian dress. The group halts in front of the brick wall. The men in military uniform line up and, at an order from the officer, fire and presumably kill the four civilians. This film is a reproduction of an incident that probably happened but was not filmed at the time.

See also: Cuban Ambush

Shooting Long Sault Rapids

AM&B © H30742 Apr. 24, 1903

Location: St. Lawrence River [?]

25 ft. FLA3390 (print) FRA0687 (neg.)

The camera was positioned low to the edge of a body of water, on which an excursion boat can be seen at a considerable distance. The vessel nears the camera position, and what appears to be a kayak or small canoe can be seen being paddled in the distance. The length and condition of the film, coupled with the distance of the camera from the subject, do not allow further clarification.

Shooting the Chutes

AM&B © H23789 Nov. 11, 1902

Location: Boston

Date: 1897 [?]

18 ft. FLA3127 (print) FRA2883 (neg.)

The camera was located to show the entry into the water of the boats used to carry passengers down a shoot-the-chute slide in an amusement park. During the film, five cars with at least two passengers each can be seen as they make their descent into the water, each passing by the camera position.

Shooting the Chutes at Luna Park

AM&B © H32296 May 29, 1903

Cameraman: G. W. Bitzer

Location: Coney Island, N.Y. *Date:* May 19, 1903

46 ft. FLA4876 (print) FRA2881 (neg.)

About ten boats are shown as they slide into a small pond built at the bottom of a shoot-the chutes in an amusement park. There is a bridge over the pond, where spectators can watch the participants as they slide down the chute and into the water.

Shooting the Chutes, Luna Park

AM&B © H34521 Aug. 13, 1903

Cameraman: G. W. Bitzer

Location: Coney Island, N.Y. *Date:* July 3, 1903

42 ft. FLA4877 (print) FRA2880 (neg.)

The camera was positioned to view the shoot-the-chutes concession from the best location. A special added attraction for the entertainment of the spectators is a man in a swimming suit who rides down the shoot-the-chutes on one ski.

Shortening and Furling Sails

AM&B © H19652 July 2, 1902

Cameraman: G. W. Bitzer

Location: Annapolis, Md. *Date:* Apr. 29, 1901

44 ft. FLA4878 (print) FRA1883 (neg.)

The camera was positioned at an altitude and distance to show what appears to be sail-furling exercises on a large sailing vessel outfitted like a training ship. The full-rigged ship is tied to a dock and very little of the hull is visible. AM&B production records say the ship is the U.S.S. Chesapeake.

Shot in the Excitement

Keystone © LP3619 Oct. 26, 1914

Producer and Author: Mack Sennett

Cast: Al St. John, Alice Howell, Joe Swickard, Eddie Cline (one of two policemen)

Location: Back lot of Keystone studio, Los Angeles

329 ft. FLA6138 (print)

Father (Joe Swickard) and daughter (Alice Howell) are painting a fence when one of her suitors (Al St. John) comes by with a box of candy. While they embrace, they are being watched through a hole in the fence by a jealous second suitor. He initiates a number of pranks to disturb the couple, such as pouring water down a rain spout which lands on the father instead. The father climbs up on the roof in pursuit and is accidentally shot by Al St. John. Both men are ordered off the place by the father. The rejected suitor goes to the park, rigs a cannon to a park bench, and sends a fake note to the lovers to meet there. When they do, somehow suitor number one pushes suitor number two against the rigged park bench, causing the cannon to go off. From there on, there is a series of persons being chased by a cannon ball, culminating in suitor number two falling off a cliff, followed by a cannon ball and the two policemen, while the father/and the two lovers peer down at them.

Shredded Wheat Biscuit, no. 1
AM&B © H44656 Apr. 18, 1904
Cameraman: A. E. Weed
Location: Studio, N.Y.C. *Photographed:* Mar. 9, 1904
30 ft. FLA4326 (print) FRA1474 (neg.)

The single-camera position shows a man and a woman sitting at a small table on which there is a paper box bearing the words, "Shredded Wheat Biscuit." The woman places a biscuit from the box on a dish and hands it to the man, who consumes it with gusto.

Shriners' Conclave at Los Angeles, Cal., May, 1907
Miles Brothers © H94996 June 8, 1907
Cameraman: Herbert J. Miles [?]
Location: Los Angeles
24 ft. FLA3573 (print) FRA0846 (neg.)

A flat area where some men are executing close-order drill formations is shown. The camera was placed at a distance that does not allow much identification, either of persons or background. The title on the original paper print film includes the line "Turkish Patrol Drilling at Ascot Park."

Shuffleboard on S.S. "Deutschland"
Edison © H19315 June 25, 1902
27 ft. FLA4057 (print) FRA1242 (neg.)

A shipboard game called shuffleboard is played by a mixed group of adults on the deck of a large ocean liner. The camera was positioned so that the playing was directed at the camera.

See also: S.S. "DEUTSCHLAND" titles

Shut Up!
AM&B © H21502 Sept. 5, 1902
Cameraman: Robert K. Bonine
Location: Studio, N.Y.C. *Date:* Aug. 4, 1902
20 ft. FLA3889 (print) FRA1111 (neg.)

A woman is asleep in a Murphy bed. A man, walking unsteadily as though intoxicated, enters the bedroom and begins to undress. The woman wakens and begins to scold her husband, waving her arms wildly. The man is unsuccessful in attempting to quiet her. He retaliates by causing the Murphy bed to fold up against the wall with his jabbering wife inside, after which he sits down and continues his disrobing.

Si Jones Looking for John Smith
See: Looking for John Smith

Silhouette Scene
AM&B © H37831 Nov. 10, 1903
Cameraman: G. W. Bitzer
Location: Studio, N.Y.C. *Photographed:* Oct. 21, 1903
50 ft. FLA4879 (print) FRA1884 (neg.)

The story involves a man, a woman, and their serving maid. The first scene shows the man and the woman sitting and eating at a dining room table in a set. The maid comes in and starts clearing the table. The woman gets up, puts on her hat, and leaves, ending the first scene. Scene number two shows a set of the outside of a brick house. The woman, returning from her visit, sees the shadows of her bearded husband and the house maid as they embrace silhouetted against the window shade. This was accomplished by the use of trick photography. The irate wife goes inside, chases her husband around the table, and the film ends as the housemaid, dressed for the street with her bags packed, passes through the set.

Silveon and Emerie "On the Web"
AM&B © H34525 Aug. 13, 1903
Cameraman: G. W. Bitzer
Location: Studio, N.Y.C. *Photographed:* July 30, 1903
25 ft. FLA3717 (print)

This vaudeville or circus act was photographed from a single-camera position as if in the audience. One man in white tights climbs up a rope followed by another man wearing a back harness. The first man suspends the second, using his teeth, from a rope attached to the backstrap.

See: On the Flying Rings

The Silver Wedding
AM&B © H74337 Mar. 8, 1906
Cameraman: F. A. Dobson
Location: Studio, N.Y.C. *Photographed:* Mar. 1-2, 1906
264 ft. FLA5698 (print) FRA2534 (neg.)

The first scene shows individuals entering a place of business and renting costumes and accouterments for begging, etc. The second scene takes places in the home of a wealthy person where guests are looking at some wedding gifts. After the guests have gone to another room, the sliding door closes abruptly, the butler is hit on the head, and two of the persons who rented costumes for the occasion put the presents in a bag and leave. The remaining scenes show the chase and subsequent capture of the thieves by the police in a set of the interior of a sewer. During the scene where the burglars knock out the butler, the camera was moved in for a tight close-up of the gifts being stuffed into a sack, and then moved back out to the original establishing shot.

Simple Charity
Biograph © J147672 Nov. 14, 1910
Director: D. W. Griffith *Cameramen:* Arthur Marvin, G. W. Bitzer
Cast: Mary Pickford, W. Chrystie Miller, George Nicholls, Kate Bruce, Claire McDowell, William J. Butler, Edwin August, Verner Clarges, Grace Henderson
Location: Fort Lee, N.J.; Studio, N.Y.C. *Photographed:* Sept. 23–27, 1910
392 ft. FLA5699 (print) FRA6413 (neg.)

An act of charity by a young lady (Mary Pickford), a scrub woman in a tenement, toward an old couple who are less fortunate is the plot from which this film was made. An old man (W. Chrystie Miller) is discharged from his job as a cigar-maker because of his age and infirmity. He returns to his tenement home and eventually dies because of his poverty. The film ends as the tenement doctor (Edwin August) bestows a kiss on the cheek of the young scrub woman because she pawned the only treasure she had, her best dress, to help the old couple. It does not save the life of the old man, but it does bring a high point into the life of the young slavey.

The Simple Life
AM&B © H71531 Jan. 3, 1906
Cameraman: G.W. Bitzer
Location: Studio, N.Y.C. *Photographed:* Dec. 14, 1905
20 ft FLA3773 (print) FRA1017 (neg.)

On a set that appears to be a stone castle or a monastery is a table with bread, meat, a plate, and a knife and fork on it, as well as a large stein of beer. A man dressed as a friar or a member of some ecclesiastical order is sitting at the table, eating greedily, reading, and enjoying himself. For the full extent of the film, the man conveys the impression that he is thoroughly enjoying both eating and reading.

See also: The Jolly Monks Of Malabar, and Wine, Women and Song

Single Harness Horses
Edison © 60564 Oct. 25, 1897
Location: Long Branch, N.J.
25 ft. FLA3020 (print) FRA0086 (neg.)

A track at either a fairground or a racecourse is shown. Apparently a show or exhibit of show horses is in progress. Approaching the camera position are two-wheeled carriages pulled by harness horses. Several carriages pass.

La Sirene
See: The Mermaid

6th Cavalry Assaulting South Gate of Pekin
AM&B © H16739 Apr. 18, 1902
Cameraman: Raymond Ackerman
Location: Peking *Date:* Jan. 26, 1901
20ft FLA4078 (print) FRA1263 (neg.)

The film is in poor condition and grainy. Its short length and its condition present little chance for detailed explanation. However, men in uniform can be seen passing the camera position carrying firearms. A section of a Chinese city, obviously under attack, can be seen in the background.

69th Regiment, N.G.N.Y.
Edison © H32488 June 10, 1903
Cameraman: Edwin S. Porter
Location: Fifth Avenue and 26th Street, N.Y.C. *Photographed:* May 30, 1903
67 ft. FLA4880 (print) FRA1885 (neg.)

The film begins from a camera position over the heads of spectators lining a street to watch a parade of the N.Y. National Guard in full dress. The mounted officers wear hats feathered fore and aft while the headpieces of the enlisted personnel are steel and plumed.

Skating on Lake, Central Park
AM&B © H21313 Aug. 25, 1902
Cameraman: F. S. Armitage
Location: 72nd Street and Central Park, N.Y.C. *Date:* Feb. 5, 1900
28 ft. FLA3853 (print) FRA1064 (neg.)

The film, photographed from a single-camera position, shows a large number of persons of all ages skating on a frozen lake in Central Park in New York City.

Skee Club
AM&B © H16725 Apr. 18, 1902
Cameraman: Robert K. Bonine
Location: Quebec, Canada *Date:* Feb. 14, 1902·
10 ft. FLA3187 (print) FRA0513 (neg.)

The length of the film gives little opportunity for description. A snow-covered field can be seen where several preadolescent children are playing on skis. There is a small jump, and one of the skiers falls into the snow for the benefit of the camera.

Skeleton Dance, Marionettes
Edison © 59207 Oct. 7, 1898
26 ft. FLA3219 (print) FRA0543 (neg.)

The film was photographed from the audience's point of view in a theater where a puppet show was in progress. The light used was so brilliant that the details of the stage and the marionettes cannot be distinguished very well. The action consists of establishing a simulated human skeleton which then begins to dance.

See also: Balloon Ascension, Marionettes and Dancing Chinaman, Marionettes

Skidoo Brothers, 23
AM&B © H78534 June 1, 1906
Cameraman: G. W. Bitzer
Location: Studio, N.Y.C. *Photographed:* May 23-25, 1906
230 Ft. FLA5700 (print) FRA2677 (neg.)

This film is an elaboration of a vaudeville act consisting of two young men and their escapades. The climax of each incident is made possible by the use of stop-action photography, and each scene is preceded by a title. The film begins with the two young men dressing to call on some young ladies whose butler throws them out. They get into an automobile that blows up, and the last scene shows them in a hospital bed.

Skiing in Montreal
Edison © H14063 Feb. 10, 1902
Location: Montreal
30 ft. FLA3349 (print) FRA0657 (neg.)

The camera was positioned at the bottom of an incline of a snow-covered hill. Preadolescent boys slide down the hill toward the camera on sleds, skis, or toboggans. In two instances, they just run. The film is underexposed, which does not allow much opportunity for detail.

Skiing Scene in Quebec
Edison © H14294 Feb. 17, 1902
Location: Quebec
25 ft. FLA3336 (print) FRA0647 (neg.)

The camera was positioned to view a snow-covered field. At a distance is a ski jump about five feet high. A man skis toward the camera. He nears the incline, makes the jump, and falls. Several people can be seen skiing down the hill or going back up the incline.

Skinflint Treats Jones
See: How Jones Lost His Roll

Skinflint's Cheap Wine
See: How Jones Lost His Roll

Skirmish Between Russian and Japanese Advance Guards
Edison © H44263   Apr. 8, 1904
Cameraman: Edwin S. Porter
Location: Forest River Hill, N.J. *Photographed:* Apr. 2, 1904
232 ft.   FLA6701 (print)   FRA2374 (neg.)
[Russo-Japanese War]

The scenes were photographed and assembled to convey the idea of the rigors of infantry and artillery skirmishes in the Russo-Japanese War. There are four chapters in the reproduction of an event that possibly could have occurred. One is an establishing scene titled "Japanese Outpost on the Yalu River," and is followed by "The Attack," "The Capture," and "The Retreat." The picture begins with the Japanese soldiers of the infantry outpost doing calisthenics and raising the flag. Gestures indicate the enemy is near, and the group begins firing the field piece (approximately 75mm). As the film progresses, they are attacked by a larger groups of men dressed as Russian infantry, who demolish the camp and tear down the Japanese flag. The remaining two scenes show the regrouping and attack and recapture of the Japanese position by Japanese soldiers. The Russian flag is hauled down, and the Japanese flag is run up on the mast as the picture ends. All the scenes were photographed from a single-camera position.

Skirmish Fight
AM&B © H34812   Aug. 19, 1903
20 ft.   FLA4147 (print)   FRA1317 (neg.)

The action consists of a company of infantrymen attacking the camera position as if it were a bastion. The poor condition of the film and its short length do not permit much detail, not even the identification of the nationality or type of uniforms the soldiers wear. It is possible to see the trees through which they run, but little else.

Skirmish of Rough Riders
Edison © 38516   June 10, 1899
Cameraman: William Paley
Location: Cuba
35 ft.   FLA3973 (print)   FRA1181 (neg.)
[Spanish-American War]

Skirmish Between Russian and Japanese Advance Guards, a 1904 Edison film.

Details are difficult to describe inasmuch as the quality and graininess of the film do not permit much separation between black and white. However, as the film begins, it is possible to see in the immediate foreground three men struggling to hold down a horse. One of the three men occasionally discharges a pistol. A man who appears to be an American officer can be seen in full regalia astride a horse behind the crouched men. He carries an American flag. As the film ends, other mounted soldiers pass the camera position.

The Skyscrapers

AM&B © H86424 Dec.11, 1906

Cameraman: F. A. Dobson

Location: 12th Street and Broadway and Studio, N.Y.C.
  Photographed: Nov. 8, 14, and 15, 1906

284 ft. FLA5702 (print) FRA2682 (neg., copy 1) FRA2683 (neg., copy 2)

The subject of this melodrama is built around and during the actual construction of a skyscraper in New York City. The story begins with the antipathy of a construction foreman for one of his crew. He ultimately fires the workman, which leads the disgruntled employee to steal. The exemployee causes the blame to be put on the foreman, but he is exonerated when the thief is exposed. All of this conflict is woven in and around the actual construction of the building as the work is in progress. There is even one scene of a hand-to-hand fight between the foreman and the villain that takes place on the unprotected ledge of the steel framework of the building.

Sky Scrapers of New York City, From the North River

Edison © H32025 May 20, 1903

Cameraman: J. B. Smith

Location: North River, N.Y. *Photographed:* May 10, 1903

85 ft. FLA5208 (print) FRA2131 (neg.)

The film begins with a view of the New York skyline, buildings, bridges, etc., from the waterfront. The camera platform is a boat. The itinerary includes some of the best combinations of railroad and steamship docks then in existence. Most of the large buildings behind the New York waterfront dock area can be seen clearly.

The Slave

Biograph © J129866 July 30, 1909

Director: D. W. Griffith *Cameraman:* G. W. Bitzer

Cast: Florence Lawrence, James Kirkwood, Harry Salter, Mary Pickford, William J. Butler, Owen Moore, Henry B. Walthall, Mack Sennett, Kate Bruce, Gladys Egan, Marion Sunshine, Arthur Johnson

Location: Studio, N.Y.C. *Photographed:* June 22–23, 1909

373 ft. FLA5703 (print) FRA2535 (neg.)

This drama, which takes place in early Roman times, tells the story of an attractive young woman (Florence Lawrence) who declines to marry a noble (Harry Salter). She marries instead a poor sculptor (James Kirkwood). As time goes by, she is faced with illness and extreme poverty, and finally sells herself into slavery. An agent of the noble buys her for his master, who takes her back to her husband and gives her to him. The last scene was a special camera effect. It shows a dark screen with the light slowly coming up to photographic value and lighting up the faces of James Kirkwood and Florence Lawrence to show their happiness, then the lights go back down, leaving them in total darkness.

The Sleeper

AM&B © H22086 Sept. 27, 1902

21 ft. FLA3225 (print) FRA0549 (neg.)

A man is sitting on a park bench in front of a backdrop painted as a park. He appears to be sound asleep when two young boys stealthily approach him. They light firecrackers and other explosive materials under his feet, but fail to disturb him. The boys repeat their prank twice to no avail when a policeman arrives. He shakes the sleeping man to awaken him and points out that his coattail is on fire, just as the film ends. All of the film was photographed outdoors.

Sleeping Child

AM&B © H18893 June 12, 1902

Cameraman: F. S. Armitage

Location: Roof studio, N.Y.C. *Date:* June 11, 1901

8ft. FLA3796 (print) FRA1033 (neg.)

Two women wearing leotards are standing before a curtain in front of which there is a sign reading "Sleeping Child." They draw the curtain open to show a young girl in repose on some fake grass. The film ends as they close the curtains.

The Sleepy Soubrette

AM&B © H57147 Feb. 28, 1905

Cameraman: G. W. Bitzer

Location: Studio, N.Y.C. *Photographed:* Feb. 18, 1905

23 ft. FLA3771 (print) FRA1015 (neg.)

In the foreground of a set of a chorus girl's dressing room is a woman sleeping beneath a comforter. Two women enter through the door of the set, discover her, and proceed to tease her. They remove her blanket, and expose her bare legs. By the end of the film, the sleeper has been awakened by their tickling her feet and ear.

Sleighing in Central Park, New York

Edison © H43006 Mar. 4, 1904

Cameraman: Edwin S. Porter

Location: Central Park, N.Y.C. *Photographed:* Feb. 8, 1904

46 ft. FLA4883 (print) FRA1888 (neg.)

Photographed from a single-camera position, the film shows an intersected path in a wooden area on which horse-drawn sleighs can be seen traveling over the snow.

Sleighing Scene

Edison © 73462 Dec. 16, 1898

Location: West Side Drive, Central Park, N.Y.C.

23 ft. FLA3300 (print) FRA0614 (neg.)

The film, photographed from a single-camera position, shows what looks like a main road in a public park. Many people in various kinds of sleighs ride by the camera. Only two pedestrians appear.

Sleighing Scene, Boston

AM&B © H26855 Jan. 9, 1903

Location: Boston *Date:* 1898 [?]

20 ft. FLA3272 (print) FRA0288 (neg.)

The camera was placed in an area covered with snow to show people driving by in one- and two-horse sleighs. Because the cameraman started and stopped his camera, several horse cars and sleighs disappear and reappear, which adds a note of amusement.

Sleighs Returning After a Spin
AM&B © H26852 Jan. 9, 1903
Location: Boston [?] *Date:* 1898 [?]
17 ft. FLA3560 (print) FRA0836 (neg.)

The camera was located at the edge of a snow-covered thoroughfare. Approximately twenty horse-drawn sleighs pass by. The title on the original paper print film, Sleighers Returning After a Spin, evidently was a working title.

Slide for Life, Luna Park
AM&B © H36554 Oct. 6, 1903
Cameraman: G. W. Bitzer
Location: Coney Island, N.Y. *Photographed:* Sept. 26, 1903
60ft. FLA5209 (print) FRA2879 (neg.)

This shows an acrobatic team performing on a revolving flying ring unit suspended between the towers at Luna Park. During the film, the two female aerialists exhibit several feats of strength, daring, and skill, such as hanging by their teeth, feet, or fingers while revolving around the axis of the trapeze.

Sliding Down Ice Mound at Niagara Falls
Edison © H40908 Jan. 15, 1904
Cameraman: Edwin S. Porter
Location: Niagara Falls, N.Y. *Photographed:* Jan. 10, 1904
68 ft. FLA5210 (print) FRA2165 (neg.)

The camera was positioned on top of the ice bridge over Niagara Falls. The first scene is a pan shot of the suspension bridge that joins Canada and the United States. As the camera continues to pan, buildings on the bank are visible, as well as a group of about one hundred young boys sliding down the natural incline made by the snow and ice.

The Slippery Slide
AM&B © H32785 June 17, 1903
Cameraman: Robert K. Bonine
Date: May 6, 1901
10 ft. FLA3542 (print) FRA0818 (neg.)

The camera was positioned to show approximately fifty steps in front of a large public building. At the edge of the picture frame, a package slide down which many children are sliding can be seen. The children run up the stairs and slide down the slide, then repeat the action.

The Slocum Disaster
AM&B © H47443 June 22, 1904
Cameramen: G. W. Bitzer, F. A. Dobson
Location: East River, N.Y.C. *Date:* June 14 and 16, 1904
117 ft. FLA5211 (print) FRA2166 (neg.)

The *Slocum* disaster occurred on June 15, 1904, when an excursion vessel of that name exploded and capsized in Hell Gate, East River, New York. One thousand and thirty persons lost their lives in the catastrophe. This newsreel film shows bodies being recovered from the water.

Small Gun Drill, St. John's Academy
AM&B © H43625 Mar. 23, 1904
Cameraman: G. W. Bitzer
Location: Manlius, N.Y. *Photographed:* Mar. 12, 1904
26 ft. FLA3512 (print) FRA0790 (neg.)

The area encompassed by the camera is covered with snow. Two companies of boys dressed in military uniforms enter the camera area. Each company is pulling a two-wheeled field piece or small wagon. As they approach the camera position, they turn the weapon, load it, and execute a firing drill. Each weapon fires two rounds before the film ends.

Smallest Train in the World
AM&B © H32559 June 12, 1903
Cameraman: G. W. Bitzer
Date: June 29, 1899
13 ft. FLA3491 (print) FRA0772 (neg.)

The short length of the film does not allow much description beyond the fact that the camera was positioned to allow the viewer to see approximately two hundred feet of narrow track on which a miniature steam locomotive approaches the camera from a distance. It is pulling nine passenger cars. The locomotive was probably five feet long.

A Smoked Husband
AM&B © H115986 Sept. 21, 1908
Director: D. W. Griffith *Cameraman:* G. W. Bitzer
Cast: Florence Lawrence, John Cumpson, Robert Harron, Linda Arvidson, Robert Harron, Mack Sennett
Location: Studio and West 12th Street, N.Y.C. *Photographed:* Aug 26–27, 1908
172 ft. FLA5704 (print) FRA2536 (neg.)

This comedy starts when the poor husband is upset over his wife's extravagance and is further enraged when he finds that her dress has a slit on the side which shows his wife's leg. The plot is then confused by adding a maid whose boyfriend is a crook. The husband finds a note to the maid arranging a rendezvous, thinks it is from his wife's lover, and hides in the fireplace to spy. The fireplace is lit, the wife calls the police when she discovers the maid has packed some things to give to her boyfriend; the husband in the fireplace climbs out on the roof. He falls of the roof and lands on the heads and shoulders of two men standing near a large cement mixer. Another in a group of comedies known as the Jones series.

The Smoker
Biograph © J140142 Apr. 4, 1910
Director: D. W. Griffith *Cameraman:* Arthur Marvin
Cast: John Cumpson, Frank Opperman, Jack Pickford, Lottie Pickford, Mary Pickford, Billy Quirk, Dorothy West
Location: Glendale, Calif.; Studio, Los Angeles. *Photographed:* Feb. 4, 10, 11, and 21, 1910
235 ft. FLA5705 (print) FRA2537 (neg.)

The wife (Mary Pickford) objects to her husband (Billy Quirk) smoking in the house. Forced to give in or give up, he rents a retreat from a farmer so he can enjoy his pipe in peace. The scent he uses to hide the smell of the smoke makes his wife suspicious that there is another woman. The film ends with the wife sitting on her husband's lap outside the house, where he is smoking his pipe.

The Smoky Stove
AM&B © H37320 Oct. 26, 1903
Cameraman: A. E. Weed
Location: Studio, N.Y.C. *Photographed:* Sept. 30, 1903
56 ft. FLA5212 (print) FRA2167 (neg.)

The set is a fashionable living room, with a stove intended for heating it. A well-dressed young woman standing in front of the stove shows she is worried because it is not operating properly. A maid is summoned who works on the stove, lifting lids and so on. An explosion occurs, completely demolishing everything in the room. Before the explosion, a dummy is substituted for the maid, who returns after the debris stops falling. The worried lady of the house calls a policeman who, as the film ends, picks up the maid from the wreckage and helps her to leave the set.

A Snare for Lovers
AM&B © H43573 Mar. 22, 1904
Cameraman: A. E. Weed
Location: Studio, N.Y.C. *Photographed:* Mar. 7, 1904
19 ft. FLA3509 (print) FRA0787 (neg.)

A young man and a young woman are embracing in front of a set of a two-story house. A window directly above the lovers opens, and a woman can be seen peering down at them. She leaves the window and returns with a large coil of rope which she drops over the couple, pinning them in the cagelike device at the end of the rope. As the rope closes around the lovers, the first-floor door opens and a man brandishing a stick runs out and begins hitting the suitor over the head. This continues until the end of the film.

See also: Novel Way of Catching a Burglar

The Sneeze
See: Edison Kinetoscopic Record of a Sneeze, January 7, 1894

Snow Storm
Edison © 25337 Apr. 21, 1898
27 ft. FLA3101 (print) FRA0438 (neg.)

The film, photographed from a single-camera position, shows an area with a house in the background completely covered by snow. It is snowing. Two horse-drawn vehicles approach and go by the camera position, and one man carrying an umbrella walks by.

Snowballing the Coasters
Edison © 12176 Feb. 17, 1898
Location: Newark, N.J. [?]
26 ft. FLA3123 (print) FRA0457 (neg.)

The film, photographed from a single-camera position, shows about twenty-five preadolescent boys throwing snowballs. The target is not shown.

The Snowman
AM&B © H106282 Feb. 17, 1908
Director: Wallace McCutcheon, Sr. *Cameraman:* G. W. Bitzer
Cast: Wallace McCutcheon, Florence Auer

Location: Studio, N.Y.C. *Photographed:* Jan. 30-31, 1908
282 ft. FLA5706 (print) FRA2538 (neg.)

The subject of the film is an obstreperous snowman made by a group of children. When it becomes dark and the moon rises (shown by special effects), the snowman comes to life. The snowman frightens a black chicken stealer into turning the chickens loose, drinks whiskey from a bottle, smokes a pipe, becomes intoxicated, steals the stove from the schoolhouse, and does many other things during the night. When the children return in the morning, they find him asleep in the snow. He wakens and frightens the children and the schoolmistress. The picture ends as the frightened group of people, led by the equally frightened black man, hit the snowman with a pipe that turns him immediately into a human being.

Society Ballooning, Pittsfield, Mass.
AM&B © H76605 May 3, 1906
Cameraman: G. W. Bitzer
Location: Pittsfield, Mass. *Date:* April 14 and 18, 1906
211 ft. FLA5707 (print) FRA2539 (neg.)

At the beginning of the film, a group of men can be seen gathered around a flat area near a large municipal gas tank. Most of the group are attending to the skin of a big balloon in the foreground near the camera. The remainder of the film shows the balloon being filled with gas until it is buoyant enough to become airborne, the mounting of the suspended basket, the release of the balloon, and the actual flight. The balloon was the Centaur, which set the world's record of 1,193 miles in thirty-five hours during the contest at the Paris Exposition. Count Henri de la Vaulx, French aeronaut, and members of the Aero Club of America can be seen.

The Society Palmist
AM&B © H65051 Aug. 30, 1905
Cameraman: G. W. Bitzer
Location: Studio, N.Y.C. *Photographed:* July 20, 1905
22 ft. FLA3907 (print) FRA1127 (neg.)

A woman suspects her fortune-teller husband of adding a little romance to each palm reading. She enters a door of a set of the inner and outer parts of an office and goes behind a screen in the inner office and hides. A man dressed as a swami enters and sits down at a small table. At the same time, two young ladies enter the premises; one sits down to wait while the other has her palm read. The palmist begins to kiss her as his wife peers over the top of the screen. The second woman arrives; the performance is repeated. The first young lady reappears and the palmist kisses both to the annoyance of the woman behind the screen. She comes out and confronts the three of them, ordering the young women to leave at once.

The Society Raffles
AM&B © H69578 Dec. 7, 1905
Cameraman: F. A. Dobson
Location: Studio N.Y.C. *Photographed:* Nov. 24, 1905
28 ft. FLA3967 (print) FRA1176 (neg.)

The scenes are enacted on a set of a living room. In the first action, a man approaches a window in the foreground of the camera position and speaks to a man dressed as a burglar who is outside the window. Another man and a

Society Ballooning, Pittsfield, Mass. (1906) shows Count Henri de la Vaulx, holder of the distance record for ballooning, and the Centaur.

woman enter the scene and stand talking for a moment. The second man leaves, and the woman sits on the sofa in front of the window. The villain joins her and during an embrace, lifts a tiara from her head and hands it to his confederate outside. The picture ends when the woman discovers her jewelry is missing and swoons on the sofa.

The Soldier

See: The Seven Ages

Soldiers Washing Dishes

Edison © 38243 June 22, 1898

28 ft. FLA4366 (print) FRA1505 (neg.)

[Spanish-American War]

The photographer filmed, from a single-camera position, a line of men as they near a water source to wash their food implements. Some of the men are clothed in military recruit uniforms, while others wear civilian dress. The actual washing is not shown.

Some Dudes Can Fight

AM&B © H27383 Jan. 22, 1903

Date: 1898 [?]

11 ft. FLA3286 (print) FRA0602 (neg.)

This film was photographed from an audience point of view. The backdrop is painted to represent an ocean scene. A man acting the part of a tough pushes a well-dressed man as he walks by. A fight ensues and the "dude" trounces the tough.

The Somnambulist

AM&B © H39216 Dec. 10, 1903

73 ft. FLA5213 (print) FRA2168 (neg.)

A young lady is sleeping in a narrow bed that is part of a set of a woman's bedroom. Then, clad only in a nightgown and with her hair hanging down her back, she gets out of bed and starts out through the French doors. She is seen from several camera positions as she walks along the roof edges and apartment ledges. She then walks off the edge of one of the buildings and, by the use of stop action photography and a dummy, falls to the street below. At this point, she takes the place of the dummy and is shown being carried away by a policeman and a bystander. As the film ends, the woman is back in her bedroom, falling out of her own bed.

Song of the Shirt

AM&B © H118293 Nov. 14, 1908

Director: D. W. Griffith *Cameraman:* G. W. Bitzer

Cast: Florence Lawrence, Linda Arvidson, Harry Salter, Frank Gebhardt, Mack Sennett
Location: Studio, N.Y.C. Photographed: Oct. 19–20, 1908
221 ft. FLA5708 (print) FRA2540 (neg.)

There are six scenes in this picture, beginning in the poverty-stricken room of a young woman (Florence Lawrence) who is desperate because her mother (Linda Arvidson) is near death's door and she has no money for food or medicine. She attempts to obtain employment from a hardhearted clothing manufacturer and is finally given some clothing to take home to stitch. The remainder of the film alternates between scenes of the young woman working frantically over the sewing machine as her mother gets worse and worse and scenes of the manufacturer drinking, eating, and generally living it up in the company of loose women, squandering the money his employees have made for him. The film ends with the death of the mother and the daughter. AM&B bulletin says of this film, "Beautiful portrayal of Thomas Hood's famous poem."

The Song of the Wildwood Flute
Biograph © J148128 Nov. 25, 1910
Director: D. W. Griffith Cameraman: G. W. Bitzer
Cast: Mary Pickford, Dark Cloud, Dell Henderson
Location: Fishkill, N.Y.; Westfield, N.J. Photographed: Oct. 1–17, 1910
346 ft. FLA5709 (print) FRA2541 (neg.)

All of the scenes were photographed outdoors in what was supposed to be an Indian camp. A young Indian maiden (Mary Pickford) is courted by two Indian braves, and marries one. Her husband goes hunting and falls into a deep bear pit; his rival sees him there, but he is still jealous and suffering from unrequited love, so he leaves him in the pit. When he returns to camp and sees the young maiden suffering over the absence of her husband, the brave relents and helps to rescue his rival.

The Son's Return
Biograph © H128255 June 12, 1909
Director: D. W. Griffith Cameramen: G. W. Bitzer, Arthur Marvin
Cast: Mary Pickford, Charles West, Tony O'Sullivan, Frank Powell, Edwin August, Mack Sennett, Clara T. Bracey
Location: Studio, N.Y.C.; Coytesville and Leonia, N.J. Photographed: May 5, 7, and 8, 1909
278 ft. FLA5710 (print) FRA2542 (neg.)

A young man takes leave of his sweetheart and his aged parents and goes off to make his way in the world. Subsequent scenes show him making money, and years later he returns home. He goes to his starving parents' inn, but they do not recognize him and decide to rob him. There is a fight; the old people think they have killed him, and they drag the body outside. When they look through the loot, they discover a miniature and realize they have attacked their own son and become frantic. They rush outside, and the body is gone. He had been found and helped by his sweetheart from long ago. As the film ends, his parents are asking their son for forgiveness.

La Sorcellerie Culinaire
Méliès © H45443 May 7, 1904
Creator: Georges Méliès Cast: Georges Méliès
Location: Montreuil, France Date: Spring 1904
U.S. title: The Cook in Trouble
111ft. FLA5214 (print) FRA2169 (neg.)

Three men are at work preparing food on a kitchen set with a two-oven stove and caldrons of washtub size steaming on top of the stove when a man dressed as a beggar enters. He asks for food but is repeatedly rejected and finally booted out by the chef. This is the signal for objects to appear and disappear, boxes to change size, acrobats to emerge from soup caldrons or ovens. The whole make-up of the film is illusion created by stop-action photography. A cast of approximately twenty persons in various costumes that are basically leotards take part in the nonsense. The picture ends with a large explosion.

Sorcellerie Culinaire
See: The Cook in Trouble

Le Sorcier
See: The Witch's Revenge

The Sorrows of the Unfaithful
Biograph © J144636 Aug. 23, 1910
Director: D. W. Griffith Cameraman: G. W. Bitzer
Cast: Henry B. Walthall, Mary Pickford, W. Chrystie Miller, Eddie Dillon
Location: Highlands, N.J.; Studio, N.Y.C. Photographed: July 12–13, 1910
622 ft. FLA5901 (print) FRA6443 (neg.)

Set in a fishing village, this two-part film starts out by showing a boy and a girl whose families encourage them to associate with one another. When the two grow up, they become engaged. The young man (Henry B. Walthall) rescues another man from a raft. This man becomes enamored of the girl (Mary Pickford), and she encourages him. The young men have a dramatic fight, culminating in the murder of the man who had been rescued. When the young man discovers a note saying the other man had intended to leave again, he runs into the waves and attempts to save his victim, but apparently he drowns too.

Sorting Refuse at Incinerating Plant, New York City
Edison © H32038 May 20, 1903
Cameraman: Edwin S. Porter
Location: N.Y.C. *Photographed:* May 9, 1903
49 ft. FLA4884 (print) FRA2861 (neg.)

The film begins with a scene involving approximately thirty men and boys who are busily sorting what appears to be combustible refuse. There is only a single-camera position and no indication as to the next step in the proceedings.

Soubrettes in a Bachelor's Flat
AM&B © H29474 Mar. 18, 1903
Cameraman: Arthur Marvin
Location: Roof studio, N.Y.C. *Date:* Oct. 13, 1900
18 ft. FLA3630 (print) FRA0887 (neg., copy 1) FRA0888 (neg., copy 2)

Three scantily clad women carouse and drink with a man in dinner clothes. As they continue their capers, gestures indicate that someone is knocking at the door of the apartment. Immediately, the three women rush behind a screen, change their clothes, and emerge dressed as Salvation Army lassies, each with a tambourine, just as the police break into the flat. When the policemen leave, the host and his guests return to their revelry.

The Soubrette's Slide
AM&B © H42175 Feb. 15, 1904
Cameraman: A. E. Weed
Location: Studio, N.Y.C. *Photographed:* Jan. 29, 1904
29 ft. FLA4043 (print) FRA1230 (neg.)

Four young ladies can be seen in front of a wall constructed to appear as if it were a drawing room. They are gathered around a large mahogany table. As if on signal, one of the four young women climbs onto the table. The remaining three pick up one side of the table and tilt it, converting it into a slide. For the full extent of the film, one after another of the young ladies climbs up and slides down the table tilted by her companions' efforts.

Soubrette's Troubles on a Fifth Avenue Stage
Edison © H7986 Aug. 21, 1901
Location: N.Y.C.
34 ft. FLA3404 (print) FRA0698 (neg.)

There is a wide street visible with a large unidentified building in the background. Passing from right to left and left to right are horse-drawn hansom cabs. From camera left, and stopping in the immediate camera foreground, is a large four-wheeled horse-drawn double decker bus or stage. A man dismounts from the second level to the street and reaches up in an attempt to aid a young woman. She refuses his hand and climbs down unaided, showing a great deal of her left ankle, knee, and thigh in the process. The film ends as she and her escort walk away from the stage in apparent high dudgeon.

A Sound Sleeper
AM&B © H125502 Apr. 8, 1909
Director: D. W. Griffith
Cameramen: G. W. Bitzer, Arthur Marvin
Cast: Arthur Johnson, Mack Sennett, Robert Harron, Billy Quirk
Location: Fort Lee, N.J. *Photographed:* Mar. 18, 1909
81 ft. FLA5215 (print) FRA2170 (neg.)

A man dressed as a tramp enters the scene and, with a brick for a pillow, goes to sleep on a pile of lumber. Two thugs decide to steal from him, but they are interrupted by a third man who starts a fight that involves at least ten more people. The melee is broken up by several policemen. The tramp sleeps throughout the commotion and wakens naturally, yawns, stretches, and goes on his way. He finds an ash barrel and decides he needs another nap. The barrel is put on a two-wheeled trash wagon and hauled to the city dump, where our hero is seen rising from the ashes, bewildered but otherwise unharmed. He yawns, stretches, and walks out of the picture.

South Spring Street, Los Angeles, Cal.
Edison © 13568 Feb. 24, 1898
Location: Los Angeles
36 ft. FLA4379 (print) FRA0376 (neg.)

The film was photographed from a single-camera position located at an intersection in Los Angeles. Coming directly toward the camera are four-horse, open carriages with passengers, similar to a local bus system. In the left foreground is the marquee of the first moving picture theater in Los Angeles, Tally's. Several horse-drawn vehicles and one electric streetcar pass the camera position.

Southern Pacific Overland Mail
Edison © 60579 Oct. 25, 1897
Location: Southern Pacific Railroad's Tunnel No.9, Calif.
45 ft. FLA4885 (print) FRA1889 (neg.)

The film was photographed alongside a railroad track emerging from a tunnel opening. On the opposite side of the track from the camera position are four people standing by a handcar. Two locomotives pulling six passenger and freight cars come out of the tunnel and pass the camera position. The four people stand and watch the train as it passes into the distance.

Spanish Ball Game
Edison © 13536 Feb. 24, 1898
26 ft. FLA3035 (print) FRA0236 (neg.)

The film, photographed from a single-camera position at shoulder height, shows the long wall and the short wall of a jai-alai *fronton* court. The activities of four players can be seen, but the camera was too far away to show much detail.

Spanish Dancers at the Pan-American Exposition
Edison © H10111 Oct. 28, 1901
Location: Buffalo, N.Y.
29 ft. FLA4203 (print) FRA1375 (neg.)

The film was photographed from the area back of the midway of the Pan-American Exposition. The immediate background indicates the camera was in front of the living quarters of the gypsy dancing troupe. Several female gypsies in costume appear and dance.

A Spanish Dilemma

Biograph ©J167111 Mar. 11, 1912

Director: Mack Sennett

Cast: Fred Mace, Mack Sennett, Mabel Normand, Dell Henderson

Location: Calif. (probably Los Angeles)

188 ft. FLA5711A (print) FRA2543 (neg.)

The plot of this farce in which all of the principals wear Spanish costumes is of two brothers in love with the same girl. Most of the scenes show the competition between the two brothers (Fred Mace and Mack Sennett) for the heart and hand of the girl (Mabel Normand) who cannot make up her mind between them. A friend suggests that they fight a duel with pistols or fencing foils, or cut cards as a means of eliminating one or the other. Having finally let luck decide, the brothers go to her house to tell her and find, to their dismay, that she has fallen in love with their friend (Dell Henderson).

Sparring at the N.Y.A.C.

AM&B © H68322 Nov. 7, 1905

Cameraman: G. W. Bitzer

Location: Studio, N.Y.C. *Photographed:* Nov. 1, 1905

86 ft. FLA5216 (print) FRA2171 (neg.)

The subject is an exhibition of boxing held in a standard gymnasium. One of the boxers is dressed in boxing shorts while the other is wearing street clothes. They spar with each other for four rounds. Approximately twenty spectators can be seen in front of the wall watching the exhibition.

Sparring Match on the "Kearsarge"

AM&B © H55392 Jan. 3, 1905

Cameraman: G. W. Bitzer

Location: Oyster Bay, N.Y. *Date:* Aug. 7, 1903

27 ft. FLA4112 (print) FRA1288 (neg.)

This shows a boxing match between two sailors. The camera was placed on an abutment above the deck area where the match takes place. Approximately fifty men in U.S. Navy uniforms can be seen watching the encounter which lasts two rounds.

Special Delivery Messenger, U.S.P.O.

AM&B © H34970 Aug. 22, 1903

Cameraman: A. E. Weed

Location: Washington, D.C. *Photographed:* Aug. 7, 1903

22 ft. FLA3320 (print) FRA0634 (neg.)

As the scene opens, the front of a house, the shrubbery, a staircase, and the sidewalk are visible. From camera left, using a flying dismount, comes a bicycle rider in the uniform of a special delivery messenger. After parking his bicycle, he goes up the stairs to the front door of the house. A woman emerges, he hands her a letter, returns to his bicycle, then rides off out of the scene.

A Spectacular Start

AM&B © H17488 May 8, 1902

Cameraman: F. S. Armitage

Photographed: Oct. 19, 1899

24 ft. FLA3201 (print) FRA0527 (neg.)

In order to film this sailing event, the cameraman placed his camera on the deck of a boat in the vicinity of the official starting craft. The film shows both racing sloops approaching the camera position and making preparations to come about to cross the starting line of the America's Cup Race.

Speech by President Francis: World's Fair

AM&B © H49076 Aug. 13, 1904

Cameraman: A. E. Weed

Location: St. Louis. *Date:* Aug. 8, 1904

27 ft. FLA3539 (print) FRA0815 (neg.)

[Louisiana Purchase Exposition]

The camera was located on a level with the speaker, who is the principal in the film. President Francis stands in front of the entrance to one of the exhibit buildings of the World's Fair. He talks to an audience of several hundred. David Rowland Francis, president of the exposition, was a prominent St. Louis grain merchant who later served as ambassador to Russia.

The Speed Demon

Biograph © J171532 July 23, 1912

Director: Mack Sennett

Cast: Mack Sennett, Dell Henderson, Fred Mace

Location: Santa Monica, Calif.

177 ft. FLA5712 (print) FRA2544 (neg.)

The story line of this farce-comedy was built around the early California road race held in Santa Monica. The grandstand filled with spectators and the actual race were used as a background, although the actors had nothing whatever to do with the race itself. The humor arises from the attempts of two members of the Biograph cast to become racing drivers and win the race by cutting across a plowed field. The last scenes occur after a title that says "Hours Later," and our heroes are shown arriving in their ancient automobile on the race track late in the afternoon when all the spectators have gone home.

Speed Trials, Autoboat Challenger

AM&B © H56667 Feb. 13, 1905

Cameraman: G. W. Bitzer

Location: Lake Worth, Fla. *Photographed:* Feb. 4, 1905

50 ft. FLA5217 (print) FRA2172 (neg.)

The speed trials of a motor boat (*Challenger*) were photographed from the dock or pier, low to the water. Several right-to-left, left-to-right approaches to the camera position are shown. A small excursion boat motors by the camera.

The Spider and the Fly

AM&B © H28556 Feb. 24, 1903

Cameraman: F. S. Armitage

Location: Roof studio, N.Y.C. *Date:* Aug. 21, 1899

10 ft. FLA3136 (print) FRA0469 (neg.)

A beautiful young blonde woman in scanty attire is seen reclining in the center of a set of a spider's web. A well-dressed young man passes in front of her. She attracts his attention and encourages him to approach her. At first he is reluctant but then goes up and kisses her hand.

Spike, the Bag-Punching Dog

AM&B © H34513 Aug. 13, 1903

16 ft. FLA3722 (print) FRA0909 (neg.)

This short film shows a dog jumping at a large air-filled balloon or bag suspended above him, and was photographed as if the camera were part of a vaudeville audience.

A Spill

AM&B © H16359 Apr. 10, 1902

Cameraman: Robert K. Bonine

Location: Shrewsbury River, N.J. *Date:* Jan. 20, 1902

6ft. FLA4137 (print) FRA1307 (neg.)

The film was photographed from the edge of a lake that was frozen over. Two boys on a sloop-rigged ice boat approach the camera position. As the ice boat and its occupants come directly in front of the camera, the boys apparently lose control of the ice boat and spill out onto the lake. They get to their feet and hurry back to their boat before it sails away.

The Spirit Awakened

Biograph © J170667 June 28, 1912

Director: D. W. Griffith *Cameraman:* G. W. Bitzer

Cast: Blanche Sweet, W. Chrystie Miller, Kate Bruce, Eddie Dillon, Alfred Paget, Mae Marsh

Location: Southern Calif.

406 ft. FLA5713 (print) FRA2545 (neg.)

An impoverished farm family (W. Chrystie Miller, Kate Bruce, and Blanche Sweet) attempts to raise sufficient money to pay off the mortgage. When they finally have all the money together, the villain (Alfred Paget) steals the cash from under the old farmer's pillow. He beats up the hired hand (Eddie Dillon), steals a horse, and gallops away. The camera is positioned in several locations to show the horseback chase. The hired hand and the farmer's daughter eventually catch up with the villain, and the hero and heroine return to the farm with the mortgage money. The last scene shows the heroine kissing the hired hand, who is caught in a barn door.

Spirit of '76

AM&B © H61107 May 19, 1905

Cameraman: G. W. Bitzer

Location: Studio, N.Y.C. *Photographed:* Apr. 19, 1905

23 ft. FLA4886 (print) FRA1890 (neg.)

The first scene visible is a backdrop painted to show a battlefield. Three men dressed in the uniform of a revolutionary war fife-and-drum corps appear, march in place in front of the camera position, and leave the stage. There is a puff of smoke, after which the three men return. They are joined by another man who waves the American flag with thirteen stars.

Spirits in the Kitchen

AM&B © H19656 July 2, 1902

Cameraman: F. S. Armitage

Location: Roof studio, N.Y.C. *Date:* May 12, 1899

21 ft. FLA3792 (print) FRA1029 (neg.)

The camera was placed to best encompass an outdoor set of a kitchen. A woman is setting the table when a policeman carrying a bucket of beer enters through one of the doors.

He pours two glasses of beer and sets the bucket on the table. A man dressed as a tramp appears to the left. The policeman reaches for him with his night stick but the tramp disappears by stop-action photography and reappears under the table where he begins drinking the beer from the bucket. As the film continues, several other illusions caused by stop action take place, such as a string of frankfurters changing into an alley cat, chairs becoming tubs of water and, as the film ends, the tramp jumping into the air and disappearing, pulling the policeman with him.

A Spiritualist Photographer

Méliès © H33238 July 6, 1903

Creator: Georges Méliès

Cast: Georges Méliès *Location:* Montreuil, France *Date:* Spring 1903

Original *Title:* Le Portrait Spirite

85 ft. FLA4887 (print) FRA1891 (neg.)

In this film, Méliès reverted to his usual style of a motion picture depicting a magician at work. It begins with Méliès holding a sign lettered in both French and English reading "Spiritualistic Photo. Dissolving Effect. Obtained Without Black Background. Great Novelty." Méliès causes a woman to appear and disappear, as if she were a painting in a frame. Later in the film, the woman comes to life and walks toward the camera. Both effects were obtained by an in-camera dissolve.

Spooks at School

AM&B © H30720 Apr. 24, 1903

Cameraman: Arthur Marvin

Location: Roof studio, N.Y.C. *Date:* Sept. 19, 1900

11 ft. FLA3119 (print) FRA0454 (neg.)

The contrast and grain of the film do not permit much separation between the actors and the background, and the general quality is poor. The action is of a stage magician dressed in a white sheet and a pointed dunce cap who produces children from other dunce caps by means of stop-action photography. The act ends as he causes the children to vanish.

Sporting Blood

Lubin Mfg. Co. © J131735 July 29, 1909

234 ft. FLA5714 (print) FRA2546 (neg.)

A husband gets a telegram, tells his wife he has been called out of town on business, and goes off to the horse races. After he has left the house, his wife finds the telegram which gives her the idea he is meeting a woman named "Sweet Marie." He comes home from the races only to be told by the servants that his wife left "acting crazy," and he starts out to find her. The film shows the parallel action of the husband and his friends seeking the wife, while the wife and her friends, equipped with umbrellas, look for the errant husband. The two groups of opposite sexes finally meet in front of a large fountain. The film ends when the husband introduces his wife to "Sweet Marie," a race horse. The film starts with a head and shoulder close-up, and has an insert of the telegram. The sets and costumes indicate a high production cost.

Springtime in the Park

AM&B © H16348 Apr. 10, 1902

Cameraman: F. S. Armitage

Date: Apr. 15, 1901

20 ft. FLA4263 (print) FRA1419 (neg.)

The film was photographed from the viewpoint of an audience watching a vaudeville act. As the film begins, a man dressed as a painter is seen painting a latticed park bench located on fake grass in front of a painted backdrop. When he has finished painting the bench, he puts a sign "Wet Paint" on the bench and leaves. At this point, a man dressed in good clothing and wearing a tall silk hat approaches the bench and, unmindful of the sign, sits down. He then realizes he is sitting in wet paint, and spends the remainder of the picture attempting to examine the damage. The working title for this 20-foot comedy was How a Nearsighted Man Read the Sign.

Squires, Australian Champion in His Training Quarters

Miles Brothers © H94998 June 8, 1907

Cameraman: Herbert J. Miles [?]

19 ft. FLA3574 (print) FRA0847 (neg.)

The film begins in surroundings that appear to be the back yard of a house. Facing the camera, a muscular man can be seen jumping rope rapidly. The man is Squires, the Australian contender for the heavyweight boxing championship of the world. Tommy Burns knocked out Bill Squires in the first round of their fight on July 4, 1907, in Colma, California.

The Stage Rustler

AM&B © H112792 July 3, 1908

Director: Wallace McCutcheon *Author:* D. W. Griffith
  Cameramen: G. W. Bitzer, Arthur Marvin

Cast: Gene Gauntier, D. W. Griffith

Location: Shadyside, N.J.; Studio, N.Y.C. *Photographed:* June 10 and 13, 1908

246 ft. FLA5715A FRA2547 (neg.)

The opening scene of this Western shows two men preparing makeshift barricades and waiting for the stage they intend to rob. The next scene shows the two robbers at their hideout, when the leader's girl friend arrives to give them information on what the townspeople are doing about the hold-up. The robbers fall out over the affections of the young girl, have a fight, and arrange a truce, which ends in a saloon when one of the robbers attempts to force his attentions on the girl. The leader shoots him, but the girl is also a victim of the crossfire and dies in her lover's arms. The part of the principal hold-up man was played by D. W. Griffith.

Stalking and Shooting Caribou, Newfoundland

AM&B © H89187 Jan. 9, 1907

Cameraman: F. A. Dobson

Location: Newfoundland, Canada *Photographed:* Oct. 15, 1906

89 ft. FLA5218 (print) FRA2173 (neg.)

D. W. Griffith (center) in The Stage Rustler *(1908), which was photographed just one week before he directed his first motion picture.*

In order to film this outdoor picture, the cameraman placed his equipment close to the shores of a small lake. During the film, two caribou approach the camera position and, as if troubled by the noise, turn and go away. Someone behind the camera position shot at the second caribou, which ran to the lake and swam away. From the film, it is evident that the hunter was successful, since later two men in a canoe paddle out to the caribou's body and drag it to shore. There is a close-up of the dead caribou on the beach. This is part of a film later released under the title of A Caribou Hunt.

See also: Moose Hunt in New Brunswick.

Stallion Race
AM&B © H17040 Apr. 26, 1902
Cameraman: F. S. Armitage
Location: Boston *Date:* Oct. 3, 1900
27 ft. FLA3866 (print) FRA1078 (neg.)

The camera was positioned at the edge of the inside rail of a race track, across from the grandstand where many hundreds of spectators are watching a race between horses pulling sulkies. The camera was panned to show the large crowd. Several groups of horse-drawn sulkies pass. According to a Biograph handbill, the horses shown were "Charlie Herr," "Arion," and "Cresceus."

Stanford University, California
Edison © 60583 Oct. 25, 1897
Location: Palo Alto, Calif.
46 ft. FLA4095 (print) FRA1276 (neg.)

A group of people are shown the campus of Stanford University in Palo Alto, California, in 1897.

The Star of Bethlehem
Thanhouser no copyright Nov. 23, 1912
Director: Lawrence Marston
Cast: William Russell, Florence La Badie
Location: New Rochelle, N.Y.
106 ft. FLA5716 (print) FRA2704 (neg., copy1) FRA2705 (neg., copy 2)

The story is of the events leading up to the birth of Christ. It is difficult to tell by watching the film whether the scenes were short by design or by expediency for copyright purposes only. Contemporary reviews, however, indicate the original was three reels long. As the film exists at present, it is difficult to follow the story line since the so-called *tableau* form was used for all the scenes, which show good production value although their short length does not permit a flow of connected ideas. No copyright number appears on this film although the date, November 23, 1912, is stamped on each reel. It is possible registration processes were never completed.

Star Theatre
AM&B © H16735 Apr. 18, 1902
Cameraman: F. S. Armitage
Location: N.Y.C. *Date:* Apr. 18, 1901
50 ft. FLA4888 (print) FRA2853 (neg.)

As the film begins, the camera focuses on a large brick building with a marquee lettered "Star Theater." The camera is positioned at approximately the third floor so that it overlooks an intersection on which the building stands. As the film progresses, the building diminishes in size for it is being demolished. Judging by the different exposures of the film, production must have been in excess of thirty days. This type of photography can only be accomplished by the use of special timing devices controlling the camera. The Star Theatre was located on the corner of Broadway and Thirteenth Street, New York City.

Start of Ocean Race for Kaiser's Cup
Edison © H61182 May 20, 1905
Cameraman: Edwin S. Porter
Location: Sandy Hook, N.J. *Photographed:* May 17, 1905
161 ft. FLA5719 (print) FRA2548 (neg.)

It is self-evident from the beginning of this film that the camera was placed on a small boat that was bobbing up and down. Large seagoing sailing yachts pass the camera position, and the film shows the ships maneuvering about the starting boat.

Start of Race—"Reliance" Ahead
AM&B © H35651 Sept. 12, 1903
Cameraman: A. E. Weed
Location: Sandy Hook, N.J. *Photographed:* Aug. 27, 1903
59 ft. FLA5219 (print) FRA2174 (neg.)
[America's Cup Races: *Reliance* and *Shamrock III*]

The sailing yachts in the America's Cup Race are seen at a distance of about a thousand yards. They pass the camera position from left to right, and the yachts are on port tack, close hauled, and full rigged.

Start of the First Race, Aug. 22
AM&B © H35071 Aug. 27, 1903
Cameraman: A. E. Weed *Photographed:* Aug. 22, 1903
Location: Off Sandy Hook, N.J.
34 ft.
[America's Cup Races: *Reliance* and *Shamrock III*]

At approximately 250 yards, a large racing yacht can be seen. It passes the camera position from right to left. The condition of the film and the distance of the vessel from the camera makes further description impossible.

The Startled Lover
AM&B © H17045 Apr. 26, 1902
Date: Circa 1898
9 ft. FLA3822 (print) FRA1052 (neg.)

The camera encompasses a living room set. Immediately in front of the camera is a sofa where two young people are kissing and embracing. Suddenly, using stop-action photography, the young woman is transformed into a skeleton. The young man jumps to his feet in astonishment. The skeleton turns back into the young woman again as the film ends.

State Normal School, Missouri
AM&B © H46817 June 3, 1904
Cameraman: A. E. Weed
Location: Kirksville, Mo. *Photographed:* May 18, 1904
21 ft. FLA3668 (print) FRA0921 (neg.)

The camera was positioned above the heads of a group of young women wearing gym clothes of the era. They perform in unison a series of physical culture exercises and calisthenics. Their demonstration is directed by an older woman who is probably their instructor. The words "State Normal School, Kirksville, Missouri" appear on the wall behind the group of young women.

La Statue Animée

See: The Drawing Lesson; or, The Living Statue

Statue of Liberty

Edison © 52060 Sept. 3, 1898
Location: Bedloe's Island, New York harbor
26 ft. FLA4005 (print) FRA1206 (neg.)

A three-quarter front view of the Statue of Liberty is shown from a single-camera position. There is nothing else visible above the ground but the statue itself.

Stealing a Dinner

AM&B © H32633 June 13, 1903
Cameraman: G. W. Bitzer
Location: Roof studio, N.Y.C. *Date:* Apr. 28, 1899
19 ft. FLA3494 (print) FRA0774 (neg.)

A man with a serviette under his chin is eating some food at a small table. A large number of dogs are seated in the immediate background. The man is still eating when a dog costumed as a waitress appears walking on its hind legs. The man gives the dog an order, which it performs. The man then leaves the table to direct a trick. Two of the animals jump onto the table and begin consuming his food. This apparently infuriates the man, who pulls a pistol from his pocket and begins firing at the animals. A huge dog dressed as a policeman then walks in on its hind legs and places the man under arrest.

Stealing Bread

See: The Kleptomaniac

Steam Hammer, Westinghouse Works

See: Westinghouse Works

Steam Riding Academy

AM&B © H33539 July 18, 1903
21 ft. FLA3433 (print) FRA0719 (neg.)

The camera was positioned to encompass almost all of a large steam-operated carousel. Nothing is shown but the passengers riding on the wooden horses as the carousel turns.

Steam Tactics

AM&B © H18895 June 12, 1902
Cameraman: G. W. Bitzer
Location: Annapolis, Md. *Date:* Apr. 29, 1901
16 ft. FLA3681 (print) FRA0931 (neg.)

The camera was positioned to show several groups of small steam-propelled craft passing. All of the craft are of the naval shoreboat type and their coxswains are men in the uniform of naval cadets.

Steam Whistle, Westinghouse Works

See: Westinghouse Works

Steamboat and Great Eastern Rock

AM&B © H17967 May 21, 1902
Cameraman: G. W. Bitzer
Location: Union Pacific *Date:* Nov. 29, 1899
34 ft. FLA3810 (print) FRA1044 (neg.)

The film was photographed in the Rocky Mountains from the front of a train traveling over a single bed track of the Union Pacific Railroad line through mountainous country. During the film, the train makes two full turns in approaching some rather majestic rock formations.

Steamer "Island Wanderer"

AM&B © H30753 Apr. 24, 1903
Location: St. Lawrence River [?]
21 ft. FLA3454 (print) FRA0736 (neg.)

The title indicates that the subject of this film is a boat. What appears is the after part of one vessel in the foreground of seemingly quiet water, and a bow-on composition photograph of another vessel at a distance of five hundred yards. The quality of the development of film leaves much to be desired. This film reportedly was photographed in the Thousand Islands.

Steamer "Mascotte" Arriving at Tampa

Edison © 31438 May 20, 1898
Location: Tampa, Fla.
25 ft. FLA3122 (print) FRA0456 (neg.)
[Spanish-American War]

From a single-camera position on a dock or pier, a single-stacked steam vessel of approximately 3,500 tons can be seen approaching. The film shows nothing but the ship from the broadside on the port bow position. The distance does not allow identification of the large number of passengers visible on the main and boat decks.

Steamer "New York"

AM&B © H30743 Apr. 24, 1903
Location: St. Lawrence River [?]
27 ft. FLA3137 (print) FRA0470 (neg.)

The camera apparently was located above the main deck of a ship tied to the dock. The ship is turning over her engines. This conclusion was reached because the film shows the back of people's heads as they look over the railing of a ship tied to a dock as she creates her own wake without moving through the water. Approximately twenty people are seen at the ship's railing. Beyond them, at a distance of about thirty feet, the agitated water appears.

Steamscow "Cinderella" and Ferryboat "Cincinnati"

Edison © H32032 May 20, 1903
Cameraman: Edwin S. Porter
Location: North River, N.Y.C. *Photographed:* May 9, 1903
37 ft. FLA4889 (print) FRA1892 (neg.)

The film, photographed from a camera positioned on a dock, shows a large steam scow passing the camera location; simultaneously, a large paddle-wheel ferryboat passes in the opposite direction. The weather was not conducive to good photography; no details of either of the craft are distinct enough for further elaboration.

Steamship "Express of India"

AM&B © H25963 Dec. 31, 1902

Cameraman: G. W. Bitzer

Location: Vancouver, B.C., Canada *Date:* Oct. 19, 1899

27 ft. FLA3860 (print) FRA1072 (neg.)

At a distance of perhaps five hundred yards, the white hull of a large two-stack steamship is visible, making her way through the water toward the camera. The ship approaches to a point where only sections of her hull can be seen, and details of the boat and main decks are clear. The steamship was the *Empress of India*, incorrectly identified as the *Express of India*.

Steeplechase, Coney Island

AM&B © H32630 June 13, 1903

Location: Coney Island, N.Y. *Date:* Circa 1897

25 ft. FLA3405 (print) FRA0699 (neg.)

The film shows a mechanical ride in an amusement park, designed to allow customers to ride down an undulating incline astride wooden horses. Several groups of people are seen enjoying the ride down the incline.

Stern's Duplex Railway

AM&B © H64925 Aug. 25, 1905

Cameraman: G. W. Bitzer

Location: Dreamland, Coney Island, N.Y. *Photographed:* Aug. 13, 1905

56 ft. FLA4890 (print) FRA1893 (neg.)

The film shows an unusual type of railroad car designed to go over or under an oncoming car instead of around it, as conventional railroad cars must do. Each car not only runs on tracks but also has a set of tracks over its top, permitting on oncoming car to go over it. The camera was placed close to a platform on which the passenger-laden train ran, and the over-and-under vehicle demonstrated its unusual capabilities several times.

The Still Alarm

Edison © H32026 May 20, 1903

Cameramen: Edwin S. Porter, J. B. Smith

Location: N.Y.C. *Photographed:* May 16, 1903

56 ft. FLA4891 (print) FRA1894 (neg.)

The camera was positioned facing a city fire house and then in several other locations. At each camera position, several pieces of horse-drawn fire-fighting equipment pass the camera, either coming toward or from right to left. The equipment includes pumper wagons, hook-and-ladder carriages, hose carriers, and personnel wagons.

Still Water Runs Deep

AM&B © H25959 Dec. 31, 1902

Date: Circa 1898

9ft. FLA4051 (print) FRA1236 (neg.)

In the foreground, one can see a narrow pier in a lake in a wooden area. A small rowboat is tied to the end of the pier. A young man is seen escorting a young woman along the pier and into the boat. As soon as he is certain she is seated in the rowboat, he leaves, picks up an umbrella, unfurls it, and starts back toward the rowboat. The pier then collapses, and he falls in the water. For the remainder of the film he can be seen splashing about in the water. Advertised in a

Biograph Bulletin of September 13, 1903, as Still Waters Run Deep.

Still Waters Run Deep

See: Still Water Runs Deep

Stolen by Gypsies

Edison © H63368 July 15, 1905

Cameraman: Edwin S. Porter

Location: N.Y.C. *Photographed:* July 1, 1905

340 ft. FLA5720 (print) FRA2549 (neg.)

The film begins with a medium shot of a nursemaid dressing an infant. The next scene shows the child's parents embracing the baby and the nursemaid taking the child outdoors, where it is stolen by gypsies in a horse-drawn covered wagon. When the child is missed, a great chase of some tramps takes place, but they have ducks and not a baby in their bag. A title indicates a time lapse of a year, and some gypsies come to town and the local ladies go to have their fortunes told. One notices a pale child with the gypsies and informs the parents of the kidnapped infant. The final scene shows the police holding the gypsies at bay while the baby is returned to its mother. The backgrounds used in the film were a combination of painted backdrops and actual furniture for interiors and some exteriors.

The Stolen Jewels

AM&B © H116138 Sept. 24, 1908

Director: D. W. Griffith *Cameraman:* G. W. Bitzer

Cast: Florence Lawrence, John Cumpson, Harry Salter

Location: Studio, N.Y.C. *Photographed:* Aug. 24 and Sept. 15, 1908

230 ft. FLA5721 (print) FRA2551 (neg.)

A small child places the family's jewel collection in a new toy, a stuffed dog. The family suffers financial losses. They are hounded by people who have answered their ad offering a large reward for the return of the jewels. The family huddles together in misery watching the finance company remove their furniture, when one of the men accidentally sits on the toy dog. It breaks and the whereabouts of the jewelry is disclosed. All the scenes but one were taken on sets.

Stolen Sweets

AM&B © H28549 Feb. 24, 1903

10 ft. FLA3152 (print) FRA0484 (neg.)

We see a large black umbrella, with the legs of two women protruding from under it. The locale is a sandy beach. Off in the distance, approaching the camera position, are four girls in bathing attire. They continue to walk directly toward the umbrella and, when they reach it, lift it up. For the first time, the camera discloses two rather overweight young girls greedily eating a box of candy.

Stop Thief!

AM&B © H18748 June 7, 1902

Cameraman: F. S. Armitage

Location: Roof studio, N.Y.C. *Date:* Dec. 7, 1900

9 ft. FLA3686 (print) FRA0936 (neg.)

A backdrop consisting of a store front can be seen. In the foreground are two big barrels. A man, apparently being pursued, enters the scene and jumps into one of the barrels. He is closely followed by a policeman who looks into the barrel the thief had climbed into, but finds it empty. As the film ends, the thief can be seen emerging from the other barrel. Apparently this was accomplished by the use of stop-action photography.

Stop Thief!
Méliès © H65901   Sept. 23, 1905
Location: N.Y.C.
17 ft.   FLA4117 (print)   FRA1293 (neg.)

In order to photograph this film, the cameraman placed his equipment on a broad sidewalk in the business district of a large city, probably New York. As the action begins, a woman dressed in the fashion of the time is seen approaching the camera position. She stops in front of the window of a mercantile store. While she is scrutinizing the merchandise, a purse snatcher comes from the rear, grabs her handbag, turns, and makes off with it in the opposite direction. The woman causes quite a commotion, waves her arms and yells attracting a large crowd, including some policemen. The cameraman changed his position and the last scene shows the woman, escorted by two policemen and followed by a group of people, walking down the sidewalk into a building that might be a police station. This film was shot by the Georges Méliès company in New York.

A Storm at Sea
Edison © D16390   Aug. 9, 1900
Location: S.S. Kaiserine Maria Theresa, on the Atlantic Ocean
36 ft.   FLA3222 (print)   FRA0546 (neg.)

The film was photographed from a single-camera position from the deck of a seagoing ship during a storm. Visible at all times is the railing, with someone wearing a white coat clinging to it.

The Story of the Biograph Told
AM&B © H40719   Jan. 8, 1904
Cameraman: A. E. Weed
Location: Studio N.Y.C. *Photographed:* Nov. 30, 1903
Release title: The Story the Biograph Told
117 ft.   FLA5722 (print)   FRA2553 (neg.)

We see a set of a business office with desks, tables, chairs, and a typewriter, etc. An office boy can be seen at work. A door opens and a man comes in and puts a moving picture camera on a table. His gestures indicate he is explaining the use of the camera to the boy to satisfy the boy's curiosity. An attractive young woman and a man enter the office and take their places at their respective desks. Soon they begin embracing, to the amusement and interest of the office boy who can be seen cranking the camera. At this point, there is a film dissolve that takes the man from the previous scene into a box in a theater with a woman who is apparently his wife. They begin watching a moving picture which, strangely enough, is the one taken by the office boy of the office manager and his secretary. The wife becomes extremely annoyed and starts to admonish him. The final scene and the end of the picture take place the next morning at the office where the office force are busily engaged in performing their duties. The wife enters and discharges the female secretary, replacing her with a male secretary. To let the audience know the businessman was telephoning his wife at home, Weed double exposed a section of the film so that he, his secretary, and his wife all appear on the screen together.

The Story the Biograph Told
See: The Story of the Biograph Told

Strange Adventure of New York Drummer
Edison © 40081   June 17, 1899
26 ft.   FLA3258 (print)   FRA0580 (neg.)

An odd set is visible, with a background of black material stretched over a frame running the full width of camera range. In the immediate foreground is a couch with a white cover. Next to it is a chair. A trunk and a small table can also be seen. Throughout the entire picture, by the use of stop-action photography, one of the two male actors constantly disappears and reappears. Pieces of furniture seen earlier in the film appear and disappear. In the final act, one of the two men is stuffed in a trunk in the course of a scuffle between the two. The trunk is then tipped toward the camera to show it is empty.

A Strange Meeting
Biograph © J130279   Aug. 5, 1909
Director: D. W. Griffith *Cameraman:* G. W. Bitzer
Cast: Stephanie Longfellow, Arthur Johnson, Frank Powell, Owen Moore, Billy Quirk, John Cumpson, Lottie Pickford, James Kirkwood, H. B. Walthall, Mack Sennett, Kate Bruce, Charles Avery, Dorothy West
Location: Studio, N.Y.C. *Photographed:* June 11 and 17, 1909
353 ft.   FLA5723 (print)   FRA2550 (neg.)

An old woman attempts to rescue a loved one from a saloon by going to her minister (Arthur Johnson) for help. The minister accompanies her to the saloon, and ends up aiding a young woman (Stephanie Longfellow) who has fallen in with evil companions. There are several scenes of the young woman drinking and carousing with her friends, and others of her in church and with the minister, apparently impressed with the good life. He gives her a cross, and later in the film she goes to him to return it as she has decided to continue her wild ways. She leaves, has second thoughts, and returns. The last scene has an unusual photographic effect caused by low key incandescent lights.

A Street Arab
Edison © 25336   Apr. 21, 1898
Location: N.Y.C.
26 ft.   FLA3078 (print)   FRA0419 (neg.)

A boy is seen doing back bends, hand stands, head spins, and back handsprings. He is dressed in the conventional attire of a preadolescent boy of the era. The only other object visible in the film is the wall against which he performs.

Street Car Chivalry
Edison © H34327   Aug. 8, 1903
Cameraman: Edwin S. Porter
Location: N.Y.C. *Photographed:* July 29, 1903
27 ft.   FLA3334 (print)   FRA0645 (neg.)

The action takes place on a set of the interior of a streetcar. A young woman boards the streetcar, and several men immediately jump to their feet, remove their hats, and offer her their seats. A large washerwoman comes in and the men busy themselves reading newspapers and books, etc. The washerwoman supports herself by holding onto the strap, and finally manages to get a seat by the simple expedient of using the rocking of the streetcar as an excuse to tromp on all of the seated men's feet until they cannot stand the pain. They get up and leave and the woman not only has a seat for herself but also room for her paper bags as well. The streetcar overhead advertising signs are made up of products then manufactured by the Edison Manufacturing Company—the phonograph, electric light, and a new product, the 'Kinetoscope.'

See also: The Unappreciated Joke

Street Fight and Arrest

AM&B © H21508   Sept. 5, 1902

Date: 1898

24 ft.   FLA3890 (print)   FRA1112 (neg.)

The subject of the film is a street fight. A police officer is shown attempting to break up the fight between two men who are rolling around in the street. A great number of spectators are attracted by the commotion. The picture ends as a horse-drawn police patrol appears, and the two brawlers are led toward the wagon. Released by AM&B as A Street Fight In Chicago.

A Street Fight in Chicago

See: Street Fight and Arrest

Street Mail Car, U.S.P.O.

AM&B © H34992   Aug. 22, 1903

Cameraman: A. E. Weed

Location: Washington, D.C. *Photographed:* July 30, 1903

35 ft.   FLA4892 (print)   FRA2875 (neg.)

The first scene appears to have been taken on a main thoroughfare of a large city. In the immediate foreground is a horse-drawn U.S. mail vehicle waiting at the side of a streetcar track. Soon a streetcar approaches the camera position. It stops beside the mail vehicle and the driver unloads mail sacks from the streetcar. He then puts some sacks from his wagon onto the streetcar. As the film ends, both the streetcar and the horse-drawn mail delivery wagon leave the scene.

Street Scene at Jaffa

Edison © H32810   June 17, 1903

Cameraman: A. C. Abadie

Location: Jaffa, Syria *Photographed:* Mar. 22, 1903

27 ft.   FLA3532 (print)   FRA0808 (neg.)

The camera was positioned in the center of a well-traveled area of a large city. The many people who pass are dressed in burnooses, turbans, and fezzes, and can be seen leading camels or donkeys carrying people or packages.

Street Scene in Hong Kong

Edison © 38252   June 22, 1898

Cameramen: James H. White, W. Bleckyrden

Location: Hong Kong

26 ft.   FLA3708 (print)   FRA0956 (neg.)

The camera was positioned at the edge of a well-traveled thoroughfare in a large city. Various modes of transportation, such as rickshas, one- and two-wheeled vehicles, and

sedan chairs can be seen. In the background are several many-storied buildings.

Street Scene in Yokohama, no. 1

Edison © 38230   June 22, 1898

Cameramen: James H. White, W. Bleckyrden

Location: Yokohama, Japan

27 ft.   FLA4449 (print)   FRA1554 (neg.)

The people on a Japanese city street and several different methods of transportation are shown. There are coolie-drawn rickshas, sedan chairs carried by coolies, two-and four-wheeled vehicles being pushed and pulled, and people on bicycles, as well as horse-drawn methods of transportation.

Street Scene in Yokohama, no. 2

Edison © 38250   June 22, 1898

Cameramen: James H. White, W. Bleckyrden

Location: Yokohama, Japan

23 ft.   FLA4449 (print)   FRA1554 (neg.)

The individuals and their activities were photographed from the side of a road in what appears to be the outskirts of a large Japanese city. The cameraman and his camera attract the attention of a considerable number of people who congregate directly across the street to watch him at work. Many different modes of transportation pass between the audience and the camera.

Street Scene, San Diego

Edison © 12174   Feb. 17, 1898

Location: San Diego

25 ft.   FLA4342 (print)   FRA0377 (neg.)

The cameraman placed his camera facing east on a main thoroughfare of San Diego, California. A double-decker electric streetcar approaches and then passes the camera position. Several buildings in the background have signs such as "Furniture," etc., painted on them.

Street Scene, Tientsin

AM&B © H19222   June 20, 1902

Cameraman: Raymond Ackerman

Location: Taku Road, Tientsin, China *Date:* Jan. 14, 1901

16 ft.   FLA3316 (print)   FRA0630 (neg.)

The film shows a street scene in a city in China. The camera is placed so that the travelers along the street approach the camera position. Horse-drawn vehicles of the two-wheeled and four-wheeled variety can be seen, being driven by Chinese of both sexes. There are many people on foot, and several two-wheeled vehicles pulled by coolies. The film quality is poor, so the detail of the building in the background is difficult to see.

Street Scene, Tokio, Japan

AM&B © H36865   Oct. 19, 1903

Cameraman: Robert K. Bonine

Location: Tokyo *Photographed:* July 25, 1901

17 ft.   FLA3097 (print)   FRA0436 (neg.)

The locale is a busy intersection, where horse-drawn streetcars and coolie-pulled vehicles such as rickshas and two- and one-wheeled baggage transports are seen approaching and departing. There are many passersby in both Oriental and Occidental dress.

The Streets of New York
AM&B © H71426   Dec. 30, 1905
Cameraman: F. A. Dobson
Location: Studio, N.Y.C. *Photographed:* Dec. 22, 1905
143 ft.   FLA5222 (print)   FRA2175 (neg.)

A single-camera position film opening from an audience point of view on a set constructed to simulate a busy street corner in New York City. The film is made up of a series of vignettes, involving one or two people that turn into mob scenes, such as two men knocking one another, or a man with a potted palm bumping into an approaching man. This is followed by burglaries, fights, pocket-picking—each with an opening scene followed by a crowd surrounding one of the two participants.

Street's Zouaves and Wall Scaling
Edison © H8689   Sept. 16, 1901
Cast: Streator's Zouaves
48 ft.   FLA4893 (print)   FRA1895 (neg.)

The film shows a demonstration of close-order military drill in a building that appears to be either an armory or a large gymnasium. The camera is elevated, perhaps from a balcony. The company (approximately twenty) executes the various maneuvers for exhibition purposes rather than for military reasons. There is footage of a wall constructed for the exhibition, which allows the performers to demonstrate their skill in scaling walls. The picture ends with two of the participants waving both the British and American flags.

See also: Wall Scaling

The Strenuous Life
AM&B © H43559   Mar. 22, 1904
Cameraman: A. E. Weed
Location: Studio, N.Y.C. *Photographed:* Feb. 27, 1904
62 ft.   FLA5223 (print)   FRA2176 (neg.)

In front of a backdrop painted like the backyard of a tenement in a large city, a man dressed as a woman can be seen scrubbing clothes, while another man reads a newspaper nearby. A third person comes along and tries to sell them something. The husband and "wife" throw the intruder over the wall. Their antisocial behavior continues, for they fight anyone who comes along as well as each other. At the end of the film, the wife climbs up on the clothesline and brandishes a broom and then starts removing one article of clothing at a time as "she" stands on one foot.

The Strenuous Life; or, Anti-Race Suicide
Edison © H55129   Dec. 19, 1904
Cameraman: Edwin S. Porter
Cast: Kathryn Osterman
Location: Studio, N.Y.C. *Photographed:* Dec. 9–19, 1904
130 ft.   FLA5224 (print)   FRA2177 (neg.)

A businessman is called home from his office by telephone. He gets a hansom cab, goes over the snow-covered streets to a brownstone where he picks up another man. They continue home. The second man goes upstairs, leaving the businessman pacing nervously up and down in the living room. A maid enters with a grocery scale, places it on the table, goes upstairs, and returns with a baby. This procedure is repeated three times, and at the end of the film the man, in deep shock, is holding two infants, while two nurses each hold another. In the scenes following the one where the first baby is brought down, the camera was moved to change the composition of the picture from full figure to one-quarter figure.

Strongheart
Klaw & Erlanger © LP2488   Mar. 9, 1914
f1*Supervisor:* D. W. Griffith   *Director:* James Kirkwood
Cast: Henry B. Walthall, Lionel Barrymore, Alan Hale, Antonio Moreno, Blanche Sweet, Gertrude Robinson
Location: N.Y.C.; Cambridge, Mass.
From the play by William C. DeMille
1,144 ft.   FLA5902 (print)   FRA2768 (neg.)

Most of this three-reel film was photographed in and around Columbia University in New York City. There are scenes of student activity as well as a football game. The story concerns a reservation Indian (Henry B. Walthall) who is studying at Columbia so he can better help his tribe. There is intrigue when the star of the football team (Lionel Barrymore) is suspected of stealing football plays and giving them to the opposition. The Indian takes the blame so that the star can play and win, knowing that the true criminal will be discovered after the game. After the game is won, the Indian sadly realizes that he cannot be part of this new life. He has proposed to a fellow student who accepts him, but his tribe refuses to have anything to do with her, and white people will not tolerate him. The film was directed by James Kirkwood, supervised by D. W. Griffith.

A Subject for the Rogue's Gallery
AM&B © H41753   Feb. 2, 1904
Cameraman: A. E. Weed
Location: Studio, N.Y.C. *Photographed:* Jan. 13, 1904
25 ft.   FLA3601 (print)   FRA0866 (neg.)

The film begins on an unoccupied set of a police station photographic gallery. A photographer comes in and stands by his camera. One man dressed as a civilian accompanied by a man in police uniform bring in an attractive young woman. They seat her on the stool directly in front of the camera. She resists having her picture taken so the two men hold her head steady. At that moment, the camera begins to move directly toward the young woman and, as the camera gets closer and closer to her, it can be seen that she is grimacing and distorting her face in an attempt to disguise her identity. The camera continues to move closer toward the subject until it arrives at the point of a tight head-shot. There are several feet of "run off" film at the end apparently having no connection with the preceding action.

See also: Photographing a Female Crook

The Subpoena Server
AM&B © H75965   Apr. 24, 1906
Cameraman: G. W. Bitzer
Location: Hoboken, N.J.; Studio, N.Y.C. *Photographed:* Apr. 13, 16, and 17, 1906
251 ft.   FLA5725 (print)   FRA2554 (neg.)

The scenes in this picture are a combination of exteriors taken on city streets and interiors photographed on sets of rooms, dining cars, basements, and the interior of a dumbwaiter. The story is based on the trouble a man goes to in order to avoid being served a summons. He disguises himself as a cook and, later, as a black waiter on a train. One set looks as if scenery were moving outside the window of a train.

Subub Surprises the Burglar
Edison © H34382 Aug. 11, 1903
Cameraman: Edwin S. Porter
Location: Studio, N.Y.C. *Photographed:* July 18, 1903
26 ft. FLA3322 (print) FRA0635 (neg.)

A man can be seen sleeping in a Murphy bed in a set of a bedroom. A window in the set opens, and a man dressed as a burglar enters and begins ransacking the place. Apparently he is unsuccessful until he locates the trousers of the sleeping man. The sleeping man wakes while the burglar is going through his trousers, and causes his Murphy bed to fold up against the wall. A series of explosions, as if from gunfire, emanate from the bed. One hits the burglar causing him to disappear in a puff of smoke. The Murphy bed then returns to its original position where its occupant dances happily. NOTE: The Thomas A. Edison trademark appears on the set itself.

See also: The Burglar-Proof Bed, made by AM&B and copyrighted in 1902

Suburban Handicap, 1897
Edison © 43415 July 31, 1897
Location: Sheepshead Bay, Coney Island, N.Y. *Photographed:* 1897
82 ft. FLA4894 (print) FRA1896 (neg.)

The full scope of a day at the race track, from the paddock to the finish line, is shown in this film, which starts with the horses coming out of the paddock and heading for the post. The next scene is of the race itself, while the remainder is of the horses trotting back to the winner's circle or paddock after the finish of the race. The winner, "Ben Brush," is shown.

The Suburbanite
AM&B © H52864 Nov. 11, 1904
Cameraman: A. E. Weed
Cast: John Troiano as the suburbanite
Location: Asbury Park, N.J.; Studio, N.Y.C. *Photographed:* Oct. 21 and 22, 1904
291 ft. FLA5724 (print) FRA2555 (neg.)

The film consists of a series of humorous incidents that arise when a city man with a large family moves to the country. Each sequence is preceded by a title. The city man's dilemma begins with an altercation with the moving men who then throw all of the furniture out on the street. There are scenes of the mother-in-law interfering with the cook, which so annoys the cook that it takes several policemen to get her out of the kitchen. In the last scene, the city man puts a "To Let—Furnished" sign in front of the house and takes his large family back to the city. In one scene, some of his children are sitting on the back porch, when the camera moves into a medium close-up of them, and then moves back out again to the establishing position

after a title appears on the screen. AM&B's bulletin describes the film as "copyright 1904, both as a Picture and as a Play, by The American Mutoscope & Biograph Co."

Such a Flirtation
See: A Flirtation

The Suicide
See: The Downward Path

The Suicide Club
AM&B © H126280 Apr.28, 1909
Director: D. W. Griffith *Cameramen:* G. W. Bitzer, Arthur Marvin
Cast: Mack Sennett, Charles Craig, John Cumpson, Owen Moore, Eddie Dillon, Tony O'Sullivan, Violet Mersereau
Location: Studio, N.Y.C. *Photographed:* Mar. 25–26, 1909
106 ft. FLA5225 (print) FRA9178 (neg.)

It is evident that a meeting of the Suicide Club of America is in session. A masked man in a black cloak passes out numbered slips of paper. The man who draws the unlucky number repairs to another room, carrying a rope, a gun, and a large knife. An attractive young woman brings him a note, which he reads, and then decides life is worth living after all. The club members find no obituary in the newspaper, so they descend on him en masse to demand that he fulfill the terms of his membership and commit suicide. Our hero shows them the letter and orders them from the room.

The Suit of Armor
AM&B © H43623 Mar. 23, 1904
Cameraman: A. E. Weed
Location: Studio, N.Y.C. *Photographed:* Mar. 2, 1904
19 ft. FLA4295 (print) FRA1445 (neg.)

The camera was positioned to best take in the full area of a set of the sitting room of a large house where a young man and a young woman are sitting on a couch. The couch is between a grandfather clock and a pedestal with a suit of armor on it. The young couple hear someone approaching, rise, and the young woman hides behind the clock while her suitor gets into the suit of armor. A pajama-clad man carrying a candle walks by the armor as the hidden man moves the head gear. The man turns quickly as though he saw it move. Apparently he does not believe his eyes when one of the hands slowly changes position. He staggers, turns, and dives in panic headlong through the window in the set.

The Summer Boarders
AM&B © H64737 Aug. 19, 1905
Cameraman: G. W. Bitzer
Location: Leonia, N.J.; Studio, N.Y.C. *Photographed:* July 29, 1905
226 ft. FLA5726 (print) FRA2557 (neg.)

A farmer is pushing a wheelbarrow filled with luggage followed by a group of people dressed as city dwellers. They head toward a house with a sign "Boarders Welcome." The remainder of the picture is a series of humorous sequences based on the cook's desire to get rid of the guests by proceeding to make their lives as miserable as possible. The last portion of the film shows the cook, armed with an axe, chasing the boarders out of the house and throwing their luggage after them.

The Summer Girl
AM&B © H26951 Jan. 14, 1903
Cameraman: F. S. Armitage
Cast: Nella Bergen, from "The Girl From Up There" stage company
Date: Sept. 6, 1899
10 ft. FLA3270 (print) FRA0589 (neg.)

As the film begins, a young woman is seen reading and reclining on a mossy bank by the side of a stream. As the film continues, she removes her shoes and stockings and goes wading in the water.

A Summer Idyl
Biograph © J145067 Sept. 7, 1910
Director: D. W. Griffith *Cameraman:* G. W. Bitzer
Cast: Gertrude Robinson, Henry B. Walthall, Dorothy Bernard, Charles West, Florence Barker, William J. Butler, W. Chrystie Miller, Robert Harron, Charles Hill Mailes, Stephanie Longfellow
Location: Cuddebackville, N.Y. *Photographed:* July 26–27 and Aug. 1–3, 1910
406 ft. FLA5140 (print) FRA2824 (neg.)

A casual refusal to a proposal of marriage causes a young, socially prominent young man (Henry B. Walthall) to take a walking trip in the country where he meets a young girl (Gertrude Robinson) guarding a flock of sheep. The city man obtains lodging on the farm and falls in love with the shepherdess. The young woman who had spurned his proposal has a change of heart and sends for him. The shepherdess's grandfather (W. Chrystie Miller) is delighted, for he had been worried about being left alone in his old age. The film ends with the young man back in the city among his friends and being accepted by the young woman, while the young shepherdess lights her grandfather's pipe.

A Summer Tragedy
Biograph © J145695 Sept. 22, 1910
Cameraman: Arthur Marvin
Cast: Mack Sennett, Florence Barker, Charles West, William Beaudine, Billy Quirk, Eddie Dillon, William J. Butler, Grace Henderson
Location: Greenwich, Conn.; Studio, N.Y.C. *Photographed:* Aug. 12–18, 1910
378 ft. FLA5727 (print) FRA2552 (neg.)

A bachelor (Mack Sennett) is packing for his vacation. He goes to a resort and stays at a good hotel where he registers as a socialite. He meets an attractive young lady, and the two of them spend their vacation telling each other about their wealth and position. They become engaged and each returns home. The young woman enters a drugstore, starts to order a soda, discovers the soda jerk is her fiancé and flounces out in a huff. Disconsolate, the soda jerk enters a restaurant and orders dinner. He looks up as he places his order, and finds the waitress is the girl he met at the resort. The film ends with both of them laughing and shaking hands.

Sunday Morning in Mexico
Edison © 13538 Feb. 24, 1898
Location: Mexico
25 ft. FLA3515 (print) FRA0794 (neg.)

Photographed from a single-camera position, approximately a hundred people are shown going by a church on a plaza. A sign reading "Empressa De Sillas" is visible in the background.

Sunset Limited, Southern Pacific R.R.
Edison © 13551 Feb. 24, 1898
Location: Fingal, Calif.
57 ft. FLA4895 (print) FRA1897 (neg.)

The single-camera position was located on a railroad station platform. Judging from the lack of buildings in the background, the locale is a rural area. A train pulling six coaches approaches the camera position, and there are several persons waving from the windows. The remainder of the film is of the train going away from the camera position.

Sunshine Sue
Biograph © J147831 Nov. 17, 1910
Director: D. W. Griffith *Cameraman:* G. W. Bitzer
Cast: Marion Sunshine, Charles West, Eddie Dillon, W. Chrystie Miller, George Nicholls, Donald Crisp, William J. Butler
Location: Westfield, N.J.; Studio, N.Y.C. *Photographed:* Oct. 6–8, 1910
378 ft. FLA5728 (print) FRA2556 (neg.)

A young woman of rural upbringing goes for a ride in an automobile with a handsome summer boarder. He promises her marriage if she will spend the night at an inn. Ashamed to return home after her city friend deserts her, she wanders through the metropolis in search of work. She finds employment in a piano store but leaves when the proprietor makes advances. She returns home where her father has kept a candle burning in the window for her. The picture ends when the father is relieved to find that the hired hand wants to marry her, and the last scene shows the young couple seated close together in the parlor.

Superintendent's Office
See: The Kleptomaniac

Surf at Atlantic City
AM&B © H29154 Mar. 11, 1903
Location: Atlantic City, N.J.
28 ft. FLA3644 (print) FRA0898 (neg.)

The film, photographed from the end of a pier, shows an area of the boardwalk at the New Jersey summer resort of Atlantic City, as well as some of the bathing beach. The camera was panned in approximately a 90-degree arc to encompass nearly a mile of beach, showing several hundred bathers splashing in the surf. The distance is such that little detail is discernible.

Surf at Monterey
Edison © 60587 Oct. 25, 1897
Location: Monterey, Calif.
20 ft. FLA4155 (print) FRA1323 (neg.)

The cameraman seems to have been intrigued by the run of the surf. The only scenes are of two rocks with the surf breaking on them. This film was part of a series made with the cooperation of the Southern Pacific Company.

Surface Transit, Mexico
Edison © 13564 Feb. 24, 1898
Location: Mexico
26 ft. FLA3824 (print) FRA2884 (neg.)

The camera was placed at a streetcar stop in a large Mexican city. A horsecar, filled with passengers, is in the foreground. Passengers of all ages are shown leaving the streetcar.

Sutro Baths
Edison © 52619 Sept. 20, 1897
Location: San Francisco
24 ft. FLA3019 (print) FRA0051 (neg.)

A large indoor swimming pool is shown, as well as the walkways that separate the varying depths of the water, and a sign identifying the locale on the wall farthest from the camera position. In the immediate foreground, camera right, is a slide that begins its incline high in the air above the water and affords entrance into the water below. There are approximately a hundred persons in the scene.

See also: Lurline Baths

Sutro Baths, no. 1
Edison © 60559 Oct. 25, 1897
Location: San Francisco
26 ft. FLA4439 (print) FRA1545 (neg.)

A public bath is shown. In the background are three tiers of spectators watching the bathers. There are many people bathing and diving into the swimming pool. There is also a two-story slide down which many individuals can be seen descending into the water.

See also: Lurline Baths

Sweet and Twenty
Biograph no copyright July 20, 1909
Director: D. W. Griffith *Cameraman:* G. W. Bitzer
Cast: Mary Pickford, James Kirkwood, Florence Lawrence, Billy Quirk
Location: Greenwich, Conn.; Studio, N.Y.C. *Photographed:* June 19 and 21, 1909
312 ft. FLA5249 (print) FRA2813 (neg.)

An overamorous boyfriend (Billy Quirk) is caught kissing the sister (Florence Lawrence) of his sweetheart (Mary Pickford), which gets him a slap in the face for his impertinence. The picture proceeds by showing the boyfriend threatening to drown himself in the dark, cold water of the river. By the use of several camera positions, the despondent young man is walked across fields and fences and brought down to the river's edge where he removes one shoe but is interrupted as he is preparing to jump into the water. His girlfriend follows him and convinces him she still loves him. The film ends as the two are seen making up after the young lady succeeds in persuading him not to jump in the river.

A Sweet Little Home in the Country
AM&B © H23786 Nov. 11, 1902
10 ft. FLA3500 (print) FRA0780 (neg.)

The poor condition and the grainy quality of the film do not permit too much description of detail. It is possible to see from the opening scene, judging from the many trees and the rural terrain, that the picture was photographed in a country area. A child is standing in the midst of a flock of chickens while in one corner of the yard a man dressed as a tramp is being chased by another man wielding a large stick. As the film ends, they are just passing the camera position.

Sweet Revenge
Biograph © J135021 Nov. 20, 1909
Director: D. W. Griffith *Cameraman:* G. W. Bitzer
Cast: Marion Leonard, Arthur Johnson
Location: Central Park and Studio, N.Y.C. *Photographed:* Oct. 11 and 13, 1909
172 ft. FLA5729 (print) FRA2556 (neg.)

Most of the film is devoted to showing the mental anguish experienced by a woman (Marion Leonard) when she learns through a newspaper item that she has been jilted by the man (Arthur Johnson) she thinks loves her. She packs up his love letters to her and a photograph of them together, and dispatches them by messenger to the woman he is going to marry the next day. There are several scenes of her savoring her revenge, followed by one of the messenger boy accidentally dropping the package into the water from a bridge. He returns, admits his carelessness, and the woman is now torn between relief and annoyance that her plan did not succeed.

Sweethearts
AM&B © H22092 Sept. 27, 1902
Cameraman: Robert K. Bonine
Date: Aug. 4, 1902
16 ft. FLA3887 (print) FRA1109 (neg.)

Two infants are seated on a small settee in the yard of a large house. The babies have their arms around each other, and they are being directed by someone off camera to kiss. The quality of the film is poor.

Sweets for the Sweet
AM&B © H34507 Aug. 13, 1903
Cameraman: G. W. Bitzer
Cast: Kathryn Osterman
Location: Studio, N.Y.C. *Photographed:* July 31, 1903
19 ft. FLA3590 (print) FRA2135 (neg.)

The moment this film begins, a young woman can be seen sitting at a table. She is very well dressed and her hair is properly coiffed. The young woman and the table are artificially lighted. No background is visible. A woman dressed as a maid enters. She brings a box of chocolates which she hands to the seated woman. The remainder of the film shows the young woman opening the box of candy, reading the note, and eating several pieces of the candy while talking to the camera.

The Swimming Class
AM&B © H48622 July 28, 1904
Cameraman: G. W. Bitzer
Location: Coney Island, N.Y. *Photographed:* July 20, 1904
48 ft. FLA4896 (print) FRA1898 (neg.)

It is obvious that the cameraman placed his equipment close to the edge of a seashore. A large number of children followed by bathers can be seen running into the surf from behind the camera position. Close to the end, the camera's view is obscured as a female bather of large proportions strolls between the swimmers and the camera.

The Swimming Ducks at Allentown Duck Farm

Edison © H16122   Apr. 7, 1902
Location: Allentown, Pa.
31 ft.   FLA3938 (print)   FRA1150 (neg.)

A large group of white ducks swim in a pool of water surrounded by a fence.

Swimming Pool at Coney Island

Edison © H7983   Aug. 21, 1901
Location: Coney Island, N.Y.
25 ft.   FLA3736 (print)   FRA0982 (neg.)

The camera was positioned on the edge of a large public swimming pool. Many children jump in the water from the edge of the pool opposite the camera and swim toward the camera.

Swimming Pool, Palm Beach

AM&B © H56666   Feb. 13, 1905
Cameraman: G. W. Bitzer
Location: Palm Beach, Fla. *Photographed:* Feb. 3, 1905
63 ft.   FLA5226 (print)   FRA2179 (neg.)

The film, photographed from a single-camera position, shows a swimming pool with a white building on the far side. Several persons in bathing suits dive into the water from a springboard, as well as from the balcony above.

A Swimming Race at Coney Island

AM&B © H49074   Aug. 13, 1904
Cameraman: G. W. Bitzer
Location: Coney Island, N.Y. *Photographed:* Aug. 7, 1904
23 ft.   FLA3302 (print)   FRA0616 (neg.)

The camera was positioned on a seashore. In the distance, there is a small sailboat on which several people are standing. Two of the passengers on the small boat dive into the water and begin to swim toward the camera. Spectators in the water cheer the two swimmers. They reach the shore, walk out of the water and out of camera range. Each is wearing the insignia of the Red Cross on his swimsuit.

Swiss Village, no. 2

Edison © D18533   Aug. 29, 1900
Location: Paris
40 ft.   FLA4897 (print)   FRA1899 (neg.)

[Paris Exposition]

The film shows a compound area surrounded by architecture of Swiss design intended to interest tourists in the products of Switzerland. In the foreground, various and sundry individuals pass the camera position. Both young men and women in Swiss alpenstock costumes dance to music from concertinas. Large, healthy appearing cattle are led across the compound by people wearing Swiss costumes.

See also: Scene in the Swiss Village at Paris Exposition

Switchback on Trolley Road

AM&B © H16641   Apr. 16, 1902
30 ft.   FLA4268 (print)   FRA1423 (neg.)

The camera evidently was placed either on a moving trolley or a train, as the only thing visible is the track area where tracklayers can be seen working. The photographer was taken on a circuitous route through wooded country. The vehicle finally comes to a stop at an excavated area where switchback tracks have been laid. The cameraman kept photographing while the car on which he was riding made the stop, went back up onto the switching mechanism, and continued on its way on another track.

Symphony in "A-Flat"

AM&B © H32558   June 12, 1903
Cameramen: G. W. Bitzer, Arthur Marvin
Location: Studio, N.Y.C. *Date:* Apr. 22, 1899
15 ft.   FLA3498 (print)   FRA0778 (neg.)

The camera was placed as if it were a spectator at a vaudeville house. There is a theatrical flat representing the side of a two-story house, where a man is painting. Men can be seen in the two windows just above him. The men in the windows reach out trying to attract the attention of women in the other windows. The women assume that the painter is the culprit and throw objects at him.

Tableau

See: The Kleptomaniac

Take Mellon's Food

AM&B © H24879   Dec. 9, 1902
9 ft.   FLA3179 (print)   FRA0506 (neg.)

A young woman dressed as a maid, with a baby carriage, is sitting on a bench in front of a backdrop painted to resemble a park. A man in a policeman's uniform comes by and they exchange pleasantries. At this point, a man dressed as a tramp can be seen stealing the baby's bottle. The policeman, suddenly aware of the tramp, leads him from the scene by the scruff of his neck. Mellon's food was a popular infants' food around the turn of the century.

Taking President McKinley's Body From Train at Canton, Ohio

Edison © H9083   Sept. 26, 1901
Location: Canton, Ohio Photographed Sept. 18, 1901
29 ft.   FLA3033 (print)   FRA2132 (neg.)

This film was photographed from two camera positions, and shows the area where the guard of honor (pallbearers) is removing the casket containing the remains of President McKinley from the railroad car. The second camera position shows the pallbearers as they carry the casket to the hearse and place it inside.

Tally-Ho Departing for the Races

Edison © H7638   Aug. 14, 1901
Location: Country Club, Buffalo, N.Y.
34 ft.   FLA3979 (print)   FRA1187 (neg.)

The film shows the departure of groups of people using a type of transportation classified as a tally-ho coach. The camera was positioned so that the six horses pulling the coaches are visible in the foreground. In the background more coaches can be seen loaded with at least forty passengers. The first coach drawn by six white horses passes the camera, followed by two other coaches, and finally a buggy drawn by one horse.

Taming a Husband
Biograph © J138677 Feb. 26, 1910
Director: D. W. Griffith *Cameraman:* G. W. Bitzer
Cast: Florence LaBadie, Arthur Johnson, Dorothy West, Tony O'Sullivan, Mack Sennett
Location: Studio, N.Y.C. *Photographed:* Jan. 10 and 12, 1910
362 ft. FLA5730 (print) FRA2559 (neg.)

All of the cast are in late seventeenth-century costumes. The heroine (Florence La Badie) feels that her husband (Arthur Johnson) has grown cold, so she writes to her friend (Dorothy West) to visit her. Together they conspire to make him jealous. The friend dresses as a man and begins to pay attention to the lonesome wife. The husband's jealousy provokes him to issue a challenge to a duel, but before it can take place, some of his friends tell him that the illicit affair is in progress. Accompanied by the friends, the husband breaks down the door, and finds two young women, as the friend has now changed back to her own clothes.

Taming of the Shrew
AM&B © H118185 Nov. 11, 1908
Director: D. W. Griffith *Cameramen:* G. w. Bitzer, Arthur Marvin
Cast: Florence Lawrence, Linda Arvidson, Harry Salter, Arthur Johnson, W. J. Butler, Frank Gebhardt
Location: Coytesville, N.J.; Studio, N.Y.C. *Photographed:* Oct. 1 and 7, 1908
Based on the play by William Shakespeare
384 ft. FLA5731 (print) FRA2561 (neg.)

This film followed as closely as its short length permitted the play The Taming of the Shrew. There are several scenes of the shrew (Florence Lawrence) beating relatives, friends, and servants with various and sundry objects, including pieces of furniture, before she acquires a husband who proves to be more than a match for her terrible temper. All the scenes were photographed from a single-camera position, and all activity parallels the camera plane.

Taping Coils, Westinghouse Works
See: Westinghouse Works

Tapping a Furnace, Westinghouse Works
See: Westinghouse Works

Tarrant Fire
AM&B © H25967 Dec. 31, 1902
Cameraman: F. S. Armitage
Location: Warren and Greenwich Streets, N.Y.C. *Date:* Oct. 29, 1900
22 ft. FLA4180 (print) FRA1344 (neg.)

The short length of the film and the poor quality of the photography do not permit much description of detail, but it is evident from the amount of smoke visible that there was a fire in a building in the business district of a city. The film was reportedly photographed about an hour after an explosion wrecked Tarrant & Company's drug manufacturing plant in New York City.

The Tavern Keeper's Daughter
AM&B © H113770 July 22, 1908
Director: D. W. Griffith *Cameraman:* Arthur Marvin
Cast: Marion Leonard, Harry Salter, Frank Gebhardt
Location: Coytesville, N.J. and Studio, N.Y.C.
Photographed: July 2 and 13, 1908
159 ft. FLA5732 (print) FRA2562 (neg.)

The few scenes in this short film begin in a set that resembles a rural tavern, where the attractive tavern keeper's daughter is waiting on three customers. One of them makes advances to her, and she runs away to a friend's home, where there is a small child in a crib. The amorous admirer pursues her, and she hides behind a curtain. When the man sees the small baby in its crib, he kneels in mute awe and respect, and this cools his ardor. The last scene shows him with his hat in hand pleading with the young woman for forgiveness.

Teams of Horses
Edison © 60566 Oct. 25, 1897
Location: Long Branch, N.J. [?]
26 ft. FLA4036 (print) FRA1223 (neg.)

The film shows the edge of an exhibition area in front of a large grandstand filled with spectators. The crowd is watching mixed teams of trained carriage horses being driven by the grandstand. Several teams of horses harnessed to custom-made carriages can be seen.

Teasing
AM&B © H65319 Sept. 11, 1905
Cameraman: G. W. Bitzer
Location: Studio, N.Y.C. *Date:* Aug. 24, 1905
19 ft. FLA3984 (print) FRA1192 (neg.)

The cameraman photographed over the right shoulder of a young woman reclining on a couch while rebuffing the advances of a young man intent on kissing her. Throughout the film, the young woman eludes his advances. Finally, at the end of the picture, she seems to have accepted his persistence as sincere and she allows him to kiss her.

The Telephone
Edison © 31432 May 20, 1898
15 ft. FLA4089 (print) FRA1270 (neg.)

A plain, flat wall with a telephone affixed can be seen. A man wearing a black suit and a homburg comes up to the telephone and reads a sign that says "Don't Travel. Use the Telephone. You Can Get Anything You Want." He puts a coin in the telephone slot and is seen removing a coffee cup from the coin-return aperture and drinking coffee. He then returns to the telephone and begins talking into the mouthpiece, ending the film.

The Telephone
Edison © 40020 July 18, 1898
24 ft. FLA4090 (print) FRA1271 (neg.)

This is a primitive attempt at comedy. The set is a telephone booth with a sign on the wall reading, "You Can Get Anything By Telephone." A man approaches the telephone, inserts a coin, operates the crank, and apparently does not reach either his party or the operator. He becomes angry and pounds the phone. As the film ends, water squirts all over him out of the mouthpiece.

A Temporary Truce

Biograph © J170148 June 10, 1912

Director: D. W. Griffith *Cameraman:* G. W. Bitzer

Cast: Blanche Sweet, Claire McDowell, Charles West, W. Chrystie Miller, Alfred Paget, Walter Chrystie Cabanne, Robert Harron, Charles Gorman, Charles Hill Mailes

Location: Southern Calif.

570 ft. FLA5903 (print) FRA2769 (neg.)

The two reels of this film show how a prospector's wife is kidnapped by a no-account Mexican villain, and how her husband declares a temporary truce with him so they can fight their common enemy, the Indians. The last scene, photographed from many different camera angles, was a tight group shot showing that the principals had survived, while all the Indians were dead. Ironically, the persons who set off the Indian attack in the first place were simply some drunken drifters.

Temptation of St. Anthony

AM&B © H18047 May 23, 1902

Cameraman: Arthur Marvin

Location: Roof studio, N.Y.C. *Date:* Aug. 3, 1900

13 ft. FLA3402 (print) FRA0696 (neg.)

Photographed from a single-camera position, the film shows a man seated at a desk turning the pages of a manuscript. He turns his head toward the camera and, by the use of stop-action photography, an unclothed woman appears before him. He gets up from where he has been sitting and moves towards her. She moves away from him to the edge of the stage and turns into a skeleton. When St. Anthony sees the skeleton, he falls to the floor.

10 Ladies in an Umbrella

Méliès © H37293 Oct. 26, 1903

Creator: Georges Méliès *Cast:* Georges Méliès

Location: Montreuil, France *Date:* Summer 1903

Original titles: 10 Femmes dans un Parapluie, and La Parapluie Fantastique

75 ft. FLA5230 (print) FRA2180 (neg.)

The concept of this short but very busy film was a typical Georges Méliès fantasy. The set, in front of a painted backdrop, was designed like the stage of a theater. A performer appears and for the remainder of the film does acrobatic tricks, appears and disappears, conjures up as many as ten beautifully gowned women, waves a wand causing their costumes to change and makes them disappear.

Ten Nights in a Bar-Room: Death Of Little May

AM&B © H31693 May 5, 1903

Cameraman: F. S. Armitage

Location: Roof studio, N.Y.C. *Date:* June 19, 1901

19 ft. FLA4397 (print) FRA1526 (neg.)

The whole story was filmed from a single-camera position. The action takes place in a set of either the bedroom or the living room of some people in poor circumstances. A little girl with her head bandaged is lying on the bed in the center of the room, with a man and a woman standing over her. Judging from their gestures, they are anxious over the possible death of the young girl. As the film ends, the child falls back against the pillow as if dead. The woman attending her swoons, and the father falls on the floor in a faint.

Ten Nights in a Bar-Room: Death of Slade

AM&B © H31694 May 5, 1903

Cameraman: F. S. Armitage

Location: Roof studio, N.Y.C. *Date:* June 20, 1901

13 ft. FLA4398 (print) FRA1527 (neg.)

The first scene takes place in a set of a saloon. The first person visible is a man seated in a chair with his head rolling about as if he is completely intoxicated. He starts to rise to his feet as another man comes in. The second man's actions convey the impression that he also is intoxicated. The two men continue to act completely demoralized by alcohol. One falls down as if dead, and the film ends.

Ten Nights in a Bar-Room: The Fatal Blow

AM&B © H31692 May 5, 1903

Cameraman: F. S. Armitage

Location: Roof studio, N.Y.C. *Date:* June 19, 1901

20 ft. FLA4399 (print) FRA1528 (neg.)

The opening scene was photographed outdoors on a set of a saloon. The action begins as two men greet one another and sit down and have a drink at a table near the bar. Another man, acting intoxicated, comes in and begins insulting the bartender and guests. A fight ensues and a woman, not previously in the picture, falls down in front of the camera apparently having been struck by something that was thrown. At the end of the film, the intoxicated man is prevented from striking the bartender with a chair.

Ten Nights in a Bar-Room: Murder of Willie

AM&B © H31691 May 5, 1903

Cameraman: F. S. Armitage

Location: Roof studio, N.Y.C. *Date:* June 19, 1901

11 ft. FLA4400 (print) FRA1529 (neg.)

Two men are playing cards at a table on a set of a saloon. Behind the bar is a saloon keeper. A door opens, and a man in a linen duster enters, buys and consumes two or three drinks, and leaves. As the door closes, perhaps on signal, the two men at the table begin an altercation over what seems to be one player's cheating. A fight starts in which the bartender is rendered *hors de combat*. The man in the linen duster reenters and breaks up the fight.

Ten Nights in a Bar-Room: Vision of Mary

AM&B © H31673 May 11, 1903

Cameraman: F. S. Armitage

Location: Roof studio, N.Y.C. *Date:* June 19, 1901

16 ft. FLA3129 (print) FRA0463 (neg.)

There is one-camera position of a scene that begins with a woman walking into a sitting room accompanied by a man who embraces her. At the time of the embrace, an image of an angel with outstretched arms is superimposed.

The Tenderfoot's Triumph

AM&B © J140758 Apr. 23, 1910

Cameraman: Arthur Marvin

Cast: Arthur Johnson, Florence Barker, Charles West, Jack Pickford

Location: Verdugo, Calif. *Photographed:* Feb. 23–24, 1910

377 ft. FLA5733 (print) FRA2564 (neg.)

The men of a town are offered a double reward in the form of money and the prettiest girl. She says she will marry the man who is successful in capturing some horse-stealing bandits. The townspeople prepare to search for the bandits, and a stagecoach brings a minister (Arthur Johnson) into town. He decides to seek the rewards, and the film ends with the discouraged posse returning to town, while the minister, at whom they had laughed, captures the bandits. The last scenes show the minister riding into town while he holds a gun on the bandits and is greeted enthusiastically by the prettiest girl in town.

Tenderloin at Night

Edison © 77521 Nov. 27, 1899

56 ft. FLA4898 (print) FRA2891 (neg.)

The film begins on a saloon set. Two women are sitting at one of the two tables. The door opens and an actor dressed as a rube enters and is seated at the other table. He signals the waiter and buys a drink for the two women. During his drunkenness, one of the women steals his wallet and stuffs it in her garter. When the police are called, they do nothing to the culprits. And the additional result of his revelry is a hangover.

Tenderloin Tragedy

AM&B © H92891 Apr. 22, 1907

Cameraman: G. W. Bitzer

Location: Studio, N.Y.C. *Photographed:* Mar. 15, 1907

188 ft. FLA5734 (print) FRA2565 (neg.)

A woman is sitting in a rocking chair knitting, and a man is reading nearby. There is no explanation of why a bearded man carrying a doctor's satchel walks through the set, reappears, picks up his hat, and leaves. A clock on the wall indicates that it is 10:30. The woman leaves the room, presumably to retire, and the man dons a silk hat and starts off for a gay evening. The next scene shows him in a private dining room, drinking and dancing with two young ladies of the evening. Soon the exertion proves too much and he collapses. A doctor is summoned, but the man dies as the young women watch in horror.

10th U.S. Infantry Disembarking From Cars

Edison © 31445 May 20, 1898

43 ft. FLA3317 (print) FRA0631 (neg.)

[Spanish-American War]

The film was photographed at a railroad siding, where a railroad car can be seen in the foreground. Approaching the camera position alongside the railroad car are men in the uniform of the U.S. Army marching in columns of fours. As the men reach the end of the car, they turn and continue to march out of camera range. At least three companies of men pass the camera position. The only other people in the scene are two Pullman porters.

10th U.S. Infantry, 2nd Battalion, Leaving Cars

Edison © 31440 May 20, 1898

44 ft. FLA4899 (print) FRA1900 (neg.)

[Spanish-American War]

American infantry troops dressed in field uniforms of the Spanish-American War can be seen close to the foreground of the camera position. Three companies of men, in columns of fours, march by the camera. In the background are railroad passengers, indicating the film was photographed on a rail siding area.

Le Terrible Bourreau Turc

See: The Terrible Turkish Executioner

A Terrible Night

AM&B © H19659 July 2, 1902

Cameraman: F. S. Armitage

Location: Roof studio, N.Y.C. *Date:* Apr. 6, 1900

16 ft. FLA4033 (print) FRA1221 (neg.)

A man is seen sleeping in a bed in a bedroom set. Stop-action photography is used to materialize a man dressed as the Devil who appears and disappears from the center of the room, from the interior of trunks, and from behind a screen as he is pursued by the man who has been asleep. As the film ends, the man is sitting on the edge of the bed drinking the contents of a whiskey bottle, completely exhausted by his unsuccessful efforts to catch the Devil.

A Terrible Night

AM&B © H110869 May 22, 1908

Cameraman: G. W. Bitzer

Location: Coytesville, N.J.; Studio, N.Y.C. *Photographed:* May 12 and 13, 1908

369 ft. FLA5735 (print) FRA2568 (neg.)

The picture opens in a mountaineer's cabin where a young girl and her father are busying themselves with food and chores. A city man enters and there is a transaction of some sort. The mountaineer buries the money he has been given in the hearth. The villain has observed everything from outside, and the next scene shows him and his companion holding up a horse-drawn wagon. After overcoming the driver, one of the men hides in a sack that is delivered with others to the mountaineer. The young girl, alone in the cabin, notices the sack move and pushes it through a trap door into the cellar, but the villain frees himself and attacks the girl. The mountaineer returns just in time to shoot him and save the girl and the money. This film was released on May 26, 1908, under the title A Night of Terror, although it was copyright as A Terrible Night.

Terrible Teddy, the Grizzly King

Edison © H1402 Feb. 23, 1901

Cameraman: Edwin S. Porter

27 ft. FLA4901 (print) FRA1901 (neg.)

The film opens in a wooded area where the ground is snow-covered. There are three men who walk toward the camera. The second camera position is about twenty feet from a big tree. The man in the lead walks rapidly and carries a rifle. The two men following him are dressed in normal street apparel but wear overcoats with signs attached. One reads, "My Press Agent," and the other, "My Photographer." The man with a rifle strikes a pose as if about to shoot. The cameraman takes his position to photograph "Terrible Teddy." The gun goes off, a house cat falls to the snow beside the hunter, who takes out a knife and stabs the cat several times for the benefit of the press. He then mounts his horse, takes the trophy and rifle, and rides off toward and past camera position, with the two men walking after him on foot. The film was intended as a satire on Vice-pres. Theodore Roosevelt.

The Terrible Turkish Executioner
Méliès © H40638 Jan. 4, 1904
Creator: Georges Méliès *Cast:* Georges Méliès
Location: Montreuil, France *Date:* Winter 1903–4
Other copyright title: Le Terrible Bourreau Turc
Original title: Le Bourreau Turc
66 ft. FLA4902 (print) FRA1902 (neg.)

Four men costumed as Turks are hauled into what is presumably a market place. Their captor puts a board with a hole in it, similar to a stock, on their heads. A bearded man is notified that the time has come and with exaggerated gestures sharpens a large scimitar. The executioner, with one mighty swoop, cuts off all four heads which fall at his feet. He picks the heads up and places them in a nearby barrel. Apparently the heads do not wish to remain separated from the bodies for each in turn leaves the barrel and returns to the body from which it was severed.

Terrier vs. Wild Cat
AM&B © H73110 Feb. 9, 1906
Cameraman: G. W. Bitzer
Location: Studio, N.Y.C. *Photographed:* Jan. 30, 1906
32 ft. FLA3742 (print) FRA0988 (neg.)

This shows an arranged fight between a terrier and an alley cat. During the length of the film, the spectators harass the animals to a point where they are forced to attack one another.

The Test
Biograph © J136053 Dec. 20, 1909
Director: D. W. Griffith *Cameramen:* G. W. Bitzer, Arthur Marvin
Cast: Mary Pickford, Billy Quirk, Lottie Pickford, Arthur Johnson, Marion Leonard, John Cumpson, Lillian Gish, Charles West
Location: Coytesville, N.J.; Studio, N.Y.C. *Photographed:* Nov. 11 and 13, 1909
203 ft. FLA5736 (print) FRA2560 (neg.)

A wife (Mary Pickford), not really sure her husband (Billy Quirk) loves her, removes her photograph from his wallet just as he leaves on a business trip. He assures her the picture will be with him at all times and departs. There are scenes showing the husband overcoming the temptations of a large city and writing his wife but making the mistake of saying her picture is in front of him. Annoyed and now definitely suspicious, the wife writes and implies he is not telling the truth. He, in turn, wires his mother to send him the the picture she has of his wife, which she does. When the husband returns home, he shows his wife the picture he has, and the film ends with the wife pleading for forgiveness.

The Test of Friendship
AM&B © H119491 Dec. 10, 1908
Director: D. W. Griffith *Cameraman:* G. W. Bitzer
Cast: Arthur Johnson, Florence Lawrence, Jeanie Macpherson, Mack Sennett, Linda Arvidson, Gertrude Robinson, Violet Mersereau, Robert Harron

Location: Studio, N.Y.C.; Hoboken, N.J. *Photographed:* Nov. 6–25, 1908
288 ft. FLA5737 (print) FRA2569 (neg.)

A rich young man (Arthur Johnson), tired of his playboy life and of his friends whom he thinks are only interested in his money, announces he has lost all his money. He takes a job in a factory where he meets an attractive young woman (Florence Lawrence). He interferes in a fight in her behalf, and is injured and bedridden. The young woman visits him at the same time some medicine arrives; when he does not have any money to pay for it, she sells her long beautiful hair to get the necessary cash. As soon as the young man regains his health, he proposes to the young woman he is sure loves him for himself alone, and they are married. After the wedding, he tells her of his wealth and can be seen bedecking her in jewels and finery.

Testing a Rotary, Westinghouse Works
See: Westinghouse Works

Testing Large Turbines, Westinghouse Works
See: Westinghouse Works

"Teutonic" and "Noordland"
AM&B © H18045 May 23, 1902
21 ft. FLA3445 (print) FRA1550 (neg.)

The camera position was on the deck of a boat, and the film shows two large ships as they pass by at approximately fifteen knots.

The "Texas" Naval Parade
Edison © 52055 Sept. 3, 1898
Location: Hudson River, N.Y.C. *Date:* Aug. 20, 1998
26 ft. FLA4111 (print) FRA1287 (neg.)
[Spanish-American War; New York City Welcome to Admiral Sampson's Fleet After the Battle of Santiago Bay]

This film shows the U.S. battleship *Texas* anchored fore and aft in the Hudson River off New York City. The short length of the film includes only one view of the ship and that is from abaft the beam on the port side. The camera was located on some sort of boat at a distance that allowed the full ship's silhouette to be seen at one time, but it was too far away for detailed description. The *Texas* was part of Admiral Sampson's North Atlantic squadron which had just returned from fighting in the Pacific.

That Chink at Golden Gulch
Biograph © J146413 Oct. 12, 1910
Director: D. W. Griffith *Cameraman:* G. W. Bitzer
Cast: Charles West, Dell Henderson, Gertrude Robinson, W. Chrystie Miller, Tony O'Sullivan
Location: Cuddebackville, N.Y. *Photographed:* Aug. 25–31 and Sept. 1, 1910
369 ft. FLA5738 (print) FRA2563 (neg.)

A group of ruffians led by the villain (Dell Henderson) molest a Chinese laundryman in small gold-mining town. At the height of the harassment, the hero (Charles West) and his girl interfere and save him. The townspeople are seeking a holdup man who has robbed the pony express on five occasions, and they offer a reward. The laundryman becomes suspicious of the villain and begins to follow him.

He witnesses a holdup and cuts off his queue and uses it to tie up the villain. The laundryman turns the holdup man over to the local constabulary, collects the reward, presents it to his friends as a wedding dowry, and leaves the town.

That Little Band of Gold

Keystone © LP4745 Mar. 13, 1915
Producer and Author: Mack Sennett
Cast: Roscoe Arbuckle, Mabel Normand, Alice Davenport, Ford Sterling, Ethel Madison, Charles Arling, Al St. John, Charles Chase, Glen Cavender, Frank Hayes, Estelle Allen, Billie Brockwell, Edgar Kennedy, Dora Rogers, Slim Summerville
Location: Interior of Alexandria Hotel, the Mason Opera House and the Keystone studio area in Los Angeles
879 ft. FLA6139-6140 (print)

Fatty and Mabel get married and her mother (Alice Davenport) lives with them. One evening, the two women are waiting for Fatty to come home, but when he does get there, he is decidedly drunk. But they attend the opera anyway, where a bored Fatty spies an acquaintance with a lovely girl, Ethel Madison. He makes signs to the man, Ford Sterling, and at intermission meets them in a restaurant. Sterling, upset at losing his girl to Fatty, calls Mabel at the opera. When Mabel and her mother arrive, a free-for-all occurs. Mother insists Mabel divorce a chastened Fatty, but when Mabel and Fatty meet outside the courthouse after the divorce, they rush inside to get married again.

That Poor Insurance Man

Paley & Steiner © H52170 Oct. 27, 1904
7 ft. FLA4420 (print) FRA1537 (neg.)

A woman, a man, and some half-grown children are standing on the steps of the front porch of a modest house. A man in a dark suit at the bottom of the stairs is being pelted with vegetables and water from pots and buckets by the family on the porch. The man of the house rushes down the stairs, grabs the man in the dark suit by the seat of his trousers, and escorts him off the property, ending the film.

That Springtime Feeling

Keystone © LP4554 Feb. 25, 1915
Producer and Author: Mack Sennett
Cast: Sydney Chaplin, Cecile Arnold, Jimmy Finlayson, Hugh Fay
Location: Griffith Park, Los Angeles
375 ft. FLA6141 (print)

Cecile Arnold, an attractive nursemaid, is sitting in the park minding an infant boy who manages to crawl into a large metal barrel. Just then, Sydney Chaplin happens along and extricates the child. He flirts unsuccessfully with the nursemaid and consequently becomes the target of disfavor of a policeman. The balance of the film is taken up with his fights with the policeman, interspersed with the antics of a drunk (Hugh Fay) who also takes on the policeman. Both wind up, heads down, in the same barrel where the infant was found at the beginning of the picture.

Thaw-White Tragedy

AM&B © H80229 July 5, 1906
Cast: Gene Gauntier
Cameraman: G. W. Bitzer

Location: Studio, N.Y.C. *Photographed:* June 27, 1906
30 ft. FLA4041 (print) FRA1228 (neg.)

The film opens on a set of a fashionable restaurant, where several men and women are sitting at tables. Their clothing is modish and they are applauding a performer who is not shown in the picture. A man in a full-length overcoat makes a dramatic entrance from camera left. With a great flourish, he pulls a pistol from his pocket and fires several times at one of the seated spectators, who falls to the floor. The scene ends as someone covers the body on the floor with a white cloth. This is a reconstruction of the murder of Stanford White by Harry K. Thaw, June 25, 1906, at a restaurant on the roof of Madison Square Garden.

Theatre Hat

AM&B © H26848 Jan. 9, 1903
Date: 1897 [?]
11 ft. FLA3276 (print) FRA0593 (neg.)

The camera was positioned as if behind the seats of a theater. Immediately in the camera foreground are several men sitting in back of a row of women wearing enormous hats, which obstruct the men's view of the performance, which seems to be a jumping clown. At the end of the film, one of the men is trying to peer around the women's huge hats with a telescope.

Theatre Hats Off

AM&B © H26849 Jan. 9, 1903
Date: 1897 [?]
10 ft. FLA3157 (print) FRA0485 (neg.)

This was photographed as if from the audience at a vaudeville show. Between the stage and the camera are the backs and heads of a number of people watching a woman doing an acrobatic tap dance. The camera does not move during the film, while the dancer remains in almost her original position and dances until the film ends.

Theatre Road, Yokohama

Edison © 38213 June 22, 1898
Cameraman: James H. White, W. Bleckyrden
Location: Yokohama, Japan
27 ft. FLA4313 (print) FRA1462 (neg.)

The cameramen who photographed the film were thwarted by the numerous small children who were attracted to the equipment they had placed on the edge of a busy thoroughfare in Japan. Almost at the beginning of the film, at least three urchins are inquisitive about their actions. By the time the film was completed, the only sight to be seen is approximately twenty small children standing close enough to the camera to block out everything in the background.

Their First Kidnapping Case

Biograph © J168045 Apr. 10, 1912
Director: Mack Sennett
Cast: Mack Sennett, Fred Mace, Eddie Dillon
Location: Southern Calif.
189 ft. FLA5739 (print) FRA2570 (neg.)

The plot of this farce consists of a series of situations in which two detectives (Mack Sennett and Fred Mace) find themselves when they mistakenly assume that a baby with a contagious disease is the kidnapped baby they have been hired to find. The film ends with the two detectives and their self-appointed assistant (Eddie Dillon) quarantined in a hospital by the Public Health Department.

Their Social Splash
Keystone © LP5198 Apr. 26, 1915
Producer and Author: Mack Sennett
Cast: Dixie Chene, Slim Summerville, Charles Murray, Polly Moran, Harold Lloyd, Frank Hayes, Estelle Allen
Location: Keystone studio and downtown Los Angeles
533 ft. FLA6142 (print)

Polly Moran and her husband, Charles Murray, are guests at an engagement or wedding party of Dixie Chene and Slim Summerville. There are several scenes of the group ballroom dancing, one of which ends in a fight between Murray and Summerville, with a ferocious Polly Moran taking part. All three eventually wind up on the roof and are shown as they cross from one building to another in the business section of Los Angeles. Somehow, the three fall through a skylight into a swimming pool around which the party has been taking place. The picture ends with a bemused Charles Murray standing waist high in water holding a baby crocodile.

Theodore Roosevelt Leaving the White House
AM&B © H27382 Jan. 22, 1903
Location: Washington, D.C.
13 ft. FLA3351 (print) FRA0688 (neg.)

This film, photographed from a single-camera position, shows the White House in the background. From camera left, Theodore Roosevelt appears and walks toward the camera, and then turns. AM&B production records give the title as Hon. Theo. Roosevelt, Asst. Sec'y, U.S. Navy leaving White House.

They Found the Leak
AM&B © H24889 Dec. 9, 1902
Cameraman: Robert K. Bonine
Location: Roof studio, N.Y.C. *Date:* May 31, 1902
14 ft. FLA3765 (print) FRA1010 (neg.)

A man accompanied by another, dressed as a fire inspector, walk down a flight of stairs on a cellar set. They appear to be looking for something with a lighted candle. There is an explosion, wrecking the basement, and the film ends as a policeman and a woman are extricating the two men from the wreckage.

They Meet on the Mat
AM&B © H79738 June 19, 1906
Cameraman: G. W. Bitzer
Location: Studio, N.Y.C. *Photographed:* May 25, 1906
20 ft. FLA3839 (print) FRA1099

Two young women wearing black gymnasium clothes can be seen standing on a white mat in the beginning stance of a wrestling match. A man in the background appears to be directing them as to what to do. The two come to grips with one another and for the remainder of the film push and pull and twist, each attempting to win the wrestling match.

They Would Elope
Biograph © J130485 Aug. 10, 1909

Director: D. W. Griffith *Cameramen:* G. W. Bitzer, Mr. Higgin
Cast: Mary Pickford, Billy Quirk, James Kirkwood, Kate Bruce, Mack Sennett, Arthur Johnson, Owen Moore, W. J. Butler
Location: Little Falls, N.J.; Studio, N.Y.C. *Photographed:* June 24, 25 and July 15, 1909
216 ft. FLA5740 (print) FRA6444 (neg.)

This situation comedy shows a series of events that begin when a young girl (Mary Pickford) and a boy (Billy Quirk) elope. They leave a note and start out in a buggy that breaks down, and continue on foot. They hitch a ride in an automobile that blows up. Fearing their pursuers are close behind, they start running. The girl collapses from exhaustion, and the boy borrows a wheelbarrow from a passing farmer (Mack Sennett) and they continue until they come to a boat landing, get in a canoe, start paddling, and manage to fall out. In sheer disgust, they return home, only to find her mother and father have invited all their friends to a wedding feast and even have the minister there. The last scene shows the two muddy, sodden youngsters being married.

The Thief and the Pie Woman
AM&B © H28675 Feb. 26, 1903
Cameraman: Arthur Marvin
Location: Roof studio, N.Y.C. *Date:* May 24, 1900
10 ft. FLA3163 (print) FRA0493 (neg.)

An old woman is seen sitting beside a homemade concession stand with a sign on it that reads "Pies and Cakes for Sale." The woman is knitting when she is accosted by a man who seems to be fleeing and who asks for help. The old woman allows him to hide under her covered stall, which he does. A policeman appears on the scene and questions the old woman who points off stage. While the old woman is engaged in misdirecting the policeman, the pie stall gets up and slowly walks off, being propelled by the man who had hidden under it.

The Thirteen Club
AM&B © H69185 Nov. 29, 1905
Cameramen: G. W. Bitzer, F. A. Dobson
Location: Studio, N.Y.C. *Photographed:* Nov. 16–18, 1905
230 ft. FLA5741 (print) FRA2571 (neg.)

A black waiter is setting a table at a club under a sign on the wall reading "Friday, the 13th." Shaking in his boots, the waiter continues setting thirteen places. The members file in, and each opens an umbrella indoors before seating himself. The remainder of the film shows how each of the members of the club dies violently because he flouts superstition. The last scene takes place in the same club room with the table again set for thirteen, and at each seat is a skeleton instead of a live person.

Thompson's Night Out
AM&B © H111067 May 26, 1908
Cameraman: G. W. Bitzer
Location: Studio, N.Y.C. *Photographed:* May 1 and 5, 1908
274 ft. FLA5742 (print) FRA2572 (neg.)

A man is dictating letters to his secretary when a customer enters. After a conversation, a messenger is summoned and each man telegraphs his wife that he will not be home that night. The scene shifts to a saloon where there is entertainment. Our heroes imbibe too much and are thrown out. The host takes his guest home where his wife beats him on the head. Our hero then tries to enter his own house. Unable to open the door, he tries a ladder, falls off it into wet cement, finally makes it up the ladder but a policeman sees him entering and thinks he is a robber. The policeman follows him up the ladder; by this time his wife has wakened and a free-for-all begins.

Those Awful Hats

AM&B © H122037 Jan. 27, 1909

Director: D. W. Griffith *Cameraman:* G. W. Bitzer

Cast: Flora Finch, Linda Arvidson, Mack Sennett, Arthur Johnson, John Cumpson, Florence Lawrence

Location: Studio, N.Y.C. *Photographed:* Jan. 11–12, 1909

85 ft. FLA5233 (print) FRA2181 (neg.)

The first scene opens in a theater and the camera is positioned as if in the back row. There is no action on the stage or movie screen. One woman enters with an exceptionally large hat and blocks the view of everybody seated in back of her, much to their annoyance. There is some stop-action photography that may not have been planned as such. In the final scenes, the clam shell of a steam shovel comes down from the ceiling and snatches the oversize hat. The picture ends as the clam shell picks up the woman as well as her hat.

Those Bitter Sweets

Keystone © LP5622 June 7, 1915

Producer and Author: Mack Sennett

Cast: Mae Busch, Harry McCoy, Dell Henderson, Ivy Crosthwaite

Location: Venice and San Pedro, Calif, as well as the area around the Keystone studio in Los Angeles

442 ft. FLA6143 (print)

Mae Busch and her boyfriend, Harry McCoy, are enjoying a ride in his Chevrolet Sportster when they are interrupted by Dell Henderson, another suitor. An irritated McCoy makes them both get out of the car, and Mae takes Dell home to meet her father. She entertains him by playing the piano, while Dell sings. McCoy comes by the house with his dog, who howls while Dell is singing. Dell is very upset and leaves. Outside he knocks McCoy down. Mae and Harry go off to the drugstore to have some ice cream. Dell is a clerk there, and when Mae finds out, she spurns him. To get even, Dell fills each chocolate in a box with poison and has it delivered to Mae who gives it to some friends on their way to the beach. Dell suddenly realizes the enormity of his act and the rest of the picture is devoted to his and other people's attempts to reach the beach-bound group before anyone eats a poisoned chocolate. Mae and Harry arrive first, and when Dell gets there, he is chased into the water where he has to dive under the waves to avoid being hit by the rocks the rest are throwing at him.

Those Boys

AM&B © H121795 Jan. 19, 1909

Director: D. W. Griffith *Cameramen:* G. W. Bitzer, Arthur Marvin

Cast: Linda Arvidson, Florence Lawrence, Clara T. Bracey

Location: Studio, N.Y.C. *Date:* Jan. 5, 1909

133 ft. FLA5743 (print) FRA2566 (neg.)

A mother is knitting while surrounded by two young boys and three teen-age daughters, when a man, presumably the father, enters with another child. He opens some packages and discloses a revolver and cartridges, which he demonstrates in a humorous way and puts down on the table. The girls go upstairs, and the two boys are left alone. They pick up the gun, load it, find a target and pin it on a closet door. The director shows a portion of two rooms split by a wall, with the three girls reading letters behind the door where the boys place the target. Mother discovers the revolver and cartridges are missing and a frantic search begins, ending just as the two boys are about to fire the pistol at the target.

Those College Girls

Keystone © LP5425 May 29, 1915

Producer and Author: Mack Sennett

Cast: Charles Murray, Polly Moran, Billie Brockwell (headmistress), Slim Summerville. College Girls: Dixie Chene, Vivian Edwards, Josephine Stevens, and others

Location: Keystone studio, Los Angeles

796 ft. FLA5744-5745 (print)

In this lively comedy, Polly Moran and Charles Murray play a couple in charge of house cleaning at a girls' college. Slim Summerville is the bellboy in love with one of the students, Vivian Edwards. Billie Brockwell tries with very little success to maintain order. In one scene, Charles Murray, who has been banished by an irate Polly Moran to the bedroom, plays a tune on a flutelike instrument, using the characters in a Hebrew newspaper as musical notes. While he is playing, Polly Moran dances and forgets entirely about a cake in the oven which burns. Murray puts the fire out with the hose, wrecking the kitchen in the process. Slim Summerville persuades one of the girls to meet him at eleven p.m. so that they can elope. The other students play a joke on Slim by painting his face with lampblack while he sleeps. This causes endless confusion and chases, in one door and out another. Murray, Moran, and Summerville are finally fired by the long-suffering house mother, ending the picture.

Those Hicksville Boys

Biograph © J167692 Apr. 1, 1912

Director: Mack Sennett

Cast: Dell Henderson, Fred Mace, Grace Henderson, Mack Sennett, William Beaudine, Robert Harron, Eddie Dillon, Charles Hill Mailes

Location: Southern Calif.

191 ft. FLA5747 (print) FRA2574 (neg.)

The situations in this split-reel comedy begin with two young men of rural background who decide to give the city the benefit of their acting ability, and the first scene shows them on their way. They get a job that ends with "the hook." The remainder of the film shows the would-be comics wandering down the railroad track toward their home town, hungry and bedraggled. A fruit picker's lunch tempts them, and they eat it, infuriating the fruit pickers who then throw their trunk in the water. One of the partners thinks the other is in the trunk and gets the fruit pickers to help him with the rescue, only to find the trunk empty when they retrieve it. The last scene shows the remaining would-be comic splashing about in the water where he has been thrown by the fruit pickers.

Those Wedding Bells Shall Not Ring Out

AM&B © H23811 Nov. 11, 1902

Cameraman: Arthur Marvin

Location: Studio, N.Y.C. *Date:* July 16, 1900

11 ft. FLA3690 (print) FRA0939 (neg.)

The film begins on a set of a church pulpit and railing. A priest or minister is conducting a wedding ceremony. The bride and groom come up to the altar and just before the conclusion of the ceremony, the groom falls to the floor with his hand to his heart.

Thou Shalt Not

Biograph © J140639 Apr. 20, 1910

Director: D. W. Griffith *Cameraman:* G. W. Bitzer

Cast: Henry B. Walthall, Marion Leonard, Charles West, George Nicholls, W. Chrystie Miller, Gladys Egan

Location: Studio, Los Angeles; Hollywood and Pasadena, Calif. *Date:* March 3-11, 1910

380 ft. FLA5395 (print) FRA2818 (neg.)

The lead (Henry B. Walthall) is in love, but he is told by his doctor that he has tuberculosis and cannot marry. His fiancée (Marion Leonard) does not agree with this edict and insists they should go through with the ceremony. The doctor and the ill young man trick the girl into believing there is another woman in his life by hiring an actress to play the part. The fiancée sees them embracing, and this convinces her that the cause is hopeless. There is one panoramic scene photographed from a hilltop overlooking Hollywood.

The Thread of Destiny

Biograph © J138986 Mar. 9, 1910

Director and Author: D. W. Griffith

Cast: Mary Pickford, Henry B. Walthall, George Nicholls, Linda Arvidson, Tony O'Sullivan, W. Chrystie Miller

Location: San Gabriel, Calif. *Photographed:* Jan. 28, 1910

543 ft FLA5904 (print) FRA6445 (neg.)

This film is significant as it is the first moving picture D. W. Griffith made in California. He not only directed it but also wrote the story, using the word "greaser," as a derogatory term in the titles. The story is of a well-born Spaniard (Henry B. Walthall) who comes to the aid of a young orphan (Mary Pickford) of good family who is mistaken for a common woman while in a saloon on a mission of mercy. The outraged local men form a lynching party to get the "greaser," and the young lady helps him to escape. They fall in love, and the local padre marries them. A combination of interior and exterior scenes was used.

Three Acrobats

Edison © 20772 Mar. 20, 1899

Cast: The Buffons

26 ft. FLA3858 (print) FRA1070 (neg.)

This film is of a vaudeville act photographed from the audience. The act itself consists of two male and one female clown-acrobats who made use of a constructed "break-away" wall of spring-hinged windows and doors. The three acrobats enter and reenter the spring doors, entangling one another, throughout the entire film.

Three Cavaliers of the Road

AM&B © H58986 Apr. 7, 1905

Cameraman: F. S. Armitage

Location: Studio, N.Y.C. *Photographed:* Mar. 28, 1905

11 ft. FLA4200 (print) FRA1363 (neg.)

As the film begins, and for its compete extent, the cameraman photographed three men wearing make-up and clothed as tramps. The area of the camera frame used shows them only from their waists up, and they continue to stare directly into the camera, barely moving for the full run of the film.

Three Girls in a Hammock

AM&B © H41043 Jan. 20, 1904

Cameraman: A. E. Weed

Location: Studio, N.Y.C. *Photographed:* Dec. 18, 1903

20 ft. FLA4335 (print) FRA1481 (neg.)

The film was photographed as if from the audience at a vaudeville show. Two women are pushing a third to and fro in a hammock suspended from the wings in front of a backdrop painted as an outdoor scene. As the rocking continues, a man appears and indicates by gestures that all three should get into the hammock so he can swing it. The two girls follow his suggestion. The film ends as the hammock breaks spilling all three girls to the floor of the stage.

Three Little Maids

AM&B © H48218 July 18, 1904

85 ft. FLA5234 (print) FRA2182(neg.)

This film shows the sadistic antics of three young girls, and it ends in retribution. First, they take a piece of cake away from a younger girl; then they play jokes on a man and cause him to fight with another. By placing a purse on the sidewalk, the three are responsible for two persons bumping heads, and they steal a tramp's hat. Then, they roll down a grassy slope, unaware that there is a mud puddle at the bottom. The last scene shows the three girls walking toward the camera completely covered from head to foot with mud.

Threshing Scene

AM&B © H70259 Dec. 19, 1905

97 ft.

The film bearing this title has been identified as a film called The Henpecked Husband, released by AM&B on January 27, 1906, but which apparently was not copyrighted under that title.

See also: The Henpecked Husband

Through Austin Glen, Catskill Railway

See: A Trip on the Catskill Mt. Ry.

Through the Breakers

Biograph © J135642 Dec. 8, 1909

Director: D. W. Griffith *Cameraman:* G. W. Bitzer

Cast: James Kirkwood, Billy Quirk, Marion Leonard, Kate Bruce, Gladys Egan, Robert Harron, Charles West, Grace Henderson, Linda Arvidson, George Nicholls.

Location: Edgewater, N.J.; Studio, N.Y.C. *Photographed:* Oct. 29–30 and Nov. 1–10, 1909

387 ft.   FLA5746 (print)   FRA2674 (neg.)

The hero (James Kirkwood) proposes to the heroine (Marion Leonard) at a party. The next scene, preceded by the title "God's greatest gift" shows the heroine with a baby in her arms. The child grows up to about ten years of age, but is so neglected by both of her very social parents that she dies from lack of love. There are scenes of the mother attending whist parties and of the father at his club. After her death, the couple separates, since the father blames his wife for the tragedy. The last scene shows the mother placing flowers on the grave. The father arrives and there is a reconciliation.

Through the Key-Hole in the Door
AM&B   © H28563   Feb. 24, 1903
Cameraman: Arthur Marvin
Location: Roof studio, N.Y.C. *Date:* Oct. 14, 1900
18 ft.   FLA3555 (print)   FRA0831 (neg.)

This comedy was photographed from a single-camera position. The locale is private room of a restaurant. A man and a woman seated there are waited on by an inquisitive waiter who believes he will see things that should be done only in private. After leaving the dining room, the waiter looks through a keyhole. The guest, evidently feeling this would happen, pulls open the door and causes the waiter to land in the room in a very awkward position.

Throwing Mail Into Bags, U.S.P.O.
AM&B   © H34976   Aug. 22, 1903
Cameraman: A. E. Weed
Location: Washington, D.C. *Photographed:* Aug. 7, 1903
26 ft.   FLA3876 (print)   FRA1087 (neg.)

This film concerns the separation of mail parcels before distribution. A semicircular rack of mail bags, each tagged with a different location, is placed on a set of the interior of a postal building. Two postal employees throw packages of envelopes brought to them by another employee into the marked mail bags.

Throwing the Sixteen Pound Hammer
Edison   © H35624   Sept. 11, 1903
Cameraman: Edwin S. Porter
Location: Caledonian Games, N.Y.C. *Photographed:* Sept. 7, 1903
51 ft.   FLA4903 (print)   FRA1903 (neg.)

The film is of a competitive event called "throwing the hammer," that was part of a track-and-field meet. During the film, photographed from a single-camera position, several participants compete, each executing the throw in his own style.

Tied to Her Apron Strings
AM&B   © H40817   Jan. 12, 1904
Cameraman: A. E. Weed
Location: Studio, N.Y.C. *Photographed:* Dec. 15, 1903
23 ft.   FLA3716 (print)   FRA0963 (neg.)

This was photographed as if from the audience at a vaudeville skit. Against a background of an outdoor scene is a park bench. A woman dressed as a nursemaid can be seen pushing a baby carriage. A policeman follows her, and they both sit on the bench. A small boy can be seen skulking behind the bench. He suddenly yells "Police!" and another policeman arrives as the first it attempting to untie the maid's apron strings from his belt.

The Tired Tailor's Dream
AM&B   © H98848   Aug. 27, 1907
Cameramen: F. A. Dobson, G. W. Bitzer
Location: Studio, N.Y.C. *Photographed:* May 31, 1907
245 ft.   FLA5748 (print)   FRA2573 (neg.)

The action takes place in a tailor shop set. A customer enters and orders a suit at the point of a gun, gesturing to the clock and indicating he will be back in one hour. The tailor's dilemma ends at that moment. The camera is relocated from a full establishing shot of the set to a close-up of a tailor's work bench. No people can be seen as a complete suit of clothes is made on the bench by the use of stop-action photography. The material unrolls, the chalk marks, the scissors cut, a sewing machine comes into view and stitches—and the suit is assembled, pressed, and hung on a rack in time for the unreasonable customer.

'Tis an Ill Wind That Blows No Good
AM&B   © H126009   Apr. 20, 1909
Director: D. W. Griffith *Cameramen:* G. W. Bitzer, Arthur Marvin
Cast: Florence Lawrence, Mack Sennett, Arthur Johnson, Tony O'Sullivan, John Cumpson, Charles Avery, William J. Butler
Location: Fort Lee, N.J.; Studio, N.Y.C. *Photographed:* Mar. 20, 24 and Apr. 6, 1909
329 ft.   FLA5749 (print)   FRA2575 (neg.)

The film begins in a busy shoe factory where the villain (Mack Sennett, who also plays two other parts) harasses an attractive shipping clerk. The hero (unidentified) comes to her aid and is fired for his trouble. He is next thrown out of his room for nonpayment of the rent. He goes to a restaurant to beg for food, and finally steals a pie. A chase starts and a policeman (Arthur Johnson) follows him to an empty room where the hero forces the policeman to exchange clothes with him. The scene changes to the house of a drunken laborer who is beating his wife and kicking his children. The wife runs out for aid and encounters the pseudo-policeman. He arrests the laborer and takes him off to the police station. There he is rewarded with a job for his courageous act. The film ends as he goes, in his new uniform, to the factory, and walks out with the attractive shipping clerk.

Tit For Tat; or, A Good Joke With My Head
See: Un Prêté Pour un Rendu; ou, Une bonne Farce Avec Ma Tête

To Save Her Soul
Biograph no copyright reg.   Dec. 27, 1909
Director: D. W. Griffith *Cameramen:* G. W. Bitzer, Arthur Marvin
Cast: Mary Pickford, Arthur Johnson, W. Chrystie Miller, George Nicholls, Caroline Harris (Mrs. R. Barthelmess), Mack Sennett, James Kirkwood, Owen Moore, Kate Bruce, William Beaudine, Robert Harron, Billy Quirk, Blanche Sweet
Location: Fort Lee, N.J.; Studio, N.Y.C. *Photographed:* Nov. 22–27, 1909

385 ft. FLA5248 (print) FRA2812 (neg.)

A young lady (Mary Pickford) who is an accomplished small-town choir singer is noticed by a big city impresario who convinces her she is wasting her talents. The village curate (Arthur Johnson) unsuccessfully pleads with her not to become a professional entertainer. She is a hit, and the curate, curious as to what effect her success has had on her, goes to see her perform. He is dismayed to find she is leading a fast and loose life. He takes her home from a party where she has been drinking, and threatens to kill her with his gun. The film ends as the curate and the performer return home, kneel in the vestry of the church, and pray.

Toboganning in Canada
Edison © H14064 Feb. 10, 1902
Location: Montreal, Canada
85 ft. FLA5236 (print) FRA2184 (neg.)

The film, photographed from several camera positions, shows large, snow-covered fields where many people are pulling toboggans. They appear to be headed toward the summit of a toboggan slide, and toboggan tracks can be seen in the snow. Many persons can be seen climbing or crossing the toboggan course.

Tom Tight et Dum Dum
See: Jack Jaggs & Dum Dum

Tom, Tom, the Piper's Son
AM&B © H57387 Mar. 9. 1905
Cameraman: G. W. Bitzer
Location: Studio, N.Y.C. *Photographed:* Feb. 12, 1905
269 ft. FLA5750 (print) FRA2576 (neg.)

This elaborate version of a nursery rhyme uses many camera changes to take a crowd from the opening scene at a street fair to the well where Tom and the stolen pig are finally captured after a chase. The director moves the camera three times from the exterior to the interior and then out again to show the pursuers entering a building, what they do inside, and their exit. All the actors are in costume and many wear masks. There are several sets that are two stories high and dimensional. The Nihilists and Tom, Tom, The Piper's Son both evince production standards, direction, costumes, and sets of a creative nature not shown at AM&B either before March 1905 or again until the arrival of D. W. Griffith some three years later.

Tomboy Bessie
Biograph © J170132 June 8, 1912
Director: Mack Sennett
Cast: Mabel Normand, Mack Sennett, William J. Butler
201 ft. FLA5751 (print) FRA2577 (neg.)

This shows an obstreperous tomboy (Mabel Normand) who is the neighborhood pest. Her older sister is being courted by the town oaf (Mack Sennett). The climax of the film is a chase that starts when the tomboy's pet chicken gets lost and runs into a farmer's pen. He thinks she is stealing his chickens and starts chasing her with a shotgun, and succeeds only in hitting the town oaf, who has been assigned the task of minding the young girl.

Tommy Atkins, Bobby and Cook
Edison © 27965 Apr. 22, 1899

24 ft. FLA4348 (print) FRA0233 (neg.)

A set of dining room-kitchen furnished with a table and a large folding screen is seen. The door in the set opens and a man in military uniform enters and embraces the woman, apparently the cook, who opens the door. The cook seats the man at a table and gives him some food. The door opens again and in comes a man dressed in a policeman's uniform. At the sight of the policeman, the military man hides behind the screen. Another woman enters and the policeman becomes aware of the soldier behind the screen, all of which results in a humorous scene.

Le Tonnerre de Jupiter
Méliès © H37627 Oct. 22, 1903
Creator: Georges Méliès
Cast: Georges Méliès
Location: Montreuil, France *Date:* Summer 1903
U.S. title: Jupiter's Thunder-Bolts, or The Home of the Muses
95 ft. FLA5509 (print) FRA2640 (neg.)

The scene opens on a trick sky. After an explosion, a man appears with a sign on him reading "Zeus." Zeus conjures up lightning and thunder, as well as dancing girls on pedestals, and then causes them to disappear. For a finale, he blows himself up, only to reappear and cause fires to burn on the pedestals where the maidens were dancing.

A Too Ardent Lover
AM&B © H33413 July 13, 1903
Cameraman: G. W. Bitzer
Location: Studio, N.Y.C. *Date:* July 2, 1903
19 ft. FLA3518 (print) FRA0797 (neg.)

The scene begins on a set of the living room of a modest home. Directly camera center is a young lady sitting in a large armchair with a young man who is embracing her. The ardent wooing continues until a man clad in pajamas enters the scene and scolds the two young lovers for staying up so late. The young man apparently disagrees with the protectiveness of the father. The film ends when the pajama-clad father throws the suitor through the window.

Too Much Johnson
AM&B © H34816 Aug. 19, 1903
Cameraman: Arthur Marvin
Location: Roof studio, N.Y.C. *Date:* Sept. 11, 1900
9 ft. FLA3640 (print) FRA0896 (neg.)

Two young women attired in bathing costumes of the era are sitting on a small pile of papier-mâché rocks. The painted backdrop behind them shows the seashore. A man in summer clothes walks up to the two girls and attempts to take their picture with his portable camera. The women show annoyance and one of them, a very large woman, takes the photographer by the scruff of his neck, throws him to the sand, and places one of the larger rocks on top of him. She then sits on the rock. The film ends as her companion is seen photographing her.

Too Much of a Good Thing
AM&B © H29475 Mar. 18, 1903
Cameraman: Arthur Marvin
Photographed: July 6, 1900

11 ft. FLA4299 (print) FRA1449 (neg.)

A man is handed three infants, one at a time, by a huge nurse, who comes out of a door on a set constructed to appear as a hospital waiting room. After being handed the third child, he falls over backward.

Toodles and Her Strawberry Tart
AM&B © H37385 Oct. 28, 1903
Cameraman: A. W. Weed *Photographed:* Oct. 19, 1903
Location: Studio, N.Y.C.
22 ft. FLA5717 (print) FRA2714 (neg.)

A woman and a small girl are sitting on a bench on a streetcar set. The woman helps the child remove a large tart from a paper bag the child places on the seat beside her. A well-dressed man in a top hat and tailcoat comes in, sits down on the tart, and starts to flirt with the woman. The child begins to cry and point at the bench where the man is sitting. The man gets up in a hurry, and then attempts to clean the tart off his coat tails.

See also: Toodles Recites A Recitation, and Toodle's Tea-Party

Toodles Recites A Recitation
AM&B © H37682 Nov. 6, 1903
Cameraman: A. E. Weed
Location: Studio, N.Y.C. *Photographed:* Oct. 28, 1903
50 ft. FLA5237 (print) FRA2185 (neg.)

A little girl is standing beside a desk behind which a small boy is seated. They are approximately five years of age. The girl appears to be reciting, and the boy is turning the pages of a picture book. A dark-colored object is thrown from off camera, hitting the little girl and leaving a dark stain on her dress. She goes around the desk and berates the boy, who was paying attention to nothing but his picture book. The remainder of the film shows the girl harassing the boy, and it ends with the little girl in tears.

Toodle's Tea-Party
AM&B © H37681 Nov. 6, 1903
Cameraman: A. E. Weed
Location: Studio, N.Y.C. *Photographed:* Oct. 28, 1903
41 ft. FLA4906 (print) FRA1905 (neg.)

A small boy and a small girl are sitting on a small chair in front of a miniature table with tiny cups and saucers at a children's tea party. A well-dressed young woman enters and places some food on the table and the children start eating. At the end of the film, the little girl gets up and starts beating the little boy, who sits there staunchly and takes his punishment and never stops eating.

The Topers
AM&B © H62507 June 22, 1905
Cameraman: G. W. Bitzer
Location: Studio, N.Y.C. *Photographed:* June 14, 1905
22 ft. FLA3908 (print) FRA1128 (neg.)

Two men are sitting at a table in front of a curtain similar to a theater curtain. Two bottles of whiskey, a seltzer bottle, and two glasses stand on the table between the two men who evidently have been drinking already. One of the men falls asleep, his head rolls back and his mouth opens. His companion sees an opportunity to play a prank and picks up a bottle of seltzer intending to squirt it into his friend's open mouth. Somehow his coordination seems to have been affected by his drinking, for the seltzer squirts all over him instead.

Torpedo Attack on Port Arthur
Selig © H43184 Mar. 12, 1904
11 ft. FLA3933 (print) FRA1145 (neg.)
[Russo-Japanese War]

The poor quality and short length of this film do not permit detailed description. The only elements of interest are some table-top model ships firing upon an equally diminutive model of Port Arthur built on a miniature lake.

Torpedo Boat "Dupont"
AM&B © H32787 June 17, 1903
Cameraman: F. S. Armitage
Photographed: Oct. 17, 1899
15 ft. FLA3531 (print) FRA0807 (neg.)

This film is too short to permit the subject, the trial of a three-stack U.S. Navy torpedo boat, to be described in much detail. The full silhouette of the vessel is shown as it steams by the camera position. Some of the crew members are visible at their stations on deck.

Torpedo Boat "Morris" Running
Edison © D10162 May 12, 1900
Location: Newport, R. I.
35 ft. FLA4907 (print) FRA1906 (neg.)

Approximately a third of the film is of a calm ocean or bay. Only water is visible until, in the upper part of the film, the bow of an oncoming vessel approximately one hundred feet long can be seen. It turns camera left going out of camera range just as the film ends.

Tossing Eggs
Edison © H16117 Apr. 7, 1902
Location: White House, Washington, D.C. *Photographed:* Apr. 1, 1900
30 ft. FLA3807 (print) FRA1042 (neg.)

The film, photographed from a single-camera position, shows a group of adults and adolescents on what appears to be the side of a hill in a pine grove, tossing and retrieving eggs. There is good footage of the participants' apparel.

See also: Scrambling for Eggs

A Total Accident
AM&B © H34823 Aug. 19, 1903
Cameraman: Wallace McCutcheon
Date: Aug. 11, 1903
15 ft. FLA4202 (print) FRA1365 (neg.)

The film begins with the display of a large contraption manufactured for the amusement of a group of spectators. The design of the device is a slide approximately one hundred feet long with a loop at the bottom. Several hundred people can be seen at the edge of a pier watching a man standing upright, as if he were skiing, descend the incline toward the loop at the bottom. The man is successful in traversing the loop, but when he reaches the bottom, he is brought to an abrupt halt by an unexplained mechanical failure. The film ends as six men carry the prone body of

William Gorham from the scene. Although it is not clear in the film, Gorham was on a bicycle.

A "Tough" Dance
AM&B © H24891   Dec. 9, 1902
Cast: Kid Foley, Sailor Lil
16 ft.   FLA4808 (print)   FRA1907 (neg.)

Two people imitate the celebrated dance of the French apache. As the film begins, a man dressed in rough clothing approaches a woman, also dressed in tattered garments, who is standing near the center of the camera position. They begin to accentuate their shoulder movements and, at the end of the film, are hitting one another and rolling about on the floor. The participants were Kid Foley and Sailor Lil, who claimed to be the champion performers of this popular Bowery dance.

Tough Kid's Waterloo
AM&B © H19653   July 2, 1902
Cameraman: Arthur Marvin
Location: Roof studio, N.Y.C. *Date:* July 18, 1900
10 ft.   FLA3798 (print)   FRA1035 (neg.)

On a set of a corner drugstore, a newsboy can be seen hawking his wares. Another boy, wearing a velvet sailor suit and carrying a balloon, walks by and the newsboy punctures the balloon. As the film ends, the two of them are rolling around on the sidewalk in front of the painted backdrop.

The Tourists
Biograph © J172002   Aug. 7, 1912
Director: Mack Sennett
Cast: Mabel Normand, Charles West, Tony O'Sullivan, Frank Evans, Grace Henderson, Mack Sennett
Location: Albuquerque, N.M.
143 ft.   FLA5754 (print)   FRA2578 (neg.)

The plot of this split-reel farce begins when some tourists stop between trains at the Albuquerque, New Mexico railroad depot and examine the wares for sale by Indians. One of the tourists (Mabel Normand) becomes bored with the peddlers and goes sightseeing on her own. She sees an Indian chief of rather large proportions and becomes very interested in him. He returns her interest, much to his squaw's dismay. The squaw solicits aid among the other Indian wives of the neighborhood and is successful in recruiting quite a few. The last scenes show the tourists being chased by the irate Indian women as they rush to board the train. The back shot shows all of the Indian women armed with various kitchen utensils shaking them at the departing train.

Tourists Arriving at Wawona Hotel
AM&B © H31667   May 11, 1903
Cameraman: Robert K. Bonine
Location: Wawona, Calif. *Date:* Nov. 15, 1901
15 ft.   FLA3153 (print)   FRA0378 (neg.)

A large, three-story wooden building can be seen. Arriving at the entrance is a coach pulled by four white horses. Several people dismount from the coach and enter the building. More horse-drawn vehicles of various kinds fol-low. The camera was too distant from the hotel to show further detail.

See also: Wawona, Big Tree and Cascade Near Wawona, Cal.

Tourists Embarking at Jaffa
Edison © H32797   June 17, 1903
Cameraman: A. C. Abadie
Location: Jaffa, Syria *Photographed:* Mar. 22, 1903
50 ft.   FLA4909 (print)   FRA1908 (neg.)

The camera was positioned on a dock close to the water, where several rowboats can be seen. The boats are being loaded with people and suitcases by men wearing fezzes, burnooses, wrap-around pants, and pullover sweaters with the word "Cooks" on the chest.

Tourists Going Round Yellowstone Park
Edison © 2467   Jan. 4, 1899
Location: Yellowstone Park, Wyo.
25 ft.   FLA4273 (print)   FRA1428 (neg.)

Several tourist coaches, each drawn by four horses, are shown on a road in Yellowstone National Park. Five coaches laden with passengers go by the camera position.

Tourists Landing at Island of Capri, Italy
Edison © H32508   June 11, 1903
Cameraman: A. C. Abadie *Photographed:* April 1, 1903
Location: Capri, Italy
38 ft.   FLA 4910 (print)   FRA1909

The film, photographed from a single-camera position near a ramp or sea wall, shows shore boats being rowed by ship's personnel. Passengers can be seen embarking from the rowboats and getting out onto the sea wall.

Tourists Landing at Island of Capri, Italy
Edison © H32508   June 11, 1903
Cameraman: A. C. Abadie *Photographed:* April 1, 1903
Location: Capri, Italy
11 ft.   FRA1911 (neg.)

The film, photographed from a dockside, shows a large number of tourists endeavoring to land on the island of Capri from small rowboats. See also: the previous film of the same title, for a longer version.

Tourists Playing Shuffleboard on "Prinzessen Victoria Luise"
Edison © H30398   Apr. 8, 1903
18 ft.   FLA3721 (print)   FRA0968 (neg.)

A game of shuffleboard was photographed on the after deck of a large ocean liner, and several people can be seen.

Tourists Returning on Donkeys From Mizpah
Edison © H32805   June 17, 1903
Cameraman: A. C. Abadie
Location: Mizpah, Syria *Date:* Mar. 17, 1903
45 ft.   FLA4911 (print)   FRA1910 (neg.)

The camera was positioned amid the rocks and brush of desolate countryside in order to show some tourists pass-ing. All are mounted on donkeys, each led by a man who appears from his attire to be a native. Approximately twenty tourists riding donkeys pass.

Tourists Starting for Canton

Edison © 38209 June 22, 1898
Cameramen: James H White, W. Bleckyrden
Location: Canton, China
24 ft. FLA3371 (print) FRA0674 (neg.)

The film, photographed from a single-camera position, shows Chinese bearers transporting passengers on their shoulders in sedan chairs. The movement is toward the camera and six chairs are visible. The immediate location is a grove of trees. Most of the bearers are barefoot and naked from the waist up.

Tourists Starting on Donkeys for the Pyramids of Sakkarah

Edison © H32801 June 17, 1903
Cameraman: A. C. Abadie
Location: Sakkarah, Egypt *Photographed:* Mar. 28, 1903
35 ft. FLA3552 (print) FRA0828 (neg.)

People can be seen walking down a gangway onto a pier or docks where there are many donkeys led by natives. Several of the tourists apparently make arrangements to ride the donkeys. They can be seen mounting the donkeys and being led away.

Tourists Taking Water From the River Jordan

Edison © H32809 June 17, 1903
Cameraman: A. C. Abadie
Location: Jericho, Palestine *Photographed:* Mar. 16, 1903
22 ft. FLA3453 (print) FRA0734 (neg.)

A large party of tourists can be seen on the banks of the River Jordan. They are being handed bottles of water by two women who stand in a boat and dip water from the river.

Tracked

See: Capture of Yegg Bank Burglars

The Tragedy of a Dress Suit

Biograph © J172321 Aug. 17, 1912
Director: Mack Sennett
Cast: Dell Henderson, William Beaudine, Mabel Normand, Eddie Dillon, Ford Sterling, William J. Butler, Grace Henderson, Kate Bruce
197 ft. FLA5778 (print) FRA2579 (neg.)

The theft of a suit of formal wear by a fortune-hunting roommate motivates the action in this picture. The slick villain (Dell Henderson) borrows his roommate's fulldress suit to attend a dinner party given by an eligible young heiress (Mabel Normand). His reason for attending is to propose marriage to her, which he does during the course of the party. The roommate, who also had planned to attend, discovers that his dress suit is missing. He goes to the party to search for both it and his roommate. Finding them, he demands the return of his suit, which causes a furor, ending the film. The film was photographed both indoors and out.

Tragic Love

AM&B © H122691 Feb. 8, 1909

Director: D. W. Griffith *Cameramen:* G. W. Bitzer, Arthur Marvin
Cast: Arthur Johnson, Linda Arvidson, Jeanie Macpherson, Mack Sennett, John Cumpson, Clara T. Bracey, Charles Inslee, Kate Bruce
Location: Fort Lee, N.J.; Studio, N.Y.C. *Photographed:* Dec. 31, 1908 and Jan. 12, 1909
334 ft. FLA5755 (print) FRA2580 (neg.)

This film is made up of many scenes, both indoors and out. The first scene shows the lead (Arthur Johnson), encountering a man and a woman who are fighting on the street. He goes to the aid of the wife, who drops her purse. His action on her behalf starts a chain of events that leads to a man robbing him of the woman's purse, and to the husband's murder by the thief. The hero thinks he has committed the murder while drunk, but the film ends after a series of scenes that exonerate him of any guilt in the murder. The last scene is of the hero embracing the woman (Linda Arvidson) he protected from her husband's beating.

Train Hour in Durango, Mexico

Edison © 13543 Feb. 24, 1898
Location: Durango, Mexico
25 ft. FLA3871 (print) FRA1082 (neg.)

The camera was positioned over the heads of a large crowd waiting for a passenger train. A locomotive and some passenger cars are seen stopping at a distance of approximately fifty yards from the camera. Passengers get on and off the train.

Train of Sugar Cane

AM&B © H18041 May 23, 1902
Cameraman: Robert K. Bonine
Location: Honolulu *Date:* Aug. 1, 1901
19 ft. FLA4141 (print) FRA1311 (neg.)

During the short course of the film, it is possible to see a small steam locomotive pulling approximately eight freight cars piled with cut sugar cane. The quality of the film does not permit further detail.

See also: Cutting Sugar Cane and Loading Sugar Cane

Train Taking Up Mail Bag, U.S.P.O.

AM&B © H36399 Oct. 1, 1903
Cameraman: A. E. Weed
Location: St. Georges, Md. *Photographed:* Sept. 21, 1903
25 ft. FLA3583 (print) FRA0857 (neg.)

The subject of this Postal Department documentary is "snatching" the mail bag from the suspended post by the railroad mail clerk. As the film begins, a man climbs the steps leading to the device that suspends the mail bag in the air. A train can be seen in the distance approaching the mail bag. At the end of the film, the mail bag is just being snatched from the suspension device.

Trained Cavalry Horses

Edison © 38235 June 22, 1898
28 ft. FLA3971 (print) FRA1179 (neg.)
[Spanish-American War]

From a single-camera position, we see eight horses ridden by U.S. cavalrymen. The riders put the horses through a training course that includes making them lie down on their sides. During the film, several horses lie down while mounted and, on command, get to their feet. These horses were part of Troop F, 6th U.S. Cavalry.

Tramp and Dump Cart
Paley & Steiner © H56272 Jan. 20, 1905
1 ft. FLA4426 (print) FRA1539 (neg.)

Only twelve inches of this film were submitted for copyright purposes; consequently it is too short to describe, except to say that the subject was dumping ashes.

The Tramp and the Bathers
AM&B © H34807 Aug. 19, 1903
10 ft. FLA4136 (print) FRA1306 (neg.)

The edge of a small lake is visible, and a man bathing a short distance from the shore. Another man, dressed in the tattered costume of a tramp, appears, walks over to a pile of clothing on the bank, picks it up, and runs. The bather waves frantically and attempts to pursue him. The bather finds an empty barrel on the shore, puts it on, and starts off after the tramp.

The Tramp and the Muscular Cook
AM&B © H16341 Apr. 10, 1902
Date: Circa 1898
10 ft. FLA3026 (print) FRA0144 (neg.)

A woman can be seen rolling out a pie crust in the center of a table on a set of a kitchen. A pie is cooling on the sideboard. As the woman continues her work, the door opens and a big man dressed as a tattered tramp enters and gestures a request for food. The woman replies by hitting him with her rolling pin, knocking him to the floor. The door opens again admitting two women with brooms who aid in administering a beating to the tramp.

The Tramp and the Nursing Bottle
Edison © H7981 Aug. 21, 1901
31 ft. FLA3780 (print) FRA1022 (neg.)

The photographer placed his camera on the edge of a small lake in order to film this picture. A woman dressed as a nursemaid is sitting on a bench alongside a four-wheeled perambulator. A policeman is sitting at the other end of the bench talking with her. A ragged tramp sizes up the situation, sneaks up to the perambulator, kneels out of sight of the policeman and begins drinking the contents of the baby's bottle. Suddenly the policeman notices the tramp, takes him by the seat of his ragged trousers, and throws him into the lake. A man in a rowboat attempts to rescue the tramp but the film ends before the rescue is completed.

The Tramp in the Kitchen
Edison © 69082 Nov. 26, 1898
19 ft. FLA3929 (print) FRA1143 (neg.)

A woman is setting a table on a kitchen set when the door of the set opens and a man dressed in the ragged attire of a tramp comes in, begs for a meal, and is asked to sit at the table. As the woman passes him, the tramp grabs her, pulls her to his lap, and kisses her. She resents his advances and chases him out of the kitchen. As soon as the tramp gets through the door, she stops for a moment to think about it, and takes off after him, ending the film.

Tramp on a Farm
Paley & Steiner © H52172 Oct. 27, 1904
8 ft. FLA4427 (print) FRA1540 (neg.)

The short length of this film does not permit too much description. It is made up of a series of short scenes and there is no way to tell whether this was done in the editing or in the original photographing. The film starts with a tramp being thrown off a streetcar. Then there are a series of scenes lasting a fraction of a second. They are: the tramp hides in a pig sty, drinks the farmer's whiskey, frightens some women, and is run off by the farmer. All the scenes were filmed out of doors.

A Tramp on the Roof
AM&B © H44206 Apr. 6, 1904
Cameraman: A. E. Weed
Location: Studio, N.Y.C. *Photographed:* Mar. 19, 1904
44 ft. FLA4913 (print) FRA1912 (neg.)

There are three scenes in this film. The action shows the tramp climbing over the edge of a set of a building and going down through the skylight. The second scene shows him entering a bedroom, sizing up the situation and getting into bed. A woman appears, sees the tramp asleep in the bed, folds the bed up against the wall, and calls the police. They let the bed down, arrest the tramp, and take him away. The final scene shows a close-up of the tramp wearing an unhappy expression on his face, in the barred window of a jail. The title was changed to Nervy Nat.

The Tramp's Dream
Edison © H4079 May 6, 1901
39 ft. FLA4914 (print) FRA1913 (neg.)

A man dressed as a tramp walks up to a bench in a park set, stretches and yawns, and then lies down on the bench. The second scene takes place on a set of part of the backdoor of a house and a garden. The tramp enters the garden and knocks on the door. When a woman answers, he indicates he is hungry and the woman points to a pile of wood and a saw horse. The tramp shakes his head. A bulldog appears, fastens its teeth to the seat of the tramp's trousers, and the tramp attempts to dislodge it by going around and around in a circle. The tramp loses his balance, falls to the ground, and the woman starts to beat him with her broom. The scene immediately shifts. The tramp is once more back on his bench, but now he is being beaten on the soles of his feet by a policeman, who escorts him off.

The Tramp's Miraculous Escape
Edison © H7328 July 31, 1901
37 ft. FLA4915 (print) FRA1914 (neg.)

A tramp seated on a railroad track is hit by a passing locomotive. Two stretcher bearers come to pick up the remains. They are carting him off when he comes back to life, takes a drink out of a bottle and walks away, to the consternation of the two stretcher bearers. At the beginning of the film, the tramp is seen to sit at the edge of the railroad track and presumably fall asleep. By the use of stop-action photography, he is replaced by a dummy. The same procedure, in reverse, is applied at the end of the film.

Tramp's Strategy That Failed
Edison © H4370 May 15, 1901

25 ft. FLA3465 (print) FRA0747 (neg.)

A man dressed as a tramp is being propelled through the swinging doors of a set of a saloon. A dog waits by the swinging doors and it sets upon the tramp. The tramp leaves the set with the dog in pursuit, with the bartender urging him on. The tramp reappears wearing a barrel and a box and carrying a stick which he uses to hit the dog. When his impromptu costume falls apart, the dog again attacks him. Note that the copyright notice appears in this film.

See also: How the Dutch Beat the Irish

The Tramp's Unexpected Skate

Edison © H4567 May 23, 1901
22 ft. FLA3481 (print) FRA0762 (neg.)

A tramp is leaning against a railing that protrudes from a painted backdrop of a public park. Two teen-age boys skate in front of the camera position on the stage. They remove their skates, put them on the sleeping tramp, and awaken him. He immediately starts to attack the boys but the skates prevent him from gaining any traction and he falls down several times. As the film ends, he has just landed on his back with his feet in the air.

Transport Ships at Port Tampa

Edison © 38242 June 22, 1898
Location: Tampa, Fla.
29 ft. FLA3247 (print) FRA0570 (neg.)
[Spanish-American War]

The film, photographed from a single-camera position located at the land end of a large dock, shows the hulls of two steamships in the background. In the foreground, between the ships and the camera position, military troops can be seen walking about. Some of the men are carrying bedrolls while others are moving cargo, etc.

Transport "Whitney" Leaving Dock

Edison © 31447 May 20, 1898
26 ft. FLA3340 (print) FRA0650 (neg.)
[Spanish-American War]

The foreground is obscured by the size of a cover on the paddle wheel of a large military transport. Alongside the paddle-wheel cover are two men in military uniform. The steamer backs away from the camera. As the film ends, most of the hull of the ship is visible.

Transporting Internal Rev. Stamps, U.S.P.O.

AM&B © H34994 Aug. 22, 1903
Cameraman: A. E. Weed
Location: Washington, D.C. *Photographed:* Aug. 5, 1903
27 ft. FLA4916 (print) FRA1915 (neg.)

The film shows a two-horse postal delivery wagon backed against a ramp, where two men are unloading the contents of the wagon into a delivery chute.

A Trap for Santa Claus

Biograph © J136186 Dec. 23, 1909
Director: D. W. Griffith *Cameraman:* G. W. Bitzer
Cast: Marion Leonard, Henry B. Walthall, Mack Sennett, Gladys Egan, W. Chrystie Miller, William J. Butler, Kate Bruce

Location: Fort Lee, N.J.; Studio, N.Y.C. *Photographed:* Nov. 13, 15, 16, and 20, 1909
412 ft. FLA5756 (print) FRA2582 (neg.)

This melodrama concerns a family of four who are reduced to unhappy circumstances, which causes the husband to turn to drink, and finally to desert his wife and children. At the family's lowest ebb, a legacy from the wife's aunt elevates them to a good home and a modest income, and they make plans for the forthcoming Christmas. The house is without a chimney and the children, upset by this, set a trap for Santa Claus in front of the window. The father, in the meantime, has turned to burglary and inadvertently selects the new home of his family for his first attempt. The film ends as he once more becomes a member of his beloved family and enacts the role of Santa for his children.

Trap Pigeon Shooting

AM&B © H92138 Mar. 29, 1907
Cameraman: G. W. Bitzer
Location: Riverside, Mass. *Photographed:* Feb. 9, 1907
347 ft. FLA5757 (print) FRA2581 (neg.)

The full film is devoted to members of a gun club who leave from the downtown station in a city for a rural area where the film was photographed. The members were photographed as they shot mechanical quail (skeet). The camera was placed in five different positions while the members were shooting, but at no time was the camera close enough to the men firing the shotguns to identify anyone or the type of weapons used.

Trapeze Disrobing Act

Edison © H10634 Nov. 11, 1901
45 ft. FLA4917 (print) FRA1916 (neg.)

This was photographed as if from the audience at a vaudeville show. The scope of the lens encompassed not only the stage but also a box on the left. As the action begins, a fully clothed woman is seen seated on a trapeze suspended above the stage. To the great amusement and enjoyment of the man in the box, she begins to remove her clothing. By the end of the film, she has removed all of her clothing except her leotard as she continues demonstrating her skill on the high bar.

Trappers Crossing Bald Mountain

AM&B © H35882 Sept. 21, 1903
Cameraman: Wallace McCutcheon
Location: Adirondack Mountains, N.Y. *Photographed:* Sept. 12, 1903
48 ft. FLA4908 (print) FRA1917 (neg.)

From a single-camera position, a dirt ridge can be seen through some thick foliage that appears to be on a mountain top. Approaching the camera, walking on the ridge clearing, are Indians of various ages and sexes. They walk by the camera.

See also: Indians Leaving Bald Mountain

Travels of a Lost Trunk

Paley & Steiner © H58836 Apr. 4, 1905
8 ft. FLA4163 (print) FRA1331 (neg.)

A number of perhaps intentionally very short scenes make up this film. They are as follows: a man in front of a house attempts to sneak past a huge dog; a man standing on a ladder kisses a woman through a window; the same man embraces the woman in her boudoir while she is sitting on his lap. Several other scenes follow, ending with a man getting out of a trunk that has just rolled down a large flight of stairs. He is the same man who was seen in the woman's boudoir. How he got in the trunk is not shown.

Treloar and Miss Marshall, Prize Winners at the Physical Culture Show in Madison Square Garden

Edison © H40945 Jan. 16, 1904

Cameraman: Edwin S. Porter

Location: Studio, N.Y.C. *Photographed:* Jan. 4, 1904

59 ft. FLA4919 (print) FRA1918 (neg.)

This shows two winners of a physical culture show in Madison Square Garden, New York City. During the course of the film, the woman, attired in white leotards, demonstrates the grace and loveliness that won her the title, while the man exhibits his muscle separation and development by a series of exercises.

See also: Al Treloar in Muscle Exercises

Trial Marriages

AM&B © H89469 Jan. 17, 1907

Cameraman: G. W. Bitzer

Location: Studio, N.Y.C. *Photographed:* Dec. 19-22, 1907

308 ft. FLA5758 (print) FRA2583 (neg.)

The story line of this film is built around a newspaper article about a woman who advocates trial marriages. The first camera position shows a man reading the article, and the second camera position moves to a close-up of an insert, two columns wide, of the beginning of the newspaper story. The remainder of the film is a series of scenes of what happens to the man after he decides to experiment with trial marriages. Each series of scenes is preceded by a title describing the type of "wife" our unknown actor has selected this time. All scenes end in violence to him, and the last scene is a close-up of the actor in a hospital bed with bandages about this hands and head.

The Trials and Troubles on an Automobilist

Paley & Steiner © H52166 Oct. 27, 1904

51 ft. FLA4920 (print) FRA1919 (neg.)

The film begins with a street scene. There is a pushcart next to an automobile in the immediate foreground. As the car starts to move, it knocks over the pushcart, precipitating a series of "chase" situations that culminate in eight different scenes of violent activity. The pushcart peddler chases the people in the automobile and they, in order to protect themselves, create other situations that add more people to the chase. A riot ends the picture, and the police and patrol wagon arrive. The film shows lots of foreground activity between moving vehicles and people against a good background of buildings.

Trick Bears

Edison © 77519 Nov. 27, 1899

50 ft. FLA3049 (print) FRA0341 (neg.)

As the film opens, several large bears are performing and, as it continues, they can be seen sitting in chairs, standing on their hind legs, carrying broomsticks as swords or rifles, marching in unison, and wearing hats, scarves, and coats.

There are several men visible in the picture, urging the bears to continue with the act.

The Trick Cyclist

Edison © H8693 Sept. 16, 1901

44 ft. FLA3829 (print) FRA1057 (neg.)

The cameraman placed his equipment high above what appears to be a schoolyard to film the exhibition of some trick bicycle riders. One of the three members of the act performs as a comic and is constantly falling or demolishing furniture as part of the act. The other members of the team demonstrate their skill doing difficult feats such as jumping rope on a bicycle or riding on one pedal.

A Trick on the Cop

AM&B © H43408 Mar. 17, 1904

Cameraman: A. E. Weed

Location: Studio, N.Y.C. *Photographed:* Feb. 26, 1904

72 ft. FLA5238 (print) FRA2186 (neg.)

This comedy is built around the attempt by a young boy and a girl to play a trick on the cook's boyfriend, a policeman. They construct a device over one of the two doors of the kitchen set. The cook appears and bribes them to leave with a piece of pie. A policeman enters and is received warmly by the cook who gives him a bottle of beer. The cook notices the thread leading from the flour box over the doorway and disengages it. The children reenter the kitchen to warn the policeman that his sergeant is coming, and it is the sergeant who gets the flour dumped all over him as the film ends.

The Trick That Failed

Biograph © J135517 Dec. 3, 1909

Director: D. W. Griffith *Cameraman:* G. W. Bitzer

Cast: Mary Pickford, Arthur Johnson, Mack Sennett, Grace Henderson, Kate Bruce, George Nicholls, Tony O'Sullivan, Gertrude Robinson, Billy Quirk

Location: Studio, N.Y.C. *Photographed:* Oct. 23, 1909

236 ft. FLA5759 (print) FRA6446 (neg.)

A young woman who thinks she is a consummate painter agrees to marry a wealthy young man (who considers her work mediocre) as soon as most of her work is sold. The rich young man employs all of his friends to buy his girlfriend's paintings from a gallery and bring them to his home. Impressed with her success, the young artist goes to her suitor's home to brag, and there discovers, through the carelessness of his valet, that it was he who bought her paintings. Her shame and anger, mixed with pride, force her to leave indignantly, and the film ends as she is being placated by another young man.

A Trip Around the Pan-American Exposition

Edison © H4968 June 8, 1901

Location: Buffalo, N.Y.

261 ft. FLA5760 (print) FRA2885 (neg.)

The entire film was photographed from an excursion vessel traveling through all of the waterways surrounding the Exposition. The major exhibit buildings and amusement attractions of the fair can be seen as the boat makes its way through the area, going through tunnels and under bridges.

The Trick That Failed (1909) features Mack Sennett as a valet whose fumbling has ruined his employer's chances with Mary Pickford. Until Sennett went to the West Coast most of his parts were of a secondary nature.

A Trip Down Mt. Tamalpais

Miles Brothers © H75870 Apr. 21, 1906

Cameraman: Herbert Miles [?]

Location: Marin County, Calif.

219 ft. FLA5761 (print) FRA2584 (neg.)

The subject is a train preceding the one on which the camera was positioned, as it goes down a winding single-track railroad hewn from the side of a mountain. The film shows the especially constructed observation cars being pulled by a small locomotive. The full trip from the top to the bottom is shown, ending at a station platform at the foot of the grade.

A Trip on the Catskill Mt. Ry.

AM&B © H77051 May 9, 1906

Cameraman: G. W. Bitzer

Location: The Catskill Mountains, N.Y. *Photographed:* Apr. 29, 1906

269 ft. FLA5762 (print) FRA2586 (neg.)

The subject is a trainload of tourists traveling over a circuitous route from the bottom to the top of an excursion railroad route in the Catskill Mountains. The photographer had his equipment on the following train. Most of the film is of the people standing on the observation platform of the rear car. There are some scenes taken from a funicular ascending and descending the steepest part of the mountain. There are some bridges, overpasses and underpasses shown. The funicular was the "famous Otis Elevating Railroad to the Mountain House," according to an AM&B handbill. The film was released under the title Through Austin Glen, Catskill Railway.

A Trip to Berkeley, Cal.

AM&B © H79820 June 23, 1906

Cameraman: O. M. Gove

Location: Berkeley, Calif. *Photographed:* May 24, 1906

71 ft. FLA5239 (print) FRA2187 (neg.)

In the beginning of the film, a streetcar passes in front of the camera position. The camera starts to move, indicating that it was on a streetcar since it is in the same position as the car in the first scene. All of the film was photographed from the streetcar. The scenes were taken in the metropolitan area, and there are four turns on the track. Several old houses can be seen as well as people and carts on the street. A man saunters on the track ahead of the streetcar. As the scene progresses, it is obvious that the camera has stopped moving. The conductor and the motorman grapple with the saunterer and finally persuade him to leave the tracks after a woman spectator hits them over the head with her umbrella. Further down the street, an automobile is trying to go up the hill. It is being passed by overloaded horse-drawn vehicles. The streetcar then proceeds, making one more turn before the picture ends.

A Trip to Salt Lake City

AM&B © H61569 June 5, 1905
Cameraman: G. W. Bitzer
Location: Studio, N.Y.C. *Photographed:* May 23, 1905
79 ft. FLA5240 (print) FRA2188 (neg.)

The film begins with a full photograph of a set of the interior of a Pullman sleeping car. The first action is a woman carrying a small child down the aisle toward the camera. She puts her child in an upper berth. A second woman, also carrying a small child, enters and proceeds down the aisle toward the camera and puts her child in the berth across the aisle. Following in close succession are several more women of various sizes and shapes, each carrying a child whom they deposit in a berth. The last person to arrive in the sleeping car is a man with a small child. The father promptly does the bidding of the child by giving him a horseback ride. At that moment, all of the other children in the sleeping car wish to get a drink of water and everyone crawls all over him. In a fit of anger and annoyance, the man leaves the sleeping car, pulls the drinking container from its mounting, drags it into the sleeping car, and puts it on the floor. He then climbs into his berth.

Triumphal Bridge, Pan-American Exposition

AM&B © H29163 Mar. 11, 1903
Cameraman: Arthur Marvin
Location: Buffalo, N.Y. *Date:* June 14, 1901
37 ft. FLA4921 (print) FRA1920 (neg.)

This is a boat-mounted camera excursion around the waterways of the Pan-American Exposition in Buffalo, New York. It provides a good view of the buildings.

Troop Ships for the Philippines

Edison © 38210 June 22, 1898
Location: San Francisco [?]
66 ft. FLA4922 (print) FRA1921 (neg.)
[Spanish-American War]

The first camera position is located on a dock or a structure associated with a dock. A steam, steel-hulled vessel of approximately 5,000 tons is seen departing. The second camera position shows the bow of the vessel, on which the name *Australia* can be seen, and the third camera position shows the ship out in the mainstream of the unidentified harbor proceeding downstream, escorted by two medium-sized harbor tugs. People are waving from the decks in all of the scenes.

Troops at Evacuation of Havana

Edison © 7258 Jan. 20, 1899
Location: Havana, Cuba
73 ft. FLA5241 (print) FRA2189 (neg.)
[Spanish-American War]

The first camera position was from over the heads of spectators who partially obscure a parade of American troops passing in front of a large public building as they embark upon a transport. They are leaving Havana for the United States. Some officers are mounted and some are not. All of the marching troops are in correct military formation and in proper uniform of the period.

Troops Embarking at San Francisco

Edison © 38256 June 22, 1898
Location: San Francisco
28 ft. FLA3079 (print) FRA0420 (neg.)
[Spanish-American War]

This film was photographed from a single-camera position over the heads of a crowd of people at the Embarcadero shed. In the background of the film, troops in full pack are mounting a ship via the gangway.

Troops Making Military Road in Front of Santiago

Edison © 52059 Sept. 3, 1898
Cameraman: William Paley
Location: Santiago, Cuba
26 ft. FLA4003 (print) FRA1204 (neg.)
[Spanish-American War]

The camera was positioned to photograph the activities of U.S. military troops building a road through the jungle in Cuba during the Spanish-American War. The men are shown working with pickaxes and shovels.

Tropisk Kaerlighed

See: Love in the Tropics

Trouble in Hogan's Alley

AM&B © H34515 Aug. 13, 1903
Cameraman: Arthur Marvin
Location: Roof studio, N.Y.C. *Date:* July 24, 1900
10 ft. FLA3588 (print) FRA0859 (neg.)

A little girl is playing with her doll while a little boy leans against a fabricated wall in a set of an alley area of a city. A larger boy arrives, takes the girl's face in his hands and kisses her, which evidently annoys the smaller boy because he starts a fight. This commotion brings the face and shoulders of a woman through a window and she shakes her fist at another woman across the court. Before the film ends, there is a melee involving several other women and children. A policeman carrying a nightstick attempts to break up the fight but is met with the anger of all of the participants, and he is forced to turn and leave the alley.

Troubles of a Manager of a Burlesque Show

AM&B © H41027 Jan. 19, 1904
Cameraman: A. E. Weed
Location: Studio, N.Y.C. *Photographed:* Dec. 14, 1903
49 ft. FLA4923 (print) FRA1922 (neg.)

A man is sitting at a desk in front of a set of a theater manager's office. Several women in street clothes enter from camera right; they are carrying packages of clothing; they show them to the man at the desk, and then exit camera left. A scantily clad woman enters the office. The man, apparently enamored, attempts to embrace her. She breaks from him and is chased around the desk. She picks up an ink bottle and throws the contents on her pursuer, which ends the film.

The Troublesome Baby

Biograph © J147936 Nov. 21, 1910

Cameraman: Arthur Marvin

Cast: William J. Butler, Flora Finch, Jeanie Macpherson, Florence LaBadie

Location: Highlands, N.J. *Photographed:* Sept. 30, 1910

184 ft. FLA5763 (print) FRA2587 (neg.)

This comedy is made up of a series of situations beginning with an insert of a telegram summoning a man to New York. He misses the train and goes to a nearby bench to read the paper while he waits for another train. A woman hands him her baby while she goes to correct another child, and his troubles begin. The mother does not return, and he tries to abandon the baby in several places, but a tall, slender woman notices him and calls a policeman. The man deposits the baby on the bench where he had been sitting, the mother returns, and everybody shakes hands. The camera was moved many times during the filming.

The Troublesome Fly

AM&B © H17228 May 1, 1902

Cameraman: Arthur Marvin

Location: Roof studio, N.Y.C. *Date:* May 14, 1900

16 ft. FLA4140 (print) FRA1310 (neg.)

A man is sleeping in a bed in a set that appears to be a hotel room. From the contented expression on his face, the man is sound asleep. A large "prop" fly floats into the room and begins harassing the man by buzzing about his head, and by pulling the bedclothes from the bed and biting him, etc. The man wakes, jumps from his bed, picks up a shotgun, and shoots the insect. The film ends at this point.

A Troublesome Satchel

AM&B © H12529 Apr. 14, 1909

Director: D. W. Griffith *Cameramen:* G. W. Bitzer, Arthur Marvin

Cast: John Cumpson, Mack Sennett, Arthur Johnson, Harry Salter, W. Chrystie Miller, Florence Lawrence, Clara T. Bracey

Location: Fort Lee, N.J. *Photographed:* Mar. 18, 1909

79 ft. FLA5242 (print) FRA2190 (neg.)

The plot involves a man (John Cumpson) who, having purchased a suitcase at an auction, does not want it or its contents and so tries to abandon it or throw it away. Each time, a policeman or some citizen reminds him of the suitcase. Finally, two thugs chase him, catch him, and rob him. When the thugs see the contents of his satchel, they feel sorry for him and return his money and his watch and go about their business. The film ends as the man walks away from the suitcase happily.

Trout Fishing

AM&B © H24877 Dec. 9, 1902

Cameraman: F. S. Armitage

Location: Muskoka Lakes, Canada *Date:* June 6, 1900

18 ft. FLA3766 (print) FRA1011 (neg.)

The camera was positioned close to the edge of a small stream in a heavily wooded area in order to take this film of two men standing in a rowboat fishing. During the course of the film, one of the men catches a fish and, in the excitement of attempting to land it, is pushed by his companion into the water. The film ends as the fully clothed and very wet man splashes water on his dry friend in the boat.

Trout Fishing, Rangeley Lakes

AM&B © H71525 Jan. 3, 1906

Cameraman: G. W. Bitzer

Location: Rangeley Lakes, Me. *Photographed:* Oct. 1905

333 ft. FLA5764 (print) FRA2588 (neg.)

The subject is a trip to a fishing camp by train, boat and pack route. All the necessary operations to prepare guests for their stay at a then well-advertised fishing camp are shown. Catching and netting trout, as well as preparing it for food are demonstrated. The purpose of the film was to advertise the area as a paradise for fishermen.

See also: Salmon Fishing Nipissisquit River

Trout Poachers

AM&B © H24878 Dec. 9, 1902

Cameraman: F. S. Armitage

Location: Muskoka Lakes, Canada *Date:* June 6, 1900

19 ft. FLA3183 (print) FRA0510 (neg.)

The camera was positioned on the bank of a river and angled down toward the water, which shows little more than the area around some men in rubber waders and hip boots who are standing in the water scooping fish into pans with their nets.

The Truants

AM&B © H92290 Apr. 4, 1907

Cameraman: G. W. Bitzer

Location: Studio, N.Y.C. *Photographed:* Jan. 24, 29, 30 and Feb. 4, 1907

259 ft. FLA5765 (print) FRA2589 (neg.)

The story line concerns the pranks of two boys, beginning with a medium close-up of them as they tie a balloon to the tail of a large dog and ending with the scene of them being chastised by a spanking in the judge's chambers. Both boys laugh heartily during the spanking because they had the forethought to put boards in the seat of their trousers. There are three scenes where trick photography is used, and several where the camera is moved to better indicate the beginning of the scene.

A True Patriot

Lubin Mfg. Co. © J134300 Sept. 9, 1909

Location: Philadelphia

285 ft. FLA5766 (print) FRA2590 (neg.)

This film is set in the period of the American Revolution and begins with a father and son draping a picture of George Washington with a flag and swearing patriotism. Unbeknownst to the father, the son is offered money to guide the British. He reports this to the American commander who asks him to take the money and lead the British into a trap. While the son is folding the money, his father challenges him as to his patriotism and strikes him. The film ends with the father holding his dead son in his arms after he learns that the son was a hero instead of a turncoat. The scenes were photographed both indoors and out.

Trying to Fool Uncle

Biograph © J171147 July 12, 1912

Director: Mack Sennett

Cast: Dell Henderson, Claire McDowell, William J. Butler, Sylvia Ashton, Frank Opperman

Location: Los Angeles

212 ft. FLA5767 (print) FRA2591 (neg.)

A ne'er-do-well nephew (Dell Henderson) is banished by his rich uncle. He marries a waitress (Claire McDowell) and gets a job as a clerk at a foundry. One day the nephew takes a snapshot of his employer's home and sends it to his uncle saying it is his own. The uncle decides to visit him, and the frantic nephew tells his employer all. The employer lends him his home and staff, but the plot to get back in the uncle's good graces backfires when he changes his will to leave his money to charity in view of his nephew's great success in the world.

Trying to Get Arrested

AM&B © H125118 Mar. 31, 1909

Cameramen: G. W. Bitzer, Arthur Marvin

Cast: Florence Lawrence, Owen Moore, Arthur Johnson, John Cumpson, Kate Bruce, Mack Sennett, Jeanie Macpherson

Location: Palisades Park, N.J. *Photographed:* Jan. 13, and Feb. 26, 1909

121 ft. FLA5243 (print, copy 1) FLA5374 (print, copy 2) FRA2191 (neg.)

This comedy is about the many unsuccessful attempts of a tramp (John Cumpson) to get himself arrested and into jail. The first scene shows a man dressed in rags sitting on a park bench and attempting to keep warm. Several couples pass by but refuse him aid. The tramp vows to get shelter even if it means jail, and he starts out by kicking a policeman. Instead of jailing him, the policeman holds him at arm's length and kicks him repeatedly. This begins a series of situations, each ending with the poor tramp being beaten or trod upon, but never arrested. The film ends as the tramp passes a construction site with a "Men Wanted" sign in front, and a policeman guides him unceremoniously toward the employment office.

Tub Race

Edison © H35325 Sept. 1, 1903

Cameraman: A. C. Abadie

Location: Wilmington, Del. *Photographed:* Aug. 25, 1903

25 ft. FLA4290 (print) FRA1941 (neg.)

Eighteen spectators stand on the bank of a narrow body of water opposite the camera, which photographed six small boys attempting to propel themselves in what appears to be wooden brine tubs. Each of the boys seems to be attempting to compete with the others as to the speed and distance he can travel under his own power.

Tugthusfangerne nr. 10 og 13

See: The Two Convicts

Tunnel Number Three

AM&B © H16926 Apr. 22, 1902

Cameraman: G. W. Bitzer

Location: Union Pacific R.R., Wyo. [?] *Date:* Dec. 2, 1900

22 ft. FLA3267 (print) FRA0586 (neg.)

The film shows a railroad track, a steel cantilevered bridge, and a tunnel under construction in the Rocky Mountains. The camera was positioned on a train proceeding over the track (passing workmen laboring on the bridge) in through the tunnel, and out the other side. This is one of several short films which show part of the Union Pacific Railroad.

The Tunnel Workers

AM&B © H84943 Nov. 10, 1906

Cameraman: F. A. Dobson

Cast: Kate Toncray, Guy Hedlund, Jim Slevin

Location: Studio and Pennsylvania R.R. [?] Tunnel, N.Y.C. *Photographed:* Oct. 14, 24–26, 1906

330 ft. FLA5768 (print) FRA2885 (neg.)

Much of this film was photographed on actual location, one side of the "superstructure of the Pennsylvania Tunnel between New York and Long Island—the greatest engineering feat the world has ever known." The producing company used a film of workers changing shifts for background of a drama involving a foreman and his superintendent. The foreman knows the superintendent is paying clandestine visits to his wife, and there are several well-constructed sets where the fight between the foreman and the superintendent was filmed. There is an explosion, and the two are buried under rocks. After the subsequent breakthrough by fellow workers, the two men set aside their jealousy and anger because of having suffered so much together.

Turkish Dance, Ella Lola

Edison © 59210 Oct. 7, 1898

25 ft. FLA4361 (print) FRA1500 (neg.)

A woman performs a rather suggestive dance with abdominal gyrations.

See also: Ella Lola, a la Trilby

Turkish Patrol Drilling at Ascot Park

See: Shriners' Conclave at Los Angeles, Cal., May, 1907

Turning the Tables

Biograph © J148648 Dec. 10, 1910

Cameraman: Arthur Marvin

Cast: Stephanie Longfellow

Location: Fort Lee, N.J.; Studio, N.Y.C. *Date:* Nov. 25–27, 1910

161 ft. FLA4179 (print) FRA1343 (neg.)

The hero receives what his wife suspects is a prearranged telephone call summoning him to the side of a sick friend. Instead, he joins his cronies in a saloon to play cards, and she follows him. The alert bartender raps on the wall of the room where the men are playing, and the husband leaves by a back entrance. He rushes home and decides to teach his wife a lesson. He turns the clock ahead and gets into bed. When his wife arrives angry and convinced her husband has been lying, she finds him asleep. The film ends as the husband is scolding his wife for being out so late at night, and she pleads with him for forgiveness. There is a split set with a bar of a saloon on one side and card tables with people playing on the other side.

Turning the Tables

Edison © H35327 Sept. 1, 1903

Cameraman: A. C. Abadie

Location: Wilmington, Del. *Photographed:* Aug. 24, 1903

32 ft. FLA5769 (print) FRA2592 (neg.)

The cameraman placed his equipment on a bank overlooking a portion of a lake, where there is a sign, "No Swimming Allowed." Several small boys walk to the edge of the lake, remove their clothing, and jump in. A policeman appears, brandishes his nightstick, and admonishes the boys for swimming. He orders them to get out of the water. All of the boys comply. They surround the policeman and, as the film ends, throw him into the water.

The Twentieth Century Tramp, or, Happy Hooligan and His Airship

Edison © H13363 Jan. 27, 1902

Cameraman: Edwin S. Porter

38 ft. FLA4924 (print) FRA1923 (neg.)

This particular film was unique for the time inasmuch as the producer or cameraman attempted to show that a man riding a bicycle suspended from a small gas bag could propel himself about and above New York City. The "in camera" horizontal split screen process was accomplished by covering the lower half of the lens while the tramp was pumping his bicycle and the picture was photographed. The lens was then covered, the film was reversed, and the upper half exposed while the cameraman photographed the panorama of the city. The actor riding the bicycle suspended from the airship represents a comic strip character called "Happy Hooligan."

25th Infantry

AM&B © H17963 May 21, 1902

Cameraman: Raymond Ackerman

Location: Philippine Islands *Date:* Mar. 23, 1900

22 ft. FLA3813 (print) FRA2856 (neg.)

The short length of the film, its poor condition, and bad photographic circumstances make description difficult. The subject appears to be more than one company of soldiers marching along a dusty road. The title indicates they are American troops, but no identification is possible.

Twenty Mule Team, St. Louis Exposition

AM&B © H46315 May 24, 1904

Cameraman: A. E. Weed

Location: St. Louis, Mo. *Photographed:* May 14, 1904

40 ft. FLA4925 (print) FRA1924 (neg.)

[Louisiana Purchase Exposition]

What appears to be a park or recreation area can be seen. In the distance, making a turn into the camera position, are ten teams of mules harnessed to a large freight wagon, with a water tanker behind. The twenty-mule team approaches and passes the camera so that the animals, their type of harness, the construction of the wagon, and the water tank are clearly visible.

Twin Brothers

AM&B © H125730 Apr. 14, 1909

Director: D. W. Griffith *Cameraman:* Arthur Marvin

Cast: Arthur Johnson, Tony O'Sullivan, John Cumpson, Owen Moore, Clara T. Bracey, Charles Avery

Location: Studio, N.Y.C. *Photographed:* Mar. 10 and 12, 1909

165 ft. FLA5770 (print) FRA2567 (neg.)

Twin brothers go out into the world to seek their fortunes, each in a different way. The film begins as they say goodbye to their aged father. One of the twins is employed as a gorilla by the proprietor of a dime museum. As the film progresses, spectators can be seen watching the animal acts, which include a lion in a cage adjoining the gorilla. After the show is over and the spectators have departed, the proprietor counts his money, and the man in the lion's suit removes his head at the same time as the man in the gorilla costume does. Each finds, to his amazement, his twin brother.

The Twisted Trail

Biograph © J139618 Mar. 28, 1910

Director: D. W. Griffith *Cameraman:* G. W. Bitzer

Cast: Mary Pickford, Arthur Johnson, George Nicholls, Kate Bruce, W. Chrystie Miller, Mack Sennett, William J. Butler, Dell Henderson, Tony O'Sullivan

Location: Los Angeles studio and Sierra Madre, Calif. *Photographed:* Feb. 15–18, 1910

477 ft. FLA5771 (print) FRA6417 (neg.)

This film was made on D. W. Griffith's first trip West. The young daughter (Mary Pickford) of a ranch owner is sent East to a finishing school. Before she goes, her father's foreman (Arthur Johnson) kisses her on the cheek. This leads to several rows, culminating in the rancher's death from a heart attack. Judged guilty of murder by his coworkers, the foreman heads for the hills where he encounters the returning daughter being attacked by bandits. The foreman is presented with a dilemma; if he saves the girl he loves, he will be lynched. He chooses to rescue her and take her home, but he encounters the posse, who tell the girl of her father's death. She orders the foreman hung quickly. Just before the posse can carry out their plan, they learn that the rancher died of natural causes.

2 A.M. in the Subway

AM&B © H62448 June 20, 1905

Cameraman: G. W. Bitzer

Location: Studio, N.Y.C. *Photographed:* June 5, 1905

21 ft. FLA3910 (print) FRA2892 (neg.)

The film opens as if the viewer were in a theater audience looking at a subway platform. A policeman, acting fatigued, is sitting on a box. As the film proceeds, two rather flashily dressed women act as though they are having a hilarious time. One of them raises her very voluminous skirt above her knees while her escort ties her shoe. The two women and the escort, with persuasive help from the policeman, board the subway. To the right of the frame can be seen female legs protruding from the subway train window. The film ends as the subway policeman throws the two women off the train.

Two Bottle Babies

AM&B © H48984 Aug. 9, 1904

Cameraman: G. W. Bitzer

Location: Sea Gate, Coney Island, N.Y. *Photographed:* Aug. 3, 1904

31 ft. FLA3293 (print) FRA0609 (neg.)

The camera was positioned on the sand facing the ocean, where a young girl is seated on a chair immediately in front of the camera. A black-and-white puppy, which she is feeding from a bottle with a nipple, sits on her lap. A little boy stands by her chair, watching.

The Two Brothers

Biograph © J141292 May 14, 1910
Director: D. W. Griffith *Cameramen:* G. W. Bitzer, Arthur Marvin
Cast: Kate Bruce, Arthur Johnson, Marion Leonard, W. Chrystie Miller, George Nicholls, Mary Pickford, Mack Sennett, Henry B. Walthall
Location: Mission at Capistrano, Calif. *Photographed:* Mar. 25-29 and Apr. 4, 1910
404 ft. FLA5772 (print) FRA6415 (neg.)

This is the story of two quite different brothers, the sons of a wealthy landowner (Kate Bruce). The serious older son (George Nicholls) becomes engaged to the "Rose of Capistran," played by Marion Leonard. The younger son (Arthur Johnson) is sent away by his mother because of his unseemly behavior. He falls in with bad companions who convince him to help them hold up his brother's wedding group. The two brothers engage in a fist fight which Mary Pickford breaks up. Through her good influence, the younger brother reforms, rejoins the church, and wins the forgiveness of his mother.

Two Chappies in a Box

Edison © H36498 Oct. 3, 1903
Cameraman: Edwin S. Porter
Location: N.Y.C. *Photographed:* Sept. 16, 1903
26 ft. FLA4926 (print) FRA1925 (neg.)

The film shows two men sitting in a theater box and causing a considerable disturbance as they watch a young woman singing on the stage. The film was photographed on a stage set, and the camera was placed to view both the stage and the occupants of the box. The young singer bows and leaves the stage just as the theater manager removes the two boisterous spectators from their box by the scruffs of their necks. A sign bearing the Thomas A. Edison copyright notice can be seen in the lower left-hand corner of the motion picture frame.

Two Companies, Royal Canadian Regiment

AM&B © H16643 Apr.16, 1902
Cameraman: Arthur Marvin
Location: Montreal or Ottawa *Date:* Aug. 15, 1899
28 ft. FLA4927 (print) FRA1926 (neg.)

The film shows a Canadian infantry recruit training center. The camera was positioned to film two companies of infantry marching past. In the immediate background is a large cluster of white canvas tents.

The Two Convicts

Great Northern © Oes J168441-42 Apr. 22, 1912
Director: August Blom *Script:* Nicolai Brechling
Cast: Frederik Christensen, Nicolai Brechling, Karen Lund, Zanny Petersen, Einar Zangenberg, Thorkild Roose, Henry Seemann, Dagny Schyberg

Location: Denmark
Original Titles: Politimesteren, and Tugthusfangerne nr. 10 og 13
Alternate U.S. Title: Adventure While Strolling
Based on a play by Jens Christian Hostrup
713 ft. FLA5905 (print) FRA2765 (neg.)

Two men dressed in prison uniforms are on a rooftop making their escape from prison. There is no chase by the prison authorities. The prisoners obtain food and clothing from a farmer. As the story continues, it becomes more complicated. Perhaps the film is incomplete, as the finale shows two men dressed in white flannel trousers, blue coats, and straw hats sitting on park benches with two young ladies. The sun is setting in the background. These two characters first are seen walking along a road, wearing knapsacks. They meet two young women when something falls from the carriage in which the women are traveling and the men retrieve it for them. There seems to be a gap in the picture at this moment because the film does not make it clear whether these two characters are the same as those wearing the white flannel trousers. If this is so, then the prisoners did make good their escape.

Two Cousins

Lubin Mfg. Co. © J134164 July 15, 1909
Location: Philadelphia
406 ft. FLA5773 (print) FRA2593 (neg.)

This one-reel motion picture has a plot involving jealousy, conspiracy, and attempted theft by use of hypnotism. The principals are two girls whose wealthy uncle plans to leave the bulk of his estate to the one whose marriage is imminent. The other cousin is to receive an established, rather small sum of money. She conspires with a hypnotist to influence her cousin to prevent the marriage. There is a short chase, and the culprits are brought to justice. The guilty cousin is charged with her crimes, swoons to the floor, and the picture ends.

Two Hours After the Chickens Leave the Shells

AM&B © H16923 Apr. 22, 1902
Cameraman: Raymond Ackerman
Date: Sept. 1, 1899
17 ft. FLA3486 (print) FRA0766 (neg.)

This is a single-camera position film of a tray filled with newly hatched chicks. Prominently displayed over the back end of the tray of chicks is a sign, "Monitor Incubator Improved."

See also: Eggs Hatching

Two Is Company, Three a Crowd

Paley & Steiner © H52168 Oct. 27, 1904
3 ft. FLA4409 (print) FRA1534 (neg.)

The exceedingly short length of this film indicates that possibly the producer sent only enough for copyright purposes rather than the entire film. A young man in summer attire can be seen sitting on a park bench with two young women. He pushes one of them off onto the grass and then begins running out of camera range pursued by the female he pushed off the bench.

Two Little Waifs

Biograph © J147286 Nov. 3, 1910

Director: D. W. Griffith *Cameraman:* G. W. Bitzer

Cast: Verner Clarges, Grace Henderson, William J. Butler, Alfred Paget, Lottie Pickford, Jeanie Macperson, Kate Bruce, Claire McDowell, Jack Pickford, Joe Graybill, Adele De Garde, Gladys Egan

Location: Greenwich, Conn.; Studio, N.Y.C. *Photographed:* Sept. 16–21, 1910

417 ft. FLA5774 (print) FRA2672 (neg.)

The story line concerns a mother who is grief-stricken at the loss of her child, and the sorrow of two little girls who have lost their mother. The two little girls are turned over to an orphanage, but they run away to try to find their mother. Eventually they arrive on the front porch of the wealthy woman who is grieving for her little girl. She considers them an answer to a prayer, and the last scene shows them asleep in her child's bed, while the woman prepares to adopt them legally. The subtitle on the film reads, "A Modern Fairy Tale."

Two Memories

Biograph © H127384 May 22, 1909

Director: D. W. Griffith *Cameraman:* G. W. Bitzer

Cast: Marion Leonard, Owen Moore, Mary Pickford, Mack Sennett, Clara T. Bracey, Florence Lawrence, John Cumpson, Tony O'Sullivan

Location: Studio, N.Y.C. *Photographed:* Apr. 23, 27 and May 1, 1909

130 ft. FLA5244 (print) FRA2192 (neg.)

This film begins with a quarrel between two young lovers over the girl's having a picture of another man. The boy leaves in a temper. Her attitude of "I don't care," is shown by her going to parties. Meanwhile, the rejected lover decides that life is not worth living, so he sends a note to the young woman to that effect. The party is interrupted while she reads his letter aloud. The revellers, carrying champagne bottles, decide to pay him a call but they are too late, for he has committed suicide. The last scene shows the remorseful heroine kneeling as she prays for forgiveness.

Two Old Cronies

AM&B © H28558 Feb. 24, 1903

Cameraman: F. S. Armitage

Location: Studio, N.Y.C. *Date:* Nov. 20, 1900

11 ft. FLA3166 (print) FRA0496 (neg.)

Two men, well past middle age, are sitting at a small table on which can be seen a whiskey bottle, a seltzer bottle, and two glasses. The actions of the men indicate they are friends; each drinks, smokes cigars, and talks rapidly throughout the film. The film was photographed with artificial light, and only the two men and the table are visible.

The Two Paths

Biograph © J150122 Jan. 4, 1911

Director: D. W. Griffith *Cameraman:* G. W. Bitzer

Cast: Dorothy Bernard, Grace Henderson, Wilfred Lucas, Alfred Paget, Donald Crisp, Adolph Lestina, Gertrude Robinson, Harry Hyde, Dell Henderson

Location: Studio, N.Y.C. *Photographed:* Nov. 19–22, 1910

403 ft. FLA5775 (print) FRA26666 (neg.)

This drama, a story of contrasts, was costumed and played in a manner that accentuates the parts. Two young women, burdened with caring for an old woman, choose to go different ways. One yields to temptation in the form of a dissolute and wealthy man, who later throws her out on the street. She dies alone in a hotel room. The other marries her neighborhood suitor, a carpenter, and has two children. Her economic circumstances do not progress a great deal, but the last scene shows the contented family group in front of the fireplace. The light from the fireplace is the key light, and the rest of the room is lighted by fill light.

Two Women and a Man

Biograph © J134952 Nov. 17, 1909

Director: D. W. Griffith *Cameraman:* G. W. Bitzer

Cast: Mack Sennett, Frank Powell, Kate Bruce, Owen Moore, George Nicholls, Florence Barker, Arthur Johnson

Location: Fort Lee, N.J.; Studio, N.Y.C. *Photographed:* Sept. 25 and Oct. 6 and 12, 1909

391 ft. FLA5776 (print) FRA2594 (neg.)

A young couple gets married. By the time they are middle aged, the husband has earned great wealth. They move to luxurious quarters in the big city, become part of its social life, and the husband becomes interested in a chorus girl. He divorces his wife to marry her, then loses all his money in a stock market crash. He asks his new bride to return the jewels he gave her so he can recoup his fortunes, but she refuses. In the last scenes, the husband returns to his former modest home, and when his former wife comes home, she finds him asleep in his old rocking chair.

Two's Company

AM&B © H16353 Apr. 10, 1902

Cameraman: F. S. Armitage

Location: Studio, N.Y.C. *Date:* Nov. 7, 1900

10 ft. FLA4261 (print) FRA1417 (neg.)

On a park set with a painted backdrop is a long stone bench divided by a pillar. On one side of the pillar, a man garbed as a friar is sitting, apparently sleeping. On the other side, a man dressed as a toreador is attempting to make passionate love to a woman in a Spanish costume of the thirteenth century. This disturbs the friar who shows he is displeased by the young man's actions. To circumvent the interference of the friar, the young man opens an umbrella over the heads of himself and the young woman and returns to his ardent wooing. AM&B described this film as an "animated reproduction of a famous painting by Vergilio Tojetti."

Tying Up Bags for Train, U.S.P.O.

AM&B © H34971 Aug. 22, 1903

Cameraman: A. E. Weed

Location: Washington, D.C. *Photographed:* Aug. 7, 1903

28 ft. FLA4064 (print) FRA1248 (neg.)

The camera shows the actions of two postal employees as they remove mail sacks from the semicircular rack where they are placed so they can be filled with mail for their respective locations. The two postal employees stack the mail sacks on a cart in preparation for dispatch elsewhere.

The Typewriter

AM&B © H23771 Nov. 11, 1902

Date: 1897 [?]
10 ft. FLA3457 (print) FRA0739 (neg.)

On a business office set, a young woman is sitting at a desk in front of a typewriter and taking dictation from an elderly man. They become interested in one another, and the old gentleman kisses the secretary. The door opens and a woman brandishing an umbrella enters. She starts beating the old man on his head. The film ends as he is being propelled from the office by the viselike grip of his wife on his ear. Released as The Pretty Typewriter.

The Ugly Tempered Tramp
AM&B © H29468 Mar. 18, 1903
Cameraman: F. S. Armitage
Location: Studio, N.Y.C. *Date:* Nov. 16, 1900
13 ft. FLA3642 (print) FRA0897 (neg.)

The set of the back stoop of a house in a rural community was built out-of-doors. A tramp appears and goes up to the back door of the house and knocks. A woman comes to the door, sees him, and closes the door. The tramp knocks on the door again, and this time the woman comes out with a container in her hands. She empties the contents of the container over the tramp and starts hitting him with a broom. A man, probably her husband, also throws a large pan of water on the tramp.

The Unappreciated Joke
Edison © H34328 Aug. 8, 1903
Cameraman: Edwin S. Porter
Location: Studio, N.Y.C. Photographed; July 29, 1903
21 ft. FLA3324 (print) FRA0637 (neg.)

The film begins on a set of the interior of a streetcar. Two men and a woman are sitting on the bench. One of the men is reading a risqué magazine and laughing as he tells the man next to him what he sees. While he is laughing raucously, his neighbor leaves the car and is replaced by a woman, which he does not notice. As the film ends, the woman is wearing a very displeased expression as she knocks him off the bench. NOTE: In the space where advertising cards are usually seen, are cards giving the names and addresses of firms that sell Edison phonographs, records, and Kinetoscopes.

See also: Street Car Chivalry

The Unchanging Sea
Biograph © J141155 May 7, 1910
Director: D. W. Griffith *Cameraman:* G. W. Bitzer
Cast: Linda Arvidson, Arthur Johnson, Gladys Egan, Mary Pickford, Charles West
Location: Port Los Angeles (Santa Monica) *Photographed:* Mar. 16–17, 1910
355 Ft. FLA5777 (print) FRA2595 (neg.)

This drama, inspired by Charles Kingsley's poem "The Three Fishers," was photographed in the then fishing village of Santa Monica, California. The fisherman husband (Arthur Johnson) goes to sea, is shipwrecked, and is washed up on the beach with no recollection of his past. During his absence, there are several scenes of his faithful wife (Linda Arvidson) returning to the lookout for news. During the course of the film, their daughter (Mary Pickford) grows up and marries another fisherman (Charles West). The husband is finally restored to health and joins a fishing

expedition. The familiar work and scenes bring back his memory. The last scene shows him embracing his now aged but always loyal wife.

Uncle Josh at the Moving Picture Show
Edison © H13364 Jan. 27, 1902
Cameraman: Edwin S. Porter
Cast: Uncle Josh was played by Charles "Daddy" Manley.
47 ft. FLA4931 (print) FRA1930 (neg.)

The plot of this film is a simple one about a country bumpkin who is so overwhelmed by watching his first motion picture from a stage box that he tears down the screen in an enthusiastic attempt to help the heroine of one of the films. Porter combined previously photographed film projected on a screen, to which he added double exposure and matte shots. Some of these effects were achieved by using an optical printer manufactured at Edison. The three films Porter used are Black Diamond Express, copyrighted December 12, 1896; Parisian Dance, copyrighted January 15, 1897; and Country Couple, probably made expressly for the picture as it was not copyrighted separately.

Uncle Josh in a Spooky Hotel
Edison © D6367 Mar. 21, 1900
Cameraman: Edwin S. Porter
30 ft. FLA4932 (print) FRA1931 (neg.)

The set is of a bedroom in a small hotel, with the camera placed to encompass three walls of the room. The room is furnished with a bed and two chairs. The action begins when a man dressed like a country bumpkin is being shown the room by the hotel manager. After the man has inspected the room, the manager offers him a chair. Through the use of stop-action photography, a person dressed as a ghost with the mask of a skeleton appears behind the guest. As the guest turns his head, the apparition disappears and reappears in back of the hotel manager. For the remainder of the film, the ghost appears and disappears, causing mischief between the two men, who begin fighting.

Uncle Josh's Nightmare
Edison © D6366 Mar. 21, 1900
Cameraman: Edwin S. Porter
Cast: Charles "Daddy" Manley
57 ft. FLA4933 (print) FRA1932 (neg.)

On a set of a man's bedroom, a woman can be seen helping a middle-aged man to retire. As soon as he falls asleep, an apparition appears at the edge of the room. The man begins to grapple with the vision and feels reasonably certain he has it in his power because he exerts a great deal of energy and gets it tied in a sheet. He then puts it in a trunk, only to have it reappear outside the trunk. The ghost appears and disappears throughout the film, as do articles of furniture, annoying the man who had been trying to sleep.

Uncle Reuben at the Waldorf
AM&B © H37384 Oct. 28, 1903
Cameraman: A. E. Weed
Location: Studio, N.Y.C. *Photographed:* Oct. 19, 1903
30 ft. FLA4934 (print) FRA1933 (neg.)

The film begins with three people, two at one table and one at another, in a restaurant set. The waiter comes in and serves the couple, ignoring the irascible old gentleman. The waiter continues to leave and reenter the room while serving the couple, and completely ignores the old man who uses many tactics to attract attention. Finally, as the waiter comes in carrying a tray of food by the old man's table, he is tripped and falls on his face, spilling the food and breaking the dishes. The old gentleman leaves the set with a triumphant brandish of his umbrella.

Uncle Tom's Cabin

Edison © H34001 July 30, 1903
Cameraman: Edwin S. Porter
Location: Studio, N.Y.C. *Photographed:* July 27, 1903
507 ft. FLA5913 (print) FRA2869 (neg.)

Uncle Tom's Cabin, made at least four months before The Great Train Robbery, follows the story line of the famous classic as closely as the facilities of the era would allow. Porter endeavored to show how motion pictures could provide greater scope than a stage for presenting a play. Each scene of the film is preceded by an explanatory title, the earliest such found in the Paper Print Collection. The finest special effects, set construction, and management of actors were used, even though all the scenes were photographed from the point of view of a theater audience. Porter also added a race between two paddle-wheel steamers, using miniature ships, floating on a made-to-scale Mississippi River, complete with a devastating thunderstorm and lightning. Painted slides depicting the end of the Civil War were incorporated into the finale of Porter's film. For this period, Uncle Tom's Cabin provides extraordinary use of special camera effects.

Under the Bamboo Tree

AM&B © H62506 June 22, 1905
Cameraman: G. W. Bitzer
Location: Studio, N.Y.C. *Photographed:* June 14, 1905
20 ft. FLA3899 (print) FRA1120 (neg.)

Several well-dressed young men and women are at a party. A couch is in the immediate foreground, between a potted palm and a drape running halfway across the camera area. A young man on the couch is behaving shyly when a young woman attempts to kiss him. At that moment, another young man joins them, and the man on the couch jumps up in embarrassment to the amusement of the others. He goes off to get some refreshments, and the second young man sits down beside the young woman and begins kissing her. The first young man returns carrying a tray, stumbles over the potted palm, and lands face down, causing all the other guests to laugh.

Under the Mistletoe

Edison © H39740 Dec. 19, 1903
Cameraman: Edwin S. Porter
Location: Studio, N.Y.C. *Photographed:* Dec. 14, 1903
34 ft. FLA3528 (print) FRA0804 (neg.)

Two women can be seen arranging furniture in a set of the living room of a modest house. A mature man enters the scene and is instructed by one of the women to get a ladder, which he does. This starts the pandemonium that continues throughout the picture. As the man enters the room with the ladder, he manages to dislodge or break every picture,

statue, bust, or table decoration in the room, to the dismay of the two women. At the end of the picture, they are still holding the wreath that is never hung.

Under the Old Apple Tree

AM&B © H101833 Oct. 30, 1907
Cameraman: G. W. Bitzer
Location: Studio, N.Y.C. *Photographed:* Oct. 22, 1907
147 ft. FLA5780 (print) FRA2596 (neg.)

The set on which this film was made was the backyard of a house. There is a painted backdrop of a rural scene, with a white picket fence and an apple tree around which a bench had been built. The whole film was taken from a single-camera position, and the story is a series of attempts of a young girl to carry on romantically with her sailor friend. Six suitors appear, one by one. Each time the sailor climbs up in the tree and disposes of them by dropping apples or other objects on them. The film ends when the young woman's father returns, sits on the bench, and in his near blindness, kisses the hand of an obese black household servant.

Under the Tree

AM&B © H43563 Mar. 22, 1904
Cameraman: A. E. Weed
Location: Studio, N.Y.C. *Photographed:* Mar. 3, 1904
20 ft. FLA4322 (print) FRA1470 (neg.)

The set of a wooded glade has a tree trunk with a seat encircling it. A small boy carrying a bucket appears and places the bucket on the bench. He climbs the tree and pulls the bucket up after him. At that moment, a young couple enters. They seat themselves on the bench. The picture ends as the contents of the bucket are spilled on the heads of the two young people who are embracing.

Unexpected Female

See: An Unprotected Female, no. 2

An Unexpected Guest

Lubin Mfg. Co. © J132277 Aug. 12, 1909
Location: Philadelphia
361 ft. FLA5781 (print) FRA2694 (neg.)

A socially conscious father persuades a young nurse with whom his son has been intimate to write a note breaking their engagement. The camera moves to a close insert showing the father cutting off the postscript where the nurse asks the son to see her once more. From her hospital bed, where she is dying after giving birth, the nurse reads an announcement of her former lover's forthcoming wedding to a socially prominent young woman. The nurse contacts the bride-to-be who rushes to the hospital. The last scene shows the young woman confronting her fiancé with his child by another woman. All of the sets are artificially lighted.

Unexpected Help

Biograph © J143826 July 30, 1910
Director: D. W. Griffith *Cameraman:* G. W. Bitzer
Cast: Arthur Johnson, Gladys Egan, Dell Henderson, George Nicholls, W. Chrystie Miller, Florence Barker, "Spike" Robinson
Location: Oil fields and studio, Los Angeles

390 ft. FLA5782 (print) FRA2665 (neg.)

The story line of this one-reel drama is built around a man (Arthur Johnson) who is employed by an oil company. He is drugged, and the company money in his possession is stolen by an impoverished gambler and his associate. The climax comes when two clergymen enter a saloon where the gambler-turned-bandit is enjoying his ill-gotten gains, proceed to place him in custody, at the point of a revolver, remove the stolen money, and return the money to its rightful custodian. They then nonchalantly walk out of camera range reading the Bible.

An Unexpected Knockout

AM&B © H16345 Apr. 10, 1902
Cameraman: F. S. Armitage
Location: Roof studio, N.Y.C. *Date:* June 7, 1901
17 ft. FLA3335 (print) FRA0646 (neg.)

The theme of this film of a vaudeville act is that the innocent bystander must accept the damage. It begins on a set where two boys are playing marbles. There is a large sack of flour beside them. The two boys start an altercation over their game of marbles. A gentleman in a tall silk hat and frock coat attempts to act as arbitrator. One of the boys seizes the sack of flour intending to hit his playmate who ducks, and the old gentleman gets all the flour in his face.

The Unfaithful Odalisque

AM&B © H29472 Mar. 18, 1903
Cameraman: Arthur Marvin
Location: Roof studio, N.Y.C. *Date:* Aug. 3, 1900
10 ft. FLA3616 (print) FRA0876 (neg.)

The set represents a corner of a harem. A woman clothed in a harem costume is reclining on a divan next to a tall palm tree. She is languidly fanning herself. A turbaned man dressed as a Middle Eastern potentate enters and, judging from his gestures, accuses her of some action she denies. The turbaned man, evidently unconvinced, summons someone from off camera. A man dressed as a Nubian slave with a cat-o'-nine-tails appears and begins lashing the young woman.

The Unfaithful Wife: Part 1, The Lover

AM&B © H33877 July 28, 1903
Cameraman: G. W. Bitzer
Cast: Kathryn Osterman
Location: Studio, N.Y.C. *Photographed:* July 14, 1903
19 ft. FLA4096 (print) FRA1277 (neg.)

A well-dressed young woman and an equally well-dressed young man are sitting at a living room table in a set of a modest house. The curtains at the back of the set open, admitting a man who appears very upset by the couple. His wife ignores his displeasure in a haughty manner, while her husband pleads his love for her. She seems unmoved by his pleading and seats herself at the table and begins reading a magazine as the film ends.

The Unfaithful Wife: Part 2, The Fight

AM&B © H33878 July 28, 1903
Cameraman: G. W. Bitzer
Cast: Kathryn Osterman
Location: Studio, N.Y.C. *Photographed:* July 14, 1903

25 ft. FLA4097 (print) FRA1278 (neg.)

The film opens on a set of the interior of a restaurant; several people are sitting at one table while a young couple is at another. The couple, in evening dress, is the subject of intense scrutiny by a man who is standing in the doorway. He walks up to their table and starts an argument that grows into a fist fight, and the two men are evicted from the restaurant. The first man returns, brushes himself off, and sits down at the table with the young woman.

The Unfaithful Wife: Part 3, Murder and Suicide

AM&B © H33879 July 28, 1903
Cameraman: G. W. Bitzer
Location: Studio, N.Y.C. *Photographed:* July 14, 1903
20 ft. FLA4098 (print) FRA1279 (neg.)

The opening scene shows a living room set. A woman with her hair unbound comes through some curtains at the back of the set and runs around the table as if frightened. A man dressed in dinner clothes follows her, seizes her by the throat, and begins to choke her. The assault continues for a considerable period of the film, and then she is thrown to the ground. The man whips out a pistol and shoots her three times, turns the gun on himself, and falls to the floor dead.

Ungdommens Ret

See: The Rights of Youth

Union Iron Works

Edison © 16436 Mar. 10, 1898
26 ft. FLA4374 (print) FRA2860 (neg.)

The single-camera position shows a gate in front of what appears to be a large factory with many men either entering or emerging from the gate. A large percentage of these persons are interested in the motion picture camera photographing them.

A Unique Race Between Elephant, Bicycle, Camel, Horse, and Automobile

AM&B © H16378 Apr. 12, 1902
Cameramen: G. W. Bitzer, Arthur Marvin
Location: Ridgewood Park, N.J. *Date:* May 4, 1899
22 ft. FLA3280 (print) FRA0597 (neg.)

What appears to be the center of an exercise ring in a large stabling area is shown. Approaching the camera at a distance of about a hundred yards can be seen the participants in a race. There is no apparent winner, but the race is repeated for the benefit of the camera. The automobile in the race is designed like a hansom cab.

U.S. Battleship "Indiana"

Edison © 25322 Apr. 21, 1898
26 ft. FLA3060 (print) FRA0405 (neg.)
[Spanish-American War]

The film begins from a single-camera position. The camera platform moves parallel to the anchored position of the battleship *Indiana*, but the distance of the subject from the camera precludes interpretation of much of the detail. The film does show the general outline of the ship, the structural detail on the starboard side, and a "stores" lighter alongside, which the crew is unloading. Nothing in the background indicates the location of the anchorage.

U.S. Battleship "Iowa"

Edison © 25321 Apr. 21, 1898
21 ft. FLA3240 (print) FRA0563 (neg.)
[Spanish-American War]

The film begins from a camera positioned on a moving platform that is proceeding parallel to the course line of the anchored battleship *Iowa*. The ship is shown from the midship line, proceeding aft; the cameraman repeated so that the film shows the full superstructure profile of the ship. The film ends with a picture of the bow, as if the photographer was rectifying his earlier mistake, and there are two complete trips alongside the vessel. Bedding is lashed to the starboard railing. The side cleaner's craft are tied to the stern, and two officers' transportation boats can be seen.

U.S. Battleship "Oregon"

AM&B © H35637 Sept. 12, 1903
14 ft. FLA3338 (print) FRA0649 (neg.)
[Spanish-American War]

To photograph this film, the camera was placed on a boat that was part of the reception for the battleship *Oregon*. The course of the camera boat was parallel to, but in the opposite direction from the battleship as she proceeded up the waterway, which probably accounts for the shortness of the film. However, it is possible to see the full profile of the vessel and to distinguish members of her crew stationed at "quarters." There are a few scenes of small escort vessels.

U.S. Battleship "Oregon"

Edison © 52050 Sept. 3, 1898
Location: N.Y.C. *Photographed:* Aug. 20, 1898
62 ft. FLA4928 (print) FRA1927 (neg.)
[Spanish-American War: New York City Welcome to Admiral Sampson's Fleet After Battle of Santiago Bay]

The camera position was a boat. The outline of the U.S. battleship *Oregon* can be seen as she proceeds up river under her own power. Her crew is at "quarters" and several unidentified naval vessels are in full reception dress (bunting and signal flags in the rigging). Several times during the course of the film, portions of the battleship are obscured by passenger-laden excursion steamers. There are two paddle-wheel excursion boats nearly as long as the battleship they are greeting. The last scene is of the reception committee and escort vessels.

U.S. Cavalry Supplies Unloading at Tampa, Florida

Edison © 31431 May 20, 1898
Location: Tampa, Fla.
25 ft. FLA3052 (print) FRA0382 (neg.)
[Spanish-American War]

The film shows the unloading of military supplies from railroad freight cars. The camera was positioned to show men in the uniform of the American cavalry unloading wagons without machinery to aid them. Judging from the hoop stakes, the type of wagon is a supply carrier.

U.S. Cruiser "Brooklyn" Naval Parade

Edison © 52049 Sept. 3, 1898
Location: N.Y.C. *Photographed:* Aug. 20, 1898
18ft. FLA4233 (print) FRA1391 (neg.)

[Spanish-American War; New York City Welcome to Admiral Sampson's Fleet After Battle of Santiago Bay]

The camera was placed high above the waterway. The beginning of the film shows a seagoing vessel at anchor. Five seconds later, the bow and forward structure of a vessel can be seen on the right of the film. As the film ends, it is possible to see the full hull profile of a large seagoing vessel with three small stacks. The distance from the camera does not permit absolute identification.

See also: Close View of the "Brooklyn."

U.S. Cruiser "Nashville"

Edison © 25329 Apr. 21, 1898
23 ft. FLA3075 (print) FRA0416 (neg.)
[Spanish-American War]

The camera was placed in a boat alongside the cruiser *Nashville* while it was at anchor. The weather, plus the camera position with relationship to the sun, do not allow much identification or description of the vessel. The silhouette shows a two-stack, two masted vessel with no armament visible.

U.S. Cruiser "Olympia" Leading Naval Parade

Edison © 72835 Nov. 7, 1899
Location: N.Y.C. *Photographed:* Sept. 29, 1899
87 ft. FLA4929 (print) FRA1928 (neg.)

This film was photographed from a single-camera position. It begins with a large white vessel approaching the camera position. The vessel is escorted by many others of indeterminate size. The camera is then directed at the naval vessel close to the camera position, which can be identified as the cruiser *Olympia*. Three other naval vessels follow the *Olympia*.

U.S. Cruiser "Raleigh"

Edison © 27967 Apr. 22, 1899
23 ft. FLA3034 (print) FRA0203 (neg.)
[Spanish-American War]

The film begins by showing the forward port quarter of a large naval vessel. As the film progresses, the camera, which was mounted on a boat, shows various sections of the anchored vessel from various camera positions. The film ends as most of the hull can be seen in silhouette, and alongside can be seen a commercial shore boat.

United States Government Gun Test

AM&B © H29005 Mar. 6, 1903
19 ft. FLA3739 (print) FRA0985 (neg.)

The camera was placed to show a profile of a large cannon before and during the firing demonstration. As the film continues, the cannon fires and the film ends with an explosion as if the projectile had hit the target.

U.S. Infantry Supported by Rough Riders at El Caney

Edison © 37442 June 5, 1899
44 ft. FLA4930 (print) FRA1929 (neg.)
[Spanish-American War]

The cameraman filmed what appears to be a reconstruction of a news event or at least an event that might have occurred during the Spanish-American War. A squad of seven men dressed in American military uniforms approaches the camera position. At a distance of approximately a hundred yards, they kneel and fire directly at the camera. They repeat this action twice and then, at the end of the film, a group of mounted horsemen attired as U.S. cavalrymen rides after them.

U.S.S. "Castine"

Edison © 25328 Apr. 21, 1898
23 ft. FLA4311 (print) FRA1460 (neg.)

The bow section of a large vessel can be seen approaching the camera, which was located on a boat moving toward the vessel being photographed. The camera position was higher than the main deck of the photographed ship. The condition of the film is poor and therefore details cannot be interpreted. It is possible to see the full profile of the ship and to make out a vessel with a displacement of approximately a thousand tons, with a single stack and a low superstructure.

U.S. Troops and Red Cross in the Trenches Before Caloocan

Edison © 37441 June 5, 1899
31 ft. FLA3863 (print) FRA1075 (neg.)
[Spanish-American War]

As the film begins, a ditch or trench can be seen in a heavily wooded area. A man attired in a U.S. Army infantry officer's uniform jumps into the ditch and brandishes a sword indicating that others should follow. Soon the trench is filled with approximately twenty men wearing American infantry uniforms. They fire their rifles over the rim of the trench, gesture as if cheering, and proceed to leave the trench. The film ends as two of the men fall wounded, and two women dressed in Red Cross nurses' uniforms are seen bending over them.

U.S. Troops Landing at Daiquiri, Cuba

Edison © 46690 Aug. 5, 1898
Cameraman: William Paley
Location: Daiquiri, Cuba *Photographed:* June 22, 1898
25 ft. FLA3513 (print) FRA0791 (neg., copy 1) FRA0792 (neg., copy 2)
[Spanish-American War]

The film was photographed from the shore side of a dock used to land troops. The dry dock is close to a large harbor and can be seen in the background, while the troops disembark, and as they march toward the camera position.

Unloading Halibut

AM&B © H29162 Mar. 11, 1903
Cameraman: Arthur Marvin
Location: Gochester, Mass. *Date:* Mar. 8, 1901
18 ft. FLA3646 (print) FRA0900 (neg.)

The film, photographed from a single-camera position, shows the unloading operations of a halibut fishing boat. The film is so short that nothing is identifiable.

See also: Drawing a Lobster Pot

Unloading Lighters, Manila

AM&B © H34818 Aug. 19, 1903
Cameraman: Raymond Ackerman

Location: Manila *Date:* Dec. 21, 1899
17 ft. FLA4154 (print) FRA1322 (neg.)

The short length of the film does not allow the subject matter to be described in detail. The camera was positioned on a pier or unloading dock, and photographed ox-drawn two-wheeled carts as they pulled away material being removed from a military lighter that apparently had come in from a supply ship. The film is too short for further description.

Unlucky at Cards, Lucky at Love

AM&B © H65317 Sept. 11, 1905
Cameraman: G. W. Bitzer
Location: Studio, N.Y.C. *Photographed:* Aug. 24, 1905
21 ft. FLA3785 (print) FRA1026 (neg.)

Two young people are playing cards. Both are dressed in evening attire. As the film progresses, the cards change hands more than once. As the film reaches its climax, the man is seen embracing and then kissing the young woman, with only a medium amount of resistance on her part.

An Unlucky Lover

AM&B © H29159 Mar. 11, 1903
Cameraman: F. S. Armitage
Location: Roof studio, N.Y.C. *Date:* May 25, 1901
22 ft. FLA3625 (print) FRA0882 (neg.)

On a set of the living room of a modest house, an elderly gentleman is cautioning a young woman. Just as the old gentleman leaves through one door, a young man comes in through another and begins embracing her. Apparently they hear someone approach for they separate. She recommends he hide in a large box in the room. A man wearing overalls comes in, lifts the lid of the box, and empties a sack of coal on the young man hidden there. The lover comes out of the coal box and renews his amorous advances to the young woman when they hear someone else, and this time he hides in the fireplace. Just as the lover is out of sight, the old gentleman returns and lights a fire in the fireplace, routing the young man once more.

See also: The Lovers, Coal Box and Fireplace

An Unprotected Female

AM&B © H33026 June 20, 1903
Location: Studio, N.Y.C. *Date:* June 15, 1903
28 ft. FLA4935 (print) FRA1934 (neg.)

The actor in this film is made up to resemble the cartoon character "Happy Hooligan." The action shows Happy Hooligan entering the yard behind a house. After a cursory examination, he walks directly toward the back door and knocks. A woman comes to the door and gives him some food, which he eats. He then prepares to leave, but the film ends as the woman of the house is shown pointing a double-barreled shotgun at him while Happy is rapidly sawing wood.

An Unprotected Female, no. 2

AM&B © H33205 July 2, 1903
Cameraman: G. W. Bitzer *Photographed:* June 15, 1903
Location: Studio, N.Y.C.
23 ft. FLA4936 FRA1935

The actor in this film is made up as the cartoon character "Happy Hooligan." As the film begins, he enters a set of the back of a farmhouse. He peers through the window, and then knocks on the door and gestures to the woman of the house that he is hungry. He eats, and then turns to walk away from the house. The woman comes out with a double-barreled shotgun and points it directly at his head. Happy apparently understands what she means for he immediately picks up a bucksaw and hastily begins sawing wood, continuing until the end of the film.

The Untamable Whiskers

See: Le Roi du Maquillage

Unveiling of the Pennsylvania Monument on the Battlefields of Petersburg, Virginia, May 19, 1909

Columbia Photograph Company no copyright reg.
Location: Petersburg, Va. *Photographed:* May 19, 1909
345 ft. FLA5784 (print) FRA2689 (neg., copy 1) FRA2690 (neg., copy 2)

The film shows the crowds that congregated to view and hear speakers dedicate a monument to the memory of the Civil War dead who lost their lives on the battlefields of that area. Several camera positions show marching military, both of the Union and Confederate armies, field equipment used by both sides, several pieces of firefighting equipment with the accompanying volunteer firemen, open landau carriages containing such celebrities as President Taft and his entourage, and several women making speeches. There are several groups of people in the parade: a large group of men on horseback who appear to be hunt club members, members of fraternal groups, and so on.

See also: Reception of President Taft, almost but not quite the same film.

An Unwelcome Visitor

Edison © 16430 Mar. 10, 1898
20 ft. FLA3966 (print) FRA1175 (neg.)

The camera was placed as though it were looking through a window into a bedroom where a man is asleep in a bed. As the film begins, a man costumed as a monkey can be seen harassing the sleeping man, which he continues to do throughout the film. Finally, however, the man becomes annoyed, and gets out of bed and starts boxing with the monkey.

Up a Tree

Biograph © J141018 Apr. 30, 1910
Cameraman: Arthur Marvin
Cast: Florence Barker, Billy Quirk, Charles West, Mack Sennett
Location: Glendale, Calif. *Photographed:* Mar. 3-4, 1910
379 ft. FLA5785 (print) FRA2597 (neg.)

A country yokel (Billy Quirk) tricks several people into climbing up a ladder into a tree to retrieve the hat that he placed there. Once the person is in the tree, the yokel removes the ladder, marooning the person. During the film, he plays this prank four times. One of the persons he tricks owns a horse and buggy, which the yokel promptly sells. He spends the proceeds at a local pub. All the marooned individuals are eventually rescued. They band together to find the prankster, force him out on the limb of a tree, and abandon him.

Upper Falls of the Yellowstone

Edison © H4084 May 6, 1901
Location: Yellowstone Park, Wyo.
32 ft. FLA3495 (print) FRA0775 (neg.)

The film shows a waterfall photographed from a single-camera position. The composition of the film takes in only a portion of the falls.

Upper Rapids [Niagara Falls] From Bridge

See: A Nymph of the Waves

The Usurer

Biograph © J144488 Aug. 18, 1910
Director: D. W. Griffith *Cameraman:* G. W. Bitzer
Cast: Claire McDowell, Kate Bruce, Henry B. Walthall, George Nicholls, Alfred Paget, Tony O'Sullivan, Grace Henderson, Charles Craig, Charles Avery, Dell Henderson, Gladys Egan, William J. Butler
Location: Studio, N.Y.C. *Date:* July 11-15, 1910
382 ft. FLA5786 (print) FRA2598 (neg.)

The greed and avarice of a money-mad landowner (George Nicholls) and his heartless treatment of his tenants is the theme of this film. Several scenes showing destitute people being evicted from their lodgings, or their furniture being repossessed by employees of the miserly landlord are contrasted with scenes of the landlord entertaining lavishly at social functions. A tenant (Kate Bruce) goes to his office to plead with him for more time, faints, and accidentally locks him a safe equipped with a time lock, where he suffocates surrounded by his money.

The Vaidis Sisters, Luna Park

AM&B © H36552 Oct. 6, 1903
Cameraman: G. W. Bitzer
Location: Coney Island, N.Y. *Photographed:* Sept. 25, 1903
13 ft. FLA3131 (print) FRA0465 (neg.)

The tops of some buildings are visible in the background. The camera was elevated several stories above the ground. In the immediate foreground, close to the camera position, is a cable that has been stretched across the amusement park midway from the tops of the buildings. Someone hanging by the teeth from a pulley on the wire approaches the camera, and the film ends there.

The Valet's Wife

AM&B © H118992 Nov. 28, 1908
Director: D. W. Griffith *Cameramen:* G. W. Bitzer, Arthur Marvin
Cast: Arthur Johnson, Mack Sennett, Mabel Stoughton, Robert Harron, Florence Lawrence, Harry Salter, Charles Avery
Location: Studio, N.Y.C. *Photographed:* Nov. 10 and 13, 1908
186 ft. FLA5787 (print) FRA2599 (neg.)

The series of scenes that constitute this comedy begin with an exterior scene of a man (Mack Sennett) painting out the word "Bachelors" from a sign that said "Bachelor's Apartments." An old man (Arthur Johnson) who has just married, insists that he and his wife adopt a baby. Sennett dispatches a nurse (Florence Lawrence) to an orphan asylum to get a baby. Her return with the infant is shown in a group shot from a single-camera position. The camera then moved in to a tight close-up of the baby, who turns out to be black. The film ends with much hilarity and pandemonium.

The Vampire Dancer

Great Northern © Oes J168228-9 Apr. 17, 1912

Director: August Blom *Script:* Valdemar Hansen

Cast: Carl Schenstrøm, Clara Wieth, Robert Dinesen, Julie Henriksen, Birger von Cotta Schonberg, Frederik Jacobsen, Henry Seemann, Agnes Norlund, Frederik Christensen, Ingeborg Bruhn Bertelsen, Svend Bille, Otto Lagoni

Location: Denmark *Photographed:* Oct. 23, 1911

Original title: Vampyrdanserinden

670 ft. FLA5907 (print) FLA5907 (print, copy 2) FRA2766 (neg.) FRA2766 (neg., copy 2)

The picture opens in a hotel room in a large city where an impresario is discussing the needs and basic requirements of a dancing partner for the heroine. A young man answers the advertisement, is auditioned and selected as the partner for the exotic dancer. He falls in love with her. The dancer does not permit her partners to become lovers and therefore thwarts his every advance. He becomes so frustrated he buys poison, takes it, and, as the dance is finished, dies on the stage.

Vampyrdanserinden

See: The Vampire Dancer

Vanishing Lady

Edison © 73463 Dec. 16, 1898

19 ft. FLA3244 (print) FRA0567 (neg.)

A single-camera position from the audience shows a vaudeville act where stop-action photography is used to create the illusion that a woman sitting in a chair and covered with a drape somehow vanishes.

The Vaquero's Vow

AM&B © H116506 Oct. 3, 1908

Director: D. W. Griffith *Cameraman:* G. W. Bitzer

Cast: Frank Evans, Arthur Johnson, Florence Lawrence, Harry Salter, Mack Sennett

Location: Studio, N.Y.C. *Photographed:* Aug. 31 and Sept. 1, 1908

298 ft. FLA5788 (print) FRA2601 (neg.)

All of the actors are in Spanish or early California-Mexican clothes, and the sets are designed accordingly. A young girl, loved by two men, chooses one and they are married. Her other admirer attends the wedding and bestows his blessing and a gift. The wedded couple returns home where the husband finds a note to his wife from the former suitor. He becomes so jealous he beats her and departs for the local saloon. There he becomes interested in a girl which angers the former suitor, and a fight begins. The exsuitor has the husband at a disadvantage when the wife enters and begs for his life. The picture ends as she leaves the saloon, not with her new husband, but with her former suitor. Natural lighting was used for all the scenes, and they were photographed from a single-camera position.

The Vatican Guards, Rome

AM&B © H35644 Sept. 12, 1903

Cameraman: W. K. L. Dickson [?]

Location: Rome *Photographed:* 1898 [?]

31 ft. FLA4122 (print) FRA1298 (neg.)

From the camera position, mounted uniformed men can be seen approaching. They are identified as Vatican guards. A company of foot guards in full regalia and carrying spears follow the mounted guards.

Vaulting Contest, Meadowbrook Hunt

AM&B © H28678 Feb. 26, 1903

Location: Meadowbrook Hunt Club, Westbury, L.I. *Date:* Apr. 24, 1898

22 ft. FLA3175 (print) FRA0502 (neg.)

A four-rail wing jump is shown from a camera positioned near the foreground. Horses and their riders were photographed from several camera positions as they jump over the rails.

Vengeance

Great Northern © Oes J166581-83 Feb. 12, 1912

Director: August Blom *Script:* Valdemar Hansen

Cast: Henry Seemann, Valdemar Psilander, Edith Buemann, Augusta Blad, Gerhard Jessen, Carlo Wieth, Thorkild Roose, Frederik Jacobsen, Svend Bille, Axel Boesen, Frederick Skondrup, H. C. Nielsen, Valdemar Hansen, Ella la Cour

Photographed: Aug. 10, 1911

Original title: Haevnen, or Haevnet

1,021 ft. FLA5908 (print, copy 1) FLA5909 (print, copy 2) FRA2767 (neg.)

The story is built around an ingenue, an army officer who woos her too well and abandons her, another army officer who also loves her but whose love is rejected, and a supporting cast of about seventeen. When the film begins, a tête-à-tête is in progress in the garden between the villainous army officer and the ingenue. He loves her and leaves her, after promising marriage. The result of this affair puts both the young woman and her family in an embarrassing position. To right the wrong, a man of the cloth, the villain's commanding officer, and the commanding general are introduced into the picture. The final scenes take place in the gaming room of the officers' quarters where the officers are playing cards when the villain enters. The spurned lover, filled with righteous indignation, pulls a revolver from the back pocket of his dinner clothes and shoots the villain. Then he goes into the sitting room, asks the ingenue for forgiveness, takes leave of her, and enters another room, where he shoots himself. His actions cause much consternation, and the film ends.

Venice in America

AM&B © H33280 July 8, 1903

Cameraman: Arthur Marvin

Location: Buffalo, N.Y. *Date:* June 15, 1901

22 ft. FLA3412 (print) FRA0703 (neg.)

The camera was positioned on the bow of a boat sailing through the canals of the Pan-American Exposition. The camera was directed at shore establishments.

Venskab og Kaerlighed

See: Love and Friendship

A Versatile Villain

Keystone © LP5503 May 29, 1915

Producer and Author: Mack Sennett

Cast: Charles Chase, James T. Kelly, Louise Fazenda, Joseph Swickard, William Sheer

Location: Keystone studio and surrounding area, Los Angeles

400 ft. FLA6146 (print)

A pair of baggage clerks (Chase and Kelly) meet a train to pick up an envelope containing a large sum of money. A debonair crook (William Sheer) observes them as he stands outside an open window. Chase shows off his skill as a pickpocket, removing a watch from the sheriff's (Swickard) pocket and then giving it back. The crook, a real pickpocket, steals the key to the safe and puts it in Chase's pocket, leading to his arrest when it is discovered there. The sheriff's daughter, Louise Fazenda, on her way to deliver her father's lunch, is kidnapped by the crook. A posse is formed to catch the criminal who has taken Louise to a little shack. Although she fights valiantly he ties her to a chair, attaches a fuse to some blasting powder, and lights a candle connecting both. Chase manages to get Louise out of the shack just in time, but the dynamite explosion blows the crook up through the roof. His umbrella opens causing him to float right into the arms of the waiting lawmen.

A Victim of Circumstantial Evidence

AM&B © H33398 July 6, 1903

Cameraman: G. W. Bitzer

Location: Studio, N.Y.C. *Date:* June 25, 1903

20 ft. FLA3428 (print) FRA0715 (neg.)

On a set of the front of a house, a woman, followed by two men, can be seen passing between the house and the camera position. Two boys carrying slingshots appear and fire rocks at the window, breaking them. They apparently become frightened for they drop their slingshots and run. An old gentleman in a top hat and tailcoat walks into the scene and notices and picks up the slingshot just as the owner of house with the broken windows emerges. He takes the old gentleman into custody, summons the law, and, as the film ends, the old man is being taken off to jail.

A Victim of Jealousy

Biograph © J142237 June 11, 1910

Director: D. W. Griffith *Cameraman:* G. W. Bitzer

Cast: Mary and Lottie Pickford, James Kirkwood, Grace Henderson, Charles West, Mrs. Charlotte Smith, Jeanie Macpherson, Mack Sennett, Tony O'Sullivan, William J. Butler, Florence Barker, Gertrude Robinson, Charles Craig

Location: Studio, N.Y.C. *Photographed:* May 6-7, 1910

393 ft. FLA5789 (print) FRA2668 (neg.)

A well-to-do man (James Kirkwood) is insanely jealous of his wife Florence Barker, and asks his valet to report her every move. She accompanies her friends to a painter's studio, and the valet reports this trip to the husband who rushes there. The wife's sister (Mary Pickford) learns of the predicament, and changes places with her sister. The husband, on finding his sister-in-law in the studio of the artist, goes home, too, where his wife is packing. She threatens to leave him. The last scene shows the two being reconciled while the husband promises never to be jealous again.

The Victorious Battle for the Conquest of Mergheb, Africa

Luca Comerio © Savoy Film Exchange MP3 Sept. 23, 1912

56 ft. FLA5790 (print) FRA2695 (neg.)

The subject is troop deployment during a skirmish between the Italian Army and the Arabians and Turks. The scenes are quite short and each is preceded by a title that explains more than the film shows.

Victorious Squadron Firing Salute

Edison © 50857 Aug. 30, 1898

Location: Hudson River, at Grant's Tomb, N.Y.C. *Photographed:* Aug. 20, 1898

73 ft. FLA4937 (print) FRA1936 (neg.)

[Spanish-American War]

The camera that filmed the scenes showing some ships of the U.S. Navy going up the Hudson River was positioned on the New York side. Three ships of the battleship class are escorted by tugs, excursion boats, and other vessels carrying interested passengers. The smoke of gunfire can be discerned on two occasions. The three ships were the *New York*, the *Massachusetts*, and the *Oregon*, all part of Admiral Sampson's North Atlantic Squadron.

Viewing Sherman Institute for Indians at Riverside, Cal.

Keystone © MP302 Mar. 29, 1915

Author: Mack Sennett

Location: Riverside, Calif.

115 ft. FLA6147 (print)

The title refers to this film as "educational," and it certainly is a straight recording of the happenings in a day at the Sherman Institute. Each short scene is preceded by a title indicating the action, such as, "Breakfast," "Manual Training," and "Recreation."

Views in San Francisco

AM&B © H77927 May 19, 1906

Cameraman: Otis M. Gove

Location: San Francisco *Date:* May 9, 1906

160 ft. FLA5791 (print) FRA2602 (neg.)

[San Francisco Earthquake]

Scenes in and around the metropolitan area of the city of San Francisco, immediately after the earthquake and fire of 1906, are shown. The cameraman placed his equipment in a position that would enable him to pan the camera and cover much of the disaster area. The film shows that at the time it was taken some public utilities were in working order. However, most of the buildings seen were not suitable for occupation.

The Village Cut-up

AM&B © H79739 June 19, 1906

Cameramen: G. W. Bitzer, F. A. Dobson

Cast: Sidney Olcott, Eddie Dillon

Location: Studio, N.Y.C.; Clayton [?] Conn. *Photographed:* June 1, 6, and 7, 1906

238 ft. FLA5792 (print) FRA2604 (neg.)

The picture begins with a head and shoulders close-up of a man being fitted into a photographer's head-rest. He distorts his face and grimaces as if in agony. The same man, dressed ridiculously and with an oafish air, is seen in four vaudeville turns, each on a set in front of a backdrop. An outdoor chase starts when the comic disturbs four men who are fishing in a tranquil stream. They catch up with him after he jumps into a river from a bridge, which ends the film.

The Violin Maker of Cremona
AM&B © H128159 June 9, 1909
Director: D. W. Griffith *Cameraman:* G. W. Bitzer
Cast: Mary Pickford, David Miles, Owen Moore, Mack Sennett, Arthur Johnson, Violet Mersereau, Tony O'Sullivan, John Cumpson, Clara T. Bracey, Herbert Pryor
Location: Studio, N.Y.C. *Photographed:* Apr.21–23, 1909
352 ft. FLA5793 (print) FRA2603 (neg.)

The film begins on a set of the living quarters of an Italian violin maker in the early eighteenth century. The story deals with the conflict between two apprentice violin makers (David Miles and Owen Moore) over the love of a young girl (Mary Pickford), as well as their rivalry as violin makers. There is a contest for the best violin, part of the prize being the prettiest girl in the village. One apprentice wants the prize so badly that he takes his rival's violin and leaves his own. He wins both the girl and the gold chain, and, although he admits his crime to his rival, the other man does not divulge the information. The picture ends in a photographic fadeout.

Vision of Mary
See: Ten Nights in a Bar-Room

A Visit to Baby Roger
AM&B © H25969 Dec. 31, 1902
Cameraman: Arthur Marvin
Location: Providence, R.I. *Date:* Oct. 20, 1900
30 ft. FLA4193 (print) FRA1356 (neg.)

The cameraman positioned his camera in a paved area that resembles a yard or park. A public building can be seen in the background as the film begins, and two horse-drawn public conveyances come into view. Many children accompanied by adults disembark from the conveyances. A baby elephant enters the camera view and walks around in a circle accompanied by an attendant. As the film ends, the children are circling around the elephant. AM&B records indicate the children attended Stade School in Providence.

"Vizcaya" Under Full Headway
AM&B © H30741 Apr.24, 1903
16 ft. FLA3470 (print) FRA0752 (neg.)

This short film, photographed from a pier or dock, shows a large, single-stack seagoing liner as it passes the camera position. The distance and the condition of the film do not permit much detailed description. However, the ship appears to be making great speed.
See also: Wreck of the "Vizcaya."

A Voice From the Deep
Biograph © J167394 Mar. 21, 1912
Director: Mack Sennett
Cast: Eddie Dillon, Fred Mace, Dell Henderson, Marguerite Loveridge
Location: Venice and Ocean Park, Calif.
202 ft. FLA5794 (print) FRA2600 (neg.)

The locale of this farce was a California beach and amusement pier, and the story line is built around a prank played by a man upon his friend. The two young men attempt to make the acquaintance of some young ladies at the beach and end up in a fight. One pushes the other off the pier. The man in the water decides to scare his friend and does not surface, which causes the friend to assume he is dead. There are a few scenes showing the anguish the prank causes the friend who feels he has committed murder. The film ends when the man in the water allows himself to be hauled up onto the pier.

The Voice of the Violin
AM&B © H124289 Mar. 17, 1909
Director: D. W. Griffith *Cameramen:* G. W. Bitzer, Arthur Marvin
Cast: Arthur Johnson, Marion Leonard, Clara T. Bracey, Gladys Egan
Location: West Twelfth Street and Studio, N.Y.C. *Photographed:* Feb. 19 and 23, 1909
367 ft. FLA5795 (print) FRA2605 (neg.)

The film begins with a young man (Arthur Johnson) instructing a young girl (Marion Leonard) to play the violin. The young lady has her maid along as a chaperone, but nevertheless, her father takes her away. Two anarchist friends of the violin teacher induce him to join their group, and he draws a number that makes him a participant in a bombing. The house selected is the one owned by the father of his former pupil. Arriving on the scene and preparing to execute the crime, the violin teacher realizes he would be blowing up someone he loves. He fights with his companion, and is knocked unconscious and tied up, but by wriggling his body he manages to extinguish the bomb fuse. The picture ends when the heroic violin teacher embraces his pupil while her adoring father watches.

The Waders
AM&B © H35099 Aug. 28, 1903
Cameraman: A. E. Weed
Location: Coney Island, N.Y. *Photographed:* Aug. 18, 1903
36 ft. FLA4938 (print) FRA1937 (neg.)

The subjects are waders, and for the extent of the film, several children are shown wading in the surf. Some of the children wear bathing suits, while others are in conventional clothing. A large sailing vessel under full sail can be seen on the ocean.

The Wages of Sin
Klaw & Erlanger © LP3034 June 4, 1914
Cast: William J. Butler, Charles Hill Mailes, Walter Miller, Franklin Ritchie, Irene Howley, Isabel Rea, William Jefferson, Lewis Wells
1,200 ft. FLA5873 (print)

This three-reel film concerns a young woman working in a mill who is ruined by the villain. He later promises marriage if she will lie about a young minister. She carries out her part but is betrayed. Her lie causes a delayed wedding and unhappy circumstances for the daughter of the mill owner as well as for his adopted daughter. Most of the film was photographed on sets; however, there are several outdoor scenes, and a considerable number of people are involved in the action.

The Wages of Sin: Murder—Part 1

AM&B © H34511   Aug. 13, 1903
Cameraman: G. W. Bitzer
Location: Studio, N.Y.C. *Photographed:* July 24, 1903
19 ft.   FLA4384 (print)   FRA1519 (neg.)

Two roughly dressed men are admiring a piece of jewelry while sitting at a small table in the center of a set of the interior of a lower class dwelling. One of the two men leaves the room while the other goes to a door and opens it. He roughly pulls a woman standing there into the room. She attempts to break away from her captor, who puts his hands on her throat and begins choking her. The man continues his assault on the woman until he realizes he has killed her. This is the first reel of two-episode drama.

The Wages of Sin: Retribution—Part 2

AM&B © H34512   Aug. 13, 1903
Cameraman: G. W. Bitzer
Location: Studio, N.Y.C. *Photographed:* July 24, 1903
20 ft.   FLA4385 (print)   FRA1520 (neg.)

The film was photographed from a single-camera position on a set of impoverished living quarters. As the action begins, a man who appears intoxicated is seated at a small table. A body is lying on a pallet in the corner. The door opens and a man dressed as a minister enters, removes his hat and coat, and proceeds to beat up the drunken man. Another man with a pistol in his hand enters. He is followed by a policeman. As the gun goes off, one man falls down as if dead and the policeman escorts the other out.

Wagon Supply Train En Route

Edison   © 38244   June 22, 1898
24 ft.   FLA4345 (print)   FRA1489 (neg.)
[Spanish-American War]

The photographer placed his camera close by the route a supply train was to pass. As the film begins, a heavily laden wagon pulled by six mules passes by, followed by several other wagons of the same basic design. Before the film ends, other types of vehicles of lighter construction and drawn by only one animal also can be seen.

Wagons Loading Mail, U.S.P.O.

AM&B   © H34995   Aug. 22, 1903
Cameraman: A. E. Weed
Location: Washington, D.C. *Photographed:* July 29, 1903
27 ft.   FLA3888 (print)   FRA110 (neg.)

The photographer placed his camera to encompass as much of the loading ramp of a mail delivery building as possible. As the film begins, several horse-drawn postal transportation vehicles are backed up to the ramp. At the end of the film, a postal delivery wagon pulled by one horse enters the scene and is backed against the ramp.

The Waif

AM&B   © H44209   April 6, 1904
Cameraman: A. E. Weed *Photographed:* March 24 and 25, 1904
Location: Studio, N.Y.C.
254 ft.   FLA5796 (print)

The opening scene of this melodrama shows a poorly furnished tenement room where a baby is seated on the floor. A shabbily dressed woman enters and quickly goes to a basket near the baby on the floor. She busies herself with the basket, lifts out a smaller infant, wraps it carefully, places the infant in another basket, and leaves the room with the child. The camera changes position to show her out on the street where it is snowing. The woman carries the basket containing the baby to a wealthy neighborhood and leaves it on the front porch where it is discovered by a servant who takes the basket containing the infant into the house.

The next scene shows the household and their servants looking over the infant.

Now the camera cuts back to the room from which the shabbily dressed woman is being evicted. Some men take her furniture and her remaining baby outside and place them on the sidewalk in the snow. Soon a policeman comes by and picks up the infant. The film ends as the mother of the child identifies herself to the policeman and takes the child from him.

AM&B production records show another title in parenthesis—it is Out in the Street.

Waiter No. 5

Biograph   © J147562   Nov. 10, 1910
Director: D. W. Griffith *Cameraman:* G. W. Bitzer
Cast: Mary Pickford, Charles West, Kate Bruce, George Nicholls, Grace Henderson, Claire McDowell, Eddie Dillon, Alfred Paget, William J. Butler, Dell Henderson, Adolph Lestina, Jack Pickford
Location: Studio, N.Y.C. *Photographed:* Sept. 19–22, 1910
360 ft.   FLA5797 (print)   FRA6441 (neg.)

This film is about a man who is forced to leave a commanding military position in Russia and become a waiter in America in order to save his wife. He does not tell his son (Charles West) of his reduced circumstances. The climax comes when his son and new daughter-in-law (Mary Pickford) go to the restaurant where his father is employed as a waiter, and they confront one another. The disturbance brings him to the attention of another military man, who recognizes him, and the end of the film shows the waiter being restored to his former military rank, which allows him the position in society he wants for his son.

Waiting at the Church

© Belcher & Waterson H90028   Feb. 1, 1907
Cast: Vesta Victoria
70 ft.   FLA5245 (print)   FRA2193 (neg.)

The camera was placed from the audience point of view and shows a painted backdrop of wood paneling. A young man in a tuxedo enters from the wings, talks directly to the camera, as if introducing someone, and then leaves. A young lady comes on stage and begins reciting. She is dressed as a bride and carries a bouquet. Judging from her gestures her recital was a lament at being jilted. Toward the end of the film, the woman makes a circle in front of the camera, exposing a sign on her back that reads "To Let," ending the film. The entertainer is probably the British vaudeville star, Vesta Victoria, who introduced both Waiting at the Church and Poor John, to the American public.

See also: Poor John

Waiting for Bill

AM&B © H39909   Dec. 23, 1903
Cameraman: A. E. Weed
Location: Studio, N.Y.C. *Photographed:* Dec. 9, 1903
35 ft.   FLA4939 (print)   FRA1938 (neg.)

The camera was placed in the audience at a vaudeville show. The backdrop was painted like a park, and a soldier is marching back and forth. An attractive young lady comes on stage, and the soldier attempts to make her acquaintance. A lieutenant arrives, orders the private to leave, and tries to talk to the young woman. Another man of higher rank appears and orders the lieutenant to depart. This performance is repeated until finally a young man in a striped sweater and slouch hat, who looks like a bum appears. He knocks down the military man, apparently impressing the young woman, as she leaves the stage on his arm.

Waiting for Santa Claus

AM&B © H18892   June 12, 1902
Cameraman: F. S. Armitage
Location: Roof studio, N.Y.C. *Date:* June 11, 1901
14 ft.   FLA3803 (print)   FRA1038 (neg.)

This sideshow act was photographed from a single-camera position as if in the audience. Two women in tights act as curtain openers. The curtains part to show two nude children in front of a fireplace apparently waiting for Santa Claus.

See also: The Pouting Model, and Sleeping Child

A Wake in "Hell's Kitchen"

AM&B © H32563   June 12, 1903
Cameraman: Arthur Marvin
Location: Roof studio, N.Y.C. Dates: July 26, 1900
18 ft.   FLA3502 (print)   FRA0782 (neg.)

Photographed from a one-camera position, this shows a room with a coffin and two people drinking the health of the departed; a woman is serving drinks. The coffin lid is off. Someone rises up out of the coffin and drinks a glass of beer from the table nearby, thereby causing a disturbance.

Wall Scaling

Edison © 60589   Oct. 25, 1897
19 ft.   FLA3018 (print)   FRA0025 (neg.)

The action consists of several fully outfitted army infantry personnel climbing over walls provided for this sort of training. The camera was placed so that both sides of the scaling wall are visible and, during the course of the film, several men can be seen aiding one another up and over the wall.

Wand Dance, Pueblo Indians

Edison © 13563   Feb. 24, 1898
Location: Arizona [?]
27 ft.   FLA3254 (print)   FRA0576 (neg.)

The single-camera position shows a group of Pueblo Indians, some with full feathers, some with no headdress at all, going in a circle around a man beating a drum. The circling Indians are executing various steps as they progress in time to the drum. Each brandishes a stick or wand.

Wanted, A Child

Biograph © J132957   Oct. 2, 1909
Director: D. W. Griffith *Cameraman:* G. W. Bitzer
Cast: Kate Bruce, George Nicholls, Gladys Egan, Adele De Garde
Location: Studio, N.Y.C. *Date:* Aug. 31, 1909
97 ft.   FLA5798 (print)   FRA2606 (neg.)

The first scene takes place on a set of the interior of a laborer's house. The room is filled with children playing, and there is a woman (Kate Bruce) preparing food, when a man (George Nicholls) enters. He has a downcast expression as if overburdened with so many children to support. A postman arrives with a letter that apparently asks for one of their children. The parents go into the rooms where the children are asleep, look each one over, as if trying to make a decision. The last scene shows the man holding a small child in his arms as he rocks her gently.

Wanted: A Dog

AM&B © H58987   Apr. 7, 1905
Cameramen: F. S. Armitage, Wallace McCutcheon
Cast: Sidney Olcott
Location: Deal, N.J.; Studio, N.Y.C. *Photographed:* Mar. 22, 27, and 28, 1905
304 ft.   FLA5799 (print)   FRA2607 (neg.)

A young widow living in a rural area is molested by tramps so she puts an ad in the paper for a dog to scare the tramps away. The ad brings quick and unexpected results, and the film shows the woman's front porch crowded with about fifty persons with dogs on leashes. The woman becomes hysterical and begins to run. The remainder of the film is devoted to a chase through hill and dale, through fields and streams, until the young woman, still ahead of her pursuers, arrives at the gate of an insane asylum, where she begs admission from the attendant.

Wanted—A Nurse

AM&B © H83223   Sept. 27, 1906
Cameraman: F. A. Dobson
Location: Studio and Morris Heights, N.Y.C. *Photographed:* Sept. 15 [?], 1906
329 ft.   FLA5800 (print)   FRA2608 (neg.)

An old man, his head bandaged, is sitting in a chair on a living room set. A white haired man enters and sits opposite him. Their conversation is depicted by the use of balloon cartoons on the wall, and one word at a time appears in a balloon. The friend suggests placing an ad for a nurse, which is done. A large group of women answer the ad, and the frightened old man runs off, with the entire group in close pursuit. Two finally catch him and drag him home. The following scenes show the old man attempting to escape by various means, but he is caught every time and brought back home. Finally, his friend arrives, and the old man leaves him to cope with the two nurses. The original paper print film bears the title Nurse Wanted, but was copyrighted under the above title.

War Canoe Race

Edison © H46579 May 28, 1904

Cameraman: A. C. Abadie

Location: Toronto *Photographed:* May 21, 1904

37 ft. FLA3674 (print) FRA0924 (neg.)

The film, photographed from several camera positions, shows some large canoes being paddled by crews of white people. The motor boats following the canoes bear Canadian flags.

War Correspondents

Edison © 25320 Apr. 21, 1898

22 ft. FLA4231 (print) FRA1389 (neg.)

[Spanish-American War]

Photographed from a single-camera position, the film shows a street bordered by wooden one- and two-story buildings. There is nothing to indicate the locale, although it seems to have been taken either at a summer resort or in Cuba. The people running toward the camera are unidentified, and none is close enough to identify.

The War of Wealth

Klaw & Erlanger © LP3429 Sept. 24, 1914

Cast: Linda Arvidson, Charles Perley, Violet Reid, Robert Drouet, Jack Brammall

Location: Southern Calif.

1,227 ft. FLA5838-5840 (print) FRA2652-2654 (neg.)

The story line of this three-reel drama begins during the Civil War and ends with a run on a bank which is averted because of a relationship that began at the Battle of Fredricksburg between a drummer boy and his commanding officer. The first scenes show battle maneuvers between the Confederate and Union armies. There are a few scenes showing the two leading actors making money after the war, as well as scenes taken on well-groomed estates and expensive interiors. There is a set of an interior of a bank where as many as one hundred extras were used.

A Warm Occasion

AM&B © H42041 Feb. 11, 1904

Cameraman: A. E. Weed

Location: Studio, N.Y.C. *Photographed:* Jan. 26, 1904

22 ft. FLA4319 (print) FRA1467 (neg.)

One woman is in bed while another is smoking a cigarette and fixing her hair in a set of a woman's boudoir. The door in the set opens and a third young woman with a top hat and overcoat over her pajamas enters. She appears to be drunk and exhibits her inability to walk as she attempts to traverse the set. Her female companions seize her, place her on a table, and spank her. She is carried bodily to the bed and then unceremoniously dropped to the floor, where she remains as the film ends.

Was Justice Served?

Biograph © H128592 June 19, 1909

Director: D. W. Griffith *Cameramen:* G. W. Bitzer, Arthur Marvin

Cast: James Kirkwood, Mack Sennett, Frank Powell, Arthur Johnson, William J. Butler, Adele De Garde, Charles Avery, Tony O'Sullivan, Billy Quirk, John Cumpson, Harry Salter

Location: Englewood, N.J.; Studio, N.Y.C. *Photographed:* May 20, 21, and 24, 1909

345 ft. FLA5802 (print) FRA2609 (neg.)

The first scene shows a man (James Kirkwood) being released from jail and returning to his wife, child, and mother. The next morning he goes out to look for work. He asks the way from two men on the street, who go their way. Another man (Frank Powell) comes along, sees a wallet on the sidewalk, picks it up, extracts the money, and throws the wallet down in front on the employment office where the hero sees it. A policeman and the man who lost the wallet arrive and the hero is arrested. The balance of the film show his trial by jury. One member of the jury is the man who actually took the money from the wallet, and he is the lone holdout for acquittal. The jury continues to argue, and finally the man admits his guilt to the foreman. The hero is released. The film makes much use of the cutback technique.

Wash-Day

AM&B © H21506 Sept. 5, 1902

Cameraman: Robert K. Bonine

Date: Aug. 5, 1902

16 ft. FLA3125 (print) FRA0459 (neg.)

The single-camera position shows what appears to be the backyard of a nursery school. There are ten or twelve children under ten years of age being instructed or playing at washing and ironing clothes, supervised by two adult women.

Wash Day in Mexico

Edison © 13544 Feb. 24, 1898

Location: Durango[?], Mexico

25 ft. FLA4172 (print) FRA1337 (neg.)

The camera was positioned next to a running stream to show approximately twenty women on their hands and knees at the edge of the water washing clothes. The entire film is devoted to the women laundering their clothing.

Washing Clothes at Sicily

Edison © H32553 June 11, 1903

Cameraman: A. C. Abadie

Location: Syracuse, Sicily *Date:* Mar. 26, 1903

27 ft. FLA3538 (print) FRA0814 (neg.)

As the film begins, approximately twenty women are washing clothes in what appears to be a community clothes washing center. The cameraman did not move his camera during the extent of the film, so the only action is of the women laundering their clothing.

Washing Gold on 20 Above Hunker, Klondike

Edison © H4080 May 6, 1901

Cameraman: Robert K. Bonine

Location: Klondike, Yukon Terr., Canada

24 ft. FLA3996 (print) FRA1200 (neg.)

[Alaska Gold Rush]

From a single-camera position, mountainous terrain and jerry-built sluice boxes can be seen. There are several men working along the sluice box raking the mud and water through the trough into a puddle. There is a horse-drawn sled on which material from the puddle is moved to a crusher.

Washing the Baby
AM&B © H26950 Jan. 14, 1903
Photographed: 1897 [?]
22 ft. FLA3315 (print) FRA0629 (neg.)

The single-camera position shows an artificially lighted scene with a woman lifting an infant out of a wash basin and proceeding through the stages of drying and dressing it.

Washington Bridge and Speedway
AM&B © H30751 Apr. 24, 1903
Cameraman: F. S. Armitage
Location: Harlem River, N.Y.C. *Date:* June 20, 1901
27 ft. FLA3158 (print) FRA0486 (neg.)

The camera, on the bow of a vessel that is proceeding on the waterway under a large suspension drawbridge, shows the drawbridge opening. The remainder of the film is devoted to the suspension portion. A few unidentified vessels also are seen.

The Washwoman's Daughter
AM&B © H32865 June 20, 1903
Photographed: 1898 [?]
12 ft. FLA3431 (print) FRA0718 (neg.)

One woman is sitting on a chair watching another at work over a washboard. The door in the set opens, and a third woman joins them. The woman at the washboard stops her work and pours a drink for the latest arrival who drinks it and immediately begins haranguing the seated woman. This starts an altercation that ends when the woman who had the drink gets hit on the head with the washboard.

Water Buffalo, Manila
AM&B © H34819 Aug. 19, 1903
Cameraman: Raymond Ackerman
Location: Manila, Philippine Is. *Date:* Mar. 1, 1900
26 ft. FLA4145 (print) FRA1315 (neg.)

In order to make this film, the photographer placed his camera on a dock or a pier. During the film, several two-wheeled carts pulled by water buffaloes pass the camera. These activities are watched by some men dressed as dock laborers. An American soldier on horseback expedites the movement of the ox carts.

Water Duel
AM&B © H27983 Feb. 7, 1903
Cameraman: G. W. Bitzer
Location: Guttenberg, N.J. *Date:* Sept. 11, 1900
22 ft. FLA3147 (print) FRA0480 (neg.)

The subject is a contest between two firemen who are squirting water on one another from fire hoses. The two firemen play the fire-hose nozzles on one another. Along the curbing of the street, where the contest is taking place there are several spectators. The spray from the water prohibits identification of anything else in the picture. According to AM&B production records, the "duel" was between farmers and firemen.

Water Nymphs
AM&B © H21504 Sept. 5, 1902
Cameraman: Robert K. Bonine
Date: Aug. 5, 1902
26 ft. FLA3954 (print) FRA1165 (neg.)

Photographed from a single-camera position is a cobble-stone water fountain in which three children, clothed in their underwear, are standing knee-deep. One of the children splashes water on the other two.

Waterfall in the Catskills
Edison © 43413 July 31, 1897
Location: Haines Falls, Catskill Mountains, N.Y.
28 ft. FLA3064 (print) FRA0407 (neg.)

The waterfall shown was photographed from a camera too close to encompass the full drop of the water. The foliage on each side of the falls, however, inhibited the cameraman from placing his camera to get a better view of the complete drop.

Watermelon Contest
Edison © D13285 June 28, 1900
64 ft. FLA4940 (print) FRA1939 (neg.)

Four black men eating watermelon halves were photographed from a single-camera position. Their actions indicate some sort of a race to finish first. The man who finishes first apparently wants more, because he takes another contestant's watermelon from him. The ensuing scuffle last until the end of the picture.

Wawona, Big Tree
AM&B © H30739 Apr. 24, 1903
Cameraman: G. W. Bitzer
Location: Wawona, Calif. *Photographed:* Sept. 28, 1901
14 ft. FLA3392 (print) FRA0690 (neg.)

This short film was photographed from a single-camera position. It begins by showing the base of the trunk of a large sequoia or California redwood tree. The center has been carved out to allow passage of a road through it. The last part of the film shows a horse-drawn coach going through the cavity.

See also: Cascade Near Wawona, Cal. and Tourists Arriving at Wawona Hotel

The Way of Man
Biograph © J129205 June 28, 1909
Director: D. W. Griffith *Cameraman:* Arthur Marvin
Cast: Mary Pickford, Florence Lawrence, Arthur Johnson, Kate Toncray, Tony O'Sullivan, Mack Sennett, James Kirkwood
Location: Edgewater, N.J.; Studio, N.Y.C. *Photographed:* May 13–24, 1909
357 ft. FLA5803 (print) FRA6428 (neg.)

A young woman (Florence Lawrence), engaged to a young man (Arthur Johnson) who has left home to seek his fortune, meets with an accident that leaves her face disfigured. The fiancé returns, tries to accustom himself to the new circumstances, but then meets her cousin (Mary Pickford). The unlucky young woman resigns herself to the situation and disappears, leaving a note that she plans to take her life. Instead, she hides behind a cliff and leaves her clothes on the water's edge. When her family and friends rush to her rescue, she watches them and decides her cousin and exfiancé are really in love. The following scenes show the cousin and the young man being married. The last scene indicates that the disfigured young woman has found a new life as a nursemaid in the "Bide-A-Wee" children's home.

The Way of the World
Biograph © J140899 Apr. 27, 1910
Director: D. W. Griffith *Cameraman:* G. W. Bitzer
Cast: Dorothy West, Tony O'Sullivan, Charles West, Mack Sennett, George Nicholls, Henry B. Walthall, Dell Henderson, Florence Barker
Location: Glendale and San Gabriel, Calif. *Photographed:* Mar. 12–14, 1910
374 ft. FLA5804 (print) FRA2610 (neg.)

The film begins with a silhouette of the San Gabriel Mission bells. The photographer opened the diaphragm of his lens until the exposure of the interior equalled that of the exterior. A lay priest is seen tolling the bell. A newly ordained young priest goes out in the world and works hard with laborers in the field, who only mock him. A young woman (Florence Barker) is set upon by the people of the town because they consider her a bad influence, and the young priest befriends her. To his dismay, he finds that people he had helped turn against him, and he takes her back to the mission to seek the advice of the old father. The woman of the streets is converted, and the last scene shows her embracing religion.

The Way to Sell Corsets
AM&B © H42036 Feb. 11, 1904
Cameraman: A. E. Weed
Location: Studio, N.Y.C. *Photographed:* Jan. 29, 1904
28 ft. FLA3959 (print) FRA1169 (neg.)

This peep-show comedy opens in a set of a department store. The signs indicate that women's undergarments are for sale. A customers enters and the proprietor orders a model to come out. Just before the end of the film, the proprietor lifts off the model's head. A dummy was substituted for the live model. Special effects and stop-action photography were used.

See also: A Busy Day for the Corset Models

The Weary Hunters and the Magician
Edison © H13361 Jan. 27, 1902
24 ft. FLA3329 (print) FRA0640 (neg.)

This was photographed as if from above the heads of spectators at a vaudeville show. The action begins on a set representing a forest where two men dressed as hunters and carrying shotguns appear. They are followed by a man in a top hat and tails, and from the gestures, it is evident the three are striking a bargain. The man in the top hat pulls a large sack from behind him. He bends over, and apparently removes and throws something from the sack, and the hunters discharge their weapons alternately. This is continued for some time, and, as the film ends, the two hunters can be seen stringing dead jack rabbits on a pole and leaving the stage.

Weary Willie and the Gardener
Edison © H7982 Aug. 21, 1901

19 ft. FLA4254 (print) FRA1410 (neg.)

The picture begins outdoors where a young man is watering the lawn in front of a house. A tramp approaches him and the gardener shows his displeasure by squirting water on the tramp, who runs away. But he then returns and crimps the hose to restrict the flow of water. The tramp waits until the gardener bends down and looks into the hose and then releases the restriction. Water squirts into the young man's face. As the tramp attempts to flee, a policeman apprehends him.

Weary Willie Kidnaps a Child
Edison © H46907 June 7, 1904
Cameraman: Edwin S. Porter
Location: N.Y.C. *Photographed:* May 24, 1904
58 ft. FLA4941 (print) FRA1940 (neg.)

A maid, her small charge, and a tramp can be seen sitting on a park bench in a park. The tramp is asleep on one end of the bench. A policeman comes along and talks with the maid. They depart, leaving the child. The tramp wakes up, sees the little girl, and leads her off into the wooded area of the park. He dresses the child in ragged clothing and starts her begging. A policeman searching for the little girl arrests the tramp just as the child is being given some money by a sympathetic passerby.

The Wedding
AM&B © H61108 May 19, 1905
Cameraman: G. W. Bitzer
Location: Brick Church, N.J.; Studio, N.Y.C. *Photographed:* May 3-5, 1905
209 ft. FLA5805 (print) FRA2611 (neg.)

The opening scene was photographed in a set of the dressing room adjacent to a wedding chapel, where a bride is being helped to dress by her bridesmaids. The camera shifts to a room where a man is hurriedly attempting to dress himself. He finally opens the door to his room and a messenger hands him a dress suit, which he puts on rapidly. The camera shifts to an exterior shot where the man, now completely dressed, is running for a carriage. He stumbles and falls in full view of the camera but manages to get in a hansom cab. The camera again shifts back to the waiting room of the chapel, and shows the groom arriving. The wedding ceremony is shown, and the bride and groom's departure by train. AM&B applied for a copyright for this title as a "Dramatic Production."

Weighing the Baby
AM&B © H36558 Oct. 6, 1903
Cameraman: G. W. Bitzer
Location: Studio, N.Y.C. *Photographed:* Sept. 19, 1903
38 ft. FLA3092 (print) FRA0431 (neg.)

In the foreground of the camera position, a young man is sitting at a table reading. A man and a woman carrying an infant come in and place the baby on the table. During the remainder of the film, the action shows the steps necessary to properly raise the baby in a sling, making it possible to weigh the infant with a hand scale.

A Welcome Burglar
AM&B © H121797 Jan. 19, 1909
Director: D. W. Griffith *Cameraman:* G. W. Bitzer

Cast: Marion Leonard, Mack Sennett, Harry Salter
Location: Fort Lee, N.J.: Studio, N.Y.C. *Photographed:* Dec. 11, 12, and 29, 1908
292 ft. FLA5806 (print) FRA2612 (neg.)

The first scene takes place on a front porch and shows a man convincing a young woman to run away with him. The next scene shows them living together. She faints when he tells her he is leaving. The young woman gets a job, her employer falls in love with her, and they get married. Her former lover discovers her whereabouts and writes a note to the husband urging his presence elsewhere. The camera shows the exterior of the house and a burglar entering through the window just before the former lover arrives. The former lover begins to molest the wife, the burglar takes her part and shoots him. The wife allows the burglar to escape through the window before her husband returns home.

Welding the Big Ring
AM&B © H45002 Apr. 28, 1904
Cameraman: G. W. Bitzer
Location: East Pittsburgh, Pa. [?] *Photographed:* Apr. 18, 1904
146 ft. FLA5246 (print) FRA2194 (neg.)

The subject is the efforts of several blacksmiths in a large manufacturing plant (Westinghouse) to shape and weld together the ends of a large iron circle. Several men working on the task are photographed from several camera positions as they speedily go about their work. The film shows the circle supported by a big block-and-tackle and guided by a half dozen workmen while the ends to be welded are in a forge being heated. As the film ends, some of the men are applying sledges to the heated portion.

See also: Westinghouse Air Brake Co., and Westinghouse Works

A Welsh Rabbit
AM&B © H33206 July 2, 1903
Cameraman: G. W. Bitzer
Cast: Kathryn Osterman
Location: Studio, N.Y.C. *Date:* June 24, 1903
37 ft. FLA4942 (print) FRA1941 (neg.)

The film was photographed from a single-camera position on a kitchen set. A woman en déshabillé is busily preparing the ingredients to go into a chafing dish on the sideboard. She puts them into the chafing dish and covers it. Then she lifts the lid but, instead of anything edible, finds a tiny white rabbit which she cuddles to her neck. The action is repeated and, as the film ends, the second live baby rabbit is removed from the chafing dish. Released as Making a Welch Rabbit.

A Welsh Rabbit
AM&B © H33880 July 28, 1903
Cameraman: G. W. Bitzer
Cast: Kathryn Osterman
Location: Studio, N.Y.C. *Photographed:* July 15, 1903
25 ft. FLA4087 (print) FRA1269 (neg.)

A woman wearing an off-the-shoulder evening gown is engaged in preparing what appears to be a Welsh rarebit. She combines the ingredients, and then places them in a chafing dish. She lifts the lid of the chafing dish and removes not food but a white baby rabbit which she holds up to full view of the camera.

West Indian Boys Diving for Money
Edison © H27647 Jan. 28, 1903
Location: St. Thomas, D.W.I.
48 ft. FLA4943 (print) FRA1942 (neg.)

The camera was placed on a pier or a dock. Several native boys swim toward the camera from a distance of approximately a hundred yards. As they approach the immediate vicinity of the camera, they stop and tread water as if waiting for someone to throw something to them. They remain in this position until the film ends.

West Indian Girls in Native Dance
Edison © H30404 Jan. 28, 1903
Location: St. Thomas, D.W.I.
41 ft. FLA3379 (print) FRA0680 (neg.)

Four women can be seen at a distance of approximately fifty feet in a wooded locale. The single-camera position shows the women are fully clothed and all are wearing bandanas around their heads. One of the women holds the corner of her apron. There is some indication this is a dance as the women attempt to wiggle their posteriors. The film has an Edison patent warning.

West Point Cadets
AM&B © H26847 Jan. 9, 1903
Cameraman: F. S. Armitage
Location: N.Y.C. *Date:* Sept. 30, 1899
41 ft. FLA3301 (print) FRA0615 (neg.)
[Spanish-American War; Dewey Homecoming, New York City]

From a single-camera position, located over the heads of the spectators on the streets, military personages in full dress on horseback can be seen approaching the camera. Following closely behind the mounted officers is a full corps of cadets of the U.S. Military Academy at West Point. They are marching in company-front order. In the background, some public buildings are visible. The grain of the film does not allow detailed identification.

West Point Cadets
Edison © 65372 Oct. 7, 1899
Location: N.Y.C. *Photographed:* Sept. 30, 1899
35 ft. FLA3232 (print) FRA0556 (neg.)
[Spanish-American War; Dewey Homecoming, New York City]

The subject is a parade. The camera was situated overlooking the crowd lining the streets to watch the parade. The action begins with the full corps of cadets from the U.S. Military Academy at West Point passing by the camera position in company-front formation.

West Point Cadets, St. Louis Exposition
AM&B © H47333 June 18, 1904
Cameraman: A. E. Weed
Location: St. Louis, Mo. *Photographed:* June 8, 1904
78 ft. FLA5247 (print) FRA2195 (neg.)

In the foreground is a large paved area. In the background are the columns of an exhibit building at the World's Fair in

St. Louis. As the film progresses, people can be seen in the background watching men in the military uniform of the U.S. Military Academy approach from camera right. Judging from the number of companies passing the camera position, the parade must have consisted of the full corps. Immediately after the West Point cadets comes a color guard of the U.S. Army, followed by a large horse-drawn float. As the film ends, four open carriages, each drawn by four horses, stop in the reception area; the distance from the camera does not allow identification of the passengers. On this occasion, the cadets were escorting the Liberty Bell.

Western Stage Coach Hold Up

Edison © H46143 May 18, 1904

Cameraman: A. C. Abadie

Location: Bliss, Okla. Terr. *Photographed:* May 9, 1904

60 ft. FLA4944 (print) FRA1943 (neg.)

The cameraman placed his equipment in a rural area. Approximately ten men in Western attire with large chaps and hats can be seen in the immediate foreground as they crouch behind some scrub trees. A stagecoach drives up and passes them, and the men emerge from behind the trees and hold up the coach. At the end, the men who robbed the coach mount their horses and ride off into the distance.

Westinghouse Air Brake Co. Westinghouse Works

See: Westinghouse Works

Westinghouse Air Brake Co. Westinghouse Co. Works (Casting Scene)

See: Westinghouse Works

Westinghouse Air Brake Co. Westinghouse Co. Works (Moulding Scene)

See: Westinghouse Works

Westinghouse Works

AM&B © various as listed below

Cameraman: G. W. Bitzer *Photographed:* April 13–May 16, 1904

Location: East Pittsburgh, Wilmerding, and Trafford, Pa.

Contents:

Panorama Exterior Westinghouse Works, H45157, May 2, 1904
    FLA 5896   FRA 2846

Steam Whistle, Westinghouse Works, H45952, May 13, 1904
    FLA 5896   FRA 2940

Girls Taking Time Checks, Westinghouse Works, H45400, May 6, 1904
    FLA 5896   FRA 2941

Girls Winding Armatures, H45003, April 28, 1904
    FLA 5896   FRA 2942

Taping Coils, Westinghouse Works, H45461, May 7, 1904
    FLA 5896   FRA 2943

Coil Winding Machines, Westinghouse Works, H45401, May 6, 1904
    FLA 5896   FRA 2944

Coil Winding Section E, Westinghouse Works, H45402, May 6, 1904
    FLA 5896   FRA 2945

Tapping A Furnace, Westinghouse Works, H48416, July 23, 1904
    FLA 5896   FRA 2946

Casting a Guide Box, Westinghouse Works, H48415, July 23, 1904
    FLA 5896   FRA 2947

Westinghouse Air Brake Co. Westinghouse Co. Works (Moulding Scene),
    H48414, July 23, 1904   FLA 5897   FRA 2939

Steam Hammer, Westinghouse Works, H45953, May 13, 1904
    FLA 5897   FRA 2937

Westinghouse Air Brake Co. Westinghouse Works, H48417, July 23, 1904
    FLA 5897   FRA 2936

Panorama of Machine Co. Aisle Westinghouse Co. Works, H48410,
    July 23, 1904   FLA 5897   FRA 2935

Panorama View Street Car Motor Room, H45147, May 2, 1904
    FLA 4897   FRA 2998

Assembling a Generator, Westinghouse Works, H45598, May 10, 1904
    FLA 5897   FRA 2934

Testing a Rotary, Westinghouse Works, H45460, May 7, 1904
    FLA 5897   FRA 2933

Testing Large Turbines, Westinghouse Co. Works, H48411, July 23, 1904
    FLA 5897   FRA 2932

Assembling and Testing Turbines, Westinghouse Works, H48412, July 23, 1904
    FLA 5897   FRA 2931

Panoramic Views Aisle B., Westinghouse Works, H45597, May 10, 1904
    FLA 5897   FRA 2930

647 ft. (reel 1)   FLA 4896 (print)
775 ft. (reel 2)   FLA 5897 (print)

The film begins with the camera mounted on a train passing the Westinghouse Works, the manufacturing plant of the Westinghouse Air Brake and Electric Motor Company. The film shows the personnel of the factory, mostly women, performing tasks.

See also: Welding the Big Ring

Whaling in the Far North Off the Coast of Alaska in the Treacherous Bering Sea

M. H. Crawford © MP13 Nov. 9, 1912

Location: Alaska

296 ft. FLA5807 (print) FRA2658 (neg.)

A bearded man is standing abaft the trigger mechanism of a cast-iron harpoon gun. Throughout the film there are scenes of loading a harpoon cannon, firing the cannon, the harpoon line attached to a whale, and towing the whale into the rendering station. There is a scene of a group of sailing vessels equipped to render whales into the main product, oil. The last scene shows salmon swimming in Ketchikan, Alaska. The film is titled Hunting the Largest Game in the World.

Wharf Scene and Natives Swimming at St. Thomas, D.W.I.

Edison © H30405 Apr. 8, 1903
Location: Charlotte Amalie, St. Thomas, D.W.I.
28 ft. FLA3607 (print) FRA0870 (neg.)

The camera was positioned on a dock adjacent to a pier where a large ocean liner can be seen moored. In the immediate vicinity, between the camera position and the side of the ocean liner, is a group of native boys in the water diving for coins thrown to them by liner passengers.

Wharf Scene, Honolulu

Edison © 38222 June 22, 1898
Cameramen: W. Bleckyrden, James H. White
Location: Honolulu
30 ft. FLA4441 (print) FRA1547 (neg.)

The camera was placed on a moored ship adjacent to a dock where several hundred people are welcoming or saying goodbye to passengers on a liner. Between the people on the pier and the camera position, approximately a dozen native children are waiting in the water for the passengers to throw coins for them to retrieve.

What Age?

See: The Seven Ages

What Are the Wild Waves Saying, Sister?

AM&B © H35097 Aug. 28, 1903
Cameraman: A. E. Weed
Location: Coney Island, N.Y. *Photographed:* Aug. 18, 1903
20 ft. FLA3727 (print) FRA0974 (neg.)

The cameraman placed his equipment on the sand close to the ocean. Between the camera position and the water are a little boy in overalls and a little girl in a long dress and a sunbonnet. Each is carrying a sand pail, and they are holding hands. They do nothing but stand with their backs to the camera and stare at the ocean. At the end of the film, they turn, head toward the camera, and walk past it.

See also: A Little Teaze [sic]

What Boys Will Do

AM&B © H32784 June 17, 1903
18 ft. FLA4158 (print) FRA1326 (neg.)

A peculiarly constructed set apparently intended to represent the front door of a house can be seen as the picture begins. The door in the set opens and a woman appears, looks across the stage, turns and reenters the house. Two small boys, one carrying a bucket, appear. One aids the other onto the roof over the door. As the film ends, the contents of the bucket are being spilled on the woman, who has again come outside.

What Burglar Bill Found in the Safe

AM&B © H40722 Jan 8, 1904
Cameraman: A. E. Weed
Location: Studio, N.Y.C. *Photographed:* Dec. 21, 1903
56 ft. FLA4945 (print) FRA1944 (neg.)

A man is writing at a desk in a set of a business office. A large double-doored safe stands against the wall. A young and attractive woman enters and is greeted affectionately by the man. She sits down and they are talking when the man is informed that his wife is outside. The man, in desperation, hides his visitor in the safe and he and his wife leave, turning out the lights. Shortly thereafter a burglar arrives and sets off an explosion to open the safe. When the smoke clears, the young woman comes out of the safe. The burglar falls on his knees, pleading for forgiveness.

What Demoralized the Barbershop

Edison © 73465 Dec. 16, 1898
17 ft. FLA3066 (print) FLA5964 (35mm pos.) FPA0097 (35mm neg.) FRA0409 (neg.)

In a set of a barbershop, a number of men are either waiting for the barber or being shaved. The shop is in the basement and has sidewalk-level windows. As the film progresses, the feet and legs of passersby can be seen by the occupants of the barbershop. Just as the film is ending, two females walk by the window. They stop and, as they do, the men in the barbershop evidence excitement by doing ridiculous things or nudging one another with their elbows. Although the film has a copyright date of 1897, the Library of Congress catalog gives 1898 as the copyright date.

See also: next film, same title, and Barber's Dee-light

What Demoralized the Barber Shop

Edison © H8587 Sept. 11, 1901
36 ft. FLA4946 (print) FRA6409 (neg.)

This is a farce and a typical peep show. It shows several men in a basement barbershop who become excited by women walking past the window. The ankles and knees of the passersby are visible to the men below, causing pandemonium among the barbershop customers.

See also: previous film, same title, and Barber's Dee-light

What Drink Did

Biograph © H127702 May 28, 1909
Director: D. W. Griffith *Cameraman:* G. W. Bitzer
Cast: Florence Lawrence, Gladys Egan, Adele De Garde, David Miles, Mack Sennett, Tony O'Sullivan, Harry Salter, George Nicholls, John Cumpson
Location: Fort Lee, N.J.; Studio, N.Y.C. *Photographed:* Apr. 19 and 28, 1909
341 ft. FLA5808 (print) FRA2615 (neg.)

The story begins with a father (David Miles) enthusiastically relating a cowboy-and-Indian story to his two small girls (Gladys Egan and Adele De Garde) while his pleased wife (Florence Lawrence) watches. The father goes off to work and, at the end of the day, joins his friends at a saloon. He continues this habit, completely forgetting his family. The older daughter goes to the saloon and attempts to persuade her father to come home, and is accidentally killed in a brawl that results. The last scene shows the father leaving the factory with his former drinking companions and gesturing to them that he will never drink again.

What Happened in the Tunnel

Edison © H37683 Nov. 6, 1903
Cameraman: Edwin S. Porter

Location: Fort Lee, N.J.; Studio, N.Y.C. *Photographed:* Oct. 30–31, 1903

23 ft. FLA3660 (print) FRA0913 (neg.)

The first scene takes place on a set of a passenger car on a moving train. Seated beside her black maid is the heroine; behind her is the hero. The young lady is reading and drops her handkerchief. It is immediately retrieved by the hero, who returns it to her but continues holding her hand. The hero starts to kiss the heroine just as the train enters a tunnel. The picture ends as the train has come out of the tunnel. We find that our hero has embraced the black maid and not the young lady.

What Happened on Twenty-Third Street, New York City

Edison © H7985 Aug. 21, 1901

Location: N.Y.C.

37 ft. FLA4947 (print) FRA1945 (neg.)

A single-camera position shows the district indicated by the title. A man in summer attire and a woman in a light organdy, ankle-length dress walk toward the camera. As they approach a grated manhole in the sidewalk, the escaping air blows the woman's dress to her knees.

What Happened to Jones

AM&B © H28560 Feb. 24, 1903

Photographed: 1899 [?]

13 ft. FLA3164 (print) FRA0494 (neg.)

On a set of a woman's bedroom, a bandit can be seen entering through the window in the wall farthest from the camera. He glances furtively about the room, acts as if he hears someone approaching, and dives under the bed. A woman in a nightgown and cap enters through the door, sits down and removes her slippers, and notices the burglar under the bed. She waves her arms and shouts until a policeman arrives, pulls out the burglar (now a dummy), hits it on the head, and leaves the room. The woman can be seen sitting on the edge of the chair crying as the film ends.

See also: The Disappointed Old Maid

What the Daisy Said

Biograph © J143189 July 13, 1910

Director: D. W. Griffith *Cameraman:* G. W. Bitzer

Cast: Mary Pickford, Gertrude Robinson, Owen Moore, Joe Graybill, Kate Bruce, George Nicholls, Charles West, Mack Sennett, Tony O'Sullivan

Location: Delaware Water Gap, N.J. *Photographed:* June 8–9, 1910

390 ft. FLA5809 (print) FRA6425 (neg.)

All of the scenes in this film of two young girls and their experiences with a gypsy fortuneteller were taken in a rural area. One young girl (Mary Pickford) goes to the encampment and has her fortune told by an attractive young male gypsy (Owen Moore). He romances her, and later, her sister (Gertrude Robinson), when she goes to have her fortune told. The father finds the gypsy making advances to one of his daughters and hits him with a stick. The gypsy retaliates and the old man falls to the ground. The citizens of the town are outraged and order the gypsy to leave town, which he does. The film ends as the gypsy takes care to pass the back door of the house of the girls he courted. The last scene shows Mary Pickford making up with her former

boyfriend. There is a considerable amount of camera movement in this film.

What the Doctor Ordered

Biograph © J172003 Aug. 7, 1912

Director: Mack Sennett

Cast: Mack Sennett, Mabel Normand, Jack Pickford, Eddie Dillon, William J. Butler

Location: Rubio Canyon and Mt. Lowe, Calif.

257 ft. FLA5810 (print) FRA2614 (neg.)

The plot of this farce is built around a hypochondriac (Mack Sennett) who is a trial to his family because he will not move out of the rocking chair in front of his house. The doctor orders him to go to the mountaintop for his health. The comic situations that develop when he and his family go to the top of the mountain via a funicular, and when he rides a small donkey, are just about the whole film. There are a few scenes showing the actor-director, Mack Sennett, lost in the snow, but basically the scenery was more the reason for the film than the plot.

What's Your Hurry?

Biograph © J134043 Nov. 1, 1909

Director: D. W. Griffith *Cameraman:* G. W. Bitzer

Cast: Mary Pickford, Billy Quirk, Lottie Pickford, Mack Sennett, Gladys Egan, Kate Bruce, George Nicholls, Florence Barker, Adele De Garde

Location: Fort Lee, N.J.; Studio, N.Y.C. *Photographed:* Sept. 21–27, 1909

160 ft. FLA5811 (print) FRA2616 (neg.)

At a birthday party, the father of the house (George Nicholls) is given a double-barreled shotgun, over which he is most enthusiastic. This is followed by an insert of a letter his daughter (Mary Pickford) receives, indicating that her boyfriend (Billy Quirk) will be home from college early. The remainder of the scenes are of a comical nature that arise out of a misunderstanding the young man has about Mary's father and the shotgun. He runs into people, knocks them down, breaks things, and finally is brought back into the young lady's arms by the father he had feared was going to shoot him.

When a Man Loves

Biograph © J150480 Jan. 9, 1911

Director: D. W. Griffith *Cameraman:* G. W. Bitzer

Cast: Mary Pickford, Dell Henderson, Tony O'Sullivan, Charles West, Eddie Dillon

Location: Westfield, N.J.; Studio, N.Y.C. *Photographed:* Oct. 22–31, 1910

402 ft. FLA5812 (print) FRA2617 (neg.)

This film was photographed in a rural area where a farmer's young daughter (Mary Pickford) and her fiancé (Charles West) are frustrated in their attempt to elope when an old friend of her father's arrives and is given the young lady's room for the night. The fiancé climbs into the bedroom and finds the father's friend instead. The rich old man then helps them to elope in his automobile, even though he had wanted to marry the girl himself. Several different camera positions were used. One was a close-up of the eloping couple in the back seat of an automobile, filmed from a camera located in the front of the moving car. Another position was from a moving horse and buggy pursuing the automobile.

When Ambrose Dared Walrus
Keystone © LP5823 July 12, 1915
Producer and Author: Mack Sennett
Cast: Mack Swain, Vivian Edwards, Chester Conklin, Billie Brockwell, Estelle Allen, Billie Bennett, Joseph Swickard
Location: Keystone studio and Glendale Boulevard, Los Angeles
847 ft. FLA6148–6149 (print)

Chester (Walrus) and his wife (Billie Brockwell) own a run-down hotel and most of their guests are broke. Among the guests are an acrobat (Mack Swain) and his lovely wife (Vivian Edwards) of whom Walrus becomes enamored. The fire insurance is about to be cancelled for nonpayment of premium, a situation Walrus remedies by taking out his gun and visiting various guests. Just then, he notices a fire in a waste basket but instead of putting the fire out, he rushes off to the insurance agent, just in time to prevent cancellation of the policy. By the time he returns to the hotel, the firemen are there. Ambrose (Swain) becomes a hero when he saves some guests by becoming a human bridge, but when Walrus accidentally retrieves his coat which the firemen are using in lieu of a net for Ambrose, a fight ensues between the two. Walrus puts the cash he has just received in payment of his policy on the window sill, the firemen turn the hose on it, and the money is lost. The final scene shows Ambrose with his arm around Walrus, trying to console him.

When Kings Were the Law
Biograph © J169418 May 20, 1912
Director: D. W. Griffith *Cameraman:* G. W. Bitzer
Cast: Dorothy Bernard, Claire McDowell, Wilfred Lucas, David Miles, William J. Butler
Location: Wentworth Hotel, Santa Monica, Calif. *Date:* May 4–5, 1912
422 ft. FLA5813 (print) FRA2619 (neg.)

The actors are wearing costumes of Louis XIV's era and the plot greatly resembles *The Three Musketeers* by Alexandre Dumas. A good deal of thought went into the production, and some scenes have a considerable number of people. Close-ups are used in three instances to show the transfer of jewelry, which is indispensable to the story.

When Knights Were Bold
AM&B © H110506 May 13, 1908
Director: Wallace McCutcheon *Cameraman:* G. W. Bitzer
Cast: Ann Lorley
Location: Studio, N.Y.C. *Photographed:* Apr. 22, 1908
335 ft. FLA5814 (print) FRA2620 (neg.)

The actors are wearing sixteenth-century English clothes, and the sets reflect the same period. The story is a heavy drama involving knights and conspiracies. The heroine, in love with a man of whom the king does not approve, tries to run away, and disguises herself as a boy to do so. The hero performs an act of heroism, and the king blesses them both.

When Love Took Wings
Keystone © LP4955 Apr. 1, 1915
Producer and Author: Mack Sennett

Cast: Estelle Allen, Roscoe Arbuckle, Al St. John, Joe Bordeaux, Frank Hayes, Glen Cavender
Location: Los Angeles
FLA6150 (print)

The daughter (Estelle Allen) has a suitor (Joe Bordeaux), but the father (Frank Hayes) objects until Joe says they are engaged. The doorbell rings and it is a second suitor (Fatty Arbuckle) with flowers for Estelle. Father decides he is better than Joe and kicks Joe out. The doorbell rings again; this time it is Al St. John, the son of a neighbor, carrying a note explaining he is of marrying age and has come for the hand of Estelle. Father tries to persuade Estelle that Al St. John is the one for her, but she remains obdurate. Fatty persuades her to run away with him, and they leave in a car, go to an airport, and take off in a biplane with a LeRhone engine. When they are followed by the Keystone police, the father, and a preacher, the plane is put through some advanced aerobatics for the time. The plane lands, and everybody goes back to the house. Estelle and Fatty are about to be married when he knocks against her, dislodging her wig. Fatty rushes outside and sends Al St. John in, who also discovers the wig and leaves. It is now Joe's turn, and the Father sees to it that he marries Estelle. Fatty and Al St. John shake hands and leave. Aviator De Lloyd Thompson was engaged especially for this picture.

When the Fire-Bells Rang
Biograph © J169194 May 13, 1912
Director: Mack Sennett
Cast: Fred Mace, Eddie Dillon, Dell Henderson, William J. Butler, Kate Bruce, Sylvia Ashton, Claire McDowell, Joseph Swickard, Harry Hyde
Location: Hollywood area, Calif.
221 ft. FLA5815 (print) FRA2621 (neg.)

This farce starts when a stage manager, told by the director to get help to play Roman soldiers, goes to a nearby firehouse and enlists the aid of the firemen. One is left behind to guard the firehouse and he thinks it would be fun to ring the firebell in the middle of the big scene. The camera shows the firemen, clad in Roman togas, pulling the fire apparatus to the scene of the fire. They discover it is a false alarm and return to the stage. The house of the fireman who played the prank catches fire, and the last scene shows him crying over the ruins when the firemen, under the impression it is another trick, refuse to answer his frantic summons.

When the Flag Falls
Lubin Mfg. Co. © J132278 Aug. 2, 1909
Location: Philadelphia
383 ft. FLA5816 (print) FRA2622 (neg.)

During the revolutionary war, a young woman, very much in love with her soldier sweetheart, is determined to get into the enemy's camp unnoticed. Once there, she empties the rifles that were going to be used by a firing squad to execute him. The soldier-sweetheart was to have delivered a message to George Washington, and the girl had sewn the real message in his trousers, while he carried a false one in his dispatch case, anticipating capture. After he is captured, he sends his sweetheart a message, and she saves his life by telling him to drop as though shot when he faces the firing squad. He does as instructed, and she removes his supposedly dead body. The last scene shows the lovers embracing after he has safely delivered the real dispatch. Most of the scenes were photographed outdoors.

When We Were in Our Teens
Biograph © J144497 Aug. 19, 1910
Cameraman: Arthur Marvin
Cast: Mary Pickford, Billy Quirk, Joe Graybill, Mack Sennett
Location: Coytesville, N.J. *Photographed:* July 15–16, 1910
172 ft. FLA5817 (print) FRA6424 (neg.)

The film opens with a young girl (Mary Pickford) standing at an easel painting. A young man (Billy Quirk) enters and begins to deprecate her work, and she becomes furious. The young man spends the rest of the picture attempting to prove his taste in painting is better than hers. He bribes the butler (Mack Sennett), and takes a picture that he attempts to show to an art critic who is not interested in it as he has become enamored of the young lady. The young man then dresses as a peddler and shows the painting to the art critic who agrees that it lacks merit. This still does not convince the young lady who goes off in a huff. All the scenes were photographed from a single-camera position, and the indoor and outdoor scenes were equally distributed. There was a good deal of actor movement left and right across the camera position.

When We Were Twenty-One
AM&B © H17227 May 1, 1902
Cameraman: F. S. Armitage
Date: Nov. 7, 1900
11 ft. FLA4133 (print) FRA1305 (neg.)

This was photographed as if in the audience at a vaudeville show. A young couple can be seen sitting on a pseudo-stone bench against a backdrop of a park. The young man and the young woman are arguing violently, while a tramp watches them. When the argument reaches its climax, the young man abruptly walks away, leaving the young lady alone. The tramp, sizing up the situation, sits down next to her. She thinks her boyfriend has returned, puts her head on the tramp's shoulder, and then discovers who it is. As the film ends, she is running after the young man.

Where Breakers Roar
AM&B © H115623 Sept. 15, 1908
Director: D. W. Griffith *Cameramen:* G. W. Bitzer, Arthur Marvin
Cast: Linda Arvidson, Arthur Johnson, Marion Leonard, Florence Lawrence, Mack Sennett
Location: Studio, N.Y.C.; a seaside resort *Photographed:* Aug. 21 and 25, 1908
212 ft. FLA5818 (print) FRA2618 (neg.)

The camera was moved many times to organize the suspense and relate it to the chases in the film. The story starts with a young city couple (Linda Arvidson and Arthur Johnson) at the seashore, where they are disturbed by friends who want to dunk them in the water. The young woman runs from her friends and gets into a rowboat. A homicidal maniac who has just made his escape from an insane asylum, arrives from another direction at the water's edge at the same time as she does, and he takes over the boat. Now the chase is twofold—the guards after the killer, and the young woman's friends and rescuers. After an exciting chase on the water, the young woman is saved.

While Strolling in the Park
AM&B © H40804 Jan. 12, 1904
Cameraman: A. E. Weed
Location: Studio, N.Y.C. *Photographed:* Dec. 31, 1903
87 ft. FLA5252 (print) FRA2196 (neg.)

In front of a painted backdrop of a park, a man made up as a fat black woman is sitting on a bench built around a tree. A policeman comes along and she asks him for directions and leaves. A nurse with a baby in a perambulator arrives, and she and the policeman sit down on the recently vacated bench. While they are talking, a tramp comes up, steals the baby's bottle, consumes the contents, and leaves. The nurse, policeman, and the baby leave, and the tramp returns and stretches himself out on the bench. The policeman comes back and tries to awaken the tramp. Finally he takes hold of one of the tramp's shoes but gets instead a wooden leg, which so annoys him that he chases the tramp away.

The White Caps
Edison © H65546 Sept. 14, 1905
Cameraman: Edwin S. Porter
Location: Fort Lee and Demarest, N.J. *Photographed:* Aug. 30–31, 1905
320 ft. FLA5819 (print) FRA2623 (neg.)

The opening scene shows the corner of a house in a rural section. Two men carrying rifles and wearing white hoods creep up to the house. The camera shifts to the interior where a women and a little girl are siting. A man enters and begins beating the woman. She takes the child and flees to a nearby house for help. The remainder of the film is devoted to the white-hooded men who seek out the wife beater, tie him to a tree, pour tar over him, and feather him. They then ride him out of town on a rail.

White Fox Motor Boat
AM&B © H78532 June 1, 1906
Cameraman: G. W. Bitzer
Location: Stamford, Conn. *Photographed:* May 18, 1906
23 ft. FLA3598 (print) FRA0863 (neg.)

The subject is the demonstration of a motor boat of early design that permitted operation by one person. The camera was placed on a dock. The film begins in an area that was probably adjacent to a yacht club. A motor boat approximately twenty feet long approaches the camera position. The boat passes the camera, turns, and proceeds away.
See also: Maneuvering a Small Motor Boat

White Horse Rapids
Edison © D7246 Apr. 4, 1900
Location: Klondike, Yukon Terr.
22 ft. FLA4212 (print) FRA1374 (neg.)
[Alaska Gold Rush]

The film is too short to permit much description. It was photographed from the edge of a rapidly running river; only the shallow portion was filmed. As the film ends, a man appears in front of the camera and seems to be watching a large raft shoot the rapids.

White Roses
Biograph © J149494 Dec. 24, 1910

Cameraman: Arthur Marvin

Cast: William J. Butler, Eddie Dillon, Kate Bruce, Joe Graybill, W. Chrystie Miller, Jack Pickford, Lottie Pickford, Mary Pickford, Spike Robinson

Location: Studio, N.Y.C.; Fort Lee, N.J. *Photographed:* Nov. 7 and 9, 1910

213 ft.   FLA5820 (print)   FRA6427 (neg.)

A young man is proposing to a young woman. After spending a considerable amount of time on his knees, the shy young man runs from the room. He goes to a florist, buys some white roses, writes a note, and sends them to the young lady. A messenger boy loses the box, a kind-hearted philanthropist buys him another, and that night the young lady wears the roses. When her suitor arrives and finds her wearing roses but not the white ones he bought her, he leaves and proposes to the first woman he meets, a cleaning woman. She guides him to a justice of the peace. The lost box of roses, with the letter of proposal, is finally delivered to the young woman, who arrives just in time to save the young man from marrying the charwoman.

White Star S.S. Baltic Leaving Pier on First Eastern Voyage

Edison   © H48202   July 16, 1904

Cameraman: Edwin S. Porter

Location: N.Y.C. *Photographed:* July 13, 1903

66 ft.   FLA4948 (print)   FRA1946 (neg.)

The film was photographed from a camera placed high over the heads of a crowd of people collected to wish a bon voyage to a large seagoing liner on her maiden trip east across the Atlantic. The first action is in the stern area of the ship, where numerous people are waving. The ship begins to back away from the mooring area and, as the film ends, the complete silhouette of the ship can be seen as she begins to get under way on her voyage.

White Wings on Review

Edison   © H32033   May 20, 1903

Cameraman: J. B. Smith

Location: N.Y.C. *Photographed:* Apr. 29, 1903

94 ft.   FLA5253 (print)   FRA2197 (neg.)

The camera was located on a street in the business district of a large city. Row upon row of men wearing white uniforms are passing in front of the camera. Each group has a police escort. The parade of uniformed men continues until several hundred pass the camera position. Immediately following the marching men come approximately a hundred horse-drawn two-wheel carts in formation of fours, and after the two-wheel carts come a few four-wheeled vehicles, each with a driver.

Whittier School, Calisthenics

AM&B   © H45148   May 2, 1904

Cameraman: A. E. Weed

Scenes with Mary Pickford and her younger sister Lottie together are not common; here we see them in the 1910 Biograph comedy White Roses — Mary (center) and Lottie (right).

Location: Kansas City, Mo. *Photographed:* Apr. 18, 1904
19 ft. FLA3109 (print) FRA0445 (neg.)

Three rows of preadolescent children are standing before a large outdoor blackboard on which the name "Kansas City, Mo." is visible as the film begins. Throughout the film, the schoolchildren exhibit their ability to do calisthenics and muscle developing exercises in unison.

Who Pays for the Drinks?
AM&B © H37379 Oct. 28, 1903
Cameraman: A. E. Weed
Location: Studio, N.Y.C. *Photographed:* Oct. 17, 1903
35 ft. FLA4949 (print) FRA1947 (neg.)

A bartender is reading when three customers enter the saloon. Two of them are supporting the third, who leans against the bar. The two indicate the third will pay for their drinks and leave. The bartender is unsuccessful in his attempt to get money from the remaining member of the trio and starts hitting him with a "bung starter." When the bartender begins his assault, a dummy is substituted and takes the beating. At the end of the picture, the dummy comes to life, punches the bartender in the nose, and knocks him cold. Then he steps behind the bar and helps himself to a bottle of whiskey, which he takes with him as he leaves the set.

Who Said Chicken?
AM&B © H30738 Apr. 24, 1903
Cameraman: Arthur Marvin
Location: Roof studio, N.Y.C. *Date:* July 18, 1900
7 ft. FLA3146 (print) FRA0479 (neg.)

A large woman dressed in the conventional attire of a black servant is seen sweeping the walk in front of a set of the side of a house. A box marked "Coal Bin" stands in front of the house. Just as the servant finishes her sweeping, a man made up as a black appears, holding a chicken by its legs, and looks furtively about for a hiding place. He spies the coal bin and gets inside. A policeman appears, realizes the fugitive is in the coal bin, and sits on the lid, gesturing for help. The lid of the coal bin flies up, throwing the policeman over backward behind the bin, and the man carrying the chicken makes good his escape.

The Whole Dam Family and the Dam Dog
Edison © H61456 May 31, 1905
Cameraman: Edwin S. Porter
Location: Studio, N.Y.C. *Photographed:* May 22–23, 1905
138 ft. FLA5254 (print) FRA2198 (neg.)

The picture begins with a title of cut out letters that spell the words "Do You Know This Family?" On two occasions during the picture, letters scramble and unscramble themselves to spell out illustrative ideas, including a cut out of an animated dog. After the title, each member of the family is introduced; the camera shows only the head of each. The family consists of mother, father, older sister, two younger sisters, their brother, and an infant boy. There is one picture of them as a group and another of them seated at a dining room table on a set of a dining room. Then the family dog gets in a fight, pulls the table cloth off, and ends the picture.

Who's Got the Red Ear?
AM&B © H28552 Feb. 24, 1903
Date: 1899
11 ft. FLA3176 (print) FRA0503 (neg.)

The camera was placed in a barnyard in order to photograph two young women and a man shucking ears of corn. They are surrounded by ducks and chickens apparently hoping to be fed. For no reason shown to the audience, the young man stands up, pushes away the fowl that are about his feet, grabs one of the young women, throws her on the ground, and begins kissing her. This continues for the remainder of the film, while the other young woman watches in high glee. (According to a country custom, the finder of an ear of red corn is entitled to a kiss.)

From the AM&B production number, it would seem that this short comedy was made during March of 1899.

Who's Looney Now?
Klaw & Erlanger © LP 3431 Sept. 24, 1914
Cast: Bob Nolan, Dave Morris, Alan Hale, Gertrude Bambrick, Kate Toncray, Jack Mulhall
850 ft. FLA5910 (print) FRA2771 (neg.)

This comedy concerns two pleasant mentally disturbed escapees from a private mental home and their effect upon the world. As the title indicates, they encounter people who are just about ready to be committed themselves. The burlesqued costumes of the actors in the film further complicate the chases that take place. The film ends with the two escapees returning to the mental institution of their own volition.

Why Curfew Did Not Ring
AM&B © H29000 Mar. 6, 1903
Cameraman: Arthur Marvin
Date: Sept. 7, 1900
11 ft. FLA3705 (print) FRA0953 (neg.)

The first scene shows a belfry on a stage in front of a backdrop of a rural area. A woman with long black hair starts to climb up the belfry to reach the clapper. As the woman grasps the bell clapper and rests her weight on it, the bell, belfry, and all tumble down about her out of camera sight. The next scene consists of an insert from a magazine page of a moon with a painted face and the words "Guess That Will Hold Her For a While."

Why Foxy Grandpa Escaped A Ducking
AM&B © H33401 July 6, 1903
Cameraman: G. W. Bitzer
Cast: Joseph Hart as Foxy Grandpa
Photographed: June 26, 1903
20 ft. FLA3600 (print) FRA0865 (neg.)

Two small boys are creeping toward the stoop of a set of a two-story apartment house or flat. They are carrying a bucket of water that they fasten above the doorway so that if the door is opened, the contents would spill on the person going through the doorway. Their actions are observed by an old gentleman who waits until they are finished, and then rearranges the tripping mechanism. When the boys return, the water spills all over them.

Why Jones Discharged His Clerks

Edison © D780 Jan. 9, 1900

38 ft. FLA4950 (print) FRA1948 (neg.)

Two clerks are playing a game of poker when they are surprised by their employer who enters his office, which is screened off from the clerks. An attractive young woman is ushered into the employer's office, and as soon as she sits down the man begins to make advances to her. The two clerks stand on a box on one side of the screen and peer over the top, but they become so engrossed in the romancing that they lean too heavily and the screen falls over on the couple. The outraged employer begins pommeling the clerks, hitting them on the head with pieces of furniture, and ending the film.

Why Mr. Nation Wants a Divorce

Edison © H1495 Mar. 1, 1901

39 ft. FLA4951 (print) FRA2907 (neg.)

The set consists of a combination living room and bedroom where a man in a nightshirt and a bed cap is sitting on the edge of the bed. Nearby is a small child in a crib and a larger child is in the bed. Soon the responsibilities of caring for the two children overwhelm the man, who begins to drink from a bottle. The door opens, and a severely dressed woman enters, admonishes him, and then turns him over her knee and spanks him. This was evidently intended as a satire on Carrie Nation, who was very active then.

Why Mrs. Jones Got a Divorce

Edison © D1727 Jan. 17, 1900

27 ft. FLA4029 (print) FRA1219 (neg.)

A woman is convinced her husband is carrying on a flirtation with the cook because of two handprints on the back of his coat left by flour-covered hands. The complete action of the film takes place in a kitchen set where a woman in a cook's uniform is preventing a small boy from putting his hands in the dough she is kneading. The boy, annoyed, hides behind the door. The door opens, and a man dressed in an overcoat, gloves, and a homburg hat enters. He begins a conversation with the cook, who apparently is happy to see him for she places her flour-covered hands on his shoulders. The woman of the house enters the kitchen, sees the evidence of her husband's flirtation, and becomes angry. Before the picture ends, the kitchen has been demolished, and the wife has overturned the flour bin on her husband's head.

See also: How The Cook Made Her Mark

Why Papa Can't Sleep

AM&B © H33409 June 13, 1903

Date: 1897

11 ft. FLA3411 (print) FRA0702 (neg.)

On a bedroom set, a baby in a crib and a man and a woman sleeping in a bed alongside can be seen. As the film progresses, a man in a nightshirt gets out of the bed, walks over to the crib, takes the crying infant out and starts pacing the floor.

The Widow and the Only Man

AM&B © H50221 Sept. 8, 1904

Director: Wallace McCutcheon *Cameraman:* G. W. Bitzer

Location: Brooklyn and Coney Island, N.Y. *Photographed:* Aug. 9 and 11, 1904

318 ft. FLA5821 (print) FRA2625 (neg.)

The first two scenes are close-ups preceded by titles, of a widow and the "only man." The next scene shows a group of women sitting on the veranda of a resort hotel. First the woman arrives, and later the man. The film then shows their friendship progressing, as they dine together, ride in a carriage together, and boat together. When they are boating, the boat turns over, and the man rescues the widow. A later scene shows a box of flowers being delivered to the widow, and the camera moves in to a close-up of the woman as she admires each flower, and back out to show the arrival of her suitor. The denouement takes place later in a dry goods store. The widow walks in and promptly faints when she discovers that the ribbon clerk is none other than her gallant summer beau.

The Wife

Klaw & Erlanger © LP3032 May 28, 1914

Cast: Linda Arvidson, Charles West, Dorothy Gish, Robert Drouet, Jack Brammall, William J. Butler, Mrs. LaVarnie, Charles Perley

1,196 ft. FLA5911-5912 (print) FRA2772-2773 (neg.)

This three-reel drama is complicated by the lies of a woman who wants to possess a man (Charles West) who is in love with another woman (Linda Arvidson). At the beginning, her lies break up a romance, and the woman marries another man. Her first suitor continues to encounter her socially, and the woman who wants him does all she can to spread more tales. The wife, when pressed by her husband, admits she is still in love with the man she did not marry. The last scene shows the despairing husband, head in his hands, announcing he has accepted a foreign mission. But the wife discovers that she really loves her husband and not the man she did not marry.

Wifey Away, Hubby at Play

Lubin Mfg. Co. © J132441 Aug. 23, 1909

Location: Philadelphia

126 ft. FLA5255 (print) FRA2199 (neg.)

There are several well-constructed sets of the interior of a house and the interior of a restaurant in this film about a man out playing while his wife visits her mother in the country. The films begins with the husband protesting the imminent departure of his wife. He escorts her to the train and, when the train leaves, kicks up his heels and rushes to call his paramour. The next scene shows them drinking champagne and dancing in a private dining room. There is an outdoor scene of the wife in the country receiving a letter from her "lonesome" husband and deciding to return at once. At the end of the film, the husband is shown kicking himself for having influenced his wife to cut her visit short.

Wifey's Mistake

Edison © H42202 Feb. 16, 1904

Cameraman: Edwin S. Porter

Location: Studio, N.Y.C. *Photographed:* Feb. 4, 1904

29 ft. FLA3741 (print) FRA0987 (neg.)

A set of reception hall and living room in the house of a wealthy man can be seen. A man in a silk hat and tailcoat enters. Another man dressed as a butler appears, and takes his cane, hat, and tailcoat. The master is handed a smoking jacket that he dons and then leaves the set. The servant puts on the tailcoat and top hat and is admiring himself in the mirror when a woman comes in and embraces him. The husband returns, throws the woman to the floor, and beats the butler.

A Wild Turkey Hunt
AM&B © H71523 Jan. 3, 1906
Cameraman: G. W. Bitzer
Location: Pinehurst, N.C. *Photographed:* Nov. 23, 1905
120 ft. FLA5256 (print) FRA2200 (neg.)

The first scene shows the front of a cabin in the wilderness. A roughly dressed man with a hunting pouch over his shoulder, carrying an old-fashioned muzzle-loading Kentucky squirrel rifle, pauses by the gate in the fence and proceeds to load the rifle. He also tears some patches for further loads. The next camera position shows the hunter entering the underbrush in search of his quarry. He cups his hands in front of his mouth, apparently making a turkey call. A large tom turkey appears, the hunter fires at it, runs to capture it and, as the film ends, is seen approaching the camera carrying the turkey head down. One of six films made for the New England Forest, Fish & Game Association.

Wilful Peggy
Biograph © J144684 Aug. 26, 1910
Director: D. W. Griffith *Cameraman:* G. W. Bitzer
Cast: Mary Pickford, Henry B. Walthall, Claire McDowell, Kate Bruce, Verner Clarges, Robert Harron
Location: Cuddebackville, N.Y.; Studio, N.Y.C. *Photographed:* July 19 and 22, 1910
312 ft. FLA5822 (print) FRA6442 (neg.)

A high-spirited young woman (Mary Pickford) attracts the attention of an Irish nobleman who marries her. She is quickly bored by high society and is also the butt of ridicule because of her ignorance of social graces. A young man challenges her to a horseback ride, and her husband thinks he has lost her to a younger rival. But the last scene shows the young girl returning home to her husband. She is now meek and mild, having realized that she really loves him. There are an equal number of indoor and outdoor scenes in the film, and there is a considerable amount of camera movement.

Will He Marry the Girl?
AM&B © H23778 Nov. 11, 1902
12 ft. FLA3559 (print) FRA0835 (neg.)

The quality of the film, its short length, and the fact that the action does not seem to be connected with the title, make it difficult to describe. The full film is devoted to two people in a rowboat. The man is rowing the boat while the woman is a passenger in the stern. They stand up, causing the boat to overturn, and fall into the water. At the end of the film, they can be seen swimming together.

Willful Ambrose
Keystone © LP4595 Mar. 1, 1915
Producer and Author: Mack Sennett

Cast: Mack Swain, Louise Fazenda, Vivian Edwards, Joe Bordeaux, Dixie Chene, Joseph Swickard·
Location: Hollenbeck and Griffith Parks, Los Angeles
421 ft. FLA6151 (print)

When the picture opens, Mack Swain, his wife (Louise Fazenda), and their daughter Pansy (Vivian Edwards) are in the kitchen watching father clean his gun. Mother insists father take Pansy out to play. The father is an excellent marksman, and he persuades Pansy to set up apples for targets. Unfortunately, the mother comes through the door with a huge beer stein she has bought as a surprise, and the bullet shatters it. Father takes Pansy to the park, where he becomes involved in trying to buy a replacement stein. He also becomes involved with a young couple (Dixie Chene and Joe Bordeaux) who also wants to buy a stein. There is considerable confusion, during which Bordeaux kisses Pansy, while Mack spies Dixie all by herself and insists on kissing her. Louise arrives at the park at this point and hits Mack over the head with a baseball bat, after which she hugs him.

Willful Murder
AM&B © H47464 June 23, 1904
101 ft. FLA5257 (print) FRA2207 (neg.)

An attractive young woman is walking down a path toward the camera in a parklike area when a man accosts her. She rejects his advances but he becomes more insistent and grabs her arm. Another man appears and knocks him down, and the woman and her rescuer walk off together. The rejected man, now armed with a shotgun, follows them and shoots the hero. The woman screams, attracting a number of people, all of whom begin to chase the murderer, who is eventually cornered. The villain shoots two more people and is about to shoot the third; then the woman from the first scene strikes his wrist, knocking the gun out of his hand, and he is captured.

Willie and Tim in the Motor Car
See: Fine Feathers Make Fine Birds

Willie Becomes an Artist
Biograph © J171804 July 30, 1912
Director: Mack Sennett
Cast: Eddie Dillon, Vivian Prescott, William J. Butler, Kate Toncray
Location: Southern Calif.
204 ft. FLA5823 (print) FRA2626 (neg.)

Willie, playboy son of a well-to-do father, borrows money from his father to study painting, but instead of painting pictures, paints the town with the help of some gay companions. One day, the father asks his son to show him one of his paintings, and the son borrows one for the purpose. The father, impressed, takes his son out to the tranquil countryside, where a cow is grazing, and insists on the son painting a landscape. The remaining scenes show the young man and two girlfriends desperately attempting to produce the landscape. The cow, interested in the painting, switches its tail across the canvas many times, and when the father arrives, accompanied by an art expert, the boy is proclaimed a genius and congratulated by all on his "masterpiece."

Willie Westinghouse and the Doctor's Battery
AM&B © H31953   May 15, 1903
Cameraman: G. W. Bitzer
Date: May 11, 1903
30 ft.   FLA4952 (print)   FRA1949 (neg.)

The picture begins with the discovery by a small boy of a box marked "Battery." He takes the battery from the sitting room into the kitchen. The boy hooks the terminal of the battery to the legs of a turkey the cook is preparing. The cook picks up the electrified turkey and cavorts wildly about the room, to the amusement of the prankster hidden under the table.

Willie's Camera
AM&B © H33400   July 6, 1903
Cameraman: G. W. Bitzer
Photographed: June 29, 1903
27 ft.   FLA3536 (print)   FRA0812 (neg.)

A single-camera position shows a drawing room set. Two little boys are actively engaged in building a simulated camera with a box, a tube of pipe, etc. The door opens, and an elaborately dressed woman with a picture hat enters. She sits down in front of camera on a chair. After one of the small boys pulls some sort of lever, there is an explosion that blows black smoke all over the woman's white dress. The irate woman chases them about the room.

Willie's First Smoke
Edison © 10649   Feb. 4, 1899
17 ft.   FLA4456 (print)   FRA1559 (neg.)

Two men dressed in ordinary business suits converse with one another in what appears to be an alley (the film is artificially lighted). The gestures of the two men indicate their conversation has ended; one puts his cigar butt on the edge of a railing and they leave. A small boy picks up the butt and smokes it. The two men return to the scene as if in search of the cigar and find the small boy smoking it. One of the men turns the boy over his knee and begins spanking him. The other man jumps on his companion, and as the film ends, walks out of camera position smoking the cigar.

Willie's Hat
AM&B © H23784   Nov. 11, 1902
Photographed: 1897
10 ft.   FLA3501 (print)   FRA0781 (neg.)

In a drawing room set, four young women are frolicking about. There is a silk hat on the table and one of the young women picks it up and holds it above her head, while the remaining three girls attempt to reach the hat by kicking high over their heads. One of them apparently overextends herself for she falls over, landing flat on her back as the film ends.

Willie's Vacation
Paley & Steiner © H52714   Nov. 8, 1904
14 ft.   FLA4432 (print)   FRA1542 (neg.)

This film was a series of not-too-well-connected vignettes intended to convey a story. The first scene shows the hero saying goodbye on the front porch of a house. This is followed by a scene in a hen yard with a lovely young lady, then a scene with a cow; the last three are of a chase with someone shooting at the hero. The reason for the shooting is not explained. The film ends as the hero jumps into a pond to escape his pursuers.

A Windy Day on the Roof
AM&B © H44207   Apr. 6, 1904
Cameraman: A. E. Weed
Location: Roof studio, N.Y.C.   *Photographed:* Mar. 18, 1904
25 ft.   FLA4125 (print)   FRA1299 (neg.)

The camera was placed in such a way as to make a composition out of a set of the edge of a building roof, where a woman can be seen hanging out wash. Below the edge of the roof, a man peers up at her while painting the eaves. The director, in order to add zest to the film, had threads attached to the hem of the woman's garments to make it appear as though the wind was blowing her skirts and allowing the painter to see what he should not. The woman hanging out the wash suddenly discovers the illicit observer, picks up a bucket filled with soapy water, and throws it upon him.

The Wine Opener
AM&B © H62447   June 20, 1905
Cameraman: G. W. Bitzer
Location: Studio, N.Y.C.   *Photographed:* June 13, 1905
23 ft.   FLA3903 (print)   FRA1123 (neg.)

The film begins in a dining room set in a small house. Seated at a table, earnestly endeavoring to remove the cork from a bottle of champagne, is an attractive young woman in an evening gown. Most of the film shows her grimaces and facial contortions as she continues to be thwarted. Before the film ends, she is successful and drinks a glass of wine from the bottle.

Wine, Women & Song
AM&B © H71530   Jan. 3, 1906
Cameraman: G. W. Bitzer
Location: Studio, N.Y.C.   *Photographed:* Dec. 14, 1905
23 ft.   FLA3982 (print)   FRA1190 (neg.)

The film concerns the illicit relations between a woman dressed as a serving maid and a man dressed in the robes of a friar. They are seen drinking from beer steins and embracing when another man, also dressed as a friar or monk, enters the room. The second friar orders the first to leave, and the young woman remains. After a cursory glance about the premises, the second friar sits down on the bench with the young woman and begins wooing her.

See also: Jolly Monks of Malabar, and Simple Life

Wine, Women & Song, no. 2
AM&B © H71425   Dec. 30, 1905
Cameraman: F. A. Dobson
Location: Studio, N.Y.C.   *Photographed:* Dec. 23, 1905
21 ft.   FLA4015 (print)   FRA1211 (neg.)

A man wearing the robes and skull cap of a friar and a woman dressed in the conventional garments of a household maid can be seen drinking wine from a bottle on a table in a set of a rough stone castle. The woman pours several glasses of wine for her companion, and when she hands him another glass, he takes her hand, pulls her down on the bench beside him and begins embracing her. The drinking and embracing continue until the film ends.

See also: Jolly Monks of Malabar, and Simple Life

Winning Back His Love
Biograph © J149495 Dec. 24, 1910

Director: D. W. Griffith *Cameraman:* G. W. Bitzer

Cast: Stephanie Longfellow, Wilfred Lucas, Vivian Prescott, Donald Crisp, Jeanie Macpherson, Alfred Paget, Spike Robinson, William Beaudine, Edwin August

Location: Studio, N.Y.C. *Photographed:* Nov. 1–3, 1910

389 ft. FLA5824 (print) FRA2627 (neg.)

A man of means goes out for the evening, leaving his wife at home alone. The next scene shows him meeting an actress outside a stage door; several other clandestine meetings are shown. The actress sends the husband a note at home which he accidentally drops, and his wife learns of the affair. A male friend suggests that he escort the wife to the same restaurant, and the two couples are shown at the restaurant, each aware that the other is there. They leave separately. The husband realizes that the love of his wife means a great deal to him, so he goes home and begs her forgiveness. The picture ends with their embrace.

Wished on Mabel
Keystone © LP5062 Apr. 19, 1915

Producer and Author: Mack Sennett

Cast: Mabel Normand, Roscoe Arbuckle, Alice Davenport, Joe Bordeaux, Edgar Kennedy, Glen Cavender

Location: Photographed in Exposition Park and the Los Feliz areas of Los Angeles

388 ft. FLA6152 (print)

Mabel Normand and her mother (Alice Davenport) are sitting on a park bench. The mother is reading aloud to her daughter. The daughter sees her boyfriend, Fatty Arbuckle, and he joins them; they leave Alice happily reading her story. A park bum (Joe Bordeaux) is rudely awakened from his sleep on a park bench by a policeman (Edgar Kennedy) who wants the bench so he can take a nap. Bordeaux spies Alice and notices a watch worn from a ribbon around her neck. He sits down next to her, engages her in conversation, and steals her watch. He later loses it. The watch is found by Fatty who gives it to Mabel. She does not recognize it as her mother's, but Alice comes along just in time to retrieve it from Bordeaux, who is claiming it as his. Bordeaux is recognized as the thief he is and taken off to jail, while Alice, Mabel, and Fatty embrace happily.

The Witch's Revenge
Méliès © H33235 July 6, 1903

Creator: Georges Méliès *Cast:* Georges Méliès

Location: Montreuil, France *Date:* Spring 1903

Original title: Le Sorcier

81 ft. FLA5258 (print) FRA2202 (neg.)

Judging from the backdrop of a courtyard, the first scene was evidently photographed from a single-camera position. The plot is difficult to follow. However, it has excellent stop-action photography. People and props appear and disappear and reappear. In one scene, a large frame is brought in and put before a person to impress him. With double exposures, a tableau of one sitting woman and one standing appear life size in the frame. At a wave of the magician's hand, two more actors appear inside the frame, and act as ladies-in-waiting to the original two as they walk out of the frame and into the picture, where they come to life, and join the group.

With Her Card
Biograph © J130708 Aug. 17, 1909

Director: D. W. Griffith *Cameraman:* G. W. Bitzer

Cast: Marion Leonard, Frank Powell, Owen Moore, Henry B. Walthall, Mack Sennett, John Cumpson, Verner Clarges

Location: Studio, N.Y.C. *Photographed:* July 7, 1909

366 ft. FLA5826 (print) FRA2631 (neg.)

An attractive society belle (Marion Leonard) accepts one suitor (Owen Moore) and rejects the other (Frank Powell), both of whom are stockbrokers. But then Moore tells her he is marrying another woman. There is a market crash, and in spite of pleas to the other broker for more time, Moore is ruined financially. The heroine feels sorry for her former suitor and asks the successful broker to underwrite his credit, which he magnanimously does. The final scene takes place in the heroine's apartment, where the man she has aided proposes marriage. She thanks him and tells him there is now another man in her life. The film ends with her embracing the man she once rejected. Two sets were used in this film, and all the scenes were photographed from a single-camera position.

With the Enemy's Help
Biograph © J172418 Aug. 22, 1912

Director: D. W. Griffith

Cast: Blanche Sweet, Mary Pickford, Charles West, Charles Gorman, Charles Hill Mailes

Location: Southern Calif.

399 ft. FLA5827 (print) FRA2632 (neg.)

A gold prospector (Charles West) is discouraged in his search for gold, and his children pray for him. He tries once more, and this time is successful. But a man and a woman with unsavory reputations jump the claim and injure the miner. "Faro Kate," the wife (Mary Pickford) of the claim jumper, starts out on horseback for the recording office. The miner's wife (Blanche Sweet) also goes on the same errand but her wagon breaks down, and Faro Kate, unaware of the woman's identity, lets her ride into town on the back of her horse. Faro Kate, popular with the miners, is detained by them, and the prospector's wife gets the claim registered first, much to Faro Kate's chagrin. All the scenes were photographed outdoors.

The Wolf Hunt
Oklahoma Natural Mutoscene Company © H120454 Dec. 28, 1908

372 ft. FLA5825 (print) FRA2630 (neg.)

The film shows a man on horseback with hunting dogs attempting to capture or run down coyotes or wolves. Most of the film shows one or more men either riding toward or away from the camera over uncultivated terrain. The last scene shows them riding into an area filled with tents where several women and children are preparing a meal.

Woman Against Woman
Klaw & Erlanger © LP2565 Mar. 30, 1914

Director: Travers Vale
Cast: Vivian Prescott, Lionel Barrymore, Alan Hale, Charles West, Betty Gray, Mrs. Lawrence Marston, Louise Vale, Millicent Evans
1,210 ft. FLA5939 (print) FRA2802 (neg.)

This three-reel drama tells the story of two sisters who leave their small town for the city after their father dies and leaves them penniless. A neighbor of theirs, jealous because the man she loves prefers one of the sisters, accompanies them and brings about the ruin of the sister she hates. But then, the man repents on his deathbed and marries her, making their child legitimate. By the end of the film, the compromised sister has married a wealthy man, while her sister returns home and marries the town blacksmith. After some misunderstandings, the blacksmith and his wife adopt the sister's child. The several sets show a great deal of production, and many extras were used. The picture, however, was photographed from a single-camera position.

The Woman From Mellon's

Biograph © J138028 Feb. 5, 1910
Director: D. W. Griffith *Cameraman:* G. W. Bitzer
Cast: Mary Pickford, Billy Quirk, Gertrude Robinson, George Nicholls, Lottie Pickford, Tony O'Sullivan, Mack Sennett, Dorothy Bernard, James Kirkwood, Mrs. Charlotte Smith
Location: Studio, N.Y.C. *Photographed:* Dec. 22–24, 1909
348 ft. FLA5828 (print) FRA2628 (neg., copy 1) FRA6426 (neg., copy 2)

A father, annoyed with the suitor (Billy Quirk) his daughter (Mary Pickford) has chosen, hires a detective agency to prove he is no good, and the detective agency employs the suitor as the investigator. He dresses as a woman and keeps the young lady under scrutiny. While he is supposed to be working, he continues wooing the daughter. The two elope, and the last scene takes place in a hotel room where a minister conducts the marriage ceremony with Quirk still dressed as a woman while waitresses hold the door closed against the outraged father.

The Woman Hater

Lubin Mfg. Co. © J132446 Sept. 2, 1909
Location: Philadelphia
342 ft. FLA5829 (print) FRA2629 (neg.)

The whole picture was filmed from a single-camera position that showed two walls of a business office set. The senior partner, a woman hater, goes off on vacation, and his junior partner fires the male stenographer and replaces him with an attractive young lady. The junior partner turns her into a good secretary, and when the senior partner returns, whispers to her to be kind to him. The senior partner becomes aware of the young woman's charm and grace and ends by proposing marriage to her.

The Woman in Black

Klaw & Erlanger © LP3245 Aug. 5, 1914
Cast: Lionel Barrymore, Alan Hale, Charles Hill Mailes, Mrs. Lawrence Marston, Marie Newton, Millicent Evans, Hector V. Sarno, Jack Drumier, Frank Evans
1,257 ft. FLA5940 (print) FRA2803 (neg.)

The young woman in this three-reel film is the victim of her father's dishonesty as well as of the lust of the man who aids her father and then blackmails him. The villain, in another casual afternoon adventure, takes advantage of the daughter of a gypsy fortuneteller, who then diligently searches out the man who wronged her child. At the last minute, the gypsy's wronged daughter, covered by her bridal veil, is married to the unsuspecting villain while the daughter of the dishonest man marries the man she loves. The sets were well-assembled, and a large number of extras was used. Two scenes of a construction site were photographed. Wall Spence wrote the play on which this film is based.

A Woman's Way

AM&B © H118461 Nov. 18, 1908
Director: D. W. Griffith *Cameraman:* Arthur Marvin
Cast: Arthur Johnson, Charles Craig, Harry Salter
Location: Coytesville and Little Falls, N.J. *Photographed:* Oct. 3 and 6, 1908
257 ft. FLA5830 (print) FRA2633 (neg.)

Every scene was photographed outdoors in a wooded area. A trapper sells his daughter to another trapper, and she rebels. Early in the film, the chase begins, and the young woman runs through the woods pursued closely by her purchaser-suitor. The camera changes position many times to bring the young woman and her pursuer into the camp of some tourists. They protect the young girl at gun point. The next day, while out for a bucket of water from the stream, she is captured, put in a canoe, and tied to a tree. The tourists who had befriended her earlier attempt to come to her rescue. At the peak of the fight, the young woman acquires a gun, and turns it on her suitor's enemies, for she decides to marry him after all.

Women of the Ghetto Bathing

AM&B © H24897 Dec. 9, 1902
23 ft. FLA4373 (print) FRA1512 (neg.)

The subject is a group of women bathing in a public swimming pool. The camera was placed on the edge of the pool and the full extent of the film shows the women in the pool. Only the heads and shoulders of most of the women are visible but it is possible to see they are wearing rented bathing attire.

Won By a Fish

Biograph © J168477 Apr. 22, 1912
Director: Mack Sennett
Cast: Mary Pickford, Eddie Dillon, Dell Henderson, Kate Bruce, William J. Butler, Charles Hill Mailes, Kate Toncray, Charles Avery
Location: Santa Monica pier, Calif.
197 ft. FLA5831 (print) FRA6440 (neg.)

This split-reel comedy starts with the father (Dell Henderson) admonishing his daughter (Mary Pickford) not to see her boyfriend (Eddie Dillon). He then goes off to fish from a nearby pier. The youngsters, searching for an answer to their dilemma, pass a fish market and see a huge fish on display. The young man buys the fish, goes down to the dock, where his girl friend takes a picture of her sleeping father. The boyfriend ties the fish to the line of the sleeping man. In the last scenes, the proud father displays a photograph of himself with the fish to a roomful of people he has invited to eat it. The youngsters snatch the joyous moment from the old man by showing their snapshot, and force him to agree to their marriage. There are an unusual number of cutbacks as well as much camera movement in this picture.

The Wooden Leg
AM&B © H123745 Mar. 8, 1909
Director: D. W. Griffith *Cameramen:* G. W. Bitzer, Arthur Marvin
Cast: Florence Lawrence, John Cumpson, Joe Graybill
Location: Studio, N.Y.C. *Photographed:* Feb. 13 and 19, 1909
87 ft. FLA5259 (print) FRA2203 (neg.)

An attractive young woman (Florence Lawrence) wants to marry one man, while her father has another in mind. The hero and the heroine scheme to make her unattractive to the father's choice, who is due to arrive at any moment. They find a tramp with a wooden leg and rent it from him. The girl hides it under her billowing dress. When the father's choice arrives and notices the wooden leg, he not only withdraws his proposal of marriage, but strikes the father and leaves, while the girl and her beloved dance around in happiness.

Working Rotary Snow Ploughs on Lehigh Valley Railroad
Edison © H14065 Feb. 10, 1902
Location: Auburn Division, Lehigh Valley R.R.
118 ft. FLA5260 (print) FRA2204 (neg.)

The camera was positioned to show how effective a rotary snow plow could be in deep drift snow. The action consists of a train pushing its way through snow, and the camera presents not only a head-on shot but also a circle shot.

Working the Breeches Buoy
Edison © H10110 Oct. 28, 1901
Location: Buffalo, N.Y.
40 ft. FLA4039 (print) FRA1226 (neg.)

A crew of men dressed in the uniform of navel cadets are rigging a line-throwing cannon on a dock of what appears to be part of a naval training station compound. The sailors are supervised by a chief petty officer as they run through the various stages of the drill, beginning with the firing of the line-throwing gun. At the end of the film, the breeches buoy they rigged can be seen in operation.

The Would-Be Shriner
Biograph © J171805 July 30, 1912
Director: Mack Sennett
Cast: Mack Sennett, Sylvia Ashton, Kate Bruce, Fred Mace, William J. Butler, Jack Pickford, Henry "Pathe" Lehrman, Charles West, Eddie Dillon
Location: Los Angeles
209 ft. FLA5832 (print) FRA2634 (neg.)

This farce is built around a series of situations that happen to a man who wants to march in a Shriner's parade. He joins the fraternal organization, takes the oath, buys the costumes, and phones his wife to watch the parade. He rushes out of the office in his new costume, complete with turned up shoes, fez, and scimitar. As the parade goes down the street, our hero (Mack Sennett) attempts to join his fraternal brothers. His efforts are thwarted by the police at each intersection. The film ends when the annoyed policemen take him to an insane asylum, where they put him in a cage with "Napoleon" and an "Indian chief."

Photographs of the 1912 Shriners' convention in Los Angeles were used.

Wounded Soldiers Embarking in Row Boats
AM&B © H30727 Apr. 24, 1903
Date: 1898 [?]
18 ft. FLA3416 (print) FRA0705 (neg.)
[Spanish-American War]

A short pier extending out to the water is visible. On the short pier are twenty-five or thirty men in American military uniforms who are attempting to get into a rowboat alongside the pier. They are having difficulty because of the small surf that is running.

The Wrath of a Jealous Wife
AM&B © H36630 Oct. 8, 1903
Cameraman: A. E. Weed
Location: Studio, N.Y.C. *Photographed:* Oct. 1, 1903
26 ft. FLA3115 (print) FRA0451 (neg.)

A woman dressed for the street and a man in a business suit are sitting at a dining room table in a dining room set of a large house of well-to-do owners. As the action begins, the woman gets up from the table, draws on her gloves, walks to her husband, kisses him on the forehead, and then leaves the room. A young lady dressed as a maid comes in from the opposite direction and, as she goes by the man's chair, he reaches out and pulls her to his lap and begins kissing her. At this moment, the wife returns, sees the maid on her husband's lap and, in righteous indignation, takes the maid by the ear and leads her from the room. The wife then returns, chases her husband around the table until she catches him, knocks him down and, as the scene ends, is seen knocking his head against the floor and pulling his hair.

A Wreath in Time
AM&B © H122692 Feb. 8, 1909
Director: D. W. Griffith *Cameraman:* G. W. Bitzer
Cast: Mack Sennett, Florence Lawrence, Harry Salter, Jeanie Macpherson, Robert Harron, Clara T. Bracey, Linda Arvidson
Location: Eighth Avenue and 14th Street; and Studio, N.Y.C. *Photographed:* Dec. 1-8, 1908
203 ft. FLA5833 (print) FRA2635 (neg.)

A man (Mack Sennett) takes leave of his wife (Florence Lawrence) and goes off to a saloon, where his friends and the liquor influence him into going to a burlesque show. In order to make the night out legitimate, the men send messages to their wives saying they have gone to a fraternal conclave. In one scene, the camera moves in close to a theater box where the men are enjoying the dancers. The camera shifts to the man's home where his wife reads of a train wreck, assumes he is killed, and goes to the undertaker to buy a wreath. The last scene shows the erring husband returning home to find his wife wearing widow's weeds, and the wife is both happy and angry, but the film ends in an embrace.

A Wreath of Orange Blossoms
Biograph © J151388 Jan. 31, 1911
Director: D. W. Griffith *Cameraman:* G. W. Bitzer

Cast: Florence Barker, Edwin August, Kate Bruce, Grace Henderson, Jeanie Macpherson, Donald Crisp, Dell Henderson, Adolph Lestina, William J. Butler
Location: Studio, N.Y.C. *Date:* Nov. 7, 8, and 10, 1910
408 ft. FLA5834 (print) FRA2636 (neg.)

A young lady (Florence Barker) delivers some of her seamstress mother's (Kate Bruce) work to a customer. She falls in love with the customer's son (Edwin August), and they are married. The day of the wedding, the bridegroom places a wreath of orange blossoms on the bride's head, and she carefully puts it in her hope chest. Her husband loses his money, and the villain (Dell Henderson) attempts to lure the wife away from her poverty-stricken life. As she packs her bag to go off with him, she finds the wreath of orange blossoms. She changes her mind and orders the tempter out of the house. The husband comes home with good news. The last scene shows them embracing over his good fortune.

Wreck of the Battleship "Maine"
Edison © 25323 Apr. 21, 1898
Location: Havana, Cuba
24 ft. FLA3243 (print) FRA0566 (neg.)
[Spanish-American War]

The camera was positioned on the deck of a ship that made a half circle around the nearly submerged hulk of the battleship *Maine,* sunk in Havana Harbor in 1898.

The Wreck of the Steamer Richmond Off the Coast of New Jersey
See: Neptune's Daughters and Davey Jones' Locker

Wreck of the "Vizcaya"
AM&B © H30726 Aug. 24, 1903
Location: Santiago, Cuba *Photographed:* 1898 [?]
19 ft. FLA3150 (print) FRA0483 (neg.)
[Spanish-American War]

The forward portion of a ship's hull can be seen. The camera is stationed on board a boat that moves toward and alongside the hull and, as the film progresses, more of the hull is visible and is shown to be resting on the bottom in shallow water. There is a harbor tug at the bow of the vessel. The hull above the water is intact and the main deck and superstructure can be seen in toto as well as some of the armament. Only the port side of the derelict can be seen.
See also: Vizcaya Under Full Headway

Wrestling at the New York Athletic Club
AM&B © H68324 Nov. 7, 1905
Cameraman: G. W. Bitzer
Location: Studio, N.Y.C. *Photographed:* Nov. 1, 1905
74 ft. FLA5261 (print) FRA2205 (neg.)

Several teams of wrestlers in action were photographed from a single-camera position on the set of the gymnasium of the New York Athletic Club.

Wrestling Yacht
AM&B © H23782 Nov. 11, 1902
30 ft. FLA4953A (print) FRA1950 (neg.)

An inland waterway can be seen, with a capsized sailing dinghy in the foreground. Four young members of the crew are hard at work trying to right the boat. They succeed. The little sailing boat with its single mast and small sail is seen sailing away from the camera area.

A (W)ringing Good Joke
AM&B © H27377 Jan. 22, 1903
Photographed: 1898 [?]
18 ft. FLA4309 (print) FRA0623 (neg.)

A man can be seen sleeping on a chair on a kitchen set in a modest house. A washtub and wringer stand on the floor a short distance from him. A small boy enters the room, ties a string to the chair of the sleeping man, fastens the other end to a piece of wet wash in the tub, and leaves the set. A woman carrying a bundle of clothes enters the set and begins cranking the clothes wringer which pulls the sleeping man over backward, causing him to knock over the tub of water, which spills over him. As the film ends, he shakes his fist at the woman.

A Wringing Good Joke
Edison © 29258 Apr. 28, 1899
17 ft. FLA4340 (print) FRA1485 (neg.)

As the picture begins, a rather large woman is bending over a washtub, and a man is sitting nearby reading a newspaper with his feet up on a table in a rather small set of the kitchen of a house of a day laborer. A boy with a dog enters and, sizing up the situation, ties a piece of string to the back of the man's chair and to an article of clothing about to go through the wringer on the washtub. As the film progresses, the inevitable happens. The washerwoman cranks the clothes wringer pulling the man over, knocking the props out from under the washtub and spilling the contents on top of the man, to the amusement of the youngster.

A Wringing Good Joke
Edison © D23738 Dec. 28, 1900
Cameraman: Edwin S. Porter
23 ft. FLA4341 (print) FRA1486 (neg.)

The quality of this film does not permit detailed description. However, some of the action is visible. The locale was a set of a kitchen or back porch of a laundress's home. During the length of the film, the washerwoman has one problem after another, including winding her husband's shirt tail in the wringer and pulling him over backward, which earns her a blow on the head.

Wrinkles Removed
AM&B © H21500 Sept. 5, 1902
Cameraman: Robert K. Bonine
Location: Studio, N.Y.C. *Date:* July 21, 1902
9 ft. FLA3922 (print) FRA1138(neg.)

The film begins by showing the neck and head of a young woman being massaged by a man standing behind her chair. During the course of this treatment, he attempts to turn her head to see her better or to kiss her. Each time the masseur does this, the young woman contorts her face to make herself as unattractive as possible, and this continues throughout the film.

The Wrong Room

AM&B © H43562 Mar. 22, 1904

Cameraman: A. E. Weed

Location: Studio, N.Y.C. *Photographed:* Mar. 2, 1904

18 ft. FLA3626 (print) FRA0883 (neg.)

The film begins on a set of the hallway of a hotel. Two doors with room numbers face the camera. A hotel bellhop and a man whose luggage he is carrying walk up to one of the doors and enter. The bellhop leaves, closing the door after him. The occupant of the room emerges with a water pitcher in his hand, leaves the stage area and returns, but enters the wrong room. The film ends as the door he has just entered bursts open showing him being forcibly expelled by a tall female in a nightgown. She is brandishing an umbrella and hollering for help.

Yacht Race—Finish

AM&B © H32947 June 25, 1903

Photographed: 1899 [?]

15 ft. FLA3520 (print) FRA0798 (neg.)

The camera was positioned on board a vessel located on the finish line of the America's Cup Races. The two contenders can be seen approaching the finish line. The camera pans back to the judge's boat at the finish line and photographs the two contenders as they cross it.

The Yacht Race Fleet Following the Committee Boat "Navigator" Oct. 4th

Edison © H9498 Oct. 9, 1901

Location: Off Sandy Hook, N.J. *Photographed:* Oct. 1901

28 ft. FLA4110 (print) FRA1285 (neg., copy 1) FRA1286 (neg., copy 2)

[America's Cup Races, Columbia vs. Shamrock III]

The complete film consists of what can be seen from the stern of a vessel proceeding through an area designated as a yacht racecourse. The vessels shown are large steam yachts and one Coast Guard cutter.

Yacht Race—Start

AM&B © H32869 June 20, 1903

Cameraman: Francis S. Armitage

Photographed: Oct. 5, 1899 [?]

20 ft. FLA3477 (print) FRA0758 (neg.)

[America's Cup Races]

Two racing yachts of the America's Cup class can be seen just before the start of the race. Both boats are under full canvas for the set of the wind. The camera position is from the lee judge's vessel anchored on a direct line from the judge's barge. The film shows the two vessels very clearly as they cross the starting line.

The Yale Laundry

AM&B © H101825 Oct. 30, 1907

Cameraman: G. W. Bitzer

Location: Studio, N.Y.C. *Photographed:* Oct. 7–9, 1907

316 ft. FLA5835 (print) FRA2637 (neg.)

The producer joined together a series of humorous scenes based on a mix-up of bundles of laundry. A group of college boys play pranks on their professors. Some scenes in the interior of the laundry show people falling into tubs, and metal ducts of soap powder spilling on unsuspecting people. To show surprise adequately on the screen, the camera was moved in for a close-up on two occasions. Once the camera was moved from the interior of the laundry to the exterior and back to the interior to follow the action.

A Yard of Frankfurters

AM&B © H32789 June 17, 1903

Cameraman: Arthur Marvin

Location: Roof studio, N.Y.C. *Date:* June 14, 1900

10 ft. FLA3530 (print) FRA0806 (neg.)

A man dressed as a sidewalk peddler is standing in front of a saloon set. A sign on his stand reads "Hot Puppies." A man in a clown's costume comes up and purchases something from the peddler. On closer inspection, his purchase turns out to be a string of large frankfurters, which he starts to eat, but the frankfurters turn into a small dog. The clown drops the dog on the floor, ending the film.

A Yard of Puppies

AM&B © H35094 Aug. 28, 1903

Cameraman: Wallace McCutcheon

Location: Studio, N.Y.C. *Date:* Aug. 10, 1903

16 ft. FLA3546 (print) FRA0821 (neg.)

Six very young black, curly haired puppies are wandering about in an enclosed area. Occasionally, they eat from a saucer.

Ye Olden Grafter

Keystone © P4498 Feb. 18, 1915

Producer and Author: Mack Sennett

Cast: Mae Busch, Harry Gribbon, Mack Swain, Eddie Cline

Location: Griffith Park, Los Angeles

246 ft. FLA6153 (print) FRA2638 (neg.)

The title of this comedy proclaims "Supervised by Mack Sennett." The actors wear 18th-century costumes. Each of the titles throughout the picture begins with the word "Ye." The action starts with Mae Busch sitting on a park bench, crocheting and flirting with a foppish young man, Harry Gribbon, seated nearby. Mack Swain, whom a title characterizes as "Ye Always Broke," spies them and sits down on a bench adjoining Mae. While Mae and Harry are flirting, Swain steals Mae's purse. Gribbon vows to get it back for her and he involves Eddie Cline in a scheme to trap Mack Swain. They succeed in retrieving the purse, making Mae very happy.

The Yellow Peril

AM&B © H106924 Mar. 3, 1908

Cameraman: G. W. Bitzer

Location: Studio, N.Y.C. *Photographed:* Feb.19-20, 1908

201 ft. FLA5836 (print) FRA2838 (neg.)

A woman finds her husband making advances to the housemaid and vows never to employ a female servant again. She hires a Chinese man, and pandemonium breaks loose. During the remaining scenes, the Chinese man alienates everybody involved in the running of the house. He manages to be thrown out of a window, beaten up by a policeman, and set on fire. The film ends with a scene in which he walks into the kitchen with a rat in a trap, causing all the women to climb onto chairs and tables, just as the stove blows up.

You Will Send Me to Bed, Eh?
AM&B © H37382 Oct. 28, 1903
Cameraman: G. W. Bitzer
Location: Studio, N.Y.C. *Photographed:* Oct. 22, 1903
44 ft. FLA5262 (print) FRA2206 (neg.)

A woman and a pre-teen-age boy are sitting at a table on a set of a well-to-do person's living room. A butler announces a visitor, and the boy is sent to bed. When he refuses to go, the butler carries him out. The boy returns and hides behind a screen. The visitor appears and makes a proposal of marriage. The youngster sneaks out from behind the screen and runs a thread from the young lady's hair to the lights above. The woman gets up to accept the proposal, and her wig is pulled from her head. Her suitor runs from the room, and the film ends.

Young America
AM&B © H34808 Aug. 19, 1903
Photographed: 1897
20 ft. FLA4146 (print) FRA1316 (neg.)

This was photographed from a single-camera position and shows two young people socializing in the backyard of a house. A boy approaches the man and ties a smoke bomb to the tail of his coat, and then lights it. There is lots of smoke. When it clears, the adult can be seen spanking the prankster, while in the background we can see that a woman has fainted.

The Zulu's Heart
AM&B © H116155 Sept. 25, 1908
Director: D. W. Griffith *Cameraman:* G. W. Bitzer
Cast: Mack Sennett, Florence Lawrence, John Cumpson, Harry Salter, Adele De Garde
Location: Cliffside, N.J. *Photographed:* Aug. 28-29, 1908
292 ft. FLA5837 (print) FRA2639 (neg.)

The opening scene shows a man and a woman whose bodies are painted to resemble African natives. They enact a burial ritual over the body of their dead child. Another native approaches their camp and indicates that there is some quarry near at hand. The camera shifts to show a covered wagon driven by an old man who is accompanied by a woman (Florence Lawrence) and a small child. The remainder of the film shows the natives attacking the wagon, capturing the woman and her child, and taking them off to camp. One of the Zulus wants to keep the child, which conflicts with the interests of the other natives, and there is a fight. The native shown in the first scene wins and releases the white woman and her child.

INDEXES

Credits

Actors and Actresses

Aitken, Spottiswoode
Alden, Mary
Allen, Estelle
Allen, Phyllis
Americus Quartet
Anderson, Augusta
Anderson, "Broncho" Billy
Arbuckle, Roscoe
Arling, Charles
Arnold, Cecile
Arvidson, Linda
Ashbrook, Florence
Ashton, Sylvia
Auer, Florence
August, Edwin
Avery, Charles
Bambrick, Gertrude
Barclay, Don
Barker, Florence
Barnes, George
Barr, Clarence
Barriscale, Bessie
Barrymore, Lionel
Beaudine, William
Beban, George
Bech, Philip
Beckley, Beatrice
Bennett, Billie
Beqnon, Bleuette
Bernard, Dorothy
Bernard, Harry
Bernhardt, Sarah
Bertelsen, Ingeborg Bruhn
Billie, Svend
Blackton, J. Stuart
Blad, Augusta
Blair
Blom, Agnete
Boesen, Axel
Booker, Harry
Booth, Elmer
Bordeaux, Joe
Borzage, Frank
Boyd, Aline
Bracey, Clara T.
Brammall, Jack
Brechling, Nicolai
Briscoe, Lottie
Brockwell, Billie
Brockwell, Gladys
Browne, Kenneth
Bruce, Kate
Bruun, Cajus
Buck, Frederik

Buemann, Edith
Buffons, The
Burbridge, Elizabeth
Burby, Gordon
Burke, J. Frank
Burt, Laura
Busch, Mae
Butler, W. J.
Butler, William J.
Cabanne, Walter Chrystie
Callahan, Tom
Carroll, William
Cashman, Harry
Cavender, Glen
Chaplin, Charles
Chaplin, Sydney
Chase, Charles
Chene, Dixie
Christensen, Frederik
Christensen, Richard
Clarges, Verner
Clark, May
Clarke, Vergie
Clausen, Hilmar
Cline, Eddie
Cogley, Nick
Cole, Thornton
Conklin, Chester
Connelly, E. J.
Connors, Chuck
Cotton, Lucy
Coulter, Frank
Courtney, Helen
Craig, Charles
Crane, Frank
Crisp, Donald
Crosthwaite, Ivy
Cumpson, John
Dark Cloud
Davenport, Alice
Davenport, Dorothy
Davenport, Kenneth
De Garde, Adele
DeMar, Carrie
Dethlefsen, Otto
Dillon, Eddie
Dillon, Jack
Dinesen, Johanne
Dinesen, Robert
Dougherty, Lee
Dowling, James
Drouet, Robert
Drumeir, Jack
Dunn, Billy
Dunn, Bobby

Durfee, Minta
Edeson, Robert
Edwards, Vivian
Egan, Gladys
Egleston, Ann
Elsky, H.
Emerie; *see* Silveon and Emerie
Evans, Frank
Evans, Millicent
Faust, August
Fay, Hugh
Fazenda, Louise
Felumb-Friis, Mrs.
Fido
Fields, Eleanor
Finch, Flora
Finlayson, Jimmy
Fisher, George
Fitz-Allen, Adelaide
Fitzhamon, Lewin
Foley, Kid
Fønss, Aage
Fønss, Olaf
Fougère, Eugenie
French, C. K.
French, Charles
Fröhlich, Else
From, Elna
Fuller, Charles
Funder, Tronier
Gauntier, Gene
Gebhardt, Mrs.
Gebhardt, Frank
Gebhardt, George
Gilbert, Billy
Gish, Dorothy
Gish, Lillian
Glaum, Louise
Gorman, Charles
Grandon, Frank
Grapewin, Charles E.
Gray, Betty
Graybill, Joe
Greene, Kempton
Gribbon, Harry
Griffith, Mrs.
Griffith, D. W.
Hackett, James K.
Haines, Mina Gale
Hale, Alan
Hale, Walter
Hamilton, Shorty
Hanaway, Frank
Hansen, Valdemar
Harris, Caroline

Harron, Robert
Hart, Joseph
Hart, William S.
Hatton, Raymond
Hauber, W. C.
Hayes, Frank
Hearn, F.
Hedlund, Guy
Held, Anna
Henderson, Dell
Henderson, Grace
Hendry, Anita
Hennessy, George
Henriksen, Julie
Hepworth, Barbara
Hepworth, Cecil
Hepworth, Mrs. Cecil
Hertel, Aage
Hertel, Tage
Hickman, Howard
Holck, Christel
Holden, Arthur C.
Hollingsworth, A.
Holloway, Sidney
Howell, Alice
Howley, Irene
Hunn, Bert
Hyde, Harry
Ince, Thomas
Inslee, Charles
Ivans, Elaine
Iversen, Jon
Jacobsen, Frederik
Jefferson, Joseph
Jefferson, Thomas
Jefferson, William
Jennings, Al
Jensen, Arnold
Jessen, Gerhard
Johnson, Arthur
Keller, Gus
Kelly, James T.
Kennedy, Edgar
Kern, H. C.
Kershaw, Eleanor
Kerzog, F.
King, Rose
Kirby, Audrey
Kirkwood, James
Kornbeck, Ellen
Krum-Hunderup, Johannes
la Cour, Ella
LaBadie, Florence
Lagoni, Otto
Laidlaw, Roy
Lañoe, J. J.
Launsdale, Harry
Lauritzen, Carl
Lauritzen, Henny
Lauritzen, Julie
LaVarnie, Mrs.
Lawrence, Florence
Lee, Florence
Lehrman, Henry "Pathé"
Leonard, Marion

Lestina, Adolph
Lewis, Walter
Little Anita
Lloyd, Harold
Longfellow, Stephanie
Lorley, Ann
Loveridge, Marguerite
Lucas, Wilfred
Lund, Karen
Lupone, Dolly
Lyndon, Clary
McCoy, Harry
McCutcheon, Wallace
McDermott, Joseph
MacDonald, Wallace
McDowell, Claire
Mace, Fred
MacEvoy, Tom
Macpherson, Jeanie
Madison, Ethel
Mailes, Charles Hill
Manley, Charles "Daddy"
Markey, Enid
Marsh, Mae
Marston, Mrs. Lawrence
Maude, Arthur
Maxudian, M.
Mayall, Herschel
Méliès, Georges
Mersereau, Violet
Miles, David
Miles, Herbert
Miles, Mrs. Herbert
Miller, Rube
Miller, W. Chrystie
Miller, Walter
Mitchell, Rhea
Montgomery, David Craig
Moore, Owen
Moran, Polly
Moreno, Antonio
Morris, Dave
Morris, Reggie
Morrison, Louis
Mulhall, Jack
Murray, Charles
Murray, Marie
Myers, Harry
Nairs, Phineas
Nathansen, Kamma Creutz
Neilan, Marshall
Newburg, Frank
Newton, Marie
Nicholls, George
Nichols, Norma
Nidermann, Marie
Nielsen, H. C.
Nielsen, Peter
Nolan, Robert
Norcross, Frank
Nørlund, Agnes
Normand, Mabel
Olcott, Sidney
Olsen, Lauritz
O'Neill, James

Opperman, Frank
Orth, Louise
Osterman, Kathryn
O'Sullivan, Tony
Ott, Fred
Paget, Alfred
Papillon, Zizi
Parmalee, Philip
Pearce, Peggy
Perley, Charles
Petersen, Zanny
Pickford, Jack
Pickford, Lottie
Pickford, Mary
Pierce, G.
Pio, Elith
Pixley, Gus
Powell, Baden
Powell, Frank
Prescott, Vivian
Prior, Herbert
Psilander, Valdemar
Quimby, Harriet
Quirk, Billy
Randall, William P.
Rasow, Knud
Ray, Charles
Rea, Isabel
Red Wing, Princess
Reed, Walter
Reid, Violet
Reumert, Poul
Reymann, Thyra
Rising, W. H.
Ritchie, Franklin
Robinson, George
Robinson, Gertrude
Robinson, W. C. "Spike"
Roeber, Ernest
Rogers, Dora
Romain, Mlle.
Roose, Thorkild
Ross, Milton
Ruben, Jose
Ruhlin, Gus
Russell, William
St. Elmo
St. John, Al
Salter, Harry
Sarno, Hector V.
Saroni, Gilbert
Schade, Fritz
Schenstrøm, Carl
Schmidt, Aage
Schønberg, Birger von Cotta
Schultz, Charles E.
Schyberg, Dagny
Seemann, Henry
Sennett, Mack
Shannon, Frank
Sheer, William
Sherry, J. Barney
Shumway, Leonard C.
Silveon and Emerie
Skondrup, Frederik

Slevin, Jim
Sloane, William
Smith, Mrs.; *see* Mrs. Charlotte
  Smith
Smith, Mrs. Charlotte
Smith, Sebastian
Smith, Mrs. Sebastian
Smith, Vola
Sterling, Ford
Stevens, Josephine
Stewart, Jane
Stewart, Lucille Lee
Stone, Fred
Storm, Jerome
Stoughton, Mabel
Streator's Zouaves
Strøm, Axel
Summerville, Slim
Sunshine, Marion
Swain, Mack
Sweet, Blanche
Swickard, Joe
Tansy, John
Teddy
Tellegen, Lou
Theby, Rosemary
Thomas, Nona
Thompson, Margaret
Thomsen, Ebba
Toncray, Kate
Torrence, David
Tracy, Clyde
Trask, Wayland
Troiano, John
Vale, Louise
Vaughan, Vivian
Victoria, Vesta
Voijere, George
Vosburg, Harold
Walthall, Henry B.
Wells, Lewis
West, Charles
West, Dorothy
White, Arthur
White, James H.
White, Thomas
Whittier, Robert
Wieth, Carlo
Wieth, Clara
Williams, Bert

Williams, Clara
Williams, Kathlyn
Yost, Herbert
Young Deer, James
Zangenberg, Einar

Cameramen

Abadie, A. C.
Ackerman, Raymond
Armitage, F. S.
Bitzer, G. W.
Bleckyrden, W.
Bonine, Robert K.
Casler, H.
Congdon
Cronjager, Henry
Dickson, W. K. L.
Dobson, F. A.
Frawley, Jack
Gove, O. M.
Hemment, J. C.
Higgin, Mr.
Jamison, W. L.
Kent, J. B.
McCutcheon, Wallace
Marvin, Arthur
Miles, Herbert J.
Newhard, Robert
Paley, William
Poore, A. L.
Porter, Edwin S.
Smith, J. B.
Weed, A. E.
White, Arthur
White, James H.

Directors

Anderson, G. M. ("Broncho" Billy)
Arbuckle, Roscoe
Avery, Charles
Barker, Reginald
Bitzer, G. W.
Blom, August
Collins, Alfred
Fitzhamon, Lewin
Gad, Urban
Griffith, D. W.
Harrington, Mr.
Hart, William S.
Henderson, Dell

Hepworth, Cecil
Kirkwood, James
Lee, William
McCutcheon, Wallace, Sr.
McCutcheon, Wallace
Macdonald, J. Farrell
Marston, Lawrence
Mercanton, Louis
Olcott, Sidney
Porter, Edwin S.
Powell, Frank
Rose, Frank Oaks
Schnedler-Sørensen, Edward
Sennett, Mack
Stow, Percy
Urban, Charles
Vale, Travers
West, Raymond B.
White, James H.

Scriptwriters and Authors

Akeley, Carl E.
Belasco, David
Brechling, Nicolai
Christoffersen, Gerda
Clifford, William H.
Cogley, Nick
DeMille, Henry C.
DeMille, William C.
Fich, Otto V.
Garde, Axel
Gauntier, Gene
Griffith, D. W.
Hall, Emmett Campbell
Hansen, Valdemar
Hepworth, Mrs. Cecil
Ince, Thomas H.
Kjerulf, Alfred
Méliès, Georges
Møller, Louis
Nobel, Christian
Norris, Frank
Pickford, Mary
Rostock, Xenius
Schnedler-Sørensen, Edward
Stewens, Helga
Sullivan, C. Gardner
Taylor, Stanner E. V.
Wallace, Lew
Woods, Frank

Names and Subjects

This index contains entries for subject categories, company names, and persons' names. Each indexed entry is followed by the pertinent film titles which are arranged in alphabetical order in the catalog. The names of actors and actresses, cameramen, directors, and scriptwriters and authors who appear in this index are also listed in the credits index. Prominent persons are not always identified by profession, but whenever provided this information follows the person's name. The place names are usually, but not always, where the films were photographed.

Abadie, A. C., cameraman

Annual Baby Parade, 1904, Asbury Park, N.J.
Arabian Jewish Dance
The Baby Review
Boxing Horses, Luna Park, Coney Island
Brush Between Cowboys and Indians
Bucking Broncos
Capsized Boat
Cowboys and Indians Fording River in a Wagon
Crossing the Atlantic
Driving Cattle to Pasture
Eating Macaroni in the Streets of Naples
Egyptian Boys in Swimming Race
Egyptian Fakir with Dancing Monkey
Egyptian Market Scene
Elephants Shooting the Chutes, Luna Park, Coney Island, no. 2
Emigrants [i.e. Immigrants] Landing at Ellis Island
Excavating Scene at the Pyramids of Sakkarah
Feeding Pigeons in Front of St. Mark's Cathedral, Venice, Italy
Flood Scene in Paterson, N.J.
Going to Market, Luxor, Egypt
The Great Fire Ruins, Coney Island
Herd of Sheep on the Road to Jerusalem
Herding Horses Across a River
Inter-Collegiate Athletic Association Championships, 1904
Jerusalem's Busiest Street, Showing Mt. Zion
A Jewish Dance at Jerusalem
Judge Parker Receiving the Notification of His Nomination for the Presidency
King Edward and President Loubet Reviewing French Troops
King Edward's Visit to Paris
Lake Lucerne, Switzerland

Market Scene in Old Cairo, Egypt
Maypole Dance
Miniature Railway at Wilmington Springs, Del.
Move On
Outing, Mystic Shriners, Atlantic City, New Jersey
Panorama of Ruins from Baltimore and Charles Street
Panorama of Ruins from Lombard and Charles Street
Panorama of Ruins from Lombard and Hanover Streets, Baltimore
Panorama of Tivoli, Italy, Showing Seven Falls
Panoramic View of Beyrouth, Syria Showing Holiday Festivities
Parade, Mystic Shriners, Atlantic City, New Jersey
Passengers Embarking from S.S. "Augusta Victoria" at Beyrouth
Policemen's Prank on Their Comrades
Primitive Irrigation in Egypt
Princeton and Yale Football Game
Razzle Dazzle
Rounding Up and Branding Cattle
Rube and Fender
A Scrap in Black and White
Shearing a Donkey in Egypt
Street Scene at Jaffa
Tourists Embarking at Jaffa
Tourists Landing at Island of Capri, Italy
Tourists Returning on Donkeys From Mizpah
Tourists Starting on Donkeys for the Pyramids of Sakkarah
Tourists Taking Water From the River Jordan
Tub Race
Turning the Tables
War Canoe Race
Washing Clothes at Sicily
Western Stage Coach Hold Up

Ackerman, Raymond, cameraman

Aguinaldo's Navy
Attempt to Escape That Led to Misfortune
The Bengal Lancers
Charge by 1st Bengal Lancers
Cossack Cavalry
Eggs Hatching
The Escalta, Manila
Fancy Driving
The Forbidden City, Pekin
The 14th Sikhs
The Fourth Ghorkhas
General Chaffee in Pekin
An Historic Feat
Hot Meals at All Hours
Li Hung Chang and Suite: Presentation of Parlor Mutoscope
The 9th Infantry, U.S.A.
Pack Train, Gen. Bell's Expedition
Reilly's Light Battery "F"
Review of Russian Artillery
Russian Sharp Shooters
Scene in Chinatown
6th Cavalry Assaulting South Gate of Pekin
Street Scene, Tientsin
25th Infantry
Two Hours After the Chickens Leave the Shells
Unloading Lighters, Manila
Water Buffalo, Manila

Actors; see name of person

Advertising

Admiral Cigarette
Chauncey Explains
Eclipse Car Fender Test, no. 1-2
Eggs Hatching
An Englishman's Trip to Paris from London
The Gold Dust Twins
Her First Cigarette
Hold-Up in a Country Grocery Store

The Kentucky Squire
Mellin's Food, no. 1
Mellin's Food, no. 2
The Non-Union Bill-Poster
A Romance of the Rail
Shredded Wheat Biscuit, no. 1
Street Car Chivalry
Trout Fishing, Rangeley Lakes
Two Hours After Chickens Leave
the Shells
The Unappreciated Joke
White Fox Motor Boat

Africa

Military Drill of Kikuyu Tribes and
Other Native Ceremonies
Paul J. Rainey's African Hunt
Victorious Battle for the Conquest
of Mergheb, Africa
see also Cairo, Egypt; Luxor, Egypt;
Sakkarah, Egypt

Afro-Americans; *see* Blacks

Airplanes and balloons

The Aeroplane Inventor
Aviator's Generosity
Balloon Race
Balloon Ascension, Marionettes
The Billionaire
Bird's-Eye View of San Francisco,
Cal., From a Balloon
A Dash Through the Clouds
Ludlow's Aerodrome
Ludlow's Aeroplane, no. 2
Society Ballooning, Pittsfield, Mass.
The Twentieth Century Tramp or,
Happy Hooligan and His Airship
The Victorious Battle for the Con-
quest of Mergheb, Africa
When Love Took Wings

Aitken, Spottiswoode, actor

Liberty Belles

Akeley, Carl E., author

Military Drill of Kikuyu Tribes and
Other Native Ceremonies

Alaska

Panoramic View of the White Pass
Railroad
Whaling in the Far North off the
Coast of Alaska in the Treacher-
ous Bering Sea

Alaska Gold Rush

The Darkening Trail
First Avenue, Seattle, Washington
Horses Loading for Klondike, no. 9
Loading Baggage for Klondike, no.
6
Pack Train on the Chilcoot Pass
Packers on the Trail
Panoramic View of the White Pass
Railroad

Poker at Dawson City
Rocking Gold in the Klondike
S.S. "Williamette" Leaving for
Klondike
Washing Gold on 20 Above Hunker,
Klondike
White Horse Rapids

Alberta, Canada

Royal Train with Duke and Duchess
of York, Climbing Mt. Hector

Albuquerque, New Mexico

The Tourists

Alcoholism; *see* Socially signifi-
cant themes

Alden, Mary, actress

Lord Chumley

Alger, Russell A.

General Wheeler and Secretary Alger

Allabad

Allabad; the Arabian Wizard

Allen, Estelle, actress

Ambrose's Lofty Perch
Crossed Love and Swords
Fatty's Chance Acquaintance
Gussle's Wayward Path
Hash House Mashers
Hogan's Mussy Job
The Home Breakers
Love in Armor
Mabel, Fatty and the Law
Mabel Lost and Won
That Little Band of Gold
Their Social Splash
When Ambrose Dared Walrus
When Love Took Wings

Allen, Phyllis, actress

Caught in a Park
Cursed by His Beauty
Dough and Dynamite
Fatty's Plucky Pup
Gentlemen of Nerve
Gussle Rivals Jonah
Gussle Tied to Trouble
Gussle's Backward Way
Gussle's Day of Rest
Gussle's Wayward Path
A Lover's Lost Control

Allentown, Pennsylvania

The Swimming Ducks at Allentown
Duck Farm

Altona, Washington

Horses Drawing in Seine
Horses Drawing Salmon Seine
Men Taking Fish From Salmon
Seine

Ambulances

Ambulance at the Accident
Drill, Ambulance Corps
Red Cross Ambulance on Battlefield

American Film Manufacturing
Company

The Fall of Black Hawk

American Indians

Admiral Cigarette
Attack on Fort Boonesboro
The Battle at Elderbush Gulch
The Broken Doll
Brush Between Cowboys and
Indians
Buck Dance
Buffalo Bill's Wild West Parade
The Call of the Wild
Carrying Out the Snakes
Circle Dance
Club Swinging, Carlisle Indian
School
Comata, the Sioux
Cowboy Justice
Cowboys and Indians Fording River
in a Wagon
Eagle Dance, Pueblo Indians
The Englishman and the Girl
The Fall of Black Hawk
The Female of the Species
Firing the Cabin
The Gambler of the West
The Girl and the Outlaw
Hogan Out West
The Indian
Indian Day School
The Indian Runner's Romance
Indians Leaving Bald Mountain
Iola's Promise
Kentuckian
Kit Carson
Leather Stocking
Line-Up and Teasing the Snakes
Man's Lust for Gold
The Massacre
The Mended Flute
A Midnight Phantasy
A Mohawk's Way
Moki Snake Dance by Wolpi Indians
Panoramic View of Moki-Land
Parade of Buffalo Bill's Wild West
Show, no. 1
Parade of Snake Dancers Before the
Dance
Procession of Mounted Indians and
Cowboys
Ramona
The Red Girl
The Redman and the Child
The Redman's View
Rescue of Child from Indians
A Romance of the Western Hills
Rose O'Salem-Town
A Round-up in Oklahoma

Serving Rations to the Indians no. 1
Serving Rations to the Indians no. 2
Sham Battle at the Pan-American Exposition
The Song of the Wildwood Flute
Strongheart
A Temporary Truce
The Tourists
Trappers Crossing Bald Mountain
Viewing Sherman Institute for Indians at Riverside, Cal.
Wand Dance, Pueblo Indians
see also Eskimos

American Mutoscope & Biograph Company

The Abductors
Academy of Music Fire
An Acadian Elopement
Accidents Will Happen
The Accomodating Cow
Across the Subway Viaduct, New York
The Adjustable Bed
Adventures of Dollie
An Affair of Honor
After Many Years
After the First Snow
Aguinaldo's Navy
Airy Fairy Lillian Tries on Her New Corsets
Al Treloar in Muscle Exercises
Algy's Glorious Fourth of July
Allabad; the Arabian Wizard
Almost a King
Alone
Alphonse and Gaston
Alphonse and Gaston, no. 1
Alphonse and Gaston, no. 2
Alphonse and Gaston, no. 3
Alphonse and Gaston Helping Irishman
Always Room for One More
American Falls, Goat Island
American Falls, Luna Island
The American Soldier in Love and War, no. 1
The American Soldier in Love and War, no. 2
The American Soldier in Love and War, no. 3
Ameta
The Amorous Militiaman
And a Little Child Shall Lead Them
And Pat Took Him at His Word
Animated Picture Studio
Anna Held
Another Name Was Maude
An April Fool Joke
Arab Act, Luna Park
The Arbitrator
The Armenián Archbishop of Rome
Around the Flip-Flap Railroad
Around the Mulberry Bush
Arrest of a Shoplifter

Arrival of Emigrants [i.e. Immigrants], Ellis Island
Arrival of Train at Muskoka Wharf
Arrival of Train, Cheyenne
Arrival of Train, Tien-Tsin
Arrival of Train, Tokio, Japan
The Art of Making Up
Art Studies
The Artist's Dream
Artist's Point
The Artist's Studio
As In a Looking Glass
As Seen On the Curtain
Asakusa Temple, Tokio, Japan
Asia in America, St. Louis Exposition
At the Altar
At the Dressmaker's
At the Foot of the Flatiron
At the Fountain
At the French Ball
The Athletic Girl and the Burglar, no. 1
The Athletic Girl and the Burglar, no. 2
Atlantic City Fire Department
An Attack by Torpedo Boats
Attack on Fort Boonesboro
Attempt to Escape That Led to Misfortune
Aunt Jane and the Tobasco [sic] Sauce
Aunt Jane's Experience with Tobasco [sic] Sauce
Auto Boat Race on the Hudson
Automobile Race for the Vanderbilt Cup
Automobiling Among the Clouds
An Awful Moment
The Babies' Quarrel
The Baby
The Baby and the Puppies
Baby in a Rage
Baby Lund and Her Pets
Baby Merry-Go-Round
Baby Playing in Gutter
Baby's Day'
A Baby's Shoe
Baby's Tooth
The Bad Boy and the Grocery Man
A Bad (K)Night
The Badger Game
Balked at the Altar
The Ballet Rehearsal
Balloon Race
A Ballroom Tragedy
Bally-Hoo Cake Walk
The Bamboo Slide
The Bandit's Waterloo
The Barbarian Ingomar
The Barber's Dee-light
The Barber's Pretty Patient
The Barber's Queer Customer
Bargain Day
Bargain Day, 14th Street New York

The Barnstormers
Basket Ball, Missouri Valley College
Bass Fishing
Bathing Girls' Hurdle Race
Bathing in Samoa
Battery Park
Battle Flags of the 9th U.S. Infantry
The Battle of Mt. Ariat
The Battle of the Yalu, No. 1–4
Battleship "Indiana" in Action
Battleship "Odin"
Battleships in Action
Battleships "Iowa" and "Massachusetts"
Bayonet Exercises
Be Good
The Bench at Coney Island
Beginning of a Skyscraper
Behind the Scenes
Behind the Screen
The Belles of the Beach
The Bench in the Park
The Bengal Lancers
Bertha Claiche
Betrayed by Hand Prints
Betsy Ross Dance
Between the Dances
The Bewitched Traveller
Ein Bier
The Bigamist's Trial
Biograph's Improved Incubator
Birth of the Pearl
The Black Hand
A Black Storm
The Black Viper
Blackmail
Blessed Is the Peacemaker
A Blessing From Above
Blind Man's Buff
The Blizzard
A Bluff From a Tenderfoot
The Boarding House Bathroom
A Boarding School Prank
Boat Race
Boating Carnival, Palm Beach
Boats Under Oars
Bobby's Kodak
The Boer War
The Bold Soger Boy
A Boomerang
The Borrowing Girl
Borrowing Girl and the Atomizer
Boston School Cadets, 3rd Regiment
A Bowery Cafe
The Bowery Kiss
The Boy Detective
The Boy in the Barrel
The Boy Under the Table
Boys Diving, Honolulu
The Boys Help Themselves to Foxy Grandpa's Cigars
The Boys Still Determined, Try It Again on Foxy Grandpa, With the Same Result

The Boys Think They Have One on Foxy Grandpa, But He Fools Them
The Boys Try to Put One Up on Foxy Grandpa
Boyville Fire Brigade
Brannigan Sets Off the Blast
A Break for Freedom
The Bridal Chamber
Bridal Veil Falls
Bridge Traffic, Manila
Bringing Up a Girl in the Way She Should Go, no. 1
Bringing Up a Girl in the Way She Should Go, no. 2
British Light Artillery
Broadway & Union Square, New York
The Broadway Massage Parlor
The Broker's Athletic Typewriter
Brook Trout Fishing
The Brooklyn Handicap—1904
Brothers of the Misericordia, Rome
Bubbles!
A Bucket of Cream Ale
A Bucking Broncho
Bucking the Blizzard
Buffalo Bill's Wild West Parade
Buffalo Fire Department
The Burd [i.e., Bund] Shanghai
The Burglar
The Burglar and the Bundle
The Burglar-Proof Bed
A Burglar's Mistake
A Busy Day for the Corset Models
Butt's Manual, St. John's School
Buying Stamps from Rural Wagon, U.S.P.O.
Cake Walk
A Cake Walk on the Beach at Coney Island
A Calamitous Elopement
Calisthenic Drill, Missouri Commission
The Call of the Wild
The Camel at Luna Park
The Camera Fiend no. 1
The Camera Fiend no. 2
Cancelling Machine, U.S.P.O.
Canoeing at Riverside
Capt. Boynton Feeding His Pets
Capuchin Monks, Rome
Cardinal Gibbons
A Career of Crime, no. 1
A Career of Crime, no. 2
A Career of Crime, no. 3
A Career of Crime, no. 4
A Career of Crime, no. 5
Carrie Nation Smashing a Saloon
Carriers at Work, U.S.P.O.
Carriers Leaving Building, U.S.P.O.
Carriers Leaving Building, U.S.P.O.
Cascade Near Wawona, California
Casey's Christening
A Catastrophe in Hester Street

Catch-as-Catch-Can Wrestling
A Catch of Hard Shell Crabs, Part 1
Cat's Cradle
Caught by Wireless
Caught in the Undertow
A Cavalry Charge
Central High School, Gymnastic Drill
Central Park After Dark
A Champion Beer Drinker
Champion Pony "Midget"
Changing Horses at Glen
Changing Horses at Linden
"Chappie" and "Ben Bolt"
Charge by 1st Bengal Lancers
Charge of the Light Brigade
Chauncey Explains
Chicks to Order
The Ch-ien-men Gate, Pekin
The Child Stealers
Children Feeding Ducklings
Children in the Surf, Coney Island
Children Rolling Down Hill
Children's Hour on the Farm
Chimmie Hicks at the Races
The Chimney Sweep and the Miller
The Chinese Rubbernecks
The Chorus Girl and the Salvation Army Lassie
The Christmas Burglars
Christmas Morning
The Christmas Party
Chums
Church "Our Lady of Grace," Hoboken
Clarence, the Cop
Clarence, the Cop, on the Feed Store Beat
Classmates
Clerks Casing Mail for Bags, U.S.P.O.
Clerks Tying Bags, U.S.P.O.
Clerks Tying Up for Bags, U.S.P.O.
Cleveland Fire Department
Clever Horsemanship
Climbing the American Alps
A Close Shave
Club Swinging, Carlisle Indian School
The Clubman and the Tramp
Coach at Rural Post Office, U.S.P.O.
Coaching for a Record
Coaching Party
Coaching Party, Yosemite Valley
Coal Heavers
The Coal Strike
Coaling a Steamer, Nagasaki Bay, Japan
A Cold Supper With a Hot Finish
Collecting Mail, U.S.P.O.
A College Girl's Affair of Honor
"Columbia" and "Defender" Rounding Stake-Boat
"Columbia" Close to the Wind
"Columbia" vs. "Defender"

Comedy Cake Walk
Committee on Art
Company Drill, St. John's Military Academy
Concealing a Burglar
Condensed Milk
The Coney Island Beach Patrol
The Coney Island Bikers
Coney Island Police Court
Confidence
Contrary Wind
The Converts
The Convict's Bride
The Convict's Escape
A Convict's Punishment
The Cook in the Parlor
The Cord of Life
A Corner in the Play Room
Corpus Christi Procession, Orvieto
"Corsair" in Wake of Tugboat
The Corset Model
Cossack Cavalry
Cosy Corner Dance
Cotton Spinning
Council Bluffs Bridge Station
A Country Courtship
The Country Schoolmaster
A Couple of Lightweights at Coney Island
The Course of True Love
The Cowboy and the Lady
Cowboy Justice
The Creators of Foxy Grandpa
The Criminal Hypnotist
The Critic
Crossroads of Life
Crowd Entering Futurity Day
Cruelty to Horses
The Cruise of the "Gladys"
The Crushed Hat
The Curtain Pole
A Customer Drops In
Cutting Sugar Cane
The Dairy Maid's Revenge
Daly of West Point Winning Hurdle Race
Dance, Franchonetti Sisters
A Dance in Pajamas
A Dance on the Pike
The Dandy Fifth
The Danger of Dining in Private Dining Rooms
The Darling of the Gallery Gods
Davey Jones' Locker
The Deadwood Sleeper
Deaf Mute Girl Reciting "Star Spangled Banner"
The Deceived Slumming Party
The Deception
Decoyed
Deer Stalking With Camera
Delivering Mail From Sub-Station
Delivering Newspapers
A Delusion

384

Johnny's in the Well
A Joke at the French Ball
A Joke on Whom?
The Jolly Bill Poster
The Jolly Monks of Malabar
Jones and His New Neighbors
Jones and the Lady Book Agent
Jones at the Ball
Jones Entertains
The Joneses Have Amateur Theatricals
Judge Alton B. Parker and Guests
Jumbo, Horseless Fire-Engine
Just Before the Raid
A Juvenile Elephant Trainer
Juvenile Stakes
Karina
Katzenjammer Kids and the School Marm
The Katzenjammer Kids Have a Love Affair
Kent House Slide
Kentuckian
A Kentucky Feud
The Kentucky Squire
Kicking Football—Harvard
The Kidnapper: At Work [Part 1]
The Kidnapper: In the Den [Part 2]
The Kidnapper: The Rescue [Part 3]
The Ki-Ki Dance
Kindergarten Ball Game
Kindergarten Dance
King and Queen Diving Horses
The King of Detectives
The King of the Cannibal Island
King of the Detectives
The King's Messenger
A Kiss and a Tumble
A Kiss in the Dark
Kiss Me!
Kit Carson
"Kronprinz Wilhelm" Docking
Ladies' Saddle Horses
Lady Bountiful Visits the Murphys on Wash Day
Lady Helen's Escapade
The Lamp Explodes
Landing of U.S. Troops Near Santiago
A Large Haul of Fish
The Last Round Ended in a Free Fight
The Late Senator Mark Hanna
Lathrop School, Calisthenics
Latina, Contortionist
Latina, Dislocation Act
Latina, Physical Culture Poses, no. 1
Latina, Physical Culture Poses, no. 2
Laughing Ben
Launch of Battleship "Connecticut"
Launch, U.S. Battleship "Kentucky"
Launching U.S.S. "Illinois"
Lawn Party
A Legal Hold-Up
Let Uncle Reuben Show You How

Levi & Cohen, the Irish Comedians
Li Hung Chang and Suite: Presentation of Parlor Mutoscope
Lifting the Lid
The Light That Didn't Fail
The Linen Draper's Shop
Linwood School, Calisthenics
A Little Bit Off the Top
A Little Man
A Little Mix-Up in a Mixed Ale Joint
A Little Piece of String
A Little Ray of Sunshine After the Rain
A Little Teaze
Lively Brushes on Speedway
Living Pictures
The Llamas at Play
The Loaded Cigar
Loading Mail Car, U.S.P.O.
Loading Sugar Cane
Logging in Maine
The Lone Highwayman
Lonesome Junction
Looking for John Smith
The Lost Child
Love and Jealousy Behind the Scenes
Love at 55
Love Finds a Way
Love in a Hammock
Love in the Cornfield
Love in the Dark
Love in the Suburbs
Love Me, Love My Dog
The Love Microbe
The Lover's Knot
The Lover's Ruse
A Lover's Yarn
Love's Perfidy
Love's Young Dream
Lower Broadway
Lucky Jim
Lucky Kitten
Ludlow's Aerodrome
Ludlow's Aeroplane, no. 2
Lure of the Gown
McKinley and Party
McKinley Funeral on Way to Church
McKinley Funeral: Panorama of McKinley Home
Madison Square, New York
Mailing Platform, U.S.P.O.
Making an Impression
The Man and the Woman
Man in the Box
Man Overboard
Maneuvering a Small Motor Boat
The Maniac Barber
The Maniac Cook
The Manicure Fools the Husband
Manual of Arms, St. John's Military Academy
Market Street Before Parade
Married for Millions
The Masqueraders

Mass. State Militia Encampment
The Matron Stakes
Mayor Van Wyck and General Miles
Me and Jack
The Meadowbrook Hunt
Meadowbrook Steeplechase
The Mechanical Toy
The Medicine Bottle
Mellin's Food, no. 1
Mellin's Food, no. 2
Men Taking Fish From Salmon Seine
The Messenger Boy and the Ballet Girl
The Meteor
Metropolitan Handicap
A Midnight Phantasy
Midwinter Bathing, L Street Bath, Boston
Mike Got the Soap in His Eyes
A Mile in 56 Seconds
Military Parade, St. Louis Exposition
Military Tactics
Milking Time
The Minister's Hat
The Minister's Wooing
Mischievous Monkey
Mischievous Willie's Rocking Chair Motor
A Misdirected Ducking
The Mis-Directed Kiss
The Misplaced Signs
Mr. Butt-In
Mr. Easymark
Mr. Gay and Mrs.
Mr. Hurry-Up of New York
Mr. Jack Caught in the Dressing Room
Mr. Jack Entertains in His Office
Mr. Jack in the Dressing Room
Mr. Jones Has a Card Party
Mixed Babies
Mixed Bathing
Model Posing Before Mirror
The Model That Didn't Pose
A Modern Sappho
Money Mad
Monkey Business
Monkey's Feast
M. Lavelle, Physical Culture, no. 1
M. Lavelle, Physical Culture, no. 2
The Moonshiner
Moose Hunt in New Brunswick
Mother's Angel Child
Moulin Rouge Dancers
Mount Stephen
A Moving Picture
Multicycle Race
Murphy's Wake
Musical Bayonet Exercises
Musical Calisthenics
Must Be in Bed Before Ten
Mutiny on the Black Sea
The Mysterious Midgets

388

Spike, the Bag-Punching Dog
A Spill
Spirit of '76
Spirits in the Kitchen
Spooks at School
Springtime in the Park
The Stage Rustler
Stalking and Shooting Caribou, Newfoundland
Stallion Race
Star Theatre
Start of Race—"Reliance" Ahead
Start of the First Race, Aug. 22
The Startled Lover
State Normal School, Missouri
Stealing a Dinner
Steam Riding Academy
Steam Tactics
Steamboat and Great Eastern Rock
Steamer "Island Wanderer"
Steamer "New York"
Steamship "Express of India"
Steeplechase, Coney Island
Stern's Duplex Railway
Still Water Runs Deep
The Stolen Jewels
Stolen Sweets
Stop Thief!
The Story of the Biograph Told
Street Fight and Arrest
Street Mail Car, U.S.P.O.
Street Scene, Tientsin
Street Scene, Tokio, Japan
The Streets of New York
The Strenuous Life
A Subject for the Rogue's Gallery
The Subpoena Server
The Suburbanite
The Suicide Club
The Suit of Armor
The Summer Boarders
The Summer Girl
Surf at Atlantic City
A Sweet Little Home in the Country
Sweethearts
Sweets for the Sweet
The Swimming Class
Swimming Pool, Palm Beach
A Swimming Race at Coney Island
Switchback on Trolley Road
Symphony in "A-Flat"
Take Mellon's Food
Taming of the Shrew
Tarrant Fire
The Tavern Keeper's Daughter
Teasing
Temptation of St. Anthony
Ten Nights in a Bar-Room: Death of Little May
Ten Nights in a Bar-Room: Death of Slade
Ten Nights in a Bar-Room: The Fatal Blow
Ten Nights in a Bar-Room: Murder of Willie

Ten Nights in a Bar-Room: Vision of Mary
Tenderloin Tragedy
A Terrible Night
Terrier vs. Wild Cat
The Test of Friendship
"Teutonic" and "Nördland"
Thaw-White Tragedy
Theatre Hat
Theatre Hats Off
Theodore Roosevelt Leaving the White House
They Found the Leak
They Meet on the Mat
The Thief and the Pie Woman
The Thirteen Club
Thompson's Night Out
Those Awful Hats
Those Boys
Those Wedding Bells Shall Not Ring Out
Three Cavaliers of the Road
Three Girls in a Hammock
Three Little Maids
Through the Key-Hole in the Door
Throwing Mail Into Bags, U.S.P.O.
Tied to Her Apron Strings
The Tired Tailor's Dream
'Tis an Ill Wind That Blows No Good
Tom, Tom, the Piper's Son
A Too Ardent Lover
Too Much Johnson
Too Much of a Good Thing
Toodles and Her Strawberry Tart
Toodles Recites a Recitation
Toodle's Tea-Party
The Topers
Torpedo Boat "Dupont"
A Total Accident
A "Tough" Dance
Tough Kid's Waterloo
Tourists Arriving at Wawona Hotel
Tragic Love
Train of Sugar Cane
Train Taking Up Mail Bag, U.S.P.O.
The Tramp and the Bathers
The Tramp and the Muscular Cook
A Tramp on the Roof
Transporting Internal Rev. Stamps, U.S.P.O.
Trap Pigeon Shooting
Trappers Crossing Bald Mountain
Trial Marriages
A Trick on the Cop
A Trip on the Catskill Mt. Ry
A Trip to Berkeley, Cal.
A Trip to Salt Lake City
Triumphal Bridge, Pan-American Exposition
Trouble in Hogan's Alley
Troubles of a Manager of a Burlesque Show
The Troublesome Fly
A Troublesome Satchel

Trout Fishing
Trout Fishing, Rangeley Lakes
Trout Poachers
The Truants
Trying to Get Arrested
Tunnel Number Three
The Tunnel Workers
25th Infantry
Twenty Mule Team, St. Louis Exposition
Twin Brothers
2 A.M. in the Subway
Two Bottle Babies
Two Companies, Royal Canadian Regiment
Two Hours After the Chickens Leave the Shells
Two Old Cronies
Two's Company
Tying Up Bags for Train, U.S.P.O.
The Typewriter
The Ugly Tempered Tramp
Uncle Reuben at the Waldorf
Under the Bamboo Tree
Under the Old Apple Tree
Under the Tree
An Unexpected Knockout
The Unfaithful Odalisque
The Unfaithful Wife: Part 1, The Lover
The Unfaithful Wife: Part 2, The Fight
The Unfaithful Wife: Part 3, Murder and Suicide
A Unique Race Between Elephant, Bicycle, Camel, Horse, and Automobile
U.S. Battleship "Oregon"
United States Government Gun Test
Unloading Halibut
Unloading Lighters, Manila
Unlucky at Cards, Lucky at Love
An Unlucky Lover
An Unprotected Female
An Unprotected Female, no. 2
The Vaidis Sisters, Luna Park
The Valet's Wife
The Vaquero's Vow
The Vatican Guards, Rome
Vaulting Contest, Meadowbrook Hunt
Venice in America
A Victim of Circumstantial Evidence
Views in San Francisco
The Village Cut-Up
A Visit to Baby Roger
"Vizcaya" Under Full Headway
The Voice of the Violin
The Waders
The Wages of Sin: Murder—Part 1
The Wages of Sin: Retribution—Part 2
Wagons Loading Mail, U.S.P.O.
The Waif

Waiting for Bill
Waiting for Santa Claus
A Wake in "Hell's Kitchen"
Wanted: A Dog
Wanted—A Nurse
A Warm Occasion
Wash-Day
Washing the Baby
Washington Bridge and Speedway
The Washwoman's Daughter
Water Buffalo, Manila
Water Duel
Water Nymphs
Wawona, Big Tree
The Way to Sell Corsets
The Wedding
Weighing the Baby
A Welcome Burglar
Welding the Big Ring
A Welsh Rabbit
West Point Cadets
West Point Cadets, St. Louis Exposition
Westinghouse Air Brake Company
Westinghouse Works
What Are the Wild Waves Saying, Sister?
What Boys Will Do
What Burglar Bill Found in the Safe
What Happened to Jones
When Knights Were Bold
When We Were Twenty-One
Where Breakers Roar
While Strolling in the Park
White Fox Motor Boat
Whittier School, Calisthenics
Who Pays for the Drinks?
Who Said Chicken?
Who's Got the Red Ear?
Why Curfew Did Not Ring
Why Foxy Grandpa Escaped a Ducking
Why Papa Can't Sleep
The Widow and the Only Man
A Wild Turkey Hunt
Will He Marry the Girl?
Willful Murder
Willie Westinghouse and the Doctor's Battery
Willie's Camera
Willie's Hat
A Windy Day on the Roof
The Wine Opener
Wine, Women & Song
Wine, Women & Song, no. 2
A Woman's Way
Women of the Ghetto Bathing
The Wooden Leg
Wounded Soldiers Embarking in Row Boats
The Wrath of a Jealous Wife
A Wreath in Time
Wreck of the "Vizcaya"
Wrestling at the New York Athletic Club

Wrestling Yacht
A (W)ringing Good Joke
Wrinkles Removed
The Wrong Room
Yacht Race—Finish
Yacht Race—Start
The Yale Laundry
A Yard of Frankfurters
A Yard of Puppies
The Yellow Peril
You Will Send Me to Bed, Eh?
Young America
The Zulu's Heart
see also Biograph Co.

American Mutoscope Co.; see American Mutoscope & Biograph Co.

America's Cup Races

After the Race—Yachts Returning to Anchorage
"Columbia" and "Defender" Rounding Stake-Boat
"Columbia" and "Shamrock II" Finishing Second Race
"Columbia" and "Shamrock II" Jockeying and Starting
"Columbia" and "Shamrock II" Start of Second Race
"Columbia" and "Shamrock II" Starting in the Third Race
"Columbia" and "Shamrock II" Turning the Outer Stake Boat
"Columbia" Close to the Wind
"Columbia" vs. "Defender"
"Columbia" Winning the Cup
"Corsair" in Wake of Tugboat
"Grandrepublic" Passing "Columbia"
Jockeying and Start of Yacht[s], Aug. 25th
Jockeying for the Start, Aug. 20
Jockeying for the Start, Aug. 22
Panorama of Excursion Boats
Panoramic View of the Fleet After Yacht Race
Pictures Incidental to Yacht Race
"Reliance" and "Shamrock III" Jockeying and Starting in First Race
"Reliance" Crossing the Line and Winning First Race
"Reliance" vs. "Shamrock III," Aug. 20
"Shamrock" After Carrying Away Topsail
"Shamrock" and "Columbia" Rounding the Outer Stake Boat
"Shamrock" and "Columbia" Yacht Race—First Race
"Shamrock" and "Columbia" Yacht Race—1st Race, no. 2
"Shamrock" and "Erin" Sailing
A Spectacular Start
Start of Race—"Reliance" Ahead

Start of the First Race, Aug. 22
The Yacht Race Fleet Following the Committee Boat "Navigator" Oct. 4th
Yacht Race—Start

Americus Quartet

Cake Walk

Ameta, dancer

Ameta

Amusement areas

Ambrose's Fury
Annual Baby Parade, 1904, Asbury Park, N.J.
Arab Act, Luna Park
Around the Flip-Flap Railroad
Asia in America, St. Louis Exposition
Atlantic City Floral Parade
The Bamboo Slide
Bathing at Atlantic City
The Beach at Coney Island
Boarding School Girls
Boxing Horses, Luna Park, Coney Island
The Boys Try to Put One Up on Foxy Grandpa
A Cake Walk on the Beach at Coney Island
The Camel at Luna Park
Capt. Boynton Feeding His Pets
Captain Nissen Going Through Whirlpool Rapids, Niagara Falls
Children in the Surf, Coney Island
Coney Island at Night
Dial's Girls' Band, Luna Park
The Diving Horse
Double Ring Act, Luna Park
Electric Tower
The Elephant's Bath
Elephants Shooting the Chutes at Luna Park
Elephants Shooting the Chutes, Luna Park, Coney Island, no. 2
Fatty's Plucky Pup
Fighting the Flames
Fighting the Flames, Dreamland
Fire and Flames at Luna Park, Coney Island
The Golden Chariots
Gussle Rivals Jonah
Head-on Collision at Brighton Beach Race Track, July 4th, 1906
The Helping Hand
Hippodrome Races, Dreamland, Coney Island
Ice Skating in Central Park, N.Y.
June's Birthday Party
Las Vigas Canal, Mexico
Las Vigas Canal, Mexico City
The Leading Man
The Lucky Wishbone
Mabel's Wilful Way

Miniature Railway at Wilmington Springs Del.
Mystic Shriners' Day, Dreamland, Coney Island
Opening of Belmont Park Race Course
Outing, Mystic Shriners, Atlantic City, New Jersey
Palace of Electricity
Panorama From the Moving Board-walk
Panorama of Eiffel Tower
Panorama of Esplanade by Night
Panorama of the Paris Exposition, from the Seine
Panoramic View of Beyrouth, Syria Showing Holiday Festivities
Panoramic View of Charleston Exposition
Panoramic View of Electric Tower from a Balloon
Parade of Shriners, Luna Park
The Racing Chutes at Dreamland
Razzle Dazzle
Rube and Mandy at Coney Island
Settled at the Seaside
Sham Battle at the Pan-American Exposition
Shoot the Chutes Series
Shooting the Chutes
Shooting the Chutes at Luna Park
Shooting the Chutes, Luna Park
Skating on Lake, Central Park
Slide for Life, Luna Park
Speech by President Francis: World's Fair
Steam Riding Academy
Steeplechase, Coney Island
Stern's Duplex Railway
Surf at Atlantic City
Sutro Baths
Sutro Baths, no. 1
Swimming Pool at Coney Island
A Swimming Race at Coney Island
Those Bitter Sweets
A Total Accident
The Vaidis Sisters, Luna Park
A Voice from the Deep
West Point Cadets, St. Louis Exposition
Wished on Mabel
see also Coney Island, N.Y.; Fairs and expositions; Merry-go-rounds

Ancient Honourables Artillery of London

Ancient and Honourable Artillery of London
Ancient and Honourable of London Homeward Bound
The Honourable Artillery Company of London

Anderson, Augusta, actress

Seven Days

Anderson, G. M. ("Broncho" Billy), actor

The Great Train Robbery
Raffles, the Amateur Cracksman

Animals

Allabad; the Arabian Wizard
Buster's Joke on Papa
Capt. Boynton Feeding His Pets
A Catch of Hard Shell Crabs, Part 1
Common Beasts of Africa
The Enchanted Well
Fatty and Mabel's Simple Life
Fatty's New Role
Fishing at Faralone Island
The Fox Hunt
From Patches to Plenty
The Gambler of the West
Glimpses of Yellowstone Park
Gloomy Gus Gets the Best of It
Gussle the Golfer
Line-up and Teasing the Snakes
Llamas at Play
Mabel and Fatty's Wash Day
The Mermaid
Military Drill of Kikuyu Tribes and Other Native Ceremonies
Moose Hunt in New Brunswick
[On] A [Good Old] Five Cent Trol-ley Ride
Paul J. Rainey's African Hunt
The Primitive Man
Rube and Mandy at Coney Island
A Rube Couple at a County Fair
The Sea Lions' Home
Stalking and Shooting Caribou, Newfoundland
The Star of Bethlehem
Their Social Splash
Tourists Going Round Yellowstone Park
A True Patriot
Twin Brothers
A Versatile Villain
West Point Cadets, St. Louis Exposi-tion
Whaling in the Far North Off the Coast of Alaska in the Treacher-ous Bering Sea
When the Flag Falls
The Wolf Hunt
The Would-Be Shriner
Won by a Fish
see also Specific types

Annapolis, Maryland

Boats Under Oars
John Paul Jones Ceremonies
Shortening and Furling Sails
Steam Tactics

Apes

Do-Re-Mi—Boom
The Educated Chimpanzee

Egyptian Fakir with Dancing Mon-key
Grandpa's Reading Glass
The Jealous Monkey
Joe, the Educated Orangoutang
Mabel and Fatty's Married Life
Mischievous Monkey
Monkey Business
Monkey's Feast
An Unwelcome Visitor

Arbuckle, Roscoe, actor

Fatty and Mabel at the San Diego Exposition
Fatty and Mabel's Simple Life
Fatty's Chance Acquaintance
Fatty's Faithful Fido
Fatty's New Role
Fatty's Plucky Pup
Fatty's Reckless Fling
Fatty's Tintype Tangle
Hogan's Romance Upset
The Little Teacher
Mabel and Fatty Viewing the World's Fair at San Francisco, Cal.
Mabel and Fatty's Married Life
Mabel and Fatty's Wash Day
Mabel, Fatty and the Law
Mabel's Wilful Way
Miss Fatty's Seaside Lovers
That Little Band of Gold
When Love Took Wings
Wished on Mabel

Arizona

The Bargain
The March of Prayer and Entrance of the Dancers
Moki Snake Dance by Wolpi [Walpa-pi] Indians
Panoramic View of Moki-Land
Parade of Snake Dancers Before the Dance
Wand Dance, Pueblo Indians

Arling, Charles, actor

The Cannon Ball
Court House Crooks
Do-Re-Mi—Boom!
Droppington's Devilish Deed
A One Night Stand
That Little Band of Gold

Armitage, F. S., cameraman

Across the Subway Viaduct, New York
Algy's Glorious Fourth of July
Ameta
Anna Held
An April Fool Joke
Around the Flip-Flap Railroad
Art Studies
The Artist's Dream
As In a Looking Glass

Aunt Jane's Experience with Tobasco [sic] Sauce
The Babies' Quarrel
Baby Lund and Her Pets
Baby's Tooth
A Bad (K)Night
Bargain Day, 14th Street, New York
Ein Bier
Birth of the Pearl
A Bluff From a Tenderfoot
A Boomerang
Brook Trout Fishing
Buffalo Bill's Wild West Parade
Buffalo Fire Department
Cake Walk
Capt. Boynton Feeding His Pets
Carrie Nation Smashing a Saloon
"Chappie" and "Ben Bolt"
Children's Hour on the Farm
Chimmie Hicks at the Races
A Close Shave
"Columbia" and "Defender" Rounding Stake-Boat
"Columbia" vs. "Defender"
Comedy Cake Walk
Contrary Wind
"Corsair" in Wake of Tugboat
The Corset Model
A Customer Drops In
The Dairy Maid's Revenge
The Dandy Fifth
Davey Jones' Locker
The Dewey Arch
Diving Through Hoops
Drill, Ambulance Corps
Drill by the Providence Police
Eclipse Car Fender Test, no. 1–2
The Evidence Was Against Him
"Exempt" of Brooklyn, N.Y.
Fancy Driving
15th Infantry
Finish of Futurity, 1901
Finishing Touches
Five Minutes to Train Time
A Flock of Export Sheep
The Foster Mother
Fougere
The Fresh Lover
Full Rigged Ship at Sea
A Gay Old Boy
Getting Ready to Entertain Harvesters
A Good Shot
Governor Roosevelt and Staff
Governor's Foot Guards, Conn.
"Grandrepublic" Passing "Columbia"
He Forgot His Umbrella
Her First Cigarette
His Masterpiece
Hot Mutton Pies
How Little Willie Put a Head on His Pa
How the Young Man Got Stuck at Ocean Beach

How'd You Like to Be the Iceman?
Johnny's in the Well
A Joke on Whom?
King and Queen Diving Horses
Ladies' Saddle Horses
A Legal Hold-Up
A Little Piece of String
A Little Ray of Sunshine After the Rain
Love in a Hammock
A Lover's Yarn
The Maniac Barber
Mayor Van Wyck and General Miles
A Midnight Phantasy
M. Lavelle, Physical Culture, no. 1
M. Lavelle, Physical Culture, no. 2
Naval Parade
Neptune's Daughters
The New Maid
The Nihilists
A Non-Union Paper Hanger
Noon Hour, Hope Webbing Co.
Nora's Fourth of July
A Nymph of the Waves
"Oceans" Fire Company
On the Benches in the Park
Panoramic View of Niagara Falls
Parade of "Exempt" Firemen
Parade of Shriners, Luna Park
Parke Davis' Employees
Pawtucket Fire Department
A Plate of Ice Cream and Two Spoons
The Poster Girls
The Pouting Model
The Price of a Kiss
The Prince of Darkness
Prize Fight
A Quick Recovery
Reproduction of Corbett-McGovern Fight
Rhode Island Light Artillery
S.S. "Chippewa"
Sailors of Atlantic Fleet, Dewey Parade
The "St. Paul" Outward Bound
The Sandwich Man
Sarnia Tunnel
Scene in Chinese Restaurant
Sea Gulls in Central Park
The Serenaders
Seventh Regiment, N.Y.
71st Regiment, Camp Wyckoff
"Shamrock" After Carrying Away Topsail
Skating on Lake, Central Park
Sleeping Child
A Spectacular Start
The Spider and the Fly
Spirits in the Kitchen
Springtime in the Park
Stallion Race
Star Theatre
Stop Thief!
The Summer Girl

Tarrant Fire
Ten Nights in a Bar-Room: Death of Little May
Ten Nights in a Bar-Room: Death of Slade
Ten Nights in a Bar-Room: The Fatal Blow
Ten Nights in a Bar-Room: Murder of Willie
Ten Nights in a Bar-Room: Vision of Mary
A Terrible Night
Three Cavaliers of the Road
Torpedo Boat "Dupont"
Trout Fishing
Trout Poachers
Two Old Cronies
Two's Company
The Ugly Tempered Tramp
An Unexpected Knockout
An Unlucky Lover
Waiting for Santa Claus
Wanted: A Dog
Washington Bridge and Speedway
West Point Cadets
When We Were Twenty-One
Yacht Race—Start

Armour and Company, Chicago

Armour's Electric Trolley

Army; *see* Military

Arnold, Cecile, actress

Ambrose's Nasty Temper
Ambrose's Sour Grapes
Caught in a Park
Caught in the Act
Crossed Love and Swords
Cursed by His Beauty
Dough and Dynamite
From Patches to Plenty
Gussle's Backward Way
Gussle's Day of Rest
His Luckless Love
Mabel and Fatty's Married Life
That Springtime Feeling

Arvidson, Linda, actress

Adventures of Dollie
After Many Years
An Awful Moment
A Baby's Shoe
Balked at the Altar
Betrayed by Hand Prints
Beverly of Graustark
The Broken Doll
A Calamitous Elopement
The Call to Arms
The Cardinal's Conspiracy
A Child's Stratagem
Classmates
The Cloister's Touch
The Clubman and the Tramp
Comata, the Sioux
Concealing a Burglar

Confidence
The Converts
The Cord of Life
A Corner in Wheat
The Cricket on the Hearth
The Curtain Pole
The Dancing Girl of Butte
The Death Disc
The Deception
The Drunkard's Reformation
The Eavesdropper
Edgar Allen [i.e. Allan] Poe
Effecting a Cure
The Face at the Window
A Fair Rebel
The Fascinating Mrs. Francis
The Fatal Hour
Fate's Turning
Father Gets in the Game
The Feud and the Turkey
A Fool's Revenge
For a Wife's Honor
The French Duel
The Gambler of the West
Gold Is Not All
Greaser's Gauntlet
The Helping Hand
His Trust
In a Hempen Bag
In Life's Cycle
In Old Kentucky
The Indian
The Last Deal
Leather Stocking
The Light That Came
Lines of White on a Sullen Sea
A Lucky Toothache
The Man and the Woman
The Medicine Bottle
The Mills of the Gods
The Peach-Basket Hat
Pippa Passes
The Pirates Gold
The Planter's Wife
Politician's Love Story
The Redman and the Child
Resurrection
The Rocky Road
The Roue's Heart
Rural Elopement
The Sacrifice
A Smoked Husband
Song of the Shirt
Taming of the Shrew
The Test of Friendship
Those Awful Hats
Those Boys
The Thread of Destiny
Through the Breakers
Tragic Love
The Unchanging Sea
The War of Wealth
Where Breakers Roar
The Wife
A Wreath in Time

Asbury Park, New Jersey

Annual Baby Parade, 1904, Asbury Park, N.J.
The Elopement
The King's Messenger
The Suburbanite

Ashbrook, Florence, actress

A Fair Rebel

Ashton, Sylvia, actress

A Close Call
A Dash Through the Clouds
Helen's Marriage
Neighbors
Trying to Fool Uncle
When the Fire-Bells Rang
The Would-Be Shriner

Athletics

The Athletic Girl and the Burglar, no. 1
The Athletic Girl and the Burglar, no. 2
Basket Ball, Missouri Valley College
Bayonet Exercises
The Broadway Massage Parlor
Butt's Manual, St. John's School
Calisthenic Drill, Missouri Commission
Central High School, Gymnastic Drill
Emerson School Calisthenics
Filipino Scouts, Musical Drill, St. Louis
Free Arm Movement, All Schools, Missouri Commission
French Acrobatic Dance
Getting Strong
Girls' Acrobatic Feats
Girls Jumping Rope
Girls Playing See-Saw
Gymnasium Exercises and Drill at Newport Training School
Her Morning Exercise
How Would You Like a Wife Like This?
Hyde Park School Graduating Class
Hyde Park School, Room 2
In a Boarding School Gym
Japanese Acrobats
Japanese Fencing
Japanese Village
Kindergarten Ball Game
Linwood School, Calisthenics
On the Flying Rings
The Prentis Trio
School Girl Gymnastics
Skirmish Between Russian and Japanese Advance Guards
Slide for Life, Luna Park
Spanish Ball Game
A Street Arab
Whittier School, Calisthenics
see also Specific types

Atlantic City, New Jersey

Atlantic City Fire Department
Atlantic City Floral Parade
Bathing at Atlantic City
Caught in the Undertow
Down Where The Wurzburger Flows
Outing, Mystic Shriners, Atlantic City, New Jersey
Parade, Fiftieth Anniversary Atlantic City, N.J.
Parade, Mystic Shriners, Atlantic City, New Jersey
Seashore Frolics
Surf at Atlantic City

Atlantic Highlands, New Jersey

After Many Years

Auburn, New York

Execution of Czolgosz, with Panorama of Auburn Prison

Auer, Florence, actress

Eradicating Aunty
The Snowman

August, Edwin, actor

A Beast at Bay
A Child's Remorse
The Fugitive
Getting Even
The Girl and Her Trust
The Golden Supper
Happy Jack, A Hero
His Lesson
The Lesser Evil
The Lesson
Muggsy Becomes a Hero
The Old Actor
Oh, Those Eyes!
One Is Business, the Other Crime
The Primitive Man
The Renunciation
The Sands of Dee
The School Teacher and the Waif
Simple Charity
The Son's Return
Winning Back His Love
A Wreath of Orange Blossoms

Authors; see name of person

Automobiles

An Acadian Elopement
The Aeroplane Inventor
An Affair of Hearts
Automobile Parade
Automobile Parade on the Coney Island Boulevard
Automobile Race for the Vanderbilt Cup
Automobiling Among the Clouds
The Aviator's Generosity
A Baby's Shoe
A Beast at Bay

The Billionaire
Boarding School Girls
The Brave Hunter
A Change of Heart
Crowd Entering Gates, Futurity Day
The Cup of Life
Curses! They Remarked
A Dangerous Play
The Deceived Slumming Party
The Devil
The Elopement
The Engagement Ring
The Evil Art, (or), Gambling Exposed, parts 1–3
The Ex-Convict
Faithful
The Fatal Wedding
Fine Feathers Make Fine Birds
For Better—But Worse
From Patches to Plenty
The Genius
The Gentlemen Highwaymen
Gentlemen of Nerve
Gold Is Not All
A Gold Necklace
Gussle's Day of Rest
A Hash House Fraud
Helen's Marriage
Help! Help!
Her Face Was Her Fortune
Her Father's Pride
Homeless
How Brown Got Married
A Human Hound's Triumph
The Interrupted Elopement
The Italian
Jim Jeffries on His California Ranch
Jimmie Hicks in Automobile
Lifting the Lid
The Little Railroad Queen
The Lonely Villa
Love and Friendship
Love in the Tropics
Love, Loot and Crash
A Lover's Lost Control
Ludlow's Aerodrome
Mass. State Militia Encampment
Merely a Married Man
Midsummer-Tide
New York Athletic Club Games, Travers Island
Not So Bad As It Seemed
Ormond, Florida Auto Races
An Outcast Among Outcasts
Panoramic View of Monte Carlo
Panoramic View of the Champs Elysees
Peace Envoys at Portsmouth, N.H.
The Poor Sick Men
The Power of Love
A Race for a Kiss
A Rich Revenge
The Rocky Road
Runaway Match

Scenes and Incidents, Russo-Japanese Peace Conference, Portsmouth, N.H.
Skidoo Brothers, 23
The Speed Demon
Sunshine Sue
That Little Band of Gold
They Would Elope
Those Bitter Sweets
The Trials and Troubles of an Automobilist
A Trip to Berkeley, Cal.
Trying to Fool Uncle
A Unique Race Between Elephant, Bicycle, Camel, Horse, and Automobile
Unveiling of the Pennsylvania Monument on the Battlefields of Petersburg, Virginia, May 19, 1909
The Vampire Dancer
The Wages of Sin
The War of Wealth
When a Man Loves
When Love Took Wings
The Widow and the Only Man
The Wife
Woman Against Woman
The Woman in Black
The Would-Be Shriner

Automobile races

Automobile Race for the Vanderbilt Cup
Automobiling Among the Clouds
Ormond, Florida Auto Races
A Unique Race Between Elephant, Bicycle, Camel, Horse, and Automobile

Avalon, Catalina Island, California

Gussle Rivals Jonah

Avery, Charles, actor

Fatty's New Role
Gussle Tied to Trouble
Gussle's Backward Way
The Helping Hand
Hogan the Porter
Hogan's Mussy Job
Neighbors
A Strange Meeting
'Tis an Ill Wind That Blows No Good
Twin Brothers
The Usurer
The Valet's Wife
Was Justice Served?
Won By a Fish

Avon, New Jersey

High Diving

Bahama Islands

Native Woman Washing a Negro Baby in Nassau, B.I.

Baiquiri, Cuba

Mules Swimming Ashore at Baiquiri, Cuba
U.S. Troops Landing at Daiquiri, Cuba

Balboa, California

The Sands of Dee

Baldwin, Lucky Ranch

California Limited, A.T. & S.F.R.R.

Balloons; *see* Airplanes and balloons

Baltimore, Maryland

The Great Baltimore Fire
Panorama of Ruins From Baltimore and Charles Street
Panorama of Ruins From Lombard and Charles Street
Panorama of Ruins From Lombard and Hanover Streets, Baltimore
Panorama of Ruins From Water Front

Bambrick, Gertrude, actress

The Billionaire
The Genius
Liberty Belles
The Rejuvenation of Aunt Mary
Who's Looney Now?

Banners; *see* Flags, banners, and pennants

Barges; *see* Ships and watercraft

Barker, Admiral

President Roosevelt's Visit to Admiral Barker

Barker, Florence, actress

An Affair of Hearts
An Awful Moment
The Call
A Child's Faith
Choosing a Husband
The Course of True Love
The Dancing Girl of Butte
Effecting a Cure
Faithful
A Fool's Revenge
Getting Even
Gold Is Not All
The Gold Seekers
Happy Jack, A Hero
Her Father's Pride
Her Terrible Ordeal
The Impalement
In Little Italy
The Kid
A Knot in the Plot

The Love of Lady Irma
The Message
A Midnight Cupid
The Newlyweds
The Oath and the Man
The Passing of a Grouch
A Summer Idyl
A Summer Tragedy
The Tenderfoot's Triumph
Two Women and a Man
Unexpected Help
A Victim of Jealousy
The Way of the World
What's Your Hurry?
A Wreath of Orange Blossoms

Barker, Reginald, director

The Bargain
The Devil
The Italian
On the Night Stage

Barnes, George, actor

The Great Train Robbery

Barr, Clarence, actor

The Rejuvenation of Aunt Mary

Barriscale, Bessie, actress

The Cup of Life
The Devil

Barrymore, Lionel, actor

Classmates
Men and Women
The Power of the Press
Strongheart
Woman Against Woman
The Woman in Black

Bartho, Cathrina

A Nymph of the Waves

Baseball

The Ball Game
Casey at the Bat
Christy Mathewson, N.Y. National
League Baseball Team

Bath Beach, New York

Diving Through Hoops

Bay Shore, New York

Fancy Driving

Battleships; see Ships and water-
craft

Bayonne, New Jersey

Burning of the Standard Oil Co.'s
Tanks, Bayonne, N.J.
The Course of True Love

Bears

The Brave Hunter
Feeding the Bear at the Menagerie

Feeding the Russian Bear
Fun in Camp
Oh, Those Eyes!
Trick Bears

Beaudine, William, actor

A Close Call
Neighbors
A Summer Tragedy
Those Hicksville Boys
To Save Her Soul
The Tragedy of a Dress Suit
Winning Back His Love

Beaumont, Texas

New Sunset Limited

Beban, George, actor

The Italian

Bech, Philip, actor

Homeless

Beckley, Beatrice, actress

The Prisoner of Zenda

Bedloe's Island

Statue of Liberty

Beirut

Arabian Jewish Dance
Passengers Embarking From S.S.
"Augusta Victoria" at Beyrouth
Panoramic View of Beyrouth, Syria,
Showing Holiday Festivities

Belasco, David, author

The Charity Ball

Belcher and Waterson

Poor John

Belmont Park, New York

Crowd Entering Futurity Day

Bennett, Billie, actress

Ambrose's Fury
Beating Hearts and Carpets
Court House Crooks
Curses! They Remarked
Droppington's Family Tree
Fatty's Chance Acquaintance
Gussle's Wayward Path
Hash House Mashers
Love in Armor
A Lover's Lost Control
A Lucky Leap
Mabel, Fatty and the Law
Miss Fatty's Seaside Lovers
Peanuts and Bullets
The Rent Jumpers
When Ambrose Dared Walrus

Beqnon, Bleuette, actress

The Fairyland, or, the Kingdom of
the Fairies

Berkeley, California

A Trip to Berkeley, Cal.

Bernard, Dorothy, actress

An Awful Moment
The Black Sheep
The Cord of Life
Fate's Turning
The Female of the Species
The Final Settlement
A Flash of Light
The Girl and Her Trust
The Girls and Daddy
The Goddess of Sagebrush Gulch
Heaven Avenges
Her First Biscuits
His Lesson
Iola's Promise
A Midnight Adventure
One Is Business, the Other Crime
The Root of Evil
A Summer Idyl
The Two Paths
When Kings Were the Law
The Woman From Mellon's

Bernard, Harry, actor

Dirty Work in a Laundry

Bernhardt, Sarah, actress

Queen Elizabeth

Bertelsen, Ingeborg Bruhn, ac-
tress

The Vampire Dancer

Beverly Hills, California

Gentlemen of Nerve

Bicycles

Bicycle Paced Race
Bicycle Trick Riding, no. 2
Carriers Leaving Building, U.S.P.O.
Colored Villainy
The Coney Island Bikers
The Dude and the Bathing Girls
Fatty's Plucky Pup
Girls Playing See-Saw
His First Ride
Multicycle Race
Neighbors
New York Police Parade, June 1st,
1899
On the Road
Paced Bicycle Race
Panoramic View of the Champs
Elysees
Parke Davis' Employees
Professional Handicap Bicycle Race
Ruhlin in His Training Quarters
Special Delivery Messenger,
U.S.P.O.
Stanford University, California
Street Scene in Yokohama, no. 1
Those Bitter Sweets

The Passing of a Grouch
The Peach-Basket Hat
Pippa Passes
A Plain Song
The Poor Sick Men
Pranks
The Primitive Man
The Proposal
The Punishment
The Purgation
Ramona
The Recreation of an Heiress
The Redman's View
The Renunciation
The Restoration
Resurrection
A Rich Revenge
The Rocky Road
A Romance of the Western Hills
The Root of Evil
Rose O' Salem-Town
A Salutary Lesson
The Sands of Dee
The School Teacher and the Waif
The Sealed Room
Serious Sixteen
1776, or, the Hessian Renegades
The Seventh Day
Simple Charity
The Slave
The Smoker
The Song of the Wildwood Flute
The Son's Return
The Sorrows of the Unfaithful
A Spanish Dilemma
The Speed Demon
The Spirit Awakened
A Strange Meeting
A Summer Idyl
A Summer Tragedy
Sunshine Sue
Sweet and Twenty
Sweet Revenge
Taming a Husband
A Temporary Truce
The Tenderfoot's Triumph
The Test
That Chink at Golden Gulch
Their First Kidnapping Case
They Would Elope
Those Hicksville Boys
Thou Shalt Not
The Thread of Destiny
Through the Breakers
To Save Her Soul
Tomboy Bessie
The Tourists
The Tragedy of a Dress Suit
A Trap for Santa Claus
The Trick That Failed
The Troublesome Baby
Trying to Fool Uncle
Turning the Tables
The Twisted Trail
The Two Brothers

Two Little Waifs
Two Memories
The Two Paths
Two Women and a Man
The Unchanging Sea
Unexpected Help
Up a Tree
The Usurer
A Victim of Jealousy
The Violin Maker of Cremona
A Voice From the Deep
Waiter No. 5
Wanted, A Child
Was Justice Served?
The Way of Man
The Way of the World
What Drink Did
What the Daisy Said
What the Doctor Ordered
What's Your Hurry?
When a Man Loves
When Kings Were the Law
When the Fire-Bells Rang
When We Were in Our Teens
White Roses
Wilful Peggy
Willie Becomes an Artist
Winning Back His Love
With Her Card
With the Enemy's Help
The Woman From Mellon's
Won By a Fish
The Would-Be Shriner
A Wreath of Orange Blossoms
see also American Mutoscope and
  Biograph Co.

Birds

Allabad; the Arabian Wizard
An Animated Luncheon
As It Is in Life
Biograph's Improved Incubator
A Bird's a Bird
Children Feeding Ducklings
The Children's Friend
Edgar Allen [i.e. Allan] Poe
Feeding Geese at Newman's Poultry
  Farm
Feeding Pigeons in Front of St.
  Mark's Cathedral, Venice, Italy
Feeding Sea Gulls
The Feud and the Turkey
A Filipino Cock Fight
Grandpa's Reading Glass
How Duck's Are Fattened
Lena and the Geese
[On] A [Good Old] Five Cent
  Trolley Ride
Ostrich Farm
Ostrich Farms at Pasadena
Ostriches Feeding
Ostriches Running, no. 1
Ostriches Running, no. 2
Pigeon Farm at Los Angeles, Cal.
Quail Shooting at Pinehurst

A Raid on a Cock Fight
Schneider's Anti-Noise Crusade
Sea Gulls Following Fishing Boats
Sea Gulls in Central Park
Stolen by Gypsies
A Sweet Little Home in the Country
Tomboy Bessie
Two Hours After Chickens Leave
  the Shells
Who Said Chicken?
Who's Got the Red Ear?
A Wild Turkey Hunt
Willie's Vacation

Bitzer, G. W., cameraman

The Abductors
The Adjustable Bed
After Many Years
Airy Fairy Lillian Tries on Her New
  Corsets
Al Treloar in Muscle Exercises
Alone
Always Room for One More
The American Soldier in Love and
  War, no. 1– no. 3
And a Little Child Shall Lead Them
Another Name Was Maude
Arab Act, Luna Park
An Arcadian Maid
Arrival of Emigrants [i.e. Immi-
  grants], Ellis Island
Arrival of Train at Muskoka Wharf
Arrival of Train, Cheyenne
The Artist's Studio
As It Is In Life
As the Bells Rang Out
At the Altar
At the Dressmaker's
At the French Ball
The Athletic Girl and the Burglar,
  no. 1
The Athletic Girl and the Burglar,
  no. 2
Attack on Fort Boonesboro
Auto Boat Race on the Hudson
Automobile Race for the Vanderbilt
  Cup
Automobiling Among the Clouds
The Awakening
The Baby
The Baby and the Puppies
Baby in a Rage
Baby Playing in Gutter
Baby's Day
A Baby's Shoe
The Bad Boy and the Grocery Man
The Badger Game
A Ballroom Tragedy
The Bamboo Slide
The Banker's Daughters
The Barbarian Ingomar
The Barber's Dee-light
The Barber's Pretty Patient
The Barnstormers
The Battle at Elderbush Gulch

400

The Modern Prodigal
A Modern Sappho
A Mohawk's Way
Money Mad
Monkey Business
The Moonshiner
Moose Hunt in New Brunswick
Mount Stephen
The Mountaineer's Honor
The Narrow Road
The Necklace
The Necromancer
Nevada Falls
New Brooklyn Bridge
A New Trick
New York Athletic Club Games, Travers Island
N.Y. Fire Department Returning
The Newlyweds
A Night at the Haymarket
The Night of the Party
The Note in the Shoe
Nursing a Viper
The Oath and the Man
Obstacle Race
Oh, Uncle!
The Old Actor
Old Isaacs the Pawnbroker
On the Beach at Brighton
On the Flying Rings
On the Reef
On the Road
One Busy Hour
One Is Business, the Other Crime
One Night and Then
One Thousand Mile Tree
One Touch of Nature
The Open Gate
Opening Day, Jamestown Exposition
Opening the Williamsburg Bridge
Ore the Banster
Ormond, Fla. Auto Races
Orphan Children on the Beach at Coney Island
"Osler"-ising Papa
'Ostler Joe
An Outcast Among Outcasts
The Outlaw
Over Silent Paths
Over the Hills to the Poorhouse
Overland Limited
A Pair of Queens
The Pajama Girl
Panorama From the Tower of the Brooklyn Bridge
The Paymaster
Peace Envoys at Portsmouth, N.H.
The Peach-Basket Hat
Peeping Tom in the Dressing Room
Pennsylvania Tunnel Excavation
Personal
The Physical Culture Girl, no. 1
The Physical Culture Girl, no. 2
The Physical Culture Girl, no. 3

Physical Culture Lesson
The Pillow Fight, no. 2
A Pipe Dream
A Pipe Story of the Fourth
Pippa Passes
The Pirate's Gold
A Plain Song
The Planter's Wife
Play Ball on the Beach
Pole Vaulting
Police Raid at a Dog Fight
Politician's Love Story
Polo Game: Myopia vs. Dedham
Pompey's Honey Girl
Poor Hooligan, So Hungry Too
A Poor Place for Love Making
President McKinley Leaving Observatory, Mt. Tom, Holyoke, Massachusetts
President Roosevelt Addressing Crew of "Kearsarge"
President Roosevelt at Lynn, Mass.
President Roosevelt's Arrival at "Kearsarge"
President Roosevelt's Departure from "Kearsarge"
Pres. Roosevelt's Fourth of July Oration
President Roosevelt's Homecoming
President Roosevelt's Visit to Admiral Barker
The Prima Donna's Understudy
The Princess in the Vase
The Professor of the Drama
The Providence Light Artillery
The Prussian Spy
Pulling Off the Bed Clothes
The Punishment
The Purgation
Quail Shooting at Pinehurst
The Racing Chutes at Dreamland
A Raid on a Cock Fight
Ramona
The Rat Trap Pickpocket Detector
Reading the Death Sentence
Reception of British Fleet
The Reckoning
The Redman's View
The Rehearsal
The Renunciation
Reproduction, Nan Paterson's Trial
Reproduction of Jeffries-Corbett Contest
The Restoration
Resurrection
Returning to China
Reuben in the Subway
A Rich Revenge
The River Pirates
Robbed of Her All
Rock Drill at Work in Subway
The Rock of Ages
The Rocky Road
Romance of a Jewess
Romance of an Egg

A Romance of the Western Hills
The Root of Evil
The Rose
Rose O' Salem-Town
The Roue's Heart
Rough House in a New York Honky-Tonk
Rube in an Opium Joint
A Rube in the Subway
A Rude Hostess
Run of N.Y. Fire Department
Rural Elopement
The Sacrifice
Sailors Waltzing
Salmon Fishing Nipissisquit
A Salutary Lesson
The Salvation Army Lass
San Francisco Disaster
The Sands of Dee
Scene in a Rat Pit
Schneider's Anti-Noise Crusade
The School Teacher and the Waif
Scrubbing Clothes
The Sculptor's Nightmare
The Sealed Room
A Search for the Evidence
The Seashore Baby
Seeing Boston
Serious Sixteen
1776, or, the Hessian Renegades
The Seventh Day
She Fell Fainting Into His Arms
Sheep and Lambs
Sherman Hill Tunnel
Shooters' Parade, Philadelphia
Shooting the Chutes at Luna Park
Shooting the Chutes, Luna Park
Shortening and Furling Sails
Silhouette Scene
Silveon and Emerie "On the Web"
Simple Charity
The Simple Life
Skidoo Brothers, 23
The Slave
The Sleepy Soubrette
Slide for Life, Luna Park
The Slocum Disaster
Small Gun Drill, St. John's Academy
Smallest Train in the World
A Smoked Husband
The Snowman
Society Ballooning, Pittsfield, Mass.
The Society Palmist
Song of the Shirt
The Song of the Wildwood Flute
The Son's Return
The Sorrows of the Unfaithful
A Sound Sleeper
Sparring at the N.Y.A.C.
Special Delivery Messenger, U.S.P.O.
Speed Trials, Autoboat Challenger
The Spirit Awakened
Spirit of '76
The Stage Rustler

Stealing a Dinner
Steam Tactics
Steamboat and Great Eastern Rock
Steamship "Express of India"
Stern's Duplex Railway
The Stolen Jewels
A Strange Meeting
The Subpoena Server
The Suicide Club
The Summer Boarders
A Summer Idyl
Sunshine Sue
Sweet and Twenty
Sweet Revenge
Sweets for the Sweet
The Swimming Class
Swimming Pool, Palm Beach
A Swimming Race at Coney Island
Symphony in "A-Flat"
Taming a Husband
Taming of the Shrew
Teasing
A Temporary Truce
Tenderloin Tragedy
A Terrible Night
Terrier vs. Wild Cat
The Test
The Test of Friendship
That Chink at Golden Gulch
Thaw-White Tragedy
They Meet on the Mat
They Would Elope
The Thirteen Club
Thompson's Night Out
Those Awful Hats
Those Boys
Thou Shalt Not
Through the Breakers
'Tis an Ill Wind That Blows No Good
To Save Her Soul
Tom, Tom, the Piper's Son
A Too Ardent Lover
The Topers
Tragic Love
A Trap for Santa Claus
Trap Pigeon Shooting
Trial Marriages
The Trick That Failed
A Trip on the Catskill Mt. Ry
A Trip to Salt Lake City
A Troublesome Satchel
Trout Fishing, Rangeley Lakes
The Truants
Trying to Get Arrested
Tunnel Number Three
The Twisted Trail
2 A.M. in the Subway
Two Bottle Babies
The Two Brothers
Two Little Waifs
Two Memories
The Two Paths
Two Women and a Man
The Unchanging Sea

Under the Bamboo Tree
Under the Old Apple Tree
Unexpected Help
The Unfaithful Wife: Part 1, The Lover
The Unfaithful Wife: Part 2, The Fight
The Unfaithful Wife: Part 3, Murder and Suicide
A Unique Race Between Elephant, Bicycle, Camel, Horse, and Automobile
Unlucky at Cards, Lucky at Love
An Unprotected Female
An Unprotected Female, no. 2
The Usurer
The Vaidis Sisters, Luna Park
The Valet's Wife
The Vaquero's Vow
A Victim of Circumstantial Evidence
A Victim of Jealousy
The Village Cut-Up
The Violin Maker of Cremona
The Voice of the Violin
The Wages of Sin: Murder Part 1
The Wages of Sin: Retribution Part 2
Waiter No. 5
Wanted, A Child
Was Justice Served?
Water Duel
Wawona, Big Tree
The Way of the World
The Wedding
Weighing the Baby
A Welcome Burglar
Welding the Big Ring
A Welsh Rabbit
Westinghouse Air Brake Company
Westinghouse Works
What Drink Did
What the Daisy Said
What's Your Hurry?
When a Man Loves
When Kings Were the Law
When Knights Were Bold
Where Breakers Roar
White Fox Motor Boat
Why Foxy Grandpa Escaped a Ducking
The Widow and the Only Man
A Wild Turkey Hunt
Wilful Peggy
Willie Westinghouse and the Doctor's Battery
Willie's Camera
The Wine Opener
Wine, Women & Song
Winning Back His Love
With Her Card
The Woman From Mellon's
The Wooden Leg
A Wreath in Time
A Wreath of Orange Blossoms

Wrestling at the New York Athletic Club
The Yale Laundry
The Yellow Peril
You Will Send Me to Bed, Eh?
The Zulu's Heart

Black Maria Studio, West Orange, N.J.

Bowery Waltz
Crissie Sheridan
Edison Kinetoscopic Record of a Sneeze, January 7, 1894
Poker at Dawson City

Blacks

The American Soldier in Love and War, no. 3
Bally-Hoo Cake Walk
A Bucket of Cream Ale
Cake Walk
A Close Call
Colored Troops Disembarking
Colored Villainy
Comedy Cake Walk
Cotton Spinning
Dancing Darkey Boy
Dixon-Chester Leon Contest
Everybody Works But Father (Black-face)
The Feud and the Turkey
The 'Gator and the Pickaninny
The Gold Dust Twins
The Guerrilla
A Hard Wash
His Trust
His Trust Fulfilled
How Charlie Lost the Heiress
A Kiss in the Dark
Laughing Ben
Military Drill of Kikuyu Tribes and Other Native Ceremonies
The Mis-Directed Kiss
Mixed Babies
Native Woman Washing a Negro Baby in Nassau, B. I.
Nellie, the Beautiful Housemaid
A Nigger in the Woodpile
Pompey's Honey Girl
A Scrap in Black and White
The Seeress
The Snowman
The Subpoena Server
The Thirteen Club
Uncle Tom's Cabin
Under the Old Apple Tree
The Unfaithful Odalisque
The Valet's Wife
Watermelon Contest
What Happened in the Tunnel
While Strolling in the Park
Who Said Chicken?
The Zulu's Heart

Blackton, J. Stuart, actor and producer

The Enchanted Drawing
Humorous Phases of Funny Faces

Blad, Augusta, actress

Midsummer-Tide
Vengeance

Blair, dog

Rescued by Rover

Bleckyrden, W., cameraman

Honolulu Street Scene
Kanakas Diving for Money, no. 1
Kanakas Diving for Money, no. 2
S.S. "Coptic"
S.S. "Coptic" Coaling
S.S. "Coptic" Lying To
S.S. "Coptic" Running Against the Storm
S.S. "Coptic" Running Before a Gale
S.S. "Doric"
S.S. "Doric" in Mid-Ocean
S.S. "Gaelic" at Nagasaki
Shanghai Police
Shanghai Street Scene, Scene 1
Shanghai Street Scene, Scene 2
Sheik Artillery, Hong Kong
Street Scene in Hong Kong
Street Scene in Yokohama, no. 1
Street Scene in Yokohama, no. 2
Theatre Road, Yokohama
Tourists Starting for Canton
Wharf Scene, Honolulu

Bliss, Oklahoma Territory

Brush Between Cowboys and Indians
Bucking Broncos
Cowboys and Indians Fording River in a Wagon
Driving Cattle to Pasture
Herding Horses Across a River
Rounding Up and Branding Cattle
Western Stage Coach Hold Up

Blom, Agnete, actress

Love and Friendship

Blom, August, actor

The Aeroplane Inventor
Desdemona
The Little Railroad Queen
Love in the Tropics
Midsummer-Tide
The Power of Love
The Rights of Youth
The Two Convicts
The Vampire Dancer
Vengeance

Boat races

America's Cup Race

Auto Boat Race on the Hudson
Boat Race
Boats Under Oars
Cornell-Columbia-University of Pennsylvania Boat Race at Ithaca, N.Y., Showing Lehigh Valley Observation Train
Ice-Boat Racing at Red Bank, N.J.
Ice Boating on the North Shrewsbury, Red Bank, N.J.
Ice Yacht Racing
Ice Yachting
Inter-Collegiate Regatta, Poughkeepsie, New York, 1904
A Mile in 56 Seconds
New York Athletic Club Crew at Phila., Pa.
Start of Ocean Race for Kaiser's Cup
War Canoe Race
see also America's Cup Race

Boats; see America's Cup Races; Boat races; Ships and watercraft

Boer War

Battle of Mafeking
Boer Commissary Train Treking
The Boer War
Boers Bringing in British Prisoners
Capture of Boer Battery
Capture of Boer Battery by British
Charge of Boer Cavalry
English Lancers Charging
Red Cross Ambulance on Battlefield

Boesen, Axel, actor

The Fire of Life
Love and Friendship
Vengeance

Bonine, Robert K., cameraman

The Accomodating Cow
Alphonse and Gaston
Alphonse and Gaston Helping Irishman
Around the Mulberry Bush
Arrival of Train, Tien-Tsin
Arrival of Train, Tokio, Japan
Artist's Point
Asakusa Temple, Tokio, Japan
At the Fountain
Beginning of a Skyscraper
Biograph's Improved Incubator
The Bowery Kiss
Boys Diving, Honolulu
The Boys Help Themselves to Foxy Grandpa's Cigars
The Boys, Still Determined, Try It Again on Foxy Grandpa, With the Same Result
The Boys Think They Have One on Foxy Grandpa, But He Fools Them

The Boys Try to Put One Up on Foxy Grandpa
Bridge Traffic, Manila
The Burd [i.e. Bund], Shanghai
Cascade Near Wawona, California
The Ch-ien-men Gate, Pekin
Chums
Church "Our Lady of Grace," Hoboken
Coaching Party, Yosemite Valley
Coaling a Steamer, Nagasaki Bay, Japan
A Corner in the Play Room
The Creators of Foxy Grandpa
Crowd Entering Futurity Day
Cutting Sugar Cane
A Delusion
The Draped Model
Eeling Through Ice
Excavation for Subway
A Filipino Cock Fight
Foxy Grandpa and Polly in a Little Hilarity
Foxy Grandpa Shows the Boys a Trick or Two With the Tramp
Foxy Grandpa Tells the Boys a Funny Story
Fun in [A] Photograph Gallery
Futurity
Glacier Point
The Gold Dust Twins
Grandpa's Reading Glass
Horses Loading for Klondike, no. 9
Ice Yacht Racing
In a Manicure Parlor
In a Massage Parlor
Japanese Fencing
Kent House Slide
The King of Detectives
The Lamp Explodes
Lawn Party
The Light That Didn't Fail
A Little Mix-Up in a Mixed Ale Joint
Lively Brushes on Speedway
Loading Baggage for Klondike, no. 6
Loading Sugar Cane
The Lover's Knot
Lower Broadway
The Manicure Fools the Husband
The Meteor
A Mile in 56 Seconds
Milking Time
Old Volunteer Fire Department
Ox Carts, Tokio, Japan
Pack Train on the Chilcoot Pass
Packers on the Trail
Panorama From Incline Railway
Panorama From Running Incline Railway
Panorama, Golden Gate
Panorama of Flatiron Building
Panorama of Kobe Harbor, Japan
Parade of Horses on Speedway
A Poet's Revenge

A Potato Bake in the Woods
President Roosevelt's Inauguration
Prince Henry at West Point
A Private Supper at Hellar's
Quebec Fire Dept. on Runners
Rex's Bath
Rickshaw Parade, Japan
Rocking Gold in the Klondike
A Romp on the Lawn
S.S. "Williamette" Leaving for Klondike
Sampans Racing Toward Liner
She Meets With Wife's Approval
Shut Up!
Skee Club
The Slippery Slide
A Spill
Street Scene, Tokio, Japan
Sweethearts
They Found the Leak
Tourists Arriving at Wawona Hotel
Train of Sugar Cane
Wash-Day
Washing Gold on 20 Above Hunker, Klondike
Water Nymphs
Wrinkles Removed

Booker, Harry, actor

The Cannon Ball
Do-Re-Mi—Boom!
Droppington's Family Tree
From Patches to Plenty
A One Night Stand

Bookmiller, E. V.

Battle Flags of the 9th Infantry

Booth, Elmer, actor

A Beast at Bay
The Narrow Road

Bordeaux, Joe, actor

Fatty and Mabel's Simple Life
Fatty's Faithful Fido
Fatty's New Role
Fatty's Plucky Pup
Fatty's Tintype Tangle
From Patches to Plenty
Gentlemen of Nerve
The Little Teacher
Mabel and Fatty's Wash Day
Mabel, Fatty and the Law
Mabel's Wilful Way
Miss Fatty's Seaside Lovers
When Love Took Wings
Willful Ambrose
Wished on Mabel

Borzage, Frank, actor

The Cup of Life

Boston, Massachusetts

Admiral Dewey at State House, Boston

Ancient and Honourable Artillery of London on Parade
Ancient and Honourables of London Homeward Bound
The Boston Horseless Fire Department
Boston School Cadets, 3rd Regiment
Canoeing at Riverside
Canoeing on the Charles River, Boston, Mass.
Canoeing Scene
Midwinter Bathing, L Street Bath, Boston
Paced Bicycle Race
Panoramic View of Boston Subway From an Electric Car
Seeing Boston
Shooting the Chutes
Sleighing Scene, Boston
Sleighs Returning After a Spin
Stallion Race

Boxer Rebellion

The Bengal Lancers
Bombardment of Taku Forts, by the Allied Fleets
British Light Artillery
A Cavalry Charge
Cossack Cavalry
English Lancers Charging
The Forbidden City, Pekin
The Fourth Ghorkhas
Hong Kong Regiment nos. 1 & 2
Review of Russian Artillery
Russian Sharp Shooters
Shanghai Police
Sheik Artillery, Hong Kong
6th Cavalry Assaulting South Gate of Pekin
see also Peking, China; Shanghai, China; Tien-Tsin, China

Boxing

The Billionaire
Boxing for Points
Boxing Horses, Luna Park, Coney Island
Comedy Set-to
Dixon-Chester Leon Contest
Expert Bag Punching
A Fight for a Bride
Gans-Nelson Contest, Goldfield, Nevada, September 3rd, 1906
Gordon Sisters Boxing
Hogan's Romance Upset
Impersonation of Britt-Nelson Fight
International Contest for the Heavyweight Championship: Squires vs. Burns, Ocean View, Cal., July 4th, 1907
Jack Johnson vs. Jim Flynn Contest for the Heavyweight Championship of the World, Las Vegas, New Mexico, July 4, 1912

Jeffries [i.e. Jeffreys] and Ruhlin Sparring Contest at San Francisco, Cal. Nov. 15, 1901—Five Rounds
Jeffreys in His Training Quarters
Jim Jeffries on His California Ranch
The Last Round Ended in a Free Fight
The Lucky Wishbone
Mr. Butt-In
Nelson-Britt Prize Fight
O'Brien-Burns Contest, Los Angeles, Cal., Nov. 26, 1906
One-Round O'Brien
Prize Fight
Reproduction of Corbett-McGovern Fight
Reproduction of Jeffries-Corbett Contest
Ruhlin in His Training Quarters
A Scrap in Black and White
Sparring at the N.Y.A.C.
Sparring Match on the "Kearsarge"
Squires, Australian Champion, in His Training Quarters

Boyd, Aline, actress

The Kleptomaniac

Boynton, Capt.

Capt. Boynton Feeding His Pets

Bracey, Clara T., actress

At the Altar
A Baby's Shoe
The Cord of Life
The Curtain Pole
Edgar Allen [i.e. Allan] Poe
Eloping with Aunty
A Fair Rebel
The Feud and the Turkey
The Girls and Daddy
The Helping Hand
Her First Biscuits
I Did It, Mamma
The Joneses Have Amateur Theatricals
Lady Helen's Escapade
Lure of the Gown
The Maniac Cook
The Medicine Bottle
The Note in the Shoe
A Peach-Basket Hat
Pippa Passes
Resurrection
The Salvation Army Lass
Schneider's Anti-Noise Crusade
The Son's Return
Those Boys
Tragic Love
A Troublesome Satchel
Twin Brothers
Two Memories
The Violin Maker of Cremona
The Voice of the Violin

A Wreath in Time

Brady, William A.

The Creators of Foxy Grandpa

Brammall, Jack, actor

Beverly of Graustark
A Fair Rebel
The Gambler of the West
The War of Wealth
The Wife

Brechling, Nicolai, actor

Desdemona
The Two Convicts

Bremen, Germany

Flying Train

Brentwood, California

Never Again!

Brick Church, New Jersey

The Wedding

Bridges and trestles

Ambrose's Little Hatchet
Aunt Sallie's Wonderful Bustle
Bridge Traffic, Manila
Circular Panorama of Suspension
  Bridge and American Falls
Council Bluffs Bridge Station
The Course of True Love
Crossing Ice Bridge at Niagara Falls
Duke of York at Montreal and
  Quebec
Frankenstein's Trestle
Gap Entrance to Rocky Mountains
The Georgetown Loop
Grand Hotel to Big Indian
In the Valley of the Esopus
Into the Heart of the Catskills
Las Vigas Canal, Mexico
The Little Teacher
Lively Brushes on Speedway
Love, Speed and Thrills
New Brooklyn Bridge
New Brooklyn to New York via
  Brooklyn Bridge, no. 1
New Brooklyn to New York via
  Brooklyn Bridge, no. 2
On to Brooklyn, no. 1
Opening of New East River Bridge,
  New York
Opening the Williamsburg Bridge
Panorama from Gondola, St. Louis
  Exposition
Panorama, Golden Gate
Panorama, Great Gorge Route Over
  Lewiston Bridge
Panorama of Gorge Railway
Panorama Water Front and Brook-
  lyn Bridge from East River
Panoramic View Near Mt. Golden
  on the Canadian Pacific R.R.

Panoramic View of Brooklyn Bridge
Panoramic View of Charleston Ex-
  position
Panoramic View of the Golden Gate
Panoramic View of the Place de
  l'Concord
Panoramic View of the White Pass
  Railroad
Parade of Horses on Speedway
Paris from the Seine
Police Boats Escorting Naval Parade
Pontoon Bridge Building
Prince Henry Arriving at West Point
Prince Henry at Niagara Falls
The Racing Chutes at Dreamland
Rapids Below Suspension Bridge
Seeing New York by Yacht
Shooting the Chutes at Luna Park
Sky Scrapers of New York City,
  From the North River
Sliding Down Ice Mound at Niagara
  Falls
Sweet Revenge
A Trip Around the Pan-American
  Exposition
A Trip on the Catskill Mt. Ry
Triumphal Bridge, Pan-American
  Exposition
Tunnel Number Three
The Village Cut-up
Washington Bridge and Speedway

Brighton Beach, New York

Beach Race Track, July 4, 1906
Bertha Claiche
The Boer War
General Cronje & Mystic Shriners
Head-on Collision at Brighton
  Beach Race Track, July 4th, 1906
Ludlow's Aerodrome
Ludlow's Aeroplane, no. 2

Briscoe, Lottie, actress

She Would Be an Actress

Britt, Jimmy, boxer

Impersonation of Britt-Nelson Fight
Nelson-Britt Prize Fight

Brockwell, Billie, actress

Droppington's Devilish Deed
Droppington's Family Tree
Hash House Mashers
His Luckless Love
Hogan Out West
Hogan's Aristocratic Dream
Hogan's Mussy Job
Hogan's Romance Upset
The Little Teacher
Love in Armor
Settled at the Seaside
That Little Band of Gold
Those College Girls
When Ambrose Dared Walrus

Brockwell, Gladys, actress

On the Night Stage

Brooklyn, New York

Academy of Music Fire
Automobile Parade on the Coney
  Island Boulevard
"Exempt" of Brooklyn, N.Y.
Funeral of Hiram Cronk
Human Apes From the Orient
Launch of Battleship "Connecticut"
The Lost Child
New Brooklyn to New York Via
  Brooklyn Bridge, no. 1
New Brooklyn to New York Via
  Brooklyn Bridge, no. 2
"Oceans" Fire Company
Parsifal: Parsifal Ascends the
  Throne, Ruins of Magic Garden,
  Exterior of Klingson's Castle,
  Magic Garden, Interior of the
  Temple, Scene Outside the Tem-
  ple, Return of Parsifal In the
  Woods
Polo Game, Myopia vs. Dedham
Return of Troop C, Brooklyn
Sheep and Lambs
The Widow and the Only Man

Browne, Kenneth, actor

Rumpelstiltskin

Bruce, Kate, actress

All on Account of the Milk
An Arcadian Maid
As It Is In Life
At the Altar
The Awakening
An Awful Moment
The Battle at Elderbush Gulch
Behind the Scenes
The Better Way
The Broken Doll
The Broken Locket
A Change of Heart
The Child of the Ghetto
Choosing a Husband
The Cloister's Touch
A Close Call
Confidence
The Converts
A Corner in Wheat
The Country Doctor
A Dash Through the Clouds
The Duke's Plan
Effecting a Cure
The Engagement Ring
The Englishman and the Girl
Examination Day at School
A Fair Exchange
The Fugitive
The Furs
Gold Is Not All
A Gold Necklace
The Gold Seekers

Golden Louis
Greaser's Gauntlet
Happy Jack, A Hero
Her Father's Pride
His Duty
His Last Burglary
His Lost Love
His Own Fault
His Trust
His Wife's Sweethearts
Homefolks
Hot Stuff
How Hubby Got a Raise
The Iconoclast
The Impalement
In a Hempen Bag
In Old Kentucky
In the Watches of the Night
An Indian Summer
The Italian Barber
Judith of Bethulia
Just Like a Woman
A Knot in the Plot
The Leading Man
Lena and the Geese
The Light That Came
Lines of White on a Sullen Sea
The Little Teacher
A Lucky Toothache
The Masher
May and December
A Midnight Adventure
The Midnight Marauder
The Modern Prodigal
The Mountaineer's Honor
Muggsy Becomes a Hero
The Newlyweds
The Old Actor
One Is Business, the Other Crime
One Night and Then
The Open Gate
A Plain Song
The Poor Sick Men
The Punishment
Ramona
The Rocky Road
A Romance of the Western Hills
The School Teacher and the Waif
1776, or, the Hessian Renegades
Simple Charity
The Slave
The Spirit Awakened
A Strange Meeting
The Tragedy of a Dress Suit
They Would Elope
Through the Breakers
To Save Her Soul
Tragic Love
A Trap for Santa Claus
The Trick That Failed
Trying to Get Arrested
The Twisted Trail
The Two Brothers
Two Little Waifs
Two Women and a Man

The Usurer
Waiter No. 5
Wanted, A Child
What the Daisy Said
What's Your Hurry?
When the Fire-Bells Rang
White Roses
Wilful Peggy
Won By a Fish
The Would-Be Shriner
A Wreath of Orange Blossoms

Bruun, Cajus, actor

Midsummer-Tide

Bryan, William Jennings

President McKinley's Speech at the Pan-American Exposition
The Sculptor's Nightmare

Buck, Frederik, actor

The Power of Love

Buemann, Edith, actress

Love in the Tropics
Vengeance

Buffalo, New York

Bally-Hoo Cake Walk
Buffalo Fire Department
Buffalo Fire Department in Action
Buffalo Police on Parade
Buffalo Stockyards
Circular Panorama of Electric Tower
Cotton Spinning
Electric Tower
Esquimaux Game of Snap-the-Whip
Esquimaux Leap-Frog
The Esquimaux Village
A Flock of Export Sheep
Horse Parade at the Pan-American Exposition
Japanese Village
Laughing Ben
The Mob Outside the Temple of Music at the Pan-American Exposition
Opening, Pan-American Exposition
Ostrich Farm
Pan-American Exposition by Night
Panorama of Esplanade by Night
Panoramic View of Electric Tower From a Balloon
President McKinley Reviewing the Troops at the Pan-American Exposition
President McKinley's Funeral Cortege at Buffalo, New York
President McKinley's Speech at the Pan-American Exposition
Sham Battle at the Pan-American Exposition
Spanish Dancers at the Pan-American Exposition

Tally-Ho Departing for the Races
A Trip Around the Pan-American Exposition
Triumphal Bridge, Pan-American Exposition
Venice in America
Working the Breeches Buoy

Buffalo Bill; see Cody, William

Buffons, The

Three Acrobats

Buggies; see Carriages, coaches and buggies

Buildings

The Abductors
Academy of Music Fire
An Acadian Elopement
Admiral Dewey at State House, Boston
Advance Guard, Return of N.J. Troops
Another Job for the Undertaker
Around New York in 15 Minutes
Arrest in Chinatown, San Francisco, Cal.
Arrival of Train, Cheyenne
Arrival of Train, Tien-Tsin
Arrival of Train, Tokio, Japan
Asakusa Temple, Tokio, Japan
Astor Battery on Parade
At the Altar
At the Foot of the Flatiron
A Baby's Shoe
Basket Ball, Missouri Valley College
Battery Park
Beginning of a Skyscraper
The Bessemer Steel Converter in Operation
The Billionaire
Bird's-Eye View of San Francisco, Cal., From a Balloon
The Black Hand
The Blizzard
Boarding School Girls
Bold Bank Robbery
The Boy Detective
Buffalo Police on Parade
The Burd [Bund], Shanghai
A Cable Road in San Francisco
A Calamitous Elopement
Carriers Leaving Building, U.S.P.O.
Champs de Mars
Charleston Chain-Gang
A Child's Strategem
Church "Our Lady of Grace," Hoboken
Circular Panorama of Electric Tower
Circular Panorama of Suspension Bridge and American Falls
Cleveland Fire Department
Confidence
Corner Madison and State Streets, Chicago

The Power of the Press
President Reviewing School Children
President Roosevelt at the Canton Station
Raffles, the Dog
Reuben in the Subway
Rickshaw Parade, Japan
Run of New York Fire Department
St. Patrick's Cathedral and Fifth Avenue on Easter Sunday Morning
Scenes in San Francisco
Secretary Taft's Address & Panorama
Seeing Boston
Shanghai Street Scene, no. 1
Sheep Run, Chicago Stockyards
Shooters' Parade, Philadelphia
Sky Scrapers of New York City, From the North River
South Spring Street, Los Angeles, Cal.
Sporting Blood
Star Theatre
Street Scene, San Diego
Street Scene, Tokio, Japan
The Subpoena Server
That Little Band of Gold
Their Social Splash
The Trials and Troubles of an Automobilist
The Vampire Dancer
What Happened on Twenty-Third Street, New York City
White Wings on Review
The Would-Be Shriner
see also Specific cities

Butler, Nicholas Murray

Installation Ceremonies of President Butler

Butler, W. J., actor

Beverly of Graustark
A Corner in Wheat
Jealousy and the Man
The Message of the Violin
A Mohawk's Way
One Night and Then
Taming of the Shrew
They Would Elope

Butler, William J., actor

As It Is In Life
As the Bells Rang Out
A Child's Impulse
The Day After
Examination Day at School
The Fickle Spaniard
Happy Jack, A Hero
Helen's Marriage
Help Wanted
His Sister-in-Law
The Honor of His Family

The Iconoclast
In Life's Cycle
In Old Kentucky
In the Border States
An Interrupted Elopement
Iola's Promise
Little Angels of Luck
The Little Waifs
Lord Chumley
Man's Lust for Gold
The Message of the Violin
A Midnight Cupid
Mr. Jones' Burglar
Not So Bad As It Seemed
One-Round O'Brien
An Outcast Among Outcasts
A Plain Song
The Poor Sick Men
The Primitive Man
The Purgation
A Rich Revenge
The Root of Evil
The Sealed Room
Serious Sixteen
1776, or, the Hessian Renegades
Simple Charity
The Slave
A Summer Idyl
A Summer Tragedy
Sunshine Sue
'Tis an Ill Wind That Blows No Good
Tomboy Bessie
The Tragedy of a Dress Suit
A Trap for Santa Claus
The Troublesome Baby
Trying to Fool Uncle
The Twisted Trail
The Usurer
A Victim of Jealousy
The Wages of Sin
Waiter No. 5
Was Justice Served?
What the Doctor Ordered
When Kings Were the Law
When the Fire-Bells Rang
White Roses
The Wife
Willie Becomes an Artist
Won By a Fish
The Would-Be Shriner
A Wreath of Orange Blossoms

Buzzard's Bay, Massachusetts

Rip Van Winkle

Cabanne, Walter Chrystie, actor

The Goddess of Sagebrush Gulch
The Punishment
A Temporary Truce

Cache, Oklahoma

The Bank Robbery

Cairo, Egypt

Egyptian Fakir with Dancing Monkey
Egyptian Market Scene
Fording the River Nile on Donkeys
Market Scene in Old Cairo, Egypt
Panoramic View of an Egyptian Cattle Market
Primitive Irrigation in Egypt
Shearing a Donkey in Egypt

California

The Black Sheep
California Oil Wells in Operation
California Orange Groves, Panoramic View
California Volunteers Marching to Embark
The Fatal Wedding
Feeding Sea Gulls
The Female of the Species
The Fickle Spaniard
The Girl and Her Trust
The Goddess of Sagebrush Gulch
Going Through the Tunnel
Heaven Avenges
His Lesson
Hogan Out West
Hotel Del Monte
An Indian Summer
Jim Jeffries on His California Ranch
Just Like a Woman
Lick Observatory, Mt. Hamilton, Cal.
Man's Genesis
Mount Tamalpais R.R., no. 1
Mount Tamalpais R.R., no. 2
Mount Taw R.R., no. 3
Neighbors
The Old Actor
An Outcast Among Outcasts
Panoramic View of Rubio Canyon, Mt. Low R.R.
Panoramic View of the Great Cable Incline, Mt. Low
The Punishment
Ramona
The School Teacher and the Waif
Southern Pacific Overland Mail
The Spirit Awakened
A Temporary Truce
Their First Kidnapping Case
Those Hicksville Boys
A Trip Down Mt. Tamalpais
The Two Brothers
The War of Wealth
What the Doctor Ordered
Willie Becomes an Artist
With the Enemy's Help
see also specific cities, towns, and geographic locations

In Old Kentucky
In the Border States
Military Maneuvers, Manassas, Va.
Reception of President Taft in Petersburg, Virginia, May 19th, 1909
Unveiling of the Pennsylvania Monument on the Battlefields of Petersburg, Virginia, May 19, 1909
The War of Wealth

Claiche, Bertha

Bertha Claiche

Clarendon Film Co.

The Convict's Escape
Fine Feathers Make Fine Birds
A Kiss and a Tumble
The Pig That Came to Life

Clarges, Verner, actor

As the Bells Rang Out
The Banker's Daughters
A Child's Impulse
The Cloister's Touch
Comata, the Sioux
Examination Day at School
The Face at the Window
A Fair Exchange
A Flash of Light
His Trust Fulfilled
The Honor of His Family
The Iconoclast
The Impalement
In Old Kentucky
The Lesson
The Little Darling
The Marked Time Table
Not So Bad As It Seemed
The Passing of a Grouch
The Recreation of an Heiress
Simple Charity
Two Little Waifs
Wilful Peggy
With Her Card

Clark, May, actress

Rescued by Rover

Clarke, Vergie

The Battle at Elderbush Gulch

Clausen, Hilmar, actor

A Dangerous Play

Clayton, Connecticut

The Village Cut-Up

Cleveland, Ohio

Cleveland Fire Department

Clifford, William H., scriptwriter, author

The Bargain

Cliffside, New Jersey

The Zulu's Heart

Cline, Eddie, actor

Ambrose's Little Hatchet
Caught in the Act
Gussle the Golfer
Gussle's Day of Rest
Hash House Mashers
Hogan the Porter
Hogan's Mussy Job
Our Dare Devil Chief
Peanuts and Bullets
Shot in the Excitement
Ye Olden Grafter

Coaches; *see* Carriages, coaches, and buggies

Coal

Coal Heavers
Coaling a Steamer, Nagasaki Bay, Japan
Giant Coal Dumper
Mining Operations, Pennsylvania Coal Fields
Native Women Coaling a Ship and Scrambling for Money

Cody, William Frederick

Buffalo Bill's Wild West Parade
Parade of Buffalo Bill's Wild West Show, no. 1
Parade of Buffalo Bill's Wild West Show, no. 2

Cogley, Nick, actor, scriptwriter/author

Colored Villainy
Cursed by His Beauty
Dough and Dynamite
For Better—But Worse
A Hash House Fraud
Hash House Mashers
His Luckless Love
A Hound's Triumph
Love in Armor
Love, Loot and Crash
A Lucky Leap
Peanuts and Bullets
The Rent Jumpers
Settled at the Seaside

Cole, Thornton, actor

Lord Chumley
Man's Enemy

Colleges; *see* Missouri State Normal School; Missouri Valley College

Collins, Alfred, director

The Eviction
The Pickpocket
Raid on a Coiner's Den
Runaway Match

Colma, California

Nelson-Britt Prize Fight

Colorado

Denver Fire Brigade
The Georgetown Loop
Royal Gorge
Serving Rations to the Indians, no. 1
Serving Rations to the Indians, no. 2

Columbia Photograph Company

The American Fleet in Hampton Roads, 1909, After Girdling the Globe
Reception of President Taft in Petersburg, Virginia, May 19th, 1909
Unveiling of the Pennsylvania Monument on the Battlefields of Petersburg, Virginia, May 19, 1909

Columbia University

Cornell-Columbia-University of Pennsylvania Boat Race at Ithaca, N.Y., Showing Lehigh Valley Observation Train
Installation Ceremonies of President Butler
104th Street Curve, New York, Elevated Railway
Strongheart

Comedies

An Acadian Elopement
Accidents Will Happen
The Accomodating Cow
The Adjustable Bed
The Affair of an Egg
An Affair of Hearts
An Affair of Honor
After the Ball
Airy Fairy Lillian Tries on Her New Corsets
Algy, the Watchman
Algy's Glorious Fourth of July
All on Account of the Milk
Almost a King
Alphonse and Gaston
Alphonse and Gaston, no. 1
Alphonse and Gaston, no. 2
Alphonse and Gaston, no. 3
Alphonse and Gaston Helping Irishman
Always Room for One More
Ambrose's Fury
Ambrose's Little Hatchet
Ambrose's Lofty Perch
Ambrose's Nasty Temper
Ambrose's Sour Grapes
The Amorous Militiaman
And Pat Took Him at His Word
An Animated Luncheon
Animated Painting
Animated Picture Studio

413

Dr. Dippy's Sanitarium
The Doctor's Favorite Patient
Dog Factory
The Donkey Party
Do-Re-Mi—Boom!
Dough and Dynamite
Down Where the Wurzburger Flows
The Drawing Lesson, [or,] The Living Statue
The Dressmaker's Accident
Drill, Ye Tarriers, Drill
A Drop of Ink
Droppington's Devilish Deed
Droppington's Family Tree
The Dude and the Bathing Girls
The Dude and the Burglars
A Dull Razor
The Easy Chair
Eccentricities of an Adirondack Canoe
Effecting a Cure
The Elopement
Elopement on Horseback
The Elopers Who Didn't Elope
Eloping with Aunty
The Enchanted Well
L'Enchanteur Alcofrisbas
The Engagement Ring
The Englishman and the Girl
An Englishman's Trip to Paris From London
Eradicating Aunty
An Escape From the Flames
The Escaped Lunatic
European Rest Cure
Everybody Works but Father (Blackface)
Everybody Works but Father (Whiteface)
Everybody Works but Mother
The Eviction
The Evidence Was Against Him
Examination Day at School
The Extra Turn
Facial Expression
A Fair Exchange Is No Robbery
The Fairyland, or, the Kingdom of the Fairies
Faithful
Fake Beggar
A False Alarm in the Dressing Room
Family Troubles
The Farmer and the Bad Boys
Farmer Oatcake Has His Troubles
The Fat and Lean Wrestling Match
Fat Bather and Treacherous Springboard
The Fat Girl's Love Affair
The Fate of a Gossip
Father Gets in the Game
Fatty and Mabel at the San Diego Exposition
Fatty and Mabel's Simple Life
Fatty's Chance Acquaintance
Fatty's Faithful Fido

Fatty's New Role
Fatty's Plucky Pup
Fatty's Reckless Fling
Fatty's Tintype Tangle
Female Crook and Her Easy Victim
The Fickle Spaniard
A Fight for a Bride
Fight in the Dormitory
Fine Feathers Make Fine Birds
The Finish of Bridget McKeen
A Fire in a Burlesque Theatre
Firing the Cook
Fisherman's Luck
Five Minutes to Train Time
A Flirtation
Flour and Feed
Follow the Leader
For Better—But Worse
Four Beautiful Pairs
The Fox Hunt
Foxy Grandpa Shows the Boys a Trick or Two With the Tramp
Foxy Grandpa Tells the Boys a Funny Story
Foxy Grandpa Thumb Book
Free Show on the Beach
The French Duel
The Fresh Lover
A Friend in Need Is a Friend Indeed
From Patches to Plenty
From Show Girl to Burlesque Queen
A Frontier Flirtation
Fun in a Bakery Shop
Fun in a Butcher Shop
Fun on the Joy Line
The Furs
The 'Gater and the Pickanniny
A Gay Old Boy
Gay Shoe Clerk
The Genius
Gentlemen of Nerve
A Gesture Fight in Hester Street
Getting Even
Getting Ready to Entertain Harvesters
Getting Strong
Getting up in the World
The Gibson Goddess
The Giddy Dancing Master
The Girl and the Cat
Girl at the Window
The Girls and the Burglar
The Girls, the Burglar, and the Rat
Gloomy Gus Gets the Best of It
A Gold Necklace
A Good Shot
A Good Time with the Organ Grinder
"Goodbye John"
The Gossipers
Grand Hotel to Big Indian
Grandfather as a Spook
Grandma and the Bad Boys
A Guardian of the Peace

Gussle Rivals Jonah
Gussle the Golfer
Gussle Tied to Trouble
Gussle's Backward Way
Gussle's Day of Rest
Gussle's Wayward Path
The Hairdresser
Halloween
Halloween Night at the Seminary
Hammock Over Water
Happy Hooligan
Happy Hooligan April-Fooled
Happy Hooligan in a Trap
Happy Hooligan Surprised
Happy Hooligan Turns Burglar
Happy Hooligan's Interrupted Lunch
Happy Jack, a Hero
A Hard Wash
A Hash House Fraud
Hash House Mashers
The Haunted Hat
"He Cometh Not," She Said
He Forgot His Umbrella
He Got into the Wrong Bath House
He Loves Me, He Loves Me Not
He Wouldn't Stay Down
Hearts and Planets
The Heavenly Twins at Lunch
The Heavenly Twins at Odds
Helen's Marriage
Help! Help!
Help Wanted
The Henpecked Husband
Her Face Was Her Fortune
Her First Biscuits
Her New Party Gown
His Day of Rest
His First Ride
His Last Dollar
His Luckless Love
His Move
His Name Was Mud
His New Lid
His Own Fault
His Wife's Mother
His Wife's Sweethearts
His Wife's Visitor
Hogan Out West
Hogan the Porter
Hogan's Aristocratic Dream
Hogan's Mussy Job
Hogan's Romance Upset
Hold-Up in a Country Grocery Store
The Hold-Up of the Rocky Mountain Express
The Home Breakers
A Home-Breaking Hound
The Home-Made Turkish Bath
Hooligan as a Safe Robber
Hooligan in Jail
Hooligan's Christmas Dream
Hooligan's Roller Skates
The Hoop and the Lovers

414

The Hoopskirt and the Narrow Door
Hot Mutton Pies
Hot Stuff
A Hot Time at Home
How a French Nobleman Got a Wife Through the New York Herald Personal Columns
How Bridget Made the Fire
How Brown Got Married
How Buttons Got Even with the Butler
How Charlie Lost the Heiress
How Hubby Got a Raise
How Jones Lost His Roll: Jones Meets Skinflint (Part 1 of 7)
How Jones Lost His Roll: Skinflint Treats Jones (Part 2 of 7)
How Jones Lost His Roll: Invitation to Dinner (Part 3 of 7)
How Jones Lost His Roll: Skinflint's Cheap Wine (Part 4 of 7)
How Jones Lost His Roll: Game of Cards (Part 5 of 7)
How Jones Lost His Roll: Jones Loses (Part 6 of 7)
How Jones Lost His Roll: Jones Goes Home in Barrel (Part 7 of 7)
How Little Willie Put a Head on His Pa
How Millionaires Sometimes Entertain Aboard Their Yachts
How Old Is Ann?
How the Athletic Lover Outwitted the Old Man
How the Cook Made Her Mark
How the Dutch Beat the Irish
How the Old Woman Caught the Omnibus
How the Young Man Got Stuck at Ocean Beach
How They Fired The Bum, Nit
How They Rob Men in Chicago
How Would You Like a Wife Like This?
How'd You Like to Be the Iceman?
Hulda's Lovers
A Human Hound's Triumph
The Hungry Actor
The Hypnotists Revenge
I Had to Leave a Happy Home for You
Illusions Fantasmagoriques
The Impossible Convicts
In a Boarding School Gym
In a Manicure Parlor
In a Massage Parlor
In a Raines Law Hotel
In the Dressing Room
In the Haunts of Rip Van Winkle
In the Springtime, Gentle Annie!
In the Tombs
In the Valley of the Esopus
An Indian Summer
Indiana Whitecaps

The Inn Where No Man Rests
An Innocent Conspirator
An Innocent Victim
The Insurance Collector
The Insurance Solicitor
The Interrupted Bathers
An Interrupted Elopement
An Interrupted Kiss
The Interrupted Picnic
Invisible Fluid
It's a Shame to Take the Money
It's Unlucky to Pass Under a Ladder
Jack and Jim
Jack Jaggs and Dum Dum
Jealousy and the Man
A Jersey Skeeter
The Johnie and the Telephone
Johnny's in the Well
A Joke at the French Ball
Joke on Grandma
A Joke on Whom?
The Jolly Bill Poster
The Jolly Monks of Malabar
Jones and His New Neighbors
Jones and His Pal in Trouble
Jones and the Lady Book Agent
Jones at the Ball
Jones Entertains
Jones' Interrupted Sleighride
Jones Makes a Discovery
Jones' Return From the Club, Part 1, 2 & 3
The Joneses Have Amateur Theatricals
Just Before the Raid
Just Like a Girl
Kansas Saloon Smashers
Katchem Kate
Katzenjammer Kids and School Marm
The Katzenjammer Kids Have a Love Affair
The Kentucky Squire
The Kid
The King of the Cannibal Island
The Kiss
A Kiss and a Tumble
A Kiss in the Dark
Kiss Me
A Knot in the Plot
Lady Bountiful Visits the Murphys on Wash Day
Lady Helen's Escapade
The Lamp Explodes
The Last Round Ended in a Free Fight
Laughing Ben
The Leading Man
A Legal Hold-Up
Let Uncle Reuben Show You How
Liberty Belles
Lifting the Lid
The Light That Didn't Fail
The Linen Draper's Shop
A Little Bit Off the Top

The Little Darling
Little German Band
A Little Mix-Up in a Mixed Ale Joint
A Little Piece of String
A Little Ray of Sunshine After the Rain
The Little Teacher
The Loaded Cigar
Lonesome Junction
Looking for John Smith
The Lost Child
Love at 55
Love by the Light of the Moon
Love Finds a Way
Love in a Hammock
Love in Armor
Love in Quarantine
Love in the Cornfield
Love in the Dark
Love in the Suburbs
Love, Loot and Crash
Love Me, Love My Dog
The Love Microbe
Love, Speed and Thrills
The Lovers, Coal Box and Fireplace
The Lover's Knot
A Lover's Lost Control
The Lover's Ruse
A Lover's Yarn
Love's Perfidy
Lucky Jim
Lucky Kitten
A Lucky Leap
A Lucky Toothache
The Lucky Wishbone
Mabel and Fatty Viewing the World's Fair at San Francisco, Cal.
Mabel and Fatty's Married Life
Mabel and Fatty's Wash Day
Mabel, Fatty and the Law
Mabel Lost and Won
Mabel's Wilful Way
The Magic Lantern
Making an Impression
The Maniac Barber
Maniac Chase
The Manicure Fools the Husband
Married for Millions
The Masher
The Masqueraders
Maude's Naughty Little Brother
May and December
Me and Jack
The Mechanical Toy
Merely a Married Man
The Mermaid
Mesmerist and Country Couple
The Messenger Boy and the Ballet Girl
The Messenger Boy's Mistake
A Midnight Adventure
A Midnight Cupid
Midnight Intruder
The Midnight Marauder

A Midnight Phantasy
Mike Got the Soap in His Eyes
Military Tactics
Milking Time
The Mills of the Gods
The Minister's Hat
The Minister's Wooing
Mischievous Monkey
Mischievous Willie's Rocking Chair Motor
A Misdirected Ducking
The Mis-Directed Kiss
The Misplaced Signs
Miss Fatty's Seaside Lovers
Mr. Butt-In
Mr. Easymark
Mr. Gay and Mrs.
Mr. Hurry-Up of New York
Mr. Jack Caught in the Dressing Room
Mr. Jack Entertains in His Office
Mr. Jack in the Dressing Room
Mr. Jones' Burglar
Mr. Jones Has a Card Party
Mrs. Jones' Lover
Mixed Babies
Mixed Bathing
Model Posing Before Mirror
The Model That Didn't Pose
Monkey Business
The Monster
Mother's Angel Child
A Moving Picture
Muggsy Becomes a Hero
Muggsy's First Sweetheart
Murphy's Wake
Must Be in Bed Before Ten
The Mysterious Cafe
The Mystical Flame
Nearsighted Mary
The Necromancer
Neighbors
Nellie, the Beautiful Housemaid
Nervy Nat Kisses the Bride
Never Again!
Never Touched Him
The New Maid
A New Trick
The Newest Woman
The Newlyweds
Next
A Nigger in the Woodpile
A Night at the Haymarket
Night Duty
The Night of the Party
No Liberties, Please
No Salad Dressing Wanted
No Wedding Bells for Him
A Non-Union Paper Hanger
Nora's Fourth of July
Not So Bad As It Seemed
The Note in the Shoe
A Novel Way of Catching a Burglar
Off His Beat
Office Boy's Revenge

The Office Boy's Revenge
Oh, Those Eyes!
Oh, Uncle!
An Old Bachelor
Old Gentleman Spinkles
Old Maid and Fortune Teller
The Old Maid and the Burglar
The Old Maid Having Her Picture Taken
The Old Maid in the Horsecar
The Old Maid's Disappointment
The Old Maid's Picture
An Old Story with a New Ending
[On] A [Good Old] Five Cent Trolley Ride
On the Beach at Brighton
On the Benches in the Park
On the Window Shades
One Busy Hour
A One Night Stand
One-Round O'Brien
The Oracle Of Delphi
Ore the Banster
"Osler"-ising Papa
The Other Side of the Hedge
Our Dare Devil Chief
Our Deaf Friend, Fogarty
The Over-Anxious Waiter
A Pair of Queens
The Passing of a Grouch
The Peach-Basket Hat
Peanuts and Bullets
Peeping Tom in the Dressing Room
Personal
The Photographer's Mishap
Photographing a Country Couple
Photographing a Female Crook
Physical Culture Lesson
Pie, Tramp and the Bulldog
Pierrot, Murderer
The Pig That Came to Life
The Pillow Fight, no. 2
A Pipe Dream
A Pipe Story of the Fourth
Pity the Blind, no. 2
A Plate of Ice Cream and Two Spoons
Play Ball on the Beach
A Poet's Revenge
Poker at Dawson City
Policemen's Prank on Their Comrades
Politician's Love Story
Pompey's Honey Girl
Poor Hooligan, So Hungry Too
A Poor Place for Love Making
The Poor Sick Men
The Porous Plaster
Postman Whitewashed
The Pouting Model
The Power of Authority
Pranks
The Price of a Kiss
The Prima Donna's Understudy
The Princess in the Vase

A Private Supper at Hellar's
The Professor
The Professor of the Drama
The Proposal
Pull Down the Curtains, Susie
Pulling Off the Bed Clothes
Pumpkin Eater
Putting Up the Swing
The Quarrelsome Washerwoman
A Quick Recovery
Quick Work for the Soubrettes
A Race for a Kiss
Raffles, the Dog
Rainmakers
The Rat Trap Pickpocket Detector
The Recreation of an Heiress
The Rehearsal
The Rejuvenation of Aunt Mary
The Rent Jumpers
The Renunciation
Le Revenant
A Rich Revenge
The Rivals
The Road to the Heart
Robbed of Her All
The Rock of Ages
The Roller Skate Craze
Romance of an Egg
Rooms for Gentlemen Only
The Rose
Rough House in a New York Honky-Tonk
Rube and Fender
Rube and Mandy at Coney Island
A Rube Couple at a County Fair
Rube in an Opium Joint
A Rube in the Subway
Rubes in the Theatre
Runaway Match
Sailors Ashore
Sampson and Schley Controversy—Tea Party
The Sandwich Man
Saturday's Shopping
The Sausage Machine
Saved!
Scarecrow Pump
A Scene Behind the Scenes
Schneider's Anti-Noise Crusade
School Girl Athletes
School Girl Gymnastics
School Master's Surprise
The School Teacher and the Waif
A Scrap in the Dressing Room
The Sculptor's Nightmare
See-Saw Scene
The Seeress
The Serenaders
Serious Sixteen
Settled at the Seaside
Seven Days
The Seventh Day
She Fell Fainting into His Arms
She Kicked on the Cooking
She Meets with Wife's Approval

She Wanted to Rise in the World
She Would Be an Actress
Sherlock Holmes Baffled
The Shocking Stockings
Shoo Fly
Shot in the Excitement
Shut Up!
Silhouette Scene
The Simple Life
The Sleeper
The Sleepy Soubrette
A Smoked Husband
The Smoker
The Smoky Stove
A Snare for Lovers
The Snowman
The Society Palmist
La Sorcellerie Culinaire
Soubrettes in a Bachelor's Flat
The Soubrette's Slide
Soubrette's Troubles on a Fifth Avenue Stage
A Sound Sleeper
A Spanish Dilemma
The Speed Demon
Spirits in the Kitchen
Sporting Blood
Springtime in the Park
The Startled Lover
Still Water Runs Deep
Stolen Sweets
The Story of the Biograph Told
Strange Adventure of New York Drummer
Street Car Chivalry
Street Fight and Arrest
The Strenuous Life; or, Anti-Race Suicide
A Subject for the Rogue's Gallery
The Subpoena Server
Subub Surprises the Burglar
The Suburbanite
The Suicide Club
The Suit of Armor
The Summer Boarders
A Summer Tragedy
Sweet and Twenty
A Sweet Little Home in the Country
Sweets for the Sweet
The Swimming Class
Take Mellon's Food
Taming of the Shrew
Teasing
The Telephone
10 Ladies in an Umbrella
The Tenderfoot's Triumph
Tenderloin at Night
A Terrible Night
Terrible Teddy, the Grizzly King
The Terrible Turkish Executioner
The Test
That Little Band of Gold
That Poor Insurance Man
That Springtime Feeling
Theatre Hat

Theatre Hats Off
Their First Kidnapping Case
Their Social Splash
They Found the Leak
They Would Elope
The Thief and the Pie Woman
The Thirteen Club
Thompson's Night Out
Those Awful Hats
Those Bitter Sweets
Those College Girls
Those Hicksville Boys
Three Cavaliers of the Road
Three Girls in a Hammock
Three Little Maids
Threshing Scene
Through the Key-Hole in the Door
Tied to Her Apron Strings
The Tired Tailor's Dream
Tom, Tom, the Piper's Son
Tomboy Bessie
Tommy Atkins, Bobby and Cook
Le Tonnerre de Jupiter
A Too Ardent Lover
Too Much Johnson
Toodles and Her Strawberry Tart
Toodle's Tea-Party
The Topers
A "Tough" Dance
Tough Kid's Waterloo
The Tourists
The Tragedy of a Dress Suit
Tramp and Dump Cart
The Tramp and the Bathers
The Tramp and the Muscular Cook
The Tramp and the Nursing Bottle
The Tramp in the Kitchen
Tramp on a Farm
A Tramp on the Roof
The Tramp's Dream
The Tramp's Miraculous Escape
Tramp's Strategy That Failed
The Tramp's Unexpected Skate
Trapeze Disrobing Act
Travels of a Lost Trunk
Trial Marriages
The Trials and Troubles of an Automobilist
A Trick on the Cop
The Trick That Failed
A Trip to Berkeley, Cal.
A Trip to Salt Lake City
Trouble in Hogan's Alley
Troubles of a Manager of a Burlesque Show
The Troublesome Baby
The Troublesome Fly
A Troublesome Satchel
Trout Fishing
The Truants
Trying to Fool Uncle
Trying to Get Arrested
Turning the Tables
The Twentieth Century Tramp, or, Happy Hooligan and His Airship

Twin Brothers
Two Chappies in a Box
Two Is Company, Three a Crowd
Two Old Cronies
Two's Company
The Typewriter
The Ugly Tempered Tramp
The Unappreciated Joke
Uncle Josh at the Moving Picture Show
Uncle Josh in a Spooky Hotel
Uncle Josh's Nightmare
Uncle Reuben at the Waldorf
Under the Bamboo Tree
Under the Mistletoe
Under the Old Apple Tree
Under the Tree
An Unexpected Female
An Unexpected Knockout
Unlucky at Cards, Lucky at Love
An Unlucky Lover
An Unprotected Female
An Unwelcome Visitor
Up a Tree
The Valet's Wife
A Versatile Villain
A Victim of Circumstantial Evidence
The Village Cut-Up
A Voice From the Deep
Wanted: A Dog
Wanted—A Nurse
A Warm Occasion
The Washwoman's Daughter
The Way to Sell Corsets
The Weary Hunters and the Magician
Weary Willie and the Gardener
Weary Willie Kidnaps a Child
The Wedding
A Welsh Rabbit
What Are the Wild Waves Saying, Sister?
What Boys Will Do
What Burglar Bill Found in the Safe
What Demoralized the Barbershop
What Happened in the Tunnel
What Happened to Jones
What the Daisy Said
What the Doctor Ordered
What's Your Hurry?
When a Man Loves
When Ambrose Dared Walrus
When Love Took Wings
When the Fire-Bells Rang
When We Were in Our Teens
When We Were Twenty-One
While Strolling in the Park
White Roses
Who Pays for the Drinks?
Who Said Chicken?
The Whole Dam Family and the Dam Dog
Who's Got the Red Ear?
Who's Looney Now
Why Curfew Did Not Ring

417

Why Foxy Grandpa Escaped a
   Ducking
Why Jones Discharged His Clerks
Why Mr. Nation Wants a Divorce
Why Mrs. Jones Got a Divorce
Why Papa Can't Sleep
The Widow and the Only Man
Wifey Away, Hubby at Play
Wifey's Mistake
Wilful Peggy
Will He Marry the Girl?
Willful Ambrose
Willie Becomes an Artist
Willie Westinghouse and the Doc-
   tor's Battery
Willie's Camera
Willie's First Smoke
Willie's Hat
Willie's Vacation
A Windy Day on the Roof
The Wine Opener
Wine, Women & Song
Wine, Women & Song, no. 2
Wished on Mabel
The Witch's Revenge
The Woman From Mellon's
The Woman Hater
Won by a Fish
The Wooden Leg
The Would-Be Shriner
The Wrath of a Jealous Wife
A Wreath in Time
A (W)ringing Good Joke
A Wringing Good Joke
Wrinkles Removed
The Wrong Room
The Yale Laundry
A Yard of Frankfurters
Ye Olden Grafter
The Yellow Peril
You Will Send Me to Bed, Eh?
Young America

Comstock, Laura

Laura Comstock's Bag-Punching
   Dog

Coney Island, New York

Alone
Arab Act, Luna Park
Around the Flip-Flap Railroad
The Baby and the Puppies
Baby Class at Lunch
Baby Merry-Go-Round
The Bamboo Slide
Bathing Girls' Hurdle Race
The Beach at Coney Island
Boarding School Girls
Boxing Horses, Luna Park, Coney
   Island
A Cake Walk on the Beach at Coney
   Island
The Camel at Luna Park
Capt. Boynton Feeding His Pets
Children in the Surf, Coney Island

Coney Island at Night
Coney Island Beach Patrol
Coney Island Bikers
A Couple of Lightweights at Coney
   Island
Dial's Girl's Band, Luna Park
The Diving Horse
Double Ring Act, Luna Park
Elephants Shooting the Chutes at
   Luna Park
Elephants Shooting the Chutes,
   Luna Park, Coney Island no. 2
Fighting the Flames
Fighting the Flames, Dreamland
Fire and Flames at Luna Park,
   Coney Island
The First Baby
The Great Fire Ruins, Coney Island
Hippodrome Races, Dreamland,
   Coney Island
King and Queen Diving Horses
A Little Tease
Ludlow's Aerodrome
Ludlow's Aeroplane, no. 2
Mystic Shriners' Day, Dreamland,
   Coney Island
Orphan Children on the Beach at
   Coney Island
Orphans in the Surf
Parade of Shriners, Luna Park
The Racing Chutes at Dreamland
Rube and Mandy at Coney Island
The Sand Baby
The Sand Fort
The Seashore Baby
Shoot the Chute Series
Shooting the Chutes at Luna Park
Slide for Life, Luna Park
Steeplechase, Coney Island
Stern's Duplex Railway
Suburban Handicap, 1897
The Swimming Class
Swimming Pool at Coney Island
A Swimming Race at Coney Island
Two Bottle Babies
The Vaidis Sisters, Luna Park
The Waders
What Are the Wild Waves Saying
   Sister?
The Widow and the Only Man

Congdon, cameraman

Football Game: West Point vs.
   Annapolis
"Kronprinz Wilhelm" Docking
McKinley Funeral: Panorama of
   McKinley Home
A Perilous Proceeding
President Roosevelt Crossing the
   Field

Conklin, Chester, actor

Ambrose's Sour Grapes
A Bird's a Bird
The Cannon Ball

Curses! They Remarked
Do-Re-Mi—Boom!
Dough and Dynamite
Droppington's Devilish Deed
Droppington's Family Tree
Gentlemen of Nerve
A Hash House Fraud
Hearts and Planets
The Home Breakers
Love, Speed and Thrills
A One Night Stand
When Ambrose Dared Walrus

Connecticut; see specific cities and towns

Connelly, E. J.

The Devil

Connors, Chuck, actor

Scene in Chinese Restaurant

Construction; see Work sites

Copenhagen, Denmark

A Dangerous Play

Corbett, James J. prizefighter

Reproduction of Corbett-McGovern
   Fight Reproduction of Jeffries-
   Corbett Contest

Cornell University

Cornell–Columbia–University of
   Pennsylvania Boat Races at Itha-
   ca, N.Y., Showing Lehigh Valley
   Observation Train

Corruption; see Socially signifi-cant themes

Cos Cob, Connecticut

The Barbarian Ingomar
The Ingrate

Cotton, Lucy, actress

The Fugitive

Coulter, Frank, actor

The Prisoner of Zenda

Courtney, Helen, actress

The Kleptomaniac

Cows, cattle, bulls, and oxen

The Accomodating Cow
Branding Cattle
Bridge Traffic, Manila
The Bull and the Picknickers
Bull Fight, no. 1
Bull Fight, no. 2
Bull Fight, no. 3
Calf Branding
Cattle Driven to Slaughter
Cattle Fording Stream
Cattle Leaving the Corral
Condensed Milk

Driving Cattle to Pasture
Herd of Cattle
Hogan's Aristocratic Dream
Jack and the Beanstalk
Lassoing Steer
Milking a Cow
Ox Carts, Tokio, Japan
Panoramic View of an Egyptian Cattle Market
A Round-up in Oklahoma
Rounding up and Branding Cattle
Swiss Village, no. 2
Unloading Lighters, Manila
Water Buffalo, Manila
Willie Becomes an Artist

Coytesville, New Jersey

The Better Way
The Broken Doll
The Call of the Wild
The Death Disc
The Final Settlement
The French Duel
The Guerrilla
Her Father's Pride
His Last Burglary
The Honor of His Family
The House With Closed Shutters
Kentuckian
The Masher
A Midnight Cupid
Mr. Jones' Burglar
Muggsy Becomes a Hero
An Old Story With a New Ending
The Open Gate
The Outlaw
Rural Elopement
The Son's Return
Taming of the Shrew
The Tavern Keeper's Daughter
A Terrible Night
The Test
When We Were in Our Teens
A Woman's Way

Craig, Charles, actor

As the Bells Rang Out
A Child's Impulse
The Englishman and the Girl
Her First Biscuits
Her Terrible Ordeal
In Little Italy
Lucky Jim
The Massacre
The Newlyweds
The Rocky Road
The Suicide Club
The Usurer
A Victim of Jealousy
A Woman's Way

Crane, Frank, actor

Men and Women

Crawford, M. H., producer

Whaling in the Far North Off the Coast of Alaska in the Treacherous Bering Sea

Crime and criminals; see Socially significant themes

Crisp, Donald, actor

Fate's Turning
Help Wanted
The Poor Sick Men
Sunshine Sue
The Two Paths
Winning Back His Love
A Wreath of Orange Blossoms

Croker, Chief

Annual Parade, New York Fire Department

Croker, Dick

Dick Croker Leaving Tammany Hall

Cromwell, Oliver

The Death Disc

Cronjager, Henry, cameraman

Lord Chumley
The Road to Yesterday

Cronje, General

General Cronje & Mystic Shriners

Cronk, Hiram

The Funeral of Hiram Cronk

Crosthwaite, Ivy, actress

Those Bitter Sweets

Cruisers; see Ships and watercraft

Cuba

Major General Shafter
Mules Swimming Ashore at Baiquiri, Cuba
Pack Mules With Ammunition on the Santiago Trail, Cuba
Packing Ammunition on Mules, Cuba
Shooting Captured Insurgents
Skirmish of Rough Riders
see also Havana, Cuba; Santiago, Cuba; Spanish-American War

Cuddebackville, New York

The Broken Doll
Comata, the Sioux
A Fair Exchange
Fools of Fate
A Gold Necklace
In Life's Cycle
In Old Kentucky
The Indian Runner's Romance
Leather Stocking

The Little Darling
The Mended Lute
The Modern Prodigal
The Mountaineer's Honor
Muggsy Becomes a Hero
1776, or, the Hessian Renegades
A Summer Idyl
That Chink at Golden Gulch
Wilful Peggy

Culver City, California

A Dash Through the Clouds

Cumpson, John, actor

At the Altar
A Calamitous Elopement
The Clubman and the Tramp
Coney Island Police Court
Confidence
The Cord of Life
The Cricket on the Hearth
The Dancing Girl of Butte
The Fascinating Mrs. Francis
A Fool's Revenge
The French Duel
Getting Even
Her First Biscuits
The Hindoo Dagger
His Wife's Mother
In Little Italy
Jones and His New Neighbors
Jones and the Lady Book Agent
Jones at the Ball
Jones Entertains
The Joneses Have Amateur Theatricals
Lady Helen's Escapade
Lonely Villa
Lucky Jim
Lure of the Gown
The Mills of the Gods
Mr. Jones' Burglar
Mr. Jones Has a Card Party
Mrs. Jones' Lover
The Note in the Shoe
On the Reef
One Busy Hour
The Peach-Basket Hat
Resurrection
The Road to the Heart
Romance of a Jewess
The Sacrifice
The Salvation Army Lass
Schneider's Anti-Noise Crusade
The Smoked Husband
The Stolen Jewels
A Strange Meeting
The Suicide Club
The Test
Those Awful Hats
'Tis an Ill Wind That Blows No Good
Tragic Love
A Troublesome Satchel
Trying to Get Arrested

Twin Brothers
Two Memories
The Violin Maker of Cremona
Was Justice Served?
What Drink Did
With Her Card
The Wooden Leg
The Zulu's Heart

Curaçao

Panorama of Willemstadt, Curaçao, Taken from the River

Curley, Jack, producer

Jack Johnson vs. Jim Flynn Contest for Heavyweight Championship of the World, Las Vegas, New Mexico, July 4, 1912

Czolgosz, Leon F.

Execution of Czolgosz, With Panorama of Auburn Prison

Danbury, Connecticut

Miss Lillian Shaffer and Her Dancing Horse
A Rube Couple at a County Fair

Dance

Ameta
Animated Picture Studio
Arabian Jewish Dance
Around the Mulberry Bush
The Artist's Dilemma
At the French Ball
The Ballet Master's Dream
The Ballet Rehearsal
Bally-Hoo Cake Walk
Betsy Ross Dance
Bowery Waltz
The Boys Think They Have One on Foxy Grandpa, But He Fools Them
Buck Dance
Cake Walk
A Cake Walk on the Beach at Coney Island
Calisthenic Drill, Missouri Commission
Carrying Out the Snakes
Charity Ball
Circle Dance
Comedy Cake Walk
Cosy Corner Dance
Crissie Sheridan
Crossed Love and Swords
Cupid and Psyche
Dance, Franchonetti Sisters
A Dance in Pajamas
A Dance on the Pike
Dancing Boxing Match, Montgomery and Stone
Dancing Chinaman, Marionettes
Dancing Darkey Boy
The Day After

Deyo
The Downward Path: The New Soubrette
Eagle Dance, Pueblo Indians
Ella Lola, a la Trilby
The Extra Turn
Fatty and Mabel at the San Diego Exposition
Fatty's Faithful Fido
Flag Dance
Fougere
Foxy Grandpa and Polly in a Little Hilarity
French Acrobatic Dance
Geisha Dance
The Gerry Society's Mistake
Getting Even
The Giddy Dancing Master
A Good Time with the Organ Grinder
Hogan Out West
Hogan's Mussy Job
Hold-up in a Country Grocery Store
How Millionaires Sometimes Entertain Aboard Their Yachts
How Would You Like a Wife Like This?
The Impalement
The Indian Runner's Romance
Jack Jaggs and Dum Dum
A Jewish Dance at Jerusalem
June's Birthday Party
Just Before the Raid
Karina
The Ki-Ki Dance
Kindergarten Dance
Leander Sisters
Line-Up and Teasing the Snakes
Little Lillian, Danseuse
Lure of the Gown
Mabel Lost and Won
The Magic Lantern
The March of Prayer and Entrance of the Dancers
Maypole Dance
The Messenger Boy and the Ballet Girl
A Midnight Phantasy
Miss Jessie Cameron, Champion Child Sword Dancer
Miss Jessie Dogherty, Champion Female Highland Fling Dancer
Moki Snake Dance by Wolpi [Walpa-pi] Indians
Moulin Rouge Dancers
Murphy's Wake
Neptune's Daughters
A Night at the Haymarket
A Nymph of the Waves
Old Fashioned Scottish Reel
Parade of Snake Dancers Before the Dance
Pompey's Honey Girl
Princess Rajah Dance
A Rube Couple at a Country Fair

Scene in the Swiss Village at Paris Exposition
She Would Be an Actress
Skeleton Dance, Marionettes
Spanish Dancers at the Pan-American Exposition
Swiss Village
Tenderloin Tragedy
Theatre Hats Off
Their Social Splash
Those College Girls
Le Tonnerre de Jupiter
A "Tough" Dance
The Tourists
Turkish Dance, Ella Lola
Uncle Tom's Cabin
The Vampire Dancer
Wand Dance, Pueblo Indians
West Indian Girls in Native Dance
Who Said Chicken?
Wifey Away, Hubby at Play

Dark Cloud, actress

The Song of the Wildwood Flute

Davenport, Alice, actress

Ambrose's Fury
A Bird's a Bird
Cursed by His Beauty
Dirty Work in a Laundry
From Patches to Plenty
Gentlemen of Nerve
The Home Breakers
Mabel and Fatty's Wash Day
Mabel, Fatty and the Law
Mabel Lost and Won
Mabel's Wilful Way
That Little Band of Gold
Wished on Mabel

Davenport, Dorothy, actress

A Mohawk's Way

Davenport, Kenneth, actor

The Road to Yesterday

Deal, New Jersey

Wanted: A Dog

Dedications

Christening and Launching Kaiser Wilhelm's Yacht "Meteor"
Duke of York at Montreal and Quebec
H.R.H. the Prince of Wales Decorating the Monument of Champlain and Receiving Addresses of Welcome From the Mayor of Quebec, the Governor General of Canada and Vice-President Fairbanks, Representative of the United States
Installation Ceremonies of President Butler
John Paul Jones Ceremonies

His Sister-in-Law
Hot Stuff
Hulda's Lovers
An Interrupted Elopement
The Little Teacher
A Lucky Toothache
The Massacre
The Message of the Violin
The Midnight Marauder
Muggsy Becomes a Hero
Oh, Those Eyes!
One Busy Hour
A Plain Song
The Purgation
The Road to Yesterday
The Sorrows of the Unfaithful
The Spirit Awakened
The Suicide Club
A Summer Tragedy
Sunshine Sue
Their First Kidnapping
Those Hicksville Boys
The Tragedy of a Dress Suit
The Village Cut-Up
A Voice From the Deep
Waiter No. 5
What the Doctor Ordered
When a Man Loves
When the Fire-Bells Rang
White Roses
Willie Becomes an Artist
Won By a Fish
The Would-Be Shriner

Dillon, Jack, actor

The Duke's Plan
Seven Days

Dinesen, Johanne, actress

Midsummer-Tide

Dinesen, Robert, actor

A Dangerous Play
The Rights of Youth
The Vampire Dancer

Directors; *see* name of person

Disasters

Academy of Music Fire
Bird's-Eye View of Dock Front, Galveston
Burial of the "Maine" Victims
Burning of the Standard Oil Co's Tanks, Bayonne, New Jersey
Flood Scene in Paterson, N.J.
The Great Baltimore Fire
The Great Fire Ruins, Coney Island
The Great Toronto Fire, Toronto, Canada, April 19, 1904
Launching a Stranded Schooner From the Dock
Panorama of East Galveston
Panorama of Galveston Power House

Panorama of Orphans Home, Galveston
Panorama of Ruins From Baltimore and Charles Street
Panorama of Ruins From Lombard and Charles Street
Panorama of Ruins From Lombard and Hanover Streets, Baltimore
Panorama of Ruins From Water Front
Panorama of the Paterson Fire
Panorama of Wreckage of Water Front
Panoramic View of St. Pierre
Panoramic View of Tremont Hotel
Paterson Fire, Showing the Y.M.C.A. and Library
Ruins of City Hall, Paterson
San Francisco Disaster
Scenes in San Francisco
Searching Ruins on Broadway, Galveston, for Dead Bodies
The Slocum Disaster
Views in San Francisco
Wreck of the Battleship "Maine"

Diving; *see* Swimming and diving

Divorce; *see* Socially significant themes

Dixon, George, prizefighter

Dixon-Chester Leon Contest

Dobson, F. A., cameraman

The Boer War
Brannigan Sets Off the Blast
Casey's Christening
Climbing the American Alps
The Coal Strike
The Convict's Bride
The Course of True Love
The Critic
The Cruise of the "Gladys"
Everybody Works But Mother
An Execution by Hanging
A Fight for a Bride
The Fox Hunt
The Great Jewel Mystery
The Henpecked Husband
In the Tombs
The Jolly Monks of Malabar
The Lone Highwayman
Looking for John Smith
The Love Microbe
Mother's Angel Child
Mutiny on the Black Sea
No Wedding Bells for Him
The Old Swimming Hole
A Reprieve From the Scaffold
Rooms for Gentlemen Only
The Silver Wedding
The Skyscrapers
The Slocum Disaster
The Society Raffles

Stalking and Shooting Caribou, Newfoundland
The Streets of New York
The Thirteen Club
The Tired Tailor's Dream
The Tunnel Workers
The Village Cut-Up
Wanted—A Nurse
Wine, Women & Song, no. 2

Documentaries

The "Abbot" & "Cresceus" Race
Academy of Music Fire
Across the Subway Viaduct, New York
Admiral Dewey at State House, Boston
Admiral Dewey Landing at Gibraltar
Admiral Dewey Leading Land Parade
Admiral Dewey Leading Land Parade, no. 2
Admiral Dewey Passing Catholic Club Stand
Admiral Dewey Receiving the Washington and New York Committees
Admiral Dewey Taking Leave of Washington Committee on the U.S. Cruiser "Olympia"
Admiral Sampson on Board the Flagship
Advance Guard, Return of N.J. Troops
Advance of Kansas Volunteers at Caloocan
"Africander" Winning the Suburban Handicap, 1903
After Launching
After the First Snow
After the Race—Yachts Returning to Anchorage
Afternoon Tea on Board S.S. "Doric"
Aguinaldo's Navy
Alone
Ambulance at the Accident
Ambulance Call
American Falls, Goat Island
American Falls, Luna Island
American Flag
The American Fleet in Hampton Roads, 1909, After Girdling the Globe
Ancient and Honourable Artillery of London on Parade
Ancient and Honourables of London Homeward Bound
Anna Held
Annual Baby Parade, 1904, Asbury Park, N.J.
Annual Parade, New York Fire Department
Arabian Gun Twirler
Arabian Jewish Dance
The Armenian Archbishop of Rome

Armour's Electric Trolley
Around New York in 15 Minutes
Around the Flip-Flap Railroad
Around the Mulberry Bush
Arrest in Chinatown, San Francisco, Cal.
Arrival of Emigrants [i.e., Immigrants], Ellis Island
Arrival of McKinley's Funeral Train at Canton, Ohio
Arrival of Prince Henry and President Roosevelt at Shooter's Island
Arrival of the Governor General, Lord Minto, at Quebec
Arrival of Tokyo Train
Arrival of Train at Muskoka Wharf
Arrival of Train, Cheyenne
Arrival of Train, Tien-Tsin
Arrival of Train, Tokio, Japan
The Art of Making Up
Artist's Point
Asakusa Temple, Tokio, Japan
Asia in America, St. Louis Exposition
Astor Battery on Parade
At the Foot of the Flatiron
At the Fountain
Atlantic City Fire Department
Atlantic City Floral Parade
An Attack by Torpedo Boats
Attack on Fort Boonesboro
The Attack on Port Arthur
Auto Boat Race on the Hudson
Automobile Parade
Automobile Parade on the Coney Island Boulevard
Automobile Race for the Vanderbilt Cup
Automobiling Among the Clouds
Babe and Puppies
The Babies' Quarrel
Babies Rolling Eggs
The Baby
The Baby and the Puppies
Baby Class at Lunch
Baby in a Rage
Baby Lund and Her Pets
Baby Merry-Go-Round
Baby Playing in Gutter
The Baby Review
Baby's Day
Baby's Tooth
The Badger Game
Balloon Race
The Bamboo Slide
Bargain Day, 14th Street, New York
Basket Ball, Missouri Valley College
Bass Fishing
Bathing at Atlantic City
Bathing in Samoa
Battery B Arriving at Camp
Battery B Pitching Camp
Battery K Siege Guns
Battery Park
Battle Flags of the 9th Infantry

Battle of Confetti at the Nice Carnival
Battle of Flowers at the Nice Carnival
Battle of Mafeking
Battle of Mt. Ariat
The Battle of the Yalu, no. 1–4
Battleship "Indiana" in Action
Battleship "Odin"
Battleships in Action
Battleships "Iowa" and "Massachusetts"
Bayonet Exercises
Beach Apparatus-Practice
The Beach at Coney Island
Beginning of a Skyscraper
The Belles of the Beach
The Bengal Lancers
The Bessemer Steel Converter in Operation
Bicycle Paced Race
Bird's-Eye View of Dock Front, Galveston
Bird's-Eye View of San Francisco, Cal., From a Balloon
Blanket-Tossing a New Recruit
The Blizzard
Boat Race
Boat Wagon and Beach Cart
Boating Carnival, Palm Beach
Boats Under Oars
Boer Commissary Train Treking
The Boer War
Boers Bringing in British Prisoners
Bombardment of Taku Forts, by the Allied Fleets
The Boston Horseless Fire Department
Boston School Cadets, 3rd Regiment
Boxing Horses, Luna Park, Coney Island
Boys Diving, Honolulu
Boyville Fire Brigade
Branding Cattle
Breaking of the Crowd at Military Review at Longchamps
Bridal Veil Falls
Bridge Traffic, Manila
British Light Artillery
Broadway & Union Square, New York
Broncho Busting Scenes, Championship of the World
Brook Trout Fishing
The Brooklyn Handicap—1904
Brothers of the Misericordia, Rome
Bubbles!
Buck Dance
A Bucking Broncho
Bucking Broncos
Bucking the Blizzard
Buffalo Bill's Wild West Parade
Buffalo Fire Department
Buffalo Fire Department in Action

Buffalo Police on Parade
Buffalo Stockyards
Building a Harbor at San Pedro
Bull Fight, no. 1
Bull Fight, no. 2
Bull Fight, no. 3
The Burd [i.e. Bund], Shanghai
Burial of the "Maine" Victims
The Burning of Durland's Riding Academy
Burning of St. Pierre
Burning of the Standard Oil Co's Tanks, Bayonne, N.J.
Butt's Manual, St. John's School
Buying Stamps from Rural Wagon, U.S.P.O.
A Cable Road in San Francisco
A Cake Walk on the Beach at Coney Island
Calf Branding
California Limited, A.T. & S.F. R.R.
California Oil Wells in Operation
California Orange Groves, Panoramic View
California Volunteers Marching to Embark
Calisthenic Drill, Missouri Commission
The Camel at Luna Park
Cancelling Machine, U.S.P.O.
Canoeing at Riverside
Canoeing on the Charles River, Boston, Mass.
Canoeing Scene
Cañon of the Rio Grande
Canton River Scene
Canton Steamboat Landing Chinese Passengers
Capsize of Lifeboat
Capsized Boat
Capt. Boynton Feeding His Pets
Captain Nissen Going Through Whirlpool Rapids, Niagara Falls
Capture of Boer Battery
Capture of Boer Battery by British
Capture of Trenches at Candaba [Candabar]
Capuchin Monks, Rome
Cardinal Gibbons
Carrie Nation Smashing a Saloon
Carriers at Work, U.S.P.O.
Carriers Leaving Building, U.S.P.O.
Carrying Out the Snakes
Cascade Near Wawona, California
Casey at the Bat
Catch-as-Catch-Can Wrestling
Cattle Driven to Slaughter
Cattle Fording Stream
Cattle Leaving the Corral
A Cavalry Charge
Central High School, Gymnastic Drill
Champion Pony "Midget"
Champs de Mars
Champs Elysees

Two Hours After Chickens Leave the Shells
Tying up Bags for Train, U.S.P.O.
Union Iron Works
A Unique Race Between Elephant, Bicycle, Camel, Horse, and Automobile
U.S. Battleship "Indiana"
U.S. Battleship "Iowa"
U.S. Battleship "Oregon"
U.S. Cavalry Supplies Unloading at Tampa, Florida
U.S. Cruiser "Brooklyn" Naval Parade
U.S. Cruiser "Nashville"
U.S. Cruiser "Olympia" Leading Naval Parade
U.S. Cruiser "Raleigh"
U.S.S. "Castine"
United States Government Gun Test
U.S. Troops Landing at Daiquiri, Cuba
Unloading Halibut
Unloading Lighters, Manila
Unveiling of the Pennsylvania Monument on the Battlefields of Petersburg, Virginia, May 19, 1909
Upper Falls of the Yellowstone
The Vatican Guards, Rome
Vaulting Contest, Meadowbrook Hunt
Venice in America
The Victorious Battle for the Conquest of Mergheb, Africa
Victorious Squadron Firing Salute
Viewing Sherman Institute for Indians at Riverside, Cal.
Views in San Francisco
A Visit to Baby Roger
"Vizcaya" Under Full Headway
The Waders
Wagon Supply Train en Route
Wagons Loading Mail, U.S.P.O.
Wall Scaling
Wand Dance, Pueblo Indians
War Canoe Race
War Correspondents
Wash Day in Mexico
Wash-Day
Washing Clothes at Sicily
Washing Gold on 20 Above, Hunker, Klondike
Washing the Baby
Washington Bridge And Speedway
Water Buffalo, Manila
Water Duel
Water Nymphs
Waterfall in the Catskills
Watermelon Contest
Wawona, Big Tree
Weighing the Baby
Welding the Big Ring
West Indian Boys Diving for Money

West Indian Girls in Native Dance
West Point Cadets
West Point Cadets, St. Louis Exposition
Westinghouse Air Brake Co.
Westinghouse Works
Whaling in the Far North Off the Coast of Alaska in the Treacherous Bering Sea
Wharf Scene and Natives Swimming at St. Thomas, D.W.I.
Wharf Scene, Honolulu
White Horse Rapids
White Star S.S. Baltic Leaving Pier on First Eastern Voyage
White Wings on Review
Whittier School, Calisthenics
A Wild Turkey Hunt
The Wolf Hunt
Women of the Ghetto Bathing
Working Rotary Snow Ploughs on Lehigh Valley Railroad
Working the Breeches Buoy
Wounded Soldiers Embarking in Row Boats
Wreck of the Battleship "Maine"
Wreck of the "Vizcaya"
Wrestling at the New York Athletic Club
Wrestling Yacht
Yacht Race—Finish
The Yacht Race Fleet Following the Committee Boat "Navigator" Oct. 4th
Yacht Race—Start
A Yard of Puppies

Dogherty, Jessie

Miss Jessie Dogherty, Champion Female Highland Fling Dancer

Dougherty, Lee, actor

Politician's Love Story

Dogs

Babe and Puppies
The Baby and the Puppies
Baby Lund and Her Pets
The Burglar's Slide for Life
Buster Brown Series: Buster and Tige Put a Balloon Vender Out of Business
Buster Brown Series: Buster Brown and the Dude
Buster Brown Series: Buster Makes Room for His Mama at the Bargain Counter
Buster Brown Series: Buster's Dog to the Rescue
Buster Brown Series: Pranks of Buster Brown and His Dog Tige
Casey's Christening
The Children's Friend
Children's Hour on the Farm
Chums

A Cold Supper With a Hot Finish
Cross Country Running on Snow Shoes
Crossed Love and Swords
Dog Factory
A Dog Fight
Dogs Playing in the Surf
The Esquimaux Village
Fatty's Faithful Fido
Fatty's Plucky Pup
Flock of Sheep
For Better—But Worse
The Foster Mother
The Fox Hunt
Frank J. Gould's Dogs
A Friend in Need Is a Friend Indeed
Fun in a Butcher Shop
Going to the Hunt, Meadowbrook
Gussle's Wayward Path
Help! Help!
Her First Adventure
A Home-Breaking Hound
How the Dutch Beat the Irish
Jerusalem's Busiest Street, Showing Mt. Zion
Laura Comstock's Bag-Punching Dog
Leaping Dogs at Gentry's Circus
Love Me, Love My Dog
Me and Jack
The Meadowbrook Hunt
Military Drill of Kikuyu Tribes and Other Native Ceremonies
Off for the Rabbit Race
On the Benches in the Park
Packers on the Trail
Paul J. Rainey's African Hunt
The Paymaster
Pie, Tramp and the Bulldog
Police Raid at a Dog Fight
Poor Hooligan, So Hungry Too
Quail Shooting at Pinehurst
Raffles the Dog
Rescued by Rover
Rex's Bath
Rights of Youth
A Romp on the Lawn
Sausage Machine
Scene in a Rat Pit
Sheep and Lambs
Spike, the Bag-Punching Dog
Stealing a Dinner
Terrier vs. Wild Cat
Those Bitter Sweets
The Tramp's Dream
Tramp's Strategy That Failed
Travels of a Lost Trunk
Two Bottle Babies
Wanted: A Dog
The Whole Dam Family and the Dam Dog
The Wolf Hunt
A Wringing Good Joke
A Yard of Frankfurters
A Yard of Puppies

431

Donkeys and mules

Another Name Was Maude
Beginning of a Skyscraper
Bridge Traffic, Manila
The Ch-ien-men Gate, Pekin
Children's Hour on the Farm
Cowboys and Indians Fording River in a Wagon
A Donkey Party
The Donkey Party
The Electric Mule
A Farmer's Imitation of Ching Ling Foo
The Female of the Species
Fording the River Nile on Donkeys
Grandpa's Reading Glass
Gussle's Backward Way
An Historic Feat
Jerusalem's Busiest Street, Showing Mt. Zion
Man's Lust for Gold
Mexico Street Scene
Mules Swimming Ashore at Daiquiri, Cuba
Pack Mules With Ammunition on the Santiago Trail, Cuba
Pack Train on the Chilcoot Pass
Packing Ammunition on Mules, Cuba
Primitive Irrigation in Egypt
Prize Winners at the Country Fair
Shearing a Donkey in Egypt
Street Scene in Jaffa
The Tenderfoot's Triumph
Tourists Returning on Donkeys from Mizpah
Tourists Starting on Donkeys for the Pyramids of Sakkarah
Twenty Mule Team, St. Louis Exposition
Wagon Supply Train En Route
What the Doctor Ordered

Dowling, James, actor

The Bargain

Downey, Wallace

Arrival of Prince Henry and President Roosevelt at Shooter's Island

Dramas

The Abductors
Adventures of Dollie
The Aeroplane Inventor
After Many Years
The American Soldier in Love and War, no. 1
The American Soldier in Love and War, no. 2
The American Soldier in Love and War, no. 3
And a Little Child Shall Lead Them
An Arcadian Maid
Arrest of a Shoplifter
An Artist's Dream

The Artist's Studio
As It Is In Life
As the Bells Rang Out
At the Altar
Avenging a Crime, or Burned at the Stake
The Aviator's Generosity
The Awakening
An Awful Moment
A Baby's Shoe
A Ballroom Tragedy
The Bandit King
The Bandit's Waterloo
The Bank Robbery
The Banker's Daughters
The Barbarian Ingomar
The Bargain
The Battle at Elderbush Gulch
Battle of Chemulpo Bay
Be Good
A Beast at Bay
Behind the Scenes
Bertha Claiche
Betrayed by Hand Prints
The Better Way
Between the Dances
Beverly of Graustark
The Black Hand
The Black Sheep
The Black Viper
Bold Bank Robbery
The Boy Detective
A Break for Freedom
The Broken Doll
The Broken Locket
Brush Between Cowboys and Indians
A Burglar's Mistake
The Call
The Call of the Heart
The Call of the Wild
The Call to Arms
Capture of the Biddle Brothers
Capture of Yegg Bank Burglars: Capture & Death (H50924); Cellar Scene (H50925); Dive Scene (H50927); Tracked (H50926)
The Cardinal's Conspiracy
A Career of Crime, no. 1
A Career of Crime, no. 2
A Career of Crime, no. 3
A Career of Crime, no. 4
A Career of Crime, no. 5
Carmen
Caught by Wireless
Caught in the Undertow
The Cavalier's Dream
A Change of Heart
The Chariot Race
The Charity Ball
The Child of the Ghetto
The Child Stealers
The Children's Friend
A Child's Faith
A Child's Impulse

A Child's Remorse
A Child's Stratagem
The Christmas Burglars
Classmates
The Cloister's Touch
Comata, the Sioux
The Coney Island Beach Patrol
Confidence
The Converts
The Convict's Bride
The Convict's Sacrifice
The Cord of Life
A Corner in Wheat
The Count of Monte Cristo
The Country Doctor
The Course of True Love
Cowboy Justice
The Cricket on the Hearth
The Criminal Hypnotist
Cripple Creek Bar-Room Scene
Crossroads of Life
Cuban Ambush
The Cup of Life
The Damnation of Faust
The Dancing Girl of Butte
The Danger of Dining in Private Dining Rooms
A Dangerous Play
The Darkening Trail
The Death Disc
The Deception
Decoyed
Desdemona
The Devil
Discovery of Bodies (The Pioneers)
The Divorce: Detected
The Divorce: On the Trail
The Divorce: The Evidence Secured
The Doctor's Bride
Down the Hotel Corridor
The Downward Path: The Fresh Book Agent
The Downward Path: She Ran Away
The Downward Path: The New Soubrette
The Downward Path: The Girl Who Went Astray
The Downward Path: The Suicide
Drunkard's Child
The Drunkard's Reformation
Duel Scene, "By Right of Sword"
Duel Scene from "Macbeth"
The Duke's Plan
The Eavesdropper
Edgar Allen [i.e. Allan] Poe
The Ex-Convict
Execution of Czolgosz, with Panorama of Auburn Prison
The Expiation
The Face at the Window
Faded Lilies
A Fair Exchange
A Fair Rebel
The Fall of Black Hawk
A Famous Escape

432

Queen Elizabeth
Raffles, the Amateur Cracksman
Raid on a Coiner's Den
A Railway Tragedy
Ramona
Reading the Death Sentence
The Reckoning
The Red Girl
The Redman and the Child
The Redman's View
A Reprieve from the Scaffold
Reproduction, Nan Paterson's Trial
Rescue of Child from Indians
Rescued by Rover
The Restoration
The Resurrection
Revenge!
The Rights of Youth
Rip Van Winkle
The River Pirates
The Road to Yesterday
The Rocky Road
Romance of a Jewess
A Romance of the Western Hills
The Root of Evil
Rose O'Salem-Town
The Roue's Heart
Rounding Up of the "Yeggmen"
A Rude Hostess
Rumpelstiltskin
Rural Elopement
The Sacrifice
A Salutary Lesson
The Salvation Army Lass
Sampson-Schley Controversy
The Sands of Dee
The Sealed Room
A Search for the Evidence
Settler's Home Life
The Seven Ages
1776, or, The Hessian Renegades
The Silver Wedding
Simple Charity
The Skyscrapers
The Slave
The Society Raffles
The Somnambulist
Song of the Shirt
The Song of the Wildwood Flute
The Son's Return
The Sorrows of the Unfaithful
The Spirit Awakened
The Stage Rustler
The Star of Bethlehem
Stolen by Gypsies
The Stolen Jewels
Stop Thief!
A Strange Meeting
Strongheart
A Summer Idyl
Sunshine Sue
Sweet Revenge
Taming a Husband
The Tavern Keeper's Daughter
A Temporary Truce

Ten Nights in a Bar-Room: Death of Little May
Ten Nights in a Bar-Room: Death of Slade
Ten Nights in a Bar-Room: The Fatal Blow
Ten Nights in a Bar-Room: Murder of Willie
Ten Nights in a Bar-Room: Vision of Mary
Tenderloin Tragedy
A Terrible Night
The Test of Friendship
That Chink at Golden Gulch
Thaw-White Tragedy
Those Boys
Those Wedding Bells Shall Not Ring Out
Thou Shalt Not
The Thread of Destiny
Through the Breakers
'Tis an Ill Wind That Blows No Good
To Save Her Soul
Tragic Love
A Trap for Santa Claus
A True Patriot
The Tunnel Workers
The Twisted Trail
2 A.M. in the Subway
The Two Brothers
The Two Convicts
Two Cousins
Two Little Waifs
Two Memories
The Two Paths
Two Women and a Man
The Unchanging Sea
Uncle Tom's Cabin
An Unexpected Guest
Unexpected Help
The Unfaithful Odalisque
The Unfaithful Wife: Part 1, The Lover
The Unfaithful Wife: Part 2, The Fight
The Unfaithful Wife: Part 3, Murder and Suicide
An Unprotected Female
The Usurer
The Vampire Dancer
The Vaquero's Vow
Vengeance
A Victim of Jealousy
The Violin Maker of Cremona
The Voice of the Violin
The Wages of Sin
The Wages of Sin: Murder [Part 1]
The Wages of Sin: Retribution [Part 2]
The Waif
Waiter No. 5
Wanted, a Child
The War of Wealth
Was Justice Served?

The Way of Man
The Way of the World
A Welcome Burglar
Western Stage Coach Hold Up
What Drink Did
When Kings Were the Law
When Knights Were Bold
When the Flag Falls
Where Breakers Roar
The White Caps
The Wife
Willful Murder
Winning Back His Love
With Her Card
With the Enemy's Help
Woman Against Woman
The Woman in Black
A Woman's Way
A Wreath of Orange Blossoms
The Zulu's Heart

Dresden, Germany

Clever Horsemanship

Drifton, Pennsylvania

Mining Operations, Pennsylvania Coal Fields

Drouet, Robert, actor

Beverly of Graustark
The Charity Ball
A Fair Rebel
The Gambler of the West
The War of Wealth
The Wife

Drumeir, Jack, actor

The Charity Ball
The Woman in Black

Dunn, Billy, actor

Fatty's New Role

Dunn, Bobby, actor

Ambrose's Little Hatchet
Fatty's New Role
Hogan Out West
Hogan the Porter
Hogan's Aristocratic Dream
Hogan's Mussy Job
Hogan's Romance Upset
Mabel's Wilful Way
A One Night Stand

Durango, Mexico

Bull Fight, no. 1
Bull Fight, no. 2
Bull Fight, no. 3
Train Hour in Durango, Mexico
Wash Day in Mexico

Durfee, Minta, actress

A Bird's a Bird
Court House Crooks
Dirty Work in a Laundry

California Limited, A.T. & S.F. R.R.

California Oil Wells in Operation

California Orange Groves, Panoramic View

California Volunteers Marching to Embark

Canoeing on the Charles River, Boston, Mass.

Canoeing Scene

Cañon of the Rio Grande

Canton River Scene

Canton Steamboat Landing Chinese Passengers

Capsize of Lifeboat

Capsized Boat

Captain Nissen Going Through Whirlpool Rapids, Niagara Falls

Capture of Boer Battery

Capture of Boer Battery by British

Capture of the Biddle Brothers

Capture of Trenches at Candaba [Candabar]

Capture of Yegg Bank Burglars: Capture & Death (H50924); Cellar Scene (H50925); Dive Scene (H50927); Tracked (H50926)

Carrying Out the Snakes

Casey and His Neighbor's Goat

Casey at the Bat

Casey's Frightful Dream

Catching an Early Train

Cattle Driven to Slaughter

Cattle Fording Stream

Cattle Leaving the Corral

The Cavalier's Dream

Champs de Mars

Champs Elysees

Charge of Boer Cavalry

Charity Ball

Charleston Chain-Gang

Children Bathing

Chinese Procession, no. 12

Chinese Shaving Scene

Ching Ling Foo Outdone

Christening and Launching Kaiser Wilhelm's Yacht "Meteor"

Circle Dance

Circular Panorama of Electric Tower

Circular Panorama of Housing the Ice

Circular Panorama of Suspension Bridge and American Falls

Circular Panorama of the Horse Shoe Falls in Winter

Circular Panoramic View of Jones & Laughlin's Steel Works Yard

Circular Panoramic View of Whirlpool Rapids

City Hall to Harlem in 15 Seconds via the Subway Route

Close View of the "Brooklyn" Naval Parade

The Clown and the Alchemist

Coaches Arriving at Mammoth Hot Springs

Coaches Going to Cinnabar from Yellowstone Park

Coasting

Coasting Scene at Montmorency Falls, Canada

Cohen's Advertising Scheme

Colonel Funstan [i.e. Funston] Swimming the Baglag River

Colored Troops Disembarking

"Columbia" and "Shamrock II" Finishing Second Race

"Columbia" and "Shamrock II" Jockeying and Starting

"Columbia" and "Shamrock II" Start of Second Race

"Columbia" and "Shamrock II" Starting in the Third Race

"Columbia" and "Shamrock II" Turning the Outer Stake Boat

"Columbia" Winning the Cup

Comedy Set-to

Coney Island at Night

Congress of Nations

The Cop and the Nurse Girl

The Cop Fools the Sergeant

Cornell-Columbia-University of Pennsylvania Boat Race at Ithaca, N.Y., Showing Lehigh Valley Observation Train

Corner Madison and State Streets, Chicago

Cowboys and Indians Fording River in a Wagon

Cripple Creek Bar-Room Scene

Cripple Creek Floats

Crissie Sheridan

Cross Country Running on Snow Shoes

Crossing Ice Bridge at Niagara Falls

Crossing the Atlantic

Cruiser "Cincinnati"

Cruiser "Detroit"

Cruiser "Marblehead"

Cuban Ambush

Cuban Refugees Waiting for Rations

Cuban Volunteers Embarking

Cuban Volunteers Marching for Rations

Cupid and Psyche

Cutting and Canaling Ice

Dancing Chinaman, Marionettes

Dancing Darkey Boy

A Day at the Circus

Decorated Carriages, no. 11

Denver Fire Brigade

"Deutschland" Leaving New York at Full Speed

Dewey Arch—Troops Passing Under Arch

Dewey Parade, 10th Pennsylvania Volunteers

Dick Croker Leaving Tammany Hall

Discharging a Whitehead Torpedo

The Diving Horse

Dog Factory

Dogs Playing in the Surf

The Donkey Party

Down Where the Wurzburger Flows

Drills and Exercises, Schoolship "St. Mary's"

Driving Cattle to Pasture

Duke and Duchess of Cornwall and York Landing at Queenstown, Ontario

Duke of York at Montreal and Quebec

A Dull Razor

Eagle Dance, Pueblo Indians

The Early Morning Attack

An East River Novelty

East Side Urchins Bathing in a Fountain

Eating Macaroni in the Streets of Naples

Edison Kinetoscopic Record of a Sneeze, January 7, 1894

The Educated Chimpanzee

Egyptian Boys in Swimming Race

Egyptian Fakir with Dancing Monkey

Egyptian Market Scene

Eiffel Tower From Trocadero Palace

The Electric Mule

Electrocuting an Elephant

Elephants Shooting the Chutes at Luna Park

Elephants Shooting the Chutes, Luna Park, Coney Island, no. 2

Ella Lola, a la Trilby

Elopement on Horseback

Emigrants [i.e. Immigrants] Landing at Ellis Island

Empire State Express, the Second, Taking Water on the Fly

The Enchanted Drawing

English Lancers Charging

Esplanade des Invalides

Esquimaux Game of Snap-the-Whip

Esquimaux Leap-Frog

Esquimaux Village

European Rest Cure

The Ex-Convict

Excavating Scene at the Pyramids of Sakkarah

Excursion Boats, Naval Parade

Execution of Czolgosz, with Panorama of Auburn Prison

Exhibition of Prize Winners

Exploding a Whitehead Torpedo

The Extra Turn

Facial Expression

A Fair Exchange is No Robbery

Fake Beggar

Falls of Minnehaha

The Farmer and the Bad Boys

Farmer Kissing the Lean Girl

Fast Mail, Northern Pacific R.R.
The Fat and Lean Wrestling Match
Faust and Marguerite
Faust Family of Acrobats
Feeding Geese at Newman's Poultry Farm
Feeding Pigeons in Front of St. Mark's Cathedral, Venice, Italy
Feeding Sea Gulls
Feeding the Bear at the Menagerie
Filipinos Retreat From Trenches
The Finish of Bridget McKeen
Fire and Flames at Luna Park, Coney Island
Fireboat "New Yorker" Answering an Alarm
Fireboat "New Yorker" in Action
Firing by Squad, Gatling Gun
First Avenue, Seattle, Washington
Fisherman's Luck
Fisherman's Wharf
Fishing at Faralone Island
Fishing Smacks
Flagship "New York"
The Fleet Steaming Up North River
Flood Scene in Paterson, N.J.
Follow the Leader
Fording the River Nile on Donkeys
14th U.S. Infantry Drilling at the Presidio
Free-for-All Race at Charter Oak Park
Freight Train
Fun in a Bakery Shop
Fun in a Butcher Shop
Fun in Camp
Funeral Leaving the President's House and Church at Canton, Ohio
Game of Shovel Board on Board S.S. "Doric"
Gatling Gun Crew in Action
Gay Shoe Clerk
General Lee's Procession, Havana
German and American Tableau
Giant Coal Dumper
The "Glen Island" Accompanying Parade
Going Through the Tunnel
Going to Market, Luxor, Egypt
Going to the Yokohama Races
The Golden Chariots
Goo Goo Eyes
Gordon Sisters Boxing
Government House at Hong Kong
Governor Roosevelt and Staff
Grandma and the Bad Boys
The Great Bull Fight
The Great Fire Ruins, Coney Island
The Great Train Robbery
Gun Drill by Naval Cadets at Newport Training School
Gymnasium Exercises and Drill at Newport Training School
Halloween Night at the Seminary

Happy Hooligan April-Fooled
Happy Hooligan Surprised
Happy Hooligan Turns Burglar
Harry Thompson's Immitations of Sousa
The Heavenly Twins at Lunch
The Heavenly Twins at Odds
Heaving the Log
Herd of Sheep on the Road to Jerusalem
Herding Horses Across a River
High Diving by A. C. Holden
Hindoo Fakir
Hippodrome Races, Dreamland, Coney Island
Hockey Match on the Ice
Hold-Up in a Country Grocery Store
Hong Kong Regiment, no. 1
Hong Kong Regiment, no. 2
Hong Kong, Wharf-Scene
Honolulu Street Scene
Hooligan Assists the Magician
Horse Parade at the Pan-American Exposition
Horses Loading for Klondike, no. 9
Horticultural Floats, no. 9
Hotel Del Monte
Hotel Vendome, San Jose, Cal.
How Jones Lost His Roll: Jones Meets Skinflint (Part 1 of 7)
How Jones Lost His Roll: Skinflint Treats Jones (Part 2 of 7)
How Jones Lost His Roll: Invitation to Dinner (Part 3 of 7)
How Jones Lost His Roll: Skinflint's Cheap Wine (Part 4 of 7)
How Jones Lost His Roll: Game of Cards (Part 5 of 7)
How Jones Lost His Roll: Jones Loses (Part 6 of 7)
How Jones Lost His Roll: Jones Goes Home in a Barrel (Part 7 of 7)
How Old is Ann?
How the Dutch Beat the Irish
How They Do Things on the Bowery
Ice-Boat Racing at Redbank, N.J.
Ice Boating on the North Shrewsbury, Red Bank, N.J.
Ice Skating in Central Park, N.Y.
Indian Day School
Inter-Collegiate Athletic Association Championships, 1904
Inter-Collegiate Regatta, Poughkeepsie, New York, 1904
The Interrupted Bathers
The Interrupted Picnic
Jack and the Beanstalk
Japanese Acrobats
Japanese Sampans
Japanese Village
The Jealous Monkey

Jeffreys [i.e. Jeffries] and Ruhlin Sparring Contest at San Francisco, Cal. Nov. 15, 1901—Five Rounds
Jeffreys in His Training Quarters
Jerusalem's Busiest Street, Showing Mt. Zion
A Jewish Dance at Jerusalem
Joke on Grandma
Jones and His Pal in Trouble
Jones' Interrupted Sleighride
Jones Makes a Discovery
Jones' Return from the Club, Parts 1, 2 and 3
Judge Parker Receiving the Notification of His Nomination for the Presidency
Judging Tandems
June's Birthday Party
Kaiser Wilhelm's Yacht, "Meteor," Entering the Water
Kanakas Diving for Money, no. 1
Kanakas Diving for Money, no. 2
Kansas Saloon Smashers
King Edward and President Loubet Reviewing French Troops
King Edward's Visit to Paris
The Kiss
The Kleptomaniac (11 parts)
"Kronprinz Wilhelm" With Prince Henry on Board Arriving in New York
Ladies's Saddle Horses
Lake Lucerne, Switzerland
Landing Wharf at Canton
Larks Behind the Scene
Las Vigas Canal, Mexico
Las Vigas Canal, Mexico City
Lassoing Steer
Launch of Japanese Man-of-War "Chitosa"
Launch of Life Boat
Launch of Surf Boat
Launching, no. 2
Launching a Stranded Schooner From the Docks
Laura Comstock's Bag-Punching Dog
Leander Sisters
Leaping Dogs at Gentry's Circus
Lehigh Valley Black Diamond Express
Lick Observatory, Mt. Hamilton, Cal.
Life of an American Fireman
Life Rescue at Long Branch
Line-Up and Teasing the Snakes
Little German Band
The Little Train Robbery
Loading a Vessel at Charleston
Loading Baggage for Klondike, no. 6
Loading Horses on Transport

Fire, Adams Express Office
Fire and Flames at Luna Park, Coney Island
Fire Department, Fall River, Massachusetts
A Fire in a Burlesque Theatre
The Fire of Life
Fireboat "New Yorker" Answering an Alarm
Fireboat "New Yorker" in Action
The Fire-Bug
Firing the Cabin (The Pioneers)
The Goddess of Sagebrush Gulch
The Great Baltimore Fire
The Great Fire Ruins, Coney Island
The Great Toronto Fire, Toronto, Canada, April 19, 1904
Hearts and Planets
The Honor of Thieves
How Bridget Made the Fire
Jumbo, Horseless Fire-Engine
Life of an American Fireman
The Lone Highwayman
Money Mad
Montreal Fire Department on Runners
Mt. Pelee in Eruption and Destruction of St. Pierre
N.Y. Fire Department Returning
"Oceans" Fire Company
Old Volunteer Fire Department
The Outlaw
Panorama of Ruins from Baltimore and Charles Street
Panorama of Ruins from Lombard and Charles Street
Panorama of Ruins from Lombard and Hanover Streets, Baltimore
Panorama of Ruins from Water Front
Panorama of the Paterson Fire
Panoramic View of St. Pierre, Martinique
Parade, Fiftieth Anniversary Atlantic City, N.J.
Parade of "Exempt" Firemen
Paterson Fire, Showing the Y.M.C.A. and Library
Pawtucket Fire Department
The Power of Love
Quebec Fire Dept. on Runners
The Rights of Youth
Ruins of City Hall, Paterson
Run of N.Y. Fire Department
San Francisco Disaster
Scenes in San Francisco
The Still Alarm
Tarrant Fire
They Found the Leak
Those College Girls
Unveiling of the Pennsylvania Monument on the Battlefields of Petersburg, Virginia, May 19, 1909
Water Duel

When Ambrose Dared Walrus
When the Fire-Bells Rang
The Yellow Peril
see also Disasters

Fisher, George, actor

The Darkening Trail
Rumpelstiltskin

Fishers Island, New York

Battleships in Action

Fishing

An Acadian Elopement
Adventures of Dollie
Bass Fishing
The Child of the Ghetto
Drawing a Lobster Pot
Eeling Through Ice
Fisherman's Luck
Fishing at Faralone Island
Fishing Smacks
The 'Gater and the Pickanniny
Hauling a Shad Net
Horses Drawing in Seine
Horses Drawing Salmon Seine
The Jolly Monks of Malabar
A Large Haul of Fish
Men Taking Fish from Salmon Seine
Mexican Fishing Scene
Salmon Fishing Nipissisquit River
Sea Gulls Following Fishing Boats
Trout Fishing
Trout Fishing, Rangeley Lakes
Trout Poachers
Unloading Halibut
The Village Cut-up
Whaling in the Far North Off the Coast of Alaska in the Treacherous Bering Sea
Won by a Fish
see also Ships and watercraft

Fishkill, New York

The Fugitive
The Song of the Wildwood Flute

Fitz-Allen, Adelaide, actress

Parsifal: Parsifal Ascends the Throne, Ruins of Magic Garden, Exterior of Klingson's Castle, Magic Garden, Interior of the Temple, Scene Outside the Temple, Return of Parsifal, In the Woods

Fitzhamon, Lewin, director and actor

The Bewitched Traveller
Decoyed
An Englishman's Trip to Paris From London
An Interrupted Honeymoon
The Lover's Ruse
The Other Side of the Hedge

A Race for a Kiss
Rescued by Rover

Flags, banners, and pennants

Advance of Kansas Volunteers at Caloocan
American Flag
Battle Flags of the 9th Infantry
Battle of Mafeking
The Battle of the Yalu, no. 1–4
Boat Race
Boating Carnival, Palm Beach
The Burglar-Proof Bed
Burial of the "Maine" Victims
Chinese Procession, no. 12
Climbing the American Alps
Congress of Nations
Deaf Mute Girl Reciting "Star Spangled Banner"
"Deutschland" Leaving New York at Full Speed
Drill, Ambulance Corps
The Early Morning Attack
English Lancers Charging
Filipino's Retreat from Trenches
First Avenue, Seattle, Washington
The Flag
The Flag Dance
German and American Tableau
In Old Kentucky
Jack Jaggs and Dum Dum
Marching Scene
Morning Colors on U.S. Cruiser "Raleigh"
Mystic Shriners' Day, Dreamland, Coney Island
Old Glory and the Cuban Flag
Parade of Chinese
Pictures Incidental to Yacht Race
Prince Henry Reviewing the Cadets at West Point
Raising Old Glory Over Morro Castle
Return of 2nd Regiment of New Jersey
Reviewing the "Texas" at Grant's Tomb
Rout of the Filipinos
The Sand Fort
Sarnia Tunnel
"Shamrock" and "Columbia" Rounding the Outer Stake Boat
"Shamrock" and 'Columbia" Yacht Race—First Race
Skirmish Between Russian and Japanese Advance Guards
Skirmish of Rough Riders
Spirit of '76
Street's Zouaves and Wall Scaling
A True Patriot
U.S. Battleship "Oregon"
War Canoe Race

Floods and hurricanes

Bird's-Eye View of Dock Front, Galveston
Flood Scene in Paterson, N.J.
Launching a Stranded Schooner from the Dock
Panorama of East Galveston
Panorama of Galveston Power House
Panorama of Wreckage of Water Front
Panoramic View of Tremont Hotel
Searching Ruins on Broadway, Galveston, for Dead Bodies
see also Disasters

Florida; *see* Lake Worth, Florida; Ormond, Florida; Palm Beach, Florida; Tampa, Florida

Flynn, Jim, prizefighter

Jack Johnson vs. Jim Flynn Contest for Heavyweight Championship of the World, Las Vegas, New Mexico, July 4, 1912

Folding beds; *see* Murphy beds

Foley, Kid, actor

A "Tough" Dance

Fønss, Olaf, actor

Love and Friendship

Football

Classmates
Football Game: West Point vs. Annapolis
Harvard-Pennsylvania Football Game
Kicking Football—Harvard
Princeton and Yale Football Game
Strongheart

Foreign films

The Aeroplane Inventor
Animated Picture Studio
Les Apparitions Fugitives
Au Clair de la Lune
The Aviator's Generosity
The Ballet Master's Dream
The Bewitched Traveller
Bob Kick, l'Enfant Terrible
Bob Kick, The Mischievous Kid
The Child Stealers
The Convict's Escape
The Cook in Trouble
The Damnation of Faust
A Dangerous Play
Desdemona
The Drawing Lesson, [or,] The Living Statue
The Enchanted Well
L'Enchanteur Alcofrisbas
An Englishman's Trip to Paris From London
The Eviction
The Fairyland, or, The Kingdom of the Fairies
Faust aux Enfers
Faust et Marguerite
Fine Feathers Make Fine Birds
The Fire of Life
The Fisherman and His Sweetheart
Homeless
How the Old Woman Caught the Omnibus
Illusions Fantasmagoriques
The Inn Where No Man Rests
An Interrupted Honeymoon
Jack and Jim
Jack Jaggs and Dum Dum
A Kiss and a Tumble
Little Lillian, Toe Danseuse
The Little Railroad Queen
Love and Friendship
Love in the Tropics
The Lover's Ruse
The Magic Lantern
The Melomaniac
The Mermaid
Midsummer-Tide
The Monster
The Mystical Flame
The Oracle of Delphi
The Other Side of the Hedge
Petticoat Lane on Sunday
The Pickpocket
Pierrot, Murderer
The Pig That Came to Life
The Power of Love
Un Prêté Pour un Rendu, ou, Une Bonne Farce Avec Ma Téte
Queen Elizabeth
A Race for a Kiss
Raid on a Coiner's Den
A Railway Tragedy
Reproduction, Coronation Ceremonies—King Edward VII
Rescued by Rover
Le Revenant
Revenge!
The Rights of Youth
Le Roi du Maquillage
Runaway Match
Saturday's Shopping
A Spiritualist Photographer
The Terrible Turkish Executioner
Tommy Atkins, Bobby and Cook
Le Tonnerre de Jupiter
The Two Convicts
The Vampire Dancer
Vengeance
The Victorious Battle for the Conquest of Mergheb, Africa

Forest Hills, New York

[On] a [Good Old] Five Cent Trolley Ride

Forest River Hill, New Jersey

Skirmish Between Russian and Japanese Advance Guards

Fort Boonesboro, Kentucky

Attack on Fort Boonesboro

Fort Lee, New Jersey

The Affair of an Egg
All on Account of the Milk
Balked at the Altar
The Call
The Convict's Sacrifice
The Course of True Love
The Cricket on the Hearth
The Curtain Pole
Eradicating Aunty
The Fatal Hour
The Final Settlement
The Fire-Bug
The Gentlemen Highwaymen
The Girl and the Outlaw
The Girls and Daddy
Happy Jack, A Hero
Her Terrible Ordeal
The Hindoo Dagger
His Trust
His Trust Fulfilled
In Life's Cycle
In Little Italy
In the Window Recess
The Italian Barber
Jealousy and the Man
The King of the Cannibal Island
The Lesson
Lonely Villa
Love in Quarantine
Lure of the Gown
The Man and the Woman
The Massacre
The Midnight Marauder
Not So Bad As It Seemed
One Busy Hour
The Peach-Basket Hat
The Poor Sick Men
The Proposal
The Salvation Army Lass
Simple Charity
A Sound Sleeper
'Tis an Ill Wind That Blows No Good
To Save Her Soul
Tragic Love
A Trap for Santa Claus
A Troublesome Satchel
Turning the Tables
Two Women and a Man
A Welcome Burglar
What Drink Did
What Happened in the Tunnel
What's Your Hurry?
The White Caps
White Roses

Fort Hamilton, New York

The Lost Child

Fotorama

Homeless

Fougère, Eugenie, dancer

Fougere

Fountains

At the Fountain
East Side Urchins Bathing in a
    Fountain
Fatty and Mabel at the San Diego
    Exposition
Feeding Pigeons in Front of St
    Mark's Cathedral, Venice, Italy
Panorama from German Building,
    World's Fair
Sporting Blood
Water Nymphs

France

Queen Elizabeth
see also Montreuil, France; Nice,
France; Paris, France; Vincennes,
France

Franchonetti Sisters

Dance, Franchonetti Sisters

Francis, David Rowland

Speech by President Francis:
    World's Fair

Frankenstein, New Hampshire

Frankenstein Trestle

Fraternal Orders

Atlantic City Floral Parade
Funeral of Hiram Cronk
General Cronje & Mystic Shriners
Mystic Shriner's Day, Dreamland,
    Coney Island
Native Daughters
New Year's Mummies (Mummers)
    Parade
New York Caledonian Club's Parade
Outing, Mystic Shriners, Atlantic
    City, New Jersey
Parade, Fiftieth Anniversary Atlantic
    City, N.J.
Parade, Mystic Shriners, Atlantic
    City, New Jersey
Parade of Chinese
Parade of Eagles, New York
Parade of Shriners, Luna Park
Parade of the Pikers, St. Louis
    Exposition
President Roosevelt's Inauguration
Shooters' Parade, Philadelphia
Shriners' Conclave at Los Angeles,
    Cal., May, 1907

Unveiling of the Pennsylvania Mon-
    ument on the Battlefield of Pe-
    tersburg, Virginia, May 19, 1909
The Would-Be Shriner

Frawley, Jack, cameraman

Bold Bank Robbery
Great Train Robbery

Freighters; *see* Ships and watercraft

French, C. K., actor

Crossroads of Life

French, Charles, actor

The Cord of Life
Lucky Jim

Fröhlich, Else, actress

The Fire of Life
The Little Railroad Queen
Love in the Tropics
The Rights of Youth

From, Elna, actress

The Little Railroad Queen

Fuller, Charles, actor

Seven Days

Fullerton, California

The Kid

Funder, Tronier, actor

Love and Friendship

Funston, Frederick

Colonel Funstan [i.e. Funston]
    Swimming the Baglag River

Gad, Urban, director

The Aviator's Generosity

Gallitzin, Pennsylvania

Running Through Galitzen Tunnel,
    Penna. R.R.

Galveston, Texas

Bird's-Eye View of Dock Front,
    Galveston
Jimmie Hicks in Automobile
Launching a Stranded Schooner
    From the Dock
Panorama of East Galveston
Panorama of Galveston Power
    House
Panorama of Orphans Home, Gal-
    veston
Panorama of Wreckage of Water
    Front
Panoramic View of Tremont Hotel
    Galveston
Searching Ruins on Broadway, Gal-
    veston, for Dead Bodies

Gambling

The Evil Art [or] Gambling Exposed

Gans, Joe, prizefighter

Gans-Nelson Contest, Goldfield,
    Nevada, September 3rd, 1906

**Garde, Axel, scriptwriter/au-
thor**

Midsummer-Tide

Gaumont, L., & Company

The Child Stealers
The Eviction
How to Disperse the Crowd
The Pickpocket
Pierrot, Murderer
Raid on a Coiner's Den
A Railway Tragedy
Revenge!
Runaway Match

**Gauntier, Gene, actress, script-
writer/author**

The Chariot Race
Hulda's Lovers
The Paymaster
The Stage Rustler
Thaw-White Tragedy

Gebhardt, Mrs., actress

Adventures of Dollie

Gebhardt, Frank, actor

Balked at the Altar
A Calamitous Elopement
The Devil
The Fatal Hour
The Feud and the Turkey
Greaser's Gauntlet
The Hindoo Dagger
The Man and the Woman
One Touch of Nature
Romance of a Jewess
Song of the Shirt
Taming of the Shrew
The Tavern Keeper's Daughter

George V, king of England

H.R.H. the Prince of Wales Decorat-
    ing the Monument of Champlain
    and Receiving Addresses of Wel-
    come from the Mayor of Quebec,
    the Governor General of Canada
    and Vice-President Fairbanks,
    Representative of the United
    States
H.R.H. the Prince of Wales Viewing
    the Grand Military Review on the
    Plains of Abraham, Quebec

Germany

Clever Horsemanship
Flying Train
German Railway Service

Gerry Society

The Gerry Society's Mistake

Gibbons, James

Cardinal Gibbons

Gibraltar

Admiral Dewey Landing at Gibraltar

Gilbert, Billy, actor

Miss Fatty's Seaside Lovers

Gilbert, Mrs. H. A.

Reception of President Taft in Petersburg, Virginia, May 19th, 1909

Gish, Dorothy, actress

A Fair Rebel
Liberty Belles
The Wife

Gish, Lillian, actress

The Battle at Elderbush Gulch
Judith of Bethulia
Lord Chumley
Man's Enemy
The Test

Glaum, Louise, actress

The Cup of Life
The Darkening Trail

Glen, New Jersey

Changing Horses at Glen

Glen Island, New York

Battleship "Indiana" in Action
Feeding the Russian Bear
An Impartial Lover
A Juvenile Elephant Trainer
The Llamas at Play

Glendale, California

His Last Dollar
Hogan Out West
The Smoker
Up a Tree
The Way of the World

Gloucester, Massachusetts

Unloading Halibut

Gold mining; *see* Alaska gold rush

Goldfield, Nevada

Gans-Nelson Contest, Goldfield, Nevada, September 3rd, 1906

Gordon Sisters

Gordon Sisters Boxing

Gorham, William

A Total Accident

Gorman, Charles, actor

The Cord of Life
Father Gets in the Game
Mexican Sweethearts
A Temporary Truce
With the Enemy's Help

Gove, O. M., cameraman

An Acadian Elopement
Scenes in San Francisco
A Trip to Berkeley, Cal.
Views in San Francisco

Governors Island, New York

15th Infantry

Grand Canyon, Arizona

The Bargain

Grand Island, Nebraska

Overland Limited

Grandon, Frank, actor

The Duke's Plan
The Englishman and the Girl
In Old California
Ramona

Grant, Major General Frederick D.

Opening Day, Jamestown Exposition

Grantwood, New Jersey

Invisible Fluid
The Nihilist

Grapewin, Charles E., actor

Chimmie Hicks at the Races
Jimmie Hicks in Automobile

Gravesend, New York

The Brooklyn Handicap

Gray, Betty, actress

The Power of the Press
Woman Against Woman

Graybill, Joe, actor

The Face at the Window
A Flash of Light
The Fugitive
Happy Jack, A Hero
Help Wanted
The House With Closed Shutters
The Italian Barber
The Last Deal
The Lesson
The Marked Time Table
An Old Story With a New Ending
The Root of Evil
Two Little Waifs
What the Daisy Said
When We Were in Our Teens
White Roses

Great Forepaugh and Sells Bros. Combined Four-Ring Circus

A Day at the Circus

Great Northern Films Co.

The Aeroplane Inventor
The Aviator's Generosity
A Dangerous Play
Desdemona
The Fire of Life
The Fisherman and His Sweetheart
Homeless
The Little Railroad Queen
Love and Friendship
Love in the Tropics
Midsummer-Tide
The Power of Love
The Rights of Youth
The Two Convicts
The Vampire Dancer
Vengeance

Greene, Kempton, actor

She Would Be an Actress

Greenwich, Connecticut

The Cardinal's Conspiracy
A Change of Heart
The Country Doctor
The Golden Supper
The Little Teacher
The Message
A Summer Tragedy
Sweet and Twenty
Two Little Waifs

Gribbon, Harry, actor

Ambrose's Sour Grapes
Fatty and Mabel at the San Diego Exposition
Mabel, Fatty and the Law
A One Night Stand
Ye Olden Grafter

Griffith, Mrs. Beverly, actress

Droppington's Family Tree
Fatty's Reckless Fling

Griffith, D. W., actor

At the Altar
At the French Ball
Balked at the Altar
The Black Viper
A Calamitous Elopement
Classmates
A Close Call
Crossroads of Life
The Girls and Daddy
Heart of Oyama
Helen's Marriage
'Ostler Joe
The Princess in the Vase
The Sculptor's Nightmare
The Stage Rustler

Griffith, D. W., author

The Battle at Elderbush Gulch
The Massacre
'Ostler Joe
Over the Hills to the Poorhouse
The Primitive Man
The Stage Rustler
The Thread of Destiny

Griffith, D. W., director

Adventures of Dollie
An Affair of Hearts
After Many Years
And a Little Child Shall Lead Them
An Arcadian Maid
As It Is In Life
As the Bells Rang Out
At the Altar
The Awakening
An Awful Moment
A Baby's Shoe
Balked at the Altar
The Bandit's Waterloo
The Banker's Daughters
The Barbarian Ingomar
The Battle at Elderbush Gulch
A Beast at Bay
Behind the Scenes
Betrayed by Hand Prints
The Better Way
The Black Sheep
The Broken Doll
The Broken Locket
A Burglar's Mistake
A Calamitous Elopement
The Call
The Call of the Wild
The Call to Arms
The Cardinal's Conspiracy
A Change of Heart
The Child of the Ghetto
The Children's Friend
A Child's Faith
A Child's Impulse
A Child's Remorse
A Child's Stratagem
Choosing a Husband
The Christmas Burglars
The Cloister's Touch
The Clubman and the Tramp
Comata, the Sioux
Concealing a Burglar
Coney Island Police Court
Confidence
The Converts
The Convict's Sacrifice
The Cord of Life
A Corner in Wheat
The Country Doctor
The Course of True Love
The Cricket on the Hearth
The Criminal Hypnotist
The Curtain Pole
The Dancing Girl of Butte
The Day After

The Death Disc
The Deception
The Devil
The Drunkard's Reformation
The Duke's Plan
The Eavesdropper
Edgar Allen [i.e. Allan] Poe
Effecting a Cure
Eloping with Aunty
The Englishman and the Girl
Eradicating Aunty
Examination Day at School
The Expiation
The Face at the Window
Faded Lilies
A Fair Exchange
Faithful
The Fascinating Mrs. Francis
The Fatal Hour
Fate's Interception
Fate's Turning
Father Gets in the Game
The Female of the Species
The Feud and the Turkey
The Fight for Freedom
The Final Settlement
A Flash of Light
Fools of Fate
A Fool's Revenge
For a Wife's Honor
For Love of Gold
The French Duel
The Fugitive
Getting Even
The Gibson Goddess
The Girl and Her Trust
The Girl and the Outlaw
The Girls and Daddy
The Goddess of Sagebrush Gulch
Gold Is Not All
A Gold Necklace
The Gold Seekers
Golden Louis
The Golden Supper
Greaser's Gauntlet
The Guerrilla
Heart of Oyama
Heaven Avenges
The Helping Hand
Her Father's Pride
Her First Biscuits
Her Terrible Ordeal
The Hindoo Dagger
His Duty
His Last Burglary
His Lesson
His Lost Love
His New Lid
His Sister-in-Law
His Trust
His Trust Fulfilled
His Ward's Love
His Wife's Mother
His Wife's Visitor
Homefolks

The Honor of His Family
The Honor of Thieves
I Did It, Mamma
The Iconoclast
The Impalement
In a Hempen Bag
In Life's Cycle
In Little Italy
In Old California
In Old Kentucky
In the Border States
In the Watches of the Night
In the Window Recess
The Indian Runner's Romance
An Indian Summer
The Ingrate
The Inner Circle
Iola's Promise
The Italian Barber
Jealousy and the Man
The Jilt
Jones and His New Neighbors
Jones and the Lady Book Agent
Jones at the Ball
Jones Entertains
The Joneses Have Amateur Theatricals
Judith of Bethulia
Just Like a Woman
Kentuckian
Lady Helen's Escapade
The Last Deal
Leather Stocking
Lena and the Geese
The Lesser Evil
The Lesson
The Light That Came
Lines of White on a Sullen Sea
Little Angels of Luck
The Little Darling
The Little Teacher
A Lodging for the Night
Lonely Villa
Love Among the Roses
Love Finds a Way
Lucky Jim
Lure of the Gown
The Man
The Man and the Woman
Man in the Box
The Maniac Cook
Man's Genesis
Man's Lust for Gold
The Marked Time Table
The Massacre
May and December
The Medicine Bottle
The Mended Lute
The Message
The Message of the Violin
Mexican Sweethearts
A Midnight Adventure
A Midnight Cupid
The Mills of the Gods
Mr. Jones' Burglar

Mr. Jones Has a Card Party
Mrs. Jones' Lover
The Modern Prodigal
A Mohawk's Way
Money Mad
The Mountaineer's Honor
Muggsy Becomes a Hero
The Narrow Road
The Necklace
Never Again!
A New Trick
The Newlyweds
The Note in the Shoe
Nursing a Viper
The Oath and the Man
Oh, Uncle!
The Old Actor
Old Isaacs the Pawnbroker
On the Reef
One Busy Hour
One Is Business, the Other Crime
One Night and Then
One Touch of Nature
The Open Gate
An Outcast Among Outcasts
Over Silent Paths
The Peach-Basket Hat
Pippa Passes
The Pirate's Gold
A Plain Song
The Planter's Wife
Politician's Love Story
Pranks
The Primitive Man
The Prussian Spy
The Punishment
Ramona
The Reckoning
The Red Girl
The Redman and the Child
The Redman's View
The Renunciation
The Restoration
Resurrection
A Rich Revenge
The Road to the Heart
The Rocky Road
Romance of a Jewess
A Romance of the Western Hills
The Root of Evil
Rose O' Salem-Town
The Roue's Heart
A Rude Hostess
The Sacrifice
A Salutary Lesson
The Salvation Army Lass
The Sands of Dee
Schneider's Anti-Noise Crusade
The School Teacher and the Waif
The Sealed Room
1776, or, the Hessian Renegades
The Seventh Day
Simple Charity
The Slave
A Smoked Husband

The Smoker
Song of the Shirt
The Song of the Wildwood Flute
The Son's Return
The Sorrows of the Unfaithful
A Sound Sleeper
The Spirit Awakened
The Stolen Jewels
A Strange Meeting
The Suicide Club
A Summer Idyl
Sunshine Sue
Sweet and Twenty
Sweet Revenge
Taming a Husband
Taming of the Shrew
The Tavern Keeper's Daughter
A Temporary Truce
The Test
The Test of Friendship
That Chink at Golden Gulch
They Would Elope
Those Awful Hats
Those Boys
Thou Shalt Not
The Thread of Destiny
Through the Breakers
'Tis an Ill Wind That Blows No
  Good
To Save Her Soul
Tragic Love
A Trap for Santa Claus
The Trick That Failed
A Troublesome Satchel
Twin Brothers
The Twisted Trail
The Two Brothers
Two Little Waifs
Two Memories
The Two Paths
Two Women and a Man
The Unchanging Sea
Unexpected Help
The Usurer
The Valet's Wife
The Vaquero's Vow
A Victim of Jealousy
The Violin Maker of Cremona
The Voice of the Violin
Waiter No. 5
Wanted, A Child
Was Justice Served?
The Way of Man
The Way of the World
A Welcome Burglar
What Drink Did
What the Daisy Said
What's Your Hurry?
When a Man Loves
When Kings Were the Law
Where Breakers Roar
Wilful Peggy
Winning Back His Love
With Her Card
With the Enemy's Help

The Woman From Mellon's
A Woman's Way
The Wooden Leg
A Wreath in Time
A Wreath of Orange Blossoms
The Zulu's Heart

Griffith, D. W., scriptwriter

'Ostler Joe
Over the Hills to the Poorhouse

Griffith, D. W., supervisor

Classmates
Men and Women
Strongheart

Groton, Massachusetts

Circular Panorama of Housing the
  Ice
Cutting and Canaling Ice
Loading the Ice on Cars, Conveying
  It Across the Mountains and
  Loading It Into Boats

Guttenberg, New Jersey

Love in the Suburbs
Water Duel

Gypsies

Adventures of Dollie
An Awful Moment
The Child Stealers
Greaser's Gauntlet
A Gypsy Duel
Her First Adventure
Old Maid and Fortune Teller
The Peach-Basket Hat
Rescued by Rover
Spanish Dancers at the Pan-Ameri-
  can Exposition
Stolen by Gypsies
What the Daisy Said
The Woman in Black

Hackensack, New Jersey

The Rocky Road

Hackett, James K., actor

The Prisoner of Zenda

Haines, Mina Gale, actress

The Prisoner of Zenda

Hale, Alan, actor

The Power of the Press
Strongheart
Who's Looney Now?
Woman Against Woman
The Woman in Black

Hale, Walter, actor

The Prisoner of Zenda

**Hall, Emmett Campbell, script-
  writer/author**

His Trust

His Trust Fulfilled

Hamilton, Shorty, actor

On the Night Stage

Hampton Roads, Virginia

The American Fleet in Hampton Roads, 1909, After Girdling the Globe

Hanaway, Frank, actor

The Great Train Robbery

Hanna, Mark

The Late Senator Mark Hanna

Hansen, Valdemar, actor

The Vampire Dancer
Vengeance

Harrington, Mr., director

The Paymaster

Harris, Caroline, actress

The Necklace
To Save Her Soul

Harron, Robert, actor

At the Altar
At the French Ball
The Banker's Daughters
The Battle at Elderbush Gulch
Bobby's Kodak
The Boy Detective
A Burglar's Mistake
A Child's Impulse
Examination Day at School
Fate's Interception
The Girl and Her Trust
The Girls and Daddy
The Helping Hand
The Hindoo Dagger
Homefolks
In a Hempen Bag
The Inner Circle
The Italian Barber
Jones and the Lady Book Agent
Judith of Bethulia
The Little Darling
Man's Genesis
Man's Lust for Gold
The Massacre
The Message
Not So Bad As It Seemed
The Note in the Shoe
An Old Story With a New Ending
One Busy Hour
A Plain Song
Pranks
The Primitive Man
The Sands of Dee
The School Teacher and the Waif
The Smoked Husband
A Sound Sleeper
A Summer Idyl

A Temporary Truce
A Test of Friendship
Those Hicksville Boys
Through the Breakers
To Save Her Soul
The Valet's Wife
Wilful Peggy
A Wreath in Time

Hart, Joseph, actor

The Boys Help Themselves to Foxy Grandpa's Cigars
The Boys, Still Determined, Try It Again on Foxy Grandpa, With the Same Result
The Boys Think They Have One on Foxy Grandpa, But He Fools Them
The Boys Try to Put One Up on Foxy Grandpa
The Creators of Foxy Grandpa
European Rest Cure
Foxy Grandpa and Polly in a Little Hilarity
Foxy Grandpa Shows the Boys a Trick or Two With the Tramp
Foxy Grandpa Tells the Boys a Funny Story
Foxy Grandpa Thumb Book
Why Foxy Grandpa Escaped a Ducking

Hart, William S., actor, director

The Bargain
The Darkening Trail
On the Night Stage

Hartford, Connecticut

Free-for-All Race at Charter Oak Park

Hartsdale, New York

The Horse Thief

Hatton, Raymond, actor

Oh, Those Eyes!

Harvard University

Harvard-Pennsylvania Football Game
Prince Henry Visiting Cambridge, Mass. and Harvard University

Hastings-on-Hudson, New York

The River Pirates

Hauber, W. C., actor

A Bird's a Bird
Hash House Mashers
Love in Armor
Love, Loot and Crash
A Lucky Leap
Mabel and Fatty's Wash Day
Mabel, Fatty and the Law
An Outcast Among Outcasts

Settled at the Seaside

Havana, Cuba

General Lee's Procession
Morro Castle, Havana Harbor
Panorama of Morro Castle, Havana, Cuba
Troops at Evacuation of Havana
Wreck of the Battleship "Maine"

Haverstraw, New York

Haverstraw Tunnel

Hawaii; *see* Honolulu

Hayes, Frank, actor

Ambrose's Nasty Temper
Ambrose's Sour Grapes
Beating Hearts and Carpets
Droppington's Family Tree
Fatty's Chance Acquaintance
Fatty's Faithful Fido
Fatty's New Role
Fatty's Reckless Fling
He Wouldn't Stay Down
Hogan Out West
Hogan the Porter
Hogan's Aristocratic Dream
Hogan's Mussy Job
The Little Teacher
A Lover's Lost Control
Mabel, Fatty and the Law
Mabel Lost and Won
That Little Band of Gold
Their Social Splash
When Love Took Wings

Hearn, F., actor

Men and Women

Hedlund, Guy, actor

The Cord of Life
Her First Biscuits
Hulda's Lovers
The Iconoclast
The Light That Came
A Modern Prodigal
Romance of a Jewess
Rural Elopement
The Tunnel Workers

Held, Anna, actress

Anna Held

Helena, Montana

Overland Express Arriving at Helena, Mont.

Hemment, J. C., cameraman

Paul J. Rainey's African Hunt

Henderson, Dell, actor, director

Algy, the Watchman
As the Bells Rang Out
The Brave Hunter

The Broken Doll
The Broken Locket
The Call to Arms
A Child's Impulse
A Close Call
The Course of True Love
The Engagement Ring
The Fickle Spaniard
For Better—But Worse
The Furs
The Genius
Gold Is Not All
The Gold Seekers
Golden Louis
Happy Jack, A Hero
Helen's Marriage
Help! Help!
His Trust
Hot Stuff
The Impalement
The Last Deal
The Leading Man
Liberty Belles
Little Angels of Luck
The Love of Lady Irma
The Marked Time Table
The Massacre
Oh, Those Eyes!
The Passing of a Grouch
A Plain Song
The Poor Sick Men
The Purgation
The Rejuvenation of Aunt Mary
The Song of the Wildwood Flute
A Spanish Dilemma
The Speed Demon
That Chink at Golden Gulch
Those Hicksville Boys
The Tragedy of a Dress Suit
Trying to Fool Uncle
The Twisted Trail
The Two Paths
Unexpected Help
The Usurer
A Voice From the Deep
Waiter No. 5
The Way of the World
When a Man Loves
When the Fire-Bells Rang
Won By a Fish
A Wreath of Orange Blossoms

Henderson, Grace, actress

As the Bells Rang Out
A Corner in Wheat
The Face at the Window
Happy Jack, A Hero
The Helping Hand
His Trust Fulfilled
His Wife's Sweethearts
The House With Closed Shutters
How Hubby Got a Raise
The Iconoclast
In a Hempen Bag
Just Like a Woman

Lena and the Geese
Little Angels of Luck
Love in Quarantine
The Marked Time Table
The Masher
The Message of the Violin
A Midnight Cupid
Muggsy Becomes a Hero
Not So Bad As It Seemed
On the Reef
The Poor Sick Men
The Purgation
The Recreation of an Heiress
The Sands of Dee
Simple Charity
A Summer Tragedy
Those Hicksville Boys
Through the Breakers
The Tourists
The Tragedy of a Dress Suit
The Trick That Failed
Two Little Waifs
The Two Paths
The Usurer
A Victim of Jealousy
Waiter No. 5
A Wreath of Orange Blossoms

Hendry, Anita, actress

The Road to the Heart

Hennessy, George, actor

A Child's Remorse

Henriksen, Julie, actress

The Fire of Life
Midsummer-Tide
The Vampire Dancer

Henry, Prince of Prussia

Arrival of Prince Henry and President Roosevelt at Shooter's Island
Christening and Launching Kaiser Wilhelm's Yacht "Meteor"
Deutschland Leaving New York at Full Speed
German and American Tableau
"Kronprinz Wilhelm" With Prince Henry on Board Arriving New York
Prince Henry Arriving at West Point
Prince Henry Arriving in Washington and Visiting the German Embassy
Prince Henry at Lincoln's Monument, Chicago, Illinois
Prince Henry at Niagara Falls
Prince Henry at West Point
Prince Henry Reviewing the Cadets at West Point
Prince Henry Visiting Cambridge, Mass. and Harvard University
Sailing of the "Deutschland" with Prince Henry on Board

Hepworth, Barbara, actress

Rescued by Rover

Hepworth, Cecil, actor, director, producer

The Bewitched Traveller
Rescued by Rover
Saturday's Shopping

Hepworth, Mrs. Cecil, actress

Rescued by Rover

Hepworth & Co.

Decoyed
An Englishman's Trip to Paris From London
How the Old Woman Caught the Omnibus
An Interrupted Honeymoon
The Lover's Ruse
Petticoat Lane on Sunday
A Race for a Kiss
Rescued by Rover
Saturday's Shopping

Hertel, Aage, actor

A Dangerous Play
Love and Friendship
The Rights of Youth

Hertel, Tage, actor

The Fire of Life
Love and Friendship
Midsummer-Tide

Hickman, Howard, actor

The Cup of Life

Higgin, Mr., cameraman

Pippa Passes
They Would Elope

High Bridge, New Jersey

The Course of True Love

Highlands, New Jersey

The Gibson Goddess
Lines of White on a Sullen Sea
A Salutary Lesson
The Sorrows of the Unfaithful
The Troublesome Baby

Highwood Park, New York

A Potato Bake in the Woods
A Romp on the Lawn

Historical dramas; *see* Period dramas

Hoboken, New Jersey

The Boy Detective
Church "Our Lady of Grace," Hoboken
The Reckoning
S.S. "Deutschland" Leaving Her Dock in Hoboken

452

Iversen, Jon, actor

The Fire of Life

Jacobsen, Frederik, actor

A Dangerous Play
Love and Friendship
Midsummer-Tide
The Vampire Dancer
Vengeance

Jaffa, Syria

Street Scene at Jaffa
Tourists Embarking at Jaffa

Jamaica

Railroad Panorama Near Spanishtown, Jamaica

Jamaica, New York

A Corner in Wheat

Jamestown, Virginia

Opening Day, Jamestown Exposition

Jamestown Tricentennial

Opening Day, Jamestown Exposition

Jamison, W. L., cameraman

Mining Operations, Pennsylvania
Coal Fields
Panoramic View of an Egyptian
Cattle Market

Japan

S.S. "Coptic" Coaling
see also Kobe, Japan; Kyoto, Japan;
Nagasaki, Japan; Tokyo, Japan;
Yokohama, Japan

Jefferson, Joseph, actor

Rip Van Winkle

Jefferson, Thomas, actor

Classmates

Jefferson, William, actor

Man's Enemy
The Power of the Press
The Wages of Sin

Jeffries, James J., prizefighter

Jeffreys [i.e. Jeffries] and Ruhlin
Sparring Contest at San Fran-
cisco, Cal. Nov. 15, 1901—Five
Rounds
Jeffreys in His Training Quarters
Jim Jeffries on His California Ranch
Reproduction of Jeffries-Corbett
Contest

Jennings, Al, actor

The Bank Robbery

Jensen, Arnold, actor

The Fire of Life

Jericho, Palestine

Tourists Taking Water From the
River Jordan

Jerusalem, Palestine

Jerusalem's Busiest Street, Showing
Mt. Zion
A Jewish Dance at Jerusalem

Jessen, Gerhard, actor

Vengeance

Johnson, Arthur, actor

Adventures of Dollie
All on Account of the Milk
And a Little Child Shall Lead Them
At the Altar
The Awakening
A Baby's Shoe
Balked at the Altar
The Bandit's Waterloo
The Better Way
The Broken Locket
A Change of Heart
The Christmas Burglars
The Cloister's Touch
The Clubman and the Tramp
Comata, the Sioux
Concealing a Burglar
Confidence
The Converts
A Corner in Wheat
The Criminal Hypnotist
The Curtain Pole
The Day After
The Death Disc
The Deception
The Drunkard's Reformation
Edgar Allen [i.e. Allan] Poe
Eloping with Aunty
Eradicating Aunty
The Expiation
Faithful
Fate's Turning
The Final Settlement
For a Wife's Honor
The French Duel
The Gibson Goddess
The Girls and Daddy
Greaser's Gauntlet
The Helping Hand
Her First Biscuits
The Hindoo Dagger
His Duty
His Ward's Love
His Wife's Mother
The Impalement
In Old California
In the Window Recess
The Indian Runner's Romance
The Ingrate
Jealousy and the Man

The Jilt
Jones at the Ball
Lady Helen's Escapade
The Light That Came
Lines of White on a Sullen Sea
The Little Darling
The Little Teacher
Love Among the Roses
Love Finds a Way
Lucky Jim
The Mended Lute
The Mills of the Gods
Mr. Jones' Burglar
Mr. Jones Has a Card Party
Money Mad
The Mountaineer's Honor
The Necklace
A New Trick
The Newlyweds
The Note in the Shoe
Nursing a Viper
One Touch of Nature
Over Silent Paths
Pippa Passes
The Planter's Wife
Politician's Love Story
Pranks
The Prussian Spy
The Redman's View
The Renunciation
Resurrection
A Romance of the Western Hills
A Rude Hostess
The Sacrifice
The Sealed Room
1776, or, the Hessian Renegades
The Seventh Day
The Slave
A Sound Sleeper
A Strange Meeting
Sweet Revenge
Taming a Husband
Taming of the Shrew
The Tenderfoot's Triumph
The Test
The Test of Friendship
They Would Elope
Those Awful Hats
'Tis an Ill Wind That Blows No
Good
To Save Her Soul
Tragic Love
The Trick That Failed
A Troublesome Satchel
Trying to Get Arrested
Twin Brothers
The Twisted Trail
The Two Brothers
Two Women and a Man
The Unchanging Sea
Unexpected Help
The Valet's Wife
The Vaquero's Vow
The Violin Maker of Cremona
The Voice of the Violin

Was Justice Served?
The Way of Man
Where Breakers Roar
A Woman's Way

Johnson, Jack, prizefighter

Jack Johnson, vs. Jim Flynn Contest for Heavyweight Championship of the World, Las Vegas, New Mexico, July 4, 1912

Jones, John Paul

John Paul Jones Ceremonies

Jones & Laughlin

Circular Panoramic View of Jones & Laughlin's Steel Works Yard

Jordan, Palestine

Herd of Sheep on the Road to Jerusalem

Kalem Company

The Chariot Race

Kansas City, Missouri

Central High School, Gymnastic Drill
Emerson School Calisthenics
Hyde Park School Graduating Class
Hyde Park School, Room 2
Kindergarten Ball Game
Kindergarten Dance
Lathrop School, Calisthenics
Linwood School, Calisthenics
Whittier School, Calisthenics

Keller, Gus

Expert Bag Punching

Kelly, James T., actor

Crossed Love and Swords
Dirty Work in a Laundry
Droppington's Devilish Deed
Droppington's Family Tree
A Hash House Fraud
He Wouldn't Stay Down
A One Night Stand
Our Dare Devil Chief
A Versatile Villain

Kennedy, Edgar, actor

Ambrose's Sour Grapes
Curses! They Remarked
Fatty and Mabel at the San Diego Exposition
Fatty's New Role
Fatty's Plucky Pup
Fatty's Reckless Fling
Fatty's Tintype Tangle
His Luckless Love
Mabel's Wilful Way
Miss Fatty's Seaside Lovers
That Little Band of Gold
Wished on Mabel

Kent, J. B., cameraman

The Bank Robbery
A Round-up in Oklahoma

Kentucky

Attack on Fort Boonesboro

Kern, H. C., actor

Rumpelstiltskin

Kershaw, Eleanor, actress

The Course of True Love

Kerzog, F., actor

Men and Women

Keyport, New Jersey

A Salutary Lesson

Keystone Film Company

Ambrose's Fury
Ambrose's Little Hatchet
Ambrose's Lofty Perch
Ambrose's Nasty Temper
Ambrose's Sour Grapes
Beating Hearts and Carpets
The Beauty Bunglers
A Bird's a Bird
The Cannon Ball
Caught in a Park
Caught in the Act
Colored Villainy
Court House Crooks
Crossed Love and Swords
Cursed by His Beauty
Curses! They Remarked
Dirty Work in a Laundry
Do-Re-Mi—Boom!
Dough and Dynamite
Droppington's Devilish Deed
Droppington's Family Tree
Fatty and Mabel at the San Diego Exposition
Fatty and Mabel's Simple Life
Fatty's Chance Acquaintance
Fatty's Faithful Fido
Fatty's New Role
Fatty's Plucky Pup
Fatty's Reckless Fling
Fatty's Tintype Tangle
For Better—But Worse
From Patches to Plenty
Gentlemen of Nerve
A Glimpse of the San Diego Exposition
Gussle Rivals Jonah
Gussle the Golfer
Gussle Tied to Trouble
Gussle's Backward Way
Gussle's Day of Rest
Gussle's Wayward Path
A Hash House Fraud
Hash House Mashers
He Wouldn't Stay Down
Hearts and Planets

His Luckless Love
Hogan Out West
Hogan the Porter
Hogan's Aristocratic Dream
Hogan's Mussy Job
Hogan's Romance Upset
The Home Breakers
A Home-Breaking Hound
A Human Hound's Triumph
The Little Teacher
Love in Armor
Love, Loot and Crash
Love, Speed and Thrills
A Lover's Lost Control
A Lucky Leap
Mabel and Fatty Viewing the World's Fair at San Francisco, Cal.
Mabel and Fatty's Married Life
Mabel and Fatty's Wash Day
Mabel, Fatty and the Law
Mabel Lost and Won
Mabel's Wilful Way
Merely a Married Man
Miss Fatty's Seaside Lovers
A One Night Stand
Our Dare Devil Chief
Peanuts and Bullets
The Rent Jumpers
Settled at the Seaside
Shot in the Excitement
That Little Band of Gold
That Springtime Feeling
Their Social Splash
Those Bitter Sweets
Those College Girls
A Versatile Villain
Viewing Sherman Institute for Indians at Riverside, Cal.
When Ambrose Dared Walrus
When Love Took Wings
Willful Ambrose
Wished on Mabel
Ye Olden Grafter

Kicking Horse Canyon, Canada

Down Western Slope
Panoramic View, Kicking Horse Canyon
Panoramic View, Lower Kicking Horse Canyon
Panoramic View, Lower Kicking Horse Valley
Panoramic View Near Mt. Golden on the Canadian Pacific R.R.
Panoramic View, Upper Kicking Horse Canyon

Kid Foley

The Bowery Kiss

King, Rose, actress

The Necklace
The Seventh Day

M. Lavelle, Physical Culture, no. 2

Lawrence, Florence, actress

After Many Years
At the Altar
The Awakening
A Baby's Shoe
The Bandit's Waterloo
The Barbarian Ingomar
Behind the Scenes
Betrayed by Hand Prints
The Call
The Call of the Wild
The Cardinal's Conspiracy
The Christmas Burglars
The Clubman and the Tramp
Comata, the Sioux
Concealing a Burglar
Confidence
The Country Doctor
The Criminal Hypnotist
The Curtain Pole
The Deception
The Devil
The Drunkard's Reformation
Eloping with Aunty
Eradicating Aunty
The Fascinating Mrs. Francis
The Feud and the Turkey
The Girl and the Outlaw
The Girls and Daddy
Heart of Oyama
Her First Biscuits
His Ward's Love
His Wife's Mother
The Honor of Thieves
The Ingrate
Jealousy and the Man
The Jilt
Jones and His New Neighbors
Jones and the Lady Book Agent
Jones at the Ball
Jones Entertains
The Joneses Have Amateur Theatricals
Lady Helen's Escapade
Lure of the Gown
The Medicine Bottle
The Mended Lute
Mr. Jones' Burglar
Mr. Jones Has a Card Party
Mrs. Jones' Lover
Money Mad
The Note in the Shoe
One Touch of Nature
The Peach-Basket Hat
The Planter's Wife
The Prussian Spy
The Reckoning
The Red Girl
Resurrection
The Road to the Heart
Romance of a Jewess
The Roue's Heart
The Sacrifice

The Salvation Army Lass
Schneider's Anti-Noise Crusade
The Slave
A Smoked Husband
Song of the Shirt
The Stolen Jewels
Sweet and Twenty
Taming of the Shrew
The Test of Friendship
Those Awful Hats
Those Boys
'Tis an Ill Wind that Blows No Good
A Troublesome Satchel
Trying to Get Arrested
Two Memories
The Valet's Wife
The Vaquero's Vow
The Way of Man
What Drink Did
Where Breakers Roar
The Wooden Leg
A Wreath in Time
The Zulu's Heart

Leander Sisters, dancers

Cupid and Psyche
Leander Sisters

Lebanon; *see* Beirut

Lee, Fitzhugh

Opening Day, Jamestown Exposition

Lee, Florence, actress

The Rejuvenation of Aunt Mary
Seven Days

Lee, William, director

The Fall of Black Hawk

Lehrman, Henry "Pathé," actor

Gussle Rivals Jonah
Gussle the Golfer
A Lover's Lost Control
Nursing a Viper
The Would-Be Shriner

Leo XIII, Pope

Pope in His Carriage
Pope Passing Through Upper Loggia
Renovare Production Company "Special"

Leon, Chester, prizefighter

Dixon-Chester Leon Contest

Leonard, Marion, actress

And a Little Child Shall Lead Them
As It Is In Life
At the Altar
An Awful Moment
The Bandit's Waterloo
The Broken Locket
A Burglar's Mistake

The Call
The Call to Arms
The Children's Friend
The Christmas Burglars
The Cloister's Touch
Comata, the Sioux
The Converts
The Cord of Life
The Criminal Hypnotist
Crossroads of Life
The Day After
The Death Disc
The Drunkard's Reformation
The Duke's Plan
The Eavesdropper
The Expiation
The Fascinating Mrs. Francis
Fools of Fate
The Gibson Goddess
Gold Is Not All
Golden Louis
Greaser's Gauntlet
Her First Biscuits
The Hindoo Dagger
His Duty
His Last Dollar
His Lost Love
In Little Italy
In Old California
In the Watches of the Night
In the Window Recess
The Indian Runner's Romance
The Jilt
The Joneses Have Amateur Theatricals
The Light That Came
Lines of White on a Sullen Sea
Lonely Villa
Love Among the Roses
Love Finds a Way
Lucky Jim
Lure of the Gown
The Maniac Cook
The Medicine Bottle
The Mills of the Gods
A New Trick
The Note in the Shoe
Nursing a Viper
On the Reef
Over Silent Paths
The Peach-Basket Hat
Pippa Passes
Politician's Love Story
Pranks
The Prussian Spy
The Restoration
The Roue's Heart
A Rude Hostess
The Sacrifice
The Salvation Army Lass
The Sealed Room
Sweet Revenge
The Tavern Keeper's Daughter
The Test
Thou Shalt Not

Through the Breakers
A Trap for Santa Claus
The Two Brothers
Two Memories
The Voice of the Violin
A Welcome Burglar
Where Breakers Roar
With Her Card

Leonia, New Jersey

His Wife's Sweethearts
The Little Teacher
The Son's Return
The Summer Boarders

Leonia Junction, New Jersey

Her First Adventure

Lestina, Adolphe, actor

The Cord of Life
The Two Paths
Waiter No. 5
A Wreath of Orange Blossoms

Levi and Cohen

Levi & Cohen, the Irish Comedians

Lewis, Walter, actor

A Fair Rebel

Lexington, Massachusetts

Children's Hour on the Farm

Li Hung Chang

Li Hung Chang and Suite: Presentation of Parlor Mutoscope

Lincoln, Robert

Prince Henry at Lincoln's Monument, Chicago, Illinois

Linden, New Jersey

Changing Horses at Linden

Lipton, Sir Thomas

Jockeying and Start of Yacht[s], Aug. 25

Little Anita

Betsy Ross Dance
Cosy Corner Dance

Little Falls, New Jersey

The Barbarian Ingomar
The Planter's Wife
Pranks
The Red Girl
The Redman and the Child
The Restoration
Romance of an Egg
They Would Elope
A Woman's Way

Lloyd, Harold, actor

Court House Crooks
Miss Fatty's Seaside Lovers

Their Social Splash

Loeb, William, Jr.

Opening Day, Jamestown Exposition

Logging

Logging in Maine

Lola, Ella, dancer

Ella Lola, a la Trilby
Turkish Dance, Ella Lola

London, England

The Pickpocket
Runaway Match
Petticoat Lane On Sunday

Long, John Davis

Secretary Long and Captain Sigsbee

Long Beach, California

The Sands of Dee

Long Branch, New Jersey

Exhibition of Prize Winners
Life Rescue at Long Branch
Sea Waves
Single Harness Horses
Teams of Horses

Longfellow, Stephanie, actress

As the Bells Rang Out
The Banker's Daughters
The Better Way
The Convict's Sacrifice
The Country Doctor
Effecting a Cure
Eradicating Aunty
The Impalement
In Life's Cycle
The Lesson
The Man
The Message of the Villain
The Rocky Road
A Strange Meeting
A Summer Idyl
Turning the Tables
Winning Back His Love

Lorley, Ann, actress

When Knights Were Bold

Los Angeles, California

Ambrose's Fury
Ambrose's Little Hatchet
Ambrose's Lofty Perch
Ambrose's Nasty Temper
Ambrose's Sour Grapes
As It Is In Life
A Beast at Bay
Beating Hearts and Carpets
The Cannon Ball
Caught in a Park
Caught in the Act

Colored Villainy
Court House Crooks
Crossed Love and Swords
Cursed by His Beauty
Curses! They Remarked
Dirty Work in a Laundry
Do-Re-Mi—Boom!
Dough and Dynamite
Droppington's Devilish Deed
Fatty and Mabel's Simple Life
Fatty's Chance Acquaintance
Fatty's Faithful Fido
Fatty's New Role
Fatty's Plucky Pup
Fatty's Tintype Tangle
For Better—But Worse
From Patches to Plenty
The Furs
Gussle the Golfer
Gussle's Day of Rest
Gussle's Wayward Path
Help! Help!
His Luckless Love
Hogan's Mussy Job
Hogan's Romance Upset
The Home Breakers
A Home-Breaking Hound
A Human Hound's Triumph
Iola's Promise
Judith of Bethulia
Lena and the Geese
The Little Teacher
Love in Armor
Love, Loot and Crash
Love, Speed and Thrills
Mabel and Fatty's Married Life
Mabel and Fatty's Wash Day
Mabel, Fatty and the Law
The Newlyweds
Our Dare Devil Chief
Peanuts and Bullets
Pigeon Farm at Los Angeles, Cal.
Ramona
Shriners' Conclave at Los Angeles, Cal., May, 1907
South Spring Street, Los Angeles, Cal.
A Spanish Dilemma
That Little Band of Gold
That Springtime Feeling
Their Social Splash
Those Bitter Sweets
Trying to Fool Uncle
Unexpected Help
A Versatile Villain
When Ambrose Dared Walrus
When Love Took Wings
Willful Ambrose
Wished on Mabel
The Would-Be Shriner
Ye Olden Grafter

Loubet, Emile

King Edward and President Loubet Reviewing French Troops

The Weary Hunters and the Magician
Welding the Big Ring
Western Stage Coach Hold Up
Westinghouse Air Brake Company
Westinghouse Works
Whaling in the Far North off the Coast of Alaska in the Treacherous Bering Sea
What Drink Did
What Happened in the Tunnel
What the Doctor Ordered
White Star S.S. "Baltic" Leaving Pier On First Eastern Voyage
A Wild Turkey Hunt
Working the Breeches Buoy
The Yale Laundry

McKinley, William, president, U.S.

Arrival of McKinley's Funeral Train at Canton, Ohio
Execution of Czolgosz, with Panorama of Auburn Prison
McKinley and Party
McKinley Funeral on Way to Church
McKinley Funeral: Panorama of McKinley Home
McKinley's Funeral Entering Westlawn Cemetery, Canton
The Mob Outside the Temple of Music at the Pan-American Exposition
Panoramic View of the President's House at Canton, Ohio
President McKinley and Escort Going to the Capitol
President McKinley Leaving Observatory, Mt. Tom, Holyoke, Massachusetts
President McKinley Reviewing the Troops at the Pan-American Exposition
President McKinley Taking the Oath
President McKinley's Funeral Cortege at Buffalo, New York
President McKinley's Funeral Cortege at Washington, D.C.
President McKinley's Speech at the Pan-American Exposition
President Roosevelt at the Canton Station
Taking President McKinley's Body From Train at Canton, Ohio

McKinley, Mrs. William

President McKinley Leaving Observatory, Mt. Tom, Holyoke, Massachusetts

Macpherson, Jeanie, actress

An Affair of Hearts
The Call
The Clubman and the Tramp
Concealing a Burglar

Confidence
A Corner in Wheat
The Curtain Pole
The Day After
The Death Disc
The Devil
Faded Lilies
Father Gets in the Game
A Flash of Light
A Gold Necklace
The Iconoclast
Jones at the Ball
Jones Entertains
Lady Helen's Escapade
The Lesson
The Medicine Bottle
A Midnight Adventure
A Midnight Marauder
Mr. Jones Has Card Party
The Newlyweds
The Peach-Basket Hat
The Rude Hostess
The Seventh Day
The Test of Friendship
Tragic Love
The Troublesome Baby
Trying to Get Arrested
Two Little Waifs
A Victim of Jealousy
Winning Back His Love
A Wreath in Time
A Wreath of Orange Blossoms

Madison, Ethel, actress

That Little Band of Gold

Mailes, Charles Hill, actor

Algy, the Watchman
The Battle at Elderbush Gulch
A Beast at Bay
The Billionaire
A Close Call
The Fatal Wedding
Fate's Interception
The Girl and Her Trust
The Goddess of Sagebrush Gulch
Homefolks
The Inner Circle
Judith of Bethulia
Just Like a Woman
Lena and the Geese
The Lesser Evil
A Lodging for the Night
Lord Chumley
Man's Genesis
The Massacre
May and December
The Narrow Road
The Old Actor
The Primitive Man
The Root of Evil
The Sands of Dee
The School Teacher and the Waif
Seven Days
A Summer Idyl

A Temporary Truce
Those Hicksville Boys
The Wages of Sin
With the Enemy's Help
The Woman in Black
Won By a Fish

Maine

Drawing a Lobster Pot
Logging in Maine
Trout Fishing, Rangeley Lakes

Major cities; see Buildings; Business districts; specific cities

Manassas, Virginia

Military Maneuvers, Manassas, Virginia

Manhattan Field, New York

"Chappie" and "Ben Bolt"
Ladies' Saddle Horses

Manila, Philippine Islands

Aguinaldo's Navy
Bridge Traffic, Manila
The Escalta, Manila
A Filipino Cock Fight
Unloading Lighters, Manila
Water Buffalo, Manila

Manley, Charles "Daddy," actor

Uncle Josh at the Moving Picture Show
Uncle Josh's Nightmare

Manlius, New York

The Battle of the Yalu, no. 1–4
Butt's Manual, St. John's School
Company Drill, St. John's Military Academy
Dress Parade, St. John's Academy
The Hero of Liao Yang
Manual of Arms, St. John's Military Academy
Small Gun Drill, St. John's Academy

Mannie, himself, a dog

Laura Comstock's Bag-Punching Dog

Marblehead, Massachusetts

Rose O'Salem-Town

Marceline

Marceline, the World-Renowned Clown of the N.Y. Hippodrome

Marionettes; see Puppets

Markey, Enid, actress

The Cup of Life
The Darkening Trail

Marsh, Mae, actress

The Battle at Elderbush Gulch

464

A Beast at Bay
Homefolks
An Indian Summer
The Inner Circle
Judith of Bethulia
Just Like a Woman
Lena and the Geese
The Lesser Evil
Man's Genesis
One Is Business, the Other Crime
The Primitive Man
The Sands of Dee
The School Teacher and the Waif
Serious Sixteen
A Spirit Awakened

Marshall, Miss

Treloar and Miss Marshall, Prize Winners at the Physical Culture Show in Madison Square Garden

Marshall, Missouri

Basket Ball, Missouri Valley College
Fencing Class, Missouri Valley College

Marston, Lawrence, director

The Fatal Wedding
The Star of Bethlehem

Marston, Mrs. Lawrence, actress

The Fatal Wedding
The Power of the Press
The Road to Yesterday
Woman Against Woman
The Woman in Black

Martinique; see St. Pierre, Martinique

Marvin, Arthur, cameraman

Accidents Will Happen
Adventures of Dollie
The Affair of an Egg
An Affair of Hearts
After Many Years
After the Ball
All on Account of the Milk
Allabad; the Arabian Wizard
Arrest of a Shoplifter
The Art of Making Up
At the Altar
An Awful Moment
A Baby's Shoe
Balked at the Altar
Bally-Hoo Cake Walk
The Bandit's Waterloo
The Barber's Queer Customer
Bargain Day
Bass Fishing
Behind the Scenes
Betrayed by Hand Prints
A Black Storm
A Bowery Cafe

Broadway & Union Square, New York
The Burglar-Proof Bed
A Burglar's Mistake
A Calamitous Elopement
The Call of the Wild
A Career of Crime, no. 1
A Career of Crime, no. 2
A Career of Crime, no. 3
A Career of Crime, no. 4
A Career of Crime, no. 5
Central Park After Dark
A Champion Beer Drinker
A Child's Impulse
The Chimney Sweep and the Miller
The Chinese Rubbernecks
The Cloister's Touch
Club Swinging, Carlisle Indian School
Coaching for a Record
Confidence
A Convict's Punishment
The Cord of Life
Cotton Spinning
The Course of True Love
The Cricket on the Hearth
Crossroads of Life
Deaf Mute Girl Reciting "Star Spangled Banner"
The Deceived Slumming Party
Delivering Newspapers
A Dog Fight
The Downward Path: The Fresh Book Agent
The Downward Path: She Ran Away
The Downward Path: The New Soubrette
The Downward Path: The Girl Who Went Astray
The Downward Path: The Suicide
Drawing a Lobster Pot
Drill, Ye Tarriers, Drill
The Eavesdropper
Eccentricities of an Adirondack Canoe
Effecting a Cure
The Elopement
Eloping with Aunty
Eradicating Aunty
Escape from Sing Sing
Execution of a Spy
Exhibition Drill, New York Firemen, Union Square
Faithful
Family Troubles
Farmer Oatcake Has His Troubles
A Farmer's Imitation of Ching Ling Foo
The Fatal Hour
The Feud and the Turkey
The Final Settlement
A Flirtation
A Fool's Revenge
For a Wife's Honor
For Love of Gold

48th Highlanders Regiment
The French Duel
The 'Gater and the Pickanniny
A Gesture Fight in Hester Street
The Girl and the Outlaw
The Girls and Daddy
A Gold Necklace
The Gold Seekers
Golden Louis
A Good Time with the Organ Grinder
Greaser's Gauntlet
The Guerrilla
Happy Jack, A Hero
Heart of Oyama
Help Wanted
The Helping Hand
His Duty
His Last Dollar
His Name Was Mud
His New Lid
His Wife's Mother
His Wife's Sweethearts
The Honor of His Family
How Bridget Made the Fire
How Charlie Lost the Heiress
How Hubby Got a Raise
How They Fired the Bum, Nit
How They Rob Men in Chicago
The Impalement
Indiana Whitecaps
The Ingrate
Installation Ceremonies of President Butler
A Jersey Skeeter
The Jilt
Kentuckian
The Kid
A Knot in the Plot
A Large Haul of Fish
Laughing Ben
Leather Stocking
The Little Teacher
Love Among the Roses
Love at 55
Love Finds a Way
Love in Quarantine
The Love of Lady Irma
Love's Young Dream
Lucky Jim
A Lucky Toothache
Lure of the Gown
McKinley Funeral on Way to Church
The Man and the Woman
Man in the Box
The Masher
May and December
The Message
A Midnight Adventure
The Midnight Marauder
Mr. Gay and Mrs.
Mr. Jones' Burglar
Muggsy Becomes a Hero
A Mystic Re-Incarnation
The Necklace

Help Wanted
Not So Bad As It Seemed
The Suicide Club
The Test of Friendship
The Violin Maker of Cremona

Mexico

Mexican Fishing Scene
Mexican Rurales Charge
Sunday Morning in Mexico
Surface Transit, Mexico
see also Durango, Mexico; Mexico
  City, Mexico

Mexico City, Mexico

The Great Bull Fight
Las Vigas Canal, Mexico
Las Vigas Canal, Mexico City
Market Scene, City of Mexico
Mexico Street, Scene
Repairing Streets in Mexico

Mianus, Connecticut

The Paymaster

Mice; see Rodents

Michigan; see Detroit, Michigan

Miles, Senator

Glimpses of Yellowstone Park

Miles, David, actor

The Drunkard's Reformation
The Eavesdropper
The Maniac Cook
The Road to the Heart
The Violin Maker of Cremona
What Drink Did
When Kings Were the Law

Miles, Herbert, actor

The Feud and the Turkey
Lady Helen's Escapade

Miles, Mrs. Herbert, actress

His Wife's Mother

Miles, Herbert J., actor, cameraman, producer

Head-On Collision at Brighton
  Beach Race Track July 4th, 1906
Horses Drawing in Seine
Horses Drawing Salmon Seine
International Contest for the Heavy-
  weight Championship: Squires vs.
  Burns, Ocean View, Cal., July 4th,
  1907
Jim Jeffries on His California Ranch
Market Street Before Parade
Men Taking Fish From Salmon
  Seine
O'Brien-Burns Contest, Los
  Angeles, Cal., Nov. 26th, 1906
Over Route of Roosevelt Parade in
  an Automobile
Panorama of Beach and Cliff House

Panorama, Union Square, San Fran-
  cisco
President Reviewing School Chil-
  dren
The President's Carriage
Shriners' Conclave at Los Angeles,
  Cal., May, 1907
Squires, Australian Champion in
  His Training Quarters
A Trip Down Mt. Tamalpais

Miles, Nelson

Mayor Van Wyck and General Miles

Miles Brothers, producer

Gans-Nelson Contest, Goldfield,
  Nevada, September 3rd, 1906
Head-On Collision at Brighton
  Beach Race Track July 4th, 1906
International Contest for the Heavy-
  weight Championship: Squires vs.
  Burns, Ocean View, Cal., July 4th,
  1907
Jim Jeffries on His California Ranch
Nelson-Britt Prize Fight
O'Brien-Burns Contest, Los
  Angeles, Cal., Nov. 26th, 1906
Shriners' Conclave at Los Angeles,
  Cal., May, 1907
Squires, Australian Champion in
  His Training Quarters
A Trip Down Mt. Tamalpais

Military

Admiral Dewey at State House,
  Boston
Admiral Dewey Landing at Gibraltar
Admiral Dewey Leading Land Pa-
  rade
Admiral Dewey Receiving the Wash-
  ington and New York Committees
Admiral Dewey Taking Leave of
  Washington Committee on the
  U.S. Cruiser "Olympia"
Admiral Sampson on Board the
  Flagship
Advance Guard, Return of N.J.
  Troops
Advance of Kansas Volunteers at
  Caloocan
Aguinaldo's Navy
The American Fleet in Hampton
  Roads, 1909, After Girdling the
  Globe
Ancient and Honourable Artillery of
  London on Parade
Arrival of Prince Henry and Presi-
  dent Roosevelt at Shooter's Island
Astor Battery on Parade
An Attack by Torpedo Boats
The Attack on Port Arthur
Battery B Arriving at Camp
Battery B Pitching Camp
Battery K Siege Guns
Battle Flags of the 9th U.S. Infantry

Battle of Mafeking
Battle of Mt. Ariat
The Battle of the Yalu, Nos. 1–4
Battleship "Indiana" in Action
Battleship "Odin"
Battleships in Action
Battleships "Iowa" and "Massachu-
  setts"
Bayonet Exercises
Beach Apparatus-Practice
The Bengal Lancers
Blanket-Tossing a New Recruit
Boat Race
Boating Under Oars
Boat Wagon and Beach Cart
Boer Commissary Train Treking
The Boer War
Boers Bringing in British Prisoners
Bombardment of Taku Forts, by the
  Allied Forces
Boston School Cadets, 3rd Regi-
  ment
British Light Artillery
Burial of the "Maine" Victims
Butt's Manual, St. John's School
California Volunteers Marching to
  Embark
Capsize of Lifeboat
Capture of Boer Battery
Capture of Boer Battery by British
Capture of Trenches at Candaba
  [Candabar]
A Cavalry Charge
Charge by the 1st Bengal Lancers
Charge of Boer Cavalry
Classmates
Close View of the "Brooklyn" Naval
  Parade
Colonel Funstan [i.e. Funston]
  Swimming Baglag River
Colored Troops Disembarking
Company Drill, St. John's Military
  Academy
Cossack Cavalry
Cruiser "Cincinnati"
Cruiser "Detroit"
Cruiser "Marblehead"
Cuban Ambush
Cuban Volunteers Embarking
Cuban Volunteers Marching for
  Rations
The Dandy Fifth
Dewey Arch—Troops Passing Un-
  der Arch
Dewey Parade, 10th Pennsylvania
  Volunteers
Discharging a Whitehead Torpedo
Dress Parade of Scouts, St. Louis
  Exposition
Dress Parade, St. John's Academy
Drill, Ambulance Corps
Drill by Naval Militia
Drilling an Awkward Squad
Drills and Exercises, Schoolship "St.
  Mary's"

468

Return of 2nd Regiment of New Jersey
Return of Troop C, Brooklyn
Review of Cadets at West Point
Review of Cadets, West Point
Review of Russian Artillery
Reviewing the "Texas" at Grant's Tomb
Rhode Island Light Artillery
Roosevelt's Rough Riders
Roosevelt's Rough Riders Embarking for Santiago
Rout of the Filipinos
Russian Sharp Shooters
Sailors of Atlantic Fleet, Dewey Parade
Sailors Waltzing
Scrubbing Clothes
2nd Special Service Battalion, Canadian Infantry, Embarking for So. Africa
2nd Special Service Battalion, Canadian Infantry—Parade
1776, or, the Hessian Renegades
Seventh Regiment, N.Y.
71st New York Volunteers Embarking for Santiago
71st Regiment, Camp Wyckoff
Sham Battle at the Pan-American Exposition
Shanghai Police
Sheik Artillery, Hong Kong
Shelter Tent Drill
Shooting Captured Insurgents
6th Cavalry Assaulting South Gate of Pekin
69th Regiment, N.G.N.Y.
Skirmish Between Russian and Japanese Advance Guards
A Skirmish Fight
Skirmish of Rough Riders
Small Gun Drill, St. John's Academy
Soldiers Washing Dishes
Sparring Match on the "Kearsarge"
Steam Tactics
Steamer "Mascotte" Arriving at Tampa
Street Zouaves and Wall Scaling
10th U.S. Infantry Disembarking from Cars
10th U.S. Infantry, 2nd Battalion, Leaving Cars
The "Texas" Naval Parade
Torpedo Attack on Port Arthur
Torpedo Boat "Dupont"
Torpedo Boat "Morris" Running
Trained Cavalry Horses
Transport Ships at Port Tampa
Transport "Whitney" Leaving Dock
Troop Ships for the Philippines
Troops at Evacuation of Havana
Troops Embarking at San Francisco
Troops Making Military Road in Front of Santiago
25th Infantry

Two Companies, Royal Canadian Regiment
U.S. Battleship "Indiana"
U.S. Battleship "Iowa"
U.S. Battleship "Oregon"
U.S. Cavalry Supplies Unloading at Tampa, Florida
U.S. Cruiser "Brooklyn" Naval Parade
U.S. Cruiser "Nashville"
U.S. Cruiser "Olympia" Leading Naval Parade
U.S. Cruiser "Raleigh"
United States Government Gun Test
U.S. Infantry Supported by Rough Riders at El Caney
U.S.S. "Castine"
U.S. Troops and Red Cross in the Trenches Before Caloocan
U.S. Troops Landing at Daiquiri, Cuba
Unveiling of the Pennsylvania Monument on the Battlefields of Petersburg, Virginia, May 19, 1909
Vengeance
The Victorious Battle for the Conquest of Mergheb, Africa
Victorious Squadron Firing Salute
Wagon Supply Train En Route
Wall Scaling
Water Buffalo, Manila
West Point Cadets
West Point Cadets, St. Louis Exposition
When the Flag Falls
Working the Breeches Buoy
Wounded Soldiers Embarking in Row Boats
Wreck of the Battleship "Maine"
Wreck of the "Vizcaya"
see also Ships and watercraft

Miller, W. Chrystie, actor

The Battle at Elderbush Gulch
The Broken Doll
The Call
A Change of Heart
The Cloister's Touch
The Converts
The Dancing Girl of Butte
The Day After
The Duke's Plan
Examination Day at School
The Goddess of Sagebrush Gulch
Gold Is Not All
The Gold Seekers
Heaven Avenges
Her Father's Pride
Her Terrible Ordeal
His Wife's Sweethearts
The Honor of His Family
In Life's Cycle
In Little Italy

In Old California
In the Border States
An Indian Summer
The Lesson
Lines of White on a Sullen Sea
Lord Chumley
A Lucky Toothache
Man's Genesis
The Marked Time Table
The Massacre
A Midnight Cupid
The Modern Prodigal
The Newlyweds
The Oath and the Man
The Old Actor
An Old Story With a New Ending
On the Reef
An Outcast Among Outcasts
Over Silent Paths
A Plain Song
The Redman's View
The Renunciation
The Rocky Road
Rose O'Salem-Town
The Sands of Dee
Simple Charity
The Sorrows of the Unfaithful
The Spirit Awakened
A Summer Idyl
Sunshine Sue
A Temporary Truce
That Chink at Golden Gulch
Thou Shalt Not
The Thread of Destiny
To Save Her Soul
A Trap for Santa Claus
A Troublesome Satchel
The Twisted
The Two Brothers
Unexpected Help
White Roses

Miller, Walter, actor

The Fatal Wedding
The Road to Yesterday
Seven Days
The Wages of Sin

Minneapolis, Minnesota

Falls of Minnehaha

Minnesota

Falls of Minnehaha

Minto, Lord

Arrival of the Governor General, Lord Minto, at Quebec

Missouri; *see* Kansas City, Missouri; Kirksville, Missouri; Marshall, Missouri; St. Joseph, Missouri; St. Louis, Missouri

Missouri Commission

Calisthenic Drill, Missouri Commission

470

Morris, Dave, actor

Ambrose's Fury
Ambrose's Little Hatchet
Ambrose's Lofty Perch
Ambrose's Nasty Temper
The Billionaire
Crossed Love and Swords
From Patches to Plenty
Liberty Belles
Merely a Married Man
The Rejuvenation of Aunt Mary
Seven Days
Who's Looney Now?

Morris, Reggie, actor

Liberty Belles
The Rejuvenation of Aunt Mary

Morris Park, New York

Juvenile Stakes
Meadowbrook Steeplechase
Metropolitan Handicap

Morrison, Louis, actor

Rumpelstiltskin

Motor Vehicles; see Automobiles; Motorcycles

Motorboats; see Ships and watercraft

Motorcycles

Fine Feathers Make Fine Birds
A Human Hound's Triumph
Love, Loot and Crash

Mules; see Donkeys and mules

Mulhall, Jack, actor

The Rejuvenation of Aunt Mary
Who's Looney Now?

Murphy beds

The Burglar-Proof Bed
He Wouldn't Stay Down
Shut Up!
Subub Surprises the Burglar
A Tramp on the Roof

Murray, Charles, actor

Beating Hearts and Carpets
The Beauty Bunglers
Caught in the Act
Cursed by His Beauty
From Patches to Plenty
Hogan Out West
Hogan the Porter
Hogan's Aristocratic Dream
Hogan's Mussy Job
Hogan's Romance Upset
Their Social Splash
Those College Girls

Murray, Marie, actress

The Great Train Robbery
A Romance of the Rail

Myers, Harry C., actor

The Cannon Ball
The Guerrilla

Nagasaki, Japan

Coaling a Steamer, Nagasaki Bay, Japan
S.S. "Gaelic" at Nagasaki

Nairs, Phineas, actor

The Kleptomaniac

Naples, Italy

Eating Macaroni in the Streets of Naples

Nassau, B.I.

Native Woman Washing a Negro Baby in Nassau, B.I.

Nathansen, Kamma Creutz, actress

Homeless

Nation, Carrie

Carrie Nation Smashing Saloon
Why Mr. Nation Wants a Divorce

National parks; see Tourist attractions; Yellowstone Park, Wyoming

Native American; see American Indians and Eskimos

Navy; see Military; Ships and watercraft

Negroes; see Blacks

Nebraska; see Central City, Nebraska; Grand Island, Nebraska; and Omaha, Nebraska

Neilan, Marshall, actor

Classmates
Men and Women

Nelson, "Battling"

Gans-Nelson Contest, Goldfield, Nevada, September 3rd, 1906
Impersonation of Britt-Nelson Fight
Nelson-Britt Prize Fight

Nevada

Gans-Nelson Contest, Goldfield, Nevada, September 3rd, 1906

New Brunswick, Canada

Moose Hunt in New Brunswick
Salmon Fishing Nipissisquit River

New Castle, Delaware

Hot Meals at All Hours

New England Forest, Fish & Games Association

A Wild Turkey Hunt

New Hampshire

Automobiling Among the Clouds
Fastest Wrecking Crew in the World
see also Frankenstein, New Hampshire; Portsmouth, New Hampshire; and Rye Beach, New Hampshire

New Haven, Connecticut

Princeton and Yale Football Game

New Jersey

Ambulance at the Accident
Ambulance Call
Eeling Through Ice
The Great Train Robbery
Ice Yacht Racing
Life of an American Fireman
A Mile in 56 Seconds
A Romance of the Rail
Rounding Up of the "Yeggmen"
A Spill
see also specific cities and towns

New London, Connecticut

Drills and Exercises, Schoolship "St. Mary's"

New Mexico

Serving Rations to the Indians, no. 1
Serving Rations to the Indians, no. 2
see also Albuquerque, New Mexico; Isleta, New Mexico; and Las Vegas, New Mexico

New Rochelle, New York

The Star of Bethlehem

New Suffolk, New York

Holland Submarine Boat Tests

New York (state)

Automobile Race for the Vanderbilt Cup
The Camera Fiend, no. 1
"Columbia" and "Defender" Rounding Stake-Boat
"Columbia" vs. "Defender"
Discovery of Bodies (The Pioneers)
Fastest Wrecking Crew in the World
Feeding Geese at Newman's Poultry Farm
Firing the Cabin (The Pioneers)
The Fleet Steaming up North River
Going to the Hunt, Meadowbrook
In the Haunts of Rip Van Winkle
In the Valley of the Esopus
Indians Leaving Bald Mountain
Into the Heart of the Catskills
The King of the Cannibal Island
Kit Carson
The "Massachusetts" Naval Parade
Panorama From Incline Railway
Panorama From Running Incline

Panorama, Great Gorge Route over Lewiston Bridge
Panorama of Gorge Railway
Panoramic View of the Gorge R.R.
Rapids Below Suspension Bridge
Reception of British Fleet
The Redman's View
Rescue of Child From Indians
Rounding up of the "Yeggmen"
Settler's Home Life
Trappers Crossing Bald Mountain
A Trip on the Catskill Mt. Ry
Waterfall in the Catskills
see also specific cities, towns, and geographic locations

New York City, New York

Across the Subway Viaduct, New York
Admiral Dewey Leading Land Parade
Admiral Dewey Leading the Land Parade no. 2
Admiral Dewey Passing Catholic Club Stand
Admiral Dewey Receiving the Washington and New York Committees
Admiral Dewey Taking Leave of Washington Committee on the U.S. Cruiser "Olympia"
Admiral Sampson on Board the Flagship
Annual Parade, New York Fire Department
Around New York in 15 Minutes
Astor Battery On Parade
At the Foot of the Flatiron
At the Fountain
Automobile Parade
An Awful Moment
A Baby's Shoe
A Bad Boy's Joke on the Nurse
Bargain Day, 14th Street, New York
Battery K Siege Guns
Battery Park
Battle Flags of the 9th Infantry
Bayonet Exercises
Beginning of a Skyscraper
The Black Hand
The Blizzard
Brannigan Sets Off the Blast
Broadway & Union Square, New York
Buffalo Bill's Wild West Parade
Capture of Yegg Bank Burglars: Capture & Death; Cellar Scene; Dive Scene; Tracked
A Child's Remorse
The Christmas Burglars
City Hall to Harlem in 15 Seconds via the Subway Route
Close View of the "Brooklyn" Naval Parade
The Clubman and the Tramp
The Dandy Fifth

The Deceived Slumming Party
Delivering Newspapers
Departure of Peary [and the] Roosevelt from New York
"Deutschland" Leaving New York at Full Speed
The Dewey Arch
Dewey Arch—Troops Passing Under Arch
Dewey Parade, 10th Pennsylvania Volunteers
Dick Croker Leaving Tammany Hall
East River Novelty
East Side Urchins Bathing in a Fountain
Elevated Railroad, New York
The Escaped Lunatic
European Rest Cure
The Ex-Convict
Excavating for a New York Foundation
Excavation for Subway
Excursion Boats, Naval Parade
Exhibition Drill, New York Firemen, Union Square
Fancy Driving
Father Gets in the Game
Fire, Adams Express Office
Fireboat "New Yorker" Answering an Alarm
Fireboat "New Yorker" in Action
48th Highlanders Regiment
A Friend in Need Is a Friend Indeed
Funeral of Hiram Cronk
The "Glen Island" Accompanying Parade
Golden Louis
Governor Roosevelt and Staff
Governor's Foot Guards, Conn.
The Helping Hand
His Wife's Mother
The Honor of Thieves
How a French Nobleman Got a Wife Through the New York Herald Personal Columns
The Hypnotist's Revenge
Ice Skating in Central Park, N.Y.
Interior N.Y. Subway, 14th St. to 42nd St.
The Jilt
Jones and His New Neighbors
The Kleptomaniac
"Kronprinz Wilhelm" Docking
"Kronprinz Wilhelm" With Prince Henry on Board Arriving in New York
Lifting the Lid
Lower Broadway
Madison Square, New York
Maniac Chase
Mayor Van Wyck and General Miles
Miss Jessie Cameron, Champion Child Sword Dancer
Miss Jessie Dogherty, Champion Female Highland Fling Dancer

Mr. Hurry-Up of New York
Mr. Jones Has a Card Party
Mixed Babies
Money Mad
Move On
The Narrow Road
Naval Parade
New Brooklyn Bridge
New York Caledonian Club's Parade
New York City Dumping Wharf
New York City "Ghetto" Fish Market
New York City in a Blizzard
New York City Police Parade
New York City Public Bath
N.Y. Fire Department Returning
New York Harbor Police Boat Patrol Capturing Pirates
N.Y. Journal Despatch Yacht "Buccaneer"
New York Police Parade, June 1st, 1899
Old Fashioned Scottish Reel
104th Street Curve, New York, Elevated Railway
Opening Ceremonies, New York Subway, Oct. 27, 1904
Opening Ceremony of New York Subway
Opening of New East River Bridge, New York
Opening the Williamsburg Bridge
Panorama at Grant's Tomb, Dewey Naval Procession
Panorama From the Tower of the Brooklyn Bridge
Panorama From Times Building, New York
Panorama of Blackwell's Island, N.Y.
Panorama of Flatiron Building
Panorama of Riker's Island, N.Y.
Panorama Water Front and Brooklyn Bridge From East River
Panoramic View of Brooklyn Bridge
Panoramic View of Floral Float "Olympia"
Panoramic View of the Hohenzollern
Parade of Eagles, New York
Parade of "Exempt" Firemen
Parade of Horses on Speedway
Pennsylvania Tunnel Excavation
A Perilous Proceeding
Personal
Pilot Boats in New York Harbor
Pole Vaulting
Politician's Love Story
Pontoon Bridge Building
Raffles, the Dog
Reviewing the "Texas" at Grant's Tomb
Romance of a Jewess
Rounding Up of the "Yeggmen"
Sea Gulls in Central Park

472

Seeing New York by Yacht
Seventh Regiment, N.Y.
Shelter Tent Drill
69th Regiment, N.G.N.Y
Skating on Lake, Central Park
Sky Scrapers of New York City, From the North River
The Skyscrapers
Sleighing in Central Park, New York
Sleighing Scene
The Slocum Disaster
The Smoked Husband
Sorting Refuse at Incinerating Plant, New York City
Soubrette's Troubles on a Fifth Avenue Stage
Star Theatre
Statue of Liberty
Steamscow "Cinderella" and Ferryboat "Cincinnati"
The Still Alarm
Stolen Gypsies
Stop Thief!
A Street Arab
Street Car Chivalry
Strongheart
Sweet Revenge
Tarrant Fire
The "Texas" Naval Parade
Throwing the Sixteen Pound Hammer
The Tunnel Workers
Two Chappies in a Box
U.S. Battleship "Oregon"
U.S. Cruiser "Brooklyn" Naval Parade
U.S. Cruiser "Olympia" Leading Naval Parade
Victorious Squadron Firing Salute
The Voice of the Violin
Wanted—A Nurse
Washington Bridge and Speedway
Weary Willie Kidnaps a Child
West Point Cadets
What Happened on Twenty-Third Street, New York City
White Star S.S. Baltic Leaving Pier on First Eastern Voyage
White Wings on Review
A Wreath in Time
see also Brooklyn, New York

New York Motion Picture Co.

The Bargain
The Cup of Life
The Darkening Trail
The Devil
The Italian
On the Night Stage
Rumpelstiltskin

Newark, New Jersey

Coasting
The Heavenly Twins at Lunch
The Heavenly Twins at Odds

Life of an American Fireman
Snowballing the Coaster

Newburg, Frank, actor

Man's Enemy

Newfoundland, Canada

Stalking and Shooting Caribou, Newfoundland

Newhard, Robert, cameraman

The Bargain
On the Night Stage

Newport, Rhode Island

Discharging a Whitehead Torpedo
Exploding a Whitehead Torpedo
Gun Drill by Naval Cadets at Newport Training School
Gymnasium Exercises and Drill at Newport Training School
Naval Apprentices at Sail Drill on Historic Ship Constellation
Naval Sham Battle at Newport
Panoramic View of Newport
Torpedo Boat "Morris" Running

Newport News, Virginia

Launch, U.S. Battleship "Kentucky"

Newport Training School

Gun Drill by Naval Cadets at Newport Training School
Gymnasium Exercises and Drill at Newport Training School
Naval Apprentices at Sail Drill on Historic Ship Constellation
Naval Sham Battle at Newport

Newsreels; *see* Documentaries

Newton, Marie, actress

The Woman in Black

Niagara Falls, New York

American Falls, Goat Island
American Falls, Luna Island
Captain Nissen Going Through Whirlpool Rapids, Niagara Falls
Circular Panorama of Suspension Bridge and American Falls
Circular Panorama of the Horse Shoe Falls in Winter
Circular Panoramic View of Whirlpool Rapids
Crossing Ice Bridge at Niagara Falls
Niagara Falls Winter
Panoramic View of Niagara Falls
Prince Henry at Niagara Falls
Sliding Down Ice Mound at Niagara Falls

Nice, France

Battle of Confetti at the Nice Carnival

Battle of Flowers at the Nice Carnival
Procession of Floats and Masqueraders at Nice Carnival

Nicholls, George, actor

An Arcadian Maid
As It Is In Life
As the Bells Rang Out
A Baby's Shoe
Behind the Scenes
The Child of the Ghetto
A Child's Faith
A Child's Impulse
The Cloister's Touch
The Cricket on the Hearth
The Day After
The Englishman and the Girl
A Fair Exchange
A Flash of Light
The Gibson Goddess
Gold Is Not All
The Gold Seekers
Help Wanted
Her First Biscuits
Her Terrible Ordeal
His Last Burglary
His Wife's Visitor
The Iconoclast
In Life's Cycle
In Little Italy
In the Watches of the Night
In the Window Recess
Iola's Promise
The Jilt
The Last Deal
Leather Stocking
The Light That Came
Lines of White on a Sullen Sea
Little Angels of Luck
The Little Darling
The Little Teacher
The Marked Time Table
The Message of the Violin
A Midnight Cupid
A Modern Prodigal
A Mohawk's Way
The Mountainer's Honor
The Newlyweds
Nursing a Viper
The Oath and the Man
The Open Gate
Pippa Passes
The Punishment
The Restoration
A Rich Revenge
The Rocky Road
Rose O'Salem-Town
The Sealed Room
1776, or, the Hessian Renegades
Simple Charity
Sunshine Sue
Thou Shalt Not
The Thread of Destiny
Through the Breakers

To Save Her Soul
The Trick That Failed
The Twisted Trail
The Two Brothers
Two Women and a Man
Unexpected Help
The Usurer
Waiter No. 5
Wanted, A Child
The Way of the World
What Drink Did
What the Daisy Said
What's Your Hurry?
The Woman From Mellon's

Nichols, Norma, actress

Curses! They Remarked
Dough and Dynamite
Fatty's Tintype Tangle
Gentlemen of Nerve

Nidermann, Marie, actress

Homeless

Nielsen, H. C., actor

Love and Friendship
Midsummer-Tide
Vengeance

Nielsen, Peter, actor

Homeless

Nissen, N. P.

Captain Nissen Going Through
Whirlpool Rapids, Niagara Falls

**Nobel, Christian, scriptwriter/
author**

The Aviator's Generosity

Nolan, Robert, actor

The Charity Ball
A Poor Relation
Who's Looney Now?

Norcross, Frank, actor

Men and Women

**Nordisk Film Co.; see Great
Northern Film Co.**

Nørlund, Agnes, actress

The Vampire Dancer

Normand, Mabel, actress

The Brave Hunter
A Dash Through the Clouds
The Engagement Ring
Fatty and Mabel at the San Diego
Exposition
Fatty and Mabel's Simple Life
The Fickle Spaniard
The Furs
Gentlemen of Nerve
Helen's Marriage
Help! Help!

Hot Stuff
An Interrupted Elopement
Katchem Kate
The Little Teacher
Mabel and Fatty Viewing the
World's Fair at San Francisco,
Cal.
Mabel and Fatty's Married Life
Mabel and Fatty's Wash Day
Mabel, Fatty and the Law
Mabel Lost and Won
Mabel's Wilful Way
Neighbors
Oh, Those Eyes!
A Spanish Dilemma
That Little Band of Gold
Tomboy Bessie
The Tourists
The Tragedy of a Dress Suit
What the Doctor Ordered
Wished on Mabel

Norris, Frank, author

A Corner in Wheat

North Beach, New York

A Country Courtship

**North Carolina; see Edenton,
North Carolina; Pinehurst,
North Carolina**

O'Brien, Jack, prizefighter

O'Brien-Burns Contest, Los
Angeles, Cal., Nov. 26th, 1906

**Occidental and Oriental S.S.
Co.**

Arrival of Tokyo Train

Ocean Park, California

The Cannon Ball
Mabel's Wilful Way
A Voice From the Deep

**Ocean voyages; see Ships and
watercraft**

**Oes, Ingvald C., film company
executive**

The Aeroplane Inventor
The Aviator's Generosity
A Dangerous Play
Desdemona
The Fire of Life
The Fisherman and His Sweetheart
Homeless
The Little Railroad Queen
Love and Friendship
Love in the Tropics
Midsummer-Tide
The Power of Love
The Rights of Youth
The Two Convicts
The Vampire Dancer
Vengeance

**Ohio; see Canton, Ohio; Cleve-
land, Ohio; and Youngstown,
Ohio**

Oklahoma

The Bank Robbery
A Round-up in Oklahoma
see also Bliss, Oklahoma; Cache,
Oklahoma; and Wichita Forest
and Game Reserve, Oklahoma

**Oklahoma Natural Mutoscene
Company**

The Bank Robbery
A Round-Up in Oklahoma
The Wolf Hunt

Olcott, Sidney, actor, director

The Chariot Race
The Village Cut-Up
Wanted: A Dog

Olsen, Lauritz, actor

The Aeroplane Inventor

Omaha, Nebraska

Council Bluffs Bridge Station

**Omnibuses; see Buses; and Car-
riages, coaches and buggies**

O'Neill, James, actor

The Count of Monte Cristo

Opperman, Frank, actor

Colored Villainy
Curses! They Remarked
A Fair Rebel
Hash House Members
A Home-Breaking Hound
A Human Hound's Triumph
The Little Teacher
A Lodging for the Night
Love in Armor
A Lucky Leap
Man's Lust for Gold
The Old Actor
An Outcast Among Outcasts
The Rent Jumpers
The School Teacher and the Waif
The Smoker
Trying to Fool Uncle

Orange, New Jersey

The Ex-Convict
The Fox Hunt
Life of an American Fireman

Orangutan; see Apes

Ormond Beach, Florida

Ormond, Fla. Auto Races

Orth, Louise, actress

Man's Enemy
Seven Days

474

Orvieto, Italy

Corpus Christi Procession, Orvieto

Osterman, Kathryn, actress

The Art of Making Up
Chicks to Order
Girl at the Window
"He Cometh Not," She Said
He Loves Me, He Loves Me Not
In My Lady's Boudoir
The Lost Child
Lucky Kitten!
The Rose
A Search for the Evidence
The Strenuous Life; or, Anti-Race
  Suicide
Sweets for the Sweet
The Unfaithful Wife: Part 1, The
  Lover
The Unfaithful Wife: Part 2, The
  Fight
The Unfaithful Wife: Part 3, Murder
  and Suicide
A Welsh Rabbit

O'Sullivan, Tony, actor

After the Ball
As It Is In Life
The Awakening
The Banker's Daughters
A Calamitous Elopement
The Convict's Sacrifice
The Day After
The Duke's Plan
The Englishman and the Girl
A Fair Exchange
The Final Settlement
Getting Even
The Gibson Goddess
The Goddess of Sagebrush
The Gold Seekers
Her First Biscuits
Her Terrible Ordeal
The Honor of His Family
How Hubby Got a Raise
Hulda's Lovers
The Iconoclast
In Life's Cycle
In Little Italy
In the Border States
In the Watches of the Night
The Jilt
Katchem Kate
The Light That Came
The Little Teacher
A Lodging for the Night
The Mills of the Gods
Mr. Jones' Burglar
Mrs. Jones' Lover
The Mountaineers Honor
The Narrow Road
The Newlyweds
The Note in the Shoe
An Old Story With a New Ending
On the Reef

An Outcast Among Outcasts
Pippa Passes
A Plain Song
Pranks
The Proposal
The Red Girl
A Rich Revenge
The Rocky Road
Schneider's Anti-Noise Crusade
The Son's Return
The Suicide Club
Taming a Husband
That Chink at Golden Gulch
The Thread of Destiny
'Tis an Ill Wind That Blows No
  Good
The Tourists
The Trick That Failed
Twin Brothers
The Twisted Trail
Two Little Waifs
The Usurer
A Victim of Jealousy
The Violin Maker of Cremona
Was Justice Served
The Way of Man
The Way of the World
What Drink Did
What the Daisy Said
When a Man Loves
The Woman From Mellon's

Ott, Fred, actor

Edison Kinetoscopic Record of a
  Sneeze, January 7, 1894

Ottawa, Canada

Two Companies, Royal Canadian
  Regiment

Outcault, James, cartoonist

Section of Buster Brown Series,
  Showing a Sketch of Buster by
  Outcault

Oyster Bay, New York

President Roosevelt Addressing
  Crew of "Kearsarge"
President Roosevelt's Arrival at
  "Kearsarge"
President Roosevelt's Departure
  From "Kearsarge"
President Roosevelt's Homecoming
President Roosevelt's Visit to Admi-
  ral Barker
Scenes and Incidents, Russo-Japa-
  nese Peace Conference, Ports-
  mouth, N.H.
Sparring Match on the "Kearsarge"

Pacific Coast Life Saving Ser-
vice

Capsize of Lifeboat
Launch of Life Boat
Launch of Surf Boat

Return of Lifeboat

Pacific Palisades, California

A Lover's Lost Control

Paget, Alfred, actor

As the Bells Rang Out
The Banker's Daughters
The Battle at Elderbush Gulch
A Beast at Bay
The Black Sheep
The Broken Doll
A Child's Faith
A Close Call
A Dash Through the Clouds
The Face at the Window
The Gambler of the West
The Girl and Her Trust
The Goddess of Sagebrush Gulch
Gold Is Not All
The Gold Seekers
The Golden Supper
Help! Help!
Her Father's Pride
His Trust
The Iconoclast
In Life's Cycle
In the Border States
The Indian
The Inner Circle
An Interrupted Elopement
Iola's Promise
Judith of Bethulia
The Lesser Evil
Little Angel's of Luck
A Lodging for the Night
The Marked Time Table
The Masher
The Massacre
The Message of the Violin
A Midnight Cupid
The Modern Prodigal
A Mohawk's Way
The Narrow Road
The Newlyweds
The Oath and the Man
One Is Business, the Other Crime
Politician's Love Story
The Primitive Man
The Redman's View
A Romance of the Western Hills
The Root of Evil
Rose O'Salem-Town
A Salutary Lesson
The School Teacher and the Waif
A Spirit Awakened
A Temporary Truce
Two Little Waifs
The Two Paths
The Usurer
Waiter No. 5
Winning Back His Love

Observation Train Following Parade

Old Volunteer Fire Department

Opening, Pan-American Exposition

Opening the Williamsburg Bridge

Over Route of Roosevelt Parade in an Automobile

Panorama at Grant's Tomb, Dewey Naval Procession

Panorama from Gondola, St. Louis Exposition

Panoramic View of Floral Float "Olympia"

Parade, Fiftieth Anniversary Atlantic City, N.J.

Parade, Mystic Shriners, Atlantic City, New Jersey

Parade of Buffalo Bill's Wild West Show, no. 1

Parade of Buffalo Bill's Wild West Show, no. 2

Parade of Chinese

Parade of Coaches

Parade of Eagles, New York

Parade of "Exempt" Firemen

Parade of Floats, St. Louis Exposition

Parade of Horses on Speedway

Parade of Marines, U.S. Cruiser "Brooklyn"

Parade of Shriners, Luna Park

Parade of the Pikers St. Louis Exposition

Parade of Women Delegates; World's Fair

Police Boats Escorting Naval Parade

President McKinley Reviewing the Troops at the Pan-American Exposition

President McKinley's Funeral Cortege at Buffalo, New York

President Reviewing School Children

President Roosevelt at Lynn, Mass.

President Roosevelt Reviewing the Troops at Charleston Exposition

Pres. Roosevelt's Fourth of July Oration

President Roosevelt's Inauguration

The President's Carriage

Prince Henry at Lincoln's Monument, Chicago, Illinois

Prince Henry at West Point

Prince Henry Reviewing the Cadets at West Point

Prince Henry Visiting Cambridge, Mass. and Harvard University

Procession of Floats

Procession of Floats and Masqueraders at Nice Carnival

Procession of Mounted Indians and Cowboys

The Providence Light Artillery

Reception of President Taft in Petersburg, Virginia, May 19th, 1909

Return of 2nd Regiment of New Jersey

Return of Troop C. Brooklyn

Review of Cadets, West Point

Roosevelt's Rough Riders

Sailors of Atlantic Fleet, Dewey Parade

St. Patrick's Cathedral and Fifth Avenue on Easter Sunday Morning

2nd Special Service Battalion, Canadian Infantry—Parade

Seventh Regiment, N.Y.

71st Regiment, Camp Wyckoff

Shooters' Parade, Philadelphia

Shriners' Conclave at Los Angeles, Cal., May, 1907

69th Regiment, N.G.N.Y.

Street's Zouaves and Wall Scaling

The "Texas" Naval Parade

Troops at Evacuation of Havana

U.S. Battleship "Oregon"

U.S. Cruiser "Brooklyn" Naval Parade

U.S. Cruiser "Olympia" Leading Naval Parade

Unveiling of the Pennsylvania Monument on the Battlefields of Petersburg, Virginia, May 19, 1909

West Point Cadets

West Point Cadets, St. Louis Exposition

White Wings on Review

The Would-Be Shriner

Paris, France

Breaking of the Crowd at Military Review at Longchamps

Champs de Mars

Champs Elysees

Eiffel Tower from Trocadero Palace

Esplanade des Invalides

King Edward's Visit to Paris

Palace of Electricity

Panorama From the Moving Boardwalk

Panorama of Eiffel Tower

Panorama of Place de l'Opera

Panorama of the Moving Boardwalk

Panorama of the Paris Exposition from the Seine

Panoramic View of the Champs Elysee

Panoramic View of the Place de l'Concord

Paris From the Seine

Scene From the Elevator Ascending Eiffel Tower

Scene in the Swiss Village at Paris Exposition

Swiss Village

Paris Exposition

Champs de Mars

Eiffel Tower from Trocadero Palace

Esplanade des Invalides

Palace of Electricity

Panorama From the Moving Boardwalk

Panorama of Eiffel Tower

Panorama of the Moving Boardwalk

Panorama of the Paris Exposition From the Seine

Scene From the Elevator Ascending Eiffel Tower

Scene in the Swiss Village at Paris Exposition

Swiss Village

Parker, Alton B.

Judge Alton B. Parker and Guests

Judge Parker Receiving the Notification of His Nomination for the Presidency

Parks; see Amusement areas; Tourist attractions; Yellowstone Park, Wyoming

Parmalee, Philip

A Dash Through the Clouds

Pasadena, California

Beverly of Graustark

Gold Is Not All

Ostrich Farms at Pasadena

Ostriches Feeding

Ostriches Running, no. 1

Ostriches Running, no. 2

Parade of Coaches

Procession of Floats

A Romance of the Western Hills

Thou Shalt Not

Patterson, Nan

Reproduction, Nan Paterson's Trial

Paterson, New Jersey

The Call to Arms

Flood Scene in Paterson, N.J.

The Oath and the Man

Panorama of the Paterson Fire

Paterson Fire, Showing the Y.M.C.A. and Library

Ruins of City Hall, Paterson

Pawtucket, Rhode Island

Noon Hour, Hope Webbing Co.

Pawtucket Fire Department

Pearce, Peggy, actress

Beating Hearts and Carpets

Gentlemen of Nerve

Gussle Rivals Jonah

Gussle Tied to Trouble

Gussle's Wayward Path

A Lover's Lost Control

Peary, Robert

Departure of Peary [and the] Roosevelt from New York

Peekskill, New York

Climbing the American Alps
Pollywog 71st Regiment, N.G.S.N.Y. Initiating Raw Recruits

Peep shows

The Animated Poster
As Seen On the Curtain
The Ball Game
Behind the Screen
Boxing for Points
Cake Walk
Christmas Morning
The Christmas Party
Cripple Creek Floats
Crissie Sheridan
Davey Jones' Locker
Deyo
A Dog Fight
A Donkey Party
Escape From Sing Sing
A Filipino Cock Fight
The Flag
Flag Dance
Goo Goo Eyes
Hanging Stockings on Christmas Eve
Her Morning Exercise
Hooligan to the Rescue
Hooligan's Thanksgiving Dinner
How to Disperse the Crowd
Love's Young Dream
The Martyred Presidents
Merry-Go-Round
Monkey's Feast
Neptune's Daughters
A Nymph of the Waves
One Way of Taking a Girl's Picture
The Pajama Girl
The Picture the Photographer Took
Pie Eating Contest
A Pillow Fight
Police Raid at a Dog Fight
A Raid on a Cock Fight
Raising Old Glory Over Morro Castle
S.S. "Chippewa"
Santa Filling Stockings
Scene in a Rat Pit
The Spider and the Fly
The Summer Girl
Terrier vs. Wild Cat
Torpedo Attack on Port Arthur
U.S. Infantry Supported by Rough Riders at El Caney
U.S. Troops and Red Cross in the Trenches Before Caloocan
Waiting for Santa Claus
What Demoralized the Barber Shop

What Happened on Twenty-Third Street, New York City

Peking, China

The Bengal Lancers
Charge by 1st Bengal Lancers
The Ch-ien-men Gate, Pekin
The Forbidden City, Pekin
General Chafee in Pekin
Li Hung Chang and Suite: Presentation of Parlor Mutoscope
The 9th Infantry, U.S.A.
Reilly's Light Battery "F"
6th Cavalry Assaulting South Gate of Pekin

Pennants; *see* Flags, banners, and pennants

Pennsylvania

Panoramic View, Horseshoe Curve From Penna. Ltd.
Panoramic View, Horseshoe Curve, Penna. R.R., no. 2
A Ride Through Pack Saddle Mountains, Penna. R.R.
A Romance of the Rail
see also Specific cities and towns

Period dramas

The Barbarian Ingomar
The Better Way
Beverly of Graustark
The Call to Arms
The Cardinal's Conspiracy
The Cavalier's Dream
The Chariot Race
The Cloister's Touch
The Death Disc
The Duke's Plan
A Fair Rebel
A Famous Escape
Faust and Marguerite
A Fool's Revenge
The Fugitive
Golden Louis
The Golden Supper
The Guerrilla
His Trust
His Trust Fulfilled
The Honor of His Family
The House with Closed Shutters
In Old Kentucky
In the Border States
The King's Messenger
Leather Stocking
Love Among the Roses
Love Finds a Way
The Love of Lady Irma
Man's Genesis
The Nihilists
Nursing a Viper
The Oath and the Man
Parsifal: Parsifal Ascends the Throne, Ruins of Magic Garden, Exterior of Klingson's Castle,

Magic Garden, Interior of the Temple, Scene Outside the Temple, Return of Parsifal, In the Woods
The Pirate's Gold
Queen Elizabeth
The Road to Yesterday
Rose O'Salem-Town
The Roue's Heart
The Sealed Room
1776, or, the Hessian Renegades
The Slave
Spirit of 1776
A True Patriot
Uncle Tom's Cabin
An Unfaithful Odalisque
The Violin Maker of Cremona
The War of Wealth
When Kings Were the Law
When Knights Were Bold
When the Flag Falls
White Wings on Review
Ye Olden Grafter

Perley, Charles, actor

Beverly of Graustark
Edgar Allen [i.e. Allan] Poe
A Fair Rebel
The Gambler of the West
The Indian
The War of Wealth
The Wife

Petersburg, Virginia

Reception of President Taft in Petersburg, Virginia, May 19th, 1909
Unveiling of the Pennsylvania Monument on the Battlefields of Petersburg, Virginia, May 19, 1909

Petersen, Zanny, actress

Desdemona
The Fisherman and His Sweetheart
Homeless
Love and Friendship
Midsummer-Tide
The Rights of Youth
The Two Convicts

Petroleum; *see* Industries

Philadelphia, Pennsylvania

Bold Bank Robbery
Cake Walk
Comedy Cake Walk
Delivering Mail From Sub-Station
The Doctor's Bride
Drill, Ambulance Corps
Football Game: West Point vs. Annapolis
Great Train Robbery
Harvard-Pennsylvania Football Game
Her Face Was Her Fortune

How Brown Got Married
The Hungry Actor
Inter-Collegiate Athletic Association
Championships, 1904
Nearsighted Mary
New Year's Mummies Parade
New York Athletic Club at Phila., Pa.
The Newest Woman
President Roosevelt Crossing the
Field
The "St. Paul" Outward Bound
Shooters' Parade, Philadelphia
A True Patriot
When the Flag Falls

Philippine Islands

Advance of Kansas Volunteers at
Caloocan
Aguinaldo's Navy
Battle of Mt. Ariat
An Historic Feat
Pack Train, Gen. Bell's Expedition
25th Infantry
see also Manila, P.I.; Spanish American War

Phoenicia, New York

The Hold-Up of the Rocky Mountain Express

Photography; *see* Trick effects; Unusual camera uses

Physical culturists

Al Treloar in Muscle Exercises
Chest and Neck Development
A College Girl's Affair of Honor
Expert Bag Punching
Faust Family of Acrobats
Fencing Class, Missouri Valley College
Getting Strong
Her Morning Exercise
Lathrop School, Calisthenics
Latina, Contortionist
Latina, Dislocation Act
Latina, Physical Culture Poses, nos.
1 and 2
Lukens, Novel Gymnast
Midwinter Bathing, L Street Bath,
Boston
M. Lavelle, Physical Culture, no. 1
M. Lavelle, Physical Culture, no. 2
The Pajama Girl
A Phenomenal Contortionist
The Physical Culture Girl
The Physical Culture Girl, no. 1
The Physical Culture Girl, no. 2
The Physical Culture Girl, no. 3
Physical Culture Lesson
Sandow
School Girl Athletes
State Normal School, Missouri
Treloar and Miss Marshall, Prize
Winner at the Physical Culture
Show in Madison Square Garden

see also Athletics

Pickford, Jack, actor

A Child's Stratagem
A Dash Through the Clouds
Examination Day at School
His Trust Fulfilled
In Life's Cycle
An Indian Summer
The Inner Circle
Katchem Kate
The Kid
Liberty Belles
The Modern Prodigal
Muggsy Becomes a Hero
The Narrow Road
The Oath and the Man
The Passing of a Grouch
A Plain Song
The Poor Sick Men
The School Teacher and the Waif
Seven Days
The Smoker
The Tenderfoot's Triumph
Two Little Waifs
Waiter No. 5
What the Doctor Ordered
White Roses
The Would-Be Shriner

Pickford, Lottie, actress

The Broken Locket
The Call to Arms
A Child's Stratagem
Examination Day at School
Fate's Interception
Fate's Turning
Happy Jack, A Hero
His Lost Love
His Sister-in-Law
Lena and the Geese
The Little Darling
A Midnight Marauder
The Necklace
The Newlyweds
An Old Story With a New Ending
The Passing of a Grouch
The Redman's View
Serious Sixteen
The Smoker
A Strange Meeting
The Test
Two Little Waifs
A Victim of Jealousy
What's Your Hurry?
White Roses
The Woman From Mellon's

Pickford, Mary, actress, scriptwriter/author

All on Account of the Milk
An Arcadian Maid
As It Is In Life
The Awakening
A Beast at Bay

The Broken Locket
The Call
The Call to Arms
The Cardinal's Conspiracy
A Child's Impulse
The Country Doctor
The Englishman and the Girl
Examination Day at School
Faded Lilies
The Female of the Species
Getting Even
A Gold Necklace
Her First Biscuits
His Lost Love
His Wife's Visitor
Homefolks
In Old Kentucky
In the Watches of the Night
The Indian Runner's Romance
An Indian Summer
The Inner Circle
Iola's Promise
The Italian Barber
Just Like a Woman
Lena and the Geese
The Light That Came
The Little Darling
The Little Teacher
A Lodging for the Night
Lonely Villa
Love Among the Roses
A Lucky Toothache
May and December
A Midnight Adventure
The Mountaineer's Honor
Muggsy Becomes a Hero
The Narrow Road
The Necklace
Never Again!
Oh, Uncle!
The Old Actor
The Peach-Basket Hat
A Plain Song
Ramona
The Renunciation
The Restoration
A Rich Revenge
A Romance of the Western Hills
The School Teacher and the Waif
The Sealed Room
1776, or, the Hessian Renegades
The Seventh Day
Simple Charity
The Slave
The Smoker
The Song of the Wildwood Flute
The Son's Return
The Sorrows of the Unfaithful
Sweet and Twenty
The Test
They Would Elope
The Thread of Destiny
To Save Her Soul
The Trick That Failed
The Twisted Trail

The Two Brothers
Two Memories
The Unchanging Sea
A Victim of Jealousy
The Violin Maker of Cremona
Waiter No. 5
The Way of Man
What the Daisy Said
What's Your Hurry?
When a Man Loves
When We Were in Our Teens
White Roses
Wilful Peggy
With the Enemy's Help
The Woman From Mellon's
Won By a Fish

Pierce, G., actor

A Fair Rebel

Pigs

Hot Meals at All Hours
Jack and Jim
The Pig That Came to Life
Tom, Tom, the Piper's Son

Pinehurst, North Carolina

Deer Stalking with Camera
Quail Shooting at Pinehurst
A Wild Turkey Hunt

Pio, Elith, actor

The Fire of Life
Love and Friendship
Midsummer-Tide

Piru, California

Ramona

Pittsburgh, Pennsylvania

Circular Panorama View of Jones &
    Laughlin's Steel Works Yard
Panoramic View from Pittsburgh to
    Allegheny
Welding the Big Ring
Westinghouse Works

Pittsfield, Massachusetts

Society Ballooning, Pittsfield, Mass.

Pixley, Gus, actor

The Honor of His Family
Lord Chumley

Poe, Edgar Allan

Edgar Allen [i.e., Allan] Poe

Police

Almost a King
Annual Baby Parade, 1904, Asbury
    Park, N.J.
Arrest in Chinatown, San Francisco,
    Cal.
As the Bells Rang Out
The Astor Tramp

At the Altar
The Bad Boys' Joke on the Nurse
The Banker's Daughters
The Bigamist
The Black Hand
Blessed Is the Peacemaker
Bobby's Kodak
Bold Bank Robbery
The Boy Detective
Buffalo Police on Parade
The Burglar
The Burglar in the Bed Chamber
A Burglar's Mistake
A Calamitous Elopement
The Camera Fiend, no. 2
A Career of Crime, no. 4
A Catastrophe in Hester Street
Caught by Wireless
Central Park After Dark
The Child of the Ghetto
The Child Stealers
Clarence, the Cop
Clarence the Cop, on the Feed Store
    Beat
The Coal Strike
The Coney Island Beach Patrol
Coney Island Police Court
The Convict's Escape
The Cop and the Nurse Girl
The Cop Fools the Sergeant
The Cord of Life
The Course of True Love
The Deceived Slumming Party
Down the Hotel Corridor
The Downward Path: The Girl Who
    Went Astray
Drill by the Providence Police
The Dude and the Burglars
The Eviction
The Evidence Was Against Him
The Ex-Convict
Fake Beggar
The Farmer and the Bad Boys
The Fatal Hour
Fatty and Mabel at the San Diego
    Exposition
Fatty's Chance Acquaintance
Fatty's Plucky Pup
Fatty's Reckless Fling
Fine Feathers Make Fine Birds
Firing the Cook
The Gentlemen Highwaymen
Gentlemen of Nerve
The Gerry Society's Mistake
A Gesture Fight in Hester Street
The Girls and Daddy
A Good Time with the Organ
    Grinder
The Great Jewel Mystery
A Guardian of the Peace
Gussle the Golfer
Happy Hooligan
Happy Hooligan Turns Burglar
A Hash House Fraud

The Heathen Chinese and the
    Sunday School Teachers
His Duty
His Name Was Mud
His Wife's Sweethearts
Hong Kong, Wharf-Scene
The Honor of Thieves
Hooligan as a Safe Robber
Hooligan in Jail
Hooligan to the Rescue
Hooligan's Roller Skates
How Brown Got Married
How the Cook Made Her Mark
How the Dutch Beat the Irish
How the Young Man Got Stuck at
    Ocean Beach
The Hungry Actor
The Hypnotist's Revenge
In a Raines Law Hotel
In the Watches of the Night
In the Window Recess
Invisible Fluid
It's a Shame to Take the Money
Jack Johnson vs. Jim Flynn Contest
    for Heavyweight Championship of
    the World, Las Vegas, New Mexi-
    co, July 4, 1912
Jones and His New Neighbors
Jones and His Pal in Trouble
Jones at the Ball
Kansas Saloon Smashers
The Kidnapper: The Rescue [Part 3]
The Kleptomaniac
A Legal Hold-up
The Lesson
The Little Train Robbery
The Lost Child
Love in the Suburbs
Love, Loot and Crash
Love, Speed and Thrills
A Lover's Lost Control
Mabel and Fatty's Married Life
Mabel and Fatty's Wash Day
Mabel, Fatty and the Law
Man in the Box
The Maniac Cook
The Masher
Merely a Married Man
A Midnight Adventure
Move On
The Narrow Road
New York City Police Parade
New York Harbor Police Boat Patrol
    Capturing Pirates
New York Police Parade, June 1st,
    1899
A Night at the Haymarket
Night Duty
Nora's Fourth of July
A Novel Way of Catching a Burglar
Off His Beat
On the Benches in the Park
One Touch of Nature
Opening Ceremony of New York
    Subway

480

Our Dare Devil Chief
Peanuts and Bullet
Photographing a Female Crook
The Pickpocket
Pierrot, Murderer
Police Boats Escorting Naval Parade
Police Raid at a Dog Fight
Policemen's Prank on Their Comrades
President McKinley's Funeral Cortege at Buffalo, New York
A Race for a Kiss
A Raid on a Cock Fight
Raid on a Coiner's Den
Revenge!
The River Pirates
A Rude Hostess
Seven Days
Shanghai Police
Shot in the Excitement
The Silver Wedding
The Sleeper
A Smoked Husband
The Smoky Stove
The Somnambulist
Soubrettes in a Bachelor's Flat
Spirits in the Kitchen
Stealing a Dinner
Stolen by Gypsies
Stop Thief!
Street Fight and Arrest
A Subject for the Rogue's Gallery
The Suburbanite
Take Mellon's Food
Tenderloin at Night
That Springtime Feeling
They Found the Leak
The Thief and the Pie Woman
Thompson's Night Out
Tied to Her Apron Strings
'Tis an Ill Wind That Blows No Good
Tommy Atkins, Bobby and Cook
The Tramp and the Nursing Bottle
A Tramp on the Roof
The Tramp's Dream
The Trials and Troubles of an Automobilist
A Trick on the Cop
Trouble in Hogan's Alley
The Troublesome Baby
A Troublesome Satchel
Try to Get Arrested
Turning the Tables
2 A.M. in the Subway
A Versatile Villain
A Victim of Circumstantial Evidence
The Wages of Sin: Retribution [Part 2]
The Waif
Was Justice Served?
Weary Willie and the Gardener
Weary Willie Kidnaps a Child
What Happened to Jones
When Love Took Wings

While Strolling in the Park
Who Said Chicken?
Wished on Mabel
The Would-Be Shriner
The Yellow Peril

Poore, A. L., cameraman

An Acadian Elopement

Popes; *see* Leo XIII, Pope

Porter, Edwin S., cameraman, director

After the Race—Yachts Returning to Anchorage
Animated Painting
The Animated Poster
Annual Parade, New York Fire Department
The Artist's Dilemma
An Artist's Dream
Aunt Sallie's Wonderful Bustle
Babe and Puppies
Baby Class at Lunch
Bad Boy's Joke on the Nurse
Battle of Chemulpo Bay
The Bull and the Picknickers
The Burglar's Slide for Life
Burlesque Suicide
Buster Brown Series: Buster and Tige Put a Balloon Vendor Out of Business
Buster Brown Series: Buster Brown and the Dude
Buster Brown Series: Buster Makes Room for His Mama at the Bargain Counter
Buster Brown Series: Buster's Dog to the Rescue
Buster Brown Series: Pranks of Buster Brown and His Dog Tige
Canoeing on the Charles River, Boston, Mass.
Capture of the Biddle Brothers
Capture of Yegg Bank Burglars: Capture & Death (H50924); Cellar Scene (H50925); Dive Scene (H50927); Tracked (H50926)
Casey and His Neighbor's Goat
Casey's Frightful Dream
Catching an Early Train
Circular Panorama of Electric Tower
Circular Panorama of the Horse Shoe Falls in Winter
City Hall to Harlem in 15 Seconds via the Subway Route
The Clown and the Alchemist
Cohen's Advertising Scheme
"Columbia" Winning the Cup
Coney Island at Night
Congress of Nations
The Cop Fools the Sergeant
The Count of Monte Cristo
Crossing Ice Bridge at Niagara Falls
Dog Factory

Down Where the Wurzburger Flows
An East River Novelty
East Side Urchins Bathing in a Fountain
The Electric Mule
Elephants Shooting the Chutes at Luna Park
Empire State Express, the Second, Taking Water on the Fly
Esquimaux Game of Snap-the-Whip
Esquimaux Leap-Frog
Esquimaux Village
European Rest Cure
The Ex-Convict
The Extra Turn
The Fat and Lean Wrestling Match
Faust and Marguerite
The Finish of Bridget McKeen
Fire and Flames at Luna Park, Coney Island
Fun in a Bakery Shop
Fun in a Butcher Shop
Gay Shoe Clerk
The Great Train Robbery
Halloween Night at the Seminary
Happy Hooligan Turns Burglar
The Heavenly Twins at Lunch
The Heavenly Twins at Odds
Hippodrome Races, Dreamland, Coney Island
Hold-Up in a Country Grocery Store
How a French Nobleman Got a Wife Through the New York Herald Personal Columns
How Jones Lost His Roll: Jones Meets Skinflint (Part 1 of 7)
How Jones Lost His Roll: Skinflint Treats Jones (Part 2 of 7)
How Jones Lost His Roll: Invitation to Dinner (Part 3 of 7)
How Jones Lost His Roll: Skinflint's Cheap Wine (Part 4 of 7)
How Jones Lost His Roll: Game of Cards (Part 5 of 7)
How Jones Lost His Roll: Jones Loses (Part 6 of 7)
How Jones Lost His Roll: Jones Goes Home in a Barrel (Part 7 of 7)
How Old is Ann?
Ice Boating on the North Shrewsbury, Red Bank, N.J.
Ice Skating in Central Park, N.Y.
Inter-Collegiate Athletic Association Championships, 1904
Inter-Collegiate Regatta, Poughkeepsie, New York, 1904
Jack and the Beanstalk
Japanese Acrobats
The Kleptomaniac
Lehigh Valley Black Diamond Express
Life of an American Fireman
Little German Band

The Little Train Robbery
Love by the Light of the Moon
The Lovers, Coal Box and Fireplace
Maniac Chase
The Martyred Presidents
The Messenger's Boy Mistake
Midnight Intruder
Miss Jessie Cameron, Champion Child Sword Dancer
Miss Jessie Dogherty, Champion Female Highland Fling Dancer
Miss Lillian Shaffer and Her Dancing Horse
The Mysterious Cafe
The Mystic Swing
Nervy Nat Kisses the Bride
New York Caledonian Club's Parade
New York City Public Bath
New York Harbor Police Boat Patrol Capturing Pirates
The Offices Boy's Revenge
Old Fashioned Scottish Reel
Old Maid and Fortune Teller
[On] a [Good Old] Five Cent Trolley Ride
Opening Ceremonies, New York Subway, Oct. 27, 1904
Opening of Belmont Park Race Course
Opening, Pan-American Exposition
Orphans in the Surf
Pan-American Exposition by Night
Panorama of Blackwell's Island, N.Y.
Panorama of Esplanade by Night
Panorama of Riker's Island, N.Y.
Panorama Water Front and Brooklyn Bridge From East River
Panoramic View of Electric Tower From a Balloon
Parsifal: Parsifal Ascends the Throne, Ruins of Magic Garden, Exterior of Klingson's Castle, Magic Garden, Interior of the Temple, Scene Outside the Temple, Return of Parsifal, In the Woods
A Phenomenal Contortionist
The Photographer's Mishap
Photographing a Country Couple
The Physical Culture Girl
Pictures Incidental to Yacht Race
Pie, Tramp and the Bulldog
President Roosevelt's Inauguration
The Prisoner of Zenda
Raffles, the Dog
Railroad Smashup
A Romance of the Rail
Rounding Up of the "Yeggmen"
Rube and Mandy at Coney Island
A Rube Couple at a County Fair
Scarecrow Pump
Scenes and Incidents, Russo-Japanese Peace Conference, Portsmouth, N.H.

Scenes in an Infant Orphan Asylum
Seashore Frolics
Section of Buster Brown Series, Showing a Sketch of Buster by Outcault
The Seven Ages
"Shamrock" and "Columbia" Rounding the Outer Stake Boat
"Shamrock" and "Columbia" Yacht Race—First Race
"Shamrock" and "Columbia" Yacht Race—1st Race, no. 2
"Shamrock" and "Erin" Sailing
69th Regiment, N.G.N.Y.
Skirmish Between Russian and Japanese Advance Guards
Sleighing in Central Park, New York
Sliding Down Ice Mound at Niagara Falls
Sorting Refuse at Incinerating Plant, New York City
Start of Ocean Race for Kaiser's Cup
Steamscow "Cinderella" and Ferryboat "Cincinnati"
The Still Alarm
Stolen by Gypsies
Street Car Chivalry
The Strenuous Life; or, Anti-Race Suicide
Subub Surprises the Burglar
Terrible Teddy, the Grizzly King
Throwing the Sixteen Pound Hammer
Treloar and Miss Marshall, Prize Winners at the Physical Culture Show in Madison Square Garden
The Twentieth Century Tramp, or, Happy Hooligan and His Airship
Two Chappies in a Box
The Unappreciated Joke
Uncle Josh at the Moving Picture Show
Uncle Josh in a Spooky Hotel
Uncle Josh's Nightmare
Uncle Tom's Cabin
Under the Mistletoe
Weary Willie Kidnaps a Child
What Happened in the Tunnel
The White Caps
White Star S.S. Baltic Leaving Pier on First Eastern Voyage
The Whole Dam Family and the Dam Dog
Wifey's Mistake
A Wringing Good Joke

Portland, Maine

Moose Hunt in New Brunswick

Portsmouth, New Hampshire

An Acadian Elopement
Obstacle Race
Peace Envoys at Portsmouth, N.H.

Scenes and Incidents, Russo-Japanese Peace Conference, Portsmouth, N.H.
Scrubbing Clothes

Poughkeepsie, New York

Inter-Collegiate Regatta, Poughkeepsie, New York 1904

Powell, Baden, actor

The Message

Powell, Frank, actor, director

All on Account of the Milk
The Broken Locket
The Cardinal's Conspiracy
The Children's Friend
The Cloister's Touch
A Corner in Wheat
The Country Doctor
Faded Lilies
Fools of Fate
His Duty
His Wife's Visitor
The Honor of Thieves
The Impalement
In Old Kentucky
The Kid
A Knot in the Plot
Lines of White on a Sullen Sea
The Love of Lady Irma
The Man
The Message
Mr. Jones' Burglar
The Necklace
The Newlyweds
A Note in the Shoe
Nursing a Viper
The Oath and the Man
Over Silent Paths
The Rocky Road
A Rude Hostess
The Seventh Day
The Son's Return
A Strange Meeting
Two Women and a Man
Was Justice Served?
With Her Card

Prentis Trio

The Prentis Trio

Prescott, Vivian, actress

The Billionaire
A Flash of Light
A Fool's Revenge
Katchem Kate
Man's Enemy
The Old Actor
The Power of the Press
The Proposal
A Salutary Lesson
Willie Becomes an Artist
Winning Back His Love
Woman Against Woman

Princeton, New Jersey

Coaching for a Record
Princeton and Yale Football Game

Presidents; see McKinley, William; Roosevelt, Theodore; Taft, William H.; Public Events

Prior, Herbert, actor

After Many Years
The Cricket on the Hearth
The Violin Maker of Cremona

Prize fights; see Boxing

Processions; see Parades and processions

Producers, motion pictures; see Name of company

Prostitution; see Socially significant themes

Providence, Rhode Island

Drill by the Providence Police
The Honourable Artillery Company of London
The Providence Light Artillery
Rhode Island Light Artillery
A Visit to Baby Roger

Psilander, Valdemar, actor

Desdemona
The Fire of Life
The Little Railroad Queen
Love in the Tropics
Midsummer-Tide
The Rights of Youth
Vengeance

Public events

Admiral Dewey at State House, Boston
Admiral Dewey Receiving the Washington and New York Committees
The Armenian Archbishop of Rome
Arrival of McKinley's Funeral Train at Canton, Ohio
Arrival of Prince Henry and President Roosevelt at Shooter's Island
Attack on Fort Boonesboro
Babies Rolling Eggs
The Baby Review
Battery K Siege Guns
Breaking of the Crowd at Military Review at Longchamps
Burial of the "Maine" Victims
Cardinal Gibbons
Classmates
Democratic National Committee at Esopus
Fleet Steaming up North River
H.R.H. the Prince of Wales Viewing the Grand Military Review on the Plains of Abraham, Quebec

The Inauguration of President Roosevelt
Installation Ceremonies of President Butler
Judge Parker Receiving the Notification of His Nomination for the Presidency
King Edward and President Loubet Reviewing French Troops
King Edward's Visit to Paris
The Late Senator Mark Hanna
McKinley Funeral on Way to Church
McKinley Funeral: Panorama of McKinley Home
McKinley's Funeral Entering Westlawn Cemetery, Canton
Mayor Van Wyck and General Miles
Military Maneuvers, Manassas, Va.
Opening Ceremonies, St. Louis Exposition
Opening Day, Jamestown Exposition
Peace Envoys at Portsmouth, N.H.
Pope in His Carriage
Pope Passing Through Upper Loggia
President McKinley
President McKinley Taking the Oath
President McKinley's Funeral Cortege at Buffalo, N.Y.
President McKinley's Funeral Cortege at Washington, D.C.
President McKinley's Speech at the Pan-American Exposition
President Reviewing School Children
President Roosevelt Addressing Crew of "Kearsarge"
President Roosevelt at Lynn, Massachusetts
President Roosevelt at the Canton, Station
President Roosevelt Crossing the Field
President Roosevelt's Arrival at "Kearsarge"
President Roosevelt's Departure from "Kearsarge"
President Roosevelt's Fourth of July Oration
President Roosevelt's Homecoming
President Roosevelt's Inauguration
President Roosevelt's Visit to Admiral Barker
The President's Carriage
Prince Henry Arriving at West Point
Prince Henry Arriving in Washington and Visiting the German Embassy
Prince Henry at Lincoln's Monument, Chicago, Illinois
Prince Henry at Niagara Falls
Prince Henry at West Point
Prince Henry Visiting Cambridge, Mass. and Harvard University

Reception of British Fleet
Reception of Pres. Taft in Petersburg, Virginia, May 19th, 1909
Renovare Production Company "Special"
Reproduction, Coronation Ceremonies—King Edward VII
Scenes and Incidents, Russo-Japanese Peace Conference, Portsmouth, N.H.
Secretary Taft's Address & Panorama
Speech by President Francis: World's Fair
Tossing Eggs
Unveiling of the Pennsylvania Monument on the Battlefields of Petersburg, Virginia, May 19, 1909
see also specific types of events

Public services

New York City Dumping Wharf
Repairing Streets in Mexico
Sorting Refuse at Incinerating Plant, New York City
see also Buses; Fires and fire services; Police; Streetcars and subways

Public transportation; see Buses; Carriages, coaches, and buggies; Horses; Railroads; Ships and watercraft; Streetcars and subways; Transportation

Puppets

Balloon Ascension, Marionettes
Dancing Chinaman, Marionettes
Davey Jones' Locker
The Mysterious Midgets
Skeleton Dance, Marionettes

Quebec, Canada

Arrival of the Governor General, Lord Minto, at Quebec
Duke of York at Montreal and Quebec
H.R.H. the Prince of Wales Decorating the Monument of Champlain and Receiving Addresses of Welcome from the Mayor of Quebec, the Governor General of Canada and Vice-President Fairbanks, Representative of the United States
H.R.H. the Prince of Wales Viewing the Grand Military Review on the Plains of Abraham, Quebec
Kent House Slide
Quebec Fire Dept. on Runners
Skee Club
Skiing Scene in Quebec

Overland Limited
Panorama From Incline Railway
Panorama From Running Incline Railway
Panorama, Great Gorge Route Over Lewiston Bridge
Panorama of Gorge Railway
Panoramic View, Albert Canyon
Panoramic View Between Palliser and Field, B.C.
Panoramic View, Horseshoe Curve From Penna. Ltd.
Panoramic View, Horseshoe Curve, Penna. R. R., no. 2
Panoramic View, Kicking Horse Canyon
Panoramic View, Lower Kicking Horse Canyon
Panoramic View, Lower Kicking Horse Valley
Panoramic View Near Mt. Golden on the Canadian Pacific R.R.
Panoramic View of Mt. Tamalpais
Panoramic View of Mt. Tamalpais Between Bow Knot and McKinley Cut
Panoramic View of Rubio Canyon, Mt. Low R.R.
Panoramic View of the Canadian Pacific R.R. Near Leauchoil, B.C.
Panoramic View of the Golden Gate
Panoramic View of the Gorge R.R.
Panoramic View of the Great Cable Incline, Mt. Low R.R
Panoramic View of the White Pass Railroad
Panoramic View, Upper Kicking Horse Canyon
Paul J. Rainey's African Hunt
Pennsylvania Tunnel Excavation
Philadelphia Express, Jersey Central Railway
The Photographer's Mishap
A Plain Song
The Power of Love
President Roosevelt's Homecoming
Prince Henry at Niagara Falls
Railroad Panorama Near Spanishtown, Jamaica
Railroad Smashup
Railroad View—Experimental
A Railway Tragedy
A Ride Through Pack Saddle Mountains, Penna. R. R.
The Rivals
A Romance of the Rail
Rounding Up of the "Yeggmen"
Royal Gorge
Royal Train With Duke and Duchess of York, Climbing Mt. Hector
Rube and Fender
Running Through Galitzen Tunnel, Penna. R.R
Sarnia Tunnel
Sherman Hill Tunnel

Sky Scrapers of New York, from the North River
Smallest Train in the World
Southern Pacific Overland Mail
Steamboat and Great Eastern Rock
Stern's Duplex Railway
The Suburbanite
Sunset Limited, Southern Pacific R.R
Switchback on Trolley Road
Taking President McKinley's Body from Train at Canton, Ohio
10th U.S. Infantry Disembarking From Cars
10th U.S. Infantry, 2nd Batallion, Leaving Cars
The Tourists
Train Hour in Durango, Mexico
Train of Sugar Cane
Train Taking Up Mail Bag, U.S. P.O.
The Tramp's Miraculous Escape
A Trip Down Mt. Tamalpais
A Trip on the Catskill Mt. Ry.
A Trip to Berkeley, Cal.
A Trip to Salt Lake City
Trout Fishing, Rangeley Lakes
Tunnel Number Three
U.S. Calvalry Supplies Unloading at Tampa, Florida
The Vampire Dancer
The Wedding
What Happened in the Tunnel
What the Doctor Ordered
Wifey Away, Hubby at Play
Working Rotary Snow Plows On Lehigh Valley Railroad
see also Bridges and trestles; Streetcars and subways

Rainey, Paul J., producer

Common Beasts of Africa
Military Drill of Kikuyu Tribes and Other Native Ceremonies
Paul J. Rainey's African Hunt

Randall, William P., actor

The Prisoner of Zenda

Rasow, Knud, actor

Love and Friendship

Rats; *see* Rodents

Ray, Charles, actor

The Cup of Life

Rea, Isabel, actress

The Genius
The Wages of Sin

Red Bank, New Jersey

Ice-Boat Racing at Redbank, N.J.
Ice Boating on the North Shrewsbury, Red Bank, N.J.

Red Cross

Red Cross Ambulance on Battlefield
U.S. Troops and Red Cross in the Trenches Before Caloocan

Red Wing, Princess, actress

The Mended Lute

Redondo Beach, California

Neighbors

Reed, Walter, actor

Miss Fatty's Seaside Lovers

Reid, Violet, actress

The Charity Ball
The Indian
The War of Wealth

Religious events and themes

The Armenian Archbishop of Rome
Battle of Confetti at the Nice Carnival
Battle of Flowers at the Nice Carnival
Brothers of the Misericordia, Rome
Capuchin Monks, Rome
Cardinal Gibbons
The Chorus Girl and the Salvation Army Lassie
Church "Our Lady of Grace," Hoboken
The Converts
Corpus Christi Procession Orvieto
The Death Disc
The Jolly Monk's of Malabar
Pope in His Carriage
Pope Passing Through Upper Loggia
Renovare Production Company "Special"
Rock of Ages
The Salvation Army Lass
The Simple Life
The Star of Bethlehem
Temptation of St. Anthony
The Way of the World
Wine, Women & Song
Wine, Women & Song, no. 2

Renovare Company

Renovare Production Company "Special"

Reproductions

Advance of Kansas Volunteers at Caloocan
Ambulance at the Accident
Ambulance Call
Attack on Fort Boonesboro
The Attack on Port Arthur
The Barnstormers
Battle of Chemulpo Bay
Battle of Mafeking
Battle of Mt. Ariat

The Battle of the Yalu, no. 1–4
Bertha Claiche
The Black Hand
Boers Bringing in British Prisoners
Bombardment of Taku Forts, by the
Allied Fleets
Brush Between Cowboys and
Indians
Burning of St. Pierre
Capture of Boer Battery
Capture of Boer Battery by British
Capture of Trenches at Candaba
[Candabar]
Carrie Nation Smashing a Saloon
Charge of Boer Cavalry
Colonel Funstan [i.e. Funston]
Swimming the Baglag River
Cuban Ambush
The Early Morning Attack
English Lancers Charging
Eruption of Mt. Vesuvius
Escape From Sing Sing
An Execution by Hanging
Execution of a Spy
Execution of Czolgosz, with Panora-
ma of Auburn Prison
A Famous Escape
Filipinos Retreat from Trenches
The Hero of Liao Yang
Impersonation of Britt-Nelson Fight
A Kentucky Feud
Landing of U.S. Troops Near Santi-
ago
The Lost Child
Mt. Pelee in Eruption and Destruc-
tion of St. Pierre
Mt. Pelee Smoking Before Eruption
Mutiny on the Black Sea
Naval Battle, St. Louis Exposition
On to Brooklyn, no. 1
On to Brooklyn, no. 2
Raising Old Glory Over Morro
Castle
Reading the Death Sentence
A Reprieve From the Scaffold
Reproduction, Coronation Ceremo-
nies—King Edward VII
Reproduction, Nan Paterson's Trial
Reproduction of Corbett-McGovern
Fight
Reproduction of Jeffries-Corbett
Contest
The River Pirates
Rout of the Filipinos
Sampson and Schley Controversy—
Tea Party
San Francisco Disaster
Shooting Captured Insurgents
Skirmish Between Russian and Japa-
nese Advance Guards
Skirmish of Rough Riders
Tenderloin Tragedy
Thaw-White Tragedy
Torpedo Attack on Port Arthur

U.S. Infantry Supported by Rough
Riders at El Caney
U.S. Troops and Red Cross in the
Trenches Before Caloocan
A Wild Turkey Hunt

Reumert, Poul, actor

The Aviator's Generosity
The Fire of Life

Revere, Massachusetts

Railroad Smashup

Revolutionaries; *see* Socially significant themes

Revolutionary War

1776, or, the Hessian Renegades
Spirit of '76
A True Patriot
When the Flag Falls

Reymann, Thyra, actress

Desdemona

Rhode Island; *see* Newport, Rhode Island; Pawtucket, Rhode Island; and Providence, Rhode Island

Rider, Bill

Moose Hunt in New Brunswick

Ridgewood Park, New Jersey

A Unique Race Between Elephant,
Bicycle, Camel, Horse, and Automobile

Riker's Island, New York

Panorama of Riker's Island

Rising, W. H., actor

The Kleptomaniac

Ritchie, Franklin, actor

The Charity Ball
Man's Enemy
The Wages of Sin

Riverside, California

Viewing Sherman Institute for
Indians at Riverside, Cal.

Riverside, Massachusetts

Trap Pigeon Shooting

Road Bridge, Virginia

Bass Fishing

Robinson, George, actor

Man's Enemy

Robinson, Gertrude, actress

The Affair of an Egg
As the Bells Rang Out
Beverly of Graustark
Classmates

The Day After
The Death Disc
The Englishman and the Girl
Examination Day at School
The Face at the Window
Men and Women
A Midnight Cupid
Nursing a Viper
The Oath and the Man
An Old Story With a New Ending
The Open Gate
Pippa Passes
A Plain Song
The Purgation
1776, or, the Hessian Renegades
Strongheart
A Summer Idyl
The Test of Friendship
That Chink at Golden Gulch
The Trick That Failed
The Two Paths
A Victim of Jealousy
What the Daisy Said

Robinson, W. C. "Spike," actor

Help Wanted
The Inner Circle
Man's Genesis
The Power of the Press
Unexpected Help
White Roses
Winning Back His Love

Rodents

Fun in a Bakery Shop
The Girls, the Burglar, and the Rat
Halloween
The Lost Child
Scene in a Rat Pit

Roeber, Ernest, wrestler

Roeber Wrestling Match

Rogers, Dora, actress

Ambrose's Lofty Perch
Ambrose's Sour Grapes
Crossed Love and Swords
Droppington's Family Tree
The Home Breakers
Love, Loot and Crash
Mabel Lost and Won
Peanuts and Bullets
That Little Band of Gold

Rogers, May

An Execution by Hanging

Rolph, James, Jr.

Mabel and Fatty Viewing the
World's Fair at San Francisco,
Cal.

Romain, Mlle., actress

Queen Elizabeth

Troops Embarking at San Francisco
Views in San Francisco

San Gabriel, California

The Converts
A Lodging for the Night
The Thread of Destiny
The Way of the World

San Jose, California

Hotel Vendome, San Jose, Cal.

San Pedro, California

Building a Harbor at San Pedro
From Patches to Plenty
He Wouldn't Stay Down
Those Bitter Sweets

Sandow, Eugene

Sandow

Sandy Hook, New Jersey

After the Race—Yachts Returning to Anchorage
Finish of the First Race, Aug. 22
Finish of Yacht Race, Aug. 25th
Firing 10 Inch Gun
An Ice-Covered Vessel
Jockeying and Start of Yacht [s], Aug. 25th
Jockeying for the Start, Aug. 20
Jockeying for the Start, Aug. 22
Panorama of Excursion Boats
Panoramic View of the Fleet After Yacht Race
Pilot Leaving "Prinzessen Victoria Luise" at Sandy Hook
Projectile From 10 Inch Gun Striking Water
"Reliance" and "Shamrock III" Jockeying and Starting in First Race
"Reliance" Crossing the Line and Winning First Race
"Reliance" vs. "Shamrock III," Aug. 20
S.S. "Morro Castle"
"Shamrock" After Carrying Away Topsail
"Shamrock" and "Columbia" Rounding the Outer Stake Boat
"Shamrock" and "Columbia" Rounding the Outer Stake Boat
"Shamrock" and "Columbia" Yacht Race—First Race
"Shamrock" and "Columbia" Yacht Race—1st Race, no. 2
Start of Ocean Race for Kaiser's Cup
Start of Race—"Reliance" Ahead
Start of the First Race, Aug. 22
The Yacht Race Fleet Following the Committee Boat "Navigator" Oct. 4th

Santa Anita, California

California Limited, A.T. & S.F. R.R.

Santa Monica, California

Ambrose's Fury
A Hash House Fraud
On the Night Stage
Rumpelstiltskin
Settled at the Seaside
The Speed Demon
The Unchanging Sea
When Kings Were the Law
Won By a Fish

Santiago, Cuba

Troops Making Military Road in Front of Santiago
Wreck of the "Vizcaya"

Sarnia, Ontario, Canada

Sarnia Tunnel

Sarno, Hector V., actor

Man's Enemy
The Woman in Black

Saroni, Gilbert, actor

Goo Goo Eyes
The Old Maid Having Her Picture Taken
The Old Maid in the Horsecar

Savoy Film Exchange

The Victorious Battle for the Conquest of Mergheb, Africa

Sayre, Pennsylvania

Lehigh Valley Black Diamond Express

Scarsdale, New York

The Moonshiner

Schade, Fritz, actor

Dough and Dynamite

Schenectady, New York

Electric Locomotive Tests, Schenectady
The Electric Mule
Empire State Express, the Second, Taking Water on the Fly

Schenstrøm, Carl, actor

The Vampire Dancer

Schley, Winfield Scott

Close View of the "Brooklyn" Naval Parade
Sampson-Schley Controversy [Parts 1 and 2 of 3]
Sampson and Schley Controversy—Tea Party [Part 3 of 3]

Schmidt, Aage, actor

Homeless

Schnedler-Sørensen, Edward, director

A Dangerous Play
The Fire of Life
Homeless

Schønberg, Birger von Cotta, actor

The Vampire Dancer

Schools, secondary

Calesthenic Drill, Missouri Commission
Central High School, Gymnastic Drill
Club Swinging, Carlisle Indian School
Emerson School, Calisthenics
Free Arm Movement, All Schools, Missouri Commission
High School Field Exercises, Missouri Commission
Hyde Park School Graduating Class
Hyde Park School Room 2
Indian Day School
Kindergarten Ball Game
Kindergarten Dance
Lathrop School, Calisthenics
Linwood School Calisthenics
President Reviewing School Children
Viewing Sherman Institute for Indians at Riverside, Cal.
Whittier School, Calisthenics

Schultz, Charles E.

The Creators of Foxy Grandpa

Schumann-Heink, Ernestine

Mabel and Fatty Viewing the World's Fair at San Francisco, Cal.

Schyberg, Dagny, actress

A Dangerous Play
The Two Convicts

Scott, George, and Company

The Great Toronto Fire, Toronto, Canada, April 19, 1904

Scriptwriters; see Name of person

Sea Breeze, New Jersey

The Children's Friend

Sea Bright, New Jersey

After Many Years
The Pirate's Gold

Seattle, Washington

First Avenue, Seattle, Washington

Horses Loading for Klondike
Loading Baggage for Klondike, no. 6

Seduction; *see* Socially significant themes

Seemann, Henry, actor

The Two Convicts
The Vampire Dancer
Vengeance

Selig, William N., producer

The Attack on Port Arthur
The Bandit King
The Count of Monte Cristo
The Girl From Montana
His First Ride
Pres. Roosevelt at the Dedication Ceremonies, St. Louis Exposition
The Roller Skate Craze
Torpedo Attack on Port Arthur

Sennett, Mack, actor

An Affair of Hearts
After the Ball
All on Account of the Milk
An Arcadian Maid
As It Is In Life
As the Bells Rang Out
At the Altar
The Awakening
An Awful Moment
A Baby's Shoe
Balked at the Altar
The Better Way
The Brave Hunter
The Broken Doll
The Broken Locket
A Burglar's Mistake
The Call
The Call of the Wild
The Call to Arms
The Cardinal's Conspiracy
A Child's Faith
Choosing a Husband
The Christmas Burglars
The Cloister's Touch
The Clubman and the Tramp
Colored Villainy
Concealing a Burglar
The Converts
The Convict's Sacrifice
The Cord of Life
A Corner in Wheat
The Cricket on the Hearth
The Criminal Hypnotist
The Curtain Pole
The Dancing Girl of Butte
The Day After
The Death Disc
The Deception
The Drunkard's Reformation
Effecting a Cure
Eloping with Aunty
The Englishman and the Girl

Examination Day at School
The Expiation
The Face at the Window
A Fair Exchange
Faithful
The Fascinating Mrs. Francis
Father Gets in the Game
The Feud and the Turkey
A Flash of Light
A Fool's Revenge
The French Duel
The Furs
Getting Even
The Gibson Goddess
The Girls and Daddy
Gold Is Not All
A Gold Necklace
The Gold Seekers
Golden Louis
The Guerrilla
Happy Jack, A Hero
Helen's Marriage
The Helping Hand
Her First Biscuits
His Lost Love
His Trust
His Wife's Mother
His Wife's Sweetheart
Homefolks
The Honor of Thieves
Hot Stuff
In a Hempen Bag
In Little Italy
In Old California
In Old Kentucky
In the Watches of the Night
In the Window Recess
The Italian Barber
The Jilt
Jones and His New Neighbors
Jones and the Lady Book Agent
Jones at the Ball
The Joneses Have Amateur Theatricals
A Knot in the Plot
Lady Helen's Escapade
Leather Stocking
The Light That Came
The Little Darling
The Little Teacher
Lonely Villa
Love Among the Roses
Love Finds a Way
Love in Quarantine
The Love of Lady Irma
Lucky Jim
A Lucky Toothache
Lure of the Gown
The Maniac Cook
The Marked Time Table
The Mended Lute
Mexican Sweethearts
A Midnight Adventure
A Midnight Cupid
The Mills of the Gods

Mr. Jones' Burglar
Mr. Jones Has a Card Party
A Mohawk's Way
Money Mad
The Mountaineer's Honor
Muggsy Becomes a Hero
The Necklace
Neighbors
Never Again!
A New Trick
The Newlyweds
Not So Bad As It Seemed
The Note in the Shoe
Nursing a Viper
One Busy Hour
One Night and Then
The Passing of a Grouch
Pippa Passes
Politician's Love Story
The Prussian Spy
The Purgation
The Reckoning
Resurrection
The Road to the Heart
Romance of a Jewess
The Roue's Heart
A Rude Hostess
Rural Elopement
The Sacrifice
The Salvation Army Lass
The Sculptor's Nightmare
Serious Sixteen
1776, or, the Hessian Renegades
The Seventh Day
The Slave
A Smoked Husband
Song of the Shirt
The Son's Return
A Sound Sleeper
A Spanish Dilemma
The Speed Demon
A Strange Meeting
The Suicide Club
A Summer Tragedy
Taming a Husband
The Test of Friendship
Their First Kidnapping Case
They Would Elope
Those Awful Hats
Those Hicksville Boys
'Tis an Ill Wind That Blows No Good
To Save Her Soul
Tomboy Bessie
The Tourists
Tragic Love
A Trap for Santa Claus
The Trick That Failed
A Troublesome Satchel
Trying to Get Arrested
The Twisted Trail
The Two Brothers
Two Memories
Two Women and a Man
The Valet's Wife

The Vaquero's Vow
A Victim of Jealousy
The Violin Maker of Cremona
Was Justice Served?
The Way of Man
The Way of the World
A Welcome Burglar
What Drink Did
What the Daisy Said
What the Doctor Ordered
What's Your Hurry?
When We Were in Our Teens
Where Breakers Roar
With Her Card
The Woman From Mellon's
The Would-Be Shriner
A Wreath in Time
The Zulu's Heart

Sennett, Mack, author

Ambrose's Fury
Ambrose's Little Hatchet
Ambrose's Lofty Perch
Ambrose's Nasty Temper
Ambrose's Sour Grapes
Beating Hearts and Carpets
The Beauty Bunglers
A Bird's a Bird
The Cannon Ball
Caught in a Park
Caught in the Act
Colored Villainy
Court House Crooks
Crossed Love and Swords
Cursed by His Beauty
Curses! They Remarked
Dirty Work in a Laundry
Do-Re-Mi—Boom!
Dough and Dynamite
Droppington's Devilish Deed
Droppington's Family Tree
Fatty and Mabel at the San Diego
    Exposition
Fatty and Mabel's Simple Life
Fatty's Chance Acquaintance
Fatty's Faithful Fido
Fatty's New Role
Fatty's Plucky Pup
Fatty's Reckless Fling
Fatty's Tintype Tangle
For Better—But Worse
From Patches to Plenty
Gentlemen of Nerve
A Glimpse of the San Diego Exposi-
    tion
Gussle Rivals Jonah
Gussle the Golfer
Gussle Tied to Trouble
Gussle's Backward Way
Gussle's Day of Rest
Gussle's Wayward Path
A Hash House Fraud
Hash House Mashers
He Wouldn't Stay Down
Hearts and Planets

His Luckless Love
Hogan Out West
Hogan the Porter
Hogan's Aristocratic Dream
Hogan's Mussy Job
Hogan's Romance Upset
The Home Breakers
A Home-Breaking Hound
A Human Hound's Triumph
The Little Teacher
Lonely Villa
Love in Armor
Love, Loot and Crash
Love, Speed and Thrills
A Lover's Lost Control
Mabel and Fatty Viewing the
    World's Fair at San Francisco,
    Cal.
Mabel and Fatty's Married Life
Mabel and Fatty's Wash Day
Mabel, Fatty and the Law
Mabel Lost and Won
Mabel's Wilful Way
Merely a Married Man
Miss Fatty's Seaside Lovers
A One Night Stand
Our Dare Devil Chief
The Rent Jumpers
Settled at the Seaside
Shot in the Excitement
That Little Band of Gold
That Springtime Feeling
Their Social Splash
Those Bitter Sweets
Those College Girls
A Versatile Villain
Viewing Sherman Institute for
    Indians at Riverside, Cal.
When Ambrose Dared Walrus
When Love Took Wings
Willful Ambrose
Wished on Mabel
Ye Olden Grafter

Sennett, Mack, director

Algy, the Watchman
The Brave Hunter
A Close Call
A Dash Through the Clouds
The Engagement Ring
The Fickle Spaniard
The Furs
Helen's Marriage
Help! Help!
His Own Fault
Hot Stuff
An Interrupted Elopement
Katchem Kate
The Leading Man
The Masher
Neighbors
Oh, Those Eyes!
One-Round O'Brien
A Spanish Dilemma
The Speed Demon

Their First Kidnapping Case
Those Hicksville Boys
Tomboy Bessie
The Tourists
The Tragedy of a Dress Suit
Trying to Fool Uncle
A Voice From the Deep
What the Doctor Ordered
When the Fire-Bells Rang
Willie Becomes an Artist
Won By a Fish
The Would-Be Shriner

Sennett, Mack, producer

Ambrose's Fury
Ambrose's Little Hatchet
Ambrose's Lofty Perch
Ambrose's Nasty Temper
Ambrose's Sour Grapes
Beating Hearts and Carpets
The Beauty Bunglers
A Bird's a Bird
The Cannon Ball
Caught in a Park
Caught in the Act
Colored Villainy
Court House Crooks
Crossed Love and Swords
Cursed by His Beauty
Cursed! They Remarked
Dirty Work in a Laundry
Do-Re-Mi—Boom!
Dough and Dynamite
Droppington's Devilish Deed
Droppington's Family Tree
Fatty and Mabel's Simple Life
Fatty's Chance Acquaintance
Fatty's Faithful Fido
Fatty's New Role
Fatty's Reckless Fling
Fatty's Tintype Tangle
For Better—But Worse
From Patches to Plenty
Gentlemen of Nerve
Gussle Rivals Jonah
Gussle the Golfer
Gussle Tied to Trouble
Gussle's Backward Way
Gussle's Day of Rest
Gussle's Wayward Path
A Hash House Fraud
Hash House Masher
He Wouldn't Stay Down
Hearts and Planets
His Luckless Love
Hogan Out West
Hogan the Porter
Hogan's Aristocratic Dream
Hogan's Romance Upset
The Home Breakers
A Home-Breaking Hound
A Human Hound's Triumph
The Little Teacher
Love in Armor
Love, Loot and Crash

Love, Speed and Thrills
A Lover's Lost Control
Mabel and Fatty Viewing the World's Fair at San Francisco, Cal.
Mabel and Fatty's Married Life
Mabel and Fatty's Wash Day
Mabel, Fatty and the Law
Mabel Lost and Won
Mabel's Wilful Way
Merely a Married Man
Miss Fatty's Seaside Lovers
A One Night Stand
Our Dare Devil Chief
The Rent Jumpers
Settled at the Seaside
Shot in the Excitement
That Little Band of Gold
That Springtime Feeling
Their Social Splash
Those Bitter Sweets
Those College Girls
A Versatile Villain
When Ambrose Dared Walrus
When Love Took Wings
Willful Ambrose
Wished on Mabel
Ye Olden Grafter

Shadyside, New Jersey

The Bandit's Waterloo
The Black Viper
The Feud and the Turkey
The Fight for Freedom
Greaser's Gauntlet
The Renunciation
The Stage Rustler

Shaffer, Lillian

Miss Lillian Shaffer and Her Dancing Horse

Shafter, William

Major General Shafter

Shanghai, China

The Burd [i.e. Bund], Shanghai
The 14th Sikhs
The Fourth Ghorkhas
Shanghai Police
Shanghai Street Scene, Scene 1
Shanghai Street Scene, Scene 2

Shannon, Frank, actor

The Prisoner of Zenda

Sheep and goats

Casey and His Neighbor's Goat
A Fair Exchange Is No Robbery
A Flock of Export Sheep
Flock of Sheep
Herd of Sheep on the Road to Jerusalem
Sheep and Lambs
Sheep Run, Chicago Stockyards

A Summer Idyl

Sheepshead, New York

Finish of Futurity, 1901
The Futurity
Racing at Sheepshead Bay

Sheer, William, actor

A Versatile Villain

Sheridan, Crissie, dancer

Crissie Sheridan

Sherman Institute

Viewing Sherman Institute for Indians at Riverside, Cal.

Sherry, J. Barney, actor

The Bargain
The Cup of Life
The Devil
Raffles, the Amateur Cracksman
Rumpelstiltskin

Ships and watercraft

After Launching
Afternoon Tea on Board S.S. "Doric"
The American Fleet in Hampton Roads, 1909, After Girdling the Globe
Ancient and Honourables of London Homeward Bound
Arrival of Prince Henry and President Roosevelt at Shooter's Island
Arrival of the Governor General Lord Minto, at Quebec
Arrival of Train at Muskoka Wharf Battery Park
Battle of Chemulpo Bay
The Beach at Coney Island
The Billionaire
Boating Carnival, Palm Beach
Boys Diving, Honolulu
Building a Harbor at San Pedro
The Camera Fiend, no.1
Canoeing at Riverside
Canoeing on the Charles River, Boston, Mass.
Canoeing Scene Canton Steamboat Landing Chinese Passengers
Canton River Scene
Capsize of Lifeboat
Capsized Boat
Caught in the Undertow
Children in the Surf, Coney Island
A Child's Remorse
Christening and Launching Kaiser Wilhelm's Yacht "Meteor"
Close View of the "Brooklyn"
Coaling a Steamer, Nagasaki Bay, Japan
Colored Troops Disembarking
"Corsair" in Wake of Tugboat
The Count of Monte Cristo

The Course of True Love
Crossing the Atlantic
The Cruise of the "Gladys"
Cruiser "Cincinnati"
Cruiser "Detroit"
Cruiser "Marblehead"
Davey Jones' Locker
Departure of Peary [and the] "Roosevelt" from New York
"Deutschland" Leaving New York at Full Speed
A Dip in the Mediterranean
Down the Hudson
Drills and Exercises, Schoolship "St. Mary's"
Duke and Duchess of Cornwall and York Landing at Queenstown, Ontario
An East River Novelty
Eccentricities of an Adirondack Canoe
Eeling Through Ice
The Electric Mule
Emigrants [i.e. Immigrants] Landing at Ellis Island
An Englishman's Trip to Paris from London
European Rest Cure
Excursion Boats, Naval Parade
Ferryboat Entering Slip
Fireboat "New Yorker" Answering an Alarm
Fireboat "New Yorker" in Action
The Fisherman and His Sweetheart
Fisherman, Eels or Snakes
Fisherman's Luck
Fisherman's Wharf
Fishing at Farlone Island
Fishing Smacks
Flagship "New York"
Fleet Steaming up North River
A Flying Wedge
The Forecastle of the "Kearsarge" in a Heavy Sea
Full Rigged Ship at Sea
Fun on the Joy Line
Game of Shovel Board on Board S.S. "Doric"
German Torpedo Boat in Action
The "Glen Island," Accompanying Parade
Gussle Rivals Jonah
He Wouldn't Stay Down
Heaving the Log
Hogan's Romance Upset
Holland Submarine Boat Tests
Horses Loading for Klondike, no. 9
How Millionaires Sometimes Entertain Aboard Their Yachts
Human Apes from the Orient
An Ice Covered Vessel
The Italian
Japanese Sampans

Troop Ships for the Philippines
Troops Embarking at San Francisco
Trout Fishing
Trout Fishing, Rangeley Lakes
Tub Race
U.S. Battleship "Indiana"
U.S. Battleship "Iowa"
U.S. Battleship "Oregon"
U.S. Cruiser "Brooklyn" Naval Parade
U.S. Cruiser "Nashville"
U.S. Cruiser "Olympia" Leading Naval Parade
U.S. Cruiser "Raleigh"
U.S.S. "Castine"
U.S. Troops Landing at Daiquiri, Cuba
Unloading Lighters, Manila
Victorious Squadron Firing Salute
Vizcaya Under Full Headway
The Waders
War Canoe Race
Washington Bridge and Speedway
Whaling in the Far North Off the Coast of Alaska in the Treacherous Bering Sea
Wharf Scene and Natives Swimming at St. Thomas, D.W.I.
Wharf Scene, Honolulu
Where Breakers Roar
White Fox Motor Boat
White Star S.S. "Baltic" Leaving Pier on First Eastern Voyage
The Widow and the Only Man
Will He Marry the Girl
A Woman's Way
Wounded Soldiers Embarking in Row Boats
Wreck of the Battleship "Maine"
Wreck of the "Vizcaya"
Wrestling Yacht
see also America's Cup races; Boat races; Military

Shooter's Island, New York

Arrival of Prince Henry and President Roosevelt at Shooter's Island
Christening and Launching Kaiser Wilhelm's Yacht "Meteor"
Kaiser Wilhelm's Yacht, "Meteor," Entering the Water

Shumway, Leonard C., actor

She Would Be an Actress

Sicily

Washing Clothes at Sicily

Sierra Madre, California

The Gold Seekers
The Man
A Romance of the Western Hills
The Twisted Trail

Sigsbee, Charles Dwight

Secretary Long and Captain Sigsbee

Silveon and Emerie

On the Flying Rings
Silveon and Emerie "On the Web"

Skiing; *see* Winter sports

Skondrup, Frederik, actor

Desdemona
The Fire of Life
The Little Railroad Queen
Love and Friendship
Midsummer-Tide
Vengeance

Sleighs, sleds, and toboggans

After the First Snow
Capture of the Biddle Brothers
Coasting
Coasting Scene at Montmorency Falls, Canada
Cross Country Running on Snow Shoes
The Esquimaux Village
Jones' Interrupted Sleighride
Kent House Slide
A Mid-Winter Brush
Packers on the Trail
Prince Henry Arriving at West Point
Skiing in Montreal
Sleighing in Central Park, New York
Sleighing Scene
Sleighing Scene, Boston
Sleighs Returning After a Spin
Toboganning in Canada
Washing Gold on 20 Above Hunker, Klondike
see also Winter sports

Slevin, Jim, actor

The Paymaster
The Tunnel Workers

Sloane, William, actor

The Rejuvenation of Aunt Mary

Smith, Mrs. Charlotte, actress

All on Account of the Milk
Getting Even
The Little Darling
A Victim of Jealousy
The Woman From Mellon's

Smith, J. B., cameraman

Fireboat "New Yorker" Answering an Alarm
Fireboat "New Yorker" in Action
New York City Dumping Wharf
New York City "Ghetto" Fish Market
New York Harbor Police Boat Patrol Capturing Pirates
Opening of New East River Bridge, New York

"Reliance" and "Shamrock III" Jockeying and Starting in First Race
"Reliance" Crossing the Line and Winning First Race
Sky Scrapers of New York City, From the North River
The Still Alarm
White Wings on Review

Smith, Sebastian, actor

Rescued by Rover

Smith, Mrs. Sebastian, actress

Rescued by Rover

Smith, Vola, actress

The Charity Ball
Liberty Belles
A Poor Relation

Socially significant themes

The American Soldier in Love and War, no. 1
The American Soldier in Love and War, no. 2
The American Soldier in Love and War, no. 3
A Career of Crime, no. 1
A Career of Crime, no. 2
A Career of Crime, no. 3
A Career of Crime, no. 4
A Career of Crime, no. 5
A Convict's Punishment
A Corner in Wheat
The Cripple Creek Bar-Room Scene
The Cup of Life
The Danger of Dining in Private Dining Rooms
The Divorce: Detected
The Divorce: On the Trail
The Divorce: The Evidence Secured
The Downward Path: The Girl Who Went Astray
The Downward Path: She Ran Away
The Downward Path: The Fresh Book Agent
The Downward Path: The New Soubrette
The Downward Path: The Suicide
The Drunkard's Reformation
The Evil Art, or, Gambling Exposed
The Ex-Convict
The Fate of the Artist's Model
Fights of Nations
The Gerry Society's Mistake
The Heathen Chinee and the Sunday School Teachers
Heaven Avenges
His Madonna
His Trust
His Trust Fulfilled
How They Do Things on the Bowery
How They Rob Men in Chicago

The Iconoclast
In a Raines Law Hotel
The Italian
Kansas Saloon Smashers
The Kleptomaniac
The Lesson
The Nihilists .
The Non-Union Bill-Poster
On To Brooklyn
One is Business, the Other Crime
Song of the Shirt
2 a.m. in the Subway
The Two Cousins
The Two Paths
Uncle Tom's Cabin
The Usurer
The Voice of the Violin
Why Mr. Nation Wants a Divorce
The White Caps

Sonyea, New York

Epileptic Seizure, nos. 1–9

Sound Beach, Connecticut

Adventures of Dollie
The Country Schoolmaster
Dr. Dippy's Sanitarium
The Great Jewel Mystery
A Kentucky Feud
Looking for John Smith
The Masqueraders
No Wedding Bells for Him

South Carolina; *see* Charleston, South Carolina

South Orange, New Jersey

Rounding Up of the "Yeggmen"

Spanish-American War

Admiral Dewey Landing at Gibraltar
Admiral Dewey Leading Land Parade
Admiral Dewey Leading the Land Parade, no. 2
Admiral Dewey Passing Catholic Club Stand
Admiral Dewey Receiving the Washington and New York Committees
Admiral Dewey Taking Leave of Washington Committee on the U.S. Cruiser "Olympia"
Admiral Sampson on Board the Flagship
Advance Guard, Return of N.J. Troops
Advance of Kansas Volunteers at Caloocan
Aguinaldo's Navy
Battery B Arriving at Camp
Battery B Pitching Camp
Battery K Siege Guns
Burial of the "Maine" Victims
California Volunteers Marching to Embark

Capture of Trenches at Candaba [Candabar]
Close View of the "Brooklyn" Naval Parade
Colonel Funstan [i.e. Funston] Swimming the Baglag River
Colored Troops Disembarking
Cruiser "Cincinnati"
Cruiser "Detroit"
Cruiser "Marblehead"
Cuban Ambush
Cuban Refugees Waiting for Rations
Cuban Volunteers Embarking
Cuban Volunteers Marching for Rations
The Dandy Fifth
The Dewey Arch
Dewey Arch—Troops Passing Under Arch
Dewey Parade, 10th Pennsylvania Volunteers
The Early Morning Attack
Excursion Boats, Naval Parade
Filipinos Retreat From Trenches
Flagship "New York"
The Fleet Steaming Up North River
General Lee's Procession, Havana
General Wheeler and Secretary Alger
"Glen Island" Accompanying Parade
Governor Roosevelt and Staff
An Historic Feat
Landing of U.S. Troops Near Santiago
Loading Horses on Transport
Love and War
Major General Shafter
The "Massachusetts" Naval Parade
Military Camp at Tampa Taken From Train
Monitor "Terror"
Morning Colors on U.S. Cruiser "Raleigh"
Morro Castle, Havana Harbor
9th and 13th U.S. Infantry at Battalion Drill
9th Infantry Boys' Morning Wash
9th U.S. Cavalry Watering Horses
Observation Train Following Parade
Pack Mules With Ammunition on the Santiago Trail, Cuba
Packing Ammunition on Mules, Cuba
Panorama at Grant's Tomb, Dewey Naval Procession
Panoramic View of Floral Float "Olympia"
Parade of Marines, U.S. Cruiser "Brooklyn"
Police Boats Escorting Naval Parade
President Roosevelt and the Rough Riders

Raising Old Glory Over Morro Castle
Return of 2nd Regiment of New Jersey
Return of Troop C, Brooklyn
Reviewing the "Texas" at Grant's Tomb
Roosevelt's Rough Riders
Roosevelt's Rough Riders Embarking for Santiago
Rout of the Filipinos
Sailors of Atlantic Fleet, Dewey Parade
Sampson-Schley Controversy [Parts 1 and 2 of 3]
Sampson and Schley Controversy—Tea Party [Part 3 of 3]
Secretary Long and Captain Sigsbee
Seventh Regiment, N.Y.
71st New York Volunteers Embarking for Santiago
Shooting Captured Insurgents
Skirmish of Rough Riders
Soldiers Washing Dishes
Steamer "Mascotte" Arriving at Tampa
10th U.S. Infantry Disembarking From Cars
10th U.S. Infantry, 2nd Battalion Leaving Cars
The "Texas" Naval Parade
Trained Cavalry Horses
Transport Ships at Port Tampa
Transport "Whitney" Leaving Dock
Troop Ships for the Philippines
Troops at Evacuation of Havana
Troops Embarking at San Francisco
Troops Making Military Road in Front of Santiago
U.S. Battleship "Indiana"
U.S. Battleship "Iowa"
U.S. Battleship "Oregon"
U.S. Cavalry Supplies Unloading at Tampa, Florida
U.S. Cruiser "Brooklyn" Naval Parade
U.S. Cruiser "Nashville"
U.S. Cruiser "Olympia" Leading Naval Parade
U.S. Cruiser "Raleigh"
U.S. Infantry Supported by Rough Riders at El Caney
U.S. Troops and Red Cross in the Trenches Before Caloocan
U.S. Troops Landing at Daiquiri, Cuba
Victorious Squadron Firing Salute
Wagon Supply Train En Route
War Correspondents
West Point Cadets
Wounded Soldiers Embarking in Row Boats
Wreck of the Battleship "Maine"
Wreck of the "Vizcaya"

Spanishtown, Jamaica

Railroad Panorama Near Spanishtown, Jamaica

Special effects; *see* Trick effects; Unusual camera uses

Specials; *see* Name of person

Speeches; *see* Public events

Squires, Bill, prizefighter

International Contest for the Heavyweight Championship: Squires vs. Burns, Ocean View, Cal., July 4th, 1907

Squires, Australian Champion in His Training Quarters

Stagecoaches; *see* Carriages, coaches, and buggies

Stamford, Connecticut

The Impalement
Maneuvering a Small Motor Boat
White Fox Motor Boat

Standard Oil Company

Burning of the Standard Oil Co's Tanks, Bayonne, N.J.

Stanford University

Stanford University, California

Steamships; *see* Ships and watercraft

Steel; *see* Industries

Sterling, Ford, actor

Court House Crooks
Dirty Work in a Laundry
He Wouldn't Stay Down
Hogan's Romance Upset
An Interrupted Elopement
Our Dare Devil Chief
That Little Band of Gold
The Tragedy of a Dress Suit

Stevens, Josephine, actress

Fatty's Plucky Pup
Those College Girls

Stewart, Jane, actress

The Kleptomaniac

Stewart, Lucille Lee, actress

His New Lid

Stewens, Helga, scriptwriter/author

Love in the Tropics

Stone, Fred A.

Dancing Boxing Match, Montgomery and Stone
Goodbye John

Storm, Jerome, actor

The Cup of Life

Storms; *see* Floods and hurricanes

Stoughton, Mabel, actress

Balked at the Altar
The Valet's Wife

Stow, Percy, director

The Convict's Escape
How the Old Women Caught the Omnibus
A Kiss and a Tumble

Streetcars and subways

Across the Subway Viaduct, New York
Ambulance at the Accident
Arrival of Emigrants [i.e. Immigrants], Ellis Island
The Blizzard
Broadway & Union Square, New York
The Burning of Durland's Riding Academy
City Hall to Harlem in 15 Seconds via the Subway Route
Collecting Mail, U.S.P.O.
Corner Madison and State Streets, Chicago
Crowd Entering, Futurity Day
Delivering Mail From Sub-Station
Delivering Newspapers
The Dewey Arch
Eclipse Car Fender Test, no. 1–2
The Escalta, Manila
Excavation for Subway
First Avenue, Seattle, Washington
For Better—But Worse
Honolulu Street Scene
Interior N.Y. Subway, 14th St. to 42nd St.
Lower Broadway
Madison Square, New York
Market Street Before Parade
Mexico Street Scene
No Wedding Bells for Him
[On] A [Good Old] Five Cent Trolley Ride
Opening Ceremonies, New York Subway, October 27, 1904
Opening Ceremony of New York Subway
Panorama of Place de l'Opera
Panoramic View from Pittsburgh to Allegheny
Panoramic View of Boston Subway from an Electric Car
Panoramic View of the Champs Elysees
Parade, Mystic Shriners, Atlantic City, New Jersey
Paterson Fire, Showing the Y.M.C.A. and Library

Reuben in the Subway
Rock Drill at Work in Subway
Rube and Fender
A Rube in the Subway
Scenes in San Francisco
Seeing Boston
South Spring Street, Los Angeles, Cal.
Street Car Chivalry
Street Mail Car, U.S.P.O.
Street Scene, San Diego
Street Scene, Tokio Japan
Surface Transit, Mexico
Switchback on Trolley Road
Toodles and Her Strawberry Tart
Tramp on a Farm
A Trip to Berkeley, Cal.
2 A. M. in the Subway
The Unappreciated Joke
A Visit to Baby Roger
see also Buses; Carriages, coaches, and buggies; Business districts; and Railroads

Streator's Zouaves

Street's Zouaves and Wall Scaling

Strøm, Axel, actor

The Little Railroad Queen
The Power of Love

Stuart, Ralph, actor

Duel Scene, "By Right of Sword"

Submarines; *see* Ships and watercraft

Subways; *see* Streetcars and subways

Sugar industry; *see* Industry

Sullivan, C. Gardner, scriptwriter/author

The Darkening Trail

Summerville, Slim, actor

The Beauty Bunglers
Caught in a Park
Caught in the Act
Cursed by His Beauty
Dough and Dynamite
Fatty's New Role
Gentlemen of Nerve
Gussle the Golfer
Gussle's Day of Rest
The Home Breakers
That Little Band of Gold
Their Social Splash
Those College Girls

Sunshine, Marion, actress

The Helping Hand
The Italian Barber
The Poor Sick Men
The Red Girl
The Slave

Sunshine Sue

Svendsen, Robert, aviator

The Aviator's Generosity

Swain, Mack, actor

Ambrose's Fury
Ambrose's Little Hatchet
Ambrose's Lofty Perch
Ambrose's Nasty Temper
Ambrose's Sour Grapes
Caught in a Park
Fatty's New Role
Gentlemen of Nerve
Gussle the Golfer
Hogan's Romance Upset
The Home Breakers
A Human Hound's Triumph
Love, Speed and Thrills
Mabel Lost and Won
When Ambrose Dared Walrus
Willful Ambrose
Ye Olden Grafter

Sweet, Blanche, actress

All on Account of the Milk
Choosing a Husband
Classmates
A Corner in Wheat
The Day After
A Flash of Light
Homefolks
Judith of Bethulia
The Lesser Evil
Man's Lust for Gold
The Massacre
Men and Women
One Is Business, the Other Crime
One Night and Then
An Outcast Among Outcasts
The Punishment
The Rocky Road
A Romance of the Western Hills
A Spirit Awakened
Strongheart
A Temporary Truce
To Save Her Soul
With the Enemy's Help

Swickard, Joe, actor

Ambrose's Lofty Perch
Dirty Work in a Laundry
Droppington's Family Tree
Gentlemen of Nerve
Gussle the Golfer
Hash House Mashers
Hearts and Planets
Hogan the Porter
Hogan's Romance Upset
A Home-Breaking Hound
A Human Hound's Triumph
Love, Loot and Crash
A Lover's Lost Control
Mabel, Fatty and the Law
The Rent Jumpers

Shot in the Excitement
A Versatile Villain
When Ambrose Dared Walrus
When the Fire-Bells Rang
Willful Ambrose

Swimming and diving

Bathing at Atlantic City
The Beach at Coney Island
The Beauty Bunglers
Belles of the Beach
Boarding School Girls
Boys Diving, Honolulu
The Camera Fiend
Caught in the Undertow
Children Bathing
Children in the Surf, Coney Island
Colonel Funstan [i.e. Funston]
    Swimming the Baglag River
The Diving Horse
Diving Through Hoops
Drills and Exercises, Schoolship "St.
    Mary's"
The Dude and the Bathing Girls
Egyptian Boys in Swimming Race
The Elopement
Fancy Driving
Fat Bather and Treacherous Spring-
    board
Gossle Rivals Jonah
He Wouldn't Stay Down
High Diving
High Diving by A. C. Holden
In a German Bath
The Interrupted Bathers
June's Birthday Party
Just Like a Girl
Kanakas Diving for Money, no. 1
Kanakas Diving for Money, no. 2
King and Queen, Diving Horses
Life Rescue at Long Branch
The Little Teacher
Love in the Tropics
Lurline Baths
Mexican Fishing Scene
Midwinter Bathing, L Street Bath,
    Boston
Miss Fatty's Seaside Lovers
Mixed Bathing
The Modern Prodigal
New York City Public Bath
The Old Swimming Hole
Orphan Children on the Beach at
    Coney Island
Orphans in the Surf
Panorama of Beach and Cliff House
Pranks
The Reversible Divers
S.S. "Gaelic"
A Salutary Lesson
A Seashore Gymkana
Settled at the Seaside
Surf at Atlantic City
Sutro Baths
Sutro Baths, no. 1

The Swimming Class
Swimming Pool at Coney Island
Swimming Pool, Palm Beach
A Swimming Race at Coney Island
Those Bitter Sweets
The Tramp and the Bathers
Turning the Tables
West Indian Boys Diving for Money
Wharf Scene and Natives Swimming
    at St. Thomas, D.W.I.
Wharf Scene, Honolulu
Will He Marry the Girl
Women of the Ghetto Bathing

Switzerland

Lake Lucerne, Switzerland

Syracuse, Sicily

Washing Clothes at Sicily

Syria; see Beirut, Jaffa, Syria; and Mizpah, Syria

Taft, William Howard, president, U.S.

Reception of President Taft in
    Petersburg, Virginia, May 19th,
    1909
The Sculptor's Nightmare
Sec'y Taft's Address & Panorama
Unveiling of the Pennsylvania Mon-
    ument on the Battlefields of
    Petersburg, Virginia, May 19,
    1909

Talbot, Henry

Bass Fishing

Tampa, Florida

Military Camp at Tampa Taken
    From Train
Steamer "Mascotte" Arriving at
    Tampa
Transport Ships at Port Tampa
U.S. Cavalry Supplies Unloading at
    Tampa, Florida

Tansy, John, actor

The Redman and the Child

Taylor, Stanner E. V., author

Lines of White on a Sullen Sea

Teddy, himself, a dog

Hogan's Aristocratic Dream
Mabel and Fatty's Wash Day

Tellegen, Lou, actor

Queen Elizabeth

Texas; see Beaumont, Texas; and Galveston, Texas

Thanhouser Film Corporation

The Star of Bethlehem

Thaw, Harry K.

Thaw-White Tragedy

Theby, Rosemary, actress

The Cannon Ball
Do-Re-Mi—Boom!
A Home-Breaking Hound

Thomas, Nona, actress

The Darkening Trail

Thompson, De Lloyd, aviator

When Love Took Wings

Thompson, Harry

Harry Thompson's Immitations of
Sousa

Thompson, Margaret, actress

Rumpelstiltskin

Thomsen, Ebba, actress

The Fisherman and His Sweetheart

Tidal waves; *see* Disasters

Tientsin, China

Arrival of Train, Tien-Tsin
Cossack Cavalry
Review of Russian Artillery
Russian Sharp Shooters
Street Scene, Tientsin

Tivoli, Italy

Panorama of Tivoli, Italy, Showing
Seven Falls

Toboggans; *see* Sleighs, sleds,
and toboggans

Tokyo, Japan

Arrival of Tokyo Train
Arrival of Train, Tokio, Japan
Asakusa Temple, Tokio, Japan
Street Scene, Tokio, Japan

Toncray, Kate, actress

Heaven Avenges
The Helping Hand
His Lesson
The Little Darling
The Renunciation of Aunt Mary
The Sands of Dee
The Tunnel Workers
The Way of Man
Who's Looney Now?
Willie Becomes an Artist
Won By a Fish

Toronto, Canada

Capsized Boat
The Great Toronto Fire, Toronto
Canada, April 19, 1904

Torpedoboats; *see* Ships and watercraft

Torrence, David, actor

The Prisoner of Zenda

Tourist attractions

American Falls, Goat Island
American Falls, Luna Island
Arab Act, Luna Park
Around the Flip-Flap Railroad
Asakusa Temple, Tokio, Japan
Asia in America, St. Louis Exposi-
tion
Atlantic City Floral Parade
Bathing at Atlantic City
Boarding School Girls
Bridal Veil Falls
Cascade Near Wawona, California
Champs de Mars
Children in the Surf, Coney Island
Circular Panorama of Electric Tow-
er
Circular Panorama of Suspension
Bridge and American Falls
Circular Panorama of the Horse
Shoe Falls in Winter
Circular Panoramic View of Whirl-
pool Rapids
Coaches Arriving at Mammoth Hot
Springs
Coaches Going to Cinnabar From
Yellowstone Park
Coney Island at Night
Crossing Ice Bridge at Niagara Falls
Dials' Girls' Band, Luna Park
Dress Parade of Scouts, St. Louis
Exposition
Eiffel Tower from Trocadero Palace
Electric Tower
Esplanade des Invalides
Esquimaux Game of Snap-the-Whip
Esquimaux Leap-Frog
The Esquimaux Village
Falls of Minnehaha
Feeding Pigeons in Front of St.
Mark's Cathedral, Venice, Italy
Fighting the Flames
Fighting the Flames, Dreamland
Filipino Scouts, Musical Drill, St.
Louis
Fire and Flames at Luna Park,
Coney Island (New York)
Flying Train
Glacier Point
Glimpses of Yellowstone Park
Gussle Rivals Jonah
Hotel Del Monte
Japanese Village
Midway of Charleston Exposition
Military Parade, St. Louis Exposi-
tion
Moonlight on Lake Maggiore
Mount Tamalpais R.R., no. 1
Mount Tamalpais R.R., no. 2
Mount Taw R.R., No. 3

Old Faithful Geyser
Opening Ceremonies, St. Louis
Exposition
Opening Day, Jamestown Exposi-
tion
Palace of Electricity
Panorama from German Building,
World's Fair
Panorama from Gondola, St. Louis
Exposition
Panorama from the Moving Board-
walk
Panorama of Eiffel Tower
Panorama of Esplanade by Night
Panorama of Race Track Crowd, St.
Louis
Panorama of the Moving Boardwalk
Panorama of the Paris Exposition,
from the Seine
Panorama, St. Louis Exposition
Panoramic View of Charleston Ex-
position
Panoramic View of Electric Tower
from a Balloon
Panoramic View of Mt. Tamalpais
Panoramic View of Mt. Tamalpais
Between Bow Knot and McKinley
Cut
Panoramic View of Niagara Falls
Panoramic View of Rubio Canyon,
Mt. Low R.R.
Panoramic View of the Great Cable
Incline, Mt. Low R.R.
Parade of Floats, St. Louis Exposi-
tion
Parade of the Pikers, St. Louis
Exposition
Paris from the Seine
Prince Henry at Niagara Falls
The Racing Chutes at Dreamland
Rapids Below Suspension Bridge
Reviewing the "Texas" at Grant's
Tomb
Riverside Geyser, Yellowstone Park
Scene from the Elevator Ascending
Eiffel Tower
Scene in the Swiss Village at Paris
Exposition
Sham Battle at the Pan-American
Exposition
Speech by President Francis:
World's Fair
Statue of Liberty
Sutro Baths, no. 1
Swiss Village, no. 2
Tourists Arriving at Wawona Hotel
Tourists Going Round Yellowstone
Park
A Trip Around the Pan-American
Exposition
A Trip Down Mt. Tamalpais
Triumphal Bridge, Pan-American
Exposition
Upper Falls of the Yellowstone
The Vaidis Sisters, Luna Park

Waterfall in the Catskills
Wawona, Big Tree
West Indian Girls in Native Dance
West Point Cadets, St. Louis Exposition
see also Amusement areas; Fairs and expositions; specific geographic locations

Townsend and Downey Ship Building Co.

Arrival of Prince Henry and President Roosevelt at Shooter's Island
Christening and Launching Kaiser Wilhelm's Yacht "Meteor"
Kaiser Wilhelm's Yacht, "Meteor," Entering the Water

Track meets

Cross Country Running on Snow Shoes
Daly of West Point Winning Hurdle Race
High School Field Exercises, Missouri Commission
Inter-Collegiate Athletic Association Championships, 1904
New York Athletic Club Games, Travers Island
Pole Vaulting
Throwing the Sixteen Pound Hammer

Tracy, Clyde, actor

Rumpelstiltskin

Trafford, Pennsylvania

Westinghouse Works

Trams; *see* Streetcars and subways

Transportation

Adventures of Dollie
Arrest in Chinatown, San Francisco, Cal.
Arrival of Train Tokio, Japan
Battle of Flowers at the Nice Carnival
Beach Apparatus-Practice
Boer Commissary Train
Bridge Traffic, Manila
The Burd [Bund], Shanghai
Burial of the "Maine" Victims
Champs Elysees
Changing Horses at Glen
Charge of the Light Brigade
The Ch-ien-men Gate, Pekin
Church "Our Lady of Grace," Hoboken
Coach at Rural Post Office, U.S.P.O.
Coaches Arriving at Mammoth Hot Springs
Coaching Party
Collecting Mail, U.S.P.O.
The Cop Fools the Sergeant

Corner Madison and State Streets, Chicago
A Country Courtship
Cowboys and Indians Fording River in a Wagon
The Curtain Pole
Delivering Newspapers
The Dewey Arch
Dirty Work in a Laundry
The Electric Mule
The Escalta, Manila
Excavation for Subway
Exchange of Mail at Rural P.O., U.S.P.O.
Exhibition of Prize Winners
Flood Scene in Paterson, N.J.
Flying Train
For Better—But Worse
General Cronje & Mystic Shriners
Going to the Hunt, Meadowbrook
Going to the Yokohama Races
Hong Kong, Wharf-Scene
Horticultural Floats, no. 9
Hotel Vendome, San Jose, Cal.
How They Do Things on the Bowery
Iola's Promise
Judging Tandems
A Kiss and a Tumble
Loading Baggage for Klondike, no. 6
Loading Mail Car. U.S.P.O.
Love, Speed and Thrills
A Lucky Leap
Madison Square, New York
Mailing Platform, U.S.P.O.
Man's Lust for Gold
Market Street Before Parade
The Massacre
Miles Canyon Tramway
New York City Dumping Wharf
New York Police Parade, June 1st, 1899
A Night at the Haymarket
Ox Carts, Tokio, Japan
Panorama of Field Street, St. Joseph
Panorama of 4th St., St. Joseph
Panorama of Place de l'Opera
Panorama of Ruins from Lombard and Charles Street
Panorama of the Moving Boardwalk
Panorama of Wreckage of Water Front
Panoramic View from Pittsburgh to Allegheny
Panoramic View of the Champs Elysees
Panoramic View of the Place de l'Concord
Parade, Mystic Shriners, Atlantic City, New Jersey
Parade of Buffalo Bill's Wild West Show, no. 1
Parade of Horses on Speedway
Parade of Shriners, Luna Park

Parade of the Pikers' St. Louis Exposition
Paris from the Seine
The Pickpocket
A Pipe Story of the Fourth
Pope Passing Through Upper Loggia
Post Man Delivering Mail, U.S.P.O.
The Power of the Press
President Roosevelt's Homecoming
Procession of Mounted Indians and Cowboys
Review of Russian Artillery
Rickshaw Parade, Japan
Romance of an Egg
A Round-up in Oklahoma
Rural Wagon Delivering Mail, U.S.P.O.
Rural Wagon Giving Mail to Branch, U.S.P.O.
St. Patrick's Cathedral and Fifth Avenue on Easter Sunday Morning
Shanghai Street Scene 1
Shanghai Street Scene 2
South Spring Street, Los Angeles, Cal.
Stolen by Gypsies
Street Fight and Arrest
Street Mail Car, U.S.P.O.
Street Scene in Hong Kong
Street Scene in Yokohama, no. 1
Street Scene in Yokohama, no. 2
Street Scene, Tientsin
Street Scene, Tokio, Japan
The Tenderfoot's Triumph
Tourists Arriving at Wawona Hotel
Tourists Starting for Canton
Transporting Internal Rev. Stamps, U.S.P.O.
The Trials and Troubles of an Automobilist
A Trip to Berkeley, Cal.
Twenty Mule Team, St. Louis Exposition
U.S. Cavalry Supplies Unloading at Tampa, Florida
Unloading Lighters, Manila
Vengeance
Wagon Supply Train En Route
Wagons Loading Mail, U.S.P.O.
Water Buffalo, Manila
What the Doctor Ordered
White Wings on Review
The Zulu's Heart
see also Specific types

Trask, Wayland, actor

A Lover's Lost Control

Travers Island, New York

New York Athletic Club Games, Travers Island

499

Star Theatre
The Startled Lover
Stop Thief!
The Story of the Biograph Told
Strange Adventure of New York Drummer
The Subpoena Server
Temptation of St. Anthony
10 Ladies in an Umbrella
Ten Nights in a Bar-Room: Vision of Mary
A Terrible Night
The Terrible Turkish Executioner
They Would Elope
The Tired Tailor's Dream
Tom, Tom, the Piper's Son
Le Tonnerre de Jupiter
Torpedo Attack on Port Arthur
The Tramp's Miraculous Escape
The Truants
The Tunnel Workers
The Twentieth Century Tramp, or, Happy Hooligan and His Airship
Uncle Josh at the Moving Picture Show
Uncle Josh in a Spooky Hotel
Uncle Josh's Nightmare
Uncle Tom's Cabin
Vanishing Lady
Wanted—A Nurse
The Way to Sell Corsets
A Welsh Rabbit
What Happened in the Tunnel
What Happened to Jones
Who Pays for the Drinks?
The Whole Dam Family and the Dam Dog
The Witch's Revenge
see also Unusual camera uses

Troiano, John

The Suburbanite

Trolleys; *see* Streetcars and subways

Union Iron Works

Union Iron Works

U.S. Army; *see* Military

U.S. Military Academy

Daly of West Point Winning Hurdle Race
Football Game: West Point vs. Annapolis
Prince Henry Arriving at West Point
Prince Henry at West Point
Prince Henry Reviewing the Cadets at West Point
Review of Cadets at West Point
Review of Cadets, West Point
West Point Cadets
West Point Cadets, St. Louis Exposition

U.S. Naval Academy

Football: West Point vs. Annapolis
John Paul Jones Ceremonies

United States Naval Training School

Drills and Exercises, Schoolship "St. Mary's"

United States Navy; *see* Military

United States Post Office

Buying Stamps from Rural Wagon, U.S.P.O.
Cancelling Machine, U.S.P.O.
Carriers at Work, U.S.P.O.
Carriers Leaving Building, U.S.P.O.
Clerks Casing Mail for Bags, U.S.P.O.
Clerks Tying Bags, U.S.P.O.
Clerks Tying Up for Bags, U.S.P.O.
Coach at Rural Post Office, U.S.P.O.
Collecting Mail, U.S.P.O.
Delivering Mail from Sub-Station
Exchange of Mail at Rural P.O., U.S.P.O.
Loading Mail Car, U.S.P.O.
Old Mail Coach at Ford, U.S.P.O.
Post Man Delivering Mail, U.S.P.O.
Routing Mail, U.S.P.O.
Rural Wagon Delivering Mail, U.S.P.O.
Rural Wagon Giving Mail to Branch, U.S.P.O.
Special Delivery Messenger, U.S.P.O.
Street Mail Car, U.S.P.O.
Throwing Mail into Bags, U.S.P.O.
Train Taking up Mail Bag, U.S.P.O.
Transporting Internal Rev. Stamps, U.S.P.O.
Tying up Bags for Train, U.S.P.O.
Wagons Loading Mail, U.S.P.O.

Universal Film Manufacturing Company

His Madonna

Universities; *see* Columbia University; Cornell University; Harvard University; Princeton University; Stanford University; University of Pennsylvania; Yale University

University of Pennsylvania

Cornell-Columbia-University of Pennsylvania Boat Race at Ithaca, N.Y., Showing Lehigh Valley Observation Train

Unusual camera uses

An Animated Luncheon
Animated Painting
Animated Picture Studio
The Animated Poster

Annual Baby Parade, 1904, Asbury Park, N.J.
Another Job for the Undertaker
Another Name Was Maude
Les Apparitions Fugitives
The Artist's Dilemma
An Artist's Dream
The Artist's Dream
As Seen on the Curtain
At the Altar
At the French Ball
The Attack on Port Arthur
Au Clair de la Lune
Aunt Sallie's Wonderful Bustle
An Awful Moment
Baby's Day
A Baby's Shoe
The Ballet Master's Dream
Bathing in Samoa
Battle of Chemulpo Bay
Be Good
A Beast at Bay
Betrayed by Hand Prints
The Bewitched Traveller
The Black Hand
Bob Kick, l'Enfant Terrible
Bob Kick, the Mischievous Kid
Bombardment of Taku Forts, by the Allied Fleets
The Bowery Kiss
The Boy Detective
Brannigan Sets Off the Blast
The Broker's Athletic Typewriter
The Burglar's Slide for Life
Burlesque Suicide
Burning of St. Pierre
Capture of Boer Battery by British
Casey's Frightful Dream
Catching an Early Train
Caught by Wireless
The Cavalier's Dream
Charity Ball
Le Chauldron [i.e., Chaudron] Infernal
Chauncey Explains
City Hall to Harlem in 15 Seconds Via the Subway Route
Climbing the American Alps
The Clock Maker's Dream
The Clown and the Alchemist
Coney Island at Night
Congress of Nations
The Cook in Trouble
The Corset Model
The Country Doctor
The Cowboy and the Lady
The Cricket on the Hearth
The Critic
The Curtain Pole
The Damnation of Faust
The Darling of the Gallery Gods
Davey Jones' Locker
Desdemona
The Devil
A Discordant Note

Si Jones Looking for John Smith
The Silver Wedding
Simple Charity
Skeleton Dance, Marionettes
The Slave
A Smoked Husband
The Snowman
The Somnambulist
La Sorcellerie Culinaire
A Spiritualist Photographer
Sporting Blood
Star Theatre
A Strange Meeting
The Strenuous Life; or, Anti-Race
   Suicide
A Subject for the Rogue's Gallery
Subub Surprises the Burglar
The Suburbanite
Sweet and Twenty
Teasing
Temptation of St. Anthony
10 Ladies in an Umbrella
The Terrible Turkish Executioner
Thompson's Night Out
Those Awful Hats
The Tired Tailor's Dream
To Save Her Soul
Tom, Tom, The Piper's Son
Le Tonnerre de Jupiter
Travels of a Lost Trunk
Trial Marriages
The Truants
The Tunnel Workers
The Twentieth Century Tramp, or,
   Happy Hooligan and His Airship
The Twisted Trail
The Two Paths
Uncle Josh at the Moving Picture
   Show
Uncle Josh's Nightmare
Uncle Tom's Cabin
An Unexpected Guest
The Valet's Wife
The Vampire Dancer
The Village Cut-Up
The Violin Maker of Cremona
A Voice From the Deep
Wanted—A Nurse
The way of the World
The Way to Sell Corsets
The Wedding
What Burglar Bill Found in the Safe
When a Man Loves
When Kings Were the Law
Where Breakers Roar
The Whole Dam Family and the
   Dam Dog
Why Curfew Did Not Ring
The Widow and the Only Man
Winning Back His Love
The Witch's Revenge
The Yale Laundry
see also Trick effects

Urban, Charles, director

Reproduction, Coronation Ceremonies—King Edward VII

Vaidis Sisters

The Vaidis Sisters, Luna Park

Vailsburg, New Jersey

High Diving by A. C. Holden

Vale, Louise, actress

Woman Against Woman
The Woman From Mellon's

Vale, Travers, director

Woman Against Woman

Van Wyck, Robert Anderson

Admiral Dewey Leading Land Parade
Mayor Van Wyck and General Miles

Vancouver, Canada

Returning to China
Steamship "Express of India"

Vanderbilt, W. K., Jr.

Auto Boat Race on the Hudson

Vaudeville acts

Acrobatic Monkey
An Affair of Honor
Al Treloar in Muscle Exercises
Allabad; the Arabian Wizard
Alphonse and Gaston, no. 3
Ameta
Les Apparitions Fugitives
Arab Act, Luna Park
Arabian Gun Twirler
As In a Looking Glass
Au Clair de la Lune
Balloon Ascension, Marionettes
The Bench in the Park
Betsy Ross Dance
Bicycle Trick Riding, no. 2
Ein Bier
Biograph's Improved Incubator
Birth of the Pearl
The Boy in the Barrel
The Boys Think They Have One on
   Foxy Grandpa, But He Fools
   Them
Central Park After Dark
Charity Ball
Chicks to Order
Chimmie Hicks at the Races
Ching Ling Foo Outdone
Comedy Cake Walk
Congress of Nations
Cosy Corner Dance
The Creators of Foxy Grandpa
Dance, Franchonetti Sisters
A Dance in Pajamas
A Dance on the Pike

Dancing Boxing Match, Montgomery and Stone
Dancing Chinaman, Marionettes
The Darling of the Gallery Gods
Dog Factory
The Draped Model
A Drop of Ink
Ella Lola, a la Trilby
Expert Bag Punching
Farmer Kissing the Lean Girl
A Farmer's Imitation of Ching Ling
   Foo
Faust Family of Acrobats
Fights of Nations
Finishing Touches
Fougere
Foxy Grandpa and Polly in a Little
   Hilarity
French Acrobatic Dance
A Frontier Flirtation
Fun in [A] Photograph Gallery
Girls Dancing Can-Can
Girls Swinging
Gordon Sisters Boxing
Harry Thompson's Imitations of
   Sousa
Hindoo Fakir
Hooligan Assists the Magician
A Hustling Soubrette
Jack Jaggs and Dum Dum
Japanese Acrobats
Japanese Village
Kansas Saloon Smashers
Karina
The Ki-Ki Dance
King and Queen, Diving Horses
Larks Behind the Scene
Latina, Contortionist
Latina, Dislocation Act
Latina, Physical Culture Poses, no. 1
Latina, Physical Culture Poses, no. 2
Laura Comstock's Bag-Punching
   Dog
Leaping Dogs at Gentry's Circus
Levi & Cohen, the Irish Comedians
Little Lillian, Toe Danseuse
Lukens, Novel Gymnast
The Magic Lantern
The Magician
Marceline, the World-Renowned
   Clown of the N.Y. Hippodrome
The Mechanical Toy
The Melomaniac
The Mermaid
The Minister's Wooing
Miss Lillian Shaffer and Her Dancing Horse
The Monster
The Mysterious Midgets
A Mystic Re-Incarnation
The Mystic Swing
The Mystical Flame
On the Benches in the Park
On the Flying Rings
On to Brooklyn, no. 1

503

On to Brooklyn, no. 2
The Oracle of Delphi
The Pajama Statue Girls
A Phenomenal Contortionist
The Physical Culture Girl
Pierrot's Problem
A Pipe for a Cigar
Play Ball on the Beach
Poor Girl, It Was a Hot Night and the Mosquitos Were Thick
Poor John
The Poster Girls
The Pouting Model
The Prentis Trio
Un Prêté Pour un Rendu, ou, Une Bonne Farce Avec Ma Téte
Princess Rajah Dance
Le Roi du Maquillage
Sandow
Saved!
The Serenaders
Silveon and Emerie "On the Web"
Skeleton Dance, Marionettes
Skidoo Brothers, 23
Sleeping Child
Slide for Life, Luna Park
Some Dudes Can Fight
Spike, the Bag-Punching Dog
A Spiritualist Photographer
Spooks at School
Springtime in the Park
Stealing a Dinner
Stop Thief!
The Strenuous Life
Symphony in "A-Flat"
Theatre Hats Off
Three Acrobats
Three Girls in a Hammock
Too Much of a Good Thing
The Tramp's Unexpected Skate
Trapeze Disrobing Act
Treloar and Miss Marshall, Prize Winners at the Physical Culture Show in Madison Square Garden
The Trick Cyclist
Turkish Dance, Ella Lola
An Unexpected Knockout
The Vaidis Sisters, Luna Park
Vanishing Lady
Waiting at the Church
Waiting for Bill
A Wake in "Hell's Kitchen"

Utah

Devil's Slide

Vaughan, Vivian, actress

Life of an American Fireman

Vaulx, Count de la, balloonist

Society Ballooning, Pittsfield, Mass.

Venice, California

Ambrose's Fury
The Cannon Ball

Fatty's Plucky Pup
Mabel's Wilful Way
Miss Fatty's Seaside Lovers
Never Again!
Settled at the Seaside
Those Bitter Sweets
A Voice From the Deep

Venice, Italy

Feeding Pigeons in Front of St. Mark's Cathedral, Venice, Italy

Verdugo, California

An Affair of Hearts
A Knot in the Plot
May and December

Versailles, Pennsylvania

The Little Train Robbery

Victoria, Vesta, singer

Poor John
Waiting at the Church

Vincennes, France

King Edward and President Loubet Reviewing French Troops

Virgin Islands; *see* St. Thomas, Virgin Islands; and St. Vincent, Virgin Islands

Virginia; *see* Hampton Roads, Virginia; Jamestown, Virginia; Manassas, Virginia; Newport News, Virginia; Petersburg, Virginia; and Road Bridge, Virginia

Vitagraph Company of America

H.R.H. the Prince of Wales Decorating the Monument of Champlain and Receiving Addresses of Welcome from the Mayor of Quebec, the Governor General of Canada and Vice-President Fairbanks, Representative of the United States
H.R.H. the Prince of Wales Viewing the Grand Military Review on the Plains of Abraham, Quebec
Humorous Phases of Funny Faces
The Miner's Daughter
Nellie, the Beautiful Housemaid
Raffles, the Amateur Cracksman

Voijere, George, actor

The Kleptomaniac

Volcanos; *see* Disasters

Vosburg, Harold, actor

The Moonshiner

Wagons; *see* Transportation

Wales, Prince of

H.R.H. the Prince of Wales Decorating the Monument of Champlain

and Receiving Addresses of Welcome from the Mayor of Quebec, the Governor General of Canada and Vice-President Fairbanks, Representative of the United States
H.R.H. the Prince of Wales Viewing the Grand Military Review on the Plains of Abraham, Quebec

Wallace, Lew, author

The Chariot Race

Walthall, Henry B., actor

The Banker's Daughters
The Battle at Elderbush Gulch
The Better Way
The Broken Locket
The Call
The Call to Arms
The Child of the Ghetto
Choosing a Husband
Classmates
The Cloister's Touch
The Converts
The Convict's Sacrifice
A Corner in Wheat
The Day After
The Face at the Window
His Last Burglary
Homefolks
The Honor of His Family
The House With Closed Shutters
The Iconoclast
In Life's Cycle
In Little Italy
In Old California
In Old Kentucky
In the Border States
Judith of Bethulia
The Kid
Leather Stocking
The Little Darling
Lord Chumley
The Mills of the Gods
The Oath and the Man
On the Reef
One Night and Then
Pranks
Ramona
Rose O'Salem-Town
The Sealed Room
The Slave
The Sorrows of the Unfaithful
A Strange Meeting
Strongheart
A Summer Idyl
Thou Shalt Not
The Thread of Destiny
A Trap for Santa Claus
The Two Brothers
The Usurer
The Way of the World
Wilful Peggy
With Her Card

505

The Hoopskirt and the Narrow Door
A Hot Time at Home
How the Cook Made Her Mark
A Hustling Soubrette
Hyde Park School Graduating Class
Hyde Park School, Room 2
An Ice-Covered Vessel
In a Boarding School Gym
In the Dressing Room
In the Springtime, Gentle Annie!
Inside Car, Showing Bag Catcher
Jockeying and Start of Yacht[s], Aug. 25th
Jockeying for the Start, Aug. 20
Jockeying for the Start, Aug. 22
The Johnie and the Telephone
A Joke at the French Ball
The Jolly Bill Poster
Just Before the Raid
The Kentucky Squire
Kindergarten Ball Game
Kindergarten Dance
A Kiss in the Dark
Kiss Me
Lady Bountiful Visits the Murphys on Wash Day
Lathrop School, Calisthenics
Launch of Battleship "Connecticut"
Let Uncle Reuben Show You How
Linwood School, Calisthenics
A Little Bit Off the Top
A Little Teaze
The Loaded Cigar
Loading Mail Car, U.S.P.O.
Love and Jealousy Behind the Scenes
Mailing Platform, U.S.P.O.
The Mechanical Toy
Military Parade, St. Louis Exposition
The Minister's Hat
A Misdirected Ducking
The Mis-Directed Kiss
Mr. Easymark
Mr. Jack Caught in the Dressing Room
Mr. Jack Entertains in His Office
Mr. Jack in the Dressing Room
The Model That Didn't Pose
Musical Bayonet Exercises
Musical Calisthenics
Naval Battle, St. Louis Exposition
Never Touched Him
Next
Nigger in the Woodpile
A Novel Way of Catching a Burglar
Off His Beat
An Old Bachelor
Old Mail Coach at Ford, U.S.P.O.
On the Window Shades
One Way of Taking a Girl's Picture
Opening Ceremonies, St. Louis Exposition
Our Deaf Friend, Fogarty

The Over-Anxious Waiter
The Pajama Statue Girls
Panorama From German Building, World's Fair
Panorama From Gondola, St. Louis Exposition
Panorama of Excursion Boats
Panorama of Field Street, St. Joseph
Panorama of 4th St., St. Joseph
Panorama of Race Track Crowd, St. Louis
Panorama of 3rd Street, St. Joseph
Panorama, St. Louis Exposition
Parade of Eagles, New York
Parade of Floats, St. Louis Exposition
Parade of the Pikers, St. Louis Exposition
Parade of Women Delegates, World's Fair
Photographing a Female Crook
The Picture the Photographer Took
A Pipe for a Cigar
Pity the Blind, no. 2
Poor Girl, It Was a Hot Night and the Mosquitos Were Thick
The Porous Plaster
Post Man Delivering Mail, U.S.P.O.
The Power of Authority
Princess Rajah Dance
Pull Down the Curtains, Susie
Quick Work for the Soubrettes
"Reliance" vs. "Shamrock III," Aug. 20
The Rival Models
Routing Mail, U.S.P.O.
Rural Wagon Delivering Mail, U.S.P.O.
Rural Wagon Giving Mail to Branch, U.S.P.O.
S.S. "Morro Castle"
Sailors Ashore
The Sand Baby
The Sand Fort
Saved!
A Scene Behind the Scenes
School Girl Athletes
School Girl Gymnastics
A Scrap in the Dressing Room
Sec'y Taft's Address & Panorama
Seeing New York by Yacht
The Seeress
She Kicked on the Cooking
She Wanted to Rise in the World
Shelter Tent Drill
The Shocking Stockings
Shredded Wheat Biscuit, no. 1
The Smoky Stove
A Snare for Lovers
The Soubrette's Slide
Special Delivery Messenger, U.S.P.O.
Speech by President Francis: World's Fair
Start of Race—"Reliance" Ahead

Start of the First Race, Aug. 22
State Normal School, Missouri
The Story of the Biograph Told
Street Mail Car, U.S.P.O.
The Strenuous Life
A Subject for the Rogue's Gallery
The Suburbanite
The Suit of Armor
Three Girls in a Hammock
Throwing Mail Into Bags, U.S.P.O.
Tied to Her Apron Strings
Toodles and Her Strawberry Tart
Toodles Recites a Recitation
Toodle's Tea-Party
Train Taking Up Mail Bag, U.S.P.O.
A Tramp on the Roof
Transporting Internal Rev. Stamps, U.S.P.O.
A Trick on the Cop
Troubles of a Manager of a Burlesque Show
Twenty Mule Team, St. Louis Exposition
Tying Up Bags for Train, U.S.P.O.
Uncle Reuben at the Waldorf
Under the Tree
The Waders
Wagons Loading Mail, U.S.P.O.
The Waif
Waiting for Bill
A Warm Occasion
The Way to Sell Corsets
West Point Cadets, St. Louis Exposition
What Are the Wild Waves Saying, Sister?
What Burglar Bill Found in the Safe
While Strolling in the Park
Whittier School, Calisthenics
Who Pays for the Drinks?
A Windy Day on the Roof
The Wrath of a Jealous Wife
The Wrong Room

Wells, Lewis, actor

The Indian
The Wages of Sin

West, Charles, actor

As It Is In Life
As the Bells Rang Out
Beverly of Graustark
The Black Sheep
A Child's Impulse
The Christmas Burglars
A Corner in Wheat
The Face at the Window
A Fair Rebel
The Fascinating Mrs. Francis
Fate's Turning
The Female of the Species
A Flash of Light
The Gambler of the West
The Genius
The Goddess of Sagebrush Gulch

A Gold Necklace
The Gold Seekers
The Golden Supper
Heaven Avenges
Helen's Marriage
Her Father's Pride
His Last Dollar
His Lesson
The House With Closed Shutters
The Iconoclast
The Impalement
In Life's Cycle
In Old California
The Lesser Evil
The Lesson
A Lodging for the Night
Lord Chumley
Love Finds a Way
A Lucky Toothache
The Marked Time Table
The Masher
The Massacre
The Message of the Violin
A Midnight Cupid
The Newlyweds
One Is Business, the Other Crime
One Night and Then
An Outcast Among Outcasts
The Peach-Basket Hat
A Plain Song
The Purgation
The Recreation of an Heiress
A Romance of the Western Hills
A Salutary Lesson
The Son's Return
A Summer Idyl
A Summer Tragedy
Sunshine Sue
A Temporary Truce
A Tenderfoot's Triumph
The Test
That Chink at Golden Gulch
Thou Shalt Not
Through the Breakers
The Tourists
The Unchanging Sea
A Victim of Jealousy
Waiter No. 5
The Way of the World
What the Daisy Said
When a Man Loves
The Wife
With the Enemy's Help
Woman Against Woman
The Would-Be Shriner

West, Dorothy, actress

At the Altar
An Awful Moment
The Banker's Daughters
The Child of the Ghetto
A Child's Impulse
The Cricket on the Hearth
The Deception
Examination Day at School

Fate's Turning
The Fugitive
The Girls and Daddy
The Golden Supper
His Last Burglary
His Trust Fulfilled
The House With Closed Shutters
Lady Helen's Escapade
Lines of White on a Sullen Sea
The Little Darling
The Little Teacher
The Medicine Bottle
Not So Bad As It Seemed
Nursing a Viper
One Touch of Nature
The Recreation of an Heiress
Rose O' Salem-Town
The Roue's Heart
A Salutary Lesson
The Salvation Army Lass
1776, or, the Hessian Renegades
The Smoker
A Strange Meeting
Taming a Husband
The Way of the World

West, Raymond B., director

Rumpelstiltskin

West Orange, New Jersey

Capture of Boer Battery
Capture of Boer Battery by British
Casey at the Bat
Edison Kinetoscopic Record of a
  Sneeze, January 7, 1894
see also Black Maria Studio, West
  Orange, N.J.

West Point, New York

Daly of West Point Winning Hurdle
  Race
Prince Henry Arriving at West Point
Prince Henry at West Point
Prince Henry Reviewing the Cadets
  at West Point
Review of Cadets at West Point
Review of Cadets, West Point

Westbury, New York

The Meadowbrook Hunt
Vaulting Contest, Meadowbrook
  Hunt

Westfield, Massachusetts

Mass. State Militia Encampment

Westfield, New Jersey

An Arcadian Maid
The Child of the Ghetto
A Child's Impulse
A Child's Stratagem
Examination Day at School
His New Lid
His Sister-in-Law
A Lucky Toothache

A Plain Song
The Purgation
The Song of the Wildwood Flute
Sunshine Sue
When a Man Loves

Westinghouse

Welding the Big Ring
Westinghouse Air Brake Co.
Westinghouse Works

Westminster, Maryland

Buying Stamps from Rural Wagon,
  U.S.P.O.
Exchange of Mail at Rural P.O.,
  U.S.P.O.
Rural Wagon Delivering Mail,
  U.S.P.O.
Rural Wagon Giving Mail to Branch
  U.S.P.O.

Whaling

Whaling in the Far North Off the
  Coast of Alaska in the Treacherous Bering Sea

Wheeler, Joseph

General Wheeler and Secretary Alger

White, Arthur, actor, camera-
man

Circular Panorama of Electric Tow-
  er
Esquimaux Game of Snap-the-Whip
Esquimaux Leap-Frog
Esquimaux Village
Life of an American Fireman
Pan-American Exposition by Night
Panorama of Esplanade by Night
Panoramic View of Electric Tower
  From a Balloon

White, James H., actor

Jones and His Pal in Trouble
Jones' Interrupted Sleighride
Jones' Return from the Club, parts
  1, 2 and 3

White, James H., cameraman

Arrival of Tokyo Train
Capture of Boer Battery
Capture of Boer Battery by British
Carrying Out the Snakes
Charge of Boer Cavalry
Circle Dance
Congress of Nations
"Deutschland" Leaving New York at
  Full Speed
Eagle Dance, Pueblo Indians
English Lancers Charging
Hong Kong Regiment, no. 1
Hong Kong Regiment, no. 2
Hong Kong, Wharf-Scene
Honolulu Street Scene

Japanese Sampans
Jones Makes a Discovery
Kanakas Diving for Money, no. 1
Kanakas Diving for Money, no. 2
"Kronprinz Wilhelm" with Prince Henry on Board Arriving in New York
Landing Wharf at Canton
Line-Up and Teasing the Snakes
The March of Prayer and Entrance of the Dancers
Moki Snake Dance by Wolpi [Walpapi] Indians
Prince Henry Arriving at West Point
Prince Henry Arriving in Washington and Visiting the German Embassy
Prince Henry at Lincoln's Monument, Chicago, Illinois
Prince Henry at Niagara Falls
Prince Henry Reviewing the Cadets at West Point
Prince Henry Visiting Cambridge, Mass. and Harvard University
S.S. "Coptic"
S.S. "Coptic" Coaling
S.S. "Coptic" Lying To
S.S. "Coptic" Running Against the Storm
S.S. "Coptic" Running Before a Gale
S.S. "Doric"
S.S. "Doric" in Mid-Ocean
S.S. "Gaelic" at Nagasaki
Sailing of the "Deutschland" With Prince Henry on Board
Shanghai Police
Shanghai Street Scene, Scene 1
Shanghai Street Scene, Scene 2
Sheik Artillery, Hong Kong
Street Scene in Hong Kong
Street Scene in Yokohama, no. 1
Street Scene in Yokohama, no. 2
Theatre Road, Yokohama
Tourists Starting for Canton
Wharf Scene, Honolulu

White, James H., Company

Love and War

White, James H., director

Love and War

White, Stanford

Thaw-White Tragedy

White, Thomas, actor

Jack and the Beanstalk

Whittier, Robert, actor

Parsifal: Parsifal Ascends the Throne, Ruins of Magic Garden, Exterior of Klingson's Castle, Magic Garden, Interior of the Temple, Scene Outside the Temple, Return of Parsifal, In the Woods

Wichita Forest and Game Reserve, Oklahoma

The Bank Robbery

Wieth, Carlo, actor

The Power of Love

Wieth, Clara, actress

The Aeroplane Inventor
Love and Friendship
The Power of Love
The Vampire Dancer
Vengeance

Willemstad, Curaçao

Panorama of Willemstadt, Curacao, Taken From the River

Williams, Bert, actor

The Indian

Williams, Clara, actress

The Bargain
The Devil
The Italian

Williams, Kathlyn, actress

Politician's Love Story

Wilmerding, Pennsylvania

Westinghouse Works

Wilmington, Delaware

The Baby Review
Maypole Dance
Policemen's Prank on Their Comrades
Rube and Fender
A Scrap in Black and White
Tub Race
Turning the Tables

Wilmington Springs, Delaware

Miniature Railway at Wilmington Springs, Del.
Razzle Dazzle

Winter sports

After the First Snow
Coasting
Coasting Scene at Montmorency Falls, Canada
Cross Country Running on Snow Shoes
Hockey Match on the Ice
Ice-Boat Racing at Redbank, N.J.
Ice Boating on the North Shrewsbury, Red Bank, N.J.
Ice Skating in Central Park, N.Y.
Ice Yacht Racing
Ice Yachting
Kent House Slide
A Mile in 56 Seconds

Skating on Lake, Central Park
Skee Club
Skiing in Montreal
Skiing Scene in Quebec
Sleighing in Central Park, New York
Sleighing Scene
Sleighing Scene, Boston
Sleighs Returning After a Spin
Sliding Down Ice Mound at Niagara Falls
A Spill
Tobogganing in Canada
see also Sleighs, sleds, and toboggans

Winthrop Moving Picture Company

Christy Mathewson, N.Y. National League Baseball Team
Dancing Boxing Match, Montgomery and Stone
"Goodbye John"
Marceline, the World-Renowned Clown of the N.Y. Hippodrome

Winthrop Press

The Auto-somnambulist
Chest and Neck Development

Woods, Frank, scriptwriter/author

Mr. Jones' Burglar
Mr. Jones Has a Card Party
Mrs. Jones' Lover

Work sites

Beginning of a Skyscraper
Building a Harbor at San Pedro
The Convicts Sacrifice
Excavating for a New York Foundation
Excavating Scene at the Pyramids of Sakkarah
Excavation for Subway
Fastest Wrecking Crew in the World
Panorama of Riker's Island, N.Y.
Panoramic View of Boston Subway from an Electric Car
Panoramic View of Mt. Tamalpais
Panoramic View of the Great Cable Incline, Mt. Low
Pennsylvania Tunnel Excavation
A Perilous Proceeding
Pontoon Bridge Building
Razing a Brick Building
Rock Drill at Work on Subway
Seeing Boston
The Skyscrapers
Star Theatre
Switchback on Trolley Road
Tunnel Number Three
The Tunnel Workers
The Woman in Black

World's Fairs; *see* Fairs and expositions

Wrestling

Catch-as-Catch-Can Wrestling
Roeber Wrestling Match
They Meet on the Mat
Wrestling at the New York Athletic Club

Writers; *see* Name of person

Wyoming

Arrival of Train, Cheyenne
Flock of Sheep
Sherman Hill Tunnel
Tunnel Number Three
see also Yellowstone Park, Wyoming

Wysock, Pennsylvania

New Black Diamond Express

Yachts; *see* Ships and watercraft

Yale University

Princeton and Yale Football Game

Yellowstone Park, Wyoming

Coaches Arriving at Mammoth Hot Springs
Coaches Going to Cinnabar from Yellowstone Park
Glimpses of Yellowstone Park

Lower Falls, Grand Canyon, Yellowstone Park
Old Faithful Geyser
Riverside Geyser, Yellowstone Park
Tourists Going Round Yellowstone Park
Upper Falls of the Yellowstone

Yokohama, Japan

Going to the Yokohama Races
Railway Station at Yokohama
Returning from the Races
S.S. "Doric"
Street Scene in Yokohama, no. 1
Street Scene in Yokohama, no. 2
Theatre Road, Yokohama

York, Duke and Duchess of Cornwall and York

Duke and Duchess of Cornwall and York Landing at Queenstown, Ontario
Duke of York at Montreal and Quebec
Royal Train with Duke and Duchess of York, Climbing Mt. Hector

Yosemite Valley, California

Artist's Point
Bridal Veil Falls
Coaching Party, Yosemite Valley
Glacier Point
Nevada Falls

Yost, Herbert, actor

At the Altar
The Deception
Edgar Allen [i.e., Allan] Poe
Faded Lilies
The French Duel
The Guerrilla
The Light That Came

Young Deer, James, actor

The Mended Lute

Youngstown, Ohio

Dumping Iron Ore

Yukon Territory, Canada

Miles Canyon Tramway
Rocking Gold in the Klondike
Washing Gold on 20 Above Hunker, Klondike
White Horse Rapids

Zangenberg, Einar, actor

The Aeroplane Inventor
The Aviator's Generosity
The Fisherman and His Sweetheart
The Rights of Youth
The Two Convicts

Zukor, Adolph, producer

The Count of Monte Cristo